The Papers of Henry Clay
Ashland Edition

By Charles T. Wade *From a wood engraving*

ASHLAND
Home of Henry Clay

The Papers of

HENRY CLAY

The Papers of
HENRY CLAY

James F. Hopkins, *Editor*

Mary W. M. Hargreaves, *Associate Editor*

VOLUME 1

THE RISING STATESMAN

1797-1814

UNIVERSITY OF KENTUCKY PRESS

Library of Congress Catalog Card No. 59-13605

Printed in the United States of America
at the University of Kentucky, Lexington, Kentucky

"My ambition is that we may enter a new and larger era of service to humanity."

Dedicated to the memory of
JOSIAH KIRBY LILLY
1861-1948
President of Eli Lilly and Company
Founder of Lilly Endowment, Inc.

Whose wisdom and foresight were
devoted to the service of
education, religion, and
public welfare

INTRODUCTION

The Papers of Henry Clay covers a period beginning near the close of the eighteenth century, when a fledgling lawyer ventured westward from Virginia to seek his fortune, and ending more than fifty years later with the death of an elder statesman in Washington, near the legislative halls where he had long been a powerful figure. Recognized by the United States Senate in 1957 as one of its five most outstanding members to date, Speaker of the House of Representatives longer than any other individual save one, Secretary of State under President John Quincy Adams, and thrice himself a candidate for the presidency, Clay was at the center of the American political stage for nearly half a century. In addition to giving a detailed view of his political life, Clay's papers reveal his progress in the legal profession, his role as a gentleman farmer, his participation in manufacturing and commerce, his relationship with his family, his service to his community, and his friendship with men and women in all walks of life. The editors hope that their work will contribute to a better understanding of both Clay and the exciting times in which he lived, when locally, regionally, and nationally his environment was rapidly maturing; they believe that it may also reveal something of the great personal charm that endeared "Harry of the West" to many of his contemporaries.

The present volume, the first of a set of ten in which the papers are to be published, covers the great Kentuckian's career through the signing of the Treaty of Ghent in December, 1814. The arrangement of materials throughout the series is to be chronological, with one exception. Realizing that additional documents may be discovered too late for inclusion in proper order, and hoping that such manuscripts will come to light, we plan to publish them in the last volume, together with undated items which cannot be inserted even with approximation at an earlier point. Each volume will include an index of names of people, organizations, blooded livestock, estates, taverns, and watering places. A general index will be published at the conclusion of the work.

The compilation is designed to present both the incoming and outgoing correspondence; personal business papers, accounts, and receipts; legislative proposals, including committee reports for which Clay bore identifiable responsibility; diplomatic papers which represent a personal contribution; and reported speeches and manuscript notes or drafts of such public utterances. Many formal documents, such as land deeds, reports of various kinds, and diplomatic notes are summarized; others, considered of more routine nature, are merely noted by title entries. Also noted in this manner are certain speeches, legislative bills, resolutions, and motions of which no copy is known to exist. Purely routine matters and transcripts by Clay of documents known to have been composed by other persons are omitted. Clay's court work for clients has also been generally excluded—much of it was formal, much of it was dictated by facts and circumstances unrelated to Clay, and much of it was too specialized to warrant coverage in a work of general appeal. Court files on the local, state, and national levels contain many items in Clay's hand, of which only those that relate to him personally are here reproduced. Cases in which he was involved as attorney are discussed in the notes merely to explain references in documents that are being printed; no effort has been made to trace every suit in which he was employed.

Since Clay is the central figure, the heading for each entry indicates the relationship of that particular item to him. When correspondents are not specifically identified by salutation, superscription, or address, their names are bracketed. Each document bears a date in the upper righthand corner, usually already there in correspondence, but transferred to that position when found standing separately at the end of the text, and supplied in brackets when not originally at either beginning or end. Every entry is followed by an unnumbered note indicating, by conventional symbols when possible, the nature and location of the original document. This note may also include addresses not found in the superscriptions of letters, meaningful endorsements either not attached to the body of the text or not related directly to Clay, and data pertaining to the context of the document. Numbered footnotes are added when needed to provide explanation of specific references.

Upon the first mention of a person, place, or specialized subject, brief identification or explanation is provided; thereafter, except in particular instances, no editorial comment is offered. The index will provide guidance to additional information.

When editorial comment is based very largely upon a specific authority, citation of that source is provided. In most instances, however, information has been gleaned from many channels, including the *Dictionary of American Biography*, *The National Cyclopædia of American Biography*, *Dictionary of National Biography*, *Biographical Directory of the American Congress*, *The Biographical Encyclopædia of Kentucky*, *Biographical Cyclopedia of the Commonwealth of Kentucky*, other works of a biographical nature, court and other official records, city directories, state and local histories, Dr.

Willard Rouse Jillson's voluminous indexes to the Kentucky land records, G. Glenn Clift's *"Second Census" of Kentucky,* the Kentucky Historical Society *Register, The Filson Club History Quarterly,* and other historical journals. Each of these works is cited in full when first used; thereafter it is identified only when related to some statement of special significance. Our procedure is usually to omit bibliographic reference to normal sources for the kind of data provided.

Most of the documents presented have been made available to the editors as photographic reproductions of the originals. Manual or printed copies have not been used when other sources have been found. When several contemporary copies, but not the original letter of delivery, have been discovered, that which most closely approximates the form identified with the sender has been used. When there are several versions of a manuscript in the inscriber's hand, that which most closely represents his final intent has been accepted. With respect to speeches, the version first reported has been chosen, but with annotation on significant changes, attributable to Clay, in later versions. Previous publication of documents in major compilations, with which comparison may be sought, has been noted, as has the fact of contemporary publication in Clay's hometown journals. No attempt has been made, however, to record the broad extent of coverage given to Clay's public utterances in the contemporary press.

At one highly important stage between raw material and printed page, each document has been transcribed by a typist whose objective was to make a copy as nearly like the original as possible. Spelling, capitalization, words run together, abbreviations, interlineations, punctuation, and raised letters were taken as found. Even deletions, in so far as they could be deciphered, were copied.

At the next stage, the preparation of the material for the printer, certain modifications became necessary in the interests of clarity and economy. With respect to correspondence, the salutation and date of each letter have been placed on the same line regardless of their position in the manuscript, and the same principle has been followed relative to the complimentary closing and signature. In all documents the original spelling and capitalization have been retained, except that in copies from printed sources, obvious typographical errors have been corrected. Superior numbers and letters have been lowered, with the result that slight changes have occurred in abbreviations and punctuation in certain instances. For example, "Mr." in our text may have been written originally with the "r" above the line and a period, double period, ditto marks, colon, a short dash, or two parallel dashes under the elevated letter. Circumflex or linkage lines over abbreviated words have been dropped. Periods and braces have been supplied for "L. S." and "Seal" following signatures on legal documents. Otherwise, punctuation and abbreviations remain as found.

Words linked together in the original have been separated, and interlineations have been pulled down to the line, with an explanatory footnote if the change seems important. Deletions have been noted if any significance has been discovered in the omission. Brackets have been used to enclose words supplied by the editors and any editorial comment within the body of a document. Missing or indecipherable words are thus inserted, usually in roman letters but in italics when the emendation is more speculative. In some cases brackets enclose dots, while a footnote indicates the approximate number of words missing or illegible. Braces have been substituted for brackets found in the original documents. The use of "*sic*" has been strictly limited in the finished product, although, for the peace of mind of copyists and editors, our typescripts are generously peppered with this reassuring adverb.

It is impossible in a brief statement of this nature to make proper acknowledgment to all who have aided the project, but without the help of these many persons and institutions the work could not have been carried to its present stage. We are indebted to the newspapers and scholarly journals that have published appeals for manuscripts and other notices of the work, to those individuals who have given leads to material, to the Henry Clay Memorial Foundation (dedicated to the preservation of "Ashland") for its special interest and encouragement, and to the archivists, librarians, curators of historical societies and museums, manuscript collectors, members of the Clay family, and the many other individuals who have responded generously to requests for documents. By far the most extensive help of this nature has come from the National Historical Publications Commission, under Dr. Philip M. Hamer, Executive Director. Not only has the Commission furnished photocopies of documents in the National Archives, but by special arrangement with the Library of Congress it has also filmed for us a tremendous amount of material located in that treasure house of manuscripts. Our obligation to the Commission has been made greater by the efforts of Miss F. Helen Beach, Archivist, who has most ably attended our interests in Washington.

A salute should be given also to those who have purchased manuscripts largely for the purpose of making them available to us. Dr. Thomas D. Clark, director and godfather of the project, has time and again come to our aid in this manner, while the University of Kentucky Library Associates have the distinction of donating the only original Henry Clay manuscript actually owned by the project.

To the University of Kentucky Library and its staff we owe a special debt of gratitude. The Department of Archives, under Dr. Jacqueline Bull, has rendered invaluable service in helping to obtain material, in adding pertinent items to its growing manuscript collections, and in aiding the solution of specific problems. Dr. Lawrence S. Thompson, Director of Libraries, has been most considerate, not only for assistance in locating documents, but also for providing working space conveniently near research materials, when his building is already seriously overcrowded.

Our sincere thanks go to those who have rendered financial aid. At crucial moments Mr. Barry Bingham of Louisville and the late Mr. Guy Huguelet of Lexington provided donations that were urgently needed. Our most consistent backer has been the University of Kentucky Research Fund Committee, which from the limited funds at its disposal has repeatedly made grants to enable the project to continue. Since the fall of 1957, Lilly Endowment, Inc., of Indianapolis, Indiana, has generously provided funds which have made possible the employment of a staff of adequate size to bring the work to completion and assure its publication.

For their willingness to discuss our problems and to make helpful suggestions we are indebted to the members of the Advisory Commission of *The Papers of Henry Clay*: Thomas D. Clark, chairman, Barry Bingham, Leo M. Chamberlain, J. Winston Coleman, Edward S. Dabney, Bruce F. Denbo, Frank G. Dickey, Herman L. Donovan, Joseph C. Graves, Gene Markey, Manning M. Pattillo, Frank D. Peterson, Herman E. Spivey, William H. Townsend, and J. Stephen Watkins.

We are grateful, too, for the advice and meticulous editorial work of the University of Kentucky Press, particularly of Mrs. Evalin Douglas, who has handled most of our copy.

I cannot fail to note my own appreciation to all who have at one time or other been members of our staff. To the succession of students who have served as part-time clerks and typists, to the graduate students who have been employed at various times as research assistants, and to Mrs. Susan Ball, Miss Maureen M. Shade, Mrs. Mary Ada Sullivan, and Mrs. Bethania Smith, who have been long-term fellow workers, I express sincere thanks for their immeasurable contributions to the work.

A special tribute is due to the associate editor, Dr. Mary Wilma Hargreaves, who has been with the project from the beginning, who has on occasion carried on alone, and who is to a large degree responsible for whatever merit these volumes have.

J. F. H.

SYMBOLS

The following symbols, one of which appears at the beginning of the unnumbered note found immediately after each document copied from a manuscript source, have been used to describe the nature of the original.

AD	Autograph Document
AD draft	Autograph Document Draft
ADS	Autograph Document Signed
ADS copy	Autograph Document Signed, copied by writer
ADS draft	Autograph Document Signed, draft
AE	Autograph Endorsement
AEI	Autograph Endorsement Initialed
AES	Autograph Endorsement Signed
AL	Autograph Letter
ALI	Autograph Letter Initialed
ALI copy	Autograph Letter Initialed, copied by writer
ALS	Autograph Letter Signed
ALS copy	Autograph Letter Signed, copied by writer
ALS draft	Autograph Letter Signed, draft
AN	Autograph Note
ANS	Autograph Note Signed
Copy	Copy not by writer (indicated "true" if so certified)
D	Document
DS	Document Signed
EI	Endorsement Initialed
ES	Endorsement Signed
LI	Letter Initialed
LI copy	Letter Initialed, copied by writer
LS	Letter Signed
NS	Note Signed

The following, from the *Symbols Used in the National Union Catalog of the Library of Congress* (7th ed., rev.; Washington, 1959), appear in this volume after the description of the document to indicate the location of the original in libraries and institutions of the United States. To the symbol for the Library of Congress we have added letters to distinguish between the two collections of Henry Clay papers in that depository.

CSmH	Henry E. Huntington Library and Museum, San Marino, California
CtY	Yale University, New Haven, Connecticut
DLC	United States Library of Congress, Washington, D. C.
DLC-HC	Library of Congress, Henry Clay Collection
DLC-TJC	Library of Congress, Thomas J. Clay Collection
DNA	United States National Archives Library, Washington, D. C. Following the symbol for this depository, the letter M means Microcopy; R, Reel; and RG, Record Group.
ICHi	Chicago Historical Society Library, Chicago, Illinois
ICU	University of Chicago, Chicago, Illinois
IHi	Illinois State Historical Society, Springfield, Illinois.
InHi	Indiana Historical Society, Indianapolis, Indiana
InU	Indiana University, Bloomington, Indiana
KyBB	Berea College, Berea, Kentucky
KyBgW	Western Kentucky State College, Bowling Green, Kentucky
KyHi	Kentucky Historical Society, Frankfort, Kentucky
KyLoF	Filson Club, Louisville, Kentucky
KyLx	Lexington Public Library, Lexington, Kentucky
KyLxT	Transylvania College, Lexington, Kentucky
KyU	University of Kentucky, Lexington, Kentucky
MB	Boston Public Library, Boston, Massachusetts
MH	Harvard University, Cambridge, Massachusetts
MHi	Massachusetts Historical Society, Boston, Massachusetts
MdHi	Maryland Historical Society, Baltimore, Maryland
MeHi	Maine Historical Society, Portland, Maine
MiD-B	Detroit Public Library, Burton Historical Collection
MiU-C	University of Michigan, William L. Clements Library, Ann Arbor, Michigan
NBuHi	Buffalo Historical Society, Buffalo, New York
NHi	New York Historical Society, New York City
NN	New York Public Library, New York City
NNP	Pierpont Morgan Library, New York City
NRU	University of Rochester, Rochester, New York
NcD	Duke University, Durham, North Carolina
NcU	University of North Carolina, Chapel Hill, North Carolina
OCHP	Historical and Philosophical Society of Ohio, Cincinnati, Ohio
PHC	Haverford College, Haverford, Pennsylvania
PHi	Historical Society of Pennsylvania, Philadelphia, Pennsylvania

PPL-R	Library Company of Philadelphia, Ridgeway Branch, Philadelphia, Pennsylvania
PPPrHi	Presbyterian Historical Society, Philadelphia, Pennsylvania
RPB	Brown University, Providence, Rhode Island
THi	Tennessee Historical Society, Nashville, Tennessee
ViU	University of Virginia, Charlottesville, Virginia
WHi	State Historical Society, Madison, Wisconsin

HENRY CLAY, *age 65*

A portrait by Manuel Joachim de França

Presented to the Henry Clay Memorial Foundation,
Lexington, Kentucky
by Robert Hall McCormick, III, of Chicago

Writing of this work, Clay observed: "Mr. Franconia [*sic*] . . . has made a portrait of me, which, as far as I can judge, is a good likeness. He has succeeded in some features, in respect to which most of the artists have failed."

To Hamilton H. Jackson
April 20, 1842

The Papers of
HENRY CLAY

Bond for Land Purchased from Warner Lewis

[August 22, 1797]

Know all men by these presents that I. Warner Lewis of Warner Hall in the County of Gloucester,[1] in consideration of One hundred dollars to me in hand paid, do hereby bind myself & my heirs to make to Henry Clay or his assigns a sure fee simple title with general Warranty against the claims of myself or any other person, whatever to a certain tract of Land lying and being in the County of Nelson in the State of Kentucky Surveyed for Mathew Walton[2] by virtue of part of a treasury warrant number 20,086, containing fifteen hundred and forty two acres, lying on the Waters of Willson Creek and Cane run as by the said Survey will appear.

Given under my hand and seal this 22nd day of August 1797.

Witness Signed WARNER LEWIS {SEAL}

The word fee simple first enterlined

EDM RANDOLPH.[3]

Copy. DLC-TJC (DNA, M212, R15). Endorsed on verso, November 10, 1804, by George M. Bibb, Lexington lawyer (later Chief Justice of the Kentucky Court of Appeals, United States Senator, and, briefly, Secretary of the Treasury), who certified that the tract was largely "broken Land, intersperced with small bottoms," worth an average of fifty cents per acre, on part of which there was an earlier claim.

In a second endorsement, dated November 21, 1804, Buckner Thruston certified that the attestation on the original document was in the handwriting of Edmund Randolph.

1 Virginia.

2 A native of Virginia who engaged in land speculation in Kentucky on a large scale, General Walton settled in Washington County and represented that district in the Kentucky Constitutional Convention of 1792, the State legislative assemblies of 1792, 1800-1803, and the United States Congress, 1803-1807.

3 Edmund Randolph had returned to the practice of law in Virginia after serving as United States Attorney General and, later, as Secretary of State under President Washington.

Settlement of Accounts of Henry Watkins

[October 27, 1797]

Henry Clay To Henry Watkins. Dr.

1797	To Cash paid Spencer Watkins[1] as	
July 28	pr. your Order	£30: 0.0
	To Commissioners for Collecting the Hire	

of your negro Boy Sam[2] for the year 1794	
1795 & 1796	£ 1-10
	31-10..0
	30:10-0
Contra Cr.	£ 1" 0"0
By Cash recd. from P. Caldwell[3] for the	
year 1794 & 1795	£15-10
for the hire of your negro Boy Sam	
By Do. from Peyton Short[4] for Do. for the	
year 1796	£15
	£30-10

Woodford County To wit,

Agreeable to an order of the Court of said County to us directed we have settled the accounts of Henry Watkins Guardian to Henry Clay for the year 1794, 1795 and 1796 and find that there is due said Watkins from the estate of said Clay the sum of twenty shillings, Given under our hands this 27th. day of Oct., 1797

RICH. YOUNG
CHARLES RAILEY[5]

Woodford County (Kentucky), Will Book B, 54-55. The account was approved and ordered to record at the sitting of the Woodford County Court on December 4, 1797. Watkins, Clay's stepfather, who had moved his family to Kentucky in 1791, had been appointed guardian by the Woodford Court in 1794. *Ibid.*, Order Book C, 20. Young Clay, left behind in Virginia, did not follow until November, 1797.

1 A relative of Clay's stepfather, possibly a nephew, who stayed in Woodford County for a time before leaving the State in 1804.

2 Two Negro boys, James and "Little Sam," were left to Henry Clay by the will of his father John Clay, dated November 4, 1780, probated February 7, 1782. Zachary F. Smith and Mary R. Clay, *The Clay Family* (Filson Club *Publication* no. 14; Louisville, 1899), 56.

3 Possibly Philips Caldwell, Frankfort merchant.

4 Younger brother of diplomatist William Short, Peyton had come west before Kentucky attained statehood, and engaged in mercantile business, downriver trade, and land speculation. At one time he was a business associate of James Wilkinson.

5 Young and Railey, native Virginians, came to Kentucky in 1783 and 1796 respectively. William E. Railey, *History of Woodford County* (Frankfort, 1928), 69, 260.

License to Practice Law

Virginia to wit [November 6, 1797]

Whereas we have been appointed by the General assembly to examine into the Capacity ability and fitness of persons applying for Licences to practice as attorneys at Law in the Courts of this Common Wealth, And Henry Clay Gentleman hath made application for that Purpose, and having produced the legal Certificate from the County of Henrico;[1] We have examined him touching his Capacity, ability and fitness and having found him duly qualified: This is therefore to licence and permit the said Henry Clay to practice as an Attorney at Law in the Courts of this Common Wealth— Given under our hands and seals the sixth day of November, One thousand seven hundred and ninety seven

P CARRINGTON {SEAL}
WM. FLEMING {SEAL}
SPENCER ROANE[2] {SEAL}

ADS by Carrington, with additional signatures. DLC-HC (DNA, M212, R1).

1 Clay had studied law under Robert Brooke in Richmond, county seat of Henrico.

2 Paul Carrington, Fleming, and Roane were members of the Virginia Court of Appeals.

Receipted Bill from Edmund Randolph

Henry Clay [*ca.* November 6, 1797]

To Edmund Randolph—	Dr.
To my fee in the suit in the High Court of chy. M. Clay agt. McKeand's executor[1]	£ 5„ –
To my advice in the case of the mortgage of Wm. Hix to John Clays exor[2]	1„ 2„6
To Cash	3„17„6
	£10„ 0„0

Received in full.
EDM: RANDOLPH.
Nov. 6. 1797

DS. DLC-TJC (DNA, M212, R15).

1 This case was not reported. It apparently involved Matthew Clay, a brother of Green, cousins of Henry's father, and John McKeand, who had held a tract on the townsite of Richmond, Virginia.

2 The mortgage has not been found.

Record of Permit to Practice Law

[March 20, 1798]

Henry Clay Esquire, produced in Court a License and on his motion is permitted to practise as an Attorney at Law, in this Court, And thereupon took the several Oaths by Law prescribed

Fayette Circuit Court, Order Book A (1796-1798), 94. Similar entries, all subsequent to this, may be found in order books for other circuit courts in which Clay practiced.

To the Electors of Fayette County

FELLOW CITIZENS: Lexington, 16 April, 1798.

THE time approaching at which you are to decide, in pursuance of the invitation of your *immediate* representatives upon the all-important question with respect to a convention, it becomes the duty of every man to form an impartial and candid judgment; it is not only his duty to quiet his own mind, but to contribute, as far as he can, towards placing the question in a fair and dispassionate point of view, before the public. In attempting this, suffer me to state to you the reasons which have been offered against summoning a convention, and the defects which, it is conceived, make an alteration in our constitution necessary.

That there exist defects in the constitution is not denied by the most violent opposers of a convention. But it is said, that, if we attempt an alteration of it now, we shall expose it to the attacks of the wicked and designing, and that, by endeavouring to expunge the defective parts, we hazard a loss of the perfect. An appeal too is made to the tranquility of the state, and it is asked, with exultation, if every one is not happy under the present form of government; whether the weight of oppression bows down the neck of any one. A grave refutation of these arguments is only necessary, from the respectability of the persons who urge them, and from the influence they have acquired.

How do we endanger the good parts of the constitution, by a convention? Those who urge this objection seem to suppose that, instead of an assemblage of the most wise and enlightened citizens of the state, canvassing the constitution and availing themselves of the lessons of experience, and the dictates of reason, we are to expect a convention of the most wicked and ignorant, shaking government and attacking property. They pay but a poor compliment to the discernment and integrity of the people. They appear to have forgotten that the members of the convention will be chosen by the voluntary suffrages of a free people. That the persons thus chosen, elevated by the dignity of their station, assemble together for the discussion of subjects, in which they are equally interested with their constituents. That they will have no motive for abusing the confidence of the public. And they seem unaware of the extent of their argument, it striking at all representative government, since if we cannot trust our delegates in establishing fundamental or elementary principles, they are equally unfit for the purpose of ordinary legislation. Has it ever been known that the cause of truth was hurt by enquiry and investigation? If not, why are we to apprehend that the sound parts of our constitution will be endangered by a convention? But it is said that it is yet too young to be touched. Its infancy is a powerful reason for amending it at the present time. It has not yet acquired that strength, that maturity, which will enable it to resist the efforts of reformation.

The first dawn of disease is the moment for remedy. The longer it continues, the more difficult is cure. The longer a government operates, the greater is the difficulty of change. Habit, the creation of new offices, their influence, a thousand relations and tyes combine to oppose a reform of abuses in an old government. We have innumerable examples of the truth of this idea. Virginia affords a recent one. There, notwithstanding their constitution is as defective as one can be, all amendatory attempts have proved abortive.

But, compelled to abandon this ground of opposition as untenable, the enemies to a convention assume a bolder aspect upon the other, the supposed happiness of the people. It may not be improper here to remark that arguments of this kind, if founded in fact, prove nothing. Because we find that it is a principle of our nature to endeavour to be contented with present situation. The inhabitant of the most dismal dungeon, the parent who has lost the most affectionate and promising child, after the first paroxisms of grief, cease their unavailing complaints. The subjects of the most despotic prince, the African who has the most ruthless and inexorable master, seem contented and happy, and rarely heave a sigh of misery. The true question with the philosopher and statesman should be, not whether men are contented, for there is a tranquility of the mind, which has the countenance of happiness, but can the present sum of human happiness, by the reform of corrupt institutions, or the change of licentious manners, be increased.

It is not however true that the people of Kentucky are contented and happy under the present government. The vote of so large a number, in favor of a convention, at the last election, and the present stir in the country, prove the contrary. Can any humane man be happy and contented when he sees near thirty thousand of his fellow beings around him, deprived of all the rights which make life desirable, transferred like cattle from the possession of one to another; when he sees the trembling slave, under the hammer, surrounded by a number of eager purchasers, and feeling all the emotions which arise when one is uncertain into whose tyrannic hands he must next fall; when he beholds the anguish and hears the piercing cries of husbands separated from wives and children from parents; when in a word, all the tender and endearing ties of nature are broken asunder and disregarded; and when he reflects that no gradual mode of emancipation is adopted either for these slaves or their posterity, doubling their number every twenty-five years. To suppose the people of Kentucky, enthusiasts as they are in the cause of liberty, could be contented and happy under circumstances like these, would be insulting their good sense.

Having thus obviated the objections against a convention, permit me to hint at some of the alterations which appear to me to be necessary to our constitution.

In addition to other misrepresentation, to which the enemies to a convention, despairing of success by a fair mode of reasoning, have had recourse, they have addressed themselves insidiously to the fears of the slaveholders, and held out as the object of the friends to a convention, an immediate and unqualified liberation of slaves. However just such a measure might be, it certainly never has been the intention of any one to attempt it; and the only motive in ascribing it to them has been to awaken the prejudices, and mislead the judgment of the public. But it is the wish of some of them, that a gradual plan of emancipation should be adopted. All America acknowledges the existence of slavery to be an evil, which while it deprives the slave of the best gift of heaven, in the end injures the master too, by laying waste his lands, enabling him to live indolently, and thus contracting all the vices generated by a state of idleness. If it be this enormous evil, the sooner we attempt its destruction the better. It is a subject which has been so generally canvassed by the public, that it is unnecessary to repeat all the reasons which urge to a conventional interference. It is sufficient that we are satisfied of this much, that the article prohibiting the legislature from making any provision for it, should be expunged, and another introduced either applying the remedy itself, or authorising the legislature at any subsequent period to do it. There can be no danger in vesting this power in them. They can have no motive but public good to actuate them, and there will be always a number of them who will themselves hold slaves. The legislature of Virginia possess this power without abusing it. The next objection which I shall mention to the present constitution, is the senate, a body which to me seems adverse to republican principles, and to be without use.[1] I am aware that I shall be opposed by the examples of all nations, who enjoy any portion of liberty. Fortunately however the present enlightened age is not to be seduced into an opinion by precedent alone: reason must be addressed and satisfied before any is embraced. The division of the legislature into two chambers, has been founded upon the principle of two classes of men, whose interests were distinct, living under the same government. It was necessary that the rights of the nobility and commonalty should be guarded and protected by a body of legislators, representing each. These distinctions not existing in America, the use of the senate has ceased. What is the object of a representative legislature? It is to collect the will of the people, and to assemble the intelligence of the state, for the purpose of legislation. It is not necessary to this end that there should be two separate bodies of delegates. But if it be, as the object certainly is, the assemblage of wisdom, and as there is a greater chance of wise men being in a large assembly than in a small one, each chamber should be composed of an equal number of members. If the will of the people is to be the governing principle of decision, certainly that will is better expressed by the lower house, since the members of that are more numerous and come more immediately from the body of the people. Is it not against the principles of all just calculation, against the spirit of democracy, to suppose that fifteen men above, are equally well qualified to understand and manage the interests of a nation, with fifty-six below? if it be true that the farther we go from the people, we get men better acquainted with, and more competent to decide upon, the affairs of the republic, why stop at fifteen, why not descend to two or one?

With respect to the check which the senate is supposed to impose upon the impetuosity and precipitancy of the lower house, this scarcely deserves an audience. To it I answer first, the will of the enlightened representatives of a free people should not be checked by any power upon earth, except it be the people themselves. And secondly, that it is not true that the senate is composed in general of men less impetuous and more wise than the other house. Is it not like the upper house composed of men? Do not these men possess the same passions, the same prejudices with the others? Have not they the same inclinations to gratify? Oh, but the senate is composed of fewer members, and the sway of passion is proportionate to the numbers in assemblies. The objection, then conducts us to the aristocratic plan of managing the people by a few. Besides there is danger that the senate may impede the progress of good laws as well as bad ones. I cannot conceive how the lower house, depending upon the people for an annual election, and responsible to them, can be induced to pass laws detrimental to the public, since they are a part of that public, and since the laws equally affect them.

I confess that these objections against the existence of a senate are hazarded with diffidence; but it is the diffidence arising from a veneration for the opinions of those wise men who have thought a senate necessary;—opinions which, though they ought not to be conclusive in any case are certainly entitled to our respect. But if the senatorial branch of the legislature should be retained, we are certain that ours is so badly constituted as to claim popular interference. It is unnecessary to dwell upon imperfections which are obvious to every one.

Having attempted to shew, and I think succeeded in manifesting, in the preceding observations, that there exists no good reason why a convention should not be summoned; that there ought to be a gradual mode of emancipation established, or, at least, that the legislature should be invested with the power of forming one, when the situation of the country should render it necessary; and that the senate should abolished or at least reformed. I shall conclude by observing to you fellow citizens, that the present is the moment for coming forward, and that it is impossible to foresee the consequences of inactivity. SCAEVOLA.[2]

Lexington *Kentucky Gazette,* April 25, 1798. Kentucky's first constitution, adopted in 1792, provided that in 1797 and again in 1798 the voters should consider the desirability of holding a convention to revise that document. If the advocates of change were successful, the legislature was authorized to call a convention in 1799. Dissatisfaction with the original constitution appeared soon after it went into effect, and the cry of "aristocracy" heightened agitation against it. Conservatives, mainly large landowners and slaveholders, defended it. The question was argued orally, in newspapers, and in handbills. Before the election of 1798 Clay aligned himself with the more radical group. This letter is notable for his early expression of hostility to slavery. His general argument was answered in a letter from "The People" to "Messrs. Voter, Gracchus, Scaevola, Keiling and other Inspired Penmen, who have wrote in favor of a convention," April 30, 1798 (Printed Broadside, DLC).

1 Under the constitution of 1792 the governor and senators were chosen by electors rather than by direct vote of the people.

2 For the identification of Scaevola as Henry Clay, see Calvin Colton, *The Life and Times of Henry Clay* (2d ed., New York, 1846), I, 187.

Newspaper Advertisement

Lexington, August 19, 1798.

LOST, some short time past, between Winchester and this place, A RED MOROCCO POCKET BOOK, containing sundry papers, which can only be useful to the subscriber. It is unnecessary to describe them particularly, as any of them will shew to whom the book belongs.—I will give Five Dollars to any person who will deliver the book to me, or secure it so that I get it again. HENRY CLAY.

Lexington *Kentucky Gazette,* August 29, 1798.

Bond for Costs of Legal Suits

[October 31, 1798]

[Whereas certain suits are about to be commenced against Robert Russell[1] in the Quarter Sessions Court of Madison County at the complaint of: first, Andrew Torbert and John Niblow; second, Samuel Holstein; third, Alexander Henderson; and fourth, John Niblow as assignee of John Jones—the plaintiffs being non-residents[2] of Kentucky—they with Henry Clay are bound to pay the costs and damages if the afore-mentioned suits be adjudged for the defendant.]

ADS, by Clay as attorney for the plaintiffs. Madison Circuit Court, Box 13 (Bundle 25). An endorsement indicates that the suits were dismissed in February, 1799. The first and the last were brought for trespass and for debt, respectively; the nature of the others is not known. Fee bills from the Madison County Clerk to Clay, dated March and April, 1799 (ADS. DLC-TJC [DNA, M212, R15]), carried charges amounting to 25 cents for "Order of Dismission against Russel" and 54 cents for other fees in the suits brought by Holstein, by Torbert and Niblow, and by Niblow.

1 Of Madison County.

[2] Holstein may have been the resident of that name in the Valley Forge district of Pennsylvania. Henderson resided in Dumfries, Virginia. The others have not been found.

To David Bullock

Dr Sir Lexington December 27h 1798.

I will thank you to issue the following writs, if the defts reside in your County. I forget whether it is not Richard Jones who lives and keeps a tavern in Mount Sterling[1] If it is you will farther oblige me by forwarding the memorandum for the Writ to Capt. Harrison.[2] And you will do the same in the case of Winn if he shd. reside in Montgomery.[3]

William Leavy[4] vs Richard Jones Case Dam. £12. Indorse "This is an action upon the Case brought to recover the value of goods wares &c. furnished by the plt to the deft."

Same vs Thomas Winn Case Dam. £20. Same indorsement. I am Dr Sir Yr mo. ob. HENRY CLAY

ALS. NN. Addressed: "David Bullock Esqr clerk of Clarke." That is, Clark County, Kentucky.

[1] Jones was a resident of Montgomery County, Kentucky.

[2] Micajah Harrison, Clerk of Montgomery County for nearly thirty years.

[3] Thomas Winn lived in Clark County. Neither case found.

[4] Leavy, a native of Ireland, came to Lexington in 1788 and shortly became one of the leading merchants of the town. According to his son, Leavy found Clay "prompt in his attention to . . . business," and directed to the young lawyer "a Considerable amount of business from his [Leavy's] friends in Philadelphia." William A. Leavy, "A Memoir of Lexington and Its Vicinity," ed. by Nina M. Visscher, in Kentucky State Historical Society, *Register*, XL (1942), 266.

Bill of Complaint

Woodford County to wit [1799]

Elijah Pepper[1] complains of John Harris in custody &c. For that whereas on the day of in the year of our Lord 1799 at the parish of Kentucky and in the County aforesaid, two negro slaves, the property of the said John Harris,[2] by the command, with the knowledge and consent of the said John, with force & arms to wit staves &c. one Bay horse the property of the said plaintiff then and there being found, did beat wound & ill-treat so that he died, and other wrongs & injuries to the said plaintiff did, against the peace and dignity of the Commonwealth, and to the damage of the said plt £50 and therefore he brings suit &c

Pledges J Doe
&
R Roe

H. CLAY p.q.[3]

ADS. ViU—Alderman Library. Endorsed vertically on verso: "We of the Juror find for the Defendant John Christoph." John Christopher was a Woodford County farmer.

The document is included as representative of Clay's early legal work and because of the personalities involved.

1 The first of his family in Kentucky to engage in the distilling industry, in connection with which the name became famous.

2 Probably the John Harris whose daughter Judith was the wife of John Crittenden and mother of John Jordan Crittenden.

3 *Pro Querente*, "for the plaintiff."

Bond for Conveyance of Land Deed

[1799]

In consideration of the services of Henry Clay in managing a suit brought in Fleming Court against us and several others,[1] as the heirs of John Constant, by Isaac Constant & Jacob Constant, we Thomas Constant and Jacob Dawson do bind ourselves to convey to said Clay by deed with warranty against the heirs of the said Constant, sixty six acres of land, which have been sold by the said Isaac and Jacob Constant under a pretended claim, and are now in the possession of Sargent, which land was sold for one hundred and forty or one hundred and fifty pounds.

In witness whereof we have hereunto set our hands and seals the day of 1799. THOMAS CONSTANT {SL}

DS, in Clay's hand. KyLxT.

1 The nuncupative will of John Constant recorded in Bourbon County, Kentucky, October 21, 1788, had divided his property among unnamed children. Kentucky State Historical Society, *Register*, XLIII (1945), 351-52. Clay lost the case, which was argued in the September, 1800, term of Fleming Circuit Court and decided in the April, 1801, term. Fleming County (Kentucky) Circuit Court, Order Book A, 278-79.

To the Citizens of Fayette

[February, 1799]

A MEETING has been held at Bryan's station and a set of principles, and a plan for establishing them, dictated to you.[1] Before the public mind could judge of the propriety of either, a friend of them both, conscious of their frailty, undertook an apology for them. One of your countrymen, under the signature of "A Voter," who felt the hesitation which ought to accompany all new plans, recommended to your deliberation, and suggested to you doubts; but, instead of being answered with the coolness of dispassionate reason, he has been attacked by "Another Voter," with all the virulence of heat and animosity, and has been attempted to be barked off the ground before he had assumed a position. This is a consequence which might have been foreseen, and which alone forms a sufficient objection to pre-concerted plans. The country will be rent into parties, animosities will arise, and the seeds of perpetual enmity will be sown. And for what? To establish principles, without which you are told you will be inevitably ruined. But is the majority of the meeting at Bryan's station alone capable of piloting us through the ocean of danger—of perceiving principles which are inseparable from your happiness? Do they alone watch and the rest of the state sleep? Is not every freeman competent to judge of his own happiness, and capable of fixing upon the delegate who deserves his confidence? Does the author of the resolutions, and their apologist, wish to establish some new truth? Committees are not the organs for enlightening the public mind. Does he wish to preserve some old principle? The press is open, and the state will be his audience. Truth seeks not the prop of combination; her strength is internal, it is error alone that demands the support of intrigue and of external force.

The committee plan is an insult to your understanding. It amounts to this: The people of Fayette are ignorant of their own interests; or if they know them, like the orphan, or the lunatic, they want a guardian to preserve them; they are not to be trusted—the committee shall think for them. What is the consequence of this plan? The poor man will be entirely excluded from all share in the Bryan station government. He has not leisure to be travelling about to meetings and to committee elections. Engaged at home in pursuit of his daily labor, he can with difficulty yield to the superior calls of annual elections, & of courts. The wealthy man, who lives by the sweat of others, can alone attend them. In the habit of oppressing one race of men, when the poor are thus excluded, the transition to their oppression is short. This is not an imaginary fear. Nay, it is justified by the resolution of the meeting. Not a sentence, not a syllable, is uttered about the qualification of an elector. Although the resolutions embrace some of the first principles of government, not one glance is made to the situation of the poor. May we not fairly conclude that the object of the majority of the meeting is to make the possession of a freehold a necessary qualification? If not why thus silent? If this should be the fact how will the case stand —suppose the county contains 2100 voters, 1500 of whom should be in favor of universal suffrage, and 600 for a freehold qualification. If these 1500 who are inactive, should be equally divided between three tickets, and the 600 should be united in favor of one, they will effectually exclude every man in the state from the right to vote, if he does not possess a freehold. But further—the meetings of the militia and religious societies have been heretofore extremely partial. Upon the most liberal calculation, not above 600 will meet to elect committee men. These 600 then, upon the statement before made, will have it in their power to carry *any* measure they please.

The author of the answer to the voter seems extremely regardful of decorum. He wishes to enjoy the exclusive right of insulting your understandings. He offers you the grossest insult, at the moment when he expresses the greatest respect for you. Affecting popular witticism, and alluding to juvenile sports, he treats you as if you were devoid of common sense, and boys in reality. Can any thing be more consumately absurd than the alarm which he attempts to make about property? Had he confined his efforts to the malevolence of a whisper, or the insinuation of a nod, they might have been pitied and despised. But when he abuses the press by making it the vehicle of such foul terrors and calumny, respect for this barrier of freedom, and a desire of his own reformation will force a reply. He writes to establish a belief that the friends of gradual emancipation, (for I dare him to name an individual of influence who supports an immediate one) are actuated by improper motives, and that if they succeed all property will be endangered. I might dispense with any other answer than stating the principles of each party and appeal to the world for a decision as to the purity of motive. As to the danger of property this I again repeat is a contemptible subterfuge. Justice and policy both recommend a gradual emancipation. But say those who oppose it, admitting this to be the case, we are afraid to trust the convention; we have no security against encroachment upon other property; they will go farther, if you suffer them to emancipate your slaves gradually; they will divide all property. This argument, in plain English amounts to this: I have important business for my agent to do at Paris, but I have no assurance that he will say, when he gets there, "here will I stop," he may proceed on to Washington,[2] I will not therefore trust him to go at all. The legislature shall not possess a power of doing what justice and policy both dictate, that is gradual emancipation, lest it will do what neither justice nor policy recommends but what both of them forbid, that is pass laws for dividing property. Now my fellow citizens when an argument like this is urged to cheat posterity, out of their rights, you must conclude that the person who insists upon it, is either a lawyer, or that he thinks you are fools.

But to pursue the argument further. I presume it will be admitted that neither justice nor policy does recommend a division of all the property in the state, by agarian laws. It will not be denied that the man who manifests a disposition hostile to society, the murderer, ought to be lopped off. The legislature possess a power of inflicting, by the judiciary, this punishment. Nay they possess the most unlimited power over our lives. They can condemn the man who makes use of the argument I am now exposing to death for his absurdity. But, at the framing of any constitution, did you ever hear that the convention objected to give the legislature power to punish the criminal, lest it should abuse it, and order the death of an innocent man?—Again: whatever arguments are made use of upon this subject must be intended to produce conviction upon the minds of the people, because it is the people who act, it is they who govern; no law can be passed without their consent. Now let us suppose the whole state to be met, by their convention, and to listen to the argument about the danger of property. It would assume this shape: We the people being sovereign, are about to form ourselves into a political society, in order to secure our happiness, we may make our own laws by our delegates annually chosen; and if they dont please us, we can repeal them. There is a part of the people who are deprived of their rights, and who are degraded below brutes. The justice which is due from us and the good of the state, require that we should emancipate their posterity. But, as they have been called property, we think it unsafe to meddle with them, lest we should destroy other property, to which we owe no justice, and which the good of the state requires should be held sacred. We will not put the posterity of the present race of negroes in possession of their rights, because if we do, we are not sure but we may afterwards proceed farther and emancipate all the hogs in the state, or divide them amongst ourselves. We will therefore tye up our hands. We have no confidence in ourselves. This is precisely the way in which the author of the above piece would have you reason. He is afraid to trust you. If he is not where is the danger to other property, by your complying with the calls of humanity and justice? If he is not why this clamor about the danger of property; why cannot he trust you with the power of making any law upon the subject of emancipation, which you may now or hereafter think proper? To be consistent he ought to require the insertion of an article in the constitution forbidding the legislature to inflict the punishment of death upon any person but the criminal, lest they should extend it to the honest man. But he is so completely absorbed by considerations of property that he is not only willing to yield up liberty, but life itself to the protection of it.

The truth is, a constitution which ought to embrace fundamental eternal principles, should be confined to the enumeration and distribution of powers. If it descends to the regulation of minutia there is no end. It will encircle the whole business of legislation. If it undertakes, the patronage of one species of property, all other property will have a right to demand the same protection, and it must then engage in all the perplexity of regulating the hereditary succession, the transfer, the transmutation, and all the other incidents to which property is subject, and there will be no use for ordinary legislatures.

The author above mentioned, affects to believe that the object of the friends of emancipation, is an immediate one, although they expressly declare the contrary. And he deduces this belief from their reasoning which he says will apply as forcibly to an immediate as to gradual emancipation. The rights of man must always be the same. The same reasons urged by the present, might have been urged by the past, and may by the future generations in favor of their liberty. But, although rights are immutable, cases may be conceived in which the enjoyment of them is improper. That of the present race of negroes is one. Thirty thousand slaves, without preparation for enjoying the rights of a freeman, without property, without principle, let loose upon society would be wretched themselves, and render others miserable. But from the most of these objections will their posterity be exempt. They may receive the education of the poor orphan, which instilling principle, will qualify them for the exercise of the rights of a citizen. So that a man may advocate a gradual and oppose an immediate emancipation (as is actually the case,) upon principle.

If my fellow citizens you believe with me, that the committee measure will certainly produce some, and if it is an object to render a freehold qualification necessary, may produce great, evil, you will reject the plan as a dangerous novelty, and with the boldness and independence of freemen vote undismayed by the insidious cry of alarm, and undeluded by the whine of interest. SCAEVOLA.

Lexington *Kentucky Gazette,* February 28, 1799. As the date for electing delegates to the constitutional convention drew near, debate became warmer and numerous anonymous contributors discussed the issue.

1 On January 26 a meeting of the conservative faction, held at Bryan's Station in preparation for the election of delegates from Fayette County, agreed that "the only proper and honest object of a convention, in a state enjoying a regular organized government, is by amendments made to the existing constitution, more effectually to secure the liberties and every species of property, which the free citizens of that state are entitled to and possessed of; and not to impair, or destroy them, or any of them." In addition, it proposed a plan whereby "each religious society, and the free male inhabitants above the age of twenty-one years, living within the bounds of each militia company within this county" would elect two delegates to meet as a committee at Lexington on the third Saturday in March for the purpose of choosing "a general ticket of proper persons" to represent Fayette County in the convention. Lexington *Kentucky Gazette,* January 31, 1799.

2 Paris and Washington, Kentucky.

Promissory Note to William Irvine

[February 8, 1799]

For value received I promise to pay or cause to be paid to William Irvine or order on the tenth day of September next one hundred and twenty dollars. As witness my hand and seal this 8h. day of February 1799.

Test HENRY CLAY {L.S.}

JAMES SPEED JR.[1]

ADS. DLC-TJC (DNA, M212, R15). Irvine was the first Clerk of the Madison County (Kentucky) Court.

1 Probably the son of Judge James Speed of the Mercer County (Kentucky) Court of Quarter Sessions.

Fee Bill from Thomas Bodley

Henry Clay Esqr.	1799. March.
To the Clerk of Lexington District Court	Dr.
Copy of a Deed from Smarts to Bradley with Indorsments 100. Copy of 3 bonds and Assignments & Certificates[1] 112½	212½
E.E.	$2 " 12½

THOS. BODLEY C.L.D.C.

ADS. DLC-TJC (DNA, M212, R15). Bodley was later Clerk of the Fayette Circuit Court for many years.

Fee bills are numerous among the Clay papers in DLC-TJC. They will hereafter be entered only when of particular interest.

1 Robert and George Smart, watchmakers, to Robert Bradley, tavernkeeper, all of Lexington, an assignment of bonds, the assignment dated February 13, 1799, recorded March 1, 1799. Fayette District Court, Deed Book B, 230-31.

Endorsement on Fee Bill from Thomas Bodley to Peacock Wrenshall and Company

[March, 1799]

I am not Security for the Plts; but if I get any money of theirs (as it is probable I may) I will pay this. H. CLAY

AES. DLC-TJC (DNA, M212, R15). On verso of Bodley's bill against Peacock Wrenshall and Company, a Philadelphia mercantile firm, for $5.47, covering his charges in their case against Edward West and Jesse Guthrie, merchants of Lexington. In February, 1800, Clay endorsed another fee bill involving the same parties, "H Clay to pay" (AN. DLC-TJC [DNA, M212, R15]), amounting to 75 cents.

Property Deed from Thomas Hart to Samuel Young

[May 15, 1799]

[Indenture by which Thomas Hart of Lexington transfers to Dr. Samuel Young of Hagerstown, Maryland, for the sum of £600, a house and lot of 25-foot frontage, adjoining a brick house "wherein Doctor Pindle[1] now lives," near the Public Square in Hagerstown. Recorded May 18, 1799, before Thomas Bodley, Clerk of Lexington District Court.]

DS, in Clay's hand. KyU-Wilson Collection. The document is representative of many such deeds drawn by Clay. It holds particular interest in that Clay had become Hart's son-in-law on April 11.

Hart, like Clay, a native of Hanover County, Virginia, had lived in North Carolina during his early years and had moved, first to Maryland, where he had been the mercantile partner of Nathaniel Rochester, and then, in 1794, to Kentucky, where as one of the organizers of the Transylvania Company, he held extensive property, mercantile, and manufacturing interests.

1 Dr. Richard Pindell (1755-1823), a surgeon in the Revolutionary War, married Eliza Hart, sister of Mrs. Henry Clay, and attained prominence as a physician at Hagerstown. In 1813 he moved to Lexington and began practice there, subsequently entering into partnership with Dr. Frederick Ridgely.

Fee Bill from William Irvine

[June, 1799]

ADS. DLC-TJC (DNA, M212, R15). Endorsed: ". . . H. Clay Esqr. will pay." The fees, amounting to $2.71, directed against John McClenahan, relate to the case of McClenahan *vs.* Patrick Hamilton, a suit to collect on a note dated March 4, 1774, for payment on a 1000-acre patent to land on Muddy Creek in Madison County, Kentucky. Opened in Madison Circuit Court in April, 1799, with Clay as one of two attorneys for the plaintiff (bill of complaint, ADS by Clay), the case was finally dismissed in March, 1808, for want of prosecution, the defendant protesting that he had not received patent to the tract. Madison Circuit Court, Box 27 (Bundle 54). Hamilton at the signing of the note lived on the Monongahela River in western Virginia; McClenahan, a resident of Augusta County, Virginia, held large tracts in Kentucky under surveys made prior to opening of the Virginia land office.

Newspaper Advertisement

To be Leased, July, 1799.

FOR a term of years, one thousand acres of land on Poages creek—one thousand acres on Pleasant run, and five hundred and fifty-six acres on Highland creek, all in Logan county, the property of Francis Brooke.[1] The object of these leases is to put the land, or a part of it, in a state for cultivation. Advantageous contracts may be made by applying in Lexington, to HENRY CLAY.

Lexington *Kentucky Gazette,* July 11, 1799.

1 Francis Taliaferro Brooke, who became a distinguished jurist in his native Virginia, was a younger brother of Robert Brooke, under whom Clay studied law and in whose home he lived for a time. The friendship which sprang up between Clay and the younger Brooke endured until the death of the latter in 1851.

As a result of his services in the Revolutionary War, Brooke received in 1784 a military warrant for 2,666⅔ acres of land in Kentucky. He actually acquired 2,556⅔ acres, surveyed early in 1785. Willard R. Jillson (comp.), *The Kentucky Land Grants: A Systematic Index to All of the Land Grants Recorded in the State Land Office at Frankfort, Kentucky, 1782-1924* (Filson Club *Publication* no. 33; Louisville, 1925), 26; Willard R. Jillson (comp.), *Old Kentucky Entries and Deeds: A Complete Index to All of the Earliest Land Entries, Military Warrants, Deeds and Wills of the Commonwealth of Kentucky* (Filson Club *Publication* no. 34; Louisville, 1926), 319.

Order on Gwyn R. Tompkins

Mr. Tomkins Sheriff of Fayette [July 8, 1799]

I have this 8h. day of July 1799 sold to Mr. Henry Clay the Judgment which I obtained at the last Quarter Sessions Court of Fayette agt. James Wallace for one hundred dollars and Costs in a

Mess James and Richard Smith

To Henry Clay Atto at Law Dr—

1801	To my fee for you in your suit against Nancarrow & Bastrop	£3:
	To my fee for you in your suit agt Janüary (being dismissed)	1:10:
	To Taxes upon the writs in the above cases.	:6:
		£4:16

Received of John W. Hunt Esqr. the above in full.

H Clay

Lexington —

Original in the Hunt-Morgan Collection, Margaret I. King Library, University of Kentucky.

Gent

Mr. James Ogilbie, on the 7th inst., inclosed to me $400, the proceeds of two of his orations recently pronounced in Lexington, deducting incidental charges, with a request to apply the same to the use of the Lexington Library. Accompanying his letter was a list of books which he recommended ~~[illegible]~~ as worthy of a place on your shelves. I have taken measures to procure immediately such of them as you do not already possess, and when received I will have the pleasure of delivering them to the Librarian & submitting a statement of their cost &c.

Yr. ob. Servt.

H. Clay

12th. July 1811

Reproduced through the courtesy of the owner, Thomas D. Clark, Lexington, Kentucky.

suit of assault & battery,[1] you will therefore pay the amount of the said Judgment to said Clay. I am Sir Yr mo ob.

Teste WILLIAM JAMESON

ANDREW GREEN[2]

DS, in Clay's hand. DLC-TJC (DNA, M212, R15). Tompkins subsequently represented Fayette County in the State legislature.

1 Case not found. In 1800 Wallace owned property in both Henderson and Scott counties; Jameson had holdings in Logan and most of the Bluegrass counties.

2 Married in Fayette County in 1803.

Assignment by Henry Williams

[September 10, 1799]

Having heretofore assigned to Henry Clay the bond of which this is a substantial copy; and as the same was assigned to me & Philip Roberts[1] jointly, and as I have purchased the Philip Roberts interest in the said Bond, I do hereby for value received of Henry Clay assign the whole of the said Bond to him. In witness whereof I have hereunto set my hand & affixed my seal this 10h. Septr. 1799.

his

Test HENRY X WILLIAMS {L.S.}

RICHD HENDERSON[2] mark

ES, in Clay's hand. DLC-TJC (DNA, M212, R15). Williams was a resident of Montgomery County, Kentucky. The assignment is written on verso of a copy of a bond, the original of which, dated October 18, 1791, bound "Matthew Payne of Davidson County in North Carolina" (now Tennessee) to "Richard Gordan of Madison County in Virginia" (now Kentucky) in the sum of £100 Virginia money to insure delivery by Payne of a "good and sufficient Deed" to one hundred acres of land in Madison County. The bond was assigned by Gordon to one William Bryant, and by him to Williams and Roberts.

1 Also of Montgomery County.

2 Possibly the Richard Henderson of Harrison County, Kentucky.

To James Hughes

Saturday morning [September 14, 1799]

H. Clay encloses Mr. Hughes the last letter from P. Short,[1] to the propositions contained in which H. C. requests an answer.

AN. DLC-Short Family Papers (DNA, M212, R22). Addressed: "James Hughes Esqr. Present." Endorsed on cover: "Copy of Shorts letter respecting State lands—to Henry Clay & my Answer.—Septr. ye. 14th 1799." Hughes was one of the outstanding lawyers in Lexington and was the compiler (in 1803) of the first Kentucky law reports.

1 Peyton Short. His letter has not been found.

Promissory Note to Jesse Bledsoe

[October 26, 1799]

Six months after date I promise to pay to Jesse Bledsoe or order with Interest from the time it becomes due 'till paid the sum of sixty pounds Current money.

As witness my hand & seal this 26h Octr. 1799

Attest HENRY CLAY {L.S.}

JAMES H. STEWART[1]

[Endorsements on verso][2]

Credit on the within Note for Ten Dollars. J. BLEDSOE

. . .

Recd. on accot of the within One Hundred Dollars Lexington April 1. 1800 $100, WILLIAM MOTT[3]

Received this 12. Feby 1801 of H. Clay £28.2.9½ the balance of the within for W. Mott— JNO. M BOGGS[4]

ADS. DLC-TJC (DNA, M212, R15). Endorsed on verso: "Clay to Bledsoe Note. 200.$ & R[eceipt]." Bledsoe, a native of Virginia and a graduate of Transylvania University, was an attorney in Lexington. He subsequently served as Secretary of State for Kentucky, United States Senator, State Senator, circuit judge, and professor of law at Transylvania.

1 Printer and merchant, editor of the Lexington *Kentucky Herald*.

2 All AES.

3 William Mott, Philadelphia cloth merchant, to whom Bledsoe had assigned the note.

4 Lexington merchant, tailor, and town trustee, who had on other occasions served as agent for nonresident owners of Kentucky lands.

Bond for John Clay

Thomas Kennedy Plaintiff [October 30, 1799]
against In Debt
John Clay Defendant

Henry Clay of Fayette County came into Court and undertook for the Defendant that in case he shall be cast in this suit he shall satisfy and pay the Costs and Condemnation of the Court or render his body to prison in execution for the same or in failure thereof that he the said Henry will pay it for him.

Fayette Circuit Court, Order Book A, 262. John Clay, Henry's older brother, was at this time a merchant in Lexington. The suit apparently resulted from his purchase of a horse from Kennedy, of Madison County.

To William Taylor

Dr Sir, Lexington 16th. November 1799

Yours of the 24th last month I received[1] by the last Mail and should have answered it immediately by the return of the post, but was desirous of first obtaining some information for you as to the circumstances of Adam Shepherd and Heugh & Ralstone.[2]

Before this time you must have received my letter acknowledging the receipt of Satterwhites note,[3] and also another letter informing you that by the advice and direction of Mr. Andrew Holmes[4] I had taken a mortgage of Satterwhite upon two houses and lots in this place and a negro fellow to secure your debt and one due to Mr. Holmes himself, and had in consequence thereof extended to Satterwhite a farther credit. And by my last letter I requested of you to inform me whether you would take produce of any description (but more particularly cordage) in payment of your debt, as Satterwhite had a prospect of selling the house for that article; this request I beg leave again to repeat, observing however at the same time that you need not be induced to take it under any apprehension that the debt is insecure, because it is now unquestionably safe, and if he should fail to pay at the times agreed on I shall be able to recover a Judgment and get the money during the next fall in the common course of business.

From the information I have received with respect to Adam Shepherd, I have no doubt of his ability to pay any sum under £10.000. As to the circumstances of Heugh & Ralstone they are more doubtful. It is said that Heugh has made over his property to Ralstone, and intends leaving the State, but this will not operate against your debt, and I am induced to believe from what I have heard that they are at present fully competent to pay any debt within moderate bounds. Heugh & Ralstone have settled near Louisville.

Neither of these houses is immediately within the circuit of my practice, but I will nevertheless attend to the collection of your debts against them.

It is proper for me to inform you that in the collection of all debts, it is customary with the Attos. in this Country to have a commission upon the amount, of 5 P Cent at least.

The sooner you forward me your claims if you conclude to send them on to me, against those houses the better, as our Courts begin very early in the year. I am Dr Sir Yr. mo. ob HENRY CLAY

ALS. DLC-HC (DNA, M212, R1). Addressed: "William Taylor Esqr. Merchant Baltimore." Endorsed: "... Henry Clay 23 January, 1800." Taylor at this time enjoyed an extensive trade, both foreign and domestic.

1 Not found.

2 Shepherd, in partnership with Austin Hubbard, conducted a mercantile business in Bardstown, Kentucky. John Heugh and Alexander Ralston were merchants in Louisville.

3 Mann Satterwhite operated a general store opposite the Market House in Lexington.

4 A Lexington merchant, who also operated a brewery on Mulberry (Limestone) Street. The mortgage was recorded as Satterwhite to Andrew and Jonathan Holmes, for two town lots and slaves, dated October 31, 1799. Fayette District Court, Deed Book C, 26.

To John Overton

Dr Sir Lexington 10th. December 1799.

In behalf of Col Hart I inclose you two Judgments against

Drumgole, Stewart and Jones, obtained by him and Saml. Price (since deceased.) in the District Court of this place.[1] His wish is to have suits commenced against Drumgole, who lives in your State, and who is the only man of property amongst them. I believe the Copies are authenticated in the manner prescribed by Congress.[2] As the Judgments were obtained by confession, copies of them only, without the whole of the record, appeared to me to be sufficient. There are some credits which you will find indorsed on the Judgments. Shortly after they were obtained Drumgole, who lived near the line between this State and yours, moved over on the other side, and carried with him his personal property. Executions have been issued and the money which has been received was made by virtue of them. We shall continue to issue executions in order to seize any property which may come in the way.

Col. Hart has understood that Drumgole designs leaving Tenassee and intends going to Natchez. This, if it be true, will make it necessary to use all possible dispatch, and that the officer who serves the writs should be particular in taking sufficient bail.

I am authorized by Col Hart to assure you that besides a liberal fee, you shall be handsomely compensated for any extraordinary exertions you may make.

Drumgole I believe lives near the line on the road between Nashville and Logan.

It will be advisable to conceal the intention of bringing suits against him, as he may fly should he know it. I am Dr Sir Yr. mo. ob.

HENRY CLAY.

P.S. Should security for the costs of the suits be necessary Mr. J. Coleman of Nashville will do me the favor to become security.[3] I presume as Mr. Price is dead, the suit will be brought in Col Hart's name only. If however it is necessary to bring it in the name of his representative, you will insert the name of Thomas Hart junr.[4] who is his administrator.

ALS. PHC-Charles Roberts Autograph Collection. Addressed: "John Overton Esqr. Atto. at Law near Nashville Care of Mr. Bradford." A native of Virginia, John Overton studied law in Mercer County, Kentucky, 1787-1789, and for the next fifteen years practiced in Nashville, Tennessee. He became a judge and, largely through land speculation, reputedly the wealthiest man in Tennessee. He was a business associate and warm friend of Andrew Jackson. Joshua W. Caldwell, *Sketches of the Bench and Bar of Tennessee* (Knoxville, 1898), 77-79.

1 James Dromgoole (spelling varies), an early settler in Logan County, Kentucky, was a merchant in Russellville, had extensive land holdings, and held at least one minor political office. A son-in-law of the notorious Philip Alston, he is said to have had connections with one or more of the outlaw gangs of that era. Ayers Stewart and Richard Jones were for a time Dromgoole's business partners. Alex C. Finley, *The History of Russellville and Logan County* (Russellville, 1878, 1879, 1890), Book I, 45; Book II, 40; Edward Coffman, *The Story of Russellville* (Russellville, 1931), 9, 11, 13; Margaret B. Stratton, *Place-Names of Logan County and Oft-Told Tales* (Russellville, 1950), 10. Price was the husband of Hart's daughter Susannah. While on a trip to New Orleans in the fall of 1799, he succumbed to yellow fever.

2 "An Act to prescribe the mode in which the public Acts, Records, and judicial Proceedings in each State, shall be authenticated so as to take effect in every other State," approved May 26, 1790. 1 *U. S. Stat.* 122.
3 Joseph Coleman later became the first mayor of Nashville.
4 Clay's brother-in-law.

Power of Attorney from Peacock Wrenshall and Company

[January 15, 1800]

Know all men by these presents That we Peacock Wrenshall and Company have nominated, Constituted, and appointed and by these presents Do Nominate Constitute and appoint Henry Clay of Lexington in Kentucky our true and lawful Attorney for us and in our names to demand sue for recover and receive whatever Sum or Sums of money may be due to us by Bond, bill, Note, or otherwise from Edward West and Jesse Guthrie or either of them of the Said Town of Lexington And we do further Authorise and empower the said Henry Clay to make any Contract with the said West and Guthrie or either of them which he may deem most to our Interest for securing the said debt or debts or any part thereof which may be so due as aforesaid by Compounding the same or granting indulgence or in any other manner which to his discretion and Judgement may seem proper And when the said debt or debts are so Collected to grant Acquittances and discharges for the same Hereby Ratifying and confirming whatever our said Attorney may do for us in the premisses— In Testimony whereof we have hereunto set our hands and Seals this 15th. day of January 1800—

Signed Sealed & Delivered In presence of
THOS BODLEY

JOHN WRENSHALL {L.S.}[1]
for
Peacock Wrenshall & Co.

Fayette District Court, Deed Book C, 98. Recorded January 15, 1800.
1 A native of England who had moved to Philadelphia in 1794 and, soon afterward, to Pittsburgh. He later returned to Philadelphia, then went back to Pittsburgh; he operated as a merchant in both places.

Receipt from Thomas Y. Bryant

[February 14, 1800]

Received this 14 Feby. 1800 of Henry Clay thirty five dollars being the price of a Carpet purchased by him from Mrs. Hare belonging to the estate of the late A. Hare.

For M. Hare
T. Y. BRYANT

DS, in Clay's hand. DLC-TJC (DNA, M212, R15). Thomas Y. Bryant resided in Lexington at this time; shortly thereafter he moved to Frankfort. He had received power of attorney from Andrew Hare, Lexington merchant, October 23, 1799. Fayette District Court, Deed Book C, 140.

Memorandum of Suits Given to Clay by John Breckinridge

20th. Feby. 1800

Dale vs Campbell &c. Chy[1]—Contract inclosed in the papers; by which I am get ¼. I am not certain, but I am security of the Costs of suit—Mr. Clay may have my whole Intr. in this claim; he standing exactly in my shoes. The land is of great value if obtained.

Hardin vs Sholls Heirs &c. Chy.[2]—The contract is inclosed—I am to get 1/3—I will divide the spoil with Mr. Clay—Hardin ought immediately to ansr. Sholls intos. & the suit set for hearing

C. Douglas vs David Hughes[3]—This demand is founded on an arbitration bond for 1000 acres of Land—I am to get 1/3.—Contract inclosed. Mr. Clay may have my whole Intr.—No suit is yet commenced. Hughes lives on Flat Creek in Montgomery.

Z. South's papers vs. Spurr &c.[4]—Contract which is inclosed will show the nature of the demand. Mr. Clay may have my whole Intr.—No suit is yet brought—South lives near the contested premises in the neighbourhood of Boones Station.

Robt. Clarke ads Hinds	Chy[5]
Matson vs Paytons Devisees	Chy[6]
Gatewoods Exrs vs Campbell	Do.[7]
E. Smith vs McDiffit	Do.[8]
Hunter ads Shriver	Do.[9]
Castle ads Spiers	Do.[10]
Tanner vs Clay	Do.[11]
Wm. Frazer ads Steel	Do.[12] this you are already empd. in by Steel.

These last 8 Suits I wish Mr. Clay to take charge of. None of them are ready for trial. I wish them made ready, & taken off my Hands. I have recd fees in most of them; altho small. It may be still understood by the Clients, that I will assist at the argument; & I will endeavour to get them to give *refreshing* fees (they are nearly all suits from the late Court of appeals) ; and if they do,—Mr. Clay shall have what may hereafter be advanced by them.

For J. BRECKINRIDGE

Mr. Henry Clay.

DS. DLC-TJC (DNA, M212, R15). Endorsed on verso by Clay: "... all in the Lexington Dist. Court; & its bounds. ..." Breckinridge, who had studied law under Chancellor Wythe, Clay's early mentor, had emigrated from Virginia and settled near Lexington in 1792. He was one of the authors of the Kentucky Resolutions, in 1801 was chosen United States Senator from Kentucky, and in 1805 became Attorney General of the

United States. His sudden death the following year cut short his promising career at the age of 46.

1 William Dale, Breckinridge's client, was resident in Georgia, but owned property in Woodford County, Kentucky. His suit against John Campbell and James Speed was continued until the March Term, 1804, when it was dismissed. Fayette Circuit Court, Order Book A (1798-1800), 502-503; Order Book B, *passim*; Order Book A (1803-1804), 453. Colonel John Campbell, a native of Ireland, had emigrated to America at an early age and become one of the earliest Kentucky land speculators. His vast holdings included part of the Louisville townsite. He was a member of the Virginia legislature for several terms, of the Kentucky Constitutional Convention in 1792, and thereafter of the Kentucky legislature. He died in Fayette County in 1799.

2 Enos Hardin, Breckinridge's client, of Franklin County, *vs.* the heirs of William Scholl (spelling varies). Dismissed by mutual consent of the litigants in September, 1801. Fayette Circuit Court, Order Book B, 212. Depositions in Clay's hand dated August 2, 1800, answering Scholl's interrogatories, are located CSmH.

3 Not found.

4 Zedikiah South, heir of John South, deceased, brought suit against Richard Spurr *et al.*, in 1801, but the case thereafter drops from sight. Fayette Circuit Court, Order Book B, 167.

5 In view of the death of Andrew Hynes, his case against Robert Clarke *et al.* was revived at the September Term, 1801, in the name of Armistead Churchill *et al.*, Hynes' heirs; but no subsequent action was reported. Fayette Circuit Court, Order Book B, 194. Clarke was Justice of the Court of Quarter Sessions of Clark County, Kentucky, 1795-1796.

6 The case of James Matson against George Martin *et al.*, heirs and devisees of Timothy Peyton, a land dispute begun in 1795, was decided in favor of Matson in September, 1803.

7 In 1801 Margaret Gateswood, executrix of Andrew Gateswood, brought suit against John Campbell, James Sullivan, and Alexander Robinson on a land claim. The case was subsequently revived against Richard Taylor, executor, and the heirs of John Campbell, deceased. Judgment was rendered in favor of the plaintiff at the June Term, 1803; Campbell's cross suit, instituted at this time, was apparently dropped. Fayette Circuit Court, Order Book B (1801), 51-52; Order Book A (1803-1804), 205, 278, 396, 407-408, 513.

8 Enoch Smith, Breckinridge's client, one of Henderson's company of adventurers to Kentucky, 1775, and subsequently a resident of Montgomery County, had for many years been in litigation against John McDiffit *et al.* on a land claim in Scott County. Smith won judgment at the September Term, 1801. Fayette Circuit Court, Order Book A (1800), 391; B (1801), 212.

9 Not found. 10 Not found.

11 The case had been running at least five years, with Breckinridge representing Green Clay, of Madison County, Kentucky, a cousin of Henry's father. In February, 1801, John Tanner and Eli Cleveland brought a chancery action against Clay, in Fayette Circuit Court. The case was remanded to the rule docket, and thereafter apparently dropped.

12 In 1803 William Steele brought suit against William Frazier, Breckinridge's client, in Fayette Circuit Court on a land dispute, a longstanding action transferred at this time from the District Court. Frazier, who lost the case, then appealed and won before the Kentucky Court of Appeals in May, 1804. Fayette Circuit Court, Order Book A (1803-1804), 70; 2 *Ky. Reports* (Sneed) 334-35.

Memorandum of Court Action

[March, 1800]

Wm. Taylor John Blackford & Wm. Young Lewis late merchants & partners trading under the Form of Blackford Lewis & Co.[1] v John Heugh, and Alexr Ralston, Merchants and partners under the firm of Heugh & Ralston Case $4,079:7 Dam $10,000. Indorse this is an action on the Case: Mr J Martin[2] Pays Costs. H. CLAY.

United States District Court of Kentucky, Memorandum Book for Thomas Tunstall, Clerk, 1799 to and including the March Term, 1801, p. 63, KyLoF. Neither the note nor the signature is in Clay's hand.

[1] Of Baltimore. Taylor was now in business alone.
[2] Possibly John Martin, Virginia veteran of the Revolution, pioneer Lexingtonian, Judge of the Court of Quarter Sessions.

To John Overton

Dr Sir Lexington Sunday morning [March, 1800]

Col. Hart will hand you the Transcripts of the Records against Dromgoole &c.[1] If there should be any error in the proceedings it will not avail them; because by an Act of the Assembly of this State, to reduce into one the several acts for preventing vexatious suits & regulating proceedings in civil cases, § 44. a Judgment by confession is rendered equal to a release of errors.[2]

Col. Hart will also deliver to you my note against Mathew Payne. I believe I mentioned to you that in taking the note I omitted to mention what Currency, altho' I intended this Currency. If you have an opportunity I will thank you either to write or speak to him in such a way as to draw from him a confession of the true amount, as I am not sufficiently acquainted with him to know whether he has honesty enough to correct the error. I have no positive way of proving it. I had a demand against him on account of Land. A suit was brought against him in the County Court of Davidson in the name I think of Richard Gordon,[3] and the depositions which are filed in that cause (brought for my benefit) make the value of the land 500 dollars. This estimate he consented to, and when I was at Nashville,[4] agreed to pay me between 90 and 100 dollars, which he did in Cash & a watch and executed his Note for the balance, which with the Costs amounted to $411:50.

Mr. McBean,[5] who was at Nashville a few days since, & whom I had requested, to call & see Payne, informs me that he promised to have 200 dollars ready by the first of this month.

If the circumstances & the character of the man are such that there is no danger of losing the money, I do not wish you to distress him by a suit, provided he makes a partial payment immediately. In this case you will be so good as to forward me whatever he pays (after deducting your fee) by the first safe opportunity.

Wishing you a pleasant return, I am Sir Yr. mo ob.

HENRY CLAY

ALS. THi. Addressed: "John Overton Esqr." Endorsed, presumably by Overton: "Henry Clay Mar. 1800."

[1] See above, Clay to Overton, December 10, 1799.
[2] The act, approved December 19, 1796, may be found in William Littell (comp.), *The Statute Law of Kentucky* (5 vols., Frankfort, 1809-1819), I, 481-502.
[3] For the origins of this controversy, involving Clay, Payne, and Gordon, see above, Assignment by Williams, September 10, 1799, note.
[4] During the previous autumn. Bernard Mayo, *Henry Clay, Spokesman of the New West* (Boston, 1937), 93n.

5 William MacBean, a native of England, was at this time a partner in a firm that operated stores in Lexington and Nashville.

Receipt from John Overton

March 4h. 1800.

Recd. of Henry Clay Esqr. of Lexington a Bond executed by Mathew Payne to said Clay for one hundred and twenty three pounds nine Shillings payable on demand, and dated the 16h. October 1799 –The said Bond under under [*sic*] Seal and attested by Joseph Coleman–Received the above for the purpose of collecting the same of Payne JNO. OVERTON

DS. DLC-TJC, 2d Series, vol. 3.

Bond for John Clay

[March 18, 1800]

Henry Clay of Lexington in Fayette County this day came into Court and undertook for the Defendants[1] that in case they shall be cast in this Suit they shall satisfy and pay the condemnation of the Court or render their bodys to prison in execution for the same or on failure thereof that the said Henry Clay will do it for them.

United States District Court of Kentucky, Book B, 305 (Ky-U, microfilm from the original then in U.S. District Court, Frankfort, Kentucky).

1 In the suit brought by Alexander Fulton of Baltimore against John Clay and Company.

Authorization to Practice in Federal District Court

[March 20, 1800]

On the motion of Henry Clay he is permitted to practice as an attorney at law in this Court, who thereupon took the Oath to support the Constitution of the United States, and also the Oath of an attorney at Law.

United States District Court of Kentucky, Book B, 312.

To Peyton Short

Dr Sir Lexington 21st. March 1800

I returned last evening from Frankfort. With some difficulty I procured a continuance of the motion which was intended to have been made by Jackson & Young to dissolve your injunction. From a perusal of their answers, in which they positively affirm that it was by your express permission, that they received assignments of the whole of the three bonds, I am fearful that we shall be unable to sustain the injunction. Their answer too is corroborated by the deposition of Ro. Haskins,[1] the Green river witness, who swears that in his presence you gave to Trabue the most unqualified authority to transfer your bonds.[2] And the whole of this is strengthened & in some measure confirmed by your letters, one of which, exhibited in the cause, apologizes for your not paying the *whole* of the bonds and seeks farther forbearance.

Under this statement of the case, equity, regarding Jackson and Young as fair purchasers, acting in confidence of your permission and promises, in reliance upon which they extended to you some indulgence, and viewing you as being a *lite pendente* purchaser of a disputed tract of land,[3] with a full knowledge of the dispute, will feel itself disposed to withhold the relief which you have sought for against Jackson and Young; more especially as admitting your equity to be equal with theirs, you have security from Trabue, whose circumstances it is said have become doubtful.

If however you can destroy the evidence of Haskins, or by any other means prove that you only permitted Trabue to assign one of the bonds, I am still of opinion that you may be relieved as to the other two. At any rate if the injunction should be dissolved, we can obtain in this same suit a decree against Trabue for the value of the lossed land. For this purpose I have obtained an order directing the surveyor to ascertain the quantity of land lossed, which you will have executed, previously giving notice, by the next Court. You will also take affidavits, giving notice also, to prove the value of the land as connected with the other part of your purchase.

In Ormsbys & Rhea's Suits[4] I confessed Judgments for you, upon the plaintiffs Counsel consenting to stay execution three months, and upon a reservation of equity. For this suspension of the execution you are more indebted to a disposition in Col. Todd,[5] their Counsel, to oblige you than to any effort of mine; because it was problematical whether I should ha[ve] got the suits continued. If you will obtain Copies of the Judgments, by the May Woodford Court, I will examine them in conjunction with you, and if they be for too much we will then obtain Injunctions. Yr's with respect H. CLAY

P. S. your suit with Fowler is in the Court of Appeals[6]—carried there since I last conversed with you about it. H. C.

ALS. DLC-Short Family Papers (DNA, M212, R22). Addressed on verso: "Peyton Short Esqr. Green-field Woodford [County]."

1 Robert Haskins, of Green County, Kentucky.

2 Earlier, Short had purchased two tracts of land from Trabue, giving bonds as part of the transaction. Short contested payment of the bonds, which had been assigned by Trabue to Jackson and Young, on the ground that part of the land for which the bonds had been given had been lost through a decree, by the District Court of

Franklin County, to adverse claimants. Short attempted through litigation to have his contract with Trabue vacated or to obtain compensation for the lands to which he did not obtain title. The Court of Appeals sustained a decision of the lower court against him. He had not actually been evicted from the land in question, nor had he presented evidence concerning the area of land allegedly lost. Peyton Short *vs.* John Jackson *et al.*, 2 *Ky. Reports* (Sneed) 192-95. John Jackson, a native of Scotland, was a pioneer merchant of Versailles, Woodford County. His associate in this litigation may have been his father-in-law, Col. Richard Young.

3 Purchaser of land involved in a pending suit.

4 Cases not found. They probably involved either Stephen or Peter Ormsby, long prominent in Louisville, Kentucky, and John Rhea, a lawyer and early settler of eastern Tennessee, member of Congress, 1803-1815, 1817-1823.

5 Thomas Todd of Frankfort, Clerk of the Court of Appeals; appointed Associate Justice of the United States Supreme Court, March 3, 1807.

6 Case not found. John Fowler, native of Virginia and Revolutionary War veteran, pioneer Kentuckian and early resident of Lexington, was a member of Congress, 1797 to 1807, and postmaster of Lexington, 1814 to 1822. He speculated heavily in land and for many years operated "Fowler's Gardens," a commercial recreation center, including a racetrack, on the outskirts of Lexington.

To William Taylor

Mr William Taylor Lexington 30h. March 1800

When I went to the Fœderal Court a few days past I found that the Marshall had omitted to execute the Writ upon Heugh & Ralston.[1] The apology he made was that the Court was so near, and the place of their residence so distant, that he was apprehensive he should not meet with them, and in that case he should have to defray the expences of the journey without a reimbursement. I found that this last objection was most influential and in order to obviate it, I proposed to one of his Deputies that if he would go and execute the Writ during the then Court I would give him, besides his legal fees, ten dollars, and that if he did not meet with the defendants his expences should be defrayed him. He went accordingly and I am glad to inform you succeeded in executing the Writ, and took bail which is said to be very good, George Wilson and John Estain.[2] I was the more anxious to get the Writ executed, because I had understood that one of the parties designed leaving the State, and some of their other Creditors were extremely urgent in the prosecution of suits against them. The amount of bail which we have taken is $5000.

I am satisfied that it was for your interest that I should give the additional ten dollars to the officer and have no doubt that you will approve of it.

According to the laws of this State, an affidavit taken without notice annexed to the bottom of an account, is not legal evidence of the justness of the account. But the witness must be examined to prove it, under a commission issuing from the Court, and in pursuance of notice given to the adverse party. For this purpose I have obtained the inclosed commission directed to the Mayor of

Baltimore, requiring him to take the deposition of John McDonogh Junr.[3] And I shall have notice given to Heugh & Ralston that his deposition will be taken at the house of the Mayor on the 10h day of May next. I will inclose you the notice by the next post or the one succeeding that. I should prefer your having a full account of particulars made off against Heugh and Ralston, and let Mr. McDonogh swear to the delivery of them, at the prices mentioned in the account. If there were any acknowledgment made to him let that be sworn to also. I will give you more particular instructions in my next. I am Dr Sir Yrs with respect HENRY CLAY

ALS. NN. Directed to Baltimore. Endorsed: "... Henry Clay 22 May."

1 See above, Memorandum of Court Action, March, 1800. The matter was settled on November 22 of the same year when the defendants acknowledged a debt of $4,332.97 and agreed to pay costs. U. S. District Court Records, 1789-1800 (KyU, microfilm).

2 Wilson and John Eastin of Louisville were partners in the river trade to New Orleans. Reminiscences of Maunsel White in WHi-Draper MSS., 27CC11 (KyU, microfilm).

3 A young man employed by Taylor. In time he became a wealthy merchant in New Orleans and is remembered for his philanthropy, particularly in connection with aid to education in New Orleans and Baltimore.

Memorandum of Receipt to Daniel Williams

[April, 1800]

Received fifty dollars the day of April 1800 as per my receipt in Williams hands. H. CLAY.

AES. Madison Circuit Court, Box 7 (Bundle 13). Two months earlier Clay, as attorney for Josephus Perrin of Harrison County, Kentucky, had won a judgment against Williams, a resident of Madison County. The litigation, initiated in the previous year, stemmed from a note for $400, dated January 13, 1798, given by Williams to Andrew Goff, Davidson County, Tennessee, as pledge to pay $200. Although several payments in small amounts had been made, Perrin, to whom the note had been assigned, had brought suit for $400, including damages.

Receipt from William Mott

[April 1, 1800]

Attached to Promissory Note, October 26, 1799.

Power of Attorney

[April 3, 1800]

[Thomas Anderson of North Carolina authorizes Henry Clay of Kentucky to collect money due from William Armstrong of Kentucky by bond dated June 25, 1798, given to William Griffith,[1] since deceased, in consideration of a tract of land supposed to contain 136 acres, sold by Griffith as agent for Anderson to Armstrong. Clay is also empowered to make a deed to Armstrong in accordance with a bond which Griffith is supposed to have given for execution of the deed to the 136 acres, excepting general warranty. Clay may have the land surveyed, if necessary; and he may execute deed with the tract more or less than 136 acres, as it shall be found.

Clay is authorized to sell the land if necessary in order to collect the money due from Armstrong, and to make deed accordingly. Signature of Thomas Anderson acknowledged before Thomas Bodley, May 3, 1800.]

Fayette District Court, Deed Book C, 211-12.
1 Both Armstrong and Griffith were residents of Bourbon County.

To John Overton

Dr Sir Lexington 28h. April 1800.

The importance of the Debt due from Drumgold,[1] and Col. Hart's anxiety as to its safety have induced him to send a special messenger, Mr. Young,[2] to ascertain its fate. Mr. Young is directed to afford any assistance which may be necessary, either to the officers of this State to collect the Debt, or to the officers of Tennassee to take the person of Drumgold. You will be so good as to inform Mr. Young whether any thing has been done in your State, and to make any use of his services which you may think proper. If the Writs have been executed the Debt I presume is out of danger. Should Drumgold not yet have descended the River, I think some chance still remains of seizing his boat & property as they pass through this State.

I will thank you to inform me by Mr. Young whether you have been able to do any thing for me with Mr. Payne;[3] and should you have received any money for me I will thank you to forward it to me by Mr. Young. If Payne can furnish me with a good horse I will take him at its value. I am Dr Sir Yr. mo ob. Hble Servt.

HENRY CLAY

Mr. Hart requests to know whether you have Seen Majr. White[4] and what is to be expected from that Gentn.

ALS (postscript not in Clay's hand). THi. Addressed on attached sheet: "John Overton Esqr. Atto at Law near Nashville."
1 James Dromgoole.
2 Possibly John D. Young, later Clerk of the Fayette County Court.
3 Matthew Payne. 4 Possibly Hugh Lawson White, Overton's brother-in-law.

To Anthony Foster

Dr Sir Lexington 1st May 1800

I yesterday received your letter covering Bryants bond.[1] I will in the course of a few days apply to those gentlemen for payment. You shall be informed of what measures I may take i[n d]ue time.

Mr. Overton has a bond of mine upon Mathew Payne which has been due for some time. It has occurred to me that as it is about the same amount as yours an exchange might be a mutual accommodation. If it is not collected, nor no part of it by Mr. Overton I will give it to you for your bond upon Bryants, and pay you the difference, which is only 8 or ten dollars whenever I collect Bryants bond. But as I know Payne to be good, & am unacquainted with the Bryants, if we make the exchange I must consider you liable in case of their insolvency or if the amount of the bond is not due[,] being willing to be responsible, in case of Paynes insolvency or if the amount of his bond is not due. If a part only of the money is collected Mr. Young who will hand you this letter is directed to bring it for me. And in that case whatever balance may remain, I will transfer to you for an equal sum in Bryants bond.

If you accede to my proposal you will write me to that effect by Mr. Young and in that case you may consider this letter as an assignment of Payne's bond.

Be Pleased to make my respects to Mr Coleman[2] and believe me to be With esteem Yr's HENRY CLAY

ALS. THi. Addressed: "Anthony Foster Esqr. Merchant Nashville Care of Mr. Young." Endorsed: "Septem 2nd. 1800 Recd from John Overton the bond on Mathew Payne above alluded to for Anthony Foster & Co Robt Searcy. . . . From. H. Clay 8h. May 1800." Searcy was Foster's partner.

1 John and William G. Bryant of Lancaster, Kentucky.

2 Joseph Coleman.

To [Thomas Arnold]

Dr Sir Lexington 3d. May 1800

Be pleased to issue a Writ Thomas Anderson assignee of Sarah Griffith Administratrix of William Griffith deceased vs William Armstrong Debt £272 Damage £272. Indorse this is an action of Debt on a Bond. As the Plaintiff is a Non-resident you will enter me as Security for the Costs and consider this as my bond as such. I will thank you to desire the Sheriff to execute the Writ if he can; and if he cannot by all means not to neglect leaving a Copy at the house of Mr. Armstrong.[1] Yr's H CLAY {L.S.}

ALS. Bourbon Circuit Court, File 123 (which also includes legal papers, ADS by Clay). Arnold was Clerk of the Bourbon Circuit Court. Clay acted under authority of the power of attorney from Anderson, above, April 3, 1800.

1 Unable to execute the writ requiring Armstrong's presence at the November Term of Bourbon Circuit Court, the Sheriff left a copy as Clay directed. When Armstrong failed to appear at the appointed time, the Court ordered that his estate pay £272 and costs. The order was confirmed May, 1801. The judgment, against which three earlier payments were now credited, remaining unpaid, Armstrong was again ordered to appear at the October Term, 1802, but the Sheriff reported that he was not an inhabitant of the County. The case was continued for several months, after which no further record has been found.

To James Taylor

Dr Sir Lexington 26h. May 1800

B Thruston Esqr.[1] declining to offer at the next Session of the Assembly for the Clerkship of the Senate, I have determined to become a Candidate for that office.[2] Not having the pleasure of a personal acquaintance with Mr. Sanford,[3] the Senator of your County, I take the liberty, upon the score of my acquaintance with you, to request that you will make me known to him. I am Dr Sir Yr. mo ob. HENRY CLAY

ALS. KyHi. Addressed: "James Taylor Esqr. Newport Campbell [County]." Taylor was for many years a personal friend and political supporter of Clay. He served as clerk of the courts of Campbell County, held the rank of major general in the Kentucky Militia, and became wealthy through land speculation.

1 Buckner Thruston had been Clerk of the Kentucky Senate since its first session. He later became United States Senator from Kentucky and, from 1809 until his death in 1845, served as a judge of the United States Circuit Court of the District of Columbia.

2 Clay was defeated. Frankfort *Palladium,* November 4, 1800.

3 General Thomas Sandford, a Revolutionary War veteran who settled near Covington in 1792, served several terms in the State legislature and was a member of Congress from 1803 to 1807.

Mortgage Deed from John Clay

[May 31, 1800]

This Indenture made this 31st. day of May in the year of our Lord 1800 Between John Clay of the Town of Lexington of the one part and Henry Clay of the same place of the other part, Witnesseth that for and in consideration of the undertakings of the said Henry Clay hereinafter mentioned, as Security for the said John Clay, and also for and in consideration of the sum of five shillings to the said John Clay in hand paid by the said Henry Clay, he the said John Clay hath bargained and sold, and by these presents doth bargain and sell unto the said Henry Clay two lotts with the houses and other improvements thereon, situate lying and being in the said Town of Lexington, one purchased by the said John Clay of James Brown Esqr.[1] being the yellow house now in the occupation of James H Stewart Esqr., lying on the Main street in the said Town, opposite to Robert Megowan's Tavern;[2] and the other being also a yellow house, near the house occupied by the said James Brown Esqr. as a dwelling house, purchased by the said John Clay of Kenneth McCoy, a part of which last mentioned yellow house is also occupied by the said Brown as an office;[3] together with all and singular the appurtenances to the said houses and lotts belonging or in any wise relating: To have and to hold the said houses and lotts with the appurtenances aforesaid to him the said Henry Clay his heirs and assigns forever. Provided nevertheless and upon the express conditions following: That whereas the said Henry Clay has become bail for the said John Clay in a Suit commenced against him in the Fœderal Court by Joseph H. Daveiss[4] for and has, with Henry Watkins, become security for the said John Clay to Stewart Wilkins[5] in the sum of £1500 or thereabouts; and this day has again become Security for the said John Clay to Mess. Cochran & Thirsby[6] in the sum of 489 Dollars & thirty six Cents: and whereas the said John Clay is also indebted to Henry Clay in several sums of money the amount of which is not now accurately known: Now if the said John Clay shall indemnify & save harmless in the first place the said Henry Clay against his several undertakings and securityships aforesaid & pay to him in the second place the amount of the several sums of money aforesaid which he the said John Clay is now owing the said Henry Clay, then this deed of conveyance shall cease determine and be void. And the said John Clay doth covenant and agree to and with the said Henry Clay that he will at all times hereafter make such further or other conveyances of the lotts and houses before mentioned, for the purposes aforesaid, as he the said Henry Clay shall desire or request.

In testimony whereof the said John Clay hath hereunto set his hand and affixed his seal the day and year first written.

Signed Sealed & Delivered
In presence of JOHN CLAY {L.S.}
JAMES MEGOWAN
ROBT. MEGOWAN
MARTHA WATKINS[7]

DS, in Henry Clay's hand. DLC-TJC (DNA, M212, R10).

1 A prominent Lexington lawyer, professor of law and politics at Transylvania University 1799-1804, and Clay's brother-in-law, the husband of Nancy Hart. He moved to Louisiana in the summer of 1804.

2 This house was located on the north side of Main Street, between Upper and Limestone. Megowan's tavern was on the south side of Main Street.

3 The second house was on the west side of Mill Street, two doors above Short. Captain Kenneth McCoy was a veteran of the Revolutionary War and of Indian fighting in the West.

4 Remembered primarily for his accusations against Aaron Burr some years later, Daveiss in 1800 had been appointed United States District Attorney for Kentucky by President John Adams.

5 Of Woodford County, Kentucky.

6 The partnership of A. Cochran and Edward Thursby, Philadelphia merchants, was formed in 1796. Thursby to John W. Hunt, December 16, 1796, KyU-Hunt Papers.

7 James Megowan, a cabinetmaker, was Robert's son. Martha Watkins was Clay's half sister.

From Elijah Craig

June 17th. 1800

Mr. Brackenrig, Mr. James Brown, or Mr. H. Clay will be so kind as to advise Mr. Herndon, and Mr. Davis[1] With respect to the South frankfort Companys Stoping my ferry road, and take such Steps to Procure me Justice as may be most advisable and Depend on me for Generas Satesfaction and oblige Their h,ble Servt.

ELIJAH CRAIG

ALS. DLC-Breckinridge Papers (DNA, M212, R20). Addressed on verso to "John Brakenrig," Brown, or Clay. Craig, a Baptist minister, land speculator, and entrepreneur in numerous commercial ventures, had received legislative authorization in 1798 to establish a ferry across the Kentucky River at his ropewalk, one mile above Frankfort. Operators of a competing ferry, which had been established in 1786, aroused Craig's anger by obstructing the road leading to his crossing. He had the road reopened and, shortly after writing the above letter, stated in the columns of the Frankfort *Palladium* (July 3, 1800) that if his competitors continued "arbitrarily to obstruct the highway, and that on land where by their patent they can have no claim, or in the streets; I hope a grand jury and district court, in a free country will be sufficient to administer justice."

1 Henry Herndon, an employee of Craig's; Davis, not identified.

Receipt from Edmund Thomas

Registers Office June 26. 1800

Receivd of Gab. Maupin Sr.[1] by Henry Clay Twelve Shillings Tax on 1400 Acres 3d rate Land in Logan County on bay s Creek entd. Survd. & patd for G. Maupin—also 600 Acres same County & Water Course—

12— EDM. THOMAS Reg.

DS. DLS-TJC, 2d Series, vol. 3. Thomas, formerly a member of the Kentucky House of Representatives from Nelson County, was Register of the Kentucky Land Office, 1798-1803.

A number of similar receipts indicate that in succeeding years Clay paid taxes on Kentucky lands regularly for Samuel Franklin, Francis Brooke, Matthew Clay, Wade Moseby and occasionally for other non-residents.

1 Gabriel Maupin, Williamsburg, Virginia, held several thousand acres on Bays Creek and the adjacent Trammell's Creek, in south-central Kentucky. Jillson (comp.), *Kentucky Land Grants*, 207; Jillson (comp.), *Old Kentucky Entries and Deeds*, 512.

On June 27 the Kentucky Auditor's Office gave Clay, as agent for Maupin's heirs, a receipt for twelve shillings nine pence, tax and interest for the years 1798 and 1799 on 1,000 acres of land in Logan County. DLC-TJC (DNA, M212, R10).

To Ninian Edwards

Dr Sir Lexington 9th. July 1800.

At the request of Col. Hart, I take the liberty of answering your favor of the 4h. Instant, for which he feels himself very much obliged.

He is happy to learn that you had recourse to Attachments. And the Court certainly did right in deciding against Pitts and Hunter.[1] With respect to the books notes and accounts of Drumgole,[2] I should imagine that attachments, sued out against him, and the Creditors summoned as garnishees, would be the most speedy, as well as the safest remedy. No doubt can exist but that Drumgole is completely within the description of an absconding Debtor. As to the books of

Drumgole & Co., I would recommend Attachments against their Creditors as garnishees also, provided in this measure you can obtain the concurrence of the other members of the Company: the reason which you mention in favor of this mode of recovery, to wit that the Statute of limitations could be obviated, since they would, upon their oaths, acknowledge the Debts, would be alone sufficient to give it the preference. To remove any difficulty which may hereafter arise as to the evidence of the Debts, I inclose you Copies of the Judgments. The sale of the property to Pitts was unquestionably illegal, and may be set aside upon motion to the Court, which possesses a power of superintending the execution of its Judgments and correcting errors which may happen. The last Section of the Law regulating the mode of suing out Attachments expressly directs, that goods attached shall be sold in the same manner as goods taken by virtue of a Fifa,[3] which cannot be unless they are in the possession of the Shf 20 days after the writ is served (and by analogy after the order of Court, which is the substitute of the writ, is given to him & he has by virtue of it taken the property), and after they have been advertized at least 10 days at the Courthouse door, and the most public places in the County. Mr. Ewing[4] I presume must have been unapprized of his duty; because as he has always discovered the greatest alacrity to serve Col. Hart, it would be ungenerous to ascribe a different motive. Besides what the Law expressly requires, the practice so far as my knowledge of it extends, has been invariable to retain the property 20 days before it is sold. The sale you will be good enough to set aside, and have the property sold again, and purchase it in, if it is likely to be sacrificed, for Col. Hart. In this, as in all other instances where property is sold, you will, by virtue of the power of Attorney which is inclosed,[5] be pleased to purchase it for Col. Hart, if it should be about to be sacrificed. And, after you have made purchases, you will do with the property as is most for his advantage, either by selling it upon a Credit, bartering it or retaining it.

The proposition of the bail is readily and cheerfully acceded to. Proceedings against them upon the Scire facias[6] shall be stopped, until the fate of their adventure is determined. And Col. Hart and myself will co-operate with them in any measures which may be deemed necessary to ensure success. With respect to the history of Drumgole's elopement, and Certificates of the integrity and respectability of the Bail, they must come from your quarter. From your knowledge of both, you will be the best person to furnish them, and other gentlemen, I suppose will join in giving the Certificates. The infamy of the Character of the Alstons, (the old man in particular) is well known to Col. Hart.[7] He was long a resident of N. Carolina, and I believe there was no doubt there, but besides almost every other species of Crime, he counterfeited every emission of paper money which took place during his residence there. But depositions will go with more propriety and with greater effect from the neighbourhood in which he last lived. These the bail I presume will procure. I have no doubt but that the governor will lend any aid in his power; more especially if he finds that your name is in the Certificates. It might perhaps be better to authorize the bail to collect the debt in that Country; but as Col Hart is not sufficiently acquainted with them, to know whether they can be safely confided in, he leaves this entirely to your discretion. If they are invested with such a power it will be most advisable to take Security from them for a faithful exercise of it.

With respect to Harrisons[8] purchase of D's Tennessee land, there is no doubt upon your statement but that he may be made to pay the amount of the purchase money. And you are right in supposing a Suit in Chancery the proper remedy. This you will be good enough to bring immediately. Besides the other necessary statements, let the bill alledge that the conveyance to Alston is fraudulent; that it is for the benefit of Drumgole; that a sale was made by Drumgole to Harrison after the conveyance; and that he is to receive the purchase money. The prayer of the bill (in which Drumgole, Alston and Harrison should all be made defendants) ought to be that Alston and Harrison may be injoined and restrained from paying away, secreting, or otherwise disposing of any estate, debts or effects in their hands belonging to Drumgole, until the further order of the Court; that Alston be compelled to execute to Harrison a deed of conveyance for the land purchased by him of Drumgole; and that Harrison be compelled to pay the purchase money to the Complainant. Upon the Subpoena which issues, it is usual in such cases to make an indorsement to this effect: "To injoin the defts Harrison and Alston from paying away, secreting, or in any other manner disposing of, the effects or estate in their hands, belonging to Drumgole, or the debts by them owing to him; he being indebted to the Complainant;" and if after they are served with this notice, they pay away any debts they may owe to Drumgole, or any of his effects in their hands, they are liable out of their own estates. At the return day of the Subpoena an order of Court should be made similar to the indorsement upon the Subpoena. And you will obtain an order of publication against the Nonresidents.

I am sorry that Gilbert is released at Law.[9] It appears upon an examination of the papers, that there is but one Recognizance of the Special bail forwarded. But the Clerk has entered up in both Suits that Recognizances were filed. A confession of Judgment (which took place in these suits) is a discharge of the appearance bail; because his undertaking is, that the deft shall appear and give Special bail, if ruled thereto. And a confession of Judgment (which might have been prevented without Special bail had been previously given) necessarily supposes an appearance, and if no Special bail is given, it will be implied that none was required. But altho' he is discharged at law, I am inclined to think equity will afford relief. It was certainly a *mistake* in the Clerk to enter Special bail in both causes, when a Recognizance in one only had been filed. This mistake deceived the plaintiffs Counsel who would not have suffered a Confession of Judgment without Special bail. Equity therefore, will interfere and place the parties in the same situation in which they would have stood, had no mistake occurred. This reasoning, which I believe to be correct, in addition to what will no doubt suggest itself to you, may be employed with Gilbert to prevail on him to give his assistance. And if other attempts fail, we will try a suit in Chancery against him.

It is Col. Harts wish that you shall be most amply compensated for your services in his business, which I am persuaded has already given you a great deal of trouble. You can for this purpose appropriate such sums, out of any money of his which may come to your hands, as may be thought proper.

You must certainly attend to any prior engagements which you may have made that interfere with Col Harts business. But where such an interference happens he will be much obliged to you, if you can get yourself released so as to appear for him.

I received your note requesting me to appear for you in a suit against E. Holland.[10] Mr. Brown had before put the papers into my hands, as he did not practice in Scott, where H. resides. I have brought suits, and if the Records are properly authenticated shall get Judgments at the next August Court.[11] If they are not, I will inform you. H. says nothing is due; but he has a talent for lying.

I am happy to hear that we are anxious for the election of the same President. It is now almost certainly ascertained that Mr. Jefferson will be elected. The Election of Representatives in New York, has been in his favor, and he will it is affirmed certainly get every Vote in that State. You have no doubt heard that Pickering is dismissed and McHenry resigned.[12] The violent friends of administration seem to be quitting public service. Harper is no longer a Candidate and Sedgwick the speaker has also declined offering.[13]

Permit me to inform you that as Mr. Thruston declines offering for the Clerkship of the Senate, I shall amongst many others be a Candidate, for that office.[14] Having lived in the Clerks office of the High Court of Chancery of Virginia, and acted some time as the

Amanuensis of the Chancellor, I have been induced to believe that I can discharge the duties of that office. Should you have it in your power to render me any service and think me deserving it, I will be much obliged to you for the favor. I am Dr Sir Yr. mo. ob.

HENRY CLAY

ALS. ICHi. Published in Elihu B. Washburne (ed.), *The Edwards Papers* (Chicago Historical Society's *Collection,* III; Chicago, 1884), [17]-23. Edwards, a native of Maryland, was at this time a rising young lawyer in Russellville, Logan County, Kentucky. In 1803 he was appointed a judge of the General Court. He held various other judicial posts prior to becoming Chief Justice of the Kentucky Court of Appeals in 1808, at the age of thirty-two. His appointment as Governor of Illinois Territory in 1809 took him from Kentucky and started him on a political career in another setting.

1 Probably of Logan County. 2 James Dromgoole.

3 *Fieri facias,* a writ commanding that a judgment for money be satisfied by levy on the goods and chattels of the person against whom the judgment is directed.

4 Probably Urbin Ewing, Sheriff of Logan County.

5 Not found.

6 A writ, and the proceeding under it, based on some public record.

7 Philip Alston is reputed to have been alternately a notorious counterfeiter and a respectable planter. One of his sons became an outlaw in his own right, while two others were good citizens. Finley, *Russellville and Logan County,* I, 20-25, 27, 30, 44; II, 2-6, 30, 34, 39-40.

8 Possibly William Harrison, who settled on the southern branch of Red River in Logan County in 1786.

9 John Gilbert, husband of one of Philip Alston's daughters, was Dromgoole's brother-in-law.

10 Ephraim Holland, who owned land in Scott and Woodford counties.

11 James Brown.

12 Timothy Pickering and James McHenry, Hamiltonian Federalists, were ousted from Adams' Cabinet in May, 1800.

13 Robert Goodloe Harper, Congressman from South Carolina, was elected as a Republican. Upon turning Federalist, he lost the support of his constituents and did not seek reelection. In 1801 he moved to Maryland. Theodore Sedgwick retired from Congress in 1801 and in the next year became a member of the Massachusetts Supreme Court.

14 See above, Clay to Taylor, May 26, 1800.

Agreement with Richard Jenkins

[July 19, 1800]

In consideration of the trouble to which Henry Clay may be at in investigating my claim agt. Geo. Winn[1] to about one acre of land at the Cross plains,[2] for which a suit has been brought by J. Brown Esqr. and is now depending in Fayette Q. S. Court against Geo. Winn Loyd Homes[3] &c; I do hereby agree to give to said Clay one half of whatever may be recovered in said suit. As witness my hand & seal this 19h. day of July 1800. RICHARD JENKINS {L.S.}

Witness

MARTHA WATKINS

DS, in Clay's hand. KyLxT. Jenkins, probably the Virginia veteran of the Revolution granted warrants to some 300 acres in Kentucky, paid taxes on property in Fayette County in 1800.

1 George Winn owned property in both Clark and Fayette counties.

2 Now Athens, in Fayette County.

3 Lloyd Holmes was a tailor in Lexington.

Receipt from Samuel Ayres

Augt. 7h. 1800

Received of H. Clay five dollars his subscription to the Cotton Machinery of Mr. John Jones & John Williamson[1] SAML AYRES

DS, in Clay's hand. DLC-TJC (DNA, M212, R15). Ayres was a Lexington silversmith.

[1] Jones was an inventor, tavern keeper, and cotton manufacturer. He, John Williams, and William Tod were cotton spinners on Water Street in Lexington.

From Hugh Brent

Mr. Henry Clay	Paris 10th. Augt 1800
To your note payable 1st. Decm 1797 for	£30. 0.0
To Interest on same till 1st. Jany 1800	3. 2.6.
To Int. £27 from 1st. Jany till 10th. Augt.	.16.9
	£33„19.3
Supra Cr—	
1800	
Jany 1st. Fee on a Suit	3„ 0.0
Bal due ——	30.19.3

Mr. Henry Clay
Sir

Mr. Langhorne[1] waits on you for the above Ballance due on a note Given Jno. Allen Esqr[2] which I have Recd. as Cash from Mr Allen in discharge of a debt due me, as I Intend leaveing this for Baltimore in a few days, I hope you will not fail in payment, as it will be a serious dissappointment to me if you do—I am Sir Yr. Mt Obt Set

HUGH BRENT

[Endorsement on verso][3]

Received on account of the within forty dollars this 10h. Augt. 1800 which is also indorsed on the Note. JOHN T LANGHORNE

ADS. DLC-TJC (DNA, M212, R15). Endorsed on verso, in Clay's hand: "H. Brent to H. Clay Order. & Rect. Paid 50 dollars & Rect." No second receipt found. Brent was a prominent merchant in Paris, Kentucky.

[1] The bearer of this communication was probably a brother-in-law of Hugh Brent, who had married a daughter of Maurice Langhorne, Paris, Kentucky, tavern keeper. John T. Langhorne later became proprietor of the Eagle Tavern in Maysville.

[2] A lawyer and a veteran of the Revolutionary War, Allen had come to Kentucky from his native Virginia in 1786. After living for a short time in Lexington, he settled at Paris, where he served as a judge of the district and circuit courts.

[3] ES, in Clay's hand.

To William Taylor

Dr Sir Lexington 31st. August 1800

The Mayor's Certificate that the Deposition in your suit against Hough [*sic*] and Ralston was taken at his house (agreeably to my former directions) and authenticated in the manner mentioned in your's of the 14h. instant, which I this day received,[1] will answer my object.

I think it is probable that the object of Heugh and Ralston in obtaining leave to take the depositions mentioned in my former letter is procrastination. But you may rest assured that they shall meet with no countenance from any relaxation of mine, and our Fœderal Judge[2] is not much disposed to admit of frivolous delay.

You are right in supposing that no additional power is necessary for me to act upon your claim against Adam Shepherd & Co. I have already informed you that Shepherd, upon my first application to him, through the medium of a letter, promised to make a considerable payment in the course of this summer, and also offered to give any security which you or myself might deem necessary for the safety of your demands. I wrote to him some weeks ago (he lives about 90 miles from this place) requesting him to appoint a time for me to meet him and receive the payment & security promis[ed.] He appointed a time accordingly.[3] But as it happened to interfere with a Court in which I practised I could not attend myself and therefore employed a young gentleman to go for me, giving him particular and full instructions. He accordingly met both Sheppard & his partner Hubbard; but to my astonishment received no money, and could only get security from Sheppard for his individual debt. Some dispute arising between Sheppard and Hubbard, the latter contending that he paid up to the former the whole of his proportion of your demand, this was employed as an excuse for evading giving security, until a settlement, which it was pretended could not then take place, should be entered into. My dispatching a messenger to them has however effected this good purpose, it has rendered the proof of your demand much easier; for they both acknowledged that the whole of it was just, except compound interest, which they say you have improperly charged upon about £20.

From the best information I can get I think you may consider the Debt as perfectly secure. The character which I have received of Sheppard is that he has the means, tho' not generally the disposition, to pay his debts with ease. I have therefore determined to institute suits immediately, or at least a Suit against the Company, and wish you to send me by the first opportunity their written acknowledgment of your demand, with a statement of your account against them, and also Shepherds bond. Without this last paper I cannot safely bring a suit against him for his private debt. I think there is not much danger of entrusting these papers to the Mail, because should they even be lost we have sufficient proof to establish the demands.

Satterwhite having failed to comply with his bond, I instituted suit against him in our last Quarter Sessions Court. He confessed Judgment, upon my allowing him the same length of time for the stay of the execution as he would have got by a defense. I can have an execution sued out against him at any time after the second monday in November. I have had some thought of purchasing the house which is mortgaged to you by him. Should I conclude to do so, would you have it in your power to give me any small indulgence for the payment of your demand against him, provided you are made safe by either personal or real security or both?

I am sorry that I cannot give you as much satisfaction respecting the Drennon's lick land[4] as I could wish. It will be impossible to form any correct idea of its value without a view of it, and it is situated 70 or 80 miles from this place. The land upon that creek is very different, some tolerably good, and a great deal very bad. That just around the lick is of the latter description. The whole of the good land would not I imagine average more than 2 dollars per acre. With respect to the title, I can form no judgment of that without I was in possession of the papers and records on which it depends. It was suggested to me that Mr. Hollingsworth was not authorized by Judge Sebastion to sell upon a general warranty.[5] If this be the fact, Mr. Sebastion will of course not be bound to make such a conveyance. I happened to meet with Mr. Hollingsworth this morning and mentioned the subject to him. He informed me that since the land was sold by him, he has heard, what he did not then know, that about 1500 acres of it are in dispute; but he does not think the interfering claim dangerous. He says that he has been upon the land and that about 1/3 or 1/4 of it is good, the remainder hilly and bad. But he also expressed a wish that the contract should be annulled. This gentleman at present is reputed to be in bad circumstances; a good deal of his property has been sacrificed at Sheriffs sales; so that if in making the sale for Mr. Sebastion he exceeded his power, the trustees of Gittings & Smith[6] will have to depend upon Jesse Hollingsworth entirely.

Upon the whole, from the information I have received, I think I shall not err in recommending it to you to cancel the contract, if you can get the money advanced returned. Upon the subject of this land however I can give you more correct information at a future day. I am Dr Sir Yr. mo. ob. Hble Servt. HENRY CLAY

P.S. I will thank you not to shew that part of this letter which relates to the circumstances of Mr. Hollingsworth, whose situation is not accurately known by myself. H C.

ALS. DLC-HC (DNA, M212, R1). Directed to Baltimore. Endorsed: "... *Henry Clay. 25 Novemb. 1800.*" Cf. above, Clay to Taylor, November 16, 1799, March 30, 1800.

[1] Not found. [2] Harry Innes. [3] The letter has not been found.

4 On Drennon's Creek, in Henry County, Kentucky.
5 Jesse Hollingsworth, originally from Baltimore, claimed land in central, western, and southwestern Kentucky. Judge Benjamin Sebastian, of the Kentucky Court of Appeals, was himself a large landowner.
6 Probably of Baltimore.

Receipt from Samuel Ratcliff

[September 23, 1800]

Received this 23d. Septr. 1800 of Henry Clay forty dollars, which with ten retained by said Clay for his fees in a suit in Woodford against Perrin,[1] and in the suit in Madison said Perrin against Williams,[2] and for his Commission for collection make fifty dollars received by said Clay of said Williams for said Perrin
Teste SM. RATCLIFF
JAMES H. STEWART.

DS, in Clay's hand. DLC-TJC (DNA, M212, R15). This receipt is on verso of a letter written from Cynthiana, September 1, 1800, by Josephus Perrin of Harrison County, to Ratcliff, a resident of Woodford County. Perrin, eager to obtain funds, appealed to Ratcliff to "Exert every power to do what you can, Call on . . . Clay make Every edge cut,—I am sick, Betty is sick and Edna and Cephus also."
1 Not found.
2 Cf. above, Memorandum, April, 1800.

Memorandums of Court Actions

[November, 1800]

William Taylor a Citizen of the Commonwealth of Maryland against Adam Shepherd and Austin Hubbard late merchants and partners under the firm of Adam Shepherd & Company[1] Case Damage $6000—an action of assumpsit on an account. No bail.
H. CLAY pq.

Samuel Willison and Rebecca his wife, Citizens of the Commonwealth of Georgia against Jonathan Taylor[2] Detinue for the detention of a negro fellow named Benjamin, of the value of $500 Damage $500—Indorse
This is an action of Detinue—Bail required[3] H. CLAY

Samuel Willison and Rebecca his wife, Citizens of the Commonwealth of Georgia against Jacob Spiers[4] Detinue for the detention of the following slaves, Kate, of the value of $500, Lemerich of the value of $500, Joe of the value of $500, Nero of the value of $500, and Chamont of the value of $500—Damage $3000
Indorse This is an action of Detinue. No bail required.
H. CLAY

Each is an ANS. Memorandum Book for Thomas Tunstall, Clerk of the U. S. District Court of Kentucky, 1799 to and including the March term, 1801, pp. 116-18, KyLoF.

These items are not dated, but on each side of Clay's entries are others bearing the notation, "Novr Term, 1800."

1 See above, Clay to Taylor, November 16, 1799, August 31, 1800.

2 Jonathan Taylor (possibly more than one) has been found as a Captain in the U. S. Army (1799), taxpayer in Clark and Lincoln counties (1800), operator of a river boat to New Orleans (1805), owner of property used as a meat inspection station on Pond River in Hopkins County (1805, 1808), and trustee of Jefferson Academy (1804) and Union Academy (1814).

3 Bail was provided by Jacob Spiers, of Lincoln County.

4 For a brief history of this case, see Clay to Charles Tait, June 25, 1818.

Agreement With Charles Morgan

[November 7, 1800]

Whereas Charles Morgan as locator, is entitled to one half of whatever land may be secured, under the following entries to wit, one in the name of Daniel Gaines for 9300 acres, made the 24h. January 1783, eight thousand eight hundred acres whereof have been surveyed, and are patented in the name of Abijah Hunt and said Morgan,[1] one in the name of Samuel Lyle for 3000 acres made the 6h. day of February 1783, one in the name of Jane Lyle assee. of 2000 acres made the same day; one in the name of Elizabeth Lyle of 2000 acres made the same day; one in the name of Samuel McDowell and James Lyle of 2006 acres made the same day; one in the name of Samuel McDowell of 590 acres made the same day; one in the name of William McKee of 1072½ acres made the same day; one in the name of John McClung of two hundred and seventy six acres made the same day: which said entries have been surveyed, and all, except the one first mentioned, patented as is believed, in the names of those for whom they were respectively made:

It is this day agreed between the said Charles Morgan and Henry Clay that the said Clay shall undertake the investigation of the claims aforesaid, at his own proper costs and charges, without any expence to the said Charles Morgan: that he shall proceed in this investigation with such dispatch as the circumstances of the case, and the conduct of those who have claims depending in a similar situation, shall make it appear proper to the said Clay. And the said Morgan doth hereby agree, in consideration of said Clay's undertaking aforesaid, to convey to him one fourth part of whatever of the said Morgan's share as locator shall be saved, after the investigation aforesaid: and he doth agree to make to the said Clay deeds of conveyance for his proportion in any one particular tract so soon as that tract shall be investigated:

But it is understood between the parties aforesaid that in case any interference with any of the claims aforesaid shall be deemed by the said Clay to be superior to that under which the said Morgan claims aforesaid the said Clay shall not be bound to incur the costs of a suit with such superior claim.

In testimony whereof the parties aforesaid have hereunto set their hands and seals this 7h. day of Novr. 1800.

In presence of — C. MORGAN {L.S.}
JAMES M. BRADFORD[2] — HENRY CLAY {L.S.}

ADS, signed also by Morgan. KyLxT. Charles Morgan had earlier served as a magistrate in Fayette County. Records of dates of entry, dates of survey, and locations of the lands mentioned in this document may be found in Jillson's two compilations, *Kentucky Land Grants* and *Old Kentucky Entries and Deeds.*

1 See below, Deed from Morgan, March 16, 1802.

2 Son of John Bradford.

Memorandums of Court Action

[December, 1800]

Wm Granger and Thomas Wheelan Merchants and Partners under the firm of Granger and Wheelan Citizens of the State of Maryland[1] against George Mara[2] Debt of $147 Dam $100 Indorsement:

This is an action of Debt on a note bail reqd. H. CLAY. p.q

Anthony Foster and Robert Searcy Surviving partners of Anthony Foster and Company, who were assignees of Benjamin Rawlings all of them Citizens of the Commonwealth of Tennessee, against William G. Bryant and John Bryant Debt $866..66 2/3 Damage $500[3] Indorsement This is an action of Debt on a note bail reqd.

H. CLAY pq

U. States v Wm. Orear[4]
The Same v Same } Copy of the Writs, Declons & Bonds, for $2..29
H CLAY

Wilison & Wife v Taylor — Copy Writs for
Same v Spiers[5] — Same. $1 - -

Neither the notes nor the signatures are in Clay's hand. Memorandum Book for Thomas Tunstall, Clerk of the U. S. District Court of Kentucky, 1799 to and including the March Term, 1801, pp. 129-30, KyLoF. These items are not dated, but just above them is an entry dated "5 Dec 1800."

1 William Grainger and Thomas Whelan also opened a general store in Lexington in 1799. Lexington *Kentucky Gazette,* August 22, 1799.

2 Of Harrodsburg, Kentucky.

3 See above, Clay to Foster, May 1, 1800.

4 Of Montgomery County.

5 See above, Memorandums, November, 1800.

Power of Attorney from Thomas Norvell

[December 13, 1800]

[Thomas Norvell, of Richmond, Virginia, gives to Henry Clay of Lexington, power of attorney to sell and convey by deed, or deeds, with general or special warranty, as may seem proper, 2,000 acres of land in Montgomery County, conveyed to Norvell by Chapman Austin[1] under deed of June 10, 1799, the tract being the remainder of a 4,000-acre holding patented by the Commonwealth of Virginia to Austin on February 1, 1786. Clay is also authorized to recover from Samuel P. Duvall[2] deeds of conveyance for military land on the northwest side of Ohio agreeable to a bond given by Duvall and his father, William Duvall, to Norvell on April 16, 1800, the property to be valued by Lucas Sullivan,[3] Nathaniel Massie,[4] and William Lytle,[5] according to the terms of the bond. Clay is also empowered to appoint one or more attorneys under him. Norvell's signature acknowledged before Thomas Bodley, Clerk, December 13, 1800.]

Fayette District Court, Deed Book C, 396. Clay paid to Thomas Bodley fees of $1.25 for certifying and recording this document (ADS. DLC-TJC [DNA, M212, R15]).

1 Of Hanover County, Virginia, Austin had several land claims in Kentucky. By deed of March 23, 1810, he conveyed the tract here mentioned to James Smith, Jr., Philadelphia merchant. Fayette District Court, Deed Book D, 33-35.

2 Formerly of Harrodsburg.

3 A native of Virginia, in 1787 he became a deputy surveyor of the land office at Falls of Ohio under the Ordinance of 1787; he was also one of four deputy surveyors for the Virginia Military District Northwest of the Ohio.

4 A surveyor of the Virginia military lands, who had become prominent in the political and economic development of the Northwest Territory.

5 Indian fighter and western pioneer, who had come to Kentucky in 1779 as a boy of nine. A surveyor most of his life, Surveyor General of Ohio, Indiana, and Michigan under President Jackson, Lytle had laid out the town of Williamsburg, Ohio, and served as first Clerk of the Court of Common Pleas for Clermont County under appointment of December 9, 1800. He removed to Cincinnati in 1810.

Agreement with Thomas Bodley

[December 18, 1800]

Articles of agreement made this 18h. day of Decr. 1800.—Between Thomas Bodley of the town of Lexington of the one part and Henry Clay of the same place of the other part, Witness That the said Clay hath sold to the said Bodley the house and lott at present in the occupation of James H. Stewart, lying on Main Street in the said town of Lexington;[1] and doth hereby covenant to cause a deed to be made to the said Bodley for the same on the payment of the last instalment herein after mentioned by the said Bodley:

In consideration whereof the said Bodley doth covenant to pay to the said Clay in hand four hundred dollars; on the tenth day of August next four hundred dollars; and on the first day of September next four hundred dollars; and to deliver at Limestone, or at some warehouse on the Kentucky river, on the first day of March in the year 1802 so much flour, of a merchantable quality, as at the Current market price in Lexington, if delivered on the Kentucky, and in Washington if delivered at Limestone,[2] will amount to eight hundred dollars. and the said Bodley doth further covenant that he will execute a bond with good security for the payment of the said four hundred dollars on the first day of September next, which bond shall be given within thirty days from the date hereof—

And the said Clay doth further covenant to give an order on James H Stewart for the possession of the said house on the 25h. of this month; and to use all exertions in his power to produce a compliance therewith.

In witness whereof the parties afd. hereunto set their hands & affix their seals the day & year first written.

HENRY CLAY {L.S.}
THOS. BODLEY {L.S.}

[Endorsement][3]

Received Mr. Bodleys bond, this 23d. March 1801 for the payment on the first of Septr. next— H. CLAY

ADS, signed also by Bodley. DLC-TJC (DNA, M212, R15).
1 Cf. above, Mortgage Deed, May 31, 1800.
2 Washington and Limestone (now Maysville) are in Mason County, Kentucky.
3 AES.

To John Breckinridge

Dr Sir Lexington 18th. Decr. 1800.

Mr. Tompkins[1] this moment handed me your's of the 16h. instant.[2]

I did not see Col. Massie[3] prior to his leaving this neighbourhood, for the Assembly of the N. W. T., altho' I kept a constant look out for him. I was at Col. Mead's the day before yesterday, and his lady informed me that she should continue to expect him until his arrival. The Legislature of that Territory has adjourned and Mrs. Massie told me that by appointment he was to have been at home on tuesday evening last. So soon as he does come, I will see him or hear from him if I have to go or send to Col. Meads, tho' I expect I shall meet with him in this place; and will immediately acquaint you with the result of the application.

I thank you for the information you have given me relative to the measures of our assembly—they have indeed attempted much and done little; but I have heard it remarked, perhaps not improperly, that this is the best evidence of their superior wisdom.

Yrs. with respect— HENRY CLAY.

ALS. DLC-Breckinridge Family Papers (DNA, M212, R20). Addressed: "John Breckenridge Esqr. Frankfort," where Breckinridge, Speaker of the House, was attending a meeting of the legislature.
1 Probably Gwinn R. Tompkins. 2 Not found.
3 Nathaniel Massie, who was a member of the first General Assembly of the Northwest Territory, which met in adjourned session at Chillicothe from November 5, 1800,

until it was closed December 9, 1800, by order of Governor St. Clair. Earlier in this same year Massie had married Susan Everard Meade, daughter of David Meade, whose home, "La Chaumiere du Prairie," located nine miles south of Lexington, was noted for its lavish hospitality. David M. Massie, *Nathaniel Massie, A Pioneer of Ohio* ... (Cincinnati, 1896), 29, 47-49, 66-84, 106; Willard R. Jillson, *Some Kentucky Obliquities in Retrospect: Meade, Rafinesque, Wilkinson* (Frankfort, 1952), 16-17.

Receipt from Robert Megowan

[December 24, 1800]

Received this 24h. Decr. 1800 of Henry Clay eleven pounds six shillings and five pence being the balance in full for the rent of my house for the present year—[1] ROBT, MEGOWAN

DS, in Clay's hand. DLC-TJC (DNA, M212, R15).

1 Apparently the brick residence next to Megowan's tavern on Main Street.

Receipted Account Against James and Richard Smith

[1801]

	Mess James and Richard Smith To Henry Clay Atto. at Law	Dr—
1801	To my fee for you in your suit against Nancarrow & Bastrop[1]	£3:
	To my fee for you in your suit agt. January[2] (being dismissed)	1:10:
	To Taxes upon the writs in the above cases.	: 6:
	Received of John W. Hunt Esqr.[3] the above in full.	£4:16

H. CLAY
Lexington—

ADS. KyU-Hunt-Morgan Papers. The Smiths were a Philadelphia mercantile firm.

1 John Nancarrow and Philip Henry Neret, Baron de Bastrop, were business partners in Lexington. Bastrop, a refugee from Holland, later became well known through his sale of Louisiana lands to Aaron Burr.

2 Case not found. James B., Samuel, and Thomas January all owed money to the Smiths at this time. KyU-Hunt-Morgan Papers.

3 Pioneer Lexington merchant and manufacturer, postmaster from 1799 to 1804, who acted as agent for the Smiths.

Agreement with Alexander Black

[January 17, 1801]

Whereas Alexander Black has a deed from Jacob Myers[1] for one thousand and fifty acres of land, lying in Montgomery County, being part of an entry of 2000 acres made in the name of the said Myers on the waters of Licking; which deed is recorded in Clarke or Montgomery Court; and a part of the said land is in dispute—

This agreement between said Black and Henry Clay witnesseth,

That the said Black has this day employed said Clay to attend as attorney to any suits which may be brought in consequence of said dispute; and said Clay doth covenant to attend accordingly; in consideration whereof the said Black doth covenant to make to said Clay a deed with special warranty for one half of whatever of the said 1050 acres of land are interfered with, and may be disputed. And the parties aforesaid agree to bear mutually the legal fees of officers which may accrue in consequence of said suits. In witness whereof they hereunto set their hands & seals this 17h. Jany 1801.

HENRY CLAY {L.S.}
ALEXDR. BLACK {L.S.}

ADS, signed also by Black, a resident of Fayette County near the Pisgah area of Woodford. DLC-TJC (DNA, M212, R15).

1 Originally of Baltimore, he was one of the early settlers in the West—a large speculator in lands, a merchant, operator of an iron furnace in Kentucky, and proprietor in 1793 of the first packet line between Cincinnati and Pittsburgh.

Agreement with George G. Taylor

[February 2, 1801]

I have this day agreed to pay Henry Clay fifty dollars, provided in a certain suit brought by Elisha O. Williams against me a verdict & Judgment are obtained in my favour[1]—And also ten pounds provided in a suit brought by me against Lindsey (both of which suits are depending in the District Court of Lexington) a decree is obtained in my favor—[2]

As witness my hand & seal this 2d. day of Feby 1801

Teste GEORGE G. TAYLOR {L.S.}
JOHN W. HUNT

DS, in Clay's hand. DLC-TJC (DNA, M212, R15). Taylor was a resident of Clark County.

1 The suit, Elisha O. Williams vs. George G. Taylor, for debt, was discontinued June 19, 1804. Fayette Circuit Court, Order Book B (1804-1805), 111.

2 A case in which Taylor, heir of Edmund Taylor, deceased, brought suit against James Lindsey and eventually recovered several parcels of land. Fayette Circuit Court, Order Book A (1798-1800), 372, 396; Order Book B (1801), 25, 457, 580-81; Order Book A (1803-1804), 526-27.

Receipt from John M. Boggs

February 12, 1801

Attached to Promissory Note, October 26, 1799.

To Ninian Edwards

Dr Sir Lexington 28th. Feby 1801

Yours' of the 16th. Instant I received yesterday—[1]

With respect to the Debt due from Dromgold to Harrison,[2] it is Col. Harts wish that it may continue bound to him until the fate of his suits at Nashville shall be decided. This I presume may be done. He regrets that his execution agt. the McKeys[3] should have arrived too late, but I enclose another. He does not wish to purchase their land, because he is so distant from it & is in such want of money that it would be no object to him.

Col. Hart is pleased to hear of the prospect of some money being collected; nothing is so desirable to him at present. I am Dr Sir Yr mo. ob. H. CLAY.

The following are all the returns which have been made on executions sent to your country—

On one of the executions returnable to 13th. Novr. 1799—The Sheriff says: "The property could not be exposed to sale agreeably to the within command, by reason of one of the Commissioners being absent on the day of sale." U.E.S.L.C.[4]

On the other returnable at the same time: "Executed one Cupboard, one Table and six chairs the property of Ayers Stewart, but too late to expose to sale before the return day of the execution. U. Ewing, S.L.C."

On one of the executions returnable to 18. Octr. 1799—"Levied on 200 acres of Dromgolds land; would not sell for ¼ its value; also 100 acres in dispute between D. & Lane,[5] given to Lane by a Jury; also two lotts in Russells'ville of Stewarts which the Commissioners refused to value, one of them being Stewarts brother and but three in the County U.E.SLC."

On the other returnable at the same time: "Exd & sold 150 acres of deft. D. Military Land and made £79:0:4 exclusive of Sheriffs Commission & Costs. UE. SL.C."

On the execution returnable to 10h. Apl. 1800—The within named J.D. &. A.S. have no property to be found in my bailiwick whereby I can make any part of the within sum of money. Jesse Ford S. Livingston[6]

On the other returnable same time—"Sold 200 acres of D.s military land for £64:2:6—Also 200 acres head right land for £7:5:2 in all amounting to £71:7:8 exclusive of Shf's. Commissions; Also 2 houses and lotts of A.S. for 115 dollars to Robt. McReynolds[7] at 3. months credit. Also one mare lately exd. sold for 12½ dolls. exclusive of costs—Also collected from deft & Co. £10:18:7, the whole amountg. to £120:11:3. U.E. SL.C.

On the exon to June 11h. 1800—"James D. no inhabitant of this State—Not executed on A.S. by order of the plt.— U.E. S.L.C."

On the one to 16 July 1800 "Exd on 100 acres of land & sold the same at 3. months credit for £103:18:0 including the Shf's fees—Also exd. on one feather bed and the sale stayed by the plt. U.E.S.L.C.

H. CLAY

P.S. You will be pleased to pay Mr. Caldwell[8] such fees as may be legally due to him

ALS. ICHi. Published in Washburne (ed.), *Edwards Papers,* 24.

1 Not found.

2 See above, Clay to Edwards, July 9, 1800.

3 Possibly Thomas and William McKey, who paid taxes on land in Logan County in 1800. G. Glenn Clift, *"Second Census" of Kentucky—1800. A Privately Compiled and Published Enumeration of Tax Papers* (Frankfort, 1954), 188.

4 Urbin Ewing, Sheriff of Logan County.

5 Possibly Robert Lane, of Livingston County, Kentucky.

6 Ford was Sheriff of Livingston County.

7 Of Logan County.

8 Probably Samuel Caldwell, clerk of the court in Logan County.

Memorandum of Court Action

[March, 1801]

William Taylor v. Adam Shepherd debt $3768:16 Cents.[1] Dam $3000. Ind. This is an action of debt on a bond under Seal—Bail reqd. H. CLAY p.q

Memorandum Book for Thomas Tunstall, Clerk of the U. S. District Court of Kentucky, 1799, to and including the March Term, 1801, p. 140, KyLoF. Neither the document nor the signature is in Clay's hand. This entry is undated, but others on either side are identified as "March Term, 1801."

1 See above, Clay to Taylor, November 16, 1799, and August 31, 1800.

Bond of George Anderson to Execute a Property Deed

[March 10, 1801]

I do hereby promise to make to Henry Clay or his assigns a deed for the yellow house and lott in the town of Lexington adjoining the house and lott purchased by James Brown of John Clay, which said yellow house and lott were late the property of Kenneth McCoy, whenever required—[1]

As witness my hand & seal this 10h. March 1801—

R W DOWNING[2] GEO. ANDERSON {L.S.}

DS, in Clay's hand. DLC-TJC (DNA, M212, R15). Anderson was a merchant on Main Street, near the Market House, in Lexington.

1 See above, Mortgage Deed, May 31, 1800.

2 Richard W. Downing, Lexington physician.

Receipt from John Allcorn

[March 12, 1801]

Received this 12h. March 1801 of H Clay ten dollars, being money

collected by him for J. Smith,[1] of Tyler & Chinn[2]
Teste JOHN ALLCORN
BENJN GRIMES[3]

DS, in Clay's hand. DLC-TJC (DNA, M212, R15). Allcorn (signature doubtful) not identified.
1 Possibly James Smith. 2 Not identified. 3 Of Lexington.

Receipt from John Arthur

March 15th. 1801

Received of Henry Clay Seventy Dollars on account of the Trustees of Lexington JNO ARTHUR
C. to the Boad [*sic*] of Trustees—

ADS. DLC-TJC, 2d Series, vol. 4. On March 2 the Lexington Board of Trustees had directed Arthur to "call on Henry Clay atto. for the amount of a Judgment he obtained against John Kiezer [*sic*] on behalf of the trustees." Lexington, Kentucky, Trustees Record Book, 1781-1811 (2 vols., photostats in KyU), 1A, 140.
Arthur, a native of Scotland, was a merchant, as well as clerk of the Board of Trustees. John Keiser was a Lexington innkeeper.

Receipt from Thomas Bodley

[March 23, 1801]

Attached to Agreement, December 18, 1800.

Power of Attorney from Samuel Wooldridge

[April 11, 1801]

[Samuel Wooldridge, being about to descend the river to New Orleans, authorizes Henry Clay to divide with other legatees of the estate of Wooldridge's father, and for this purpose to draw by lot or adopt any other plan which may appear proper for effecting the division. When the division is ascertained, Clay is empowered to investigate titles to such land as may fall to Wooldridge, by bringing suits, referring disputes to arbitration, or in any other manner deemed proper, and to dispose of the land for cash or such property as Clay may find acceptable. Signature of Wooldridge acknowledged before Thomas Bodley, April 18, 1801.]

Fayette District Court, Deed Book C, 455. Wooldridge was a son of Edmund Wooldridge of Woodford County, Kentucky, who had left a will appointing John Watkins (his wife's brother and the brother of Clay's stepfather) as one of his executors.

Agreement with Maddox Fisher

[April 23, 1801]

An agreement Between Maddox Fisher and Henry Clay made this 23d. April 1801—

The said Clay intending to build a house in Lexington,[1] the said Fisher covenants to build the brick and stone part of the same, that is to make & lay the brick, furnish the lime & all attendance, purchase the stone & have the same laid by a skilful mason, in like manner furnishing the lime & all attendance, at the price of forty five shillings per thousand for the brick work, and 11/3 per perch for the stone foundation—He further covenants that the ends of the said house shall be faced with neat sand brick—And as the said Clay intends to have the house fronted with stock brick, the said Fisher covenants to procure the same, at the cost of the said Clay, and lay them, in like manner furnishing cement & attendance. The said Fisher farther covenants to set about the making of the bricks for the above house immediately or so soon as the weather will permit, and to continue with all his force steadily at work until the same is completed; and that the whole of the work above mentioned shall be completed in a workmanlike manner—

In consideration whereof the said Clay covenants to pay to the said Fisher at the above rates of 45/- per thousand for the brick; and 11/3 for the stone work, in the following manner towit £30 in Cash upon the completion of the work, £50 or £60 in nails, including twenty penny brads & ten penny & 8d. nails at 1/6 per pound, to be paid immediately, and the balance in merchandize to be paid from time to time as the work progresses.[2]

In witness whereof the parties aforesaid have hereunto set their hands & seals the day and year first mentioned.

MADDOX FISHER {L.S.}
HENRY CLAY {L.S.}

The words "and stone" in the fourth line on the other side first interlined before execution in presence of THOMAS HART

[Endorsement][3]

Received September 1st. 1801. of Henry Clay fifty four dollars in money being the balance in full of the Cash payment within mentioned— MADDOX FISHER

ADS, signed also by Fisher. KyLxT.

1 Probably on Mill Street. Cf. below, Deed from Hart, February 10, 1802.

2 Clay had ready access to nails through his relationship to Thomas Hart, who operated a nail factory as well as a general mercantile establishment in Lexington.

3 ES, in Clay's hand.

Acknowledgment of Debt by Samuel Wooldridge

April 24h. 1801—

I have this day borrowed of Henry Clay fifteen Dollars—

SAML. WOOLDRIDGE

DS, in Clay's hand. DLC-TJC, 2d Series, vol. 4.

Receipt from Andrew F. Price

[April 27, 1801]

Received Lexington April 27th 1801 of Henry Clay Esqr One hundred Dollars on Account of Cochrane & Thursby.

$100. for John Jordan Junr & Co.[1] ANDW. F PRICE

ADS. DLC-TJC (DNA, M212, R15). Price, of Lexington, presumably at this time an employee of John Jordan, Jr., was later business agent for eastern firms operating in Kentucky.

1 Jordan was a merchant, speculator, and, from 1802 to 1813, postmaster in Lexington.

Agreement with Thomas Donnell

[May 11, 1801]

I do hereby acknowledge that I have this 11h. day of May 1801. agreed with Henry Clay that he shall have one fourth of whatever is recovered upon a bond of William McConnells[1] dated the 1st. Decr. 1781 for three hundred acres of Land lying on the waters of the East branch of Licking, given to me, which bond I have this day placed in said Clay's hands to bring suit on—This I have agreed to give him in consideration of his prosecuting the said suit & paying all Costs—

In witness whereof I hereunto set my hand & seal—

Teste THOMAS DONNELL {L.S.}

BENJAMIN BLACKFORD[2]

DS, in Clay's hand. KyLxT. Donnell was a resident of Bourbon County, Kentucky.

1 One of the early explorers of Kentucky, among the first settlers and land claimants in the vicinity of Lexington. No suit found between him and Donnell.

2 At this time a resident of Lexington, apparently for only a brief period.

To Ninian Edwards

P.S. [May 27, 1801]

You mentioned to me the name of the gentleman to whom the two judgments placed by you in Mr. Brown's[1] hands belonged—I have forgotten it; be pleased to inform me that I may write to him upon that subject; also the place of his residence H CLAY

ANS. IHi. This postscript was added to a letter, written by Clay, from Thomas Hart to "Ninion Edwards Esqr. Russilsville favor'd by Mr. Frazer." The letter, which also includes an "N.B." in Hart's handwriting (and is endorsed: "Rect for money paid Frazier of Harrison 50 for the Whiskey") follows:

"I received your's of the 10h. Instant—I was extremely glad to learn that you expected to get & would have ready as soon as I could send for it four or five hundred dollars—My wants are such that I hastened immediately to look out for a proper person to send for it, and having engaged one, he was just about to start when Mr. Frazier arrived and informed me that your expectations had been frustrated—As his message was somewhat imperfect, since he did not inform me in what respect you were disappointed, I was at a loss to know what to do, but at length concluded to postpone sending for a couple of weeks—At the end of that time I shall send Mr. Tevis and hope you will in the mean time collect as much as possible for him—

"I very chearfully accept of your offer to transfer the balance of the execution against McKey, you taking the Land, & paying me the amount of the execution—And will make the assignment when & in what manner you may desire it—But the Sheriff is unquestionably answerable for this debt—It was his business to have taken sufficient security in the first instance, and as I was not at liberty to object to such as he did take it was his duty to guard against an eventual loss—

"Drumgole, who has written me two lengthy epistles from the Jail in Nashville, states that when Mr. Reading gave the mortgage to Mr. Price he agreed to release the Company from his proportion of the Debt—I do not know that such is the fact—But I will thank you to speak to Mr. Reading and inform him that I shall expect to hear from him shortly, and that if he does not make some provision, disagreeable it will be, I must order suit against him—

"Will it be worth while to issue an execution against Ayers Stewart & to proceed against the bail; or can nothing be got out of them? I trust you will relax in no exertions in you [*sic*] power to secure me this debt, or as much of it as possible.

"I mean to authorize Mr. Tevis, the gentleman whom I shall send, to take some good horses for the balance of what you may not secure—You will be good enough to inform Stewart & Russell & Reading of this so that they may make arrangements to meet Mr. Tevis— . . . N B Mr. Frazer who will deliver you this letter has lodged with a Bond for twenty Six pounds Eight Shillings which I have agreed to take and desire you will pay him So much Out of Dromgoles debt"

Edwards' messenger was possibly George Frazer of Logan County, Kentucky. Robert Tevis, Colonel Hart's agent, resided near Boonesborough in Madison County. William Reading, a native of Maryland, was reputedly the first lawyer, the first Commonwealth's Attorney, and the first Surveyor of Logan County. For a time around 1795 he, Dromgoole, and Ayres Stewart operated the principal mercantile establishment in Russellville. The "Price" mentioned was Samuel.

1 James Brown.

To the Public

[June, 1801]

WE the subscribers, being prompted, in consequence of a report, which has been propagated through the country that the SMALL-POX has been lately introduced in this Town; have made every possible enquiry respecting it, and are happy to have it in our power to say, that the report is not only unfounded, but neither that, nor any other infectious disease has existed here for several years.

Being convinced, that this report, must derive its origin from malicious motives: The subscribers, as well as the citizens of Lexington at large, will consider it as an act of Justice in any person to inform them of the name or names of the propagators thereof.

JAMES MORRISON, GEORGE POYZER. JAMES MACCOUN,
WILL. MORTON, C. COYLE, GEORGE TEGARDEN,
JOHN JORDAN, JUN. JOHN POSTLETHWAIT, ALEX. PARKER,
ANDW. M'CALLA. ARCH. M'ILVAIN, SEN. THOMAS WALLACE,
JOHN BRADFORD, THOS. BODLEY, JOHN A. SEITZ,
HENRY MARSHALL, JAMES TROTTER, BENJAMIN STOUT,
JOHN M'NAIR, G. R. TOMPKINS, THOMAS WHITNEY,
HENRY CLAY, WILLIAM ROSS. GEORGE MANSELL,

Lexington *Kentucky Gazette,* June 8, 1801. The same paper carried another notice, signed by four "practicioners of medicine," denying the existence of smallpox in Lexington. McIlvaine and Whitney were cabinetmakers, Ross was a shoemaker, and Tegarden was a merchant on Main Street. The others are identified elsewhere.

Bill of Sale from William Orear

[June 11, 1801]

Know all men by these presents that I William Orear have this day bargained & sold to Henry Clay, for the consideration of eighty pounds to me paid, one negro boy named Simon–And do hereby for myself & my representatives warrant & defend the title to the said boy to the said Clay his heirs & assigns for ever, against the claim of all persons whatsoever

In testimony whereof I hereunto set my hand & affix my seal this 11h. June 1801.

Teste WILL, OREAR {L.S.}

SAML VENABLE[1]

DS, in Clay's hand. DLC-TJC (DNA, M212, R15).

1 Lawyer, who for a time practiced in Lexington.

To William Taylor

Dr Sir Lexington June 17h. 1801.

Mr. Ralston of the house of Heugh and Ralston, on his way to Baltimore, called upon me yesterday for a letter to you upon the subject of your claim against that house–I wrote you that, in consequence of his giving me his bond with two good securities to pay the whole amount of your debt, including interest & costs, on the 25h. day of August next, I had agreed to a suspension of the execution against him until that time[1]–He has now gone in for the express purpose, as he informed me, of collecting some funds, on which he could certainly rely, to pay you $2000–

I farther wrote you that I had received $400 of Satterwhite's[2] debt; that I expected the balance in the course of this or early in the next month; and that I had also received $700 of the debt due you from Sheppard and Hubbard.[3] These sums I stated I should have remitted, if I had been able to procure drafts–I also informed you that a gentleman, who had sent a Cargo to Orleans this Spring, was notified by his Super Cargo of the sales of the produce, and of his intention to go round by water with the proceeds to Philadelphia or Baltimore;–and that he had promised me a letter directing the Super cargo to pay you $1100. This letter, containing such a direction, is now inclosed to you[4]–Mr. Tho. Hart who has written it, informs me that he directed his Super cargo Mr. Will. Hart,[5] that in case he should go round by water, to call at the post office in Baltimore for a letter from him, whatever port he might land at. Mr. W. Hart, unless accident prevents him, will be in Baltimore in three weeks after the receipt of this; because about this time he will sail from

Orleans. I wrote you farther that, if we should be disappointed in this arrangement, and any opportunity should offer by which you could draw the above $1100 & also the $500 from this Country, I would thank you to avail yourself of it—Indeed if such an opportunity should occur immediately after the receipt of this, you may take advantage of it, without waiting the expiration of the three weeks within which Mr. Hart's arrival is expected;—and should he call after you may have drawn, you may nevertheless receive from him the $1100; because if a Surplus should get into your hands, above the amount of your funds received by me, it may be easily drawn out by a draught upon you, for which I could always get a ready market. The moment you receive this, you will be pleased to deposit at the post office a letter, with your address, directing Mr. Will. Hart to call upon you for the letter of Mr. Thomas Hart—

Should you be disappointed both in procuring an opportunity of drawing on me & in meeting with Mr Will. Hart, you will be good enough to say whether I may purchase bank notes at 2½ or 3 per Cent (the price at which they are generally sold here) and transmit them by the Mail—I am Dr Sir Yr. mo. obt. HENRY CLAY

ALS. DLC-HC (DNA, M212, R1). Directed to Baltimore. Endorsed: ". . . Henry Clay 2 July. 1801"

1 This letter has not been found.

2 Mann Satterwhite.

3 Adam Shepherd and Austin Hubbard.

4 The letter from Thomas Hart, Jr. (see William Hart to John W. Hunt, March 18, 1801 [KyU-Hunt Morgan Papers]), not found.

5 Nephew of Colonel Thomas Hart and cousin of Thomas Hart, Jr. Later a Lexington blacksmith.

Agreement with Stephens and Winslow

[July 3, 1801]

It is this day further agreed[1] between Henry Clay and Stevens & Winslow upon the subject of said Clay's house[2] as follows:

That in addition to and alteration of the work agreed upon by the parties in their former agreement the Stair case of the said Clay's house shall begin as that in the brick house of Mess Trotter and Scott[3] and to be rampt & kneed having a square well hole, and the remaining work of the said stair case corresponding therewith—That the said Stevens & Winslow shall erect an arch in the passage of said Clay's house somewhat better than that in the passage of said Trotter & Scott's house—A sub-base and base in the passage like that in the lower front room of Mr. Lytle's house[4]—Four doors and two windows in the passage to be cased with a double architrive—

The front room in the lower story of said Clay's house shall be finished off as follows—There shall be two windows like those in the house of Col Hart, in the partition between the two lower rooms, except that the sashes shall correspond with the rest of the sashes in the room—The whole six windows to be cased with a double architrive & set upon pedestals similar to those of the lower front room of Mr. Lytle's house—the base and sub-base also to be similar to those in the said room—the windows all to be recessed—The door to be cased also with double architrive—

For the above work, which the said Stevens and Winslow agree shall be executed in a workmanlike manner, the said Clay agrees to pay said Stevens & Winslow fifty pounds—

And as to the whole payments of the said house it is agreed between the parties that they shall be made as follows: one hundred pounds, fifty pounds in cash & fifty pounds in merchandize, to be paid upon the completion of the work, or if the finishing of it shall be prevented by the said Clay's neglect to furnish materials, then the said payment of one hundred pounds shall be made on the first day of November next—One hundred pounds in Cash to be paid the first day of November following—And the remainder on the first day of November 1803 in Cash—

In witness whereof the parties aforesaid have hereunto set their hands & seals this 3d. July 1801— HENRY CLAY {L.S.}
LR. STEPHENS & CO {L.S.}

[Endorsement][5]
Received this 23d. Nov. 1801 of Henry Clay twenty four pounds ten shillings being the balance of the cash payment to be made this fall—
LR. STEPHENS & CO.

ADS, signed also by a representative of Luther Stephens & Company. KyLxT. Luther Stephens and Hallet M. Winslow, carpenters and builders, later became merchants in Lexington.

1 The earlier agreement has not been found.

2 See above, Agreement with Fisher, April 23, 1801.

3 On Main Street. Alexander Scott and George Trotter were Lexington merchants. Their partnership was dissolved in 1803, but Trotter reorganized the business with his son-in-law, John Tilford, in 1806, later operating as Trotter and Tilford, of Lexington, and as Scott, Trotter & Company (Scott, Trotter, and Tilford) of Philadelphia, coterminously.

4 On Short Street between Market and Upper, opposite the public square.

5 ES, in Clay's hand.

Agreements with William Hopper and James Gay

[July 3, 1801]

Articles of agreement between William Hopper and Henry Clay—

The said Clay is about to commence for Wm Degraffenridt[1] a suit against the said Hopper and others for the said Degraffenridts proportion of an entry of 3925 acres of land, lying on Red River,[2] made in the name of William Jones; and in case of the said Degraffenridts being successfull in the said suit the said Clay is to receive one half of his part of the said entry, which it is supposed will amount to 1462½ acres—And as the said Hopper is desirous of holding 500 acres of the said land in case the said Degraffenridts claim should be established it is this day agreed between the said Clay and Hopper as follows:

The said Clay covenants to sell of his proportion of the said Degraffenridts claim, should it be supported, to the said Hopper five hundred acres; in consideration whereof the said Hopper covenants to pay to the said Clay one dollar per acre for the said five hundred acres of Land—fifty dollars in cash to be paid in hand, fifty dollars in cash to be paid on the decision of the suit, and the remainder of four hundred dollars to be paid in mares or geldings between 3 and 9 years old, and of a value from twenty pounds upwards, two of the said mares or geldings to be paid on the decision of the said suit, and the remainder on the first day of September 1802—The said mares or geldings to be valued by men chosen by the parties if they cannot agree—

It is expressly understood that the said Clay only disposes of and warrants his right as derived from William Degraffenridt—And is not to be in any manner responsible in case after the said Degraffenridts claim shall prove successfull against the said Hopper and others, it shall be taken by any other contending claim. The said Clay also agrees to refund the fifty dollars which he now receives, should the said W. Degraffenridt be cast in the said suit, but without paying interest.

In testimony whereof we have hereunto set our hands & seals this 3d. July 1801—

Teste — W HOPPER {L.S.}
MADDOX FISHER — HENRY CLAY {L.S.}

[Endorsements][3]

Recd. April 4th. 1809 of Willm. Hopper three horse Beasts in part the within agreement (viz)

one Bay Mare at .... £22.. 6..0
one Sorrell horse at ..... 20..16..0
one Brown horse .... 27..10..0
all amounting to .... £70..12..0

Teste JEREMIAH DAVIS[5] — MARTIN his X mark COONS[4]

It is agreed between James Gay[6] and H. Clay that in case the said William Degraffenridt should recover in the suit referred to in the foregoing agreement the said Gay shall have 230¼ acres of land, being the balance of the said Clay's part of 1462¼ acres, the proportion as is supposed of William Degraffenridt; for which the said Gay covenants to pay 230¼ dollars in cash, fifty to be paid now in hand, and the remainder on the decision of the said suit—

It is expressly understood that the said Clay only disposes of and warrants his right as derived from William Degraffendridt—And is not to be responsible in any shape in case the said land should be taken by any interfering claim—

Should the said Degraffenridt not succeed the said Clay is to return the fifty dollars which he now receives, without interest—Witness our hands & seals this 3d July 1801—

test— JAMES GAY {L.S.}
MADDOX FISHER HENRY CLAY {L.S.}

ADS, signed also by Hopper, who in the previous year had paid taxes in both Madison and Montgomery counties. DLC-TJC (DNA, M212, R10).

1 Of Lunenburg County, Virginia.

2 The Red River, a tributary of the Kentucky, rises in Wolfe County, crosses Powell, and forms the boundary between Estill and Clark, all in Kentucky.

3 The first, ES, in Davis' hand; the second, AES, signed also by Gay.

4 Of Fayette County, Kentucky.

5 Of Mount Sterling, Montgomery County, Kentucky.

6 Of Woodford County, Kentucky.

To Ninian Edwards

Dr Sir Lexington 4h. July 1801

In consequence of the verbal message which Col Hart received from you by Mr. Frazier he has hitherto delayed sending for the money which you wrote him to send for. I have lately engaged in a very expensive building,[1] and to assist me in this undertaking Col. Hart has given me one half of Drumgoles Debt—

My wants are therefore very pressing, as i[ndee]d are his—I trust you will, my dear Sir, d[o] what you possibly can to assist us—Mr. Tevis is sent by us for the special purpose of receiving what you can raise, and to endeavour to draw this very troublesome business to a close—

In your last[2] you said nothing relative to the attachment against Harrison—Be pleased to let me know whether this debt is likely to be secured—Mr. Tevis will proceed on from Logan.[3] to Nashville for the purpose of seeing if any thing can be done with Dromgole, and if you can give him any information which may be serviceable to him, you will oblige us—

Col. Hart has been lately informed that Mr. Price agreed to release Mr Jones and take Mr. Reading for one third of the Debt due from Dromgole & Company—Will you be good enough to examine the mortgage from Mr. Reading to Saml Price & Co.? It is either in Mr. Ewing[4] the late Sheriff's possession or recorded in Logan Court—

Should it throw any light upon this subject be pleased to forward it or a copy—Yrs. HENRY CLAY

ALS. ICHi. Published in Washburne (ed.), *Edwards Papers*, 24-25.
[1] See above, agreements with Fisher and Stephens and Winslow, April 23, July 3, 1801. [2] Not found. [3] Logan County, Kentucky. [4] Urbin Ewing.

To John Overton

Dr Sir Lexington 4h. July 1801.

Col. Hart nor myself has not had the pleasure of receiving a letter from you upon the subject of his claim against Dromgole, since your favour of the 5h. Feby.[1] So that he is ignorant of what success you may have had in the prosecution of his demand—He has had indeed the honor of receiving from Mr. Dromgole himself two very lengthy epistles, the contents of which however he paid but little respect to—The records, authenticated as the act of Congress directs, have been long since sent to you[2] and I presume received—

In consequence of a probability which Col. Hart has been informed exists of Dromgoles making payment in property, he has engaged the bearer Mr Tevis to go to Nashville for the purpose of ending if possible this lengthy business by taking property, if it can be procured. He wishes Mr. Tevis to consult you and be governed by your friendly advice—Horses, negroes, or indeed whatever property you may recommend him to take, will be received—You will be able I presume by this time to say what will probably be the ultimate fate of this debt—The thought of losing it is unpleasant; and the prospect of gaining it has hitherto been unflattering—

If any thing should be received you will be pleased to pay yourself for your trouble—And whatever assistance you may afford Mr Tevis will be thankfully received—I am Dr Sir Yr. mo ob. H. CLAY

ALS. THi. Addressed to Overton "near Nashville," and entrusted to "Mr. Tevis" for delivery. [1] Not found. [2] See above, Clay to Overton, December 10, 1799.

From William Lytle

July 8th. 1801.

Mr. Clay, will plese to let Mr. Benj: Stout have the amount of my Bond with Costs &C. which I put into your hands to collect, on Wm Huston & oblige Sir, Yours &C.[1] WM. LYTLE

ANS. OCHP-Lytle MSS.
[1] Both Stout and Huston were saddlers in Lexington, where somewhat earlier Stout had conducted a general mercantile business.

Agreement with Michael Stoner

[July 21, 1801]

An agreement between Michael Stoner and Henry Clay—made this 21st July 1801—

The said Stoner has this day employed said Clay to prosecute a claim of his to five hundred acres of Land founded on an instrument of writing given to said Stoner by the executors of Robert Todd deceased,[1] dated the 10h. Septr. 1793—And hereby invests the said Clay with full power and authority to settle the same by suit compromise or otherwise as he may judge most proper—And the said Clay covenants to prosecute the said claim as aforesaid at his own proper costs & charges.

In consideration whereof the said Stoner covenants and agrees to allow to said Clay for his services aforesaid one fourth part of whatever may be obtained from said claim—

In witness whereof the parties aforesaid have hereunto set their hands and seals the day & year afd.

Signed Sealed & Delivered
In presence of (being previously read to said Stoner by me).
JAMES HOUSTON[2]

his
MICHAEL S STONER {L.S.}
mark
HENRY CLAY {L.S.}

ADS, signed also by Stoner, a notable figure in pioneer Kentucky, one of the early settlers in Bourbon County. DLC-TJC (DNA, M212, R15).

1 A surveyor, who, when returning home from the Green River country in 1792, had been killed by Indians on the outskirts of Frankfort.

2 Of Bourbon County.

Receipt to Edward Payne

[July 25, 1801]

Received this 25h. day of July 1801 of Mr. Edward Payne five hundred dollars being money which he assumed to pay me for Mann Satterwhite, at his request— HENRY CLAY

ADS. Owned by J. Winston Coleman, Jr., Lexington, Kentucky. Payne, a merchant and farmer, had sold the ancestral manor in Fairfax County, Virginia, and settled near Lexington in 1785.

Promissory Note from John Bostick

[August 11, 1801]

On or before the tenth day of November next I promise to pay to H. Clay ten Dollars: to which payment well & truly to be made I bind myself &c. in the penal sum of twenty dollars—Augt. 11h. 1801— As witness my hand & seal—

Teste JOHN BOSTICK {L.S.}
A BEATTY[1]

DS, in Clay's hand. DLC-TJC (DNA, M212, R10). Bostick was a resident of Fayette County.

1 Adam Beatty, who became a close personal and political friend of Henry Clay, was at this time studying law with Clay's brother-in-law, James Brown. Shortly afterward Beatty moved to Mason County to practice his profession. He represented that district in the State legislature in 1809 and, in 1811, became a circuit judge. After holding the latter post for fifteen years, he sat at various times in both the Kentucky House and Senate. He was defeated in congressional campaigns in 1829 and 1831.

Assignment of Judgment by Thomas Peebels, Agent for Peter Hull

[August 22, 1801]

For value received and as agent of Peter Hull I do hereby assign to Henry Clay a Judgment recovered by the said Peter Hull against the administratrix of John[1] Hull at the last Court of Quarter Sessions for Fayette County, by the confession of the said administratrix[2] And I do for the said Peter Hull and for myself covenant with the said Clay, that the said Judgment is founded on a just debt no ways discharged or extinguished, and that if the contrary should appear the said Peter Hull & myself shall be answerable to the said Clay for the amount of the said Judgment—But neither the said Peter Hull nor myself is to be answerable in any manner for the solvency of the said John Hulls Estate—

As witness my hand & seal this 22d Augt. 1801—

Teste (the word John first interlined)
C. MORGAN

THOS PEEBELS {L.S.}
for Peter Hull
THOS PEEBELS {L.S.}

DS, in Clay's hand. KyLxT. Endorsed by Clay at bottom of page: "Write to Mr. P. Hull—Franklin town Pendleton County, Virginia or Stauntoun." Although Peebels owned property in Fayette County, he appears to have lived in Mount Sterling, Kentucky. 1 Interlined. 2 Catherena Hull.

Receipt from Nathan Adams

[August 27, 1801]

Received 27h. Augt. 1801 of Henry Clay thirty dollars on account of plank contracted for with me by Mr. Winslow, said Clays Carpenter—

Test
JNO. HAWKINS[1]

NATHAN ADAMS

DS, in Clay's hand. DLC-TJC (DNA, M212, R15). Adams was a resident of Scott County.

1 Of Fayette County, member of the Kentucky House of Representatives, 1792.

Receipt from Maddox Fisher

[September 1, 1801]

Attached to Agreement, April 23, 1801.

Agreement with William Price

[September 4, 1801]

An agreement between William Price & Henry Clay—made this 4h. Sept. 1801—

The said Price has this day employed said Clay to conduct a suit which he is about bringging to investigate the claim of Charles Price's 1000 acres of Land, below the mouth of Hickman, adjoining Arwalker Johnson[1]—And hereby agrees to pay said Clay ten pounds certain before the trial of the said suit, and at the rate of ten dollars per hundred for whatever part of the said land, now interfered with, shall be saved, whether by suit, by compromise, or by the party holding the interference giving up without a suit; to be paid whenever the land is obtained by any of the means aforesaid—

In witness whereof we have hereunto set our hands & seals the day & year aforesaid— WILLIAM PRICE {L.S.}

H. CLAY {L.S.}

Wm Price, Robert Price, Elizabeth Price, Susannah Price & Leonard Price infants under the age of 21 by William Price their next friend, heirs at Law of Charles Price deceased—

ADS, signed also by Price. DLC-TJC (DNA, M212, R15). Price first came to Kentucky in 1781 with the "Traveling Church." He returned to Virginia briefly, then settled in Jessamine County. Bennett Henderson Young, *A History of Jessamine County, Kentucky, from Its Earliest Settlement to 1898* (Louisville, Ky., 1898), 31.

1 Both Charles Price and Johnson entered claims in 1780 for land on Hickman Creek, which rises in Fayette County east of Lexington and joins the Kentucky River at Camp Nelson in Jessamine County.

To William Price

Lexington 4h. Septr. 1801.

Mr. Price will apply to the Surveyor of Jessamine County, or to any other accurate Surveyor, whom he can get, and have a connection representing the interferences between his claim & those of Lewis and Craig,[1] made out—

Let the Surveyor first lay down the claim of Arwalker Johnson as surveyed, then Mr. Price's as it adjoins him—And then the claims of Lewis & Craig, or such parts of them as interfere with Mr. Price's—

Let the connection also represent the head spring of the branch on which A Johnson has surveyed his claim—And have the distance from the mouth of Hickman creek to where that branch empties into the Kentucky River, both in a strait line and with the meanders of the river, accurately ascertained—

Mr. Price will also ascertain whether there is any other branch running into the Kentucky "about two miles below the mouth of Hickman", except that on which the claim of Arwalker Johnson has been surveyed; and if there be which of the two is nearest the distance of two miles to the mouth of Hickman, and whether this other branch be a permanent one, or only a stream rising in wet weather—He will also make this latter inquiry with respect to the branch on which Johnson has surveyed—

Having ascertained the interferences between the above claims, Mr. Price will inquire & find one who has the legal [ti]tles (that is deeds) for the parts of Lewiss & Craigs claims which interfere with him, in order that we may know against whom to bring suit—

I suppose that the claims of Lewis & Craig may be laid down, as also some of the lines of Prices, without going entirely around the Surveys—This will lessen the expence— H CLAY

ADS. IHi. Endorsed by Clay: "Instructions for Mr. Price."

1 Probably William Lewis and Lewis Craig, both of whom owned land in this area. Craig, like his brother Elijah a Baptist minister and leader of the "Traveling Church," also speculated extensively in land. First active in central Kentucky, he moved to Mason County in 1792.

Receipt from John Arthur

Sept 16h. 1801

Received of Henry Clay his Town Tax in full to this day—Received also his Store account in full to this day— JOHN ARTHUR

DS, in Clay's hand. DLC-TJC, 2d Series, vol. 4.

Promissory Note from Robert Elder and William Allexander

[September 22, 1801]

On or before the tenth day of February next we promise to pay H. Clay for value received ten pounds—As witness our hands & seals this 22 day of Septr. 1801—

Teste: ROBT. ELDER {L.S.}
JOHN GOODMAN[1] WM. ALLEXANDER {L.S.}

DS, in Clay's hand. DLC-TJC, 2d Series, vol. 4. Elder and Allexander were residents of Scott County, Kentucky.

1 Lexington cabinet maker.

From Thomas Anderson

Dr Sir, Chesterfield County Virga Septr 26th 1801

I Recd. yours dated 30th June 1801.[1] wherein you inform me that Mr Armstrong[2] had paid you three hundred Dollars &C. This is to Request you to pay the said sum to Mr William Branch[3] and what else you have collected of Him for me, reserving for your self 5PCent for collecting as stipulated by us. You will oblige me to send a statement of the business. Mr Branches recipt shall be good for what you send by him. From your Hble Servant

THOMAS ANDERSON

[Endorsement][4]

Received at Lexington this 19h. day of October 1801. of Henry Clay three hundred dollars in pursuance to the above letter.

$300 Witness WILLIAM BRANC[H]

N G HART[5]

ALS. DLC-TJC (DNA, M212, R12). Addressed: "Mr. Henry Clay Attorney at Law Lexington Kentucky." Endorsed: "Judgment Anderson vs Armstrong Bourbon Court—"

1 Not found.

2 William Armstrong.

3 Of Chesterfield County, Virginia.

4 ES, in Clay's hand.

5 Nathaniel G. S. Hart, Clay's brother-in-law, second son of Col. Thomas Hart.

Receipt to Colonel Thomas Hart

[October, 1801]

Received of Col. Hart a note of which the within is a Copy[1] to forward by post to Baltimore. H CLAY

ADS. DLC-TJC (DNA, M212, R10).

1 The enclosure was a copy of a note written in Lexington, October 1, 1801, signed "S Wante," promising to pay Thomas Hart $395.64 in Baltimore, 90 days after date. Charles Peter Stephen Wante was a Baltimore merchant who owned land in Kentucky.

Receipt from William Branch

[October 19, 1801]

Attached to letter from Anderson, September 26, 1801.

Order Drawn by Nathan Estes

october the 20. 1801

Sir pleas to pay Mr Franks[1] for the timber you had of him [. . .][2] and you yours NATHAN ESTES

Mr. H Clay

[Endorsement on verso][3]

As Mr Estes got the timber referred to for me I accept this order. H CLAY

DS. KyU-Charles R. Staples Papers. Estes has not been identified.

1 Probably John Franks, a resident of the southern district of Fayette County.

2 Ink blot, possibly obliterating several words.

3 AES.

Assignment from John Fowler

[October 27, 1801]

For and in consideration of Attorneys fees which I have and may contract with Henry Clay I do hereby assign and transfer to him the balance of my Interest in a Judgment obtained in the Mason Court of Quarter Sessions in the name of Patrick Doran[1] against Simon Kenton,[2] by James Brown Esqr., and which is now tyed up by Injunction in the District Court of Washington in the name of the said Simon Kenton and John Kenton;[3] which Interest was originally one half; but is liable to sundry deductions–

As witness my hand & seal this 27h. day of October 1801.

JOHN FOWLER {L.S.}

DS, in Clay's hand. DLC-TJC (DNA, M212, R15).

1 Of Mercer County, Kentucky.

2 Famous Kentucky pioneer, who moved to Ohio in 1799.

3 Simon's brother, founder of a station adjacent to his near Washington, Mason County, Kentucky. The case, not found.

Promissory Note from Hugh Duffin

[November 21, 1801]

On demand I promise to pay to Henry Clay five pounds for value recd.–As witness my hand & seal this 21. Nov. 1801–

Teste H. DUFFIN {L.S.}
WM. HUNTER[1]

DS, in Clay's hand. Bourbon Circuit Court, File 154. At the July Term, 1804, of Bourbon Circuit Court Clay won judgment against Duffin, a resident of that county, in a suit instituted earlier in the year to collect this note.

1 Of Fayette County.

Receipt from Luther Stephens and Company

[November 23, 1801]

Attached to Agreement, July 3, 1801.

To William Taylor

William Taylor Esqr. Lexington 8h. Decr. 1801.

Dr Sir

By the last Mail I forwarded you [5]00 Dollars in Bank notes, the numbers, dates, [a]mount &c of which I now enclose you a list[1]– As I hope you will receive that letter and the notes safely I have nothing upon the subject of your debts in this Country farther to add at this time–

Inclosed is an accepted bill of Exchange for $250, payable in Carlisle at Foster's Tavern[2] on the first day of February next—You will have it if you please presented on the day; & should you receive the amount I can reimburse myself out of some of the payments which Shepherd[3] may make, or Heugh & Ralston—John Armstrong,[4] the payer, is a man of probity & punctuality & will not occasion any disappointment, if he can avoid it—Should any occur you can contrive probably to have application made to him at his own house, agreeably to the memo. on the bill—I am Dr Sir Yr. mo. ob

HENRY CLAY

ALS. DLC-John Brown Papers (DNA, M212, R20). Endorsed: "Henry Clay 25 December."

1 The earlier letter and the list have not been found.

2 Foster's was "the best inn" in the town of Carlisle, Pennsylvania. Fortescue Cuming, *Sketches of a Tour to the Western Country* (Pittsburgh, 1810), 31.

3 Adam Shepherd.

4 A merchant of Maysville, Kentucky.

To Nathaniel Massie

Col. Nath Massie Lexington 11th. Decr. 1801.

Dr Sir

I am sorry to inform you that I have not been able yet to recover the money due you from the Bullocks and Simpson,[1] and that I fear the prospect of getting it shortly is but dull—Simpson's person was taken in confinement some time ago, and he remained in Jail twenty days, at the end of which time as no person appeared to give bond & security for his prison bound fees, as our Laws require, he was liberated—You will recollect that I informed you that Mr. Breckenridge left the balance of his Judgment against you with me for collection,[2] and directed how the money, when received, should be applied; and that you promised if the amount of your Judgment against the Bullocks could not be shortly obtained, to make some other arrangement to pay Mr. Breckenridge—The persons whom he directed the payment of this money to have grown extremely impatient, so much so that I have been compelled to advance out of my own pocket upwards of $100 to one of them, which will probably increase the clamor of [. . .][3]

course of 8 or 10 days pass through your town for the Fœderal City, whither he is going—I shall give him an order on you, and I hope you will not fail to pay it—It is possible that Mr. Brown[4] may change his mind & go the other rout—And if you do not see him in a fortnight you may count upon his having done this: In that event I beg you will remit the amount to me—For if you do not I fear that the pressing applications of those to whom Mr. Breckenridge gave orders will oblige me to take the disagreeable measure of issuing an execution against your Security, which I assure you would not be more disagreeable to you than to Dr Sir Yr. friend & hble Servt.

HENRY CLAY

ALS. Ross County Historical Society, Chillicothe, Ohio. Addressed: "Col Nathaniel Massie Chilicothe."

1 In February, 1799, Josias and Patterson Bullock with William Simpson, all then identified as of Fayette County, signed a note to pay £77/5s to Chesley Gates, also of Fayette. The note was assigned and reassigned until it passed to Massie on March 17, 1800. Josias Bullock was at this time a boatbuilder at Silver Creek, on the Kentucky River; and both he and Patterson Bullock were at various times Trustees of the Winchester Academy, in Clark County. Following judgment of the Fayette Circuit Court ordering payment to Massie, order for arrest of both the Bullocks and Simpson was issued in Clark County, the warrant bearing endorsement on verso, in Clay's hand: "Memo To be executed on Patterson Bullock only—Bail required Henry Clay pq" Bail bond was executed on March 29, 1802. Matthew [*sic*] Massie *vs.* Bullocks and Simpson, Fayette Circuit Court, File 50 (1802). Cf. below, Clay to Ridgely, January 31, 1804, note.

2 Probably a judgment in the series of cases, Floyd's devisees *vs.* Massie, Massie *vs.* Sebastian, and Breckinridge *vs.* Sebastian, all related to a land contest brought against Massie by John Floyd's widow, remarried to Alexander Breckinridge, brother of John. The issue was not finally settled until 1816. 7 *Ky. Reports* (4 Bibb) 427-37.

3 MS. torn; half a page missing.

4 John Brown, brother of James, was United States Senator from Kentucky, 1792-1805.

Receipt from John M. Franks

[December 12, 1801]

Received 12h. Decr. 1801 of H. Clay three dollars on account of Timber got by Mr Estes[1] for him

JOHN M. FRANKS

DS, in Clay's hand. DLC-TJC, 2d Series, vol. 4.

1 Nathan Estes.

Agreement with Samuel Burton

[December 19, 1801]

I have this day employed H Clay to bring a suit for me agt. John Halley[1] for 140 acres of Land on which I live—If he succeeds in getting me a deed for the Land, or if I get the value of it in hand I agree to pay said Clay whenever either of those events happens thirty dollars, otherwise nothing—The suit is to be conducted at my Costs—As witness my hand & seal this 19h. Decr. 1801—

Witness SAMUEL BURTON {L.S.}

RICHD. OLDHAM[2]

DS, in Clay's hand. DLC-TJC (DNA, M212, R15). Burton was a resident of Madison County, Kentucky.

1 A pioneer trader and speculator, who had numerous claims to lands in central Kentucky.

2 Probably of Madison County.

Power of Attorney from Benjamin Netherland

[December 23, 1801]

Know all men by these presents that I Benjamin Netherland of the County of Jessamine have nominated constituted and appointed, and by these presents do nominate constitute and appoint George Walker[1] of the same County and Henry Clay of the town of Lexington my true and lawfull attorneys for me and in my name to settle and adjust by suit compromise or arbitration all my titles or claims to lands in the state of Kentucky; by Contract or otherwise and to transact all my land business of whatever nature or description, in this state hereby Conferring upon them an irrevocable power to do and act for me in my said business just as they shall think proper for my Interest or as I myself could do—And I do moreover empower my said attornies to sell & dispose of any of my said lands upon such terms as they shall Judge proper—and further I do hereby authorize and empower them to appoint for the above purpose or any of them one or more attornies substitute under them;—Hereby ratifying and confirming whatever my said attornies or their substitute or substitutes shall do and transact in the premises In Testimony whereof I have hereunto set my hand and seal this 23d. day of December 1801.

Signed sealed and delivered B NETHERLAND {L.S.}

In presence of
THOS. B SCOTT[2]

Jessamine County Court, Deed Book A, 306-307. Acknowledged and ordered to record at the December Quarter Session Court, 1801. Netherland, a Virginia veteran of the Revolution, had come to Kentucky toward the end of the war and participated in numerous encounters with the Indians, including the Battle of Blue Licks, August 19, 1782. He had been a pioneer settler in the area that became Jessamine County, where he operated a tavern and for about a quarter of a century was postmaster at Nicholasville.

1 A Virginian who had come to Kentucky in 1794 and begun the practice of law in Jessamine County in 1799. He was a member of the State legislature, 1808-1814, and of the United States Senate in 1814, when he was appointed to fill the vacancy caused by the resignation of George M. Bibb.

2 Of Nicholasville, Jessamine County.

To Ninian Edwards

Dr Sir Lexington 25th. Decr. 1801.

Col. Hart placed your letter some short time after he received it in my hands to be answered. From a variety of causes, of business, absence from home &c. better conceived than described., I have hitherto omitted, what I now sit down to do, to write you an answer—

Inclosed is an execution against Hendley Russell. I thought that one might have been obtained against Stewart[1] also—But to my surprize when I applied for it I found that the Scire facias was not executed upon him—And have therefore sent an Alias, to the service of which be pleased to attend.

Should any property of Russell be taken you will be pleased to advise Col. Hart or me of it, and whether it would be advantageous for him to purchase it—It is unnecessary to observe how solicitous he is to get as much as possible of this debt, and that you should urge payment from Harrison[2] & Blackburn[3]—

Col. Hart & myself have supposed that six per Cent upon the amount of what you have or may collect for him, together with a fee of 30/—for every case in which you shall have appeared for him, either before a Jury in the Country, or in Court, would be a sufficient compensation for your services, which have been so useful to him—The usual commission in this part of the Country is five per Cent, but he supposes six ought to be allowed you in consideration of extraordinary trouble—You will be good enough to say whether you think your services will be sufficiently rewarded—

An order of Court has been made in the suit against Dromgold in Tennessee requiring the production by Col. Hart of the Mortgages given by Dromgole, Ayers Stewart & William Reading—They are I believe all recorded in the office of Logan—You will be good enough to obtain Copies of them, or of such as may be there, and send them to John Overton Esqr.—I will thank you also to send me a Copy of the one given by Mr. Reading, and to jog that gentleman's memory about paying his proportion of the Debt, for which it seems Dromgole is about to contend for a Credit.[4]

I believe I some time ago informed you that Ephraim Holland had filed a bill of Injunction against Edward Gwinn[5]—Inform me to whom I shall send it to procure an answer—

A Friend of min [*sic*] Francis Brooke Esqr. in Virginia,[6] feels extremely solicitous to have some Land of his in your quarter of the Country remarked & processioned, so as to preserve the boundaries against fraud or accident—He has written to me to have it accomplished if possible for him—I must trouble you so far as to ascertain whether you [ca]n get it done—Mr. Reading[7] I suppose can do it—I should prefer he would to any other person—I will thank you to speak to him and know whether [he] c[a]n do it & write me what he will charge by post—They are two tracts of 1000 acres each, one lying on Cliff Creek a branch of the Ohio surveyed in 1785—The other on the waters of Poagues Creek surveyed in 1785 also—Copies of the boundaries shall hereafter be sent—Perhaps if Mr Reading cannot some [other] p[erson] can be procured to do it[. Be] p[lea]sed to attend to this for me par[ticularly.] I am Dr Sir Yrs with esteem H. CLAY

P.S You will find inclosed an assignment of the Execution agt. McKey[8]—H C.

ALS. ICHi. Addressed: "Ninian Edwards Esq Atto at Law. Russellsville." Postmarked: "Lex. K. Jan. 7." Published in Washburne (ed.), *Edwards Papers,* 25-27.

1 Ayres Stewart. 2 William Harrison.

3 Not identified.
4 See earlier letters from Clay to Overton and to Edwards.
5 Holland was a resident of Georgetown, Kentucky. Gwinn was now a resident of Davidson County, Tennessee.
6 See above, Advertisement, July, 1799.
7 William Reading.
8 See above, letter to Edwards, May 27, 1801, note.

From William Taylor

Henry Clay Esqr Baltimore 25h December 1801.
Lexington
Dear Sir

I wrote you The 17th. Inst acknowledging your favor of The 4h. Inst[1] enclosing Five Hundred Dollars in Bank Note[s]—Amongst which was The enclosed Twenty Dollar Counterfeit note which I hope you can get from the endorser J Crawford.[2] I am astonished any person did not discover This note to be a counterfeit—

I have now y'r favr of The 8th. Inst with John Armstrongs acceptance for Two hundred & fifty Dollars payble at Fosters Tavern at Carlisle on The 1/4 Feby—I shall forward it to a Friend for payment. But if not paid I don't know how I can get it protested—I request you not to take any more Bills on Inland Towns as it is so Trouble [*sic*] to get Them negotiated—I wou'd preferr for all my money to pay some discount for Bank Notes.

I hope Mr. Short will comply with his promise and call on me to settle Edwards draft[3]—I hold The original for that purpose. a Doctor Williams of Shepherdstown has wrote me he expects in January or February to receive some money from Thomas Sprigg[4] for account of Mrs. Swearingin[5] and shou'd it be The Case he will pay me. 250 £ or 666 67/100 $ on account of Edwards drft—if This is done I will Instantly inform you. But I have but a slender relyance on The punctuality of people in The Country That pay no attention to such Things altho' They may be wealthy.

I am sorry for what is said of Heugh & Ralstons Case—you will take care of my Interest and do all That is possible, and not allow the security to be released.

When in your power to make me remitances I shall thank you and They will be very acceptable. With esteem & regard I am Dr Sir Yr obt. Sert WM. TAYLOR

ALS. DLC-TJC (DNA, M212, R15).
1 These two letters have not been found.
2 Possibly James Crawford of Lexington.
3 In July, 1801, Haden Edwards drew a bill of exchange for $1450 on Mrs. Swearingen, in favor of Peyton Short of Lexington, who endorsed it to Taylor. The bill was protested on August 27, 1801. See below, Clay to Short, March 17, 1802, enclosure. Edwards, who lived for several years in Kentucky after leaving his native Virginia, emigrated to Louisiana about 1822, and soon afterward figured in early Texas history.
4 Of Frederick, Maryland. 5 Not identified.

To Francis Taliaferro Brooke

Dr Sir Lexington 30th. December 1801

I have received as well your letter by Mr. H. Taylor,[1] as the one written a few days after by the post—You need not have remitted the money you sent by that gentleman, as a surplus still remains of what I have heretofore received—

I wrote by a few mails ago to a gentleman, living in Logan County,[2] not very far from your Land, and requested him to use his best endeavours to employ some capable person to procession your Land, so as to preserve the boundaries against fraud or accident; but desired him to inform me previously of what it could be a[ccompli]shed for—So soon as I receive an answer you shall be apprized of its contents—

The business of Field & Son agt. Barbours shall be attended to—[3] And I will write to Col. Anderson by the first opportunity for the information you wish—[4]

I must now request the favour of you to execute a small commission for me—The acts of the Virginia Legislature, passed prior to the separation of this State, are extremely difficult to be procured, even by collecting fugitive acts, in this Country; but few indeed of the public offices possess entire collections—Will you be so obliging as to obtain for me, if you can, the old revisal, which reache[s] I believe to year 1766, the Chancellors Revisal, and the acts passed since that in a regular series to the year 1792? The last is most desired, but I could wish to possess all—Your revisal of 1794 would not answer my purpose, because it contains laws not in force in this Country, &, if my recollection serves me, omits to give the respective dates of the passage of each law, all important in many cases—These books you will be pleased to forward to William Taylor Esqr. Merchant in Baltimore, from whence I can easily procure them, or to either of our Representatives in Congress, Mr. Brown, Mr Breckenridge, Fowler or Davis,[5] who will contrive some mode for them to get to me—I suppose they may be obtained from the Council Chamber—

What has become of the Son of my much regretted friend your brother?[6] I feel myself under obligations of gratitude to the father which I should be happy of having an opportunity of discharging to the son—What is the progress he has made in his education? We have in this place an university in a very flourishing condition—Could you not spare him to me in this Country for two or three years? I li[ve but a] short dis[ta]nce from the [buil]dings, have a small family, and need not add that from the cheapness of living in this Country, his expence to me would be extremely inconsiderable. We have too a distant hope of getting Mr. Madison from William &

Mary to take the management of our Seminary[7]—Be pleased to let me hear from you upon this subject—And believe me to be Sincerely yr friend HENRY CLAY

ALS. KyU. Addressed: "Francis Brooke Esqr. Atto at Law Fredericksburg Virginia." Postmarked: "... DEC. 29 [*sic*]" Published in Calvin Colton (ed.), *The Private Correspondence of Henry Clay* (New York, 1855), 9-10; and St. George Tucker Brooke, "The Brooke Family," *Virginia Magazine of History and Biography,* XIX (1911), 208.

1 Hubbard Taylor, brother of General James Taylor, moved to Kentucky from Virginia at an early date, lived first in Fayette County, then settled in Clark County. He was a land speculator and acted as agent for several Virginians who had claims to lands in Kentucky. The letters here mentioned have not been found.

2 Ninian Edwards.

3 John Field and Son were Philadelphia merchants with trade connections in Kentucky. "Barbours" was possibly James Barbour, merchant of Danville, Kentucky.

4 Col. Richard Clough Anderson, veteran of the Revolution, principal surveyor of Virginia's military bounty lands in Kentucky, and for several terms Jefferson County representative in the Kentucky legislature.

5 John Brown, John Breckinridge, John Fowler, and Thomas Terry Davis. Davis, of Mercer County, was a Congressman from Kentucky from 1797 to 1803, when he became United States judge of Indiana Territory.

6 Richard, the only child of Robert Brooke, had been about ten years old at the time Clay resided in the Brooke home. The boy later became a merchant in Richmond, Virginia. Brooke, "The Brooke Family," *Virginia Magazine of History and Biography,* XIX (1911), 209.

7 James Madison, cousin of President James Madison, was president of William and Mary College from 1777 to his death in 1812. On the effort to bring him to Lexington as president of Transylvania University, see below, Pledge, April, 1802.

John Coburn and John Allen to Clay and Jesse Bledsoe

[*ca.* 1802]

The Court is of opinion that the little & very unecessary flame enkindled between Messrs. Clay & Bledsoe be extinguished, as they are not only friends but men of honor a want of compliance will incur the displeasure of this Court.[1] JNO. COBURN
To Messrs. Clay & Bledsoe. JOHN ALLEN

ANS by Coburn, signed also by Allen. WHi-Draper MSS., 31CC195. Coburn, a native of Pennsylvania, had been a merchant in Lexington before moving to Maysville in 1794. He was a District Court judge and from 1802 to 1805, with Allen, a judge of the Circuit Court. In the latter year Coburn became Judge of the Territory of New Orleans.

1 No additional reference to the dispute has been found.

Bond for Slaves Hired by Thomas Hart, Jr.

[January 7, 1802]

Know all men by these presents that I Thomas Hart Junr. of the County of Fayette am held and firmly bound unto Henry Clay of the same County in the just and full sum of five hundred pounds: to be paid to the said Clay his heirs executors administrators or assigns: to which payment, well and truly to be made, I bind myself my heirs executors, and administrators firmly by these presents. Sealed with my seal and dated this 7h day of January 1802.

The Condition of the above obligation is such That whereas the said Thomas Hart Junr. hath hired of the said Henry Clay, for the space of five years, commencing upon the first day of this present January, three negro boys to wit Sam, at the price of twenty pounds per annum, Aaron[1] at the price of fifteen pounds per annum, and Simon at the price of seven pounds ten shillings per annum: and whereas the said Thomas Hart hath agreed, in consideration of the prices aforesaid, for the length of time aforesaid, to put the said boys to the trade of nailing, so that they may acquire a knowledge thereof: Now if the said Thomas Hart shall on the first day of January 1803, and so on that day every ensuing year for the space of five years, counting as aforesaid from the first day of this present January, pay to the said Henry Clay his heirs or assigns the said sum of twenty pounds for Sam, fifteen for Aaron and seven pounds ten shillings for Simon; and shall keep the said boys during the time aforesaid to the business of nailing, unless either of them should discover on full and fair trial inability to learn the said trade (in which case he may be taken from it) and shall at the end of the said term of five years return the said boys, cloathed as hired servants usually are, then this obligation to be void otherwise to remain in full force and virtue.

THOS. HART JUNR. {L.S.}

DS, in Clay's hand. DLC-TJC (DNA, M212, R10).
1 Aaron Dupuy, husband of Charlotte and father of Charles—the father and son acting as Clay's personal servants throughout his public life.

Receipt from John M. Franks

[February 8, 1802]

Received 8th Feby 1802 of H. Clay five dollars on account of timber—procured by Mr. Estes—[1] JOHN M. FRANKS

DS, in Clay's hand. DLC-TJC, 2d Series, vol. 4.
1 Nathan Estes.

Property Deed from Thomas Hart, Sr.

[February 10, 1802]

This Indenture made this tenth day of February in the year of our Lord one thousand eight hundred and two Between Thomas Hart Senr. of Lexington in the State of Kentucky of the one part and Henry Clay of the same place of the other part Witnesseth that the said Thomas Hart Senr. for and in consideration of the sum of five shillings to him in hand paid by the said Henry Clay, the receipt whereof he doth hereby acknowledge, hath granted bargained and sold and by these presents doth grant bargain and sell unto the said

Henry Clay one lott or parcel of land lying and being in the said town of Lexington fronting Mill Street Beginning on the said street one hundred feet South West from the East corner of the house this day sold and conveyed by Thomas Hart Senr. to Thomas Hart Junr. thence North forty five West at right angles from the said Mill street, two hundred and one feet with the line of Thomas Hart Junr. thence from the corner with the line of the said Thomas Hart Junr. South forty five degrees West about one hundred feet to where running a line at right angles will strike the East corner of Stout and Ashton's lott[1] in a line of the said Thomas Hart Junior's lott, thence to said corner North forty five degrees West about ten feet, thence from their said corner and with their line South forty five degrees West sixty six feet and two thirds of a foot to a corner of the lott of the said Stout and Ashton, thence South forty five degrees East one hundred and twenty nine and a half feet to the West corner of the lott sold and conveyed by the said Thomas Hart Senr. to Samuel Wilkerson,[2] thence with his line North forty five degrees East sixty six feet and two thirds of a foot to his North corner, thence with his line North forty five degrees East about eighty one and a half feet to Mill street, thence with the said street about one hundred feet to the Beginning—Also one other lott or parcel of ground Beginning at the West corner of the aforesaid lott conveyed to the said Clay, being also a corner of the said Stout and Ashton's lott, thence South forty five degrees West to the Ally on which the stable of James Brown Esqr stands, thence with the said Ally North forty five East ten feet, thence a line running parallel to the first described line so far as will intersect the line of the said lott conveyed to the said Henry Clay, thence with that line North forty five West ten feet to the Beginning: To have and to hold the said lotts or parcels of ground, with all and singular the appurtenances thereunto belonging or in any wise appurtaining: To have and to hold the said lotts or parcels of ground to the said Henry Clay his heirs and assigns forever and to their only proper use and behoof: Reserving however to Thomas Hart Junr. and to the said Thomas Hart Senr. their heirs, and assigns the right and priviledge of using the latter mentioned parcel of ground which is to be converted into an ally, and so much of the first mentioned parcel as will continue the said ally ten feet wide from the said second parcel to the ally which is now opened—And the said Thomas Hart Senr. doth for himself and his heirs covenant and agree to and with the said Henry Clay that he will warrant and forever defend the right and title to the two parcels or lotts of ground hereby conveyed, to the said Clay his heirs and assigns forever, against the claim of and [*sic*] every person whatsoever—

In testimony whereof the said Thomas Hart Senr. hath hereunto set his hand and affixed his seal the tenth day of February 1802 aforesaid.

Signed Sealed & Delivered THOMAS HART {SEAL}
In presence of— SUSANNAH HART {SEAL}
THOS. BODLEY

DS, in Clay's hand. KyLxT. Recorded February 10, 1802. Clay lived on the Mill Street property before moving to Ashland, his estate on the outskirts of Lexington.

1 John W. Stout and Richard Ashton, coachmakers on Limestone Street, who had recently come to Lexington from Philadelphia.

2 Samuel Wilkinson, whitesmith.

From Jesse Bledsoe and John Geoghegan

[March 3, 1802]

In the question Submitted by Mr. Armstrong and H. Clay Esqr. as Agent for Thos. Anderson[1] to us to decide which of them shall pay the Costs of the last Survey as by Mr. Clays Letter to Jno. Geohagen. We are of Opinion that Mr. Clay as Agent for sd. Anderson Ought to pay the Costs of sd. Survey last Made. Armstrong has been correct in his Statemt. of the quantity and appears to have been guilty of no fault. It was Andersons business to have the Land Ascertained & Convey it to Armstrong, consequently he ought to pay the costs of doing what he is bound to do. J: BLEDSOE

March 3d. 1802. JNO. GEOGHEGAN

[Endorsements on verso][2]

1802

Henry Clay Esqr. to John Geoghegan Dr
To Surveying attendance &c. on a Survey
Anderson to Armstrong &c. 0„12„0

Recd. of Henry Clay Esqr. as agent for Thomas Anderson Twelve Shillings being the amot. Of the above Accot. JNO. GEOGHEGAN

DS. DLC-TJC (DNA, M212, R15). Geoghegan, a taxpayer in Nicholas County, Kentucky, was apparently a surveyor.

1 For the transaction involving Armstrong, Anderson, and Clay, see above, Power of Attorney, April 3, 1800. 2 The first, AE; the second, AES.

Receipt from Jacob Adams

March 15. 1802

Received of Henry Clay three pounds nineteen shillings for 295 feet of Cherry plank & 700 feet of Ash plank purchased for him by Mr. Winslow[1] of Mr. Nathan Adams—

his
Teste JACOB X ADAMS
THOS. MOSELEY[2] mark

DS, in Clay's hand. DLC-TJC, 2d Series, vol. 4. Adams was probably a resident of Scott County. [1] Hallet M. Winslow. [2] Of Montgomery County.

Property Deed from Charles Morgan

[March 16, 1802]

[Indenture by which for the sum of five shillings, paid and acknowledged, Charles Morgan of Muhlenburg County, Kentucky, conveys to Henry Clay one equal, undivided moiety of 8,800 acres lying, it is supposed, in Montgomery County, patented in the names of Charles Morgan and Abijah Hunt on June 22, 1799 and surveyed on March 26, 1787. Title warranted only against claimants under this patent. Signature of Morgan attested by Thomas Bodley, March 16, 1802.]

Fayette District Court, Deed Book D, 63-64. See above, Agreement, November 7, 1800.

To Peyton Short

Dr Sir Lexington 17th. March 1802

I have examined the papers in your suit with Rhea and believe I entirely understand them[1]—You do appear to be in danger of suffering evident injus[tice.] The only mode in which you can be relieved is by Injunction, which will suspend the operation of the Judgment as to all but that part which you [admit] to be justly due. I have spoken upon the subj[ect to] Col. Todd,[2] who supposes some mistake has [been] committed. To ascertain this it becomes necessary [to get] a copy of the last execution together with a [list of] credits indorsed thereon, which you may obtain from the Clerk—This you will bring up with you to this place, and Col. Todd consents that if we cannot correct the error without applying for an Injunction he will dispense with notice, and the application may be made to one of the Judges who are attending the District Court here—But you must be here so as to have the business someway accomplished on tomorrow or the next day early, as Col Todd will leave this place early on friday, and wishes to be present—

I inclose you a statement of the amount of Edwards[3] bill, interest damages and charges of protest—Upon this subject I feel the greatest anxiety. It is now nearly a year since the bill was drawn—The money which I paid for it was collected on account of an old stale debt due Mr. Taylor, which had been a long time unjustly withheld—a circumstance which will in his mind aggravate the delay which has arisen in the payment of the bill—In addition to this, relying upon the certainty [of the a]cceptance and payment of the bill, in [consequ]ence of my confidence in you, I trespassed [against] Mr.Mr. Taylor's order, which was to purchase [bank no]tes and not to receive bills—The bill being protested necessarily attached some degree of censure to my agency, which the subsequent delay in the payment is by no means calculated to remove, especially as I have foreborne, at the hazard of his total displeasure, to commence suit —Confiding as I do upon a punctual discharge of the duties of my profession for the accomplishment of all my future prospects, I conjure you to extricate me from the reproaches of Mr. Taylor by the most immediate & prompt discharge of the bill—I am Dr Sir Yr friend &c HENRY CLAY.

[Enclosure][4]

Dr. Peyton Short and Haden Edwards Esqrs To William Taylor—

1801		
July 15	To amount of the draft by Mr. Edwards on Mrs. Swearingen, in favour of Mr. Short, and endorsed by him to me bearing this date for $1450	£435: 0: 0.
	To interest thereon from the 27h. day of August 1801, the time when the said bill was protested, to the 16h. March 1802 @ 6 P Cent P annm. 6 months & 17 days	13:14: 2
	To 10 P Cent damages on the amount of the sd. bill	43:10: 0
	To Charges of protest $5:79	1:14: 9
		493:18:11

E. Excepted[5]

P Henry Clay agent for Wm.
Taylor — — 16 March 1802

ALS. DLC-Short Family Papers (DNA, M212, R22). Addressed on verso: "Peyton Short [Esq]r. Frankfort Care of Mr Burnes." Burnes not identified. MS. ragged.

1 See above, Clay to Short, March 21, 1800.

2 Thomas Todd. 3 Haden Edwards.

4 ADS, DLC-Short Family Papers (DNA, M212, R22). At the bottom of the page a calculation subtracting £120 from the total of this account indicates that a payment was made. 5 Errors Excepted.

Conditional Pledge to Transylvania University

[April, 1802]

Understanding that a Board of the Trustees of the Transylvania University is called for the purpose of taking into consideration the propriety of inviting James Madison Esqr. to the management thereof; and being informed that the principal, if not the only, obstacle to the success of the said measure, for which we feel extremely anxious, arises from a supposed deficiency in the funds of the said Institution; and being further informed that provided the Tuition money is raised from four pounds, its present price, to twenty dollars, and fifty students annually should attend the said University, there will be no cause to apprehend the said deficiency: We the subscribers do hereby bind and oblige ourselves to the Trustees of the said University, our heirs &c, that if Mr. Madison shall undertake the superintendence thereof, and the tuition money shall be raised as aforesaid, we will warrant, and upon the said contingencies happening, do hereby warrant that the Tuition money, to be received at the said University, for and during the term of five years, to commence from the day that Mr. Madison begins his presidency, shall amount annually to the sum of one thousand dollars: And we do covenant and agree that if there should be a deficiency in that sum during any one of the said years, we will make up the said deficiency; the advance so to be made by us to be returned in case of a surplus above that sum during any other of the said years, or so much thereof as such surplus shall discharge.[1]

In witness whereof we have hereunto set our hands & seals this day of April 1802.

THOMAS TODD	{L.S.}	JOSEPH HAMN. DAVEISS.	{L.S.}
JOHN POPE.	{L.S.}	ISHAM TALBOTT	{L.S.}
GEORGE MUTER	{L.S.}	JOHN ROWAN–	{L.S.}
BEN: SEBASTIAN–	{L.S.}	HENRY CLAY–	{L.S.}
THOS. TUNSTALL	{L.S.}	JOHN. L. BRIDGES.	{L.S.}
JOHN LOGAN	{L.S.}	GREEN CLAY	{L.S.}
J: BLEDSOE	{L.S.}	EDM THOMAS–	{L.S.}
JOHN DRAKE–	{L.S.}	ACHILLES SNEED.	{L.S.}
LOUIS MARSHALL JR	{L.S.}	CHRISTO. GREENUP	{L.S.}
HENRY C BRUCE	{L.S.}	THOS. BODLEY	{L.S.}
JAMES KNOX	{L.S.}	CUTH: BANKS	{L.S.}
J HUGHES	{L.S.}	CHS. WILKINS	{L.S.}
JAS BLAIR	{L.S.}	THOS. DEYE OWINGS	{L.S.}
THOMAS HART	{L.S.}	J POSTLETHWAIT	{L.S.}
JOHN W. HUNT	{L.S.}	JOHN JORDAN JR	{L.S.}
NATHL. HART	{L.S.}	JAMES MORRISON	{L.S.}

DS. PPPrHi. The signers were all residents of Lexington or central Kentucky.

[1] The tuition fee was raised to $20, but Madison did not accept the proffered post.

From William Taylor

Henry Clay Esqr. Baltimore April. 14th. 1802.

Dear Sir,

I have for a year past had repeated applications from John Laird to purchase The Debt of Heugh & Ralstone, But he never wou'd offer me near its value—He has this day by his agents come so near my terms That I have accepted as expressed in The foregoing letter

—The Copy of The Judgment you sent me about a year ago was .4,360.28/100 $ you received by y'r letter 26 Jany.[1] 1000$ and you was to get payment .500$ more the 1t. of this month. That will leave a Balance of about .3000$ after The Interest is added if The .500$. is paid. On Receipt of this do me The favour to forward a Correct Statement of The Judgment, a Calculation of Interest & Costs with a Credit for The Payments & Strike The Balance due—it may be proper That the Clerke of The Court date & Sign it—and I wish you to notice if The Interest is properly Stated to The time. on geting That I shall receive my money deducting a discount of 10PrCt— which may be best considering The uncertainty & delays of The Law; and you will oblige me by not delaying a mail. Armstrongs[2] note is not yet paid—I have not heard further of The money deposited at Beards Town[3] from Shepherd[4]—nor no payment from any person for The Bill on Mrs. Swearingen—I hope soon to hear from you & am Yrs Sincerely WM. TAYLOR

ALS. DLC-TJC (DNA, M212, R12). Taylor enclosed herewith, as the first page and a half of this MS., a copy of his letter to Ferguson and Robertson dated August 14, 1802 [*sic*], agreeing to give them an assignment of that part of Heugh and Ralston's debt yet unpaid in return for their acceptance of John Laird's draft for $2,000 as part payment. Ferguson and Robertson were apparently acting as agents of Laird, a merchant of Georgetown, D. C.

1 Not found. 2 John Armstrong.

3 Bardstown, Kentucky, was named for David Baird, one of the original proprietors of the land on which it stands.

4 Adam Shepherd.

Assignment from William Dailey

15h. Apl 1802—

I do hereby assign the within to Henry Clay for value received—

Teste

WM MORTON[1] WM. DAILEY {L.S.}

ES, in Clay's hand. DLC-TJC (DNA, M212, R15). This assignment is on verso of an agreement whereby James Russell and Thomas Irwin rented to Dailey, a free mulatto, "the Field of grass on the Maine Street of Lexington called the race Field f[or] the Term of seven Years. . . ." Russell, the husband of Colonel John Todd's daughter, Mary Owen, died later in the year. Irwin, who had married Jane, Colonel Todd's widow, had been a Lexington merchant. The property had been part of the estate of Todd, who was killed in the Battle of Blue Licks in 1782.

1 Lexington merchant, several times deputy sheriff of Fayette County, first president of the Kentucky Insurance Company.

Property Deed from George Johnson

[May 11, 1802]

[In consideration of the sum of $1,000 paid by Clay, George Johnson sells to Clay "one equal undivided moiety of three several tracts of land," containing a total of 16,000 acres, located in Mason

County, Kentucky, and patented to Johnson on June 2, 1800. On one of the tracts were "the Salt Springs now in the occupation of and claimed by Graham on Little Sandy."[1] Title warranted against claims through Johnson or Richard Ridgely,[2] but against no other. Recorded in the office of the Clerk of the Court of Appeals, Frankfort, July 14, 1802.]

DS, in Clay's hand. DLC-TJC (DNA, M212, R15). Johnson, a Caroline County, Virginia, speculator in Kentucky lands, settled in Mason County two years later.

1 John Graham, originally from Virginia, one of several claimants to the land where these salt springs were located, in 1799 had brought in kettles and other equipment to begin the manufacture of salt. He later became a merchant, banker, judge, and representative in the Kentucky legislature. John Graham to Nathaniel Massie, May 29, June 6, 1799, in Massie, *Massie,* 148-49. 2 Owner of an adjoining tract.

Promissory Note from Hugh Miller

[May 15, 1802]

I do hereby promise to pay to Henry Clay on demand twenty five dollars. Witness my hand & seal this 15h. day of May 1802.

Teste HUGH MILLER

MATTHEW TALBOT[1]

DS, in Clay's hand. DLC-TJC, 2d Series, vol. 4. Miller was a resident of Harrison County, Kentucky. 1 Frankfort lawyer.

Bill of Complaint

Lexington District [June, 1802]

Fayette County to wit

Cæsar (a pauper) complains of Nathl Lowry[1] in custody &c. For this to wit that the said defendant on the day of in the year of our Lord at the parish of Kentucky in the County aforesaid with force & arms &c on him the said plt did make an assault and him the said plt then & there did beat wound, take & imprison for a long time to wit for the space of 24 hours next ensuing without any reasonable & lawful cause & against the Laws of the State & oth[erwis]e[2] illtreat so that his life was greatly despaired of; and other injuries to him the said plt then and there did against the peace & dignity of the Commonwealth & to the damage of the said plt £100: and therefore he brings suit &c H. CLAY for plt

Pledges J. DOE
&
R. ROE

ADS. NHi. Endorsed vertically: "We of the Jury find for the Plaintiff and one penny Damages.—Green Clay."

1 The plaintiff was a free Negro; the defendant, a hatter on Main Cross Street (Broadway) in Lexington. 2 MS. torn.

To William Taylor

William Taylor Esqr. Lexington 1st. June 1802—
Dr Sir

Inclosed is a list of Notes &c which [I][1] forwarded to you by the Mail on the 11h. May. Having [t]hat same day set out for Frankfort, where I continued almost ever since until saturday last, I did not transmit it before to you.

You will also find inclosed bank notes amounting to $250, for which I had to give the usual premium here of 2½ P Cent. I shall continue to expect with anxiety to hear from you until I receive accounts of the safe arrival of both remittances. I am Dr Sir Yrs.

HENRY CLAY

ALS. DLC-HC (DNA, M212, R1). Directed to Taylor at Baltimore.
1 MS. torn.

From Rebeccah Willisson

Sir. Augusta 4th June 1802

On the 4th of June [*sic*] wrote in answer to yours of the 30h of April[1] expressing my intention of calling on Colo. Taylor & his Son Mr John Taylor for an explanation of those objections stated in your letter which they refused to comply with—observing that they were guided wholly by the direction of Mr Spiers & if an error was committed it was not intentional

A Certificate of Mr Daniel[2] one of the Commissioners directed to the Court for Kentucky District accompanies this expect from the manner of this Certificate that it will be rejected as illegal, in the event of which wou'd it not be prudent to apply for a Commission to examine other Evidences—

Mrs Gildart who resides in the Neighborhood of Captn. Wormeley[3] is my Sister and tho' not present at the time of the consumation of my marriage no doubt recollects the time that it became public— There is no record or register of my Marriage, My Father being the only person at that time Commissioned for granting Licence and the nature of this transaction render'd it inconvenient to apply to him—

Shall regret extremely the necessity for another postponment of my Suits but submit the management of this entirely to your direction possessing the most perfect confidence in your Judgment Remain with Great Friendship RE WILLISSON

This post conveys to your friend Mr Clay[4] £50—

ALS. DLC-HC (DNA, M212, R1). Addressed to Henry Clay at Lexington; postmarked at Augusta, Ga. June 17 [*sic*]. See above, Memorandum, November, 1800.
1 Neither letter has been found.

2 Probably Walker Daniel, Attorney General for the District of Kentucky from March, 1783, to his death in the next year.
3 Possibly John Wormeley of Frederick County, Virginia.
4 Matthew Clay. Cf. below, Willisson to Clay, April 28, 1806.

Receipt from John C. Allen

[June 5, 1802]

Received the full amount of the Clerks & Sheriffs fees In the Suid [*sic*] lately determined In Green County wherein Henry Clay was Plaintiff and John Luke[1] was deft
This 5th day of June 1802.
Test JOHN C ALLEN CGC
ROBERT WICKLIFF [*sic*][2]

ADS. DLC-TJC, 2d Series, vol. 4. Allen, Clerk of Green County and holder of a succession of local offices, had been one of the early settlers in central Kentucky.
1 Of Green County.
2 Born in Pennsylvania when his parents were moving from Virginia to the West, Robert Wickliffe had been brought up in Nelson County, Kentucky. He had studied law under George Nicholas and practiced that profession with great success. After moving to Lexington in 1811, he repeatedly represented Fayette County in the General Assembly, served on the Transylvania University Board of Trustees, and was active in State and local politics. In later life he was widely known as the "Old Duke."

Receipted Account from Richard Ashton and John W. Stout

[June 13, 1802]

June th13:1802	Dr.
Henry Clay To Ashton & Stout	£ S d
to 1½ Yds Cloth at 18/6 per Yd	1.. 7. 9
One Paper of 8 Oz taches	4. 6
¼ Yard of Yellow Cloth	4. 6
to Painting Chair Boddy	2.10. 0
to Painting Chair Carriage	12 –
to Lineing Chair Boddy	1.10 –
to 150 Brass nails –	2: 6
to Makeing Bridle for hors	12
to a new Pad and to sprits	– 11 3
to the Black Smith Work	1. 1..0
	8.15..6
Cr. by Cash 2.2..0	2.. 2..0
Ballance Due	6.13..6

[Endorsement][1]
Received on a/c of the above fifteen dollars 17h. June 1802.
JAMES CONOVER

D. DLC-TJC (DNA, M212, R15).
[1] ES, in Clay's hand. Presumably at this time Conover was employed by Ashton and Stout; he was, a few years later, a saddler on North Main Cross Street (Broadway).

Receipt to William Smith

[June 14, 1802]

Received 14h. June 1802 of Mr. William Smith executor of Benjamin Smith & Mary Smith fifteen Shillings for my advice respecting his duty as executor. H CLAY Atto at Law

ADS. Owned by Henry H. Harned, Frankfort, Kentucky. Benjamin Smith had owned a small farm about six miles from Lexington. William also lived in Fayette County.

Agreement with Martin Nall

[June 16, 1802]

Memorandum of an agreement between Martin Nall and Henry Clay: The said Martin owns a settlement and preemption on the Ohio, which interferes with a military survey, made in the name of Daniel McDonald,[1] and which is also claimed by some person as assignee of John Cape[2] under a contract between the said Cape and Nall for the said settlement and preemption; and the said Martin Nall hath agreed, in consideration of the said Clay's undertaking to defend his right—against both of the said claims, and to bear all the expences that may be incurred in the prosecuting or defending any suit or suits which may be brought respecting the said claims or either of them to give & convey to him one third of the land which may be finally left to him after the said disputes are settled, according to quantity and quality—And the said Henry also agrees to give his advice and directions, & if they are brought in any Court in which he practices his personal services also in two disputes which the said Martin is likely to have one with John Waller[3] and the other with Moses Thomas.[4] Given under our hands & seals this 16h June 1802.

Teste MARTIN NALL {L.S.}
PORTER CLAY HENRY CLAY {L.S.}

[Endorsement][5]
I agree to take one third only of what shall be finally saved from all interfering claims as well those mentioned above as any others.
HENRY CLAY

ADS, signed also by Nall, a resident of Scott County, Kentucky. DLC-TJC (DNA, M212, R15).
[1] Of Culpeper County, Virginia. [2] Of Lexington.
[3] A Virginian who had built the blockhouse at Maysville, Kentucky, in 1784, represented Bourbon County in the first session of the Kentucky legislature in 1792, and owned property in both Washington and Bourbon counties at the turn of the century.
[4] Who had settled in Kentucky around 1776 and owned property in Bourbon and Nelson counties in 1800. [5] AES.

Receipt from James Conover

[June 17, 1802]

Attached to Account, June 13, 1802.

Receipt to Sheriff's Office

[July 11, 1802]

Received 11h. July 1802 of C. Carr[1] ninety two dollars on account of the execution Hull against Hull—[2] HENRY CLAY

ADS. KyHi.

1 Charles Carr, Sheriff of Fayette County.

2 See above, Assignment, August 22, 1801.

To William Taylor

Wm. Taylor Esq. Lexington 23d. July 1802.

Dr Sir

The last mail brought me the unpleasing intelligence of the protest of Douglass's[1] Note—But I shall have no difficulty in getting the money returned with interest & costs, damages we cannot claim—I am informed that it is ready when I call for it—The amount together with a very handsome sum which I expect every day to receive on account of Shepherd[2] shall be remitted the very moment I can procure bankbills; but such has been the demand upon this Country for money lately that it is almost exhausted of all the light money, and I fear I shall meet with great difficulty in procuring notes[3]—Be pleased to retain Douglass's note until otherwise directed—

I received some mails ago the papers relative to Mr. Wantes' affair[4]—The absence of Mr. Daviess[5] from town ever since they came to hand has prevented me from presenting the order. The answer however I can easily anticipate—It will be that he has no funds & bad prospects—On his return you shall again hear from—Yrs.

HENRY CLAY

ALS. Owned by J. Winston Coleman, Jr., Lexington, Kentucky.

1 Samuel Douglass, of Madison County, Kentucky.

2 Adam Shepherd.

3 Western businessmen faced great difficulty in making remittances to their creditors along the seaboard. "Light money," in the form of bills and bank notes, could be transported much more easily than specie, but it was extremely scarce. For several years local contractors for Army supplies did an extensive business in selling bills to merchants. Notes from eastern banks were rare, and Kentucky had no bank until the establishment in December, 1802, of the Kentucky Insurance Company, with banking privileges. Leavy, "Memoir of Lexington," in Kentucky State Historical Society, *Register*, XL (1942), 373; Elmer C. Griffith, "Early Banking in Kentucky," Mississippi Valley Historical Association, *Proceedings, 1908-1909,* II, 173.

4 See below, Clay to Taylor, March 8, 1803.

5 Joseph Hamilton Daveiss.

Receipt from Herman Bowmar

July 31st. 1802

I Certify that Henry Clay Esqr Credited me in Settlement with him by Fifty Dollars on acct. of Mr Henry Watkins, which said sum was lent the said Watkins by the said Clay HERMAN BOWMAR

ADS. DLC-TJC, 2d Series, vol. 4. Major Bowmar, brought to Kentucky by his parents at an early age, became a prominent citizen and large slaveholder of Woodford County. He fought in the Indian wars, served as deputy sheriff and sheriff and was elected to two terms in the State Senate, 1814-1817. He died in 1855 at an advanced age.

To William Taylor

Dr Sir Lexington 10h. August 1802

Inclosed are four hundred dollars in bank notes [. . .] part of the $500 I some days ago received from [Mr. Adam Shep]herd—I could procure no more bank notes, and [. . .] had to give 3 PCent.—I fear I shall be unable [*to procure*] any more of this kind of money, such is [. . .] The fall in the price of horses to the Eastwa[rd *& the in*]considerable sum which we get for our exported [. . .] leave the balance of trade at this time greatly against us; the consequence of which is that the Country is quickly drained of Notes. Shall I meet with your approbation in packing the money? I believe it may be done with less expense than giving the premium for notes—One horse will carry about $2000, and if he can only be sold for first Cost there will be a considerable saving—I expect to receive $2000 from Shepherd this week, of which you shall receive due notice—

Mr. Daviess has not yet returned to this place, in which he resides —I must defer therefore any information respecting Wantes affair to a future day—Yrs with esteem HENRY CLAY

ALS. NcD. MS. torn and a few words missing. Cf. above, Clay to Taylor, July 23, 1802.

To Henry Messonier and William Taylor

Lexington 7h. Septr. 1802.

Mess. Henry Messonier & William Taylor
Gent.

Your's of the 14h. June last reached me some time since.[1] It should have been answered at an earlier period had not the absence of Mr. Daviess from this place, where he resides, prevented me from gaining that full information which I desired, and from presenting to him the order drawn by Mr. Wante. You have now inclosed Mr. Daviess's answer in writing. Permit me to add, from my knowledge of this business, notwithstanding Mr. Daviess's confidence of ultimate success (in which I have no doubt he is entirely sincere) you should not permit yourselves to be too sanguine in your calculations. Bastrop has made two distinct assignments of his property, one to Morehouse, which is prior in date, the other through his agent to Mr. Owings, which is attended with the most formality. Between these two assignments, whether the first shall finally be decided in favour of Mr. Wante or Morehouse, a dispute exists. Which will prevail is a question of difficulty in the solution of which our best attornies differ. Independent of this embarrassment, you know I presume, that Morehouse & Wante are disputing about the assignment from the former to the latter. Admitting however that the assignment to Morehouse from Bastrop is superior to that of Owings, and that the transfer from Morehouse to Wante is valid, the property itself is claime[d] by other persons under different titles, and I fear will not nett any considerable sums in the sales. You will easily perceive that before all these disputes are adjusted a length of time will elapse; so that I fear the day is very remote before any money will be obtained.

No original papers are necessary for me to have to act upon—The order is accepted by Mr. Daviess, and as soon as any money is received by me it shall be remitted to you—In the mean time if any thing shall occur which appea[rs] to be necessary for you to know, it shall be communicated by Gent Yr. Obt. Servt. HENRY CLAY

ALS. KyU-Wilson Collection. Messonier, like Taylor, was a Baltimore merchant. See below, Clay to Taylor, March 8, 1803, in which Clay attempts to explain the complicated business involving Wante, Bastrop, Morhouse, Daveiss, and Owings.
1 Not found.

To [James Taylor]

Dr Sir Lexington 19h. September 1802

Major Morrison[1] of [this] place having given me his bond for £271:14:6 pay[abl]e in land in the North Western Territory at its valuation by two men & their umpire, I have taken the liberty on my part to nominate you. He has appointed Mr. William Lytle. The land lies as the Majr. informs me about 25 or 30 miles from you. Knowing that you have frequently business on the other side of the river, I presume that you & Mr. Lytle can make such an arrangement as will accommodate both of you. But if your own business should not lead you to the quarter in which the land lies, I must get the favour of you to take some leisure moment to go & see it; for I need not add that without viewing it justice cannot be done to both parties. Whatever shall be deemed a liberal compensation I will with pleasure pay you. The land was located & is to be shewn by Mr. Lytle. To enable you to estimate it upon the principles which we have agreed on, I herewith send you a Copy of the bond which is to be your guide.

With respect to the suits in the Bourbon District Court of Boone &c. & Beans heirs,[2] I intended long since to have written you. I did not, when I was employed in the last, know that the same claim was involved therein as in the former. And when I received this information I should have got released if in my power—I should at all events if there had been any inconsistency in the engagements. But in the one case you rely upon the age of your patent alone, in the other on the strength of your entry—No argument can arise where one depends upon his patent only with respect to his entry, and of course as I have in one instance engaged to defend you upon one of these grounds, no inconsistency can take place when the other is controverted—I have mentioned the subject to Capt. Fowler[3] who has returned & who promises to prepare for trial in Baines suit at the n[ex]t term—[4]

Be pleased to let me hear from you as soon as convenient, & believe me to be Yr's sincerely HENRY CLAY

Copy of the Condition referred to

The Condition of the above obligation is such that if the said James Morrison shall by a good & sufficient deed, with a general warranty, convey to the said Clay within twelve months from this time military land lying between Deerfield & Williamsport in the North Western Territory,[5] sufficient at its cash valuation, which is to be made by two men, one to be chosen by each party, and if they disagree their umpire, to pay the sum of £271:14:6, then this obligation &c.

Indorsed on the bond—

"Memo. It is understood that the valuers who are to estimate the land within mentioned are to value it at its real money value, under the impression that the consideration is to be paid twelve months from the present time: for example if they were to value it to day, they are to estimate it at what it would sell for in money, payable twelve months hence; if they value it three months hence, they are then to estimate it at what it would sell for in money on a credit of nine months—And the said Morrison is to shew the land & have it surveyed 18h. Septr. 1802. JAMES MORRISON {L.S.}
H CLAY {L.S.}

ALS. KyHi.

1 James Morrison, prominent Lexingtonian—a land commissioner, navy agent, and army contractor, until his death in 1823 a close friend of Clay.

2 Suits not found.

3 Congressman John Fowler.

4 Suit not found.

5 Probably on Deer Creek, a branch of the Scioto River, in either Ross or Pickaway County (or in both).

From William Taylor

Henry Clay Esqr. Baltimore September. 25th. 1802.
Lexington.
Dear Sir,

I have received your esteemed favr of the 7th. Instant and notice its Contents; In consequence of The difficulty you have met with in remiting The money you have recovered for me I have this day drawn on you Two Bills

one to John Brown at five days sight for .500$
one to Henry Abbett[1] at five days sight for 500$

together making one thousand Dollars which do me the favour to honour at all events and if Convenient please to pay these Bills at sight as I have told The holders of Them it is probable it may be The Case.

If you have packed my money and sent it on, I trust in your good management to pay These Bills on you by my other funds which are in your hands & if no better can be done draw on me to Cover their payment and negotiate The Bills to The best advantage which Shall meet due honour. I have allowed 2½ P Cent Discount on The amount of These Bills which is better Than packing The money.

Mr. Short[2] is in Virginia—I have not seen him. I hope he will call on me before his return & I will advise you Thereof. I am, most respectfully Dear Sir, Yr mo. obt. Sert WM TAYLOR

ALS. DLC-TJC (DNA, M212, R12). Endorsed by Clay: ". . . giving me inform of his drafts fav. Brown and Abbott for . . . $1000."

1 By whom Taylor sent this letter. Abbott or Abbett has not been identified.

2 Peyton Short.

Assignment of Bond and Power of Attorney from William Patterson

[September 25, 1802]

Know all men by these presents that I William Patterson of Fayette County Kentucky have this 25h. day of Sept. 1802, for value received, assigned to Samuel Douglass & Henry Clay a bond given by David McCready[1] to me, upon which is due about one hundred dollars, and which is now in the hands of James Holmes of Washington County in Pennsylvania, but without recourse—And I do hereby nominate constitute & appoint the said Clay & Douglass my true & lawful Attornies for me & in my name to demand sue for & recover from the said James Holmes possession of, & from the said David McCready payment for, the said bond, principal and interest—And I do hereby empower my said Attornies to appoint for this purpose one or more attornies under them—Hereby ratifying

& confirming whatever my said Attornies or their Substitutes shall do for me in the premises.

In witness whereof I have hereunto set my hand & seal the day & year first written—

Signed Sealed & Acknowledged WILLIAM PATTERSON {L.S.}
In presence of—
WM CHILES[2]
NATL MOORE[3]

DS, in Clay's hand. DLC-TJC (DNA, M212, R15). In an agreement between Patterson and Douglass on September 18, 1802 (DS, in Clay's hand. DLC-TJC [M212, R15]), Patterson had promised to assign this bond to Douglass.

1 Not identified.

2 Of Montgomery County, Kentucky.

3 Taxpayer in Franklin County, Kentucky, in 1800; by 1810 a resident of Fayette.

Property Deed from William and Sarah Patterson

[September 25, 1802]

[William Patterson and Sarah, his wife, of Fayette County, for five shillings, paid and acknowledged, sell to Clay and Samuel Douglass, "one equal undivided moiety" of a tract of 1,000 acres in Mason County which had been patented to Patterson on September 19, 1800.[1] Title warranted only against persons claiming through the Pattersons.]

DS, in Clay's hand. DLC-TJC (DNA, M212, R15).

1 By an agreement dated September 18, 1802, Patterson had promised to convey to Douglass within one month the land which he now deeds to Douglass and Clay (DS, in Clay's hand. DLC-TJC [DNA, M212, R15]).

Reversal of Judgment Imposing Fine

NOVEMBER 3, 1802.

Henry Clay *v.* Quarter Sessions Court of Fayette county.
Upon a writ of error to reverse a judgment of the said Court imposing a fine of ten pounds on the said Henry Clay.

. . . .

It does not appear that the contempt alleged to have been committed was committed in the presence of the court, or that the said Clay was present when the fine was imposed, and if not, he ought to have been brought into court by summons or attachment to answer the charge. Therefore, it is considered by the court that the judgment aforesaid be reversed and set aside, and that the plaintiff recover of the defendants his costs in this behalf expended, which is ordered to be certified to the said court.

2 *Ky. Reports* (Sneed), 189-90.

Receipt from Andrew F. Price

[November 13, 1802]

Received Lexington November 13th. 1802 of Henry Clay Esqr. by the hands of Mr. William Akin[1] Five hundred Dollars in full of money lent him.

ANDW. F PRICE.

ADS. DLC-TJC (DNA, M212, R15).

[1] Of Mercer County, Kentucky.

Agreement with William Huntley

[November 24, 1802]

I have this day employed H. Clay. to bring a Suit for me on an Injunction bond given by B. Netherland and William Murray[1] as his Security in a suit in the District Court of Lexington brought by said Netherland against me & others, lately decided. And I do hereby agree to give said Clay one third of whatever may be recovered on said bond, & pay the Costs of Suit.

Witness my hand & seal this 24h. Nov. 1802.

Teste WILLIAM HUNTLEY {L.S.}

STEPHEN TRIGG[2]

DS, in Clay's hand. DLC-TJC (DNA, M212, R15). Huntley has not been identified.

[1] Lexington lawyer, a prominent Federalist and Masonic leader, and, earlier, State Attorney General and a member of the Kentucky House of Representatives. He left Kentucky about 1803 and died in Natchez two years later.

[2] Of Madison County, Kentucky. After Estill County was formed, he was one of the founders of the town of Irvine and, in 1816 and 1817, member of the State legislature.

Property Deed from William Trigg and Others

[November 30, 1802]

[William Trigg, his wife Susanna, and Phillip Caldwell sell to Clay "all that part of the lott in the town of Frankfort No. 51 binding on St Clair street ninety nine feet, on Broadway Sixty feet . . . being the corner lott & opposite to the Market house. . . ." General warranty of title.]

DS, in Clay's hand. DLC-TJC (DNA, M212, R15). Endorsement notes fees for recording, in Franklin County Court, Commissioners' Deeds, 1795-1807, pp. 165-66. Trigg, a magistrate of Frankfort, son of the Colonel Stephen Trigg who was killed at the Battle of Blue Licks, 1782, was married to Susanna, daughter of Francis and Ann (Preston) Smith.

Petition Relating to Sessions of Federal District Court

1st. Decr. 1802

To the Honbl. Congress of the United States of America

The undersigned who are the Counsellors at Law practising in the District Court of the united States for Kentucky

Respectfully Represent That from their Experience in the said Court and in the Superior Courts of the State, they Consider it more advantageous to Suitors that the Said District Court should be held only twice in each year: The terms to commence on the third mondays of May and November and continue as long as the business before the Court should Require

They therefore petition that a Law may pass accordingly &c.

JOSEPH H. DAVEISS. JOHN ALLEN J HUGHES
JAS BLAIR ISHAM TALBOT.
JAMES BROWN JOHN ROWAN
HENRY CLAY H. MARSHALL

DS. DLC-Breckinridge Family Papers (DNA, Microcopy Supp.).

From George Clark

Dear Sir Frankfort Dec 17: 1802

Wm Fenwick surviving partner of Heathcote & F[1] has an acct of which I inclose the Statemt, agt Jno Craig.[2] Security was given for the debt, in a mortgage, or Bill of Sale, on 60000 Acres of land; the mortgage was forfeited, & land sold, as pr Acct. Jno Craig's bond (Copy inclosed) [3] was given, previous to this, as a farther Security– The Sale of the land not discharging the whole debt, Col Todd[4] brought Suit in behalf of F[enwic]k, but, instead of bringing it for the balance, brought it, for the amt of the Collateral Security, on the bond. Judgmt was obtained on the bond, and still, as pr Acct, a balance remained due W Fenwick–For this I wish you to bring Suit in what shape I leave to your judgmt, though I presume it will be best answered by a Bill in Chancery–

Receive with these an acct deld by Col Quarles[5] agt Fenwick who accepts the Credit therein allowed, and allows the Cash Charges, but refuses to pay Quarles's demand for Services done for W Fenwick, considering it so exorbitant.[6] The charge for Services done for Banks,[7] is, as p Note Subjoined to Quarles acct, left optional with Fenwick to pay or not as Suits him–I fear this Suit must also be brought in Chancery, as we know, by experience, that if we carry it at Common law, our friend Quarles will move to the former Court–

I recommend Pollards Suit to your attention likewise Trotter & Allens Exon agt him, fresh Suit do vs do,[8] Browns judgmt vs Owens[9] –Sonne vs Jones[10]–I am your friend & Svt GEORGE CLARK

PS Do not hazard the conveyance of the 2 Certificates inclosed by Post, but after obtaining Colemans Signature advise me of it by Post.

ALS. DLC-TJC (DNA, M212, R15). Addressed to Clay at Lexington. Clark, who resided in Lexington for a brief period, served as agent for Virginians with interests in Kentucky.

1 Heathcote has not been identified. William Fenwick resided in Frankfort at this time.

2 Of Boone County, Kentucky, a brother of Lewis and Elijah Craig. A few years earlier John had been a member of the State legislature. The statement has not been found.

3 Not found.

4 Thomas Todd.

5 Colonel John Tunstall Quarles settled near Pisgah Church in Woodford County in 1789.

6 Fenwick won a suit against Quarles in Fayette Circuit Court in 1805, which, however, did not settle their differences.

7 Probably Cuthbert Banks.

8 These suits have not been found.

9 James Brown had obtained a judgment against Owings (probably John Cockey Owings) on a note given in payment for land. Owings maintained that Brown, who had acquired the land from Wade Mosby of Powhatan County, Virginia, had not been able to convey title. The Court of Appeals in 1827 finally ended the prolonged litigation by directing that the original contract be rescinded. 21 *Ky. Reports* (5 T. B. Monroe) 462-64.

10 Not found.

Settlement with Maddox Fisher

Dr. H. Clay— 17h. Decr. 1802.

To balance upon Settlement
respecting dwelling house pavement &c. £1:16:10
To amount of Account for
Stable smoakhouse necessary pave
ment &c — — — 105: 0:11
106:17: 9

Contra Cr—
By hire of Sam[1]— £18
By Cash pd. John Fisher[2] 10:7.
By Order on Baylor[3] 27:0.
By Cash from yr. Wife 0:3:
By Cash 4¼dollars & 9d. 1:7.9
56:17: 9.
£50: 0: 0

Mr. Fisher and myself have this day had a Settlement in full of all accounts when the above balance (subject to a deduction or addition for any errors which may hereafter be discovered) is found due to him, one half of which I will pay at Christmas & the other on the first day of April next— H. CLAY

NB. It is understood he is to finish off my house—pencelling, pointing, stopping holes &c. of Stable &c. H. CLAY

[Endorsement][4]
thare is 15/ to be deducted £ 105„15„11
15.
105„ 0„11

[Endorsements on verso][5]

Decem 28 then recevid of harrey Clay 50 Doll. in part pay of the with in by me MADDOX FISHER

1803

June 1 then Recevid of Mr. Clay ten pounds Cash in part paey a Cradit By T.. Hart Juner £13..10.0 of the within by me M. FISH

ADS. DLC-TJC, 2d Series, vol. 4. See above, Agreement, April 23, 1801.

1 Clay's slave

2 Lexington bricklayer and, later, brickmaker; probably a brother of Maddox Fisher.

3 Probably Walker Baylor, a Virginia veteran of the Revolution who had moved from Caroline County to Lexington, where he had opened a tavern in 1796, received an appointment as justice of the peace in the next year, and subsequently engaged in mercantile business.

4 AE, by Fisher.

5 The first two, AES; the third, AE, by Fisher.

Receipted Order from Nathan Adams

[*ca.* December 18, 1802]

Mr Clay pleas pay Mr Jacob Adams twelve dollars and three Quarters that is the Ballans for the plank: I sent you 200 and Eighty---feet more to make A lod for the wagon Acord in to your order

NATHN ADAMS

[Endorsement on verso][1]

Recd. 18h. Decr. ten dollars & a quarter on account of the within JACOB ADAMS

ADS. DLC-TJC, 2d Series, vol. 4.

1 ES, in Clay's hand.

Receipt to Sheriff's Office

Lexington 29th Decr. 1802

Recd. of Charles Carr Ds Fayette County twenty Pou[nd]s on A/c of an Exon. obtaind Fayettee Court Peter Hull vs Hull.[1]

Teste HENRY CLAY

JOS. GRAY[2]

DS. KyHi.

1 See above, Assignment, August 22, 1801.

2 Lexington merchant, at this time in partnership with Alexander Parker.

To Joseph Hamilton Daveiss

SIR, [January, 1803]

When an individual offers himself for the suffrages of the people, that people have a right to demand an honest avowal of his political opinions. As their dearest interests, their political honor and consistency are placed at his disposal, it is their right, it is their duty to make the enquiry, and he can have no negative right to dissent from it. If he refuses, you must admit, the presumption arises that his opinions do not accord with those of the people, and that he believes a declaration of them would be detrimental to his election. For if this were not your opinion, why would your political confession of faith, have accompanied the letter, which announced your pretensions to a seat in congress?[1] You have too much knowledge not to be informed that no people ever rejected a man, because his opinions were similar to their own; and too much understanding to believe that a free people will ever elect a candidate to office whose political opinions are avowedly opposed to their own.

In pursuance then of the duties which the high character of a citizen imposes upon me, I now call upon you for a more full and explicit avowal of your political opinions, than has yet appeared before the public. I am anxious that my representative should carry into the bosom of congress those principles which every republican would cherish. And I cannot be silent when a candidate is about to enter that body in a dubious character.

The voice of fame hath declared that your political opinions have vibrated; and that you have neither been consistent with yourself, nor at all times friendly to the politics of Mr. Jefferson. Satisfactory information must therefore be given whether you are displeased with Mr. Adams because he is out of office, or pleased with Mr. Jefferson because he is in it. I am well aware sir, that it is natural for *some* characters to worship the rising sun; but I do not therefore conclude that it is generous to kick at the fallen. I wish you to give me some information upon this subject. And perhaps you will without my requesting it, tell me when, or how, or for what good reason, you *so suddenly* have acquired all this attachment to the present administration.

To return to the voice of fame. It further instructs me to enquire, whether you did not at Danville, make a long speech in defence of the British treaty?[2] Whether you have not considered the Alien and Sedition Bills as constitutional? Whether you did not approve the administration of John Adams? And have not repeatedly declared your disapprobation of that of Mr. Jefferson? Whether you have not declared the law repealing the act which authorised John Adams' midnight appointments to be unconstitutional?—And when elected into congress intend to oppose the present administration?

If your opinions upon these subjects are conformable to those of the people, you can have no objection to declare them; because the declaration would promote your election. If, however, you give no answer, I shall consider you unable to make a satisfactory one. I shall consider you an outward republican, and at heart a federalist. I shall believe you have used the general expressions of Mr. Jefferson, which all parties affect to admire, to cloak your real principles. And I shall conclude that as you have commenced your career with deceit, you will end by betraying. SCAEVOLA.

Lexington *Kentucky Gazette*, February 1, 1803. In a reply addressed *"To the Editors of the Kentucky Gazette, and Guardian of Freedom,"* published in the *Kentucky Gazette*, February 14, 1803, Daveiss commented that he would state his political tenets in public addresses, since the circulation of newspapers in the district for which he stood was too limited to reach "the twentieth part of the electors. . . . Not to mention the obvious impropriety of entering into newspaper controversies with impertinent and calumniating scribblers, whose opposition is manifestly personal, not political, and who delight in traduction and abuse, so long as their fictitious names secure them from responsibility."

1 Daveiss had announced his candidacy through the medium of a letter in the Frankfort *Palladium*, December 25, 1802. Quoting a portion of Jefferson's first inaugural address, he had pledged himself to "a faithful observance" of the principles stated therein. Although Daveiss' Congressional District did not include Fayette County, Clay was apparently outraged by this effort of the Federalist leader to identify himself with Republicanism. 2 The Jay Treaty.

Receipt to [William] Stephenson

8. Jany. 1803

Received of Mr Stephenson two notes given to Mr J. Breckenridge one by Reuben Field[1] for fifty dollars, and the other by Danl. Spangler, Richard Dictum & Lewis Craig Jr[2] upon which there are 33 dollars & some Interest due to bring suit on. H CLAY

ADS. DLC-Breckinridge Papers (DNA, M212, R20). Endorsed by Breckinridge on verso: "Mr. Clay's rect. for Fields Note £15.–Spangler's–9.18.0" William Stephenson was (or had been earlier) a student in John Breckinridge's law office.

1 Of Bourbon County, Kentucky. 2 All of Woodford County.

Receipt from John James Dufour

[January 28, 1803]

Received 28 Jan. 1803 of H Clay Twenty dollars. on account of a share in the Vineyard Association. J J DUFOUR

DS, in Clay's hand. DLC-TJC, 2d Series, vol. 4. Dufour, a Swiss, was manager of the vineyard established on the Kentucky River, near the mouth of Hickman Creek, by the "Directors and Society for promoting the cultivation of the Vine," incorporated in 1799.

Judgment: John Franks *vs.* Clay

Fayette County Court. [February 3, 1803]

John Franks Complt. ves. Henry Clay Deft.

Judgment for the complt. for three pounds fifteen shillings and cost given under my hand this 3 day of February. 1803

Thomas Hart as Security WALKER BAYLOR.

ADS. Owned by J. Winston Coleman, Jr., Lexington, Kentucky.

Appeal Bond: John Franks *vs.* Clay

[February 3, 1803]

Know all men by these presents that we Henry Clay and Thomas Hart Junr. are held and firmly bound unto John Franks in the just and full sum of ten pounds Current money; to be paid to the said John Franks his heirs executors or administrators; to which payment well & truly to be made we bind ourselves our heirs executors and administrators jointly & severally, firmly by these presents. Sealed with our seals & dated this 3 day of February 1803.

The Condition of the above obligation is such That whereas the said John Franks hath recovered before Walker Baylor, a Justice of the peace for Fayette County, a Judgment against the said Henry Clay. for the sum of three pounds fifteen shillings and Costs; from which the said Henry Clay hath appealed to the next County Court of Fayette County: Now if the said Clay shall pay the amount of the said Judgment & Costs should it be confirmed by the said County Court then this obligation to be void, otherwise to remain in full force & virtue.

Signed Sealed & Delivered HENRY CLAY
In presence of— THOS. HART JR
SOPHIA GROSH[1]

ADS, signed also by Hart. Owned by J. Winston Coleman, Jr., Lexington, Kentucky.
[1] Sister of Mrs. Thomas Hart, Jr. In April, 1804, Miss Grosh married Henry Clay's younger brother, Porter, at this time a cabinet-maker in Lexington.

To Levi Todd

Dr Sir [*ca.* February 3, 1803]

I send you a Judgment given by a magistrate, with an appeal bond[1]—I will thank you to send me a summons for the appellee & a blank Subpoena for witnesses—Yrs.

Lexington H. CLAY

ALS. Owned by J. Winston Coleman, Jr., Lexington, Kentucky. Addressed to Todd, Clerk of the Fayette County Court. The summons, for Franks to appear in Fayette County Court on the second Monday in February, was issued by Todd on February 8, 1803. At the April Term of the Court the original judgment in favor of Franks was confirmed. Fayette County Court, Order Book no. 1, p. 17 (April 11, 1803).
[1] In the case John Franks *vs.* Clay.

Lease to Isaac Wilson

[February 28, 1803]

An agreement between Isaac Wilson and Henry Clay entered into this 28h. day of Feb. 1803.

The said Wilson has this day rented of the said Clay the house on

Main Street and the piece of ground inclosed adjoining, being part of the Race ground for one year.[1] And the said Wilson covenants to deliver at the end of that time the said house in as good order as it shall be when the repairs hereafter mentioned are made, and the said lott in as good order as it is at present (natural decays excepted). And the said Wilson further covenants to pay to the said Clay at the end of the said year[2] Seventy dollars for the use of the said house & lott, for the security of which (in addition to the said Clays right of distress) the said Wilson agrees to enter into bond with good security in one month. And the said Clay covenants to permit the said Wilson to put any repairs on the said house which he may think proper, not exceeding in value ten dollars, for the amount of which repairs the said Wilson is to receive a credit against the said Seventy dollars. And the said Wilson is to have possession of the premisses to day, and to return them as aforesaid on the 28 day of Feb. 1804.

Witness our hands & Seals.

Teste (being first interlined) HENRY CLAY {L.S.}
JOHN MCKINNEY JR[3] ISAAC WILSON {L.S.}

ADS, signed also by Wilson. KyLxT. Wilson was the founder of the Lexington Grammar School in 1787 and first "grammar master" of Transylvania Seminary after its removal to Lexington. Only one month later Clay rented the same property to William Palmateer.

1 Cf. above, Assignment, April 15, 1802. In 1793 the town trustees confined horse racing to Water Street west of Main Cross Street (Broadway). Charles R. Staples, *The History of Pioneer Lexington (Kentucky), 1799-1806* (Lexington, 1939), 96.

2 The last seven words interlined.

3 Possibly at the time Clay's law clerk; later Clerk of the Woodford County Court for many years.

Account with William Morton

[*ca.* February 28, 1803]

Henry Clay Esqr— To Will. Morton —Dr—

1800			
June 13th	To	1. empty tight barl	£ 0. 6. 0
1801			
Nov. 2.—	"	1. yd swansdown 24/. 3 yds drab cloth @ 11/	2.17. 0
1802			
Decr— 6 —	"	6 lb white Lead p. Stephens[1]	0.12. 0
1803			
Jany. 4 —	"	7½ yds 5/4 Irish sheeting ... 3/9 ...	1. 8. 1½
Feby. 14 —	"	2 7/8 yds supr. black cloth @ 36/- Lin. &c 15/11	5.19. 5
28 —	"	2 gall. Mada—wine 30/	3. 0. 0
			£14. 2. 6½

Contra . . . . . . Cr.

1802			
Mar 23	By cash recd of Dounton for your certificat from Colo. Beatty[3] 15 2/3.$.		4.14. 0
	due W. M.	£	9. 8. 6½

D. DLC-TJC (DNA, M212, R15).

1 Luther Stephens, of the firm, Stephens and Winslow.

2 Richard Downton, of Lexington, appointed by the town Trustees later this year to enforce the local laws against nuisances.

3 Cornelius Beatty, Lexington merchant.

Fee Bill from Levi Todd

[*ca.* February, 1803]

1803.	Henry Clay Esquire Dr	Cents
Feby.	filing and docketting appeal agt. Franks[1]	25.
	summons 18. endorsement 10. subpoena 18.	46
	Bond to prosecute 25 Order for Continuance 25.	50
	filing papers 18.	18
Jany.	To six blank writs	3.00
		4„39

Teste LEVI TODD Cl. Fayette.

ADS. DLC-TJC, 2d Series, vol. 4.

1 John M. Franks.

To William Taylor

William Taylor Esq. Lexington 1 March 1803.

Dr Sir

Having in vain endeavoured to procure bank bills, the scarcity of which is increased by the inauspicious circumstances in which the Commerce of our Country is placed and the fall in the price of horses to the Eastward,[1] I thought it best to take the inclosed drafts which I know are safe. The small one is drawn by an intimate acquaintance, who paid the Taxes on the land of Dr. McClurg, a man of wealth & eminence in Richmond.[2] The large one is drawn by the Contractor for supplying the Troops of the United States, on his agent Genl. Mason,[3] in favour of James Morrison, Supervisor of this State; all men of wealth and respectability. Such drafts I should myself prefer to bills at the premium of 2½ per Cent, with the risk attending their remittance; for I had to give no premium on the drafts:

I have not yet received the balance of your money; but expect to get it in a few days—

I wait also for an answer to my last[4]—I am Dr Sr Yr. mo. ob. Hble Servt. HENRY CLAY

ALS. NcD.

1 Kentucky trade suffered greatly not only from the general business depression following the peace of Amiens, but also as a result of the suspension of the right of deposit at New Orleans, under a ruling by Spanish officials during the previous October.

2 Dr. James McClurg, physician of Richmond, Virginia.

3 General John Mason, of Analostan Island, in the Potomac River at Georgetown. Revolutionary officer and commandant of the militia for the District of Columbia, second president of the Bank of Columbia, farmer and stock-breeder. He was Superintendent of the Indian trade in 1807.

4 Not found.

Receipt from Thomas Tunstall

Lexington 3d. March 1803

Recevd. of Henry Clay Esq twenty two dolls. and fifty seven Cents the amt. of my fees agains [*sic*] DeGraffendriet[1] from 1801. to Decemr. 1802 inclusive which fee bill includes copy of and [*sic*] ansrs. delivered this year. THOS TUNSTALL CK.DC

ADS. DLC-TJC, 2d Series, vol. 4.

1 William DeGraffenridt. Cf. below, Confirmation of Contract, August 6, 1803.

To Thomas Hockley

Thomas Hockley Esqr. Lexington 4h. March 1802.
Dr Sir Say 1803 [*sic*]

Both of your last, one covering the anonymous letter to you, and the other acknowledging the receipt of mine of the first of January last have been received.[1] The suit against Edwards[2] is depending in the Washington Circuit Court, distant about sixty miles from this place, and in which I do not practice myself. Mr. Davis[3] employed Mr. Bledsoe[4] a gentleman of respectable talents & attention to business your attorney. I have seen him since the receipt of the anonymous letter & placed that together with such other papers as related to Mr. Edwards and which you sent out by Mr. Leavy[5] in his hands. Having resided in the same town with Calderwood[6] he as well as another gentleman acquainted with him & to whom I shewed that singular production, is of opinion that it was written by Calderwood. And Mr. Bledsoe is moreover of opinion that Edwards has attached this rascal to his interest; because having summoned him at the last Court, Edwards informed him that he need not produce Calderwood as he would swear that nothing was due you; in consequence of which Mr. Bledsoe continued the cause. We will take care to make such use of the letter as to invalidate his testimony if he is produced on the trial. I believe we shall be compelled for proof of your account to resort to Mr Davis, to whom Edwards acknowledged it. Edwards has a variety of his receipts, which I have instructed Mr. Bledsoe to possess himself of, and give him in their place an aggregate receipt.

As soon as Mr Davis arrives I will wait on him & do the best I can for you—

Tom January[7] promises immediate payment, which if he disappoints me in I will sue him—I am Dr Sir Yrs— HENRY CLAY

ALS. Owned by Thomas D. Clark, Lexington, Kentucky. Addressed on attached sheet: "Thomas Hockley Esqr. Merchant Philadelphia." Endorsed: "Lexington Kenty 4th Mar: 1803 Henry Clay Esqr. recd. March 17th—"

1 Not found.

2 Haden Edwards. Washington is in Mason County.

3 Not identified.

4 Jesse Bledsoe.

5 William Leavy.

6 Possibly James Calderwood, a Virginia veteran of the Continental Line. Bledsoe was from Culpeper County, Virginia.

7 Lexington merchant and manufacturer.

To William Taylor

William Taylor Esq. Lexington 8h. March 1803.

Dr Sir

By the last mail but one I inclosed you the first numbers of two setts of Exchange,[1] of which I now send you the second. My inability to procure notes and the high confidence I have in the drawers & payers of these bills induced me to accept them; and indeed having got them without premium, they are in my estimation more valuable than Notes at 2½ P Cent: for although one of the bills is at Ninety days. I presume the bank will discount it at 1½ P Cent.

The last mail brought me your favour of the 10 February[2] covering the acknowledgment of Mr. Mickle[3] of the receipt of three hundred dollars

I am glad to hear that you have received the amount of Armstrong's bill,[4] but am sorry that you sustained a loss on it. Mr. Short[5] has returned to this Country and as soon as I can see him (which will probably be the case shortly) I will endeavour to get the balance from him. The Judgment against him is in full force. In the course of the week after next I will forward a statement of our a/c by the Mail.[6]

I will attempt to explain to you the situation in which Mr. Wante's & Bastrop's business stands.[7] Mr. J. C. Owings of Baltimore[8] has an incumbrance upon part of Bastrop's property, which is mortgaged also to Morehouse & to Wante, whose mortgages include not only what was conveyed to Mr. Owings but the whole of Bastrop's property in this Country.[9] Mr. Wante has obtained from Morehouse an assignment of his lien, which is prior in date to any other, but is deficient in form and is moreover believed to be fraudulent. Morehouse contests the assignment made to Mr. Wante, against whom he alledges a violation of the contract in pursuance of which it was made. A suit is commenced by Mr. Wantes Atto.[10] first to establish the assignment; but that failing to set aside the mortgage to Morehouse as fraudulent, and in the mean time to prevent a Sale of the property under a decree obtained in Morehouse's name, by virtue of which sales were about to be made at which he no doubt would be the purchaser. Before I received your letter & Mr. Messoniers,[11] I had been engaged as Counsel for Mr. Owings. But in the present stage of the business I do not feel any incompatability in this engagement with any service I can render you. In the case hereafter of any contest between Wante & Owings my prior engagement to the latter must prevail. But at this time both Wante & Owings are equally interested in defeating Morehouse; and if his incumbrance is entirely vacated I presume no contest will take place between Mr. Owings & Wante, because the mortgage to the former is prior to that of the latter & possesses every requisite solemnity. So united have I considered the interests at this time of Mr. Owings & Wante, that I have felt myself bound to appear in the suit of the latter, in case any assistance should be necessary, which may probably be not the case as a gentleman of respectable talents is engaged particularly for Mr. Wante. Whatever shape the contest may assume, I can at least receive the money under your's & Mr. Messonier's draft & transmit it to you, in case any money is ever recovered. But so complicated & involved are the property & incumbrances, that I fear several years will expire before any thing is made. And when every conflicting claim is investigated and decided on, the intrinsic value of the property is extremely questionable. You may rely on my aid—and should it so turn out that I cannot with propriety serve you, I will give you due notice. Did you & Mr. Messonier not receive my letter covering one from Mr. Daviess on this subject?[12] I am Dr Sir Yr. mo. ob.

HENRY CLAY

ALS. NBuHi. Directed to Baltimore. Endorsed: "... Henry Clay seconds of Masons & Mc. Clurg's Bill An'd 22 March."

1 See above, Clay to Taylor, March 1, 1803.

2 Not found.

3 Probably Robert Mickle, of Baltimore.

4 John Armstrong.

5 Peyton Short.

6 See below, Account, April 5, 1803.

7 In addition to his activities in Louisiana, where in 1795 he acquired from the Spanish governor a huge land grant on the Ouachita River, Bastrop engaged in business in Lexington and became deeply indebted to Charles Peter Stephen Wante for merchandise. Bastrop also acquired lands in Kentucky that were mortgaged in 1801 to John Cockey Owings. Wante contended that this mortgage was fraudulently made to prevent his taking the land to satisfy his claim on Bastrop. Meanwhile, Bastrop's Kentucky land had also been mortgaged to Abraham Morhouse, a New Yorker who lived in Kentucky before moving to Louisiana. The litigation arising from this situation continued for many years. See Bastrop papers in KyU-Samuel M. Wilson Collection; and above, Clay to Messonier and Taylor, September 7, 1802.

8 John Cockey Owings was a large speculator in Kentucky lands, a proprietor of the town sites of Bardstown, in Nelson County, and Owingsville, in Bath County, where he engaged in numerous business ventures.

9 That is, in Kentucky. Bastrop also had legal difficulties with Wante, Morhouse, and others in Louisiana.

10 Joseph Hamilton Daveiss.

11 Not found.

12 See above, Clay to Messonier and Taylor, September 7, 1802.

Agreement with John Coons

[March 9, 1803]

For value received, I have this day agreed to give Henry Clay fifty dollars out of whatever may be recovered by me in a suit in Chancery I am about to bring in the Circuit Court of Fayette against John Arthurs, Joseph Hostuttur & David Stout[1]—And if I dismiss, discontinue or compromise the said Suit I am to pay the said fifty dollars.[2]

Witness my hand & seal this 9h. day of March 1803.

Teste [. . .][3] JOHN COONS {L.S.}

JOHN MCKINNEY JR

DS, in Clay's hand. DLC-TJC (DNA, M212, R15). Coons, who had come to Kentucky from Berkeley County, Virginia, was a Lexington coppersmith.

1 Hostetter, a German, operated a butcher shop on Water Street. Stout, who lived on Mulberry (Limestone) Street, was a carpenter and a member of the town Board of Trustees.

2 When the case was heard, in 1805, after having been redocketed several times, the Court dismissed Coons' bill and ruled that the defendants should recover costs. Fayette Circuit Court, Order Book C, 174.

3 Illegible.

Assignment by Luther Stephens and Company

[March 17, 1803]

For value received we have this day assigned to Henry Clay One hundred pounds of a note due to us from Thomas Tunstall[1] and on which a Suit is now depending in the Circuit Court of Fayette County. It is understood that the interest which has already accrued on the said one hundred pounds is not transferred to said Clay, but that the interest which may hereafter accrue is for the said Clay's benefit.

Witness our hands & seals this 17h. March 1803.

Teste LR. STEPHENS & CO {L.S.}

JOHN MCKINNEY JR—

DS, in Clay's hand. DLC-TJC (DNA, M212, R15).

1 By decree of the Fayette Circuit Court, June Term, 1803, Stephens and Winslow had been awarded a judgment for $500 (£150) against Thomas Tunstall. At the June Term, 1804, Tunstall agreed to pay 10 per cent of the above amount in lieu of prosecuting an appeal. Fayette Circuit Court, Order Book B (1804-1805), 102.

From John Wrenshall

Mr. Henry Clay Pittsburgh 21. March 1803
Sir

Your favour dated 17th. of Feby 1803[1] I received in course. I have consulted my partner Mr. Ralph Peacock respecting the propriety of takeing Lands or cash for our part of West & Guthries Debt, who agrees with me in prefering the latter.

We hope you will add the interest to the principle and gurantee to us the punctual payment of said money on the 18th. of September next the time you mention—I informd you by letter some time ago that Edward West had paid the sum of fifty dollars in part of said bond, and to Mr. Wm Boggs[2] Seventy dollars in Cash and a Dirk value fifteen dollars totall amount eighty five dollars—for these payments he had receipts which he will no doubt produce at the time,—as we are anxious to close the business of Peacock Wrenshall & Co. shall thank you to observe the above request with punctuallity—in expectation of which I am Sir Yours very respectfully

JOHN WRENSHALL

ALS. DLC-TJC (DNA, M212, R12).
1 Not found. 2 Probably of Philadelphia.

Rental Agreement with William Palmateer

[March 31, 1803]

Know all men by these presents that I William Palmateer of the town of Lexington am held and firmly bound unto Henry Clay in the just and full sum of two hundred pounds; to be paid to the said Clay his heirs executors administrators or assigns: to which payment well and truly to be made I bind myself my heirs executors and administrators firmly by these presents. Sealed with my seal and dated this 31st. day of March 1803.

The Condition of the above obligation is such that whereas the said Clay hath rented to the said Palmateer the lott or parcel of ground lying in the said town of Lexington on Main Street and near the lower end thereof, being that part of the Race ground which is now inclosed,[1] taken off from the remainder by the opening of the New Street,[2] until the first day of November 1807, for which the said Palmateer is to pay at the rate of twenty pounds per year, and at the end of the said term is to return the said ground and the house & fence thereon[3] to the said Clay in as good order as they are at present, natural decays excepted: Now if the said William Palmateer shall on the first day of November next pay to the said Clay the sum of eleven pounds thirteen shillings and four pence, and shall pay to the said Clay half yearly thereafter at the rate of twenty pounds per year until the expiration of the term aforesaid; and shall moreover keep on the said premises property sufficient to enable the said Clay to distrain in case of nonpayment of the rent, and shall at the end of the term aforesaid return the said property in as good order as it is at present, natural decays excepted, then this obligation to be void otherwise to remain in full force and virtue.

Signed Sealed & Delivered
being first interlined
in presence of
SAMUEL WILKINSON.

his
WILLIAM X PALMATEER {L.S.}
mark

Memorandum It is understood that in case the said lott of ground should be recovered from M. O. Russell[4] before the expiration of the term within mentioned, the said Palmateer is only to pay for the time he has it, and the said Clay is to be liable to no damages.

31 March 1803.
Teste
SAMUEL WILKINSON.

his
WILLIAM X PALMATEER {L.S.}
mark
HENRY CLAY {L.S.}

DS, in Clay's hand. KyLxT. Palmateer, or Palmeter, was a stonequarrier.

1 This property had been rented to Isaac Wilson one month earlier.

2 Locust Street, between High and Water. The ground for this street was relinquished to the town by Robert Patterson in December, 1802. Lexington Trustees Book, I, 162.

3 Last six words interlined.

4 Mary Owen Todd Russell. A claim to the property had been entered by James Hughes and John Fowler, the litigation continuing for many years.

Assignment from Catherine Woods

[April 4, 1803]

For value received I do hereby assign to Henry Clay the Judgment I recovered against Christopher Greenup in the late Fayette Court of Quarter Sessions, which was afterwards affirmed in the Court of Appeals; and also the bond given by the said Greenup on suing out the writ of Error, and the bond which he gave when he obtained the Injunction which was lately dissolved in Fayette Circuit Court[1]— And I do also assign to said Clay all damages interest & Costs to which the said Greenup is subject in consequence of said Judgment or the steps which he has taken to put off the payment of it—

I do hereby also give the said Clay an irrevocable authority to prosecute any suit in my name which he may deem necessary to recover the said demand.

Witness my hand & seal this 4h. day of April 1803.

Signed Sealed & Delivered
In presence of
HALLET M WINSLOW

CATH. WOOD {L.S.}

DS, in Clay's hand. KyLxT. Catherine Woods, a widow, was for a time engaged in mercantile business in Lexington. Greenup became Governor of Kentucky in 1804.

1 Fayette Circuit Court, Order Book A (1803-1804), 21.

William Taylor's Account

[April 5, 1803]

Dr. William Taylor Esq.	To Henry Clay	Doll.	Cents
1800	To Cash paid the Marshall for extraordinary exertions to serve the Capias on Heugh and Ralstone[1]	17	25
1801			
15 July.	To a bill of exchange drawn by Edwards on Mrs. Swearingen[2]	1450	"
4 Decr.	To Cash remitted you by the post in notes[3]	500	"
	To premium of $2\frac{1}{2}$ P Cent paid for exchanging $320 into notes	8	"
1802.			
Jany 26.	To this day remitted you by the post in bank notes	810	"
	To premium of 2 P Cent for exchanging $800 into notes	16	"
10 May	To this day remitted you by the post	500	"
	To premium of 3 P Cent on $470 light money	14	"
1 June	To this day remitted you by the post	250	"
	To premium of $2\frac{1}{2}$ P Cent thereon for light money	6	25
10 Augt.	To this day remitted you by the post in notes	400	"
	To premium of 3 P Cent thereon	12	"
28 Septr.	To this day remitted you by post	500	"
	To prem. of 3 P Cent for light money	15	"
22 Octr	To your bills on me in favour of Abbot & Brown[4]	1000	"
1803.			
1 March	To a bill on Genl. Mason favor D. Vertner[5]	460	"
	To do. on Dr. McClurg drawn by B. Howard[6]	58	"
	To Stephen Wante's note due 31 Decr. 1801[7]	395	64
	To paid you by Tho. Hockley for me[8]	200	"
	To Armstrong's bill[9]	250	"
	To Marshalls Commission on your execution agt. Heugh & Ralstone $97 & some Cents, which are forgotten as the bill was forwarded to you	97	"
	To original Costs of suit & of last execution	29	44

	To postage on sundry letters, on depositions in Heugh & Rs. suit &c	10	"
	To my Commission on $7444:29 collected by me at 5 P Cent	372	21
	To do. on $3332:97 the bal. of Heugh & Ralstones debt received by you	166	64
		7537	43

Contra Cr.

1801			
	By Cash received of Satterwhite[10] as P Statement A	960	68
June—			
	By do. of A. Shepherd[11] per statement B ...	1796	18
	By do. of Heugh & Ralstone	1000	"
	By do. of Shepherd & Hubbard[12] P statemt C	3287	43
	By do of Short a/c of Edwards' protested bill	400	"
		7444	29
	By a bank note retd. Counterfeit	20	"
	By paid Mr. Mickle[13] for me	300	"
		$7764	29

Bal. due by H.C. $226:86. N.B. I have given Mr. Taylor credit by the whole sum due from Shepherd & Hubbard. In January last all was paid to me except $435 some Cents, for which I took the engagement of a gentleman—The whole of this is not yet paid, but I consider myself answerable for it. H C

A

Mann Satterwhite (guarranteed by A. Holmes) .[14]
To Wm. Taylor ..... Dr.

1795		
17 March	To amount of your note this day due in Maryland Currency	£455: 1:11
	To Int. thereon to the 10 August 1796	37:18: 8
		493: 0. 7
1796		
10 Augt.	By Cash Recd. through Orr[15]	213:15: 0
		279: 5: 7
	To Int. thereon to the 10 June 1801	80:19: 6
		£360: 5: 1

Equal to $960.68—

Mr. Satterwhite still owes a small balance which I take on myself—

B.

Dr. Shepherd & Hubbard To Wm. Taylor.

1797		
26 Oct.	To bal. this day due me in M.[16] Currency £960:6:9–	$2560:91
	To Int thereon to the 25 May 1801	550:40
		3111:31.
1801		
25 May	By Cash paid H. Clay	700: 4
		2411:27
	To Int. thereon from the 25 May to 1 Decr. 1801	74:38
		2485:65
1 Decr.	By Cash pd. H.C.	500: 0.
		1985:65
	To Int. thereon to the 24 March 1802	37:22
		2022:87.
1802		
24 Mar	By Cash paid H.C.	334: 0
		1688:87.
	To Int. thereon to the 24 Apl.	8:34.
		1697:21
24 April	By Cash paid the Marshall	246:29.
		1450:92
	To Int. thereon to 22 Octr. 1802	43:45
		1494:37.
22 Octr.	By Cash paid the Marshall	380.
		1114:37.
	To Int. thereon to the 1 Jan. 1803	12:73
	By Cash paid the Marshall	1127:10

C.

Dr. Adam Shepherd To William Taylor–

1797		
Nov. 10.	To your bond of this date payable one half in six the other in twelve months	$1884:16
	To Int. thereon from the times it became due to the 3 Augt. 1802	449: 4
		2333:20
1802		
3. Augt.	By Cash this day paid to the Marshall	1460: 0
		873:20

	To Int. thereon to the 22 October		11:64
			884:84
22 Octr.	By Cash this day paid to the Marshall		190:
			694:84
	To Int. thereon to the 1 January 1803		8:10
			702:94.
	By Cash paid to W.T. as per receipt in the hands of Shepherd 1 April 1798.	$433:32*	
	By Int. thereon from that time to the 1 January 1803	123:44	556:76
			146:18
1803 1 January	By Cash in full paid the Marshall		146.18

* In allowing this Credit I was governed by a receipt in Mr. Taylors hand writing in Shepherd's possession—It differs from the account forwarded to me— E E. HENRY CLAY

ADS. DLC-HC (DNA, M212, R1). See below, Taylor to Clay, April 25, 1803.
1 See above, Clay to Taylor, March 30, 1800.
2 See above, Taylor to Clay, December 25, 1801.
3 See above, Clay to Taylor, December 8, 1801.
4 See above, Taylor to Clay, September 25, 1802.
5 Cf. above, Clay to Taylor, March 1, 1803. Daniel Vertner, Mason County business man, formerly a clerk for Charles Wilkins, in Lexington, later a resident of Mississippi.
6 See above, Clay to Taylor, March 1, 1803. Benjamin Howard, Lexington lawyer, Kentucky legislator (1801-1802) and Congressman (1807-1810), Governor of Louisiana Territory (1810-1812), and Brigadier General, U. S. Army, 1813 till his death in 1814.
7 See above, Receipt to Hart, October, 1801, note.
8 See below, Clay to Taylor, June 3, 1803.
9 See above, Clay to Taylor, March 8, 1803.
10 Mann Satterwhite.
11 Adam Shepherd.
12 Austin Hubbard.
13 See above, Clay to Taylor, March 8, 1803.
14 See above, Clay to Taylor, November 16, 1799.
15 Possibly Alexander Dalrymple Orr, resident near Maysville, Kentucky, member of Congress, 1792-1797.
16 Maryland.

Assignment from Samuel Wooldridge

[April 24, 1803]

Whereas H. Clay has this day agreed to become my security to Alexander Parker[1] & Thomas Wallace[2] for the payment of somewhere about two hundred dollars—In order to secure him against his said undertaking I do hereby assign to said Clay two Judgments obtained by me as the assignee of William Hawkins[3] one against John H. Craig,[4] and the other against Lewis Craig—And if any accident should happen whereby the said Clay shall become bound to pay the said debts to Parker & Wallace, and the Judgments hereby assigned should prove from any cause insufficient to indemnify him,

I do hereby mortgage to him such a portion of my interest in my fathers estate as will secure and save harmless the said Clay.

Witness my hand & seal this 24 April 1803.

Teste SAML. WOOLDRIDGE {L.S.}

JOHN MCKINNEY JR

DS, in Clay's hand. DLC-TJC (DNA, M212, R15).

1 A Pennsylvanian who became a merchant in Lexington and, later, president of the Kentucky Insurance Company.

2 Merchant and director of the Kentucky Insurance Company.

3 Probably a resident of Franklin County, Kentucky.

4 A justice of the peace in Boone County, son of John Craig.

From William Taylor

Henry Clay Esqr. Baltimore April. 25th. 1803.

Lexington

Dear Sir.

Since I wrote you The 22d. March I have your favr of the 5th. inst; Inclosing your account with a Statement of Satterwhites, Shepherd & Hubbards & Adam Shepherd's.[1] The only Credit on my Books to Adam Shepherd was two Specialties left me to Collect in
April. 97. £50 Maryd. [*cash time*][2] deductions
100 to ditto ditto.
The sum does not disagree above 40$ which is no great object. But I wish I had a Copy of The receipt to detect the error.

You charge me 200$. p'd by Thomas Hockley which I never received. I have this day wrote him again on the Subject.

The Balance of Edwards I am yet laying out of—Mr Sprigg will not pay the order Mr Short left with me,[3]—Before he gets his Title to The land and a Chancery Suit will be tedious & expensive—The young man I sent to Mr. Sprigg's lately assures me he appeared decided and Obstinate—He is able and only wants The Title to pay what is due—Mr. Sprigg lives near Frederick Town and there my young man met with a monied Character that offered him .650$ Cash for that order of 850$ and to take his chance of its Payment. I cannot afford such a loss. B[ut if Mr.] Short or Mr. Edwards cannot make up The Balance to you, I think [I] had better accept it —at any rate I beg you to urge payment.

The Balance due me please to remit as soon as convenient—The Bank notes of your Incorporated Insurance Company[4] will not answer here. I notice you charge me a full commission on The full amount of Heugh & Ralstones debt—considering The sacrifice I made here to get The money, and you had not the Trouble to receive & pay it away. I shall leave it to yourself to re-consider The subject —you also charge me a full commission on 400$ received of Short on account of Edwards Bill which Bill was received on account of money & recovered by you on which you charged a Commission in the first Instance—

Altho' I make these remarks to yourself for consideration, I assure you they are done in perfect Harmony—and I declare I consider your Conduct as highly satisfactory in my Business and That you are a Character of as much merit in your profession as any I have ever had experience with. Mr. Messionnier[5] lately wrote Mr. Banks[6] and enclosed him some papers respecting Mr. Wantes Character &ca, which be so kind as to request him to give you a sight of. Mr. Messionnier is determined to stick to Mr Wantes Interest & if you can aid it, you shall reccieve [. . .][7] acknowledgments. I am. Dr Sir, Yr mo. obt. Sert. WM. TAYLOR

ALS. DLC-TJC (DNA, M212, R12).
1 See above, Account, April 5, 1803. The letters have not been found.
2 Words obliterated.
3 See above, Taylor to Clay, December 25, 1801.
4 The Kentucky Insurance Company.
5 Henry Messonier.
6 Joseph Hamilton Daveiss and Cuthbert Banks held power of attorney from Charles Peter Stephen Wante to manage his affairs in Kentucky. KyU-Bastrop Papers, Samuel M. Wilson Collection. Banks was an early resident of Lexington, at various times a merchant, partner in the Kentucky Iron Works and the Madison Hemp and Flax Mill Company, tavernkeeper and proprietor of the Olympian Springs.
7 Illegible.

Agreement with Lewis Castleman

[May 19, 1803]

An agreement between Samuel Dew of Virginia by [his] agent Lewis Castleman of Woodford County of the one part and Henry Clay of Fayette of the other part Witnesseth:

That the said Clay hath this day covenanted to commence a Suit against the heir of Daniel Sullivan[1] deceased or other his legal representatives upon a bond given by the said Sullivan to the said Dew on the 27h. day of Septr. 1780 for two tracts of land of four hundred acres each, one of which said tracts was to include Sullivan's Spring: which said suit is to be conduced at the proper Costs and charges of said Clay:

That the said Dew hath covenanted to give the said Clay one fourth of whatever shall be recovered in the said suit, whether it be money or land: And that he will not dismiss, discontinue or compromise the said Suit without the consent of the said Clay; but if he should he will pay the said Clay the said fourth.

In witness whereof the parties aforesaid have hereunto set their hands & seals this 19th day of May 1803.

Teste LEWIS CASTLEMAN {L.S.}
JAC. CASTLEMAN[2] HENRY CLAY {L.S.}

ADS, signed also by Castleman, a prosperous farmer, tanner, and distiller of Woodford County, who had come to Kentucky from Virginia in 1790. DLC-TJC (DNA, M212, R15).

1 Pioneer settler of Jefferson County, Kentucky. Suit not found.

2 Jacob, son of Lewis Castleman.

To William Taylor

Wm. Taylor Esq. Lexington 3. June 1803.

Dr Sir

Mr. Purviance[1] not having set out as soon as I expected and meeting with the inclosed bank notes I procured them at [a prem]ium of 2½ P Cent, that is for the $200 I gave [. . .]$.[2]

Mr. Hockley writes me from Philadelphia that he has transmitted you the $200, which I long ago expected had been paid.[3] I hope you have received it.

I calculate upon seeing Mr. Short[4] in the course of the next week and receiving from him what he owes you or a part of it at least; of which you shall be duly advised.

In my last[5] I promised you an account of the situation of Mr. Wante's Suit with Morehouse and Bastrop. You have been already informed that Morehouse obtained from the Baron an assignment or conveyance of all his property in this Country:[6] that a Suit was commenced on this instrument & a decree for a Sale of the property obtained by Morehouse: [A]nd that the claim of Morehouse was purchased by Mr. Wante: He however contends that in this Sale he was deceived and defrauded by Wante, who agreed to pay him a certain Sum in Cash, and instead of it when the writing was executed, presented him with his own paper given to Lanthois Petot & Co.,[7] & which he alledges he had paid. Mr. Wante by his agents applied to the Court which had pronounced the above decree & insisted upon being placed, in consequence of his purchase from Morehouse, in his shoes. This was refused him, and the Court permitted the Sale to proceed for the benefit of the former. To prevent this the agents of Mr. Wante filed a bill and obtained an Injunction in the General Court, stating his claim first under the aforesaid purchase, and next under the conveyance obtained by himself from the Baron, while in Louisiana; and praying that if his said purchase should not be ratified, the instr[umen]t itself might be declared void as being frau[dulently] procured by Morehouse. In opposition to his rig[ht] under Morehouse's deed, a Mr. Blanton[8] also sets up a claim by virtue of a prior transfer of the same paper. He was made therefore a deft. to Wante's bill. And both he & M filed their answers to it, and at the Genl. Court which sat in last month dissolved the Injunction obtained by Wante—So far they have then been successful—The Suit is not yet decided. And I fear very much that Morehouse & Blanton have so contrived to inveloppe in darkness their transactions that Mr. Wante will be finally defeated, notwithstanding I am convinced he has justice on his side. His attorney however is still sanguine, and I do not altogether despair of his succeeding against thos[e] men.

By the dissolution of the Injunction, the Sale will proceed, and whatever it produces will be pocketed by M. & Blanton—If however Mr. Wante should ultimately prevail the sale will be voided.

Be pleased to communicate so much of this letter as relates to Mr. Wante to Mr. Messonier.[9] And believe me to be Dr Sir Yr's

HENRY CLAY

ALS. DLC-HC (DNA, M212, R1). Endorsed: "Henry Clay. rf S Wante. June 24. 1803."

1 Henry Purviance, who had come to Lexington from Washington, Pennsylvania, around 1797 and become one of the developers of the townsite of Henderson, a merchant and magistrate of Lexington, one of the organizers of the Kentucky Insurance Company, and a trustee of Transylvania University. He died in Lexington in 1811.

2 MS. torn; words obliterated at several points.

3 See above, Account, April 5, 1803. Hockley's letter has not been found.

4 Peyton Short.

5 Probably the letter of April 5, not found.

6 See above, Clay to Taylor, March 8, 1803.

7 Lanthois, Pitot and Company, a New Orleans firm, commission agents for Taylor.

8 John Blanton of Shelby County, Kentucky.

9 Henry Messonier.

From Joseph Wingate

Sir wednesday—15h. June, 1803

I am run very hard for a little money, and my only resource is you, when the work is finished which I have on hands for you, I will make any reasonable deduction, if you will be so oblidgeing as to let Messrs. Wilson & Anderson,[1] have Fifteen Dollars,

Henry Clay E. JOSEPH WINGATE

15 $ –

Teste. JOHN CAMPBELL[2]

[Endorsement on verso][3]

Recd. 11h. July 1803 of H. Clay the amount of the within order

JOHN ANDERSON

ALS. DLC-TJC (DNA, M212, R15). Wingate was a blacksmith on Short Street, Lexington.

1 James Wilson and John Anderson, Lexington carpenters.

2 A resident of Lexington.

3 ES, in Clay's hand.

Acceptance of Mortgage from Alexander MacGregor

18 June 1803.

Accepted in behalf of John Evans & Evans and Emslie

HENRY CLAY {SEAL}

Agent for Evans & Evans & Emslie—

AES. Owned by Henry H. Harned, Frankfort, Kentucky. Attached to a mortgage (DS, in Clay's hand) on 613 acres of land in Mason County, Kentucky, given by MacGregor, of Lexington, to a long list of creditors. Evans was a resident of Philadelphia; his partner was possibly Alexander Elmslie, Philadelphia merchant.

Receipt from John Anderson

[July 11, 1803]

Attached to Wingate to Clay, June 15, 1803.

To [William Taylor]

Dr Sir. Lexington 27 July 1803.

I received a few days ago of Mr. Short[1] $200 and have a prospect of exchanging it for bank notes this week.

The balance he assures me I shall get in a few weeks.

Your letter[2] acknowledging the receipt of $200 some time since remitted you has been received. Yrs Sincerely HENRY CLAY.

ALS. Owned by Gregg M. Sinclair, President Emeritus of the University of Hawaii.
1 Peyton Short.
2 Not found. See above, Clay to Taylor, June 3, 1803.

Confirmation of Contract with William de Graffenreidt

[August 6, 1803]

I do hereby ratify and confirm a contract made between Genl Walton[1] & Henry Clay, whereby the said Walton agreed in my behalf to give said Clay one half of the land which I claim on Red River & to establish which claim a Suit is now depending in the Fœderal Court in my name against Allen Degraffenreidt,[2] James Gay & others—

As witness my hand & Seal this 6h. August 1803.

Teste WILLIAM DE GRAFFENREIDT {L.S.}

RICHD. H. GAINES.[3]

DS, in Clay's hand. DLC-TJC (DNA, M212, R15).
1 The Walton agreement has not been found, but relative to it cf. above, Agreement with Hopper and Gay, July 3, 1801.
2 Of Lunenburg County, Virginia—either the younger half-brother or uncle of William.
3 Of Danville, Kentucky.

Bill of Sale from Allen Davis

[August 9, 1803]

I have this day sold to H. Clay a pair of bay horses about Sixteen hands high, four years old, at the price of two hundred & thirty dollars, eighty in a horse; and the balance in Cash.

Witness my hand & Seal this 9h. Augt. 1803.

ALLEN DAVIS {L.S.}

DS, in Clay's hand. DLC-TJC (DNA, M212, R15). Davis was a bricklayer on Mulberry Street, Lexington.

Agreement with John Fisher

[August 18, 1803]

An agreement Between John Fisher and Henry Clay entered into this 18h. August 1803.

The said Fisher undertakes & covenants to build an office for the said Clay,[1] and to do whatever is necessary to erect the said building, except furnishing the Brick, which are to be procured by said Clay— And the said Fisher covenants to have the said office finished so early this fall that it may be covered in & protected against the Frost—The said Fisher likewise covenants to erect for said Clay if he shall require it, a Necessary & in like manner to furnish every thing for it except the brick & complete it as aforesaid. The said Fisher further covenants to pave for the said Clay in front of his office, and to do this also so early as to prevent injury by the frost.

In consideration whereof the said Clay covenants to furnish the brick for the purposes aforesaid, without hindrance to the said Fisher, and to pay him, at the rate of nineteen shillings per thousand for the brick actually laid in the said Office & necessary, and the usual prices for the arches over the windows, and to pay for the said pavement one shilling per square yard; to be paid in the following manner—Forty dollars to be paid by the said Clay to the said Fisher on the first day of January next, and the balance in a horse or horses on or before the last day of November next, to be valued by two men to be chosen by the parties—Should the said horse or horses overgo or fall short of what the said Clay may owe after deducting the said forty dollars, fifteen or twenty dollars, the excess is to be paid by the said Fisher or the deficiency by the said Clay as the case may be—

In witness whereof we have hereunto Set our hands & Seals.

Teste JOHN FISHER {L.S.}

DANL. MCVICAR[2] HENRY CLAY {L.S.}

[Endorsement on verso][3]

Received on account of the within One hundred dollars in a horse Cash and Note which Note was before receipted for. 14 Feb. 1804.

JOHN FISHER

ADS, signed also by Fisher. DLC-TJC (DNA, M212, R15).

1 On Mill Street, across from his dwelling. Clay acquired title to the property by deed, below, July 27, 1804.

2 Of Montgomery County.

3 ES, in Clay's hand.

To John Breckinridge

Dr Sir Lexington 27 August 1803.

I have examined the papers in Porters suit against you,[1] and satisfied my mind as to what ought to be the result.

Porter clearly holds your obligation, subject to all the defects with which, in the hands of Isaac Robinson, it was encumbered. Was any other principle to prevail, the holder of an equity, obtained by the grosset [*sic*] fraud, would have nothing to do to accomplish his purpose but to pass it off to an innocent purchaser, concealing from him the defects.

If then Isaac Robinson could not, Porter cannot, coerce a specific execution of the contract. That he could not I think may be proven without much difficulty. The principle is well settled that he who is guilty of fraud, unfair or unconscientious dealing, shall not be aided in equity. That principle is adopted by the Courts of law. In 1 Vol Esp. p. 91 § 5[2] it is extended so far that even where *third* persons have been defrauded, the plaintiff shall not recover. The reason is interwoven with the existence of all Courts—Being established to do justice, they will not degrade themselves so much as to become instrumental to those who have violated law, honesty, or upright dealing. It remains then only to be shewn that Isaac Robinson practised a fraud. This is defined to be either the suggestion of a falsehood, or the suppression of the truth. It is fraudulent and will vitiate the contract, if the vendor conceals that which, being disclosed, would prevent the sale, diminish the price of the subject, or change materially the terms of the contract. It was therefore fraudulent in Robinson to conceal from you the *mere* report that his father had been before married, and that he had an elder brother living.[3] That he knew of the report is so strongly to be inferred that no one can doubt it: It was his duty to have said to you "My title to this land may not be good: my fathers intimate acquaintances inform me that he was married before he married my mother, and that he has a son living older than myself." Had he made this communication, you would either have refrained from buying, given a price proportionate to the risk, or before compleating the sale, demanded an indemnity.

If I am correct a complete answer is furnished to almost the whole of Mr. Hughes's[4] argument. He contends that there ought to be proof of a former marriage and the birth of a son—that without this it does not appear that you would have been injured—and that from the lapse of time it is presumable no such older Son exists. Let it be absolutely conceded that there was neither a former marriage nor an older son, still *there was such a report,* and the failure by Robinson to disclose that, being a fraud, must deprive him of the interposition of a Court of Equity. That you were actually injured by the existence only of such a report is well established—Your land was less esteemed by yourself—less valuable in market—and has been sold for a less price. Mr. Hughes's principle as to the proof of a marriage is correct whenever it comes directly in controversy, as in actions of crim con,[5] and contests about inheritance. But that will not render Robinson the less guilty of a fraud. And the proof you have adduced is sufficient to raise such a presumption of an older son and previous marriage as will in this case, where these facts come indirectly into dispute, prevent A Court of Equity from enfcorcing [*sic*] the contract.

But whatever doubt might exist as to this part of the cause, no one can hesitate to say that he practised a fraud in holding up his title as one by devise. There is no legal evidence shewing that a will ever existed at all—it is all hearsay. If it ever did exist his title under it was only momentary, the will never having been established and being destroyed by fire. In holding out that he was devisee, you must have understood that he claimed under an *established* will, committed to record. But the transitory existence of his title under the will—the destruction by fire of that instrument—and its never being established, were all concealed from you. So that if you ever had heard of the report of an older son (a supposition that the cause does not permit us to indulge) you must have been entirely lulled by the false information he gave you about his claim as devisee.

Robinson then has been guilty of fraud within every member of the definition—he has suggested what was not true—that he was devisee—he has suppressed the truth—relative to his older brother and the will. That you have been injured by the fraud is sufficiently proven by Mr. Smith and others.[6] But even if you had not been, it would be inconsistent with the purity and dignity of a Court of conscience to give countenance to a man, who has so wantonly violated those maxims which are made its guide. That a Court of Chancery possesses a discretionary power to enforce or not contracts is sound doctrine; and from my view of the cause I am clearly of opinion that the Court of Q.S. should have dismissed the bill, leaving the Complt. to his legal remedy.

If the writ of error is sued out by Graham and Robinson only, the decree being divisible as between you and Porter can not I think be changed: for a W. Error is in the nature of an original suit, and consequently cannot affect those who are not parties, unless from necessity. But I understand from Mr. Brown,[7] who is counsel for Graham, that Porter has also sued out a Writ of Error, which takes the whole cause before the Court of Appeals.

With respect to the Error committed by the Commissioners in

laying off the land, I do not think it the proper subject of a bill of review. The Court of Appeals, by their decision in Logan and Boyd,[8] have only declared what the law was, and consequently no "new" matters (which refer rather to matters of fact than law) have arisen since the final decree. The Judgment too in Logan and Boyd could not be used in your Suit with Porter, because of the difference of parties. As well as I recollect that determination you have been misinformed respecting it. The Court of Appeals does not declare what is the boundary between Barnes and Boyd, but that as they adjoin, Logan cannot be between them, leaving the line of separation for themselves to ascertain. But I think you are relievable against the error. The day of payment to you having passed, Porter before he can compel you to convey must either commence a new suit, or apply to the Court to prolong the time of payment. Whenever he does one or the other, the cause will be placed in such a situation as to enable you to rectify the mistake. Should the decree be reversed and the cause sent back, it will afford you another opportunity of being relieved. But not being bound to warrant any but 500 acres, even should you convey, and Boyd eject Porter, could he recover of you, that quantity being left him? It will be better however to leave nothing open to future litigation. I am Dr Sir Yr's Sincerely HENRY CLAY

ALS. DLC-Breckinridge Papers (DNA, M212, R20). Addressed: "John Breckenridge Esq. Fayette."

1 This suit was based on transactions that began in 1787, when Isaac Robinson of Botetourt County, Virginia, sold to John Breckinridge 356 acres of land on Tinker Creek in Botetourt County. In part payment Breckinridge gave to Robinson his bond to execute a deed to certain lands on Elkhorn Creek, Fayette County (now Kentucky). The Tinker Creek land declined in value, owing to a rumor that Robinson's title was not valid, and Breckinridge sold it for only £250 in 1789. Meanwhile, Breckinridge's bond for the Elkhorn Creek land had passed from Robinson to Francis Graham, who transferred it to William Porter.

A suit brought by Porter in 1798 to force Breckinridge to convey the land resulted in an interlocutory decree to the effect that Porter should pay Breckinridge by February 1, 1799, the sum of £272, 17s, 3½d, with interest from September 29, 1787, after which Breckinridge should convey to Porter the land specified in the bond. Porter was authorized to recover from Graham and Robinson the money that he was directed to pay to Breckinridge. Commissioners appointed by the Court "to lay off the land" in question filed their report in May, 1801, when a decree was pronounced, upholding the interlocutory decree but extending the time for payment of the money and conveyance of the land.

A decision by the Kentucky Court of Appeals was reached in the Spring Term, 1805, in connection with two writs of error brought in an effort to reverse the earlier ruling. In Porter against Breckinridge the Court of Appeals found that there was no error in fixing the sum to be paid by Porter but that the lower court had erroneously fixed the date at which interest should begin. The case was remanded to the Fayette Circuit Court with directions to correct the date, and to set the time of payment of the money as well as the date when the conveyance should be made. In Graham and Robinson against Porter the appellate court reversed the decision of the inferior court, at the same time, however, reserving to Porter the right to amend his bill or to bring a new suit. Botetourt County, Virginia, Deed Book IV, 1, 368-70 (microfilm at KyU); 3 *Ky. Reports* (Hardin) 23-30. Thereafter the controversy was resumed in the Fayette Circuit Court and continued for several years.

2 Johnson *vs.* Mason, 170 *English Reports* 289, 290 (King's Bench, 1794). Isaac Espinasse was the original reporter.

[3] It was this report which led to questioning of the validity of Robinson's title to the Tinker Creek land.
[4] Probably Attorney James Hughes. [5] Criminal conversation (adultery).
[6] Not identified. [7] Probably James Brown. [8] Not found.

Receipt from John J. Dufour

[August 27, 1803]

Received of Henry Clay this 27. Augt. 1803. Fifty dollars on account of the Vineyard Association.

$50. J. J. DUFOUR

DS, in Clay's hand. DLC-TJC, 2d Series, vol. 4.

To Samuel Johnston, and Others

Gent. Lexington 29h. Augt. 1803.

A notice was this day delivered to me from John Instone[1] stating that on the first day of October next at the house of Mr. Fulton[2] corner of Market and Howard Streets in Baltimore, he will take the deposition of Joseph B. Smith, to be read as Evidence in your Suit as McGruders & Co, Trustees against him.[3] I believe the object of this testimony is to prove that a partnership existed between Mr. Smith and himself, and that a Note of McGruders, which he now attempts to offset against your demand, came into the hands of his Concern, before the date of the deed of Trust. I do not think such Testimony if procured will avail him, but perhaps it will be well enough to attend the examination and write me if you can counteract his Testimony—The Cause will be tried I expect in December. I am Gent., Yrs HENRY CLAY

ALS. Owned by Thomas D. Clark, Lexington, Kentucky. Addressed on attached sheet: "Samuel Johnston, David Williamson James Somerville, William Lorman and Charles G Mequire Esquires Baltimore." Johnston was a lawyer. Lorman and Williamson were merchants.

[1] A Frankfort merchant, appointed Cashier of the Bank of Kentucky in November, 1807. The notice has not been found.

[2] Probably Alexander Fulton, who had Lexington connections somewhat later as agent for Luke Tiernan & Company.

[3] Suit not found. The Magruders, with John Read Magruder of Upper Marlboro as the leading member at this time, were a prominent mercantile family in Prince George's County, Maryland.

To [David Bullock]

Dr Sir Lexington 12h Sept. 1803

Inclosed are two declarations which I will thank you to file and take the necessary steps to have the causes tried at the next Court. I am not certain whether the Suits are brought in the name of Miles or Crosthwait; if they are in the latter I will thank you to give them to Mr. James Clarke[1] and request him to alter the declarations accordingly.

Be pleased to issue writs agreeably to the following memoranda:

Robert Elder agt. Peter Dewitt[2] Debt £ 10:10. Dam. £ 10—Indorse This is an action of debt Bail reqd.

John Elder & Phebe his wife agt. Peter Dewitt[3] Case. Dam. £ 100—Indorse Case. No Bail reqd.

Elijah Craig agt. John Taylor[4] Debt £ 8:4. Dam. £ 8:4. Indorse This is debt Bail reqd. Yrs. H. CLAY

ALS. NcD. Not addressed, but apparently directed to the Clerk of the Clark County Court.

1 Lawyer in Winchester, Kentucky, and long-time friend of Clay, Clark was a member of the Kentucky legislature, 1807-1808, 1832-1835: judge of the Kentucky Court of Appeals, 1810-1812; member of Congress, 1813-1816, 1825-1831; judge of the Circuit Court of Kentucky, 1817-1824; and Governor of Kentucky, 1836-1839. The suits have not been found.

2 Clay's client, Elder, was attempting to collect the amount of a promissory note dated December 27, 1802. The case, begun in the October Term, 1803, of Clark Circuit Court, was settled in 1806 when the defendant, a resident of Clark County, confessed judgment. Clark Circuit Court, File 49.

3 An action on a plea of trespass, continued from October 1803 through 1806, when it was apparently dropped. Clark Circut Court, File 76. John Elder was a Lexington bricklayer.

4 Begun in October, 1803, this case was continued until October, 1806, when, the defendant not being found, the suit was dismissed at the request of the plaintiff. Clark Circuit Court, File 66.

Property Deed from Montgomery Bell

[September 24, 1803]

[Indenture by which Montgomery Bell for the sum of $1,000, paid and acknowledged, conveys to Henry Clay a tract on Hickman Creek in Jessamine County, containing 164 acres bounded beginning at a hickory and an elm at the mouth of Wimer's Branch, running thence North 20° East 94 poles to two white oaks and a red oak, thence South 63° East 149 poles to an elm on the east bank of the west fork of Hickman, thence down that stream 36 poles to the forks, thence with the middle of the creek as it meanders to the beginning, which property is part of 1,000 acres patented by the Commonwealth of Virginia to General Adam Stephens,[1] June 21, 1780, and by him divided, this portion having been sold to Nathaniel Rochester[2] and by Rochester to Bell under deeds recorded in the late Lexington District Court. General warranty of title. Bell's signature witnessed by Patterson Bain,[3] John McKinney, Jr., and Porter Clay, the last two of whom certified the signature for record before Samuel H. Woodson, Jessamine County Clerk, August 8, 1808.]

Jessamine County Court, Deed Book B, 378-80. Bell, formerly a Lexington hatmaker and proprietor of the Hickman Mills on Hickman Creek, had recently moved to Nashville, Tennessee.

[1] General Adam Stephen, a native of Scotland, a resident of Berkeley County, Virginia, a veteran of the French and Indian War and of the Revolution, had died in Martinsburg, Virginia, in 1791.

[2] Former business partner of Col. Thomas Hart in North Carolina and Maryland, and a large speculator in lands, particularly in western New York, where he moved from Hagerstown in 1810. A veteran of the Revolution, Rochester held minor political offices in North Carolina, Maryland, and New York and was a founder of the city named for him in New York.

[3] Lexington hatter.

Agreement with Montgomery Bell

[September 24, 1803]

An agreement between Montgomery Bell and Henry Clay—

The said Bell has this day sold to the said Clay a lott of one hundred & Sixty four acres of land on Hickman in Jessamine County, and executed a deed therefor—

In consideration whereof the said Clay has delivered to the said Bell one horse and mare and further Covenants to pay to John Jordan Jr. one hundred dollars, and to pay for said Bell to Rice Jones three hundred dollars with Interest thereon for which the said Jones has obtained a decree against said Bell at the present Septr. Term of the Circuit Court of Fayette, and also the Costs of the said Suit and moreover to pay to the said Jones for said Bell the further Sum of two hundred dollars in May next.[1]

And whereas there may be a dispute between the Repts or Trustees of Genl. Lawson[2] and said Clay respecting five or six acres of the land conveyed by said Bell to said Clay, it is agreed between the parties aforesaid that the said Clay shall be and is hereby vested with whatever right the said Bell possesses to compel an alteration of the lines of the 200 acres laid off by said Lawson off of Genl. Stevens'[3] Survey on Hickman, and that the said Bell shall not be liable for any damage that may accrue to said Clay by the said Lawson's representatives compelling a change of the lines of the said Clay's 164 Acres, provided the said alteration is not so made as to deprive the said Clay of his said quantity.

In witness whereof the parties aforesaid have hereunto Set their hands & Seals this 24h. day of Septr. 1803.

Teste M. BELL {L.S.}
JOHN MCKINNEY JR H. CLAY {L.S.}

ADS, signed also by Bell. DLC-TJC (DNA, M212, R15).

[1] In a chancery suit in Fayette Circuit Court, September Term, 1803, Clay won for Jones a judgment for £120, plus interest, against Bell, who failed to appear in court. Jones, Attorney General of Indiana Territory, was a controversial figure in early Indiana history.

[2] Brigadier General Robert Lawson, prominent in the Southern campaign of the Revolutionary War, who died in Richmond, Virginia, in 1805.

[3] General Adam Stephen.

Account with Alexander Parker and Company

[*ca.* September 26, 1803]

Henry Clay Esqr. To Alexander Parker & Co Dr.

1802					
March 13	To Cash pd Carriage on a barrel & box from Philada 251 lbs @ 5 3/4	6	"	"
Augst. 17	To 12 lbs. white Lead pr. Montelle[1] @ 1/8	1	"	"
" "	3 lbs Spanish Brown[2] .... " 1/3	"	3.	9
" "	1½ lbs Whitening ...... " 1/3		1	10½
" 19	6 lbs white Lead .... " 1/8		10	—
" "	1 Quart Common Varnish " 4/6		4	6
" 20	6 lbs white Lead .... " 1/8	"	10	—
Sepr. 3.	30 lbs white ditto pr. Order " 1/8	2	10	—
" 15	29 lbs ditto ditto p order . " 1/8	2	8	4
1803				
January 10.	1 pair Shovel & Tongs pr. self ..30/	1	10	—
March 4.	To Merchandize dld Mr. Menteele 35/3	1	15	3
April 19	12 lbs white Lead pr Menteele .. 1/10	1	2	—
Sepr. 22	6 lbs Spanish Brown pr Anthy Bless[3] 1/-	"	6	—
" 26	8 3/4 lbs ditto ditto pr Anthony Bless 1/-	"	8	9
		£18	10	5½

D. DLC-TJC (DNA, M212, R15).

1 Augustus Waldemarde Mentelle, refugee from the French Revolution, was at this time in partnership as a house painter in Lexington. He also conducted classes in French and dancing, and later, with his wife, Charlotte, maintained a select boarding school for young ladies in their home across the road from "Ashland."

2 A natural earth pigment.

3 Three years later Anthony Blest was listed in the *Lexington Directory* as an innkeeper on Main Street.

Sight Draft from David B. Langhorne

19h Nov. 1803,

At sight pay Henry Clay or order Thirty three dollars value received. D. B. LANGHORNE

Accepted ISHAM TALBOT[1]

DS, in Clay's hand. Fayette Circuit Court, File 135 (1808). Endorsed by Clay on verso: "on a/c. of Langhornes Subscription to the Vineyard. . . ." Langhorne was probably a resident of Bourbon County, Kentucky.

1 A native of Virginia who grew up in Harrodsburg, Kentucky, studied law and practiced for a time in Versailles before settling in Frankfort. He was a member of the State Senate, 1812-1815, and of the United States Senate, 1815-1819, 1820-1825.

To John Breckinridge

Dr Sir Frankfort 21st Nov. 1803.

I am indebted to you for various communications and inclosures during the present Session of Congress, for which be pleased to accept my sincere thanks.

We argued your suit with Porter several weeks ago,[1] but no opinion has been yet expressed by the Court, nor any thing fallen from them which can authorize a conclusion as to the event of it. I still hope for success and heard nothing on the argument which shakes the opinion I first formed. The Court intend having a recess until the first monday in December. So soon as their Judgment shall be pronounced I will communicate it to you.

Our Assembly commenced its Session on the day appointed by law:[2] And various new projects were very soon suggested. But the arrival of the News from Washington, relative to the Expedition to New Orleans, has called the public attention from every other object & placed it on this great National concern.[3] Armies, Sieges and Storms completely engross the public mind, and the first interrogatory put on every occasion is Do you go to New Orleans? If all who answer in the affirmative should really design to go, Government will find it necessary to restrain the public Ardor, instead of resorting to coercion to raise the 4000 called for. You will have heard that General Hopkins[4] is appointed commander in chief, and Generals Adair and Russell his Brigadiers.[5] The Regiments will be commanded by Colonels Price, Hickman, Calloway, Deshai, Payne, Guthrie, Stewart & Terrill.[6] Having been honored by Genl. Hopkins with the appointment of one of his Aids I shall go with the croud to endeavour to share the glory of the expedition.

The accounts from Tennassee are not so flattering. Rumour says that the governor of that State has lately become disgraced in the public estimation in an affair with Genl. Jackson and has made such unpopular appointments that no Volunteers can be had.[7] Perhaps this account is not to be implicitly relied on, but I fear there is some truth in it.

You mention in your last that the Atlantic members are opposed to the Sales of land in Louisiana and the settlement of the Country. Will they be averse to the settlement of those lands which had been unconditionally granted by the former governments of that Country? Or does not the Treaty secure to the proprietors of those grants the rights of settlement and sale of these lands?[8] Be pleased to give me whatever information relative to this subject you may be possessed of, as it may be highly useful to me in case I should go to Orleans.

I think it likely this Session of the Assembly will terminate without any thing of importance being done. Should any thing occur in the course of it worth communicating to you, I shall do myself the pleasure of writing you it; and shall be happy in the continuance of that correspondence on your part by which I have been already so much obliged and honored. I am Dr Sir Yr's Sincerely

HENRY CLAY

ALS. DLC-Breckinridge Papers (DNA, M212, R20). Addressed: "The Honble John Breckenridge Senator in Congress From Kentucky Washington." Endorsed: "Ansd. 14 Decr.," but no answer has been found.

1 See above, Clay to Breckinridge, August 27, 1803.

2 Clay began his political career as representative for Fayette County in the session of the Kentucky General Assembly which opened on November 7, 1803. No report of the House action is known to exist.

3 On the possibility that Spain would refuse to give up Louisiana, which the United States had just purchased from France, President Jefferson had ordered a concentration of troops on the lower Mississippi and requested 4,000 men from Kentucky, 2,000 from Tennessee, 500 from Ohio, and 500 from the Mississippi Territory. Lexington *Kentucky Gazette*, November 22, 1803; Joseph Allen Thacker, Jr., "The Kentucky Militia from 1792 to 1812" (M.A. thesis, University of Kentucky, 1954), 67-68.

4 Samuel Hopkins, Revolutionary War veteran from Virginia, had purchased land from Richard Henderson and Company and moved to the Green River area, where he served as agent of the company. Lawyer as well as soldier, Hopkins was repeatedly a member of the Kentucky legislature and served one term in Congress, 1813-1815.

5 John Adair, a native of South Carolina and a veteran of the Revolution, had settled in Mercer County, Kentucky, in 1786; served as a member of the Kentucky legislature for many years, as a member of the Kentucky delegation in Congress, 1805-1806, 1831-1833, and as Governor of the State, 1820-1824. William Russell, born in Virginia and an early Kentucky pioneer, had had long experience in the Revolution and as a frontier Indian fighter. He commanded a regiment of the United States army on the northwestern frontier during the War of 1812. Russell had been a member of the Virginia legislature in 1789, was subsequently Fayette County representative in the Kentucky General Assembly for thirteen sessions and the defeated candidate for Governor in 1824.

6 William Price of Jessamine County, Richard Hickman of Clark, Richard Calloway of Madison, Joseph Desha of Mason, John Payne of Scott, Adam Guthrie of Nelson, Abraham Stewart of Christian, and Edmund Terril of Garrard. Desha later served as a major general and Payne, the younger half brother of Edward Payne, as a brigadier general in the War of 1812.

7 A bitter dispute between Jackson and John Sevier, based on charges of fraud in land speculation and on political and military rivalry, had culminated in a challenge issued by Jackson in October, 1803. Sevier, who had just returned to the Governorship of Tennessee after a lapse of two years, refused to fight a duel within the State and the encounter did not take place.

8 The treaty provided for the cession of "all public lots and Squares, vacant lands and all public buildings . . . and other edifices which are not private property" and guaranteed that "the inhabitants of the ceded territory" should be "protected in the free enjoyment of their liberty, property and the Religion which they profess."

Act for Choosing Presidential Electors

[December 24, 1803]

[For the purpose of choosing electors for President and Vice-President of the United States the State shall be divided into two districts: all that part lying north of the Kentucky River, together with Madison County and the segments of Franklin and Gallatin counties lying south of the river shall compose one district; all that part lying south of the river except the above-mentioned areas shall compose the other district. Four persons, to be residents of the respective districts, are to be elected and certified by the county sheriffs meeting in each of the districts.]

Ky. Gen. Assy., *Acts, 1803,* ch. LXXI (app. December 24, 1803), 100-102. This was partisan legislation, reducing the electoral districts from six to two and thus eliminating the possibility of a single Federalist vote in the generally strongly Republican state. Clay's introduction of this measure, and his fear of mounting Federalist strength growing out of factional controversy among the Republicans, is discussed in Mayo, *Henry Clay,* 153.

To John Breckinridge

Dr Sir Lexington 30th. Decr. 1803.

Your's of the 14h. instant came safely to hand,[1] and I am much obliged by the information which it contains.

The Court of Appeals adjourned a few days ago without determining your suit with Porter.[2] The General Court has also risen, your suit with Ross and Carneal being previously continued.[3]

The Assembly closed its Session on tuesday last. It continued two days longer than was intended in expectation of receiving the amendment to the Constitution. This fortunately arrived on sunday, and in the course of the two next days received the unanimous approbation of our Legislature.[4] The Acts which distinguish the present Session are

The passage of a law for the appointment of Electors, by which the State is divided into two Districts, separated by the Kentucky, and four are to be chosen in each[5]—The aportionment of the Representation, by which 600 is fixed on as a ratio, and one member is added to the lower house—The instalment of the debt due from the Settlers South of Green river, under the Act of 1800, by which it is to be paid in six equal annual payments with Interest.[6] And the passage of a law for the publication of the Revisal of the Criminal common law, by Toulmin and Blair.[7] It is to receive such weight in the Courts as it shall be found to deserve. A bill passed the Senate by which it was to have authority, exclusive of all other books. An amendment was proposed in the lower house giving it concurrent authority, but even this was deemed dangerous, and it was finally placed on the foundation of its merit. An attempt was made to remove the Seat of Government to Lexington, but it failed 31 for 29 agt. it.[8]

I am happy to learn that the conduct of Kentucky has raised her in the estimation of our Eastern friends. It would have given me individual pleasure to visit New Orleans, but I nevertheless sincerely rejoice that the affair has terminated pacifically.[9] You must no doubt be considerably perplexed in adopting a government for our newly acquired territory. I believe no difference in sentiment will exist between the people of this Country and the other parts of the Union relative to the settlement of Louisiana. It is desirable that a settlement to such a degree should be tolerated as would protect the navigation of the river against piracy and robbery. But this will be attained probably by the settlement of those grants which have been made by the different governments possessing that Country Farther than this I have heard no one express a wish. While on this subject permit me to mention that if in the distribution of offices in New Orleans it should happen that one could be procured for John Clay, I should be much indebted to you. His residence in that place for three years,—his knowledge of the French language and acquaintance with the inhabitants and their manners may give him some claim to a subordinate post. But I beg you to give yourself no particular trouble, much less add to the perplexity of the situation of the Executive, already I learn overwhelmed by the multitude of applications.

Be pleased to inform me when you are entirely at leisure whether the Repeal of the Bankrupt law takes immediate effect, and when the president approved it.[10] Yr's Sincerely HENRY CLAY

ALS. DLC-Breckinridge Papers (DNA, M212, R20). Directed to Washington.

1 Not found.

2 William Porter.

3 Thomas Carneal of Frankfort served as Kentucky agent for David Ross of Richmond, Virginia, large-scale speculator in lands of Kentucky and Ohio. In December, 1809, a judgment of the Kentucky General Court awarded Breckinridge's heirs title to the land in controversy. The case was then carried to the Court of Appeals but not further reported. Ky. General Court, Order Book C (1809-1811), 164, 166.

4 The Twelfth Amendment to the United States Constitution was ratified by the Kentucky General Assembly on December 27, 1803.

5 See above, Act, December 24, 1803.

6 By the act of 1800 the price of the land was to have been paid in nine annual instalments; the present measure, designed to relieve those who had failed to meet the payments, provided for prorating the debt over the period. Ky. Gen. Assy., *Acts, 1803,* ch. XXXII (app. December 23, 1803) pp. 42-45. This subject regularly engaged the legislature, and Clay, for many years.

7 Harry Toulmin and James Blair, respectively Secretary of State and Attorney General of the Commonwealth.

8 Lexington, which had served briefly as the State Capital in 1792, remained a contender for this role long after compromise among the aspirants had fixed upon Frankfort as the site.

9 See above, Clay to Breckinridge, November 21, 1803.

10 The act repealing the bankruptcy law of 1800 was approved on December 19, 1803. The measure was effective immediately, but it provided that "the repeal of the said act shall in no wise affect the execution of any commission of bankruptcy which may have been issued prior to the passing of this act." 2 *U.S. Stat.,* 248.

From John Vance

January 6th 1804

Sir you please to let Major William Bradford[1] have what Money you have Collected on the note you undertook to Collect for Thomas Irwin[2] that was put in to your hands by me.

Mr Henry Clay Esq. JOHN VANCE

[Endorsement on verso][3]

Received this 10h. Jan. 1804 of H. Clay forty dollars on a/c of the within

$40 WM. BRADFORD

ANS. DLC-TJC (DNA, M212, R15). Vance, who owned land in Barren and Fayette counties in 1800, had been a pioneer Kentuckian, one of the founders of the town of Falmouth in Pendleton County, Kentucky, and of Cincinnati, Ohio.

1 A pioneer settler of Muhlenberg County and representative of that county in the Kentucky legislature for several terms.

2 Of Muhlenberg County or, possibly, the resident of that name in Fayette.

3 ES, in Clay's hand.

Power of Attorney from Samuel Wooldridge

[January 24, 1804]

[Samuel Wooldridge authorizes Henry Clay to demand, sue for, and recover whatever Wooldridge may be entitled to from his deceased father's estate, to divide with other legatees, and to execute instruments for such division.

Clay is also empowered to recover any money due Wooldridge in the State of Kentucky, and he may make any arrangement deemed advisable with Wooldridge's debtors. Clay may appoint one or more attorneys under him for these purposes. Signature of Wooldridge attested by Thomas Bodley, January 24, 1804.]

Fayette Circuit Court, Deed Book A, 269-70.

Advertisement of Reward

200 Dollars reward. [January 25, 1804]

The above sum will be given to any person who will give information to either of the Subscribers, by which they may be enabled to discover the mother of a Female Child, left at the door of James Morrison, in Lexington, on the morning of the 9th instant—They pledge themselves in the most sacred manner, not to divulge the name of the person giving the information, if required to keep it secret. They will receive information either verbally, or through the medium of a letter, addressed to either of them, by post; and on the fact being ascertained, the money shall be transmitted in bank notes to the address required, and no questions asked—Or, if the mother will come forward, the above sum will be given to her, or appropriated to the support and education of the child, as she may think proper.

The above reward is offered with a view of rescuing the reputation of several innocent females from the unjust suspicion of being the mother of the child. It is a primary duty with every honest citizen, to do justice, and relieve the innocent from aspersions calculated to wound the reputation, which, to a female of delicacy and sensibility, is dearer than life. Under these circumstances, the subscribers have the utmost confidence that exertions will be used to discover the mother, and give them the information required.

HENRY CLAY,	JAS. MACCOUN,	JAS. MORRISON,
W. MACBEAN,	WILLIAM WEST,	THOS. BODLEY,
TH. HART, JR.	G. ANDERSON,	JAS. FISHBACK,
J. W. HUNT,	J. POSTLETHWAIT,	THOS. WALLACE,
J. BRADFORD,	WILL. MORTON,	JOHN POPE,
ALEX. PARKER,	SAM. BROWN,	W. WARFIELD[1]
J. JORDAN, JR.	JAS. BROWN,	

Lexington *Kentucky Gazette*, January 31, 1804; also printed as a broadside (WHi-Draper MSS., 3 MM 122).

1 All prominent Lexington business and professional men.

To Dr. Frederick Ridgely

Dr Sir Lex: 31. Jan. 1804

I think you may receive of Blackmore[1] what he may be disposed to pay without impairing your claim to the residue, taking care however so to express the receipt as that it may not be inferred that it was designed as full satisfaction. Until I see you I cannot advise whether the Suit should be brought agt. Carneal or Black:[2]

Inclosed is a memorandum shewing the amount due to Massie.[3] You ought to call on me when you next come to Town relative to this business: It will at the same time afford me the pleasure of seeing you, and learning what sort of a farmer the physician makes. Yr's Sincerely HENRY CLAY

ALS. PHi-Dreer Collection. Addressed to Ridgely in Woodford County, Kentucky. A native of Maryland and a veteran of the Revolution, Ridgely began practice in Lexington in 1792. When the Transylvania Medical School was opened in 1799, he was one of its two professors. Shortly before this letter was written he had moved to Woodford County.

1 Probably John Blackmore, of Woodford County.

2 Thomas Carneal and Alexander Black. In March, 1808 (no earlier suit found), Ridgely sued Carneal in Fayette Circuit Court. The case was referred to arbitration, docketed again in March, 1809, and thereafter dropped. Fayette Circuit Court, Order Book E, 112, 259, 273, 499.

3 In the suit, Massie *vs.* Bullocks and Simpson (see above, Clay to Massie, December 11, 1801), Ridgely was required to pay the debt of Josias Bullock, for whom he was special bail. Fayette Circuit Court, File 76 (1804).

From William Taylor

Henry Clay Esqr. Baltimore February. 13. 1804

Dear Sir,

I have yr favr of The 31 Ultimo—I wrote you on The 28th. ulto.[1]

informing you That Peyton Skipwith[2] had remited me a Bill for Four hundred Dollars which had been paid and was placed to The Credit of Payton Short on The 17 January 1804—This is to Confirm The contents of my last letter to acknowledge yours [a]nd to request That you will now make a final Settlement with Mr Short & remit me The Balance.

In settleing with Mr. Short please to calculate The Interest & Charge The Damages and you will notice 11. 50/100$ Charges I paid here on The Bill he left me on Sprigg.[3]

The Bill was 1450 $
Interest . . . . . .
Damages . . .
Charges pd here Bill on Spriggs 11 50/100$

The only payments made are I believe, he pd me 22 Oct 1802—400—
settled by you April. 1803— 400—
order from Skipwith Jany 17. 1804—400—
$.1,200

From this short sketch which I believe correct There must be yet a considerable Balance due on That Bill—I thank you for taking measures to prevent the Judgment from Expiring and I request you now to take Those to obtain what is due. With sentiments of high respect I am, Dr Sir, Yrs truly WM. TAYLOR

ALS. DLC-HC (DNA, M212, R1). [1] These letters have not been found. [2] Possibly of Mecklenburg County, Virginia. [3] Thomas Sprigg.

Commissioner's Bond for Samuel Blair

[February 13, 1804]

Know all men by these presents that we Saml Blair & Henry Clay are held & firmly bound unto James Garrard Esquire Governor of the commonwealth of Kentucky in the just and full sum of 2000 Dollars to which payment well and truly to be made to the said Governor & his successors we and each of us bind ourselves & every of our heirs executors & administrators jointly & severally firmly by these presents sealed and dated this
13th day of February 1804.

The condition of the above Obligation is such that whereas the above bound Saml Blair has this day been appointed commissioner of the tax in the 9th. Regiment in this county under the Revenue Law,[1] now if the said Samuel Blair shall well & truly discharge his duty according to law then the above Obligation to be void otherwise to remain in full force

Executed in court SAML. BLAIR {SEAL}
DAVID TODD D.C.[2] HENRY CLAY {SEAL}

DS. Owned by Henry H. Harned, Frankfort, Kentucky. Blair was for some time a member of the Board of Trustees of the Town of Lexington, one of the justices of Fayette County, and, later, treasurer of Transylvania University.

[1] Revenue Act of 1799. Littell (comp.), *Statute Law of Kentucky*, II, 316-33. That part of Fayette County within the Ninth Regiment included the town of Lexington. Thacker, "Kentucky Militia," 9.

[2] Deputy under his father, Levi Todd, Clerk of the Fayette County Court. Young Todd, admitted to the bar in 1810, sat in the Kentucky legislature from 1810 to 1814, and in 1819 became the first judge of the northwestern circuit of Missouri Territory.

Commissioner's Bond for Hezekiah Harrison

[February 13, 1804]

DS. Owned by Henry H. Harned. This document, almost identical to the one above, was signed by Clay and Harrison. The latter, appointed Commissioner of the Tax in the 8th Regiment of Fayette County (the area between the Limestone and Tate's Creek roads), was not always aligned with Clay politically. He had been a member of the conservative group during the constitutional struggle in 1799. Subsequently a member of the State legislature for several years, he was defeated, on charges of Federalism, by Clay in 1808.

Receipt from Arthur T. Taul

13. Feb. 1804

Received of H. Clay the Sum of Six pounds Nineteen Shillings & Six pence being the balance in full of three Decrees & Costs Ar. T. Taul Jonath. Taul & Jesse Coffer agt. Bell.

Teste. ARTHUR T. TAUL

DAVID TODD

DS, in Clay's hand. DLC-TJC (DNA, M212, R15). In chancery actions of the March and June Terms of the Fayette Circuit Court, 1803, Clay had won debt suits against Montgomery Bell for Arthur T. Taul and Jonathan Taul, of Fayette County, and Jesse Cofer, of Clark County.

Guardian's Bond

[February 13, 1804]

KNOW all men by these presents, that we Henry Clay Benjn Howard & John H. Morton are held and firmly bound unto Saml Blair Wm. Dudley Leonard K Bradley & Ro. S. Russell—Gentlemen, Justices of the county of Fayette in the just and full sum of £300—current money; to the payment of which well and truly to be made to the said Justices and their successors, we and each of us bind ourselves and every of our Heirs, Executors and Administrators, jointly and severally, firmly by these presents, sealed and dated this 13th day of February 1804

THE CONDITION of this Obligation is such, that if the above bound Henry Clay his Heirs, Executors and Administrators, shall well and truly pay and deliver John Watkins Wooldridge & Powettan Wooldridge Orphans of Edmond Wooldridge deceased, of whom he is appointed Guardian, all such Estate as now is or shall hereafter appear to be due from him to the said Orphan, when he shall attain to lawful age, to demand the same, or when thereunto required by the Justices of the said county for the time being; and also faithfully execute his office herein in such a manner as to save harmless and indemnify the first above-mentioned Justices, their Heirs, Executors and Administrators, from all trouble or damage that may arise about the said Estate—then this Obligation to be void, else to remain in full force.

	HENRY CLAY {SEAL}
Teste	BENJA. HOWARD {SEAL}
DAVID TODD	JOHN H MORTON {SEAL}

Fayette County, Guardians Bonds, 1803-17, p. 15.

Receipt from John Fisher

[February 14, 1804]

Attached to Agreement, August 18, 1803.

Receipted Account with Lewis Sanders

Mr. Henry Clay [*ca.* February 20, 1804]

To Lewis Sanders Dr.

1803	Octo. 3d.	¼ yd. Striped Cassimere delivd. Coyle[1]			£ 0. 4. 6
1804	Jany 6	1 ps. 4/4 Irish Linen 25 yd.	6/6.	£8. 2.6	
	—	2 doz. Green edged. Plates	13/6.	1. 7—	
	—	1 doz do do Do.	12/.	0.12—	
	—	2 yds. Dimity	4/6.	. 9—	
	.	2 Loaves Sugar 12 lb.	2/9.	1.13 .	
					12. 3. 6
	" 8	1 doz White plates	9/.	. 9—	
	—	½ doz. do do	12/.	6—	
	—	1 doz. Soupe do	12/.	12—	
	—	2½ yds. Country Linen	2/6.	6.3	
		½ yd. Calico	3/6.	1.9	
					1.15. 0
	14—	1 Blanket per order—			16. 6
	Feby 11—	Locks & Hinges per Bill deld. Winslow[2]			1. 5.10½
	20.	5 doz. Screws per	Ditto @ 9d.		3. 9
			E E.		£16. 9. 1½

Received the amount in full for Lewis Sanders

LITTLEBERRY HAWKINS[3]

DS. DLC-TJC (DNA, M212, R10). Sanders, a native of Virginia and a son-in-law of George Nicholas, was active in Lexington and Fayette County as a merchant, manufacturer, stock breeder, and speculator. His declining years were spent at "Grass Hills," his estate in Carroll County, Kentucky.

1 Cornelius Coyle, a native of Ireland who had come to Lexington about 1789 and subsequently acquired a considerable fortune as a Main Street tailor.

2 Hallet M. Winslow.

3 At this time apparently a clerk in Sanders' store; later in partnership with his brother, a proprietor of a dry-goods store in Lexington.

Opinion Regarding Conflicting Land Claims

23 February 1804

In considering the claim of James Govens for two thousand Acres of land, under an entry made the 16h. day of May 1780, it is necessary previously to determine the validity of Jarrard Hopkins's entry for the same quantity, made on the same day:

Hopkins's entry is to lay on a branch of Licking, called Holder's Creek, emptying into Hingston's fork, Beginning at a Spring about 2 miles from Lydia's mount, emptying in on the East side of the Creek, to run down on both sides of the Creek for quantity. The creek, then denominated Holder's, shortly after exchanged its name for that of Huston, which it has ever since borne, and by which it has been most generally known: It discharges itself into a Creek, then called Gess's, now Stoner; and this latter stream unites with Hingston. John Holder proves Lydia's mount, but he does not state that it was an object of general notoriety, among persons conversant with that quarter of the Country. A spring is shewn on the east side of Holder's or Huston's creek two miles and sixteen poles distant from Lydia's mount.

If I were to give an opinion as to Hopkins's entry, upon the papers which have been shewn me, to wit, Holder's and Strother's depositions, the entry itself, and the connected platt, I should pronounce it to be bad. To establish this entry it will be necessary to prove that Lydia's mount when the entry was made[1] was generally known by the early adventurers and persons acquainted in the year 1780 in that quarter of the Country; and it will further be necessary to prove that Huston was also then generally known by the name of Holder's Creek. This latter fact I am informed can be established, but whether the former can or not I have not learnt. The entry will also be rendered bad, by shewing any other Spring answering equally well as to distance and description with that which is claimed as being the one alluded to in Hopkin's entry: for although Holder is positive that the Spring contended for is the one which the locator of Hopkins's entry *intended,* this will not be sufficient to maintain the entry, unless that intention is so *expressed* in the entry as to exclude all other Springs emptying in on the East side of Holder's creek and lying about 2 miles from Lydia's mount: This might have been done by calling for the marked tree, spoken of by Holder, but it will be recollected that it has not been done. But, it being proven that Lydia's mount and Holder's Creek were objects in the year 1780 of general notoriety, and it not being shewn that there is any other Spring corresponding with the one called for so well as that shewn (such testimony, if it is produced) the entry of Hopkins will be deemed a good one. I think he has been surveyed right or very nearly so. And Govens s entry, depending upon Hopkins's, would also be established, upon the production of the before mentioned Testimony.

The next enquiry will be as to the claims with which Govens's interferes. The papers laid before me are not sufficient to determine the validity of all of them. It may be confidently asserted however that McDowell's military claims are superior to Govens. They cover all of his entry except about 758 Acres. The principal interferences with this are the claims of Joseph Early, John Grant, John Green and Richard Graham, as to all of which Govens' entry being prior in date, is superior. As to William Marklands preemption I can give no opinion for the want of the necessary papers and information.

The result of the whole is, that James Govens has no prospect of recovering any part of the land under his entry, except what is not covered by McDowell, to wit 758 Acres or thereabouts, and his recovering this depends upon his being able to produce, in support of Hopkins s entry, the testimony mentioned in the preceding statement. HENRY CLAY

[Endorsement][2]

Received 23 February 1804 of Wm. Kelly[3] Esq. Ten dollars for the above opinion. HENRY CLAY

ADS. CSmH. The land involved lies in Bourbon County, Kentucky.
1 The qualifying phrase interlined.
2 AES.
3 Partner of Hugh Brent in a store on Main Street in Paris, Bourbon County.

Bill from Maddox Fisher

[*ca.* February 28, 1804]

1803	Henry Clay To Maddox Fisher Dr	£ " " S " D
	To 150 paving Bricks for your pump @ 3/pr	0" 4" 6—
	To tendance taken up and paving Round your pump @ 9/	0" 9" 0—
1804		
Jany 21	To 325 feete of kill dried ash florring @ 12/ pr h	1"19" 0

	To Cutting one Dore through To your kitchen @ 4/6	0„ 4„ 6–
25	To 29 feete of Scantling @ 2d per foot 4/10	0„ 4„10–
Febr 24	To 67 feete of ash floring kill Dried @ 12/pr	0„ 8„ 0–
	To 9½ feete of Scantling @ 2d pr foot by winslow[1]	0„ 1„ 7–
27	To 293 feete of ash flowring @ 9/ pr hundred	1„ 6„ 4–
28	To 720 feete of ash florring @ 9/ pr hund.	3„ 4„ 9–
		£8„ 2„ 6
	To 27 feete of Dried walnut @ 12/ pr hundred	0„ 3„ 3
		£8„ 5„ 9

AD, by Fisher. DLC-TJC (DNA, M212, R15). [1] Hallet M. Winslow.

Receipt from Andrew F. Price

[March 10, 1804]

Received 10. March 1804 of Henry Clay for T. D. Owings[1] Two hundred dollars
$200. on acct. of H Cadbury[2] ANDW. F PRICE

DS, in Clay's hand. DLC-TJC, 2d Series, vol. 4.

[1] Thomas Deye, son of John Cockey Owings, had come from Maryland to Kentucky at an early age to manage his father's extensive land holdings. The younger Owings, for whom the town of Owingsville in Bath County was named, served as a colonel of the 28th Regiment, United States Infantry, in the War of 1812 and was several times a member of the Kentucky legislature. He fought in the Texas Revolution and died in Texas in 1853.

[2] Henry Cadbury, with William Blythe (Blieth, Blith, Blyth), had contracted to buy some goods from the Philadelphia mercantile firm Elisha Fisher and Company. When the $500 note accepted for the goods was not paid at the due date in six months, Fisher and Company brought suit in Fayette Circuit Court to recover the money from Price, Owings, and James Morrison, who were supposed to hold money or other effects belonging to the debtors, no longer residents of Kentucky. Owings at the March Term, 1804, acknowledged his possession of such a sum and agreed to pay it at the judgment of the court. The court then ordered payment amounting to $500.13 with interest from December 3, 1801, until the debt was extinguished. Fayette Circuit Court, File 60 (1804). Cadbury had moved to Cincinnati by 1802.

Receipted Account with John Postlethwait

Henry Clay Esqr. [March 18, 1804]

1803	To John Postlethwait	Dr
May –23	To wine & billiards 6/9 (31st.) wine & billiards 7/8	.. 14. 7
June– 2	To wine & billiards 13/6. 4th. wine &. Do 6/9	–1 – 3
17	" wine & billiards 6/9 20th.. Do.. & . Do .12/11	– 19. 8
"	" 1 Demijohn 30/- Sangaree & billiards 5/10	-1. 5 10
24	" wine & billiards 14/- 27th Sangar & Do. 10/4	1. 4 4

	28	"	wine & billiards 6/9 billiards 1/ - - -	— 7. 9
	30	"	dinner 1/6 (July 9th.) Supper & wine 7/6 -	— 9 —
July	17	"	Punch 4/6 1 Elegant Card Box 48/	2 12. 6.
"		"	3 days diet Mr. Gains[1]	— 9. —
Augt—	1	"	Punch 4/6 billiards 8d	— 5. 2
	12	"	Punch & billiards 5/3 wine & billiards 6/9	— 12 —
	15	"	dinner & club 25/- (16th.) wine & billiards 3/4	-1. 8. 4
	20	"	billiards 1/8 Punch 6/	— 7. 8
	29	"	wine & billiards 11/1. dinner 1/6 - -	— 12. 7.
	31	"	Punch & billiards 11/4	— 12 4
Sept	1	"	billiards 2/4 . (3d.) wine 6/..	.. 8. 4
	10	"	Do .2/- wine 6/- billiards 1/4 . .	— 9. 4
	28	"	wine .2/- wine & billiards 6/9 . —	— 8. 9
Octor	—3.	"	billiards 1/- (8th. billiards 1/- .. ---	— 2 —
Decr.	3	"	Supper & club 6/- (10th.) Supper & club 6/.	.. 12 —
"		"	2 pts. wine 12/- (17th. Supper & club 6/ ..	— 18. —
	24	"	Supper & club 6/- wine 1/6	.. 7. 6
Jany	5	"	J. Clay[2] club at dance	.. 18. —
	7	"	Supper & club 6/- billiards 1/ . . .	.. 7. —
	13	"	wine 15/- 30th. wine & billiards 9/. .	1. 4. —
	31	"	wine & billiards 6/9	.. 6. 9
Februy.				
	13	"	billiards 1/8 (15th.) wine & billiards 3/9 .	.. 5. 7.
	15	"	wine 15/- brandy 1/6 wine & billids. 9/9.	1. 6. 3
				20.14. 6.
			To Amount of Debit brought over—	20.14. 6.[3]
1804				
Febry.	25	To	Supper & club 6/-	.. 6 —
March	2	To	billiards 2/- (7th.) wine 12/-	— 14 —
	8th.	"	wine & bitters	— 3. 4
				£21.17.10
			Supra Cr.	
			By Cash 20 dollars	6 — —
				£15.17.10

Recd. Payment in full of the above a/c
Lexington March 18th. 1804 J POSTLETHWAIT

DS. DLC-TJC (DNA, M212, R15). Postlethwait had been in partnership with his brother Samuel as a Lexington merchant for about a decade before 1800. John was now, and intermittently for nearly thirty years, proprietor of a tavern on the southeast corner of Main and Mulberry streets, Lexington, where the Phoenix Hotel today stands. He was also in 1806 Cashier of the Kentucky Insurance Company.

1 Possibly Richard H. Gaines.

2 John Clay, who had moved to Louisiana several years earlier, returned to Lexington for a visit in the winter of 1803-1804.

3 Heading of p. 2.

From Christopher Greenup

Sir. Frankfort March 19th. 1804.

Inclosed you'll receive a letter from Mr. Walter Beale as also one from Mr. Ths. T. Davis to me respecting a Judgment against me by Knox & Henderson,[1] concerning the unfortunate Iron Works business;[2] I was to have been exonerated from those contracts, but they have in every instance almost, turned the demands against me, Mr. Owings I expect will pay it as soon as Mr. Nancarrow[3] arrives or give you a draft on Some house in Baltimore or Philadelphia, he is my Security in the Replevin Bond and was to have settled the Debt. If you cou'd suspend your demand against Davis until about the first of May (when I shall return from the Green River Circuit) I know the Money can be raised, part of which will be due me from Mr John Jourdan But I pledge myself that the money shall be soon raised after my return whether I get it from, the Company or not.

I set out the day after tomorrow on the Circuits and shall be at home the last week in April. I am Sir Yr Hble Servt.

CHRISTO. GREENUP

ALS. DLC-TJC (DNA, M212, R10). Addressed: "Henry Clay Esquire Lexington." Greenup, who was apparently riding circuit as a lawyer, was elected Governor later in the year.

1 The letters from Beall and Thomas T. Davis, the latter recently appointed a Federal judge in Indiana Territory, have not been found.

David Knox, James Henderson, and William Deas were a firm of Philadelphia merchants, trading under the name Knox, Henderson and Company. Henderson had died several years before the judgment here mentioned.

2 In 1791 Jacob Myers of Baltimore, Maryland, began the construction of a furnace for the production of iron on land in what is now Bath County, Kentucky. Later in the same year he sold most of his interest in the enterprise to John Cockey Owings, Greenup, Walter Beall of Nelson County, and Willis Green of Lincoln County. In 1803 control of the heavily mortgaged property passed to Owings and his son, Thomas Deye. The latter acquired his father's interest in the iron works in 1811 and operated the business until he became bankrupt in 1822.

3 John Nancarrow.

Agreement with John Jordan

[March 31, 1804]

An agreement between John Jordan Jr and H. Clay.

The said Clay agrees to sell and binds himself to convey with general warranty one hundred & Sixty four & ½ Acres of land that he purchased of Montgomery Bell on Hickman at Seven dollars per acre—

In Consideration whereof the said Jordan agrees to sell and binds himself to convey by deed with general warranty one third of the ground he owns fronting the public square[1] beginning at the upper corner of his house next to Majr. Morrisons[2] and extending to the lower corner of Smiths lott, which said third is to extend back from the said front to the Ally, of which the said Clay is to have the use—

And the said parties agree that the aforesaid third of the said ground which the said Clay is to have shall be the third next to Smith, if Charles Wilkins[3] should choose to have the middle third, and if he does not the said Clay shall have the middle third—

And they further agree that the said ground so to be conveyed by the said Jordan shall be valued by two men one to be chosen by each of the parties and their umpire if they cannot agree And whatever the said ground shall be valued at shall be credited against the said land—If it should be valued to more than the price of the land, the said Clay shall pay the balance in good Cash notes or bonds now due—If to less the said Jordan shall make up the deficiency in like notes or bonds—

In witness whereof the parties have hereunto set their hands & seals this 31. March 1804.

Witness JOHN JORDAN JR {L.S.}
WILL JORDAN[4] HENRY CLAY {L.S.}

[Endorsement on verso][5]

The lott within mentd. was valued 31 March 1804 by John Bradford,[6] John Postlethwait & James Morrison to forty Six dollars per foot.

ADS, signed also by Jordan. KyLxT.
1 On Upper Street, between Main and Short.
2 James Morrison.
3 Lexington merchant and, from 1808, for many years president of the Lexington branch of the Bank of Kentucky. He was the son of John Wilkins, founder of a Pittsburgh mercantile firm, and brother of John, Jr., who continued the family business and opened the trans-Allegheny branch of the Bank of Pennsylvania in 1804.
4 Lexington attorney.
5 AE, by Clay.
6 Pioneer Kentucky printer, founder (with his brother Fielding) of the *Kentucky Gazette,* and prominent in local politics. William Bradford was another brother.

From James Brown

Dear Sir Frankfort April 30. 1804

Inclosed is a Bill[1] on which I wish you to commence suit in the Genl. Court and foreclose the Mortgage Mr John Beckley[2] is interested and will Correspond with you on the subject—The whole of the fees you will charge as I have received nothing

Among the papers of Beekham and Reese[3] (see Bundle of Letters & federal Court papers) you will discover a Bond due them from Wm. Craig & Wm Bell of Scott County—Craig is dead—I commenced suit some time ago but found I had made the wrong party admr. and was obliged to take back the Writ—I am to day informed that John Craig and Elijah Craig sons of Toliver Craig admd. on Wm. Craig's estate[4]—Will you be so good as to commence immediately and explain to Mr Reese the cause of the delay—

I ordered suit for Beekham and Reese against Robert. Caldwell[5] of Madison Case Dam=$2000 on an acct–He procured me about 400 Dollars and promised to pay the ballance if I would delay till April–He has not paid–give him no further time–Of the 400 Dollars I have given Mr Leavy[6] a draft to be paid in Phia. for $200 –I wish Mortons 120 applied the same way and Doctor Brown will pay 30 more leaving me $50 for the management of their business–[7]

If you have management address or influence to settle with Mansill[8] you will oblige me if [. . .][9] it can be done *at a loss*–I wish to lea[ve] no man in Kentucky disatisfied with my conduct in pecuniary matters–Do not value fifty or a hundred Dollars for the sake of having me off the Dockett–

Wishing often to hear from you, and most fervently praying that you and your much beloved fa[mily] may have your measure of felicity filled to the bri[m.] I am Dr Sir Your affte friend

Henry Clay Esqr. JAMES BROWN

ALS. DLC-HC (DNA, M212, R1). Published also in James A. Padgett (ed.), "Letters of James Brown to Henry Clay, 1804-1835," *Louisiana Historical Quarterly*, XXIV (October, 1941), 922-23.

1 Not found.

2 Probably John Beckley of Philadelphia, Clerk of the United States House of Representatives, an intimate of the Jeffersonian political leaders, and a speculator in Kentucky land; however, a John Beckley of Wilkes County, Georgia, one of the early Kentucky explorers, had recently engaged in legal action in Fayette County. See Fayette Circuit Court, Order Book B (1802), 172, 402.

3 Bickham and Reese, a Philadelphia mercantile firm.

4 Toliver Craig and his wife, Polly, had accompanied several of their children in a removal from Virginia to Kentucky about 1781, stopping first at Bryan Station where they had helped withstand the famous siege of 1782. Shortly afterward they had moved with their son, Captain John Craig, to what became Woodford County, and there Toliver had died in 1795 at an advanced age. William Craig, formerly a justice of the peace and militia captain in Scott County, was not a member of the immediate family of Toliver Craig.

5 No suit found. Caldwell was one of the leading citizens of Richmond, formerly a justice of the peace and member of the Kentucky legislature.

6 William Leavy.

7 The references are probably to William Morton and Dr. Samuel Brown.

8 Probably George Mansell.

9 MS. torn; possible omission.

From Francis T. Brooke

Dr Sir June 2d 1804–

Some months past I Sent you the three Latest revisions of the Virginia Laws by a Mr George Johnson who when he Left this intended to go to Lexington but who I am informed is settled in Washington in your State–Let me know if you have received the Books–Genl Posey[1] some time since promised to find my other Tract of Land and to give me some account of it–if you see him or write him be so good as remind him of it Colol Anderson has given me no acct of my warrants that were to be located in the other side of the

River. I am sorry again to Trouble you on this subject[2]—you will please excuse it and Believe me yours with Much Respect & Regard

FR BROOKE

ALS. DLC-HC (DNA, M212, R1). Addressed to Clay at Lexington; postmarked at Richmond, Virginia, June 6.

1 Thomas Posey, reputedly the natural son of George Washington. A Virginia veteran of the Revolutionary War and of General Anthony Wayne's campaign against the Indians in the Northwest, Posey had later settled in Kentucky, whence, after serving as State Senator and Lieutenant Governor (1804-1806), he removed to Louisiana. He was appointed to fill a vacancy in the United States Senate in 1812 and upon the expiration of his term the following year was named Governor of Indiana Territory.

2 See above, Clay to Brooke, December 30, 1801.

To William Taylor

Wm. Taylor Esq. Lexington 19h. June 1804.

Dr Sir

It has been so long since you have heard from me that I fear you have had reason to apprehend that I had entirely forgotten you. The truth is that it has been entirely owing to my not having collected from Mr. Short the balance of Edwards'[1] ill fated draft. Perhaps I ought in strictness to have issued an execution and before now have coerced payment. But such have been the promises of Mr. Short, founded upon what he and I believed, were certain resources, that I have hitherto foreborne issuing execution, and verily believe you would have done the same under similar circumstances.

Inclosed are $200 in notes, obtained at a premium of 2½ P Cent. This money is received of Mr. Short, from whom I have the strongest assurances of payment of the balance in the course of a week or two. If I am again disappointed I will issue an execution. I am Dr Sir Yr. ob Servt.

HENRY CLAY

ALS. DLC-HC (DNA, M212, R1). Endorsed: "... Henry Clay. 7 July, 1804."

1 Peyton Short and Haden Edwards.

Agreement with James Barbour

[June 29, 1804]

An agreement between James Barbour and Henry Clay

The said Barbour agrees to sell to the said Clay his one third of the thousand Acres of land including the Upper Blue Lick on Licking,[1] the other two thirds being owned by William Lynn[2] and John Williams;[3] for which said land a suit is now depending in the Fœderal Court; & covenants to make the said Clay a deed therefor on demand, warranting only that the said third is legally derived from Lynn.

In Consideration whereof the said Clay doth covenant to pay to the said Barbour in horses not older than eight years nor less than three the sum of eight hundred dollars, on or before the first day of Octr. next, in Lexington; the horses to be valued if the parties cannot agree—

And the said Barbour further agrees to take at any time that the said Clay may request him before the said first of Octr horses as the said Clay may receive them—

It is also agreed that the said Clay is to receive whatever rents may be recovered, if any should be for the use of the Land & Salt Springs. N.B. The parties understand that no Stud horse is to be delivered.

In witness where of they hereunto set their hands & seals this 29 June 1804.

Jas. Barbour {l.s.}
Henry Clay {l.s.}

Teste
Len K Bradley
Th. Holt[4]

ADS, signed also by Barbour. KyLxT. Col. James Barbour, originally of Culpeper County, Virginia, one of the Virginia Land Commissioners appointed in 1779 to quiet title to lands entered prior to opening of the Kentucky Land Office, had subsequently moved to Lancaster, Kentucky, where he died later in this year.

1 In Nicholas County. Salt was manufactured at both the Upper and the Lower Blue Licks.

2 William Lynn had been awarded a preemption to the whole trace in 1779, by virtue of his earlier improvements. "Certificate Book of the Virginia Land Commission, 1779-80," in Kentucky State Historical Society, *Register,* XXI (1923), 53.

3 Probably the clerk to the Virginia Land Commission.

4 Thomas Holt, Harrison County, Kentucky.

From John Clay

My dear Brother New Orleans, July 6th. 1804—

I have had the pleasure of addressing you twice since my arrival to this place; since which I have not the pleasure of hearing a word from you, or any of my relatives, which has been the source of much uneasiness to me.[1] I mentioned in my former espistles that nothing had transpired as to my welfare, except that I had undertook to transact business as a Clerke under Messrs West & Siddins in which employment I still continue.[2]—I have been since appointed by this Govenor Inspector of Flour, Salt provisions & Hemp, this appointment for the present year will produce nothing to me. & some time must elapse ere it is productive; I have been in hopes & am not entirely out of them now, that yourself & my friends in Kentucky will thro. your influence procure me an appointment of more importance & which will be more congenial with my feelings. I am more flattered with this expectation lately as I am told that Mr Monroe will certainly be the Govenor to this Province.[3] for Godsake keep a strick look out for with Mr Breckenridge on your side you can do any thing.[4]

Mr John A. Seitz,[5] who arrived in this place about three weeks ago dyed on the 4th. Inst. much regretted by many of his friends here & must be more sincerely & extensively felt with you, he appeared to have been possession [*sic*] of a presentiment of his fate, his case baffled the united skill of the phisians of this place, his untimely fate has no doubt been hastened from the situation which his mind was in, appeared to have been extremely gloomy & thoughtfull for many months previous to his death—he dyed after an illness of sixteen days, underwent much pain, with a fever Common to this Climate: he was burryed yesterday afternoon attended by all of the Respectable Americans of this place with many strangers.

In a letter which I addressed you hastily from Louisvill I mentioned my wish that you would obtain from the Grand Lodge of Lexington a Cerfcte of my being a member of. that the expense attending it you would pay Majr. Morrison having previously mentioned that he would see that there should no difficulties arise on that head & that he would give you every assistance in obtaining it[6]—I beg leave again to impress it upon you, that you would attend to that business early as possible.

You mentioned to me while with you that it would be in your power the ensuing Spring to render me some assistance in the way of Shipping some produce, must beg leave to hold you in rememberance of that promise; let it be whisky Horses. Hemp. or Tobacco. it will be a like acceptiable—I have already stated to you how dependant I am & how much I am mortifyed for the want of some little funds: you might am sure send me a Boat consisting of any of the above articles without feeling it; as to the expense attending the transportation, should be able to pay ere it could arrive; many are the little speculations & turns I could make was I invested with some little funds—don't forget the negro Boy.

Nothing has transpired of importance lately in in [*sic*] this Province; some arrivals from different parts of Europe but bring nothing interesting. The 4th of July was spent here with great eclat. the Militia Corps joind with those of the Military made a parade of about 2000 men which was conducted with a pleasing regularity. Watkins[7] deliverd an oration in English & Monsr. Derbigny,[8] the prensent Interpeter of the Govenor, one in french, both of which displayed much ingenuity & was listened to with much attention—they are not as yet Published or would send them by this Oppy.

My respectful comps. to Lucretia. & all our friends. expecting shortly to hear from remain D Bro Sincerely yrs JOHN CLAY

ALS. DLC-TJC (DNA, M212, R10).

1 See above, Account, March 18, 1804, note. The two letters that he mentions have not been found.

2 See below, John Clay to Henry Clay, August 18, 1804.

[3] William C. C. Claiborne had served as Governor of Louisiana from the beginning of American occupation. Upon the division of the province into two parts he, rather than James Monroe, became Governor of the Territory of Orleans, effective October 1, 1804.

[4] Henry had already approached Breckinridge in this connection. See above, Clay to Breckinridge, December 30, 1803.

[5] A native of Germany, who with Frederick Lauman had opened a store in Lexington in 1792 or 1793.

[6] In 1794, and as late as 1802, John was listed among the "Entered apprentices" of Lexington Masonic Lodge No. 25. At the former date James Morrison was Master of the Lodge. J. Winston Coleman, Jr., *Masonry in the Bluegrass* (Lexington, 1933), 35, 52.

[7] Dr. John Watkins, who at an earlier date had practiced in Lexington, Kentucky, was important in Louisiana politics. He was a member of the first territorial Legislative Council and later became Mayor of New Orleans.

[8] Pierre Auguste Charles Derbigny, who had resigned the office of Secretary of the Municipality of New Orleans to become official interpreter of the territorial government under Claiborne.

From George Walker

D Sir 15 July 1804

you will oblige me by accepting an order on me for $ ten dollars in favour of Seth Thruston Esqr.[1] I am Sir

Mr. Henry Clay GEO. WALKER

ALS. DLC-TJC (DNA, M212, R15).

[1] Of Jessamine County. Thruston's order to Walker for payment to Clay is attached to this document and dated "16th [*sic*] July 1804."

To the Public

July 16th, 1804.

I certify that as a practising attorney in Fayette circuit court, I was present during the trial of the presentment against Mr. James Payne; that in my opinion the exposition of the act of Assembly as given by Judge Thruston was just; that it appeared to me that on that, as upon all similar occasions, the Judge was actuated solely by the desire of preserving the morals of society, and suppressing a pernicious practice, made by law his particular duty to reprove; and that the discharge of Mr. Payne without security, at the instance of one [of] the members of the bar, was rather an act of lenity than of strict right.[1] HENRY CLAY.

Lexington *Kentucky Gazette*, July 24, 1804.

[1] On July 3 "Jammy Payne," son of Edward Payne, had published in the *Kentucky Gazette* a diatribe against Judge Buckner Thruston, who had obtained in magistrate's court a conviction of the younger Payne and one Elijah Grimes for assault. Payne's anger had apparently stemmed from a trial over which Judge Thruston had presided in the March Term of court, when the former had been charged with keeping a gaming table. Clay's letter refers to the March trial. A similar statement, published at the same time, was signed by three other prominent Lexington lawyers.

Property Deed from George and Mary Ann Shepherd

[July 27, 1804]

[Indenture by which George Shepherd and Mary Ann his wife,

of Mason County, Kentucky, for six shillings current money of Kentucky, paid and acknowledged, convey to Henry Clay a tract in Lexington bounded as follows: beginning on Mill Street at the corner of Stephens and Winslow's lot, thence with Mill Street north 45° east four poles, thence southeastward half way to Market Street, thence southwest four poles, thence northwest to the beginning; also a tract lying on the northeast side of the above property, binding on Mill Street and from thence back the same distance as the aforesaid lot. These tracts are identified in the plat of McDermid's Square by numbers 44 and 45. Title warranted only against claimants through Shepherd's title. Signatures of the Shepherds attested by Thomas Bodley, July 27, 1804.]

DS. DLC, TJC, 2d Series, Vol. 5. Before marriage Mrs. Shepherd had been Mary Ann McDermid of Lexington.

1 The two tracts conveyed lay on the northeast side of Mill Street, between Short and Second, and comprised part of lot "F" in the original town plat. Lot "F," in turn, was a part of "McDermid's Square," which was bounded on the northeast by Mulberry Street and extended from Short to Second. One hundred feet of the Mill Street frontage here acquired, lot 45 and part of lot 44, became identified as Clay's "office lot."

From Thomas Norvell

Dear Sir Lynchburg August 3rd. 1804

Your favor of the 6th. June[1] I received at this place a few days Since, I am greatly obliged by your polite attention to my request. and your kind offers to Serve me.

Since I last wrote to you I have Seen Mr Carneal[2] and procured from him a new deed which is entirely Satisfactory and paid him all the taxes on my proportion, Subsequent to my purchase. So that I shall not have occasion to trouble you farther with that business

The information you have been pleased to give respecting the Selection of Messrs. P.[3] or their agent is interesting and for which you have my grateful acknowledgements. I am fully impressed with the delicacy of your Situation. and shall not disclose the Source of my information. I have written to the Messrs. P. on the Subject. and requested that they would give Some instructions to have Some man living near the land appointed to make Sale in a manner Suitable to purchasers—I mentioned to them that I would authorise Some friend in Lexington to cooperate in the appointment, and as you have been so polite as to tender your Services, my interest Strongly recommends the propriety of troubling you with it. with an impression that it may also prove to your interest. for if sales are made, it certainly shall be so—you will therefore be pleased to Search out Some man who you may think best calculated to execute our wishes, and give him what authority may be necessary for the purpose in conjunction with the agent of Messrs. P.—I shall be thankful to have this appointment made as early as possible as I wish Sales made immediately.

I am very desirous of having the title to the Land I purchased of Austin[4] ascertained. I am fearful I shall be pressed in the chancery court before it is done, as they may aledge I have had a Sufficient time &C. Will you have the goodness to inform me what will be the most ready mode to bring the business on. if it is not already done. for when it is once depending in a court in your State the Chancelor here. no doubt will wait for a decission there. and if they find nothing is done towards the investigation of the title, I fear it may in Some way operate vs me.—Direct to me if you please at this place—I shall always be proud in finding an opertunity of rendering you any Services in this quarter.—Be pleased to present my respectful compliments to yr Lady I am respectfully Yr Mo. ob. Se—

THOM NORVELL

ALS. DLC-TJC (DNA, M212, R12).

1 Not found.

2 Thomas Carneal.

3 Israel and John Pleasants, Baltimore merchants.

4 Norvell had acquired 2000 acres at Great Beaver Points on the Red River, a branch of the Kentucky, from Chapman Austin of Hanover County, Virginia, by deed of June 10, 1799. Fayette District Court, Deed Book D, 34.

Receipted Account with Dr. John M. Scott

H. Clay esqr. to Jno M Scott Dr [August 9, 1804]

1803.		
April 14	Visits. Vivisect & attendance & Medicine till 17th. inclusive	£ 2„14. 3
	By Cash	1. 10. 0
June.		£ 1„ 4„ 3

Mr Clay. You will oblige me very mu[ch] if its convenient, to pay the above ballance at this time, as I have paid all the cash I brought up & have not as much as will clear me out. Yrs respectfully

JNO M SCOTT—
at Mr Bradleys[1]

Recd the full amt of the above a/ct. 9th Augt. 1804.

JNO M SCOTT.

ADS. DLC-TJC (DNA, M212, R15). Dr. Scott, a native of Pennsylvania, had been an army surgeon with the northwestern expeditions under Generals Josiah Harmar and Anthony Wayne before settling at Frankfort, Kentucky, where he practiced his profession and served for a time as Sheriff of Franklin County. He held the rank of colonel in the militia, and, despite the ill-health that caused his death in 1813, he was appointed to the command of the First Regiment of Kentucky Volunteers, organized August 15, 1812.

1 Robert Bradley at this time operated "Traveler's Hall," a tavern on Short Street, opposite the public square in Lexington.

Receipt from James Barbour

[August 11, 1804]

Received 11 August 1804 of Henry Clay in horses one hundred and forty five pounds ten shillings on account of my Interest in the Upper blue Licks sold to him. JAS. BARBOUR

DS, in Clay's hand. KyLxT. See above, Agreement, June 29, 1804.

From John Clay

My dear Brother New Orleans August 18th. 1804

I had the pleasure of addressing you yesterday[1] P Mail & meeting to day with this Opportunity P Mr. Briggs[2] who goes thru yr. Place— & not knowing what to attribute my not receiving any letters *from* you—since leaving Kentucky: fearful that my letters have met the fate they heretofore have done, I have thought proper to address you again by this Private conveyance.

I had an offer last evening from Mr Benjamin F West (who you are well acquainted with) of joining him in Business; he has been in the Commercial Business here since february last & has made $5000 & his business is increasing—several Vessels are now loading to his Consignment to Liverpool & London. he had commenced business here at first with a Mr Siddins, who has lately got disgusted with the Climate & has disolved with him & left the Country: when Mr. W. made the proposition with me: I was obliged to be candid with him & tell my real situation[3] he was aware of it in part. his reply was that my advantages in being well acquainted in the Comn line my speaking the french Language' would over balance that defect, but that it would be necessary for me to be possessed of some Capital say from 1000 to 1500 dollars for equipping myself such as aiding in the building of Stores &c. for the reception of produce &c that to participate with him completely I must have at least that Capital. that if it was paid by next Spring in any kind of Kentucky produce. it will be sufficient You will readily see the advantages that would arise from a connexion with Mr West, he stands as high if not higher than any Merchant in this Country: To you then I must look up to for to be placed in this eligible situation. if Mr Seitz[4] had have lived to so see you he would have been able to have convinced you that any thing done to this end would not have been in vain I beg you will reflect upon it & give me your answer as early as possible. I wish you to keep this subject close till it may take effect.

This City is still very unhealthy. I shall leave it in a few days for the Country. let me hear from you shortly Yrs sincerely

Henry Clay Esq JOHN CLAY

ALS. DLC-TJC (DNA, M212, R10). [1] This letter has not been found.
[2] Possibly Isaac Briggs, surveyor of lands of the United States south of Tennessee.
[3] Unsuccessful in business in Lexington, he was deeply in debt when he left Kentucky. [4] John A. Seitz.

From Samuel Putnam

Sir. Salem Aug. 22. 1804.

Instead of a grant of our permission to Mr. West to sell two thirds of *his* Patent to Messrs. Morrison & Mansell, Mr. W. has sent us a Form which would operate as a grant of *our Patent* Right to him.[1] If we should execute it [we] should be obliged to ask *his* permission to use *our own* Machinery.

I inclose to you Mr. Wests Assignment of Mr. Morrisons Bond[2] and his Grant of one half of one third of his Patent,[3] which you will please to forward to him[, wi]th the original Bond in your Possession, and the inclosed form of a Gran[t][4] (which is the only one we can make) from us. If *tha[t]* will answer his purpose we will execute upon receipt of your letter which shall inclose the Assignment of the Bond & his grant of one half of one third of his Patent, and informing us that the original bond had been *re*delivered to you indorsed for our use.[5] If this form will not avail him, Mr. West must keep his own papers which you are to send him—and that must be the end of this troublesome business. We are much obliged by your Services and shall take care that you are compensated to your satisfaction. You will be so obliging as to communicate the result to me.[6]

I am Sir very respectfy. Yr mo. obedt. Serv SAM. PUTNAM
Henry Clay Esq. for the A.N.F.C.

ALS. DLC-TJC (DNA, M212, R12). Putnam was a lawyer in Salem, Massachusetts, and, later, a member of the Supreme Court of that State.

[1] Edward West, inventor of machinery for making nails, in May, 1802, contracted to sell the rights to his invention to James Morrison and George Mansell for $9,375. West agreed to obtain patents without delay and to assign them to the purchasers. On July 7 the patents were granted, but in September the original contract was replaced by another under which West, Morrison, and Mansell should become partners in the machine upon payment by Morrison and Mansell of two-thirds of the price originally fixed. Subsequently it developed that "a Mr. Perkins" had already patented a machine constructed on the same principle as West's. Putnam's letter apparently was written in response to an attempt by West to compromise with the holders of the Perkins patent.

[2] On July 16, 1804, West had assigned to Putnam and to Abel Lawrance and William Ward, also of Salem, Massachusetts, James Morrison's bond dated September 20, 1802, for $2500 secured by such a quantity of land on Bear Creek, in Hardin County, Kentucky, as would at the cash price to be determined by designated appraisers amount to $1162.86. (DS, in Clay's hand. DLC-TJC [DNA, M212, R15]).

[3] Also dated July 16, 1804 (DS, in Clay's hand. DLC-TJC [DNA, M212, R15]), it provided that for $1000 to be paid by Lawrance, Ward, and Putnam, "for the use of the Amesbury Nail Factory Company," West sold one half of all the "money, estate, benefit and advantage whatsoever," that he held on one third of the patent.

[4] The "form of a Grant" has not been found.

[5] The bond was not re-endorsed for their use. For a second assignment of part of Morrison's bond, see below, October 20, 1804.

[6] No subsequent correspondence with Putnam has been found.

From Montgomery Bell

Dear Sir Cumberland Furnace August 25th 1804

When in Lexington you mention to me the necessity of your having an evidence of what you were to have for Settleing my Business with the executors of Co,l Nicholas,[1] I shall consider myself one hundred dollars in your debt when you establish to my credit the paper of Co,l Nicholas I left in your hand for discount and I am a[c]quited from it. You also mention to me the probability of Selling the Hickman Mills[2] for whisky. I am now disposed to take whisky for them my price is 27,000 gallons 9000 gallons paid the first of may next 9000 gallons paid the first of May 1806 and 9000 gallons the first of May 1807 all delivered in good barrels at Bolers warehouse,[3] if a sale of that kind can be effected by you I will forward paper that may be necessary for that purpose I am Sir with respect your Obed,t Serv,t MONTGOMERY BELL

I have made a purchase of most valuable tract of land since my arivel at this place

ALS. DLC-TJC (DNA, M212, R12). Addressed to Clay at Lexington. Postmarked: "NASHVILLE T August 28."

1 George Nicholas, Virginia lawyer and statesman, came to Kentucky in 1788 and settled in Lexington a few years later. He played a major role in the framing of the first Kentucky Constitution, in establishment of the State capital, and in the agitation which gave rise to the Virginia and Kentucky Resolutions of 1799. He was the first incumbent of the professorship of law and politics at Transylvania University, but died in July, 1799, shortly after his appointment. The administration of his heavily encumbered estate occasioned protracted litigation.

2 On Hickman Creek, in Jessamine County.

3 Not located.

Agreement with Daniel Bryan

[September 7, 1804]

An agreement Between Daniel Bryan & Henry Clay.

The said Clay agrees to appear for the said Bryan in any suit which may be necessary to be brought against the Trustees of the Transylvania University or which may be brought by them against him relative to his Settlement & preemption on the waters of Hickman & Elkhorn.[1]

In consideration whereof said Bryan agrees to pay said Clay Seven pounds; and one dollar per acre for whatever may be saved of the said Settlement & preemption, excepting that part of the settlement which is not in dispute with the Trustees & excepting that part of the preemption which the said Bryan has conveyed to Levi Todd.

In Testimony whereof the parties have hereunto set their hands & affixed their Seals this 7. Septr. 1804. HENRY CLAY {L.S.}

DAN'L. BRYAN {L.S.}

[Endorsement on verso][2]
I acknowledge that I have heretofore recd. of Mr. D. Bryan in full satisfaction for the within agreement fifty dollars. 3. Septr. 1808.
$50. H. CLAY

ADS, signed also by Bryan, a landholder in both Fayette and Scott counties. KyLoF.
1 Southeast of Lexington in Fayette County.
2 AES.

Account with Dr. Samuel Brown

[*ca.* September 8, 1804]

Henry Clay Esqr. To Saml. Brown Dr.

1800			
		To Amount of your for 1800 & part of 1801.	19 19 9
		To yr. Acct. for Part of 1801.. 2 & Part of 1803	12 5 3
			£32 5 0
1801		Cr.	
July	22	By Cash	6 16 6
		Ballance Due	£25 8 6
1803		To yr. Acct. for Part of 1803.	11 6 9
			£36„15„3
		To yr. Acct for Part of 1803	8 19 3
			£45 14 6
		To yr. Acct for Part of 1803 & Part 1804	4 17 3
			£50 11 9
1803		Cr.	
Augt	19	By Cash $50	15 0 0
Septr.	3	3 1 oz. Phials Returned 2/6	„ 2 6
			£15 2 6
			£35„ 9„3
Septr 1804	8	By Asst. for Mrs Jackson[1] 10$	3 0 0
		Ballance Due S Brown	£32„ 9„3

[Endorsement on verso][2]
Lexington March 1st 1806
Recd. the within Acct in full for Dr S. Brown J OVERTON[3]

D, in James Overton's hand. DLC-TJC, 2d Series, vol. 6. Document torn across bottom, one or more lines missing. Brown, who had followed his brother James to Lexington in 1797, had become a professor of medicine at Transylvania University and introduced vaccination for smallpox to Kentucky in 1802. In 1806 he moved to New Orleans, then lived in Mississippi and Alabama before returning in 1819 to a professorship at Transylvania, where he served until his retirement to his home in Alabama in 1825.
1 Probably Clay's client, Susannah Jackson. See below, Order, March 26, 1809.

[2] AES.

[3] James Overton, who was probably studying medicine with Dr. Brown. In 1809 Dr. Overton was "appointed to the chair of Materia Medica and Botany" in Transylvania University, and upon the reorganization of the medical faculty in 1815 he became professor of theory and practice. He moved from Lexington to Nashville, Tennessee, in 1818. Robert Peter, *The History of the Medical Department of Transylvania University* (*Filson Club Publications* no. 20, Prepared for Publication by Johanna Peter; Louisville, 1905), 26-28.

Agreement with Cuthbert Banks

[September 13, 1804]

An agreement entered into between C. Banks & H. Clay this 13th. day of September 1804.

The said Banks covenants to sell to the said Clay and to make him therefor a deed with general warranty his plantation near Lexington on Todd's road[1] lately occupied by Elisha Winters,[2] now by Slayback[3] & supposed to contain one hundred and twenty five acres; and covenants to deliver possession thereof to the said Clay on the expiration of the Case of Slayback

The said Clay covenants to pay the said Banks for the said plantation at the rate of eight pounds per acre for every acre therein to be ascertained by actual admeasurement and to be paid in the following manner: Two hundred & fifty pounds in Thomas Bodley's bonds carrying interest from the date hereof, and payable at the end of two years from this date: an out lott lying between Limestone & Main cross streets adjoining on one side the lott belonging to the estate of John McNair and the other the lott of Robert Holmes,[4] at the price of one hundred & fifty pounds: an order on Thomas Todd Esqr. for Thirty two pounds: a Judgment on James Morrison rendered on the thirty first day of March last for two hundred & seventy one pounds fourteen shillings and six pence with Int. thereon from the 18h. day of Septr. last till paid: and whatever balance remains after the deduction of these several payments the said Clay is to pay within four years from this date, with legal interest thereon to be paid annually.

And whereas the said James Morrison contests the payment of the said Judgment and has filed a bill enjoining the same[5] it is therefore further agreed that if the said Morrison shall finally prevail in preventing the payment thereof or shall compel the said Clay to receive it in any thing but money, that in either of those cases the amount of the said Judgment shall be paid by the said Clay within the said term of four years from the date hereof; with Interest to be paid annually as aforesaid; and it is also agreed that the said Clay shall attend to the recovery of the said Judgment.

And it is further agreed by the parties that the said Banks shall whenever demanded make a deed to the said Clay for the plantation, upon the said Clay's giving him good security to comply on his part with the present contract.

And the said Clay covenants to deliver to the said Banks immediate possession of the said out lott and to make him a title therefor on demand.

In Testimony whereof the said Banks & Clay have hereunto set their hands & seals the day & year first written.

Signed Sealed &c CUTHB: BANKS {L.S.}
In presence of HENRY CLAY {L.S.}
J WILSON[6]

[Endorsements][7]

Recd. of H. Clay T. Bodleys bond agreeably to the foregoing agreement for Two hundred & fifty pounds 25 March 1805.

CUTHB: BANKS

On a final settlemt. I have recd. paymt in full of H. Clay for the land within sold, & Mr. Bodley is requested to make him a deed for the Land.[8] 26 Nov. 1809 CUTHB: BANKS.

ADS, signed also by Banks. KLxT. This transaction was the beginning of Clay's control of land that later became part of "Ashland."

1 Usually referred to as "Boone's Road," which passed Levi Todd's estate southeast of Lexington.

2 Prominent merchant and manufacturer, who on February 1, 1800, deeded to Thomas Hart 150 acres of land on the "Boon's Station" road (DS, in Clay's hand. KyU-Wilson Collection). Hart, in turn, on April 2, 1800, transferred 123 acres of this tract to Thomas Bodley, from whom Banks contracted to buy it. Fayette District Court, Deed Book C, 174-75, 248-49.

3 Probably Solomon Slayback of Fayette County.

4 McNair and Holmes, the latter a wheelwright and furniture maker on the northeast corner of Short and Main Cross (now Broadway), were both extensive property holders in Lexington. The tract in question is not sufficiently delineated for identification, and no record of the property transfer by Clay has been found.

5 See below, Wrenshall to Clay, June 13, 1807, note.

6 Joshua Wilson, recently come to Lexington from Bardstown, Kentucky, was now the proprietor of Postlethwait's Tavern.

7 Both ES, in Clay's hand.

8 Deed dated October 11, 1811.

From James Brown

WASHINGTON,[1] September 16, 1804.

DEAR SIR,—Your last letter was dated at the Springs,[2] where you were reveling in the enjoyments of ease, mirth, and engaging society. Since that time you have probably experienced the bustle and solicitude attendant on an election, for I discover your name at the head of the list of successful candidates.[3]

. . . .

Nancy was delighted at finding that Lucretia had overcome her repugnance to writing, and by the next post replied to her letter.[4] She begs me to press upon you the task of urging her to write more frequently, and authorizes me to declare that although her correspondents are numerous, Lucretia's letters shall ever receive prompt answers.

I have written to so many of my friends to-day, that I have, much against my inclination, defrauded you of your share. My affectionate wishes for the happiness of yourself and family wait upon you.

Colton (ed.), *Private Correspondence of Henry Clay,* 10. Brown, newly appointed Secretary of the Territory of Orleans, left Lexington in May, 1804, but halted at Natchez until the end of the yellow fever season before proceeding to New Orleans. J[ohn] Brown to Thomas Jefferson, August 10, 1804, in James A. Padgett, "The Letters of Honorable John Brown to the Presidents of the United States," Kentucky State Historical Society, *Register,* XXXV (1937), 22; Claiborne to James Madison, October 3, 1804, in Dunbar Rowland (ed.), *Official Letter Books of W.C.C. Claiborne, 1801-1816* (Jackson, Miss., 1917), II, 345-46.

1 Mississippi Territory.

2 Probably Olympian Springs (formerly "Mud Lick"), a resort in Montgomery County owned by Thomas Hart. Clay's letter, to which Brown refers, has not been found.

3 During the previous month Clay had been re-elected as a member of the Kentucky General Assembly.

4 Ann Brown and Lucretia Clay were sisters.

To Israel and John P. Pleasants

Mess. Israel & John P. Pleasants Lexington 24 Sept. 1804.
Gent.

I received yours' of the 7h. Inst.[1] and I have since seen Mr. Boggs.[2] The deed of trust from Norvel[3] to you has been received and he informed me that he would have it recorded in the proper office. I can give you no certain information as to the probability of effecting a Sale of the Land; the nearest is 50 and the farthest tract upwards of 70 or 80 miles from this place. Speaking from conjecture only, I fear the prospect of a speedy Sale is not very good. Land is every where now in this State sold with difficulty. And lands, acquired as Mr. Norvell purchased this, at the public Sales for taxes, have not yet obtained in the public estimation much value; it may however have happened that both as to title and value he made a fortunate bargain. This can only be ascertained upon farther investigation. I will endeavour to seek out a proper character to attend to the agency of Selling the Land. I am Gent. Yr. ob. Servt.

HENRY CLAY

ALS. MdHi. 1 Not found.

2 Probably John M. Boggs, who had on other occasions served as agent for non-resident owners of Kentucky lands. 3 Thomas Norvell.

Agreement with John Wrenshall

[September 24, 1804]

It is agreed between Peacock Wrenshall & Co. & H. Clay as follows:

The said Clay undertakes the collection of the debts due from Hughes, Allen,[1] Metcalfe, Barlow,[2] Pigman[3] and Holmes[4] to the said Company.

He will also endeavour to get himself released from any prior obligation, and undertake the collection of the debt due from Williams[5] to said Company.

In Consideration whereof the said Company agree to allow to said Clay a Commission of five per Cent upon Hughes & Allen's debts—of ten per Cent upon Metcalfe & Barlows—and of fifteen per Cent upon Pigmans—For the Collection of Holmes's the said Company has already paid: And they agree to allow him one third of whatever may be obtained from Williams; & one half of whatever may be recovered from David Duncan,[6] whose debt is also placed in said Clay's hands for Collection.

In Witness whereof the parties hereunto Set their hands & Seals this 24 Septr. 1804.

Teste JOHN WRENSHALL {L.S.}
JOHN MCKINNEY JUNR HENRY CLAY {L.S.}

ADS, signed also by Wrenshall. DLC-TJC (DNA, M212, R15).

1 James Hughes; John Allen (of Paris, Kentucky).

2 Possibly William Barlow, a carpenter of Scott County, and Thomas Metcalfe, at this time a stone-mason of Nicholas County, later a member of the Kentucky legislature (1812-1816, 1834-1838) and of the United States Congress (1819-1828, 1848-1849), and Governor of Kentucky (1828-1832).

3 Ignatius Pigman, a Methodist preacher, had moved to Kentucky about 1788, settling in that part of Hardin County from which Ohio County was formed. He engaged heavily in land speculation until his failure in that business, after which he moved to New Orleans around 1806. For comment on his debt to Wrenshall see below, Bartlet and Cox to Clay, November 11, 1811.

4 At the September Term, 1802, of Fayette Circuit Court, in a suit brought against him by John Wrenshall and Ralph Peacock, surviving partners of Peacock, Wrenshall and Company, Andrew Holmes had confessed a debt of $1,951.12½ (United States money) plus £585, 6s, 9d (Kentucky Currency), with interest from April 15, 1801, until paid. The plaintiff, represented by Clay, had agreed to a stay of execution for two months. When Holmes died December 13, 1803, the claim became involved in the settlement of his estate.

5 Not identified.

6 Merchant of Washington, Kentucky.

Power of Attorney from Peacock Wrenshall and Company

[September 25, 1804]

[Peacock Wrenshall and Company, by John Wrenshall, grant power of attorney to Henry Clay to demand, sue for, recover, and receive any money or property due or belonging to them in Kentucky; power to compromise or arbitrate any dispute they may have, and where their claim may be doubtful to give up a part so as to obtain the remainder; power to sell and dispose of any property under terms he thinks proper; and in order to effect collection of any such debt, power to transfer any security or securities held by the firm against said debtors. Clay is also authorized to substitute an attorney or attorneys under him. Certification of Wrenshall's signature before Thomas Bodley, Fayette Circuit Clerk, September 25, 1804.]

Fayette Circuit Court, Deed Book B, 2.

Receipt from James Smith

29. Septr. 180.4

Received of H Clay for Col. Barbour in horses Two hundred & Sixty Six dollars & Sixty Six Cents.

Teste JAMES SMITH

J. P. WAGNON[1]

DS, in Clay's hand. KyLxT. See above, Agreement, June 29, 1804. Smith was probably from Mercer County. [1] A Lexington innkeeper.

To John Breckinridge

Dr Sir. [*ca.* October 1, 1804]

I have been furnished by Col. Greenup[1] and others with several letters of recommendation in favour of my brothers application for the office of Collector or Surveyor of the Port of New Orleans, and I am promised some others. These together with the one you were good enough to promise me, I wish to forward immediately. As Col. Sandford[2] will be upon the spot I have thought it advisable to enclose them to him that he may place them in the proper channel. I will thank you for your opinion on this subject. And am Dr Sir Yrs.

Monday morning— H CLAY

ALS. DLC-Breckinridge Family Papers (DNA, M212, R20). Addressed to Breckinridge. [1] Christopher Greenup. [2] Thomas Sandford.

Receipt from Ambrose Young

8. Oct. 1804

Recd. of H. Clay Fifty dollars on a/c. of the Vineyard Association.

Teste AMBROSE YOUNG

JNO. MCKINNEY JR

DS, in Clay's hand. DLC-TJC (DNA, M212, R15). Young lived in the southern part of Fayette County.

From Thomas Hart

October 15th 1804

Mr. Clay will please have a Deed presented to Govr. Grenup, for the

125 Acres of Land with the appurtenances, & Agreable to the inclosed Bond[1] and If Ramsey is indebted for any part of the Consideration Money (by leting me know it) I will Immediately discharge it as there is yet a ballance due from me to that Gentn.
he will also dispose of the five head rights and the Amt. of whatever Sum he may get for them he will Credit [m]e, for Services Already done and preformed THOMAS HART

ANS. DLC-TJC (DNA, M212, R10). 1 Not found.

Assignment of Bond by Edward West

20 October 1804

For value received I assign one third of this bond to Henry Clay.
EDWD WEST

ES, in Clay's hand. Fayette Circuit Court, File 238 (1812). On the bond, from James Morrison to West, cf. above, Putnam to Clay, August 22, 1804, note.

Agreement with Thomas Vaughan

[October 29, 1804]

An agreement between Thomas Vaughan & Henry Clay entered into this 28h [*sic*] day of October 1804.

Whereas the said Clay is the owner of two thirds of a patent which issued to William Linn, James Barbour & John Williams on the 18h. day of December 1787, by purchase from the said Barbour and the heir of the said Linn, which patent issued for one thousand acres of land including the Upper Blue Licks.[1]

The said Clay has this day covenanted to sell to the said Vaughan one of the said two thirds and to make or cause to be made a deed with special warranty only, it being clearly and expressly understood that the said Clay in the Sale does not bind himself for the goodness of the Title of the said Linn, Barbour & Williams, nor to return any part of the consideration money, if it proves bad:

In consideration of the said one third, the said Vaughan Covenants to pay the said Clay in clean dry merchantable Salt Six hundred bushels in the following manner; one hundred and fifty bushels to be delivered to said Clay in Lexington on or before the first of March next; two hundred & twenty five bushels to be delivered to said Clay at the Upper Blue Licks on or before Christmas 1805 and the remaining Two hundred & twenty five bushels on or before Christmas 1806:

It is further agreed by the parties that the said Vaughan shall have the lower end of the said Survey of one thousand Acres, exclusive of the Springs which are to be in common, and whatever part he takes is to be estimated whenever a division of the tract may be made; and if it is more valuable than the part which may be allotted to the said Clay, said Vaughan is to make up to said Clay the difference in Value if less valuable the deficiency to be made up to him out of the adjoining land.

And whereas there are two Suits depending in which the said claim is controverted, one with Finley,[2] and the other with Prestons,[3] it is agreed by the parties that the said Vaughan shall pay one third of the Costs which may attend said Suits, and shall be entitled to one third of the rents which may be recovered therein.

In Witness whereof we have hereunto Set our hands & Seals this 29h. Oct. 1804.

Signed Sealed &c THOMAS VAUGHAN {L.S.}
In presence of HENRY CLAY {L.S.}
THOMAS HART
JOHN MCKINNEY JUNR

[Endorsement][4]

Credit by the two first payments of 150 bushels & 225, except 41 lb. as per receipts & statement of Mr. Vaughan. HENRY CLAY

ADS, also signed by Vaughan, already a taxpayer in Nicholas County, where the land is located. DLC-TJC (DNA, M212, R15).

1 See above, Agreement, June 29, 1804.

2 John Finley, a Pennsylvanian, had been a member of a party that discovered the licks in 1773. After the Revolution he settled in this area and engaged in a long legal controversy with Clay on the question of ownership of the land. In the lower court Clay won the suit on the basis of his claim to the first patent, but the decision was reversed by the United States Supreme Court in view of Finley's earlier improvement on the land. WHI-Draper MSS, 12CC 238-39.

3 Not found. 4 AES.

Agreement with Jonathan Patterson

[November 1, 1804]

An agreement between Jonathan Patterson in behalf of himself and those interested in an entry of 12500 acres made in the name of Samuel Patterson on the 24 Decr. 1782,[1] of the one part, and Henry Clay of the other.

The said Clay has this day engaged to commence and prosecute Suits against the claims or such of them as in his Judgment may be recovered interfering with the aforesaid entry:

And the said Patterson for himself and Copartners for whom he is empowered, agrees in consideration of said Clay's services to allow him for every 1000 acres which shall be recovered out of Thomas Marshall entries one of 3816½ acres and the other of 6000 Acres and out of the entries or entry for 3000.0 acres or thereabouts claimed by Bodley and Hughes, the Sum of £20—For every 100

Acres that may be recovered out of the claims of Peter Johnson heir at law of Jamieson and John & Robert Walden the Sum of £20; and for every 100 Acres that may be recovered out of the preemption of Montgomery the Sum of £10[2]—The said sums to be paid by said Patterson to said Clay as the said recoveries may take place and within six months after each final decree or Judgment may be pronounced. Witness our hands & Seals this 1 Nov. 1804.

Teste JONATHAN PATTERSON {L.S.}
JOHN MCKINNEY JR HENRY CLAY {L.S.}

ADS, signed also by Patterson. KyLxT. Both Jonathan and Samuel Patterson were taxpayers in Green County, Kentucky.

1 This land lay on the Licking River.

2 A suit by Patterson and others against Thomas Bodley and James Hughes was brought before Fayette Circuit Court in the spring of 1805 (Fayette Circuit Court, Order Book C, 15); but no further action on it is reported, and no other Patterson suits with the named parties have been found.

Peter Johnson, a Revolutionary veteran of Prince Edward Court House, Virginia, as heir of Jacob Johnson claimed 1,400 acres in settlement and pre-emption grants on the buffalo road from Blue Licks to Limestone (Maysville). John Walden had entered and surveyed 1,666⅔ acres on Johnson's Fork of Licking dependent upon the location of Johnson's survey. Colonel Thomas Marshall, father of Chief Justice Marshall and first Surveyor of Fayette County, held numerous Virginia grants in that county, as then defined, including tracts of 3,816 and 6,052 acres, the former not identified as to watercourse, the latter located on Johnson's Fork. James Montgomery, veteran of the French and Indian War and a pioneer explorer from the Holston frontier, claimed 1000 acres as a Virginia grant also on Johnson's Fork. David Jamieson, a Virginia merchant who had supplied the Revolutionary forces, held thousands of acres in Virginia grants on the Licking. The complicated litigation over these overlapping entries is discussed further below, Taylor to Clay, January 4, 1807.

Nomination of William Waller

[November 5, 1804]

Clay nominated William Smith Waller as clerk for the committees on privileges, elections, propositions, and grievances. The Clay nominee was elected by a large majority. Ky. H. of Reps., *Journal, 1804*, p. [3].

Waller, of Frankfort, had been appointed clerk in the office of the state auditor, 1803; he was subsequently first clerk of the first Bank of Kentucky, 1807, and cashier of the latter institution, 1809.

Resolution Relating to State Land Sale

[November 5, 1804]

Resolved by the general assembly, that the sales of lands which were to commence this day, under the superintendence of the register be, and the same are hereby ordered to be suspended for the space of six days.

Ky. H. of Reps., *Journal, 1804*, p. 4. The resolution, suspending sale of the land for delinquent tax payments pending further legislation on the subject, was ultimately rejected in the Senate. Cf. below, Bill, November 6, 1804.

Bill Regulating Sale of Non-Residents' Lands

[November 6, 1804]

Clay reported the bill for a drafting committee which also included Felix Grundy of Nelson County, John Kercheval of Mason, William McMillan of Clark, and Samuel South of Madison. Ky. H. of Reps., *Journal, 1804,* p. 14. Clay had asked leave to present the measure following House adoption of his resolution on November 5. On November 9 he moved to bring the bill before the House, whereupon it was rejected on the question of engrossment. Cf. below, Bill, November 21, 1804.

Amendment Relating to Senatorial Election

[November 15, 1804]

If neither of the candidates has a majority of the members of the two houses on the first vote, the house shall proceed to vote again, until six successive votes are taken, unless a majority should sooner be had, and if no candidate has a majority on the last vote, the candidate having the smallest number of votes on the last vote shall be dropped, and a vote shall then be taken between the other candidates, and he who shall first obtain a majority of all the votes of both houses shall be considered as duly elected.

Ky. H. of Reps., *Journal, 1804,* p. 29. Clay had first moved to refer to Committee of the Whole the resolution and amendments prescribing the mode of voting for a Senator to Congress. When this proposal was defeated, he moved that the resolution be tabled until the end of the session. When this suggestion was also rejected, he offered the present amendment to be substituted for the whole of the original resolution and the proposed amendments. The Clay proposals were designed to modify the resolution as first adopted in the House, which had provided for dropping the least-favored candidate after the first vote. The final motion was accepted in both houses, and applied in the ensuing election. By this procedure Buckner Thruston, who was lowest on the first vote, ultimately was elected to the Senate.

From Franklin, Robinson and Company

Respected Friend New York 11 mo 19: 1804

Thy letter of 30th ultimo[1] came duly to hand, & we observe its contents. We approve of thy *employing an agent to retrace the lines of our Survey, and to warn the persons living on the lands to cease cutting the timber, and if they persist, to take coercive measures to prevent them.*

We also think well of thy paying col Suddith[2] ye. $50 for ye 700 acres of our land which he bought, and request thee to do so and draw upon us for the amount—We are, Respectfully, thy Friends

Henry Clay Esqr. FRANKLIN, ROBINSON & CO.

ALS. DLC-TJC (DNA, M212, R12).

1 Not found.

2 Probably William Sudduth, long Surveyor of Clark County.

Bill Relating to Recovery of Land Forfeited to State

[November 21, 1804]

For a drafting committee which also included John Allen (Franklin County), Richard M. Johnson (Scott), Matthew Flournoy (Shelby), James Liggett (Woodford), and Felix Grundy, Clay reported a bill "to amend the act, entitled an act to reduce into one the several acts for establishing a permanent revenue." Ky. H. of Reps., *Journal, 1804*, p. 43. On November 17 he had asked leave to present such a measure, and on November 30 he moved to bring it before the House. Enacted on December 15, it provided that lands forfeited to the State because they had not been listed for taxation might be recovered if within two years from passage of this act they were listed and all arrearages of tax paid. Littell (comp.), *Statute Law of Kentucky*, III, 192.

Resolution Relating to Adjournment

[November 21, 1804]

Resolved, That when the general assembly adjourns on Saturday the first day of December next, it will adjourn without day.

Ky. H. of Reps., *Journal, 1804*, p. 46. Clay called up his resolution on November 26, whereupon it was amended and tabled. His interest in the matter may have been dictated by a desire to forestall the discussion on the Kentucky Insurance Company which opened in the House on December 1, following Senate passage of a bill relating to the firm. He does not appear to have been concerned in the later action on adjournment.

From Thomas Hockley

Dear Sir Philad. November 22nd. 1804.

I have to acknowledge rect. of your's of 17h. Ultimo which came to hand 3 Inst.[1] Have wrote to my Friends in the State of New York for instructions respecting their lands in Kentuckey which you informe me had been sold for taxes, when I receive an answer I will perhaps trouble you again. The five hundred dollars I recd by Mr Reese[2] in July last, for which I am much obliged & thought I had acknowledged it before. I feel mortified at the dissapointment in not sending your quarter Cask of wine, the Fact is when I applied for the former one on the receipt of your letter; it was sold, Mr Lewis[3] thinking from such a lapse of time that I did not intend calling for it. I accordingly engaged another quarter Cask from Mr Robt. Morris,[4] which had been imported in pipes for the Danish Consul, 4 years, at 3½ dollrs. a gallon: both of those Gentlemen are Importers of wine. Mr Trotter[5] had fixed on his last waggons to take it in, but unfortunately his own loading was so great as to prevent him; the n[ex]t [morn]ing about 12 O Clock he sent a very decent man to my [. . .][6] [c]ould have taken it: I instant[ly] [. . .] [hi]m Mr Morris's house but he was gone out of town & the waggoner would not wait half an hour, this has obliged me to defer it to another time. I have been thus precise in order to satisfy you that it was not owing to my want of Attention, you did not receive your wine. I some time past forwarded you an account against Mr Craig;[7] as he has not made any exception to it, I conclude it is right & have settled my books accordingly.

I also wrote you some time past that Mr Walker of this City would receive from you the amount in your hands received from Davis, & if it should come to hand; in the mean time, I shall pay it over to him.[8] Our approaching winter I fear will be a gloomy one among our Merchants, we have had already some heavy failures & there is no knowing how far their effect will extend. I remain respectfully Dr Sir Your Most Obt [. . .] [THOMAS HOC]KLEY

Henr[y Clay] Esq.

ALS (mutilated, signature partially destroyed). DLC-TJC (DNA, M212, R10). Addressed to Clay at Lexington. Endorsed in Clay's hand: "Tho. Hockley."

1 Not found.

2 Of the Philadelphia firm of Bickham and Reese.

3 Probably Mordecai Lewis, Philadelphia merchant.

4 Merchant and statesman, sometimes called "financier of the American Revolution."

5 Probably George Trotter, Sr., Lexington merchant.

6 MS. torn. Possibly two words missing in each of the indicated gaps.

7 Elijah Craig.

8 A. Walker was another Philadelphia merchant. Davis has not been identified.

Bill Relating to Fayette County Records

[November 23, 1804]

For a drafting committee which also included Felix Grundy, John Kercheval, and Joshua Lewis (Jessamine County), as well as William Russell and Benjamin Graves, the other Fayette representatives, Clay reported a bill "to provide for transcribing certain record books in the surveyor's office of Fayette." Ky. H. of Reps., *Journal, 1804*, p. 54. On November 13 he had asked leave to present such a measure. It was subsequently adopted in the House, but rejected in the Senate. Clay's interest in this bill and in his resolution of December 19, 1804, doubtless stemmed from the evidence of alteration of the land records revealed in his defense of Prettyman Merry at this time. Cf. below, Memorandum of Conversation, *ca.* July, 1806, note.

Amendments to Bill Providing Tax on Billiard Tables

[November 27, 1804]

Mr. Clay from the select committee to whom was referred the engrossed bill entitled "an act to amend the several acts establishing a permanent revenue," reported the same with several amendments. The first amendment (which was to strike out two hundred dollars, and insert in lieu thereof fifty dollars, being the tax imposed on Billiard tables) being read, it was concurred in.

. . . .

The other amendments were then concurred in.

Resolved, That the said bill do pass, and that the title be amended to read "an act more effectually to suppress the practice of gaming."

Ky. H. of Reps., *Journal, 1804,* p. 63. Other members of the select committee were Felix Grundy, Samuel Caldwell, and George C. Thompson (of Mercer County, son of Colonel George Thompson and for many years a member of the Kentucky legislature, Speaker of the House, 1820-1822). The bill as initially presented had provided for a tax of $50 on billiard tables. By a close vote, in which Clay had taken no recorded stand, the measure had been amended to raise the levy to $200. At the third reading, on the following day, the bill had been sent to a select committee, with Clay as chairman, whose report is here adopted. Clay's subsequent resolution was also concurred in. As finally enacted, after Senate amendment, the tax was set at $100. Littell (comp.), *Statute Law of Kentucky,* III, 176.

Bill Relating to Fayette Circuit Court

[November 28, 1804]

Clay presented a bill to give an additional term to the Fayette Circuit Court, to handle chancery cases and to be held the following February. Ky. H. of Reps., *Journal, 1804,* p. 66. Other members of the drafting committee were William Russell, Benjamin Graves, Joshua Lewis, Henry C. Bruce (Bourbon County lawyer), and William B. Blackburn (of Woodford County, member of the Kentucky legislature much of the interval through 1828, a lawyer, and husband of Clay's half-sister, Martha Watkins). On November 26, Clay had asked leave to present such a measure. It was enacted December 15. Littell (comp.), *Statute Law of Kentucky,* III, 187-88.

From John Clay

M Henry Clay New Orleans 1st. Decemr 1804

Dear Brother

Your favour of the 22d October, came to hand[1] Seeing some part of it which required answering you should have attended to it much earlier, but have been rescently a good deal indisposed, at present (thank God I feel pretty well.

I am very thankful to you for the interest you have taken in indeavoring to procure me the Office of Collector or Surveyor of this Port. I wish you to continue to make every effort for the Office of Surveyor, as I am doubtful you will not be able to succeed for that of Collector, indeed I do not aspire to that. a Mr Brown of this place (Brother in law to the late Mr. Trist) has the unanimous recommendation of the Merchants of this Place, for the Office of Collector. I immagine ere your letters can reach Washington he will be appointed as it was forwarded very early after the death of Mr Trist.[2] I should not be so eager after this appointment my prospects being pretty good in the Commission line, but find that it can be done thro. a deputy, & finally if I should not succeed in the Commission buisness [*sic*] it is an excellent resort its emolument is worth at present about $2,500, but increasing every year, it is a very honorable appointment, & should I succed will gain me a good deal of influence—I should have gotten the Govenor Mr Brown Watkins[3] & some other freinds to have said something in my favr. but would have been too late a Mr Andrew Porter[4] who has been doing the duties of that Office for some time past had already gotten the names of many Merchants here with that of Watkins & the Governor to Recommend him before they knew of my wish to obtain it; this Recommendation in fav[or] of Porter has only sett out two weeks ago. it will arrive I immagin it [*sic*] some time after mine &

M. Brown[5] & family only arrived here on Monday last they are well. I have been buisily employed for some days past in getting them to house keeping they will not get in their house for a few days when they will have a very comodious Building nearly in the center of the City Mr Browns prospects are flattering I I [*sic*] have no doubt of his making from 10 to 15000 Dols. for the first year. I shall speak to him & get his opinion relative to my case with Hunt[6] in a few days & forwarded it to you

I wrote you very fully in October,[7] to which & several other letters upon the same subject I beg you will refer nothing but my prospects being so flattering would induce me to ask you such requests—you will readily see the necissity perhaps it will be the last of the same complexion—& the good effects produced by yr acqueising will be ever lasting

I have nothing new to address you this place is uncommonly healthy & wears a degree of *gaitti* which it has not done for six months past—Owing a number of the Legislative Council having refused their appointments, we will not have a Council for some time, we have just heard here of the death of Judge Kirby[8] (at Pencacola) one of the Judges of this District

My Compts to Lucretia & Children—& Col Hart & family Yr Affte Brother JOHN CLAY

ALS. Owned by J. Winston Coleman, Jr., Lexington, Kentucky.

1 Not found.

2 Following the death of H.B. Trist on August 29, 1804, William Brown became Collector of the Port of New Orleans and served until he absconded with public funds in 1809. Rowland (ed.), *Official Letter Books of W.C.C. Claiborne,* II, 312, 314; V, 10, 18.

3 Governor Claiborne, probably James Brown, and Dr. John Watkins.

4 A partner in the firm Robert and Andrew Porter, merchants of Lexington for a brief period beginning in 1797. Robert, a Philadelphia lawyer, later judge of the Third Judicial District of Pennsylvania, apparently figured only as backer for the operations of his younger brother. Andrew, identified primarily as a merchant in New Orleans, continued as Surveyor of the Port until his death on October 16, 1805, when he was succeeded by James Lovell.

5 James Brown.

6 Wilson Hunt, a Philadelphia merchant and brother of John W. Hunt of Lexington, had been trying for several years to collect money owed to him by John Clay. KyU-John W. and Abijah Hunt Papers.

7 This letter has not been found.

8 Ephraim Kirby, a Connecticut lawyer appointed a judge of the Superior Court of Orleans Territory in 1804.

Resolution for Relief of Chickasaws

[December 6, 1804]

Resolved, That there shall be appropriated for the use of the five

Chickasaw Indians now in Frankfort, to purchase blankets and cloathing, a sum not exceeding twenty dollars.

Ky. H. of Reps., *Journal, 1804,* p. 83. The resolution was rejected on first reading.

Bill Relating to Paving the Streets of Lexington

[December 11, 1804]

Clay reported the bill for a drafting committee which included all the Fayette County representatives. Ky. H. of Reps., *Journal, 1804,* p. 80. The measure, enacted December 18, empowered the town trustees to compel property owners to pave along their frontage on a portion of Main Street and on the remaining streets as demand arose. Littell (comp.), *Statute Law of Kentucky,* III, 207-208.

Motion Concerning Bill on Kentucky Insurance Company

[December 12, 1804]

Clay moved to table the proposed legislation until the end of the Session. Ky. H. of Reps., *Journal, 1804,* p. 95. The Kentucky Insurance Company was a Lexington firm, which had been incorporated as a monopoly with privileges for issuance of negotiable notes without explicit limitation, as well as for insurance operations. A bill amending the statute so as to repeal the provisions assuring negotiability of company notes and judicial remedy in collection of debts was one of the major items on the calendar of this legislative assembly. Clay fought the move through several days of unreported proceedings in Committee of the Whole. The proposal was defeated by one vote in an action immediately preceding that here noted, but the defeat of Clay's motion then prolonged the agitation. Though the note-issuing privileges were ultimately limited to the amount of the property *and* the capital stock of the company, and the insurance monopoly provision was repealed, the banking activities were given specific legislative recognition. Littell (comp.), *Statute Law of Kentucky,* III, 25-31, 213.

From Francis Brooke

Dr Sir Decem 12 1804

I received your Letter with the inclosure[1] and happily feel no Relation either private or public to the Business that will prevent my being your agent in it—and doing every thing in my power to make you some return for the many friendly Services rendered me—may not the representatives of Mr Lewis require some Judicial proof of the Eviction of the Title in the Land to Justify their Compliance with his warranty—I do not know who they are but have written this Day to Mr Saunders[2] of the Senate for information—

Genl Posey promised me to use his best efforts to find one of my Tracts of Land and on him I have the greatest reliance but fear his appointment to office will prevent his attention to the Business[3]—if you could aid him in any way, I should be obliged—a Mr Pitman[4] in this neighbourhood wishes to Exchange his Land here for some of mine in Kentuckey but I am at a loss to know what price to set on mine be so good as say in your next what you think Lands of their Character worth—Yours Truly F. BROOKE

ALS. DLC-HC (DNA, M212, R1). Addressed to Clay at Lexington. Postmarked: "FREDG. VA. DEC 19."

1 The bond of Warner Lewis, above, August 22, 1797; the letter not found.

2 Robert Saunders, attorney at law, Williamsburg, Virginia.

3 Thomas Posey had recently been elected to the Kentucky Senate.

4 Not identified.

Amendments to Bill Incorporating Ohio Canal Company

[December 13, 1804]

As chairman of a select committee Clay presented several unrecorded amendments to the Senate's proposed act to incorporate the Ohio Canal Company. Ky. H. of Reps., *Journal, 1804*, p. 96. The amendments were adopted in both houses, and the measure was enacted December 19, 1804. It provided for organization of a company empowered to construct canals and locks for the improvement of navigation on the Ohio River and to collect prescribed tolls for use of the waterway. A stock issue of $50,000 and a lottery for the raising of a sum not to exceed $15,000 were authorized. Littell (comp.), *Statute Law of Kentucky*, III, 221-34. Because of the inadequacy of the capital provisions, this effort to bypass the falls of the Ohio proved abortive. Cf. below, Resolution, January 12, 1807.

To Thomas Hart

Dr Sir Frankfort 14h Decr. 1804

Mr. Edwards[1] says that he was to pay you $400 by Christmas, and that he will not fail to do so.

Mr. Dufour[2] is anxious to take some of the wine produced at the Kentucky Vineyard to the President to drink with the Mammouth Cheese[3]—He cannot defray the expences himself—We have made up for him $41—19 more will do—Will you endeavour to have it raised in Lexington. Yr's respectfully H. CLAY

ALS. Owned by Miss Henrietta Clay, Lexington, Kentucky. Addressed: "Col. Tho. Hart Lexington." 1 Ninian Edwards. 2 John James Dufour.

3 Apparently a reference to the cheese weighing 1,600 lbs. presented to President Jefferson in the winter of 1801-1802 by the citizens of Cheshire, Massachusetts. Lexington *Kentucky Gazette*, July 23, 1802; Ben: Perley Poore, *Perley's Reminiscences of Sixty Years in the National Metropolis* (Philadelphia, c. 1886), I, 195.

Amendments to Bill on Bail Procedure

[December 17, 1804]

For a select committee Clay reported several unrecorded amendments to a measure, proposed early in the session and long suspended in House action, giving an additional method of requiring bail. Ky. H. of Reps., *Journal, 1804*, p. 111. The amendments were accepted; but the bill, which passed the House on the closing day of the assembly, was tabled in the Senate.

Resolution Relating to Extension of Federal Courts

[December 17, 1804]

The general assembly being impressed with the necessity of a well regulated federal judiciary, if it retains its present jurisdiction; conceiving that, as it respects this state, it is defectively organized, although they have the highest confidence in the present judge of the federal court; being fully persuaded that it is a fundamental principle of the union of the states that each member has equal rights and should enjoy equal political advantages with the others, without regard to local situation; more especially as that does not produce an exemption from general burthens, and consequently ought not to prevent a participation of general benefits; seeing that the federal court is, and will probably continue to be crouded with business, owing to the unfortunate disputes existing in the titles to land, much of which is claimed by the citizens of other states, who in general prefer this tribunal; and the magnitude of the sum litigated requisite for appeals, and the difficulties attending their prosecution, being such as almost to preclude a revision in the supreme court of the decisions of the court of this district; and moreover concerning [*sic*] the responsibility and powers of the judge of this district, too great for any one man, however virtuous and enlightened:

Resolved therefore, That it be an instruction to the senators, and a request to the representatives from this state in congress, to use their best exertions to effect an extension of the circuit courts of the United States to this state, or the establishment of a similar system adapted to our peculiar situation.

Ky. H. of Reps., *Journal, 1804,* p. 111. Clay called up his resolution the following day, and it passed unanimously. As at first enrolled, it appeared the action of the "house of Representatives," rather than of the "general assembly," no Senate stand being reported. Attributing the error to one of enrollment, Governor Christopher Greenup returned the document to the House. It was amended to the form as originally proposed, adopted by both houses, and approved by the governor on December 19, 1804.

From James Brown

Dear Sir, New Orleans, Decr. 18th. 1804

I had the pleasure of finding in the Post Office your friendly Letter of the 17th. of October,[1] and sincerely rejoice at the continuance of health, happiness, and prosperity in a family which possesses the warmest apartment in my heart. The attention you have bestowed upon the troublesome unfinished business left in your charge has been enlarged upon by both my brothers,[2] and affords one proof, among the many you have formerly given, of the sincerity of your friendship, and the interest you feel in every thing which concerns me. In a Country where my few pretensions to talents have been rewarded by applauses far beyond my merits—where my warm and social disposition has been mett by the attentions and hospitalities of the elegant and accomplished characters of the Country—where in a word every surrounding object is calculated to flatter hope, to afford delight, or to inspire contentment, my only regrets have been produced by a consciousness that my removal from Kentucky has imposed upon my friends a burthen too laborious and too irksome to be discharged without an unreasonable sacrafice of their time and feelings.

The decision of the Circuit Court of Bourbon in the case of Couchman and Thomas has I confess surprized me. I did consider Thomas's entry too vague to be established. The decree if confirmed by the Supreme Court will make a very heavy inroad upon my prospects in that Country.[3] I hope however that there exists no room to fear such a decision.

I hope you have had sufficient influence to keep me clear of Mansell[4] by some adjustment of that business. No object is more desireable than to be disengaged forever from men of his *Cast* and I pray you make sacrifices rather than not effect it—

You express an extreme desire that I should Continue my political remarks on the affairs of this Country and promise the most religious reserve—Of this I know *you* to be capable, but can I trust *myself*? If I indulge in pourtraying characters, and examining measures will not my mind dwell too much on the subject? "Out of the fullness of the heart" saith the scriptures "the mouth speaketh." Can I see folly vanity and indiscretion "walking (to use another scripture phrase) "in *high places*" and sketch it for my friend and avoid repeating in conversation the remarks which my pen has just conveyed? Besides I have been here only two weeks. Ought I not to suspend my remarks, resist my first impressions, and enquire whether reflection, and more close observation, will not remove my prepossessions, and justify the confidence of & trust of our first Magistrate?[5] The last course is surely the most prudent and I will adopt it. Some weeks hence you may expect to hear from me on the subject of public men and measures.[6]

On the score of our private affairs I can be more communicative. I can with truth assure you that we are pleased—charmed with New Orleans and its inhabitants. My residence in the Mississippi T—.[7] contributed greatly towards securing me a flattering reception here. The Citizens of New Orleans have given me credit for talents and integrity in advance; and have vied with each in rendering the place agreeable. There is not in the United States a more hospitable people than the Louisianians, nor do the inhabitants of any part of

America live in the midst of greater abundance or in greater style and elegance In obtaining a house and furniture we have been extremely fortunate, and are actually living in a style superior to that in which we lived, or could have lived in Kentucky. How often sitting at our fine dishes of fish oysters and Turtle, or enjoying the delicious sweet meats and oranges of this Country do we regret that friends so dear are not seated near us, & wish that we could exchange these Luxuries for the only article which is scarce amongst us—Butter—

We find our knowledge of the French extremely useful to us and begin to speak tolerably well—Indeed without a knowledge of both French and Spanish the practice of Law is here impossible—The proceedings are by Petition and Answer and are written in both the French and English Languages. Make my respects to my old friend Bradford and assure him that James has set out with full sails[8]—My Love to Lucretia JAMES BROWN

ALS. DLC-TJC (DNA, M212, R10). Addressed to Clay at Lexington.

1 Not found.

2 John and Dr. Samuel Brown.

3 The decision in the chancery suit between Philemon Thomas and Malachiah Couchman was ultimately reversed by the Kentucky Court of Appeals. 3 *Ky. Reports* (Hardin), 268-88 (1808).

4 George Mansell.

5 William C. C. Claiborne, Governor of Orleans Territory.

6 No such communication has been found.

7 See above, Brown to Clay, September 16, 1804.

8 James M. Bradford, son of John, early in 1804 gave up his Frankfort newspaper, *The Guardian of Freedom,* and moved to New Orleans, where the following December he began publication of *The Orleans Gazette; and Commercial Advertiser.* Clarence S. Brigham, *History and Bibliography of American Newspapers, 1690-1820* (Worcester, Mass., 1947), I, 153, 190.

Bill Explanatory of an Act on Fayette Circuit Court

[December 19, 1804]

For a drafting committee which also included William Russell and Benjamin Graves, Clay reported a bill providing specifically that the additional court term earlier authorized (above, Bill, November 28, 1804) should not alter normal arrangements for the customary March meeting. Ky. H. of Reps., *Journal, 1804,* p. 122; Ky. Gen. Assy., *Acts, 1804,* pp. 138-39.

Amendment to Bill on Repair of Jail and Penitentiary

[December 19, 1804]

As chairman of a select committee, Clay reported the Senate-originated bill with an amendment, not recorded. Ky. H. of Reps., *Journal, 1804,* p. 122. So amended, the measure then passed the House on this, the closing day of the session, but no further action was taken in the Senate.

Resolution Relating to Land Records

[December 19, 1804]

Resolved, That the register of the land office be and he is hereby instructed in the recess of the general assembly, to cause the transcript and alphabet of the entries made in the Kentucky office, commonly called May's books of entries,[1] which were begun by the late register, to be completed and examined, and that he lay his account therefor before the next legislature.

Ky. H. of Reps., *Journal, 1804,* pp. 122-23. The measure was adopted the same day. As a consequence of this action, the General Assembly at its next session conducted an investigation of the register's office. The report of a joint committee of the two houses revealed numerous erasures and interlineations, as well as the dilapidated condition of the documents.

1 Six books of entries covering the period from the opening of the Surveyor's office in Kentucky County in 1777 through December 13, 1784. Ky. Sen., *Journal, 1805,* pp. 126-27. George May was the first surveyor of Kentucky County and held that office till 1780, when he became surveyor of Jefferson County at the division of Virginia's western territory into three counties. Samuel M. Wilson, *The First Land Court of Kentucky, 1779-1780, An Address Delivered . . . before the Kentucky State Bar Association at Covington, Kentucky, July 6, 1923* (Lexington, 1923), pp. 21, 104.

To John Breckinridge

Dr Sir Lexington 22 Decr. 1804

The General Court adjourned on saturday last, your suit with Carneal,[1] and Preston vs Craig having been previously continued.[2]

On wednesday last the Legislature closed its Session. The measures either adopted or rejected, which mark this Session are the following: In the first class, the extension of the Circuit Courts to all the Counties, A provision for the promulgation of the decisions of the Court of Appeals, A continuation of the Criminal revisal, and the passage of two resolutions, one instructing our Senators and requesting our Representatives in Congress to endeavour to procure an amendment in the Fœderal Constitution limiting the powers of the Fœderal Judiciary to the enforcement of the Laws of the U. States, and the other giving a similar instruction and making a similar request to them to endeavour to procure an extension of the Circuit Courts to this State or the establishment of a system corresponding with our peculiar situation.[3] The most prominent of the rejected measures were the bill for altering the mode of summoning Juries, which passed the lower house, and was lost in the Senate by the casting voice of the Speaker, and the attempt to repeal so much of the Charter granted to the Insurance Company as authorized a Bank. This latter measure occasioned much struggling—its discussion occupied in all nearly a week, and was at length negatived by a very small majority.[4] I think however the institution has nothing to fear in future. It had to encounter and at length subdued the most unheard of prejudices. The ignorance of members on the subject was truly astonishing.

With regard to the resolutions just mentioned we feared that the object of the first at this moment was unattainable, however desirable. It is evident, upon the least reflection, that unless the amendment contemplated does take place, a dissolution of the union must be the ultimate consequence. Two independent Judiciaries, neither acknowledging the superiority of the other, may for a time subsist without inconvenience, but in the end they will come into collision, and the concussion which they will produce must destroy one or the other or the government.

The object of the latter resolution, which passed both houses unanimously, is so just that I presume you can meet with no difficulty in effecting it. It is what the Bar have much at heart: and Mr Innes, who is so much esteemed by us all, is anxious for the change.[5] The System that occurred to me as most practicable, and which is approved by others of the Bar, is the following: Let Ohio, Kentucky and Tenassee compose a Circuit; appoint two additional judges (both from this State if possible, on a/c. of our Land disputes, we being most interested) and let them with the District Judge in each of those States, constitute a Circuit Court, with the jurisdiction of the present District Courts: The district judges to remain stationary, and the additional judges permitted but not enjoined to set on the bench of the Supreme Court. The Court to hold two terms a year.

A Court somewhat like this outline I am sure would be satisfactory. Our State has been too long held in a kind of vassalage—In no other State in the Union is the Fœderal Court so important—And when you look at the immense powers of the present Judge, & the difficulty of appealing, you will see that it will relieve him much distributing his responsibility. I am Dr Sir Yr's Sincerely. HENRY CLAY

ALS. OCHP-Whelpley Autographs. Addressed to Senator Breckinridge in Washington, and endorsed that he replied on February 11. His answer has not been found.

1 Thomas Carneal.

2 This case, involving conflicting claims to land, was not settled until the Court of Appeals handed down a decision in favor of Preston in 1812. Littell (comp.), *Selected Cases,* 138-42.

3 Ky. Gen. Assy., *Acts, 1804,* pp. 7-9, 92-93, 127-28, 146-48.

4 See above, Motion, December 12, 1804, note.

5 Harry Innes, United States District Judge for Kentucky. On Clay's role in the enactment of legislation for this proposal, see below, Resolution, January 2, 1807.

To Gabriel Lewis

Dr Gabriel Lexington 23d. Decr. 1804

The Fœderal Court at the last term pronounced an interlocutory decree in your fathers suit with your friend Bledsoe,[1] by which he is compelled to take 9 per Acre for the Land—the small survey is to be divided &c.. I have not a Copy of it or I would send it to you. As it is the bottoms on Richland which occasioned the Jury to value the Land at that price, I am clearly of opinion if they are taken by superior claims Bledsoe & Co. Will have to share the loss with your father; and when you return it may be worth while to investigate this matter fully.

I sent to Genl Brooke a few weeks ago the bond I held of Warner Lewis's with a Certificate of Geo. Bibbs stating the value of the Land.[2] I also wrote him the terms on which I was willing to compromise. If you can give him any aid in this matter you will very much oblige me. If money should be obtained it may remain in the General's hands; if property I will thank you to take charge of it, or if you should have occasion to use the money you may do so

Our Legislature closed its Session last wednesday. A very formidable attack was made on the Bank[3]—It however terminated by giving in my opinion additional security to the institution. The Circuit Court System is extended to all the Counties, and Cary L. Clarke is appointed one of the Circuit Court Judges.[4] But I am troubling you with politics, for which I know you have a great aversion: Let me tell you then that A. Price has done what you ought half a dozen years ago, gotten him a wife—Miss Sally Lee: And Tho. Owings has just had what you never will unless you imitate the example of Price, a very fine Son. Alfred Grayson and Miss Breckenridge & Alexr. Frazier and Miss Oliver have also undertaken to try their hands in the same way.[5] Whilst speaking of the means of people getting into the world I ought not to omit the attempt made by Ben. Nancarrow[6] last night to get out of it He shot himself in the side just below his heart—The wound is not certainly ascertained to be mortal but is supposed so—A duel was fought opposite to Louisville about ten days ago between Geo. Strother and Dr. Luckett; the latter was killed shot through the heart.[7]

I spend [*sic*] last evening with Cox and a party of our friends at J. Postlethwaits[8]—I recollect no events worth communicating but the above & remain Yr's Sincerely HENRY CLAY

ALS. NBuHi. Addressed to Lewis at Fredericksburg, Virginia, his former home. Lewis, who had come to Lexington early in 1801 to engage in land speculation, subsequently settled at Russellville in Logan County.

1 John Lewis and Joseph Bledsoe had each entered a claim for land on Richland Creek, a tributary of the Cumberland River.

2 See above, Brooke to Clay, December 12, 1804.

3 The Kentucky Insurance Company.

4 A resident of Scott County, Clark presided over the district including Woodford, Franklin, Gallatin, Henry, and Shelby counties. Littell (comp.), *Statute Law of Kentucky*, III, 505.

5 Andrew Price of Lexington and Polly (not Sarah, her sister) Lee were married on November 11, 1804; Alfred Grayson of Washington, Mason County, and Letitia, daughter of John Breckinridge, on October 26, 1804; and Alexander Frazier and Nancy Oliver of Jessamine County, on December 20, 1804. G. Glenn Clift (comp.), "Kentucky

Marriages and Obituaries, 1787-1860," Kentucky State Historical Society, *Register*, XXXVI (1938), 160-61. Grayson had been a member of the Kentucky House of Representatives for Mason County in 1803 and 1804, but subsequently moved to Fayette County, which he represented in 1809-1810. Owings, who had married Maria, a daughter of George Nicholas, in 1803, was proprietor of a store in Lexington which served as an outlet for his iron works.

6 Probably the Benjamin Nancarrow who resided in New Orleans later in the decade.

7 John M. Luckett of Jefferson County, Kentucky, who referred to the approaching encounter in his will, dated December 13, 1804. Jefferson County, Will Book 1, pp. 156-57. His opponent has not been further identified.

8 Postlethwait's Tavern. Cox has not been identified.

Property Deed to Andrew F. Price

[January 1, 1805]

[Indenture by which Henry and Lucretia Clay for 400 pounds current money of Kentucky, paid and acknowledged, transfer to Andrew F. Price a tract of land in Lexington, containing 23 1/3 feet frontage, bounded as follows: beginning on Main Street at the western corner of Patrick McCullough's lot (no. 4), thence with Main Street north 45° west 23 1/3 feet to the corner of John Jordan's part of lot no. 3,[1] thence north 45° east 13 poles to Short Street, thence with said street south 45° east 23 1/3 feet to the northern corner of McCullough's lot, thence with it south 45° west 13 poles to the beginning—being part of In lot no. 3, the other part being this day conveyed by the Clays to John Jordan Jr.,[2] the lot having been granted by the Trustees of Lexington to Basil Duke,[3] who transferred it to Thomas Love,[4] who conveyed it to Clay by deed recorded in the Court of Appeals at Frankfort.[5] General warranty of title. Certification of signature acknowledgment by Henry and Lucretia Clay before James Bliss, Deputy Clerk, recorded by Thomas Bodley, Fayette County Clerk, January 1, 1805.]

Fayette Circuit Court, Deed Book B, 171-72.

1 In-lots 3 and 4 lay between Upper and Mulberry streets and ran from Main to Short.

2 Deed dated August 6, 1805. The cause of the discrepancy in dates is not clear.

3 Native of Maryland, who had come to Lexington in 1790 and practiced medicine in partnership with Dr. Frederick Ridgely for a few years. He had then moved to Mason County, where he engaged in mercantile business as well as the practice of his profession.

4 Lexington manufacturer and tavernkeeper, who in 1795 had moved to Frankfort, where for many years he operated a tavern.

5 Not found.

Contract with John Fisher

[January 22, 1805]

An agreement entered into between John Fisher and Henry Clay this 22d. day of January 1805.

The said Fisher covenants to make and lay the bricks necessary for two buildings which the said Clay designs erecting, one on the lot purchased by the said Clay of John Jordan,[1] and the other on the said Clay's farm purchased of C. Banks.[2] The building in Town to be of such dimensions as the said Clay may determine, and that in the Country not to exceed twenty five thousand brick: The said Fisher is to deliver the brick at the respective places aforesaid and to furnish the necessary materials (Sand excepted) for laying them: He covenants that the brick shall be of a good quality, and that the town building shall go up and be finished with the house the said Fisher is to build for David Dodge[3]—And the house in the Country shall be finished as soon as brick can be made and laid in the Spring. The house in Town shall be fronted with Stock brick, and three of the sides of that in the Country with Sand brick.

In consideration whereof the said Clay covenants to pay the said Fisher forty five Shillings per thousand for every thousand of brick which he shall actually lay as aforesaid in the following manner: He assigns to the said Fisher at this time two notes amounting to ninety four dollars: He covenants to deliver to the said Fisher at the Upper blue Licks at Christmas next fifty bushels of Merchantable Salt at two dollars per bushel:[4] He covenants to pay to the said Fisher one hundred dollars on the completion of the work; and the balance he covenants to pay in horses at their value not under three nor over nine years of age, to be paid as the work progresses: The said Clay also covenants to pay for the Stock brick four dollars per thousand over and above the forty five shillings aforesaid to be paid in the manner aforesaid—

In witness whereof the parties aforesaid have hereunto set their hands & Seals the day & year aforesaid JOHN FISHER {L.S.}
Signed Sealed &c HENRY CLAY {L.S.}
In presence of—
SUSANNAH HART[5]

[Endorsement on verso][6]

Recd. the Notes for Ninety four dollars within mentioned. 22 Jan 1805. JOHN FISHER

ADS, signed also by Fisher. KyLxT.

1 See below, Property Deed from Jordan, August 6, 1805. Exactly one year later two other Lexington builders, Maddox Fisher and John Springle, certified that they had examined Clay's house "Built by John Fisher AJoining John Jordan, and it Contains 99,,364—Bricks."

2 See above, Agreement, September 13, 1804. Apparently the structure erected on the farm in fulfilment of Fisher's contract was the center portion of "Ashland." The wings were added later.

3 A rope manufacturer on High Street, who owned, or had owned, the lot adjoining Clay's.

4 Cf. above, Agreement, June 29, 1804.

5 Clay's mother-in-law.

6 ES, in Clay's hand. Notations the opposite direction of the page, in Clay's hand, record ten payments, amounting to £285:4, made to Fisher. Cf. below, Account, [*ca.* October 28, 1805].

Tax Bill

1804 Henry Clay	[*ca.* February 1, 1805]
To the Shff of Fayette	Dr.
To Tax on 4.504 acrs. 2d. Land[1] @ 34 cents	15:52
1.000 - 3d. Ditto @ 12½	1:25
$500 value Town lotts @ 3/- pr £100	.75
6 slaves @ 12½ 9 Horses @ 4	1.11
2 wheele carriage @ 25 pr wheele	.50
County Levy on 5 Tithes[2] @ 1/-	.83
	19:96
To Bal. of Tax & Levy for 1803.	5.28½
	$25.24½

JOHN H. MORTON D. S.[3] for
J. Parker shff[4]

DS. DLC-TJC (DNA, M212, R15). Dating of tax bills is based upon the statute requiring that sheriffs "shall, from and after the first day of February, annually, collect and receive from all and every person or persons chargeable therewith, the taxes imposed by this act. . . ." Littell (comp.), *Statute Law of Kentucky,* II, 322 (December 21, 1799).

1 That is, second rate land.

2 Tithables included all males sixteen years of age and older and all female slaves of the same age group.

3 Farmer and businessman, who later served as Sheriff of Fayette County and member of the State legislature. He was the eldest son of William Morton, and brother of William R. Morton.

4 John Parker, a native of Pennsylvania who had settled on what is now the Parker's Mill Road near Lexington, had been a member of the State legislature for several terms before the turn of the century and subsequently returned to that post in 1808, 1816-1817, and 1819.

From Felix Grundy

Dr Sir Springfield [Kentucky] February 4th. 1805

We differed in opinion on the subject of the bank, during the last Session of the Legislature.[1] That difference ought not to induce either of us however to wish, or even permit a false statement to be made to the prejudice of either. I am sure it would not have that effect on me; and presume it will not on you. I am charged by some person (but who it is I have not the least suspicion) of having stated in argument on that question "*that the bank had actually issued paper to three times the amount of the money in their Coffers.*"—I know I did not state this; but on the contrary, spoke respectfully of those who at present had the management of the bank; but did urge that they had the power to issue notes to any amount; and I recollect when speaking on the great profits arising to the Stock-holders, to have observed, that a part of those profits must in my opinion arise from the interest of Paper issued over and above the sums actually deposited in the bank by the Stock-holders.

I make this application to you because it relates to my character, and not to the bank; and because you had the best opportunity of recollecting what I did say

You will oblige me by transmiting to me a certificate stating, in short, whether I did say that the bank had issued paper to three times the amount of the money which they had in the bank; and permit me if I should think it necessary to publish it.[2] I am Yrs

FELIX GRUNDY

ALS. DLC-HC (DNA, M212, R1). Addressed to Clay at Lexington. Grundy, who had been admitted to the bar in 1797, was a spokesman in the General Assembly for the Green River section of the State. After serving briefly on the Kentucky Court of Appeals (1806-1807), he moved to Nashville, Tennessee, whence he later became Clay's colleague as a Warhawk in the United States Congress.

1 Grundy had led the attempt to amend the charter of the Kentucky Insurance Company so as to take away the banking privileges of that institution.

2 If Clay replied, his letter has not been found.

From John Clay

My dear Brother New Orleans 4th Feby. 1805

I wrote you pretty leng hly some short time since[1] & this is now principally intended to beg your particular attention to some business which Mr Thomas Reilly forwards you per this Mail:[2] he will no doubt give you handsome fee if it is transacted to his satisfaction.

In my late letters to you I have given you an account of my prospects here: indeed they appear to be more flattering every day, & there appears nothing wanting to ensure me success but a little Capitol: in this I depend entirely on your goodness: you have it in your power to insure me a fortune "the greatest felicity that of rescuing me from oppressive obligations" & my eternal gratitude: Confident that you'll do every thing in your power I shall say nothing further upon the subject.

Seeing what unbounded success Mr. Brown[3] appears to reap from his profession here: I am almost induced to pursuade you to come down & reside here for a few years: Mr B has already made 5 or 6000 $ say in two months) he is infinitely the most eminant: Livinsgton [*sic*] who may be called the next is becoming a good deal in disrepute owing to his misfortunes to the Northwards which is now very public[4] the rest are mere ketch penny Lawyers. Our Society is growing very fast some very respectable families have recently settled here: a few years only 5 or 6 American families could be counted in this place: now nearly 100 may be enumerated, many rich & respectable indeed I never heard of Country which has populated so fast for the same time: this City bids fair to be one of the first Mercantile places in America—from some late accounts received here from Liverpool a War between England & Spain is inevitable:[5]

This will occasion a very great change in our comercial situation here, & will actuate in favour of the Western Country: so much that the Havana & other adjacent Spanish ports will be necessarily opened for the introduction of Neutral Vessels, & will consequently raise the price of every kind of provisions &a.

Presuming that you receive regularly the proceedings of our Legislative Council, I shall say nothing upon that head & having nothing further interesting to add after my Comps to Lucretia remain D Brother J. CLAY

ALS. DLC-TJC (DNA, M212, R10). Addressed to Henry Clay at Lexington.
1 Possibly referring to his letter of December 1, 1804.
2 Not found. Reilly, who owned property in Lexington, in 1808 brought suit in the Fayette Circuit Court against Thomas Bodley and Charles Humphreys because of the latter's failure to fulfill a contract to deliver produce to New Orleans in 1805. Reilly's attorney was James B. January, not Clay.
3 James Brown.
4 Edward Livingston formerly had been United States District Attorney for New York and Mayor of the City of New York. In 1803, after one of his agents had absconded with a large sum of Federal money, Livingston assigned his property to trustees for payment of his debts, confessed judgment in favor of the United States, and moved to New Orleans, where he arrived in February 1804. He later became United States Representative and Senator from Louisiana, United States Secretary of State, and Minister to France.
5 England and France, with whom Spain was allied, were already at war with one another, and Spain was soon involved in the struggle.

Receipt from William Akin

[February 4, 1805]

Recd. 4 Feb. 1805 of H. Clay Three hundred dollars being the sum deposited with him on a/c of the purchase of a house in Frankfort & which was to have been deposited in the K I. Office[1] for my benefit. W AKIN

DS, in Clay's hand. DLC-TJC, 2d Series, vol. 5.
1 Kentucky Insurance Company.

Bill from Stephens and Winslow

Henery Clay to Stephens & Winslow [*ca.* Feb. 5, 1805]
to work done on the new office[1]

544 ft. shetting & shingling @ 10/6	£ 2.17.–
1400 ft of framing @ 5/-; 37 ft of cornice @ 1/6	6. 5. 6
23 ft of boxing @ 10d. 46 ft. of barge board @ 4d.	1.14. 6
360 ft. of flooring @ 18/d. 76 ft. sub base @ 6d 76 ft of base @ 5d.	6.14. 6
67 ft of sash & jamb cassing with an ovold on the edge @ 10d.	2.15.10
42 ft of sing. archg. @ 6d shelving and portision for Cobbard 12/d.	1.13.–

Cobbard doors & pans. @ 3/9 hanging & putting on locks 1.13.—
52 lights of sash @ 1/- 1 Chimney Piece 24/d. 3.16.—
glazing 52 lights @ 4d. 2 front windows frames @ 18/- 2.13. 4
2 back window frames @ 15/d. 2 gabal end window frames @ 6/. 2. 2.—
10 pans. of Jam cassing @ 3/- 23 ft of Double archg. @ 9d- 2. 7. 3
1 six panl. door @ 3/d. lining the same 4/6 1. 2. 6
hanging do & putting on lock 3/- seller door frame 7/6 10. 6
3 seller gratted windows frames @ 10/6 Shutters for the same @ 3/. 2. 0. 6
1 ledge door hang & lock 10/6 outside seller doors frame & hang- 25/6 1.16.—
shades & hanging for 2 windows @ 36/- 3.12.—

work don on the dweling house[2]

putting in the weights & hangings for 11 windows @ 2/3 1. 4. 9
glazing 6 lights of glass @ 4d 1½ lb of putty @ 2/3 5. 4.½

work don on the old office

16 ft 6 of sing. archg. @ 6d 15 ft of Jam cassing with moulding @ 7d. 17.—
2 ledge doors hanging putting on locks @ 7/6 15.—

1803

April 9 to boxes to set in front of yellow house[3]— 6.—
Decr. 15 to glazing 3 large light & 8 of small- glass— 4. 2

1804
May 19th. repairs on yellow house } 9 lights of sash @ 8d. mending sashes 5/4 64 lights glazing @ 3— 1. 7. 4
reparing the sash cassing 2/-
do the Brest[4] 13/6
do cobbard & wash boards 4/6 } £1.0.0 1. 0. 0

hanging cobboard door & putting on latch 2/3 11 ft of singl. arch @ 6. 7. 9
flite of stepps 4/6 repairs on stepps 1/6 47 pailings @ 3d. .17. 9
framing the fence 2/3 64 ft of plank 7/8 9.11

£51. 8. 7½

1804
June 28h. work done on nescesary
framing floors & roof & laing the floor 25/6d. £ 1. 5. 6
putting up a portision 7/6 1 door caist 17/- 1. 4. 6
taking down & reputting up the cassing of 1 door 8. 6

wash boards 3/6 seats risers hang the leads & fitting in 15/	18. 6
making 1 door & hanging 7/6 hang 2 doors putting on lach/bolt	9. 9
barge boards & facin 8/6 shetting shingling roof 12/-	1. 0. 6
making stepps for office 6/-	6.
making rabbit box 4/6 reparing the palings 5/3	9. 9
Nov. 1st. to glazing 2/8 cutting out the old putty 1/6	4. 2
" 1½ lb. of putty @ 2/3	3. 4
1805	
Feb 5h to cutting & resetting 10 lights of glass 5/- 2 lb of putty 2/3	9. 6
	£ 7. 0. 0
	51. 8. 7½
	£58. 8. 7½
	3.12. 9
	£54.15. 9
Cr.	48. 0. 0
by tools from P. Clay[5] £ 3. 6	6:15: 9
" 37 ft of timber 6. 9	6:17: 6
3.12. 9	13:13: 3

D. DLC-TJC (DNA, M212, R10).
1 See above, Agreement, August 18, 1803. 2 On Mill Street.
3 Also located on Mill Street, the second house deeded to Clay by his brother John on May 31, 1800. 4 Breast, or window sill, molding. 5 Porter Clay.

From Thomas Whelan

Dear Sir. Baltimore February 12th. 1805

I have written to you several times,[1] respecting the business left by me in your hands, to settle and am without any answer, which places me in a very disagreeable situation. I again take up my pen to address you On the same subject, to solicite from your hands a Statement of my business in Order that I may bring it to a speedy close. The amount left in your hands for adjustment was Considerable and of course makes me very uneasy fearfull that you find it very difficult to settle Should this even be the case please inform me but as you have discretionary Orders it is in vain for me to dictate to you. for I am convinced you will do the best for me. I anticipate ere this you have recovered all for me should it be the case use any means you may think the most safe to remit it me, and be please to let An Account Accompany it in Order that I may have a final settlement, should this be too troublesome Mr. William Kelley of Paris will adjust all accounts with you, and any Money you should have of mine you may pay into his hands, and his receipt shall be good for the same, and any arrangments that you and he shall make for the speedy close of my business I shall acknowledge with thanks. I have written to Mr. William Kelley On the Subject, and have solicited him to call on you, and any thing he can help you in to do it: he being my particular friend in your Country, necessity compels the urgency of this request; With Sentiments of Repect. I remain your Obt. Servant THOMAS WHELAN

ALS. DLC-TJC (DNA, M212, R12). [1] Letters not found.

Promissory Note from Morris Morris

[February 26, 1805]

On demand I promise to pay H. Clay Twenty dollars—Witness my hand & seal this 26 Feb. 1805. MORRIS MORRIS {L.S.}
Teste JOHN M MILLIN[1]

DS, in Clay's hand. DLC-TJC, 2d Series, vol. 5. Morris was a merchant at Carlisle, Nicholas County, Kentucky.
[1] Probably the fuller and dyer of that name who had come to Kentucky in 1795 and located near Todds Ferry on the Kentucky River, in Mercer County.

Receipt from Maddox Fisher

1 March 1805.

Recd. of H. Clay his Note in full of all demands
MADDOX FISHER

DS, in Clay's hand. DLC-TJC, 2d Series, vol. 5.

Receipt for Salt Sold to Maccoun and Tilford

Mar 2nd 1805

Received of Henry Clay Esqr P the Hands of Mr Bradford[1] Six Barrels Salt. . . . for Maccoun & Tilford
W S DALLAM[2]

DS. DLC-TJC (DNA, M212, R15). Markings and weight of barrels deleted. The salt was manufactured at the Upper Blue Licks. See above, Agreement, October 29, 1804. James Maccoun and John Tilford had moved from Mercer County, Kentucky, to Lexington, where for several years they were partners in a mercantile establishment. The firm was dissolved in 1806, with Tilford then embarking in similar business with George Trotter while Maccoun resumed operations under the firm of James and David Maccoun, continuing until 1816.
[1] Possibly John Bradford's second son, Daniel, who engaged in various enterprises as manufacturer, commission merchant and auctioneer, and steward of Transylvania University (1822-1823), in addition to publishing the *Kentucky Gazette* at intermittent periods from 1802 to 1840. He was Captain of the Lexington Light Infantry Regiment in the War of 1812 and Mayor of Lexington in 1841.
[2] William S. Dallam, a native of Maryland, had settled with his father in Logan County, Kentucky, but removed to Lexington early in 1805, married Letitia Meredith of "Winton," and lived in the Blue Grass area for the next forty years.

From Jesse Bledsoe

Dear Henry. March 6th. 1805

I sent your Mare to Lexington. I was Much deceived when I represented her to you as being in good order. She was so the last time I saw her but is now to my surprise, very poor, She is in sufficient order to bring a colt but too poor to sell. You will be disappointed in her appearance but you will like her much better when you come to see her in good order

You shall have her for less than I asked, if on trial you think she is worth less. I think myself some deduction ought to be made for her plight say 20 $. If however you think that too little say how much and take her. But remember you are not to fail giving me what you think she is worth after bringing her next colt after this. In case you deduct. For I expect she will breed well, tho I do not much like the Horse she is in foal by. I send you the Ejectmt. Gists Heirs vs Robinett &C.[1] Please to mention to Mr. Allen,[2] I have taken the liberty of putting his name to it. in consequence of some conversation with him some time ago.

I also send you the Bill of Swan vs Anderson &c. Make what corrections You think proper. I should be more than glad the Spoe. could be returned to this Court & an Order of Advertisemt. agt. Massy.[3] I would enter myself Secy. for costs if I were present. If you will do so. Mr. Baylor[4] shall releive you from it. when he comes down to the court of Appeals or perhaps the bond may as well be given then. I am as ever yours Sincerely— J. BLEDSOE

ALS. DLC-HC (DNA, M212, R1). Addressed to Clay at Frankfort. Bledsoe was apparently writing from his home in Paris, Kentucky.

1 The heirs of Nathaniel Gist (including Bledsoe's wife and the wife of Lucretia Clay's brother, Nathaniel Hart) were suing to recover possession of land in Bourbon County, Kentucky, part of a tract granted to Thomas Gist for his services in the French and Indian War. The case was finally settled in favor of the plaintiffs in 1813. 6 *Ky. Reports* (3 Bibb) 2-5.

2 Probably John Allen, a native of Virginia, who had come to Kentucky at an early age and become prominent as a lawyer of Shelby County, later of Frankfort. Allen represented both Shelby and Franklin counties, at various times, in the Kentucky legislature. Colonel of the 1st Regiment of Kentucky Riflemen, he was killed at the Battle of the River Raisin in 1813.

3 Nathaniel Massie. On the case mentioned see below, Swan to Clay, March 21, 1806.

4 Probably Walker Baylor.

From Jesse Bledsoe

Dear Henry. Paris March 7th. 1805.

I send you the Bill Swan vs Anderson &c. I should have sent it earlier but had no Opportunity. Make what corrections you think necessary. I am anxious if possible the Spo. should be returned to this court. And an Order of Advertisemt. taken agt. Massy. Mr.

Baylor will enter Secy. for costs when he comes down in April. Or if required you may safely do it yourself. I send you also the Ejectmt. Gists Heirs vs Robinett &c. Pray attend to it You know how much I am interested. take the necessary Orders. And speak to Mr. Allen if you please. that I have taken the liberty of putting his name with yours to the Ejectmt. in consequence of my having formerly Spoken to him. I intend also to employ Mr. Rowan[1] if he does not feel himself engaged for Col. Todd,[2] who has undertaken to defend long since.

I have sent your Mare to Lexn. You will no doubt be surprised at her poor appearance when you see her as indeed I was for she is greatly fallen of since I last saw her. I have however written to you on the subject & by mistake sent the Letter to Lexn. I intended for you at F.[3]

Take her at what you shall think On trial she is worth.

Yrs. Sincerely. J. BLEDSOE

ALS. DLC-HC (DNA, M212, R1). Cf. above, Bledsoe to Clay, March 6, 1805.

1 Probably John Rowan, a native of Pennsylvania, whose family had moved to Kentucky in 1783 and settled at Bardstown. Rowan became an outstanding lawyer and served as Secretary of State under Governor Greenup, a member of the State legislature, a member of both houses of Congress, and, for a brief period, a judge on the Kentucky Court of Appeals. His home at Bardstown is the well known "Federal Hill" (My Old Kentucky Home) of today.

2 Thomas Todd.

3 The letter had been addressed to Frankfort.

From Joseph Hays

Dr Sir Nashville March 10th 1805

Some time Since & perhaps it is near three years, I had requested a Brother of mine (Charles Hays)[1] to Imploy you & to pay you a fee to ascertain the property & in whom the right was vested of a Negro Girl named *Fanny*. It might be proper for me to State to you the plea I have & the circumstances which lead to it—(altho I trust my freind Wm P Anderson[2] has formerly named. them) viz, that a Mr Joseph Walker of Virginia Intermaried with a Sister of mine at a time when In that State Negroes were conceived to be real property[3] My father Intailed to her & Children a Negro Woman Named *Sue* with her Isue my Sister died at an early age leaving two very young Children, Joseph Walker again maried & had by a Second Wife one Daughter at his death he Willed to the Daughter of his Second Wife the above named Negro Girl Daughter & Isue of *Sue*—I brot. on the Children of my Sister to Nashville & have long Since been apointed their Gaurdian consequently feel it my duty to do every Justice to them that is in my power, It be readily in my power to procure an attested Copy of my fathers Will Should you deem it proper from the Statement above that I ought to contend for the rights of those

Children or otherwise you will Oblidge by Intimating it by Mr Stowel who will hand you this & in a second communication I will be more particular—I have further to request you if you please to attend to the collection of a Note Hays & Dickson Holds on a Doctr Joseph Cornwell[4] formerly of Williamson County & town of Franklin in this State he left this Country in not a very Honorable way & I am told is now In Lexington Kentucky Mr Stowel will hand you the note & you will please to act as you Deem proper Should the Laws of your State require Security for the prosecution of a Suit. Mr Stowel will call on some of my freinds & procure it for you or rather for me. I am afraid Mr Stowel will not have Sufficient money to pay you your fees at present & he will name to you the cause why he has it not but at any time after this when you intimate it to me pr Mail I will forward it to you, I take the liberty to write in this manner to you in Consequence of your being recommended as a proper person (formerly) to attend to my business & provided you can make it convenient to attend to it you would truly Oblidge your Obt. &c—

JOSEPH HAYS

ALS. DLC-TJC (DNA, M212, R12). Hays was a Revolutionary officer who had fought at King's Mountain and was later active in campaigns against the Indians in Tennessee.

1 A resident of Green County, Kentucky, in 1802 and of Adair in 1803. He apparently owned several tracts of land in Kentucky.

2 Nashville lawyer, son-in-law of John Adair of Kentucky, and at one time a close friend of Andrew Jackson.

3 In Virginia, from 1705 to 1776, Negro, mulatto, and Indian slaves were considered legally as real estate. William W. Hening (comp.), *The Statutes at Large; Being a Collection of All the Laws of Virginia, From the First Session of the Legislature, in the Year 1619* (13 vols.; Richmond and Philadelphia, 1809-1823), III, 333-35; IV, 222-28; V, 432-48; IX, 226-27. Hereafter this work will be cited as Hening (comp.), *Statutes of Virginia*.

4 Stowel, Dickson, and Cornwell have not been identified further.

From James Brown

Dear Sir, New orleans March 12. 1805.

I received two mails ago your very acceptable favor of the 28th. of January[1] and should sooner have answered it but for the pressure of business arising from two Courts in Session at the same time. I rejoice at every assurance I receive of the health and happiness of a family to whom I feel every attachment which a consciousness of their worth and a recollection of their friendship can inspire—The hope of a rapturous meeting with you shortly consoles me under an absence which, without this delightful expectation, would be insupportable. With the young portion of my relations I feel confident of an interview, but poor old Colo. Hart—am I never to see him again! He has frightened me by the very circumstance which he mentions as flattering to his hopes of long life—He informs me that his weight has increased twenty three pounds since his return from the Springs—I consider this as an unfavorable omen, but will feel perfectly relieved from all apprehensions if he survives the month of March.[2]

My success as a Lawyer continues to be flattering and if the change in our government contemplated by Congress does not obscure my prospects, I hope to acquire the means of a genteel support in a few years independent of my profession. My knowledge of two or three of the modern languages has saved me from ruin, or what was as bad, a resort to Kentucky for the means of support. I stand at the head of my profession and am employed in every important case, whilst Lawyers of respectability who cannot speak French or Spanish are left without the means of a decent support. In a few months our Courts will close and I shall retire to a beautiful farm I have purchased about 24 miles above the City—This Tract has 150 acres of cleared land, and a house 75 by 40—I have some thoughts of persuading your neighbour, Majr. Wagnon[3] to come down and become my tenant—The Stage stops there—The stand is excellent for a public house, and six or eight of the genteelest families in town would join me in spending four or five months during the sickly season at that delightful retreat—If he moves he ought to be here by the 1st. of June or sooner if possible—You may sit down and tax your fancy to the extent of her powers which I know are fruitful and she cannot create such a Country as borders on the Mississippi—

I am happy to find my friend John Clay so completely cured of every wild and extravagant idea as he is at this time—His steady habits, industry, and obliging temper are gaining him many friends, and I beg of you to use your influence to gain him the confidence of the people of Lexington—I think they will find him every thing they can wish—

I am happy that the Bank has had the means of resisting the attacks of that unprincipled demagogue Grundy,[4] and of defeating the villainous speculations of that nest of rascals who have fattened under the auspices of Morrisons office[5]—Mansell was originally destined for the Gallows and nothing but a premature death will dissappoint him of the pomp of an execution—[6]

It gives me real pleasure to hear from every quarter that you stand in Kentucky at the head o[f our] profession—May you soon grow rich and be [*thus*][7] able to retire from a profession the duties [. . .] of which are too severe in that inclement [*clime*] for the most robust constitution—My retreat [from] your State saved my life—One winter more [would] have fixed upon me a confirmed consumption. Here I have renewed my youth—

Nancy has written to Lucretia—She enjoys good health, good spirits, and as you may suppose the esteem of all who know her—

Let me hear from you more frequently & believe me your most sincere friend,

Henry Clay Esqr. JAMES BROWN

ALS. DLC-HC (DNA, M212, R1). Published in Colton (ed.), *Private Correspondence of Henry Clay*, 12-13; Padgett, "Letters of James Brown to Henry Clay," *La. Hist. Quar.*, XXIV (1941), 923-25.

1 Not found.

2 Col. Thomas Hart lived several years longer. See below, Brown to Clay, September 1, 1808, note.

3 John P. Wagnon.

4 Felix Grundy.

5 James Morrison was supervisor in Kentucky of the United States direct tax on land, levied by act of July 14, 1798, amended March 16, 1802. 1 *U. S. Stat.* 597-604; 2 *U. S. Stat.* 138-39. The tax, and any special collection charges, remained a lien upon the land until discharged and greatly complicated title transfer in this locale where the confusion of non-resident entries was already overwhelming.

6 George Mansell, Morrison's deputy.

7 MS. torn.

From Henry Baldwin

Sir Pittsburgh 19th. March 1805

I inclose to you a note on Dr Charles Mayersbach,[1] on which there will be due on the 31 of this month £ 91. 8. 5. payable to Messrs Field & Son. Those Gentlemen have taken the benefit of the bankrupt law, and Mr John Field Senior is the agent of his assignees and authorised to settle his affairs—& he is indebted to me a considerable sum, and has put this note in my hands to pay in part his debt to me. Dr Mayersbach lives as I am informed, about ten miles from Lexington. I wish you would use your endeavours to secure the money. I do not wish to distress him, and if he will secure the money in one year I shall be satisfied. If you can collect the money you will please to deduct from it a liberal fee; if not you will be so good as to inform me to what amount I am indebted to you for your trouble.

yours with esteem HENRY BALDWIN

Henry Clay Esqr.

ALS. DLC-TJC (DNA, M212, R12). Baldwin, a native of Connecticut and a graduate of Yale University, had moved to Pittsburgh in 1801 and quickly attained prominence as a lawyer. He was later an iron manufacturer, a member of Congress, and an Associate Justice of the United States Supreme Court.

1 A resident of the northern district of Fayette County.

From Samuel Johnston

Dear Sir.. Baltimore March 26: 1805

I received Your favour of the 2d Inst. In my last to you,[1] I enclosed the Copy of the Inquisition, returned & filed at Richmond, as to McKee,[2] which I hope you received. Mr Pringle,[3] the Trustee for the Creditors of Mr Russell, has agreed to your proposal, that you shall have four Hundred Acres of the Land, when recovered, in the manner you propose & expect that he will write either to you or Mr Morton[4] to that purpose. As to the proofs of Mr McKees being furnished with the field Notes of a survey corresponding with the boundary contained in the deeds; or the other proofs mentioned in your Letter; I fear it will not be easy to obtain them all; Mr McKee's residence is at this time unknown to us. the practice of the Surveyors is best known in Virginia or Kentuckey. But if the Surveyor of the District at that time can be found out, he probably might give the information necessary. As to the impeachment of the Deed made by McKee to Ross, it appears to be for a valuable consideration, and made at a time when he had a right to Convey & unless *fraud* can be proved, in the transaction, I should think it hard to over set the Conveyance, in the hands of a third purchaser, for a valuable consideration. Mr Russell & his Trustee are entire Strangers to any intent of McKees, to protect his property; that is best known by McKee and Mr Ross, who then lived at Pittsburg & perhaps resides there yet. As to a Copy of the Deed of Trust, which has been recorded here in our General Court; please to let me know in what manner it is to be Certified, so that it will be admitted as proof in Your Fedral Court, & it shall be done; or as that Deed Contains several Tracts of Lands, in different States; Mr Russell will Execute a new Deed to Mr Pringle, for the said Lands in Kentuckey, to be described, Executed & Certified, as you shall direct; in either Case please to let us know. I hope your endeavours in this momentuous undertaking will be Crowned with success; & that You as well as the Creditors will have every advantage attending the same. I am Sir very respectfully—Your Obed,t Servt— SAML. JOHNSTON

ALS. DLC-HC (DNA, M212, R1). Addressed: "Henry Clay Esqr. Attorney at Law In Lexington—Kentuckey." Enclosed in Mark Pringle to Clay, March 28, 1805.

1 Neither letter found.

2 Alexander McKee, a Pennsylvanian who had remained a loyalist during the American Revolution, claimed 2,000 acres of land lying on the south fork of Elkhorn and Hickman creeks in central Kentucky. In 1780 the Virginia legislature called for the escheat of this land, as well as that of certain other loyalists, and provided that it should be vested in a board of trustees for the purpose of establishing a "publick school, or seminary of learning" in Kentucky. This act was the foundation upon which Transylvania Seminary (later Transylvania University) was established in 1784.

At an inquest of escheat, held in Lexington on July 1, 1780, the lands were declared forfeit. Owing to confusion in the surveyor's description of McKee's Kentucky property and to a claim of Alexander Ross, former Pittsburgh partner of McKee in the Indian trade, who seems to have bought McKee's holdings before their escheat, Transylvania's title was clouded. William Russell purchased certain lands, the title of which depended upon the validity of Ross's claim. After protracted litigation Russell's contest came before the United States Supreme Court, which on March 21, 1816, decided in favor of Transylvania. Lewis Collins, *History of Kentucky* (Rev. and enl. by Richard H. Collins; 2 vols., Covington, Ky., 1882), II, 176; Hening (comp.), *Statutes of Virginia,* X, 287-88; Transylvania University, Board of Trustees, "Minutes," September 26, 1806, December 1, 1813, PPPrHi-Shane Collection; Russel *vs.* Trustees of Transylvania University, 14 *U. S.* (1 Wheaton) 432-38.

3 Mark Pringle, Baltimore merchant.

4 William Morton.

Samuel Meredith to Robert Johnson or Clay

Sir Trenton [March 26, 1805]

Your favr of the 10th November dated Frankfort with the post Office mark of that place of the 30th January, I received, When the Honbl Mr Brown[1] was at Philadelphia he was so obliging as to give me his advice with Respect to the Lands I hold in Kentucky, it was that the suit should be brought in the Federal Court, which from his reasoning on the Subject I thought perfectly right & proper, he likewise said that as 2/3ds were given by me to retain only 1/3d the Expenses of suit ought to [be] borne by the Representatives of May[2] who had the 2/3ds, howeve[r] I wrote to Mr James Brown & desired him to draw on me for 100 Dollars as a particular fee of my own, not knowing who might be employed by the Representatives of May, & further assured him that in case of my success in the suit I would make him a handsome gift, I wrote the same to Mr Clay,[3] but as the sum was indefinite & not perhaps supposed binding, I now reiterate to you, that if Mr Henry Clay undertakes the suit, & is successful, I engage to pay him Five Hundred Dollars, which I think is the best mode I can fall on being unable to attend to the business, if the suit is likely to prove favourable my offer may have some weight.—An answer with the present situation of matters will be considered as a particular favr. confered on Sir Your most Humble Servant

Robert Johnson Esqr. SAML MEREDITH

ALS. DLC-TJC (DNA, M212, R12). Addressed: "Robert Johnson Esqr. or in his Absence to Henry Clay Esqr. Frankfort Kentucky." Meredith, a Pennsylvania merchant, Revolutionary War officer, member of the Continental Congress, and first United States Treasurer, had entered several large tracts of land in Kentucky. Robert Johnson was a Virginian who had settled in Kentucky during the Revolution, served in the State legislature as Senator from Woodford County, 1792-1795, and as Representative from Scott County much of the succeeding period through 1813.

1 John Brown.

2 Probably John May, brother of George. Cf. John May to Samuel Meredith and George Clymer, August 5, 1789 (DLC, TJC, 2d Series, vol. 1). John, a Virginia veteran of the French and Indian War, had come to Kentucky as early as 1775 to speculate in land. Though he continued his residence in Virginia, he had returned to Kentucky several times prior to his murder by Indians during a voyage down the Ohio in 1790. Among his properties were the tracts on which the towns of Mayslick and Maysville, Kentucky, were established.

3 Letter not found.

From Mark Pringle

Henry Clay Esquire Baltimore 28th. March 1805

Sir

I have received a letter from my friend, Mr. Wm. Morton, with yours of the 2d. instant to Mr. Johnston,[1] whose answer you will please find enclosed.[2]

As Trustee of Mr. Wm. Russell, I agree to the proposal you have made to Mr. Johnston, to accept, in lieu of Fee and all the Expences incident to the prosecution of the Suit against the Trustees of the Transylvania University, Four hundred acres of the Land if recovered, and nothing if it is not. Respecting the requisite proofs and documents you mention I beg leave to refer you to Mr. Johnston's letter, and, having the fullest reliance on your attention to the business, which is important, I have the honor to be with esteem & respect Sir Your most obedt. Servt. MARK PRINGLE

ALS. DLC-TJC (DNA, M212, R12).
1 Not found.
2 Above, March 26, 1805.

Receipt from Hart and Bartlet

[April 8, 1805]

Received Lexington April 8th 1805 of Mr. Henry Clay eight Barrels Salt Weighing Seventeen hundred & fifty eight pounds Neet—by George McIntosh[1]— HART & BARTLET

DS. DLC-TJC (DNA, M212, R15). Thomas Hart, Jr., and John C. Bartlet operated a store on Main Street in Lexington. Bartlet later moved to New Orleans, where the firm was known as Hart, Bartlet and Cox.
1 Not identified; probably a wagoner.

Agreement with Arthur Connely

[April 13, 1805]

Provided an Entry of T. Miller for Two thousand Acres of Land calling to lie 2 miles below Estills Battle ground,[1] now in Suit in Montgomery Harrow & others agt. Smith[2] shall be established, I promise to pay H Clay One hundred dollars; but if the whole entry shall not be established in said Suit, I am to pay in proportion

Witness my hand & Seal this 13. Apl. 1805.

ARTHUR CONNELY {L.S.}

DS, in Clay's hand. DLC-TJC (DNA, M212, R15). Connely lived in Montgomery County.
1 The Battle of Little Mountain, or "Estill's Defeat," had occured in March, 1782, near the present town of Mount Sterling. Thomas Miller's entries were made in 1783.
2 The statute of limitations operated in favor of Harrow, who had occupied for over twenty years the land in dispute. Smith, a Virginian who moved to Kentucky in 1803 after an earlier visit, therefore lost the case, both in the Montgomery Circuit Court and the Court of Appeals. Connely's interest apparently derived through Smith. 6 *Ky. Reports* (3 Bibb) 446-48.

Promissory Note from Thomas Rule

[April 17, 1805]

Provided Miller's Entry is set aside in the Suit now depending in the Court of Appeals between Miller's Heirs & Haws heirs,[1] I do hereby bind myself & those for whom I am authorized to act by power of Atto. to pay H. Clay on or before the first day of Octr. next Fifty dollars.

Witness my hand & seal this 17. Apl. 1805. THOS RULE {L.S.}

[Endorsement on verso][2]

Credit for the interest up to 19 Feb. 1806. H. CLAY

HENRY CLAY

DS, in Clay's hand. Bourbon Circuit Court, File 172. In August, 1806, Clay brought suit to enforce payment of this note; and Rule, a justice of the peace in Bourbon County, confessed judgment.

1 The conflicting entries, to land within five or six miles of the Lower Blue Licks, had been made in 1782 by Henry Miller, pioneer Kentucky settler and Indian fighter, and Samuel Hawes (Haws or Hawse), Revolutionary War veteran of Caroline County, Virginia. The Court of Appeals, Fall Term, 1805, affirmed the decree of the lower court, which had decided the case in favor of Hawes' heirs. 3 *Ky. Reports* (Hardin) 30. 2 AES.

From John Overton

Dear Sir Nashville May 3d. 1805

I have written to Colo Hart[1] respecting the Cost of his two Suits against Dromgole[2] for which I am security. and shall be liable to execution after the first day of June next

Having corresponded with you respecting Colo Harts business. I am encouraged to take the liberty of asking you to put the Colo in mind of the Circumstance, for it seems hard for me to pay it. after using every exertion for Colo Hart in my power to which Mr Humphreys[3] and other gentlemen Can testify

Before starting on the last circuit I wrote the Colo the amount, which I believe was some where about $140 or 150 though not certain, his letter will shew.

I cannot say that I was dissatisfied with the verdict of the jury upon the principle question, tho. Dromgole surely ought to have been subject to all Costs—This was strenuously Contended for at the trial but the judge did not give any charge to the jury, upon which they found a verdict for the defendant though the payments were proved to have been made after Suit commenced I contended that they ought to have found at least one Cent or some small sum so as to carry the Cost. You will recollect it was clearly proved at the trial that Price agreed to release Dromgole for Jones' part and take Reading in lieu of Jones[4]—

A new trial was moved for and argued without effect. At the next term a particular motion was brought before the Court. for the purpose of having the Clerk directed to expunge the sum of $90 from the taxation of Costs. which was inserted for the Goalars fees.

at 25 Cents a day for Dromgoles board while in jail and in the bounds; but without effect. We are bound to presume that Courts of justice are right, at least I have no doubt in this case but the judge thought he was, and it may be that he really was, but I do declare I cannot accord with the decision as to the Costs, particularly the Gailors fees for board—

I expected Colo. Hart would have renewed the money in Edwards[5] Hands, but he writes me that he has only about $70. for $66:66 of which Colo Hart has given me an order for my fees

Will you be so obliging as to speak to Colo Hart and write me upon the subject. and tell him that I hope he will relieve me from the inconvenience of paying the money I am Dear Sir with Sents of the higt respt yr. mo ob S JNO. OVERTON

ALS. DLC-TJC (DNA, M212, R12). Addressed to Clay at Lexington.
1 Thomas Hart.
2 James Dromgoole.
3 Parry Wayne Humphreys, later Tennessee judge and member of Congress, who had moved from Lexington to Nashville and begun practice of law in 1801.
4 Samuel Price, Richard Jones, and William Reading.
5 Ninian Edwards.

Account with Andrew McCalla

[*ca.* May 18, 1805]

Henry Clay To And. McCalla Dr.

1798				
Jan.	22	To ℥ 1 Pulv. C. B.[1]	4	
	25	℥ 1 do	4	
Febry.	11	A Tooth brush	1	6
	15	do 1„6 & P. Syringe 3„9.	5	3
	30	Box Ung. Merc.[2]	1	6
May	16	2 Tooth brushes	3	
June	15	Dose Sal Glaub.[3]		9
	26	℥ Cort. Cam.[4]	2	—
	30	2 Tooth brushes	3	—
Aug.	11	℥ ½ Tereb. Venet. & V.[5]	1	—
	22	2 Tooth brushes	3	
Novem	19	℥ 1 Ung. Merc.	1	6
Sept.	28	W. Tomkin's Fees on Doc. Hun's Suit[6]	15	
Decem	29	℥ 1 Cort. Berb.	3	9
1799				
Jany.	1	℥ 1 do	3	9
	21	℥ ½ Ung. Merc.		9
March	9	℥ ½ do		9
May	13	2 Tooth brushes	3	
June	25	ʒ 2 Sac Sat.[7]		9

1800						
Jan.	20	Extr. Tooth and one T. opiate	pro N. W.om[8]		2	3
Febr.	3	do	p N. man		1	6
Sept.	20	℥ 4 Ol. Oliv[9]			3	9
1801						
June	6	℥ 1 Ol. Beuni.[10] ℥ 2 Tamarynds			2	3
July	29	℥ 4 Olivar & V.[11]			4	6
Sept.	25	℥ ½ Turner's Cereate, ℥ 1 C. P. Fl.[12]			3	3
1802						
Jan.	13	℥ 1 Cort. Peruv. Fl.			3	9
April	17	Phlebot.	pro Uxore Domi[13]		3	
May	11	℥ 2 Vitr. Alb.[14] ℥ 2 Litharge			3	
July	30	lb 16 Lamp black at 2„3		1	16	—
Sept.	20	1 Small Kegg, Phlebot, pro N. W.			4	6
	30	Box Ung. Merc.			1	6
Nov.	28	Cutg. Glass			6	
Dec.	29	Do.			3	
				6	16	6
		Amt. carried over £6„16„6		$	22	75
		Amt. bro't over		$	22	75
Februy	28	To ℥ ½ Sac. Sat. & ℥ 1 V.				25
March	1	Grs. 30 Calmel	p se[15]			13
April	11	lb 3½ Patent Yellow	p W. Mentelle		3	50
		lb ½ Pruss. Blue	p do		3	
		lb 4 Ochre	p do		1	
Sept.	24	lb 9, ℥ 12 Lamp. Black	p Winslow[16]		3	62
Decem	13	lb 6 Putty			2	25
	14	lb 2 do				75
1804						
Februy	22	Cutg Glass	pro do			13
1805						
April	19	Extr Tooth	pro N. B. Simon[17]			25
May	18	do	pro N. Wom			25
					37	37
		Bushells 2 Blue Grass Seed at 400/100			8	
					$45	87
		Subscripn for levelg. Street			6	
					$51	87
		Supra			Cr,	
1798						
January	22	By Cash				66⅔
October	11	By Doc. Hun			5	50[18]
		By fee & Tax vs Poor			5	50
		By fee vs Wilson			5	—

By fee Clarke vs Ridgley &c in Clarke	5 –
	21 66⅔
By Cash in full in Palmateer's[19] bond	30 21

D. DLC-TJC (DNA, M212, R10). McCalla, who had come to Lexington from Philadelphia before 1790, for many years conducted an apothecary's shop at Short and Market streets. In addition, he served at various times as librarian of the Lexington Library, justice of the peace, town trustee, and assistant postmaster.

1 Powdered barberry bark. 2 Mercurial ointment. 3 Glauber's salt.
4 Camphor bark. 5 Venice turpentine and vial.
6 Dr. Anthony Hunn, suit not found. 7 Sugar of lead.
8 Negro woman. 9 Olive oil. 10 Probably oil of betony.
11 Olive oil and vial. 12 Yellow Peruvian Bark (quinine).
13 Phlebotomy (bleeding) of Mrs. Clay. 14 White vitriol (zinc sulfate).
15 For self. 16 Hallet M. Winslow. 17 Negro boy, Simon.
18 The remainder of the document is in Clay's hand. The suits mentioned have not been found. 19 William Palmateer.

To Thomas Hockley

Dr Sir Lexington 18h. May 1805

I received a few days ago your favour of the 22d. Apl.[1] I was extremely sorry to learn that your misfortunes had subjected you to the unpleasant duty of laying your affairs before your Creditors. The reflections however that a merchant, in the most honest and prudent commerce, is liable to these reverses, and that your creditors entirely acquit you of impropriety, ought and I hope will amply console you.

With regard to your situation in this quarter I fear you will be unable to get any thing from Gano.[2] I am told he is certainly & has been for some time insolvent. Craig[3] has been struggling under difficulties. Your debt due from him is quite safe, and I will endeavour to obtain immediate payment.

I received yesterday the balance of Davis's debt, of which you will be pleased to save me the necessity of writing Mr. Walker, by giving him this information.[4] At this time I am unable to get a single dollar of light money; but I am assured at the Bank that they expect some in a few days, and that I shall be supplied as soon as they receive any.

I never heard a doubt suggested of James Weir's solvency[5]—A gentleman who is engaged in extensive commerce in this place, and acts as one of the Directors of the Bank, assured me this moment that he believes him to be perfectly safe. You will therefore do as you please in regard to his Note.

I will endeavour to find out the present owner of the Land of James Reynolds sold for the Taxes; and to ascertain whether and for what he will relinquish his purchase, & advise you accordingly.[6]

Should you still have the Cask of wine which you bespoke for me, you will be pleased to have it inclosed in a second barrel, and sent to me by any of the Lexington merchants, of whom I believe Mr. Tilford[7] is now in Philadelphia, and others will be in the course of the summer. Any of them will take charge of it for me.

Yr. obt Servt. HENRY CLAY

ALS. Owned by Thomas D. Clark, Lexington, Kentucky. Addressed: "Thomas Hockley Esqr. Merchant Philadelphia." Endorsed: ". . . recd June 7th."

1 Not found.

2 Possibly Isaac E. Gano of Frankfort, who was experiencing financial difficulties at that time. Gano *vs.* Hart, 3 *Ky. Reports* (Hardin) 304-306.

3 Elijah Craig.

4 See above, Hockley to Clay, November 22, 1804.

5 Weir, a native of northern Ireland, was a prominent Lexington merchant and manufacturer.

6 Reynolds had acquired under Virginia warrants in 1784 and 1785 claims to more than 2,000 acres in Lincoln and Fayette counties of Kentucky.

7 John Tilford.

Assignment of Note by Jehoida Musick

[May 20, 1805]

Document not found; cited in Clark Circuit Court, File 55. When the note by Jacob and Henry Lander of Clark County, dated April 22, 1805, for $60 payable to Musick in three months, was not paid, Clay promptly filed suit for £40 damages on a plea of covenant broken. Judgment for the plaintiff was rendered at the April Term, 1806.

Receipt to George Heytel

[June 12, 1805]

Recd. of Mr. George Heydel One hundred & Seventy two dollars on a/c. of Isaac Hazzlehurst of Philadelphia 12h. June 1805

$172.– H. CLAY

ADS. Fayette Circuit Court, File 445 (1810). Clay, acting for Isaac Hazlehurst and Company, merchants, won by default in the Fayette Circuit Court, March Term, 1804, a suit against Heytel, a Lexington tanner, who while a resident of Philadelphia had become indebted to the firm. In addition to the cash payment here recorded, Heytel executed a land mortgage, on which Hazlehurst subsequently won a foreclosure suit. The Court of Appeals in 1815 failed to sustain the judgment, however, and remanded the case for new proceedings. 7 *Ky. Reports* (4 Bibb) 19.

Receipt to Charles Carr

[June 13, 1805]

Recd. 13. June 1805. of C. Carr Esqr. Ten dollars my fees &c Gibson vs South.[1] H. CLAY

ADS. KyHi.

1 Clay had represented Samuel Gibson in an action against John South for debt of £32, 18s, 6d, with damages of £40. Warrant had been issued for the plaintiff on September 21, 1803. Fayette Circuit Court, File 62 (1804). The Gibsons, father and son of the same name, had settled in Kentucky from frontier Pennsylvania around 1794.

They had lived for a year on the Kentucky River in Fayette County, then removed to Brush Creek in Montgomery County. John South, who had fought on the Kentucky frontier during the Revolution, had been a Justice of the Peace of Fayette County and served as a member of the Kentucky legislature for that county from 1793-1804. He was declared of unsound mind in 1807 and died shortly thereafter.

Promissory Note from Joseph Hughes and James Carothers

[June 17, 1805]

If we succeed in a suit in Chancery in Fayette Court Wherein John McCleery's Heirs & Representatives are Complts against us &c. we promise to pay H. Clay on the determination of the suit in the said Court fifty dollars.[1] Witness our hands & seals this 17h. June 1805

Teste
J. WATKINS JR—[2]

JOSEPH HUGHES {L.S.}
JAMES CAROTHERS {L.S.}

DS, in Clay's hand. DLC-TJC (DNA, M212, R15). Hughes lived in Jessamine County, Kentucky; Carothers, in Fayette.

1 The suit, begun in 1805, was continued until March, 1808, when the complainants failed to appear and were ordered non-suited. The case was reinstated a few days later but does not appear subsequently in the court records. Fayette Circuit Court, Order Books C-F, *passim.* McClary had been a resident of Woodford County.

2 Not Dr. John Watkins, then a resident of New Orleans, but Clay's half-brother John, born in Hanover County, Virginia, the eldest child of Henry and Elizabeth Clay Watkins.

Promissory Note from James Dunn

[June 17, 1805]

Two months after date I promise to pay to Henry Clay, with interest from the date hereof, Seventy pounds. Witness my hand & seal this 17th. day of June 1805

Teste
JOHN MCKINNEY JUNR.

JAS DUNN {L.S.}

DS, in Clay's hand. Fayette Circuit Court, File 266 (1813). This instrument was apparently given by Dunn, a resident of Lexington, as partial payment for certain lots on Mill Street which he had contracted to buy from Clay. Neither the agreement nor Clay's bond to make title has been found. Cf. below, Settlement and Conditional Promise, October 13, 1813.

To Thomas Hockley

Dr Sir Lexington 25h. June 1805

Your favour covering James Weirs Note.[1] came saft to hand. I immediately presented it to him and he assures me that it shall be taken up in the course of the next month.

I communicated the contents of your letter, in relation to your continuance in business, to such of the gentlemen mentioned in it as I have met with, and will to the remainder.

Inclosed is a letter[2] to Mr. A. Walker, covering a bill of Exchange for $500, which you will be pleased to deliver to him. This sum I believe will discharge the debt of Davis.[3] I however will obtain the amount from the Clerks office at Frankfort, which with your assistance will enable me certainly to ascertain; for in making remittances to you before the transfer of this debt I did it without a view to the particular debt or debts I had received. Yr ob. Servt

HENRY CLAY

ALS. Owned by Thomas D. Clark, Lexington, Kentucky. Addressed to Hockley at Philadelphia. Endorsed: ". . . recd. July 12th." 1 Not found.
2 Not found. 3 See above, Hockley to Clay, November 22, 1804.

Fee Bill to Mrs. Elizabeth Parker

[June 27, 1805]

Mrs. Parker To H. Clay Dr.

To my fee in the Suit Bodley vs Parkers heirs &c[1] £6:0:0

To advice given at various times to you in relation to the affairs of the Estate 3:0:0

£9:0:0

[Endorsement on verso][2]

Recd. payment of Mrs. Parker this 29h. June 1805 H. CLAY

ADS. Owned by Henry H. Harned, Frankfort, Kentucky. Endorsed: ". . . June 27. 1805:" Mrs. Parker was the widow of Major Robert Parker, who had died March 4, 1800. Mary Todd Lincoln was their granddaughter.

1 Robert Parker, having agreed to a speculative venture with Thomas Bodley, in 1796 had purchased a tract of land for which he had paid, with the expectation of receiving from Bodley one half the purchase price and in return granting him a half interest in the property. After Parker's death, Bodley sued to recover his share of the land from the heirs, who maintained that he had not paid his share of the purchase money. Bodley's suit was successful, but in 1815 the Court of Appeals reversed the decision of the lower court, at the same time ruling that he should be recompensed for certain payments that he had made to Parker. 7 *Ky. Reports* (4 Bibb) 102-104.

2 AES.

Order to Thomas Vaughan

29h. June 1805.

Be pleased to deliver to Mess. Stevens & Winslow or order at the Upper Blue Licks on or before the 25h. day of Decr. next Sixty two & a half bushels of merchantable Salt on a/c. of your contract with me. Yrs HENRY CLAY

Mr. Tho. Vaughan
Upper Blue Licks

ANS. DLC-TJC (DNA, M212, R15). See above, Agreement, October 29, 1804. On verso of document Stephens & Winslow direct that delivery be made to Maddox Fisher.

Bond to John Rowan

[July 18, 1805]

I have sold to John Rowan a lott of ground in Frankfort fronting Broad-way one hundred & twenty feet and running back with St. Clair Street one hundred and ninety eight feet, being the corner opposite to the Market house, which said lott I promise & bind myself to convey to said Rowan on demand. Witness my hand & Seal this 18h. July 1805. HENRY CLAY {L.S.}

[Endorsement on verso][1]

Memo. H. Clay has made me a deed agreeably to the within but at the time of executing it he was not certain that he had the legal title to the whole of the ground. Should that be the case the deed is not in any way to operate to his prejudice; nor on the other hand to release him from his obligation to convey me the legal title. 10h. Septr. 1813. H. MARSHALL

ALS. DLC-TJC (DNA, M212, R1). Under endorsement dated September 8, 1812, this obligation was assigned by Rowan to Humphrey Marshall, a Virginia veteran of the Revolution, who in 1782 had settled in Kentucky, where he became wealthy through land speculation and the practice of law. At various times a member of the State legislature and the United States Senate, Marshall attained political prominence as the foremost Federalist in the West. His *History of Kentucky*, published in 1812, was the first formal history of the State, as well as a defense of his own conduct and a castigation of his enemies.

1 ES, in Clay's hand.

Land Patent

[July 23, 1805]

[In consideration of three land office treasury warrants Christopher Greenup, Governor of Kentucky, grants to George Walker and Henry Clay, as assignees of Benjamin Netherland, and to William May[1] 3,003 acres of land in Jefferson County on the "main East branch of Floyds fork."]

DS. KyHi. Recorded in Ky. Register of Lands, Old Kentucky Grants, Book no. 16, p. 147.

1 First Clerk of Lincoln County, later a justice and surveyor of Nelson County.

Receipt for Tax on Matthew Clay's Land

[July 31, 1805]

["*Received of* Matthew Clay *by* Henry Clay *the treasurer's receipt* for ten *dollars* Sixty eight *cents,* one *mills*" for taxes, for the year 1804, on 2,000 acres of land on the Cumberland River and 1,090 acres in Madison County. John Adair, Register of the Land Office, Frankfort.]

DS. DLC-HC (DNA, M212, R1). Cf. above, Receipt, June 26, 1800.

To John Breckinridge

Dr Sir Lexington 1 Augt. 1805

The Court of Appeals having decided your cause with Porter,[1] and designing to rise this evening or tomorrow evening at four O Clock, I have dispatched the bearer to apprize you of the event. They say they do not consider the fraud sufficiently injurious to you to annul the contract, but that it entitles you to be made whole. They therefore affirm the decree of the Fayette Court except as to the time when interest is to commence, which they fix at the time you sold the Tinker Creek land Costs divided.

The Fœderal Court has admitted the Answer of Skillerns exors to be filed, but the Cause will not be determined this term[2]—

I reached here last evening from Frankft. and am this moment starting to the Springs.[3]

Be pleased to pay the bearer 1 Dollar, which I have agreed to give him for taking this letter to you Yrs H. CLAY.

ALS. DLC-Breckinridge Family Papers (DNA, M212, R20). Addressed: "John Breckenridge Esqr."

1 See above, Clay to Breckinridge, August 27, 1803.

2 A chancery suit involving on one side the executors of George Skillern, an early speculator in Kentucky lands, and on the other the executors of John May. Clay, who represented Skillern's executors, lost the case before the United States Supreme Court in 1807. 8 *U. S.* (4 Cranch) 136-41, 10 *U. S.* (6 Cranch) 267-68.

3 Olympian Springs.

Property Deed to John Jordan, Jr.

[August 6, 1805]

[Indenture by which for the sum of 500 pounds current money of Kentucky, Henry and Lucretia Clay sell to John Jordan, Jr., a tract in Lexington, bounded as follows: beginning at the southern corner of Lot no. 2, purchased by Jordan of Innis B. Brent,[1] thence south 45° east, binding on Main Street 43 feet to a corner of Lot no. 3, this day conveyed by Clay to Andrew F. Price,[2] thence north 45° east 13 poles to Short Street, and with same north 45° west 43 feet to the eastern corner of Jordan's Lot no. 2, and with it 45° west 13 poles to the beginning—being part of In Lot no. 3, granted by the Trustees of Lexington to Basil Duke, transferred to Thomas Love, and from him to Henry Clay by deed recorded in the Court of Appeals at Frankfort,[3] being all the Lot no. 3 except that part which was conveyed by Clay to Price. General warranty of title. Certification of signature acknowledged by the Clays and recorded in the Office of the Clerk, Fayette County, August 6, 1805.]

DS. Owned by Henry H. Harned, Frankfort, Kentucky; recorded in Fayette Circuit Court, Deed Book B, 417-18.

1 Tavernkeeper (for several years in partnership with Thomas Love), jailer, deputy sheriff, and first postmaster of Lexington.
2 See above, Property Deed, January 1, 1805. 3 Not found.

Property Deed from John Jordan, Jr.

[August 6, 1805]

[Indenture by which John Jordan, Jr., for five shillings, paid and acknowledged, transfers to Henry Clay a tract in Lexington fronting on the Public Square, adjoining other property of Jordan on one side and on the other the lot formerly owned by David Dodge, now by William Macbean, the transferred lot "being the same whereon the said Clay is now building a brick house" and containing in frontage about thirty feet and running back the same width 112¼ feet to an alley separating the Bank lot from those facing the Public Square.[1] Jordan and his heirs are to have use of the alley from Main to Short Streets. General warranty of title. Signatures by John and Catharine Jordan, acknowledged before Thomas Bodley, Clerk of Fayette County, August 10, 1805.]

Fayette Circuit Court, Deed Book B, 419.
1 The site was on the southeastern side of Upper Street, between Main and Short. Cf. above, Contract, January 22, 1805.

To Robert Smith

Sir Lexington (Kentucky) 7. Aug. 1805.

Among the tracts of land sold and conveyed some years ago by Kincaid[1] to you and your brother[2] is one situated in Lincoln County, and patented as containing 9000 & odd Acres. In this tract is contained a considerable surplus, to which Mr. Kincaid supposes himself entitled, having sold by the acre and not the tract in gross. This surplus he has contracted for with two gentlemen, who have engaged me as an attorney at law to investigate the claim. The land itself is not an object of much consideration from the information I have received, but there is situated upon it a Salt lick, now held and worked by the owner of an adversary title to yours, which may possibly become valuable. It is the wish of the gentlemen for whom I am engaged to adjust their claim to the surplus by compromise or arbitration rather than by a Suit, and in order to enable you to form some opinion of the nature of the controversy, as well as the strength of your own, claim I will state such information as I have received.

In this Country it was frequently practised by the Surveyors at an early period to make what has been denominated here, Chimney-corner surveys—that is Surveys made without ever going upon the ground and marking corners and boundary. It some times happened that after they had thus returned Surveys, they would go upon the ground and mark corner trees corresponding with the ideal corners which had been reported in the surveys. I am told this it is very probable is the case with regard to the survey of your tract of land before mentd. Two corners and a line are all the evidences of boundary that can be found. The marks on the corners extend through the bark only so as to prevent their age being ascertained by resort to the annulars. If no survey has ever been in reality made the claim is worthless, and the title to the surplus is prostrated with the remainder: In which case the present possessor of the Lick, or some other claimant (for I understand there is another) would hold the property.

But if the line and corners were really marked, the line, which ought to be about 1500 poles according to the patent, is ascertained to be about 2000 poles, and the lick is situated at the end of the line farthest from the beginning; so that by stopping at the patent distance the lick would not be included. We conceive therefore that as Mr. Kincaid sold at the rate of 6d. per acre a given quantity of land, you have no right to hold what he did not sell and what he has never been paid for, to wit the quantity beyond the patent distance. I understand the principle to be, that in sales of land by the acre at a price agreed upon by the parties, if the tract is, on the one hand, deficient in the supposed quantity, a proportionate abatement will be made in the consideration; whilst on the other the Vendor has a right to the Surplus, if the real is beyond the computed quantity. Should you concur in this opinion you will be pleased to authorize your agent to lay off the Surplus accordingly. If you do not you will say whether you will arbitrate, and direct on your part a nomination of referees. And if you are disposed to sell the entire tract if you will name a price it is probable those for whom I act would purchase it.

Mr. Trotter,[3] who is Kincaids security, for the return of the purchase money of such part of the land as may be lost, once expressed to me a wish to be relieved from his responsibility. If you are disposed to sell the whole of the lands bought of Mr. Kincaid it is probable if you will take the original purchase money with interest, you may sell them. I believe a great portion of them is scarcely worth the taxes, which are constantly accumulating, and perhaps never would have been taken up but for the fever of speculation whi[ch] raged with such violence some years ago

Permit me to hope for an early an[swer] and to subscribe myself with great resp[ect.] Yr. ob Servt. HENRY CLAY

ALS. DLC-Samuel Smith Papers (DNA, Microcopy Supp.). Addressed: "Robert Smith Esqr. Secretary of the Navy City of Washington." At the beginning of President Madison's administration Smith became Secretary of State.

1 James Kincaid of Madison County, Kentucky.
2 Samuel Smith, Baltimore merchant and shipper, long a member of Congress.
3 Probably George Trotter, Sr.

From John Adair

Sir Lexington Augt. 15th. 1805.

How ever unwilling I may be to submit my Conduct or Sentiments to a news paper investigation, It now appears, that Mr. Daniel Bradford is determined, I shall be the next to occupy a part of his—As I have reason to believe I have been wantonly persecuted by that family, and as I am Conscious that the truth will not opperate to my Discredit—I have only to prepare myself for such an Event—I need make no farther appology for calling your recollection to the Hand Bill that was shewn in frankfort, last November, implicating my political principle as inimical to Mr. Jefferson and republicanism[1]—from an application to Mr. Taylor[2] and others who were pressent it appears that the Conversation alluded to, took place principally between you and myself—although in pressence of Several Gentn. I wish you now to recollect as far you [*sic*] can the nature of that conversation in what manner I spoke of the Amendt. to the Foederal Constitution,[3] whether positive as bad or whether I did not merely doubt its future opperation as unfavorable to republicanism —Stating as my reason that It had been urged by they [*sic*] Foederalists under the former Administration & opposed by the party who had now carried it in opposition to them—I wish you likewise to state in what manner and by whom Genl. Pinckneys[4] name was first introduced and whether I discovered the least displeasure with the Administration or tallents or personal Character of Mr. Jefferson, on the contrary whether I did not Say I would prefer him as President to any man in the union; but observe that they people of America Ought not to think their Liberty or happiness depended on the Election of any individual; but on their Steady adherence to a Virtuous Observance of their Laws—

Your Answer by post to Frankft. will be deemed a favor by
Your most Obt. JOHN ADAIR

ALS. DLC-HC (DNA, M212, R1). Published in Colton (ed.), *Private Correspondence of Henry Clay*, 11.

1 The handbill had been circulated by Adair's opponents during the Senatorial contest of 1804. Buckner Thruston, aided by Clay, had barely defeated Adair, who was now preparing to offer for the Senate post lately vacated by John Breckinridge.

2 James and Thompson Taylor, both of Jefferson County, had been members of the House of Representatives and Richard Taylor was Sergeant at Arms of the Kentucky legislature in November, 1804.

3 The twelfth amendment.

4 Charles Cotesworth Pinckney had been Jefferson's Federalist opponent in the Presidential election of 1804.

Order to Thomas Vaughan

Lex. 17 Aug. 1805.

Be pleased to deliver to Mr. John Fisher Fifty bushels of Salt and oblige

Yrs

Mr Vaughan
Upper Blue Licks.

Henry Clay

ANS. DLC-TJC (DNA, M212, R15). See above, Agreement, October 29, 1804. Written on verso of this document is a receipt, dated August 24, 1805, to Vaughan from one William Ray for fifty-seven bushels of salt obtained for Clay.

To John Adair

Sir, Lexington 24 August 1805

Your's of the 15h. instant, addressed to me at the Olympian Springs, did not reach me until a few days ago at Paris, or it should have been earlier answered.

I recollect during the Session of the Assembly of 1803 having had one or more conversations with you relative to the amendment of the Fœderal Constitution, providing for a designation of the President and Vice President in the votes to be given for those officers. But I regret that my memory does not enable me to detail the particulars of those conversations. I remember however that you expressed doubts as to the propriety of the proposed amendment, urged some arguments to prove that the existing provision was best, and suggested your fears that a change would produce mischievous consequences. Whether your opinion was matured or not I cannot say, but I do not think you expressed one decisively. If the name of Genl. Pinckney was mentioned and how or by whom it was introduced, at the times of the conversations, or at any of them, it has escaped my memory. I have heard you speak of that gentleman I think more than once in terms of high respect and it may have been when the topic of conversation was the Amendmt., but I do not believe that you drew any parallell between Mr. Jefferson and him, or contended that he was equally well qualified to fill the presidential chair.

When I saw the hand-bill to which you allude I was surprized at some of the sentiments there ascribed to you; and am inclined to think had they been avowed in my presence and hearing that they would have made an impression which would be still fresh.

I am Sir Yr ob. Servt. H. Clay

ALS draft. DLC-HC (DNA, M212, R1). Published in Colton (ed.), *Private Correspondence of Henry Clay*, 11-12.

Promissory Note from Thomas A. Thomson

[August 26, 1805]

On demand I promise to pay H. Clay Twenty five dollars. Witness my hand & seal this 26h. Augt. 1805.

Teste THOS A. THOMSON {L.S.}
JNO. MONROE[1]

DS, in Clay's hand. Bourbon Circuit Court, File 167. Thomson (also cited as Tomson and Thompson) was a resident of Bourbon County. Clay "for the use of John Barry" brought suit to collect on this note at the February Term, 1806, of the Bourbon Circuit Court. In April a ruling of *nil debet* per specialty (he owes nothing) was issued and the decision was confirmed in May.

1 Earlier in the decade, President Jefferson's appointee as Federal attorney for the western section of Virginia; later a judge of the Fayette Circuit Court in Kentucky. In 1811 he resigned the latter post to move to Ohio, but he returned to Lexington the following year and died at Georgetown, Kentucky, in 1814.

Promissory Note from Thomas A. Thomson

[August 26, 1805]

On demand I promise to pay to Henry Clay the Sum of Twenty dollars. Witness my hand & seal this 26h. day of August 1806.

Test THOS A TOMSON [*sic*] {L.S.}
D. IRVIN[1]

DS, in Clay's hand. Bourbon Circuit Court, File 196. In December, 1807, Clay brought suit to collect on this note in Bourbon Circuit Court; he won judgment at the February Term, 1808.

1 Daniel Irvin, of Bourbon County.

From John Clay

Mr Henry Clay New Orleans September 5 1805
Dear Brother

Your favor of the 6th augt[1] reached me per last Mail too late to answer it by the return.

I have not written you for long time for many reasons. I was much mortified on the R.g of your letter inclosing a Dedimus for depositions that those Gentleman from whom I was to take them was out of Town: & living at a distance I could not have notified them in Town: upon refering to your letter upon the subject of Hunts[2] answer I cannot but be surprised at the fellows villiany. it may be true that he never took the two horses from Byrd,[3] but Byrd wrote me some years ago a long letter reproaching me for my Conduct & begging to immediately remit him the amt of the Horses Of course I have always considered myself indebted to Byrd the other horse was sent by Hunt with one of his Clerks to Pha[4] & applied to his use. If you will observe my Books you'll find that Hunt got two horses from Smith[5] one of which was paid for by him & being Security I was obliged to settle with Smith for the other by refering to Smith that fact will be assertaind tis true also that I gave an order in favr. of Madam Chabot[6] on Hunt but tis equally true that he protested it & since my arrival here I have been obliged to pay it to Madam Chabot. I have destroy that order but will soon forward you a certfe from the Lady that she never received a farthing from Hunt—Let him produce the draft: if Hunt has not recovered from Craig[7] tis not my fault. he took the note as payment. I sincerely wish the Business was closed & beg that you will exert yourself for that perpose.

I have been so extremely occupuyd during this Spring & Summer that I have not had really a moment that I could call my own notwithstanding all the fatigue of a very laborious buisness [*sic*] my Health has continued permanant add to the [*sic*] our City never being known so healthy has left me no fears as to my safety in residing here during the Summer: J Brown[8] as well as many who have reported to you my prosperity in this Country have been very extravigant tis true that my Credit is as high as I could possibly expect & that I have had more business than I had a right to expect but being obliged to encounter a heavy expence in the first year of my establishment a number of Clerks necessary to carry on my Buisness add to this being obliged to take up a number of notes from my old misfortunes (which was absolutely necessary to do to keep up my Credit) making all those deductions very little indeed will remain at the close of the first Season. However my Expectations are as flattering as perhaps ought to be more so than any New Beginour in this City. You will discover from this sketch how illy I am situated to answer a Claim of such magnitude as that of Slaybacks[9]—I have written to him that in the course of the Winter & Spring I would forwar him a part say at least $1000 If you possibly could furnish him with a tract of Land & take up my obligation you may calculate by the close of the approching Year that it shall be refunded "say 1000 by ls april $1000 1st Sept. & residue at the end of the year— do indeavor to arrange it you might do it to an advantage for yourself & very material accomodation to me—I have one other debt to pay which gives me a little concern a Mr M[. . .][10] in your neighbourhood who I am told has offord it 100 less than the amt—if so will you get it up or get T. Hart[11] to do it for me I will remit so soon as I can [*reach*] some light money I believe the claim is original for £90 I immagine it may got [*sic*] for $200—under the regulation of this Country veiwing my agreements with my Creditors I should be obliged be obliged [*sic*] to pay it before the expiration of the term spe fied as nine-tenths of them have subscribed to it thus says my Council—however to prevent it injuring my Credit I will settle with the [*calculating*] Scoundral who manifestedly cheated me with his whisky half waterd

Mr Brown & lady still remain at their plantation. I was there a few days since & left them in good health—they are enraptured with the Country—We were alarmed some time ago thro the medium of a letter to Mr Brown from one of his friends that you were in an ill state of health—as you have not mentiond this in your letter I take it for granted that you are reestablishd—I shall leave this place in 10 days for Natchez—principally to arrange some affairs for my friend Jordan[12] Perhaps I will address you before I go—if not I will from there—Comps to Lucretia—Adieu Yrs Sincerely JOHN CLAY

ALS. DLC-TJC (DNA, M212, R10). 1 Not found. 2 Wilson Hunt.

3 Charles Willing Byrd of Ohio on August 18, 1800, thanked Nathaniel Massie, his brother-in-law, for his "proposition relative to my claim against Mr. Clay. The horses I gave up to release him were valued at $180." Massie, *Massie*, 161.

4 Philadelphia.

5 Probably Senator John Smith of Ohio, preacher, farmer, and merchant, who was closely associated with Byrd, Nathaniel Massie, and others, and who became deeply indebted to Wilson Hunt's brother, John W. Hunt. Smith to John W. Hunt, December 17, 1810, KyU-Hunt Papers.

6 Of New Orleans, probably a tavernkeeper.

7 Probably Elijah Craig, who on September 12, 1798, had written to Abijah and John W. Hunt regarding his debts to them. KyU-Hunt Papers.

8 James Brown. 9 Possibly Solomon Slayback, of Fayette County.

10 Illegible. 11 Thomas Hart. 12 John Jordan, Jr.

Agreement with Arthur Patterson

[September 18, 1805]

[Arthur Patterson covenants to sell to Henry Clay one-half of Francis Patterson's preemption of 1,000 acres on Cane Run near Lexington, for which Clay agrees to pay $800 in money and horses and, nine months later, an additional sum of $200. Arthur, as one of the heirs of Francis, binds himself for conveyance of title under special warranty only, Clay agreeing to run the rest of Francis' title. Signed by Arthur Patterson and witnessed by a younger Francis Patterson, with a supplementary clause also signed by the latter, agreeing to convey title under the above arrangement.]

[Endorsements on accompanying sheet][1]

Recd. the deed agreeably to this Contract for the Land bought by me 9h. Nov. 1807. HENRY CLAY

Settled this 7 Decr. 1807 & there remains due me on a/c. of the within purchase $268 1/3 in horses. ARTHUR PATTERSON

ADS, signed also by the Pattersons. DLC-TJC (DNA, M212, R15). Francis Patterson, now deceased, holder of the preemption, had come to Kentucky from western Pennsylvania in 1787. The Francis who countersigns this document was another of the devisees of the elder Francis.

1 AES; and ES, in Clay's hand.

Receipt from Arthur Patterson

[September 24, 1805]

Recd. of H. Clay. One hundred and fifty dollars on a/c of the land, that is one half of the preemption granted to my father which I sold him the other day. Sept. 24h 1805—

$150. Arthur Patterson

Teste
Henry Lewis[1]

DS, in Clay's hand. DLC-TJC (DNA, M212, R15). 1 Of Franklin County.

Bond by Thomas Hart

[September 30, 1805]

Whereas a certain Thomas Hare[1] on the 17h. day of April 1776 placed in my hands £100 to be laid out in the purchase of lands in Transylvania; which money was vested by me in the purchase of warrants, two of which have been located to the amt. of one thousand acres with some warrants of my own on Lulbegrud,[2] as by an entry made in the name of Lawrence Thompson[3] for 2500 Acres which have been patented or conveyed to me appears; and the locations made upon the other warrants in my name cannot be found—And whereas H. Clay has purchased of the heir of the said Thomas Hare all the lands to which he the said Hare was entitled as afd.: In consideration of my receipt for the said Sum of £100 this day delivered up to me by the said H Clay I do hereby bind myself my heirs &c. to convey to the said Clay by deed with special warranty the said One thousand acres of land patented or conveyed to me as afd., to be divided according to quality & quantity; and also the other one thousand acres now lost, whenever the beginnings of the locations can be found, or whenever the said Clay shall require.

Witness my hand & Seal this 30h. September 1805.

Thomas Hart {L.S.}

DS, in Clay's hand. DLC-TJC (DNA, M212, R15). 1 Probably a Virginian.
2 Lulbegrud Creek rises in Montgomery County, Kentucky, and flows southwestward to form the boundary between Clark and Powell counties before joining the Red River.
3 Of Madison County, Kentucky.

To John Bradford and Thomas Whitney

[Between October 1 and 13, 1805]

Gentlemen, I have considered the questions proposed to Mr. Hughes Mr. Bibb and myself in your letter of the Eighteenth ultimo[1] upon an attentive examination of the acts of assembly in relation of the Subject, I am of opinion that the fee Simple to all of that part of the two acres of ground, reserved for the public buildings of the County, by the act of one thousand Seven hundred and eighty two, not Sold to the Presbyterian Congregation and upon which the market house is now built,[2] is in the County Court of Fayette and their Successors. By the act of one thousand Seven hundred and eighty two, it was vested in the Trustees of the town, and had no other act passed it would have remained in them, but by the act of December one thousand Seven hundred and ninety Six reducing into one the Several acts for establishing County Courts &c. it is provided that to every Court house already erected and established two acres of the land built upon and adjacent thereto, not having any house orchard or other immediate conveniences thereon, Shall be and remain appropriated to Such Court house; and the fee Simple thereof is hereby declared to be in the Court of the same County and their Successors." &c.[3] This latter act therefore repeals So much of that of one Thousand Seven hundred and eighty two as vested the fee Simple of the two acres in the Trustees of the town, and vests it under the exceptions contained in the act, in the County Court, and their Successors. The propriety of this construction of the two acts will be more evident, by indulging the Supposition, that no part of the public Square, had been sold to the Presbyterian congregation, or had been appropriated to the use of a market house, but had remained appropriated, as it was by the act of one thousand Seven hundred and eighty two, to the use of the bublic [*sic*] buildings of the County. In whom then by the act of one thousand Seven hundred and ninety Six would the fee Simple have been? In the County Court certainly. This construction then cannot be rendered improper by the sale to that Congregation, or the erection of the market house. Since these circumstances are provided for by the expressions contained in the act "not having any house" &c. This construction is not the less proper because the act of one thousand Seven hundred and ninety Six is a copy of the Virginia act of one thousand Seven hundred and forty eight, which was in force in Kentucky from the commencement of its government. For I consider the operations of the act of one thousand Seven hundred and ninety Six is precisely what it would have been, had it been the passage of a new, and not the re enaction of an old law—it applies to the circumstances of the Country a[s] existing in December one thousand Seven hundred and ninety Six, and not as existing in any interior [*sic*] period.

But Supposing I am mistaken in the foregoing opinion and the fee Simple is in the Trustees; I think the Security of the town in the enjoyment of their market house, would be equally provided for, in either of the two ways proposed by the Trustees and the County Court: That is; by making a Deed containing a condition that the town Shall not be molested in their market house; or by making an unconditional Deed, previously declareing upon the records of the Board of Trustees that it is ordered to be executed in consideration of the order of the County Court, providing for a renewal of the order giving the priviledge to erect the market house. It has been said that the permission to build a market house, originally given by the County Court, was illegal and a violation of their duty. Be it so, without undertaking now to decide the question of what avail will it be to withhold the title? If the County Court have a right to be vested with the fee Simple to the ground belonging to their Court house, would any Court of chancery, to whom they might apply to the Trustees to execute them a title, clog the deed with an illegal condition? I presume not. But even if the first order of the County Court was void, the acquiescence both by the County at large (for whose benefit was the two acres reserved) and the County Court itself, in that order by suffering the town without prohibition first to build a market house, and afterwards to add considerably to it, would prevent the town being disturbed. A Court of Chancery would never permit a man to be molested in his property, who purchased of a Trustee, and in the presence, and with the knowledge of the Trustee and the person for whom the trust was created has gone at great expence to improve the Subject, without the least opposition. I am Gent. Yr. ob. Servt.

John Bradford and Thomas Whitney Esqrs. HENRY CLAY.

Recorded Copy. Lexington Trustees Record Book, IB, 224-26. The document was written in response to an order of the Trustees, on September 17, 1805, "that John Bradford and Thomas Whitney be appointed a Committee to take the Opinion of James Hughes, Henry Clay & George M. Bibb esquires—whether the fee simple of the public square in the town of Lexington is in the Trustees of the town—and if it is so, & they convey that part on which the Market house stands to the county court, whether under the provision of the law establishing the town of Lexington the County Court can legally revest the Trustees so as to secure to the citizens the uninterupted use of the Market house, so long as they may choose to continue it on the ground it now stands, and whether a deed cannot be framed, as not to injure the right of the town to the Market house, and yet to satisfy the County Court." In view of Clay's statement, and a similar opinion by Hughes, the Trustees on November 4, 1805, decided to execute to the Justices of Fayette County a deed to the public ground.

1 Not found.

2 The western portion of the public square had been sold to the Presbyterians in 1790. In the same year the Trustees had decided that the public square was the proper location for the market house.

3 Hening (comp.), *Statutes of Virginia,* XI (May, 1782), 100; Littell (comp.), *Statute Law of Kentucky,* I, 375, (December 17, 1796).

Account with John Fisher, Jr.

Mr Henery Clay Dr To John Fisher Jnr [*ca.* October 28, 1805]

1804

February 4th To a ballance on account of office[1] when seteled £ 0„13„6

do	24	To building up sellor dore at 12/do . . .	12„0
	23	To 5 bushills of mortar for ditto at 1/pr bushill—	5„0
	20—	To 1 hand Cleaning out Sellor and diging out sellor dore and tending on the workman 2½ days at 4/ . .	10„0
		To paving your office Sellor flore which measures 44 yds at 1/ pr yd	2„ 4„0
		To Layin or tirning 1 trimer arch at 4/6d	4„6
		To Laying 1 harth and filld up the same at 3S/9d . .	3„9
			4„12„9
april 27		To 2 hands diging on your vault for nesesary 1 day Each at 4/ pr day	8„0
May 5		To 1 ditto do 2 days at 4/ shills pr day . .	8„0
do 12		To one ditto 3¼ days at do pr day	14„0
13		To 2 hands 1 day Each at do pr do	8 0
15		To 1 mayson 1½ day—taring down and Cleaning the bricks in a old nesesary at 6/ pr day	9„0
June 20		To Laying 7„602 bricks in nesesary at 19s/pr do	7„ 4„6
		Lime and tendane found in with the above	14— 4„3
do 21		To paving 53 yds of pavement before your yallow hous[2] at 1/ Shilling pr yard .	2„13„0
		To 1 hand 1 day wheeling on dirt at the above pavmnt	4„0
		To paving front of office 24½ yds of pavemnt at 1/—	1„ 4„6
		To Seting Stones around the two above pavement—	0„ 9„0
		To 3 posts found and Set int before office at 3/ Each	9„0
		To walling around 3 windows and found atendance and meterials	0„ 6„9
			19„10„6
1805			
June 17		To finding 23„050 bricks and Laid them on your Cantray hous[3] and found all acomadations at 45/ pr thus	51„17„0
		To 9 Singel arches at 3s/ pr arch	1„ 7„0
		To paving 12 yds of pavement in harth at 1/ Shillings Cuntry hous	0„12, 0

	To underpining harth at 4s/6d	0" 4"6
	To 3 bushells of Lime for the above harth at 9d pr do	0" 2"3
	To turning 1 trimer arch above and Laid harth at 7/6 ..	0" 7"6
October 5	To 1 hand tending 2 days at filling harth at 4/6 ..	9"0
	To building up yard wall at home at 4/6	4"6
	To Laying 2 yds of pavement at 2/ pr do [*sic*]	2"0
	To 2 bushills morter at 1/ pr do 1 hand hallf day at 4/6 pr day	4"3
	amt Caried over	75" 0"6
Amount brought over	....	£75" 0"6
October 28	To histing and Setting fier wall Stones and Extray on fier walls at the Rate 24/ Extra	1"16—
	To Laying 100"050 bricks in your town hous[4] and found them and all acomodations at the Rate of 45/Shillings pr thous	£225" 0"0
	To 5"100 Stock bricks at 24/ pr do Extray	6" 2"5
	To 7 doubel arches at 6/ Each	2" 2"0
	To 3 singel ditto at 3/ Each	9"0
		£310" 9"11

D. KyLxT.
[1] See above, Agreement, August 18, 1803. [2] On the western side of Mill Street.
[3] "Ashland." [4] See above, Contract, January 22, 1805.

Promissory Note from John Craig and John Bush

[October 28, 1805]

Twelve months after date we John Craig & John Bush of Boone County promise to pay to Henry Clay for value received Two hundred & fifty dollars. Witness our hands & seals this 28th day of October 1805.

Teste

ZENAS HILL — JOHN CRAIG {L.S.}
JOHN HUSER[1] — JOHN BUSH {L.S.}

DS, in Clay's hand. Franklin Circuit Court, File 73 (1808). Bush, a justice of the first county court of Campbell County, resided in the area from which Boone County was formed in 1798.

[1] Both witnesses probably residents of Boone County. Huser paid taxes in Campbell in 1800.

Bond from John Hardwick

[October 29, 1805]

Know all men by these presents that I John Hardwick am held

and firmly bound to H. Clay in the just and full sum of eighteen hundred Dollars to be paid to the said Clay his heirs Executors, administrators or assigns, to which payment well and truly to be made I bind myself my heirs Exors and admrs firmly by these presents, sealed with my seal and dated this 29th. day of October 1805.—The Condition of this obligation is such that if the said John Hardwick shall pay to the said Clay four hundred and twelve dollars and fifty cents on or before six months from the date hereof, and shall deliver to the said Clay mares or Geldings not under four years nor over eight years old, nor under fifty dollars value at George Webbs[1] tavern in Winchester on or before the first day of September next to the value of four hundred and twelve dollars and fifty cents, then this obligation to be void otherwise to remain in full force and virtue J. HARDWICK {SEAL}

Seald and delivered in the presence of
H. TAYLOR[2]

True copy. Clark Circuit Court, File 65. In a suit against Hardwick, Sheriff of Montgomery County, Clay at the April Term, 1807, of Clark Circuit Court won a judgment for $866.15. *Ibid.; ibid.*, Order Book B, 173.

1 Webb later represented Clark County in the State legislature.

2 Hubbard Taylor.

From James Brown

My dear Sir, New Orleans Octr. 31. 1805

I received your very agreeable letter[1] two posts ago, and should have answered it immediately had not the bustle of returning to Town, the trouble of re-establishing myself, and the pressure of business postponed during my stay in the Country, prevented me from performing my intentions. My letters from my retreat on the Coast must have from time to time assured my friends of the health and happiness which were enjoyed by my fellow adventurer and myself during the summer months. On our return we found our friends healthy, and happy to see us, and hope, if exempted from accidental and violent death to remain safe until the next Season. In fact my opinion is that the Island of Orleans is as healthy as the County of Fayette and more favorable to longevity. You are too young as yet to feel any inducements to establish yourself here founded on the latter considerations, and I am happy to hear that your own health and that of your family has greatly improved during the last year On all hands it seems agreed by such of your countrymen as visit us that you are at the head of your profession, and are rapidly growing rich—Indeed some accounts assure us that you are acquiring money "as fast as you can count it." All that I infer from this is that you are *doing extremely well* for I have long been sensible that the public rumors respecting the growing purses of Lawyers were, like most other reports, subject to great exaggeration

Mr. Leavy requested me to collect for Bickham & Reese an account amounting to about £400 Pena. Currency. Mr. Caldwell in part payment assigned an Execution against French & Stone & perhaps Evans, then injoined, but which was paid to me and delivered up to the parties[2]—The amount might be 200-300-or 400 Dollars. I paid it to Leavy before my leaving that Country as will appear by his books, by his receipt among my papers or by my check book at Bank—Upon the account I ordered suit agt. Caldwell before leaving Kentucky, at the Office of Tunstall[3] as you may see by my memorandum—and Caldwell always told me that his defence would be that he had left at the War Office for Bickham & Relse [*sic*] certain militia charges muster rolls and accounts which they had neither collected nor returned and for which he thought he ought to be credited—Mr. Leavy can explain every word of this affair to your satisfaction as at present I speak only from memory.

Smith's[4] account struck you and I do not wonder at it—However he is *my relation* & as it the [*sic*] last of the kind which he can present it shall be settled—But why impress it into the affair of Shoemaker?[5] He must pay that debt—it is upon an execution—Mr Jordan's[6] statement on his own account is correct but I have a long account which relates to the estate of my poor friend Seitz[7] which I expected to settle here which I hope Jordan will adjust. I shall send it and Mr Jordans due Bill for $160 which was given me on account of money lent by me to Mr Seitz & which I pray you to adjust—Mr Tho Hughes[8] is an *honest man* and although I do not remember to have been indebted yet I pray you to pay him out of any of my monies in the Country—My answer in Doran's case with Kenton[9] was long before leaving Kentucky sent to Adam Beatty who acknowledged the receipt and promised attention to it—

I wish my friend that I possessed some means of returning to yourself and Doctr. Brown[10] most [*sic*] substantial expressions of my gratitude for your attentions to my interests than can flow from the point of a goose quill, and I pray you to aid me in discovering the way to return the favor. Somewhat loose in the arrangement of my affairs you must have had some trouble, but I hope some period of prescription is approaching when the the [*sic*] "wicked shall cease to trouble, and the greedy be at rest." If every man in Kentucky would pay me as honestly as I have discharged my debts in that State, I should yet possess in that Country a fortune to which I could retire from labor to ease.

Present my most sincere and affectionate regards to your Lucretia & believe me unchangeably Your friend

Henry Clay Esqr. JAMES BROWN

ALS. DLC-HC (DNA, M212, R1). Published in Padgett, "Letters of James Brown to Henry Clay," *La. Hist. Quar.*, XXIV (1941), 925-27. 1 Not found.

2 See above, Brown to Clay, April 30, 1804. James French, Valentine Stone, and Peter Evans, whose business partnership had been dissolved in 1799, had agreed to pay equally in settlement of various debts to Caldwell. Madison Circuit Court, Box 10 (Bundle 19); Box 14 (Bundle 27); Fayette Circuit Court, File 44-46 (1803). French and Evans were residents of Madison County; Stone, of Montgomery.

3 Thomas Tunstall. 4 John Smith, a first cousin of Brown.

5 Edward Shoemaker, a Philadelphia merchant.

6 John Jordan, Jr. 7 John A. Seitz.

8 State Senator from Bourbon County in the preceding session of the legislature.

9 Patrick Doran and Simon Kenton. 10 Dr. Samuel Brown.

From James Smith, Jr.

Esteemed Friend [*ca.* November 2, 1805]

I received your favour of 20h Octr.[1] this evening & on opening the same I was very much disappointed in not finding inclosed the amount of Millers[2] Note—but you have explained the reason & I must bear the disappointment—but the reason of my writing now is to beg that you will send it forward as soon as you possibly can, and also Owens,[3] should he be returned—I expect I feel the disappointment more, because, having so many & such large sums out & being on all hands disappointed I cannot get sufficient money to meet the engagements that must be met here with rigid punctuality —& cannot this season, as yet remit a shilling—I therefore feel extremely uneasy about it, but am not without a hope that the amount of Millers Note will come in the course of this month, the last of which & beginning of next all the Vessels will be going—His Note I think was due 15 Sepr. & 45 days will bring it to 1t of this month—I therefore may & shall look for it by the 20 or 25h Jan—You have not mentioned the Ballance of Jordans[4] Debt

I have enquired of several persons with respect to W Wren,[5] & was told by a Mr. Piatt,[6] who lives near Cincinnati & who was here at the same time he bought his Goods, that he believes he has property sufficient to pay his Debts if he does not take measures to secrete it—I hope your exertions will be availing in securing it at least & I approve of your method of giving time—it often has a better effect than harsher methods—I beg you not to loose sight of this Debt—

I note what you say about the land & am pleased to hear you have a prospect of getting the man who can ascertain the lines—I think you have possession of the Deed made by Norvell[7] to me—He assured me the Title to the Land was unquestionable—of this you must be the best Judge & I beg you will take as much pains to ascertain & establish the same as if the land was your own—As you know it will be valuable & will be the only thing I shall ever get for so large a Debt—Inclosed you have W Wrens Note, and on the other side an

Accot of what he owes me besides,[8] which if disputed I can send you Accot qualified to—I think he must have property sufficient to pay with unless he has foolishly dissipated it—I cannot help again requesting that every thing be done that can possibly be done to get Wrens debt & am Very respectfully Yr Friend JAS SMITH JR

ALS. DLC-HC (DNA, M212, R6). Addressed to Clay at Lexington.
1 Not found.
2 Robert Miller, Lexington merchant and owner of an inn at Richmond, Kentucky.
3 Thomas Deye Owings, who was returning from Baltimore. 4 John Jordan, Jr.
5 Woodson Wren, Lexington merchant, who closed his store early in 1806 and subsequently moved to Louisiana.
6 Probably John H. Piatt, pioneer Cincinnati manufacturer, merchant, and banker.
7 Thomas Norvell.
8 D. DLC-HC (DNA, M212, R6). The note amounted to $809.01, and the account, $44.21.1, with unspecified interest charges on each.

Property Deed from John Walker Baylor

[November 4, 1805]

[Indenture by which John W. Baylor, through his attorney, Mark C. Woodford,[1] for $900, paid and secured to be paid as hereby acknowledged, transfers to Henry Clay three lots in Lexington adjoining in the whole extent the southeastern boundary of the lot of Dr. F. Ridgely, fronting Upper Street on the southeast and fronting Second Street on the northeast, lying in the corner produced by the intersection of said streets, the lots having been conveyed to John W. Baylor by Walker Baylor. General warranty of title. Signed by Mark C. Woodford in the presence of James Bliss, Deputy Clerk, and recorded by Thomas Bodley, Clerk of Fayette Circuit Court, November 4, 1805.]

Fayette Circuit Court, Deed Book B, 529. Baylor, of Albemarle County, Virginia, was the son of George Baylor of Caroline County, Virginia, and nephew of Walker Baylor. John's wife, Ann Digges Fitzhugh Baylor, in 1807 relinquished her dower rights to this property. *Ibid.*, C, 26-27.
1 Mark Catesby Woodford, also of a prominent family in Caroline County, Virginia.

Resolution Relating to Committee of Finance

[November 5, 1805]

Resolved, That a committee of finance be appointed to consist of seven members to whom shall be referred matters in relation to the revenue & who may from time to time suggest any new subject of taxation or defects existing in the revenue laws for the consideration of the house, & that the said committee shall possess the powers necessary to accomplish the foregoing objects.

Ky. H. of Reps., *Journal, 1805,* p. 10. Such a committee had not been customarily authorized in the Kentucky House of Representatives. The measure was adopted, and Clay was appointed chairman of the committee; its work, however, was routine.

Motion for Relief of Securities

[November 15, 1805]

Clay asked leave to bring in a bill for the relief of securities in certain cases. Ky. H. of Reps., *Journal, 1805,* pp. 36-37. The bill, to have been prepared by a committee under Clay's chairmanship, seems not to have been presented.

Report on Petition of Charles Dibrell

[November 18, 1805]

The committee of finance have according to order had under consideration the petition of Charles Dibrell, late sheriff of Wayne, praying to obtain a credit of twenty dollars twenty-five cents, for certain delinquents occurring in the collection of the revenue of 1803, for reasons therein assigned, and beg leave to report the following statement and resolution.

It appears to your committee that from the height of the water in Cumberland river the petitioner was prevented from passing it for some days before the first day of January last; that he sat out a few days after the first day of January, and owing to the height of Dick's river was detained there some time, that he came by Lexington for the purpose of redeeming some land sold for the direct tax, that having dispatched his business there, he reached Frankfort on the 12th of January, that by law the said petitioner was allowed the term of three months for returning his list of delinquents commencing the first day of October: and consequently that the said list having been presented not until the 14th January for adjustment was 14 days too late.

Your committee notwithstanding some degree of hardship attends the case of Mr. Debrell, are of opinion that the credit ought not to be allowed, that in such cases the individual hardship ought to yield to general good—that an ample time, during which the waters were confessedly low, was afforded the petitioner to return his list, that had he settled within a reasonable time from the first of October, the period fixed by law, the particular inconvenience would not have been felt, that too great lenity to public delinquents is injurious to the treasury and often to the delinquents themselves by inspiring false hopes, and that to legislate upon every particular case is expensive troublesome and involves a necessity to discriminate between nice shades of difference not often felt or easily perceived.

Wherefore, resolved that the said petition, be rejected.

Ky. H. of Reps., *Journal, 1805,* pp. 38-39. Other members of the committee were Matthew Flournoy, Martin D. Hardin (Madison County), Joseph Welch (Lincoln), Felix Grundy, John Allen (Franklin), and Christopher Tompkins (Muhlenberg). The report was concurred in by the House. Dibrell appears variously, as Dibrill, Debril, Debrell.

Promissory Note from George Adams

[November 21, 1805]

For value received I promise to pay Henry Clay on demand fifty dollars. Witness my hand & Seal this 21 Nov. 1805.

GEORGE ADAMS {L.S.}

DS, in Clay's hand. Fayette Circuit Court, File 120 (1807). Earlier in the year Clay had won a suit in the name of Arthur T. Taul to collect a debt for approximately this sum from Adams, probably either the tavern keeper or the hatter of that name in Lexington. *Ibid.,* File 96 (1805). In 1807 Clay brought and won an action in his own name against Adams for collection of this note. *Ibid.,* Order Book D, 462.

Bill Relating to Examining Trials

[November 21, 1805]

Clay reported the bill for a drafting committee which also included William E. Boswell (Harrison County), Martin D. Hardin, William Russell, and George Walker. Ky. H. of Reps., *Journal, 1805,* p. 46. On November 4, Clay had asked leave to present such a measure. It was now read twice and directed to the committee of the whole, after which no further action is reported. Legislation for this purpose was enacted in 1809 with Clay's support but not as his bill. It provided that in a criminal case for which the punishment would be capital, corporal, or confinement in the penitentiary, the preliminary hearing should be held before two justices of the peace, who might then remand the accused to trial at the next session of the circuit court, meanwhile releasing him on bail if the offense were bailable. Previous legislation had required special meeting of the justices of the county courts to sit at such hearings, with the accused imprisoned from five to ten days pending examination. Littell (comp.), *Statute Law of Kentucky,* III, 41-42 (December 20, 1802); IV, 67-68 (February 11, 1809).

Bill for the Benefit of Samuel Beeler

[November 22, 1805]

Clay presented the bill for a drafting committee which included also Gwyn R. Tompkins and William Russell, the other Fayette County representatives. Ky. H. of Reps., *Journal, 1805,* p. 49. Clay had asked leave to present the measure on November 5. On December 19, he moved to withdraw it from committee of the whole for further consideration by a special committee, and that same day he again reported the bill, with several unrecorded amendments. The latter were accepted, but the bill was then rejected. Two years later the Fayette County representatives submitted another bill for the benefit of Beeler, which was again defeated. Ky. H. of Reps., *Journal, 1807-1808,* p. 82. Beeler (Bealer, Bealle) lived on Cane Run, four miles from Lexington.

Resolution Relative to Payment for Green River Lands

[November 22, 1805]

Resolved, By the senate and house of representatives that provision ought to be made by law for coercing the payment of so much of the principal and interest of the debt owing by settlers south of Green river as has become due.

Ky. H. of Reps., *Journal, 1805*, p. 51. On Clay's motion the resolution was brought before the House on November 23, whereupon it was adopted after amendment to remove the specific reference to Green River settlers. Clay then requested and was given permission to offer a "bill to coerce payment of so much of the debt owing to the commonwealth for the sale of her lands, as has become due." The timing of these maneuvers is significant. The resolution, introduced the day after the House had passed a bill repealing the banking privileges of the Kentucky Insurance Company, was adopted and carried to the Senate in the midst of that body's debate on the latter measure. Inasmuch as the chief opponents of the Insurance Company represented districts most affected by tightening the administration of State land sales, the menace in Clay's action was obvious. The Senate initially passed the bill hostile to the Insurance Company despite Clay's dramatic reading of the land-payment resolution immediately before the vote. The Senate also rejected the resolution on coercing payment for the lands; cf. below, Bill and Resolution, November 26, 1805.

Bill and Resolution on Coercing Payment for State Lands

[November 26, 1805]

Resolved, That such members of this house as are owing instalments which become due for lands purchased of the commonwealth, have not a right to vote upon the bill under consideration.

Ky. H. of Reps., *Journal, 1805,* p. 59. Clay proposed the resolution as a previous question to the second reading of a bill which he had just reported for coercing payment of the debt due the State for its lands. On his authorship of the resolution see Frankfort *Argus of Western America,* September 16, 1829. The proposal was rejected, whereupon Clay moved for a recorded vote upon the question of a second reading of the bill. The latter measure, prepared by a drafting committee which also included John Allen, William B. Blackburn, William E. Boswell, Martin D. Hardin, and Richard M. Johnson (Scott County), received overwhelming support in the test vote on December 18. Final passage was delayed, however, until after Senate defeat of the effort to override the governor's veto of the legislation repealing the banking privilege of the Kentucky Insurance Company. The governor's action was upheld on December 22, whereupon Clay himself then (below, December 23, 1805) proposed amendment of the land-payment bill in a manner emasculating its punitive nature. That the continuing threat of the latter measure may have influenced the final vote relative to the Insurance Company seems indicated by the altered stand of Senators from the affected region. See Ky. Sen., *Journal, 1805,* pp. 40, 112; also Lexington *Kentucky Gazette,* December 12, 1805.

Bill Confirming Circuit Court Proceedings

[November 27, 1805]

Clay reported the bill for a drafting committee which included also John Allen (Franklin County), Fortunatus Cosby (Jefferson), Felix Grundy, and Samuel South. Ky. H. of Reps., *Journal, 1805,* p. 61. On November 9, Clay had obtained permission to offer such a measure, and it was enacted without controversy on December 26. Its purpose was to confirm proceedings conducted by judges who, for want of a meeting of the General Court the preceding May, had operated without a specific allotment among the several circuits—and to provide for continued proceedings according to the last preceding allotment in the event of a similar situation in the future. Littell (comp.), *Statute Law of Kentucky,* III, 318.

Bill Authorizing Land Sale by the Lexington Presbyterian Congregation

[November 27, 1805]

Earlier this day Clay had asked leave to present the bill. It was now reported from a drafting committee which included also Gwyn R. Tompkins and William Russell. Ky. H. of Reps., *Journal, 1805,* p. 62. The bill was enacted, without controversy, on December 16. It permitted the trustees of the Lexington Presbyterian Congregation to sell the tract of land on which their meeting house had been located and to purchase another site. Littell (comp.), *Statute Law of Kentucky,* III, 251. Need for such legislation stemmed from the fact that the original site had been acquired as a purchase from a tract of land reserved for public use, this portion having been specifically designated for church purposes. Hening (comp.), *Statutes of Virginia,* XIII, 85.

Amendments to Bill Relating to Lands of Joseph Vance and Others

[December 7, 1805]

Clay's role in connection with this measure had begun on December 2, when he moved that the House take up the bill then already engrossed. Earlier on December 7 he had asked that the bill be recommitted to a select committee (Clay, William Russell, and William B. Blackburn), for whom he now reported several amendments, not recorded. Ky. H. of Reps., *Journal, 1805,* p. 91. The latter were accepted, and the measure was enacted December 20. David Vance, Jr., and John Vance were natives of Ireland and pioneer settlers of Fayette County, Kentucky, where they had acquired large land interests. Both died intestate, with the next of kin still resident in Ireland. The petitioners, of whom two were brothers of David and John and a third was John's son, had emigrated to America in 1787, settled on the land and regularly paid the taxes, and had finally become naturalized at the Kentucky General Court of 1805. Special legislation was necessary, however, to quiet the State's claim to escheat. Ky. Gen. Assy., *Acts, 1805,* pp. 68-69. Joseph Vance, the named heir of the *Journal* record, was a member of the Lexington Light Infantry Company in the War of 1812, and later operated a tailor shop in Lexington for many years.

Bill Relating to Fayette County Court House

[December 10, 1805]

Clay reported the measure for a drafting committee which included also Gwyn R. Tompkins and William Russell, appointed this same day. Ky. H. of Reps., *Journal, 1805,* p. 97. The bill authorized the Fayette county and circuit courts to meet in any house in Lexington during the interval between the tearing down of the old court house and the erection of a new one on the same site. Amended to provide for purchase or rental of land for a stray-pen, the measure was enacted December 23. Littell (comp.), *Statute Law of Kentucky,* III, 287.

From Francis Brooke

My Dear Sir Decemr 12, 1805

I have an offer to Exchange my Lands in your State for City property at the valuation price of such Lands in Kentuckey it will be a month before it will be necessary for me to Decide on this offer—to enable me to do so I must beg the favour of you to enquire and inform me as soon as you can what the valuation price will probably be—Genl Posey[1] could give you the information in all probability—be so good as Discriminate Between a a [*sic*] Cash valuation and one on the ordinary Terms of Sale in the Country your attention to this business will add to the many obligations Conferred[2] your friend Truly F BROOKE

ALS. DLC-HC (DNA, M212, R1). Postmarked at Fredericksburg, Virginia; addressed to Clay "now at Frankfort Kentuckey—" [1] Thomas Posey.

[2] No reply from Clay has been found. Brooke did not sell the land at this time.

Report of Committee on Finance

[December 12, 1805]

The committee of finance have according to order had under consideration the several petitions to them referred and come to the following resolutions thereupon, viz.

1st, *Resolved,* That the petition of John Bearden, setting forth that he, as collector of Livingston county, had been prevented from returning a list of delinquents within the time prescribed by law and praying that the auditor may be authorised to admit and receive the same, be rejected.

2d, *Resolved,* That the petition of Joseph Charless,[1] praying that he may be exonerated from paying a tax on his book-store, and that the tax which he has already paid may be refunded to him, be rejected.

Ky. H. of Reps., *Journal, 1805,* p. 104. For other members of the committee, see above, Report, November 18, 1805. The report here presented was concurred in.

[1] A refugee from the political riots of 1795 in Ireland, Charless had removed from Philadelphia to Lexington, where he had opened a printing office and book store in 1803. He had become one of the partners in publication of a newspaper, *The Independent Gazetteer,* but had relinquished his interest within a few months. He was the publisher of Lexington's first printed city directory (1806). In May, 1806, the Fayette County Court relieved him of his taxes for the year 1805 on his book store, as "not coming under mercantile store." Fayette County Court, Order Book no. 1 (May 12, 1806), p. 379. Shortly thereafter, he moved to Louisville, and in 1808 to St. Louis, where he established the *Missouri Gazette.*

Report on Establishing a State Bank

[December 17, 1805]

For a select committee of fifteen members appointed to consider the bill as originated in the Senate, Clay reported the measure without amendment. Ky. H. of Reps., *Journal, 1805,* p. 119. In Committee of the Whole the report was amended and endorsed. After numerous efforts to delay further action until the next meeting of the legislature, the bill was finally rejected in the House. The fate of the measure was intimately related to the action on the banking privileges of the Kentucky Insurance Company, the Senate having proposed to designate the latter institution as Lexington branch of the proposed state bank. Clay opposed the proposal under such condition. A State bank, the Bank of Kentucky, was established the following year, without specific reference to the Insurance Company and after Clay had gone to the United States Senate.

Resolution and Motion on Coercing Payment for State Lands

[December 23, 1805]

Resolved, That the legislature, without the intervention of the judiciary, does possess the power to coerce payment of the debt due to the commonwealth for the sale of her lands before the expiration of the period of the last instalment, by selling the land, or otherwise.

Ky. H. of Reps., *Journal, 1805,* p. 148. Clay offered the resolution as a previous question to the vote upon the bill for coercing payment on the lands. When the resolution was passed in the affirmative, he then moved to strike out the sixth, seventh, and eighth sections of the bill, thus removing most of its punitive sting. After further amendment the measure was enacted on December 26. In final form it merely required that a statement be prepared showing the money due to the Commonwealth for sale of its lands, barred further entry on certain lands pending future action of the legislature, and terminated issuance of land certificates by the county courts. Littell (comp.), *Statute Law of Kentucky,* III, 306-308. For the significance of the original bill and of this emasculative amendment, see above, Resolution, November 22, 1805; Bill and Resolution, November 26, 1805.

To John Breckinridge

Dr Sir Lexington 5h. January 1806

Your suits in the General Court were continued as you desired, under the positive stipulation however that trials should take place at the next term. In the Fœderal Court we did no business. Can you not lend a hand in getting this Court new-modified so as to inspire a greater degree of confidence, and divide the enormous power now exercised by a single individual?[1] The honesty and many good qualities of Judge Innes are unquestionable. But the duties assigned him are too vast for one man, altho' he possessed the head of Holt or Mansfield.[2]

Our Legislature adjourned not until the day after Christmas. Much business was attempted and but little really executed. Among other measures proposed was the passage of a limitation act in Land suits.[3] This bill received the approbation of the Senate, & would I believe have been concurred in by the lower house, if it had not been postponed to so late a period in the Session as to prevent its being acted upon. The attempt to Repeal the Lexington Bank[4] is no doubt made known to you through our papers. The measure finally failed in the Senate. The State has appropriated $50000 to aid in the cutting of the Canal.[5]

By the last mail I forwarded to Mr. Thruston[6] the recommendation by Gov. Claiborne,[7] and a number of the Citizens of this place, of my brother John for the office of Navy agent at New Orleans. Will you permit me to trespass upon you so far as to request your aid in promoting my brother's wishes? I am much indebted to you for your friendship upon this subject already, but I hope you will increase the obligation a little further, and perhaps upon some future occasion I may have it in my power to lessen or discharge it. If Morrison[8] should be in Washington, as he is well acquainted with the Secretary of the Navy, his recommendation would be of considerable advantage, & I have no doubt he will chearfully give it if you will do me the favour to speak to him

We are anxious to know if a War will take place. Such an event is peculiarly interesting to this Country. I believe it would not be unpopular. Perhaps this is a fortunate moment to repress European Aggression; and to evince to the world that Americans appreciate their rights in such a way as will induce them, when violated, to engage in War with alacrity and effect.

I believe your family is well. Mr. Grayson[9] was with me this morning. Yr's Sincerely HENRY CLAY

ALS. DLC-Breckinridge Family Papers (DNA, M212, R20). Addressed to Breckinridge at Washington, where he was now Attorney General of the United States.

1 See above, Resolution, December 17, 1804; below, Resolution, January 2, 1807.

2 Sir John Holt (1642-1710) and William Murray, first Earl of Mansfield (1705-1793), Chief Justices of the King's Bench.

3 Cf. below, Clay to Crawford, May 10, 1814, note.

4 The banking priviliges of the Kentucky Insurance Company.

5 Under authority of an act approved December 20, 1805, the State subscribed for 1,000 shares in the Ohio Canal Company.

6 Senator Buckner Thruston.

7 Claiborne to Robert Smith, Secretary of the Navy, November 14, 1805. Rowland (ed.), *Official Letter Books of W. C. C. Claiborne*, III, 233.

8 James Morrison. Cf. below, Morrison to Clay, March 20, 1806.

9 Alfred Grayson, Breckinridge's son-in-law.

From Allan B. Magruder

dear Sir, Natchez, 7h. January 1806—

We arrived here yesterday, after a most disagreable Voyage of more than two months from Louisville—I am glad, however, to Inform you, that from what I can learn, the Board of Commissioners in the Opelousas, has not wanted my attendance, as yet, as agent to the Board, on the part of the U. States—The Commssioners [*sic*] have been Engaged for some time past, in receiving & submiting to Record, the various claims of Individuals.—As soon as I can acquire any information, with respect to the nature & situation of the Country of Lower Louisiana, & of the titles of Lands there, I shall, with great pleasure, make my communications to you.—I shall make out, from personal observation, a particular discription of the Opelousas & Atacapas Countries, two of the finest districts of Lower Louisiana, & send it on, to be published in Kentucky, in numbers. A Copy, I beg leave, to send to you, in manuscript; as I intend to do, to several other persons in different parts of the United States, whose good opinion I am anxious to preserve.—The Opelousas & Atacapas Countries compose a point, to which the current of Emigration is directed, from different parts of the Union; & I shou'd be happy to give my fellow Citizens of Kentucky, an Equal chance of changing their positions, upon advantageous grounds.—

I remain, dear Clay, with the most perfect Esteem, yr. friend & humle. Sert ALLAN B. MAGRUDER—

ALS. DLC-HC (DNA, M212, R1). Addressed to Clay at Lexington; postmarked at Natchez on January 10. Magruder, a Lexington lawyer, was author of *Political, Commercial and Moral Reflections, on the late Cession of Louisiana, to the United States* (Lexington, 1803). In 1805 he had been appointed United States agent for investigating land claims in the Western District of Orleans, with instructions particularly to examine claims to two large tracts on the Washita River originally granted to Baron Bastrop and the Marquis Grand Maison. Clarence E. Carter (ed.), *The Territorial Papers of the United States* (23 vols. to date; Washington, 1934-), IX, *The Territory of Orleans,* 1803-1812 (Washington, 1940), 468-69.

Assignment by James Owens

14 Jan. 1806.

Without recourse to me I assign the within Judgment to H Clay value recd.

Teste JAMES OWENS

JAMES M HAWKINS[1]

ES, in Clay's hand. DLC-TJC (DNA, M212, R15). The judgment. rendered in 1801 by the Fayette County Court of Quarter Sessions, resulted from a suit by Owens against John Clay in which the defendant through his attorney confessed debt of £118 and costs. Owens was a resident of Woodford County, Kentucky.

Another endorsement, AES by Abraham S. Barton, dated at New Orleans, May 18, 1806, acknowledges payment by John Clay of $360, "the consideration paid by Henry Clay for the within judgement." The question of interest was to be settled between the Clay brothers. Barton was a Lexington merchant, at this time clerk of the Kentucky Insurance Company, later a director of the Lexington branch of the Bank of the United States.

1 Also of Woodford County.

Acknowledgment of Debt by James Coleman, Jr.

31 Jan. 1806.

I owe H. Clay Seven pounds as a part of his fee in the suit Cleveland against me,[1] JAMES COLEMAN JUNR

D. DLC-TJC, 2d Series, vol. 5. Coleman was a resident of Loudoun County, Virginia.

1 The suit brought by George Cleveland, of Bourbon County, Kentucky, had been filed as a chancery action in Bourbon Circuit Court in May, 1805, upon complaint that Coleman had obtained a fraudulent conveyance of Cleveland's two-thirds interest in 1000 acres on Green Creek in Bourbon County, the remaining third having already passed to Coleman as the husband of Hannah Cleveland, George's sister. At the August Term, 1807, the court ruled that the lands should be reconveyed to Cleveland and that he be paid a specified sum as his proportionate return on a portion of the tract already sold. Cleveland appealed against the sum awarded, but the decision appears to have been upheld. Bourbon Circuit Court, File 190.

Tax Bill and County Levy

[*ca.* February 1, 1806]

1805	Henry Clay Esqr.	Dr.	Cents
	To Tax on 125 acres 1st. rate land @ 50 Cnts		62½

" " 4400 acrs. 2d. Ditto @ 34 .... 14.96
" " 2000 acrs. 3d. Ditto @ 12½ 2.50
$1000 value of Town Lotts @ 50 pr.
£100. 1.50
6 Slaves @ 12½ 8 Horses @ 4 ... 1.07
County Levy on 5 Tithes @ 6/- . 5 00
$25:65½

JOHN H. MORTON D.S.
for
Charles Carr Shff

DS. DLC-TJC (DNA, M212, R15).

From Richard R. Smith

Dear Sir Philada. Febry. 8th. 1806.

Your Favour of 8th. ulto[1] reached me safely and I thank you for your exertions in Mr. Seitz's[2] affairs. I am perfectly satisfied with what you have done, and you may draw on me for your charge, or can deduct it out of the Money when received from Mr. Jordan[3] —With much Esteem Your hble Servt. RICHD. R SMITH

Henry Clay Esqr.—

LS. DLC-TJC (DNA, M212, R12). Smith, a Philadelphia merchant, was associated with James Smith, Jr.

1 Not found. 2 John A. Seitz. 3 John Jordan, Jr.

To [Edward Shoemaker]

Sir Lexington 15h. Feb. 1806.

Your favour of the 9h. Jan. reached me a few days ago.[1] I equally regret with you the delay which has arisen in the receipt of the money to which you are entitled. I have heard from Mr. Brown,[2] who directs me to press the execution against Mr. Smith[3] who was to pay £100 on your account, but who claimed an offset against Mr. B. This I shall immediately cause to be done. By the time the money is received I expect to have the command of some funds of Mr. B. out of which the balance shall be discharged.

You may rely Sir that as far as any exertion of mine can contribute towards a speedy receipt of this money, out of which you have been so long kept by an unfortunate train of circumstances, it shall not be spared. And as soon as I receive it I will hasten to remit it to you. Yr. ob. Servt. HENRY CLAY

ALS. NcD. 1 Not found.

2 James Brown; letter dated October 31, 1805. 3 John Smith.

Assignment from Dr. John Barry, Jr.

[*ca.* February 15, 1806]

I assign the within to Henry Clay for value received.

Teste J. BARRY[1]

STERLING ALLEN.[2]

ES, in Clay's hand. Fayette Circuit Court, File 119 (1807). On verso of a promissory note, dated February 15, 1806, by which John Jordan, Jr., engages to pay $1000 one year later to Dr. Barry, a resident of Lexington, formerly of Paris, Kentucky. A few months later Barry, in partnership with William Garrett of Lexington, opened a mercantile business which operated only until the latter part of 1808. To collect the note here assigned, Clay brought suit against Jordan under a bill of complaint dated May 15, 1807 (ADS. *Ibid.*). Jordan acknowledged the debt at the June Term following. Fayette Circuit Court, Order Book D, 254.

1 The abbreviation "Jr." was appended to, then deleted from, the signature in the manuscript.

2 Resident of Lexington, later partner in a mercantile firm there.

Survey by Zachariah Eastin

[February 19, 1806]

[Eastin, Surveyor of Bourbon County, Kentucky, surveyed for Clay three adjoining tracts of land,[1] part of a survey of 500 acres on the Licking River, originally made for Lawrence Thompson. One tract, occupied by Thomas Current, contained 377½ acres; the second, by Charles Yelton, 65¼ acres; and the third, by William Rout, 18 acres.]

ADS, by Eastin. DLC-TJC (DNA, M212, R15).

1 This land was involved in litigation stemming from a chancery action brought in 1801 by Col. Thomas Hart against John Coburn in the Bourbon District Court (Kentucky) for recovery of lands claimed under warrants originally brought to Kentucky by Nathaniel Hart. The case had been carried to the Court of Appeals, where it was decided in Hart's favor during the Fall Term of 1805. 3 *Ky. Reports* (Hardin) 41-44.

From Francis Brooke

Dear Sir February 22d, 1806

Mr Saunders a Gentleman of the Bar who resides at Williamsburg requests to know the names of some fit persons in your State to be commissioners for taking testimony in your Behalf in the Suit against Lewis Executors[1]—you can either give him the information by Letter to him at Williamsburg or through me as may be most agreeable to yourself—I wrote you some weeks past and under the impression my Letter would find you at Frankfort addressed to you at that place—where I presume it did not find you the object chiefly was to get some more precise information of the Value of my Lands in your State as I was then on Treaty for them at Valuation—and concluded that through Genl Posey who has seen one of the Tracts and has received very Late information respecting the other from a gentleman who has been upon it, and around it, you would get more accurate knowledge of them than heretofore—it still is a very Desirable thing to me to obtain this information as I have frequent offers made for them and might possibly for want of it, sacrifice them—will you do me the favour to Communicate with the Genl and give his and your idea of the value as soon as you can—

Yours Truly F BROOKE

ALS. DLC-HC (DNA, M212, R1). Addressed to Clay at Lexington; postmarked at Fredericksburg, Virginia, February 25. See above, Brooke to Clay, December 12, 1804.

1 On May 21, 1806, Will Russell, Clerk of Williamsburg, Virginia, District Court, authorized John Jordan, William Morton, Charles Wilkins, Thomas Bodley, and Joshua Wilson, all of Lexington, to examine witnesses and take testimony on behalf of Henry Clay in his suit against John Lewis, executor of Warner Lewis, deceased. DS. DLC-TJC (DNA, M212, R15).

From James Brown

My dear Sir New Orleans Feby 27th. 1806

The mail of to day has this moment enabled me to read your very interesting and friendly letter of the 18 Ulto.[1] and although but a few minutes are allowed me before closing the return mail, I shall drop you a line acknowledging the obligations you impose upon me by the attention you pay to myself, and to my affairs in your Country—I am happy to learn that your prospects "altho exaggerated are flattering" and I most sincerely pray that your prosperity may keep pace with your merits and my good wishes.

You are right. No evidence in my reach has served to *convince me fully* that either New Orleans or Natchez is as healthy as Lexington, and much as I wish to see you display upon a new theatre talents which from frequent experience of their powers I have learned to respect, I never have advised you, I cannot *yet* advise you to change your establishment. One summer is too short to warrant favorable conclusions. We wait another and another—and then if *we* who are your harbingers can report favorably you may venture—but until then I beg of you remain where you are. Having so long escaped, there is every reason to believe that my Nancy & myself are now acclimated and may promise ourselves many happy days in the Country. We are now fearless of danger from the ordinary bilious fever, and too sensible of the horrors of yellow fever to risque that dreadful contagion. Before it can approach the town we shall have found an assylum on our farm, far beyond the reach of its ravages.

I am happy in the success of Coburns suit inasmuch as it will give my best of friends Mrs. Price a trifle which may serve as a memorial of the affection I bear her.[2] I hope the time is not far distant when I shall have the pleasure of seeing her, and of endeavoring to persuade her and her charming little girls to embark with us for this Town. From a long acquaintance with her disposition I am sure we should be happy extremely happy in the same house—May I not hope too that your Lucretia and yourself will be able shortly to change the scene and spend a winter among the gay unthinking dancing inhabitants of Louisiana? It is unnecessary to say what pleasure it would give us to see you here, and how steadily we should exert ourselves in making the place agreeable to you.

I am not so indifferent about Kentucky, and Kentucky politics as not to rejoice in the defeat and consequent mortification of that unprincipled upstart Grundy.[3] When will the day arrive when men of talents and principle will acquire due weight in your councils?

Mansel[4] *will* have law—He *shall* have my answer by the next Mail.

I have done services for Winn[5] to more than the amount claimed for the mare—He promised me fifty dollars out of her in the suit of the porters alone[6]—The rest was promised on other causes. I had bought his land for a trifle in discharge of a debt I agreed to let him redeem it—He gave me the mare as my fees and commissions in Riddle & Dalls suit[7] alone—afterwards he promised to pay those Commissions & fees in money and wished the mare taken as I have mentioned in porters suit & other fees—But when I left Kentucky I counted on being somewhat cheated in my old accounts—Settle it as well as you can and I shall be content—

I am about putting on board Riddles Boat[8] some good wine to be drank by the Judges at their June Session of the Court of Appeals—Tell my friends Todd & Sebastian that they must invite the bar and sit as President & Vice President of the Club—Wallace is too much of a Presbyterian to Preside & I should be sorry to force Muter to [dr]ink as much as a President should swallow [to] my health—[9]

Doctor Brown's[10] departure from Kentucky will oblige me to be doubly troublesome to you but I wish not to be an ungenerous Client—The earnings of many years are yet in your State. Will you take care of them for me. Can I lose so clear a cause as that in Bourbon with Thomas?[11] It is important to me to gain that suit—Gain it and take as much as you please of it. Why does not Trimble[12] write me? Is he not the honest fellow I always thought him? or have I offended him? Ask him if he has recovered 1000 Dollr. & int. which he sued Shipp for before I left Kentucky?[13] And how has he decided the the [*sic*] entry of Morly which interferes with Timberlake?[14] Remember me affly to all my friends & believe me your sincerely attached friend JAMES BROWN

ALS. DLC-HC (DNA, M212, R1). Addressed to Clay at Lexington. Published in Padgett, "Letters of James Brown to Henry Clay," *La. Hist. Quar.*, XXIV (1941), 927-30.

1 Not found.
2 On the suit, see above, Survey, February 19, 1806, note. Susannah, widow of Samuel Price, was a daughter of Thomas Hart and sister of Mrs. Brown and Mrs. Clay.
3 Felix Grundy. 4 George Mansell.
5 Adam Winn of Fayette County, brother of George.
6 Robert and Andrew Porter *vs.* Winns, Fayette Circuit Court, Order Book A (February Term, 1800), 314; *ibid.*, File 93 (1805).
7 The suit involved Joseph Riddle of Alexandria, Virginia, and James Dall, of Baltimore, operating as a mercantile firm, against George, Adam, and Thomas Winn. Fayette Circuit Court, File 11 (1798).
8 The barge *Ann,* James Riddle, master, was employed in the river trade.
9 Thomas Todd, Benjamin Sebastian, and Caleb Wallace, with George Muter as Chief Justice, then comprised the Kentucky Court of Appeals.
10 Dr. Samuel Brown. 11 See above, Brown to Clay, December 18, 1804.
12 Robert Trimble of Bourbon County, Kentucky, who had studied law under Brown and was jointly with Jesse Bledsoe to have handled Brown's remaining legal business in the Bourbon Circuit Court. Lexington *Kentucky Gazette,* April 25, 1804. Trimble had been a member of the Kentucky legislature in 1803, and was appointed a judge of the Kentucky Court of Appeals in 1808, United States District Attorney for Kentucky, 1813, a justice of the Federal District Court in 1817, and Associate Justice of the United States Supreme Court, 1826.
13 The suit of Brown *vs.* Colby Shipp, a resident of Scott County, was not initiated until April, 1807, when a plea of trespass was instituted in Scott Circuit Court on complaint that Shipp had failed to make payment as agreed for a tract of about 200 acres on the Ohio River. Clay posted bond for the costs of suit July 23, 1808 (ADS. Bourbon Circuit Court, File 246). Continued in Scott through September, 1809, the case was then carried on change of venue to Bourbon Circuit Court, where in August, 1810, it was dismissed with each party to pay his own costs. *Ibid.*
14 Suit not found.

Receipt from Dr. Samuel Brown

[March 1, 1806]

Attached to Account, *ca.* September 8, 1804.

From Allan B. Magruder

Dear Sir, Opelousas, 6h. March 1806—

I arrived at this place sometime in January last, after a most tedious & uncomfortable Voyage of near three months from Louisville—

I found, that owing to the peculiar situation of the land claims in this part of the Territory, & the absence of one of the Commissioners, nothing had been entered on.—Col Thompson,[1] the Register, had merely devoted his time to receiving into his Office the title papers of the people. When I arrived, not more than fifty or sixty claims had been presented to the Register.

The people having received their grants, and made settlements under the Spanish government, appear to have rested in perfect security, without every [*sic*] having, in numerous instances, taken the necessary steps to *complete* their titles.—Surveys, accordingly, were never made; & when they found that it was necesary to do it by the 1st. of March, or forfeit their lands to the United States,[2] a panic was excited from one end of the country to the other. This was considerably increased by the situation of the lands, during almost the whole of last winter. Very large districts were almost under water; & proper measures had not been adopted, under the infant Judicial Establishments here, to appoint Surveyors in the different counties of the territory. Innumerable complaints were made on these grounds, as to the severity of the Law in giving such little time for the return of Surveys. They have been as often silenced by our assurances, that an Amendatory act wou'd be passed by Congress, extending the term for making surveys;[3] & that it was the intention of Government to do nothing that might in the slightest degree oppress, or embarrass the people.—These assurances, together with the dignified, mild and honorable conduct of the board, have proved effectual checks to all sentiments of disgust, which might otherwise have arisen from the novelty of the Law, and the ignorance of those, upon whose property it was to operate. —Never were public Agents more respected, or the motives which regulated their conduct, deemed more pure.—

In the *structure* of the Law under which we act, it is evident that the government has been very ignorant of the real situation of the claims of the people in this part of Louisiana.—The law, it is true, gives a good deal of latitude to the Commissioners in determining cases, according to Law & Equity. But there are many of those cases not embraced by the statute; & indeed it is impossible that Congress cou'd have been possessed of that competent knowledge, relative to the nature of land claims, in every respect, necessary for the formation of a complete act, embracing every case that might occur, and guarding against all inconveniences that might arise out of the peculiar situation of the country. There are purchases made from Indians, & now held under such a title. There are settlements by virtue of *Riguets,* or written permissions of a commandant to settle a particular portion of land. These cases, & some others, have not been provided for, by the Law; & the Commissioners concur with me in opinion, that the board may receive the *Evidence* of those claims, & recommend them, in their general Report, to the Equitable Consideration of Congress. No provission has also, been made to embrace those cases, where lands are held under grant, or by actual settlement and occupancy, by *minors.* Some of those cases have occurred at the board. Upon discovering that settlements or grants of this nature had taken place many years since, that valuable improvements had been made, that the claimant had long been in peaceble possession under the spanish government, and that he had raised upon his Estate a numerous family, the Law which was to deprive him of it, at this period, was deemed less Equitable than many of its other provissions.—I am aware that some limitation of *age* was necessary to be incerted in the statute; but there are Cases, where a rigid adherence to the present act, wou'd not so well comport with Equity, or prehaps [*sic*], with sound policy. The Case I have stated is one of them.

There is no part of the Law where the intelligence of the Legislature appears to have been more defective, than where it speaks of the *extinguishment of Indian titles.* The Spaniards, in common with other European powers who have acquired territory on the continent of America, bottom their claim upon the *Right of Conquest.* In this manner was the country of Louisiana held by the French, who drove out the Indians when they took possession; and in their transfer of the Country to the Spaniards, no extinguishments of this nature, were ever contemplated by either party. The Equitable policy adopted on this subject, by the United States, was never persued by the ancient occupants of Louisiana. Such being the situation of all the lands granted or settled, under the Spanish Government, the original encumbrance of an Indian title, rests upon almost every claim in the country. It will, therefore, be readily seen, that the part of the Law respecting the *extinguishment of Indian titles,* is a mere nullity. In the mean time, the Commissioners will determine claims according to the Law as if all extinguishments had been made & leave to the Wisdom of Congress the power of ultimately deciding on this subject. Were they to confine themselves *strictly to the Law* on this point, every claim to lands in this country, wou'd be shaken to its foundations.—

The want of knowledge on the part of the Legislature has, also, been evinced as to the *period* prescribed by Law for entering Surveys with the Register. Had the act extended the term to the first of August next, it wou'd not have exceeded the time necessary for this business. Indeed, I believe that such a limitation, wou'd have been too short.—None but those who have seen this country, can form an adequate idea of the difficulties that are to be encountered in making Surveys, through Swamps that are almost impassible, & along water courses whose banks are frequently inundated by heavy rains, and by the large rivers that bound the Coast and run through the heart of the country.—But to fix the period for the meeting of the Commissioners on the 1st. of December, & thus prescribe that the Surveys shou'd be returned by the first of March following, when it wou'd take at least six months for the promulgation of the law in these remote parts, was surely a limitation too rigid, & a great oversight in the legislation.—

About three weeks since, the Board proceeded to ascertain the state of the land claims in this district. During that period, about 700 cases have been brought forward. They consist principally of claims by Virtue of Settlement, grant and Riguet, or a written permission of a Spanish commandant to settle certain quantities of Land. By far the greater part of those claims, I apprehend, will be confirmed by the Board. I cannot forbear to express my pleasure at the prospect; for I well know, that it is the true policy of the government to conciliate the affections of the people in this remote part of the Empire: and altho' bad titles might increase the quantity of public lands, yet it is infinitely better to have happy and affectionate Citizens, in the peacible enjoyment of their property, attached to the Government from the the [*sic*] mildness of its principles, and willing from this Instance of its clemency, to yield obedience to the sanctity of future laws.—

Few claims have, as yet, been brought forward from the remote parts of the district; and in the Spring, when the roads will be rendered impassible by inundations, and the difficulty of making Surveys from this circumstance increased, we have but little prospect of receiving in more, than what have already been entered.—The Marquis de Caso Calvo,[4] the Spanish Emissary to the West, has done much mischief about Natchitoches.—He has perswaded most of the people in that part of the country, that there was no necessity to survey their lands under the American Government, as a retrocession of territory wou'd certainly take place. The people, have, in general, submited to the delusion; and taken but few steps to have their claims adjusted.—

Since the expiration of the time for bringing in Surveys, we have had little or nothing to do. We wait with anxiety to hear from Congress, on the subject of an Amendatory Law.—It is beyond all question, that such a law extending the term for the Entry of Surveys in the Registers office, *ought* to be ennacted; and I have no doubt whatever, that the *necessity* of such a measure will be immediately seen by the Legislature.—

From the best calculation we can make, there cannot be less than from 5 to 6000 claims within this district; and only 700 have been exhibited.—Few Surveys of the above 6000 claims, have been made; & shou'd Congress not extend the term for this business, what will be the situation of the country? Shou'd the limitation under the first act be adhered to, the temper of the people will be aroused; and whilst a palpable act of injustice will be commited, it will never be suffered on the part of those, who sustain the injury.—

The Calculation that the land claims in this country Cou'd be adjusted within 6 or 9 months, was surely a very erroneous one; & shews how little the best informed men, in the United States, were acquainted with the State of things, under the silent and despotic operations of the Spanish Government—If the object of the mission into this country is accomplished in two years, it will not be exceeding my own expectations, and every rational calculation that can be now made on the subject.

The beauties of this country are absolutely indiscribable. I arrived here in the dead of winter, when the Earth must have been covered with ice and snow in northern climates, and found myself sourrounded by all the scenery of the spring. The fruit trees were begining to blossom, and the forrest to assume a green appearance. Such is the general aspect of winter in this part of Louisiana. The spring and summer months are exceedingly pleasant, from what I am informed, the heat being considerably attemper'd by refreshing breezes from the Gulph of Mexico, which lies about 40 or 50 miles to the south of this country. The lands, in point of fertility, are equal to any in America. They lie remarkably level, and are of a sandy nature, the evident affect of alluvion from the large Rivers which bound the Coast & run through the Country. All lower Louisiana, in my opinion has been made by vast accumulations of sand, brought down by the Rivers. This is proved by the discovery of large trees thirty feet deep in the earth, in digging wells, and in the Banks of B'ayous where the water has washed away the sand, and exposed them to the view, ten feet below the surface.

The arts here, have made but little advance towards ether Elegance, or usefulness. The Houses are all built on one plan, one story high, surrounded on all sides, very frequently, by piazzas, without glazing, & often without being plastered within.—The inhabitants, who are principally French, live on the Edges of Praries, & Cultivate Cotton. There are some very Extensive Vacheries here, which produce beef for the market at Orleans, & many parts of the atlantic States.—The French are remarkably Civil; but they do not like the Americans, who are too fond of speculation, & often take advantage of their ignorance in making a Bargain.—

I have not been able to make many observations as yet, being confined to the Board, which meets every day, where it is my duty to attend.—As soon as I can make a tour through the Country, I shall communicate my remarks to the public.[5]—

I am happy to inform you, that my situation here is a very Agreable one. Col Thompson the Register, and Mr. Francis Vacher[6] one of the Commissioners, are gentlemen & men of honour—The former is truly a man of business & a most worthy character—The latter is a young gentleman of handsome abilities, excellent Education, Inquisitive in the persuit of Knowledge & for whom time & experience will do much.

I remain, dear Sir, with very great regard & Esteem,

yr mo: Ob Sert ALLAN B. MAGRUDER

ALS. DLC-HC (DNA, M212, R1). Addressed to Clay at Lexington; postmarked: "NATCHEZ-April 8."

1 John Thompson, Lexington lawyer, had been appointed Register for the Western District of Orleans Territory in 1805.

2 See "An act for ascertaining and adjusting the titles and claims to land, within the territory of Orleans, and the district of Louisiana," 2 *U.S. Stat.*, 324-29 (March 2, 1805).

3 Such an act was passed in April, 1806. 2 *U.S. Stat.*, 391-95.

4 Casa Calvo, one of the Spanish Commissioners who had delivered the province of Louisiana to France in 1803, remained in the area until ordered by President Jefferson to leave in 1806.

5 See Allan Bowie Magruder, *A Letter . . . to His Correspondent in the State of Virginia, Dated 20th Nov. 1807* (New Orleans, 1808).

6 Vacher had been recommended for the post by "J. Brown of Kentucky" and by two New Yorkers. Carter (ed.), *Territorial Papers*, IX, *Orleans*, 613.

Agreement with William Green

[March 11, 1806]

I have put into H. Clays hands a contract between R. Patterson[1] & myself in order to recover the difference in value between two tracts of land one on Lecompts run, the other on the waters of Eagle Creek[2]—I do hereby agree to give said Clay one fifth of what may be recovered as a compensation for his services. Witness my hand & seal this 11h. March 1806. WILLIAM GREEN {L.S.}

I authorize H. Clay to compromise with Patterson.

WILLIAM GREEN

DS, in Clay's hand. KyLxT. Green, a native of Virginia, at this time a resident of Woodford County, Kentucky, was a younger brother of Willis.

1 Probably Robert Patterson, pioneer and Indian fighter, one of the founders of Lexington, who had moved to Ohio in 1804.

2 Lecomptes Run lies entirely in Scott County, Kentucky. Eagle Creek rises in that county and flows northward and westward before joining the Kentucky River a few miles above the Ohio.

Receipt from Arthur Patterson

[March 18, 1806]

Recd. 18 March 1806 of H. Clay Twenty five pounds in Cash and one black horse on account of the part of F— Patterson's preemption purchased by him ARTHUR PATTERSON.

DS, in Clay's hand. DLC-TJC (DNA, M212, R15). See above, Agreement, September 18, 1805.

From John Breckinridge

Dear Sir Washington 19, March 1806

It is but two days past, that the sense of the house of Reprs. has been so manifested, as to enable us to form any opinion what course they would pursue with respect to our relations with G. Britain. Last week, Gregg's resolutions were postponed by a very large majority, for the purpose of taking up Nicholson's; and two days ago a vote was taken on Nicholson's (precisely in the form you saw them in the news papers) yeas 87 nays 35. I have not seen the yeas & nays, but am informed, that the minority contained but eleven republican members. From the great variety of opinion that seemed to exist some weeks ago on this subject, I had no idea that such unanimity would have resulted. A bill is directed to be brought in, & will no doubt pass the H. of Reprs.; but what its fate in the Senate will be, I cannot say[1]

Few acts have passed. The bill for classing the militia was lost in the Senate, where it originated. Little is said about fortifying forts & Harbors. The 74s in the same state. War in short does not seem to be apprehended by Congress.

Gen'l. Armstrong is appointed envoy extraordinary to unite with Mr. Bowdin in negociating with Spain on the subject of our difficulties with her;[2] and I think the prospect of a favorable issue is not unpropitious.

A Bill is before the Senate for encouraging emigration to the territory of Orleans, by allowing a bounty of land to every able-bodied militia man who will settle there, by a particular day. One hundred & sixty acres is spoken of as the bounty. Should this measure be adopted,[3] it will not only effectually protect that, at present, very defenceless & vulnerable part of the Union, but enable the people there to carry on their civil government with more ease & harmony, by infusing among them a more general knowledge of our Laws, customs, &c.

The Yazo [*sic*] claim is before the Senate, but I understand, it has yet met with no discussion; therefore but imperfect conjectures can be made of its fate there. If it reaches the H. of Reprs. it will no doubt rekindle the former flame, which has hitherto accompanied it, & add to the present irritation which exists there.[4]

You will see in the last paper, the commencement of Mr. Randolph's[5] speech on British affairs. There is nothing late from Mr. Monroe: and I think it very probable that the dispatches which may be rec'd. from him after the account of the affair at Austerlitz shall have reached London, will be more favorable than heretofore.[6]

Mr. Thurston [*sic*] I presume wrote to you on the subject of your letter respecting the navy agency at Orleans.[7] The office was filled; but we signed & deposited a recommendation, which will be attended to if any thing hereafter occurs; & I beg that you will with freedom & without hesitation make known your wishes to me on such subjects; as I shall feel much pleasure in serving you, whenever it shall be in my power.

From present appearances, I do not think that Congress will

adjourn sooner than one month; consequently it will not be in my power to attend the Court of Appeals; & should they sit even one month more, I shall not be able to attend the Genl. Court; for it will take me 20 days to ride out. I want therefore my dear Sir [to] commit my concerns to your care in both those courts hoping to experience a continuance of that attention which they have hitherto received from you. You know how deeply I am interested in the case with Ross & Carseal [*sic*].[8] The appeal in the case vs. Johnson & Netherland,[9] which I directed to be sent up, will of course rest there. You recollect the conversation which passed between us on that subject. The business can be closed by us this Summer; therefore just continue the appeal.

I am, dear Sir, with much esteem &c Your friend &c

H. Clay, Esq. J. BRECKINRIDGE.

P. S.—The president has been a good deal indisposed for a few days; but is again perfectly recovered. Poor Genl. Jackson (of the Senate) from Georgia, who has been confined most of the session, I am just informed, is dead.[10] Doct. Archer from Maryland of the H. of Reprs. (& Doct. Downey's[11] old master) is also about to die.[12] We generally loose a member every session. J. B.

Typed Copy. InHi-William H. Smith Collection.

1 On January 29, 1806, Andrew Gregg of Pennsylvania introduced in the House of Representatives resolutions designed to cut off importations of British goods until "equitable and satisfactory arrangements" should be made with Great Britain relative to impressment of American seamen and violations of neutral rights. A less drastic course was recommended on February 10 by Joseph Hopper Nicholson of Maryland, who proposed that non-importation should apply only to British goods which could be manufactured in the United States or purchased elsewhere. After much debate the House on March 13 voted against consideration of Gregg's resolutions and, instead, agreed to take up Nicholson's bill, which was adopted on March 26. The Senate acted favorably on April 15 and the President gave his approval three days later.

2 John Armstrong, United States Minister to France, later Secretary of War under President Madison; and James Bowdoin, Minister to Spain.

3 Action on the bill was postponed until the next session of Congress.

4 On March 29 the bill reached the House, where it was rejected. The Yazoo claims resulted from cancellation of a 35,000,000-acre grant obtained by a group of land companies through bribery of the Georgia legislature in 1795. Since Georgia had ceded her western lands to the United States in 1802, the appeal for relief was now directed to Congress. In 1814 legislation authorized payment of over five and a quarter million dollars to the claimants. 3 *U. S. Stat.*, 116-20 (March 31, 1814).

5 John Randolph of Roanoke.

6 James Monroe, United States minister to London since 1803, had not been successful in negotiating with regard to neutral rights. Napoleon had won the Battle of Austerlitz in early December 1805.

7 See above, Clay to Breckinridge, January 5, 1806.

8 David Ross and Thomas Carneal.

9 The dispute, relating to conflicting entries for a salt lick on Middle Creek in Floyd County, Kentucky, had originated as an action of Benjamin Netherland and Robert Johnson against James Young and John Breckinridge. Decided in the lower court in favor of the plaintiffs in September, 1805, the case was appealed and later compromised. Fayette Circuit Court, Complete Record Book B, 87-152 *passim*; and below, Agreement, October 10, 1806. Young, who had manufactured salt at the lick in 1779, was living on the tract as late as 1801.

10 James Jackson died March 19, 1806.

11 Probably Dr. Richard W. Downing, a Maryland Revolutionary veteran, who had moved to Lexington about 1790.

12 Dr. John Archer, noted medical teacher, an officer in the Continental Army, founder of the Medical and Chirurgical Faculty of Maryland, and member of Congress from 1801 to 1807, survived until September 28, 1810.

From James Morrison

Dear Sir Washington March 20th. 1806

I have Just returned from a long ride of 130 Miles to J. M. Gilmore's[1]—We have been Damnly imposed on by young Graham[2] —His mother received 11 Negroes before her Mother or Brothers death, the former lived 2. years after the death of her son Dr. Ball—I have a Certificate from the Executor of Dr. Ball fully establishing the fact, and expect Depositions to the Same purport by tomorrows post—The proof is conclusive Mrs. Grahams acknowledgement to her Brother in her letter—and the Executor declares that of the four Negroes mentioned in the Will only 2. Women and 3 small Children remained over & above those which Mrs. Graham got—One of the men went off to the British, the Other went off to Mrs. Graham[3] to Dumfries, was hired by her for 2 or 3 years & afterward ran off & is now in Philaa—I blame Graham because Gilmore assures me that he shewed him all the papers—and he urged him to write to his Mother, Otherwise she would suppose he had done nothing in the business—I only know of one method of regaining our advances, viz by writing to him, that unless he makes an arrangement to repay with all expenses, that we will immediately have him arrested—He can be broke for his ungentlemanly conduct—

I have written to W. C. Nicholas[4] and requested he would enable me to give you a decisive answer as to the farm, he has been very ill, but look for his answer daily—of which you shall be duly & without loss of time notified—

I beg you may write to Graham, I believe he is with Genl. Wilkinson—[5]

I am greatly disappointed in not having rec'd your answer relative to my letter on the subject of McKees & Genl. & Robt. Smiths Land[6] —I can purchase both if I had your letter authorising the measure—

You will again hear from me as soon as I receive the papers from Gilmor[e]

I refer you to our friend Hughes[7] for the Polotics of this quarter—I will only Say, that the Administration has more friends in Kentucky, than Virga. Things do not go on well here—Muroe[8] will probable be our next President—I have scratched over this in great haste, Hughes setting out unexpectedly and I have been so unwell for a few days that I have not been out of my Room— I am Dear Sir Your sincere friend & Huml. Sert. JAMES MORRISON

Henry Clay Esqr

ALS. DLC-TJC (DNA, M212, R12).

1 Probably John Morton Gilmour of Lancaster County, Virginia.

2 The son of Reginald and Mary Graham, who had come to Kentucky from Virginia at an early date. His mother, daughter of William Ball and sister of Dr. William Ball of Lancaster County, had been married previously to John Ball.

3 Not young Graham's mother, but one of several people of this name who lived at Dumfries, Prince William County, Virginia.

4 Wilson Cary Nicholas, Congressman, United States Senator, and twelfth Governor of Virginia (1814-1816), one of the owners of a tract of 255 acres which Clay later purchased as an addition to "Ashland."

5 General James Wilkinson was in command of American troops in Orleans Territory.

6 The letter has not been found.

7 James Hughes, who had given up his law office in Lexington a few months earlier and was apparently visiting in Washington.

8 James Monroe.

From John Swan

Henry Clay Esqr. Baltimore March 21st. 1806

Sir

Mr Bledsoe informed me by Letter of the 25th April last, that you had join'd him in prosecuting a suit against Anderson & Massey[1] for the recovery of my Military Lands, and that it would be necessary to forward Colo Andersons Letters on the subject by some Conveyance, learning from the bearer Mr B Hughes,[2] that Mr Bledsoe is now in Louisiana, think it best not to loose so good an Opportunity, have therefore taken the Liberty to inclose them to you, that you will find herein enclos'd, viz two Original Letters with an order on me from Colo Anderson for surveyors fees &ca,[3] in these Letters He Constitutes himself my agent, & solicites indirectly a right to remove my Locations, long after him or some other person has not only removed them, but sold the Land, as you will see by a reference to his Location Book, an extract from which was once shewn me, how this will Comport with his Character the world will judge.

I wrote Mr. Bledsoe lately directed to Lexington not knowing of his absence, requesting his Opinion as to my situation, with respect to my present Locations that have been sold for taxes, If you should fail in the present suits this I think Cannot well happen, Yet it might be well to guard Against all Chances, Should be glade of your or Mr Bledsoe's Opinion on that subject, by one of your Merchants that will be here this Spring, by whom the Customary fee will be forwarded, this you will please let me know and own receipt of the enclos'd papers—I hope every exertion will be used to bring the present Suit to a speedy decission. Life is precarious especially at the State, the parties have arrived at. with great respect I am Sir

Your most Hble Servant JNO SWAN

ALS. DLC-TJC (DNA, M212, R12). Addressed to Clay at Lexington. Swan, a Maryland cavalry officer during the Revolution, claimed several tracts of land in Kentucky.

1 Jesse Bledsoe, Colonel Richard Clough Anderson, and Nathaniel Massie.

2 Probably James Hughes.

3 Not found.

From John Breckinridge

Dear Sir 22. March 1806

Mr. Hughes[1] called upon me two days ago, & politely took charge of some letters I had written for Kentucky to go by the Mail. Among these was a letter for you.[2] Since that I have seen a Kentucky paper in which is published some extracts of letters from Members here to their friends in Kentucky, which I incline to think will be considered as having disclosed rather too much of the business which occupied Congress with closed doors. As when writing to a friend I write without reserve, it is very probable that my letter to you may contain facts or opinions which I ought not to disclose except to a friend. I do not now recollect its contents particularly; but be that as it may, I have to request that you will consider that letter as well as others you may receive from me as committed to your confidence. My present situation makes this proper for me, & will be my apology for suggesting that, which your own prudence & Judgment rendered unnecessary. —— By accounts late last night, recd. in this place (not official) it is said & beleived, that on the 26. of Decr. Bonaparte made peace with the Emperors of Germany & Russia, the particulars of which are not stated; except that the Step son of the former is to be furnished a Wife out of the family of the Elector of Bavaria, & that electorate is to be extended at the expense of Austria; perhaps to the size & importance of a Kingdom:[3] That no attempts were made to include G. Britain in the treaty: and that Pitt died the 21 of Decr.[4] If this latter fact be true, I think it probable that our difficulties with G.B. will be acmodated. Should the opposition party or some of the most influential of them come in, we have little to fear. Indeed there is no man in that Nation, who is not more likely to act justly with us than Pitt. His hatred to this Country had become inveterate & his schemes to annoy & depress our Commerce, systematic.

Nothing has occurred in either House since I wrote to you, particularly interesting. The bill founded on Nicholsons resolutions, is committed to a Comee. of the whole & made the order of the day for monday next.[5] Adieu Yours sincerely

H. Clay esq J. BRECKINRIDGE

ALS. DLC-HC (DNA, M212, R1).

1 James Hughes.

2 Above, March 19, 1806.

3 On December 26, 1805, Napoleon forced Austria to sign the Treaty of Pressburg. Russia was not a party to the treaty. Arrangements for the marriage of Eugene Beauharnais and the daughter of the Elector of Bavaria were made immediately afterward.

4 Pitt's death occurred on January 23, 1806.

5 Nicholson's bill reached the Senate on Thursday, March 27.

From Rebecca Willisson

28th April 1806

With infinite surprize and concern have consider'd of the cause which cou'd have produced such an unusual delay in my worthy friends writing on a subject so interesting to me as that which relates to my affairs in Kentucky, eight or nine long Months have elapsed since the date of yours, enclosing Dedimus's for the examination of Witnesses in this quarter,[1] which did not arrive untill several days after the time that was specified for examination which letter was return'd with the Post Masters affidavit to that purpose, It was also stated in your letter my attendance in Virginia on the examination of Evidences was essential held myself prepared to do so for a length of of [*sic*] time and only waited your summons to be gone, flattering myself that this exertion wou'd have made a final close of this unpleasant business, and that it was only a dermire [*sic*] resort of the defendant to protract and not to strengthen his Testimony as you apprehended, not supposing that any thing which my Aunt cou'd prove wou'd invalidate my claim, having applied to her myself at the commencement of this business for information on the subject, she then declared that she did not recollect the particulars of the transaction—You will Sir add another favor to the very many which you have already conferred by writing & stating the situation of the Suits as they now stand

Mr Wormeley[2] as my agent obtain'd a Verdict in the District Court of Frederick County for several hundred dollars in my favor at Octr Term have since directed him to enforce the collection as soon as possible and pay into the hands of the Honble Mathew Clay one hundred dollars for your use which flatter myself he has e'er this received and that you [have] had advice of the same—

If there is any thing further to [be] done in the prosecution of my suits will be thankful for your directions shall be grateful for your advice & will pursue & execute your plan with diligence—

Shou'd more Cash be necessary for immediate disbursements in the prosecution of my Suits you will please signify the amount in your next that will be requisite And remain Sir With great Respt

Re Willisson

ALS. DLC-TJC (DNA, M212, R12). Addressed to Clay at Lexington; postmarked at Augusta, Georgia.

1 Clay's letter has not been found. 2 John Wormeley.

Acknowledgment of Receipt from James Coleman

29h. Apl 1806.

Including my note of $600 this day given to H. Clay & Benj. Howard

I have paid one thousand dollars on a/c. of the Judge [*sic*] Field & Sons agt. me & others, for which said Clay has given receipts to me & Henry Coleman[1]

JAMES COLEMAN

DS, in Clay's hand. DLC-TJC (DNA, M212, R15). Coleman, born in Caroline County, Virginia, was now a resident of Harrison County, Kentucky.

1 For several years a justice of the Court of Quarter Sessions in Harrison County.

Power of Attorney from Thomas Deye Owings

[May 1, 1806]

[Power of attorney from Thomas Deye Owings and his father to Henry Clay to prosecute, defend, and attend to any suit brought by or against them, or either; to sign and deliver any bond deemed necessary in such prosecution or for the suspension of any judgment against them; and during the younger Owings' absence on a projected trip to Maryland, Clay is authorized to draw on him or his father for the amount to cover any execution pressed against the Owings' property or security. Certification of signature acknowledgment by Thomas D. Owings recorded in the Office of the Clerk, Fayette County, May 22, 1806.]

Fayette Circuit Court, Deed Book B, 748-49.

Bill of Sale from A. Smith

[May 3, 1806]

I have this day sold to Henry Clay a bay mare now at the pasture of Mr. Banton,[1] called Ethe, whose pedigree I warrant as follows: She was got by the Imported horse Adventurer out of Stella who was got by the Imported horse Flimnap out of the Imported mare Britannia; and she is now in fold [*sic*] by Monticello, a medley.[2] The said mare is aged ten years or eleven.

Witness my hand & seal this 3d. May 1806.

Teste A. SMITH {L.S.}

LLOYD POSEY[3]

DS, in Clay's hand. DLC-TJC (DNA, M212, R10). Smith has not been further identified.

1 Probably William T. Banton, Lexington innkeeper, who for a time managed the stables of the Kentucky Hotel and later operated the Hotel.

2 Flimnap, a grandson of the Godolphin Arabian, had been imported into South Carolina. Britannia had been imported by Col. John Tayloe of Virginia. Henry William Herbert, *Frank Forester's Horse and Horsemanship of the United States and British Provinces of North America* (2 vols.; New York, 1857), I, 131, 458, 491. Monticello, by Diomed out of a mare by Chanticleer, was bred and owned by Thomas Jefferson. James Douglas Anderson, *Making the American Thoroughbred, Especially in Tennessee, 1800-1845* (Norwood, Mass., 1916), 38 note. The other horses have not been identified.

3 A native of Virginia, the son of Thomas Posey, and by 1810 a resident of Opelousas, Louisiana.

From Rebecca Willisson

Mr Clay Augusta 4th May 1806

Sir/

Yours of the 3d of April[1] did not arrive as you will perceive by a deposition to that effect an till the 1st of May which was after the time had expired & Mr Taylor and Spiers had left Edgefield[2] the place agreed upon to take depositions which from their tendency consider as indispensible in the prosecution of my Suit in Kentucky. Shou'd now collect the Witnesses & proceed to examination but have an impression that affidavit so taken cou'd not be shewn as evidence in your Courts, were my adversaries opposed to the measure, and the time allow'd is so short that it will be impossible for me to perform a Journey to the place of my Aunt Walkers residence before the time for examination had elaps'd also—Am extremely sorry to find that so great a misunderstanding prevails with respect to the nature of my claim to Kate and her Children & have also so compleatly fail'd in an attempt to prove the source from which my Title to Kate derived To attain this desireable purpose have now to requir[e] the favor of your particular attention & permit me to indeaver to explain the nature of the case more fully than former letters have done altho you will find on a referrence the story related much in the same way—My Grand Mother at the time of this donation had been a Widow for many Years & in the free exercise of her own will & was possess'd of a Female Slave called Betty who had a Daughter named Moll this Girl was the first Gift of my Grand Mother which was in conformity to a custom of hers to give to each of her Sons Eldest Daughters when in infancy a Negro Girl shortly after the donation was made my Father determined to move with his Family to South Carolina on this discovery Betty was in an agony of Grief at the apprehension of being forever seperated from her Child when motives of humanity induced My Grand Mother & Father to make an exchange & for the accomodation of all parties my Grandmother for the sum of £ 26 Virginia money purchased Kate of my Father who was given to me in lieu of Moll & is now the Identical Kate claim'd by me in Kentucky—You will doubtless Sir perceive that former Wills and divises has no connection with my present claim

With submission to your better Judgment suppose that to establish the above stated Facts & whether my Father as my natural Guardian in infancy had a right to make the exchange with my Grandmother are points that are to be discussd

For your better information beg leave to mention that have understood by my Grand Mothers Will Betty & Moll were devised to my Aunt Walker or one of her Daughters which produces no doubt the shyness in my Aunt to unfold the sequel being ever my

Mothers opinion that she had a perfect recollection of it as they were both present at the transaction and from a suspicion that it might hereafter involve the title of Moll

From many circumstances am confirm'd in in [*sic*] an opinion that my presence in Virginia at the time of examination is indispensible shall set out the first Week in Septr for that purpose and let the appointment be the first Monday in Octr at my Aunt Walkers residence beginning [at] the House of Capn Wormeley on the last Monday in Septr & suffer the other appointment to embrace as large an extent as possible being unacquain[t]ed with the residence of others Witness' whose Evidence is essential—Have already proven in this State my Fathers acknowledgment that the property was mine and also that it was [the] Gift of my Grand Mother—It may be expedient [to] proceed to further examination in Caroli[na—] consider the second Week in August a convenient time—Beg leave to assure you that have not been inattentive to your interest as you will find in a letter addressed on the 27th of April last—[3] Am Sir With Great Friendship And respect Yours RE WILLISSON

Henry Clay Esquire

direct to me in future Augusta Post Office

ALS. DLC-TJC (DNA, M212, R12). Postmarked at Augusta, Georgia, May 12.

1 Not found. 2 In Dinwiddie County, Virginia.

3 The letter was actually dated April 28 (above).

Promissory Note from Alexander Taylor

[May 7, 1806]

I Promise to pay or cause to be paid unto Henry Clay Fifty five dollars & fifty Cents to be discharged (on the determination of a suit now depending in the Federal Courts in which Cochran & Thersby are Complts. & Wm. Coleman[1] Deft.) provided the sd. Clay shall succeed in defending sd. Land on behalf of sd. Coleman, witness my hand & seal this 7th. day of May[2] 1806.

Atteste ALEXANDER TAYLOR {SEAL}

I KRURY[3]

DS. DLC-TJC (DNA, M212, R15). Taylor had been a taxpayer in Woodford County in 1800.

1 Of Harrison County, Kentucky, son of Henry Coleman. The suit, not found.

2 Possibly an error. This document and the two below, dated June 7, 1806, were written on the same sheet of paper. 3 Not identified.

Bill of Sale from James Condon

[May 12, 1806]

I have this day bargained sold and delivered and by these

presents do bargain sell and deliver to Henry Clay for and in consideration of four hundred & fifty dollars, a negro female slave named Charlotte[1] aged about nineteen, which said slave I warrant & defend to said Clay against the claim of all & every person whatsoever; and I likewise warrant her to be sound.

Witness my hand & seal this 12h. May 1806.

Teste JAS. CONDON {L.S.}

ISAAC WELLS[2]

DS, in Clay's hand. DLC-TJC (DNA, M212, R15). Condon, a tailor, had recently come to Lexington from Maryland.

1 Purchased because of her marriage to Clay's body servant, Aaron Dupuy, "Lottie" became nursemaid to Clay's children and many of his grandchildren. She was emancipated in 1840.

2 Of Fayette County.

From Joseph Riddle

H Clay Esqr Alexa, May 12th, 1806
Lexington
Sir

Enclosed you have Original Youngs Bond to Joseph Young[1] Dated the 15th, Decr, 1804 Conditioned for the Payt, of £ 92-8-2½ Virginia Mony & by Joseph Young Assigned to me the 31t March 1806—I am informed that O Young resides in Montgomy County near Mount Sterling Post Officc 20 or 30 Miles from Lexington—I Wish you to assertain if this is the Case & to take the shortest possible Way in your Power to secure the Debt if insecure, either by suit or otherwise—Mr Mc Law[2] informs me that you have put Wins Debt in the Way of recovery—he also says that Win Charges for a Mare or horse Delivered Mr Brown on my Acct. I presume he is *not* Correct as I understand from Mr, Mc, Law that you Informed that Mr B Did Business for Win & that you suppose he gave the Mare for fees[3]—hope you May soon get the Mony at all events by the time Mr Mc Law Returns in the fall.

Please let me hear from you On Rect, of this & Say What probability there is of getting the Mony from Young—With Respects to Col Hart I am yr Obt Svt JOSEPH RIDDLE
for Self & Late Co

ALS. DLC-TJC (DNA, M212, R12).

1 Possibly the early Kentucky settler and Indian fighter, later resident in Indiana. Original Young lived on Flat Creek in Montgomery County.

2 Not identified.

3 See above, Brown to Clay, February 27, 1806.

Promissory Note from James Coleman

[June 7, 1806]

I Promise to pay or cause to be paid unto Henry Clay Twenty two dollars and twenty five Cents to be discharged (on the determination of a Suit now depending in the Federal Courts in which Cochran & Thersby are Complts. & Wm. Coleman Deft.) provided the sd. Clay should succeed in defending sd. Land on behalf of sd. Coleman. witness my hand & seal this 7th. of June 1806.

Atteste JAMES COLEMAN {SEAL}

I KRURY

ADS. DLC-TJC (DNA, M212, R15). Cf. above, Promissory Note, May 7, 1806.

Promissory Note from John Hudelson

[June 7, 1806]

I Promise to pay or cause to be paid unto Henry Clay Twenty two dollars and twenty five Cents to be discharged (on the determination of a Suit now depending in the Federal Court in which Cochran & Thersby are Complts. & Wm. Coleman Deft.) provided the sd. Clay shall succeed in defending sd. Land on behalf of sd. Coleman, witness my hand & seal this 7th. day of June 1806

Atteste JOHN HUDELSON {SEAL}

I KRURY

DS. DLC-TJC (DNA, M212, R15). Cf. above, notes from Taylor and Coleman, May 7, June 7, 1806. Hudelson was one of the original lot owners of the town of Cynthiana, Harrison County, Kentucky.

Memorandum of Conversation with Robert Todd

[*ca.* July, 1806]

In conversation between Genl. Todd and me between this place and Lexington he stated that the warrants had been drawn from the surveyor's office for all the land except what appears from the entry in the margin[1] of the surveyor's book to have been left; and that he believed the warrants were located in Virginia about the period of 1795 when the land fever existed. H. CLAY.

Certified copy, printed. Ky. H. of Reps., *Journal, 1807-1808*, p. 201. Todd, a native of Pennsylvania and one of the original lot owners of Lexington, was a judge of the Fayette Circuit Court. The document was offered as evidence in the chancery suit of Humphrey Marshall *vs.* Prettyman Merry, probably at the July Term, 1806, of the Federal District Court of Kentucky. Marshall in his bill of complaint filed in the spring of 1803 had asserted claim to Todd's full entry, 6666⅔ acres, part of which tract was also claimed by Merry, a Virginia veteran of the Revolution and a resident of Buckingham County, Virginia (though he frequently visited Kentucky to look after large land holdings in the northern part of the State, and he died in Bourbon County in 1817). Clay was attorney for the defense—his agreement on the facts of the case and his drafts of the answer and amended answer to Marshall's bill are also printed in this source. The final outcome of the litigation, not found, was less important than the evidence indicating that the records of Todd's original plat and certificate had been defaced so as to remove a notation that the largest part of the tract had already been withdrawn from entry prior to Marshall's application for patent to the whole of it. The charge that Marshall had intentionally mutilated the documents subsequently formed one of the grounds for legislative investigation of his fitness for House membership. See below, Resolutions, February 3, 1808, note.

1 "*Amended in book* 10th page 236. *Surveyed* 300. *Surveyed* 90. 6276 2/3 withdrawn."

To John Breckinridge

Dr Sir Lexington 8h. July 1806.

I send you a transcript of the record in Key against Matson,[1] which I should have sent you before, had I not understood that you were too much indisposed to attend to business. When I left Frankfort about the time the Court of Appeals adjourned, it was doubtful whether Judge Sebastian would return before the Fall term. If he should not, the suit will not be tried before the Fall term, as Judge Todd will not set in it. I have not yet learnt if Judge Sebastian has changed his intention. Should he come up the Court (which begins to day) will set out the week, and in that event I will have Key and Matson laid over until wednesday or thursday.

Yrs Sincerely HENRY CLAY

ALS. DLC-Breckinridge Papers (DNA, M212, R20). Addressed to Breckinridge at Cabell's Dale, his home near Lexington.

1 A land case first argued before the Court of Appeals in 1804, reargued in 1805 and at the fall term of 1806. 3 *Ky. Reports* (Hardin) 76-81.

Bond as Executor of Henry Marshall

[July 14, 1806]

[Henry Clay, George M. Bibb, and Cornelius Coyle give bond of £2000 current money to Samuel Blair, David Logan, Ambrose Young, and John Parker, justices of Fayette County, as security that Clay, as executor of Henry Marshall, deceased, will render a true inventory of all the "Goods, Chattels and Credits of the said deceased, which have or shall come" to Clay's knowledge; that he will exhibit this record to the Fayette County Court as required; that he will "well and truly" administer the estate and make a just accounting; and that he will pay all legacies specified in the will. Witnessed by D. Todd, Deputy Clerk.]

DS. Fayette County Executors' Bonds, vol. 2 (1803-27), p. 34. Marshall, an inkeeper on Main Street in Lexington, had died May 30, 1806. On July 26, Clay advertised in the Lexington *Kentucky Gazette* a scheduled sale of household and kitchen furniture, "and sundry other species of property," to settle this estate.

Security for Executor's Bond

[July 14, 1806]

[Clay, Alexander Atchison, Kattrin [*sic*] Clark, Samuel Blair, and

William Gibson, bind themselves in the sum of $2000 to the Justices of Fayette County for a proper administration by the last three as executors of the estate of John Clark.[1]]

DS. Fayette County Executors' Bonds, vol. 2 (1803-27), p. 35. Catherine was the widow of the decedent. Atchison and Gibson lived in the southern district of Fayette County.

1 One of the pioneer settlers of Lexington, who had died June 26, 1806.

Receipt from Arthur Patterson

14h. July 1806.

Recd. of H. Clay One hundred & twenty dollars on a/c. of his purchase of one half of the preemption granted to my father—I also acknowledge that the black horse received by me of said Clay on same account was estimated at One hundred[1] dollars,

ARTHUR PATTERSON

DS, in Clay's hand. DLC-TJC (DNA, M212, R15). See above, Receipt, March 18, 1806.

1 The words "& twenty" following this sum, deleted.

Agreement with Charles Yelton

[August 27, 1806]

I promise & oblige myself that Tho. Hart Senr. & myself shall as soon as we obtain a title from John Coburn & upon the request of Charles Yelton convey to him 65¼ Acres of land within the boundary of the tract recovered by said Hart from said Coburn as surveyed by Mr Eastin, with condition that if the land shall be lost the sum of seven dollars per acre shall be returned to the said Yelton without interest.[1] If there is more than the said quantity of 65¼ Acres in the survey of the said Eastin it is to be accounted for by said Yelton at seven dollars per acre, if less he is to be credited therefor at the same rate. Witness my hand & seal this 27 Aug. 1806.

Teste H CLAY. {L.S.}

WM. BROWN[2]

[Endorsement][3]

Given up to H Clay in Consequence of his receiving the amount of a replevin Bond Thos. Hart against Mountjoy[4] & others

JAS. GARRARD ADM.

ADS. DLC-TJC (DNA, M212, R10).

1 See above, Survey, February 19, 1806, note.

2 Brown, a native of Virginia, had come to Bourbon County at an early age, then settled at Cynthiana, Harrison County, where he became a wealthy and influential lawyer. He served in the State legislature and in the Sixteenth Congress (1819-1821).

3 AES.

4 Probably James Garrard's brother-in-law, Alvin Mountjoy, who had moved from Bourbon County to Pendleton, where he was at this time an assistant judge of the Circuit Court.

Property Deed from George Shepherd and Others

[September 10, 1806]

[Indenture by which George Shepherd and Maryann, his wife, and Duvall Cooper and Margaret, his wife, of Mason County, Kentucky, for the sum of five shillings, paid and acknowledged, sell to Henry Clay two seventh parts of a lot in Lexington in McDermid's Square on Mill Street, no. 48, lately occupied by William Dailey and by him sold to Clay, on which Dailey erected a brick house and other improvements–to which two sevenths Cooper and Shepherd and their wives derived title through the status of the wives as heirs of Francis McDermid and Fanny Wilson, the latter being another heir of Francis McDermid. Title warranted against all claiming through McDermid, with additional provision for return of the fifty dollars paid by Clay to each of the claimants in the event that the two sevenths should be lost. Certification of acknowledgment of the signatures of the Mason County parties before Lewis Bullock and William Bryant, justices of the peace for that county, September 10, 1806; recorded by Thomas Bodley, Clerk of Fayette Circuit Court, September 19, 1806.]

Fayette Circuit Court, Deed Book C, 14-15.

Promissory note from Elijah Lacy

[September 12, 1806]

I promise to pay to H. Clay on demand Ten dollars; and if I obtain a decree in my favour in the Circuit Court of Fayette in a suit agt. the Legrands I promise to pay said Clay Two pounds more. Witness my hand & Seal this 12h. Septr. 1806. ELIJAH LACY {L.S.}

DS. in Clay's hand. DLC-TJC, 2d Series, vol. 6. The suit, growing out of an earlier land case, was brought in September, 1806, by Lacy, of Goochland County, Virginia, against Peter Legrand, Sr., and Peter Legrand, Jr., of Fayette County, Kentucky (formerly of Prince Edward County, Virginia). It was decided in the plaintiff's favor in March, 1808. Fayette Circuit Court, File 146; *ibid.*, Order Book E, 81.

Deed of Trust from John Jordan, Jr.

[September 13, 1806]

[Indenture by which John Jordan, Jr., for five shillings, paid and acknowledged, and in consideration of the undertakings of Cuthbert Banks and William Macbean for Jordan as herein mentioned, conveys to Thomas Hart, Jr., and Henry Clay the following tracts: one in Montgomery County, on the Kentucky River, amounting to 27,500 acres, which was granted to Jordan by Nelson Hackett, late

Sheriff of Montgomery County, by deed of November 30, 1799, recorded in the Montgomery County Clerk's Office, Book A, page 464; also 5000 acres on Bank Lick Creek, Campbell County, being part of 6000 acres patented by the Commonwealth of Virginia to William Jones[1] in two grants, one of 2000 acres under date of February 23, 1789, and the other of 4000 acres under date of February 25, 1789, the property conveyed by Jones to John Fowler, and 5000 acres of the tract transferred by Fowler to John A. Seitz under two deeds dated September 28, 1789, recorded in the Lexington District Court, Book B, pages 513 and 514, the land having been conveyed to Seitz for himself and Jordan trading as merchants in partnership, and Jordan by the death of Seitz having acquired a right thereto for the purposes of the partnership; also a tract of 1000 acres in an unidentified county within the area set apart for soldiers and officers of the Virginia line, the property having been conveyed to Seitz by Thomas Todd and his wife under deed of July 27, 1798, to which Jordan succeeded as above; also a tract in the area set apart for soldiers and officers of the Continental line, on the waters of Cumberland River, containing 688 acres and one rood, being part of George and Thomas Underwood's[2] Military Survey, dated November 16, 1797, conveyed to Jordan by deed of October 30, 1804, from George Underwood, recorded in the offices of the Fayette Circuit Court and of the General Court; also one other tract, in Jessamine County on Hickman Creek, Marshall's Creek, and Weimer's branch, being part of General Adam Stephens' Military Survey, amounting to 125 acres, conveyed to Jordan by deed from Montgomery Bell dated August 11, 1804, recorded in the Office of the Jessamine County Clerk; also the proceeds of a contract entered into on April 10, 1806, between Jordan and Edmond and Anderson Searcy[3] for a large quantity of staves and whiskey; together with the appurtenances to the aforementioned land—In trust that whereas Banks and Macbean are bound as securities for Jordan in two notes given to Thomas January and Henry Purviance upon which suits have been instituted in the Circuit Court of Fayette County, and Jordan wishes to protect his endorsers, therefore Hart and Clay, or the survivor, is to sell, privately or at auction, so much of the property as necessary for these purposes. Hart and Clay covenant to perform the trust faithfully to the best of their judgment.

Signatures of Jordan, Hart, and Clay acknowledged before the Clerk of Fayette Circuit Court, September 29, 1806.]

Fayette Circuit Court, Deed Book C, 173-75. Recorded also in Ky. Court of Appeals, Deed Book L, 53-56.

1 Of Bourbon County, Kentucky.

2 Both of Hanover County, Virginia.

3 Of Woodford County, Kentucky.

Bill of Exchange from William Macbean

Exche. for £ 100 Bri Sterlg. Lexington Kentucky 16 Sepr. 1806
No. 337.

Sixty days after sight of this my first of Exchange second and third of same tenor and date being unpaid pay to Henry Clay Esqr. or order in London One Hundred Pounds British Sterling for value received which place to account with or without advice from

To Gillus Macbean Esqr. W. MACBEAN.
Secy. to Admiral the Honble Lord Gardner.
Cork Irland

True copy (included in notice of protest). DLC-TJC (DNA, M212, R1). Endorsed by Clay, by John Postlethwait for the Kentucky Insurance Company, and by James Smith, Jr.—the last endorsement in the form of an order on "Tho. & Robt. Barr." Thomas T. and Robert R. Barr were sons of the pioneer Lexington merchant, Robert Barr, and took over their father's business upon his retirement. The partnership was dissolved in 1811, after which Thomas T. became a prominent lawyer and, in 1817, a member of the Kentucky legislature.

From Jemmy Payne

Mr. Clay September 29th 1806

Capt, price[1] has left a Horse with me to sell, in order to raise money for the settlement of your fee or fees—as soon as I can sell the Horse you shall the Money [*sic*] I am with Esteem. JEMMY PAYNE

ANS. DLC-TJC (DNA, M212, R15).
1 Probably one of the sons of Colonel William Price.

Property Deed from Hugh McDermid

[September 29, 1806]

[Indenture by which for the sum of $50, paid and acknowledged, Hugh McDermid of Wayne County, Kentucky, sells to Henry Clay one seventh part of lot no. 48 in the tract known as McDermid's Square on Mill Street, lately occupied by William Dailey and by him sold to Clay, on which lot Dailey had erected a brick house and other improvements—Hugh McDermid deriving title to the property as heir of Francis McDermid and Fanny Wilson, the latter another heir of Francis McDermid. Warranty of title limited to claims through Francis McDermid. Certification of acknowledgment of signature by Hugh McDermid before Thomas Bodley, Clerk of Fayette Circuit Court, September 29, 1806.]

Fayette Circuit Court, Deed Book C, 37-38. Cf. above, Property Deed, September 10, 1806.

Promissory Note from Jesse Woodroofe

Octobr 7th 1806.

Due Henry Clay Esqr on or before the twenty fifth day of December next Ensueing fifty Dollars Specia for Vallue Recd as witness my hand JESSE WOODROOFE

Teste

J: BLEDSOE[1]

ADS. DLC-TJC, 2d Series, vol. 6. Woodroofe, a Virginia veteran of the Revolution, lived in Mount Sterling, Kentucky, at this time. By 1818 he had moved to Lincoln County, Tennessee, where he died in 1826.

[1] Jesse Bledsoe.

From John Wood

Dear Sir Frankfort Thursday 9 Octr. 1806—

I have thought proper to state to you in writing, my sentiments on the subject of the conversation which we had last night; as I can explain myself more fully by this mode of communication than any other; and I am confident in addressing myself to you on paper I have not to apprehend any exposure

You have had frequent opportunities of observing the reciprocal attachment that has existed between Street and myself. Perhaps such an ardent friendship is unfortunate, as it frequently entails misery on those who are the slaves of such a strong passion; but be that as it may, it has always been my lot and probably ever shall, to confine my regard exclusively to one person. This species of solitary regard constitutes my only happiness, and when deprived of the object of my affections, I feel the most miserable of mortals. This enthusiasm was likewise a principal motive which induced us to travel from Richmond together, and had it not been for some officious interference, of your acquaintance John Robison of Richmond whom we met at Shelby,[1] I trust we should not have suffered a day's separation. My object in coming to Frankfort & joining Street in the Western World proceeded from the same motives and however deserving censure I may seem; yet I must candidly confess that a principal inducement in commencing the investigation of the Spanish conspiracy[2] were the hopes, that the arduousness of the undertaking, and the difficulties we should have to encounter, with the enmities we would incur, would be the means of binding us closer together.

This indissoluble union too, would have been produced; had not *certain individuals* of a *certain family* as remarkable for their coldness towards each other as to strangers interposed. Although J. H. Davis one of those to whom I allude, be perhaps in your opinion a person of integrity; yet his conduct when here in this respect, shall never be by me forgotten Every art of which he was master, was exerted in order to produce a distrust and breach of friendship between Street and myself. His views were evident, he saw that Street was young and candid in the extreme; and therefore he supposed if we were separated, he might influence him as he pleased. At the commencement of the paper, I certainly was inclined to have been neuter as to Federal and Antifederal politics; but the conduct of Davis alone influenced me in my numbers of the spanish association, wherever an opportunity offered itself, to make an attack upon the Federal party in hope of irritating Davis and breaking off his connexion with Street. This likewise was my sole object in republishing the Western American, and observing the prosecution was shamefully quashed; knowing it was done at the instance of Davis[3]—

You have been the sole witness to any harsh expressions which have passed between Street and myself.[4] Since that unhappy day, several such instances have occured, but only caused, I am certain by erroneous prejudices impressed in his mind by Davis against me. The conduct of the Marshalls is nearly similar. They preserve the utmost distance towards me; but do every thing in their power to keep Street along with them, and he has been for those [*sic*] two days with Alexander and Doctor Marshall.[5]

Under these circumstances, it is my sincere wish, that a total stop be put to the further developement of the Spanish Association, if not to the paper. If we proceed, we must necessarily come to the utmost variance in our opinions which finally may lead to an open rupture between us.

If you therefore could suggest any mode by which this could be done with honour to ourselves, and the satisfaction of those accused & concerned it would be highly gratifying. I shall briefly state some of those ways which have suggested themselves to me and shall be happy to have your opinion as to their correctness

1st. To inform the public that we have given the names of the persons in whose possession the principal documents respecting the Spanish Association are placed; and that the accused by applying to them if not guilty have a fair opportunity of vindicating themselves; but that from the unusual sensation which has been created among the minds of the citizens in this and other states; we deem it improper to proceed farther in the business particularly as we are informed the Executive are in possession of more documents than we have had access to; as likewise that from the early factions which prevailed in this state many misrepresentations may have taken place—

2dly. To state in the most candid manner, that from the few subscribers who have paid their subscriptions, we cannot feel ourselves justified in incurring expences which may never be defrayed.

I have now Sir, unfolded myself in a manner which I certainly would not have hazarded to any other individual; and with the certain confidence, that no advantage will be taken of the sentiments which I have expressed. The situation in which both Street & myself [*sic*] is certainly a deplorable one; but he does not see it. Those in whom he confides so far from assisting him will only urge him nearer sedition. Even John Rowan who I believe is his best friend, will I am satisfied advise to measures, which will prove equally fatal.[6] Had the same cordiality as formerly existed between Street & myself, we should have surmounted every difficulty; but the only salvation to both of us which I now can see, is the stoppage of the paper, or at least the developement of the Spanish Conspiracy.

Of those whom we have accused, there is only one, for whom I confess I entertain the slightest regard. This is Colonel Tod [*sic*]. I regret that any thing has been mentd. respecting him. Davis alone was the cause of it; for although from the information I obtained, Colonel Tod was equally zealous as the others for a *violent separation* from the Union, yet his name should have been passed over in silence, had not Davis written a small paragraph for Colonel Tod in answer to the toast of Hopkins, which I refused to insert; and the passion of contradition which I bore against Davis I am sorry to say in this instance surpassed the friendship I had for Colonel Tod.—[7]

Your advice Sir on the foregoing points will much oblige

Your most obedient Servant JOHN WOOD

ALS. DLC-HC (DNA, M212, R1). Wood, a New York "newspaper hack," and Joseph M. Street, a Virginian, established in July, 1806, the Frankfort (Ky.) *Western World*, which became the mouthpiece of Humphrey Marshall and Joseph Hamilton Daveiss. Disturbed by the growing influence of these Federalist leaders on his partner, Wood had consulted Clay in July. During the month of October, 1806, the editors employed Clay, Humphrey Marshall, and Isham Talbot as defense counsel in two suits involving defamation of character. On the advice of Clay and others, Wood finally terminated his connection with the *Western World* in December, 1806.

1 Virginia.

2 The *Western World* carried numerous articles purporting to expose treasonable activities of Kentuckians who in the 1780's were allegedly under Spanish influence seeking to separate their section of the country from the United States.

3 The *Western World* of September 20, 1806, contained an essay, written by Francis Flournoy but signed "A Western American," which had originally appeared in the Frankfort *Guardian of Freedom*, March 2, 1803. An editorial note in the *Western World* stated that a "sham prosecution" against the author of the "treasonable publication" had been "carefully quashed."

4 On one occasion in Clay's presence Wood had quarrelled with Street at Bush's Tavern in Frankfort. Wood to W. S. Hunter, June 22, 1809 (DLC-Innes Papers), quoted in Temple Bodley, "Introduction," in *Reprints of Littell's Political Transactions In and Concerning Kentucky* (Filson Club *Publications*, no. 31; Louisville, Ky., 1926), xcvi note.

5 Alexander K. and Dr. Louis Marshall, brothers of Chief Justice John Marshall, were cousins of Humphrey Marshall.

6 Elected to Congress late in 1806, Rowan continued the exposé of the Spanish Association and tried unsuccessfully in the spring of 1808 to have Judge Harry Innes impeached for his role in the intrigue. For Street's legal difficulties growing out of the Innes attack, see below, Clay to Innes, April 21, 1812, note.

7 Samuel Goode Hopkins, son of General Samuel Hopkins, at a Fourth of July celebration at Frankfort in 1806 had toasted "Those judges of the Kentucky courts, whose integrity has never been stained by Spanish gold, and who have never prostituted the dignity of their station, by holding a plurality of offices." Apparently Daveiss had written a defense of Justice Thomas Todd which Wood had not published.

Agreement with John Breckinridge

[October 10, 1806]

Whereas John Breckinridge claims the one equal moiety of 1000 acres of land patented in the name of—James Young & himself, & founded on an entry in the—name of John Green, lying on middle Creek in Floyd County & including the Salt Works now in the occupation of William Keaton tenant of the said Breckinridge:[1]

And whereas the said Breckinridge also claims a tract of 5000 acres patented in his own name[2] & which also includes the said Salt works: And whereas the said Young is indebted to the said Breckinridge about five hundred pounds (the sum not exactly recollected), and in order to secure the payment thereof has mortgaged to the said Breckinridge the aforesaid 1000 acre tract of land; as will more fully appear by the deed of mortgage, now of record in the Court of Floyd County:

And whereas Robert Johnson, Benja. Netherland, Humphrey Marshall & Henry Clay claim a tract of 192 acres, entered, surveyed & patented in the Name of the said Netherland, which tract also includes the aforesaid Salt Works; also 300 acres entered in the name of the said Johnson surveyed, adjoining or contiguous to the said tract of 192 acres; also acres entered in the name of John Moseby,[3] which is survd. adjoining or contiguous to the said tract of 300 acres: ——And the parties hereto being desireous to compromise their. aforesaid. interfering claims, have agreed as follows:

1st. The said Breckinridge agrees to convey [. . .][4] required, to the said Netherland, Johnson, Marshall & Clay or to their Assignees, one equal moiety of his right & interest in the aforesaid 1000. & 5000. acre tracts of land; and also to invest them by such transfer as they may deem proper, with a right to an equal moiety of whatever may accrue from the aforesaid mortgage.

2ndly. The said Netherland, Johnson, Marshall & Clay agree to convey at the same time to the sd. Breckinridge one equal moiety of their right & interest in the aforesd. 192, 300 and acre tracts—It is clearly understood by the parties hereto, that no warranty of title whatsoever is expected to be made by either party to the other; but the party receiving is to take such title, & such only, as the party conveying is seized of under the claim conveyed.

And 3rdly. The said Netherland, Johnson, Marshall & Clay are to be admitted to the possession of one equal half of the said lands & salt works from & after the first day of next month, & to participate in the profits thereof from that time.—They are however to account with the said Breckinridge for one half of the value of the salt kettles which may be in use at the salt works at the time they are admitted to participate in the profits as afd. Witness our Hands & Seals this 10th. day of October 1806 JOHN BRECKINRIDGE {SEAL}

Teste HENRY CLAY for {L.S.}
himself, Netherland
Johnson & Marshall.

DS, in Breckinridge's hand. DLC-TJC (DNA, M212, R10).

1 The entry had been made December 21, 1782, by Green, a resident of Virginia who frequently visited Kentucky to attend to extensive land interests. He was an elder half-brother of Willis and William Green.

2 Entered April 16, 1796.

3 Of Woodford County, Kentucky.

4 MS. torn.

Receipt from Arthur Patterson

12 Octr. 1806.

Recd. of H. Clay Twenty dollars on account of land sold him.

ARTHUR PATTERSON.

DS. in Clay's hand. DLC-TJC, 2d Series, vol. 6. See above, Agreement, September 18, 1805.

From Robert Saunders

Sir, Oct. 12h. 1806.

Untill this day I have not been able to get a Notice regularly served on the Representative of the late Warner Lewis; altho', since I received your letter dated in March last,[1] and since the Commission awarded by the Court, I have made two several Efforts—I enclose therefore the Commission and Notice[2] with a hope that they will reach you time enough to have the Commission executed agreeably to the Notice—

The cause stands at issue upon the Plea of *covenants performed* by Warner Lewis—of course no Proof is necessary as to the execution of the Paper—[3]

With respect to evidence for the increase of damages, I am at a loss, without conferring with you to give you any guide—If it could be shewn that Mr. Lewis had a title which he refused to convey, your damages ought to be estimated in proportion to the estimated value of the Land: so, if Mr. Lewis has benefitted himself by an after sale and conveyance your injury would be proportionably aggravated—I apprehend, however, he never had title; else, it would have been your course, I suppose, to obtain a specific performance.

If he had not title, can you recover upon the ground of deceit more than the sum advanced and interest—?

It will be well, I think, Sir, to prove the value of this Land, about the time of your purchase, by those who best know it; and, what has been the selling Price since:—And, if any offers have been made to you, in consequence of Mr. Lewis's Covenant, it would be proper to prove what they were—Did you tender any Deed at any time to Mr. Lewis, and can it be proved? who is in Possession of the Survey; and has a grant been obtained thereon? Perhaps a Copy of the Survey with the Register's Certificate, with the authentication of his Power will be proper:—No doubt the survey speaks of the indentical [*sic*] Land described in the covenant.

In the execution of the Commission, the Commissioners will be pleased, (at least three), to seal the same—and have the Commission certified according to the Mode prescribed by the Laws of Kentucky.

I know not whether the money spoken of in the deed will be disputed—If it is, as Edmund Randolph Esqr. is within my reach, I can easily have him summoned—

I am, respectfully, Your obed. Servt.

Virga. RO: SAUNDERS
Wmsburg

ALS. DLC-TJC (DNA, M212, R10). Addressed to Clay at Lexington.
1 Not found. 2 Not found.
3 See above, Bond, August 22, 1797.

Receipt from Robert Russell

13. Oct. 1806.

Recd. of H Clay Twenty one Dollars on account of Stone for his Stone Steps.

Gabl Lewis ROB. RUSSELL

DS, in Clay's hand. DLC-TJC, 2d Series, vol. 6. Russell, a stone cutter, was located on Short Street in Lexington.

Power of Attorney from John Cockey Owings

[October 16, 1806]

[John Cockey Owings of Baltimore County, Maryland, appoints Henry Clay and Thomas Deye Owings his attorneys, authorizing them to dispose of his Kentucky lands, to collect rents and other obligations due him, and for these purposes to substitute one or more attorneys under them. Acknowledged before a notary public of Baltimore, October 16, 1806; recorded by the Clerk of the Kentucky Court of Appeals, November 5, 1806.]

Kentucky Court of Appeals, Deed Book K, 491-93.

From Andrew Jackson

Henry Clay Esqr. Nashville October 27th. 1806

Sir By advice Just recd. from Mr. J. W. Hunt, we are informed that you are attorney for us in the suit Jackson & Hutchings vs. John. M. Garrard[1]—Mr Hunt also advises, that Mrr. [*sic*] Garrard has put in a plea relative to the Justness of our claim against him and concludes, "we had better confer with you upon the Subject," we therefore take the liberty, altho unaquainted, to write you—And beg leave to observe—that the claim on which Mr Garrard is Sued, originated, in Merchandize sold to him, in cash loaned, and in orders drew on and accepted by us—in the fall 1805—in 1806—(we believe in May) a final settlement took place, between us, and he closed his acpt" by his note with assurances that the Money Should be paid before he left this country—but contrary to our expectations and the good oppinion we had entertained of him, he went off without taking up his note, altho he carried with him at least one thousand dollars in cash—and on the day of settlement he drew an order on Major Verrell,[2] in part of the debt due us which Verrell did not accept —This is over and above the amount of his Note and for which he stands Justly indebted—we have no doubt from the conduct of John M. Garrard he is capable of doing any thing—or sugesting any thing that is either dishonest or dishonourable but it is strange to us, that such sugestions should way any thing, in a court of Justice against his own note which was given on a final settlement since which no kind of intercourse or dealings has taken place between us—you will therefore be good anough to advise us, the state and situation of that suit—the nature of the plea he has put in, and what kind of (if any) proof may be necessary for us to forward you and send on commissions for that purpose—and be good anough to draw on us for your fee, which shall be honoured on sight—

your attention to this will Much oblige yr Hble Servts

JACKSON & HUTCHING[S]

ALS, by Jackson. DLC-Andrew Jackson Papers (DNA, M212, R21). Published in John Spencer Bassett (ed.), *Correspondence of Andrew Jackson* (Carnegie Institution of Washington, *Publication* no. 371; 7 vols., Washington, 1926-1935) I, 151.

1 Jackson and John Hutchings, Mrs. Jackson's nephew, were partners in a Nashville mercantile firm. Garrard, a resident of Bourbon County, Kentucky, the son of former Kentucky Governor James Garrard, had lived for a time in Nashville, where he had been associated with Jackson in the training of race horses. Clay filed a bill of complaint, Andrew Jackson *vs.* John M. Garrard (ADS. Bourbon Circuit Court, File 224), in 1807, asking payment of a note for $193.74 and damages of $100. Judgment favoring the plaintiff was rendered in August, 1809.

2 John Verrell, of Dinwiddie County, Virginia, was a friend of Jackson and a fellow racing enthusiast.

From George Cleveland

27th Day of october 1806

Henry Clay Esqr attorney at Law for James Coleman Jur.

Sir please to take notice that I shall procede to take the Depositions of Sundry witnesses at the house of Henry Buchannan in the town of paris in the County of Bourbon in the State of Kentucky on the thirteenth Day of November 1806 Betwen the Hours of ten in the forenown and SunSet of the Same Day and to bee Continued from Day to Day untill the Depositions are all taken which Depositions I Shall offer as evidence in a Suit in Chancery Depending in the Bourbon Circuit Court State of Kentucky wherein I am Complainant and James Coleman Junr. is Defendant. I am Sir your obt Sert GEORGE CLEVELAND

To Henry Clay Esquire attorney at Law
for James Coleman Junr Lexington Kentucky

ALS. DLC-TJC (DNA, M212, R15). See above, Acknowledgment of Debt, January 31, 1806, note.

Note from John South

[November 2, 1806]

Copy, included in Bill, August 22, 1807.

From Nat Smith

Dumfries Virginia
3rd. November 1806

Estimable Acquaintance

Being actuated by the pure desire of rendering, or being instrumental in promoting the welfare and prosperity of a de[se]rving man, I have presumed to reccommed to your confidance and patronage Mr Asa Blanchard (a Silver Smith)

I lament that I cannot write to you under more *auspicious circumstances*—but the thorough knowledge of your liberality of sentiment eases me greatly on that subject—Mr Blancet I believe has a variety of recommendations from eminant and dignified characters which will (I dare believe) clearly confirm his honor and vertue as a man; and his skill and punctuality as a workman I need not suggest much to your extended & discriminateing mind of the utility and importance of having influential friends in the commencement of business among strangers; and that of a trade where the dignity of Jobs entrusted to him opens a door for the establishment of celebrity in the particular vocation—nor need I say that we are all links of one great chain, and by the laws of phylanthropy (written in the constitution of the heart of every good man) are bound to contribute our part in promoteing the felicity of a *man*—

I shall say but little more—I could wish that Mr Blanchard could come better reccommeded to you (if he has none else but mine) as I am certain he has merit Permit me here to predicate my my [*sic*] heart felt gratitude, for your magnanimous & friendly, disinterested offers when I took leave of you, at the Olympian Springs, last year, when I was unpleasantly situated.

I really wish you happiness & celebrity NAT SMITH

PS. It is late. Mr B embraces an early hour for starting, and I cannot (with out distressing my health) *copy*, and write as fair & well as I ought to you but you are not the slave of ceremony—

NS—

ALS. DLC-TJC (DNA, M212, R12). Addressed to Clay at Lexington for delivery by Blanchard, who was to become the most celebrated of the early Kentucky silversmiths.

Bill for Redemption of Lands Sold for Taxes

[November 5, 1806]

Clay reported the bill for a drafting committee which included also Samuel Hopkins, Felix Grundy, and John Pope. Ky. H. of Reps., *Journal, 1806*, p. 11. On the preceding day Clay had moved to present such a measure. After amendment by the Senate, the proposal was enacted November 28. It provided for redemption of land sold for taxes within two years from the date of sale, by payment of the amount of the tax, interest, and charges for which the land was sold, with interest thereon at the rate of 100 per cent per annum from the date of sale to the date of redemption, and by payment of taxes accrued subsequent to sale. All tracts exposed to sale which were not sold for want of sufficient bids were to be turned over to the State, subject to redemption within two years under conditions similar to those above stated, but with the interest rate lowered to 50 per cent per annum. Littell (comp.), *Statute Law of Kentucky*, III, 335. Clay's efforts to obtain such legislation, of particular applicability to non-resident landholders, had been defeated in 1804.

Committee Report Relative to Election in Green County

[November 5, 1806]

The select committee to whom was referred the petition of Elias Barbee, have come to the following resolution thereupon, to wit:

Resolved, As the opinion of this committee, that the said petition of Elias Barbee's,[1] complaining of the undue election of Samuel Brents,[2] be rejected—because the charges therein contained, are not supported by the oath or affidavit of a person having knowledge of their truth.

Ky. H. of Reps., *Journal, 1806*, p. 13. Other members of the drafting committee were Samuel McKee (Garrard County), William Russell, John Pope, John Thompson (representative from Scott County, 1803-1807, not the Lexington lawyer of that name),

Samuel Hopkins, and Felix Grundy. The report is here printed in the form adopted by the House, after minor amendment.

1 Elias Barbee, farmer, one of the first judges of the Green County Court of Quarter Sessions, and delegate in the Kentucky House of Representatives, 1800-1802, 1825-1827; in the Kentucky Senate, 1820-1823.

2 Samuel Brents, lawyer and Green County delegate in the Kentucky House of Representatives, 1803-1807, 1820, 1821, 1824.

From Aaron Burr

Sir Loves Inn[1] ½ past 3—[November 7, 1806]

At nine this Morning Mr. Jordan[2] recd. your letter in reply to one which he wrote at my request—

I have just arrived, wet and something fatigued and send to inquire whether my presence in Court is *now* deemed necessary or expedient.—

I pray you to consider yourself as my Counsel in the business moved by Mr D—[3] a more *technical* application will be made when I shall have the pleasure to see you—an early interview, at this house, would very much gratify, Yr Ob St

H. Clay Esqr. A BURR

ALS. DLC-HC (DNA, M212, R1). Published in Colton (ed.), *Private Correspondence of Henry Clay*, 14.

1 Tavern in Frankfort operated by Major Thomas Love.

2 John Jordan, Jr., whose support of Burr left him a large holder of defaulted Burr notes. Neither letter has been found.

3 Joseph Hamilton Daveiss on Wednesday, November 5, had instituted proceedings in Federal Court at Frankfort, over which Judge Harry Innes presided, charging Burr with preparing for a warlike expedition against Mexico. On November 8, Burr voluntarily appeared and a grand jury was empaneled, after which the court postponed further action until November 12. On the appointed day Daveiss, unable to produce all his witnesses, asked that the grand jury be discharged, and the court adjourned.

Promissory Note from Charles Morgan

[November 9, 1806]

I promise to pay to Henry Clay on or before the last day of April next the Sum of Twenty Six pounds. Witness my hand & Seal this 9h. Nov. 1806 at Frankfort. CHARLES MORGAN {L.S.}

DS, in Clay's hand. DLC-TJC, 2d Series, vol. 6. Endorsed on verso by Clay: ". . . Living about Sixteen miles below Pittsburg."

Bill Relating to Term of Fayette Circuit Court

[November 13, 1806]

Clay reported the bill for a drafting committee which also included John Pope and William Russell, the other Fayette representatives. Ky. H. of Reps., *Journal, 1806*, p. 40. On November 10, Clay had moved to present such a measure. Proposing to change the term from March to January, the bill was enacted without controversy on November 22. See Littell (comp.), *Statute Law of Kentucky*, III, 330.

To Noah Webster

Sir Lex. 18. Nov. 1806.

I have received several letters from you and a power of Atto.[1] in relation to a contract with Mr. Charless.[2] Execution of the contract has been delayed in consequence of Mr. Charless not having earlier received the Types. They are now received & the contract is executed. He has struck 5000 Copies of the book, & says he can vend annually 12.000. He i[s] willing to make the purchase yo[. . .][3] for the Western Country, if you will render the payments less speedy. He will give you the price asked if you will accept of annual payments of $200 each with interest. In the event of your noncurrence he says he will edit the Columbian Spelling book,[4] sales of which he thinks he can effect. Yrs. HENRY CLAY

ALS. NN-Ford Collection. Addressed to Webster at New Haven, Connecticut. Endorsed: "Answered Decr 18th. & the terms offered by Mr Charless accepted; the first payment to be forthwith—& Mr Clay to keep the note for the sums—the money to be paid to my agent in Philadelphia, David Hogan—or sent in Bank bills to me at the risk of Charless N Webster"

1 These documents have not been found.

2 Joseph Charless, who two months before the date of this letter had begun offering *Webster's Spelling Book* for sale at the price of twenty-five cents.

3 Two or three words obliterated.

4 *The Columbian Spelling and Reading Book, or an Easy and Alluring Guide to Spelling and Reading* (Philadelphia: Printed for Mathew Carey, 1798).

Nomination for United States Senator

[November 18, 1806]

Clay nominated Samuel Hopkins; Fortunatus Cosby, John Pope; and Felix Grundy, John Adair as suitable for the office of Senator to represent Kentucky in Congress. Ky. H. of Reps., *Journal, 1806,* p. 60. Clay served as chairman of the House committee which met with the delegation from the Senate to compare the votes of each house. After three ballots, the House restricted its election to the two highest candidates, Pope and Adair, whereupon Pope was elected.

Discussing this election with William Plumer, United States Senator from New Hampshire, 1802-1807, Clay commented "that Adair's supposed connection with Burr did not lose him a single vote. He [Clay] said, That Adair was never popular—that Pope was always so—& had a great advantage over Adair by being a member of the legislature who elected the Senator." Plumer, Diary, 622 (DLC, DNA Micro. Supp.).

John Pope was a member of the Kentucky House of Representatives, 1802 (Shelby County), 1806 and 1807 (Fayette County): of the United States Senate, 1807-1813; Kentucky Secretary of State, 1816-1819; member of the Kentucky Senate, 1825-1829 (Washington County); Governor of Arkansas Territory, 1829-1835; member of Congress, 1837-1843. He was the only member of the Kentucky Congressional delegation to oppose the War of 1812, and largely on this ground he was defeated by Clay for a seat in Congress in the close election of 1816.

Credentials as United States Senator

Kentucky to wit. [November 19, 1806]

The Legislature of this Commonwealth on the Nineteenth day of November one thousand eight hundred and six having in pursuance of the Constitution of the United States of America chosen Henry Clay Esquire a Senator, (in the place of John Adair resigned) I Christopher Greenup being Governor or Chief Magistrate of the Commonwealth of Kentucky, do hereby certify the same to the Senate of the United States

Given under my hand and seal of the Commonwealth this nineteenth day of November, One thousand eight hundred and six and of the Commonwealth the Fifteenth

{SEAL} CHRISTO. GREENUP

By the Governor JOHN ROWAN Secretary

DS. DNA, RG46, 11B-B2. Endorsed on cover sheet: "1806. .29 Decr. Read."

Promissory Note to John Pickett

[November 21, 1806]

On or before the first day of November next I promise to pay to John Pickett or order One hundred and fifty dollars with legal interest thereon from the 20h. day of September last—

Witness my hand & Seal this 21 Nov. 1806

Teste HENRY [CLAY {L.S.}]

WILLIAM POLLOCK[1]

ADS. DLC-TJC (DNA, M212, R15). Part of signature defaced. On March 10, 1807, Pickett, a resident of Harrison County, Kentucky, made an assignment of $118 of this note to Isaac Miller, a merchant of Cynthiana in the same county. It was then assigned by Miller to James Coleman and by the latter to Benjamin Howard.

1 A member of the State House of Representatives from Harrison County.

Receipt from William G. Sears

[November 23, 1806]

Recd. 23d. Novr. 1806 of Henry Clay bills to the amount of five hundred dollars on account of an Assumpsit made by Genl. Brooke[1] on account of said Clay to the Exors of John Hoomes[2] in the purchase of Buzzard.[3] Recd for the Exors as their Agent.

WILLIAM G SEARS

DS, in Clay's hand. DLC-TJC (DNA, M212, R15). Sears has not been identified.

1 Francis T. Brooke.

2 Wealthy planter of Caroline County, Virginia, whose will had been probated January 16, 1806.

3 See below, Advertisement, March 7, 1808.

From Michael Tiernan and Company

Mr. Henry Clay Baltimore 24th. November 1806

Dear sir Our Luke Tiernan,[1] forwarded you sometime ago. Two.

Fifty dollar Counterfeit Notes, which was paid to Jonas McPherson, by mr Thomas Eastland[2] on our account. and he has requested us to write you by mr Francisco[3] to Know if you have recovered the same, if so. you will do us a favor by Remitting the same. or advising us in what state of forwardness you have got the same

we are sir Your Friends M. TIERNAN & Co

ALS. DLC-TJC (DNA, M212, R12).

1 A native of Ireland who had come to the United States around 1783, settled first at Hagerstown, then moved to Baltimore, where he became a wealthy merchant, prominent in local civil and political affairs.

2 Partner with Joseph Akin in a mercantile firm at Greensburg, Green County, Kentucky. Both men also had connections in the Bluegrass section of the State, where Eastland held property in Woodford County at this time. McPherson has not been identified.

3 Possibly John Francisco, of Woodford County.

From Aaron Burr

Dear Sir,— Louis Ville 27 Novr 1806

Information has this Morning been given to me that Mr. Davies has recommenced his prosecution & inquiry[1]—I must intreat your professional aid in this business—It would be disagreeable to me to form a new connection & various considerations will it is hoped induce you even at some personal inconvenience to acquiesce in my request—I shall however insist on making a liberal pecuniary compensation—The sta[r]ting of your Journey to Washington for a few days cannot be very material—No business is done in Congress till after New Year[2] respectfully Yr Obt St A. BURR

I pray you to repair to Frankfort on receipt of this—

ALS. DLC-HC (DNA, M212, R1). Published in Colton (ed.), *Private Correspondence of Henry Clay*, 13. Addressed to Clay at Lexington.

1 At Daveiss' request the Federal Court on November 25 had ordered the grand jury to convene one week later to investigate Burr's conduct.

2 On November 19 the Kentucky legislature had elected Clay to the United States Senate to complete the term of John Adair. As Clay reported the circumstances to Plumer, "The next day after Pope's election, Genl Adair told Clay that as he did not possess the confidence of the Legislature he would no longer represent them in the Senate of the United States—& he accordingly sent in his resignation." Plumer, Diary, 622-23 (DLC, DNA Micro. Supp.).

From Aaron Burr

Sir, Frankfort 1. Dec. 1806.

I have no design, nor have I taken any measure, to promote a dissolution of the Union or a seperation of any one or more States from the residue—I have neither published a line on this subject nor has any one through my agency or with my knowledge—I have no design to intermeddle with the Government or to disturb the tranquility of the United States, or of its territories or any part of them. I have neither issued nor signed nor promised a commission to any person for any purpose. I do not own a musket nor a bayonet nor any single article of military stores nor does any person for me by my authority or with my knowledge.

My views have been fully explained to and approved by several of the principal officers of Government, and, I believe, are well understood by the Administration & seen by it with complacency. They are such as every man of honor & every good Citizen must approve.

Considering the high station you now fill in our national Councils I have thought these explanations proper as well to counteract the chimerical tales which malevolent persons have so industriously circulated as to satisfy you that you have not espoused the cause of a man in any way unfriendly to the laws, the Government or the interests of his Country. respectfully yr obd Servt.

The Honble. Henry Clay. A. BURR.

Copy. DLC-TJC (DNA, M212, R10). Published in Colton (ed.), *Private Correspondence of Henry Clay*, 13-14. A cover sheet, without the letter that once accompanied it, endorsed by Clay as follows: "Burr Aaron Copy disavowing all treasonable projects & purposes—" is located in DLC-HC (DNA, M212, R1). The endorsement appears to have been separated from the copy, which was prepared for Clay by Col. Isaac Coles, secretary to President Jefferson, from the original in Jefferson's files. See below, Clay to Dr. R. Pindell, October 15, 1828.

Clay explained the origin of this letter in the following conversation reported by William Plumer (Plumer, Diary, 606-608; DLC [DNA, M212, R22]):

"He [Clay] told me that Aaron Burr was present at the District court in Kentucky when Mr Davies made the second attempt to indict him for a conspiracy agt the Spanish dominions & for attempting &c to effect a disunion of the United States.—That at this second time he told Mr Burr that it was possible that there might be something in the nature of his enterprize that would militate against his (Clay's) duty as a Senator—& therefore it would be improper for him to engage as his council. Mr Burr replied That he was guilty of no hostile measures against the United States or any power in amity with them.

"Mr Clay then said to me here is a letter Mr Burr wrote & sent to me upon the subject."

From Cuthbert Banks

Sir Lexington December 2 1806

I Sold the Out Lott I purchased From you to C Kieser[1] for Which I wish you to Give Him the title for the said Lott & Obige [*sic*] your HSt

Mr H Clay CUTHBT BANKS

ADS. DLC-TJC, 2d Series, vol. 6.

1 Christopher Keiser, father of John, was a Lexington blacksmith.

Defense of Aaron Burr

[December 2, 1806]

Mr. Henry Clay, who appeared in conjunction with Mr. John Allen[1] as the counsel for Col. Burr, rose, and in reply observed, that Col. Burr was only apprehensive of delay, that it was painful, and particularly irksome to be obliged perpetually[2] to dance attendance upon such a charge in that court.

. . . .

Mr. Clay was only desirous (he said) that the attorney for the United States would pursue what the law of the land warrants. Something has been said, continued Mr. Clay, about Col. Burr's presence not being necessary; and will Mr. Daveiss tell me this after what has already passed? Is his name to be mentioned, and is he not to appear because there is no process, no deputy marshall directed to take his person?

[The attorney for the United States, Joseph H. Daveiss, reiterated his view that, without a formal indictment, neither Burr nor his attorney held legal status in court. Daveiss also contended for his right to examine witnesses before the grand jury.]

Mr. Clay observed, he understood the constitution of a grand jury to be very different—He should never cease (he said) to contend for the liberty of the country. All at once continued Mr. C. the office of public attorney springs into an importance which never before was heard of. I appeal to the practice of every other court whether or not the public attorney has the priviledge now contended for? I take the functions of the grand jury to be these, to send for what witnesses they please, and examine whom they please. They ought to retire and enquire of the proper persons to send for.

. . . . He [Daveiss] then moved for an attachment against general Adair,[3] for non-attendance. This was opposed by Mr. Clay, on the grounds that no hour had been mentioned in the summons, and consequently the attachment could not issue during the whole day to which he was summoned, until Wednesday morning; in which objection he was supported by the opinion of the judge.

Frankfort *Western World,* December 18, 1806.

1 Of Frankfort.

2 Cf. above, Burr to Clay, November 7, 1806, note.

3 John Adair had been summoned as a witness but had failed to appear.

Defense of Aaron Burr

[December 3, 1806]

Mr. Daveiss rose and stated to the grand jury, that they might call on him, if they thought proper, to assist them to examine witnesses; and was proceeding to make some remarks to the foreman, when Mr. Clay interrupted him, and addressing the court, observed, that the privilege contended for by Mr. Daveiss, was a novel one, and he hoped the court would not grant it.

. . . .

Mr. Clay said, he appealed to the practice of other courts—yesterday his honor addressed the public attorney on this subject—he was willing to give up the point, if either equity or law appeared in his favor; but he was confident that neither would warrant the demand of Mr. Daveiss.

. . . .

Mr. Clay cared not in what attitude he should be considered as standing; but he would instantly renounce Col. Burr and his cause, did he entertain the slightest idea of his guilt, as to the charges exhibited against him by Mr. Daveiss. You have heard of inquisitions in Europe, (said Mr. Clay) you have heard of the screws and tortures made use of in the dens of despotism, to extort confession; of the dark conclaves and caucuses, for the purpose of twisting some incoherent expression into evidence of guilt. Is not the project of the attorney for the United States, a similar object of terror? But all will not do; all the art of the attorney will not effect his purpose. I call upon him to produce a single instance where the public attorney has been accustomed to examine the witnesses before the grand jury; to sound the jurors and enter into all their secrets.

Frankfort *Western World,* December 18, 1806.

From John Wood

Dear Sir Frankfort Thursday 4 Decr. 1806

As I may not have an opportunity of seeing you this evening, I take the liberty of penning my ideas to you in a few lines.

I am situated at present with Mr. Street under the most distressing circumstances. He is advised and supported by certain individuals whom I need not name that are inimical to me. From language and conversation which have passed between us all hopes of reconciliation are at an end—My only ambition and object therefore are to procure such a settlement as may afford the means of carrying me to Richmond in Virginia where I know I can procure employment as as [*sic*] a Teacher. Soon after entering into partnership I gave him all the money I had, and the nature of our concern necessarily required it, even if it had been more. He is willing to give me his note with security for what may be due payable in eight months; but this will not answer my present purpose.

If it could be in your power to advance me as much as would be necessary to carry me in the Stage there I should esteem it as the most singular favour. I should deposit Mr. Streets note in your hands for security: besides I think by taking five hundred coppies of the report of the committee[1] along with me I could sell them at

Richmond & Frederick-burgh and remit the sum I owed to you immediately at Washington—I am at present so circumstance [*sic*] that there is not another individual I could apply to with any expectation of service.[2]

I am particularly anxious if I could have a meeting with Colonel Burr either at this place or Lexington; as I think I can prevail with the company at Richmond to purchase 100,000 Acres of Col. Lynch's Grant and should be happy to have his views on the subject.[3] I could also better explain to him personally my only inducement to the present unfortunate political engagement. With the utmost gratitude for your services I remain with respect Yours &c.

JOHN WOOD

ALS. DLC-HC (DNA, M212, R1). Addressed to Clay at Frankfort. Cf. above, Wood to Clay, October 9, 1806.

1 *The Report of the Select Committee, to Whom Was Referred the Information Communicated to the House of Representatives, Charging Benjamin Sebastian, One of the Judges of the Court of Appeals of Kentucky, with Having Received a Pension from the Spanish Government* (Frankfort: Press of J. M. Street, 1806).

2 Wood later stated that "Mr. Clay advanced me seventy dollars on Street's note." Wood to W. S. Hunter, June 22, 1809, in Bodley, "Introduction," *Reprints of Littell's Political Transactions*, p. xcvii, note. Humphrey Marshall charged that Wood "was seduced from" his partner "principally by the address and solicitation of Henry Clay." Humphrey Marshall, *The History of Kentucky* (2d. ed., 2 vols.; Frankfort, 1824), II, 412.

3 Charles Lynch of Shelby County, Kentucky, had acquired from Abraham Morhouse a claim to about 700,000 acres of the Washita land originally claimed by Bastrop. Burr, in turn had purchased about one half of Lynch's claim.

Receipt to William Henry

7h. Decr. 1806

Received of Wm. Henry Esq. admor of Robert Henry full satisfaction for the amount of a decree of Fayette Circuit Court in the suit in Chancery Turner & Henry agt. Hart & Dodge and also the costs of a Suit at law in Scott Court of Quarter Sessions Dodge agt. Henry & Turner.[1]

HENRY CLAY
Atto at law of Hart & Dodge

F COSBY

ADS. Fayette Circuit Court, File 96 (1805). Henry, Revolutionary veteran and Indian fighter, one of the first trustees of Georgetown, Kentucky, and a member of the second Kentucky constitutional convention, 1799, had represented Scott County in both houses of the State legislature.

1 In 1798 William Turner and Robert Henry, both of Fayette County, had agreed to purchase from David Dodge and Thomas Hart a quantity of cordage delivered at Cleveland's Landing on the Kentucky River. Samuel Price and Henry had supervised transportation of the cordage to New Orleans, where, finding no market for it, they had undertaken to ship it to an east coast port. Both Price and Henry had died during the voyage. Subsequently Hart and Dodge had brought suit against Turner and Robert Henry's administrator in Scott County Court of Quarter Sessions, where they had won judgment for £ 131:6:4¼. Turner and Henry had then obtained an injunction to stay execution while they filed a counter-suit against Hart and Dodge in Fayette Circuit Court. The latter body had finally dissolved the injunction and ordered payment of the original judgment. Fayette Circuit Court, File 96.

Advertisement

8th December, 1806

HENRY CLAY,

BEING about to leave the state for three or four months, informs his Clients, that wherever they desire a continuance of their causes until his return, he has satisfactory assurances that they will be indulged. He expects but three of the Courts in which he practises will set during his absence, Fayette, Woodford, and Bourbon at their first terms. In Fayette, Mr. Bledsoe, Mr. Barry, or Mr. January,[1] will try such causes, as his clients wish disposed of without his personal exertion, and direct orders to be made preparatory to the trial of others; in Woodford, Mr. January or Mr Blackburn;[2] and in Bourbon, Mr. Robert Trimble, Mr. Mills, or Mr. Brown,[3] will bestow similar attention upon his business in those courts.

Lexington *Kentucky Gazette*, December 15, 1806.

1 Jesse Bledsoe, William T. Barry, and James January. Barry, a Virginian whose family had settled in Lexington, had been educated at William and Mary College and Transylvania University. Successful in the practice of law and in politics, he was at various times a member of the Kentucky legislature, a United States Senator, and Lieutenant Governor of his adopted state. Once a close friend of Clay, he became in the 1820's a leader of the relief party and a follower of Jackson, who made him United States Postmaster General in 1829. January, also a Lexington lawyer, maintained an office on Short Street.

2 William B. Blackburn.

3 Benjamin Mills and William Brown. Mills, a native of Maryland, had studied medicine, then law, and had become an attorney at Paris, Kentucky. He was elected several times to the State legislature, became a circuit court judge in 1817, and three years later was elevated to membership in the Court of Appeals.

Agreement with Fortunatus Cosby

8 Decr. 1806

An agreement between Fortunatus Cosby and Henry Clay.

Whereas the said Cosby purchased of Sarah Beard[1] certain property lying at & adjacent to Louisville as will appear by a deed made about a year ago first recorded in Fayette office & then in the Jefferson for which he agreed to give her Ten thousand dollars and to pay certain debts as will appear by the agreement between the said Cosby and the sd. Sarah.

It is this day agreed between the said Cosby and Clay that the said Clay shall have one fourth of the property described in the said deed, except a half acre lot and two five acre lots which the said Cosby had previously purchased of the said Sarah—

In consideration whereof the said Clay covenants to pay to those entitled to receive it one thired [*sic*] part of the said ten thousand dollars—to pay one third part of the debts which the said Cosby stands bound to pay by his contract with the said Sarah, & in all respects to comply with one third part of his contract of purchase with her.

FORTS COSBY {L.S.}
HENRY CLAY {L.S.}

It is this day further agreed between the said Fortunatus Cosby and the said H. Clay that the interest of the said Clay in the purchase described by the preceding agreement as being made by the said Cosby from the said Sarah Beard shall be increased from one fourth to one third; in consideration whereof the said Clay binds himself to pay for the said addition upon the said terms in all respects as he bought the said fourth—that is in the same proportion for the addition as he gave for the fourth.

And it is understood by the parties that the two lots described as five acre lots in the preceding agreement are described in the plan of Louisville as Squares. 10h. Octr. 1807.

FORTS. COSBY {L.S.}
HENRY CLAY {L.S.}

[Endorsements on verso][2]
Memo.

It is understood that if the said Cosby is not bound to pay to Heirs or representatives of Sarah Beard the amount of a Sale of Twenty four Acres of land made to James Berthoud[3] in her life time; and the Sum of one thousand dollars which he agreed to give her for the three lots excepted from the said agreement, the said Clay is to be entitled to one third thereof. 10 Octr. 1807. F COSBY

Besides any payments which the said Clay may have made to the Representatives of Sarah Beard, I acknowledge to have received of him Two hundred & ninety five dollars on a/c. of his Contract with me. 10 Octr. 1807. F COSBY

ADS, signed also by Cosby. DLC-TJC (DNA, M212, R15). Cosby was a native of Georgia reared in Virginia, who had settled near Louisville, Kentucky, in 1798. A successful lawyer and land speculator, he became wealthy and prominent in affairs of that community. He was several terms a member of the Kentucky legislature and in 1810 became a judge of the Jefferson Circuit Court.

1 Widow of William Beard, half sister of John Campbell, and sister of Robert and Allen Campbell, through the last two of whom she had inherited the vast holdings of John on the site of the town of Louisville. The property amounted to about 3000 acres on the Ohio River, "all the islands in the sd. River Ohio near the sd. town of Louisville lately the property of Allen Campbell deceased, also the ground & ferry at the lower landing in Shipping port," and an unspecified number of town lots. Fayette County, Deed Book B, 284-85.

2 Both ES, in Clay's hand.

3 A Frenchman who speculated in land and operated as a commission merchant at Shippingport, Jefferson County, Kentucky.

From Benjamin Comegys

D Sir Baltimore Decr 10. 1806

I am this morning favored with your letter of the 18 Ulto.[1] handing A[2] Burrs bill on G M Ogden[3] for five hundred Dollars at

90 Days which shall in regular course appear at the credit of Dor. Rumsey.[4] I am perfectly satisfied that you will do all in yr power to bring this business to a speedy close. I am authorised by Messr P Hoffman & son[5] to request you will do every thing in yr power to secure their debt in any way you may think best without restrictive act as for yr self and be the result what it may they will be equally obliged

The bill before mentioned I have sent on for Acceptance and I will let you know its fate With much respt I am Dr Sir yr Obt s

BENJN. COMEGYS

ALS. DLC-TJC (DNA, M212, R12). Benjamin, John, and Cornelius Comegys were partners in a Baltimore mercantile firm. In 1816, Cornelius, the only surviving member of the firm, moved to Philadelphia.

1 Not found.

2 "A" superimposed on "Mr."

3 George M. Ogden was Burr's agent in New York City, and occupied "a cramped office over a small grocery store, on Water Street." Anna V. Parker, "Lewis Sanders of Grass Hills," in *Papers of the Christopher Gist Historical Society* (Covington, Kentucky), 1951-1952, p. 3.

4 Dr. Edward Rumsey, brother of James Rumsey, the inventor, had moved from Virginia to Christian County, Kentucky, shortly after 1800.

5 Baltimore merchants.

From Peter Hoffman and Son

Lexington Baltimo. 18th Decembr 1806

Henry Clay Esquire

Sir! On the 9th inst: we took the liberty of writing to you recommendatory of certain Bills of Exhg: which might fall in your way, drawn by Mr Benj. Ives Gilman of Marietta. We continue the same perfect implicit confidence in those Bills: it is however suggested to us, (a mere suspicion of possibility, without real grounds;) that Mr Gilman *may perhaps,* be somehow connected with Coln. Burr in the wild schemes lately attributed (in your country) to this Gentleman.[1] Could we immagine this at all probable, we should on no consideration whatever be induced to give him the assistance of our name or commendation. We are not ourselves *at all* aquainted with Mr Gilman. what we took the liberty of saying to you in our 9th inst. in his behalf, in relation to the credit due on his Bills, was at the instance & to serve highly respectable & substantially wealthy friends of our ins [*sic*] New York. Should you, contrary to our present belief & hopes, find Mr Gilman, directly or indirectly, concerned in the plots said to be maturing by Coln Burr we give you herewith our unequivocally pointed request to pass *totally unnoticed,* our said recommendatory Letter. It is not necessary for us to repeat that we do not really ourselves harbour a suspicion hereof. While however we confirm our continued & complete confidence in the

Bills to be drawn by him on our before alluded to friend, in New York, we deem it prudent to guard against the *possibility* of contributing in any wise, towards an attack on the unity of our common country.

Your esteemed favour in relation to our demand on Docr Edwd Rumsey we were duly favd with;[2] and are in daily anticipation of the pleasure of hearing from you, that your efforts, alluded to in said favour, for perfect security of said claim, have proven effectual. With the greatest respect We are Sir Yr mo. Ob & very Hb Sts

PETER HOFFMAN & SON

ALS. DLC-HC (DNA, M212, R1).

[1] Letter not found. Gilman was a prominent business and political figure in the Northwest Territory and early Ohio. His daughter, Jane, was the wife of Dudley Woodbridge, a boatbuilder at Marietta and a business partner of Harman Blennerhassett.

[2] Not found.

Property Deed from William and Margaret Tod

[December 19, 1806]

[For the sum of $500 William Tod and Margaret, his wife, sell to William Macbean of Madison County, Kentucky, and to James Maccoun, Robert Frazier, and Henry Clay of Lexington fifty acres of land on Silver Creek in Madison County. Clay is to receive one-sixth of the tract. General warranty of title. Certification of signature acknowledgment before Thomas Bodley, Clerk of Fayette Circuit Court, December 19, 1806.]

Fayette Circuit Court, Deed Book C, 131-32. Tod, a Scotsman, had erected machinery for spinning cotton in Lexington in 1796.

Resolution on Extension of Federal Circuit Courts

[January 2, 1807]

Resolved that a Committee be appointed to prepare and bring in a bill to extend to the Districts of Kentucky, Tennassee and Ohio, the Circuit Courts of the United States.

AD, by Clay. DNA, RG46, 11A-B2. Clay prefaced his motion for the resolution with a statement noting that over 400 suits were pending in the District Court of Kentucky and that a majority of them were chancery suits relating to land. Plumer, Diary, 628 (DLC, DNA Micro. Supp.). The motion was adopted January 5.

From John Taylor

Dr. Sir Virginia January 4. 1807. Port Royal

I am just informed that you are at Washington, and it is my wish to associate you with Mr: Key,[1] in finishing my suit with Bodley

&a.[2]—Will a fee of an hundred dollars, in case of my saving the land, in addition to what Mr: Hubbard Taylor may have engaged to pay, obtain your aid in the court of appeals? Mr: Hughes has notice that the case is to be again stired.

From a hope that you will join Mr: Key, I take the liberty to inclose you an argument, whence you will see the grounds taken at the last court. Mr: Hughes was driven to and finally relied on a single argument, namely, that Johnson's settlement was founded, neither on an actual settlement or actual improvement, but meerly on residence in the country, and was what is called a village right. If you could clear up this difficulty, none would remain in the case. It is a point, artfully concealed by the complainants, to prevent the exhibition of evidence, proving and locating Johnson's actual improvement, which would have overthrown it. Such evidence may hereafter appear, in the suit Bodley &a. agt. Ambrose Walden,[3] and if so, in case I should lose my land by construction, and Walden should save his by the fact, a strong illustration would result of the consequence of the court's deciding upon the first ground, when the artifice of the plts. defeated a recourse to the second. It would be like admiting imperfect evidence for a man, who had concealed perfect.

Further, I am very anxious that you should join Mr: Key, on account of the point depending on the doctrine of compensation as no injury, supposing my survey erroneous. The case of Johnson v Nall[4] (inclosed to Mr: Key) seems to me, perfectly in point; that of Jones v Craig I do not so well understand[5]—& that of Craig v Holeman[6] I have not seen. This point can be again introduce[d] and pushed, because Mr: Hughes at the last term, exhibited, an[d] the court admited, transcripts of records from Kentucky as author-[ity] and therefore they will hardly reject them on my part.

Ambrose Walden is now with me. He says he has written you [to] engage in his suit with Bodley &a. but has paid no fee. The poor fellow has been long deranged in his mind, but seem[s] to be now recovering. I wish to serve him. Will you do me the favor to answer this letter without delay, and to say, what fee A. Walden must remit to you? I am with great respect Sir Yr: mo: obt. St.

JOHN TAYLOR.

Will you be pleased to give the argument to Mr: Garnett[7] of the house of representatives, after you have done with it. I have no copy, and being sued in a similar case in Kentucky, it will be useful to me. This new suit was brought in a state court, & I have written to Mr: H. Taylor, to remove it to the federal court, & engage you.

ALS. DLC-HC (DNA, M212, R1). Addressed to Clay in Washington. "John Taylor of Caroline," Virginia planter, author, political philosopher, and statesman, claimed numerous tracts of land in Kentucky.

1 Philip Barton Key, Federalist Congressman from Maryland.

2 A case growing out of conflicting claims to land on the north side of Johnson's fork of the Licking River, over which tract litigation continued for half a century. In 1780 Ambrose Walden, of Caroline County, Virginia, acting for himself and as agent for John Taylor, had employed Simon Kenton to locate lands in Kentucky. As a result, Taylor had acquired a claim to 3,000 acres, but his title depended upon definition of the entry of Jacob Johnson, a pioneer settler in the area. In 1798 Thomas Bodley and others had bought from the heirs of John Tibbs a claim to part of the same land. James Hughes, Lexington attorney, had then acquired, by conveyance from Bodley, an interest in the claim. Taylor's entry antedated the other, but the segment claimed by Bodley and others had been first surveyed. In the settlement of this particular controversy, Taylor lost a part of the disputed tract. Bodley *et al. vs.* Taylor, 9 *U.S.* (5 Cranch) 191-234 (1809).

3 A detailed history of this case appears in 50 *U.S.* (9 Howard) 34-54 (1850).

4 Samuel Johnson *vs.* Martin Nall, 2 *Ky. Reports* (Sneed) 331-32 (1804).

5 Cited as a manuscript record in 9 *U.S.* (5 Cranch) 216.

6 The Heirs of Arthur Fox and John Craig *vs.* Edward Holeman, 1 *Ky. Reports* (Hughes) 399-405 (1801).

7 James Mercer Garnett, Virginia Congressman, 1805-1809.

From James Smith, Jr.

Respected Friend 6 Jany 1807—

I received your favour of 2 Inst this morning[1] covering 905 Dollars in two drfts and a One hundred Dollar Bank Note which you say is all that was recd on Accot of Millers[2] Note when you left home—The drft on Reede & Ford[3] is accepted, but the one on I Gardner Jur. & Co[4] is protested for nonacceptance—I ex[pe]ct it must be held untill due, or shall I return it to you, as it is of no use to me—You do mention the 2 Notes of Smiths[5] for which you some time ago received security & were to be paid on some persons (I forget the name)[6] return from Baltimore—I wish you to be kind enough to write to The Agent who transacts your business in Lexington to endeavour to recieve & forward to you the amount of those Notes & also the remainder of Millers, as soon as he possibly can—otherwise I fear it will be a long time before I get either, for I do not expect you will leave Washington before Congress rises which may perhaps be March or April next—I find in your letter of 20 Octr.[7] you mentioned to me that you had indulged Mr Miller by taking a good Accep at 45 days when his Note became, which was the 15 Sept. consequently this Acceptance must have become due about 1t November & I have been looking for it ever since—

I should not be this particular, were it not for the many & grevious dissappointments I have & do daily meet with It seems as if every body I deal with considers me a person that does not want money & that they can do as they please with—I have no doubt, if you write particularly to your young Men at home they will forward to you the remaining amount of Millers Note & also the money for Mr Smiths 2 Notes sent you, which I expect must be received by this time—I have another of Mr Miller's Notes becomes due in March

& one in September next 1500 Dollars each What will you give me for the two?—or do you know any monied Man that would take them at a discount

Perhaps you may find a leisure half hour to inform me whether any thing has been done with respect to the Land[8]—I feel much desirous that every effort may be made to asscertain [*sic*] the Title to this Land—

Should you visit the City it will give me pleasure to see you I hope you will attend to what is herein requested—I am very respectfully Yr Friend JAS SMITH JR

ALS. DLC-TJC (DNA, M212, R12). Addressed to Clay in Washington.

1 Not found. 2 Robert Miller.

3 John Reed and Standish Forde, Philadelphia merchants trading extensively in the Ohio Valley and New Orleans.

4 Not identified.

5 In 1805 the firm of James Smith, Jr., and Son had sold a quantity of goods to William W. Smith of Philadelphia in return for eight notes, totaling $8,226.15, all due before the end of the year. When the first of the notes was unpaid, Clay on July 15, 1805, had filed a bill of complaint in chancery and obtained writs garnisheeing payments due to W. W. Smith by numerous Kentucky merchants, including Robert Miller. Fayette Circuit Court, File 95 (1805). Many years later apparently the same William W. Smith was reportedly a resident of New Orleans.

6 Thomas Deye Owings, who for "a valuable consideration," apparently a shipment of calicoes, had given his own note for £253, 4s, dated July 12, 1805, payable in a year (DS, in Clay's hand. Fayette Circuit Court, File 196), and assumed some $850 in the shorter-term obligations of William W. Smith to James Smith, Jr.

7 Not found. 8 See above, Smith to Clay, *ca.* November 2, 1805.

Presentation of Petition for Laurient Bazadon

[January 6, 1807]

Bazadon (variously identified as Basse, Bassadon, Bassidon, Bayadone, Bazadonne) was an illiterate Spanish trader from New Orleans, who had settled at Post Vincennes in 1783. In October, 1786, George Rogers Clark had seized his goods with those of two other Spanish merchants trading at Vincennes without passport. Clark's action was subsequently repudiated by Governor Edmund Randolph, who recommended court suit for damages. WHi-Draper MSS., 53J53; Temple Bodley, *George Rogers Clark, His Life and Public Services* (Boston, 1926), 300-301, 320-21. Reimbursement amounting to about $12,000 was later awarded Bazadon; but before execution of the judgment Congress divided the Northwest Territory (under act of May 7, 1800), and the old court decree could no longer be executed in Indiana. The petition here presented asked that legislative provision be made to permit execution of the judgement in the same manner as if the change in governmental unit had never taken place. (DNA, Senate, 9A-G5).

On January 12 Clay reported (no written report found) for a committee, which also included Stephen R. Bradley and William B. Giles, that the prayer of the petitioner ought not to be granted. The report was adopted.

Resolution on Proposed Ohio Rapids Canal

[January 12, 1807]

Resolved that it is expedient and proper to appropriate a quantity of land not exceeding[1] acres at a fair cash valuation towards the

opening of the Canal proposed to be cut at the Rapids of the Ohio on the Kentucky Shore
Mr Clay

AD. DNA, RG46, 9A-B3. Published in Washington *National Intelligencer,* January 16, 1807; *Annals of Cong.,* 9 Cong., 2 Sess., XVI, 30. On the following day the proposed resolution was referred to committee. For subsequent action see below, Report, February 24, 1807. Earlier petitions for such aid had been reported upon by Congressional committees in 1805 and 1806. *American State Papers, Miscellaneous,* I, 419, 453-54.

[1] Following this word the figure 25000 was written, then deleted.

Bill Extending Federal Circuit Court System

[January 14, 1807]

Sect 1 Be it enacted by the Senate and House of Representatives of the United States of America in Congress assembled that so much of any act or acts of Congress as vests in the District Courts of the United States, in the Districts of Kentucky, Tennessee and Ohio, the powers authority and jurisdiction of the Circuit Courts of the United States shall be and the same is hereby repealed.

Sect 2 Be it further enacted that the said Districts of Kentucky, Tennessee and Ohio shall constitute and be denominated the seventh Circuit. And there shall be holden annually in each district of the said Circuit two Courts, to be called Circuit Courts, and to consist of one Justice of the Supreme Court of the United States, and the Judge of the District where such Court shall be holden. And the Sessions of the said Courts, in the District of Kentucky shall be held at Frankfort and commence on the first monday in May and November annually; in the District of Tennessee at Knoxville & Nashville alternately to commence on the first monday in April and October annually, beginning at Knoxville, and in the District of Ohio at Chillicothe to commence on the first monday in January and September annually. And the Circuit Court of Tennessee shall designate at which of the two places the said Court is hereby directed to be holden, the office of the Clerk thereof shall be kept.

Sec 3. Be it further enacted that all the authority powers and jurisdiction vested in the several Circuit Courts of the United States, or the Judges thereof or either of them, shall be and hereby are vested in, and may be exercised by, the several Circuit Courts of the seventh Circuit, and the Judges thereof: And that all actions, causes, pleas, process [*sic*], and other proceedings relative to any cause civil or criminal, which shall be returnable to, or depending in, the several District Courts of Kentucky, Tennessee and Ohio, at the time of the passage of this act, shall be and hereby are declared to be respectively transferred, returnable and continued to the several Circuit Courts constituted by this act, at the times herein appointed for the session of each of the said Courts, and shall be heard, tried, and determined therein, in the same manner and with the same effect as if no change had been made hereby in the Courts of the said Districts. And the said Circuit Courts of the seventh Circuit shall be governed by the same laws and regulations as apply to the other Circuit Courts of the United States.

Sect 4 Be it further enacted that all the authority powers and jurisdiction vested in the several District Courts of the United States, and the Judges thereof, in those Districts in which Circuit Courts are now held, shall be retained and may be exercised by the several District Courts of Kentucky, Tennessee and Ohio, and the several Judges thereof. And the Sessions of the said Districts Courts shall be as follows: in Kentucky at Frankfort two Sessions to commence on the first monday in June & December annually, in Knoxville two Sessions to commence on the fourth monday in April and October annually, and at Nashville two Sessions to commence on the fourth monday in May and November annually; and in Ohio at Chillicothe three Sessions, to commence on the first monday in February, June and October annually.

Sect 5 Be it further enacted that the Supreme Court of the United States shall hereafter consist of a Chief Justice and six associate justices, any law to the contrary notwithstanding. And for this purpose there shall be appointed a sixth associate justice, to reside in the seventh Circuit, whose duty it shall be, until he is otherwise allotted, to attend the Circuit Courts of the said seventh Circuit and the Supreme Court of the United States, and who shall take the same oath, and be entitled to the same Salary as are required of and provided for the other Associate Justices of the United States.

[Endorsement][1]

An Bill [*sic*][2]

Establishing Circuit Courts, and abridging the jurisdiction of the District Courts, in the Districts of Kentucky, Tennessee, and Ohio.

AD. DNA, RG46, 9A-B1. Other members of the committee, to which Clay's resolution of January 2 had been referred, were Abraham Baldwin of Georgia, William B. Giles of Virginia, John Quincy Adams of Massachusetts, and Stephen R. Bradley of Vermont. Though amended in both Senate and House, the measure as enacted on February 24 differed little in essence from the original version. 2 *U.S. Stat.*, 420-21.

1 AE. 2 The word substituted by Clay for "act."

To [Harry Innes]

Dr Sir City of Washington 16 Jan. 07

I am indebted to you for three letters with their inclosures, for which be pleased to accept my sincere thanks.[1] The information they afforded me, as well as the promise of further communications, was extremely gratifying. I should have earlier done myself the pleasure of writing to you, but that I wished whatever I might write you should not be from hasty & incorrect impressions. Mr Thruston, with whom & Capt. Fowler, Genl. Walton & Genl Sandford[2] I conferred as to the propriety of presenting your address to the Speaker, informed you that the result of our conference was that it was unnecessary & perhaps improper to offer it. We were all of opinion that you had acted incorruptly & not so as to subject yourself to impeachment; and that altho' you may have erred in not communicating to the Government the propositions of Spain, you could not thereby have incurred a forfeiture of your office. Your failure to make this communication, as well as the bare circumstance of the propositions being made to you, has subjected you as you will see from the papers to much censure; and in a conversation I held with Mr Randolph[3] he condemned this part of your conduct. Other gentlemen however acquit you of blame. The present moment I thought at any rate inauspicious to an investigation, by Congress, into your Conduct, if at any time it would be proper. The extraordinary circumstances which came out on Sebastian's case,[4] the agitation excited by the movements of Col Burr, & the vast preparations he is said to have been making on the Ohio & below, have thrown the public mind into such consternation, as to render a cool deliberate & impartial examination into your conduct even by Congress itself, at this moment, very improbable. I think however you have only to bear with fortitude the present crisis, that it will pass off without affecting your official situation, & that ultimately the momentary tarnish which your character is supposed by some to have received, will be obliterated.

The Government appear to be confident that Burr is engaged in treasonable projects. They speak of having received the most unquestionable evidence of his designs. The reduction of New Orleans first, the subjugation of Mexico afterwards, and ultimately the separation of the Western from the Eastern section of the Union are supposed to have been his objects. Nothing is more false than that any countenance has been given him by the administration. On yesterday a resolution passed the house of representatives calling from the Executive for such information as they possess (not deemed improper to be disclosed) of the nature and object of his treason; and of the measures which have been taken to defeat it. These I trust will have the desired effect, but should Congress suppose them insufficient to suppress any attempts to divide or distract our Country, I have no doubt that the most efficient steps will be taken. The papers will have informed you that New Orleans is put in the best possible state of defence.

I inclose you a Copy of the bill for extending to the Western States the Circuit System of the United States which I introduced into the Senate[5][. It] has had two readings, and I believe will pass without opposition in the Senate. It was the best thing I could do. I found an indisposition to vary the system in our Country from its form in other parts of the Union, but a perfect willingness to make it uniform throughout the Country.

Of our relations with Spain we have obtained no satisfactory intelligence; and how the negociation will eventuate is still uncertain.[6] I presume some information will be received before Congress closes its Session. Our affairs with Britain are said to be in a favourable train.[7]

Should the Court bill be lost (which I do not apprehend will be the case) I shall attempt a change of the term to May, agreeably to the arrangement made before I left Frankfort; Upon this & other subjects you shall again hear from Yrs. HENRY CLAY

ALS. ICU.

1 These letters, not found, apparently contained a defence of Judge Innes' conduct in relation to the "Spanish Conspiracy," for which Humphrey Marshall was attempting to have him impeached. See below, Resolutions, February 3, 1808.

2 Senator Buckner Thruston and Representatives John Fowler, Matthew Walton, and Thomas Sandford were members of the Kentucky delegation in the Ninth Congress.

3 Both John and Thomas M. Randolph were representatives from Virginia in the Ninth Congress.

4 Judge Benjamin Sebastian had recently resigned as a consequence of investigation by the Kentucky House of Representatives revealing that he had received a pension from the Spanish government. See Ky. H. of Reps., *Journal, 1806-1807,* pp. 97-114.

5 See above, Resolution, January 2, 1807, and note.

6 The United States was negotiating with Spain relative to spoliation claims and the boundary of Louisiana.

7 In April of the previous year, William Pinkney of Maryland, lawyer, diplomat, United States Attorney General (1811-1814), and United States Senator (1819-1822), had been sent to join James Monroe in London for the purpose of settling differences with Great Britain and negotiating a commercial treaty.

Presentation of Petition for John Griffin and Others

[January 21, 1807]

The petition of Griffin and other judges of Indiana Territory asked remuneration for their duties in assisting to organize the governments, establish the courts, and prepare the codes of law at the division of Louisiana into two territories. *Annals of Cong.,* 9 Cong., 2 Sess., XVI, 38. A bill to this effect, having passed the House of Representatives, was presented to the Senate and approved on March 3, 1807, without record of a report by the Senate committee. The sum granted amounted to $300 each. 2 *U.S. Stat.,* 444. Griffin had been a judge of Indiana Territory since its organization, but in March, 1806, he had resigned to become a judge of Michigan Territory.

To Thomas Todd

My Dear Col. City of Washington 24 Jan. 1807.

I have not been favoured with the pleasure of a line from you since my arrival in this place. From others I have learnt the revolutions in our State since my departure. Among these I am happy to find my friend placed in the chair of the chief justice. May this promotion be attended with as much happiness to him as I know it will advantage to our Country! Poor old Muter, I wish more justice had been done to his innocence and goodness in the provision made for his retirement.[1]

Upon reaching this place I found very different opinions prevailing from those I left in Kentucky, relative to the projects of Burr. The [A]dministration spoke of his guilt in a tone of [en]tire confidence. And I now enclose you a document[2] exhibiting the best developement of his plans yet presented to the public. However extensively criminal, I presume they have been frustrated. I do not believe that any Censure has fallen upon the Judge, or the Counsel appearing in the defence of Burr, for the result of the prosecution—I mean censure from the government. The institution [of the] prosecution, at the particular mome[nt] is supposed to have been ill-timed and injudicious. Dr. Bollman & Mr. Swartout,[3] two of the agents of Burr in the City of Orleans, have been arrested there, and have arrived at this place, having been sent on by water. They have applied to the Court of this District for a H. Corpus, which has been granted.[4] They have however not yet been produced in Court; and what disposition will be made of them remains to be decided.

Our affairs with Britain are stated to be in a train of amicable adjustment; and the most favourable result is anticipated. Of those with Spain we still continue in the dark. But War does not seem to be a necessary event—Indeed it depends wholly upon the complexion of the information to be received.

Rodney is appointed Atto. Genl.[5]

Tayloe[6] says that Buzzard is the finest horse upon the Continent—that there is no comparison between him and Dragon—[7]

I have not yet visited Richmond; but still contemplate a journey thither. Yr's Sincerely HENRY CLAY

ALS. DLC-Harry Innes Papers (DNA, M212, R21). Addressed to Thomas Todd, "near Frankfort Kentucky."

1 On December 13, 1806, Todd had been made Chief Justice of the Kentucky Court of Appeals, replacing George Muter, to whom the legislature granted an annual pension of $300.

2 Not found.

3 Justus Erick Bollman and Samuel Swartwout.

4 Efforts had been made on January 23 to enact a bill suspending the writ of habeas corpus for three months in cases of commitment made by warrants from the President, from officers directed by him, or from the governors of the several States and Territories charging "treason, misprision of treason, or other high crime or misdemeanor, endangering the peace, safety, or neutrality of the United States." William Plumer reported a conversation in which Clay observed that he thought there was no occasion for such a bill, but that he felt he could not oppose it in view of his own position as recent counsellor for Burr. Clay did support the bill and the measure passed the Senate, but it was promptly and decisively defeated in the House. Plumer, Diary,

729-30 (DLC, DNA, Micro. Supp.); *Annals of Cong.*, 9 Cong., 2 Sess., XVI, 44, 402, 424-25.

5 Caesar Augustus Rodney, of Delaware.

6 The wealthy Colonel John Tayloe of Mt. Airy, Virginia, and Washington, D.C., a well known racing enthusiast.

7 Purchased in 1806 by John W. Hunt of Lexington from Wade Hampton of South Carolina. Both horses were sired by Woodpecker, a Herod colt.

Speech Relating to Toll Bridge across the Potomac

[January 29, 1807]

The speech, cited in Plumer, Diary, 750 (DLC, DNA, Micro. Supp.), and in John Quincy Adams, *Memoirs . . . Comprising Portions of His Diary from 1795 to 1848* (Charles Francis Adams, ed., 12 vols.; Philadelphia, 1847-1877), I, 448, was not reported. It opposed a motion calling for postponement of the bill providing for such a bridge.

To [Col. Thomas Hart]

My Dear Sir, City of Washington 1 Feb. 1807

I received your agreeable favor,[1] which gave me great pleasure as it evinced a greater attention to me on your part, than I have experienced even from my younger friends. I should have answered your letter much earlier, but have been waiting to see what would be done in the House of Representatives with a bill introduced there to repeal the act of limitations against the claims of the creditors of the United States. That bill is still undisposed of, but it is believed that it will pass that house.[2] Should it become a law I will endeavor to have your claim re examined, and will promote it as much as I can consistently with my duty and propriety.

It seems that we have been much mistaken about Burr. When I left Kentucky, I believed him both an innocent and persecuted man. In the course of my journey to this place, still entertaining that opinion, I expressed myself without reserve, and it seems owing to the freedom of my sentiments at Chillicothe[3] I have exposed myself to the strictures of some anonymous writer at that place. They give me no uneasiness, as I am sensible that all my friends and acquaintances knew me incapable of entering into the views of Burr. It appears from the President's message to Congress, in answer to the resolution of the House of Representatives calling for information, that Burr had formed the no less daring projects than to reduce New Orleans, subjugate Mexico, and divide the Union. The energetic measures taken by the Administration have, I presume, entirely defeated him. Dr Bollman and Mr. Swartwout,[4] two of his most criminal agents at New Orleans, having been arrested in that city by the military authority, were sent on to this place. They have attempted to effect their liberation by a writ of Habeas Corpus, but after a full investigation of their case, they are sent to jail by one of the courts of this District for treason. Where they are to be tried is not yet decided.

I am attempting in Congress several things for the good, as I suppose, of our country. A bill at my instance has passed the Senate to extend to Kentucky and the other Western States, the circuit court system of the United States. By this measure, if it passes the other House, Kentucky, Tennesee and Ohio will have the advantage of two judges upon the Federal bench instead of one; and the circuit Judge who presides in those States, will also attend the Supreme bench, and carry with him there a knowledge of the local laws and decisions of each of those States.[5]

I have also proposed a resolution to appropriate a quantity of land to assist in opening the canal at the Falls. I fear the shortness of the session will prevent the success of this measure.[6]

My reception in this place has been equal, nay superior to my expectations. I have experienced the civility and attention of all whose acquaintance I was desirous of obtaining. Those who are disposed to flatter me say that I have acquitted myself with great credit in several debates in the Senate. But after all that I have seen, Kentucky is still my favorite country. There amidst my dear family, I shall find happiness in a degree to be met with no where else.

Present me affectionately to Mrs. Hart, Mrs. Price, Nat,[7] and all the family, and believe me to be Yours sincerely HENRY CLAY

Copy. InHi-William H. Smith Collection.

1 Not found.

2 Shortly before the date of this letter the House, in Committee of the Whole, had discussed the report submitted by a special committee on this matter. No decision was reached, and the subject was not again taken up before the end of the session.

3 In Ohio, where Clay had stopped on his way to Washington. Clay's comments at this place were not reported. At Washington, however, he had expressed his views in similar vein to William Plumer:

"Mr Clay told me, that Mr Davies, the district Atty, was zealous in carrying on the prosecution agt. Mr Burr—That the grand jurors were gentlemen of the first respectability in that State. That they were near two days engaged in the examination of witnesses & investigating the subject—That they were unanimously of opinion that Mr Burr was wholly & altogether innocent of the crimes whereof he was accused—He said but one opinion prevailed in that State as far as he could collect it—& that was in favor of Mr Burr.

"He said there was no disposition in Kentucky to attack, in this manner, the dominions of Spain—or to secede from the government of the United States. Their people were strongly attached to the Union.

"Mr Clay said his own opinion was that Mr Burr was unjustly accused. That if there was any evidence agt him he had not been able to discover it.

"That he knew Mr Burr was interested in the tract of land in Louisiana called 'Bastrops Grant'—he had examined his title with attention—& intimated he thot it legal.

"That he had heard Mr Burr say that the Marquis de Yrujo [Spanish Minister to the United States] was an enemy to the United States—& was a man not to be trusted.

"Mr Clay said he asked Mr Burr why he did not contradict in the newspapers the accounts that was published against him? He replied his enemies were industrious, & intent upon his ruin. That he had published nothing—& if he should commence the work it would be endless & unavailing—That time would set all things right.

"Mr Clay said he passed through Chilicothe (in Ohio) just at the time when Govr Tiffin had issued his orders to seize the batteau's at Marietta That Harman Blannerhassett & Tyler had fled—that they had acted imprudently he had no doubt—but not in flying—for such was the state of public opinion in Chilicothe that innocence was no security—that accusation founded on mere suspicion, was in fact equivalent to conviction & condemnation—That a mania had seized the public mind in that place.

"He told me that Burr assured him he owned only two boats or batteaus.—" Plumer, Diary, 610-13 (DLC [DNA, M212, R22]).

On orders of Governor Edward Tiffin of Ohio, fifteen boats and a quantity of supplies belonging to Burr had been seized on December 9 at Marietta. On the night of the 10th Blennerhassett, Burr's fellow "conspirator," and Comfort Tyler, who had lately arrived at Blennerhassett's island with a few boats and men, had shoved off down river to escape capture by the Virginia militia, which on the next day had taken possession of the island.

4 Justus Erick Bollman and Samuel Swartwout.

5 See above, Resolution, January 2, 1807.

6 See above, Resolution, January 12, 1807.

7 Mrs. Samuel Price and Nathaniel G. S. Hart.

To ———

[Washington, February 1, 1807]

The House of Representatives having passed a resolution, calling upon the President for information upon this subject, he sent a message to Congress in reply, which I presume you will have seen before this reaches you. It appears from this document, that Burr had grasped at the conquest of Mexico, the seizure of New-Orleans, and a separation of the states. Whatever were his plans I presume they have been defeated by the measures adopted by the administration. Dr. Bollman and Mr. Swartwout, two of his most criminal agents at N. Orleans, having been arrested at that city by the military authority, were sent on to this and placed under the control of the civil power. They moved in one of the courts of this District for a writ of Habeas Corpus to effect their discharge. But after a very lengthy discussion, a majority of the court decided that they ought to be remanded to jail for treason. The place of their trial has not been determined on.

By some arrivals lately from Europe, it appears that our differences with Britain are not in so favourable a train as they were supposed to be at the commencement of the Session. Whether this account is to be relied upon, subsequent arrivals must decide. No such official intelligence has been received by the Government.[1]

From Spain no certain information has been received as to the state of our negociation.[2]

You will see from the enclosed paper, that the Prussian power has sunk beneath the arms of Bonaparte. The battle of Jena was followed by a succession of disasters, which has terminated in the total overthrow of the Prussian monarchy, cities deemed impregnable have been reduced, and it appears as if death alone can check the career of this modern conqueror.

It is with pleasure I learn from Kentucky, that sentiments friendly to the Union, and the administration are every where expressed.—Doubts seemed to be cherished by some upon my arrival here of the fidelity of our state.—I told them I would answer with my honor and life for her attachment to the common cause, and I am happy to find that they were, and I am not deceived.

Lexington *Kentucky Gazette,* February 28, 1807.

1 The treaty signed by James Monroe and William Pinkney on December 31, 1806 (which President Jefferson subsequently rejected), had not yet arrived in this country, nor had the British order in council of January 7, 1807, which imposed further restrictions on American commerce with Europe.

2 See above, Clay to Innes, January 16, 1807, note.

Tax Bill

[*ca.* February 1, 1807]

1806. Henry Clay	Dr. Cents
To Tax on 125 acrs. 1st. rate land	75
" 4500 acrs. 2nd. Do. @ 34 Cnts.	15.30
" 2000 acrs. 3d. Do. @ 12½ —	2.50
" 8 slaves @ 12½ 15 Horses @ 4	1:60
" $2300 value T. Lotts @ 50 P. £100	3.45
" 4 Carriage wheels @ 25 p whl.	1.00
Levy on 7 Tithes @ 125 Cnts	8.75
	$ 33.35

33:35
19.49½ fees
$52:84½

[Endorsement][1]
Recd. in full
JOHN H. MORTON Shff
18th. March 1808.

DS. DLC-TJC (DNA, M212, R15).

1 ES.

Resolution on Indemnity for Indian Depredations

[February 3, 1807]

Resolved that a Committee be appointed to enquire whether any, and if any, what farther provision is necessary to secure to the Citizens of the United States suffering from Indian depredations the indemnity guarranted to them by Law.

AD. DNA, RG46, 9A-B3. Published in *Annals of Cong.,* 9 Cong., 2 Sess., XVI, 52. The resolution was adopted and a committee appointed with Clay as chairman, but no report was filed.

From James Johnson

Sir New Orleans Feby. 5th 1807

Some time since I wrote requesting you to purchase the freedom of my Brother Daniel and send him to me at this place. as before I wrote you I will pay the amount of his price to your brother John Clay;[1] if you should upon the purchase request the amount to be forwarded to you I will do so agreable to your Directions—It is with Regret that I am compel'd to ask the above favor of purchasing my brother Daniel—but there is none else in whom I can place that Confidence—Write me the particulars as soon as convenient and you'll much oblige Your Hble Servant

Henry Clay Esquire JAMES JOHNSON

P.S. Remember me to my old Mistress[2] and State that I am Well and doing something for myself I have a small Grocery and Livery Stable—Dont forget me to the whole family &Ca— —Every thinge has been and still is dull on account of rumours of Mr Burr but will soon mend I hope

ALS. DLC-HC (DNA, M212, R1). Addressed to Clay at Lexington. Johnson was probably the slave, James, bequeathed to Clay under his father's will.

1 Letter not found. Daniel had been devised to John Clay under the elder Clay's will.

2 Henry's mother, Elizabeth Clay Watkins.

From John Taylor

Dear Sir Port Royal Feb: 5. 1807

Yours of the 27th. ulo. was only yesterday received, and that directed to the Bowling Green has never come to hand.[1]

The payment of a proportion of the conditional fees "equal to the proportion of the land I may save" is undoubtedly just, and I cheerfully accede to the proposal.

I believe however that all will be saved, or all lost. The idea of compensation, arising from the parties having respectively the lands which the plaintiffes say ought to have belonged to the others, seemed to me to strike the court, and I hope you will state to them the records I sent, brought from Kentucky, as very material.

I do not probably understand the distinction between a settlement right and an actual settlement, but it seems to me to be this, so far as it affects my cases—a settlement right is to be fixed by the location; therefore it might be placed wherever the locator pleased. But an actual settlement being fixed before the location, is only described by it. The plaintiffes have used Johnson's certificate of settlement to fix and not to find the settlement, and have measured a straight line for that purpose. But if in describing his settlement, & he was describing what was already fixed, namely an actual settlement, the distance he mentions from the licks must have undoubtedly been along the road, and not through the woods. If so, his settlement could never have been where it is deemed to be by judge Innes, but must have been within his first or second survey. Be so good as to read the argument I sent you, and to consider this part of it, with the survey before you, for I think, that if Johnson's was an actual settlement, that the cause will easily and certainly be gained upon it.

The cause was argued at the last term, upon a survey drawn by a small scale, in which the different plats are so united together, as to yield a plainer view of the case. one of those I gave to each of the judges, from whom or from Mr: Key you may borrow one, because the attention of the court having been directed to this united survey, as we called it, they will understand observations refering to it, best.

I gave to Judge Washington[2] my copy of the record—will you do me the favor to get it, when the cause is over, and to return it, with the argument and the records from Kentucky &a. to Mr: Garnett, who will take charge of all the papers belonging to me.

I shall take care to give Walden notice of the fee you expect in his case. I am, Sir, Yr: mo: obt: St. JOHN TAYLOR

ALS. DLC-HC (DNA, M212, R1). Addressed to Clay at Washington. Cf. above, Taylor to Clay, January 4, 1807.

1 Neither letter has been found.

2 Bushrod Washington, Associate Justice of the United States Supreme Court.

To ------

[Washington, February 6, 1807]

THE statement in the papers that our negociation with Britain is broken off, is not credited by the administration. They have received no such official intelligence; on the contrary they are still impressed with the opinion that matters with that country are in a favourable train. We have nothing yet from Spain.

Lexington *Kentucky Gazette*, February 28, 1807. See above, Clay to -----, February 1, 1807, note.

To Henry Dearborn

Sir Senate Chamber 10h. Feb. 1807.

I am instructed by a Committee raised by the Senate "to inquire whether any, and if any, what farther provision is necessary to secure to the Citizens of the U. S. suffering from Indian depredations, the indemnity guarranteed to them by Law,"[1] to ask of you such information as your department can afford on the following points:

1. What is the amount of claims preferred by such Citizens?
2. What portion of them has been paid?
3. What sum is necessary, in addition to the fund already provided by law, to discharge those claims that remain unpaid?

I am Sir Yr. ob. Servt. HENRY CLAY
chairman

ALS. DNA, RG107, Letters Received, (3) C-235. Addressed to Dearborn, "Secretary at War."

[1] See above, Resolution, February 3, 1807.

From John Taylor

Dear Sir Virga. Port Royal- Caroline Feb: 12. 1807.

Your letter of the 13th. ulto. only reached me yesterday,—having been found in consequence of the intimation in your last,[1] at a post office, distant from my home.

Having nothing material to add I would not have wasted any of your time, except for the purpose of endeavouring to remove your idea, that the fee I proposed to pay you in my writ of error, was too low.

Mr: Brown[2] was paid £25 or more, and on his removal, he informed me, that having engaged you to finish the suit, he retained the money. He did nothing. I drew the answer, and Mr: H. Taylor attended to all business out of doors. You were paid a sum which I forget—$40 or more, and promised on success a much larger sum. Your whole trouble, was, I suppose, an argument. To Mr: Key I paid $100 & on success, I am to pay him $100 more. Him I laboured to assist. And I proposed $100 dollars eventually to you, to come into the cause after this argument, when the labour was chiefly over. My opponents only offered me £800 for my title, payable on long credit. This cause does not decide the title, a circumstance which diminishes the value involved in the case. I have yet to contend with a location claim, and also with a patent older than mine. It is therefore probable from the best information I can get, that my interest, involved in the decision, cannot, at the utmost, exceed £2000. My expences, in cash, have already exceeded $300, and in case of success will exceed $300 more, and of these $600 dollars above $500 will be paid to gentlemen of the bar, whose whole trouble will be comprised in argument, exclusive of any attorney's business. This sum, computing by the value in controversy, or the trouble sustained, will be a more liberal compensation than I ever received myself, or have known to be given in this state; and these or at least one of them, seem to me, to be scales of computation as favorable to the gentlemen of the bar, as they could wish. A similarity of fee, in all cases from Kentucky, whether the trouble is great or trifling, whether they involve the title to 1000 or 100.000 acres of land or relate to a large sum or a small one, would create a question, whether its rate ought to be settled by the scale of the major or minor cases. I hope upon a reconsideration of the subject, you will not continue to discern any parsimony in the conduct of, Sir,

Yr: mo: obt: St. JOHN TAYLOR

Walden resides in Berkely county, I think. I shall write to him, informing him of your demand, & advising him to employ you.

ALS. DLC-HC (DNA, M212, R1). Addressed to Clay in Washington. Cf. above, Taylor to Clay, January 4, 1807.
1 These letters not found.
2 James Brown.

To William Prentiss

Dear Sir: City of Washington. 13th. Feb 1807

I received your agreeable favor with its inclosure,[1] for which accept my thanks.. Your New years ode was well adapted to the object in view, and the perusal of it afforded me much pleasure.

Col Burr has supplied much fund of conversation. No doubt is now entertained here of his having engaged in schemes of the most daring and illegal kind. Having left Kentucky under a belief that he was innocent, it was with no little surprise upon my arrival here that I found that I had been deceived. Entertaining the opinion I did, I ventured at Chillicothe to speak with some freedom upon measures proposed there of a harsh character and unjustified as it appeared to me by public exigencies. It is to this cause that the strictures upon my conduct alluded to in yours are owing. They give me no pain, as I am conscious of having participated in no illegal projects of Burr, and know that I will not be suspected of having done so by any who know me.

Alexander[2] has been discharged for want of proof, Bollman and Swartout remain in custody. They applied to the Supreme Court of the U.S. now in session for a writ of habeus corpus. Some of the Judges doubted their power to grant it, as it was not included within the enumerated powers confered upon that tribunal in the Constitution. The question has been discussed and three Judges to two (Chase and Johnson) [3] have determined in favor of the application. The prisoners are to be brought before the Court to day.

The papers inform you of the great events pressing upon the European theatre. A new measure has been lately taken by Buonaparte—of a most gigantic nature—the declaration that the islands of Great Britian are in a state of Blockade.[4] It is said that our Minister at Paris[5] has written on to Government that our Commerce is not to be effected by it; I apprehend however, that it will subject it to much embarrassment.

The Session of Congress has not been so interesting as I had anticipated. No questions in relation to our foreign intercourse, involving much discussion have been agitated—every thing depends upon the result of pending negotiations, and this will not be known it is probable until the Session expires.—

I expect to be accompanied to Kentucky by two young gentlemen, one proposing the practice, and the other the study of the Law.[6] The latter will continue with me. I am glad to find that you have been getting acquainted with Strange.[7] He is a valuable reporter, but occupies a second station only in the grade of merit. I calculate upon finding you much improved in your law knowledge. Two words will make any man of sound intellect a Lawyer—*InDustry* and *Application,* and the same words with a third *Economy* will enable him to make a fortune.

My respects to your fellow students, and tell them they have been very inattentive to me in not writing. Present me also to the very amiable and sensible man with whom you reside.[8] Yours

Mr Wm Prentice H CLAY.
Lexington Ky.

Copy. OCHP. Published in Colton (ed.), *Private Correspondence of Henry Clay,* 14-15, where it is dated February 15, 1807, and where the addressee is cited as Thomas M. Prentiss. Since Colton presumably used the original manuscript, his date may be correct. It appears, however, that Clay was writing to William Prentiss, one of his Transylvania law students, rather than to Thomas M. Prentiss, who several years later opened a school in Lexington and subsequently served as librarian of the Lexington Library.

1 Not found.

2 James Alexander, who, like Samuel Swartwout, Peter V. Ogden, and Justus Erick Bollman, had been arrested in New Orleans on orders of General James Wilkinson.

3 Samuel Chase and William Johnson.

4 One of the provisions of the Berlin Decree, announced by Napoleon in November, 1806.

5 John Armstrong.

6 Not identified.

7 Sir John Strange, *Reports of Adjudged Cases in the Courts of Chancery, Kings Bench, Common Pleas, and Exchequer, from Trinity Term in the Second Year of King George I to Trinity Term in Twenty-first Year of King George II* (2 vols., London, 1855).

8 William's father, Nathaniel Prentiss, Lexington jailer and clerk of the Market House.

From Elijah Foley

Fayette County Kentucky
Honoured Sirs Feby. 17th. 1807

After informing you of my health, & that which prevails generally through this State; Also the tranquil Spirit that appears to prevail, altho, the storm had collectted. Thanks to kind providence it has broke & we appear all to be safe in the repose of peace. I am happy to have it in my power to State to you from good information, that Burr & his party are frustrated also that Burr, and[1] with the principal conspirators are in safe custody.

I have forwarded a sample of common glazed powder to you, which I want you to shew to the Secratary.[2] I want you to get a true list of the Strength of Cannon, Musket. &. C. powder that is in the magazines of the United States, & send it to me. If this sample is not sufficient I flatter myself that I can make it stronger If you can get a sample of the best powder, that is in the Secratary s possession forward it to me, which I will receive as a token of your friendship. I am Your Obedt. Humb. Servt. &. C.

The Honorable Messrs. ELIJAH FOLEY
B. Thruston, & H. Clay
Washington City

N.B. Yesterday I had a conversation with Capt Dangerfield[3] he told me that you (Mr. Thruston) was much surprised to find that the contract was confirmed with a man at 36 cents per lb. When I had offered to make it at 32 cents per lb. I am equally surprised with you. Honoured gentlemen keep this communication to yourselves E.F.

ALS. DLC-HC (DNA, M212, R1). The writer was probably associated with John Foley, who in 1803 and 1804 advertised his gunpowder, manufactured at South Elkhorn, five miles from Lexington.

1 This word may have been erased. 2 Of War.

3 William Daingerfield, of Fayette County.

Advertisement Concerning Buzzard

[February 17, 1807]

N. B. The subscribers, in order to improve their own stock, have been induced to purchase this horse, at the price of $5500, and have placed him in the hands of Maj. B. Graves, who, we doubt not, will pay the greatest attention to mares left with him.

Any mare failing to prove with foal, shall be entitled to the next season gratis, provided the mare continues the property of him who put her—supposing the horse living. ABM. BUFORD,[1]
THOS. TODD,
HENRY CLAY,
GEO. GRAVES,[2]
BENJ. GRAVES.

Frankfort *Western World,* March 5, 1807. These paragraphs were appended to a Buzzard stud advertisement signed by Benjamin Graves, Fayette County farmer, soldier, and politician.

1 Abraham Buford, Revolutionary veteran from Virginia and owner of a large body of land in Scott County, was greatly interested in horses and racing.

2 Brother of Benjamin and also a resident in the northern district of Fayette County.

Presentation of Petition of Reni Naw

[February 17, 1807]

The petition asked allowance of a drawback on certain goods exported from New York. *Annals of Cong.,* 9 Cong., 2 Sess., XVI, 69. Referred to a committee already considering the memorial of sundry Philadelphia merchants on the subject of drawbacks, Naw's petition was rejected; and the committee stand was concurred in by the Senate. Naw is unidentified.

Resolution for Amending Constitution

[February 20, 1807]

Resolved, by the Senate and House of Representatives of the United States of America in Congress assembled, (two thirds of both houses concurring,) that the following article be proposed to the Legislatures of the several states, which, when ratified by three fourths thereof, shall be valid as part of the Constitution of the said United States:

Article XIII.

"The Judicial power of the United States shall not be construed to extend to controversies between Citizens of different States; between Citizens of the same State, claiming lands under grants of different States; nor between a State or the Citizens thereof, and foreign States, Citizens or Subjects."

AD. DNA, RG46, 9A-B3. Published in Washington *National Intelligencer,* April 3, 1807; *Annals of Cong.,* 9 Cong., 2 Sess., XVI, 76. On February 26 the Senate postponed consideration of the measure until the next Session, at which time it was not revived. The proposal was not of Clay's impetus; it had passed the Kentucky legislature on motion of Felix Grundy in 1804, and had been presented to the United States Senate originally by John Breckinridge in 1805. Ky. H. of Reps., *Journal, 1804,* pp. 57-58, 62, 87; *Annals of Cong.,* 8 Cong., 2 Sess., XIV, 53.

Presentation of Memorial for Henry Cary Gist and Others

[February 23, 1807]

The memorial stated that Gist, Jesse Bledsoe, and James Morrison had discovered a valuable lead mine on the public lands bordering the Ohio in Indiana Territory and asked that they be given the exclusive right to open and develop the mine. *Annals of Cong.,* 9 Cong., 2 Sess., XVI, 76. Clay was appointed chairman of a committee to consider the memorial but no report from the committee is recorded in the *Annals.* Elsewhere it is noted that the application failed because its terms were "inadmissible." When other applicants subsequently failed to locate the mine, the Gist group renewed their application for a lease on altered terms. Though the lease was then authorized and an extension of time subsequently granted for making entry, the tract was apparently never located. Carter (ed.), *Territorial Papers of the United States,* VII, 609, 660; VIII, 257-58. Henry Cary Gist was the son of Nathaniel Gist, soldier in the French and Indian and the Revolutionary wars and pioneer Kentuckian.

Promissory Note from William M. Vein

[February 24, 1807]

On demand I promise to pay to Henry Clay One hundred and fifty dollars. Witness my hand & seal at the City of Washington 24 Feb. 1807. WM. M. VEIN {L.S.}

Teste

M. CLAY.[1]

DS, in Clay's hand. DLC-TJC, 2d Series, vol. 6. Vein (or Veirs, signature not clear) has not been identified. 1 Matthew Clay.

Speech on Land Grant to Chesapeake and Delaware Canal Company

[February 24, 1807]

In a speech, not reported, Clay supported the bill "with great ability & much eloquence." Plumer, Diary, 87 (DLC, DNA Micro. Supp.).

Report on Ohio Rapids Canal

[February 24, 1807]

The committee, to whom was referred the resolution proposing the appropriation of a quantity not exceeding acres of land, to assist in cutting out a Canal at the Rapids of the Ohio, have, according to order, had the same under consideration, and beg leave to report,

That they have attentively examined a Survey of the Rapids of the Ohio and the adjacent shores, accompanied by explanatory notes, made by a Mr. Jared Brooks,[1] who appears to be a skilful and intelligent Engineer: That this survey exhibits the scites proposed for the Canal on the Kentucky shore, and its supposed contemplated route on the Indiana side; and its accuracy is certified by nine respectable gentlemen, who, being appointed by the Kentucky legislature to promote the execution of an act for incorporating a Company for cutting the Canal in question, have themselves examined the several objects delineated. Mr. Brooks has sunk, at short and convenient distances, shafts ascertaining the nature of the ground through which the Canal is proposed to pass on the Kentucky shore [and] the various depths to the surface of the rock—and by his survey and notes has fully evinced the practicability of the object, and the superior advantages of the Kentucky over the opposite side. On the Kentucky shore, the requisite depth of the Canal will be less, its length not so great by at least one-third, a better bed afforded, firmer ground for its sides, and far better harbours at its head and foot. From these circumstances it is presumed the expense of the undertaking will not be so great, by one half, on the Kentucky as upon the opposite shore, and in Mr Brooks opinion will not exceed $200.000.[2]

To open the canal so as to admit of the passage of Vessels of any burthen capable of navigating the Ohio, the legislature of Kentucky at their Session of 1804 passed an act incorporating a Company, by the name of the Ohio Canal Company, which was amended by an act passed at their Session of 1805.[3] By the provisions of these acts, the Company is permitted to raise a Capital of 500.000$, composed of shares of fifty dollars each, is vested with suitable powers to accomplish the work, and, upon its completion, authorized to charge reasonable tolls. On their part, the Legislature of Kentucky has directed a subscription for 1000 shares, and has invited the governments of the U. States, Pennsylvania, Virginia, Maryland, Ohio and New York, all supposed to be more or less interested, to participate in the undertaking.

That the work is one of great & national importance is undeniable. The immense Country on the Ohio and its waters, above the rapids, in seeking a market for its surplus products, has to encounter the obstruction in the navigation of that stream which they present. This obstruction, never entirely free from danger, is such as to absolutely preclude the passage of vessels for several months in the year in their descent, and when laden for the whole year in their ascent of the river. The rapidity of the current (which averages at the rate of from 10 to 11 miles an hour through the falls) leaves no alternative for a safe voyage up as well as down the river, but in a Canal.

How far it is the policy of the Government to aid in works of this kind, when it has no *direct* interest—whether indeed, in such a case, it has the constitutional power of patronage and encouragement, is not necessary to be decided in the present instance. Being the proprietor of Land bordering upon the Ohio to a greater extent than any individual state, owning too an invaluable Saline near the Wabash,[4] there can be no doubt that both policy and *power* combine in favour of promoting an undertaking by which its property is to be incidentally benefited. If the value and price of land depend, as well upon the facility with which its products find a market, as upon its capacity to produce, there can be no doubt that the public lands will be increased in value, by improvements in the navigation of those streams which water them. The Saline alluded to will have its market enlarged by the opening of the proposed Canal; and those above the Rapids, as well as those below, may in time count upon it as one of the sources from whence Salt may be obtained.[5]

But as some contrariety of opinion has existed in relation to the preferable side of the Ohio for the Canal; as the information upon which your Committee has on this subject acted, is rather of an ex parte character; and as any aid this Government may think proper to give, ought only to be afforded after the most impartial and thorough investigation on the subject, they beg leave to recommend the following resolution:

Resolved that the President be authorized to appoint three Commissioners for the purpose of examining the Rapids of the Ohio to ascertain whether a Canal to avoid them be practicable, and which side of the river presents the greatest advantages for its accomplishment; and also whether the bed of the river is capable of being so cleared out as to admit of ascending & descending navigation, and the relative importance of a sluice & canal.

AD. DNA, RG46, 9A-D1. Published in Washington *National Intelligencer,* March 2, 1807; *Annals of Cong.,* 9 Cong., 2 Sess., XVI, 92-93. Other members of the drafting committee were William B. Giles of Virginia and Abraham Baldwin of Georgia. The document is erroneously ascribed to John Quincy Adams in *American State Papers, Miscellaneous,* I, 479. William Plumer reported that Clay supported the proposal "with great ability & much eloquence." Plumer, Diary, 857 (DLC, DNA Micro. Supp.). The speech was not recorded. On February 26, the report was agreed to and a committee appointed to draft the appropriate legislation. See below, Bill, February 26, 1807.

1 A surveyor and map maker, of Louisville, Kentucky.

2 J[ared] Brooks, statement of October 28, 1807, in *American State Papers, Miscellaneous,* I, 822.

3 Littell (comp.), *Statute Law of Kentucky,* III, 221-34 (app. December 19, 1804); 259-72 (app. December 20, 1805). Cf. above, Amendments to Bill, December 13, 1804.

4 The United States Saline, also called the Wabash Saline, comprising salt springs between the Wabash and Saline rivers a few miles back from the Ohio, was located on land ceded by the Indians in 1802. Established as a Federal reservation, the area had been leased for commercial development under act of March 3, 1803. 2 *U.S. Stat.,* 235.

5 In the foregoing sentence the words "some of" followed the phrase "as well as" and the phrase "so great a necessity of life," followed the word "Salt"—which omissions from the present version were deleted in the MS. Two paragraphs following at this point were also crossed out:

"Upon the whole your Committee is of opinion, that those who are jointly benefited in a scheme of this sort, ought jointly to contribute in the expences to be incurred in it, and therefore take the liberty of submitting the following resolution:

"Resolved that it is expedient to appropriate a quantity of land, not exceeding Acres towards opening a Canal at the Rapids of the Ohio on the Kentucky shore."

Bill Relating to Ohio Rapids Canal

[February 26, 1807]

A bill providing for the appointment of Commissioners to ascertain the practicability of removing the obstructions in the navigation of the Ohio at the Rapids

Be it enacted by the Senate and House of Representatives of the United States in Congress assembled, That the President of the United States be, and he is hereby, authorized to appoint three Commissioners for the purpose of examining the Rapids of the Ohio, and the adjacent shores, to ascertain the practicability of opening a Canal to avoid the obstruction in the navigation of that river produced by the Rapids; and, if it be practicable, which shore presents the fewest obstacles, and greatest advantages, for the accomplishment of the work; and also whether the bed of the river is capable of being so cleared out as to admit of the passage of vessels, descending as well as ascending, at all Seasons in which they could navigate the Canal; and the relative importance and probable expence of the two objects.

Be it further enacted that the said Commissioners with all convenient dispatch, shall proceed to perform the duties herein specified. And they are hereby authorized to appoint an Engineer to assist them in the discharge of the said duties. And the said Commissioners and Engineer shall each be entitled to receive dollars per day in full for their compensation & expences.

And Be it further enacted that a sum not exceeding dollars be and is hereby appropriated to carry into effect this act.

AD. DNA, RG46, 9A-B1. Other members of the drafting committee were Buckner Thruston and William B. Giles. The measure passed the Senate two days later but failed to emerge from Committee of the Whole in the House. *Annals of Cong.*, 9 Cong., 2 Sess., XVI, 93, 95-96, 681.

From Cornelius and John Comegys

Henry Clay Esqr. Baltimore, 7 March, 1807
Lexington Kentucky
Sir;

In October 1806 we sold to Messrs. Owen Reilly & Co. of Frankfort sundry goods as P their note herewith,[1] amounting to £373.5/. this Currency, he Owen Reilly & Clark & Anderson[2] composing said firm, and by a letter recently recd. from Reilly we have reason to believe that undue advantages have been taken of him by his said Partners, the present is to request that you will immediately on receipt hereof endeavor to get the debt paid or secured or in case of need to commence Suit against the whole of them without delay—O R. observes in his Letter to us under date of the 9 ulto—"When I purchased the Goods and entered into Partnership with Clark & Anderson I had no Idea that the debts contracted in Baltimore would have remained so long unpaid; for at that time I had the most ample & implicit Confidence in these men; but which I am sorry to say has been very much weakened by their conduct towards me—I had recd. considerable sums of money which I intended carrying on last Fall to Baltimore to discharge the debts due there; but was induced to lend it to C & A under a promise that they would return it to me when I should be ready to start and would also advance me all they could raise besides—But when I had made my arrangements for starting & applied to them for the money they told me they had not a Cent to pay me with, or to advance, and brought forward an Acct. against me for Goods sent from their Store to stand against part of the Cash I had advanced them"—So much of his Letter for your government—his object appears to be to assign over the goods and debts for the benefit of his Creditors and as we are not disposed to accept of this kind of settlement & to relinquish Clark & Anderson, unless indeed you are of opinion it will be our Interest, in this case you will act as may appear most prudent, and being on the spot can judge better than we can at this distance, and as he has written in the same way to others no time shou'd be lost on the Occasion and must beg your pointed attention on rect. hereof—Let us hear from you by first Mail,[3] interim we remain Respectfully Your Obt. Servants CORNS. & JNO. COMEGYS

ALS. DLC-HC (DNA, M212, R1). [1] Not found.
[2] Reilly, a Frankfort merchant, had apparently entered into partnership with Clark and Anderson, a Louisville mercantile firm.
[3] No reply has been found.

To ———

[Baltimore, March 10, 1807]

When I left Washington, the original treaty with Britain had not arrived, but the British minister had received a copy.[1] It does not meet the approbation of the president in two respects—First it fails to provide competent protection for our seamen; and in the second place, it was accompanied with a diplomatic note, presented to our commissioners by the British, at the time of their signing it, declaring that if France persisted in the decree of blockade,[2] and neutrals did not oppose it, Britain would hold herself at liberty to deviate from the treaty.

Extract. Frankfort *Palladium,* April 2, 1807. Identified as "from Henry Clay esq."
[1] A copy of the treaty resulting from the Monroe-Pinkney mission reached the British Minister in Washington on March 3, 1807, a few hours before Congress adjourned.
[2] The Berlin decree.

From Benjamin Comegys

Henry Clay, Esqr. Baltimore March 24, 1807
Dear Sir,

I herewith enclose you Aaron Burr's draft on George M. Ogden for $500 protested for non-payment.[1] Amt of protest $1.50 which have the goodness to get settled with the least possible delay and advise me thereof. I hope in your next to have a good account of Dr. Rumsey.

It will give me pleasure to hear of your safe arrival at your house. Accept, dear Sir, my best wishes for your long life and happiness.

BENJ. COMEGYS

New Orleans Branch notes answer here very well, and I presume they are frequently to be had in your country.

Copy. InHi-William H. Smith Collection. Cf. above, Comegys to Clay, December 10, 1806.
[1] Not found. Ogden claimed that funds promised by Burr's friends had not been provided and, consequently, he was unable to pay Burr's obligations. Parker, "Lewis Sanders of Grass Hills," *Papers of the Christopher Gist Historical Society,* 1951-1952, p. 3.

From James Brown

Dear Clay New orleans April 10th. 1807

By this time you are at your own fire side enjoying the pleasing society of your affectionate wife and the engaging prattle of your children—God grant you in the words of the spanish compliment "a thousand years" of such pure such delightful enjoyments!

We poor devils have during the winter endured every thing which tyranny could inflict. A weak Governor and despotic General[1] who appeared to agree in nothing except the terrors which they spread through our city and the Slanders of all the principal men of the western Country, have lead us a wretched life God knows—These miscreants have not dared to assail me *here* because they found me fortified in the esteem of almost every man in new Orleans but their tools have endeavored to blast my character abroad and to confound me with conspirators. How absurd the idea! and how infamous the wretches who gave rise to it! Enjoying the confidence of the administration, and the esteem of every respectable man in the Territory your friendly heart would rejoice in hearing the execrations uttered against our slanderers and against the Arch Traitor[2] of whose character I have only lately had proofs. I fear he has like old Sebastian[3] deceived me & that he has touched the "accursed thing." But we are now restored to peace; and to God and his Country I leave him.

You have taken the right side on this question. When we adhere to our excellent Constitution and laws we walk on safe ground—we cannot err. When we appeal to necessity we are at sea without a compass. Is it possible that the President will pledge his well earned popularity for the safety of a *scoundrel*[4] who has always been suspected and I fear always deserved it? I hope not. The Leader Aaron Burr has never had my confidence although I think him equal to his accuser in purity. I wish all such intriguers at the Devil. *We* are a poor weak miserable people but we thank God *you* are able and willing to protect us—

I am extremely anxious to know the fate of a claim which Bodley[5] and myself have on Indian Creek which is in the hands of Trimble[6] and of the entry in the name of Gillespie &. Brooks.[7] Trimble has brought suit for about one thousand Dollars against Shipp.[8] Is it decided—

My plantation moves on well—If in the course of your business you can buy any likely negroes of good characters I will if sent down give from 450 to five hundred & fifty dollars for them on 12 months. In descending as hands they will earn about 50 Dollars. I want about 12 more—It is probable you can speculate in them & I will take them of your hands.

We all continue healthy notwithstanding the dangerous climate— My Nancy[9] & myself love you all more than ever & pray God to bless you Your friend,

P.S. Midnight excuse this scrawl JAMES BROWN

Henry Clay, Esqr.

ALS. DLC-TJC (DNA, M212, R10).

1 Governor William C. C. Claiborne and General James Wilkinson.

2 Aaron Burr.

3 Benjamin Sebastian.

4 General Wilkinson.

5 Thomas Bodley.

6 Robert Trimble.

7 The entry of William Gillespie, of Davidson County, North Carolina (Tennessee) was located on Boggs fork of Boone's Creek, Fayette County, Kentucky. Brooks, not identified.

8 Colby Shipp.

9 Mrs. Brown.

To Benjamin Sebastian

Dr Sir Frankfort 21st. Apl. 1807.

Not meeting with the writer of the inclosed in the City of Washington, I had not an opportunity of delivering your letter to him until I went to Philadelphia, where he resides.[1] I did not go there until after Congress rose. I called at his house twice to see him personally, but was unable to do it. Whether he was absent in fact or did not wish to see Company I could not learn. Supposing the latter might be the case, I did not choose to press myself upon him, and therefore left your letter. In the course of a day or two after, the inclosed was sent to me. With its contents I am unacquainted but hope they will be satisfactory to you.

After having spent an agreeable winter, I returned home last friday in good health. I hope this letter will find you well.

Yr's truly HENRY CLAY

ALS. KyU-Sebastian Papers, microfilm copy from original in possession of the family at Bardstown, Kentucky. Addressed to Sebastian "near Louisville Kentucky." Postmarked: ". . . April 27th."

1 Not found.

Legal Advice to Lewis Sanders

26 Apl 1807

Mr. Saunders will sign the bill I have prepared.[1] It is not necessary that it should be sworn to, but if it should become so, Mr. Woodbridge[2] as his agent can do it.

He will also execute the power of Atto.[3] acknowledge it before the Notary public, and get him to certify it with his official seal.

It is proper to remark that by the Laws of Virginia a Creditor is furnished with two remedies by attachment agt. such debtors as Mr. Blennerhassett. One is by bill as suggested by Mr. Woodbridge, and which can only be used against absent *un*absconding debtors. The other is at law and may be used against absconding debtors. This latter mode where it can be resorted to is much less dilitory and more effectual than the former. According to this the Creditor before a magistrate makes oath to his demand, & that his debtor has absconded so that the ordinary process of law cannot be served upon him, and enters into an attachment bond. A warrant thereupon issues, by virtue of which the officer takes into his immediate custody any property he can find belonging to the debtor, which at the next Court is ordered to be sold and the proceeds paid over to the Creditor.

If the Slaves of Blennerhassett can be got into Virginia it will probably be best for Mr. Saunders to take this latter remedy, and his agent can make the necessary application to the Justice and give the proper bond. HENRY CLAY

ADS. MiD-B. Sanders had acquired $10,000 in bills drawn by Burr on his New York agent and endorsed by Blennerhassett. Unable to collect, Sanders looked to Blennerhassett for payment. In addition, Sanders had purchased $6000 of Burr's bills, without endorsement, which also remained unpaid. Parker, "Lewis Sanders of Grass Hills," *Papers of the Christopher Gist Historical Society*, 1951-1952, p. 3.

1 Directed "To the Honble the———Court of——————sitting in Chancery," and signed by Sanders, this document (DS, in Clay's hand. MiD-B) explains the claim against Blennerhassett, states that the latter had moved from Virginia to the Mississippi Territory, and levies a claim against an unnamed defendant in Virginia who allegedly has control of some of Blennerhassett's property.

2 Dudley Woodbridge.

3 Not found.

From John Swan

Dear Sir Baltimore May 1st 1807.

Inclos'd you will find the note[1] you gave for the Amount of Mr Campbells[2] draft on me, for which He sent the money. After receipt of Your Letter,[3] that was kept here nearly three weeks, you will perceive I knew the man & promised He would pay you but not me, when Convenient be pleased to return the receipt for the draft, or your receipt for the money in full—

You will greatly oblige me bringing forward my Suit[4] as soon as possible, If you obtain a Confirmation of my Original Location or the value of it in money, rely on an ample Compensation, gain that point & I will at least double Your Contingent fee, Shall be glade to hear occasionally the prospect of a decision, when I Can serve you here you may Command Dear Sir Your very Obedient Servt

The Hon Henry Clay Esqr J SWAN

ALS. DLC-TJC (DNA, M212, R12). Delivered by a "Mr Greer," possibly George Greer, Frankfort merchant who had Baltimore connections.

1 Not found.

2 Not identified.

3 Not found.

4 Against Richard Clough Anderson and Nathaniel Massie

From James Smith, Jr.

My friend May 2d 1807

Did I not send to you a Note of Woodson Wren's? if I did not I have either mislaid it, or sent it to a Mr. Jesse B Thomas of Lawrenceburgh[1] I recollect that shortly after I wrote you on this business —There was one of my Customers here who said that this Man had moved from Lexington to somewhere in that neighbourhood & that I had better write to the above Gentleman on the business I did send him another. Note against one William Sebrees[2]—but have no memorandum of sending him the other, I therefore conclude this business of Wrens is under your care—for I have this morning recd a letter from Wren, dated Grants Lick—Campbell County Kentucky —saying that he has sold his goods on a Credit—that he has Notes & other security by him which he is willing to give for the Debt—and begs that I may not have him confined—He also offers lands at a fair price—but this I have told him is out of the Question—If the thing is under your care which I believe it is & that you have the Note—You will know best how to manage the business—if he can make you assignments of good Notes—it certainly will be best to take them—however I rely on your doing exactly as if the Debt were your own & please to write me on the subject—I have lately received from Hart & Bartlett 400 Dollars which they desire me to place to your Credit, which is done—If you can possibly send me what you have recovered to wards those Notes of Smiths[3] & the ballance coming from Jordan[4] by an early conveyance, it will much oblige me as I never before knew the want of money so much—Another of Millers[5] notes is due & I must desire you to push for the money—or at least for undoubted security & perhaps by a little indulgence, you you [*sic*] may be able to secure both. & get part of the money for the first—The last I think is due in September—Your particular attention to this will oblige me—and will also thank you to attend to the land—as this is material —I may perhaps by proper attention have this fixed so that a Sale may be made—With much respect I am your friend

JAS SMITH JR

ALS. DLC-TJC (DNA, M212, R12). Addressed to Clay at Lexington.

1 An attorney-at-law of Lawrenceburgh, Indiana Territory.

2 Probably the captain of Kentucky militia in the War of 1812, subsequently Marshal of the District of West Florida, where he died in 1827.

3 William W. Smith.

4 John Jordan, Jr.

5 Robert Miller.

From James Smith, Jr.

Respected Friend 4h May 1807

Doctor Barry[1] informs me that you are his particular friend & will undertake to forward me a Check on the Bank of Pennsa. when the inclosed[2] becomes due, or even before it becomes due if he arrives before—clear of expence to me, as he is bound to pay me here—Will you therefore oblige both him & me by so doing?—The Doctor has been in Town some time—and all along promised me he would not leave it without paying me but he like all other mercantile Men are liable to, has been disappointed—I am sensible he has done the best he could—

I wrote you some days since & I have no doubt you will attend to the Content.[3] I am very anxious about that Tract of Land—I think if proper pains were taken—we certainly could get hold of it so as to make Sale. Norvell[4] still insists upon that the Title is clear & unexceptionable—You may perhaps find some person that will for a Commission undertake to investigate fully into this business—Please to let me hear from you as soon as convenient & I hope you will use every means to secure what money you cannot get from Miller—With much respect I am Your friend JAS SMITH JR

ALS. DLC-TJC (DNA, M212, R12). Addressed to Clay at Lexington.
1 Dr. John Barry, Jr.
2 Not found.
3 See above, May 2.
4 Thomas Norvell.

Receipt from Arthur Patterson

9h. May 1807.

Recd. of Henry Clay one bay horse at the price of forty seven pounds ten Shillings on account of a Contract between him. my brother & me relative to my fathers preemption

ARTHUR PATTERSON

DS, in Clay's hand, DLC-TJC (DNA, M212, R15). Cf. above, Agreement, September 18, 1805.

Promissory Note from Abner and Alexander Willis

[May 11, 1807]

We promise to pay to Henry Clay one hundred and fifty dollars as follows: One horse or mare at the price of one hundred dollars Cash to be delivered to said Clay in two months from this date at his farm and fifty dollars in money.

Witness our hands & seals this 11h. May 1807.

Teste ABNER WILLIS {L.S.}
WM. B. PRICE ALEXD. WILLIS {L.S.}

DS, in Clay's hand. DLC-TJC (DNA, M212, R15). All whose names appear in this document were residents of Fayette County.

From James Smith, Jr.

My Friend May 16h 1807—

In my walks up market Street I have not long since seen R Miller[1] who I suppose came to the City to purchase Goods—he did not call upon me & having a great many Debts out already I did not invite him—I expect before you receive this he must have arrived with his Goods & it will be a good time for you to obtain from him the amount of the Note that is due—which will thank you to press for as much as you can, as I want it much—The other comes round in September Should you apprehend danger I hope you will take care to secure the whole—but by all means if possible, get hold of the first 1500 & send on as soon as you possibly can—and also the money that was secured on W W Smiths[2] first Notes—I hope soon to hear something favourable of the land business—I must beg your further attention thereto—I believe I mentioned to you my having Notes of Vance & Dills—near Cincinnati[3] & if I recollect right you were to give me the name of one of your profession in that Quarter on whom I might depend—or that you would undertake the collection yourself I am told they are Men of property—& I want the money—please to let me know what you think about it & oblige Yr Friend

JAS SMITH JR

ALS. DLC-TJC (DNA, M212, R12). Addressed to Clay at Lexington.
1 Robert Miller.
2 William W. Smith.
3 Possibly Samuel C. Vance and James Dill of Lawrenceburgh, Indiana Territory.

To Leonard Jacoby

Dr Sir Lexington 18h. May 1807

Your favour of the 13h. Apl. came safely to hand,[1] covering the a/c. of Mess. Banks & Owings.[2] I have seen Mr. Owings since the receipt of it & presented him with the account, which he acknowledges to be just, except that he claims a farther Credit than what is allowed for money paid to Mr. Poyzer[3] for you. He promises to pay the balance 'ere long. You will instruct me whether Mr. Poyzer or any other person was ever authorized to receive any money for you. Mr. Owings had not the receipt and does not recollect the amt. of the Credit.

I fear the prospect is dull of getting any thing from Jordan or his indorsers.[4] He has made over his property to Trustees for the benefit of his Creditors, giving a preference to some. But it will not pay one dollar in the pound as is supposed. And his indorsers I apprehend are unable to discharge your demand. I will however do the best I can for you. Yrs H. CLAY

ALS. PHC-Charles Roberts Autograph Collection. Addressed: "Leonard Jacoby Esqr. Merchant Philadelphia." Endorsed: "... answered 2d. July." Answer not found.

1 Not found.

2 Cuthbert Banks and Thomas Deye Owings had dissolved their partnership two years earlier.

3 George Poyzer, an Englishman, had been a Lexington merchant before moving to Nashville.

4 John Jordan, Jr.

From David B. Langhorne

May 18 1807

Mr H. Clay will please give to Mr Marcus Richardson[1] the Order, I gave him some years ago, on Isham Talbot,[2] If he now has it,

D. B. LANGHORNE

ADS. Fayette Circuit Court, File 135 (1808).

1 Captain Marquis Richardson, a resident of Franklin County, who later (1818) operated a mill in Clark County, and still later removed to Montgomery.

2 Above, November 19, 1803.

Bond as Agent for Thomas Hart

[May 20, 1807]

I have sold William Rout eighteen acres of land being part of the Tract I recovered of John Coburn by decree of the Genl. Court which was afterwards affirmed by the Court of Appeals,[1] at the price of Seven dollars per acre—I bind myself upon the payment of the consideration money to make a deed for the said land containing a clause to return the purchase money without interest, if the land should be recovered from said Rout by any other claim. Witness my hand & seal this 20 May 1807. THOMAS HART {L.S.}

by H. CLAY—

I bind myself for a compliance of Tho. Hart with the above 20 May 1807. H. CLAY {L.S.}

Att

SAMUEL VANCE.[2]

ADS. KyU-Wilson Collection. Endorsements on verso assign the bond from William Rout to William Kendall, for $126, April 5, 1823; and from William Kendall to Elijah Current, for $300, January 30, 1830. Kendall, born in Fayette County, was a Harrison County farmer.

1 See above, Survey, February 19, 1806, note.

2 Possibly of Pendleton County.

From Thomas Todd

Dr Clay. May 23d. 1807.

I wished much to have seen you when in Lexington & to have advised with you, whether I should indict or [. . .][1] (or both) the ungrateful, base, & scurrillous Editor of the Western World.[2] I have written our friend Allen[3] on the Subject & wish you & him to consult on the subject & take such measures as you deem adviseable, this Editor & his Masters have passed so long with impunity, that the character of no man is safe from their malicious attacks—I have indirectly heard that they have a rod in soak for *even* you—more of this when I see you.

I must beg your Attention to my Suit with Bush &c in the Court of Appeals,[4] Also to two Suits in the Woodford Circuit Court[5]—One Stewarts devisees & oth[ers] vs. Thomas Claggett—Ejectment—get an Order of Survey—the other Trabue's Admr. vs Stewarts devisees—A demurrer was filled [*sic*] to the Bill, they may probably ask leave to amend—I took the liberty to place your name as Counsel, to the demurrer, considering you as my Counsel in all cases, whether civil or criminal, for I really fear my warm temper will so far get the ascendancy as sometime as [*sic*] to hurry me into an imprudent act wit[h] some of the villainous Junto. Yrs. Sincerely

THOMAS TODD

ALS. DLC-HC (DNA, M212, R1). Addressed to Clay as "Atto at law expected in Frankfort." 1 MS. torn; a short word missing.

2 Todd finally brought a libel suit against Joseph Street at the October Term, 1808, of Franklin Circuit Court. The case was continued until July, 1810, when it was dismissed with the defendant to assume all costs. Franklin Circuit Court, Order Book, 1808-1810, pp. 87 *et passim; ibid.*, File 100.

3 John Allen (of Frankfort, Kentucky).

4 Involving conflicting claims to land on Silver Creek, about two miles northwest of the Blue Licks, decided in Todd's favor in 1809. 4 *Ky. Reports* (1 Bibb) 64-67.

5 The case of Jane E. Trabue *vs.* Stewart's Heirs, a land dispute, was initiated in September, 1807, and settled by decree for the defendants in 1809. Woodford Circuit Court, File 77. The other suit has not been found.

Order Drawn by George Mansell

13 June 1807

Pay H. Clay One hundred dollars out of my Judgt. agt. you,[1] being the amt of his several fees in that suit.

Mr. T. D. Owings GEORGE MANSELL

[Endorsement on verso][2]

Accepted

THOS D OWINGS

DS, in Clay's hand. DLC-TJC, 2d Series, vol. 6.

1 On June 4, the Kentucky Court of Appeals had upheld a decision of Fayette Circuit Court dissolving an injunction and rendering damages and costs to Mansell, against Owings, litigation in which Clay had represented Mansell. Fayette Circuit Court, Order Book D, 376.

2 AES.

From John Wrenshall

Mr. Henry Clay

Sir Pittsburgh June 13. 1807

I flatter'd my self that your promice of a remitance immediately on your arrival in Lexington, would have render'd it unnecessary for me to write again in that stile which your unaccountable neglect justifies me in doing—if it afforded you any pleasure to keep an injur'd family in torture, and my exertions on the rack, for devizing means to save my credit from sinking on account of this delinquency, I should think you excusable, but this cannot be the case—why then Sir, do you not discharge your duty, you *can* if you *will*—and I have *paid* for the work being done more than two years ago, nor can all the manoeuvres of Bodley[1] counteract your skill if you are disposed to use it. I intreat you sir to remitt the amount of Holmes[2] debt with interest by return of mail.

The time is elaps'd when the second payment of the whisky should have been made, in case that was not done, you had my instructions to incist on cash, I hope this is effected, and that you are preparing to send it along with the above—

Hughs[3] balance of Debt and interest, and Allens note and interest, with what rent he may have received for the brick house in Paris,[4] pray let these be attended to and sent off—what is the result of Morrisons affair or West & Guthrys bond[5] you mention'd to me that it would terminate long 'ere this—it is impossable that you can be insenceable to this, that I am waiting with painfull anxiety the receipt of your promised remittance I Remain Sir Yours &c

JOHN WRENSHALL

ALS. DLC-TJC (DNA, M212, R12).

1 Thomas Bodley. 2 Andrew Holmes. 3 James Hughes.

4 John Allen, whose house in Paris, Kentucky, had been rented for use as a private school.

5 As payment under the partnership agreement of James Morrison and George Mansell with Edward West for a two-thirds interest in West's nail-cutting machine (above, Putnam to Clay, August 22, 1804, note), the inventor had agreed to credit his partners for the amount paid by them on his debt to Peacock, Wrenshall, and Company, for whom Clay was attorney and agent. Morrison, under court order at the March Term, 1804, had given Clay two bonds, payable in money and lands, and in return Clay had executed to West and Jesse Guthrie a release of the judgment obtained by Peacock, Wrenshall, and Company. When West's patent proved of little value, Morrison brought suit against Clay for recovery of the bonds. At the Spring Term, 1808, the State Court of Appeals upheld the ruling of the Fayette Circuit Court in Clay's favor. Fayette Circuit Court, Order Book B (1804-1805), pp. 17-19; 3 *Ky. Reports* (Hardin) 421-32.

Contract with Hugh McDermid

20 June 1807.

I have sold to H. Clay Francis McDermids interest in Dailey's lot in Lexington at present occupied by Wm. Barry. He has paid me Twenty six dollars on account of it, and when I send him the deed executed by said Francis (which I am to do as soon as I get home) he is to pay the balance of Twenty four dollars.

HUGH MCDERMID

DS, in Clay's hand. DLC-TJC (DNA, M212, R15). Cf. above, Property Deeds, September 10, 29, 1806.

Promissory Note to Thomas Hart, Jr.

30 June 1807.

Twelve months after date I promise to pay to Thomas Hart Jr[1] or order One hundred & forty two pounds Kentucky Currency, with Interest thereon from the 5h. day of June 1806, without defalcation; payable & negociable at the office of the Kentucky Insurance Company.

HENRY CLAY

[Supplementary endorsements on verso][2]

October 17th 1808 Recd Three Hundred Dollars on a/c of the within Bond.

for Scott Trotter & Co
L DENT[3]

Recd. the bal. in full 13 July 1809. WILL. SCOTT[4]

ADS. DLC-TJC (DNA, M212, R15). Assigned, by endorsement of same date on verso (ES, in Clay's hand), from Hart to Daniel Brodhead, Sr., Revolutionary officer and pioneer Louisville merchant.

1 Clay originally wrote the note in favor of Brodhead, then deleted and changed the name to Hart.

2 The first, an AES; the second, ES, in Clay's hand.

3 Probably Lawrence Dent, of Mason County, Kentucky.

4 Possibly the proprietor of a fulling mill near Lexington, agent for collection of debts due the early firm of Trotter and Scott. During this period several members of the family in central Kentucky carried the same name.

Security Bond for James Morrison

[July 3, 1807]

[James Morrison, Lewis Sanders, Thomas Hart, Jr., Charles Wilkins, Alexander Parker, William Morton, Henry Clay, and Peyton Short, all of Lexington, bind themselves to the United States of America in the amount of $50,000 to guarantee Morrison's compliance with a War Department contract by which he engaged to supply rations to United States troops.]

DS. KyU.

Argument Relative to Harman Blennerhassett

[July 15, 1807]

Mr. Clay, as counsel, assured the court, that he was instructed by his client to express his wish to be sent on for trial—he only wished an unnecessary rigour might not be observed, and that he might be forwarded in a manner as delicate as the nature of his situation would permit. Mr. Clay at the same time took the liberty, as a citizen, to protest against, or rather to object to the mode which had been pursued by the court–he viewed the proceedings as unprecedented and illegal–He, however, wished it to be understood that his observations were made as a citizen, and not at the instance of Mr. B.–it was his real wish to be sent on for trial. Mr. Bibb[1] stated that he had provided himself with authorities to prove the proceedings proper; but that he had that morning enquired of Mr. Clay whether any exceptions would be taken to the legality of the proceedings, and being informed that none would be taken, had neglected to bring his authorities into court–that he was now surprised to find the exceptions taken–

Mr. Clay stopped him, again to declare, that the exceptions were not by the consent of Mr. B. who he believed was really desirous of being conveyed to Richmond.

Lexington *Kentucky Gazette,* July 21, 1807, reprinted in Washington *National Intelligencer,* August 14, 1807. Upon his arrival in Lexington, July 14, 1807, Blennerhassett was arrested at the instance of Lewis Sanders (cf. above, Legal Advice, April 26, 1807, note). Before the day ended, David Meade, Jr., a deputy United States Marshal, arrived to take Blennerhassett into custody under charges of treason brought against him at Richmond, Virginia. The hearing, at which Clay served as Blennerhassett's counsel, was held the next day, and on July 20 the prisoner and his escort departed for Richmond.

1 George M. Bibb, at this time United States Attorney.

Survey of Meadows at "Ashland"

Fayette County Sct. 16th. July 1807.

Surveyed for Henry Clay Esqr. a Meadow in front of his dwelling House Containing 10 acres & twenty poles–Beginning at the Corner A on the So. West side of Boons station road, thence with the same N 46½ W 23¼ poles to Corner at (B) thence So 45 W 63½ poles to (C) thence So. 33 E. 26¼ poles to (D) thence N 43½ E. 69½ poles to the Beginning RICHD. HIGGINS S.F.C.[1]

Also one Other Meadow Containing twenty Seven Acres three quarters & twenty poles–Beginning at the Corner (A) near the Hay stacks thence So. 73¼ W. 34 poles to Corner (B) thence So 11 E 86 poles to Corner (C) thence N 80 E 26½ poles to (D) thence N 73 E. 41½ poles to E, thence N 33 W. 92 poles to the Beginning.

RICHD. HIGGINS S.F.C.

Monsieur Montell }
& Moses } C.C.[2]

[Two survey plats drawn beside text.]

ADS. DLC-TJC (DNA, M212, R15).

1 Surveyor, Fayette County. Higgins also was, or had been, a justice of the peace.

2 Not signatures. Augustus Waldemarde Mentelle and Moses (either a servant or Moses Hall) acted as the surveyor's chain carriers.

Receipted Bill for Charges on Protested Draft of William Macbean

[July 16, 1807]

1807.	Will Macbean & Henry Clay Dr. To Sundries	
July 16th.	To Thomas & Ro. Barr for amount said Macbeans bill, on Gillus Macbean, Protested	444. 4
	To General Expences. paid postage Covering bill, and charges Notary protesting	6
	To Interest 10 Pr Cent on the a[bove] from the 16 Septr. 1806 to the day—10 Mo.	36" [8]
		$487" 2

Recd. for the Kentucky Insurance Company
of Henry Clay JOHN L. MARTIN[1]

DS. DLC-HC (DNA, M212, R1). See above, Bill of Exchange, September 16, 1806. An accompanying Notice of Protest, signed by T. Heather, Notary Public, Portsmouth, England, is dated February 28, 1807.

1 Clerk, later cashier, of the Insurance Company.

Property Deed from Francis McDermid

[July 21, 1807]

[Indenture by which for the sum of $50, paid and receipt acknowledged, Francis McDermid of Wayne County, Kentucky, transfers to Henry Clay a lot in Lexington in what is called McDermid's Square, no. 48, upon which William Dailey, "a man of colour," who lately owned the lot, built a brick house which is at present occupied by William Barry—a corner lot on Mill Street, nearly opposite to Colonel Thomas Hart's lot. Warranty against all claiming through or under McDermid, but against no other claimant. Signed by Francis McDermid (his mark), the signature acknowledged in the Clerk's Office of Wayne County before Micah Taul, July 21, 1807, and subsequently produced before John D. Young in the Clerk's Office of Fayette County and recorded October 12, 1807.]

Fayette County Court, Deed Book B, 510. See above, Contract, June 20, 1807.

To [Harman Blennerhassett]

Sir Lexington July 22 1807

Your favor of the 20h.[1] was delivered to me. The apology you offer on the subject of my fee is abundantly sufficient, and the compensation you propose adequate. You will be pleased to inclose a Virginia bank note to me from Richmond, by the Mail.

I did not understand that by the agreement between Mr. Sanders & you, Mr. Miller was to be any way interested in the deed of trust upon your Island; and am pretty positive it was not agreed that he should be concerned in it, which is evident indeed from the face of the deed itself.[2] Nevertheless, you may give Mr. Miller an order upon Sanders to pay him out of the proceeds of Sale of the Island, if the [*amount*][3] exceed Mr. S. demand, and Mr. Alston[4] sho[uld *not*] be willing or forced to pay, according to [*his*] engagement. I think therefore you ought to acknowledge the deed before the Genl. Court in Virginia. You will only by refusing to do it give Mr. Sanders the unnecessary trouble of having the deed returned to be proven and certified from this place, or commencing a suit agt. you to coerce an acknowledgment. Yr. ob. Servt. HENRY CLAY

ALS. DLC-Blennerhassett Papers (DNA, M212, R20). Published in William H. Safford (ed.) *Blennerhassett Papers* (Cincinnati, 1864), 271. 1 Not found.

2 At the time of Blennerhassett's arrest in Lexington, Clay, his attorney, had worked out an agreement to extricate him from his difficulty with Lewis Sanders. Robert Miller, one of the creditors of Burr and Blennerhassett, seized certain property belonging to the latter and in addition became the principal purchaser of Blennerhassett's island. Safford (ed.), *Blennerhassett Papers,* 278; Leavy, "Memoir of Lexington," Kentucky State Historical Society, *Register,* XL (1942), 264; Norris F. Schneider, *Blennerhassett Island and the Burr Conspiracy* (Columbus, 1950), 30. 3 MS. torn.

4 Joseph Alston, Burr's son-in-law, a member of the South Carolina legislature and later Governor of that State.

Advertisement of Land Auction

[July 27, 1807]

[Henry Clay and Thomas Hart, Jr., Trustees,[1] advertise an auction to start at noon on the third Monday in September next, at Wilson's Inn,[2] in Lexington, relative to various properties: Jack Kennedy's plantation of around 100 acres, two miles from Lexington on the Woodford road; 27,500 acres on the Kentucky River in Montgomery County; 5,000 acres on Bank Lick Creek,[3] part of 6,000 acres patented to William Jones; 1000 acres in the tract set apart for officers of the Virginia Continental Line; 688 acres on the Cumberland River; and 125 acres in Jessamine County, part of Gen. Adam Stephens' military survey.]

Lexington *Kentucky Gazette,* August 18, 1807.

1 Of John Jordan, Jr. See above, Deed of Trust, September 13, 1806.

2 John Postlethwait's tavern was operated for several years by Joshua Wilson.

3 A tributary of the Licking River in what is now Kenton County, Kentucky.

Statement of Account with Benjamin Howard

August 18th 1807.

We have this day settled our accounts upon the Judgment of Fields

& son against the Colemans & in which we are equally interested, and it appears that Benjamin Howard has received only five hundred and thirty two dollars & fourteen cents towards his proportion, this includes not only what he has received through my hands but the whole which he has received on acct of said Debt.

BENJA. HOWARD
HENRY CLAY

[Endorsement on verso][1]
Augt. 18th. 1807
Recd. in full of Henry in full of accts. except as to the Jugt. of Fields & son agt. the Colemans & the situation of which is stated fairly by the the [*sic*] within writing B HOWARD

ADS, signed also by Clay. DLC-TJC (DNA, M212, R15). Cf. above, Acknowledgment of Receipt, April 29, 1806; Promissory Note, November 21, 1806, note.
1 AES.

Bill Against John South

Fayette Circuit Sct. [August 22, 1807]

Henry Clay plaintiff states that he holds a note of the defendant John South in substance as follows

On or before the first day of May next I promise to pay to Henry Clay for value received Two hundred dollars with interest from the date. Witness my hand and seal this 2d. day of Nov. 1806

Teste THOMAS C. GRAVES[1] JOHN SOUTH {L.S.}

Yet the said debt remains unpaid. Wherefore the Plaintiff prays Judgment for his debt & damages for the detention of the same together with his costs &c H. CLAY PQ

ADS. Fayette Circuit Court, File 135 (1807). At the September Court Term, 1807, the parties having reached an agreement, the suit was dismissed. Fayette Circuit Court, Order Book D, 428.
1 A resident of the northern district of Fayette County, brother of Benjamin and George.

Receipt from John Leiby

[*ca.* August 24, 1807]

Recd. of H. Clay the within sum JOHN LEIBY

ES, in Clay's hand. DLC-TJC, 2d Series, vol. 6. On verso of order for $90 drawn by Joseph Beard on Fortunatus Cosby, favor of "Mr. Leiby," August 24, 1807. Joseph, son of Sarah Beard, was a resident of the southern district of Fayette county. Leiby was a Lexington brickmaker.

Property Deed to Jacob Clear

[September 22, 1807]

[Indenture between Thomas Hart, Jr., and Henry Clay of the first part and Jacob Clear, also of Lexington, of the other part: whereas

John Jordan, Jr., by deed dated September 13, 1806, conveyed lands to Hart and Clay in trust for certain purposes mentioned in the deed, recorded in Fayette Circuit Court, and whereas the trustees by that power on September 21 at a public sale in Lexington sold two properties, one of 100 acres cornering on the "cashner"[1] field and the other a smaller adjacent tract, both having been conveyed to Jordan by deed from John Kennedy and Sally, his wife, dated September 27, 1805, recorded in Fayette Circuit Court, are now transferred to Clear subject to all previous encumbrances for the sum of $900, paid and hereby acknowledged, by Hart and Clay as trustees. Signatures acknowledged at the November Court, 1807, and the deed recorded by John D. Young, Clerk of Fayette County, August 23, 1808.]

Fayette County Court, Deed Book C, 22-23. This tract was advertised by Hart and Clay on July 27, 1807.

1 Probably Casper Karsner (otherwise cited as Kersner or Gasper Casner), a Pennsylvania German who had emigrated to Kentucky in 1780. He had died in 1797; but his property, located on the Versailles Road near Lexington, was not divided until 1813.

Property Deed to Dr. Walter Warfield

[September 22, 1807]

[Indenture between Thomas Hart Jr. and Henry Clay of the first part and Dr. Walter Warfield, also of Lexington, of the second part: whereas John Jordan, Jr., of Lexington, by deed of September 13, 1806, conveyed to Hart and Clay sundry lands, of which the following described tract is a part, in trust for purposes specified in the deed recorded in the office of the Fayette Circuit Court—And whereas the trustees by virtue of the power thus vested in them have on the date of this indenture sold by public auction in Lexington the tract of 27,500 acres on the Kentucky River in Montgomery County, which tract was conveyed to Jordan by deed from Nelson Hackett, late Sheriff of Montgomery County, by deed of November 30, 1799, recorded in the Office of the Clerk, Montgomery County—Now this indenture witnesses that for $510, paid and acknowledged, Hart and Clay as trustees convey the land to Warfield, with all the right, title, and interest of Jordan. Signatures of Hart and Clay acknowledged before Achilles Sneed, Clerk of the Court of Appeals, Frankfort, October 2, 1807; recorded by M. Harrison, Clerk of Montgomery County, October 16, 1807.]

Montgomery County Court, Deed Book 4, pp. 300-301. Recorded also in Ky. Court of Appeals, Deed Book L, 126-27. This is one of the tracts listed in the advertisement of Hart and Clay, above, July 27, 1807.

Bill of Sale for Daniel, from James Bristow

[September 26, 1807]

Know all men by these presents that I. James Bristow have this day for & in consideration of four hundred & fifty dollars to me in hand paid bargained sold and delivered to Henry Clay one negro man named Daniel purchased by me of John Clay—

Witness my hand & seal this 26 Septr. 1807.

Teste JAS BRISTOW {L.S.}

MATTW ELDER[1]

DS, in Clay's hand. DLC-TJC (DNA, M212, R15). Cf. above, Johnson to Clay, February 5, 1807. Bristow was probably a resident of Shelby County.

[1] Lexington bricklayer.

From Benjamin Parke

D. Sirs, 5th. October 1807

The enclosed certificates fell into my hands a short time since—I suspect they are quite worthless—Indeed I am not certain but the very land has again been sold—as you will be much at Frankfort this fall,[1] I would thank you to see how they stand at the office—whether they have been sold? tax now due thereon?—worth any thing or worth nothing?—If the land should be advertised for sale this year, would thank you to pay the tax for me, and I will refund to you on my return—your general acquaintance with Land claims in the state will enable you to form a tolerable opinion as to the validity of the claims—I do not wish however to purchase a Law Suit—

Health and prosperity B. PARKE

ALS. DLC-TJC (DNA, M212, R12). Addressed to Clay at Lexington. Parke, delegate to Congress from Indiana Territory (1805-1808), had lived briefly in Lexington, where he studied law. Having been admitted to the bar, he moved to Vincennes, Indiana Territory, in 1799. His career included terms as Territorial judge, 1808-1817, and Judge of the United States District Court for Indiana from 1817 to his death in 1835.

[1] Clay had again been elected to the State legislature.

Agreement, Memorandum, and Receipt from Fortunatus Cosby

[October 10, 1807]

Attached to Agreement, December 8, 1806.

Receipt from Benjamin Warfield

14 Octr. 1807

Recd. the above bal. in full for Dr. Warfield B. WARFIELD

ES, in Clay's hand. DLC-TJC (DNA, M212, R15). Attached to an illegible statement, covering the period from July 3, 1804, through October 2, 1806, from Samuel Brown and Elisha Warfield, Lexington physicians, partners until Brown's move to New Orleans early in 1806. Cf. above, Account, *ca.* September 8, 1804. The account through

September 27, 1805, is made out to the partnership, with Dr. E. Warfield assuming the balance due and continuing the statement. It includes charges for such drugs as calomel, paregoric, zinc sulphate, "aqua ophthalmia," spirits of camphor, spirits of nitre, and castor oil, as well as fees for bleeding various members of Clay's household and for vaccinating his sons, Theodore and Thomas, on January 25, 1805, and three of his Negroes the following week. Clay is credited with payment of E. Warfield's note to Thomas Hughes, principle and interest amounting to £22:18:1, and an order of John Parish (Fayette County farmer, who had recently died), £2:0:2. The total amount of the account ran to £30:1:3; the balance due at settlement, £5:3:0. Dr. Elisha and Benjamin were sons of Elisha Warfield, who had moved to Kentucky from Maryland in 1790. Dr. Elisha, who for a time taught in the medical department of Transylvania University, practiced his profession until about 1812, when he launched a mercantile business. He later devoted much attention to raising livestock, including race horses. Benjamin attended Transylvania University, practiced law, served as an officer in the War of 1812, and attained prominence as an attorney and stock raiser in Harrison and Fayette counties.

Receipt from James Kern

15 Octr. 1807.

Received of Henry Clay seventy dollars and ninety one Cents collected by him on an execution from Fayette Circuit Court Campbell vs Adams &c.[1]

Teste JAMES KERN

JOHN H. MORTON.

DS, in Clay's hand. DLC-TJC, 2d Series, vol. 6. Kern was a Lexington rope and bagging manufacturer.

1 Probably the case of Robert Campbell, assignee of Henry Lander, for the benefit of Peter Love *ads.* George Adams, wherein Clay as attorney for the defendants was awarded permission to take out an execution on the judgment which he had won for his clients in 1805 in their suit for recovery of a debt. Fayette Circuit Court, File 83 (1805), 116 (1807); *ibid.* Order Book D, 378. Campbell, a veteran of the Revolution and one of Lexington's pioneer residents, was a potter on High Street; Lander had paid taxes in both Bourbon and Clark counties in 1800; and Love was a resident of Newport, Kentucky.

Receipt from Kennedy and Cox

[October 22, 1807]

Recd. 22 October 1807 of Henry Clay Two hundred & fifty dollars on a/c. of money due Kennedy & Cox from Akin & Eastland.[1]

$250 JNO KENNEDY & COX

DS, in Clay's hand. DLC-TJC (DNA, M212, R10). John Kennedy and Benjamin Cox were Baltimore merchants.

1 Joseph Akin and Thomas Eastland.

Advertisement of Land for Sale

26th Oct. 1807.

FOR SALE,

TWO hundred and twenty-eight acres of

LAND,

Lying on Henry's Mill road,[1] between four and five miles from Lexington, and near Mr. Richardson Allen's farm.—This land is inferior to none in soil, timber, water, situation, and neighbourhood. It will be shewn to any person disposed to purchase, by Mr. Arthur Patterson, living on a part of the original tract. The bulk of the purchase money will be required in hand, and the balance on a short credit. An indisputable title, with general warranty will be made by the subscriber. HENRY CLAY.

Lexington *Kentucky Gazette,* December 29, 1807. Cf. above, Agreement, September 18, 1805. The tract was still advertised in the *Gazette* of December 6, 1808.
1 Now the Newtown Pike.

Property Deed from Fortunatus Cosby

[October 29, 1807]

This Indenture made this 29th. day of October 1807 between Fortunatus Cosby of Louisville in the State of Kentucky of the one part and Henry Clay of Lexington in the same State of the other part, whereas Sarah Beard by a deed bearing date the seventh day of July one thousand eight hundred and six recorded in the County Court of Fayette, and afterwards on the seventh day of November one thousand eight hundred and six recorded in the office of the County Court of Jefferson, conveyed to the said Fortunatus Cosby a certain tract or parcel of land lying in the said County of Jefferson adjoining the town of Louisville and containing by estimation three thousand acres of land, be the same more or less, which said land was patented to John Cornnelly,[1] and Charles De Wornsdorff[2] and also certain lots Islands ferry rents issues and appurtenances, thereunto belonging, as will by reference to the said deed more fully and at large appear, and whereas the said Cosby has heretofore sold to the said Clay one equal undivided third part of all the property with appurtenances described & conveyed by the said deed from Sarah Beard to him, except as is hereinafter excepted: Now this Indenture witnesseth that the said Fortunatus Cosby for and in consideration of the sum of one dollar to him in hand paid by the said Clay; the receipt whereof he doth hereby acknowledge, Hath granted bargained, sold and delivered, and by these presents doth grant bargain sell and deliver, unto the said Henry Clay one equal undivided third part of all the land and property of whatever discription [*sic*] contained and described in the said deed of conveyance from Sarah Beard to him, except twenty four acres of land adjoining the town of shippingport deeded to James Berthoud also an half acre lot in the town of Louisville No. 7. and the two squares in said town adjoining the half acre lots No 5, 6, 7, 8, 9, 10, 11, & 12 extending to Beargrass[3] and the river with all and singular the appurtenances to the said third part in any manner befonging [*sic*], together with the remainder and remainders, reversion and reversions rents issues and profits to the said third part in any manner appertaining, and all the right title and Inderest [*sic*] therein devived [*sic*] to the said Cosby from the said Sarah. To have and to hold the said equal undivided third part of the afore-described property, with its appurtenances, to the said Henry Clay his heirs and assigns forever: To his and their only proper use and behoof; and the said Cosby for himself and his heirs doth covenant and agree to and with the said Clay that he and they shall at any time hereafter at his request make such further or other conveyance better to vest the said Clay with the said third part of the said property as counsel may advise: and the said Cosby for himself and his heirs doth further covenant and agree to and with the said Clay that he will warrant and defend the right and title to the said equal undivided third part of the said property against the claim of all and every person whatsoever claiming by through or under him but against no other person whatsoever: it being clear by [*sic*] and expressly understood by the parties that the said Clay is to be vested with the title, such as it is, devived from Sarah Beard, and that the said Cosby is in no manner to be responsible for the goodness thereof. In testimony whereof the said Fortunatus Cosby hath hereunto set his hand and affixed his seal the day and year first Mentioned. FORTS. CORSBY [*sic*] {SEAL}

Jefferson County Court, Deed Book 8, pp. 205-206 (KyU microfilm). Recorded on October 31, 1807, by Worden Pope, Jefferson County Clerk.

1 Dr. John Connolly (also cited as Connally), a surgeon's mate in the British forces in the American colonies, had obtained patent from George III, dated September 16, 1773, for 2,000 acres lying at the foot of the falls of the Ohio River. With John Campbell he had purchased on February 11, 1774, the 2,000-acre tract adjacent, patented to Charles de Warnsdorff (below, note 2). At the same time Connolly had transferred half his original holding to Campbell, each man thus possessing title to 2,000 acres, the upper and the lower thousand acres of the combined tract going to Connolly. As a Tory, Connolly lost his holdings by escheat in 1780, and the town of Louisville was established on the upper thousand acres. Hening, *Statutes of Virginia*, 293-95 (May, 1780). Prior to this date, however, Connolly had conveyed the lower thousand acres to Campbell, making a total of 3,000 acres, the tract here under consideration.

2 Charles de Warnsdorff (also cited as Warrenstorff), an ensign in a British regiment stationed in Pennsylvania, had received patent from George III to 2000 acres at the foot of the falls of the Ohio River, September 16, 1773.

3 Beargrass Creek, a stream flowing into the Ohio River near the northeastern border of the present city of Louisville.

Assignment from Benjamin Graves

[November, 1807]

ES, in Clay's hand. DLC-TJC (DNA, M212, R15). On verso of note, dated April 26, 1807, by which William Dailey acknowledged himself "indebted to Benj. Graves agreeable to his advertisement of the celebrated horse Buzzard for the year 1807."

To Edmund W. Rootes

Dr Sir Lexington 7th. Nov. 1807

Your favor of the 16h. Octr.[1] covering the Notes of Mess. Bodley and Nicholas[2] reached me in safety this day. Neither of those gentlemen has yet returned, but both of them are daily expected. Of the responsibility of the former there is no doubt. At this particular time however he is considerably pressed, & I think an immediate payment somewhat doubtful. The other gentleman is not visibly possessed of much property, but as far as my limited knowledge of his pecuniary transactions extends he is punctual. Considering both of them as men of honor, I presume you may safely count upon payment. In this event I shall have no difficulty in making a secure and satisfactory remittance.

I thank you for the friendly expressions in your letter relative to myself. I still retain a lively recollection of the pleasure I experienced from your acquaintance, and the many agreeable hours I have spent in your Company. And it has given me much satisfaction to learn that, with the exception of one domestic loss, you have had a full tide of prosperity. For its continuance you have the wishes of

Yr. friend HENRY CLAY.

ALS. NNP. Addressed to Rootes at Richmond, Virginia, where he practiced law. He and Clay had been friends and members of the same debating society during Clay's residence in that city.

1 Not found.

2 Thomas Bodley and Robert C., son of George Nicholas. In 1809 the Fayette Circuit Court awarded Rootes $350, plus interest, in a suit against Robert C. Nicholas and Lewis Sanders. In the previous year Nicholas had become an officer in the United States Army, from which he resigned with the rank of colonel in 1819.

Receipted Account from Barry and Garrett

Mr. Henry Clay [*ca.* November 9, 1807]

1806 In Account with Barry & Garrett

Octr. 1.	To 2 large Knob locks P stephens[1] " " "		2" 2. "
Novr 1.	To Paid Mr Steel[2] P order ...... " " "		1. 9. "
1807			
June 8	To 1 Vol. Lauderdale on Wealth[3] " " "		1" 2. 6
15	To 4 41/50 Bs. Salt P Boy ..12/. " " "		2"18. 10½
16.	To 1 doz Spanish Segars .... " " "		" . 1. 6
July 21.	To Saml. Combs.[4] P Acceptance . " " "		10. 16. "
30.	To William Hanson[5] P order ... " " "		27"13. 6
Augt. 12.	To 5 yds linen 15/. 4 lb Coffee		
	12/ Miss Hall[6]	1. 7. "	
	Paid H. Atcherson[7]	6 - -	
			7. 7. "

	24	To Paid Kay[8] P order . . 50$		15. ". "
	25.	To 2½ yds Country linen P Miss Hall	" 7. 6	
		" 6 3/4 . ditto	" 16.10½	
		" 1 pr shoes 11/3 1 Pen Knife 1/6	" 12 9	
		" 1 Pair fine Scissors	" 4 6.	2. 1. 7½.
	29	" 4 yds Callicoe P Lady	" 12. "	
		" 1 Handkf 3/9 6 Tumblers 4/6	" 8. 3	1. ". 3
Sepr.	1	To Paid Winslow & Stephens P order	" " "	11. 11. 4
	8.	" 7½ yds Country linen P Miss Hall	" 16.10½	
		" 6 lb Coffee 18/ 1 pe tape 1/.	" 19 "	1"15. 10½
Oct.	6.	" 2 large Door Locks P Stephens . 27/.	2.14 "	
		" 6 small . ditto . . . . . . 10/6.	4 19. "	7"13. "
		Card. forward		£ 92"12" 5½
1807		Amount bro. forward	". ". "	92. 12. 5½
Octr.	20	To 7 pair butt Hinges . . . . 1/3.	" 8. 9	
		" 13. large ditto . . . . 1/9.	1 2 9	
		" 1 Gro. Wood screws	" 7. 6	
		" ½ Gro. large ditto	" 6 "	2 - 5. "
Novr.	3.	To Paid Fisher[9] . . . . 30$ . .	" " "	9. " "
	9	To Paid ditto . . . . 10$ . .	" " "	3. ". "
				106"17. 5½
1807				
July	21.	By Cash recd of R. Quarles[10]		6. ". "
		Dr. due	336 " 25 Cts	£100. 17" 5½
		To pd H. Atcherson .	5. "	1. 10. -
			$341 " 25 Cts	£102" 7" 5½

Errors Excpd. BARRY & GARRETT

[Endorsement on verso][11]

Recd. payment 19h. Septr. 1808. J BARRY JR

DS. DLC-TJC (DNA, M212, R15).

1 Luther Stephens.

2 Not identified.

3 James Maitland, Earl of Lauderdale, *An Inquiry into the Nature and Origin of Public Wealth, and into the Means and Causes of its Increase* (Edinburgh and London, 1804).

4 Possibly Samuel R. Combs of Clark County.

5 Lexington carpenter.

6 Sarah Hall, an Englishwoman, for more than fifty years housekeeper for the Clay family.

7 Hamilton Atchison, of Fayette County.

8 Robert Kay, Fayette County.

9 Either John Fisher, Jr., or Maddox Fisher.

10 Roger Quarles, Fayette County.

11 ES, in Clay's hand.

Property Deed from Arthur and Francis Patterson

[November 9, 1807]

[Indenture by which Arthur and Francis Patterson of Fayette County for five shillings, paid and acknowledged, transfer to Henry Clay a tract in Fayette County, part of the preemption granted to Francis Patterson, deceased, and by him devised, and also part of a tract of land recovered by the Pattersons from John Bradford,[1] and by him this day conveyed to them, beginning at a stake at the Pond Spring and including 228 and a fraction acres plus twenty poles. Title warranted only against claimants through Patterson. Signatures of Arthur and Francis Patterson and of Mary, wife of Francis, acknowledged before John D. Young, Clerk of Fayette County, at the November Court, 1807.]

Fayette County Court, Deed Book C, 20-21. See above, Agreement, September 18, 1805.

1 The settlement of the dispute between the Pattersons and Bradford had come after long years of litigation occasioned by overlapping claims to land on the north fork of Cane Run.

Receipt to Arthur Patterson

[November 9, 1807]

Attached to Agreement, September 18, 1805.

Agreement with Humphrey Marshall

[November 18, 1807]

An agreement between H. Marshall and H. Clay.

The said Marshall claiming one third part of the Land secured by virtue of a Warrant issued by Virginia No. 312, upon the assignment of Ben Netherland agrees to Sell the same to the said Clay, without recourse in any event, for One hundred pounds—And the said Clay agrees to deliver to the said Marshall his note for about £20 assigned to him by one Harrah.[1] The ballance it is agreed by the parties shall be considered as a payment in full for any professionable serv[i]ces heretofore rendered by the said Clay to the said Marshall. Witness our hands & Seals this 18th Novr. 1807.

Test H. MARSHALL {L.S.}
HENRY CLAY {L.S.}

DS, in unidentified hand. KyLxT. The land involved in this transaction was probably part of the tract mentioned above, Agreement, October 10, 1806.

1 Not identified.

To Caesar Augustus Rodney

My Dr Sir Lexington 5h. Decr. 1807

I received your favor of the 8h. Nov.[1] in which you request me to say, if I feel at liberty to act as Counsel for the U. S. agt. Burr and his associates. I am under no engagement for any of the parties, nor will I in any event appear for Col Burr. Having deceived me last winter, when I really believed him both innocent, and persecuted by Mr. Daveiss,[2] he shall not deceive me again, now that I believe him guilty and meriting punishment. But it will not be in my power to appear at Chillicothe for the government.[3] The Court there sets just at the moment when our Legislature (of which I am a member) and our Supreme State Court (the most crowded with business of any in the Country) will be in Session; and I could not think of disappointing those who have confided their business to me, by contracting new duties.

Altho' I have no hesitation as it respects Burr about appearing against him, I have some doubt whether I should not by doing so subject myself to the imputation of violating professional honor. Having once appeared for him, it will be supposed, that he imparted to me his projects &c. The fact is however otherwise, but this may not be known to or thought of by the world. Would it not be then said that by appearing for him I confidentially obtained a knowledge of his plans, means of execution, preparations &c; and that, availing myself of this information, I afterwards pressed the prosecution agt. him with more effect than I could have done?

If it should be the intention of the Government to prosecute him in this State, I will in the mean time think of my situation, and determine whether I can consistently with my own honor and reputation act agt. him. If Chillicothe is to be the place of trial I cannot attend there.

It will give me great pleasure to hear occasionally from you, when you can snatch a moment from the fatigues of office & cares of State.

Yr's Sincerely HENRY CLAY

ALS. DLC-Rodney Family Papers (DNA, M212, R22). Addressed to Rodney as "Atto. Genl. U.S. Washington." Not postmarked from Lexington until December 10.

1 Not found. 2 Joseph Hamilton Daveiss.

3 The Circuit Court convened at Chillicothe, Ohio, January 4, 1808. Though both Burr and Blennerhassett were under bond, they failed to appear.

Receipt from Arthur Patterson

[December 7, 1807]

Attached to Agreement, September 18, 1805.

Receipt from James Knox

[December 28, 1807]

Recd. 28 Decr. 1807 of H Clay Two hundred and seventy nine

dollars Sixty-Seven Cents being the Sum received of Col. Gamble[1] of Richmond by the said Clay through Mathew Clay for me

JAMES KNOX

DS, in Clay's hand. DLC-TJC (DNA, M212, R15). Knox, a native of Ireland who had acquired numerous land holdings in Kentucky, had first come into the area as one of the "Long Hunters" in 1769. He had served in the Revolution and had represented Lincoln County in the Kentucky Senate, 1795-1800. He died in Shelby County in 1822.

1 Probably Robert Gamble, merchant and Revolutionary veteran.

Nominations for House Clerks

[December 28, 1807]

Clay nominated Gabriel J. Johnston as Clerk of the House; Thomas Y. Bryant, clerk to the committees of propositions and grievances, privileges and elections; and George Blackburn, clerk to the committees of claims, religion, and courts of justice. Ky. H. of Reps., *Journal, 1807-1808,* pp. [3]-4. Johnston was a prominent lawyer of Louisville, formerly a member of the Kentucky House. Bryant was at this time a resident of Frankfort. Blackburn was probably the son of the Woodford county pioneer of the same name and the younger brother of William B. Blackburn. All the Clay nominees were defeated.

Motion Relating to Freedom Claims of Certain Slaves

[December 29, 1807]

Clay proposed that a bill be prepared to limit the time of commencing certain actions by "people of color." Ky. H. of Reps., *Journal, 1807-1808,* pp. 6-7. The measure was not introduced until after Clay had assumed the Speakership, when a bill was presented by Hezekiah Harrison, of Fayette County, and ultimately enacted. It provided that in order to terminate the uncertainty of dormant claims to freedom under the abolition acts of Pennsylvania and the Virginia law prohibiting importation of slaves, judicial suits stemming from this legislation must be instituted by colored persons within two years from passage of the Kentucky statute. Littell (comp.), *Statute Law of Kentucky,* III, 484-85.

Clay's interest in such a measure probably stemmed from a suit in Fayette Circuit Court initiated at the June Term, 1806, wherein he won damages in behalf of eight Negroes suing *in forma pauperis* against Mary Nuttall, widow of Elijah Nuttall, on a plea of trespass, assault and battery, and false imprisonment. These Negroes had been brought as the slaves of Nuttall from Pennsylvania to Kentucky around 1790 without registration of their status as required under the Virginia statute on slave importation. Kentucky law, enacted in 1794, had not required such recording of the importation of domestic slaves, but it carried no clauses applicable retroactively to the Virginia period. Fayette Circuit Court, Order Book C (1805-1806), 475; *ibid.,* File 166 (1809); Hening (comp.), *Statutes of Virginia,* XII, 182; XIII, 62, 121; Littell (comp.), *Statute Law of Kentucky,* I, 246 (December 17, 1794).

Resolution Relating to Apportionment for Representation

[December 29, 1807]

Resolved, That in the apportionment of the representation for members, to the general assembly, the ratio as at present fixed by law ought to be increased.

Ky. H. of Reps., *Journal, 1807-1808,* p. 7. The measure, tabled at this time, was taken up and adopted after Clay's assumption of the Speakership. The new ratio, set by amendment in Committee of the Whole and subsequently enacted, was 700 qualified voters for each representative, making a total House membership of 70, as contrasted with 63 under the previous ratio of 600 to 1, established in 1803. Littell (comp.), *Statute Law of Kentucky,* III, 147, 452-54.

Bill on Terms of Fayette Circuit Court

[December 30, 1807]

For a drafting committee which included also James Trotter and Hezekiah Harrison, the other Fayette representatives, Clay reported a measure providing for restoration of the Court meeting to March, as prior to the act of the last legislature (above, Bill, November 13, 1806), and for lengthening of the June Term, if necessary. Ky. H. of Reps., *Journal, 1807-1808,* p. 7; Ky. Gen. Assy., *Acts, 1807-1808,* ch. XX, p. 40. On December 29, Clay had moved to present such a bill. Amended slightly by the Senate, it was enacted January 25, 1808.

Committee Report on Petition of Robert Didlake and Others

[December 31, 1807]

The committee for courts of justice have, according to order, had under consideration the petition of Robert Didlake, Isaac Hockaday, James Parish and Patsey H. Parish, from Clarke county, and have come to the following resolution:

Resolved, As the opinion of this committee, that the said petition, be rejected.

Ky. H. of Reps., *Journal, 1807-1808,* p. 14. Other members of the drafting committee were William Blackburn, Samuel Brents, John Simpson (Shelby County), George Walker (Jessamine), Humphrey Marshall, James Clark, George Webb (Clark), and James Ferguson (Jefferson). The committee report was read twice and tabled, without further action.

Resolution on Charge Against John Kercheval

[January 1, 1808]

Resolved, That a committee of five be appointed to enquire into the truth of a charge alledged to exist against John Kercheval, a member of this house, that he hath forged an alteration, in an order drawn by George Madison,[1] in his favor on the sheriff of Mason for 333: dollars.

Ky. H. of Reps., *Journal, 1807-1808.* p. 20. The resolution was adopted, and Clay was appointed chairman of the committee, an assignment which he relinquished upon his election as Speaker. The final report, condemnatory of Kercheval (Mason County), was presented by William Blackburn. It was accepted, and Kercheval was expelled from the House.

1 A Virginia veteran of the Revolution, Madison had served since 1796 as Auditor of Public Accounts for the State of Kentucky. He served as an officer in the War of 1812 and, from June 1, 1816, to his death a few months later, as Governor of Kentucky.

Motion for Bill Moving State Capital

[January 2, 1808]

On Clay's motion it was "*Ordered,* That leave be given to bring in a bill to remove the seat of the government of this commonwealth." Ky. H. of Reps., *Journal, 1807-1808,* p. 23. No further action was reported. Clay's proposal followed defeat of efforts to move the capital to Lexington, to Danville, and to an unspecified center. Clay, it may be noted, had voted "nay" on the proposed move to Lexington.

Property Deed to Margaret January

[January 4, 1808]

[Indenture by which Henry Clay and Lucretia, his wife, for an unstated sum, paid and acknowledged, sell to Margaret January a lot in Lexington bounded on Upper and Second streets as follows: 64 feet fronting on Upper Street by 164 feet deep on Second Street —that is, one third of the tract Clay holds on Upper Street, extending his whole depth on Second. General warranty of title. Signatures of Henry and Lucretia Clay witnessed by Thomas Hart, Jr., acknowledged before John D. Young, Clerk of Fayette County, April 2, 1808.]

Fayette County Court, Deed Book C, 152-53. This property was part of the tract which Clay had purchased from the McDermids. Margaret January was the widow of Peter and the mother of Thomas.

Receipt from Richard Allen

Jan. 4, 1808.

Recd. of H. Clay ten dollars the bal. in full for four thousand feet of plank.

RICHARD ALLEN

DS, in Clay's hand. DLC-TJC, 2d Series, vol. 6. Allen lived in the southwestern area of Fayette County.

Committee Report on Logan County Court

[January 6, 1808]

The committee for courts of justice have according to order had under consideration a petition to them referred, and have come to a resolution thereupon, to wit:

Resolved, As the opinion of this committee that the petition of the justices of the county court of Logan county, praying that a law may pass legalizing their proceedings as a court, on the third Monday in February last, is reasonable.

Ky. H. of Reps., *Journal, 1807-1808,* pp. 31-32. For other members of the drafting committee see above, Committee Report, December 31, 1807. The report was adopted, and after Clay's assumption of the Speakership the action was effected by amendment of an earlier introduced bill to legalize the proceedings of several other courts. Littell (comp.), *Statute Law of Kentucky,* III, 466 (app. February 16, 1808).

Motion Relative to Fayette County Records

[January 8, 1808]

On Clay's motion it was *"Ordered,* That leave be given to bring in a bill to vest in the county court of Fayette, certain powers in relation to papers and records which have been destroyed." Ky. H. of Reps., *Journal, 1807-1808,* pp. 40-41. After Clay became Speaker, the bill was filed by James Trotter, and enacted on February 3, 1808. Fayette County records had been largely destroyed by fire at the home of Levi Todd, County Clerk, in March, 1803. Contemporary comment suggested that the fire had originated in a desire to conceal land records. WHi-Draper MSS., 13CC3. Cf. above, Bill, November 23, 1804, note. Governor James Garrard, with endorsement by the legislature on December 27, 1803, had appointed commissioners to collect evidence of the records burned. The present legislation authorized the Fayette County Court to assume the powers earlier vested in the commissioners. Littell (comp.), *Statute Law of Kentucky,* III, 446.

Motion to Increase Salary of Appellate Judges

[January 9, 1808]

On Clay's motion permission was granted to introduce a bill increasing the salary of judges of the Court of Appeals. Ky. H. of Reps., *Journal, 1807-1808,* p. 43. After Clay became Speaker, the measure was presented by John Simpson. Clay, as Speaker, broke a tie vote, affirmatively, on the question whether the bill should be carried to second reading. Thereafter the measure was dropped. Salaries of these judges had already been raised by $166.66.7 annually, at the preceding legislative session. Littell (comp.), *Statute Law of Kentucky,* III, 358.

Remarks on Assuming Speakership

[January 11, 1808]

Having attained a majority vote on the third ballot (he had at first failed to attain a plurality), Clay was declared Speaker of the Kentucky House of Representatives. Conducted to the Chair, he "made acknowledgments to the house for the honour conferred by their support, and recommended the observance and preservation of good order and decorum." Ky. H. of Reps., *Journal, 1807-1808,* p. 46. He succeeded William Logan, who had resigned to accept a judicial appointment.

Petition to Incorporate the Madison Hemp Mill Company

[January 11, 1808]

Clay, with William Macbean, Robert Frazier (Lexington watchmaker and silversmith, an emigrant from northern Ireland around the turn of the century), and

James and David Maccoun, petitioned that a law be passed to incorporate the shareholders of the existing company, located on Silver Creek in Madison County. Ky. H. of Reps., *Journal, 1807-1808,* p. 47. Committee report favorable to the petition was accepted; and a bill to this effect, introduced by William Blackburn, was enacted February 24, 1808. Littell (comp.), *Statute Law of Kentucky,* III, 532-35. The legislation provided for organization of the Madison Hemp and Flax Spinning Company and for issuance of shares at $25 each to an amount of $25,000, or, with the assent of a majority of shareholders, to a total of $37,500. The law was amended February 11, 1809, to permit handling of wool, also. Littell, *op. cit.,* IV, 74. The relationship of Clay and the Maccouns to the business prior to its incorporation is indicated below, Release, June 18, 1808. The new enterprise began with the manufacture of thread, both for direct sale and to "let out" for weaving. The firm later established a reputation as producer of excellent sail duck, but ultimately lost heavily in the venture. Lexington *Reporter,* May 19, 1810; Leavy, "A Memoir of Lexington," Kentucky State Historical Society, *Register,* XL (1942), 353.

From Henry Baldwin

Dr. *Sir* Pittsburgh 14 January 1808

I wish you would urge Dr Mayersbach to the payment of the note in your hands, He has had a reasonable indulgence; and I cannot conveniently wait longer on him. When the money is received I will thank you to pay it either to the order of George Robinson Esquire[1] of this place or remit it to him by post deducting a liberal compensation for collection—yours with esteem

Henry Clay Esquire HENRY BALDWIN

Lexington Kentucky

[Endorsements on verso][2]

Please to pay the proceeds of the within Order to S & G Trotter[3]

H Clay Esqr. GEO: ROBINSON

Recd. ($200) Two hundred dollars on a/c of the within 28 Apl 1808. SAM & GEO TROTTER

ALS. DLC-TJC (DNA, M212, R15). See above, Baldwin to Clay, March 19, 1805.

1 Later an Associate Judge of Allegheny County, Pennsylvania.

2 AES; and ES, in Clay's hand.

3 Brothers, Lexington merchants. George Trotter, Jr., later a State representative from Fayette County and a brigadier-general at the Battle of the Thames, died in 1815. Samuel then continued the business alone.

From Isaac Shelby

Dear Sir Jany. 19th. 1808

I inclose you the Connection of Surveys[1] which I spke off—Shewing the interference of Smiths claim with mine[2]—You can at once discover that his location with the Commissioners cannot cover the ground in dispute nor come within little less than two miles of it upon any rational construction—

If my survey is not made exactly agreeable to my entry—still the land in dispute is precisely in the center of my location and if I had surveyed according to entry, I should have covered more of the land which Smith afterwards located his preemption warrant upon—

You will see by this plot that three Surveys of Levi Todds are nearer Smiths Ground than any part of my tract, & Smith knows well that Levi Todd who had the management of his claim from first to last laid those State Warrants two years after his claim was Granted by the Comsrs. & then carried Smith where he now lays in order to save those three surveys which he had previously made on part of the Ground that he first intended for Smith—

My pattant lays in the Clerks office in Lexington filed in the suit of Overtons Heirs against Ferguson. You will find it older than Smiths—tho I believe that Smiths and John Shelby's[3] are of the same date—The interference of their claims is about 63 as. & to which Smith cannot have any just pretentions, as it lays near four miles from any part of Smiths claim as granted by the Comrs. & Shelbys entry a a [*sic*] special one, if his survey had been made exactly to the entry it aught to have taken more of the ground that Smith afterwards entered—but the land in dispute is in Shelbys location upon any construction that can be put upon his location—be pleased to preserve this plot—and the papers I gave you—the first time I am in Lexington will apply to you for them

I am Dear Sir Your Obedient friend ISAAC SHELBY

ALS. DLC-TJC (DNA, M212, R10). Addressed to Clay "in Frankfort." Shelby, twice Governor of Kentucky, had extensive land claims in the state, some as a result of his service in Dunmore's War. 1 Not found.

2 The conflicting claims of Horace Smith and Shelby to lands in Mercer County occasioned litigation in the Kentucky courts for many years. By decision of the Court of Appeals in 1820, when Clay was no longer identified with the case, Shelby retained his lands. 3 Isaac Shelby's uncle.

Receipted Accounts Rendered to Abijah and John W. Hunt and to John W. Hunt

Mess. Abijah & John W. Hunt	[January 21, 1808]
To H. Clay	Dr—
To my fee for you ads. Warnicks[1]	$50
To do agt. - - Whitley &c.[2]	60
	$110
To do vs Brooke &c[3]	10
	$120

Recd. payment 21. Jan. 1808. H. CLAY

Mr. J. W. Hunt To H. Clay	Dr.
To my fee ads Smith[4]	$ 20.
To do. vs Burt[5]	10:
To do vs Sutton[6]	5:

To do for drawing contract with Owings[7] & deed from him 8:

$ 43

$163

Recd. paymt. 21 Jan. 1808. H. CLAY

ADS. KyU-Hunt-Morgan Papers. The Hunts operated a store in Lexington from 1794 to 1800, when Abijah moved to Mississippi.

1 The heirs of Col. Frederick Warnicke (spelling varies) had brought suit in chancery to recover lands he had acquired for services as a Virginia officer in the Revolution but for which he had not obtained patents. After Warnicke's death, patents were obtained by the Hunts in consequence of an assignment made by a person whom the plaintiffs, residents of Idstein in the German Empire, claimed had no authority in the matter. The decision of the lower court, favorable to the heirs of Warnicke, was reversed by the Kentucky Court of Appeals, Spring Term, 1806, on the ground that aliens could not inherit lands in this state. 3 *Ky. Reports* (Hardin) 66-67.

2 Not found.

3 Probably a case involving George Brooke, of Woodford County, from whom John W. Hunt was trying unsuccessfully to collect money in 1801. KyU-Hunt Papers.

4 A suit brought by Benjamin Smith against John W. Hunt and John Brandt in 1804, continued from term to term of the Fayette Circuit Court, and finally settled out of court in 1807. Fayette Circuit Court, Order Book B, *passim;* Order Book D, 73, 266.

5 Early in 1807 Andrew Burt, of Cincinnati, drew a bill of exchange for $215 on a Natchez, Mississippi, mercantile firm in favor of Christopher Keiser, who endorsed it to John W. Hunt. When the bill was protested, Hunt brought suit against Burt and Benjamin Stout, Burt's agent. Fayette Circuit Court, File 141 (1807).

6 In January, 1807, Hunt won a suit for $29.40 against William Sutton, possibly of Scott County, when the defendant failed to appear. Fayette Circuit Court, Order Book D, 191-92.

7 Probably a contract for the management of the ironworks in Montgomery (now Bath) County and a mortgage deed to land in that area, given to John W. Hunt and Thomas Hart by John C. and Thomas D. Owings in 1803. Fayette Circuit Court, Deed Book A, 74, 76.

Speech Relating to Use of English Legal Precedents

[January 28, 1808]

No report of the speech has been found. Clay is said to have left the Speaker's chair to argue against passage of a bill, reported from Committee of the Whole, which would have barred use of English legal precedents in Kentucky courts. Thomas Hart Clay and Ellis Paxson Oberholtzer, *Henry Clay by his Grandson* (Philadelphia, 1910), 46-47. Following this debate the bill was amended on motion by John Simpson to prohibit use of English precedents dating after 1776. In this form the measure was enacted February 12, 1808. Ky. H. of Reps., *Journal, 1807-1808,* pp. 103, 119, 125; Littell (comp.), *Statute Law of Kentucky,* III, 457.

From Luke Tiernan and Company

Henry Clay Esqr. Baltimore 30h. January 1808

Dear Sir

Your Esteemed favor of the 28' Decr.[1] came to hand by last mail and are [*sic*] much pleased to find you have made a final settlement with Eastland[2]—the present state of the times makes money very scarce and collections are so dificult that very little money comes into our hands, at any other time it wou'd be much less Inconvenient to give the Indulgence you wish for, however we feel under obligations for the exertions you have made and shou'd be very thankful if you can remit us the money about the last of april or early in May; we expect you will allow Interest or make a deduction on your Comissions, if you cannot get a draft at one to one and a half Pct you will please pay the amt. to our friends Messrs. Kelly & Brent Merchts Paris,[3]

Enclosed you have Wm. Wests note[4] our favor dated 17' May 1804 and due the 17' February 1805 for $1404:57 upon which is paid $269.70/100 which payments are Endorsed thereon, we have written him repeatedly & have only received promises, in his last letter he proposes to deliver Horses which wou'd not suit us on no terms, he also proposed to deliver Bonds but of this you will be the best Judge what ought to be done, if money cou'd be had it is very desireable as we stand in great need of it at present, and we have to request you will use your best Endeavors to get the money if this cannot be done you must Bring suit in the Federal or State Courts whichever you think best or in that Court that the money can be most speedily obtained—

Mr. Alex. Fulton of this place we believe will be in Kentuckey before you receive this letter, we directed our letter for him to care of Mr. Thomas Hart as Mr. Fulton had Instructions from us to attend to this and several other a/cs we wd. wish you to inquire if Mr. Fulton has recd. any money or made a settlement with Mr. West, we wd. also wish you wd. send to Mr. West to know what arangements he can make with you, at any event you are not to delay the Business but get the money as quick as possible by suit or otherwise—we are with much regard Your friends & Sers.

LUKE TIERNAN & CO.

ALS. DLC-HC (DNA, M212, R1).
1 Not found. 2 Thomas Eastland. 3 William Kelly and Hugh Brent.
4 Not found. West, a native of Ireland, had opened a store in Lexington in 1795.

Resolutions Relating to Judge Innes

[February 3, 1808]

WHEREAS the general assembly did, at their last session, order transcripts of the evidence, taken before the committee appointed to examine into the conduct of Benjamin Sebastian to be transmitted to the president of the United States, and to the senators and representatives from this state in congress; and as the present assembly has entire confidence in the general administration and in the congress of the U. States, among whose duties is that of arraigning the public officer or private citizen, who may have violated the constitution or laws of the union: and whereas the legitimate objects which call for the attention of this legislature are themselves sufficiently important to require the exercise of all their wisdom and time, without engaging in pursuit of others, thereby consuming the public treasure and the time of the representatives of the people, in investigating subjects not strictly within the sphere of their duty: and inasmuch as the expression of an opinion by the general assembly, upon the guilt or innocence of Harry Innes, Esq. in relation to certain charges against him, would be a prejudication of his case—if in one way would fix an indellible stigma upon the character of the judge, without the forms of trial, or judicial proceeding; and if in the other might embarrass and prevent a free and full investigation into those charges: wherefore,

Resolved, by the general assembly that it is improper in them to prescribe to congress any course to be taken by that body, in relation to the said charges or to indicate any opinion upon their truth or falsehood.

Resolved, That the constitution and laws of the land, securing to each citizen, whether in or out of office, a fair and impartial trial, whether by impeachment or at common law, the example of a legislative body, before the commencement of any prosecution, expressing an opinion upon the guilt or innocence of an implicated individual would tend to subvert the fundamental principles of justice.

Frankfort *Western World,* February 18, 1808, reporting action in the Kentucky House of Representatives. The resolutions, unreported in the *Journal* of the House, were offered by Clay in Committee of the Whole as a substitute for proposals of Humphrey Marshall which called for impeachment of Judge Innes on the basis of testimony revealed in the House investigation of Judge Benjamin Sebastian the preceding year. Clay's resolutions were defeated; and others offered by William Blackburn, still condemnatory of Judge Innes, were approved by the House. Senate amendment, however, reworded the prefatory statement so as to call for an investigation of Innes without an accusation of guilt, and in this form the measure passed the House with the casting vote of Clay as Speaker. The report of a congressional committee subsequently exonerated Innes, and a sharply divided House of Representatives supported this stand in tabling further action on the report.

Following passage of the resolutions in the Kentucky House of Representatives, and before the State Senate's action on them, Marshall's opponents attempted to unseat him on charges that he had committed fraud and perjury in certain land transactions. Cf. above, Memorandum of Conversation, *ca.* July, 1806, note. Clay's involvement in the court proceedings which gave rise to the allegations suggests his interested role in the inquiry, as does the similarity of political tactics to those employed in the earlier controversy on chartering the Kentucky Insurance Company.

Nomination of James Madison

[Eagle Tavern, Frankfort, Kentucky February 17, 1808]

TO THE FREEMEN OF KENTUCKY.

FELLOW-CITIZENS,

YOU have no doubt learned that the illustrious Jefferson declines being a candidate for the Presidential Chair, at the next election. Whilst we regret the loss of his eminent services, we can but admire and approve the motives which urge him to retire. They are an additional evidence of that virtue and patriotism which have always distinguished his useful life. We are aware, fellow-citizens, that in the choice of his successor it is and ought to be your right to think and decide for yourselves.—We presume not to dictate to you, and we hope that we shall escape the imputation of arrogance, when we merely venture to recommend to your consideration, a suitable character in our judgments. In Mr. JAMES MADISON, the Secretary of State, are we believe combined all those qualifications which are requisite for the chief magistrate of the union. His superior talents, his integrity, his uniform adherence to the principles of liberty, and his knowledge of our foreign relations, are pledges that he will persevere in that course of administration, which for seven years past has shed such political happiness on the people of the United States. Entertaining this opinion, we beg leave to call your attention to him as a proper person on whom to bestow, through the Electors of this state, your suffrage.

CHRISTO. GREENUP,
Governor of this commonwealth, and President of the Meeting.

ALFRED WILLIAM GRAYSON, *Secretary of State for the state of Kentucky, and Secretary of the meeting.*
GREEN CLAY, *Speaker of the Senate.*
HENRY CLAY, *Speaker of the House of Representatives.*

Frankfort *Western World,* February 25, 1808. The journalist, attributing the statement to Clay, notes that he presented it before an assembly of Republican Senators and Representatives from the State legislature, who thereupon unanimously approved and signed it. Signatures of 77 additional legislators have been deleted.

Receipt from James T. Barbour

6th. March 1808.

Recd. of H. Clay for the Exors[1] of Jas Barbour deceased Thirty dollars on account of the purchase of the Blue Licks

JAS. T. BARBOUR

DS, in Clay's hand. KyLxT. James T. Barbour was the son of Colonel James and Frances Throckmorton Barbour, of Lancaster, Kentucky.

1 The administrators of Colonel Barbour's estate were two other sons, Richard and Thomas. Garrard County Court, Order Book 13 (November 19, 1804), p. 68.

To Thomas Worthington

D Sir Lexington 6 March 1808

I received your favor of the 26 Ulto.[1] Amongst a parcel of papers left with me by Col. Peyton[2] are the two notes referred to by you. No measures have been taken to enforce paymt., because I was informed by Col. P. that you did not wish to resort to coercion, and that I should receive your instructions.

Mrs. Beck's Academy stands very high in public estimation, and I believe very deservedly.[3] I have not had it in my power to attend her examinations; but the united testimony of all who have, gives the most favorable account of her mode of instruction, and the progress of her pupils. You will find her terms in the inclosed paper. I send you also an extract from the last Kentucky gazette, in which the writer speaks in the most flattering terms of the last public examination of her young Ladies.

Should the Miss Worthingtons come over it will afford Mrs. Clay pleasure to contribute to rendering their time agreeable, by any attentions in her power. I am told that it is most advisable for the young Ladies to board with her,[4] as she feels her responsibility increased when they do, and takes a pride in making them excel those who board elsewhere. Yr. ob Servt. HENRY CLAY

ALS. Ross County Historical Society, Chillicothe, Ohio. Addressed to Worthington at Chillicothe, where his home, "Adena," still stands. Worthington was twice a member of the United States Senate and was Governor of Ohio from 1814 to 1818.

1 Not found.

2 Possibly Colonel Francis Peyton of Loudoun County, Virginia, a veteran of the Continental Line and long a member of the Virginia legislature.

3 Mrs. Mary Beck, an Englishwoman, conducted a "female academy," said to be "the first of any eclat or distinction" in Lexington. Leavy, "Memoir of Lexington," Ky. State Hist. Soc., *Register,* XLI (1943), 345.

4 That is, with Mrs. Beck. Mary and Sarah Anne Worthington attended the Lexington school later in the year. Alfred Byron Sears, *Thomas Worthington, Father of Ohio Statehood* (Columbus, Ohio, [c. 1958]), 150.

Advertisement Concerning Buzzard

March 7th 1808.

The Celebrated Imported Turf Horse,

BUZZARD,

WILL stand the ensuing season in Lexington, to commence the 15th inst. & expire on the 15th of July next, at 40 dollars the season.

This high finished horse was imported by the late Col. John Hoomes, of the Bowling Green, in Virginia[1]—was the favourite of that gentleman, & is esteemed by the best judges to be superior to any horse on the continent. In point of form, blood, and performance, he is unrivalled in America, and has few, if any equals in England. The proprietors had intended to present to the public, a full extract from the Racing Calender[2] of all the races run by him; but as that would be tedious, and as this work is generally diffused, they beg leave to exhibit this summary of his

PERFORMANCE.

He won 34 races, and generally at New-Market, where the best horses in the kingdom are started.

[Summary of Buzzard's winning races, 1792-1794.]

From this statement it will appear that Buzzard has run with success all of the usual distances. In the advertisement of Clifden, by Dr. Thornton,[3] in the National Intelligencer of the spring 1807,[4] it is remarked, "that Clifden won ten of his twelve first races, which was unequalled by any horse in England for seven years but Buzzard." One of the proprietors has carefully examined the racing calender and has been unable to find that Buzzard, during all the period of his running, ever lost any but two races, and never paid a forfeit. Buzzard is not less distinguished as a sure and good foal getter than as a performer. Out of upwards of one hundred mares that he covered last year, but four have been heard of that did not prove with foal. The superiority of his

STOCK

Will be evinced by the Racing Calendars of England. Among the most distinguished of his colts are Hornby Lass, Peck, Quiz, Poppinjay, Surprise, Malta, Castrell, Merriman, Sophia, &c. &c. The following account of his winning colts and their prizes is extracted from the Calender.

In 1799	5	Winning colts	12	Prizes.
1800	7	- -	19	
1801	14	- -	43	
1802	16	- -	32	
1803	21		55	
1804	16		28	
1805	23		63	
1806	25		82	

BUZZARD's stock are large and finely formed.—Poppinjay is upwards of sixteen hands high, and said to be the most elegant horse in England. Quiz won the great Oatland stake, and a match over the Beacon course for one thousand guineas. In the spring 1806 the Oak stakes, one of the greatest in England, was won by a Buzzard filly, own sister to Castrell; and several of his colts are covering in England at ten guineas.

His PEDIGREE

Proves him to have descended from a long line of noble ancestry. He was got by Woodpecker, his dam (Misfortune) by Dux, grand dam (Curiosity) by Snap, great grand dam by Regulus; great great grand dam by Bartlets Childers;[5] great, great, great grand dam by Honeywood's Arabian, out of the dam of the two True Blues.

The Subscribers purchased this horse at the extraordinary price of 5500 Dollars with the view principally of improving their own stocks. They are sensible that the price at which he stands sounds high. It is however less than he ever stood at in England or America having stood at New-Market for seven years at 10 guineas, and a half guinea to the groom; and in Virginia, the first season at 10 guineas, and the next at fifty dollars.

He will be the ensuing season under the superintendance of Col. Buford, who will take care to provide good pasturage with never failing water gratis, but no responsibility.

ABRAHAM BUFORD,
THOMAS TODD,
BENJAMIN GRAVES,
GEORGE GRAVES,
HENRY CLAY,

Lexington *Kentucky Gazette,* June 14, 1808. The advertisement was also run in the Frankfort *Palladium* during this spring.

1 Buzzard was brought to America in 1804 or 1805.

2 *Racing Calendar: Containing an Account of the Plates, Matches, and Sweepstakes, Run for in Great-Britain and Ireland, &c.* (London, 1773-).

3 Dr. William Thornton, a native of the West Indies and a graduate in medicine of the University of Edinburgh, came to the United States in 1788 and attained prominence as a scientist and architect. He designed the first capitol building in Washington, D. C., and from 1802 until his death twenty-five years later was Superintendent of Patents.

4 Washington *National Intelligencer,* March 9, 1807.

5 Bartlet's Childers and Snap were of the Darley Arabian line. Regulus was the best of the Godolphin Arabian's colts.

Receipt from John H. Morton

[March 18, 1808]

Attached to Tax Bill, above, *ca.* February 1, 1807.

Bond from Nicholas Lewis and William Allen

[March 26, 1808]

Know all men by these presents that we Nicholas Lewis principal and Willm. Allen security are held and firmly bound unto Henry Clay in the just and full sum of four hundred pounds Current money; to be paid to the said Clay his heirs executors admors. or assigns; to which payment well & truly to be made we bind ourselves our heirs executors & admors jointly & severally firmly by these presents Sealed with our Seals & dated this 26h. day of March 1808.

The condition of this bond is such That if the said Nicholas Lewis shall well & truly pay to the said Clay Two hundred pounds on or before the first day of September one thousand eight hundred and nine with interest thereon from the first day of September

Last, then this obligation to be void otherwise to remain in full force & virtue

Sealed & Delivered NICHS. LEWIS {L.S.}
In presence of WM. ALLEN {L.S.}
Teste
J. DOWNING[1]

DS, in Clay's hand. Fayette Circuit Court, File 249 (1812). Lewis, earlier a tavernkeeper in Lexington, had moved to Jessamine County before 1800. Allen, also an early Lexington tavernkeeper and once a member of the town Board of Trustees, lived on the Georgetown Road. When the obligation remained unpaid, Clay filed suit to collect. Judgment against Allen was awarded at the September Term, 1810, but Lewis could not be found. *Ibid.*

1 Probably John Downing, another Lexington innkeeper.

Vote as Bank Director

[April 5, 1808]

Mr Clay one of the Directors dissenting desired his Negative should be entered on the minutes—

Bank of Kentucky, Frankfort, Record Book A, October 12, 1807-September 14, 1810, p. 82 (KyU). The Bank of Kentucky was chartered in December, 1806, and began operations on October 12 of the next year. Clay was elected one of the State's representatives on the board of directors of the institution by action of the legislature on January 6, 1808. Ky. H. of Reps., *Journal, 1807-1808,* p. 37. His vote here recorded was in opposition to the board's decision to buy land from John Instone as the site for the bank building.

From Luke Tiernan and Company

Henry Clay Esqr. Baltimore 9 April 1808—
Dear Sir

Your favor of the 16h. March[1] is received this day and are thankful for your promised remittance, as money is very scarce and much wanted in those times.

If you will look at our letter[2] that covered Mr. Wests note you will find we directed you to Bring suit, we now repeat this and request it may be done to the next Federal or State Court whichever in your Judgment is for our Interest provided you cannot procure undoubted good notes that will be regularly paid at your Bank in a short time, say from 3 to 4 months, if those can be had it will be preferable to a suit—we request this may be done or suit brought *to the first Court*—Charles P & C Buck of versailles[3] are Indebted to us for a long time and have some thought of sending you their account, we will thank you to Advise us in one or two posts your Opinion of them and if you know of any suits being Instituted against them and to what amount, we are with much regard

Your friends & Servts. LUKE TIERNAN & CO.

Since writing the within we have Concluded to draw a draft on Chs. & P. C. Buck of versaills 30 days sight for $879—in favor of Wm. Moore[4] who has Endorsed the same to you, this will aford you an opurtunity of knowing their situation, the amt. when received please remit in Bank notes or a draft at short sight, we do not wish Messrs. Bucks to know that we have adopted this mode to get part of our debt, we wish it to be Considered as a real transaction—by this post we have written them that we drew a draft in favor of Wm. Moore and requested they wd. pay the same, if you cannot get the whole in thirty days we hope it will be paid in about 45 days—Enclosed you have also a note of Messrs. Eastland & Aikens of Greensburgh Kentucky Ballance due us $38 12/100 Enclusive of Interest which please receive & forward[5]

Last fall we sent a letter to Mr. Thos. Harts care for Alex. Fulton, as he has returned request of Mr. Hart to return us the letter by first private hand, we made sale of the property taken from Mr. Eastland to Jno Jackson of versailles payable in 1 & 2 years we do not reccollect if the title to this property is made to us and if it is recorded, please Inform us on this subject we are with much regard

Your friends & Servt. LUKE TIERNAN & CO.

[Endorsement][6]

Sir

when your receive amt. of L. Tiernan & Co draft my favr please apply the amt. to their Credit & remit the same as they have directed you in the annexed letter—

Baltimore 10 April 1808— WILLIAM MOORE

ALS. DLC-TJC (DNA, M212, R12). Postmarked April 10.
1 Not found. 2 Dated January 30, 1808.
3 Charles and Peter C. Buck, of Versailles, Woodford County, Kentucky.
4 Of Baltimore. 5 Not found. 6 ES.

Receipt from Samuel and George Trotter

[April 28, 1808]

Attached to letter, Baldwin to Clay, January 14, 1808.

Promissory Note from Gilbert Pew and William L. Cox

[May 1, 1808]

One Month after date we or either of us promis to pay Henry Clay the sum of twelve dollars for the hire of negro man called Frank one month as witness our hands this firs day may 1088 [*sic*]

Teste GILBERT PEW

BENJ MERSHON[1] W. L. COX

ADS by Pew, signed also by Cox. DLC-TJC (DNA, M212, R15). Both Pew and Cox lived in Frankfort, Kentucky. 1 Of Franklin County.

From Noah Webster

Henry Clay Esq New Haven May 6. 1808

Sir.

I have just received a letter from Joseph Charless, dated at Louisville, in which he informs me that he has assigned the Contract respecting the Copy right of my Spellg. Books, to James & David Maccom Merchants of Lexington, to whom he has sold the types—& that I am to look to them as my publishers.[1] As I have been left totally in the dark on this subject, till this day, & am now utterly ignorant what are the terms of the contract, as it has been executed, I beg you to send me a copy of it without delay. I wish to know & it is indespensable that I should know, whether the Contract is that Charless or his assignees shall pay me a *Cent a copy,* for all they may publish; or whether they are to give me a thousand dollars, for the Copy right for the whole term—payable by installments—Please to let me know the particulars—& what is the amount of the Bond Charless has given for what he printed.

As I was 18 months without any advices from you or Charless, I lately wrote to Mr Bodley[2] to inquire into the facts—& if you should not be able, from extreme hurry of business, to attend to the agency, I requested him to undertake the agency. I have no preference, not being acquainted with either of the gentlemen named as suitable persons to act for me—All I want is, an agent of talents, & fidelity who will attend to my concerns, & from time to time inform me of such facts as may be necessary for me to know—I have entire confidence in you both But the subject of this letter is of immediate importance, & you will, by complying with my request, greatly oblige Sir, your most Obedt huml Servt—

NOAH WEBSTER

ALS. DLC-HC (DNA, M212, R1).

1 In a newspaper advertisement, dated May 10, 1808, J. and D. Maccoun announced that "They have . . . contracted for a few thousand copies of WEBSTER'S SPELLING BOOK . . .; to be printed in Lexington, from the standing types composed in Philadelphia. Orders from one to one hundred dozen, can, in a few weeks after this time, be filled on the shortest notice, and at a lower price, than they can be imported from Philadelphia." Lexington *Kentucky Gazette,* June 3, 1808.

2 Thomas Bodley, of Lexington.

Report of a Committee of Directors of the Bank of Kentucky

[May 10, 1808]

The Committee appointed to examine the State of the vaults

report that the following boxes to wit, No. 1. heretofore reported as containing . . . . $9000 is sealed

do.	No. 2.	9000	"	do.
"	" 3.	9000	"	do.
"	" 4.	9000	"	do.
"	" 5.	"3000		seal broke

The other boxes are opened and emptied which leaves in the vaults $39.000.

HENRY CLAY.

Bank of Kentucky, Frankfort, Record Book A (1807-1810), 119-20 (KyU). At a meeting of the board on May 3, 1808, Clay and Richard Dallam had been appointed a committee to report on the state of the vault. Clay had served on such a committee earlier in the year, but the report on that occasion is unsigned in the Bank Record Book.

Receipt to John Adair

Frankfort 14th May 1808

Recd of Genl John Adair by M Hardin fifteen dollars Seventy five cents—being refunded for the within purchases—for J. Tilford[1]

HENRY CLAY

DS, in Hardin's hand. KyHi. Mark Hardin was Adair's son-in-law, as well as his successor in the office of land register.

[1] John Tilford had bought certain lands for delinquent taxes. The sales were cancelled and the purchase price refunded when it was later discovered that the taxes had been previously paid.

"Regulus" to the People

TO THE PEOPLE. [*ca.* May 31, 1808]

The approach of the period for electing a Chief Magistrate of this Commonwealth, at all times interesting, is peculiarly so in the present crises of public affairs. Threatened with foreign war, in the event of which calls will be made upon the wisdom, vigor and patriotism of the state functionaries; distracted by intestine divisions, and cherishing in our bosom a faction which is pursuing, under numerous pretexts, with undeviating perseverance, one favorite object, the repossession of power which they had abused, and from which they were driven by the indignant voice of a magnanimous people, the claim upon you for the exercise of discernment and circumspection, in the choice you may make, has irresistable force.

Various have been, and will continue to be, the means employed to deceive and delude you. Each candidate will be marked out as the victim of some popular prejudice, and will receive his full measure of abuse and calumny. It is a melancholy truth, incidental to our representative system of government, that to become a candidate for popular patronage is to become a target for all the shafts of malice and detraction. And in proportion as the station in question is honorable and exalted, are the means base and malignant which are used to poison the minds of the electors. A free people should keep a watchful vigilance—the subjects of choice should be scrutinized and well weighed, but the arts of the calumniator ought to be detected and detested.

The writer of this address was led to these remarks by observing, in a late number of the Western World, an attack upon the public character of Mr. John Allen, made by the nominal editor of that paper.[1] Whatever merit this print might have acquired, by contributing to the exposure and removal of Mr. Sebastian,[2] it is notorious that it has now become the humble instrument of a certain high toned Federalist and his party.[3] Its object is too apparent to admit of doubt with any but those who voluntarily remain blind. Every distinguished character on the Republican list is to be villified and brought down, and the stations occupied by them, in the public estimation, are to be filled by the masked and covert, or the open and avowed Federalist. Perhaps no man had pursued a more unexceptionable public course than Mr. Allen. A firm and decided republican, but in the pursuit of an active profession calling for all his exertions, and having a growing family to provide for, he never sought distinction or preferment, by becoming the demagogue. He never availed himself of the honest prejudices of the people to excite a prejudice in his favor. He appears to have challenged attention to the acts of an uniform, consistent and honorable life, and asked to be tried by these, rather than to be tested by empty professions. In the domestic and social circle the most amiable; always firm, independent and dignified; possessed of a mind vigorous, correct and comprehensive, such a man as Mr. Allen it might have been expected, would have escaped the malevolence of those who direct the operations of the Western World. But boundless in their ambition, and regardless of the means which are to promote it, the honest fame of all who stand in their way is to be assailed, and Mr. Allen is too distinguished an object to pass unnoticed. The fruitful resources of "Burrism" and "Spanish Conspiracy" are to be appealed to, and when these fail of furnishing charges for the meditated victim, the ingenuity of federalism will resort to some other plausible expedient.

The piece signed by Mr. Street in the Western World of the 5th of May commences in artifice and progresses and ends in falsehood, perversion and misrepresentation. It affects to state that the editor is called upon by a citizen of Garrard to afford certain information relative to Mr. Allen. Although he has actually set out upon a journey to Virginia, for the purpose of visiting his very, very dear friends and relations; and had intended to remain silent during the present contest for the *gubernatorial* chair, yet he suddenly calls a halt, and continuing in Lancaster[4] several days, composes the piece alluded to. Most disinterested patriotism! After the great efforts which this pure and enlightened statesman has made to diffuse information, among the ignorant people of this Western frontier, would it not be most ungrateful to ask, whether the queries alledged to have been received from a citizen of Garrard, are really genuine? Were they not written, prior to his departure from Frankfort, by or in concert with a certain well known character in the neighbourhood of that place, before referred to? Did he feel no resentment towards Mr. Allen last winter, for giving a preference to Hunter as public printer?[5] Has he no rankling, on account of his being employed as counsel to prosecute an action for a libel, brought by Col. Todd, now depending on the docket of Franklin?[6]—Such interrogatories as these, it is hoped, should they be put to the editor of the W. World, his pride will not permit him to stoop to answer; for who can doubt the rectitude of his motives? It is time he had a very bad opinion of M. Allen; thought him "either a consummate fool, or that he defended Sebastian knowing his guilt? that he appeared for Burr, knowing the damning consequences of his scheme (of which he was not quite clear) and that he opposed an enquiry into the conduct of Innis,[7] not because he believed him innocent, but to prevent the positive proof of his guilt," but still believing that the people throughout the state were well informed of all this, Mr. Street had no intention of interfering with the present *guburnatorial* contest, until he was reluctantly drawn forth by the Garrard querist. Happy it is for this country that the patriotic citizen of that county accosted Mr. Street, just on the borders of the state,[8] in his journey to see his dear, dear friends, & obtained the well timed information in his piece.—Had he left the state, it is probable if not certain, that no other man in the commonwealth, could have detailed *the facts* contained in his address. And who is hardy enough to say that if he had departed without communicating these facts to the people, he might not upon his return, (if he should ever return) have found the *guburnatorial* chair polluted by Mr. Allen? At least it would have been as probable as that this country would have been severed from the Union, in the course of twelve months, had Sebastian continued that much longer on the bench of the Court of Appeals; and that such must have been the inevitable result of his remaining there is one of those self-evident propositions, that requires no proof. No man can seriously doubt it.

The author of these remarks commenced them for the purpose of examining into the charges preferred against Mr. Allen. He had intended to treat the subject with gravity; but as he progressed he found it impossible to repress that disposition to ridicule which the statements and reasoning of the writer of the piece, subscribed "Jos. M. Street," are so well calculated to excite. His apology will be found in their folly, extravagance and absurdity. There are two charges however contained in that singular production against Mr. Allen meriting attention. It is alledged or insinuated 1st, that he wished to screen Sebastian from punishment; and 2dly, that he knew of and participated in Burr's project.

The state of the public mind prior to the Legislative Session 1806 is within the recollection of all. Great curiosity and much agitation prevailed in relation to the developement of what was termed the Spanish Conspiracy. The characters were assailed of men long confided in by the people and believed to be virtuous. Much bold assertion had been made and but little proof offered to the public. With respect to Sebastian it is not remembered that a single particle of proof had been presented to the world, prior to the meeting of the Legislature. The denunciators themselves had stated that the persons implicated had veiled in profound secrecy their criminal transactions. Thus without information, and in a state of general ferment, the Legislature was called upon to enquire into the conduct of S. Did Mr. Allen oppose the enquiry? No. Did he stand forth "the champion of S.—argue upon the propriety of disregarding the voice of the people—of rejecting their petitions for enquiry, and of postponing the subject until the next session of the Legislature?" No. It is utterly without foundation. Mr. Street knows it. It is known by the author of this address. Mr. Sebastian by letter solicited a postponement. It was proposed immediately to reject the request, and proceed in the investigation. At this time it ought to be recollected that Mr. Allen was ignorant it is presumable of the extent and weight of proof capable of being adduced. On the one side he beheld an accusation as yet unsupported by evidence; on the other an accused, advanced in life, and who had long enjoyed the honors and confidence of his country. His profession, his habits, his experience had evinced to him the importance of circumspection and deliberation in trials. The person thus accused avowed his innocence and asks time to obtain from New Orleans, (the alledged theatre of his guilt, and from which or the Havannah alone conclusive proof of that innocence, if it existed, could be drawn,) the proof to manifest it. Had Mr. Allen advocated this application would he have been criminal? Is a man to be covered with the guilt of a traitor because he asks for him a fair trial? Is he to be denounced because he supports a motion for time to collect and let in the proofs of the accused? But Mr. Allen did not go this far. The Legislature had a character to sustain; to expose and punish the guilty was not more a duty than it was to respect the forms of justice, consecrated by the constitution and laws of the land, and to proceed without precipitation. This was all he asked;—time to reflect, and for the house to reflect upon the proper course to be taken in this very novel and unprecedented business. *No proposition* was made, by any member of the house whatever, to postpone the enquiry until the succeeding session of the Legislature. It is not true that Mr. Simpson,[9] Mr. Allen or any other member suggested the propriety of continuing it for twelve months, or for any specific time, or for any other purpose than before stated—that is deliberation. The appetite of the editor of the W. World for traduction is evident from the manner in which he mentions the names of Mr. Simpson and Mr. Clay. It is his subsistance—his bread; he would expire without it. Although the Garrard querist had called for no information in relation to those gentlemen, the editor could not forbear indulging his favorite propensity, by bes[pat]tering[10] them as he passed along.

Mr. Allen defended Burr upon a charge of *Treason*. You are entreated, fellow citizens, to attend to this statement of the editor. It displays to what lengths of misrepresentation a man, when he consents to become the tool and instrument of unprincipled ambition will proceed. Burr was *never* charged before the court in this country with *Treason*. The indictment here against him was for setting on foot an expedition against Mexico. Never until he reached Richmond was he arraigned for the former offence. The punishment of the one is death—of the other fine and imprisonment. The former is the highest and most atrocious crime known to society; the latter is denominated by the law itself a misdemeanor. It is not however intended to place Mr. Allen's vindication on the degree of Burr's guilt. What were the impressions of the moment? As late as the 10th December, 1806 but one sentiment prevailed in this country. It was believed universally that the charges against Burr were without foundation. Amidst the multitude who were attracted to Frankfort by his trials there, it is not supposed that ten of them then imagined him to be guilty. The nature of the charge; the total impracticability of the plan attributed to Burr; the reputation he had enjoyed for intellectual endowment; the ardent and sanguine disposition of the ex-attorney for the United States[11]—every circumstance of the moment gave an air of incredibility to the accusation, and combined to produce general conviction, that the prosecution was totally groundless. The Grand Jury, after much deliberation, extracting, weighing, and scrutinizing every thing like testimony laid before them, pronounced him innocent. What has the president said? That the prosecution was premature. Why? Because the requisite proofs were not and could not then be collected. It is true that shortly after his acquittal, information began to flow in, and the eyes of the people to be opened. The president's proclamation came out, the letter in cypher to Wilkinson[12] followed, and at length his treachery, in all its deformity and attrociousness, was exposed to the nation. That Burr's counsel knew what every body was ignorant of, his guilt, there is no evidence, nor reason to believe. That he laboured to deceive them is manifest from a letter which he addressed to one of them, avowing, in the strongest and most unequivocal language, his innocence.[13] And so satisfied has been the executive of the United States of their freedom from participation in his scheme, that the counsel alluded to, it has been said was solicited, long after the transactions at Frankfort, to prosecute him in behalf of the government.[14] That subsequent to his arraignment at Frankfort, he should have been proven to have been guilty, ought not to operate against Mr. Allen. He is to be judged by the circumstances of the *time* when he acted—by the information which he *then* possessed, not by testimony *afterwards* exhibited. The character of an anterior act is not to be fixed by posterior events. Mr. Allen ought not to be censured for believing, on the evidence he then possessed, that Burr was innocent, when all Kentucky, with but few exceptions, then believed him innocent.

Let, however, more be conceded than has been, or as is believed, can be shewn: that from circumstances he ought to have believed him guilty of the misdemeanor. Was he therefore to refuse to appear as his counsel? The practice of the law is his trade. He follows it as a profession, recognized, respected and honored. Would a shoemaker or taylor have been guilty of treason, if the one had made a pair of boots and the other a coat for Mr. Burr? Or had he applied to them to take his measure, did patriotism or duty require that they should kick him out of their shops? Had his counsel stepped out of the legitimate defence of their client; had they resorted to trick or chicanery to acquit him, it would have been dishonorable and reprehensible in the highest degree. This is not alledged. The constitution of the United States, almost all the state constitutions, tender of the rights of the accused, have expressly provided that they shall have the benefit of counsel for their defence. Did these instruments mean to say to the unfortunate culprit, "you shall have advocates to defend you," and to those advocates, "if you appear in the defence, you shall be deemed unworthy of public trust or confidence?" When the editors of the Western World had published a gross, scandalous and indecent libel upon the chief magistrate of this state,[15] (for which they were compelled to apologize) did they conceive the gentlemen of the bar who defended them as disgraced and forfeiting all claim to public confidence? Did no counsel volunteer for them? And if they did, were they conceived as censurable for so doing?

But Mr. Allen smiled on Burr's acquittal by the grand jury in this country. Believing him innocent, it was natural that he should have been pleased at the declaration of the jury that he was not guilty. But what an inhuman sentiment is implied in this reprobation by the editor? Who is delighted at conviction? The infamous Jefferies,[16] amidst his bloody career, assuming the semblance of virtue, would avow the wish that the victim of his oppression should be acquitted by his peers. It is made the express duty of the arraigning officer by our laws, in all the sincerity of mercy, to proclaim to the accused the hope "that God would send him a safe deliverance." Acquittal supposes innocence. The fiend then, only can rejoice at condemnation. Had the acquittal been produced by unfair means, by a packed jury, or by a suppression of evidence, or perversion of law (as is said to have happened at Richmond before the chief justice)[17] there might be complaint against Mr. Allen for expressing his satisfaction at the result. But no such imputation has been made.

He wrote the verdict of the grand jury. Never was a more false and groundless insinuation made. The records of this or any other country are challenged to exhibit a pannel composed of more respectable, intelligent and independent men than sat on Burr's trial. They would have spurned at the offer to word their verdict for them; and their capacity rendered the aid of others as unnecessary as it would have been improper. A list of their names will manifest the correct selection of the Marshal, whose honesty is proverbial; and will further shew that whilst the propagator of foul calumnies against them was "pewling [*sic*] in his nurse's arms," many of them were exposed to the tomahawk of the savage, and engaged in converting this country from a wilderness into a cultivated and civilized land. REGULUS.

Lexington *Kentucky Gazette,* May 31, 1808. Reprinted in Lexington *Reporter,* June 11, 1808, and in Frankfort *Western World,* June 23, 1808. On Clay's identity as "Regulus," see below, Dr. Hunn's Reply, *ca.* June 7, 1808. John Allen, who had been Clay's associate as Burr's legal counsel, was now a candidate for the office of Governor of Kentucky. He was defeated in the election by General Charles Scott.

1 Joseph M. Street, whose attack had been leveled at Clay as well as Allen.

2 Judge Benjamin Sebastian.

3 Humphrey Marshall.

4 The county seat of Garrard County.

5 Allen had been a member of the State Senate when William Hunter, editor of the Frankfort *Palladium,* had been chosen over Street as public printer.

6 See above, Todd to Clay, May 23, 1807.

7 When Humphrey Marshall was seeking the removal of Judge Harry Innes from office.

8 Garrard County is, of course, far from the borders of the state.

9 John Simpson.

10 Correction supplied from other printed versions.

11 Joseph Hamilton Daveiss.

12 General James Wilkinson.

13 See above, Burr to Clay, December 1, 1806.

14 See above, Clay to Rodney, December 5, 1807.

15 Governor Christopher Greenup.

16 George Jeffreys, appointed by James II to the highest judicial posts in the realm, is remembered for his cruelty and, more particularly, for the "bloody assizes" of 1685.

17 Chief Justice John Marshall had presided over the trial of Burr at Richmond, Virginia.

Dr. Anthony Hunn's Reply to "Regulus"

[*ca.* June 7, 1808]

By whatever denomination the political parties in America have been characterised, whether they have been called Federalists, Quids, Aristocrats, Tories, Republicans, or Democrats, there are really but two grand political divisions among the citizens of the United States. The one consists of all such men as believe, or affect to believe, that the great mass of the people are unfit for self-government; that a great majority of our citizens are a mob, a rabble, a "swinish multitude," who must be governed by gentlemen of a certain qualification, if the government shall not be engulphed in anarchy and confusion. Nearly all the lawyers, the foreign merchants, such Americans as have become suddenly wealthy, either by accident or by inheritance, by cheat or pilfering, without knowing what it is to become opulent by honest care and industry–belong to this class. The other division consists of such citizens as feel convinced by reason and experience, that no man or set of men, are better judges of the national interests of a people, than the people themselves, and that from the voice of the majority of the people, results the highest degree of political wisdom, attainable by human society. That the science of government, if stript of pedantry and knavery, is so simple that any citizen of common sense and common education may become acquainted with it, without having sucked pride and self-conceit in a college; without having his brain loaded with the useless knowledge of Greek or Latin; and without having his integrity corrupted at the bar. This class comprehends a great majority of the farmers, mechanics, and American merchants. They wish to be represented by plain, intelligent farmers, or other citizens whose private interests are congenial with their own and demand the strictest responsibility from all their public functionaries, whom they call their public servants, and not *rulers*. The principles and actions of these two parties are diametrically opposite to each other. The first are constantly striving to impose on the community, in order to raise a lawful aristocracy; and the second forever endeavoring to detect public impostors and to equalize the rights and emoluments of society. The first are smaller in number, but forever plotting and closely united; the last compose at least five sixths of the community, but have ever been divided, unless when some great public calamity has forced them to a temporary union. All political mischief in America has sprung from the first, and all political salvation from the last. It is the interest of the first class to fill the public offices with creatures of their own stamp, and from their action and perseverance they hardly ever have missed to effect their purposes. Thus McKean became the tyrant of Pennsylvania, and filled that otherwise so happy state with feuds and distraction.[1] Thus rose in Kentucky the abominable fraternity of Spanish conspirators, the different bands of thievish land-shoppers, and the all-corrupting junto of bar-aristocrats; and thus has lately been organised that venal and unprincipled club, which is furiously determined to leave nothing untried; to have the second McKean, mr. Allen, promoted to the powers of Governor, that he might aid to stifle all further enquiries into misdeeds of the two last legislatures, and to counteract powerfully that growing spirit of amelioration in our judiciary system, which threatens to fill up all the old goldmines of the lawyer-aristocracy. Mr. Allen like the Grand Sultan, thinks himself too far above the contest for the favor of a "swinish multitude"; but he has his Viziers, his Agas, and Janizaries to fight ought [*sic*] his battles. Mr. *Henry Clay* is his great vizier; and well chosen is the Generalissimo, for his fate is firmly linked with that of his Sultan. It was their united strength that broke the constitution in advocating the pension bill;[2] they both became champions of a traitor, when as attorneys of Burr, they publicly professed their belief in his innocence, at the same time when all the circumstances attending that sham-trial, proved them to have been conscious of his guilt. The piece, written by mr. Clay, under the name of Regulus, altho' apparently intended against the editor of the Western World, is yet so strongly corroborating all we have mentioned against the unhallowed profession of lawyers, and moreover seeks to refute some of our assertions against mr. Allen, with a tissue of such glaring falsehoods and unprincipled sophistry, that we deem it peculiarly our duty, to spread out all its deformities before the eyes of an intelligent people.

Those crooked witticisms, which in the beginning of his piece mr. Clay heaps as invectives on mr. Street, the editor of the W. World, we purposely forego to take notice of, as we believe mr. Street as willing as he is able to take his own part, to the smart of his proud adversaries. With respect to the Spanish conspiracy we will mention only, that the developement of this treachery has been of most singular advantage to the people of this state. By it they have been impressed with the necessity to distinguish accurately between men, who carry republicanism on the tongue only, and such as evince it by their actions. The business is not over with the conviction of one vile pensioner of Spain[3]—there are strong reasons to suspect several big gentlemen, who now have the effrontery to solicit the favors of a people, whose destruction they planned, and yet plan, of handling Spanish money to this very hour. Proofs are accumulating every day—tremble, ye wolves in sheep-skins! The day is not far off, when you will share the fate of Sebastian.

That part of mr. Clay's *matchless* piece, which begins to introduce Burr's treachery, and where mr. Clay speaks two words for himself and one for mr. Allen, in order to shake the weight of Burrism from their galled shoulders, is the proper place for our investigation to begin.

If mr. Clay did not in the fulness of his insuperableness think the Kentuckian people at large to be altogether destitute of common sense, he would not have ventured to assert, contrary (no doubt) to his better knowledge, that "as late as the tenth of December, 1806 it was *universally* believed in Kentucky, that the charges against Burr were without foundation." To be sure, Burr was known as a man of talents and enterprise; but after his being detected as a political swindler in the election of Jefferson, and after his subsequent horrid murder on Hamilton, no man of common sense expected any thing but devilment from his "exalted" capacities. His galloping journies through the west were early suspected and raised a foreboding sigh in the breast of many a Kentuckian citizen. But at the time, Mr. Clay speaks of, Kentucky was thrown into a general ferment. Burr had his enlisting officers in every county. An expedition against Spain was the ostensible plan, but it was constantly insinuated, that there were "something more behind"—that the present government of the U. S. could not stand, and that much money might be made by the first adventurers in a revolution. In some instances Burr was even mentioned as king and New-Orleans as the capital of the Western Monarchy. Many an ill raised chap, too ignorant to know his happiness, or too lazy or too proud to work for a living, had his horse and ammunition ready to assist in the hailing of the halcyon days of Burrish greatness. The young lawyers especially, who had found themselves deceived in the hopes of their proud hearts, the Irish merchants, with few exceptions, the old Tories, who "had told it long ago, that the Americans must have a King"; all these & perhaps many more were well wishers to the scheme of Burr. But the rest of the citizens of Kentucky were under the greatest inquietude, and tho' the flying reports of the precise extent of the conspiracy of Burr were as yet various and contradictory, yet the dismemberment of the union, and the erection of a western empire were generally believed to be contemplated by the Burrites. Influenced by this general ferment of the people, and by a report, which was communicated in some of the eastern papers, that the Kentuckians in general were friendly to Burr's schemes, mr. Grundy[4] moved on the third day of December, in the General Assembly, a resolution that was unanimously agreed to, and of which the following are extracts:

Resolved—By the general assembly, that the people of Kentucky, consider a dismemberment of the union as the greatest evil which could befal them, and would view with abhorrence any individual or set of individuals, who should attempt to separate us from those whose interests are so intimately connected with our own.

Resolved—That the people of Kentucky have no doubt but that such measures will be pursued by the present administration, as are best calculated *to secure us peace and tranquility.*

From the same reason mr. Bibb,[5] on the 5th of December, moved for a bill, "more effectually to secure the peace of this commonwealth," which at last terminated in an "act to prevent unlawful enterprises," which gives to the governor the extraordinary power to raise the militia to oppose all military enterprises against the 'peace and tranquility' of the state. (Vid. acts of the assembly, of the year 1806.) When afterwards the grand jury brought in that singular verdict, which cleared Burr and Adair[6] even of *bad intentions,* it was by authority and without delay communicated to the people—"in order to calm the public mind." The newspapers of the state inserted that verdict with the editorial hope, "that now the public mind would be restored to tranquility." All these notorious facts were known to the bottom by mr. Clay, who himself was a member of the assembly, and yet he boldly declares in the face of a whole community, who know the contrary, that as late as "the 10th of December, 1806, but one sentiment prevailed in this country. It was universally believed that the charges against Burr were without foundation." *A falsehood told with the intention to deceive is a lie.*

That mr. Clay and mr. Allen, both believed Burr guilty of the charges brought against him, when as his defenders, they expressly and publicly declared their conviction of his innocence, we conclude from the following facts. When Burr's guilt became publicly known, and mr. Clay apprehended the loss of his popularity from his having defended a notorious traitor, he attempted to excuse himself by an insertion in a Kentuckian paper,[7] in which he declared that he was deceived into a belief of Burr's innocence by a letter from Burr, of which the following is a pertinent extract:

"Considering the high station you fill, in our national councils, I have thought these explanations proper; as well to counteract the chimerical tales, which malevolent persons have so industriously circulated, as to satisfy you that you *have not espoused the cause* of a man in any way unfriendly to the laws, the government, or the interests of his country."

The same letter appeared in the National Intelligencer,[8] with the following editorial remarks, which undoubtedly flowed from the instruction of mr. Clay, who was then at Washington.

"Let it be recollected, that it was on the strength of assurance contained in this letter that mr. Clay's services actually were commanded: that without them they would not have been rendered: and that it was probably in a great measure owing to this circumstance, that Burr was acquitted by the grand jury of Kentucky."

The reader will here please to observe, that mr. Clay publicly declared that this letter convinced him of Burr's innocence, in consequence of which he had been persuaded to become his defender; and yet this very letter says: *"you have not espoused the cause" &c.* It is plain from this that mr. Clay *had already espoused Burr's cause, before he received the letter. A falsehood told, with the intention to deceive is a lie.* At Burr's trial before the grand-jury, the prosecuting attorney of the United States, mr. Joseph Daveiss, demanded the privilege of examining the witnesses. He certainly was thoroughly acquainted with the Burrite scheme. He knew that several of the witnesses were engaged Burrites. We ourselves know at least one of them to have been such. The necessity of putting the proper questions to such witnesses before *such* a grand-jury was evident. If Burr was innocent, it is impossible to say, that any harm would flow from such an examination, but the conviction of Burr must have been its certain consequence if he was guilty. Why did mr. Allen and mr. Clay plead so powerfully against that reasonable and necessary measure if they believed Burr innocent? This question can be answered but one way. They knew Burr guilty, they knew that the witnesses, Burrites, would convict Burr if properly interrogated, therefore they opposed the measure. Judge Innis, had first declared, that Daveiss should have the right of interrogating the witnesses before the grand-jury, but afterwards on the suggestions of Allen and Clay, the pliant judge revoked his opinion. Judge readers, whether we are wrong when we conclude from these circumstances that mr. Allen and mr. Clay were not only acquainted with Burr's guilt when they undertook his defence, but that they were, *if not engaged Burrites,* at least *well wishers* to his horrid scheme?

But as if conscious of the flimsiness of his arguments, mr. Clay continues saying, that if mr. Allen had even known Burr to be guilty, he could not be blamed for defending him *for that was his trade,* by which he maintained a growing family—God Almighty help us! Has lying and tricking notorious traitors out of the hands of retributive justice really become a trade among us, and that too "honored and respected"? All the accusations, which the Lamp has issued against the profession of lawyers, are flatteries compared with this confession of the mammoth Barrister, H. Clay. The law, which warrants every accused the benefit of defence, certainly supposes this defence to be subordinate to the oath of the attorney "to demean himself *honestly*" in his practice. It means that an attorney shall defend an accused as far as he can do it with honesty and truth; but not that a lawyer shall become a liar and a scoundrel, in order to screen rogues and traders from justice! But if we actually have such an "honorable" trade established by law or custom, for God's sake let us not make such 'honorable' tradesmen —Governors!!! To make a pair of shoes or a coat for Burr, could never be criminal: but a lie will not become an "honorable" truth, if even it should be told by mr. Allen for Burr!!! We concede, that under the present organization of our judiciary system, mr. Allen, or Clay, or any other lawyer, might have undertaken Burr's defence, for money, without meriting blame, if it had been carried on without breach of truth and honesty; but for an attorney to stake his honor for his belief of the culprit's innocence, when in his heart he is convinced of his guilt, and that too in a case on the right decision of which perhaps depends all the welfare of the community; to exert all his plotting, as well as oratorial powers, to defeat a proper investigation of the case—these are actions which must be considered as dishonorable even by—Lawyers.

The expression of *"unfortunate culprit,"* which from the connection, mr. Clay must have meant to apply to Burr, raises so strong a suspicion against the rectitude of mr. C's political principles, that we cannot but take notice of it here. Instead of being unfortunate, Burr has been the most *fortunate* culprit that ever was brought to trial. First to be convicted of murder, in cold blood, without receiving the slightest punishment for it;[9] then planning and actually commencing the destruction of the best of governments, then to meet with such a grand jury; such a judge and such advocates as mr. Clay and mr. Allen in Frankfort; and at last with a John Marshall at Richmond,[10] to clear him in the face of a whole condemning world—what a train of unheard of good fortunes! No other culprit will ever be so fortunate again as long as the world stands. If the expression "unfortunate culprit" has any meaning at all, it must mean, that mr. Clay thinks it unfortunate, that Burr was so unfortunately, for himself and his co-traitors, interrupted in his machinations to murder innocent citizens, & to destroy the only refuge of the world from the calamities of tyranny, the liberties of America. How *"fortunate"* it would have been to see a new empire rise from under the carnage of Burrites, in which men of such "great" talents as mr. Clay and mr. Allen, could not fail to become prime Ministers, Dons, Counts, Princes—yea perhaps even kings!! In this view only Burr could with any propriety be called "an unfortunate culprit," and—mr. Clay is understood!

A few more words on the praise which mr. Clay bestows on the *wisdom* and *integrity* of the grand jury, by whom Burr was cleared in Frankfort, and then we will conclude this lengthy investigation. This wisdom and integrity we will not, like mr. Clay, infer from their names, but from their actions, if they will bear that inference. The verdict, which declares Burr and Adair innocent, not only of facts, but even of sinister intentions, the reader will recollect, was given at a time, when Burr's manoeuvres were highly suspected throughout the union, when the jury knew, that in the State of Ohio actually military measures had been taken to capture the armed flotilla of Burr, and when our legislature in Frankfort had taken several measures to secure the state from insurrection and invasion. The reader will likewise take to proper account, that the bills of Burr on some Lexington merchants were endorsed by several of the grand jury-men, when Burr was universally known to be a bankrupt, and that they knew the means, by which Daviess was prevented to put such questions to the witnesses as he pledged himself would either perjure them, or convict Burr of the charges brought against him. Impressed by the ideas, raised by these facts, read the *verdict* itself.

"The Grand Jury are happy to inform the court, that no violent disturbance of the public tranquility, or breach of the laws has come to their knowledge.

"We have no hesitation in declaring, that having carefully examined and scrutinized all the testimony which has come before us, as well on the charges against Aaron Burr, as those contained in the indictment preferred to us against John Adair, that there has been no testimony before us which does in the smallest degree criminate the conduct of either of those persons; nor can we, from all the enquiries and investigation of the subject, discover any thing improper or injurious to the interest of the U. States, or contrary to the laws thereof, is designed or contemplated by either of them."

The usual form of verdicts is to find the culprit either guilty or not guilty. Why was that rule dispensed with in this case? The reasons will appear in the verdict itself—It was to persuade the people that they had investigated and scrutinized the business before they judged. Is this so new a thing in a grand jury, to need its being told? Or were they apprehensive, that their honest endeavors in the momentous investigation, might be doubted by the people? Why did they not consult with Daviess on the proper questions, which he wished them to put to the witnesses? They had the right to do so, and in our opinion it was their duty to do so, for Daviess declared that the prosecution must fail, unless the proper questions were put. In the latter part they not only make Burr innocent of the charges brought against him, but labor to impress the people with an idea that he and his lieutenant, Adair, did not harbor even sinister intentions. They were judges of facts, but who wanted their judgment about *intentions?* God almighty judges the heart. A man can be proved to be a thief, but who can prove that a man has no intention to steal? Whether it was absurdity or design, that made this "respectable intelligent, and independent" jury, compose such a verdict, we leave our readers to judge. At any rate, this verdict served as an excellent passport for Burr, to reach his quarters without further molestation. That desire which evidently appears to us in the singular wording of this verdict, to find and declare Burr innocent, is in our opinion altogether incompatible with that strict impartiality, which ought to characterize an American grand jury.

Whether mr. Allen worded the verdict or not, as we deem it by far the least impropriety in mr. Allens conduct, we intend from the present want of room, to investigate in a future number of the Lamp.

Fellow-citizens! We are persuaded, that we now have shewn to your satisfaction, that in the present contest not *Federalists* contend against the election of mr. Allen, but Republicans strive against the machinations of Federalists and Burrites: that all the Aristocrats in the State, with mr. Allen at their head, are now united, to make one decisive effort against the growing republicanism of Kentucky, in order to perpetuate the horrors of British lawyer-craft, to strengthen the young precedent of pensioning lazy aristocrats, to crush the further development of the Spanish conspiracy, and perhaps to smooth the way for another "unfortunate culprit" that he might convert *erect* citizens into *stooping* subjects! —We have no personal acquaintance with mr. Allen and as a private gentleman he may be "amiable" to what we know, but we detest his principles as a public character. To scrutinize boldly and impartially the public conduct of candidates for public trusts, is at all times, and urgently in the present aweful crisis of the world, *the indispensable duty of the American press.*

Frankfort *Western World,* June 30, 1808. Reprinted from *The Lamp,* a journal published by Dr. Hunn in Lincoln County. Cf. above, "Regulus" to the People, *ca.* May 31, 1808.

1 Thomas McKean, Governor of Pennsylvania from 1799 to 1808.

2 For the benefit of Judge George Muter.

3 Judge Benjamin Sebastian.

4 Felix Grundy.

5 George M. Bibb served only a few days, late in 1806, as a member of the lower house of the State legislature.

6 John Adair. See above, Defense of Burr, December 2, 1806.

7 Not found. The quotation is from Burr to Clay, December 1, 1806.

8 March 13, 1807.

9 Although indicted for murder in New Jersey and New York, following his duel with Alexander Hamilton in 1804, Burr was never brought to trial.

10 Virginia, where the Chief Justice presided over Burr's trial.

Promissory Note by Thomas Bodley

$ 527.51— due 14 & 17 July Lexington 14th June 1808

Thirty days after date I Thomas Bodley promise to pay Henry Clay or order without defalcation Five Hundred & Twenty Seven dollars fifty one Cents, payable & negotiable at the office of the Lexington Branch Bank[1] Value received. witness my hand ———

THOS. [BODLEY][2]

DS. DLC-TJC (DNA, M212, R15). Endorsed on verso in unidentified hand: "I took up H Clay note given on a/c of this for 503.75 which I gave up to him, he is entitled to Cr for the balls," followed by a calculation showing a balance of $23.76. Signatures of Henry Clay and Charles Wilkins indicate that the balance was deposited.

1 A branch of the Bank of Kentucky, established in this year.

2 MS. torn, part of signature missing.

Agreement with William L. Fisher

[June 15, 1808]

An agreement between William Fisher and Henry Clay.

The said Clay has sold to the said Fisher a gigg at one hundred and thirty five dollars, which the said Fisher agrees to pay for in laying brick in a stable[1] at sixteen shillings and six pence the thousand. The said Clay is to use his best endeavours to procure the brick so as to commence with the work on or before the 15h.

July next. Witness our hands & seals this 15 June 1808. The said Fisher is to be furnished two meals per day by the said Clay.

HENRY CLAY {L.S.}
WILLIAM L. FISHER {L.S.}

ADS, signed also by Fisher, a Lexington bricklayer. DLC-TJC (DNA, M212, R15).
1 See below, Lease of Traveller's Hall, June 24, 1808.

From Luke Tiernan & Company

Henry Clay Esqr. Baltimore 16h June 1808
Dear Sir

Your favor of the 23rd. May[1] Enclosing a Bill drawn by Jno. Pr[. . .][2] of new Orleans on Messrs. Corp Ellis & Shaw of new york sixty days sight for one thousand dolls. when paid we will pay Messrs. Hugh & Wm. young[3] four Hundred dollars debiting them one and a half pC premm. for the same—we are in hopes you will receive the money from messrs. Bucks[4] and that you will be able to remit the same in a good Bill; our last letters from new Orleans quoted Bills at par we shou'd prefer them if undoubted good ones can be had—we think you ought only to have charged a commission on $1600 which in fact was the full value of the House & Lott taken from Eastland[5]—we must request you will proceed in the recovery of Wm. Wests debt as soon as possible, so much Indulgence has been given by us that he cannot look for any further, his account be asured is Correct and has Credit on his note for allowance on Rose Blankets[6] as well as a small sum recd. of Henry messionier we are with much regard Your friends & Servs.

LUKE TIERNAN & CO.

ALS. DLC-TJC (DNA, M212, R12).
1 Not found.
2 Illegible.
3 Baltimore merchants.
4 Charles and Peter C. Buck.
5 Thomas Eastland.
6 Blankets of fine quality, of soft white wool with a stylized wheel design of colored yarn embroidered into two, sometimes all, corners.

Deed to Madison Hemp and Flax Spinning Company

[June 17, 1808]

[Indenture between William Macbean, Robert Frazier, Henry Clay, and James and David Maccoun, all of Fayette County, of the first part, and John Bradford and Luke Usher[1] of Fayette County and Thomas C. Howard of Madison County,[2] being the President and Directors of the Madison Hemp and Flax Spinning Company,[3] of the second part—by which for the sum of five shillings current money of Kentucky, paid and acknowledged, the first parties sell to the latter, in trust for the Madison County Hemp and Flax Spinning Company, and to their successors in office, a tract of fifty acres in Madison County on the waters of Silver Creek, the property having been conveyed to the first-named parties by William Tod and Margaret, his wife, under deed dated December 19, 1806, and conveyed to Tod by John Bryant and Mary, his wife, by deed of April 1, 1799, recorded in the Clerk's Office of Madison County. Title warranted only against claimants through or under the first-named parties. Signatures of Macbean, Frazier, Clay, and J. and D. Maccoun acknowledged before John D. Young, Clerk of Fayette County, June 18, 1808.]

Fayette County Court, Deed Book C, 250-51. Recorded also in Madison County Court, Deed Book F, 703-705.

1 Who came to Lexington from Baltimore in 1806 and operated in succession an umbrella factory, a brewery, a theater, and a hotel. When his hotel burned in 1819, he became steward of Transylvania University.

2 Formerly a clerk in the store of George Tegarden, of Lexington, Howard later became a wealthy merchant of Richmond, Kentucky.

3 The act of incorporation of the company had authorized the shareholders to meet in Lexington in March, 1808, to elect a president and directors.

Release of William Macbean from Mortgage

[June 18, 1808]

We do hereby acknowledge that we have received full satisfaction for debts secured by the within Mortgage,[1] and do release acquit and exonerate the said William Macbean therefrom, witness To the president and Directors of the M-H. M-Company[2]
Gent–

You will please to furnish Mr Macbean in his own name or in the name of such other as he may direct with the evidence of such shares as we may be entitled to in the Corporation excepting one hundred and eighty, of which you will make out one hundred in our joint names and the remaining eighty in the name of James D. MacCoun. Yrs

HENRY CLAY
J. & D. MACCOUN

Fayette County Court, Deed Book C, 251-52. Acknowledged and recorded in Fayette County on the same date; recorded also in Madison County Court, June 27, 1808 (Deed Book F, 705-706).

1 Not found.

2 Madison Hemp Mill Company.

Receipt to William Macbean for Shares of Stock

[June 18, 1808]

We do hereby acknowledge that we have received one hundred

shares in the Madison Hemp Mill Company of William Macbean for the purpose of indemnifying us against any debts contracts or engagements of the Madison H. M. Company, to which we may as former members of that Company be made liable if we should be so made so liable by the neglect of the said Macbean, Witness our hands this 18th. day of June 1808. Memo the above shares to be returned to Mr Macbean when the purposes of the indemnity are fulfilled. HENRY CLAY

J. & D. MACCOUN

Fayette County Court, Deed Book C, 252. Recorded by the Fayette County Clerk, June 18, 1808.

"Scaevola" to Dr. Anthony Hunn

TO DR. A. HUNN, EDITOR OF THE LAMP. [*ca.* June 18, 1808]

I have seen some fugitive numbers of the paper edited by you in Lincoln, and particularly those of the 31st May, and 7th June. The style, the sentiment, and the unprincipled assertions of this print, are such as might be expected from a legitimate descendant of the Goths and Vandals, as you are understood to be. But little known as you are to the people at large, it may not be improper to state, that you are an European by birth—a physician by profession; and what you were by practice, may be inferred from the fact of your abandoning the pursuit of medicine, which never fails to reward its meritorious disciples; and commencing the trade of slander and defamation. A temporary success in a limited section of the country, (a success resulting from the honest confidence of the people,) has given to your paper, a momentary eclat; which, however, is now gradually fading away, and will finally leave you to the scorn and contempt of all honest men. It is in vain that you resort to the vile pretext of discharging the contents of your own pistol, in your own hat, for the purpose of creating a belief, that you have been attempted to be assassinated.* It may serve for a time, to awaken the sympathies of a generous people in your behalf; but a detection of the fraud, (and no one can now seriously believe it,) will bring upon you the execrations of the whole community.

In your paper of the 31st ult. you announce, that Regulus is to make his appearance in the next Kentucky Gazette; and that you have positive proof of the real author of that production. Taking it as granted, that your statement is correct in this particular, and we have it by confession from your own mouth, that you have been guilty of the meanest treachery. How did you acquire this information? Not from the author; for whoever he may be,

I venture to pronounce, that he holds no communion, no kind of intercourse with you. But one other supposition then remains, and that is, that some of your base minions, stealing into the confidence of the unsuspicious youths of Mr. Bradford's office,[1] have obtained, no doubt under the most solemn injunctions and promises of secrecy, a knowledge of the fact, and then betrayed the trust reposed. You cannot, you dare not deny, abandoned and unprincipled as you are, that if you really possess the name of the author of Regulus, you got it in the manner I have suggested.

In your paper of the 7th June, after publishing Regulus, you offer what is termed by yourself, an answer to that piece. I presume the example was before you of that dauber, who, having delineated upon canvass, a form so wretched, and unlike any of the productions of nature, affixed to it a label, denoting the animal class to which it belonged. For it would have been impossible to have seen any thing responsive to Regulus in it, if you had not have had the goodness to tell us so. To the correct statement of facts; to the clear and perspicuous reasoning of Regulus, what do you offer in reply? A mutilated, garbled and distorted detail of circumstances; an attempt at reasoning without premises, and premises without deductions. And all this is delivered in a style of such coarse billingsgate, as to disgust the most illiterate. The elegant and gentlemanly expressions, "lie, devilment, insuperableness," &c. glitter throughout your composition, and manifest your capacity for ameliorating and ornamenting our scanty language. For shame, for shame, Doctor, take again to your ancient calling. You have mistaken your powers. Nature never designed you for a statesman, or a great political reformer. Retire into the precincts of your native gallipot, and revel and riot in your proper aliment, asafoetida. For sooner or later, your press and yourself, will be avoided, as the passing traveller avoids the carrion that annoys him as he journeys on his way. To descend to argue with you, is what I hope, Regulus will never do. Debased and degraded indeed, would Messrs. Allen and Clay be, if they or their friends paid any attention to your scurrility. This is the *first* and the *last* notice I shall take of you. The world knows, that

Superior virtue and superior sense,
To knaves and fools forever give offence.

SCAEVOLA.

*An anecdote of the Doctor not generally known deserves to be told. Riding home one night from Danville, and animated by the laudable ambition of becoming conspicuous, the expedient of raising the cry of assassination suggested itself. The success of his friend Street was before him.[2] The explosion of a pistol was

heard, and away went Gilpin's mare and away went his hat.[3] When the *affrighted* Doctor presented himself to some neighbouring family, his head was without its covering, and his mare without her bridle. His hat was sought for, and when found it was discovered to have two corresponding bullet holes, on opposite sides, perforated in such a manner as to render it singular how his head could escape. But upon examining his head critically it was found not to have been penetrated. Now either the Doctor must have discharged the piece himself, or if it were done by another his skull must be impervious, or when the ball came in contact with it, it must have kindly surmounted his head, and passed off quietly on the opposite side. Whether a skull bone may not be so thick as to repel a ball is a question of difficult solution, which I shall not pretend to decide, but submit, with great deference, to the *learned faculty.*

Lexington *Reporter,* June 18, 1808. Cf. above, Dr. Hunn's Reply, *ca.* June 7, 1808.
1 The office of the *Kentucky Gazette.*
2 Joseph M. Street was involved in several affrays as a result of his articles on the Spanish Conspiracy.
3 William Cowper, "The Diverting History of John Gilpin," first published in 1782.

Agreement with William Lytle

[June 18, 1808]

An agreement entered into this 18h. day of June 1808 Between William Lytle of the one part and Henry Clay of the other part, Witnesseth,

That the said Lytle doth covenant & agree to sell to the said Clay all his property in the Town of Lexington, consisting of the two large houses and lot & appurtenances fronting the public square and adjoining Maj Morrisons house and lot, lately occupied by John Downing as a Tavern, and the small house and lot adjoining them and adjoining Tibbatts[1] at present occupied by Maj Wagnon; and also the Stable and lot hitherto used for the purposes of the said Tavern on Market street,[2] adjoining the lot at present occupied by William T. Barry Esqr. All of which property the said Lytle covenants to deliver to the said Clay immediate possession of, except the afd. small house occupied by Wagnon, which he agrees to deliver to the said Clay in December 1810. And to the said property the said Lytle covenants to make to the said Clay a clear title, with general warranty, free from all incumbrance, on demand.

In consideration where of the said Clay doth covenant and agree to sell to the said Lytle all the property lying at and near Louisville conveyed to him by Fortunatus Cosby by deed bearing date the 29h. day of October 1807 and recorded in Jefferson County Court.

To which said property the said Clay covenants to make to the said Lytle a deed with general warranty, except for his interest in what has been generally termed the lower thousand acre tract or survey, upon which lower thousand acres there is a mortgage held by Connolly from John Campbell, and another held by from Connolly.[3] As to this lower thousand acres so encumbered, and possibly otherwise encumbered, the said Lytle agrees to take the title of the said Clay, such as it is; and that in no event whatever the said Clay is to be responsible therefor.

And should any part of the said property, for which as aforesaid the said Clay is to make a title with general warranty, be recovered from the said Lytle or his Assigns, the said Clay in that case is to pay the value of the part of which eviction shall take place in money.

In Testimony whereof the parties afd. hereunto Set their hands & seals.

WILLIAM LYTLE {L.S.}
HENRY CLAY {L.S.}

Sealed & Delivered
In presence of
NAT. G. S. HART

ADS, signed also by Lytle. Fayette Circuit Court, File 823.

1 The tavern, then known as "Traveller's Hall," was later called "The Kentucky Hotel." Thomas Tibbats was at this time a baker, later a soap and candle maker.

2 This stable, not the one newly built at this time (above, Agreement, June 15, 1808; below, Lease, June 24, and Agreement, September 3, 1808) was the subject of prolonged litigation between Clay and Robert Wickliffe from 1817 to 1834.

3 See above, Property Deed, October 29, 1807. The name here omitted was that of Charles De Warnsdorff.

"Regulus" in Reply to "A Farmer"

To the author of the piece signed "A Farmer." [*ca.* June 21, 1808]

THE respectable and imposing name you assume, and the occasional attempt at argument which you make, induces me to bestow an attention upon your publication which shall never be yielded to the ravings of the maniac editor of the Lamp,[1] or to the billingsgate of any other scribbler.

In this contest you are an unprovoked volunteer. Mr. Street had preferred certain charges against Mr. Allen.[2] They were answered in my first number, which was entirely defensive, without endeavoring in the smallest degree to lessen the character or pretensions of the two other candidates for the chief magistracy.—One of them, from his important services and his venerable years spent in obeying his country's calls, has an extensive claim upon her gratitude.[3] Whether that claim ought to be satisfied by the honours of the first office, in the gift of the people, is a question now before the public, and upon which I intend to remain perfectly silent. In adopting an anonymous signature I was influenced by the prevailing habit of the day, and by reasons sufficiently obvious. The correctness of a statement of fact, the propriety of a logical deduction, or the soundness of an argument, does not depend upon the high name or authority from which it flows. The effusions of a writer, under a fictitious name, rest upon their naked intrinsic merit, claiming attention as far only as they deserve it, and in their effect and force neither gaining, on the one hand, from the established reputation, nor losing, on the other, by the odium of the author. The object of the people is information and truth. —To them it is immaterial from whence they derive it. But responsibility ought to attach to any publication, under whatever name, it may be presented to the world. That responsibility I am prepared to meet, under any form, whenever it shall become necessary.

You attempt to impress on the public mind the false belief that I was unfriendly to the freedom of discussion, and insinuate that I am hostile to the freedom of the press. Not a sentence escaped me which, in the smallest possible degree, could authorise with any candid mind such an inference. To calumniate is one thing—to investigate another. The latter I expressly stated ought to be promoted, the former to be despised. Because a man suggests and complains of the licentiousness of calumniators is it to be asserted that he is unfriendly to the press? The only danger ever to be apprehended to this great palladium of our liberty, arises from its being committed to unworthy hands. When the time shall arrive that all parties are indiscriminately abused—that the press, instead of presenting useful and correct information to the people, teems with calumny—that public and private character is unjustly aspersed, and the most virtuous persons in the community are traduced and blackened, it is to be feared, that in some unlucky moment, all parties concurring, the unwise measure will be resorted to of abridging the freedom of the press.—There are but two correctives of the abuses to which it is incident; one is in the law, the other is in public sentiment. Legislative interference is extremely dangerous, and jeopardizes the very existence of the press; it has therefore been properly rejected ever since the repeal of the famous sedition law. The only remaining alternative is in the just sentiments of the people. To call upon them for the exercise of this high prerogative was the evident object of that part of my remarks from which you have chosen, without reason, to infer that I was inimical to free enquiry.

Having appeared the ally of the Western World and published

your address with the avowed purpose of making good the charges against Mr. Allen, I am warranted, from the whole complexion of your composition, in asserting that you are one of the aiders and abettors of that paper, and one of the faction which it has consolidated. Nor sir will the qualified approbation which you have chosen to express of its course deceive the people. Do you imagine that, by selecting a few obnoxious characters and holding them up to the public as the only persons who have been denounced by that paper, you can create the belief that, as to all others the editor has been silent, or has bountifully lavished upon them praise and commendation? But one course of calumny and detraction has characterized that paper since its first establishment. Instead of enumerating the republicans whose reputations have been assailed, let me rather ask who amongst them has escaped? The whole Democratic society in mass has been villified and abused. The crimes of disunion and treason have been imputed to them, although it was notorious that the great objects of that institution were the navigation of the Mississippi, and a change in the national councils—patriotic objects which they contributed to accomplish, and which have been effected, so much to the prosperity of America.[4] Not even the sanctuary of the grave has guarded the memory of departed worth from the aspersions of the W. World. One exception alone has distinguished its slanderous career, and that is that *not a federalist in Kentucky has been attacked.* No, the unsullied character of H. Marshall[5] has never been tarnished by the columns of the W. World. Whilst the judge of the federal court here[6] (who really had nothing further to do with Burr's discharge than to preserve decorum in court, and to keep the grand jury free from the intrusions of the attorney[7] for the U. States) has been charged over and over again with being accessory to his guilt, because the grand jury acquitted him for want of evidence. Chief Justice Marshall, by whose legal opinions he was actually acquitted,[8] has never been arraigned by the editor of the W. World. But the Chief Justice is a staunch federalist—he is the brother-in-law of H. Marshall, and it would have been very ungrateful in Mr. Street to criticize his conduct.

Becoming the advocate for the W. World you endeavour, in support of its accusation, to maintain two charges against Mr. Allen; the one applying to his Legislative conduct in the case of Sebastian,[9] the other to his professional conduct on the trial of Burr. The first shall be noticed in this number; the second in the next.[10]

Your friend Street had asserted that Mr. Allen had made or supported "a proposition to postpone the trial of Sebastian for twelve months; that he opposed enquiry; that he stood forth his champion," &c. All of this, in which there is not one word of truth, I denied. You complain that I have not made a plain, simple statement of facts. To an accusation unfounded in truth, what facts were to be opposed? That Sebastian requested a postponement, indefinate as to time, is not denied. That Mr. Allen proposed it —that he seconded such a proposition—that he advocated it—that he acquiesced in it, is positively denied. Street avers that a motion or proposition was actually made to postpone the enquiry twelve months. When this is controverted, you state it to be an *acquiescence* in Sebastian's request; and shortly after falsely construing this assumed acquiescence into an opposition for enquiry, you alledge that it *looks somewhat suspicious!* Do you, sir, who charge others with sophistry, and who have modestly set yourself up as the pure logician, pretend to offer such stuff as this to an enlightened people as correct reasoning? How did he acquiesce? Did he say so, did he vote it, or in imitation of your friend Street, this modern Lavater,[11] do you assert that he looked acquiescence? No, sir, you very well know that several propositions were made— Mr. M'Kee making one, Mr. Pope another[12]—that a diversity of opinion existed as to the manner of proceeding, and that upon this subject, and this subject alone, Mr. Allen wanted time to satisfy his mind as to the proper course to be taken. But upon some explanations being made he acquiesced not in Sebastian's request, but in the mode of prosecuting the enquiry recommended by others. The draft of Mr. Sebastian for his pension had not appeared at this time. It was rumoured about; but not until the enquiry took place before the committee was it exhibited. Was Mr. Allen to take as true this rumour, and, acting upon oath as a judge between the accused and his country, to make it the basis of his conduct? The precepts of justice are eternal and immutable; they pronounce that until conviction the presumption of innocence ought to be indulged, and the trial ought to be as circumspect in one man's case as in another. We have not yet learnt to hang a man without judge or jury. Will you dare, sir, still to persist in the assertion that Mr. Allen opposed the enquiry, after reading the letter of Genl. Hopkins which has been published?[13] His zeal in the investigation is known to have been surpassed by no other member of the legislature. He was associated with Mr. Allen on the committee of enquiry; he was an eye witness of his conduct there and in the House; he drew as is believed the report made by the committee and adopted by the house, and he unequivocally acquits Mr. Allen. After this his country will exonerate him from the charge of violating his duty as a legislator.

You profess to know the author of Regulus. I again repeat whoever he may be is immaterial as it respects the truth of his statements, or the force of his arguments. The supposed author it is well known has been marked out as a victim of the W. World faction. This I presume is the cloud you alledge is suspended over his head. Take care of your own when the storm bursts. Do not flatter yourself that the beams of popular favour, which you hope will shortly cease to shine upon him, will irradiate your brow. You are known, sir; and do not provoke a removal of that veil under which you fondly expect you are shrouded from the public indignation.

REGULUS.

Lexington *Kentucky Gazette,* June 21, 1808. In the Lexington *Reporter,* June 11, 1808, an anonymous writer, signing himself as "A Farmer," had attacked "Regulus" in an article addressed "To the People of Kentucky."

1 Anthony Hunn.

2 Joseph M. Street and John Allen.

3 General Charles Scott.

4 Sympathy for France and bitter opposition to the administration of President Washington, particularly in regard to foreign policy, had led to the organization of Democratic societies, first in Philadelphia, then elsewhere over the country. Under the leadership of John Bradford, John Breckinridge, Thomas Todd, and Thomas Bodley, the Lexington (also called the Kentucky) Democratic Society had been established in August, 1793, and at least two others had appeared in the state. The local groups, corresponding with others in Pennsylvania and Tennessee, had castigated the Federalists and collaborated with the French emissary, Edmond Genet, while devoting attention mainly to the question of opening the Mississippi River to western trade.

5 Humphrey Marshall.

6 Harry Innes.

7 Joseph Hamilton Daveiss.

8 At the trial in Richmond, Virginia.

9 Judge Benjamin Sebastian.

10 Below, *ca.* July 9, 1808.

11 John Gaspar Lavater (1741-1801), a theologian born in Zurich, became widely known through his volumes on physiognomy, published in several English translations in the late eighteenth century.

12 John Pope had introduced a substitute accepted in lieu of the original resolution presented by Samuel McKee, calling for investigation of Judge Sebastian's conduct. McKee, born and educated in Virginia, had begun the practice of law at Somerset, Pulaski County, Kentucky, about 1800, and in 1801 moved to Lancaster, Garrard County. He was a member of the State legislature for several terms both before and after service in the United States House of Representatives from 1809 to 1817.

13 Samuel Hopkins to John Allen, May 16, 1808, printed in *Kentucky Gazette,* June 14, 1808.

Receipt from William Pollock

22nd June 1808

Recd. fr Mr. Henry Clay Check on the Insurance Co. for Seventy Six Dollars in full for the hire of a negroe WM POLLOCK

ADS. DLC-TJC, 2d Series, vol. 7.

To Edward Shoemaker

Sir Lexington 23 June 1808.

I received your favor of the 24h. May.[1] I beg you Sir to believe that your business has had my attention, and as is really the case has given me a great deal of concern.

When Mr. Brown[2] left this Country he placed in my hands two demands which when collected were to be applied to the discharge of your claim on Caldwell.[3] One of them was an order for $100 on Mr. Jordan,[4] which he said he had accounts against Mr. B. to balance, and which therefore he never did pay; and the other was a Judgment for £100 this money with several years int. upon it. This Judgment had been under the management of Col. Tho. Todd not under my own. When I had the pleasure of seeing you in Philadelphia,[5] and indeed when I gave Mr. Gill[6] the memorandum, I had no doubt but that the amount of this Judgment, principal and interest would be collected by Col. Todd or his representative at the Bar. But I find now that the person against whom it is, Mr. John Smith, who is a relation of Mr. Brown, sets up some stale demands against that gentleman with which he says he will discharge the Judgment. I have no doubt in my own mind that Mr. Brown (of whose honor no one who knows him can doubt) fully believed that both of those claims would have been long since paid. And I am well persuaded that the offsets claimed by his debtors have no foundation in justice.

Prior to the receipt of your favor I had written to Mr. Brown giving him a statement of this matter.[7] He may possibly instruct me to enforce payment of the Judgment, or he may make some other provision for you. Perhaps it will be advisable for you to address a letter to him at New. Orleans. When I hear from him (which I have not yet done) you shall know the result. In the mean time I am Sir Yr. mo. ob. Servt HENRY CLAY

ALS. Owned by J. Winston Coleman, Jr., Lexington, Kentucky. Addressed to Shoemaker in Philadelphia.

1 Not found. 2 James Brown.

3 Phillip Caldwell. 4 John Jordan, Jr.

5 Clay must have visited that city in March, 1807, following his brief term in the United States Senate.

6 Presumably associated with Shoemaker's firm.

7 Letter not found.

To James Taylor

Dr Sir Lexington 23 June 1808

I have not yet the letter which you addressed to me by the Mail.[1] There is no doubt but that we can get the Ejectment delayed at the ensuing term.[2] Fowler told me that his object was that if he cast you at Richmond to have it in his power to get possession of the property at once, or to compel you at least to proceed in the investigation of your other claims, so that there might not be unnecessary procrastination after the issue of the suit in Virginia. It is possible I shall find means to continue the ejectment beyond the Nov. term, and until the decision of the suit in Richmond.

I do not see that it is necessary for you to have any of your claims laid down, unless you have the senior patent upon some one of them, which I believe you have not. Fowler can attain no object by having it shewn in the Ejectment that there a [*sic*] number of contending claims.

Even if he gets a Judgt. in the Ejectmt. I have no doubt that by filing a bill suggesting the pendency of the suit at Richmond the Court will enjoin any proceedings upon it until the result of that suit is known. Yr. friend HENRY CLAY

ALS. OCHP-Whelpley Autographs. Addressed: "Col. James Taylor, New Port (K)."

1 Not found.

2 The case, probably involving John Fowler, has not been found.

Lease of Traveller's Hall to Cuthbert Banks

[June 24, 1808]

Articles of Lease Between Henry Clay & Cuthbert Banks.

The said Clay having purchased the property in Lexington known by the name of Traveller's Hall doth hereby covenant and agree to lease the same to the said Banks, that is to say the two large houses adjoining each other lately occupied by John Downing as a Tavern, and the small house at present in the possession of Majr. Wagnon, with the lot and appurtenances (not including however the stable & lot adjoining the lot of Wm. T. Barry) [1] for the term of five years to commence on the first day of September next; and the said Clay further covenants with the said Banks to deliver him possession of the said property on the said first day of September, except the said small house occupied by Wagnon, possession of which he covenants to deliver upon the determination of the said Wagnon's lease.

In consideration whereof the said Banks covenants to pay to the said Clay the following rents to wit: on the first day of September 1809 the sum of eight hundred dollars; during the succeeding year the sum of nine hundred dollars, to be paid quarterly; and during the three succeeding years the sum of one thousand dollars per annum, to be paid quarterly. And the said Banks further covenants to pay not exceeding eighty dollars annually on each first day of September during the said term of five years, for the purpose of ensuring the said houses against fire. And should the said Banks fail to pay the said rent as it becomes due in the manner aforesaid, it is covenanted and agreed that the said

Clay may distrain therefor; and furthermore if he the said Clay thinks proper, on such default of payment, it is understood & agreed that he is at liberty to reenter & reoccupy the demised premises, & thereby determine this lease.

And whereas the said Clay hath reduced the rent upon the aforesaid property for the purpose of obtaining the personal attention of the said Banks to the said Tavern, and with the view of raising its reputation as a stand: It is therefore further covenanted and agreed between the parties that the said Banks shall not, under the condition of forfeiting this lease and giving the said Clay a right of re-entry, rent out the said property or any part thereof to any other person, but that he shall bestow his own personal attention thereon, except during the three summer months, when he is at liberty to go to the Olympian Springs,[2] by furnishing a good substitute to superintend the said Tavern. And should the said Banks die it is agreed that this lease shall determine upon that event happening, in which case rents are to be paid after the rates aforesaid up to the time of his death.

The said Clay further covenants and agrees to have made on the said lot the following improvements, that is to say, to have a stable built not less than Twenty eight feet by fifty, a smoak house, spring house, and a back portico and to have the upper story of the New house built by Ro. Bradley completed. These improvements he covenants to have made with all reasonable despatch. But it is expressly understood that no objection is to be made as to the commencement or payment of the rents on account of the time when or manner in which the said improvements shall be compleated.

And it is further covenanted and agreed by and between the parties aforesaid that the said Banks shall, at the end of the said five years, have the liberty of renting the property aforesaid two years longer at the sum of twelve hundred dollars per annum, & by paying the premium of insurance thereon against fire.

And the said Banks further covenants that upon the determination of this lease he will surrender the property hereby demised to the said Clay his heirs or assigns in good tenantable order & condition, and as much so as he the said Clay puts it in, natural decays excepted.

In Testimony whereof the parties parties [*sic*] afd. have hereunto set their hands & Seals this 24 June 1808.

Sealed & Delivered — CUTHB: BANKS {L.S.}
In presence of — HENRY CLAY {L.S.}
ROBERT MILLER
MOSES COX JR.[3]

[Endorsements][4]

In consideration of the improvements not having been completed as early as was contemplated it is agreed that the rent instead of commencing on the first day of Septr. 1808 and the lease on that day, shall be considered as commencing on the first day of Decr. 1808, and that the first day of each succeeding Decr. during the continuance of this lease shall be considered as terminating the preceding year. Witness our hands & seals 1 Decr. 1808

HENRY CLAY {L.S.}
CUTHB: BANKS {L.S.}

In addition to the rent which the said C Banks covenants to pay to the said H. Clay in and by the second clause on the first page of this lease he the said Banks covenants & agrees to pay to the said Clay the further sum of forty eight dollars per annum during the continuance of this lease payable in like time & manner as the said clause specifies for the payment of the residue of the said rent; which sum of forty eight dollars payable as aforesaid, is in consideration of the Chandeliers which the said Clay has purchased for the use of the Tavern, it being the interest only upon the price he paid for them.[5] 24 Decr. 1808. Witness our seals.

Attest CUTHB: BANKS {L.S.}
THOMAS C. GRAVES HENRY CLAY {L.S.}

ADS, signed also by Banks. Fayette Circuit Court, File 823.
1 Cf. above, Agreement, June 18, 1808.
2 Banks had purchased this resort from Col. Thomas Hart in 1807.
3 Possibly of Barren County, Kentucky.
4 Both AES, signed also by Banks.
5 See below, Agreement, November 9, 1808.

Bill of Complaint against Joseph M. Street

[July, 1808]

Henry Clay complains of Joseph M Street in custody &c. of a plea that he the said defendant render to the plaintiff the sum of seventy dollars which to him he owes and from him unjustly detains: For that defendant on the day of in the year of our Lord 180 at the Circuit aforesaid by his certain promissory note subscribed with his hand, (and which being lost or mislaid the plaintiff is unable to make protest of) the date whereof is the same day and year aforesaid, promised and bound himself[1] to the said plaintiff the sum of seventy dollars on or before the first day of July 1807: Yet the said deft tho' often required the said sum of money or either of them to the said plaintiff to pay hath not paid; but the same to him to pay hath hitherto refused and still doth refuse to the damage of the plaintiff $70 and therefore he brings suit &c. H. CLAY p p. [*sic*]

Pledges J Doe
R. Roe

[Jury verdict on verso]

ADS. Franklin Circuit Court, File 73 (1808). The case was settled in October, 1808, when the jury found for the plaintiff, awarding him the amount of the debt plus $5.25 damages.

[1] Several lines at this point deleted from the manuscript, apparently by Clay, refer to another unpaid note for $70 given by Street, July 1, 1807, to John Wood, who had assigned it to Clay (see above, Wood to Clay, December 4, 1806).

From Anthony Hunn

FELLOW CITIZENS; [*ca.* July 2, 1808]

My name has latterly been brought before you, sullied and mangled with the most savage barbarity. It is with reluctance, that I appear before you, to plead my cause, since my defence, must of necessity, assume the appearance of self-praise. But delicacy must give way to necessity. That reputation which I have acquired by a successful practice of 15 years in Kentucky, and by which alone, I did, and *now do*, maintain a helpless family, has been poisoned by the breath of a monster, under the name of *Scaevola.* I hasten to the relief of my honor: *truth* is my antidote.

I was born in Europe, where I received an academical education —witness my diploma, in which I was publicly honored with the appellation of Doctor of Medicine and Surgery—(See documents, No. 1.) An innate love of liberty, and the just renown of the American Republic, not necessity, winged me across the Atlantic. I became an American citizen. This title I claim, not only by law, but by the usefulness of my practical services to the community. To convert my European birth into a reproach, as *Scaevola* has done, is to vilify the noble characters of a Lee, Stuben, La Fayette, etc. and of your forefathers, who all came from Europe. This is the first time that my character has been measured by the place of my birth! Esteem is the birth-right of usefulness. Leaving all my relations in Europe, I have found many brothers in America, and —I boastingly proclaim it—never lost a friend! A majority of such "Scaevolas" in Congress, must inevitably curse us with another *alien law.*

For several years, I lived in Bourbon county, on my own plantation, where my chief support was an extensive medical practice. It maintained me plentifully, and whether honorably or not, the testimony of Dr. Sam. Brown will shew, with whom I had the honor of being intimately acquainted, and who, on the eve of my removal to Danville, pressed his recommendation upon me. Dr. *Ridgely Warfield* sen. and Todd,[1] in Paris, will likewise bear witness of the successes of my medical practice, and have seen me operate as surgeon. How far I was supported with honor by my medical skill, since my removal from Bourbon, and during my residence in this neighborhood, the voice of my neighbors must decide. (See No. 2) I never forsook my medical practice; and it has so little forsaken me, that all along, to this very hour, with the assistance of two physicians, I could not satisfy all the demands that are made for my medical services. The public paper, entitled "The Lamp," has never interfered with my practice as medicus. I *have no controul* over that paper. To ascribe all the pieces printed in its columns to me, is the most baseless assumption. I own, I am the author of several political pieces in the Lamp, in which I maintain, that no sovereignty is just but that of the people—that a representative is a public servant, *no ruler*—that a strict responsibility of all our public servants, is necessary to prevent our republic from sinking to the level of English corruption—that our constitutions, though they certainly create the best government on earth, are yet susceptible of much amelioration. My plans for such amendments, I have humbly laid before a self-ruling people.[2] Aided perhaps, by those publications, and certainly through the bold, republican principles maintained in the Lamp, and so congenial with the sentiments of the free-born Kentuckian, that paper soon enjoyed an unexampled patronage of the people; and so far is that patronage from "sinking," that never before the subscription for the Lamp has *increased* so fast, as it does at this very moment.

One of the avowed principles of the Lamp is, to "flash its fullest blaze into the faces of venality and corruption." The all-corrupting lawyer aristocracy in Kentucky, was accordingly detected, and many public sinners bled on the altar of public detestation: many more tremble at the approach of light. *"Hinc illae lacrymae!"* That makes Mr. Clay so sorry, and Mr. Scaevola so mad!! But there is no help for that! He dabbles in "scandal," who commits a scandalous action; not he who exposes it to public indignation. It is "billingsgate" to *tell* a lie; but to *detect* a liar is meritorious.

It is the duty of an independent American press, strictly and impartially to scrutinize the characters of public candidates. Without the right to do so, we must be slaves; and without the exercise of that right, we would *deserve* to be slaves. Mr. Allen was objected to as a candidate for the office of governor. Mr. Henry Clay, under the false name of "Regulus," undertook to defend Mr. Allen, and himself into the bargain. The information that Mr. H. Clay was the author of the piece, was received by a gentleman of veracity, *who never promised to keep it a secret.* This, the raging Scaevola calls "treachery." By what means did Mr. Clay find out, that I was the author of the answer to Regulus? But why is Mr. Scaevola, or which is the same, Mr. Regulus, or which is the same, Mr. Henry Clay, so enraged at his detection? Because he is ashamed of his work? Yes! If the card table and punch bowl have left one drop of blood in the face of Mr. Clay, he ought to blush the deepest red, for the horrid principles and glaring falsehoods contained in his piece. What else but the fear of public detestation, can make him shrink from the public eye?

The Editors of the Reporter have professed, and all along, maintained the characters of impartiality. Scaevola has introduced several unconnected expressions from the answer to Regulus, which is ascribed to me. Not till this answer has been inserted in the Reporter,*[3] its readers can judge with impartiality, whether the arguments contained in that answer be conclusive or not.

Fellow citizens! I have read in the pages of ancient history, and actually beheld in the tyrannic struggles of modern Europe, by what insidious means an unsuspecting people may be wheedled into subjection. You, native Americans, inattentive perhaps, to the approaches of aristocratical tyranny, because they are *gradual;* you may profit by the warnings of an European, who has marked down the steps of political corruption, when they were before his eyes. The desire of perpetuating the blessings of liberty to my children, and to your children, has prompted me to write in the Lamp. The enemies of liberty have never dared to encounter my principles, because they knew, that they were the principles of the people. Unable to meet me on the field of argumentation, they attack my private character as a physician: like a cunning general, who converts his siege into a blockade, to *starve* that fortress, which he cannot take by assault. I have offered proposals of a popularized medical science, adapted to the capacity of every common English scholar;[4] by which I hope to become eminently useful to you and your children. My enemies fear, that the emoluments arising from this publication, might procure me leisure to prosecute my political labours, of which they already too keenly feel the effects. This alone, can be the cause, why, instead to contest against my political principles, they attack, ruffian-like, my private character as a physician. Read, if you please, the documents annexed to this address, and then peruse again, the mad piece of Scaevola, and then say, if you can find in the whole English language another name for him, than that of a—*Liar.* ANTHONY HUNN.

[Two appended documents testify to Dr. Hunn's medical practice, and a third certifies that his hat was bullet-pierced.]

Lexington *Reporter,* July 2, 1808. Addressed: "TO THE PEOPLE." Cf. above, "Scaevola" to Hunn, *ca.* June 18, 1808.

1 Dr. Frederick Ridgely; Dr. Elisha Warfield; and either David or John Todd, both doctors in Paris, Kentucky.

2 No file of the *Lamp* is known to exist.

3 Hunn's article dated *ca.* June 7, 1808 was not reprinted in the Lexington *Reporter.* In the note here indicated the editor stated that he was unable to reprint all political disputation.

4 No such publication has been found.

Advertisement of Land Auction

[July 6, 1808]

[Henry Clay and Thomas Hart, Trustees,[1] advertise a public auction at Traveller's Hall, in Lexington, beginning at noon on the second Monday in September next, to dispose of the following properties in accordance with the terms of their trust: one equal moiety of 5,000 acres on Bank Lick Creek, part of 6,000 acres patented to William Jones, which has been conveyed by Captain John Fowler, under deed of general warranty; and one moiety of 1,000 acres in the boundary set apart for officers of the Virginia Continental Line, lying on Russell's Creek,[2] conveyed by Judge Todd[3] under deed of general warranty.]

Lexington *Kentucky Gazette,* July 12, 1808.

1 For John Jordan, Jr. See above, Deed of Trust, September 13, 1806.

2 In Green County.

3 Thomas Todd.

"Regulus" to the People

TO THE PEOPLE. [*ca.* July 9, 1808]

REGARDLESS of the attempts made to withdraw your attention from the subject of these numbers, and to fix it upon their supposed author, I proceed to execute the promise made in my last, by shewing that the objection to Mr. Allen, drawn from his professional conduct on the trial of Burr, possesses no validity. It is necessary to bear in mind, that nothing is more foreign from my intention than to lessen, in the smallest degree, the just pretensions of either of the other candidates for the office of chief magistrate. Upon this gentleman the W. World and some of its partizans have wreaked all their vengeance. Against him they have marshalled and combined their forces in hostile array, and he alone is exposed to the misrepresentations and calumnies which they are busily propagating. To check the torrent of defamation; to develope the base arts of those who, under the specious garb of public good, are seeking to gratify the worst of passions; and to assist in giving to public sentiment an unbiassed direction are the motives which have actuated me in these publications.

I further premise that no man entertains a more despicable opinion of Aaron Burr than I do. Whether his object was disunion, revolution in Louisiana, or conquest of Mexico, or all of them, there can be no doubt of his attrocious guilt. And I sincerely regret with every other good citizen that he has hitherto escaped with impunity. It will be seen hereafter that in these admissions there is nothing inconsistent with the position, that in the fall 1806, for the want of information, a general opinion prevailed that the charge against him was groundless.

The transactions at Frankfort, the evidence exhibited against Burr there, and the state of the public mind at the time he was arraigned in that place, have been so blended with subsequent events that it is impossible to form a correct judgment upon the charge in question against Mr. Allen, without making an accurate discrimination. There were two attempts made by the attorney for the U. States to arraign Burr in this country. The course which he pursued for this purpose was by application to the court for grand juries to be ordered, with a view to lay before them the proper indictments or informations. In the first instance a Grand Jury was directed, and a very able one selected. Much curiosity was excited by the procedure, and crowds flocked to Frankfort to witness the trial. When the court set and expectation was at its height, the prosecutor upon his own motion, without the smallest interference from Burr or his counsel, obtained the dismission of this Jury. Great disappointment of course ensued with those who expected to have seen an interesting trial; and from this period an opinion was taken up, that the prosecution was without foundation. The address of Burr, his commanding though diminutive appearance, the extraordinary spectacle of beholding a personage who had been the second man only in the nation, and that personage a stranger in our country, arraigned at the bar as a public culprit, excited with all at Frankfort, sympathies which no candid man can deny. On the second trial a Grand Jury having again been summoned, at the instance of the attorney of the U. States, he laid before them his indictments against Adair and Burr, not for treason, but for a military expedition against Mexico. They remained in their room for a day or two examining all the witnesses sent to them by the attorney, and sending for others, (amongst them the editors of the W. World) not named by him; and after the utmost deliberation, returned the indictments "not true bills;" and presented to the court the address, which has been published, declaring that there was no evidence offered to them authorising any apprehension for the public safety or tranquillity. The effect this had upon the great bulk of those persons who were at the seat of government, cannot be denied. With very few exceptions, the opinion formed on the first trial was confirmed, and Burr believed to be persecuted. On this last trial, the attorney professed himself to be entirely ready, witnesses for the government alone were examined, and yet an honest and intelligent Jury, not only heard no evidence to convict, but heard none warranting even alarm. This decision happened on the 5th December, and it was not until *eight or ten days after,* that the President's proclamation reached this country, and gave a different tone to public feeling & sentiment. It was still later that the letter in cypher from Burr to Wilkinson,[1] and other documents and evidence were submitted to the world; and it ought to be recollected that it is, from these only that the opinion, now prevailing of Burr's guilt was formed.

Let us now enquire what part Mr. Allen bore in these proceedings at Frankfort. It is seen that the incipient stages only of trial had taken place. The accused was not put upon his final trial before his peers. But it is only upon the final trial of a culprit that the great efforts of the advocate are to be made. Before an indictment is found by the grand jury his duty is limited and circumscribed. If any unusual steps are attempted by the prosecutor, the advocate attending to the interest of his client, is bound to oppose them. The extraordinary motion made [*sic*] by Mr. Daviess to permit him to go into the apartment of the grand jury, and interrogate the witnesses. This was opposed, as an innovation in our criminal code, and as a reflection upon the understanding of the jury. The court decided against it. And I appeal to you Fellow Citizens to say, if you have ever known an instance of the commonwealth's attorney being admitted into the jury room, after they have retired, to interrogate witnesses. No! the judge himself dare not go there. The attorney is sometimes suffered (but even that he cannot claim as a right) to go into their chamber for the purpose of throwing a presentment or indictment into proper form, but never to decide or interrogate witnesses for the jury. Mr. Daviess was however indulged in drawing up a list of interrogatories, and sending it to the jury—an indulgence believed never to have been granted before. Thus was Burr discharged, or rather the prosecution failed, (for he never was even in custody in this country,) not by any eloquent address, ingenious argument, or subtle management of his counsel, but because there was NO EVIDENCE to convict him.

In my first number[2] I had stated that as late as the 10th Dec. 1806, but one opinion existed in this country as to the charge against him. That period was mentioned because it was subsequent to his trial, and previous [to] the arrival of the President's proclamation. This position is controverted by the author of "A Farmer,"[3] who politely pronounces it one of the most gross insults to the good sense of the people ever penned. Let us examine the remarks by which he attempts to support the alledged misrepresentation. He states that early in 1805, the public prints began to teem with *suspicions* against Burr—that from the period of his intrigue about the Presidency, he began to sink, and in 1805 was universally beheld as a fallen and desperate character—that the rapidity of his movements in the West excited the most *alarming suspicions* relative to his real object—and that in the fall 1806, a general belief prevailed that he was engaged in *some* project inimical to the Union. But he admits that the real object of this adventurer, whatever it was, *seemed to be veiled in the utmost mystery*. Supposing every thing thus advanced to be true, (and I am free to admit that prior to the first trial of Burr conjecture and suspicion was busy in quest of his objects,) was counsel, acting upon the basis of these suspicions and rumours, to refuse to defend him? Is suspicion to produce condemnation? Is it a ground for denying the common rights of a fair trial, which the constitution carefully guarantees to the meanest culprit?[4] Are counsel, because a man covers with a mysterious veil his enterprizes, to reject an application to defend him? The inference deducible from the reasoning of the Farmer is this, that whenever a general prejudice is excited against an individual, whenever *suspicion* has widely diffused its poison, the person implicated is to be deprived of counsel. Let me suppose a case—the Western World and the Lamp combine to destroy the reputation of a citizen. They commence their operations by assailing his political character—they proceed to attack his moral principles, and at length ascribe to him the most infamous crimes. It is in vain that he appeals to the rectitude of his former life. The region of truth is less extensive than the region of slander: the latter moves with electric rapidity, whilst the gait of the former is slow and tardy. Credulity is a common error, and we often believe, upon the slightest evidence, the blackest crimes. The editors of the papers mentioned have two presses at their command, and have time and inclination to pursue the meditated object. The public mind thus biassed and prejudiced, their victim is *dragged* (to use the hacknied term of one of them) before a tribunal of justice. An intelligent and independent jury is collected, but their minds are already unalterably fixed, and anathemas await them if they do not convict. Are counsel awed by these denunciations, to be silenced, and to resign to an unmerited fate the unfortunate person thus unjustly surrounded by popular odium? The spirit in which they would be condemned, for vindicating such a cause, is ready to pronounce sentence against the immortal Curran for his efforts in the defence of the persecuted patriots of Ireland;[5] and to say that the defender of a Sidney and Hampden,[6] is a traitor. It is of no consequence to urge that Burr *now* appears to have been guilty. *An innocent man might have been attended with more suspicious circumstances than those under which Burr appeared in November and December* 1806: and I repeat that his counsel are to be judged by what was believed *at the time*.

When General Moreau passed through this country, the rumours that preceded and followed him cannot be forgotten.[7] The public prints *teemed with suspicions*. He appeared since his exile to be a *fallen* man. His real object seemed to be profoundly veiled. At one time it was said that he was the partizan of Burr, and that his enterprizes were to be renovated. At another time he was charged with being the secret emissary of Bonaparte, engaged to survey Louisiana and to prepare maps, &c. for invasion. These idle tales have died away, and the hero of Hohenlinden is perhaps at this moment employed in the innocent pursuits of domestic life. Had he been arrested at Louisville as the accessary of Burr, or the clandestine agent of Bonaparte, ought counsel, by refusing to defend him, to have brought upon their country the reproach of denying to a stranger ignorant of our laws and our language the benefit of a fair trial?

The objection made to the counsel who were engaged for Burr is founded upon a principle, subversive of justice and involving the most dangerous consequences. According to it the accused is to undergo two trials, one before the attorney, to whom he makes application to defend him, and the other before the court. If the attorney condemns him, he is then to be without counsel, and the effect may easily be perceived of the whole bar (for if one ought to refuse all ought to refuse to appear for him) thus prejudging a cause. Such is not the dictate of humanity, or the spirit of our mild laws. They pronounce that the temple of justice is accessible to all. Before its altar the accused presents himself without bias or prejudice. Upon the doctrine of the Farmer every counsellor is a judge, before whom the accused is to be tried, and not until he received his acquittal there, is he to have the advantage of legal advice and assistance. And indeed if he does acquit him, and the jury afterwards acquit him, if it should even subsequently appear by evidence not before *either of them* that the party was guilty, both the jury and attorney are to be condemned. Mr. Farmer appears to have forgotten that the province of the attorney is to reason, to argue, to illustrate; the province of the court and jury to decide. But how is this new jurisdiction assigned to attornies to be exercised—how are they to try their clients to know whether they may appear for them? They cannot coerce the attendance of witnesses on either side. They can present no indictment; impannel no jury, grand or petit. *Suspicions, rumour, mystery* then, according to the Farmer, are to be substituted for indictment, witness, jury, sentence; and these infallible guides are to be conclusive upon counsel!

Thus, fellow-citizens, having shewn that whatever may have been the state of the public mind, Mr. Allen was justified in becoming counsel for Burr, upon the principles of the constitution, from the benign spirit of our laws and the nature of public justice, I now undertake to make good my assertion that as late as the 10th December, 1806, the opinion was general that Burr was innocent of the charge against him. I never did assert that there were no rumours or suspicions against him. I know that they were various, but from their very variety they were not calculated to make an impression. It was said that the canal at the falls was his object—that he was about to settle in Tennessee to get into congress—that he was going to purchase out the whole of the stock of the insurance company[8]—that he was going to Ouachita,[9] &c. &c. Indeed report after report succeeded each other in idle and endless succession. But the people of this country have too much good sense to place implicit confidence in every report that is heard. Nor are the unsupported suggestions of the Western World yet taken as oracular. The public mind was drawn to no point, settled upon no opinion, prior to the trial at Frankfort. Then a definite charge was adduced, and general attention attracted. How his trial eventuated, and the effect that the result produced, has been noticed. I state these facts as conclusive evidence that at Frankfort, where an immense concourse of people had assembled and the Legislature was in session, the opinion prevailed that he was innocent.

1st. Whilst attending on his trials he was invited to dine out at several of the most respectable houses in the place, and amongst others at the governor's.

2. Visits were interchanged between him and the most distinguished members of the Legislature.

3. After the first trial, and whilst he was attending on the second, he was invited by the House of Representatives to take a seat within their chamber, among the members—a mark of respect scarcely ever before shewn to a *private citizen.*

4. Upon his last trial two general officers, members of the legislature, who had served with Burr in the revolution, and who believed him innocent, waited upon him at his lodgings and attended him to court. And

5. After the last trial, and as late as about the 7th or 8th Dec. 1806, he was honored with a public ball, at which a number of the members of the legislature was present, and the governor officiated as a manager.

Is it possible for any frank man to hesitate in believing that all these marks of civility were shewn to Burr under the full conviction of his innocence? Will the W. World dare insinuate that the Governor, the Legislature, the citizens of Frankfort who extended their hospitality to him, or who attended the ball, male and female, were partizans of Burr? No! That governor and legislature, when Jefferson's proclamation arrived, with a promptitude that does them honour, proceeded to pass and execute the most effective laws to defeat the enterprizes of Burr; and at every commanding point on the Ohio were stationed troops to intercept the passage of his boats.

Fellow-citizens inquire, read, think, decide for yourselves and say whether the charges against Mr. Allen are not made from malice, unsupported by facts, and urged for base and electioneering purposes. REGULUS.

Lexington *Reporter,* July 9, 1808, reprinted from the *Kentucky Gazette.* The same issue of the *Reporter* carried an attack on "Regulus" addressed "To the People," by "Franklin Penn." See above, "Regulus" in Reply, *ca.* June 21, 1808.

1 The letter of July 29, 1806. See Walter Flavius McCaleb, *The Aaron Burr Conspiracy* (Expanded Edition, New York, 1936), 68-69.

2 See above, "Regulus" to the People, *ca.* May 31, 1808.

3 "A Farmer" to "The People of Kentucky," Lexington *Reporter,* June 11, 1808.

4 Editorial note quoting Constitutional provisions has here been deleted.

5 John Philpot Curran, Irish politician and judge, attained renown for his speeches in behalf of Lord Edward Fitzgerald and other defendants in the state trials between 1794 and 1803.

6 Convicted of complicity in the Rye House Plot of 1683, Algernon Sidney was beheaded and John Hampden imprisoned.

7 After having been banished by Napoleon, General Jean Victor Marie Moreau, renowned for his leadership in defeat of the Austrians at Hohenlinden in 1800, lived for several years at Morrisville, Pennsylvania. His name was sometimes mentioned in connection with the Burr episode, and late in 1807 popular interest was stirred by a journey he made through the West to New Orleans. After the destruction of Napoleon's army in Russia, Moreau returned to Europe where, until his death in September, 1813, he served as adviser to the Allies on the conduct of the war.

8 The Kentucky Insurance Company.

9 Where the Bastrop lands were located.

From James Smith, Jr.

My Friend Philada. July 9h 1808—

I have to acknowledge your favour of 4 June[1] With respect to Major Davenport[2] I have received the Letters you allude to from himself and his friends, and am very sorry on both our Accounts that he has met with so great a loss—When I wrote to you I was not apprised of his situation—I have written him some time ago advising him to take the very measures that I find you say is taking [*sic*] And as he is a Man so well esteemed I make no doubt he will get up again—He owes me a large sum and if he is favoured with Health I have no doubt he will pay me as I believe him to be perfectly honest—

I am very certain that I inclosed Millers[3] Notes to you I have made a memorandum of it—I paid the postage of the letter at the time & have no doubt but you will find them—His acknowledging the Debt will answer the purpose if they are not found as they were indorsed payable to you—I am very much at a loss to determine with respect to his [*sic*] taking the property he offers —It will not suit me. I shall not know what to do with it, having already more real property than Debts or money—and the latter I want very much & cannot pay my Debts without it—I find your advise is to take it—but the Question is—what shall I do with it?— Before I determine on this I want to have from you a particular description of it—the size & dimension of the Lott & House or Houses—whether it is in your opinion an increasing property or otherwise—an old House or a new one &c—and the very lowest price he will take—Also—if I agree to take it & get a proper Deed— whether you think it will be in your power to sell it for me by giving time—accepting a part of the money—and take the premises as security & what loss, or whether any I should sustain—Also— the highest Rent that can be obtained for it on a lease to a good Tenant that will pay punctually—I declare to you that I have been so liberal in crediting, & so wretchedly deceived & disappointed— that I am much afraid in the winding up that I shall find myself worth very little more than when I began after a long toil & slaving in business—It is very discouraging & the times are gloomy indeed —Answers to the above Queries will determine me whether to take that property or not—If you really think there is a risque—I certainly had better accept it & will write you an answer immediately —but if he is paying others & wanting to put this property on me it is not fair—His Creditors gave him time, but I did not make a memorandum at the time—but I think the time as [*sic*] expired at least for the first & perhaps the second payment. As you seem to doubt his resources—I will leave it with yourself should any thing happen in the meantime—before I can hear from you & return an answer—If the property after I have taken it can be turned into money in any reasonable time & without much loss—is the Question? The sums you have remitted me are correct—but part being credited to Jordans[4] Accot & part to Millers & others—I looked over them—The post Note of Barry & Garretts is to their Accot which they should have sent themselves—& they should send me the ballance—I have written to them & if I do not shortly recieve it I must send you their Note and accot for collection—I hope you will recieve the money from Owens[5] & give me a Statement of their Notes & what they have paid that I may endeavour to get the remainder from W W Smith[6] which they have disputed—Having some other business with T Norwell—I have recieved the inclosed Letter from him[7] in answer to what I mentioned to him in mine—which was to get him if possible to throw some further light on the business—You will see by this what he says—& I must beg you to take this matter up seriously—I will make this bargain with you with respect to this land—If you ascertain the Title so that I can sell—let it bring what it will—you shall have One fourth—or nothing—if we can do nothing—But I consider it as certain that if the proper measures are pursued—We can establish the Title—& I hope you will be able so to do If any Man can—I am convinced you can —and that it is valuable there is no doubt—I am well aware that it is troublesome but I think the offer I make is liberal & worth attending to—

I hope you will be able to recover my demand against Woodson Wrenn—I beg you will attend to it, & take anything you can get—If Cotton or Tobacco could be delivered at New Orleans for me by Miller at the Market prices there or even a little higher I would rather have either than his Real Estate—or if he will send me Cordage to the amount of the Debt and suffer me to sell it for the most that can be got either in New Orleans or here—I will charge him no Commission if here—I will be guided by your opinion entirely, when I hear from you the lowest price he will take & what prospect there will be of getting it off if I take it—I mean the property in Lexington—I am with respect Your Friend JAS SMITH JR

ALS. DLC-TJC (DNA, M212, R12). Addressed to Clay at Lexington.

1 Not found.

2 Probably Major William Davenport, who lived in the southern district of Fayette County.

3 Robert Miller.

4 John Jordan, Jr.

5 John C. and Thomas Deye Owings.

6 William W. Smith.

7 Letter from Thomas Norvell not found.

Rental Agreement with Younger Grady

[July 9, 1808]

I do hereby agree to lease of James Coleman[1] & Henry Clay one Cabbin which has been pointed out to me by Jeremiah Murphy[2] lying on Short Street for the term of six months to commence from this day at two dollars per month payable monthly. In testimony whereof I hereunto set my hand & seal this 9h. July 1808.

Teste YOUNGER GRADY {L.S.}

JOHN H. MORTON

DS, in Clay's hand. KyLxT. Grady has not been identified.

1 Of Lexington, probably the resident of that name who was for a time James Morrison's clerk in the tax office and a large speculator in lands.

2 Innkeeper on Mulberry Street, Lexington.

Deed of Emancipation for Daniel

[July 11, 1808]

Know all men by these presents that I, Henry Clay a Citizen and resident of Fayette County of Kentucky for divers good considerations me there unto moveing have and by these presents do emancipate, set free and discharge from all manner of servitude a negro slave named Daniel about thirty two or three years of age formerly the property of my Brother John Clay, by him sold to James Bristow, and purchased by me of said Bristow, supposed to be now in the City of New Orleans

In Testimony whereof I have hereunto set my hand and affixed my seal this 11th day of July 1808 HENRY CLAY {SEAL}

Fayette County Court, Deed Book C, 299-300. Clay's signature acknowledged before John D. Young, Clerk of Fayette County, July 11, 1808. A fee bill from Young, dated July, 1808 (ADS. DLC-TJC [DNA, M212, R15]), amounted to $2.00 for recording, certification, and tax charges on this document. For background of the transaction see above, Johnson to Clay, February 5, 1807.

Bill of Sale from John Bush

27 July 1808.

I have sold the within mentd slave to H. Clay for value recd. & warrant the title of him JOHN BUSH {L.S.}

ES, in Clay's hand. DLC-TJC, 2d Series, vol. 7. On verso of a certificate, signed by John Madison, Deputy United States Marshal, stating that the slave, Newman, had been purchased by John Brown for $150 at a sale held at the Boone County courthouse, August 28, 1807. The sale had been ordered by the United States Circuit Court for the Kentucky District in a suit of William Fenwick against John Bush and John Craig. By endorsement dated December 25, 1807, Brown had assigned the certificate and given up the slave to John Bush.

Agreement with John Bush

27 July 1808.

Upon the receipt of a Negro man named Newman & a young sorrel horse now in Mr. Bush's possession (both of which he has engaged to send me tomorrow) I acknowledge to have received five hundred & seventy dollars in full of a note given by the said Bush and his brother[1] to W. Fenwick[2] & of a Judgment in my name in the Franklin Circuit Court agt. him & John Craig.[3]

HENRY CLAY

[Endorsements][4]

The Negro man and horse above mentioned were delivered to me this 29h. July 1808. HENRY CLAY

Mr. Talbot[5] will be pleased to transfer the Judgment or Execution in my name agt. Craig and Bush to Mr. John Bush. 29. July 1808. HENRY CLAY

ADS. Franklin Circuit Court, File 73 (1808).
1 Matthias Bush. 2 William Fenwick.
3 Clay had sued to collect $250 on the promissory note given by Bush and Craig on October 28, 1805. In July, 1808, the jury found for the plaintiff and one cent damages. Franklin Circuit Court, File 73 (1808).
4 Both AES. 5 Matthew Talbot, Clay's lawyer in this case.

Receipt from James and David Maccoun

4 Augt. 1808.

Recd. of H. Clay Two hundred & Seventy dollars on his own account & thirty for R. Allen[1] making Three hundred dollars in the whole J. & D. MACCOUN

DS, in Clay's hand. DLC-TJC, 2d Series, vol. 7. 1 Richard Allen.

Property Deed to Peter Paul, Jr.

[August 22, 1808]

[Indenture by which Henry Clay and Lucretia, his wife, for the sum of $250 current money of Kentucky, paid and acknowledged, sell to Peter Paul, Jr., a tract beginning on Upper Street at the southeast corner of a lot this day sold by Clay to Henry Purviance and running with Purviance's line 104 feet in depth to Dr. Elisha Warfield's line, thence with the latter line 32 feet, thence to Upper Street parallel with the first mentioned line for 104 feet, thence along Upper Street to the beginning—that is, Clay sells one sixth part of the land which he held on Upper Street and his whole depth back to Warfield's line. General warranty of title. Signatures of the Clays acknowledged before John D. Young, Clerk of Fayette County, August 23, 1808.]

Fayette County Court, Deed Book C, 313-15. Paul and his father, stonecutters, had come to Lexington from England in 1802.

Property Deed to Henry Purviance

[August 22, 1808]

[Indenture by which Henry Clay and Lucretia, his wife, for $500 current money of Kentucky, paid and acknowledged, sell to

Henry Purviance a lot in Lexington bounded as follows: beginning on Upper Street at the southeast corner of a lot sold by Clay to Mrs. Margaret January by deed of January 4, 1808, and running with the latter lot 104 feet in depth to the line of Dr. Elisha Warfield, thence with his line 64 feet to the line of another lot of Clay, from which he has today sold half to Peter Paul, Jr., thence with the line of this last lot 104 feet to Upper Street, and thence on Upper Street to the beginning—that is, one third of the tract Clay held on Upper Street, running his whole depth to Warfield's line. General warranty of title. Signatures of Henry and Lucretia Clay acknowledged before J. D. Young, Clerk of Fayette County, August 23, 1808.]

Fayette County Court, Deed Book C, 357-58.

Bond of Indemnity from John W. Wooldridge

[August 22, 1808]

I do hereby acknowledge to have received of Henry Clay forty nine pounds seven shillings and six pence for my brother Powhatan Wooldridge—And I do bind and oblige myself my heirs &c to indemnify & save harmless the said Clay for making payment to me of the said sum, the same having been paid under the authority of letters from my brother Powhatan

Witness my hand & seal this 22d. August 1808.

Sealed & Delivered JOHN W. WOOLDRIDGE {L.S.}
In presence of
BENJN. STOUT

DS, in Clay's hand. DLC-TJC (DNA, M212, R15).

Order from Edward P. Harrison

[August 23, 1808]

Sir plese to pay Davey six dollers and thre quarters and you will OBlige your umBle survent 1808 Mr Clay augut 23

ED P HARRISON

ADS. DLC-TJC, 2d Series, vol. 7. Harrison lived in the southern district of Fayette County.

From Luke Tiernan and Company

Henry Clay Esqr. Baltimore 30h Augt. 1808.
Dear Sir

your favor of the 8h August[1] is received, a few days previous

Mr. Neville[2] Enclosed us Mr. Wilkins[3] draft accepted and payable at the Bank of Pennsylvania for one Thousand dollars which is to your Credit, if you have received the money from Eastland & Aiken will thank you for a statement of your account and if any Ballance is in hand be so good as to forward the same, you are Credited for the premm. paid on the Bill

we beg you will use every Industry to get Judgment against Wm. West to whom we have given very great Indulgence and hope he will not thro any dificulties in the way of paying the money at Judgment Court. we are with much regard Your friends & Servs.

LUKE TIERNAN & CO

ALS. DLC-TJC (DNA, M212, R12).
1 Not found.
2 Probably Presley Neville, surveyor and land speculator, member of a Pittsburgh family long prominent in commercial and political affairs of that city.
3 Either Charles Wilkins or his brother John.

Property Deed from Thomas Deye Owings

[August 30, 1808]

[Indenture by which Thomas Deye Owings, for five shillings, paid and acknowledged, sells to Clay a tract in Lexington in the property known as McDermid's Square, on Mill Street, no. 48 in the plan of division of the Square,[1] lately occupied by William Dailey and by him sold to Clay, now occupied by William T. Barry, in which tract Owings acquired an interest by deed from William Smith and Porter Clay, dated March 18, 1808, recorded in Fayette County Court.[2] Title warranted only against claims through Owings. Signatures of Thomas D. Owings and Maria, his wife, acknowledged before John D. Young, Clerk of Fayette County, August 30, 1808.]

Fayette County Court, Deed Book C, 361-62.
1 Cf. above, Property Deeds, September 10, 29, 1806; July 21, 1807.
2 Fayette County Court, Deed Book C, 350-52. There were several William Smiths living in Fayette County in 1810; to which one the deed refers is not clear.

Property Deed to Micajah Clark

[August 31, 1808]

[Indenture by which Henry Clay for the sum of five shillings, paid and acknowledged, conveys to Micajah Clark a tract of 164 acres on Hickman Creek in Jessamine County, it being the property transferred to Clay by Montgomery Bell under deed of September 24, 1803, recorded in the Jessamine County Court. General warranty of title. John C. Walker, Deputy Clerk of Jessamine County, records the deed July 11, 1815, upon certification by John

D. Young, Fayette County Clerk, dated July 10, 1815, that John Hart[1] and William R. Morton[2] have identified the document as written in Clay's hand.]

Jessamine County Court, Deed Book C, 431-32. Clark was probably the Clark County resident of that name, formerly a magistrate there.
1 Clay's brother-in-law, the youngest son of Col. Thomas Hart.
2 Son of William and brother of John H. Morton.

Bill of Sale for Major from Thomas C. Graves

[August 31, 1808]

For value received I have sold & delivered to H. Clay a negro man slave named Major about twenty-five years of age; & do hereby warrant & defend the title to the said Clay his heirs and assigns. Witness my hand & Seal this 31 Aug. 1808.

THOMAS C. GRAVES {L.S.}

1 DS, in Clay's hand. DLC-TJC (DNA, M212, R15).

From James Brown

My dear Sir New orleans Septr. 1 re. 1808

Before I had the pleasure of your last very agreeable letter[1] the news of the death of our venerable friend had reached us.[2] Although in some degree prepared for the melancholy event by the account given in your former letter of the state of his health, I yet felt the loss with a degree of sensibility which was heightened by the regret I experienced by being forever denied the long expected pleasure of giving him a gleam of his happiness in his last days by restoring him the society of his beloved daughter. I need not tell you what she has suffered. You know the sensibility of her heart and the warmth of her gratitude and attachment to the best of fathers. Reflection however should teach us the duty of yielding to the decrees of Heaven. Our friend was not prematurely snatched away from us. He has left no needy infant orphans. He lived long and he lived well. His character is set before his family as a model of public and private virtues worthy of their imitation. Whilst they cherish his memory may they never depart from the example he has left them.

I am happy the industry and perseverance of my friend Trimble and yourself have brought the entry of Gillespie to a decision.[3] The property is valuable and I pray you to carve out until you satisfy yourselves fully for the trouble and expence this affair may have given you.

I am sorry you are become the object of the malignity of my

former enemies.[4] I know their business and have learned to dread their power from a long experience of the unprincipled lengths to which they will go in attacking their enemies or in giving vent to their malignity. In the present state of our Country no pursuit is so irksome to my feelings as the Career of politics. The Press is *free* and every scoundrel who can purchase ink and a set of types vies with his neighbour editor in the trade of blackening the reputation of every man whose talents or virtues excite envy or thwart ambition. For my own part I have imposed upon myself an eternal silence on that subject. Things are not in practice what my fancy fondly imagined.[5] I have seen men who clamored about the smallest constructive violations of the Constitution advocate the propriety of openly treading it under foot, and I have seen an administration commence with a modest waiver of its legitimate powers and end with an attempt to prostrate the Judiciary and divide its constitutional powers between the Legislative & Executive departments. Standing armies have been advocated and reprobated by the same tongues; and a fleet has been introduced in the puny and inefficient form of Gun boats by the former enemies to a navy. A Cataline has been converted into a Cicero and corruption has been Carefully covered by a Court of Inquest from which Independence was not to be expected.[6] This Important section of the Union is committed to the hands of a demi-idiot whose inability to govern his warmest friend cannot deny.[7] To approve all these things requires a complete departure from all my former principles and having warmly supported the men who have advised them I feel ashamed of taking any part against them. And do these things meet the approbation of the Republicans of Kentucky? And is it to support such measures as these that you have destroyed your peace encreased the number of your enemies, and perhaps endangered your very life which you may be forced to risque in defence of your Character? I am sorry that you do not live in better times for you have talents to adorn a public station, and to be useful to your Country. But to me character is more dear than every other thing; and can any man hope long to preserve it in the present miserable state of things? You have carried your election.[8] I am rejoiced at it. Your enemies will be wounded. But I pray you to quit public life or muster up sufficient philosophy to bear up under all the hard names with which you will be christened in the papers. You are it seems a Burrite. If Wilkinson deserves to be believed seven thousand men in your State deserved the same opprobrious title—What you may next be called is uncertain but as long as you retain your brains and your independence you will be abused. Republicanism demands that a man of talents should be kept down by detraction Too much genius, like too much wealth destroys Equality the very soul of Democracy. But I forbear. You will say I have become splenetic or rather that I have always been subject to that infirmity. Nothing is further from the fact. Ever since my arrival in this merry dancing Country, my temper has remained unruffled, with the exception of Wilkinson's Winter of horrors.[9] In domestic life I have nothing to wish and my practice has been more prosperous than I had any right to expect. It is with pleasure that I discover that your rage of electioneering has not diverted your mind from the *main point;* and that the people, whilst the [*sic*] rail at the profession of law vie with each other in filling the coffers of its professors. Happy in the bosom of your family may you long enjoy the fruits of your labors and transmit liberal Educations and competent fortunes to your descendants!

The blockhead Shoemaker sent out a debt of five hundred Dollars against P Caldwell and as his affairs were deranged advised me to do as well as I could with him.[10] He paid me about 70 Dollars which I paid to Billy Leavy and gave a draft on John Jordan for 100 and one on Smith to be paid out of some Judgmt in the hands of Todd amount uncertain. I have now Jordans note for 160 Dollars money lent to Seitz which Jordan told me Seitz would pay. I have Seitz acct. for ten years services amountg to near $1000.[11] Of John Smiths acct I never heard until at Frankft. but as he is my kinsman I requested Doctor Brown to settle with him & hoped he had done It can be no [*sic*] set off against the debt due to Shoemaker.[12] As to any balance I have never touched a cent. You have all I know of this affair. Jordans note can be sent you at any time & you will see how it conforms to his account. With this business as with most other of their Phila. Debts I had much trouble & no profit

We have been for some weeks at our farm busily engaged in finishing our Sugar house and preparing to make a small crop of fifty or sixty Hoghd. of Sugar. Of this you shall have a sample by the Winters boats and if I can procure the forms I will endeavor to send some refined

Present my affecte. regards to Lucretia & the family, & believe me Dear Clay Your sincere friend JAMES BROWN

ALS. DLC-TJC (DNA, M212, R10). Published in Colton (ed.), *Private Correspondence of Henry Clay,* 16-17. Postmarked September 5.

1 Not found.

2 Col. Thomas Hart, father-in-law of Brown and Clay, had died June 22, 1808.

3 See above, Brown to Clay, April 10, 1807.

4 The group headed by Humphrey Marshall and Joseph Hamilton Daveiss. A marginal note borders this paragraph: "for your own eye only unless the postmaster should have the curiosity to examine the contents."

5 Brown had formerly been an ardent Republican.
6 General James Wilkinson, accused of having been in the pay of Spain, requested a hearing before a military court of inquiry. After sitting for several months in 1808, the court exonerated him of wrongdoing.
7 Governor William C. C. Claiborne of Orleans Territory.
8 To the Kentucky House of Representatives in August, 1808.
9 In the winter of 1806-1807, during the hysteria that attended the Burr episode, General Wilkinson with the support of Governor Claiborne assumed command of the New Orleans militia and imprisoned several persons in defiance of the judicial processes of the Territorial courts.
10 See above, Clay to Shoemaker, June 23, 1808.
11 See above, Brown to Clay, October 31, 1805.
12 See above, notes 10 and 11, and Clay to Shoemaker, February 15, 1806.

Agreement with William M. Nash

[September 3, 1808]

An agreement Between William M. Nash of the one part and Henry Clay of the other part made this 3d. day of September 1808.

The said Nash covenants to sell & convey to the said Clay by deed with general warranty his two houses and lot lying on Upper Street, the said lot having been conveyed to him by Simon Hickey:[1] He further covenants to have the rough of the small house covered in, and not to remove or suffer to be removed the doors, or any other of the parts or materials provided for the said houses or either of them: He further covenants to deliver the said houses to the said Clay in good order on or before Christmas next, and in the mean time to suffer the said Clay or his workmen to have free access to the said houses for the purpose of completing them, and in particular for the purpose of plaistering the house in which the said Nash resides.

In consideration whereof the said Clay covenants to sell & convey to the said Nash his tract of land on Cane run, containing about two hundred and twenty-six acres, more or less, according to a deed made to the said Clay by Francis and Arthur Patterson,[2]—The deed for the said land to be with general warranty, and to be made eight months from the date hereof, upon the request of the said Nash:[3] The said Clay further covenants to pay to the said Nash on or before Christmas next the sum of two hundred dollars in money; and to deliver to the said Nash at his the said Clay's farm near Lexington, on or before the first day of October 1809 horses and mares, not exceeing [*sic*] eight years old, to the amount of eight hundred dollars, according to the valuation of two men one to be chosen by each of the parties, and their umpire, if they cannot agree.

In witness whereof the parties hereunto set their hands & seals.

Teste W M NASH {L.S.}
DANL. BRYAN HENRY CLAY {L.S.}

[Endorsements on verso][4]

Memo. The said Nash is to be at liberty to take possession immediately of the Land, except that part which is occupied by a tenant or tenants, of which he is to have possession on the expiration of the year, and they are to pay the rent to him; & the said Clay is to be at liberty to procure plank for his Stable floors at Traveller's Hall of oak, from the Land. W M NASH {L.S.}
DANL. BRYAN HENRY CLAY {L.S.}

The sum of eight hundred dollars within mentd. is to be credited by Twenty dollars for professional services rendered by said Clay to me. 3. Septr. 1808. W M NASH

The Horse debt within mentd. is to be further credited by Two hundred and seventy dollars. 8. Apl. 1809. W M NASH

Recd. 9 Jan. 1810. of H. Clay Two hundred and eighty five dollars which with former payments some mentioned & some not mentd. on this agreement is in full. W M NASH

ADS, signed also by Nash, a Lexington saddler. DLC-TJC (DNA, M212, R10).
1 A blacksmith in Lexington. For the deed, see Fayette Circuit Court, Deed Book B, 552-53.
2 Dated November 9, 1807.
3 The deed dated April 27, 1811.
4 The first, AES, signed also by Nash; the others, ES, in Clay's hand.

Property Deed from William M. Nash

[September 3, 1808]

[Indenture by which for five shillings, paid and acknowledged, William M. Nash sells to Henry Clay a lot in Lexington on Upper Street, one quarter acre bounded as follows: beginning at the corner of William Emmidon's[1] lot and running north 45° east 66 feet, thence south 45° east 10 poles, thence south 45° west 66 feet, thence north 45° west 10 poles to the beginning—known in McDermid's Addition to Lexington as no. 21, conveyed to Nash by deed from Simon Hickey dated November 13, 1805, recorded in Fayette County Court.[2] General warranty of title. Signature of Nash acknowledged before J. D. Young, Clerk of Fayette County, September 5, 1808.]

Fayette County Court, Deed Book C, 412-13.
1 William Emmons, who lived on Short Street.
2 Fayette Circuit [*sic*] Court, Deed Book B, 552-53.

Receipt from Daniel Bryan

[September 3, 1808]

Attached to Agreement, September 7, 1804.

Property Deed to John Fowler

[September 16, 1808]

[Whereas by deed of trust dated September 13, 1806, John Jordan, Jr., conveyed to Thomas Hart, Jr., and to Henry Clay two tracts: first, 5000 acres on Bank Lick Creek, now in Campbell County, part of 6000 acres patented by the State of Virginia to William Jones in two grants, one of 2000 acres under date of February 23, 1789, and the other of 4000 acres on February 25, 1789, both of which tracts were conveyed by Jones to John Fowler, and by Fowler under two deeds dated September 28, 1789, to John A. Seitz and Jordan as merchants in partnership; second, 1000 acres in an unnamed county, in the area set apart for officers and soldiers of the Virginia Continental Line, conveyed to John A. Seitz by Thomas Todd and wife under deed of July 27, 1798–to which properties Jordan succeeded upon the death of Seitz; whereas under the terms of the trust Hart and Clay on September 12, 1808, offered equal and undivided moieties of the aforesaid tracts for sale at public auction, where they were purchased by John Fowler as highest bidder for $210: now Hart and Clay for this sum convey to Fowler equal and undivided moieties of the aforesaid tracts, together with appurtenances. Title warranted against claimants through Hart and Clay only. Thomas January and Henry Purviance acknowledge receipt from Fowler of the above-mentioned $210. Hart's and Clay's signatures acknowledged before a notary public in Lexington, February 7, 1809, and the deed recorded by the Clerk of the Court of Appeals, January 15, 1810.]

Ky. Court of Appeals, Deed Book N, 146-48.

Promissory Note from John Barry, Jr.

[September 19, 1808]

On demand I promise to pay to H. Clay or order value received Two hundred & six dollars and sixty seven Cents. Witness my hand & seal this 19h. Septr. 1808. J BARRY JR. {L.S.}

DS, in Clay's hand. DLC-TJC, 2d Series, vol. 8.

Receipt from John Barry, Jr.

[September 19, 1808]

Attached to Account, November 9, 1807.

Bond from John White

[October 1, 1808]

I bind and oblige myself to pay H. Clay One hundred dollars and to deliver him at his farm near Lexington forty bushels of Salt provided the Judgt. of Fayette Circuit Court in behalf of Fox shall be reversed in the Court of Appeals where my appeal is now depending.[1]

Witness my hand & Seal 1 Oct. 1808.

C BANKS[2] JOHN WHITE {L.S.}

DS, in Clay's hand. DLC-TJC (DNA, M212, R15). White was a resident of Madison County, Kentucky.

1 Richard P. Fox, also of Madison County, had won a suit against White for malicious prosecution in a cross action to a libel suit brought by White against Fox for reporting that Green Clay's Negroes had been distributing turkey, apples, and brandy at the Madison Court House on Election Day, 1802. The Court of Appeals, in the Spring Term, 1809, affirmed the judgment of the lower court. Fayette Circuit Court, File 121 (1807); 4 *Ky. Reports* (1 Bibb) 369-75.

2 Cuthbert Banks.

From William Taylor

Henry Clay Esqr. Baltimore October. 4h. 1808.
Lexington,

Dear Sir,

I have for a number of years been trying to hear of a Mr. Joseph Kelly who moved from Virginia, and it is only this day I am told he removed to Bourbon County, Kentucky, and from there to Logan County (near Russellville, the County Town) where he now resides & is a Farmer of Considerable Property. will you do me the favor to make enquiry in This Case and write Mr. Kelly that I have the annexed claim against him as partner of Stonestreet and add it will greatly oblige me if he will take arrangements in his Affairs to make a speedy settlement with you. I hope it may be in your reach and convenient to you to attend this Claim, But if not I have heard well of a Mr. John Allen of Frankford (attorney at Law) and if you think as well of Him you can place The Application & Demand in his hands.

Mr. Kelly established Stonestreet in a Store in a partnership Concern and they bought Goods from me. In July. 1797. I settled with Thomas Stonestreet & Co. and took Their Bond due me .1278„ 20/100 Dollars. This Bond is endorsed on The back As follows. "This is to Certify that I Joseph Kelly as partner to Thomas Stonestreet do hereby bind myself and hold myself liable to Wm. Taylor in The same manner as Thomas Stonestreet for The Performance of the Within Bond. Louden County Virginia. January. 30h. 1798." signed "Joseph Kelly," Seal
Present Willm. Osbn. Payne.[1] some payments were re-

ceived, and in 1802 it was found necessary to sue Thomas Stonestreet Esqe. in Louden County and The suit was kept off as long as Stonestreet cou'd do it and finally he was taken under execution, all his property sold, he went to Goal and cleared by an act of Insolvency of The State and finally discharged in June. 1806.

By The Statement of The Bond & payments There appears due me to 1 January last (1808), .1,213„6/100 Dolls. You shall have a Copy of The account and if Mr. Kelly wishes it a Copy of The records of the Court.

The only payments ever made on the Bond were

29 July. 1797	213„00 Dollas
3 January. 1798	43– do
10 March 1798	100– do
12 March 1798	20– do
	386 Dollars [*sic*]

T. Stonestreet property sold for . . 251„55/100$

I request to hear from you as soon as you can make it convenient & as soon afterward as you can hear from Mr Kelly.

I am. very respectfully, Dear Sir Yr. obt. Servt WM. TAYLOR

I have a note of W W Whittakers of Beards Town Kentucky[2] for $ do you practice in That District or have you an acquaintance you wou'd recommend There–

ALS. DLC-TJC (DNA, M212, R12).
1 One of Taylor's clerks until about 1802. 2 Bardstown, Nelson County.

Promissory Note from Thomas Bodley

[October 15, 1808]

Three years after date I promise to pay to Henry Clay for value received the Sum of Nineteen hundred and fifty six dollars Witness my hand & seal this 15h. Octr. 1808

$1956. THOS: BODLEY {L.S.}

DS, in Clay's hand. DLC-TJC, 2d Series, vol. 8.

Receipt from Scott Trotter & Company

[October 17, 1808]

Attached to Promissory Note, June 30, 1807.

Order from Edward P. Harrison

october 18 1808

Sir plese to pay Davey for holling at the saltpit 1.18.3

ED P HARRISON

ADS. DLC-TJC, 2d Series, vol. 8.

Report of a Committee of Directors of the Bank of Kentucky

[October 28, 1808]

The Committee to whom was referr'd the letter of the President of the Bank of Pennsylvania of the 15th. Sepr last, incloseing the terms of a proposed intercourse between that institution and this, have considered the same, and beg leave to report,

That they conceive it is expedient to open the said intercourse upon the Terms proposed by the Bank of Pennsya.; and they therefore advise that the president be requested to inform the Bank of Pennsya. that the said intercourse shall be considered as commenceing on the first day of January next, and that in the mean time if it should be deem'd for the interest of this institution to draw for the whole or any part of the $20,000 proposed by the Bank of Pennsya. to be advanced to this Board, bills will be drawn payable on the 1st. day of January next.

Your Committee having further considered that in the course of the intercourse thus proposed to be established it may happen some times, from a variety of causes, that the Bank of Kentucky, calculating upon funds in the Bank of Pennsya., may be disappointed, and that their drafts founded upon such calculation would thereby be liable to be dishonored, to guard against this possible inconvenience, recommend that the president be requested to correspond with the Bank of Pennsya. on this subject, and to obtain a Stipulation on the part of that Institution that in the Case supposed they will honor the drafts of this Institution, altho' at the time they may be in advance the full $20,000 charging the Bank of Kenty however with Interest upon all such drafts until they are fully reimbursed.

Your Committee would further recommend that as there has been no limitation suggested by the Bank of Pennsya. to the duration of this intercourse, and as a sudden interruption of it might produce inconvenience, it be proposed that it shall not terminate until six months previous notice given by one or the other party.

Bank of Kentucky, Frankfort, Record Book A, October 12, 1807-September 14, 1810, pp. 187-88 (KyU). Other members of the drafting committee were John Allen (of Frankfort) and John Brown, appointed with Clay first named at the meeting of the directors on October 25, 1808.

Promissory Note from John P. Wagnon

[November 1, 1808]

Three years after date for value received I promise to pay to H. Clay or order the sum of one thousand dollars, with interest thereon from the date Witness my hand & seal this first day of Novr. 1808.

Teste PORTER CLAY J. P. WAGNON {L.S.}

Copy, in Clay's hand. Fayette Circuit Court, File 823. Cf. below, Agreement, November 9, 1808.

Agreement with John P. Wagnon

[November 9, 1808]

Henry Clay covenants and agrees to sell to John P. Wagnon the Stable and lot adjoining the lot of W. T. Barry Esqr. on Market Street, purchased by the said Clay of William Lytle,[1] for which the said Clay will make a title to the said John P. Wagnon after the payment of the consideration money as hereafter mentioned.

In consideration whereof the said John P. Wagnon covenants and agrees to pay the said Clay the sum of eighteen hundred dollars, of which he has paid eight hundred dollars in the Chandaliers formerly owned by Robert Bradley, and the balance of one thousand dollars he is to pay in three years with interest from the first day of this month, for which he has executed his note. And it is expressly agreed & understood that the said Clay is to have and hereby retains a lien upon the said Stable and lot for the payment of the said one thousand dollars and interest.

Witness our hands & seals this 9h Nov. 1808.

JAMES VANCE[2] HENRY CLAY {L.S.}
J P WAGNON {L.S.}

[Endorsements on verso][3]

I do hereby transfer the within agreement to Genl George Mathews[4] he being bound for the ballance due Mr. Clay as Stipulated and the rents and profits arrising from the Stable he is to receive, to make good the intersest [*sic*] and to secure in him in a ballance due by me of $600 Dollars in horses—17th April 1809 J. P. WAGNON

Credit 6 Septr. 1809 by one horse paid by Maj Wagnon to J. W. Hunt at thirty nine pounds And also by a bay mare formerly the property of Wilkins[5] and her Dragon Colt at forty pounds.

£79 H. CLAY

I assign the within to W. T. Barry without recourse to me or my heirs this assignment to take affect from the 16th. March 1810—Witness my hand & seal this 1st. April 1810. GEO MATHEWS

[Endorsements on separate sheet][6]

For the consideration of two thousand dollars paid me in hand by John T. Mason Jr.[7] I assign the within bond to said Mason. Witness my hand this 30th. June 1819 W. T. BARRY

For and in consideration of two thousand Dollars in hand paid to me by Robert Wickliffe I hereby assign to him the within bond. Witness my hand this 24th. August 1819–

JOHN T. MASON JR

ADS, signed also by Wagnon. Fayette Circuit Court, File 823.
1 By deed dated June 18, 1808.
2 A resident of the northern district of Fayette County.
3 The first, ES, in unidentified hand; the second and third, AES.
4 A Virginia veteran of the Revolution, Mathews had moved to Georgia, where he was appointed a brigadier general in the State militia and elected Governor, 1787 and 1793-1796, and Representative in Congress, 1789-1791. His identification with the Blount conspiracy of 1796-1797 for seizure of the Floridas and Louisiana from Spain prevented confirmation of his appointment as Governor of Mississippi Territory in 1798, and his activiteis between 1810 and 1812 in connection with Florida separatism brought further official repudiation. He died in 1812.
5 Probably Charles Wilkins.
6 Both, ES.
7 Second son of Stevens Thomson Mason of Loudoun County, Virginia. John Thomson Mason moved to Kentucky in 1812 and lived for a time in the house built by Levi Todd on the Boonesborough Road. He later moved to Owingsville and to Mt. Sterling, Kentucky, and eventually to Michigan, where he held the office of Territorial Secretary. William T. Barry was his brother-in-law.

Bill of Sale for Slaves Will and Patsy

[November 19, 1808]

By Virtue of a Vendia. Epa.[1] to me directed from the Circuit Court of Clarke County, Henry Clay, vs. John Hardwick[2] & Micajah Harrison I have exposed for Sale to the highest bidder; for ready money, two Negroes Slaves Will, and Patsey taken as the property of said Hardwick, which was knocked out to said Clay, for the sum of Five hundred Dollars he being the highest bidder; And I do by Virtue of my Office as Sheriff of Montgomery County, under the Authority aforesaid. Bargain & Sell the said Slaves, Will and Patsey to the said Clay his Heirs & assigns forever, Hereby Warranting defended the Title to said negroes against the Claim or Claims of all and every Person or Persons Whatsoever.

Witness my Hand & Seal as a Deputy Sheriff, for said County at Mountsterling Novr. 19th. 1808

HARRISON GRAVES DS– {SEAL}

DS. DLC-Slave Papers (DNA, M212, R9).
1 *Venditioni Exponas,* a writ directing the sheriff to sell goods or other property.
2 See above, Bond, October 29, 1805.

Fee Bill for Court Costs

[December, 1808]

July 1808 Henry Clay To the Shff of Franklin Dr.
To Exd: Caps. on Craig[1] & Bail ...... $ 2:25

same on Street[2] & Bail	1:12:5
To Witness vs Do	21:
To Jury vs Do	1: 4:
Decr: To levying Exon. & Reple: bond vs Street	3:26:
To same vs same second time	3:50
	$ 11:38:5

P: HICKMAN[3] D.S.

DS. DLC-TJC (DNA, M212, R15).
1 John Craig. See above, Agreement, July 27, 1808.
2 Joseph M. Street. See above, Bill of Complaint, July, 1808.
3 Paschal Hickman, a native of Virginia who had come to Kentucky as a boy and served in the Indian fighting in the nineties, was the jailer of Franklin County from early in 1808 until his death in 1813.

Agreement with Cuthbert Banks

[December 1, 1808]

Attached to Lease, June 24, 1808.

Assignment by Henry Watkins

5 Decr. 1808.

Without recourse I assign the within to H. Clay H WATKINS

ES, in Clay's hand. KyLxT. Endorsement on verso of an agreement dated November 9, 1808 (DS, in Clay's hand), between Samuel Watkins and his uncle, Henry Watkins, whereby Samuel contracted to sell his share of the estate of his father, John Watkins. The property included 150 acres of land in Woodford County, two slaves, "named Cuthburt and Phillis," blacksmith's tools, a bed, and other furniture, including a desk and bookcase. The consideration for the Watkins transaction was to have been $1200—$450 in a mortgage which Henry Watkins held from Samuel upon the land, $450 to be paid in thirty days, and the residue, $300, payable in nine months. A supplementary endorsement, dated also on November 9, 1808, and signed by Samuel Watkins, acknowledged receipt of the mortgage.

From Richard H. Wilcocks

Henry Clay Esqre Philadelphia 9th. December 1808.
Lexington Kentucky Dear Sir

Your esteemed favour of the 6th March last[1] I duly received by which I observe you had made overtures to some of the Parties concerned in the purchase of the Lands belonging to the Estate of My late Father[2] and had offered Drs. 400 for their claim which they did not seem inclined to take but that you indulged the hope that for about $600 or 700 an extinguishment of their claim could be effected. That you should endeavour to bring to a close the negotiation about a compromise in the course of a few weeks and would communicate to me the [re]sult. Since that time I have not had the pleasure of hearing from you although I have been anxiously waiting for advice. Soon after the receipt of your above mentioned letter I received one from Mr. Morrison[3] a copy of which is Enclosed.[4] I have defered answering his communication until I should hear from you. You will observe thereby after his return return [*sic*] to Lexington on running out my claim and one of 31000 acres of which he owns a moiety it was found that they interfered about 11,000 acres and that he had been induced to purchase from Mr. Coleman[5] a joint Interest with him in his claim of mine in order to strengthen himself against my interference with his claim alluded to and offering to sell or purchase the Title to the interfering part also to relinquish all the Title he has acquired and to procure a compleat release or transfer of the Title acquired by Mr. Coleman to my land for the sum of Drs. 867.50. You will observe he alludes to your offer of Drs. 400 which he says will not be acceeded to—You state there are several Gentlemen interested in the purchase of my land. I will be obliged if you would mentioned [*sic*] the names of all of them. In order that you may have a precise knowledge of the Lands I claim and wish information of and that you may particularly examine into their having been really sold for Taxes and purchased by Mr. Coleman or other Persons I now enclose you copies of two Patents Patents [*sic*] for tracts or parcels of Land situate in the County of Jefferson State of Virginia. Vizt the Tract for Thirty Thousand Acres in the forks between nolin & Green river and bounded &c. In this tract Mr Nicholas Low of New York has an undivided Interest with me he holds a Deed from John & Chamless Hart[6] for two thirds of the above Tract in common with my late Father, to whom the other equal third part of the said tract of Land was conveyed by indenture in common with Mr. Low an abstract from which I likewise enclose you. One other tract of Land for Ten Thousand acres granted by Patent to Benjamin Wynkoop[7] assignee of Robert Coleman[8] and by said Wynkoop conveyed by indenture to my late Father Mr. John Wilcocks,[9] situate on the Waters of Salt river adjoining George Wescots[10] Ten Thousand acre Survey &c. An abstract from this Deed [y]ou will also find herewith. My wish respecting those [l]ands is that you ascertain if they have been actually sold and to whom. It does not appear from any thing stated by Mr Coleman or Morrison that the Salt River tract has been sold or purchased by either of them and I would desire a careful comparison of my patents and deeds with the conveyances Mr. Coleman has obtained and thus see if those purchased by him are the identical Lands Lands [*sic*] belonging to Mr. Low and the Estate of my late Father and to ask a report whether the Sale to Coleman is conclusive and binding on Mr. Low and the Estate of my late Father so as to bar our claim both in Law and equity to examine the interfering claim for 11,000 acres to renew your treaty with Morrison and to obtain from him the lowest sum he and Coleman will take for the Title which they may have acquired and the extinguishing the interfering claim to 11000 and also the highest sum they will give us for our quit claim to give us from the best information you can obtain an estimate of the value of those Lands and whether by appointing an Agent on or near the Spot they can be sold to settlers and a[t] what price and terms of payment and finally to give us your opinion and advice what under all the circumstances it is best for us to do. If it should appear that Coleman has not purchased the Salt River tract I wish you to ascertain and inform me to whom it may have been conveyed. Enclosed I transmit you a fee of of [*sic*] Fifty Dollars of which I request your acceptance. I now answer Mr. Morrisons letter by acknowledging the receipt thereof and refering him to you. I think it well to enclose the same to you which after perusal please deliver him. I remain With respect Sir Your Obdt Hble Servt

RICHARD H WILCOCKS

United States Bank note to R Patton[11] or Bearer fifty Dollars No. 89.

ADS. DLC-TJC (DNA, M212, R12). [1] Not found.
[2] John Wilcocks, also of Philadelphia. [3] James Morrison.
[4] None of the enclosures mentioned in this letter has been found.
[5] James Coleman, of Lexington.
[6] On August 26, 1786, John Hart and wife, of Philadelphia, deeded to Nicholas Lowe 30,000 acres of land on Nolin and Green rivers in western Kentucky.
[7] Of Philadelphia.
[8] Possibly the Lancaster County, Pennsylvania, iron-master, a veteran of the Revolution, who had supplied munitions for the Continental Army, and later became active in Pennsylvania politics. His son James may have been the resident of Lexington, cited above, n. 5. Another Robert Coleman, of Culpeper County, Virginia, had entered claim to some 80,000 acres in Jefferson County, Kentucky, in 1783 and 1784.
[9] The deed was drawn August 22, 1786.
[10] Wescott was also a Philadelphian.
[11] Possibly Robert Patton of Fredericksburg, Virginia, who was himself a large-scale landowner in Kentucky.

Nomination of Committee Clerk

[December 12, 1808]

Clay nominated Daniel Todd as clerk to the committees of claims, courts of justice, and religion. Ky. H. of Reps., *Journal, 1808-1809*, p. 7. On the first ballot Todd received a plurality of the votes; but a majority being required, he was subsequently rejected.

Resolution Relating to Clerkship of W. C. Greenup

[December 14, 1808]

Resolved, That the clerkship of the committees of propositions and grievances and privileges and elections, *is yet vacant,* for that it appears to this house that the present incumbent is constitutionally and legally ineligible to that office, from the circumstance of his holding a lucrative appointment under the authority of the government of the United States.

Ky. H. of Reps., *Journal, 1808-1809,* pp. 20-21. The resolution followed acceptance of a committee report announcing that William C. Greenup, elected to the clerkship on December 12, had previously accepted an appointment as deputy surveyor under the Surveyor General of the United States. Clay had been a member of the investigating committee, but he had not presented the report. The House concurred in Clay's resolution, whereupon David Todd, Clay's recently defeated nominee for clerk of the committees of claims, courts of justice, and religion, was elected to fill the vacancy. Greenup had held the post of Secretary of State for the Commonwealth for the past year. Frankfort *Western World,* February 25, 1808.

Amendment of Resolution on Foreign Relations

[December 15, 1808]

Strike out from the word "resolved" in the original resolution, and insert the following in lieu thereof:

"That the administration of the general government, since Thomas Jefferson has been elected to the office of president, has been wise, dignified and patriotic, and merits the approbation of the country.

Resolved, That the embargo[1] was a measure highly judicious, and was the only honorable expedient to avoid war; whilst its direct tendency, besides annoying those who had rendered resort to it necessary, was to preserve our seamen and property, exposed to the piratical depredations of foreign vessels.

Resolved, That the general assembly of Kentucky would view with the utmost horror a proposition, in any shape, to submit to the tributary exactions of Great Britain, as attempted to be enforced by her orders of council, or to acquiesce in the violation of neutral rights, as menaced by the French decrees; and they pledge themselves to the general government, to spend, if necessary, the last shilling, and to exhaust the last drop of blood, in resisting these aggressions.

Resolved, That whether war, a total non-intercourse, or a more rigid execution of the embargo system be determined on, the general assembly, however they may regret the privations consequent on the occasion, will cordially approve and cooperate in enforcing the measure; for they are sensible that in the present crisis of the nation, the alternatives are—a surrender of liberty and independence, or a *bold* and *manly* resistance.

Resolved, That Thomas Jefferson is entitled to the thanks of his country, for the ability, uprightness and intelligence which he has displayed in the management both of our foreign relations and domestic concerns."

Ky. H. of Reps., *Journal, 1808-1809,* pp. 30-31. The original resolutions had been introduced by Robert Scroggin of Bourbon County. Clay's version, first presented in Committee of the Whole, abbreviated and sharpened the phrasing, but in basic content differed only in eliminating a resolution citing the evils of war as the alternative to embargo. After prolonged opposition by Humphrey Marshall, the Clay resolutions were adopted in the House with only Marshall's dissenting vote. Senate amendments, accepted by the House, substituted "an" for "the only" in the second resolution and substituted "in resisting which aggressions they pledge themselves to the general government for their most energetic support," in lieu of Clay's more militant lines following the word "decrees" in the third resolution. A Senate proposal to rephrase, less vigorously, the last line of the fourth resolution was rejected. *Ibid.,* 9-10, 23, 33, 51, 52; Ky. Sen., *Journal, 1808-1809,* pp. 33-34. On Clay's authorship see Lexington *Reporter,* December 22, 1808, citing letter to the editor November (*sic*) 16, 1808.

1 The Federal Embargo Act of December 22, 1807 (2 *U. S. Stat.,* 451-53) had evoked such bitter opposition among mercantile classes that Jefferson's own party split on the issue during the Presidential election of 1808. The Kentucky resolutions, initiated on the opening day of the legislative session, were significant in this connection. In the face of mounting protest, Congress on January 9, 1809, passed the Force Act (2 *U. S. Stat.,* 506-11), permitting Federal officials without warrant to seize goods suspected as destined for foreign trade. The subsequent outcry finally compelled repeal of the embargo, except as it related to trade with France, England, or their dependencies, on March 1, 1809 (2 *U. S. Stat.,* 531).

Debate on Foreign Relations

[December 16, 1808]

Mr. *Clay* replied to some misrepresentations or misconstructions of Mr. Marshall, observing, that he thought it unnecessary to consume time in answering that gentleman in all his lengthy detail —that he hoped the house were prepared finally to decide—were prepared when the resolutions were first introduced, and would in their unanimous decision draw the line of distinction between the American *Whig* and *Tory*.

Lexington *Reporter,* December 22, 1808, quoting a letter to the editor, November (*sic*) 16, 1808. Earlier remarks by Clay, not recorded, in answer to Humphrey Marshall's speech opposing the embargo law, were described as "pertinent, severe, and eloquent."

Further Amendment of Resolutions on Foreign Relations

[December 16, 1808]

Subjoin the following resolution:

"*Resolved,* That a copy of the foregoing resolutions be transmitted to the president of the United States, and to each of our senators and representatives in congress."

Ky. H. of Reps., *Journal, 1808-1809,* p. 31. See above, Amendment, December 15, 1808. The new proposal was also adopted.

Committee Report on Sundry Petitions

[December 16, 1808]

The committee for courts of justice have according to order had under their consideration sundry petitions to them referred, and have come to the following resolutions thereupon, to wit:

Resolved, as the opinion of this committee, that the petition of Rebecca Winchester,[1] setting forth that from a combination of adverse circumstances, therein set forth, her husband is insolvent, and apprehending that any property she might acquire by her industry or aid of friends, may be subjected to the payment of his debts, thereby depriving her of the means of personal support, and praying that a law may pass permitting her to acquire and hold property as a *feme sole;* is reasonable.

Resolved, as the opinion of this committee, that the petition of Andrew Kriesal,[2] setting forth that from his indigence and his old age and other circumstances, he is unable to pay the state price on a tract of land in Logan county, and praying that a law may pass for his relief, and granting him a right thereto; is reasonable.

Resolved, as the opinion of this committee, that so much of the petition of sundry inhabitants of this commonwealth as prays that a law may pass relaxing the usual summary course of the law for the recovery of debts; is reasonable.

And on motion,

Resolved, That the latter part of the said petition, respecting settlers &c. of head right claims south of Green river, granting them indulgence in payment of the state prices thereon; be laid over.

Resolved, as the opinion of this committee, that the petition from sundry inhabitants of this state, praying the repeal of the act of last session, entitled "an act concerning the collection of certain officers' fees," for reasons therein stated; is reasonable.

Ky. H. of Reps., *Journal, 1808-1809,* pp. 26-27. Other members of the drafting committee were James Clark, Humphrey Marshall, James Blane (Green County), Abraham Owen (Shelby), Samuel G. Hopkins, Thomas A. Covington (Warren), and John B. Campbell (Christian). The first resolution was amended so that the petition was rejected. The second and fifth resolutions were approved, and the committee was directed to prepare the necessary bills. The third and fourth petitions were tabled pending action on separately introduced bills relating to these subjects. See Littell (comp.), *Statute Law of Kentucky,* IV, 49-51 (February 8, 1809), and below, Amendment, January 2, 1809. A bill for the relief of Andrew "Kriessall" was subsequently introduced by Peyton Nowlin, of Logan County, but was rejected at first reading. A measure granting the proposed relief was ultimately enacted January 30, 1810. Ky. H. of Reps., *Journal, 1808-1809,* p. 106; Littell, *op. cit.,* IV, 159. James Clark presented the bill for repeal in part of the act of February 20, 1808, concerning the collection of sheriffs' and clerks' fees. The Clark measure, with extensive Senate amendment, was subsequently enacted. Ky. H. of Reps., *Journal, 1808-1809,* pp. 89, 101, 265, 285, 318. Neither of the latter measures occasioned further reported comment by Clay.

[1] Of Jefferson County, Kentucky; daughter of Benjamin Lawrence, also of Jefferson County.

2 Elsewhere cited as Grisal, Grissel, Grysal, Kreissal, Krisal. His tract amounted to 160 acres, surveyed April 17, 1799, on a branch of Laurel Creek, in Logan County. Jillson (comp.), *Kentucky Land Grants,* 321.

Resolution of Mourning for General Thomas Sandford

[December 16, 1808]

Resolved by the senate and house of representatives, That as a testimony of respect to the late general Thomas Sandford, the members of the general assembly and their officers will, and that the officers of the government generally, be requested to wear black crape on the left arm, as a badge of mourning, for the space of thirty days.

Ky. H. of Reps., *Journal, 1808-1809,* p. 25. The measure passed the House immediately; under Senate amendment it was enacted with deletion of the words "the late" and insertion, after the name, of the words "deceased, and late a member of the senate." Ky. Sen., *Journal, 1808-1809,* pp. 18-19. Though Sandford had been drowned in the Ohio River on December 10, the news had just reached Frankfort. Lexington *Reporter,* December 19, 1808.

Bill to Extend Time for Property Declaration

[December 17, 1808]

Clay reported the measure for a drafting committee which included also William Owsley (Garrard County) and Samuel G. Hopkins. Ky. H. of Reps., *Journal, 1808-1809,* p. 35. On December 13, Clay had asked leave to present such a bill, and it was enacted without marked controversy on December 27. It extended the period for redemption of land forfeited to the State as unlisted for taxation, until two years beyond the expiration of the act of December 27, 1806. Littell (comp.), *Statute Law of Kentucky,* IV, 5.

Bill to Benefit Certain Mechanics

[December 19, 1808]

Clay reported the bill for a drafting committee which included the other Fayette County representatives. Ky. H. of Reps., *Journal, 1808-1809,* p. 44. On December 17 he had obtained leave to offer such a proposal, and it passed the House, with the addition of a clause by way of rider; but the entire measure failed in the Senate. The effort to obtain legislation "for the benefit of mechanics" had been initiated at the Session of 1807-1808, in a measure offered by John Simpson, who presented much of the legislation in which Clay was interested while the latter was serving as Speaker. At that time, too, the bill had passed the House but failed in the Senate. Ky. H. of Reps., *Journal, 1807-1808,* pp. 91, 102, 184.

Report of Committee for Courts of Justice

[December 19, 1808]

The committee for courts of justice have, according to order, had under consideration sundry petitions to them referred, and have come to the following resolutions thereupon, to wit:

Resolved, As the opinion of this committee, that the petition of sundry inhabitants of Logan county, stating that James Karr, a citizen of said county, had obtained a certificate from the commissioners for 200 acres of land, and that from the poverty of said Karr and his having a large and helpless family, he is unable to pay the state price for said land, praying that a law may pass releasing him from the payment thereof, and directing that a grant may issue to him for the same—*is reasonable.*

Resolved, As the opinion of this committee, that the petition of Thomas Randolph, a citizen of Muhlenburg county, stating that he had paid the state price on a removed certificate, which he holds as assignee, for 200 acres of land on the south side of Green river, had been taken up by a prior grant, and praying that a law may pass directing a warrant to issue for the amount paid by him, to be applied to the payment of other lands for which he is indebted—*be rejected.*

Ky. H. of Reps., *Journal, 1808-1809,* p. 44. Other members of the drafting committee are listed above, Committee Report, December 16, 1808. House action on the present report amended the first of the resolutions and accepted the second, in such manner that both petitions were rejected.

Report on Petition of Jacob Ryman's Heirs

[December 20, 1808]

The committee for courts of justice have, according to order, had under consideration a petition to them referred, and have come to the following resolution thereupon, to wit:

Resolved, As the opinion of this committee, that the petition of the representatives of Jacob Ryman,[1] deceased, praying that a law may pass authorising said representatives to sell a certain tract of land, for reasons therein stated—*is reasonable.*

Ky. H. of Reps., *Journal, 1808-1809,* p. 49. The committee recommendation was adopted, and a bill pursuant to it was authorized. Clay, for the same committee, introduced such a measure on December 21. It passed the House without controversy, but was rejected by the Senate.

1 Jacob Ryman (or Rymond), of Fayette County.

Motion Relating to Virginia Resolution on Recall of Senators

[December 22, 1808]

On Clay's motion the Kentucky House began consideration of the Virginia proposal which provided for recall of Senators from the Congress of the United States

by action of a majority of the members of the respective State legislatures. Ky. H. of Reps., *Journal, 1808-1809,* p. 58. Thereafter a resolution was reported from Committee of the Whole as follows: "*Resolved by the general assembly of Kentucky,* That whilst they at all times feel a disposition to co-operate in the adoption of any salutary amendments to the constitution of the United States, it would in their opinion be inexpedient to adopt the amendment proposed by the state of Virginia." Clay's possible agency in this measure is suggested by his subsequent role in carrying it before the State Senate. *Ibid.,* 63-64, 94. With Senatorial amendment to append a restatement of the Virginia measure, the House proposal was adopted.

Resolution on Divorce Procedure

[December 23, 1808]

Resolved, That the committee appointed to prepare a bill regulating divorces, be instructed to draft it in such a manner as to vest the   with the jurisdiction.

Ky. H. of Reps., *Journal, 1808-1809,* p. 61. A resolution had been introduced banning divorces for any reason. This had been rejected in favor of a resolution proposing to state by law the particular ground or grounds for which divorces should be granted. *Ibid.,* 53, 54. Clay now struck at the root of the legislative concern, the crowding of the calendar with private bills on divorce petitions. With the words "circuit courts" inserted in the blank, the resolution was immediately adopted. A bill stating authorized grounds for divorce and assigning jurisdiction in accordance with this resolution was subsequently introduced by James Garrard and enacted January 31, 1809. Littell (comp.), *Statute Law of Kentucky,* IV, 19-20.

Agreement with Cuthbert Banks

[December 24, 1808]

Attached to Lease, June 24, 1808.

Receipt to Thomas Ryerson

26 Decr. 1808.

Received of James Morrison Twenty dollars my fee for Thomas Ryerson &c. against Steel &c. on a foreclosure of mortgage.[1]

HENRY CLAY

ADS. DLC-TJC (DNA, M212, R15). Endorsed on verso: ". . . Charged to Ryerson 23d. Jany. 1808."

[1] Robert Steele of Montgomery County, Kentucky, had on December 1, 1798, mortgaged to Thomas Ryerson and Caleb and Owen Folk, Philadelphia merchants, town lot no. 42 in Mount Sterling for £111, 12s, 8d current money of Pennsylvania. Fayette District Court, Deed Book B, 172.

Order on Thomas Bodley

26 Decr. 1808

Be pleased to pay to Thomas Williams Esq.[1] or order One hundred and ninety eight dollars and fifty Cents. H. CLAY

Tho. Bodley Esqr.

[Endorsement][2]
Recd. the amt of the above THOS. WILLIAMS

ADS. DLC-TJC (DNA, M212, R15).
[1] Possibly Simon Kenton's companion in early explorations of northern Kentucky, later a trustee of the town of Maysville.
[2] AES.

Order to Lewis Sanders

27 Decr. 1808.

Be pleased to let the bearer have in merchandize Ten dollars.
L. Sanders Esqr H CLAY

ADS. Owned by Miss Anna V. Parker, Ghent, Kentucky.

Property Deed from Thomas and Eleanor Hart

[December 29, 1808]

[Indenture by which Thomas Hart and Eleanor, his wife, for the sum of $1800, current money of Kentucky, paid and acknowledged, sell to Clay a tract in Lexington beginning at the "southeast" corner of a lot, no. 6 in the plat of the town; running from thence south 45° west with Mill Street two thirds of the distance from the beginning to Lewis Sanders' lot, supposed to be 44 feet; from thence north 45° west 50 feet to an alley of five feet; from thence running north 45° east with the alley, including use of the alley, to Short Street; from thence with Short Street fifty feet to the beginning. General warranty of title. Signature of Thomas Hart acknowledged before J. D. Young, Clerk of Fayette County, August 12, 1809.]

DS. DLC-TJC (DNA, M212, R15). Recorded in Fayette County Court, Deed Book D, 256-57.

To William Taylor

Dr Sir Lexington 30 Decr. 1808

I have received in safety your favor covering Mr. Whitakers note, and the record in relation to your demand upon Mr. Kelly.[1] Since I had the pleasure of addressing you before Mr. Kelly has written me a reply to my letter[2] requesting of him information as to the provision he has made to dischagre [*sic*] your demand. He also mentions that he has written to the same effect to you. He states that his property would not pay above half the debt; that if he is liable he wishes you to come and take it at valuation without suit; but he suggests that the Sheriff of Loudon had made himself responsible by indulgence to Stonestreet. I am inclined to believe that Mr. Kellys situation is not so bad as he would represent it; and his latter suggestion is contradicted by the record. I shall nevertheless wait until I hear from you again, as the suit will not at all be delayed by it, provided the writ is executed by May. I expect soon to hear from Whitaker. Yrs. H. CLAY.

ALS. DLC-HC (DNA, M212, R1). Addressed to Taylor, and postmarked January 2.
1 W. W. Whitaker and Joseph Kelly. Apparently Clay and Taylor exchanged letters not found between October 4, 1808, and the date of the present document.
2 Neither letter found.

Bill from Davey

[*ca.* December 31, 1808]

Hawling for Henry Clay

To Hawling	2 loads at 3/. per Load	0. 6 .0
To do	5 do at 3/. pr. do	0.15.0
To do	7- do at 3/. pr. do	1. 1 .0
To do	2 loads of Oak plank	0.12.0
To do	1 load of Locust Timber	0. 3 .0
To do		0.18.0
To do		0.12.0
To do		0. 6 .0
		£ 4.13.0

D. DLC-TJC, 2d Series, vol. 8. Endorsed on verso: "Henry Clay for hawling by Davey with cart 1808." Additional charges listed in the endorsement, including two orders by "Harrison" (Edward P.) and an earlier bill on Clay for hauling timber (DLC-TJC, 2d Series, vol. 8), bring the total to £12:9.9 or $41.62½. A part of this lumber probably came from the Cane Run land, sold to Nash September 3, 1808.

Bill of Sale for Slaves

Lexington Jany 1st. 1809.

Know all men by these presents that I John Hart[1] of Fayette County, Trustee for the benefit of the heirs of John Holder deceaced,[2] have this day sold and delivered to Henry Clay esqr. a negro woman called Ede & her son Giles, the former about forty years of age, & the latter about nine, for and in consideration of the Sum of five hundred dollars to me in hand paid, the receipt whereof I hereby acknowledge; which said negroes I warrant sound, & free from all incumbrance in law, & will defend them to the said Henry Clay against the claim of all and every other person or persons whatsoever

Atteste Witness my hand
JOHN F. EVANS[3] JOHN HART TRUSTEE &C

DS. DLC-TJC (DNA, M212, R15).
1 Nephew of Col. Thomas Hart and a first cousin of Lucretia Clay. Hereafter identified as John Hart, Senior.

2 A Revolutionary veteran from Virginia, captain of a company stationed at Boonsborough in 1779, Holder had been killed by Indians in Kentucky in 1792.
3 Not identified; the middle initial doubtful.

Promissory Note to John Hart, Senior

Lexington, January 1st, 1809

On the first day of January one thousand eight hundred & eleven I promise to pay to John Hart Trustee for the benefit of the heirs of John Holder, decd, or order five hundred dollars, without defalcation, for value received Henry Clay by his Agent

Atteste JOHN HART[1]

JOHN F. EVANS

[Endorsement of verso][2]

Recd. of H Clay (as per rect given) One hundred and ten pounds on a/c of the within 26 Septr. 1812 JOHN MORTON

Received the Ballance in full of this note, June 20th 1817—

LESLIE COMBS Atty[3]

ADS. DLC-TJC (DNA, M212, R15).
1 Clay's brother-in-law.
2 The first, ES, in Clay's hand; the second, AES.
3 A veteran of the War of 1812 and a rising young lawyer, later to become a General in the Texan Revolution, a Fayette County political leader, and a steadfast Clay supporter. He represented his district in the Kentucky legislature for nine terms, was Speaker of the House in 1846, and subsequently served as Clerk of the Kentucky Court of Appeals, 1860-1866.

Amendment of Senate Bill on Payment for State Lands

[January 2, 1809]

For reference to the amendment (not printed), see Ky. H. of Reps., *Journal, 1808-1809*, p. 90. So amended, the bill was enacted the following day. Because high water had made travel difficult, the measure extended for six days the time limit on completing payment for State lands without interest, as required under act of December 27, 1806. Cf. Littell (comp.), *Statute Law of Kentucky*, III, 389; Ky. Gen. Assy., *Acts, 1808*, pp. 12-13. On December 22, Clay, probably in deference to earlier progress on the Senate measure, had moved to suspend action on a House bill for this purpose. Ky. H. of Reps., *Journal, 1808-1809*, p. 56.

Resolution to Encourage Use of American Manufactures

[January 3, 1809]

Resolved by the senate and house of representatives, That from and after the day of next, the members of the general assembly will clothe themselves in productions of American manufacture, and will abstain from the use of cloth or linens of European fabric until the belligerent nations respect the rights of neutrals by repealing their orders and decrees as relates to the United States.

Ky. H. of Reps., *Journal, 1808-1809,* p. 93. The resolution, so stated, passed the House; but when subsequent Senate amendments were rejected, the measure was rephrased in conference, with Clay as a member of the committee but not as its chairman. As finally enacted, a preamble stated that whereas the belligerent powers had transgressed the rights of neutrals by their unjust orders and decrees, the national interest required that a preference be given to articles grown and manufactured in this country, and that Americans "abstain" from use of European commodities. Resolutions then provided that it be recommended to the people of the commonwealth to use every exertion to promote domestic manufactures, and that, to effect this object, the members of the General Assembly on June 20 next would clothe themselves in products of American manufacture, and would "discourage" use of European fabrics, until American rights were respected and commerce freed from restrictions. *Ibid.,* 315.

Resolution for Investigation of Fayette County Justices

[January 3, 1809]

Information having been received by this house to induce them to believe that an investigation into the official conduct of Leonard K. Bradley and Hezekiah Harrison, Esquires, justices of the peace in Fayette county, is called for as well for the sake of public justice as for the vindication of those persons if innocent: wherefore,

Resolved, That a committee of nine be appointed to enquire whether Leonard K. Bradley and Hezekiah Harrison, two justices of the peace of Fayette county, have so acted in their official characters as to call for the constitutional interposition of this house to effect their removal, or the removal of either of them.

Ky. H. of Reps., *Journal, 1808-1809.* pp. 94-95. The resolution was thereupon adopted and Clay appointed chairman of the committee. On January 12 Clay moved that the committee be discharged from further prosecution of the enquiry against Harrison (who had died on January 10). *Ibid.,* p. 122. Bradley was subsequently removed from office, but Clay was absent from the House as a result of duelling wounds when the report of the committee was filed and the consequent legislation enacted.

To Humphrey Marshall

4 Jan. 9.

After the occurrences in the House of Representatives on this day,[1] the receipt of this note will excite with you no surprize. I hope on my part I shall not be disappointed in the execution of the pledge you gave on that occasion, and in your disclaimer of the character attributed to you. To enable you to fulfill these reasonable and just expectations my friend Maj. Campbell[2] is authorized by me to adjust the ceremonies proper to be observed.

I am Sir Yrs &c HENRY CLAY

ANS. DLC-HC (DNA, M212, R1). Addressed: "H Marshall Esqr. Present."

[1] In the course of debate on the resolution to encourage use of American manufactures, the long-standing conflict between Clay and Humphrey Marshall came to a head. During a bitterly vituperative exchange, Marshall called Clay a "liar." The two were restrained from physical combat only by intervention of their colleagues. Clay, apologizing to the House for his actions, asserted that he would not have taken the liberty had his opponent been a man of honor. Marshall retorted that it was the "apology of a poltroon!" Mayo, *Henry Clay,* 338.

[2] John B. Campbell, member of the House of Representatives from Christian County.

To Thomas Hart, Junior

Dr Sir Frankfort 4. Jan. 1809

On this day in the House of Representatives a dispute arose between H. Marshall and myself which terminated by the use of language on his part to which I could not submit, & I attempted to chastise him on the spot, but was prevented by the interference of the House. I have since challenged him, and there is a prospect of his accepting it. Should he do so I shall want a brace of pistols, and know of none that I can get on which I would rely, except Mortons.[1] These I must prevail on you to procure upon any terms, by purchase or otherwise. You will have some difficulty in doing it, and must conceal from him the true purpose of them, which may be done through the agency of some person, whom he will not suspect. I must also request the favor of you to procure some of the best powder, adapted to such occasions, which can be had.

Should the pistols require cleaning I will be obliged to you to get West[2] to put them in proper order. But at any rate let the bearer return with them by tomorrow evening, or in the course of the night.

I need not suggest to you the necessity of entire secrecy on this subject. Yrs. HENRY CLAY

ALS. DLC-HC (DNA, M212, R1). Addressed: "Mr. Tho. Hart In his absence Nath G Hart Lexington."

[1] Probably John H. Morton. Marshall's biographer states that the guns used in the duel belonged to Joseph Hamilton Daveiss. A. C. Quisenberry, *The Life and Times of Hon. Humphrey Marshall* (Winchester, Ky., 1892), 103.

[2] Edward West.

From Humphrey Marshall

Sir, Janry. 4th 1809.

Your note of this date was handed me by Major Campbell, the object is understood, and without deigning to notice the insinuation, it contains as to character, the necessary arrangements are, on my part, submitted to my friend Colo. Moore.[1] Yours Sir &c.

H. MARSHALL

ALS. DLC-HC (DNA, M212, R1). Addressed to Clay at Frankfort.
[1] James F. Moore of Jefferson County, who represented Jefferson and Bullitt in the State Senate. Campbell and Moore signed the following agreement (DLC-HC [DNA, M212, R1]):
"Rules to be observed by Mr. Clay and Mr. Marshall on the *ground,* in settling the affair now pending between them.
"1. Each gentleman will take his station at ten paces distant from the other and will stand as may suit his choice with his arms hanging down, and after the words Attention! Fire! being given, both may fire at their leisure.
"2. A snap or flash shall be equivalent to a fire.
"3. If one should fire before the other, he who fires first shall stand in the position in which he was when he fired, except that he may let his arm fall down by his side.
"4. A violation of the above rules by either of the parties (accidents excepted) shall subject the offender to instant death."

Resolution of Censure against Clay and Humphrey Marshall

[January 5, 1809]

Resolved, That the conduct of Humphrey Marshall and Henry Clay, whilst in the service of the house of representatives on yesterday, was an indignity offered to the same and highly reprehensible; but having made suitable acknowledgments, the house think proper to accept the same, and proceed no further therein.

Ky. H. of Reps., *Journal, 1808-1809,* p. 103. The resolution, presented by John Lancaster, of Washington County, was adopted without recorded vote.

Amendment of Bill on Adjustment of Land Claims

[January 5, 1809]

Clay reported the amendment (not printed) for a select committee which included also Samuel South and Humphrey Marshall. Ky. H. of Reps., *Journal, 1808-1809,* p. 104. The bill, introduced by Marshall, was designed to terminate the interference of dormant claims to Kentucky lands under Virginia law. The Clay report was tabled and the bill subsequently enacted without amendment. *Ibid.,* 106, 195, 308, 318; Littell (comp.), *Statute Law of Kentucky,* IV, 55-57 (February 9, 1809).

Resolution on Fees of Judicial Clerks

[January 13, 1809]

It being deemed by the house of representatives, improper to derive revenue from litigation, and the labour of the officers concerned in it; and moreover, such resort for supplying revenue being considered as a violation of that clause of the *Bill of rights* which forbids the sale of justice: At the same time, it being deemed just, that if the labor of clerks and their compensations are not properly adjusted, the one to the other, but that their fees are too high for their services, a reduction ought to take place for the benefit of litigants themselves—Therefore,

Resolved, That it is improper to derive revenue from such a source.—And,

Resolved, That a committee be appointed, to enquire whether any, and what reduction ought to be made in the fees of clerks in this commonwealth; and whether any, and what provision ought to be made by law, to produce uniformity in their charges.

Ky. H. of Reps., *Journal, 1808-1809,* p. 155. Read once, the resolution was tabled and not revived. A bill to equalize clerk's fees, previously introduced by Humphrey Marshall, was dropped in Committee of the Whole; and a similar measure passed by the Senate also failed in the House. *Ibid.,* 56, 296-97, 312, 313.

To James Clark

Dr. Clarke: LOUISVILLE, 19 January —9.

I have this moment returned from the field of battle. We had three shots. On the first I grazed him just above the navel—he missed me. On the second my damned pistol snapped, and he missed me. On the third I received a flesh wound in the thigh, and owing to my receiving his first fire, &c., I missed him.[1]

My wound is no way serious, as the bone is unhurt, but prudence will require me to remain here some days.[2] Yours,

HENRY CLAY.

Lexington Daily Press, August 9, 1873, reprinted from *Henderson* (Ky.) *Reporter.* Addressed: "Samuel G. Hopkins or James Clarke, Esq. Frankfort."

1 Before the month was out several Kentucky newspapers published Clay's challenge, Marshall's acceptance, the rules for the duel, and the following account, written immediately after the encounter (DLC-HC [DNA, M212, R1]) and signed by John B. Campbell and James F. Moore:

"Conformably to previous arrangement Mr. Clay and Mr. Marshall attended by their friends crossed the Ohio, at Shippingport, and an eligible spot of ground presenting itself immediately below the mouth of Silver creek, ten steps, the distance agreed on, was measured off, and each gentleman took his position. The word being given, both gentlemen fired: Mr. Marshall's fire did not take effect: Mr. Clays succeeded so far as to give Mr. Marshall a slight wound on the belly: preparations were then made for a second fire: Mr. Marshall again fired without effect, Mr. Clay snapped, which agreeably to rules agreed on, was equivalent to a fire. A third preparation was made when each gentleman stood at his station waiting for the word. Mr. Marshall fired first, and gave Mr Clay a flesh wound in the right thigh: Mr. Clay fired without effect. Mr. Clay insisted on another fire, very ardently, but his situation, resulting from the wound, placing him on unequal grounds, his importunate request was not complied with. We deem it justice to both the gentlemen to pronounce their conduct on the occasion cool, determined and brave in the highest degree. Mr. Clays friend was under an impression that Mr Marshall at the third fire violated a rule which required, that he who fired first should stand in the position in which he was when he fired, but Mr. Marshalls friend being convinced, that Mr. Clay had fired previous to Mr. Marshalls moving from his position, this circumstance is considered as one in which gentlemen may be mistaken on such occasions, and is not to be noticed in this affair."

2 Clay did not return to his seat in the legislature until February 8.

Resolution of Censure for Arranging Duel

[January 24, 1809]

Whereas the practice of *duelling* merits the execration of society at large, and the disapprobation of the legislature in particular: And whereas, this house has good reason to believe that Henry Clay, Humphrey Marshall and John B. Campbell, members of this house, have been engaged while members, in making arrangements in this state for a duel, which it is believed, has been fought in another government, and consequently without the reach of this legislature. But as the arrangements have been made in this commonwealth, and such conduct deserves the most severe reprehension, Therefore,

Resolved, that the said H. Clay, H. Marshall and J. B. Campbell, deserve censure for their conduct aforesaid.

Ky. H. of Reps. *Journal, 1808-1809,* p. 203. The resolution, adopted by a vote of 55 to 7, was presented as a substitute for a measure proposed the previous day by John Parker, of Fayette County, which called for an investigation of the report that during the absence of these members they had "engaged in the heinous practice of duelling."

From James Johnson

Worthy Friend! Frankfort Jany 28th 1809

We have Just convened this morning to proceed to business as it is announced to me that Genl Breckenridge[1] will leave town to day for Louisville—This being a good opp rtunity I cannot refrain transmiting a few lines—Upon hearing of the affair nothing seemed so much to affect me as your pistol snaping the second round—This tho I feel bound to attach to the interposition of Providence rather than a failure on the part of your friend[2]—I believe and it is generally believed had your pistol fired the second time your adversary must have fallen Your firmness and courage is admited now by all parties—I feel happy to hear of the heroism with which you acted—I had rather heard of your Death than to have heard of your backing in the smallest degree—I never doubted on the subject myself, but this will serve to stop the mouths of all snivel faced Tories—I belive your freind Majr Campbell to be a Gen leman of the greatest respectability. Your interest on this occation is his interest I dec[l]are I love the man. I hope you will observe the utmost patience in your present situation dont expose yourself—One days exposure might retard your recovery a considerable time—I long to see you—I have heard you are fast recovering—I know your patriotism will make you reconsiled to your present situation without frown or complaint—I disaprove of Dueling in the general but it seems absolutely necessary sometimes for a mans dignity—If possible without endangering yourself I should be very glad to see you before we rise—We talk of rising next saturday but I think it very doubtful Yours untill Death JAMES JOHNSON

ALS. DLC-HC (DNA, M212, R1). Addressed to Clay at Louisville. James, a son of Robert Johnson, was at this time State Senator from Scott County; he subsequently served as Congressional representative from Kentucky, 1825-1826.

1 Robert Breckinridge, who lived in Louisville, a veteran of the Revolutionary War, brigadier-general of the Kentucky militia, member of the Kentucky Constitutional Convention of 1792, and Speaker of the House of Representatives in the State's first legislature. He was an older half brother of John Breckinridge.

2 Clay's second, John B. Campbell, who presumably had loaded the weapon.

From William Taylor Barry

Dr. Clay 29th. Jany. 1809—

I rejoice to hear that you are fast recovering. I hope it will not be long before I shall have the pleasure of seeing you—but of one thing I am confident that the efforts of nature & art combined cannot keep pace in healing your wound with the wishes and solicitude of your friends—*Fortune* who has hitherto accompanied you thro' life seems to have left you on the seacond fire—but no! perhaps she never was more careful of her darling Son—She interfered to save the life of a miserable sinner and give him time for repentance—And thereby has saved a feeling mind from the unpleasant reflection of hurrying into the other world a poor soul in all probability not prepared to meet his God—Genl. Breckenridge who will hand you this letter has been here for some days and can inform you of what the Legislature have been doing—I have introduced a Bill to lengthen our next June Term of Fayette Court—

As you are confined & may be unable to attend to business for some time—If it is in my power to serve you in any way I request that you will freely make known to me how I can be useful to you as it will give me pleasure to render you any service in my power—

Wishing you a speedy recovery—I remain your Obdt. Sert. & friend

WM. T BARRY

Frankfort

ALS. DLC-HC (DNA, M212, R1). Addressed to Clay at Louisville. Barry was a member of the House of Representatives from Fayette County.

Tax Bill

[*ca.* February 1, 1809]

1808	Henry Clay	Dr Cents
	Tax on 1810 acres 1st. rate Land @ 50 ..	9.05
	" 4000 acres 2nd. ditto @ 34	13.60.
	" 4333 ⅓ acres 3d ditto @ 12½..	5.42½
	" 14 Slaves @ 12½ 40 Horses @ 4	3.35
	" 6 Carriage Wheeles @ ... 25.	1:50

Levy on 11 Tithes	@ 50	5.50
		$ 38.42½

JOHN H. MORTON Shff

ADS. DLC-TJC (DNA, M212, R15).

Resolution on Quartering Militia Company

[February 9, 1809]

Resolved, that captain Geo. R. C. Floyd[1] be permitted to have for the accommodation of his company, the use of the room, lately occupied by the public printer in the state house, for a period not exceeding ten days.

Ky. H. of Reps., *Journal, 1808-1809,* p. 316. The measure was passed immediately in the House and approved the following day by the Senate and the Governor. The Kentucky militia had been mustered by Governor's proclamation of November 17, 1808, to meet Kentucky's quota under call of Congress enacted March 30, 1808. Lexington *Reporter,* November 21, December 8, 1808; 2 *U. S. Stat.,* 478.

1 Captain George Rogers Clark Floyd, a native of Jefferson County, Kentucky—son of John Floyd, pioneer Kentuckian, and brother of John Floyd, who subsequently became Governor of Virginia—was a militia officer, commander of the 4th Regiment of Infantry at the Battle of Tippecanoe, and a colonel in the War of 1812.

Order Drawn by Robert S. Russell

13 Feby 1809

Henry Clay in account	Der.	$ C
to 1500 feet of seasond ash flooring		30" 0
to 1500 feet of Sheeting at 6/ per hundred		15" 0
		$ 45" 0

Sir, Please to pay the within account to James McCoun[1]; And you will oblige Yours &c. &c.

Henry Clay Esqr. ROBT. S RUSSELL

ADS (date alone in Clay's hand). DLC-TJC (DNA, M212, R15). Russell lived on North Elkhorn in Fayette County, where he operated a distillery and a saw mill.

1 Maccoun.

Receipt from Elizabeth McGowan

Lexington Feby 15th. 1809—

Recd. of Henry Clay Esqr. in part of my mothers Estate, pr. the hands of James Morrison—One hundred & three Dollars & forty five Cents being amt my note of 31st. Decr. 1807 for One hundred Dollars to said Morrison & Interest thereon to 27th. July 1808—

Teste ROBT. SCOTT[1] ELIBETH [*sic*] MCGOWAN

DS, in Robert Scott's hand. DLC-TJC (DNA, M212, R15). Elizabeth, daughter of Sarah Beard, was the wife of Charles McGowan of Fayette County.

[1] Morrison's nephew and clerk. After Morrison's death, Scott was employed by Clay for similar duties, particularly in connection with settlement of the Morrison estate.

Agreement with John P. Wagnon

[February 28, 1809]

An agreement between H. Clay and John P. Wagnon.

The said Clay has agreed with the said Wagnon to indemnify Thomas Hart agt. his indorsement upon a note of the said Wagnon for four hundred dollars, now lying at the Insurance office[1] & to get the said Note once renewed if practicable;

In Consideration whereof the said Wagnon has executed a deed of trust to Tho. Hart for certain property therein mentd. He further agrees with the said Clay that he will put into his possession immediately the negro boy Lewis mentd. in the said deed of trust; and that upon his relieving the said Clay from his obligation to indemnify the said Hart as afd. by paying the note indorsed by him, or if it shall be renewed with the said Clay's indorsement, upon his paying the note so indorsed by the said Clay, he the said Clay may take the said boy Lewis the mare mentd. in the deed of trust & her produce (if he chooses so to do) at the price of four hundred dollars, to be credited the said Wagnon's bond held by the said Clay for one thousand dollars.

In Witness whereof the parties hereunto set their hands & Seals this 28 Feb. 1809. H. CLAY. {L.S.}

Teste D WATTS[2] J P WAGNON {L.S.}

ADS, signed also by Wagnon. DLC-TJC (DNA, M212, R15).

[1] Kentucky Insurance Company.

[2] David Watts, of Fayette County.

Advertisement for Lost Horse

Ashland,[1] 6th March, 1809.

Twenty Dollars Reward!

STRAYED or stolen, several weeks ago, from the farm of the subscriber, near Lexington, a sorrel filley, three years old this spring. Between the knee and fetlock on the side of one of her fore legs is a scar about an inch in length; in her forehead is a long star or blaze, and on close inspection, white hairs may be perceived intermingled with the sorrel. I will give the above reward to any person who will deliver her to me. HENRY CLAY

Lexington *Kentucky Gazette,* March 6, 1809.

[1] First record found of Clay's use of this name for his farm.

Property Deed from Samuel Watkins

[March 11, 1809]

This Indenture made this 11th day of March 1809 between Samuel Watkins of Woodford County of the one part and Henry Clay of Fayette County of the other part Witnesseth that where as the said Samuel Watkins made several month [*sic*] ago with Henry Watkins a contract for the sale of certain interests in his father's estate devised and bequeathed to him by his said father by his last will and testament bearing date the first day of April 1807 and recorded in Woodford County, which said contract has been assigned by the said Henry Watkins to the said Henry Clay, now in Consideration of the premises & the sum of twelve hundred dollars paid or secured to be paid to the said Samuel Watkins he the said Samuel Watkins hath bargained sold and delivered and by these presents doth bargain sell and deliver to the said Henry Clay two negro slaves named Cuthbert & Phillis bequeathd. to him by the said Will, to be held used and disposed of by the said Clay in the same manner and under the same conditions as he the said Samuel could have held used and disposed of them and whereas in the said will is this devise "my will and desire is that after the decease of my wife the land whereon I now live may be sold to the highest bidder at one or two years creadit as my executors may Judge best and the money arising from such sale be equally divided among my three children, towit,, Samuel Phebe & patsey with this express condition that patsey pay out of her part of the said money to my son John and to my daughter Polley twenty five pounds to each of them in cash" now this Indenture farther witnesseth that the said Samuel Watkins for the Condition aforesaid hath bargained and sold assigned and transferred all the land and money or either of them to which by the said Clause refered to the said samuel now is or hereafter may become entitled to, and also such portion of the profits of the tract of land in the said Clause described as he the said Samuel under the will or as one of the heirs at law of his father may be entitled to, prior to the death of his mother. To have and to hold the said land or money with the appurtenances and the said profits to the said Henry Clay his heirs and assigns forever and the said Samuel Watkins doth Covenant and agree to and with the said Henry Clay that he will warrant and defend what is conveyed and intended to be conveyed by this deed to the said Henry Clay his heirs and assigns forever against the claim of all and every person whatsoever deriving title from him.

In Testimony where of the said Samuel Watkins hath hereunto

set his hand and affixed his seal the day and year first mentioned

SAMUEL WATKINS {L.S.}

Woodford County Court, Deed Book D, 455-56. Recorded on the same date. Cf. above, Assignment, December 5, 1808.

Toast on St. Patrick's Day

[March 17, 1809]

The genuine Irish character—Frank, brave, and generous.

Lexington *Kentucky Gazette,* March 21, 1809. Delivered at a banquet in the Kentucky Hotel.

Receipted Bill for Lottery Tickets

Henry Clay, Esq. Lexington, March 20, 1809

To Managers of Lottery No. 2 for the Improvement of Main Street

To your loss on 20 Tickets in said Lottery $28, 33

Recd. payment for Managers WM. W. WORSLEY, AGENT.[1]

ADS. DLC-TJC (DNA, M212, R10).

1 Founder and publisher, with Samuel Overton, of the Lexington *Reporter.*

Order to John H. Morton

26 Mar. 1809

Mr Morton may allow Mr. Irvine fifty dollars being the amt. of Porter Clay's note assigned to me, — in the Settlemt. of Mrs. Jacksons execution agt. him[1] H. CLAY

ADS. DLC-TJC (DNA, M212, R15).

1 At the June Term, 1806, of Fayette Circuit Court, Susannah Jackson, with Clay as her attorney, had won judgment against Thomas Irvine (Irwin) for collection of a debt amounting to $99.70 with interest at six per cent dating from March 29, 1793, and her costs of suit. The plaintiff having agreed to a stay of execution, the case was revived in September, 1807; and in January, 1809, a replevy bond was filed for the payment. Fayette Circuit Court, Order Book C (1805-1806), 509; D, 408; various fee bills, DLC-TJC, 2d Series, vol. 9.

Property Deed from Deputy Sheriff of Fayette County

[March 28, 1809]

[Indenture by which William R. Morton, Deputy Sheriff of Fayette County, transfers two pieces of property for which Clay was high bidder at a sheriff's sale on executions against Christopher Keiser. The first tract, located at the corner of Main and Mulberry streets, runs northwest on Main for twenty five feet, eleven inches, and extends back to Water Street. The second parcel, only seven feet, seven inches wide, adjoins the first on the west and runs the same depth. Signature of William R. Morton acknowledged before John D. Young, Clerk of Fayette County Court, June 20, 1810.]

Fayette County Court, Deed Book E, 94-97.

Receipt from Martin Coons

[April 4, 1809]

Attached to Agreement with Hooper and Gay, July 3, 1801.

Receipt from James D. Breckinridge

6th. Apl. 1809.

Recd. of H. Clay a note given by P. B. Ormsby[1] for one hundred & seventy two dollars 60 Cents to Benj. Comegyss of Baltimore payable on demand dated 27 Septr 1805 for collection

JAMES D. BRECKENRIDGE

DS, in Clay's hand. DLC-TJC (DNA, M212, R15). Breckinridge, a Louisville lawyer, nephew of General Robert Breckinridge, was a member of the Kentucky legislature, 1809-1811, and of the United States Congress, 1821-1823.

1 Peter Benson Ormsby, a native of Ireland, settled in Louisville about 1797.

Property Deed to Peter Paul, Sr.

[April 7, 1809]

[Indenture by which Henry Clay and Lucretia, his wife, for $250, paid and acknowledged, sell to Peter Paul, Sr., a lot in Lexington, fronting Upper Street and bounded as follows: beginning on Upper Street at the southeast corner of a lot sold to Peter Paul, Jr., and running with the latter Paul's line 104 feet in depth to the lot of Dr. Elisha Warfield, thence with Warfield's line 32 feet, thence to Upper Street parallel with the first mentioned line 104 feet, thence with Upper Street to the beginning—it being the intent of Clay to convey one sixth part of the tract which he held on Upper Street, the residue thereof being conveyed to Peter Paul, Jr., and others. General warranty of title. Signatures of the Clays acknowledged before J. D. Young, Clerk of Fayette County, June 28, 1809.]

Fayette County Court, Deed Book D, 78-80.

Settlement of Accounts with Stephens and Winslow

8. Apl. 1809.

We have this day settled all accounts up to this time except H:

Clay's Subscription to the Steeple & a street; and H. Clay has passed his note & others in full H. CLAY

STEPHENS & WINSLOW

ADS, signed also by Stephens and Winslow. DLC-TJC (DNA, M212, R15). In 1808 an Episcopal Church with a tower and bell had been built at the corner of Church Alley and Market Street in Lexington. Clay was one of the original pew holders. The street subscription was probably for work on Church Alley.

Memorandum of Credit in Account with W. M. Nash

[April 8, 1809]

Attached to Agreement, September 3, 1808.

To James Madison

Sir Kentucky Frankfort 10 April 1809

Mr Boyle haveing accepted the office of Judge of the court of appeals of this state, I presume it will become necessary immediately to appoint a Govr of the Illinois Territory in his stead.[1] N Edwards Esqr chief Justice of our court of appeals is desirous of filling this vacancy, and it is with pleasure that I bestow my suffrage on his recommendation.[2] The Honorable appointments which this gentleman has held (first a Judge of our superior courts and then promoted to his present station, evince how highly he is estimated amongst us. In these he has acquitted himself with great ability and general satisfaction nor can a doubt exist of his entire fitness for the office in question I am Sir Yr ob. Servt

The President HENRY CLAY

Copy, by Ninian Edwards. ICHi.

[1] John Boyle, Kentucky Congressman for three terms, had not sought re-election in 1808. Upon the expiration of his term of office in 1809, President Madison offered him the appointment as Governor of Illinois Territory. When he reached home, however, he declined the post in favor of a judgeship on the Kentucky Court of Appeals.

[2] Edwards received the appointment.

To Robert Smith

Sir Frankfort 10 April 1809

In consequence of Mr Boyles resignation of the office of Govr of the Illinois Territory, the Administration will I presume proceed to make a new appointment. Under this impression I take the liberty of recommending the Hon N. Edwards Chief Justice of the Supreme court of our State. His political principles accord with those of the republican party. His good understanding, weight of character, and conciliatory manners give him very fair pretensions to the office alluded to. Should further information be desired in relation to him, I have no doubt that the whole representation from this state when consulted will concur in ascribing to him every qualification requisite for the office in question &c.

H. CLAY

Copy, by Ninian Edwards. ICHi. Recipient identified by Edwards.

To Caesar Augustus Rodney

Dr Rodney [April 10, 1809]

Allow me to recommend to your patronage and support for the office of Govr of the Illinois Territory rendered vacant by Boyles resignation my friend N Edwards Esqr Chief Justice of this State. His standing & character are deservedly high & his political principles are correct. He possesses an excellent understanding and his conciliating manner would I have no doubt render him a very popular and acceptable Governor. Should it be expedient to delay the appointment untill an opportunity exists of consulting the Kentuckey representation, I am persuaded that they will all concur in assigning to Judge Edwards the requisite qualifications. By promoti[ng] his wishes you will oblige Yr frid. H. CLAY

Copy, by Ninian Edwards. ICHi.

Agreement with General George Mathews

[April 17, 1809]

Attached to Agreement, November 9, 1808.

Promissory Note from Thomas Dean

[April 20, 1809]

I promise to pay to H. Clay the sum of fifty dollars, provided a decree of the County Court of Washington in a suit in Chancery between James Elder & Wife Complts agt. William Richards Zadock Richards & others shall be reversed in the Court of Appeals, where the cause is now depending—[1]

Witness my hand & seal this 20h. day of Apl. 1809.

THOS DEAN {L.S.}

[Endorsement on verso][2]

without recourse 5 July 1825 H CLAY.

DS, in Clay's hand. DLC-TJC, 2d Series, vol. 9. Dean was a resident of Washington County, Kentucky.

1 Case not reported. All the parties were taxpayers of Washington County.

2 AES.

From John P. Usher

Henry Clay Esqr Baltimore May 7th 1809

Sir I received a letter a few days since from Mr. Postlethwait,[1] by which it does not appear that he is willing to direct the Suit against Mr Hughes.[2] I must therefore allow you the customary comission for attending to it yourself and doubt not that you will exert yourself to bring this buisness to an Issue Mr. P. obseved in his letter that they had made an arrangement with the Bank of Pennsylvania, which would enable them to Issue post notes which I think would be the safes way of remitting the money—Mr P has a small claim against the Estate which I will thank you to settle.—Mr Greer[3] presented to me a few days since a fee Bill which I did not think that I would be justifiable in paying as the greater part of it was for suits that Mr. H. settled with out claiming the fees in which case Mr H & not the Admx, should be the looser particularly as they were not settled with a view of Advantageing the Estate I'll thank you to mention it Mr H & write to me by return of mail wether it will a loss [*sic*] to the Admx & Oblige Yrs Very respy

JOHN P USH[ER]

ALS. DLC-TJC (DNA, M212, R12).

1 Probably John Postlethwait.

2 James Hughes, who in 1806 had given a note, backed by a property mortgage, for $8,179 to Usher, as attorney-in-fact for Mary Usher, administratrix of the estate of Thomas Usher, Baltimore Town Commissioner and horse and furniture dealer. Hughes confessed his inability to pay the debt in 1807, and the mortgaged property was finally ordered to sale in 1811. The case was closed at the August Term of Fayette Circuit Court, 1811.

3 Possibly George Greer.

Bond to John Winn

[May 8, 1809]

I have this 8th: day of May 1809 sold to Maj: John Winn my Interest being one half in the Dower land as decreed by the Court of appeals to Henry and wife in the suit Winns against Elliott's heirs &C.[1] for Three hundred dollars and bind myself to make to him any other or further conveyance therefor HENRY CLAY

Copy. Fayette Circuit Court, Order Book L, 510. John, a brother of George Winn, was probably the Fleming County, Kentucky, lawyer of that name.

1 The Kentucky Court of Appeals at the Spring Term, 1808, had affirmed the decision of the Fayette Circuit Court in a suit brought by George and Owen Winn against the heirs of William Elliott to force conveyance of land the plaintiffs had purchased from Elliott before his death. The lower court had decreed conveyance but had permitted Elliott's widow, one of the defendants, who had become the wife of John Henry, to retain her dower. Clay had represented Elliott's heirs in the litigation. 3 *Ky. Reports* (Hardin), 490-95. Owen Winn was a brother of George and John.

Agreement, for Kennedy and Cox, with Philip Barbour

[May 12, 1809]

It is agreed between Philip Barbour & Kennedy & Cox as follows: The said Kennedy & Cox may take a Judgt. during the present term of the Foederal Court for the amount of their account & interest agt. William Taylor & Company,[1] and sue out their execution upon the same immediately: The said Barbour agrees to send up to H. Clay immediately upon his return home his bond with good security for what he deems his proportion of the said debt with interest payable at Christmas next, and which shall not be less than four thousand five hundred dollars: Upon the said bond being received, the said Kennedy & Cox shall credit the amount thereof upon the said Judgment, and shall proceed against the other partners of William Taylor & Co. for the residue of the debt, and not return upon the said Barbour but in the event of their insolvency: And whereas the said William Taylor & Co. claim certain credits which are not allowed by the said Kennedy & Cox it is clearly understood and agreed that the parties are to endeavour to adjust these credits themselves, but if they cannot do so the Judgment to be obtained as aforesaid is to constitute no bar to relief in equity. Witness our hands & seals 12 May 1809.

Teste PHILIP BARBOUR {L.S.}
THOS. BODLEY H CLAY for Kennedy & Cox {L.S.}

ADS, signed also by Barbour. DLC-TJC (DNA, M212, R15). Barbour was a Henderson, Kentucky, businessman and had represented his county in the State legislature in 1807.

1 The firm was composed of Barbour and Jonathan and William Taylor, the latter being members of a prominent and numerous family in Virginia and Kentucky, related through collateral lines to James Taylor of Newport, Kentucky, and to President Zachary Taylor.

From William M. Nash

H. Clay Esquire May 17th. 1809.

Sir

Please to pay to John H Morton or order thirty eight dollars & sixty eight cents & charge the same to Yr obt. Servt. W M NASH

ALS. DLC-TJC, 2d Series, vol. 9.

Account with John H. Morton

Dr. Henry Clay with John H. Morton [*ca.* May 17, 1809]

To Tax & Levy for the year 1808. $38.42½[1]

To Sundrey fee Bills .,..............	113.46
To Wm. M Nash's Order	38.68½
To season of three Mares to Bald Eagle[2] in 1808 @ $5	15.00
To Cash paid Porter[3] £2.6-6	7.75
Cr	$213:32
By Amt. collected on Exon Mrs Jackson vs. Tho. Irvine[4] $	138:41
	74.91
	2.25.
	72 66

D. DLC-TJC (DNA, M212, R15).
1 See above, *ca.* February 1, 1809.
2 Thoroughbred stallion sired by the imported horse Spread Eagle, raised by Col. John Hoomes, owned for a time by John Breckinridge, and sold at auction by the administrators of Breckinridge's estate early in 1808.
3 Possibly Samuel Porter. Cf. below, Summons, December 28, 1809.
4 See above, Order, March 26, 1809.

Report of Committee to Examine Bank Vault

2d. June 1809.

The Committee appointed to examine the state of the Vault and Count the cash in the hands of the Cashier Report—That they have Counted in Specie $21.271.61/100 of which they have deposited in three Boxes in the Vault . . . . $18.000.
And have left in the hands of the Cashier . . . . . . " 3.271.61
They have also counted in Eastn. Notes $ 695.
in Miami[1] Notes " 1070.
in Lexn. Br:[2] do 749.
in Insce[3] Notes 775.
in Russll.[4] Notes 117.
3406

In Notes of the Bank of Kentucky in Good order . . . 29.431
They found a packet sealed which by the report of a former Committee contains . . . . 8.018.
40.855.

They have also counted in notes of the Bank of Kentucky which are imperfect . . . . 545.
41.400.—
$ 62.671.61

H. CLAY

Bank of Kentucky, Frankfort, Record Book A, October 12, 1809-September 14, 1810, p. 271 (KyU).

1 Miami Exporting Company of Cincinnati, incorporated with note-issuing privileges in 1803.

2 Lexington Branch, Bank of Kentucky.

3 Kentucky Insurance Company.

4 Russellville Branch, Bank of Kentucky.

To James Taylor

Dr Sir Frankfort 3d. June 1809

I received your favor of the 30 Ulto.[1] I have not yet written to Mr. Botts,[2] but propose doing so upon my return home after I shall have collected such information as I can conveniently procure.

It is probable that we may find it our interest to engage in this business.[3] But I should not like to embark in it unless we would foresee some reasonable period when it might be brought to a final conclusion. Those speculations which require a life time to terminate & close do not suit my taste. We might perhaps select some of the claims from the schedule & undertake their investigation. I should like to be connected with you, and we could divide very well the labour, by your attending to the business in the Country, and my attending to it in Court.

I will write you again on this subject[4] Yr friend H. CLAY

ALS. KyHi. Addressed: "Col. James Taylor New Port."

1 Not found.

2 Possibly George W. Botts, northern Kentucky merchant and trader. The proposed letter has not been found.

3 Probably land speculation.

4 No additional letters on this matter have been found.

From James Smith, Jr.

Esteemed Friend/ Philad June 6h 1809

Not having heard from you for a long time. I am very anxious to know whether it has yet been or whether you think it will be in your power to sell my land, or to ascertain the boundaries &c so that my Title may be so fixed that I may sell it hereafter

I sincerely hope that you may, as I have always counted upon it as valuable—and I cannot see what can be the reason why Norvell[1] should not have the legal right I beg you will do all you can in the business—

I am very anxious to have all my Accots closed as soon as possible—I find, owing to mismanagement somehow, several Account [*sic*] not closed—of which you have had the care.—There is John Seitz & John Jordans Accounts—amounting together to upwards of £1000—say with Interest—to -- -- -- -- -- -- -- 1025—

There was 1st. Note of Millers[2] 1500 Interest 567.10

2 Notes taken of W W Smith[3] 1800$ & upward 675—

By my Accot. I have received in all on these Accot—from you & them—at different times—£1361—consequently there must be yet coming to me about £900—from which your Commissions are to come—I wish you to examine & see how these Accot stand & let me know as I am very anxious to have every Accot settled—

From what you formerly wrote me I have no doubt but the Notes of W W Smith have been received I forget the names of the persons who gave the Notes—

Please to let me have a statement P first Oppy when you have leisure to attend to it—as I am confident there must be something very considerable yet behind I am very respectfully Yr Friend

JAS SMITH JR

[Marginal note]

Please also to say whether you know any thing of Woodson Wrens debt—& what you think I had better do with Miller—as he yet owes me the two Notes of 1500 Dollars each which I certainly did inclose to you—

ALS. DLC-TJC (DNA, M212, R12). Addressed to Clay at Lexington. Endorsed by Clay, "Answered," but no reply has been found.

1 Thomas Norvell.

2 Robert Miller.

3 William W. Smith.

Promissory Note from James Hoskins and Others

[June 6, 1809]

Six months after date we promise to pay to H. Clay or order Seventy dollars.

Witness our hands & seals 6 June 1809

JAMES HOSKINS {L.S.}

his
WILLIAM × KEMP {L.S.}
mark

JOHN GATWOD {L.S.}

[Endorsement on verso][1]

Credit by Ten dollars.

6 June 1809. H. CLAY

DS, in Clay's hand. Woodford Circuit Court, File 82. In June, 1813, Clay won a suit, initiated over a year earlier, for the collection of this note. The defendants were all involved in more than one suit in Woodford County, in some instances against each other; but they have not been identified as residents there. Gatwod may have been John Gatewood of Fayette County, who subsequently moved to Montgomery County.

1 AES.

From James Smith, Jr.

June 20h 1809

Received June 20. 1809 of James Smith Jr One hundred and Fifty Dollars by virtue of an Order on him from Henry Clay Esq in my favour— 150 Dollars THOMAS C. GRAVES

My Friend

Your friend Greaves called upon me with a Letter[1] dated so long since as 30 Aug last requesting that I would advance him not exceeding 300 Dollars—The above is all he wants & it happens fortunate that it is so as I have been upon the borrow for several weeks myself owing to those who owe me keeping me out of money so long as they do—You will be kind enough to remitt me this 150 Dollars as soon as you receive this, and I hope it will be in your power to send me more with it—as there must be something considerable coming, from the whole of the Debts collectively—I wrote you lately[2] with a statement of what I had received—and you know the amount there was to collect—there was Seitz—Jordan—Millers note of 1500—Owens Notes &c[3]—I also do sincerely hope that something can be done with the land or it does seem very strange—It either did belong to Norwell,[4] or it did not & I should suppose this can be ascertained & let me beg of you to see into it if it is in your power—I also wish to know in what situation Miller is—You certainly have his his [*sic*] Notes for 1500 Dollars each—I sent them to you You received one 1500 besides & sent it to me—It is high time Miller did something for me—& I beg that at least he will put me on a footing with others—& not let others receive & me not Please to speak to him & tell him how badly I want the money—I actually had to borrow yesterday 2400 Dollars at 1¼ P Cent P month & this is extremely hard when I have so much due me Please to let me hear from you P first Opportunity & oblige Yr Friend

JAS SMITH JR.

ALS (the receipt is a DS, in Smith's hand). DLC-TJC (DNA, M212, R12). Addressed to Clay at Lexington.

1 Not found. Presumably from Clay.
2 Above, June 6, 1809.
3 John A. Seitz, John Jordan, Jr., Robert Miller, and Thomas Deye Owings.
4 Thomas Norvell.

From John Taylor

Dear Sir Virginia Port Royal June 26. 1809

I am much obliged to you for yours of the 1st. instant,[1] covering a plat of the decree in my case with Bodley &a., and if my land should be surveyed in conformity with your conjecture, so as to cover the land you include, I shall submit to the loss, without giving Messrs. the Compts. any farther trouble, if however the loss should be much greater, I mean to commence another process in the names of some of the Walden family, upon a prospect of being able to produce several new facts, going materially to assail the complainants' title, as well as to sustain mine; and if they succeed, however distant the period may be, I have no doubt of being able to come at the present decree, for which purpose I shall make myself a party with them, to be able to use the new testimony, and to pray for a bill of review.

This speculation however is only mentioned, to shew you that if we could, there is little cause now for re-measuring the road, or entering into a dispute about Johnson's begin ing. But I conceive that this point is settled by the decree, the court having decided "that the begin ing of Peter Johnson's[2] settlement in the proceedings mentioned *is rightly placed* in the decree of the district court." This proposition is therefore positively determined, and the determination is made the basis for the rest of the decree. In this, if I am mistaken, I concur with you in thinking that the expence and trouble of surveying the road would be needless, and that the parties had best agree to take Johnson's begining as it stands. But I have the opinion of the court of appeals, which seems to me to ascertain the intention of fixing the begining of Johnson at A as clearly as words can fix it.

As to the general course of the road, the decree is doubtful, and where there is a doubt, a party ought to assert the alternative which is in his favour, since the judge may possible [*sic*] be of that opinion. Whether we contend therefore for the general course of the whole road, or of that part binding on Johnson, ought to be the result of our interest, and if the latter opinion is most conformable to that, as it seems to be the best, it ought to be asserted; but if upon further enquiry it turns out to be the least favourable for us, the former need not be abandoned.

Ought the surveyor to lay down any lines required by either party, if they should differ. Who is to judge of the form of the survey? Not the surveyor I suppose. If it is like the case of a man's surveying his own entry, he is himself the director of the surveyor, it being at his peril to pursue that entry; so here, the decree is my entry, which I am at my peril to pursue. If this is correct, then we had best refuse to allow the complts. to obtrude any lines upon us for if you could exhibit a survey corresponding with your plat, without any rival project, the superior court would I think establish it. The first object therefore is to make the survey as we please, and if that can be accomplished, not to agree that the surveyor should lay down such lines as either party may require. If this cannot be accomplished, the second is to exhibit such a plat on the report of the surveyor as we think right, even if it is attended by a rival.

I have written largely to my friend Mr: Taylor[3] by Colo. Slaughter;[4] to those letters I refer you. The spheroidical square there spoken of, seems from your plat unnecessary; and indeed it ought not to be tried except for the sake of including the cabin, or for some very considerable object.

Will you be pleased to shew Mr: Taylor your plat, and this letter, and to confer with him on the business, which need not be delayed, as I have nothing to add, and he understands it far better than, Sir, Yr: mo: obt: St. JOHN TAYLOR

Mem: I requested Mr: Taylor to pay you $50 I think—if you can fix your plat, I will add $100 more—and if you can put him in the way of coming at a considerable amount of rents which must be [due][5] you shall have 25 per Ct. of them.

ALS. DLC-HC (DNA, M212, R1). Addressed to Clay at Lexington. Endorsed by Clay, "Answd.," but no answer has been found. See above, Taylor to Clay, January 4, February 5, 1807.

1 Not found. 2 Heir of Jacob Johnson. 3 Hubbard Taylor.

4 Probably George Slaughter, native of Culpeper County, Virginia, veteran of the Revolution, one of the original trustees of the city of Louisville. 5 MS. torn.

Property Deed, Drawn as Executor for Colonel Thomas Hart

[June 27, 1809]

[Henry Clay and Thomas Hart, Jr., executors of Colonel Thomas Hart, deceased, transfer to William T. Barry a lot on the north west corner of Mill Street and Church Alley in Lexington.]

Fayette County Court, Deed Book D, 311-12.

Deed of Trust from William T. Banton

[July 1, 1809]

[Indenture under which William T. Banton delivers to Henry Clay the following slaves: Charles, John, and James, now in possession of Banton—in trust that Clay upon request of the executors of John Hoomes, deceased, will sell the slaves at public auction to satisfy a debt owed by Banton to the aforesaid executors, amounting to $718 together with interest from this date. Certification of signatures of the parties before J. D. Young, Clerk of Fayette County, July 10, 1809.]

ADS, signed also by Banton. DLC-TJC (DNA, M212, R15).

From Robert Bywaters

Sir Lexington 3d. July 1809

Pleas pay Benjn. Adams[1] Thirty Six Shillings & Six pence for Hawling Gravel & oblige yours. &C ROBT BYWATERS

H. Clay Esqr.

ALS. DLC-TJC, 2d Series, vol. 9. Bywaters was a Lexington plasterer.

[1] Free colored resident of Lexington.

Bank Check to Richard Taylor

[July 5, 1809]

Pay to Richard Taylor or bearer forty three dollars and seventy five Cents. 5 July 1809. $43:75 HENRY CLAY

Cashier of the K. I. Co.[1]

ADS. DLC-TJC, 2d Series, vol. 9. Taylor had opened a tavern in Frankfort in October, 1805.

[1] Kentucky Insurance Company.

Agreement with William Orear

[July 8, 1809]

[Henry Clay, under power of attorney from Edward Tanner, and under authorization from John Tanner, agrees to sell to William Orear 400 acres, Rooker's settlement on Four Mile Creek in Clark County, which has been in controversy between John Tanner and Orear in the Court of Appeals,[1] for which land Orear has given bond[2] and security for $900. Title is to be such as Rooker derived from the Commonwealth, and is to be provided when the aforesaid consideration is paid. Signature of Clay witnessed by Henry B. Sanford.[3] Agreement recorded by M. Harrison, clerk of Montgomery County, April 7, 1812.]

Montgomery County Court, Deed Book 5, p. 515.

[1] In chancery proceedings Orear had defended his failure to comply with the terms of an earlier agreement with John Tanner, pioneer settler of Madison County, on the ground that the latter had failed to provide a legal title to the tract. Court decision had upheld Tanner's contention that the complaint of defect in title was unfounded. 4 *Ky. Reports* (1 Bibb) 237-39 (1808). Edward was John Tanner's son.

[2] See below, Bond, July 9, 1809.

[3] Probably of Montgomery County.

Promissory Note from Thomas N. Gist

[July 8, 1809]

Six months after date for value received I promise to pay to

Henry Clay the sum of One hundred and twenty dollars. Witness my hand & seal this 8h. July 1809. THOS. N GIST {L.S.}

DS, in Clay's hand. Clark Circuit Court, File 173. Thomas N. was a brother of Henry C. and son of Nathaniel Gist. In March, 1816, Clay won a judgment in a suit filed during the previous December to force payment of this note. *Ibid.*

Bond from William Orear, Lawrence Owens, and Benedict Couchman

[July 9, 1809]

Know all men by these presents that we William Orear, Lawrence Owens and Bennedict Couchman are held and firmly bound unto John Tanner and Henry Clay in the just & full sum of eighteen hundred dollars; to be paid to the said Tanner and Clay their heirs exors admors. or assigns: to which payment well and truly to be made we bind our selves jointly & severally our joint & several heirs exors & admors firmly by these presents. Sealed with our seals & dated this 9h. July 1809.

The Condition of this obligation is such that if the said William Orear Lawrence Owens & Bennedict Couchman shall on the first day of March next pay to the said Tanner & Clay the sum of four hundred & fifty dollars; & shall on or before the first day of March 1811 pay to the said Tanner & Clay the further sum of four hundred and fifty dollars more then this obligation to be void.

Sealed & Delivered — WILL, OREAR {L.S.}
In presence of — LAWRENCE OWENS {L.S.}
HENRY B. SANFORD — BONEDICK [*sic*] COUCHMAN {L.S.}

DS, in Clay's hand. Clark Circuit Court, File 154. See above, Agreement, July 8, 1809. Owens was a resident of Clark County; Couchman had explored in Kentucky as early as 1776, acquired claims to several thousand acres of land, and apparently settled in Clark County.

In September, 1813, Tanner and Clay won a suit against Orear, Owens, and Couchman for the amount of this note. The judgment was not paid, however, and nine years later, after Tanner and Owens had died, Clay won another suit, brought against Owens' heirs. Clark Circuit Court, File 154, 256.

Advertisement for Bids for Street Paving

Paving July 10, 1809.

The subscribers will receive proposals at the Kentucky Hotel on Saturday the 22d inst. at twelve o'clock, from any person disposed to undertake the paving of that portion of Upper Street, lying between Main Street and Short Street, and that portion of Short Street lying between Upper and Market Streets. For one moiety of the work, the county court will provide payment on the laying of their next levy; and for the residue the several proprietors, whose lots front the ground contemplated to be paved, will be responsible.

JOHN BRADFORD,
RICHARD HIGGINS. *Commissioners for the county.*
H. CLAY, *in behalf of the individual proprietors.*[1]

Lexington *Kentucky Gazette,* July 11, 1809.
[1] Clay was a property owner on Short Street.

From John Wrenshall

Sir Pittsburgh 11 July 1809

I expected, agreably to your promise, to receive an acct in Aprill last, of the final issue of our affair with Major Morrison, and presume that your omitting to inform me, is oweing to the result being favourable—I need not inform you, because the nature of our affairs in Kentucky are such, as will convince you that money with us is scarse, shall therefore be exceedingly obliged if you'l remitt us the other five hundred dollars which will compleat our quota of the two thousand recovd. Morrison—I flatter myself that by this time also, you are in funds to settle the residue of our demands against Allen, Hughs Holmes's estate, Brick House in Paris and to oblige me with general statement of our affairs—in expectation of which I remain Yours very respectfully JOHN WRENSHALL

ALS. DLC-TJC (DNA, M212, R12). Addressed to Clay at Lexington. Cf. above, Wrenshall to Clay, June 13, 1807.

From James Smith, Jr.

Esteemed Friend Philada. July 11h 1809

I have received a letter from R. Miller dated 27 June in which among other things he says—that he has sold the House he formerly offered to you for me, but does not mention the price—He further says he will give Mr Clay the Bonds together with a payment in Cash—One of the Bonds he says is not payable untill December 1810—which he fears Mr Clay will not take—I am extremely anxious to have all my old affairs settled as soon as possible, and therefore will submit it to your better judgment, whether it will not be best to accept of the said Bonds, and endeavour to get as much Cash as you possibly can & either Cotton or Saltpetre, or something worth the money for the Ballance—I find on enquiry that refined Salt petre is only worth at this time 37 Cents & consequently what is called rough cannot be worth more than from 15 to 20 Cents—I expect he means to pay the Interest on this heavy sum that he has owed me so long, & I beg you to make the best settlement for my Interest that you possibly can without delay I have answered his letter & have desired him to raise as much money as he possibly can to accompany this settlement & you will of course take care that the Bonds are secured—Should his Notes not be found in your possession—they are certainly not in mine & therefore I expect he will be content to receive a Guarrantee from you that in case they are found they shall be delivered—& I will give you the same—I believe Robt Miller to be a very honest Man & desirous of paying I therefore presume & believe that you will have but little trouble in settling with him which I beg may be done without delay. because the losses he may possibly sustain In his laudable attempts at manufacturing &c—may put it out of his power & I have lost so much & waited so long that it really has become absolutely necessary for me to make every exertion in my power to get what is due me—I have been very unfortunate in many of my Customers—I wrote you some time since requesting a statement of the business of mine under your care[1] & as soon as you have leisure, no doubt you will attend thereto—I am very confident that unless I have omitted some credits which is not very likely, there must be some moneys coming to me & I do stand much in need of all I can get—With much respect I am your Friend JAS SMITH JR

ALS. DLC-TJC (DNA, M212, R12). Addressed to Clay at Lexington.
1 Above, letters of June 6, 20, 1809.

Receipt from William Scott

[July 13, 1809]

Attached to Promissory Note, June 30, 1807.

Receipted Bill from John Harrison

[July 15, 1809]

Henry Clay Esqr Dr T John Harrison

1809		
July 15	To fitting Two Windows &	
	" Turning Arch . . .	$ 2.00
	" Laying 4 Harths.	2"00
		4.00.

Recd the above in full from Robt Bywaters

JOHN HARRISON

DS. DLC-TJC (DNA, M212, R15). Harrison was a Lexington bricklayer.

From Hugh and William Young

Henry Clay Esqr Baltimore 18 July 1809
Sir

In reply to Your Favor of the 1st Currt.[1]—The mode You adopted to get Our Claim agt. Clarke & Anderson well securd, fully meets Our approbation, But shoud the Note not be paid when due We request You will bring Suit imy. after the 1st. of Octr

On 18 Octr last We Recd. from L. Tiernan & Co. in part of the Money Collected by You for Us from Aikin & Eastland $394 which with the Premium paid by You on the Bill is equal to $400[2] by Your Statement furnishd Decr. 1807[3] the Balance in Your Hands then was $461 74/100

Shoud the Note of Clarke & Anderson's &c. be paid when due We request You will embrace the first Opy. of procuring & remiting a Bill for the proceeds & include the above small Balance with Respect We remain Sir Your Mo. Obt Sts

HU & WM. YOUNG

ALS. DLC-TJC (DNA, M212, R12). 1 Not found.
2 See above, Tiernan and Company to Clay, June 16, 1808. 3 Not found.

Memorandum of Credit for John P. Wagnon

[September 6, 1809]

Attached to Agreement, November 9, 1808.

Promissory Note from Elijah Noble

27 Septr. 1809.

Due H. Clay at Christmas next fifty dollars. ELIJAH NOBLE

DS, in Clay's hand. DLC-TJC, 2d Series, vol. 10. Noble for a short time operated a store in partnership with Robert Bywaters and, early in 1816, opened the Old Ironsides Tavern on Short Street, Lexington.

Settlement with Nathaniel Ford

4 Octr. 9

On a settlemt. of all a/ct with Nathl Ford there remains due him $70: & 83 Cents H. CLAY

[Endorsement][1]

Recd. paymt in full 7 Octr. 1809

NATHANIEL FORD

ADS. DLC-TJC, 2d Series, vol. 10. Ford was a resident of Fayette County.
1 ES, in Clay's hand.

Bill from Benijah Bosworth

		october 21st 1809
Henry Clay to B Bosworth		Dr.
to paveing 20 Square and 65 feet		
at $6 per Square -- --	$123	=90 cents
to Setting 33 yards curb Stone		
at 12½ cents per yard - - -	5	=12½ do
	$128	= 2½ [*sic*]

[Endorsements on verso][1]
october 30th 1809 received on the within a/c 25 dollars
december 26 reciv'd. 50 dollars on the within
Recd. the bal. in full 15 Jan. 1810 B Bosworth

D. DLC-TJC, 2d Series, vol. 11. Bosworth, a resident of Lexington, was a millwright.
1 E; and ES, in Clay's hand.

Deed of Trust from the Attorneys of Peyton Short to Clay and Robert Alexander

[October 24, 1809]

[Whereas Peyton Short by letter of attorney recorded in this court, October 16, 1809, appointed Charles Wilkins and Frederick Ridgely[1] his agents, they now for the sum of five shillings, paid and acknowledged, convey to Henry Clay and Robert Alexander the following property and debts: 7,500 acres near the mouth of the Big Miami River in Ohio, adjoining lands of William H. Harrison,[2] of which 7,500 acres 5,000 have been conveyed in trust to Nicholas Clarke[3] to secure a debt due William Croghan[4] by deed also recorded in this court; 1,000 acres in Indiana Territory on the Ohio River; 1,200 acres in the same Territory in three donation lots near Vincennes; 615 acres near the mouth of the Cumberland River in Kentucky; 20,000 acres in Christian County, Kentucky, a tract recently purchased by Short from George Browne;[5] all the castings which Short has on hand in Lexington and elsewhere; all debts in money, castings, or property due or to become due to Short from Thomas D. Owings; all slaves conveyed by Short to Clarke as aforesaid not sold by Short to Thomas Hart;[6] negro Betty, dairy woman; all stock of horses, cattle, hogs, and farming utensils now on Short's estate and Thomas Eastland's farm in Woodford County, Kentucky; and also all Short's household and kitchen furniture, his library, stills, and distilling utensils, together with all appurtenances to the property and debts:

In trust that Clay and Alexander will sell the property and collect the debts and from the proceeds discharge such debts as Short may have contracted with any of the banking institutions in Kentucky or for which he now stands bound under replevy bonds, thus relieving his securities in such bonds; also that they will satisfy Frederick Ridgely in a debt of about $10,000 due him from Short, for which he holds Short's paper; that they will pay Mrs. Henry, mother of the late Mrs. Short,[7] about $3,000 which Short owes her and for which she holds his paper; and finally, when these objects are accomplished, that they will render to Wilkins and Ridgely, or the survivor, any proceeds remaining. The trustees are authorized to appoint one or more attorneys under them.

Clay and Alexander agree to execute the trust to the best of their ability. Signatures of all the parties are witnessed by J. Bledsoe, Joseph Crockett, and John H. Hanna and acknowledged before the Clerk of the Court of Appeals, May 25, 1810.]

Kentucky Court of Appeals, Deed Book N, 258-60. Alexander was a prominent Woodford County farmer, member of the State Senate, 1795-1802, and first president of the Bank of Kentucky.

1 Wilkins and Ridgely were Short's brothers-in-law.

2 William Henry Harrison was at that time Governor of Indiana Territory. His wife was a sister of Peyton Short's first wife.

3 Of Jefferson County, Kentucky.

4 Revolutionary veteran from Virginia, an early settler in Kentucky, whose home, "Locust Grove," was near Louisville.

5 Persons bearing this name were found in several Kentucky counties, including Logan, Muhlenberg, Scott, Mercer, and Fayette.

6 Probably Thomas Hart, Jr.

7 Short's second wife was Jane Henry Churchill, daughter of Mrs. Mary Henry of New Jersey.

Report of Committee to Examine Bank Vaults

[October 26, 1809]

Bank of Kentucky, Frankfort, Record Book A, October 12, 1807-September 14, 1810, p. 323 (KyU). For reports essentially similar cf. above, May 10, 1808; June 2, 1809. In this account, Bank of Chillicothe (Ohio) notes are mentioned, in addition to those of the institutions cited previously.

Assignment from the Attorneys of Peyton Short

[*ca.* November 1, 1809]

We assign the within Bond to Henry Clay & Robt. Alexander—

F RIDGELY

for self & Chs Wilkins—Attornies in fact for Peyton Short—

ES. Franklin Circuit Court, File 91 (1810). Endorsement on verso of a promissory note, dated June 17, 1808, for £7, 14s, 3d, given by Clement Bell of Franklin County to Peyton Short. Cf. above, Deed of Trust, October 24, 1809. A suit, brought in Franklin Circuit Court by Clay and Alexander against Bell for collection of the note, was dismissed by the plaintiff in March, 1810. *Ibid.* Order Book, 1809-1810, p. 466.

Receipt to Robert Johnson

November 4th. 1809

Col. Robt Johnson has paid each of us twenty five dollars for our Services as arbitrators in the Suit in Chancery in the United States Court for Kentucky Wherein sd Johnson and John Craig are Complts. and Thomas Lewis & Anne[1] his wife executors of John May are Defendts.

ROBERT TRIMBLE
H. CLAY
M. D. HARDIN[2]

ADS, by Trimble, signed also by Clay and Hardin. Fayette Circuit Court, File 273 (1814).

1 Ann, widow of John May, had become the wife of Thomas Lewis, of Virginia.

2 Martin D. Hardin, brother of Mark, was a native of Pennsylvania who had moved to Nelson County, Kentucky, as a boy, studied law under George Nicholas, and practiced that profession first at Richmond, Kentucky, later at Frankfort, where he was reporter for the Court of Appeals, 1808. He was a member of the Kentucky House of Representatives from Madison County in 1805, from Franklin County, 1812, 1818-1820; and United States Senator completing an unexpired term, 1816-1817. He was Secretary of State for Kentucky, 1812-1816, but left that post to serve as major in Colonel John Allen's militia regiment during the winter of 1812-1813.

Report of Committee on Steps for Bank of Kentucky

[November 9, 1809]

Appointed on October 30 to make inquiries concerning the style and price of steps to be obtained for the entrance to the Bank, the committee, composed of Clay and Daniel Weisiger (a tavernkeeper in Frankfort and one of the founders of that town) recommended that "stone steps consisting of a treble flight one in front and one on each side should be procured for the front door on Montgomery Street." The "Keeper of the penitentiary," it was noted, would undertake to supply the steps for eighty dollars. The report, not found, is summarized in Bank of Kentucky, Frankfort, Record Book A, October 12, 1807-September 14, 1810, pp. 328-29 (KyU). The committee was thereupon ordered to engage the aforementioned official to provide the steps accordingly.

Receipt from John W. Wooldridge

[November 10, 1809]

Recd. of H Clay 10h. Nov. 1809 Thirty dollars being the balance in full of what he had in his hands as guardian of my brother Powhatan

JNO. W. WOOLDRIDGE

DS, in Clay's hand. DLC-TJC (DNA, M212, R15).

Advertisement of Trustees' Sale

[November 11, 1809]

[Robert Alexander and Henry Clay, Trustees of Peyton Short, advertise a public auction to be held at Short's "mansion house" in Woodford County, beginning at noon on November 29. Stock of all kinds—"between eighty and one hundred Horses, a large number of Hogs and horned Cattle"—household furniture, and farming utensils are to be offered for sale at "twelve months credit (to bear interest from the date if not punctually paid) for all sums above five dollars, bond and approved security being given therefor, and cash for all sums of five dollars or under."]

Lexington *Reporter*, November 14, 1809.

Settlement of Accounts with Cuthbert Banks

[November 26, 1809]

We have this day settled all accounts whatever except what is due from C. Banks to H. Clay upon the lease of the Hotel[1] executed the 24 June 1808 & except the Tavern account which the said Banks has upon the books of the Hotel agt. H. Clay;[2] upon which settlement a balance appeared in favor of C. Banks of sixty pounds 13/6 for which sum he is credited on his note held by H. Clay given to L. Sanders[3] for $400.

Witness our hands this 26 Nov. 1809. HENRY CLAY
CUTHB: BANKS

ADS, signed also by Banks. DLC-HC (DNA, M212, R9).
1 The Kentucky Hotel. 2 See below, Account, January 15, 1810.
3 Lewis Sanders.

Bond to Peyton Short's Trustees

[December 1, 1809]

TWELVE months after date, for value received, we promise to pay to *Robert Alexander* and *Henry Clay*, or the survivor of them, and the Executors and Administrators of such survivor, the sum of Twenty Dollars with interest thereon from the date; but if the principal should be punctually paid, the interest is to be remitted.

WITNESS, our hands and seals, this first day of December 1809.

Witness, PORTER CLAY {SEAL.}
WILL S DALLAM H. CLAY {SEAL.}

DS. DLC-TJC (DNA, M212, R15). Cf. above, Advertisement, November 11, 1809. An endorsement on verso shows that on November 2, 1811, Henry Watkins paid $22.30, the amount of principal and interest on this note, to Thomas Bullock, also of Woodford County and a former member of the State legislature.

To Isaac Shelby

My Dr Sir Lex. 2 Decr. 1809.

You have no doubt 'ere this heard of the melancholy loss in the death of Mr. Hart which our family has sustained.[1] He has left a will by which Mr. Hunt, Mrs. Hart, Mr. Barton, and Mr. John Hart & myself are appointed his executors.[2] We are disposed to believe from the view of his affairs which we have as yet been able to take that after paying all his debts an ample competence will remain to his family. But owing to the sudden check to the course of his business produced by this event, a momentary pressure arises against which we wish to provide. To enable us to do this it becomes necessary to obtain some pecuniary aid. Believing that you possess the disposition, & hoping that you may the means, we are induced to make application to you. We propose making ourselves personally responsible, & in addition to this giving any security, personal or real or both that may be desired. We should like to obtain a loan of Ten thousand dollars or as large a proportion of it as practicable, and we could desire to have the use of it for twelve months. Will you favor us with a reply stating whether you can supply us with any money, how much, & for what time?[3] The family will be sensible of the obligation under which you may place them, & your indemnity shall be as extensive & as safe as you can possibly ask it.

We shall be gratified also by a statement of the amount which Mr. Hart already owes you. I am Dr Sir Yr friend &c

HENRY CLAY

ALS. KyU-Darbishire Papers. Addressed to Shelby in Lincoln County.

1 Thomas Hart, Jr., died November 26, 1809. He was a first cousin of Shelby's wife, Susannah, daughter of Nathaniel Hart.

2 Eleanor Grosh Hart was the widow, John Hart a brother, and Abraham S. Barton a business partner of the deceased. The wife of John W. Hunt was the widow's sister.

3 The reply has not been found.

Nominations for Committee Clerks

[December 4, 1809]

Clay nominated David Todd as clerk to the committees of propositions and grievances, and privileges and elections; and Charles Bradford as clerk to the committees of claims, courts of justice, and religion. Ky. H. of Reps., *Journal, 1809-1810* pp. 5, 6. Todd was elected on the first ballot. Bradford, at this time engaged in a printing business with his brother Daniel, was promptly rejected. Clay then swung his support to Robert P. Henry, a young lawyer who had recently completed his studies under Clay. When Henry's name was also dropped as lowest in the balloting, Clay supported Tunstall Cox, nominee of the Mercer County representatives and the plurality candidate from the beginning, who was thereupon elected.

Resolution Relating to Hardin County Election

[December 4, 1809]

Resolved, that a committee of five, be appointed to enquire whether Samuel Haycraft,[1] or John Thomas, was constitutionally and legally elected a member of the house of representatives for the county of Hardin, at the late general election in August last; that the said committee have power to send for persons, papers, and records for their information, and report their opinion thereon specially to the house.

Ky. H. of Reps., *Journal, 1809-1810,* p. 7. The resolution was accepted and a committee appointed, with Clay as chairman. For the final report, see below, December 5, 1809.

[1] Pioneer settler of Hardin County, sheriff in 1802, a lawyer and judge of the Court of Quarter Sessions and the Circuit Court, a member of the Kentucky House of Representatives in 1801 and 1810.

Committee Report on Hardin County Election

[December 5, 1809]

The committee appointed to enquire whether Samuel Haycraft or John Thomas, was constitutionally and legally elected a member of the house of representatives, for the county of Hardin, at the general election, in August last, have, according to order, had the subject under consideration, and beg leave to report,

That the county of Hardin being entitled to two representatives, it appeared to your committee, that the votes given at the last election were, for Charles Helm[1] 436, for Samuel Haycraft 350, and for John Thomas 271: that at the time when these votes were given the said Samuel Haycraft was an assistant judge of the circuit court of Hardin; and that he did not resign that office until some time after the election was closed. From these facts the following questions arise: Is mr. Haycraft entitled to his seat? if not, is mr. Thomas?

Upon the first question, three clauses of the constitution shed some light; the first and second sections of the first article, providing for a separation, into three departments, of the powers of government; and the 26th section of the second article, interdicting amongst others, as ineligible to a seat in the general assembly, all who hold or exercise any office of profit under this commonwealth, with certain exceptions, not embracing mr. Haycraft's case.

The principle of separating, and preserving distinct, the great powers of government, ought, rather, to be enlarged than circumscribed. But this case is not one in which we have to resort to construction. On the contrary we have clear and explicit injunctions to guide us. The fact being ascertained, that mr. Haycraft held an office of profit under this commonwealth, at the time of the election, the constitutional disqualification attaches, and excludes him—he was ineligible, and therefore cannot be entitled to his seat.

It remains to enquire into the pretentions of mr. Thomas. His claim can only be supported, by a total rejection of the votes given to mr. Haycraft, as void to all intents whatever. It is not pretended that they were given by persons not qualified according to the constitution; and consequently if rejected, it must be, not for any inherent objection in themselves, but because they have been bestowed in a manner forbidden by the constitution or laws. By an act passed 18th December, 1800,[2] it is required that persons holding offices incompatible with a seat in the legislature, shall resign them before they are voted for; and it is provided, that all votes given to any such person, prior to such resignation, shall be utterly void.

This act, when applied to the case in question, perhaps admits of the construction, that the votes given to mr. Haycraft, though void and ineffectual in creating any right in him to a seat in this house, cannot affect in any manner, the situation of his competitor. Any other exposition of it, is, in the opinion of your committee, wholly inconsistent with the constitution and would in practice be extremely dangerous. It would be subversive of the great principle of free government, that the majority shall prevail. It would operate as a deception upon the people; for it cannot be doubted that the votes given to mr. Haycraft, were bestowed under a full persuasion that he had a right to receive them. And it would infringe the right of this house, guaranteed by the constitution, to judge of the qualifications of its members. It would, in fact, be a declaration that disqualification produces qualification—that the incapacity of one man, capacitates another to hold a seat in this house.

Your committee, therefore being unanimously and decidedly of opinion, that neither of the gentlemen is entitled to a seat in this house, recommend the adoption of the following resolution:

Resolved, That a writ of election issue, to authorize and cause to be elected and returned, a member of the house of representatives for the county of Hardin.

Ky. H. of Reps., *Journal, 1809-1810,* pp. 8-10. Other members of the drafting committee were James D. Breckinridge, Thomas Bullock, George C. Thompson, and Adam Beatty. The report was adopted and a new election ordered. John Thomas was ultimately awarded the seat.

1 Member of the legislature from Hardin County, 1806, 1809-1816.

2 Littell (comp.) *Statute Law of Kentucky,* II, 396.

Resolution on Treating by Political Candidates

[December 9, 1809]

Resolved, That the provision in the constitution, against a treating by candidates for the House of Representatives, as much forbids an union and agreement amongst all the candidates of a county, to treat, and divide the expence equally between themselves, with a view of affecting the election, as it does a treating by an individual candidate.

Ky. H. of Reps., *Journal, 1809-1810,* p. 40. The House concurred in the resolution unanimously. The measure related to a prohibition in Article VI, section 3, of the Kentucky Constitution of 1799. Littell (comp.), *Statute Law of Kentucky,* I, 50.

Promissory Note from Prettyman Merry

[December 15, 1809]

Having brought a suit in the Foed. Court agt. Bealls representatives[1] I promise to pay H. Clay One hundred dollars if I am entirely successful in the said suit; & at all events I promise to pay him on demand thirty dollars. Witness my hand & seal this 15 Decr. 1809. PRETTYMAN MERRY {L.S.}

DS, in Clay's hand. DLC-TJC (DNA, M212, R15).

1 Case not found. It was probably directed against the heirs of Benjamin Beall, deceased, claimants of land entered by Peter Shepherd on Hinkston Fork of Licking in Bourbon County, Kentucky, which entry conflicted with one by Prettyman Merry.

Committee Report on Petition of Isaac Rayfield

[December 18, 1809]

The committee for courts of justice, have according to order, had under consideration, a petition to them referred, and have come to the following resolution thereupon, viz.

Resolved, As the opinion of this committee, that the petition from Isaac Rayfield, setting forth—that from infirmity, and his indigent circumstances, he is unable to pay the remaining instalments on two small tracts of head right land, and praying that a law may pass for his relief—*is reasonable.*

Ky. H. of Reps., *Journal, 1809-1810,* p. 65. Other members of the drafting committee were William T. Barry, Humphrey Marshall, John Simpson, Thomas A. Covington, William Henry (of Scott County), Samuel G. Hopkins, Joel Yancey (Barren), Cyrus Talbot (Nelson), and Edward George (Henry). The report was concurred in and appropriate legislation authorized. The bill was not introduced at this session, but the petition was ultimately granted by act of January 28, 1812. Littell (comp.), *Statute Law of Kentucky,* IV, 336. Rayfield's tracts, 32 acres surveyed February 19, 1807, and 50 acres surveyed September 19, 1807, were located in Cumberland County, on the east and main forks, respectively, of Sulphur Creek. Jillson (comp.), *Kentucky Land Grants,* 390.

Resolution Relating to Holiday Adjournment

Resolved, [December 23, 1809]

By the senate and house of representatives, that when an adjournment of the two houses takes place, on this day, it shall be until Tuesday morning, ten o'clock.

Ky. H. of Reps., *Journal, 1809-1810,* p. 83. Monday was Christmas. This apparently routine action occasioned a vote requiring recorded count: 29 "Yeas" to 21 "Nays."

To James Trotter

Trans: University Dec. 26. 1809.—

Sir, We hereby request you to call a meeting of the Board of Trustees, to be held on friday to appoint a Proxy to represent the Board at a meeting of the Shareholders of the Bank of Kentucky on monday next.—[1] Yr. obt. serts.— HENRY CLAY

James Trotter esq.
Chm. of the Board
of Trustees T. U.

HENY. PURVIANCE
W. LEAVY
CH HUMPHREYS[2]
THO: T. BARR.

LS. KyLxT. An early emigrant from Virginia to Lexington, Trotter became prominent as a merchant, a magistrate, and, at widely separated intervals, a member of the State legislature. In 1797 he had retired to his farm of about 400 acres on the Tate's Creek Road, leaving his mercantile business to his sons, Samuel and George, Jr.

1 Pursuant to this request the board assembled on December 29 and authorized Edmund Bullock, Clay, and William T. Barry to represent the shares of Transylvania University in voting for directors of the Bank. PPPrHi-Shane Collection (KyU-microfilm).

2 Charles Humphreys, Lexington merchant, lawyer, jurist, and writer.

Motion Proposing Legislation

[December 28, 1809]

Clay asked permission to introduce two bills, one providing for definition of the Kentucky-Tennessee boundary, the other explaining "the privilege of the Prison bounds." Ky. H. of Reps., *Journal, 1809-1810,* p. 93. For the latter measure, see below, Bill, December 29, 1809. The legislation relating to the state boundary was introduced by John Simpson after Clay's departure for Washington. The proposal passed the House, but failed of Senate action at this time.

Summons to Magistrate's Court

[December 28, 1809]

[John H. Morton signs a warrant authorizing the sheriff or any constable to summon Henry Clay to appear before a justice of the peace to answer complaint of Samuel Porter[1] "in a plea of debt of £2"5 due by Acct." Witnessed by James Dunn.]

DS, printed form. DLC-TJC, 2d Series, vol. 10. Executed by William Fair, Constable of Fayette County, on June 15, 1810. On the same day Fair gave Morton a receipt for £2:6:6, the amount of the debt "for halling one load of sand," plus the constable's fee.

1 Pioneer Indian fighter residing in Fayette County.

Bill Relating to Prison Bounds

[December 29, 1809]

For a drafting committee which included also William T. Barry and George Walker, Clay presented a bill providing that the privilege of prison bounds should not be extended to those committed to prison for contempt or to those sentenced to "imprisonment" by judgment of any tribunal or magistrate. The measure passed without amendment. Ky. H. of Reps., *Journal, 1809-1810,* pp. 94-95; Littell (comp.), *Statute Law of Kentucky,* IV, 101-102 (January 15, 1810). The law in effect repealed the section of the act of 1796 which permitted establishment of bounds for county prisons, not exceeding ten acres of land, adjoining such prison, within which prisoners not committed for treason or felony had liberty to walk, out of the prison, "for the preservation of his or her health." Littell, *op. cit.,* I, 376 (December 17, 1796).

Motion Relating to Enquiry on William Orear

[December 30, 1809]

On Clay's motion the select committee appointed in accordance with House resolutions to institute an enquiry into Orear's conduct as surveyor of Montgomery County was discharged from further proceedings relative to the incompatibility of the offices held by Orear. Ky. H. of Reps., *Journal, 1809-1810,* p. 100. The select committee, of which Clay was a member but not chairman, had been assigned to investigate whether the duties of surveyor and justice of the peace were compatible, as well as to consider charges that Orear had abused his dual authority in these posts. Following acceptance of the Clay motion, the committee reported a recommendation to discharge Orear for want of sufficient evidence in support of the allegations.

Amendments to Bill Altering Mode of Summoning Jurors

[December 30, 1809]

For a seven-man select committee, appointed the preceding day, Clay presented several amendments (not recorded) to a Senate bill. Ky. H. of Reps., *Journal, 1809-1810,* p. 101. The amendments were approved and the measure passed the House, but it was not subsequently reported out of the Senate. A bill relating to the same subject, providing for empaneling a grand jury after discharge of one such body during a term of circuit court, was enacted at the next session of the legislature. Littell (comp.), *Statute Law of Kentucky,* IV, 267 (January 31, 1811).

Bill for Relief of Certain Mechanics

[January 2, 1810]

After moving earlier in the day to present such a bill, Clay reported it for a drafting committee which included also William T. Barry and George Walker. Ky. H. of Reps., *Journal, 1809-1810,* pp. 109, 111. The measure was amended but then rejected at third reading in the House. Cf. above, Bill, December 19, 1808.

Committee Report on Sundry Petitions

[January 3, 1810]

The committee for Courts of justice have, according to order, had under consideration, sundry petitions to them referred; and have come to the following resolutions thereupon, to wit:

Resolved,

As the opinion of this committee, that the petition of Joseph Brooks,[1] representing that he held a joint interest with the late *Col. J. F. MOORE,*[2] in certain lands lying in the Counties of Jefferson and Bullitt; which had been entered in the name of *Joseph Wynkoop,*[3] a non-resident—and sold for the tax, interest and costs due thereon; that owing to the indisposition of Col. Moore, he was prevented redeeming the same, until the lapse of that period at which, by law, lands thus sold, might be redeemed. And praying that he may yet be permitted to redeem the same, *is reasonable.*

Resolved,

As the opinion of this committee, that the petition of *John Jackson,*[4] representing his confinement in the Jail of Breckenridge county, on a charge of FELONY, and the improbability of his getting a trial there. And praying a change of venue for his trial, *is reasonable.*

Resolved,

As the opinion of this committee, that the petition of *Richard Nicholson,*[5] representing that in 1803, he had obtained from the County Court of Madison, a certificate for 400 Acres of land—

That through the mistake of the Clerk, no record was made thereof. In consequence of which the said land had been appropriated by another. And praying that a law may pass for his relief, *be rejected.*

Ky. H. of Reps., *Journal, 1809-1810,* p. 116. For other members of the drafting committee, see above, Committee Report, December 18, 1809. The present report was concurred in and appropriate legislation authorized. A bill for the relief of Joseph Brooks, introduced by William T. Barry after Clay's resignation from the legislature, was enacted January 25, 1810. Littell (comp.), *Statute Law of Kentucky,* IV, 133. A bill for John Jackson, also introduced by Barry after Clay's departure, was rejected in the House. Ky. H. of Reps., *Journal, 1809-1810,* pp. 151, 176.

1 A resident of Jefferson County and an extensive land holder in Kentucky. The tract under consideration amounted to 4,200 acres in Bullitt County, conveyed by deed of partition from Moore. Jillson (comp.), *Old Kentucky Entries and Deeds,* 400, 474, *et passim;* Ky. Gen. Assy., *Acts, 1809,* pp. 73-74.

2 James Francis Moore.

3 Of Philadelphia, who claimed 12,231 acres in Bullitt and Jefferson counties. By deed of September 5, 1807, he had transferred the property to Moore and Brooks. *Tyler's Quarterly Magazine,* III (July, 1921), 45; Ky. Gen. Assy., *Acts, 1809,* p. 73.

4 Unidentified.

5 Later in the year Nicholson acquired a tract of 200 acres on Collins Fork of Goose Creek, in Clay County. Jillson (comp.), *Kentucky Land Grants,* 379.

Resignation of Seat in Kentucky House of Representatives

Sir, *Frankfort, January* 4, 1810.

The appointment to the senate of the United States, with which

I have been recently honored, being incompatible with a seat in the house, over which you preside, I hasten to tender my resignation as a member from the county of Fayette, in order that the public service may receive no injury by a delay in filling the vacancy. It is in vain, sir, to attempt to express my gratitude to a partial country for this new mark of its esteem. No language would do justice to the sensibilities excited on the occasion. I cannot, however, refuse to myself this opportunity of bearing testimony to the frank, liberal, and honorable manner, in which, on your part, the competition between us has been conducted.

With great respect, I am, sir, Your obedient servant,

The hon. Wm. Logan, speaker of the H. CLAY:
House of Representatives.[1]

Ky. H. of Reps., *Journal, 1809-1810,* p. 121. Clay had on this day been elected to complete the unexpired term of Buckner Thruston, by a House vote of 44 for Clay to 20 for William Logan and by a joint House and Senate vote of 61 for Clay to 31 for Logan.

1 Logan, who had served as Speaker in the legislative sessions of 1805-1806, 1808, and 1809, and briefly as a judge on the Kentucky Court of Appeals in 1808, returned to the bench later this month. He was subsequently a United States Senator from March 4, 1819, through May 28, 1820, when he resigned to make an unsuccessful race for the office of Governor.

Credentials as United States Senator

[January 6, 1810]

DS by Governor Charles Scott. DNA, RG46, 11B-B2. Addressed: "The Speaker of the Senate of the United States Washington City." The text is similar to the Credentials, above, December 29, 1806.

Receipt to Robert Johnson

8. Jan 1810

Recd. of Col Johnson forty pounds ten shillings heretofore being my fees in two suits between May's representatives & Craig & Johnson

H. CLAY

ADS. Fayette Circuit Court, File 273 (1814). Cf. above, Receipt to Johnson, November 4, 1809.

Receipt from Jean Leforce

[January 8, 1810]

Recd. of H. Clay 8 Jan. 1810 his order on Geo. G. Taylor being the balance in full of the portion of rents recovered from Col. W. Robertson[1] to which my husband was entitled.

Teste JEAN LEFORCE
DAVID MCGEE[2]

DS, in Clay's hand. DLC-TJC (DNA, M212, R15). Mrs. Leforce was a resident of Clark County, Kentucky.

1 Probably William Robinson of Clark County.

2 Of Clark County.

To James D. Breckinridge

Dr Sir Ashland 8 Jan. 1810.

I send back your boy,[1] for whose services I am much obliged to you.

I forgot before I left Frankfort to furnish you with the names of the Exors of Mr. Hart. They are Eleanor Hart executrix, Henry Clay, John W. Hunt, Abraham S. Barton and Jno Hart Exors.

Yrs truly H. CLAY

ALS. KyLoF. Addressed to Breckinridge at Frankfort.

1 Jim, the bearer of the letter, presumably a slave.

Receipt from W. M. Nash

[January 9, 1810]

Attached to Agreement, September 3, 1808.

Order from Luke Usher

Sir Lexington Jan. 10. 1810

Please to pay Mr. Joseph Barby[1] Seventy five Dollars in Horses which will be in full for your Subscribtion [*sic*] in the theatre

Henry Clay Esqr. LUKE USHER

[Endorsement on verso][2]

Recd. paymt. 13 Jan. 1810 JOSEP [*sic*] BARBEE

ALS. DLC-TJC (DNA, M212, R15). Usher's connection with the theater seems to have begun in 1808, when he provided a place where plays could be staged by Noble Luke Usher, an actor, probably Luke's son. Luke Usher also controlled a theater in Frankfort and another in Louisville. Staples, *Pioneer Lexington,* 35, 238; Mabel Tyree Crum, "The History of the Lexington Theatre from the Beginning to 1860" (2 vols., unpublished Ph.D. dissertation, University of Kentucky, 1956), I, 14-21.

1 Barbee was a house-joiner and merchant in Lexington.

2 ES, in Clay's hand.

From William Taylor Barry

Dr. Sir Frankfort 11th. Jany. 1810

I was compelled to leave Lexington so early on Tuesday morning[1] that I could not see you I have a favour to ask—you have befriended me by endorseing—for me in the Bank of Kentucky—as I shall have to renew my notes again before I can well discharge them I should be glad if you deem it propper that you will authorise some one to endorse for you in your absence[2]—A Petition was sent down from the members of the Episcopal church in my absence—Grayson[3] cannot tell anything about it and the Petition is not to be found, if you have it please send it to me—or request some member of that Church to state in a letter what was the object of it[4]—I hope Sir if I can be serviceable to you in any way whilst you are absent from Kentucky—that you will without hesitation make it known—it will always give me pleasure to do you any favour in my power—

It will afford me great satisfaction to hear from you as often as leisure & convenience will admit—

Accept a tender of my friendship and esteem—with an unfeigned wish for your happiness & fame Respectfully WILL. T. BARRY

ALS. Owned by J. Winston Coleman, Jr., Lexington, Kentucky. Sent to Clay in Lexington by "Mr. Banton" (probably William T. Banton).

1 January 9. Barry, a member of the legislature, had apparently been home for the weekend. 2 While in Washington. 3 Alfred W. Grayson.

4 No further reference to the petition has been found.

Receipt from Joseph Barbee

[January 13, 1810]

Attached to Order, January 10, 1810.

From John Hart

[January 13, 1810]

Recd. 13 Jan. 1810 of H. Clay Surviving Exor of Thomas Hart. Senr. five thousand dollars on a/c of my legacy & interest in his Estate. JOHN HART.

DS, in Clay's hand. DLC-TJC (DNA, M212, R15).

Agreement as Executor of Thomas Hart, Sr. and Thomas Hart, Jr.

[January 13, 1810]

[Agreement to cancel lease on 3000 acres of Transylvania Seminary lands originally made on October 23, 1795, by Thomas Hart, Sr., Thomas Hart, Jr., and Samuel Price, under the firm name of Thomas Hart and Company. Signed by James Trotter, Chairman of the Board of Trustees of Transylvania University, and in behalf of Thomas Hart and Company by Clay, John W. Hunt, Abraham S. Barton, and John Hart, executors of Thomas Hart, Jr., and by Clay as surviving executor of Thomas Hart, Sr.]

DS. KyU-Samuel M. Wilson Collection.

Receipt from Daniel Bradford

13. Jan. 1810.

Recd. of H Clay in full for all accounts DAN BRADFORD.

DS, in Clay's hand. DLC-TJC (DNA, M212, R15).

Order on Thomas Bodley

13 Jan. 1810.

Mr. Bodley will be pleased to settle with Mr. Norton[1] for me Two hundred & four dollars, with int. thereon, out of the Replevy bond in the name of Morton agt. John Keizer[2] & me. H. CLAY.

[Endorsement on verso][3]

I have transfered to H. Clay at the request of Geo Norton, $154„7 of the principle of the within mentd. replevy bond, with Interest thereon from the 27th. day of Feby. 1809. Feby 1st 1810

THOS: BODLEY

ADS. DLC-TJC (DNA, M212, R15).

1 Probably George Norton, Lexington nail manufacturer.

2 Record of the suit not found.

3 AES. An accompanying calculation reckons the interest at $9.25.

Due Bill from William Leavy

15 Jan. 1810.

Due H. Clay one hundred and forty dollars in goods.

W. LEAVY

DS, in Clay's hand. DLC-TJC (DNA, M212, R15).

Account with Cuthbert Banks

Mr Henry Clay To Cuthbert Banks 15 Jan 1810.

1808					
Novr	27	To Dinner & Horse 2/3 ½ pt why[1] 9d	"	3	"
Decr	3	" Cash pd. for Subscription[2]	1	10	"
	16	" 2 lb Lead	"	1	6
	17	" Cash paid Orange[3]	"	3	"
	19	" Cash pd for Load Stone	"	6	"
	"	" paid Wilguss[4] in part	2	2	"
	20	" Cash paid for Glass	"	10	6
	25	" Horse 9d 26th Horse 9d	"	1	6
	27	" Horse 9d Club 3/9. Wine & Cards $5—	1	14	6
	28	" 1 doz Segars 1/6 1 pt Wine 6/.	"	7	6
	"	" Dinner 1/6 Horse 9d	"	2	3

				£	s	d
	29	"	Horse 9d Brandy 9d Dinner 1/6	"	3	"
	31	"	Horse 9d Dinner 1/6 Supper 1/6	"	3	9
	"	"	Cash paid Elder[5]	9	"	"
	"	"	Cash paid Day[6]	"	12	"
1809	"	"	Cash paid Beard[7]	24	"	"
Jany	7	"	Supper	"	1	6
	9	"	Segars 1/6 ½ pt Brandy 3/. Wine 6/.	"	10	6
		"	Dinner 1/6 Horse 3/.	"	4	6
	13	"	Keeping 2 Horses 8 Weeks @ 10/6 ea.	8	8	"
	24	"	Cash paid Elder	"	12	"
February	10	"	Cash paid for Troughs	1	19	"
	13	"	Horse 9d Barber 9d ½ pt Wine 6/. Segars 1/6	"	9	"
	"	"	Cash paid for Hawling wine	"	9	"
	"	"	Bottle Wine	"	12	"
	16	"	½ pt why 9d Dinner 1/6	"	2	3
	18	"	Dinner	"	1	6
	19	"	½ pt why	"	"	9
	21	"	Horse 9d Dinner 1/6 Toddy 2/3 Wine 6/	"	10	6
	22	"	Horse 9d Segars 1/6 Dinner 1/6 2 Suppers 3/.	"	6	9
	23	"	Horse 9d	"	"	9
	25	"	Horse 9d Dinner 1/6 Cash pd for Pullies 9/.	"	11	3
	27	"	Segars	"	1	6
March	2	"	Horse	"	"	9
	4	"	Club at Dinner	1	4	"
	"	"	Cash paid for Hawling Hay	1	1	"
	5	"	Horse 9d 2 pts Wine 12/. Dinner 1/6	"	14	3
	11	"	Horse	"	"	9
	1[*sic*]	"	Cash pd Norton[8] for Rolling Iron	"	16	4
		"	Cash paid Hart[9] for Furnace	2	2	"
			Carried Over	£ 62	"	4
			To Amount brought Over	£ 62	"	4
March	13	"	Horse 9d Dinner 1/6	"	2	3
	14	"	Horse 9d Dinner 1/6	"	2	3
	15	"	Horse 9d Dinner 1/6 1 pt. Wine 6/.	"	8	3
	16	"	Horse 9d Dinner 1/6 Wine 6/. Club 1/3	"	9	6

				£	s	d
	17	〃	Horse	〃	〃	9
	18	〃	Horse 9d Wine 6/. Supper 1/6	〃	8	3
	20	〃	Horse 9d Dinner 1/6 why 9d	〃	3	〃
	21	〃	Horse 9d Dinner 1/6	〃	2	3
	〃	〃	Cash paid Elder	〃	6	〃
	22	〃	Horse 3/. Dinner 1/6 Club at			
			Cards 19/5	1	3	1[*sic*]
		〃	Supper	〃	1	6
	23	〃	Lodging 9d Horse 9d Breckft 1/6			
			Dinner 1/6	〃	4	6
	24	〃	Horse 9d Dinner 1/6	〃	2	3
	25	〃	Horse 9d Dinner 1/6	〃	2	3
	26	〃	Horse 9d	〃	〃	9
	27	〃	Horse 9d Wine 6/. Dinner 1/6	〃	8	3
	28	〃	Horse 9d Dinner 1/6	〃	2	3
	〃	〃	Cash paid for Hawling troughs	〃	1	6
	29	〃	Horse 9d Segars 1/6 Dinner 1/6			
			Wine 6/.	〃	9	9
	30	〃	Horse 9d Dinner 1/6	〃	2	3
	31	〃	Horse 9d Dinner 1/6	〃	2	3
April	1	〃	Horse 3/. Dinner 1/6			
			1 pt Wine 6/.	〃	10	6
		〃	Club up stairs	〃	19	8
	2	〃	Lodging 9d Dinner 1/6			
			4 Glasses Toddy 6/.	〃	8	3
		〃	Toddy 6/9 Glass broke 1/.	〃	7	9
	3	〃	Lodging 9d Breckft 1/6 Segars 1/6	〃	3	9
		〃	Dinner 1/6	〃	1	6
	4	〃	Horse 9d Dinner 1/6	〃	2	3
	5	〃	Horse 9d Dinner 1/6	〃	2	3
	6	〃	Horse 9d Toddy 9d Dinner 1/6	〃	3	〃
	7	〃	Horse 9d Dinner 1/6			
			Club at Cards 12/9	〃	15	〃
	8	〃	Horse	〃	〃	9
		〃	Club of Dinner pr Mr Beard	1	7	〃
		〃	2 4/7 weeks keeping Mare @ 10/6	1	7	〃
		〃	2 4/7 weeks board pr John[10]	1	11	〃
	22	〃	Horse	〃	〃	9
	24	〃	Horse 9d Segars 1/6	〃	2	3
	17	〃	Cash paid Peter Lewis[11]	〃	9	〃
	18	〃	Cash paid for Hawling dirt	〃	10	〃
	21	〃	Cash paid Dick[12] for Hawling dirt	〃	10	3
				76	15	4
			To Amt brought forward	£76	15	4

				£	s	d
May	7	"	Horse	"	"	9
	8	"	Horse 9d Dinner 1/6	"	2	3
	13	"	Porter	"	3	"
	14	"	2 Bottles Porter	"	6	"
	15	"	Cash pd Usher[13] for Plank & Scantling	1	17	11
	20	"	1 Bottle Porter	"	3	"
	22	"	Horse 9d Dinner 1/6	"	2	3
	28	"	Horse 9d Porter 3/.	"	3	9
	29	"	Bitters	"	"	9
	"	"	Cash paid for 2 Pad Locks	"	7	6
June	3	"	Cash paid for Shingles	"	13	6
	4	"	Horse	"	"	9
	9	"	Cash paid Orange	"	18	"
		"	" Peter[14]	1	2	6
		"	" paid Dick for Hawling dirt and Work on back Yard	1	10	"
	10	"	" paid Shaw[15] for stone	"	18	"
	12	"	Horse 9d Porter 3/. why 9d Dinner 1/6	"	6	"
	13	"	Horse 9d Dinner 1/6	"	2	3
	14	"	Horse 3/. Dinner 1/6 Porter 3/.	"	7	6
	"	"	Segars 1/6 Supper 1/6	"	3	"
	16	"	Horse 9d Dinner 1/6	"	2	3
	17	"	Horse 3/. Dinner 1/6 Lodg 9d	"	5	3
	18	"	Breckft & Brandy	"	2	3
	19	"	Horse 9d Segars 1/6	"	2	3
	20	"	Horse 9d Bounce 3/. why 9d	"	4	6
	"		Dinner	"	1	6
	21	"	3 Horses 2/3 Dinner 1/6 why 9d	"	4	6
	22	"	Horse	"	"	9
	23	"	Horse 9d Toddy 3/. Dinner 1/6 Sangaree 2/3	"	7	6
	24	"	Horse	"	"	9
	26	"	Horse 9d Dinner 1/6	"	2	3
	"	"	Cash paid for Screws	"	4	7
	27	"	Horse 9d Dinner 1/6 ½ pt why 9d	"	3	"
	28	"	2 Horses 1/6 Dinner 1/6	"	3	"
	29	"	Horse 9d. Dinner 1/6 Segars 3/. Supper 1/6	"	6	9
	30	"	Horse 9d Dinner 1/6	"	2	3
July	1	"	Horse 9d Segars 1/6 Dinner 1/6	"	3	9
	2	"	Horse	"	"	9

				£	s	d
	3	"	Horse 9d Dinner 1/6 Sangaree 4/6	"	6	9
				89	8	7
		To Amt brought Over		£89	8	7
July	4	"	Horse	"	3	"
"	"		Cash paid Subscription for taking McClure[16]	"	18	"
		Segars 1/6 Leomonade 1/6		"	3	"
		Decanter 9/. Club of Wine 6/.		"	15	"
		2 Horses		"	1	6
	5	"	Segars 1/6. Dinner 1/6 Horse 9d	"	3	9
		"	1 pt Wine	"	6	"
	6	"	Horse 9d Dinner 1/6 Segars 1/6	"	3	9
	7	"	Horse 9d why. 9d Dinner 1/6	"	3	"
	8	"	Horse	"	"	9
	9	"	Horse 9d Dinner 1/6	"	2	3
	10	"	Horse 9d Dinner 1/6	"	2	3
	11	"	Horse 9d Dinner 1/6	"	2	3
	12	"	Horse 9d Dinner 1/6	"	2	3
	13	"	Horse 9d Dinner 1/6	"	2	3
	14	"	Horse 9d Sangaree 7/6 Dinner 1/6	"	9	9
	15	"	Horse 9d. Dinner 1/6 Segars 1/6 Wine 3/.	"	6	9
	16	"	Horse	"	"	9
	17	"	Horse 9d. Dinner 1/6	"	2	3
	18	"	Horse 9d Dinner 1/6	"	2	3
	19	"	Horse 9d Dinner 1/6	"	2	3
	20	"	Horse 3/. Dinner 1/6 Club at Card 21/2	1	5	8
	21	"	Lodg 9d Breckft 1/6 Dinner 1/6	"	3	9
	22	"	Horse 9d Dinner 1/6 Sangaree 2/3	"	4	6
	26	"	Horse	"	"	9
	27	"	Horse	"	"	9
	28	"	Horse 9d Dinner 1/6	"	2	3
	30	"	Horse 9d Dinner 1/6	"	2	3
	"	"	Keeping Horse 39 days @ 1/6	2	18	6
	31	"	Horse	"	"	9
August	1	"	Horse	"	"	9
	3	"	Horse 9d Dinner 1/6 Sangaree 4/6 Segars 1/6	"	8	3
	4	"	Horse 9d Dinner 1/6	"	2	3
	5	"	Horse	"	"	9
	6	"	Horse	"	"	9
	7	"	Horse 9d. Office Lock 1/6 Dinner 1/6 why 9d	"	4	6

				£	s	d
	8	"	Horse 9d why 9d Dinner 1/6	"	3	"
		"	Bottle Wine 12/. Sangaree 4/6	"	16	6
	9	"	Horse 9d Dinner 1/6			
			3 Bottles Wine 36/.	1	18	9
				102	16	3
			To Amt brought Forward	£102	16	3
August	9	"	Cash paid Elder	"	18	"
	10	"	Horse 9 Dinner 1/6 Toddy 4/6	"	6	9
	11	"	Horse	"	"	9
	21	"	Cash paid for Letters	"	4	6
	28	"	Sangaree	"	2	3
	31	"	1 Bottle Wine	"	12	"
September	2	"	Horse	"	"	9
	3	"	Horse	"	"	9
	4	"	Horse 3/. Sangaree 1/6	"	7	6
		"	Dinner 1/6 Supper 1/6	"		" [*sic*]
	5	"	Breckft	"	1	6
	11	"	Horse 9d Dinner 1/6 Brandy 1/6			
			Suppr 1/6	"	5	3
	12	"	Horse 9d Dinner 1/6	"	2	3
	13	"	Horse 9d Dinner 1/6			
			2 Bottles Wine 24/.	1	6	3
		"	Supper	"	1	6
	14	"	Horse	"	"	9
	15	"	Horse 9d Dinner 1/6	"	2	3
	16	"	Horse 9d Dinner 1/6	"	2	3
	18	"	Horse 3/. Dinner 1/6 Toddy 7/6	"	12	"
		"	Club at the Election[17]	4	7	9
		"	Club at Ball July 4th	1	4	"
		"	Club at Cards & Supper	1	2	8
	19	"	Breckft 1/6 Club at Cards 4/1	"	5	7
	20	"	Horse 9d Dinner 1/6 Brandy 9d	"	3	"
	21	"	Horse 9d Dinner 1/6	"	2	3
	22	"	Horse 9d Toddy 3/.			
			Club at ball 25/6	1	9	3
		"	Wine 12/. Sangaree 2/3 Cards 2/3	"	16	6
	23	"	Horse 9d Dinner 1/6 Segars 9d	"	3	"
	24	"	Horse 9d Gin Toddy 1/6	"	2	3
	25	"	Horse 9d ½ pt why 9d	"	1	6
	26	"	Horse 9d Dinner 1/6	"	2	3
	27	"	Horse	"	"	9
	28	"	Horse 9d Dinner 1/6 Sangaree 4/6	"	6	9
	29	"	Horse 9d Dinner 1/6			
			Cyder Royal 1/6	"	3	9

Month	Day		Item	£	s	d
	30	"	Horse 9d Dinner 1/6	"	2	3
		"	Cash pd Harry[18] for Work at payment [*sic*]	"	3	"
October	2	"	Horse 9d Cash pd for Hawling dirt for payment	"	9	9
	3		Horse 9d Dinner 1/6	"	2	3
	4	"	Horse 9d Dinner 1/6 Brandy 9d	"	3	"
		"	Cash pd for cleaning Yard	"	18	"
		"	Cash pd for Subscription of Bridge[19]	1	10	"
		"	" Hawling dirt	"	2	6
				121	13	6
			To Amt brought Over	£121	13	6
October	5	"	Horse 9d Dinner 1/6	"	2	3
	8	"	Horse	"	"	9
	9	"	Horse 9d why 9d Dinner 1/6	"	3	"
	12	"	Horse 9d Club at Cards 7/.	"	7	9
	13	"	Cash paid Orange for Hawling dirt		18	"
	14	"	Horse 3/. ½ pt Brandy 3/. Gin 6/.	"	12	"
		"	Club at Cards	"	9	11
		"	Cash paid James Biggs[20]	1	13	"
		"	your part of a Horse pd Cave[21]	9	"	"
	15	"	Cards 4/6 Sling 3/. Brakft 1/6	"	9	"
	16	"	Horse 9d Brandy 9d	"	1	6
		"	Cash pd Ben[22] for Hawling dirt	"	12	"
	22	"	Horse	"	"	9
	23	"	Horse 9d Dinner 1/6	"	2	3
	27	"	Horse 9d Brakft 1/6 Dinner 1/6	"	3	9
	28	"	Horse 1/6 Wine 6/. Club of Sundries 1/9	"	9	3
	30	"	Cash pd for Hawling Lumber	"	"	9
		"	1 pt Wine 6/. Hawling dirt 4/6	"	10	6
	31	"	Cash pd Work Hand	"	4	"
Novr	2	"	Cash paid for Nails	"	1	6
	4	"	Cash pd for hand in Yard	"	3	"
		"	Supper	"	1	6
	5	"	Horse	"	"	9
	6	"	Horse 9d Toddy 2/3	"	3	"
		"	Cash pd for plank & Nails	"	13	6
	10	"	Cash pd for Hawling dirt	"	3	"
	11	"	Horse 9d Dinner 1/6	"	2	3
	13	"	Horse 9d	*"		9[23]
		"	Cash paid Dick for Hawling dirt	"	18	"
	16	"	Cash paid Orange	"	3	"

	19	"	Horse 3 Nights @ 3/.	"	9	"
	22	"	2 Horse 1 Night	"	6	"
	24	"	2 Horse feeds	"	1	6
	25	"	Horse 9d Dinner 1/6	"	2	3
	26	"	Horse 3/. Dinner 1/6 Supper 1/6	"	6	"
	27	"	Club at Cards	"	12	4
Decr.	2	"	Horse 3/. Dinner 1/6 Segars 1/6	"	6	"
			Cash pd Springle[24] order	"	18	"
	10	"	Horse	"	"	9
	11	"	Horse 9d Dinner 1/6 why 9	"	1	6[*sic*]
	12	"	Horse 9d Dinner 1/6	"	2	3
				144	7	"
			* deduct	"	18	"
			To Amt brought forward	£144	7	"
Decr.	24	"	Horse	"	"	9
	25	"	Horse	"	"	9
1810	"	"	7 Week board p John Bowen & Jerry[25] @ 12/.	4	4	"
January	8	"	Horse 9d why. 9d	"	1	6
	10	"	Horse 9d	"	"	9
	11	"	Horse	"	"	9
	12	"	Horse 9d Dinner 1/6	"	2	3
	13	"	Horse 9d Dinner 1/6	"	2	3
		"	amt of Mr Springle's A/C	4	18	1½
	"	"	amt of Mr Robt Bywaters A/C	4	11	7½
	14	"	L Carry[26] for $3.60	1	1	7½
		"[27]				
		"	Keeping Horses 38 nights @ 1/6	2	17	"
				184	7	10½
			Over Charge	"	18	"
				183	19	10½
1808			Contra. Cr			
Decr.	30		By Cash $125. £37.10"			
1809						
March	4	"	4½ Tons Hay —9 " "	46	10	"
				£137	9	10½
			Cash paid Davis[28] for Hawling bricks by Wm. T Banton	1	14	9
				£139	4	4½
			Cr. B Paul & Sons[29] A/C deducted	21	19	6
Jany.	15	"	Horse & Dinner 2/3	£117	4	10½

[Endorsement][30]

Credit by bal. due on C. Banks'. note to L. Sanders[31]	37	0	1
	80	4	9½

The above bal. of eighty pounds 4/9½ due me on my tavern a/c. agt. H Clay is to be credited agt. the rent &c for the Hotel.[32]

CUTHBT. BANKS

D. DLC-TJC, 2d Series, vol. 10

1 Whisky. 2 See below, debit entry of October 4, 1809, this document.

3 A free Negro residing in Lexington.

4 Probably Asa Wilgus, a resident of the northern district of Fayette County.

5 Either John or Matthew Elder. 6 Joseph Day, Lexington bricklayer.

7 Probably Joseph Beard. Cf. above, Agreement, December 8, 1806.

8 George Norton. 9 Probably Will Hart.

10 Possibly John Bowen. See entry of December 25, this account.

11 Free Negro living on Market Street.

12 Either the free Negro of that name in Lexington or the one in the southern district of Fayette County. 13 Luke Usher. 14 Probably Peter Lewis.

15 John Robert Shaw, rhyming well digger and stone cutter of Lexington.

16 Not identified.

17 The election, by which Clay had been returned to the State legislature, had been held the preceding month.

18 Possibly Henry Quile, a free Negro of Lexington.

19 In March, 1808, the town trustees had appointed a committee to solicit subscriptions for funds with which to dig a new canal through the middle of Water Street and construct bridges over it. Lexington Trustees Record Book, IB, 286.

20 Not identified.

21 Probably either Thomas or William Cave, residents of the southern district of Fayette County.

22 Possibly Benjamin Adams of Lexington or Benjamin Day of the northern part of Fayette County, both free Negroes.

23 The figure "18" crossed out in the shillings column.

24 John Springle. 25 Not identified.

26 Ludwell Carey, of the southern area of Fayette County.

27 The entry, "Amt of Messrs Paul & Son A/C 21 19 6," crossed out.

28 Probably Allen Davis. 29 Peter Paul, Sr. and Jr.

30 ES, in Clay's hand. 31 Lewis Sanders. 32 The Kentucky Hotel.

Receipt to Cuthbert Banks

15 Jan. 1810.

Mr. Banks is to be credited against the rent &c. due me for the Hotel by eighty pounds four shillings and nine pence being the bal. due him upon his a/c rendered. H. CLAY

ADS. DLC-HC (DNA, M212, R9). See above, Account, this date.

Public Notice: Dissolution of Hart, Barton, and Hart

[January 15, 1810]

[Clay, with the other executors of Thomas Hart, Jr., announces dissolution of the partnership of Thomas Hart, Jr., Abraham S. Barton, and John Hart on January 13. Those having accounts with the firm are urged to settle them.]

Lexington *Reporter*, January 20, 1810.

Bill from Samuel Owens

Lexingn. Januy. 17 1810

Cr. Henry Clay Esq- To Samuel Owens Dr.
To makeing two Coats
One p of pantiloons — $7.50

[Endorsement][1]

Pay the above to Mr. Owens 16 Jan. 1810 [*sic*] H CLAY
Mr. Banks[2]

D. DLC-HC (DNA, M212, R9). Owens' tailoring shop was on Main Street in Lexington. 1 AES. 2 Cuthbert Banks.

From Thomas Hart Benton

Dear Sir, Franklin, Tenn. Feb'y 7th 1810

I received your letter of the 12th Jan'y[1] a few days since, and shortly before that had heard the very unhappy news of Mr. Hart's death.[2]

The land wh. is the subject of your enquiries, and which belongs to Col. Hart's and my father's heirs, lies in Maury county,[3] two miles from Columbia, the county town. The different parts of it are unequal in value; some parts would sell for five or six dollars an acre; other parts for much less. Perhaps the average price might be fixed at two and a half or three dollars. Sales could be made pretty readily, and cash obtained in payment, either in hand, or on reasonable credits. Two years ago it would have sold better than at present, as the expectation prevailed then very generally that the seat of justice would be fixed upon it. This expectation has failed, owing to which, the dullness of the times, and the uncertain prospect of what is to follow, and it appears to me that its price will remain stationary for some time to ensue.

I had intimated the propriety of having Col. Hart's heirs represented when an application is made for a division; not that our law requires all the parties to be present, for the contrary is the fact; but because it is proper that Col. Hart's heirs should have an opportunity of naming one half of the commissioners by which the division is to be made. It is indeed the duty of the court to see that good characters are appointed; but you know in what manner county court justices discharge their duties: and as the return of- these commissioners is to be conclusive, even against minors, the necessity is therefore the greater for paying attention to them at the time of their appointment.

For information of the law on this head, I refer to you Col. (?)

[*sic*] Whiteside,[4] of the Senate, whose advice would further be of service to you, perhaps, in pointing out proper persons as commissioners.

It will be in September, the third Monday, before an application can be made to the court; as a notice by publication in one of the newspapers for six months, must precede an application, where a personal service of notice is not given; and in this latter case, a personal service is impracticable on account of the dispersed situation of the parties.

As to the payment of taxes, our law requires those lands to be sold on the first Monday in Nov. annually on which the taxes of that year remain due, subject to be redeemed by the owner at any time within 12 months by reimbursing to the purchaser the sum paid with 50 per cent. No distinction is made in favor of non residents. But on this subject you will have no occasion for knowing the law, as I have paid the tax which has heretofore accrued on Col. Hart's land, & shall continue to do so for his heirs until you have disposed of it.

Will Congress give us war this winter? Or, will the majority still incline to trust to the chapter of accidents, and wait for chance or destiny to mend our condition?

I have the honor to be, Sir, Yours very respectfully

THOMAS H. BENTON

Copy. InHi-William H. Smith Collection. Benton, later Senator from Missouri, was a son of Jesse and Ann Gooch Benton. His mother was a niece of Thomas Hart, Sr., for whom the younger Benton was named. Thomas Hart Benton's mother and Henry Clay's wife were first cousins. [Thomas Hart Benton] *Thirty Years View* (2 vols., New York, 1859-60), I, i.

1 Not found. 2 Thomas Hart, Jr. 3 Tennessee.

4 Jenkin Whiteside, Tennessee lawyer, served in the United States Senate from April 1, 1809, to October 8, 1811.

Receipted Account from Asa Blanchard

Feby 14h. 1810

Henery Clay Esqr To Asa Blanchard Dr

1809			
July 15	To 1 pr Sugar Tongs - - - - - - ---	$5	42
	To Order on you in favour of Harrison[1]	30	
		35	42
	By Old Silver - - - - - - ---	1	56
		$33	86

Recd. the above in full of Henry Clay exor. of T. Hart Sr decd.

ASA BLANCHARD

DS. DLC-TJC (DNA, M212, R15).

1 Probably John Harrison.

Property Deed to Asa Blanchard

[February 14, 1810]

[Indenture by which Clay and Susannah Hart, surviving executors of Thomas Hart, Sr., sell to Asa Blanchard a lot in Lexington.]

Fayette County Court, Deed Book E, 101-102.

Promissory Note from Amelia Violett

[February 19, 1810]

I Milly Violet owe & promise to pay Henry Clay one hundred Dollars for Value received Witness my hand and seal this 19th. day of Feby. 1810

Teste AMELIA VIOLETT {SEAL}

WILLIAM B LONG[1]

DS. Woodford Circuit Court, File 83. Shortly after signing this note, Amelia Violett was married to Samuel H. Mitchell. A suit brought against the Mitchells for $100 was decided in Clay's favor in the September Term, 1810, Woodford Circuit Court.

1 Son of one of the early settlers of Woodford County; later (1819) a member of the State legislature.

Speech on Proposed Repeal of Non-Intercourse Act

[February 22, 1810]

Mr. President[1]—At all times embarrassed when I have ventured to address you, it is with peculiar diffidence I rise on this occasion. The profound respect I have been taught to entertain for this body—my conscious inadequacy to discuss as it deserves the question before you—the magnitude of that question—and the recent seat I have taken in this house,[2] are too well calculated to appal, and would impel me to silence, if any other member would assume the task I propose attempting. But, sir, when the regular troops of this house, disciplined as they are in the great affairs of this nation, are inactive at their posts, it becomes the duty of its raw militia, however lately enlisted, to step forth in defence of the honor and independence of the country. I voted yesterday against the amendment offered by the gentleman from Maryland,[3] because, whilst that vote did not pledge me for the ultimate passage of the bill, it would have allowed me to give it my support, if no better proposition was tendered. I did not like the bill, as sent from the house of representatives. It was a crazy vessel, shattered and leaky. But it afforded some shelter, bad as it was. It was opposition to the aggressive edicts of the belligerents. Taken from us, without a substitute, we are left defenceless, naked and exposed to all the rage and violence of the storm.

Sir, have we not been for years contending against the tyranny of the ocean? Has not congress solemnly pledged itself to the world not to surrender our rights? Has not the nation, at large, in all its capacities of meetings of the people, state and general governments, resolved to maintain, at all hazards our maritime independence? Your whole circle of commercial restrictions, including the non-importation, embargo and non-intercourse acts, had in view an opposition to the offensive measures of the belligerents, so justly complained of by us. They presented *resistance*—the *peaceful* resistance of the law. When this is abandoned, without effect, I am for resistance by the *sword*.

No man in the nation desires peace more than I. But I prefer the troubled ocean of war, demanded by the honor and independence of the country, with all its calamities, and desolations, to the tranquil, putrescent pool of ignominious peace. If we can accommodate our differences with one of the belligerents only, I should prefer that one to be Great-Britain. But if with neither, and we are forced into a selection of our enemy, then am I for war with Britain; because I believe her prior in aggression, and her injuries and insults to us were atrocious in character. I shall not attempt to exhibit an account between the belligerents of mercantile spoliations, inflicted and menaced. On that point we have just cause of war with both. Britain stands preeminent, in her outrage on us, by her violation of the sacred personal rights of American freemen, in the arbitrary and lawless impressment of our seamen—the attack on the Chesapeake—the murder, Sir, I will not dwell on the long catalogue of our wrongs & disgraces, which has been repeated until the sensibility of the nation is benumbed by the dishonorable detail.

But we are asked for the means of carrying on War; and those who oppose it triumphantly appeal to the vacant vaults of the treasury. With the unimpaired credit of the government, invigorated by a faithful observance of public engagements, and a rapid extinction of the debt of the revolution; with the boundless territories in the west, presenting a safe pledge for reimbursement of loans to any extent—is it not astonishing that despondency itself should disparage the resources of this country? You have, sir, I am credibly informed in the city & vicinity of New Orleans alone, public property sufficient to extinguish the celebrated deficit in the Secretary's report.[4] And are we to regard as nothing the patriotic offer so often made by the states to spend their last cent, and risk their last drop of blood in the preservation of our neutral priviledges?[5] Or, are we to be governed by the low, groveling parsimony of the counting room, and to cast up the actual pence in the drawer before we assert our inestimable rights? It is said, however, that no object is attainable by war with Britain. In its fortunes we are to estimate not only the benefit to be derived to ourselves, but the injury to be done the enemy. The conquest of Canada is in your power. I trust I shall not be deemed presumptuous when I state, what I verily believe, that the militia of Kentucky are alone competent to place Montreal and Upper Canada at your feet. Is it nothing to the British nation—is it nothing to the pride of her monarch to have the last of the immense North American possessions held by him in the commencement of his reign, wrested from his dominion? Is it nothing to us to extinguish the torch that lights up savage warfare? Is it nothing to acquire the entire fur trade connected with that country, and to destroy the temptation and the opportunity of violating your revenue and other laws?

War with Britain will deprive her of those supplies of raw materials and provisions, which she now obtains from this country. It is alledged that the non-intercourse law, constantly evaded, is incapable of execution. War will be a non-intercourse admitting of but partial elusion. The pressure upon her, contemplated by your restrictive laws, will then be completely realised. She will not have the game, as she will if you pass this bill without an efficient substitute, entirely in her own hands. The enterprize and valor of our maritime brethren will participate in the spoils of capture.

Another effect of war will be the re-production and cherishing of a martial spirit amongst us. Is there not danger that we shall become enervated by the spirit of avarice unfortunately so predominant? I do not wish to see that diffusive military character which, pervading the whole nation, might possibly eventuate in the aggrandizement of some ambitious chief, by prostrating the liberties of the country. But a certain portion of military ardor (and this is what I desire) is essential to the protection of the country. The withered arm, and wrinkled brow of the illustrious founders of our freedom, are melancholy indications that they will shortly be removed from us. Their deeds of glory and renown will then be felt only through the cold medium of the historic page. We shall want the presence and living example of a new race of heroes to supply their place, and to animate us to preserve unviolated what they atchieved. Am I counting too much on the valor of my countrymen, when I indulge the hope, that, if we are forced into war, the American hero now lives, who, upon the walls of Quebeck, imitating his glorious example, will avenge the fall of the immortal Montgomery?[6] But we shall at least gain the approbation of our own hearts.—If we surrender without a struggle to maintain our rights, we forfeit the respect of the world, and what is infinitely worse, of ourselves.

We are often reminded that the British navy constitutes the only barrier between us and universal dominion; and warned that resistance to Britain is submission to France. I protest against the castigation of our colonial infancy being applied in the independent manhood of America. I am willing, sir, to dispense with the parental tenderness of the British navy. I cannot subscribe to British slavery upon the water, that we may escape French subjugation upon land. I should feel myself debased and humbled as an American citizen, if we had to depend upon any foreign power to uphold our independence. And I am persuaded that our own resources, properly directed, are fully adequate to our defence. I am therefore for resisting oppression, by whomsoever attempted against us, whether maritime or territorial.

Considering then that the bill, as amended in this house, in furnishing no substitute for the law of non-intercourse which it repeals nor the propositions of the other house intended to take its place, is a total dereliction of all opposition to the edicts of the belligerents, I cannot vote for it in its present form. I move a recommitment of the bill to supply this defect.[7] What ought to be the substitute I confess I have not satisfied myself, not expecting that it would fall to my lot to make you this motion. The committee however can deliberate upon the subject and propose one.—I would suggest two for consideration.—Either a total non-importation, which our laws can doubtless enforce; or to arm our merchantmen and authorize convoys. A day may be fixed, allowing sufficient time for the last effort of negociation, and that failing, our merchants then to be permitted to arm, and to receive all the protection by convoys which the public vessels can give. This latter measure may lead to war, but it is not war. Our neutral rights are violated by the belligerents.—Each places our commerce under restrictions not warranted by the law of nations. We must then submit or protect it. Whilst we confine ourselves within the pale of that law, neither has a right to complain. When so armed, and pursuing our lawful destination, let those who attempt to molest us, take to themselves the consequences of their own violence. On our part a war thus produced, will be a war of defence.

But Mr. President if after all our deliberation it shall be deemed unwise to adopt either of these expedients, perhaps some other unexceptionable course may occur. I insist that you do not return the bill to the other branch of the legislature in its present form. They have sent you a measure I acknowledge weak. It is however not submission. It professes to oppose in form at least the injustice of foreign governments. What are you about to do? To breathe vigor and energy into the bill? No sir, you have eradicated all its vitality and are about to transmit back again the lifeless skeleton. I entreat the Senate to recollect the high ground they occupy with the nation. I call upon the members of this house to maintain its character for vigor. I beseech them not to forfeit the esteem of the country. Will you set the base example to the other house of an ignominious surrender of our rights, after they have been reproached with imbecility and you extolled for your energy? But, sir, if we could be so forgetful of ourselves, I trust we shall spare *you* the disgrace of signing with those hands, so instrumental in the revolution,[8] a bill abandoning some of the most precious rights which it secured.

Washington, D.C., *Spirit of 'Seventy-Six,* February 27, 1810 (NHi). Published also in *Annals of Cong.,* 11 Cong., 2 Sess., XX, 579-82; Lexington *Kentucky Gazette,* March 13, 1810; Lexington *Reporter,* March 17, 1810. For reference to the source here reprinted as the first publication of Clay's speech see John Pope to the People of Kentucky, June 13, 1811, in Frankfort *Palladium,* June 22, 1811.

The debate concerns provisions of the legislation antecedent to Macon's Bill No. 2, which repealed the Non-Intercourse Act but called for reinstitution of the regulations against either France or England in the event that the designated belligerent failed to revoke its edicts hostile to American shipping within ninety days after the other had so acted. The original House draft (Macon's Bill No. 1) had lifted the general trade barrier, but restricted importations from France and England to American vessels and to direct commerce with the country of manufacture, so long as the hostile decrees were levied against American shipping. Senate amendment, to which Clay refers in the second paragraph, provided for absolute repeal of the regulations. When the two houses were unable to harmonize their differences, the Macon Bill No. 2 was enacted as a substitute, May 1, 1810.

1 George Clinton, Vice-President, 1804-1812.

2 Clay had assumed his seat in the Senate on February 5.

3 Samuel Smith.

4 See Gallatin's report of December 7, 1809, in *American State Papers, Finance,* II, 374.

5 See above, Amendment, December 15, 1808.

6 Brigadier-General Richard Montgomery of New York, who had fallen in the assault on Quebec, December 31, 1775, following the capture of Montreal by New England troops under his command.

7 Clay's motion (recorded AD, by Clay. DNA, RG46, 11A-B5) was subsequently defeated by a vote of 20 to 13.

8 Clinton had commanded the defense of the Hudson Highlands and held an appointment as brigadier general in the Continental Army.

To [Thomas Smith]

[February 23, 1810]

On yesterday the bill respecting our foreign intercourse, as amended in the Senate, passed, and was sent to the House of Representatives where it is confidently believed the amendment of the Senate will be concurred in. Should this take place, all our commercial restrictions having in view the coercion of foreign governments to abrogate their edicts, will be abandoned; and our commerce once more left to its fate.

Extract. Lexington *Kentucky Gazette,* March 6, 1810. Identified as a letter from Clay to the editor. Smith had become editor of this journal in October, 1809.

From James Brown

My dear Sir New Orleans February 26. 1810

Deeply interested as you must feel in the prosperity of Kentucky you cannot have overlooked the obvious fact that its safety; tranquility; wealth and even the continuance of the form of government it enjoys depend on the destinies of the Territories on the Mississippi. Should this key to your trade fall into the hands of either of the two great nations who now figure on the European theatre, the effects would be serious, if not ruinous to your prosperity. On no object are you more deceived than as to the ease with which the Territory of Orleans could be taken by the people of Kentucky and the other states adjoining it. The Island of N. Orleans is susceptible, in the hands of those powers who have made war a trade, of being made defensible by a force of 20,000 men against an Army of 100,000, and no place is better adapted to defence against a force by sea—It is true that we have little to dread from England because her restless and powerful rival will keep her soldiers at home and give full employment to her small population in defending her present possessions. But should France succeed in her amiable, and benevolent, and disinterested, and philosophical projét of "restoring the liberty of the seas" and leaving herself no rival on that element, or in my understanding of what are her present views and will be her future policy, should she become the tyrant of the Ocean, will she not immediately annex Cuba, the Florida's and the other Spanish American possessions to her Crown of Spain, and will not the important positions of Pensacola Havanna Campeche La Vera Cruz &c give to the ambitious Emperor a compleat command of the commerce of the Gulph leaving the desireable and at present undefended point the Mississippi exposed a tempting and easy prey to her insatiable cupidity? And with the command of the Ocean and the adjoining provinces, holding a population equal to that of the United States, will she find any difficulty in seizing upon and maintaining her possession of a Territory whose population is French and who have considered themselves as only lent for a few years to the United States? The successes of the British in the Islands[1] and the struggles of Spaniards,[2] have concentrated the force of Bonaparte in this Territory. Our American population since the Cession has perhaps increased about 2,000 whilst we are indebted to the last 12 months alone for the introduction of from 10. to 15000 French[3]—The refugees from all the Islands who had sheltered themselves in the different American States or French Colonies, have collected in this City & Territory where they find their own manners, laws, and, I may add government—For the feeble authority who is nominally American here is so true to the Republican maxim of a Government by a Majority that he[4] submits to it where foreigners compose that majority and where that majority act in opposition to the most sacred principles of good policy and of the

Constitution. Indeed such is his rigid adherence to the maxim that he did not fail to yield his whole civil authority to the majority composed of Wilkinsons Army and adherents, and I am firmly persuaded that should a minion of Bonaparte's arrive to morrow at the head of an army he would advise submission upon the principle of the inviolability of the Majority—So sensible are the adherents and agents of the Emperor that this Country is undefended, and such their conviction that it will soon return to France, that they act and speak as if it was already a French province—By the terms of the Capitulation on the taking of Santo Domingo[5] the French officers were to be sent on parole to France—About fifty or sixty took their passages for New York but by some strange mistake arrived in New Orleans. The French Consul directed them to the Municipality who having a control of the immense funds of the city allowed them a weekly salary of four dollars each without any rational hope of repayment—On this allowance they remained there about two months amusing themselves and examining the Country—When ready to depart, a ship was chartered to carry them to New York—their passages were paid by our Corporation—they sailed but as the Vessel was loaded with Cotton it is said they took charge of her and proceeded direct for France. The sufferings of our own officers who died from want of Musquittoe curtains fresh provisions and other comforts in the morasses of Terre aux boeuff[6] and whose groans might have touched the heart of the humane City Council passed unheaded whilst the tricolored cockade was treated with every degree of Humanity attention and respect—Indeed it would be absurd to expect that things could be very different from what they are—The military despotism of Genl. Wilkinson who bearded the Judges in open Court,[7] Mr Jefferson's unqualified approbation of his conduct, and his more unwarrantable contempt of our Court in taking possession of the Bature by military force in opposition to their decree and injunction[8]—these public insults upon the Judicial authority have brought the Judges into such disgrace with the people that they are scarcely able to enforce their own Judgments or to preserve the peace of society—In a word we are at this moment a French Province—From the imperfect sketch of our situation you will anticipate a recommendation of a strong army at this place—You are mistaken—I have no such wish—My partiality for large armies is not much greater than when we parted—I have seen some thing of the despotism and insolence of a small one, and what I have seen is not very well calculated to induce me to wish that it had been larger—My plans for defending this Country and making it American are such as require neither Armies nor money.

The first object is to make the Councils completely American—

This is to be effected

1° By permitting the Inhabitants of West Florida to attach themselves to the American Government which they will immediately do if assured of being received and protected[9]—The title to this Country is in dispute being claimed by the Emperor,[10] by Ferdinand the 7th.[11] and by the United States under the limitless treaty of Mr Livingston[12]—In such a state of affairs there could be no impropriety in giving the possessors a choice of Masters—The thirty third degree on the North, Mobile on the East, the Sabine on the West and the Gulph would then form a State of very convenient bounds, sufficiently populous to be admitted into the Union and immensely wealthy.[13] The destinies of this place would no longer be in the hands of a French faction; because the Majority would be American This circumstance would remove many of the existing prejudices against our Country and encrease migration—

2nd Let the vacant lands be liberally given to settlers—The mode pursued under the Spanish Government was extremely simple and produced few interferences—Let a warrant of Survey issue for the required quantity and make it the duty of the Surveyor to advertize the day on which he will survey the land and put the Claimant in possession—Let the possession be given in presence of the neighbours and let them certify that the land is vacant—Should Livingston remain at the City[14] he can give you much valuable information on this subject It appears to me to afford a fine field for a man of talents, and the opportunity of distinction is the greater, as the subject is but little understood at Congress—In securing this Country and promoting its growth you serve Kentucky more effectually than by raising Cavalry there to fight the British Navy—A little of this must be done to please your constituents but you are to look for solid fame and lasting distinction in objects of higher utility—The New England members are deeply interested in the measures I have recommended—Our Markets are filled with their productions—They carry ours to market—And as this Country would form a Commercial State it is probable it would feel strongly attached to the other States of that description

Excuse this rough sketch of my ideas on this important subject You can perhaps turn it to some account

My Nancy begs to be remembered by you Your friend

JAMES BROWN

ALS. DLC-HC (DNA, M212, R1). Published in Padgett, "Letters of James Brown to Henry Clay," *La. Hist. Quar.*, XXIV (1941), 930-34.

1 The French West Indian islands.

2 Napoleon's invasion of Spain and his treatment of the Spanish royal family had aroused resentment in Latin America against the French.

3 In 1809 French refugees had poured into New Orleans. The Governor of Orleans Territory reported the city already "crowded with the unfortunate Refugees from

Cuba" and expressed apprehension that English conquests in the West Indies would cause among the French a "very general" desire to emigrate to the United States. Claiborne to Robert Smith, November 21, 1809, and to William Savage, November 10, 1809. Rowland (ed.), *Official Letter Books of W. C. C. Claiborne,* V, 1, 5.

4 William C. C. Claiborne. 5 By the English.

6 In April, 1809, General James Wilkinson had selected an elevated site at Terre-aux-Boeufs, about eight miles below New Orleans, for an encampment of the 2,000 soldiers under his command. Though he had received orders almost immediately to remove the troops farther up river, the movement was not begun until mid-September. Meanwhile, about two-fifths of his force had died of disease and a large number had deserted. Charles Gayarré, *History of Louisiana* (4th ed., 4 vols., New Orleans, 1903), IV, 221-22.

7 See above, Brown to Clay, September 1, 1808, notes.

8 The Batture, an alluvial area on the river in New Orleans which had been considered public property, had been occupied in 1807 by Edward Livingston after a victory in the local court. The people of the city had resisted Livingston's control of the property, and in January, 1808, President Jefferson had directed the Marshal of the United States to take possession of the area. Prolonged litigation followed. In the earlier suit James Brown had been one of Livingston's attorneys. Gayarré, *History of Louisiana,* IV, 185-90, 192.

9 On October 27, 1810, following a rebellion against Spain in West Florida, President Madison proclaimed the occupation of the area.

10 Napoleon. 11 Of Spain.

12 The Louisiana purchase treaty with France.

13 Brown's "State" would have included the present States of Louisiana and Mississippi and part of Alabama. Louisiana was admitted to the Union in 1812.

14 Edward Livingston, having gone to Washington early in 1809 in connection with his Batture claim, was probably still there or had returned to that city.

To John Watts

Dr Col. Wash. 4 Mar. 1810

I have the satisfaction to inform you that the Court has affirmed in all its parts your decree agt. Massie.[1] I have been very ill for a week past, indeed unable to write until yesterday, so that I have not yet seen the decision, but have learnt the above both from Mr. Key and Judge Todd.[2]

When I shall have seen the opinion I will hereafter indicate the course you are yet to pursue. Yr friend H. CLAY

ALS. CtY. Addressed: "Col John Watts near New London Virginia."

1 Conflicting claims to 1,000 acres of land adjoining Chillicothe, Ohio, had led to litigation between Watts and Nathaniel Massie. Clay and Philip Barton Key argued the case in behalf of Watts before the United States Supreme Court. 10 *U.S.* (6 Cranch) 148-70 (1810).

2 Thomas Todd.

To [Thomas Smith]

Senate Chamber, 9*th March,* 1810.

I enclose you a newspaper containing some foreign news from both France and Great Britain, of an aspect rather favourable. I will also add that a private official letter had been received from Mr. Pinckney,[1] our minister at London, stating that in a conversation with Marquis Wellesley,[2] that minister intimated a disapprobation of Jackson's conduct here,[3] and that he would be replaced by a successor of rank and standing; and moreover manifested a strong conciliatory disposition towards this country.

Contrary to expectation, the House of Representatives disagreed to the amendments made by the Senate to Mr. Macon's bill;[4] and the two houses have appointed committees of conference to produce accord between them if practicable.

Extract. Lexington *Kentucky Gazette,* March 20, 1810. Identified as from Clay to the editor. [1] William Pinkney.

[2] Richard Colley Wellesley, Marquis Wellesley, elder brother of the Duke of Wellington, was Foreign Secretary in the Perceval Cabinet.

[3] Francis James Jackson, British Minister to the United States, had been dismissed by President Madison in 1809, yet remained in the United States about a year.

[4] See above, Speech, February 22, 1810, note.

To [William Taylor]

Dr Sir Washington 11 Mar. 1810

Your's of the 9h. is duly recd.[1] I am sorry Mr. Hanna[2] has troubled you with the fee bill mentd. by you. It was contrary to my knowledge, having intended to pay it in Kentucky. The Marshall was about starting to see Kelly[3] with the execution upon your judgment, when I left Frankfort. I have not heard the result. Unless Kelly's property is removed beyond the reach of this officer I am persuaded the debt will be secured. No injury will happen by my absence to your interest, having taken the proper precautions and given the requisite instructions before my departure.

I have recd. the amt. of your claim upon Mr. Whitaker,[4] and before I left Kentucky had sent a bill to my friend in Fredericksburg[5] covering this & other monies. That bill has unfortunately after being accepted been dishonored; but I still have expectation of receiving the amt. Should I however be disappointed, it is possible that I shall have to ask your indulgence 'till my return. I hope however this will not happen.

Should I visit Baltimore (which I am not certain of at present) it will give me great pleasure to accept your friendly invitation

Yr. ob Servt H CLAY

ALS. NcD. [1] Not found.

[2] John H. Hanna, Frankfort lawyer, merchant, and banker, for many years Clerk of the United States District and Circuit Courts at Frankfort.

[3] Joseph Kelly. [4] W. W. Whitaker. [5] Probably Francis T. Brooke.

To George Thompson

Dr. Col. Senate Chamber 14 Mar. 1810.

I thank you for your favr. of the 23 Feb. I refer you to my letter to Majr. Thompson for politics.[1]

Bonaparte has repudiated the Empress. I suspect he is afraid of being denominated a fumbler, and wishes to operate on a subject more prolific than the Empress.[2] His brother's wife Miss Patterson alias the Dutchess has been figuring away here for some time, with her little son.[3] I would recommend her to imitate her brother in law's example, and take to herself a good strong back Democrat. She looks as if she wanted very much the services of such a character.

Mrs. Madison has her parties every wednesday evening. They are gay and agreeable, tho' I have been but seldom to them, owing to very bad health which I have had ever since my arrival.

I am gratified with the prospect of good prices for our produce in Kentucky, particularly hemp. We have the finest Country in the world, and he who has seen it & *doubts* it ought to receive the punishment denounced agt. unbelievers. Yr. friend H. CLAY.

ALS. DLC-HC (DNA, M212, R9). Addressed: "Col. Geo. Thompson near Harrodsburg Kentucky Via Marietta." Colonel Thompson was one of the earliest magistrates and jurists of Mercer County and also one of the original Trustees of Transylvania Seminary and of the Harrodsburg Academy. His residence, "Pleasant Fields," near Graham Springs, Harrodsburg watering-place, was one of the largest plantations in the region and noted for its lavish hospitality.

1 Neither letter has been found. Major Thompson was probably George C. Thompson.

2 Napoleon had divorced the Empress Josephine in December, 1809, and early in the next year married the Archduchess Marie Louise of Austria.

3 Elizabeth, daughter of William Patterson of Baltimore, had married Jerome Bonaparte in 1803. Napoleon had forced a separation, the Imperial Council had issued a decree of divorce, and Jerome in 1807 had become King of Westphalia and the husband of a princess of Wurtemburg.

Report of Amendments to Bill on Sale of Public Lands

In Senate of the U. States March 26. 1810.

Mr. Clay from the Committee to whom was referred the bill "To alter the terms of sale of the public lands of the U. States, and granting a right of preemption to purchasers in certain cases," reported the bill with the following

Amendments.[1]

Strike out the third condition beginning in the 19th. and ending in the 27th. line; and insert in lieu thereof the following.

"III. At the time of sale, every purchaser shall deposit one twentieth part of the purchase money with the Receiver of public monies, and within days thereafter pay the residue and produce to the Register of the Land office, at which the sale had taken place, a receipt for the payment made either to the Receiver of the public monies of such Land office, or into the Treasury of the U. States."

Strike out the fourth condition except the provisio [*sic*], and insert in place of the part stricken out the following to precede the proviso:

"IV. In case of failure to produce as aforesaid such receipt, within the said days, as directed by the preceding condition, the said deposit of the twentieth part of the purchase money shall be forfeited to the U. States; and the land bought shall revert to them; and shall & may be thenceforth disposed of at private sale, on the same terms and conditions, and in the same manner, as if it had not been previously purchased:"

AD. DNA, RG46, 11A-B2. On March 22 the Senate in Committee of the Whole had resumed consideration of "a bill granting the right of pre-emption to purchasers of public lands in certain cases," which had been reported by a select committee on January 26, recommitted on February 15, and reported again, with amendments, on March 13. Clay had not been a member of the earlier committee, but at the resumption of the debate he had moved to recommit the bill and had been named with Stephen R. Bradley (Vermont) and Michael Leib (Pennsylvania) as a select committee to give it further consideration.

The amendments which Clay reported were initially adopted in Committee of the Whole on March 27, but later that day the Senate struck out all provisions of the bill except the enacting clause and the third section and sent the measure to another select committee, of which Clay was not a member. As finally enacted, the bill contained none of Clay's suggestions and no grant of a right of pre-emption. 2 *U.S. Stat.*, 591-92.

1 Several minor word substitutions have been here deleted.

Speech on Domestic Manufactures

[March 26, 1810]

The local interest, Mr President, of the quarter of the country which I have the honor to represent will apologize for the trouble I may give you on this occasion. My colleague[1] has proposed an amendment to the bill before you, instructing the secretary of the navy, in providing supplies of cordage, sail cloth, hemp, &c. to give a preference to those of American growth and manufacture. This part of the amendment is moved by the gentleman from Massachusetts (Mr. Lloyd)[2] to be stricken out. And in the course of the discussion which has arisen, remarks have been made on the general policy of promoting manufactures. The propriety[3] of this policy is perhaps not very intimately connected with the subject before us, but is nevertheless within the legitimate and admissible scope of debate. Under this impression I offer my sentiments.

In inculcating the advantages of domestic manufactures, it never entered the head, I presume, of any one to change the habits of the nation from an agricultural to a manufacturing society. No one I am persuaded ever thought of converting the plough share and the sickle into the spindle and shuttle. And yet this is the delusive view too often taken of the subject. The opponents of the manufacturing system transport themselves to the establishments of Manchester and

Birmingham, and perceiving the indigence, vice and wretchedness prevailing there, by pushing it to an *extreme,* argue that its introduction into this country will be attended by the same mischievous consequences. But what is the fact? That England is the manufacturer of a great part of the world, and even there the numbers thus employed bear an inconsiderable proportion to the whole mass of population. If we were to become the manufacturers of other nations, effects of the same kind might result. But if we *limit* our efforts by our own wants, the evils apprehended would be found to be chimerical.—The invention and improvement of machinery, for which the present age is so remarkable, dispensing in a great degree with manual labour; & the employment of those persons, who, if we are engaged in the pursuits of agriculture alone, would be either unproductive, or exposed to indolence and immorality, will enable us to supply our wants without withdrawing our attention from agriculture; that first and greatest source of our wealth and happiness. A judicious American farmer, in the household way, manufactures whatever is requisite for his family. He squanders but little in the gewgaws of Europe. He presents in epitome what the nation ought to do. Their manufactories ought to bear the same proportion, and effect the same object in relation to the whole community that the part of his household employed in domestic manufacturing does to the whole family. It is certainly desirable that the exports of the country should continue to be the surplus production of tillage, and not become those of manufacturing establishments. But it is important to diminish our imports—to furnish ourselves with clothing made by our own indusry—and to cease to be dependent for the very coat we wear upon a foreign and perhaps inimical country. The nation that imports its cloathing from abroad is but little less dependent than if it imported its bread.

The fallacious course of reasoning urged against domestic manufactures, the distress and servitude produced by those of England, would equally indicate the propriety of abandoning agriculture itself. Cast your eyes upon the miserable peasantry of Poland. Revert back to the days of feudal vassalage, and you may thence draw copious arguments of the kind now under consideration against the pursuits of the husbandman! What would become of commerce, the favorite theme of some gentlemen, if assailed with this sort of weapon? The fraud, perjury, cupidity and corruption with which it is unhappily too often attended would at once produce its overthrow.—In short, sir, take the black side of the picture and every human occupation will be found pregnant with fatal objections.

The opposition to manufacturing institutions recalls to my recollection the case of a gentleman of whom I have heard. He had been in the habit of supplying his table from a neighbouring cook and confectioner's shop, and proposed to his wife a reform in this particular. She revolted at the idea. The sight of a scullion was dreadful, and her delicate nerves could not bear the clattering of kitchen furniture. But the gentleman persisted in his design; his table was thenceforth better and cheaper supplied, and his neighbour the confectioner lost one of his best customers. In like manner Dame commerce will oppose domestic manufactures. She is a flirting, flippant, noisy jade, and if we are governed by her fantasies we shall never put off the muslins of India and the cloths of Europe. But I trust that the yeomanry of the country, the true and genuine landlord of this tenement, called the U. States, disregarding her freaks, will persevere in reform until the whole national family is furnished by itself with the cloathing necessary for its own use.

It is a subject no less of curiosity than of interest to trace the prejudices in favor of foreign fabricks. In our colonial condition we were in a complete state of manufactural and commercial, as well as political dependence on the parent country. For many years after the war, such was the partiality for her productions, that a gentleman's head could not withstand the influence of solar heat unless covered with a London hat—his feet could not bear the pebbles or frost of this country unless protected by London shoes—and the comfort or adornment of his person was only consulted when his coat was cut out by the shears of a tailor "just from London." At length, however, the wonderful *discovery* has been made that it is not absolutely beyond the reach of American skill and ingenuity to provide these articles, combining with equal elegance greater durability. And I entertain no doubt that in a short time the no less important fact will be developed, that the domestic manufactories of the United States, fostered by government, and aided by household exertions, are fully competent to supply us with at least every necessary article of cloathing. I therefore, sir, *for one* (to use the fashionable cant of the day) am in favour of encouraging them, not to the extent to which they are carried in England, but to such extent as will redeem us entirely from all dependence on foreign countries. There is a pleasure—a pride (if I may be allowed the expression, and I pity those who cannot feel the sentiment) in being clad in the productions of our own families.—Others may prefer the cloths [of] Leeds and of London, but give me those of Humphreysville.[4]

Aid may be given to native institutions in the form of bounties and of protecting duties. But against bounties it is urged that you tax the *whole,* for the benefit of a *part* only, of the community; and in opposition to duties it is alledged that you make the interest of one part, the consumer, bend to that of another part, the manufacturer. The sufficiency of the answer is not always admitted, that the sacrifice is merely temporary, being ultimately compensated by the greater abundance and superiority of the article produced by the stimulus. But, of all practicable forms of encouragement, it might have been expected that the one under consideration would escape opposition, if every thing proposed in congress were not doomed to experience it. What is it? The bill contains two provisions—One prospective, anticipating the appropriation for cloathing for the army, and the amendment proposes extending it to naval supplies also, for the year 1811.—And the other, directing a preference to be given to home manufactures & productions whenever it can be done *without material detriment to the public service*. The object of the first is to authorize contracts to be made before hand with manufacturers, and by making advances to them, under proper security to enable them to supply the articles wanted in sufficient quantity.—When it is recollected that they are frequently men of limited capitals, it will be acknowledged that this kind of assistance, bestowed with prudence, will be productive of the best results. It is in fact, only pursuing a principle long acted upon, of advancing to contractors with government, on account of the magnitude of their engagements. The appropriation contemplated to be made for the year 1811 may be restricted to such a sum as, whether we have peace or war, we must necessarily expend. The discretion is proposed to be vested in officers of high confidence, who will be responsible for its abuse, and who are enjoined to see that the public service receives no *material detriment*. It is stated that hemp is now very high, and that contracts made under existing circumstances will be injurious to government. But the amendment creates no obligation upon the secretary of the navy to go into market at this precise moment. In fact, by enlarging his sphere of action, it admits of his taking advantage of a favorable fluctuation, and getting a supply below the accustomed price, if such a fall should occur prior to the usual annual appropriation.

I consider the amendment under consideration, of the first importance in point of principle. It is evident that, whatever doubt may be entertained as to the general policy of the manufacturing system, none can exist as to the propriety of our being able to furnish ourselves with articles of the first necessity, in time of war. Our maritime operations ought not in such a state to depend upon the casualties of foreign supply. It is not necessary that they should. With very little encouragement from government, I believe we shall soon not want a pound of Russia hemp. The increase of the article in Kentucky has been rapidly great. Ten years ago there were but two rope manufactories in the state. Now there are about 20 & between 10 and 15 of cotton bagging; and the erection of new ones keeps pace with the annual augmentation of the quantity of hemp. Indeed the Western country alone is adequate to the supply not only of whatever of this article is requisite for our own consumption, but is capable of affording a surplus for foreign markets. The amendment proposed possesses the double recommendation of encouraging at the same time the manufacture and growth of hemp. For increasing the demand for the wrought article, you increase the demand also for the raw material, and consequently present new incentives to the cultivator.

The three great subjects that claim the attention of the national legislature are the interests of agriculture, commerce and manufactures. We have had before us a proposition to afford a manly protection to the rights of commerce, and how has it been treated? Rejected!—You have been solicited to promote agriculture, by increasing the facilities of internal communication through the means of canals and roads, and what has been done? Postponed! We are now called upon to give a trifling support to our domestic manufactories, and shall we close the circle of congressional inefficiency by adding this also to the catalogue?

Washington, D. C., *Spirit of 'Seventy-Six,* April 3, 1810 (NHi). Published also in Washington *National Intelligencer,* April 6, 1810; *Annals of Cong.,* 11 Cong., 2 Sess., XX, 626-30; Lexington *Kentucky Gazette,* April 17, 1810; Lexington *Reporter,* April 21, 1810; [James B. Swain], *The Life and Speeches of Henry Clay* (2 vols., New York 1843), I, Appendix, i-iv; Daniel Mallory, *The Life and Speeches of the Hon. Henry Clay* (2 vols., Hartford, 1855), I, 251-55; and Calvin Colton, *The Life, Correspondence, and Speeches of Henry Clay* (6 vols., New York, 1864), V, 7-11. The dating of the Swain, Mallory, and Colton versions, however, seems to have been taken erroneously from the publication date of the *Intelligencer.* For reference to the source here reprinted as the first publication of Clay's speech see John Pope to the People of Kentucky, June 13, 1811, in Frankfort *Palladium,* June 22, 1811.

1 John Pope.

2 James Lloyd, Jr., of Boston, a Federalist serving in the Senate from 1808 to 1813, and subsequently from 1822 to 1826.

3 The word given as "prophecy" in the source reprinted; it is here corrected from other published versions.

4 At this time the factory at Humphreysville, Connecticut, was the largest and best-equipped woolen mill in the United States. Victor S. Clark, *History of Manufactures in the United States* (1929 edn., 3 vols., New York, 1929), I, 562.

Report on Petition of Richard Bland Lee

In Senate U States March 28 1810

The Committee to whom was referred the Petition of R. Bland Lee and the Report of the Secretary for the Department of War thereupon, have according to order had the same under consideration, and Mr Clay from the said committee makes the following

Report,

That on the 24 Apl. 1790, Henry Lee[1] executed a lease to John

Smith,[2] of two parcels of land, containing together 654 Acres, lying on the Shennandoah near Harper's ferry in Virginia, for the term of 50 years, renewable, on certain conditions, for the additional term of 20 years: That in this lease the Covenants material to the present application are 1st. That there shall be no waste on the premises, and that the timber thereon shall be used for plantation purposes *only,* except tree tops and dead wood: 2dly. That the lessee shall, at the expiration of the lease, leave on the premises untouched, one fifth of the wood land: 3dly. That at no one time shall he put on the premises more than six sub-tenants: And 4thly. That on observance by the lessee of all the covenants on his part to be fulfilled, he shall during the term be protected by the lessor in the enjoymt. of the property: That the right to this lease became vested by assignment in a certain Thomas Wilson,[3] who in Novr. 1799 demised to James McHenry, then Secretary for the Department of War, in trust for the U. States, 196 Acres and 18 poles, part of the tenement aforesaid, under such restrictions and reservations as are contained in the original lease: That the reversionary interest held by Henry Lee was conveyed on the 13h. day of March 1804 by him to the petitioner Richard Bland Lee, and Ludwell Lee;[4] and a release of Ludwell Lee to the petitioner is exhibited for that part of the afd. tenement in the occupation of the U. States, dated the 2d. day of January 1809: That it is alledged by the petitioner that whilst the U. States troops, under the command of Genl. Pinkney,[5] were stationed at Harper's ferry in 1799 & 1800, they committed great waste & destruction in the timber on the 196 Acres of land before mentd., withdrawing it from the tenement, and applying it to other than plantation uses, in violation of the restrictive covenants of the lease: In support of this allegation the petitioner exhibits the letter of Col. Thomas Parker,[6] who states that "By the direction of the Executive I purchased a lease from Thomas Wilson near Harper's ferry in the fall of 1799 for the use of the U. States: Without this purchase we should have found it extremely difficult if not impracticable to have accomodated the Troops. It afforded a great quantity of logs for building the huts and a large quantity of fuel. I do not believe that the number of logs and the quantity of firewood that was taken from the land could have been purchased for much less than $2000." And also the letter of Geo. North,[7] represented to be a respectable man, who states in substance, that when the U. States took possession of the land about 1/8h. was cleared—the residue in wood, of which one fourth was covered with lofty building pine—that the wood land would average about 20 Cords per acre, worth about fifty Cents per cord; and that the whole wooded part has been cut by the U. States & the wood taken off the land. The petitioner also produced the honble John Smith of the H. of R. who, without pretending to have an intimate knowledge of the present situation of the land, supposed it to be worth 6 dollars per acre, and if now in the state in which it was when the U. States came to the possession that it would be worth 13 1/3 dollars:

That in opposition to the claim for damages growing out of this statement it appeared to your committee from the letter of Saml. Annin,[8] a respectable man, that more than one fifth of the timber upon the entire tenement remains untouched That Thomas Wilson claims the damages, if any, to which the U. States are subject for the alledged depredations of the Army; and that the land stripped of timber, will by the expiration of the lease have been timbered as valuably as ever:

That the petitioner also alledged a breach of the lease in withdrawing from a quarry which he stated to be on the premises stone & applying it to the use of the U. States. But he offered no proof whatever on this subject.

That it is stated by the late Secretary Dearborn[9] that he had reason to believe that the leased premises have been encumbered by Henry Lee.

That the petitioner submits three propositions to the Government,

1 To take a surrender of the tenement, releasing all claim for damages.

2. To receive $1200 in full satisfaction for damages. or

3. To convey to the U. States in fee simple the 196 Acres for $2000, as a compromise of all controversy; and to satisfy the officer appointed to receive the conveyance of the removal of all incumbrances.

Your Committee not conceiving it advisable for the Government to accede to either of these proposals, recommend the following resolution.

Resolved that the Petitioner have leave to withdraw his petition.

AD. DNA, RG46, 11A-D1. On February 23, Clay had moved that Lee's petition with the related papers be sent to a select committee. William H. Crawford of Georgia and Richard Brent of Virginia were thereupon appointed to serve with Clay. Their report of March 28 was tabled two days later. Subsequently, on motion of Brent, Lee's petition was recommitted to the same committee, but no further action was reported. Lee, a member of Congress from Virginia, 1789-1795, had petitioned Congress during the preceding session for compensation for the damage caused by the United States troops stationed at Harper's Ferry.

1 "Light-Horse Harry," brother of Richard B. Lee.

2 Member of Congress from Virginia, 1801-1815.

3 Possibly of Richmond, Virginia. There were also others of this name in Virginia at the time.

4 Cousin of Richard B. Lee's father.

5 Charles Cotesworth Pinckney, appointed major general in 1798, during the reorganization of the army in anticipation of war with France.

6 Virginia veteran of the Revolution, lieutenant colonel of the Eighth Regiment of United States Infantry, 1799-1800, colonel and brigadier general of infantry during the War of 1812.

7 Brigade quartermaster under General Anthony Wayne during the Revolution.
8 Not identified.
9 Henry Dearborn.

Bill Relative to Trial and Punishment of Indians

[March 29, 1810]

A Supplement to an Act entitled "an act to regulate trade and intercourse with the Indian Tribes & to preserve peace on the frontiers."[1]

Sect. I. Be it enacted by the senate and house of Representatives of the United States of America in congress assembled, That if any Indian or Indians shall, within the Indian boundary lines now established by law, or which may hereafter be established, commit any crime misdemeanour or offence against the person or property of any citizen or inhabitant of the United States or of their territories, which would be punishable by law in any circuit or district court of the United States, if committed within the jurisdiction of such circuit or district court; such Indian or Indians, for such crime misdemeanour or offence, shall be prosecuted in the same manner & receive the same punishment to which he she or they would, by law, be subjected in case such crime misdemeanour or offence were committed within the jurisdiction of any circuit or district court of the United States.

Sec. II. And be it further enacted, That the circuit and district courts of the United States or of their territories, & the suprior [*sic*] courts of those territories in which a district or circuit court is not established by law, shall, in each district or territory, within which any offendor against this act may be apprehended, or into which he may be brought for trial, agreeably to the provisions contained in the act to which this is a supplement, or the act entitled "An act to establish the judicial courts of the United States", have full power authority & jurisdiction, to hear & determine all crimes, misdemeanours & offences against this act, in the same manner, as if such crimes misdemeanours or offences were committed within their respective jurisdictions.

D. DNA, RG46, 11A-B2. On this day Clay asked and obtained leave to present the bill, which was read and passed to the second reading. Read a second time on March 30, it was then referred to a select committee composed of Clay, Joseph Anderson of Tennessee, and Return J. Meigs, Jr., of Ohio. The committee did not submit a report.
1 Approved March 30, 1802, 2 *U.S. Stat.*, 139-46.

Agreement with W. T. Barry

[April 1, 1810]

Attached to Agreement, November 9, 1808.

Proposed Amendments to National Bank Bill

[April 4, 1810]

And upon such assignment the Stockholders of the said Bank shall become Stockholders of the Bank hereby created, to the amount of the Stock which they shall respectively hold in the present Bank, at the time of the subscription aforesaid; and shall be entitled to Certificates for shares accordingly. And there upon all and singular the lands, tenaments, goods, chattels, effects, rights, claims & demands of the said Bank shall be transferred to & vested in the Bank hereby created; & shall be held enjoyed claimed demanded & recovered by the Bank hereby created.[1] And from & after such assignment the said Bank hereby created shall be answerable at law & in equity for all demands for which the present Bank is liable or answerable.

—

Provided that, at the time of so subscribing, such person co-partnership or body politic shall pay into the Bank at Philadelphia authorized to be established by this act, for the use of the U. States
of the advance at which the Stock of the said Bank shall then be selling above par in the market of Philadelphia, upon each share which he or they may thus subscribe.

—

Be it further enacted that it shall be lawful for the incorporation of the Subscribers to the Bank of the U. S. made & established by the act entitled "An act to incorporate the subscribers to the Bank of the U. States" to subscribe the amt of their Capital Stock at par into the Bank proposed hereby to be established, & to assign the same accordingly: Provided that they pay into the public Treasury of the U. States the sum of & provided that they make their election so to subscribe on or before the day of next

AD. DNA, RG46, 11A-B2. Three separate proposals, the second of which is endorsed in another hand, "to come in at the end of the third section." James A. Bayard of Delaware, who earlier had reported a bill to establish a National Bank, offered an amendment on April 4 to permit stockholders of the existing Bank of the United States to subscribe within three years for as many shares of the proposed bank as they held of the old and to pay for them in gold, silver, or the stock of the existing bank. Clay's proposals, to be added to this amendment, were withdrawn; and on April 25 the Senate in Committee of the Whole agreed to postpone further consideration of the bill itself until the following December.

1 Following this word, Clay wrote and crossed out several phrases, all encompassed by the line "in the same manner as the Same are or could be by the present," which he also then deleted.

Resolution for Land Grants to Promote Emigration to Orleans Territory

[April 7, 1810]

Resolved that it is expedient to make provision by Law for

encouraging emigration to the Orleans Territory of American Citizens, by making a suitable donation of certain portions of the public lands, within the said Territory.

AD. DNA, RG46, S11A-B5 (1). Published in *Annals of Cong.*, 11 Cong., 2 Sess., XX, 644. No action on the motion was reported, and no such legislation was enacted. On the origin of Clay's proposal, cf. above, Brown to Clay, February 26, 1810.

Amendment Relative to Investigation of Title to the Batture

[April 14, 1810]

together with the Laws, usages edicts or customs upon which the said title may depend, and which they shall also collect & arrange

D. DNA, RG46, S11A-C2 (2). Published in Washington *National Intelligencer*, April 23, 1810; *Annals of Cong.*, 11 Cong., 2 Sess., XX, 656. See above, Brown to Clay, February 26, 1810, note. After Senate acceptance of a motion to delete the words *"together with their opinion thereon respecting the title aforesaid,"* from the section prescribing the duty of the commissioners appointed to collect testimony under a bill for investigation of the title to the Batture in front of the suburb St. Mary in New Orleans, Clay moved to insert his amendment in lieu of the deleted words. Clay's motion was also at first adopted. When, on April 18, the Senate reconsidered the bill after House rejection of the amendments, Clay moved that the proposed changes be dropped. The Senate adhered to its amendments, and the House postponed indefinitely further consideration of the bill.

Committee Report on Petition of Elisha Winters

In Senate U States April 17h 1810

The Committee to whom was referred the petition of Elisha Winters

Reported

That it appeared to your Committee that during the years 1801. 2. and 3. a daring banditti, headed by one Mason,[1] infested the wilderness road from Natchez to Tennessee and the river Mississippi: That they committed vast depredations both upon the persons & property of individuals, and were the terror of all travelling through the wilderness: That the petitioner in ascending the river, in company with his son, was robbed by them of a considerable sum of money: That their enormities at length became so great as to attract the attention of the then Governor of the Mississippi Territory, who issued a proclamation offering rewards for the Chief and his associates, according to the several degrees of their guilt: That finally the Civil authority of the Mississippi Territory obtained the custody of two of the party, who were tried, condemned & executed: That the petitioner & his son attended on their trial from the State of Kentucky, for the sole purpose of testifying against the accused; and were detained in consequence thereof several weeks in the M.

Territory: That your Committee were informed by the gentleman who prosecuted the culprits that, without the evidence of the Petitioner and his son, it would not have been practicable to convict them. That the Petitioner in travelling with his son from Kentucky for the purpose before stated, and in attending on the Court, must necessarily have incurred considerable expence, besides the loss of time; and justice would seem to require an indemnity for these sacrifices: That he states the amt. of his expences to have been between $200 & 300$, & the mileage allowed him by the Territorial Laws commenced only upon his entrance into the Territory: That the whole compensation recd. both for travelling and per diem allowance for himself & son was the evidence of a claim upon the Territorial Treasury of abt. fifty dollars, upon which he had to make a considerable discount, in order to procure money.

Your committee doubted whether the application of the Petitioner ought not to be made to the justice of the Territorial Government; but upon reflecting that the theatre of the depredations of the robbers was within the Indian boundary, under the jurisdiction of the U. States; & that they were punishable only by their laws, in the execution of which proper incentives to individual aid ought to be presented, recommend the following resolution:

Resolved that it is reasonable that the Petitioner be allowed[2] the sum of dollars to reimburse him for the expenses of himself & son & as compensation for their loss of time in attending as witnesses afd.

AD. DNA, RG46, 11A-D1. On April 10, Clay had presented Winters' petition and, with Jenkin Whiteside (Tennessee) and William H. Crawford, had been appointed to a select committee for consideration of the matter. After the report was read, no further action was taken.

1 Samuel Mason, notorious outlaw, killed in 1803 by two of his former associates, Wiley Harpe and Samuel Mays, who in turn were themselves tried and hanged for complicity in robbery of Winters.

2 Following this word Clay wrote and then deleted the line, "by law Two hundred & fifty dollars."

Amendment of Bill to Provide for State Governmnt in Orleans Territory

[April 20, 1810]

Provided further that the said Convention shall, by an article in the Constitution so to be formed, irrevocable without the consent of the United States, provide that after the admission into the union of the said Territory of Orleans as a State, the laws which such state may pass, shall be promulgated & its records of every description shall be preserved & its written judicial & legislative proceedings conducted in the language in which the laws & the written judicial & legislative proceedings of the United States are now published & conducted.

D. DNA, RG46, S11A-B2 (3). Published in Washington *National Intelligencer,* April 23, 1810; *Annals of Cong.,* 11 Cong., 2 Sess., XX, 663-64. The amendment passed the Senate and was ultimately retained in substance in the measure enacted February 20, 1811, but disagreement between the House and the Senate on other features of the bill delayed final acceptance of the proposal until the latter year. 2 *U.S. Stat.,* 642, sec. 3. On Clay's interest in such a provision, cf. above, Brown to Clay, February 26, 1810.

To Adam Beatty

WASHINGTON, April 23, 1810.

DR. BEATTY,—This day was fixed by resolution of the two Houses of Congress for its adjournment, but that resolution has been rescinded, and the session protracted one week longer. On the great subject of our foreign affairs, I believe we shall adjourn without adopting any efficient measure. A bill to augment the duties fifty per cent. has passed the House of Representatives, but I fear, like Macon's bill,[1] it will not be concurred in by the Senate. One of its valuable effects, if it passes will be the encouragement of our manufactures. As the increase is not contemplated, however, to be permanent, I should prefer a smaller augmentation, and that it should be durable.

Two committees of the House of Representatives are engaged in investigating Wilkinsons's conduct (who has at length arrived), one into the Spanish conspiracy, and the other into the causes of the mortality of the army last summer. On this latter subject it is expected a report will be made this session; upon the other a report will hardly be made before the next.[2]

Howard is appointed Governor of Louisiana.[3]

Colton (ed.), *Private Correspondence of Henry Clay,* 46-47.

[1] Macon's Bill No. 1.

[2] The report relative to the mortality of the troops at New Orleans (see above, Brown to Clay, February 26, 1810) was made April 27, 1810; the other, on May 1, 1810. *Annals of Cong.,* 11 Cong., 2 Sess., XXI, 1997, [2426-96], 2032-48, [2288-2379].

[3] Benjamin Howard had resigned his seat in Congress on April 10 to accept the appointment.

Bill Relating to Punishment of Crimes against the United States

[April 27, 1810]

Be it enacted by the Senate and House of Representatives of the U. States of America, in Congress assembled,

That on the trial of an indictment found against any person or persons for any offense or crime committed against the provisions contained in the 28h. section of the act, to which this is a supplement, it shall not be necessary to prove, for the purpose of conviction, either that such person or persons knew the diplomatic character of the party injured, or his domicil.

[Endorsement on verso][1]

A supplement to an act entitled "An act for the punishment of certain crimes against the U. States."

AD. DNA, RG46, S11A-B7 (4b). Clay had given notice on April 26 of his intention to present the measure. It was now committed to a select committee under John Pope, Clay's Kentucky colleague in the Senate, who reported the bill without amendment on April 30. While the proposal was under consideration in Committee of the Whole on May 1, a motion was approved which postponed further consideration indefinitely.

1 AE.

Agreement by Executors of Thomas Hart, Jr.

[May 11, 1810]

[Clay and other executors for the estate of Thomas Hart, Jr., agree to the sale of partnership rights of Thomas Hart, Jr., in the firm of Hart, Bartlet and Cox of New Orleans.]

Copy. DLC-TJC (DNA, M212, R10).

To the Electors of the Fifth Congressional District

Lexington, 14th May, 1810.

I tender, fellow citizens, my services to represent you in the 12th Congress.

In presenting myself to your notice, I conform to sentiments I have invariably felt, in favor of the station of an immediate representative of the people.

I am not vain enough to suppose that, in the event of receiving your approbation, I shall carry with me into the House of Representatives the ability to advance in any material degree the interests of my country. All that I dare promise is, that those political principles, which have hitherto directed me, shall continue to be my guide; and that in honest zeal to promote the welfare of the nation I yield to no one. Your obedient servant, HENRY CLAY.

Lexington *Kentucky Gazette*, May 15, 1810. Clay's district included Woodford, Fayette, Jessamine, Clark, and Montgomery counties.

Receipt from John W. Wooldridge

[May 21, 1810]

Recd. 21 May 1810 of H. Clay a bond given by Edmund Wooldridge to John & Powhatan Wooldridge for £194:11:2 dated the 27 Octr. 1810 [*sic*] payable with int. from the date, six years after date JNO. W. WOOLDRIDGE

DS, in Clay's hand. DLC-TJC (DNA, M212, R15). Cf. above, Guardian's Bond, February 13, 1804.

To Caesar A. Rodney

My Dr Sir Lexington 27 May 1810.

You were good enough to promise that I should hear from you. Suffer me to remind you of that engagement and to say that it will give me great pleasure to receive a communication of any kind from you. I trust you found, after your long absence from home, your family in good health upon your return to their bosom, as I had the happiness to find mine.

What news from abroad? Have you yet heard any thing calculated to extricate you from the embarrassments existing when we parted? I feel great solicitude for our Country & for our cause.

Chiefly upon the advice of yourself & our friend Burwell[1] I have been induced to decline offering for the Senate, altho I should I believe have encountered no opposition, and am about to take a poll for the H. of R. in the 12th. Congress, in which also it is probable I shall have no com[p]etitor.[2] Yr. friend H. CLAY

ALS. DLC-Rodney Family Papers (DNA, M212, R22). Addressed to Rodney at Wilmington, Delaware, and postmarked at Frankfort, May 31.

1 William Armisted Burwell, Representative from Virginia, formerly President Jefferson's private secretary. 2 Clay's view proved to be correct.

To [William Taylor]

D Sir Lexington 28th. May 1810

I have the pleasure to inform you that your debt agt. Kelly[1] is I think rendered safe by a replevy bond taken abt. the 1st. Feb. last with three securities, payable twelve months after date. To elude payment of your debt Kelly had made a pretended sale of all his property to his brother, but by extraordinary exertions of the Marshall (for which I have promised him an extra allowance, with your assent) the replevy bond,* with that brother & two others as securities, was obtained. You will perceive however that the payment of the debt is necessarily postponed until next February, after which if default is made, we shall be at liberty to sue out a new execution; such being the mode prescribed by our Laws.

Yr. ob. Servt. H. CLAY

* Amount 1599„40/100 $ P Jno. H. Hanna's Letter from Frankford April. 10. 1810.

ALS. DLC-HC (DNA, M212, R1). Endorsed on verso, presumably by Taylor: "Lexington 28 May 1810. Henry Clay. July 29. 1810. . . ."
[1] Joseph Kelly.

To Adam Beatty

FRANKFORT, May 31, 1810.

DR. BEATTY,—I received your favor,[1] with the specimen inclosed of your merino's fleece, and compared it with one which I took from a full-blooded merino of General Mason's,[2] and find very little difference between them. If you could send your wool, or the yarn, to a manufacturer[3] in Danville, he would make you the best piece of cloth that you could obtain from it. I do not recollect his name, but he is an Englishman, accustomed to the business, and has undertaken, for Judge Todd,[4] to make him a coat which he warrants shall not be inferior to the best imported cloth in the State. I propose sending mine to him. If, however, you prefer having it made in the neighborhood of Lexington, there will be no difficulty in getting it wove, fulled, etc.

I am glad to learn that your election to the Legislature is deemed certain.[5] Your presence there will be extremely necessary. I am solicitous for it on various accounts. You will have heard that I am no longer a candidate for the Senate, and that my successor will consequently be appointed. May not the Federalists attempt to rally in support of one of their party? This should be looked to.[6]

In offering for the House of Representatives, I was influenced by a partiality for the station, and by the wishes of some of my friends, as well here as to the East. I contemplate, however, serving out the term for which I am already appointed in the Senate, not wishing to give the trouble of supplying my place for the ensuing session, and being desirous to prevent the possibility of the State being partially represented during a considerable portion of it.

Colton (ed.), *Private Correspondence of Henry Clay*, 47. [1] Not found.
[2] John Mason owned several stock farms in Maryland and Virginia; he was one of the founders of the Columbian Society for Promotion of Domestic Economy and an importer and breeder of prize-winning merino sheep. Merino sheep had been first brought into Kentucky in 1809. Adam Beatty, *Southern Agriculture* (New York, c. 1843), 48. [3] Not identified. [4] Thomas Todd.
[5] Beatty was not elected. In the next year Governor Scott appointed him a circuit judge.
[6] George M. Bibb, a Republican and a Warhawk, was elected as Clay's successor.

Offer of Reward in Theft of Homespun

TEN DOLLARS REWARD. June 18, 1810.

On Friday night last, was stolen from the house of Mrs. Butler,[1] in Lexington, four pieces of homespun diaper,[2] three of them containing about six yards each, and the fourth about eight yards. The diaper had loops in the sides and hems in the ends, had been recently wove, was when stolen in a tub of lye whitening, and was made from a ten hundred thread.

The above reward will be given for detection of the thief, or for the linen. HENRY CLAY.

Lexington *Reporter*, June 23, 1810.
1 Possibly Mrs. Thompson Butler, of the southern district of Fayette County.
2 Linen cloth with woven pattern.

Bill in Chancery Concerning "Ashland" and Other Property

[June 18, 1810]

To the Honble the Judges of the Fayette Circuit Court in Chy. sitting: Humbly complaining shew unto your Honors your orator Henry Clay, & Thomas Hart[1] an infant by the said Clay his next friend,

That on the day of 1807 your orator Henry purchased a farm of 255 Acres of land near Lexington at public auction on which he resides, of Wilson C. Nicholas, & Saml. Smith:[2] That at the same time & at the same sale Thomas Hart now deceased purchased a house & certain lots in the town of Lexington from the same persons, on which his family now resides: That the said Hart has since departed this life & by his will devised the said house lots &c. to your orator Thomas: That the said Wilson C. Nicholas & Saml Smith derive title to the said property from the late Geo Nicholas deceased; 'tho' your orators are not exactly informed of the manner of its deduction; but they charge & believe that it is under a mortgage given by the Exors of the said Nicholas of the said property to Willis Green, under which the said property was sold & purchased at public sale by the said W. Nicholas & Smith:[3] That a certain Joseph Thornburg & Co.[4] in virtue of certain executions sued out by them upon Judgments, obtained against the said Geo. Nicholas's Exors, claim that the said property is liable to be sold to satisfy the said Executions; & for the purpose of effecting this object the said Thornburg & Co. did on the 14h. day of May last sue out Vend. Exponas's from the Clerks office of this Court, with which they or their Attorney are threatening to sell the said property: That your orators are not vested with legal titles as yet from the said Smith & Nicholas, but the said Thomas Hart deceased has paid up the consideration money for the house & lots afd and your orator Henry is ready to fulfill his contract for the purchase made by him—

That the Executions, in virtue of which the said Thornburg & Co. pretend that the said property is liable for their debt, were not as your orators are informed & believe delivered to the Sheriff until after the execution of the said mortgage to Green That if the said property is liable your orator Henry will have in his hands a sufficient sum, part of the consideration money for the purchase afd, to pay the said executions:

That situated as the property is your orators are advised that a Court of Equity will interpose, & protect your orators until the said Thornburg & Co. & Smith & W. Nicholas shall by interpleader settle between themselves how their rights stand, so that your orators may know their true situation—In tender consideration whereof &c. To the end therefore that the said Wilson C. Nicholas & Saml Smith & Joseph Thornburg & Company (all of whom your orators pray may be made defts hereto) may upon their oaths make as full answer to the allegations of this bill as if they were herein again repeated in the form of interrogatory: that the said defts may interplead between themselves & ascertain in whom the title to the said property is that in the mean time the said Thornburg & Co. may be enjoined from proceeding to sell the said property, and if ultimately it shall be found not liable to the said Executions that the said defts may be enjoined & restrained perpetually from proceeding to sell the said property & that your orators may have such relief as is proper—May it please &c H. CLAY

ADS. Fayette Circuit Court, File 442. Endorsed: "Fayette Circuit Sct. Sworn to in Open Court. June 18h 1810 Robert: S: Todd." Endorsed on verso: ". . . Injt granted bond ord on bill. . . ." An unsigned copy of the bond, for $6000, is filed, *ibid.* The case was continued from term to term until dismissed in 1819. Fayette Circuit Court, Order Book U (April 5, 1819-October 9, 1819), 294.

1 Thomas Pindell Hart, eldest son of Thomas Hart, Jr.

2 The property advertised for the auction to have been held on January 15, 1807, was described as follows:

"That elegant Farm, one mile south of Lexington, containing two hundred and fifty five acres, about one hundred acres cleared and under good fences forty acres of which is excellent meadow well set with Timothy and Clover, and the balance laid off in convenient fields and grass lots; a small dwelling-house, and good barn, and constant spring and good spring-house, together with an excellent orchard of young and growing apple trees.—The convenient situation of this farm gives it probably more advantages than any other in the neighbourhood of Lexington." Lexington *Kentucky Gazette,* December 4, 1806.

3 In 1798 George Nicholas had agreed to mortgage the property to Willis Green (pioneer surveyor in Kentucky, for many years from 1783 Clerk of the Lincoln County Court), as indemnity for Green's securityship in certain debts. Following Nicholas' death shortly thereafter, Samuel Smith and Wilson Cary Nicholas, as assignees of Green, had brought suit to obtain the property from George Nicholas' executors. By decree of the Fayette Circuit Court the land had been placed on sale and conveyed to Smith and W. C. Nicholas on January 18, 1806. Fayette District Court, Deed Book C, 283-86; Fayette County Court, Deed Book F, 525-26; Fayette Circuit Court, File 220 (1811).

4 Of Baltimore.

Property Deed to George Norton

[June 20, 1810]

[Indenture by which for the sum of five shillings, paid and

acknowledged, Clay sells to George Norton a lot in Lexington fronting on Main Street 33½ feet, beginning at the intersection of Main and Mulberry streets, extending thence on Main Street 33½ feet to the lot of John Parker, thence back with Parker's lot and Mulberry Street to Water Street. Clay will defend the title as conveyed by William R. Morton, Deputy Sheriff of John H. Morton, Sheriff of Fayette County, by deed of March 28, 1809—the title warranted only against claimants under Clay, "it being expressly understood & agreed by the parties hereto that the said Clay having no interest in the said lot or the sale of it is not to be responsible except as herein provided, if the right derived to him from the sheriff as afsd. & hereby conveyed should prove inferior to any other contending claim." Signature of Clay acknowledged before J. D. Young, Clerk of Fayette County, June 20, 1810.]

Fayette County Court, Deed Book D, 487-88.

Promissory Note from William J. Phillips and William Montgomery

[June 21, 1810]

We promise to pay H. Clay on demand Twenty dollars for value recd. Witness our seals 21 June 1810.

WM. J. PHILLIPS {L.S.}
WM MONTGOMERY {L.S.}

DS, in Clay's hand. DLC-TJC, 2d Series, vol. 11. Phillips and Montgomery were residents of Frankfort, Kentucky.

Account with Cuthbert Banks

[*ca.* June 28, 1810]

1810		Mr. Henry Clay To Cuthbert Banks	
January	16th	To 2 Horses 1/6 Dinr 1/6 . .	£ " 3 "
"	"	" Wm. T Banton	1.14. 6
February	4th.	" A. Miller[1]	5. " 6
	5th	" Cash paid Lemmons[2] . . .	1.11. 6
	6h.	" paid Luke Usher . . .	5 15 5½
	9h	" paid Hawling plank . .	" 1. 6
		" paid Usher for Plank . . .	1.12. 3
"	"	" Saml. Owings[3] (Taylor) work	2 5 "
	14th	" Nails - - - - - - . .	" 3 "
	27h.	" Barbee[4] for Smoke house Stairs	3 " "
April	9h.	" Cash paid Usher . . .	7.11.10
"	"	" Cash paid Springle[5]	

May	12th	"	Horse 9d Dinr 1/6	"	2. 3
	14th.	"	Horse 9d Dinr. 1/6 Punch 4/6	"	6 9
	20h	"	Horse 9d 25th Horse 9d . . .	"	1. 6
	31st	"	Horse 2 Nights	"	6 "
June	3rd	"	Horse 9d 10th Horse 9d - - -	"	1. 6
	11th	"	Horse 9d Dinr 1/6 - - -	"	2 3
	15h	"	Horse 9d Dinr 1/6 - -	"	2 3
	16h	"	Horse 9d Dinr 1/6 17th Horse 9d	"	3 "
	18h	"	Horse 9d Dinr 1/6 Supper 1/6	"	3 9
	19h	"	Horse 9d Dinr 1/6 Sangaree 5/3	"	7. 6
	20h	"	Horse 9d 21st Horse 3/. - - -	"	3. 9
	23rd	"	Horse 9d Dinr 1/6 - - -	"	2 3
	24h	"	Horse 9d Sangaree 5/3 . .	"	6 "
	25h	"	Horse 9d Dinr 1/6 Wine 3/.	"	5. 3
	26h	"	Horse 9d Dinr 1/6 27h Horse 9d. Dinr 1/6	"	4 6
	28h	"	Horse 9d. Dinr 1/6 1 pt. Wine 6/.	"	8/ 3
					5 3½[6]

D. DLC-TJC (DNA, M212, R15). Cf. above, Account, January 15, 1810.
[1] Possibly Aaron Miller, Fayette County.
[2] Probably James Lemon, tailor, Main Cross Street.
[3] Samuel Owens. [4] Joseph Barbee. [5] John Springle.
[6] The "5" is superimposed on "10"; the £32 total is missing.

Bank Check to the Messrs. Bullitt

No. *Lexington,* 28 June 1810

THE CASHIER OF THE KENTUCKY INSURANCE CO.

Pay to Mess Bullitts or bearer fourteen hundred & five—Dollars 71 Cents.

$1405:71/100 Dollars. H. CLAY

ADS, partially printed form. DLC-TJC, 2d Series, vol. 11. The Bullitts were probably members of the prominent Louisville family of that name.

Fee Bill from County Clerk

[July, 1810]

1810	Henry Clay Esq. Exor of Henry Marshall	D Cts
July	Order to settle 25 Copy. 18 . . .	43

J. D. YOUNG C. F. County.

ADS. DLC-TJC (DNA, M212, R15). Cf. above, Bond, July 14, 1806.

Advertisement of Hotel for Rent

Lexington, 1st July, 1810.

THE KENTUCKY HOTEL

To be Rented.

CAPTAIN BANKS, the present tenant, wishing to apply himself exclusively to his own property, the Olympian Springs, is disposed to surrender his lease of this establishment. It is therefore offered for rent. Its advantageous situation is so well known that a particular description of it is not necessary. It is sufficient to say, that its local position, in the heart of Lexington, the number, extent and convenience of the apartments in the buildings, the superiority of the stables, &c. place it unquestionably in the very first order of public establishments of this kind.

A lease for a year or term of years may be obtained, and the lessor may procure from Capt. Banks a variety of valuable furniture.

HENRY CLAY.

Lexington *Reporter,* July 7, 1810. Banks had apparently made an agreement to purchase the Springs in 1807, but cf. below, Advertisement, April 9, 1813, note.

To James D. Breckinridge

My Dr Sir. Lex. 10 July 1810.

I understand that Mr. Clarke[1] is committed to the Jail of your County at the suit of Tiernan & Co. for whom I recovered a Judgment in the Fed. Court. I conceive it my duty not to suffer his release, for want of security for the Jail fees, if it be demanded. Will you do me the favor therefore to assure the Jailor that his fees shall be paid, or if he require it enter yourself as security?

Are you likely to recover a Judgt. shortly agt. Ormsby[2] upon the note I placed in your hands? Yr. friend H. CLAY

ALS. KyLoF. Addressed: "James Breckenridge Esqr. Counseller at Law Louisville (K)."

1 Probably of Clark and Anderson. The suit has not been found.

2 Peter B. Ormsby.

Payments to Sarah Beard's Representatives

[July 14, 1810]

Acct. of payments made by H. Clay to Sarah Beard's representatives on a/c of Cosby's purchase of the Falls Estate.

1807		
13 July	To Cash paid C. Megowan[1] & wife per rect - .	$300:
18th	To do. do. do.	97:50.
13 Augt.	To do. J. & D McCoun[2] per their order - -	212:50.

16 Octr.	To do. John Kay Jr.[3] per rect	506:75
1808		
11 Apl.	To do pd. Wm. Beard[4] per rect	100 " –
29 July	To do. pd. Jo. Beard Admor per rect .	700 " –
16 do.	To do do. do. do -	50 "
29 –	To do. to Majr Morrison[5] for Megowan's note	103.47.
6 Octr.	To do. to C. Megowan per rect -	30:
"	To do. to do. by T Bodley[6] do . . .	150 "
31 Decr.	To do. by Capt. Banks[7] per rect . . .	80 "
1809		
7. Apl	To do per do . .	50 "
5 July.	To do. per do.	150 "
5 Octr.	To do to R. Byewaters[8] per J. Beards order	130 "
16 Feb.	To do. per J. Beards rect	200 "
27 Octr.	To do do do . . .	100 " .
30 .	To do. paid Mrs. Beck[9] per J. Beards order –	53:50
14 Novr.	To do. paid J. Beard per do rect.	100 " .
1810		
13. Jan	To do. paid do. per do.	50:
		$ 3163:72
14 July–	To do in a check on the Ins. Company[10]	150:
		$3313:72

I do hereby acknowledge that the payments as above stated have been made by H. Clay, amounting to $3313:72 on account of the purchase made by F. Cosby of the Falls Estate from Sarah Beard 14 July 1810.

Teste JOSEPH BEARD Extr
F COSBY– for Sarah Beard D

DS, in Clay's hand. DLC-TJC (DNA, M212, R15). See above, Agreement, December 8, 1806. 1 Charles McGowan.
2 James and David Maccoun. 3 Of Fayette County.
4 Brother of Joseph and son of Sarah Beard. He lived in the southern part of Fayette County. 5 James Morrison. 6 Thomas Bodley.
7 Cuthbert Banks. See above, Account, January 15, 1810 (entry of December 31, 1808).
8 Robert Bywaters. 9 Mrs. Mary Beck.
10 Kentucky Insurance Company.

To Adam Beatty

LEXINGTON, July 27, 1810.

DR. BEATTY,—I received your favor of the 24th June.[1] The nett yield of our merino (owing to the neglect or fraud of the shearer of him) was not sufficient to make me a coat. Mrs. Clay therefore determined to have it spun, and either applied to other uses, or retained until we could get an additional quantity. A Captain M'Call,[2] in this neighborhood, has undertaken to weave and full, for Jordan,[3] some yarn spun from the merino wool; and if you can not better dispose of yours, I have no doubt Mr. Jordan can procure him to weave and full yours also.

I learned with pleasure your decision in favor of again offering for the Legislature. Your success, I am told, is not doubted. The Republican interests will require, and, I am sure, will receive your best support. Whether the Federalists will or will not attempt a Senator of their own kind depends on the issue of the election. I believe Daviess will not be elected here; and even Humphrey dreads the result of the Franklin election.[4]

P. S. I requested a Mr. Fowke,[5] of Baltimore, to call on you for professional aid, which I hope you will afford.

Colton (ed.), *Private Correspondence of Henry Clay,* 48. 1 Not found.
2 Probably John M'Call, who operated a "Merchant mill, Saw mill, Distillery and farm," about eleven miles east of Lexington. Lexington *Reporter,* August 4, 1810.
3 Probably John Jordan, Jr.
4 Neither Joseph Hamilton Daviess nor Humphrey Marshall held a seat in the next legislature.
5 Possibly Thomas Fowke, who had entered a land claim in Kentucky in 1799.

From William Taylor

Dear Sir, Baltimore July. 29h. 1810.

I think I acknowledged The payment of *150*$ by Samuel Walker[1] on the 17h. April last for your account in part of The money you recovered of Mr. Whittaker[2]—and when convenient remit me The Balance with a statement.

I do not know that I acknowledged yr favr of The 11h March & 19h April[3] from Washington, and I have before me now that of 28h. May from Lexington. will you do me The favr to have the enclosed sealed directed & forwarded to W. F. Simrall,[4] and inform me if he is good—I may have occasion to imploy you on this Business.

I was a little disappointed at not seeing you after you left The seat of Government of The United States—I did not hear of your passing through our City.

It gives me pleasure to hear you think Kellys[5] Dbt safe—I certainly assent to your making good yr promise to The Marshal for extra allowance. But make it as moderate as you can and get my Debt or turn it into money & remit me here as soon as you can. I am, very sincerely, Yr mo. obt Sert WM. TAYLOR

I have a claim of 1177.58 agt. Simrall.

Henry Clay Esqr,

ALS. DLC-TJC (DNA, M212, R12). Endorsed by Clay: "Answd. 29 Aug." Answer not found.
1 Not identified. There were men of that name in both central Kentucky and Baltimore. 2 W. W. Whitaker. 3 This letter not found.
4 William F. Simrall, of Louisville. 5 Joseph Kelly.

Rental Agreement with John Riesman

[August 4, 1810]

I have this day rented of H. Clay, acting for himself & the others interested therein with him, the Salt lick on the waters of Big Sandy commonly called Youngs,[1] for two years, commencing the 20h. of this month—And I do hereby bind & oblige myself to deliver to the said Clay at his farm near Lexington on or before the first day of Octr. next one or two geldings to be valued at One hundred & fifty dollars; & on or before the first day of Octr. 1811 One or two geldings more to be valued likewise at one hundred. & fifty dollars. And failing in either payment the said Clay is to be at liberty to re enter & re occupy the premises. Witness my seal this 4h Aug. 1810.

Teste JOHN RIESMAN {L.S.}
C H ALLEN[2]

DS, in Clay's hand. KyLxT. Riesman not identified.
1 See above, Agreement, October 10, 1806.
2 Possibly Charles H. Allen, member of the Kentucky legislature from Henry County for many years after 1817.

To Caesar A. Rodney

My Dr Rodney Lexington 6 Aug. 1810.

Your very agreeable and friendly favor of the 18h. June[1] would have been earlier answered, but for my absence from home, attending some of the Courts.

The recent confiscation of our property in France, and the Countries subject to her control, was indeed an act of infamous treachery, if not of open robbery.[2] That it affords us just cause of reprisal no one can doubt. But I scarcely know of an injury that France could do us, short of an actual invasion of our Territory, that would induce me to go to War with her, whilst the injuries we have received from Great Britain remain unredressed. That the Feds. should endeavor to precipitate us into a War with France, whilst they are totally regardless of British aggressions, is perfectly consistent with the uniform tenor of their conduct. What will they say of the repetition upon the Vixen of the outrage committed on the Chesapeake?[3] Is not it provoking in the extreme that Trippe should have imitated so exactly the conduct of Barron?[4] After receiving two shot, that he should have stooped to ask an explanation, parleyed, or hesitated for a moment as to the part he ought to have acted is to me astonishing. A man receives a fillip on the nose, and instead of instantly avenging the insult, inquires of the person giving it what he means!

Horses already well matched and broke to the carriage are not easily to be procured in this Country of such a description as is given in your letter. The best and cheapest way of getting them is to buy them singly, and afterwards have them broken. In this manner they may be obtained for about 300$ the pair of the first quality.

I anticipate great pleasure in your society this winter, which I am happy to find we shall have more of by your contemplated residence in the City. I fear however that Mrs. Clay will not this winter participate in the gratification, as I shall be detained in this Country so late, & compelled to return so immediately after the close of Congress, that she will not be able to encounter the travelling at those seasons of the year. Yr's very sincerely

HENRY CLAY

ALS. DLC-Rodney Family Papers (DNA, M212, R22). Addressed to Rodney at Wilmington, Delaware.

1 Not found.

2 Following passage of the Non-Intercourse Act by the United States Congress in 1809, Napoleon on March 23, 1810, had issued the Rambouillet decree, to be applied retroactively, ordering the seizure and sale of all American vessels in French ports.

3 On June 24, 1810, the British warship *Moselle* had fired on the United States brig *Vixen*, which was under the command of Lieutenant John Trippe.

4 Commodore James Barron had commanded the *Chesapeake* at the time of the *Chesapeake-Leopard* affair.

From James Smith, Jr.

Esteemed Friend August 13h 1810

I have received your favour of 26 July.[1] and am much pleased to hear that you have secured the Debt due by Mr Miller[2] He has all along assured me that I never should loose either principal or Interest—But my friend—the money is the Article wanted & really wanted so much—that on some days I really have my doubts whether it is worth while to scuffle along any longer—& yet knowing that I really have on Book a good many thousand Dollars more than will pay my engagements if it could be got—I am encouraged from day to day to go on—in daily hope & expectation that money will come—. In December last I sent you a statemen [*sic*] of how I believed the Accot stands between us[3]—& as you do not notice it I presume the said letter has either not been recieved, or that it is mislaid—It is as follows

Ballance of Jordans[4] & Seitzs[5] debts as sent to March 1805 - - - - - - - - - - - - - -	808.13 6
Miller's 1t Note of - - - - - - - - - - - -	562.10
Suppose 1 years Interest on Both altho there must be more	82. 5 4
is Dollars - - - - - - - - 3875.84	

Owens Notes[6] - - - - - - -	2028.95
Supposed Interest on Owens Note	180.
	6084.79

Cr. By payments received from H Clay Esq. at different times as P his Statement, not encluding the post Note from Barry & Garrett—this being a seperate business & which ought to have been sent by them—say 730. 500. 300. 400. 300. 405

500. & 100 is - -	3585 [*sic*]	
Commissions suppose	179.25	3764.25
Ballance coming to J S jr when Owens Notes are paid		2320.54—

I wish you would examine & see whether I am not correct I think I must be as the payments are taken from your own statement & must be right—I have said so much & so frequently on the subject of money that I am ashamed to say more than earnestly to request that some may be got as soon as possible & forwarded—It is immaterial whether you or Mr Price[7] send me the money—I wrote to him with two or three Accot while you were absent, being weary with waiting & wanting money so much—in short, my good nature has nearly ruined me & instead of being worth an independant Fortune as I thought I once possessed I am reduced and obliged to borrow daily to get through—I shall therefore take it as a particular favour if you & Mr. Price will do all in your powers, as speedily as possible to put me in funds—Please to tell Mr. Miller my situation, and let him by no means think that because I am secured that I can wait—this is by no means the case—the time, as he well knows has been long enough already—& he must make every exertion for me—You do not say any thing about the Land. Is there no way that I could get possession of this—or must I give it up—Either it is mine by the Deed recieved from Norvell,[8] or it is not—Will you be kind enough to give me the best advise you can about this—perhaps if Mr Price and you consult together about this business, you may fall upon some plan whereby I may get possession It is worth while to make the attempt I should suppose—I shall be in hopes of soon hearing from you with some money & must beg you will be attentive to the business under your care as my wants are truly as represented & I am extremely anxious to get along without the mortification of being obliged to stop payment, which I must do, if not soon relieved With much respect I am Yr Friend

JAS SMITH JR

ALS. DLC-TJC (DNA, M212, R12). Addressed to Clay at Lexington.

1 Not found.
2 Robert Miller.
3 Not found.
4 John Jordan, Jr.
5 John A. Seitz.
6 Thomas Deye Owings.
7 Andrew F. Price.
8 Thomas Norvell.

Credentials as United States Congressman

[August 21, 1810]

In the name of the State of Kentucky to all who shall see these letters Greeting! Know ye that we William R Morton Deputy for Samuel Blair Sheriff of Fayette County and Peter B. Atwood deputy for Charles Railey Sheriff of Woodford County William Caldwell Deputy for James Martin Shff of Jessamine County Johnston Megowan Depupty [*sic*] for John Roberts Shff of Montgomery County—& James Sympson Sheriff of Clark County composing one entire District entitled by Law to to [*sic*] Elect a Member to the house of Representatives of the United States.[1]

do hereby Certify and make known that at an election held on the 6th 7th and 8th days of August 1810 at the Courthouse of our respective Counties persuant to Law the electors qualified to vote for members to the house of representatives Caused to be chosen Henry Clay to represent this state as a member of the House of representatives of the United States Given under our hands and seals this 21st day of August in the year of our Lord one thousand eight hundred and ten.

WILL. R. MORTON DS {SEAL}
for Saml. Blair Shff FC
P B ATWOOD {SEAL}
deputy for Charles Railey SWC
WM CALDWELL D {SEAL}
For James Martin Shff
JOHNSTON MAGOWAN D
for John Roberts Shff MC
JAMES SYMPSON Shff C C {SEAL}

DS. DNA, RG233, HR12A-H1.
1 In Atwood's hand to this point.

Property Deed from Charles Wilkins and Wife to the Executors of Thomas Hart, Jr.

[September 1, 1810]

[Charles Wilkins and his wife convey to Clay and the other executors of Thomas Hart, Jr., a lot on Market Street, running from Second to Third, in Lexington, on which property a rope walk is situated. General warranty of title. Acknowledgment of signatures before John D. Young, Clerk of Fayette County, September 18, 1810.]

Fayette County Court, Deed Book E, 112-13.

Deed of Trust from John Wilkinson and Thomas Pickett

[September 1, 1810]

[Indenture by which John Wilkinson and Thomas Pickett of Clark County, Kentucky, convey to Clay in trust a tract of land on Pretty Run, Clark County, containing 208½ acres; a tract on Howard's Creek, also in Clark County, containing 150 acres; another tract on Howard's Creek, containing 305 acres; a carriage; and twenty-six slaves to ensure payment of four bonds, or promissory notes, of $2,500 each, executed by Wilkinson and Pickett to Abraham S. Barton and John Hart, surviving partners of Hart, Barton, and Hart.]

Clark County Court, Deed Book 7, pp. 483-85.

Rental Agreement With John P. Wagnon

[September 1, 1810]

An agreement entered into this first day of September 1810. Between H. Clay of the one part and John P. Wagnon of the other part Witnesseth,

That the said Clay hath rented to the said Wagnon for one year commencing & including this day the Kentucky Hotel, & small house adjoining, with the appurtenances, and the Chandeliers in the Ball room, excepting the room only occupied by the said Clay as an office[1] & excepting one of the said Chandeliers which the said Clay is to be at liberty to remove at pleasure.

In consideration whereof the said Wagnon covenants to pay One thousand dollars in quarterly payments of Two hundred & fifty dollars each, the first to be made on the first of Decr next, the second on the first day of March next, the third on the first day of June next & the fourth on the first day of September next.

The said Wagnon further covenants to deliver up the premises at the end of the afd. term in as good order as he receives them, natural decays excepted.

It is further understood & agreed between the parties that the said Clay is to be at liberty to distrain & re enter and re occupy the premises upon failure in payment on the part of the said Wagnon of the quarterly payments aforesaid or any of them.

And whereas the said Clay expects to receive of Cuthbert Banks a number of articles of furniture household & kitchen, liquors &c. It is further agreed between the parties that the said Wagnon shall receive at valuation the same, and at the end of the term aforesaid he covenants to deliver to the said Clay on the premises a like amount at valuation of furniture and liquors, free from interest.

And the said Clay having agreed to indorse a note for the said Wagnon for about three hundred dollars, the said Wagnon further covenants to execute on request a deed of trust upon all the furniture which he may receive as aforesaid from C. Banks, and all other furniture which he may from time to time put in or on the premises & likewise upon upwards of Twenty head of horses, the object of which deed of trust is to secure fulfillment by the said Wagnon of this agreement in all its parts and to indemnify the said Clay against his said indorsement.

Witness our seals the day first mentioned.

H. CLAY {L.S.}
J P WAGNON {L.S.}

ADS, signed also by Wagnon. Fayette Circuit Court, File 823.
[1] For the location of Clay's earlier office see above, Agreement, August 18, 1803.

Receipt to Thomas Bodley and Charles Humphreys

1 Sept. 1810.

Recd. of Tho. Bodley & Charles Humphries negociable notes of the following persons.

William Mortons for	$2065:31
payable on the first of October next.	
Joseph Bartholomews[1] for — —	685:
payable on the first of October next.	
Thomas Tibbatts's for	757:50
payable on the 29h. Septr. next.	
David Megowans[2] for —- -	700 —
payable on the 4h. Octr. next . . .	
Thomas Bodleys for —- .	300:
payable sixty days after date	$4507:81

making a total of four thousand five hundred and seven dollars & 81 Cents, which being paid are to be credited as if received on the first of Octr. next on a Judgment Usher agt. Hughes.[3]

HENRY CLAY
Atto for Usher.

ADS. DLC-TJC (DNA, M212, R15).
[1] Of Jessamine County. [2] Carpenter and builder, son of Robert Megowan.
[3] See above, Usher to Clay, May 7, 1809. Bodley and Humphreys were acting as trustees for Hughes.

Land Patent

[September 8, 1810]

[Charles Scott, Governor of Kentucky, by virtue of part of

Treasury Warrant no. 12975, entered January 1, 1783, and amended July 28, 1783, grants unto George Walker and Henry Clay, assignees of Benjamin Netherland, a tract of 1320 acres by survey dated October 7, 1795, in Fayette County on the cliff of the Kentucky River,[1] opposite the mouth of Cedar Run and adjoining the property of one McMurtree,[2] together with appurtenances. Signed by Scott and by J. Bledsoe, Secretary of State.]

Ky. Register of Lands, Old Kentucky Grants, Book 17, pp. 170-71.

1 At the time of the patent in Jessamine County (formed, 1798).

2 Cedar Branch, in Mercer County, flows into the Kentucky River a short distance below the mouth of the Dix River. Both John and Samuel McMurtree (McMurtry) were early settlers and landowners in this area.

Land Patent

[September 8, 1810]

[Charles Scott, Governor of Kentucky, in consideration of part of Treasury Warrant no. 12972, entered January 4, 1783, grants to George Walker and Henry Clay, assignees of Benjamin Netherland, the last also assignee of unnamed parties, a tract of 949½ acres by survey dated September 18, 1798, in Fayette County,[1] running up the Kentucky River from a point near the mouth of Jessamine Creek,[2] together with appurtenances. Signed by Scott and by J. Bledsoe, Secretary of State.]

Ky. Register of Lands, Old Kentucky Grants, Book 17, pp. 190-91.

1 Now in Jessamine.

2 On the Kentucky River between Camp Nelson and the mouth of the Dix River.

Land Patent

[September 8, 1810]

[Charles Scott, Governor of Kentucky, in consideration of Land Office Treasury Warrant no. 14407, entered July 22, 1783, grants to John Brents,[1] George Walker, and Henry Clay, the last two as assignees of Benjamin Netherland, a tract of 133 acres by survey dated September 22, 1795, in Fayette County along Hickman Creek, adjoining properties of Jacob Hunter[2] and Robert Smith, together with appurtenances. Signed by Scott and by J. Bledsoe, Secretary of State.]

Ky. Register of Lands, Old Kentucky Grants, Book 17, pp. 193-94.

1 Not identified. Possibly a clerk's error for John Bruce (below, next document).

2 Oldest of three brothers who were among the first settlers in the area now Jessamine County. He later moved to Owen County.

Land Patent

[September 8, 1810]

[Charles Scott, Governor of Kentucky, in consideration of Land

Office Treasury Warrant no. 14409, entered January 22, 1783, grants unto John Bruce,[1] Henry Clay, and George Walker, the last two as assignees of Benjamin Netherland, a tract of 614 acres by survey dated September 21, 1795, located in Fayette County along Hickman Creek, adjoining surveys made for one Terrey[2] and for Robert Smith, together with appurtenances. Signed by Scott and by J. Bledsoe, Secretary of State.]

Ky. Register of Lands, Old Kentucky Grants, Book 17, pp. 194-95.

1 Possibly the Lexington rope and bagging manufacturer (an older John Bruce resided in Garrard County).

2 Joseph Terry, whose grant of 2000 acres on a branch of Hickman Creek had been surveyed in 1782.

Land Patent

[September 8, 1810]

[Charles Scott, Governor of Kentucky, in consideration of part of Treasury Warrant no. 12972, entered January 4, 1783, grants to George Walker and Henry Clay, assignees of Benjamin Netherland, the last named being also an assignee of unnamed parties, a tract of 1220 acres by survey dated September 27, 1798, in Fayette County[1] on the cliff of the Kentucky River at Hickman Creek, adjoining properties held by John Craig, Joseph Terry, and Samuel Johnson,[2] together with appurtenances. Signed by Scott and by J. Bledsoe, Secretary of State.]

Ky. Register of Lands, Old Kentucky Grants, Book 17, pp. 196-97.

1 Now in Jessamine.

2 Who owned land, in addition to other tracts, below the mouth of Hickman Creek on the Kentucky River, where he operated (or had operated) a ferry.

Property Deed to Jack Weaver

[September 12, 1810]

[Indenture by which Henry Clay, surviving executor of Thomas Hart, Sr., for the sum of five shillings, current money of Kentucky. conveys to Jack Weaver, of Fleming County, seventy-three and one quarter acres of land on the waters of Fox's Creek,[1] part of a 30,000-acre tract patented in the name of Littleberry Mosby, heir at law to John Mosby, and the same parcel for which Thomas Hart, Sr., by John Winn on February 8, 1804, executed bond to Jack Weaver for a title.]

Fleming County Court, Deed Book E, 343. Sometime later this month Clay noted his conveyance of this property, in an endorsement to the bond of Thomas Hart, Sr., by his attorney John Winn of Fleming County, under date of February 8, 1804, for £43, 19s, to secure transfer of the title (ADS. KyU-Samuel M. Wilson Collection).

1 In Fleming County, a tributary of the Licking River.

To John W. Hunt

Dr Sir Lexington 12 Septr. 1810.

You are privy to a wish I have some time cherished of converting the Hotel[1] into a more active Capital. In casting about upon the probable means of effecting this object it has occurred to me that you might possibly find some merchant disposed to give goods for it. From the disposition manifested by several in New York to make investments in real propert[y] in this Country, in the cases of McClelland, G[... th]at[2] City would most likely present [*someone who* w]ould make the purchase. I w[*ould take*] $20.000 in goods of the usual assortmen[t *credited at*] the accustomed whole sale prices.[3] And if it wou[ld] promote a bargain I would take an additional quantity of goods to the amount of $10 000 or $15000, paying this sum at the end of six months from the purchase in money. If the price be objected to I will submit the establishment to the valuation of good men in this place.

You are aware that this property has rented as high as $1300 per annum. When I leased it to Banks[4] for a term of five years I placed the property at a low rent with a view to give the establishment a start. But even at this reduced rate it averaged about $1100 per annum during the term. I entertain a firm persuasion th[at nothing] is requisite but a man qualified for the task, with some little Capital, to make the Hotel the first public establishment in the Western Country.

Can you not aid me in accomplishing the Sale herein proposed? If you will effect it, & receive and transport the goods for me to Pittsburgh, I will allow you a generous Commission, besides feeling very sensibly the obligation.

We have no news here. The prospect of fine [...]ns is not diminished at all sin[ce ...]n [...],[5] and the Country is alive to [the pr]os[*perity* w]hich seems at present to await it. Yr. friend

H. CLAY

ALS. KyU-Hunt-Morgan Papers. Addressed to Hunt "Of Kentucky Philadelphia." MS. torn.

1 The Kentucky Hotel.

2 McClelland not identified; the next two or three words missing.

3 Clay was interested in embarking in a mercantile venture and may already have entered a partnership, active shortly afterward, with his brother-in-law under the name John Hart and Company.

4 Cuthbert Banks.

5 One or two words missing at each of the indicated points.

Order on Alfred W. Grayson

15 Sept. 1810

Pay to Mess Tandy & Castleman[1] in Salt at nine shillings per bushel one hundred & fifty dollars on a/c of my fee in Hite vs. Grayson &c.[2]

A. W. Grayson Esq. H CLAY
or John Jordan Jr. Esq his Agent
[Endorsement][3]
Accepted For A W. Grayson JOHN JORDAN JR

ADS. Fayette Circuit Court, File 225 (1811).
1 Gabriel Tandy and David Castleman, brothers-in-law, had opened a mercantile business in Lexington in 1809 or 1810.
2 Case not found.
3 AES.

From Matthew T. Scott

Henry Clay Esqr. Bank of Kentucky Sept 15th. 1810.
Lexington Ky.
Sir

You are the payee and have endorsed a note of Alfred Wm. Grayson for four hundred Dollars dated the thirteenth day of July 1810 and made payable at the Bank of Kentucky, sixty days after date. Yesterday the last day of grace expired & the said note not having been paid was protested. I am &c M T. SCOTT &c

Copy. Bank of Kentucky, Frankfort, Letter Book A, December 7, 1807-October 16, 1810, p. 250. Scott, appointed second clerk of the Bank of Kentucky when that institution was organized, was transferred to the Lexington branch in 1810, and remained a banker until his death in 1858. In his last years he was president of the Northern Bank of Kentucky.

From Thomas H. Benton

Dr. Sir, Columbia, Septr. 18th. 1810

Mr. Price,[1] the bearer of your letter[2] has been with me some days. We have effected a division of the land held by the heirs of Col. Hart, and Jesse Benton

You are cheifly anxious, I fancy, to know the state of your title; whether it is affected by the interference of other claims. On this ground you may rest undisturbed. On the North end of it there is a small interference of 34 acres, arising out of [*some*] much younger third Parties. On South east corner there is another small claim.— Neither of these claims are of the least concern to us. They are so perfectly harmless that I would not make an account of them, a cents difference in the value of the land, or the least hesitation in the warranty of the title.

To morrow a return will be made by the commissioners of the division, and Mr. Price will then be able to see your part, and to report its value to you, if he does not sell it.

Any service which I can render you shall be cheerfully rendered.

I beg you to remember me to your lady, and my frends in your country especially to Mrs. Hart, the worthy widow of our friend Mr. Tho. Hart.

I have often pleased [*sic*] with the anticipation of spending some time among you. But eager to make something, I have engaged in a most extensive circuit, which takes up my time so completely, that an interval only of one month is left on my hands in the dead of winter, and the same space in the middle of summer.

I see you have left your seat in the seat in the [*sic*] senate, to appear in the house of representatives. I hope I augur right when I see you placing yourself at the head of that house.—You will have Grundy there in a short time.[3] I have [*sic*] most respectfully

THOMAS H. BENTON.

ALS. DLC-TJC (DNA, M212, R12). Addressed to Clay at Lexington. Cf. above, Benton to Clay, February 7, 1810.

[1] John R. Price, Surveyor of Fayette County.

[2] Not found.

[3] Felix Grundy was elected to the Twelfth and Thirteenth Congresses from Tennessee.

From Luke Tiernan & Co.

H. Clay Esqr. Baltimore 25th. Sept 1810

Dear Sir

Your favor of the 11th. Septr is received[1] with a post note on the Bank of Pennsylvania for Twelve Hundred & Eighty dollars being the Ballance in full of Wm. West account [*sic*] deducting Commission and premium on the Bill for which accept our thanks

we shall be very thankful to attend to the settlement of our Claim on Eastland & Aiken and shou'd be glad you wou'd procure Mr. John Jackson the title to the lotts received of Ths. Eastland, the sooner this is done the more agreeable to us as Mr. Jackson has paid us for the property and he will pay you for your trouble in having this done; we are with much regard Dear Sir Your friends & Servts

LUKE TIERNAN & CO

ALS. DLC-TJC (DNA, M212, R12).

[1] Not found.

Receipt from Joseph Beard

28 Septr. 1810.

Recd. of H. Clay fifty two dollars & a half on a/c of Cosby's purchase of the Falls Estate. JOSEPH BEARD Extr
for S.. Beard[2] Dcd

DS, in Clay's hand. DLC-TJC, 2d Series, vol. 11. See above, Agreement, December 8, 1806.

[1] Fortunatus Cosby.

[2] Sarah Beard.

Promissory Note from John Craig

[September 29, 1810]

On demand I promise to pay to H. Clay One hundred & forty two dollars. Witness my seal this 29h. Septr. 1810.

Attest JOHN CRAIG {L.S.}

WM GRIMES[1]

DS, in Clay's hand. DLC-TJC, 2d Series, vol. 11.

1 At about this time employed as a clerk in the store of William Leavy and in 1813 proprietor of his own general merchandise store in Lexington.

Property Deed to Joshua Wilson

[September 29, 1810]

[Whereas John Jordan, Jr., on September 13, 1806, executed a deed of trust to Henry Clay and Thomas Hart, Jr., recorded in Fayette Circuit Court on September 29, 1806, to secure Cuthbert Banks and William Macbean against certain securityships; and whereas Hart and Clay in execution of the trust on day of 1807 sold two entrusted tracts to Joshua Wilson at public auction in Lexington—now in consideration of these premises and for five shillings, paid and acknowledged, Clay as surviving trustee grants Wilson 688 acres and one rood located along the waters of Cumberland River in the boundaries set apart for officers of the Continental line, being part of George and Thomas Underwood's military survey dated November 16, 1797, conveyed to Jordan by deed of October 30, 1804, from George Underwood, recorded in the offices of Fayette Circuit Court and the General Court; also one other tract in Jessamine County on Hickman Creek, Marshall's Creek, and Weymore's branch, being part of General Adam Stephens's military survey, containing 125 acres, conveyed to Jordan by deed from Montgomery Bell, August 11, 1804, recorded in Jessamine Court, together with appurtenances. Clay's signature acknowledged before Achilles Sneed, Clerk of the Court of Appeals, October 3, 1810.]

Ky. Court of Appeals, Deed Book N, 276-77.

Receipt to John L. Martin

1 Oct 1810

Recd of John L. Martin five hundred & Eighty Eight dollars to be credited to James Hughes & his Securities in their debt to Usher's Estate H CLAY Atto for Usher

ADS. DLC-TJC, 2d Series, vol. 11. Cf. above, Receipt to Bodley and Humphreys, September 1, 1810.

Receipt to Charles Carr

1 Octr. 1810.

Recd. of C. Carr heretofore the amt of an execution for Costs from the Ct. of Appeals Grahams against Porter &c.[1] Recd. also $1472:58 the amt. of Executions Tiernan & Co. agt. Sundries[2]

H. CLAY P Q.

ADS. KyHi.

[1] See above, Clay to Breckinridge, August 27, 1803, note.

[2] See above, Clay to Breckenridge, July 10, 1810; Tiernan and Company to Clay, September 25, 1810. In addition to these cases, Tiernan had won a suit against William West in 1809. Fayette Circuit Court, Order Book F, 37; *ibid.*, File 179 (1809).

Receipt from Charles Carr

8. Oct. 1810

Recd. of H. Clay a note of N. B. Beall[1] for four hundred and twenty three dollars due 1st. Novr. next, which when collected I am to pay thereout to said Clay One hundred and seventy three dollars with the int. which may accrue on that sum. C. CARR. {SEAL}

DS, in Clay's hand. DLC-TJC (DNA, M212, R15).

[1] Norbonne B. Beall, a Virginian who had come to Kentucky about 1802 and settled at Spring Station, Jefferson County, on land owned by his father, served in the Kentucky legislature in 1810, 1811, and 1813.

Receipt from Joseph Beard

8. Octr. 1810.

Recd. of H. Clay Thirty dollars on a/c of Cosby's[1] purchase of the Falls Estate JOSEPH BEARD Extr.

for Sarah Beard D. .

DS, in Clay's hand. DLC-TJC, 2d Series, vol. 11. See above, Agreement, December 8, 1806.

[1] Fortunatus Cosby.

From Samuel Moale

Henry Clay Esqr

Sir Balto Oct 9h. 1810

I received yours of the 21st. of September last[1] and in reply beg leave to inform you that the Chancellor of Maryland by his Decree on the application to appoint agents as heretofore mentioned conceives that he hath no power to grant such agenvy=I therefore refer you to my former Letters written to you on this subject[2] and as soon as the Decree is obtained by you in Kentucky for the sale of the Lands contained in the mortgage, you will please to give me notice= I cannot as you perceive by the Chancellor's opinion authorise you to receive from the purchasers of Lands under Henry Purviance any Sum or Sums of Money but those Lands must be sold in common with the rest=As the last effort to obtain the agency I mean that the Creditors of Messrs Saml & Robt. Purviance shall apply to the Chancellor which application I hope will succeed and that you shall hear from me respectfully SAML MOALE

ALS. DLC-TJC (DNA, M212, R12). Samuel Moale, of Baltimore, was trustee of the estate of Samuel and Robert Purviance, Irish emigrants to this country in 1768 and 1763, respectively, prominent shipping merchants of Baltimore, and active proponents of the American cause during the Revolution, who had acquired a quarter interest in the 200,000-acre grant of Richard Henderson and Company at the mouth of Green River in Kentucky. Samuel had been captured and presumably killed by Indians during a voyage down the Ohio in 1788, leaving his interest in the property to Robert and to various personal heirs, including Henry Purviance, who had been authorized to manage and convey the holdings at the time of his removal to Kentucky. Robert, for many years Collector of the Port of Baltimore, had died in 1806.

In 1803 Moale had sold to Henry Purviance all interest in the estate's holdings in Kentucky and accepted in return a mortgage to secure payment. Henry Clay, Moale's attorney, in November, 1809, had filed a bill of complaint with the United States Circuit Court for the District of Kentucky (Certified copy. WHi-Draper MSS, 8CC 144-59), in reply to which Henry Purviance had admitted the execution of the mortgage and nonpayment of the debt. The Court had then decreed a sale of the land and appointed commissioners for that purpose. A second order for foreclosure of the property issued from the Court in November, 1810; litigation involving Samuel Hopkins, a purchaser of part of the land, followed; and the matter was not settled for several years. 10 *Ky. Reports* (3 A. K. Marshall) 485-89; Hopkins *vs.* Purviance, Fayette Circuit Court, File 414, Bundle 691, filed January 24, 1817.

1 Not found. 2 Not found.

Receipt from John R. Price

14h. Octr. 1810.

Recd. of H. Clay Exor of Tho. Hart Senr. sixty eight dollars for a trip to Tennessee to attend to the division of Land with Bentons heirs[1] & to endeavor to sell the same; & also for a trip to Green river below Henderson to see McFadin[2] about the Madison land.[3]

JOHN R PRICE

DS, in Clay's hand. DLC-TJC (DNA, M212, R15).

1 See above, Benton to Clay, February 7, September 18, 1810.

2 Andrew McFadden, who had established a station on the Big Barren River in 1785.

3 Lying in Madison County, Kentucky. See George Shackelford to Clay, October 22, 1815.

Promissory Note from Alfred W. Grayson

Dollars 600 Lexington, K Oct 27, 1810

Sixty days after date I promise to pay Henry Clay or order six hundred Dollars without defalcation negotiable and payable at the office of the Kentucky Insurance Company for value received

A. W. GRAYSON

Copy, by John D. Young. Fayette Circuit Court, File 203 (1811). Endorsed by Clay and Charles Carr. When presented for payment at the office of the Kentucky Insurance Company, the note was protested for lack of funds.

Receipt to Charles Humphreys and Thomas Bodley

[October 27, 1810]

Recd. 27 Oct 1810 of C Humphries & T Bodley by Benj. Sto[ut] Two hundred & twelve dollars & fifty Cents on a/c of the debt due by J. Hughes to Usher. H. CLAY

ADS. DLC-TJC, 2d Series, vol. 11. Cf. above, Receipts to Bodley and Humphreys, September 1, October 1, 1810.

Property Deed from Charles de Warnsdorff, by Achilles Sneed, Commissioner

[November 1, 1810]

This Indenture made this first day of November 1810 Between Charles De Warnsdorff otherwise called Charles Warnstoff, by Achilles Sneed hereafter mentioned to have been appointed a Commissioner, of the one part and Fortunatus Cosby and Henry Clay of the other part Witnesseth that the said Charles De Warnsdorff otherwise Charles Warnstoff by a decree of the General Court of the State of Kentucky, pronounced at the May term last in a suit in Chancery wherein the said Cosby and Clay are Complainants and the said Charles and John Connelly are defendants, is decreed to convey to the said Cosby and Clay the tract of land hereinafter described, and the said Sneed is appointed Commissioner under the act of Assembly in such cases made and provided to execute the deed:[1] Now in consideration of the premises and for and in consideration of the sum of five shillings to the said Achilles Sneed, in behalf of the said Charles De Warnsdorff in hand paid by the said Cosby and Clay, the receipt whereof is hereby acknowledged, the said Sneed as Commissioner aforesaid, for and in behalf of the said Charles De Warnsdorff otherwise called Charles Warnstoff, hath granted bargained and sold, and by these presents doth grant bargain and sell, unto the said Fortunatus Cosby and Henry Clay a certain tract or parcel of land containing by survey two thousand acres, lying and being on the Ohio river at and near the Falls there of. . . .[2] To have and to hold the said tract of land with the appurtenances to the said Cosby and Clay, that is to say two thirds thereof to the said Cosby and one third thereof to the said Clay, and their heirs and assigns forever:

And the said Achilles Sneed Commissioner as aforesaid for the said Charles De Warnsdorff otherwise Charles Warnstoff, doth covenant and agree to and with the said Cosby and Clay that he will warrant and defend the right & title to the said tract of land to the said

Cosby and Clay their heirs and assigns against all & every person whatsoever claiming by through or under him the said Charles.

In Testimony where of the said Achilles Sneed hath hereunto set his hand & affixed his seal the day and year first mentioned.

Sealed & Delivered ACHILLES SNEED {L.S.}
In presence of (37)
S KENTON D.C.C.A[3]

DS, in Clay's hand. DLC-TJC (DNA, M212, R15). Endorsed on verso: "Recd. and acknowledged by A Sneed Comr &c 2 Novr. 1810. Recorded in Book N page 295 and Examined. . . ." Achilles Sneed was Clerk of the Kentucky Court of Appeals from 1802 until his death in 1825. He was in this instance serving also as Clerk of the General Court, a State court of original jurisdiction, primarily devoted to trial of land cases and to disputes between Kentucky residents and those of other States.

1 Ky. General Court, Order Book C, 4, 234-35.

2 Boundary definition omitted by editors. For the history of this tract see above, Property Deed, October 29, 1807.

3 Simon Kenton, son of John. Simon was subsequently killed as a member of a Frankfort militia unit in the Battle of River Raisin, January 22, 1813.

Property Deed from John Connolly, by Achilles Sneed, Commissioner

[November 1, 1810]

[Whereas by a decree of the General Court of Kentucky pronounced at the May Term last in a chancery suit wherein Henry Clay and Fortunatus Cosby were plaintiffs and Charles De Warnsdorff, otherwise called Charles Warnstoff, and John Connolly were defendants, it was ordered that Connolly through Achilles Sneed, serving as commissioner, should convey to Cosby and Clay the tract here described—now on these premises and for five shillings, paid and acknowledged, Sneed gives title to 2000 acres on the Ohio River near the falls, beginning at a point opposite the head of Half Mile Island and running downstream, together with appurtenances. Two thirds of the tract is assigned to Cosby; one third, to Clay. Warranty only against claimants through Connolly. Signed by Sneed and S. Kenton, and acknowledged before the latter, the Deputy Clerk of the Court of Appeals, on November 5, 1810.]

Ky. Court of Appeals, Deed Book N, 293-94.

Deed of Trust from Charles Humphreys and Thomas Bodley

[November 12, 1810]

[Whereas James Hughes on November 30, 1808, conveyed to Charles Humphreys and Thomas Bodley, in trust, a variety of property to discharge his debts and relieve his securities, as recorded by deed in the Office of the Court of Appeals; and whereas Frederick Ridgely has become security for Hughes in certain appeal bonds entered in consequence of two judgments of Fayette Circuit Court in favor of John Darby,[1] one for $2000 and the other for $1000, exclusive of interest and costs, on trial of which appeals the judgments were confirmed—now to indemnify and secure Ridgely and in consideration of five shillings, paid and acknowledged, Humphreys and Bodley grant Henry Clay a tract of land in Mason County on the bank of the North Fork of Licking 100 poles above the forks, amounting to 1000 acres, conveyed to Hughes by George M. Bibb— In trust that Clay, whenever Ridgely may so direct, is to sell the land at public auction, after advertisement for one month in Lexington newspapers, or at private sale without advertisement, and from the proceeds to pay the debt owing to Darby, with any surplus to go to Humphreys and Bodley. Humphreys and Bodley further agree to execute additional conveyances to Clay to effect the object of this deed, as counsel may advise. Signatures of Humphreys and Bodley, as trustees of Hughes, acknowledged on March 1, 1811; that of Clay, on April 3, 1811—all before John D. Young, Clerk of Fayette County.]

Fayette County Court, Deed Book E, 384-86.

1 Of Richmond, Virginia. On February 25, 1807, Darby had sold to Hughes a tract of 9,922 acres on the North Fork of Licking River. Ky. Court of Appeals, Deed Book Q, 511. When Hughes defaulted on notes given in exchange, Darby brought suit in Fayette Circuit Court.

To [James Monroe]

Dr Sir Ashland (near Lex.) 13 Nov. 1810

I have to regret that receiving only yesterday your favor of the 20th. October,[1] and intending the day after tomorrow to take my departure for Washington, I am unable at this time to ascertain the value and practicability of selling your Goose Creek[2] lands. I fear however that the moment is inauspicious to effect a sale, the vast discoveries of Saline water on the Kanawha and Sandy having depreciated very much the price of Salt in this Country, and consequently diminished the value of lands affording Salt water or the expectation of it. Upon my return it will give me great pleasure to promote your wishes on the subject of a sale, or on any other affecting your interests.

With regard to the location made by Mr. Baker,[3] comprehending the 50 poles, which your survey fell short of including the Goose Creek Works, altho' his conduct certainly deserves reprobation, I do not think any Court can afford you relief. Supposing your survey not to embrace those fifty poles, the land was *vacant* & *unappropri-*

ated, as respects your claim, and being so was liable to be located by any one, and of course by Mr. Baker. Under the circumstances of the case, having obtained a knowledge of this vacancy whilst acting as your agent, he was I think bound on principles of honor to give you the benefit of it. But I do not think that these principles, which just & honorable men know how to appreciate, can be made the basis of judicial interposition. I need not add that the act of Mr. Baker cannot in the slightest degree impair your right, if upon another experiment Mr. Walker[4] shall be found to have been mistaken, and your survey really includes the 50 poles in question.

I thank you for the sentiment your [*sic*] are pleased to express in relation to my seat in the H. of R. Accustomed to the popular branch of a Legislature, and prefering the turbulence (if I may be allowed the term) of a numerous body to the solemn stillness of the Senate Chamber, it was a mere matter of taste that lead me, perhaps injudiciously, to change my station. I shall however continue in the Senate this Session.

Among the agreeable anticipations under which I commence my journey, I indulge the hope of having the happiness of seeing you in course of the winter. Yr's truly H. CLAY

ALS. DLC-James Monroe Papers (DNA, M212, R22).
1 Not found.
2 Goose Creek flows into the South Fork of the Kentucky River, in Clay County. The Goose Creek Salt Works were located on this stream.
3 Abner Baker of Garrard County, a former member of the Kentucky legislature and subsequently Clerk of Clay County, who managed Monroe's Goose Creek lands for more than a decade after the date of this letter.
4 Possibly John W. Walker of Madison County, who also owned land on Goose Creek.

Receipt to Charles Humphreys

13 Nov 1810

Recd of Ch Humphrys for Jas Hughs Robert Holmes negotiable note for $322:75 pay fifty days from this date on acct of Mary Usher adm. when paid. H. CLAY.

DS. DLC-TJC (DNA, M212, R15). See above, Usher to Clay, May 7, 1809.

Receipt from John P. Usher

[November 14, 1810]

Recd. 14 Nov. 1810 of H. Clay Six hundred & twenty two dollars on a/c. of the debt of James Hughes. For Mary Usher
JOHN P USHER

DS, in Clay's hand. DLC-TJC (DNA, M212, R15).

Rental Agreement with George Slaughter, Jr.

[November 14, 1810]

An agreement between Henry Clay and George Slaughter entered into this 14h. day of Nov. 1810.

The said Clay leases to the said Slaughter for one year the Hotel & appurtenances in Lexington, also the Chandeliers in the Ball room; and also a quantity of furniture which the said Slaughter is to receive from John P. Wagnon, or Cuthbert Banks, the amount of which is to be here after ascertained. The aforesaid year is to commence on the first day of next month.

In consideration where of the said Slaughter covenants to pay to the said Clay One thousand dollars, in quarterly payments, commencing with the said first day of December next. The said Slaughter further covenants at the end of the afd. year to deliver to the said Clay a quantity of furniture equal in value to what he shall receive on the said Clay's account from the said Wagnon or Banks.[1] He further covenants to deliver the property demised at the end of the said year in a state of repair equal to that in which he shall receive it, natural decay & destruction by fire excepted. He further covenants to execute, whenever the said Clay may require it, a deed of trust upon all the property he the said Slaughter may have in or upon the premises to secure fulfillment on his part of this Contract.

It is further agreed by the parties that the said Clay is to be at liberty to distrain for the said rent, whenever any part thereof shall be in arrear.

The said Clay reserves to himself the use of the office room which he at present occupies & the liberty to remove one of the Chandeliers.

Witness our Seals. H. CLAY {L.S.}
Teste GEO. SLAUGHTER JNR. {SEAL}
C BANKS

[Endorsement on verso][2]

This agreement having been rescinded by the parties, there remains due to Henry Clay on a final settlement five hundred & six dollars and forty two Cents which I promise to pay on demand. Witness my hand & seal this 15. July 1811.

GEO: SLAUGHTER {L.S.}

ADS, signed also by Slaughter. DLC-TJC (DNA, M212, R15). Cf. above, Rental Agreement, September 1, 1810.

1 On December 13, 1810, Slaughter acknowledged receipt from Major Wagnon of table and house furniture to the value of $100 left in the hotel on Clay's account. ADS. DLC-TJC (DNA, M212, R15).

2 ES, in Clay's hand.

To William S. Dallam

Dr Sir 14 Nov. 1810.

I understand that your father[1] purchased at the Register's Sales in 1807 a tract of land in the name of Sam. Thompson[2] of 750 Acres. At the time of the sale Mr. Thompson was dead, & the land had descended to his heirs, one of whom was an *infant* and two others *femes covert*. This renders the sale invalid. Mr. Thompson the bearer hereof[3] has come out for the purpose of attending to this & other lands. He is a near connexion of a particular friend of mine, & I feel very desirous that he should arrange his affairs here to his satisfaction. I have stated to him that you have probably some agency for your father, and that he will find in you a liberal disposition. Should you possess any control over the purchase in question you will perceive the propriety of receiving a reimbursement of the price of the purchase &c &c. Yr. friend H. CLAY

ALS. NcD. Addressed to Dallam.

1 Richard Dallam, a native of Maryland who had settled at Russellville in Kentucky, one of the first directors of the Bank of Kentucky, and a large investor in lands sold for delinquent taxes.

2 Thompson, a resident of southwestern Virginia, had held a Virginia grant of 1,000 acres on the Kentucky River in present day Henry County, entered in 1780 and surveyed in 1784. A guardian had been appointed for his three infant daughters in Wythe County, Virginia, 1791.

3 Not identified.

Account with John P. Wagnon

Henry Clay esqr. [*ca.* November 14, 1810]

1810..		In a/c with John P. Wagnon	Dr.
Septr	1	To Horse	£ 0. 0. 9
"	2	" Horse 9d. Segars 9d.	". 1. 6
"	8	" Supper	". 1. 6
"	9	" Hore [*sic*] 9d. Dinner.1/6.	" 2. 3
"	10	" Horse 9d	" . 9
"	11	" Horse & Dinner	" 2. 3
"	12	" Horse 9d	" " 9
"	13	" Horse & Dinner	" 2. 3
"	14	" Horse & Dinner	" 2. 3
"	15	" Horse 3/. Dinr. 1/6 2 Horses fed 1/6 .	" 6. 0
"	17	" Horse & Dinner	" 2. 3
"	18	" Horse & Dinner	" 2. 3
"	19	" Horse & Dinner	" 2. 3
"	20	" Horse 9	" " 9
"	21	" Horse & Dinner	" 2. 3
"	22	" 2 Horses 1/6 Dinner & Supper 3/- . . .	" 4. 6
"	24	" Horse 9d. Brandy 3/- Dinner 1/6 . .	" 5. 3

"	25	" Horse & Dinner 2/3 Cash lent 6/- . . .	" 8. 3
"	26	" Horse 9d 27th. Horse 9d.	" 1. 6
"	28.	Horse & Dinner	" 2. 3.
"	29.	Horse. 9d. 30th. Horse 9d	" 1. 6
Oct	1st.	Horse & Dinner 2/3 2nd. Horse 9d . .	" 3. 0
"	5.	Whiskey 9d Brandy 3/-	" 3. 9
"	6.	Horse & Dinner 2/3	" 2. 3
"	8.	Horse & Dinner 2/3 Cash lent 2/3 . . .	" 4. 6
"	11.	Horse 9d. 12th. Horse & Dinner 2/3 . . .	" 3. 0
"	13.	Horse 9 14th. Horse & Dinner 2/3 . . .	" 3. 0
		Carrd over	£ 3" 9" 9
Amt	brot	over ---- ---- ---- --	£ 3" 9. 9
Oct	21.	Dinner 1/6. 22nd Bitters 1/-	" 2. 6
	26	Horse 9d. 27 Horse & Dinner 2/3 . . .	" 3. 0
	28.	Horse & Dinner 2/3 . . - - - -	" 2. 3
Novr	3rd.	Dinner 1/6 11th. Horse 9 . - -	" 2. 3
	13th.	Horse & Dinner 2/3 Cider 9d Brandy 3/- . ".	6. 0
	14	2 Horses 1/6 Wine 24/— . - - - . -- -	1. 5. 6
	"	pd: Downing for building Stable[1] . .	21. 6. 9
	"	Horses Standing 116 days @ 25 Cts. . . .	8. 14. 0
		E E	£ 35"12" 0
	"	Pd for Glass. 16/-	" 16. 0
	"	Pd. T. Grant[2] for glazing	. 14. 3
			37. 2 3

D. DLC-TJC (DNA, M212, R15). This debt was incurred at the Kentucky Hotel. See above, Rental Agreement, September 1, 1810.

1 John Downing, Lexington carpenter, who had built a new stable on the hotel grounds. See Lexington *Kentucky Gazette*, January 3, 1809.

2 Thomas Grant, Lexington painter.

From James Smith, Jr.

My Friend Philada. 16h Nov 1810—

I am very sorry to inform you that what I have so long dreaded has become unavoidable, because I am not able to collect what has been so long due to me—I have thought most prudent to make an assignment while I believe myself able with the effects I have and debts due to me to pay what I owe—this I am extremely anxious to do & indeed my very existence depends upon it—The Assignees have appointed me Agent to effect the business, & I take the earliest Opportunity to beg you will endeavour by all means possible to collect & turn into money what is under your care—I understood you to say that Millers[1] debts was perfectly safe, & as such I have returned it—I do hope, especially if he is acquainted with my circumstances that he will pay you without having to resort to the tedious process of entering up the Mortgage &c—If not, this must be immediately attended to—I wrote you fully,[2] & gave you a Statement of what I supposed woud be coming from you, provided the Debts had all been received—that is Jordans, Seitzs, those Notes had of W W Smith,[3] the first Note of Millers &c—I cannot find any Error in the Statement sent you—What can be got from Owens,[4] please to get as soon as possible & send on—& perhaps some part of Millers may also be got, to send on with it—I sincerely hope that the Debts under the care of Andrew F Price may be recovered. I have returned them as good—and sincerely hope he has been taking & will take the most prompt measures to secure them—& the sooner either of you, or both, can send forward any money it will be particularly acceptable—for at the time of my stopping, I unfortunately owed some borrowed money to individuals which makes more noise than any thing else, & which I am extremely anxious to discharge—It has been very common for us to borrow of each other from day to day, & I have been in this practise, in daily hopes of receiving something—The Banks curtailing & no money to be had out of doors—I thought it best to take the measure, & am now extremely anxious to do the very best I can—I hope you will be as moderate as you possibly can in your charges, considering my unfortunate Circumstances & get me all the money you possibly can for me I think you mentioned to me that I might depend on Woodsons Wrens debt eventually & that you had taken some kind of security—please to say what this is—& where he lives at present It now becomes necessary, as you will perceive to settle with those I owe in the best manner I can—& some Creditors, from various motives, will accept of some Debts in part &c—Let me once more beg it, as a particular favour that you and Mr Price will do all in your power to help me & that as soon as possible—

With respect to Land taken from Norwell[5]—there being so little prospect of ever getting hold of it I wrote him that he must take it & give me something else—He has written me for answer—that he has taken some measures to endeavour to ascertain the boundaries—but that if I prefer it, he will convey me, in room thereof, 2000 Acres of military Land lying on Grose [*sic*] Creek in the State of Kentucky being as he says half of a Survey made the 20h May 1788 in the name of Elias Edmonds[6]—this he says, he is offered for the Land he first conveyed—You may perhaps know something of this land—or will you be kind enough to advise me, what I had better do—Norvell has always shewn a disposition to pay this heavy Debt, but has I believe, no other means but by Lands of some description—perhaps you may know his situation better than I do—I must endeavour to get some thing from him—Are the Titles to military Lands liable to disputes? I think I have heard not[7]—

You will please to excuse the trouble I now give you, *Hope* only keeps me alive—as my misfortunes hung heavy, having a large family —& without great attention, shall have nothing left—I hope soon to hear favourably from you & am very respectfully Yr Aflicted Friend

JAS SMITH JR

Norwell says in his letter, that he has written to you[8] & to his Agent or Surveyor—perhaps this may produce some more satisfactory information with respect to the Land first conveyed—You see the necessity of my ascertaining that I get something from Norwell & that soon— the Question is—What is best to take—

ALS. DLC-TJC (DNA, M212, R12). Addressed to Clay at Lexington, forwarded to Washington on December 3. Endorsed by Clay: "Answd," but no reply found.

1 Robert Miller. 2 Probably referring to his letter of August 13.

3 John Jordan, Jr., John A. Seitz, and William W. Smith.

4 Thomas D. Owings. 5 Thomas Norvell.

6 Virginia officer of the Revolution, who entered 4,000 acres on Goose Creek in May, 1788.

7 In an opinion of the Kentucky Court of Appeals during the Spring Term, 1808, on a case which Clay argued, the Chief Justice stated that a land claim based on a patent issued upon a survey of a military warrant was "of higher dignity in law" than a claim bottomed on a certificate for settlement and pre-emption. 3 *Ky. Reports* (1 Hardin) 365. 8 Letter not found.

From James Smith, Jr., and Richard R. Smith

Esteemed Friend Nov 23d 1810

I wrote you fully on the 16h. since which I have made another arrangement with my Creditors which is to assign them Debts—and I have this day assigned Robert Miller's note and Floyd & Grey's[1] to my friend & Kinsman Richd R Smith—You will therefore oblige both him & me to take the most speedy method in your power to get the money for Millers Notes by entering up the Mortgage or otherwise as you may think most proper—and will thank you to desire Andrew F Price to do the same with Floyd & Grey—

These are the only two Notes or Debt under either of your care that I have assigned & the mony for them when received is to be remitted to Richd R Smith—The others to witt Owens & W Breashears[2] is to come to myself & whatever Ballance there may be—that is, none but Millers & Floyd & Greys are assigned. The money is very much wanted—& I beg you will write to Richd. & myself soon on the subject & am very respectfully Yr Friend JAS SMITH JR

[Endorsement][3]

I confirm the above and shall be glad to hear from you soon with particulars—please direct to me care of Thomas Austin Mercht Philadelphia RICHD R SMITH

ALS. DLC-TJC (DNA, M212, R12). Addressed to Clay at Lexington, forwarded to Washington. Endorsed by Clay: "Answd.," but no reply found. 1 Not identified.

2 Thomas Deye Owings and, probably, Walter Brashear of Bardstown. 3 AES.

Bill from Doctors Baker and French

[*ca.* December 13, 1810]

The Hon Henry Clay Dr. To Dr. Baker & French.
1810
Decem th13 To yr. Lady Visit & Vevesect $2 –
[Endorsement on verso][1]
Recd. June 7h. 1812 the within acct in full for Baker & French
The Hon Mr. Clay ROBT. B. BELT[2]

D. DLC-TJC (DNA, M212, R15). Probably Dr. William Baker of Georgetown, District of Columbia. French has not been identified. 1 AES.

2 A clerk. He was appointed an assistant factor in the Indian trade in 1813, and assigned to Prairie du Chien, where he remained for several years.

From James Smith, Jr.

Esteemed Friend 26h Decr 1810

I have been in hourly expectation for some time to hear from you, & with something that I at present so much want, as by your letter of 26 July last[1] I had some right to expect.

In this letter you say that you had obtained Judgment against the Owens,[2] and count certainly upon the receipt of the entire, or a greater part of the money at farthest in about 3 months—our Law allowing of a replevy for that time—

Your favour received to day dated Washington 22 Inst.[3] does not say a word about it, more than that you will do all you can in my affairs—I should have hoped that before you had left Lexington, this Debt of Owens would have been recd.—& that you would have brought it—If you are certain it would be received, can you spare any part of it now—if so, it will very much delig[ht] me indeed—I do not mean without you are sure of being reimbursed, but if you are & can get hold of or have got any with you, please to spare it to me—You say that such of my Interests as under your care shall have your best attention, by which it is meant that some person must be left at home as capable of taking care as yourself—You will give directions that Millers[4] Debt must be recovered as soon as it is possible for it is given to one of my Endorsers, who has actually paid the money for me—as I wrote you. Owings Debt belongs to myself & all others except such as has been mentioned to my friends—In a late letter[5] which I perceive you have not received, I have stated our old affairs so as I think to convince you that there must be a ballance in your hands coming to me—I have requested you to give me the Dates & Sums you have remitted me & those you have received for me & I can presently discover if I am in an Error—but this I suppose cannot be done[6] while you are from home—If If [*sic*] you should not have money with you—Will you be so obliging as to write home pr first

Mail, that if Owings money is received, which I take it for granted must be the case, that they send it on to me immediately—but if you should have about the amount or even any part it will suit better—for I am sorry to say that a few days previous to my stopping, I borrowed from one friend & another expecting daily remittances—these did not come—& of course those sums must be returned & it does worry me more than any thing—I date my misfortunes almost altogether, or in a great measure to the being kept out of large sums a long time—for instance Millers Debt, upwards of 3000 & many others elsewhere to 10 or 12 times the amount & the disappointments in not receiving, when in a right to look for money is often attended with material disadvantage—for instance—by yours of 26 July last I had a right to look for a remittance a month ago at least,—but disappointments will occur—You will excuse my asking for any money you can now command on that account I would by no means do it if I were not pressed & if I did not suppose you would without any doubt receive it

I thank you for the caution a[bout the] Land I will write to Norvell[7] about it—I shall thank you if you will write home & order a statement sent me of monies received by you for me—& the Dates & remittances made me on accot thereof—& I feel confident you will oblige me in the money way if you can as I really want it much I am very respectfully Yr Friend JAS SMITH JR

ALS. DLC-TJC (DNA, M212, R10). Addressed to Clay at Washington.
1 Not found. 2 John C. and Thomas Deye Owings.
3 Not found. 4 Robert Miller. 5 Probably the letter of November 16.
6 Following this word the phrase "untill I hear from your" was written and then deleted. 7 Thomas Norvell. The bracketed words are not clear in MS.

Notes for Speech on West Florida

[*ca.* December 28, 1810]

Facts relative to Louisiana &c.

1682. La Salle & Tonti descended the Mississippi and named the Country Louisiana. Went to the mouths of the river observed their latitude & retd. to Canada Joutel XVII-XX.[1] Tonti 153[2] &c.

Soon after this some Canadians, enticed by the flattering a/cs. of the Country, settled on the Coast near the mouth of the Mississippi.
2 Dumont page 260.[3]

1696. Spain established a fort at Pensacola. 9 Raynal 128.[4]

1698. D'Iberville discovers the mouth of the Mississippi by Sea. 2. Dumont 260
Is made governor of the Colony.

1699.	Establishes a Colony at Mobile 2 Dumont 260. & Isle Dauphine
1712.-Sept 14.	Louis XIV grants the exclusive commerce of Louisiana to Crozat (See the grant.)
1716.	Crozat assigns his Charter to the W. India Co. 2. Dumont 6. 260.
1717	The Company sent some inhabitants to Isle Dauphine where were some settlers before 2. Dumont. 7.
1719.	The French take Pensacola 1 DuPratz 189.[5] 2 Dumont 9. The Spaniards retake it 191. 12. French take it again ib. 195. 18. France & Spain make peace 5 Russell 7.[6] N. Orleans laid off 30 leagues above the mouth of the Mississippi where some emigrants from Canada had already settled & the seat of Government is fixed there.
1736.	The French build a fort on Tombicbee. 1 Du Pratz 85
Bounds of Louisiana.	Du Pratz (whose book was published in 1758 & translated in 1763) says "On the East the coast is bounded by Rio Perdido & a little to the East of Mobile" &c 1 Du Pratz 216.
1712. Septr. 14	The great document establishing the boundary of Louisiana is Louis the 14h. grant of this date to Crozat. Transln. of Joutel 196.
1763.	Treaty of Paris Art. 6. France Cedes to England the river and port of Mobile and every thing on the left side of the Mississippi which she possesses or ought to possess except the island of New Orleans, and by the 19h. article Spain cedes to England all she possesses East or S. East of the Mississipi. and all English claims W. of Mi. ackd. to Spain. England divides the country South of Georgia and East of the Iberville into two provinces E. & W. Florida by the Apalachicola.
1783.	England by the 5h. article of the treaty cedes to Spain the Floridas. Spain then re-establishes the governmt. of Louisiana as before, and the government of Florida, that part of what the English had called W. Florida being under the Govr. of N. Orleans & the rest under the governr. of Florida. See the Baltimore American Patriot. Vol. 1. No. 97. This is confirmed by M D'Azara, Spanish Ambassador at Paris, who told Mr. Livingston that Mobile made a part of Louisiana—See Livingston's letter to Monroe Paris May 22. 1803.

1762. 3 Nov	France by a secret convention with Spain ceded to her that portion of Louisiana lying West of the Mississippi and including the island of N Orleans. On the same day were signed the Preliminary articles of the treaty of 10h February 1763 by which France ceded to Great Britain that portion of Louisiana lying East of the Mississippi, exclusive of the island of New Orleans..
1685. Feb. 18	La Sale landed in the Bay of St Bernard or St Louis, having been in quest of the mouth of the Mississippi. Joutel 32. 1 Dupratz 6. Tonti 245. 2 Dum. 259. —Builds a fort in that bay Tonti 245. 276. He left 130 persons there Joutel 45
June.	He makes another settlement further up the river.
1713.	By the treaty of Utrecht the 49h. degree of latitude is made the division between Louisiana & the brutish Northern possessions.
1715.	The Spaniards made a settlement at Pensacola with the view to restrict the limits of the French. 1 Dupratz 9. 13. 14.

AD. DLC-HC (DNA, M212, R6). For the speech, see next document.

1 M. Joutel, *Journal historique du Dernier Voyage que feu M. de la Sale fit dans le Golfe de Mexique, pour trouver l'embouchure, & le cours de la Rivière de Missicipi* (Paris, 1713). An English translation of this work was published in London in 1714 and was reprinted, under a different title, in 1719.

2 Henri de Tonti (supposed author), *Dernieres Decouvertes dans l'Amerique Septentrionale de M. De La Sale; Mises au jour par M. le Chevalier Tonti, Gouverneur du Fort Saint Loüis, aux Islinois* (Paris, 1697). Translated and published in London, 1698, as *An Account of Monsieur de la Salle's last expedition and discoveries in North America.*

3 George Marie Butel-Dumont, *Mémoires historiques sur la Louisiane, Contenant ce qui y est arrivé de plus mémorable depuis l'année 1687. jusqu'à présent* (2 vols., Paris, 1753).

4 Guillaume-Thomas Raynal, *Histoire Philosophique et Politique des établissemens et du commerce des Européens dans les deux Indies.* There are several editions of this work. Those appearing in nine volumes and more before the date of Clay's speech include five ten-volume sets published at Geneva from 1780 to 1793, an edition of ten volumes at Neufchâtel in 1785, another of seventeen volumes at London in 1792, and one of ten volumes at Paris in 1794.

5 M. Le Page Du Pratz, *Histoire de la Louisiane* (3 vols., Paris, 1758). An English translation, in two volumes, appeared in 1763.

6 [William Russell], *The History of Modern Europe, with an Account of the Decline and Fall of the Roman Empire . . . to the Peace of Paris, in 1763 . . . In a Series of Letters from a Nobleman to His Son* (New Edition, 6 vols.; Philadelphia, 1800-1811).

Speech on the Occupation of West Florida

[December 28, 1810]

Mr. President—it would have gratified me if some other gentleman had under taken to reply to the ingenious argument which you have just heard. But not perceiving any one disposed to do so, a sense of duty obliges me, though very unwell, to claim your indulgence whilst I offer my sentiments on this subject, so interesting to the Union at large, but particularly to the Western section of it. Allow me, sir, to express my admiration at the more than Aristidean justice, which, in a question of Territorial title between the United States and a foreign nation, induces, certain gentlemen to espouse the pretensions of the foreign nation. Doubtless, in any future negociations, she will have too much magnanimity to avail herself of these spontaneous concessions in her favor, made on the floor of the Senate of the United States.

It was to have been expected that in a question like the present, gentlemen, even on the same side, would have different views, and although arriving at a common conclusion would do so by various arguments. And hence the honorable gentleman from Vermont[1] entertains doubts with regard to our title against Spain, whilst he feels entirely satisfied of it against France. Believing, as I do, that our title against both powers is indisputable, under the treaty of St. Ildefonso between Spain and France, and the treaty between the French Republic and the U. States, I shall not enquire into the treachery by which the king of Spain is alleged to have lost his crown; nor shall I stop to discuss the question involved in the overthrow of the Spanish monarchy, and how far the power of Spain ought to be considered as merged in that of France. I shall leave the hon. gentleman from Delaware[2] to mourn over the fortunes of the fallen Charles. I have no commiseration for princes. My sympathies are reserved for the great mass of mankind, and I own that the people of Spain have them most sincerely.

I will adopt the course suggested by the nature of the subject, and pursued by other gentlemen, of examining into our title to the country lying between the Mississippi and the Rio Perdido (which to avoid circumlocution I will call West Florida, although it is not the whole of it—) and the propriety of the recent measures taken for the occupation of it. Our title depends, first, upon the limits of the province or colony of Louisiana, and secondly, upon a just exposition of the treaties before mentioned.

On this occasion it is only necessary to fix the Eastern boundary. In order to ascertain this, it is proper to take a cursory view of the settlement of the country, the basis of European title to colonies in America being prior discovery or prior occupancy.[3] In 1682, La Salle migrated from Canada, then owned by France, descended the Mississippi and named the country, which it waters, Louisiana. About 1698, D'Iberville discovered by sea the mouth of the Mississippi, established a colony at the Isle Dauphine or Massacre, which lies at the mouth of the bay of Mobile, and one at the mouth of the river

Mobile, and was appointed by France governor of the country. In the year 1717, the famous West India Company sent inhabitants to the Isle Dauphine, and found some of those who had been settled there under the auspices of D'Iberville. About the same period Baloxi, near the Pascagola, was settled. In 1719, the city of New Orleans was laid off and the seat of the Government of Louisiana was established there. In 1736, the French erected a fort on Tombigbee. These facts prove that France had the actual possession of the country as far East as the Mobile at least. But the great instrument which ascertains, beyond all doubt, that the country in question is comprehended within the limits of Louisiana is one of the most authentic & solemn character which the archives of the nation can furnish. I mean the patent granted in 1712, by Louis 14th to Crozat–[. . . .][4] According to this document, in describing the province or colony of Louisiana, it is declared to be bounded by Carolina on the East and Old and New Mexico on the West. Under this high record evidence, it might be insisted that we have a fair claim to East as well as West Florida against France at least, unless she has by some convention or other obligatory act restricted the Eastern limit of the province. It has, indeed, been asserted that by a treaty between France and Spain, concluded in the year 1719, the Perdido was expressly stipulated to be the boundary between their respective provinces of Florida on the East and Louisiana on the West; but as I have been unable to find any such treaty, I am induced to doubt its existence.[5]

About the same period, to wit, towards the close of the seventeenth century, when France settled the isle Dauphine and the Mobile, Spain erected a fort at Pensacola. But Spain never pushed her actual settlements or conquests further West than the bay of Pensacola, whilst those of the French were bounded on the East by the Mobile. Between those two points, a space of about 13 or 14 leagues, neither nation had the exclusive possession. The Rio Perdido, forming the bay of the same name, discharges itself into the gulph of Mexico between the Mobile and Pensacola, and, being a natural and the most notorious object between them, presented itself as a suitable boundary between the possessions of the two nations. It accordingly appears very early to have been adopted as the boundary by tacit if not express consent. The ancient charts and historians therefore of the country so represent it. Dupratz, one of the most accurate historians in point of fact and detail of the time, whose work was published as early as 1758, describes the coast as being bounded on the East by the Rio Perdido. In truth, sir, no European nation whatever, except France, ever occupied any portion of West Florida, prior to her cession of it to England in 1762. The gentlemen on the other side do not indeed strongly controvert, if they do not expressly admit, that Louisiana, as held by France anterior to her cession of it in 1762, reached to the Perdido. The only observation made by the gentleman from Delaware to the contrary, to wit, that the island of New Orleans being particularly mentioned could not for that reason constitute a part of Louisiana, is susceptible of a very satisfactory answer. That island was excepted out of the grant to England, and was the only part of the province east of the river that was so excepted. It formed in itself one of the most prominent and important objects of the cession to Spain originally, and was transferred to her with the portion of the province West of the Mississippi. It might with equal propriety be urged that St. Augustine is not in East Florida, because St. Augustine is expressly mentioned by Spain in her cession of that province to England: From this view of the subject I think it results that the province of Louisiana comprized W. Florida previous to the year 1762.

What is done with it at this epoch? By a secret convention of the 3d of November of that year, France ceded the country lying West of the Mississippi, and the island of New-Orleans, to Spain; & by a contemporaneous act, the articles preliminary to the definitive Treaty of 1763, she transferred West Florida to England. Thus at the same instant of time she alienated the whole province.

Posterior to this grant, Great Britain having also acquired from Spain her possessions East of the Mississippi, erected the country into two provinces, East and West Florida. In this state of things it continued until the peace of 1783, when Great Britain, in consequence of the events of the war, surrendered the country to Spain, who for the *first* time came into the actual possession of West Florida. Well, sir, how does she dispose of it? She re-annexes it to the residue of Louisiana—extends the jurisdiction of that government to it, & subjects the governors or commandants of the districts of Baton Rouge, Feliciana, Mobile and Pensacola, to the authority of the governor of Louisiana, residing at New-Orleans; whereas the governor of East Florida is placed wholly without his control, & is made amenable directly to the governor of the Havannah. And I have been credibly informed that all the concessions or grants of land, made in West Florida, under the authority of Spain, run in the name of the *government of Louisiana.* You cannot have forgotten that about the period when we took possession of New Orleans, under the treaty of cession from France, the whole country rung with the nefarious speculations which were alleged to be practising in that city, with the connivance, if not actual participation of the Spanish authorities, by the procurement of surreptitious grants of land, particularly in the district of Feliciana. West Florida, then, not only as France had held it, but as it was in the hands of Spain, made a part of the province of Louisiana; as much so as the jurisdiction or district of Baton Rouge constituted a part of West Florida.

What then is the true construction of the treaties of St. Ildefonso and of April 1803, from whence our title is derived? If an ambiguity exist in a grant, the interpretation most favorable to the grantee is to be preferred. It was the duty of the grantor to have expressed himself in plain and intelligible terms. This is the doctrine not of Coke only, (whose dicta I admit have nothing to do with the question) but of the code of universal law. The doctrine is entitled to augmented force when a clause only of the instrument is exhibited, in which clause the ambiguity lurks, and the residue of the instrument is kept back by the grantor. The entire convention of 1762, by which France transferred Louisiana to Spain, is concealed, and the whole of the Treaty of St. Ildefonso, except a solitary clause. We are thus deprived of the aid which a full view of both of those instruments would afford. But we have no occasion to resort to any rules of construction, however reasonable in themselves, to establish our title. A competent knowledge of the facts, connected with the case, and a candid appeal to the treaties, are alone sufficient to manifest our right. The negociators of the treaty of 1803 having signed with the same ceremony two copies, one in the English and the other in the French language, it has been contended, that in the English version the term 'cede' has been erroneously used instead of 'retrocede,' which is the expression in the French copy. And it is argued that we are bound by the phraseology of the French copy, because, it is declared that the treaty was agreed to in that language. It would not be very unfair to enquire if this is not like the common case, in private life, where individuals enter into a contract, of which each party retains a copy, duly executed. In such case neither has the preference. We might as well say to France we will cling by the English copy, as she could insist upon an adherence to the French copy; and if she urged ignorance on the part of Mr. Marbois,[6] her negociator, of our language, we might with equal propriety plead ignorance on the part of our negociators of her language. As this however is a disputable point, I do not avail myself of it; gentlemen shall have the full benefit of the expressions in the French copy. According to this, then, in reciting the treaty of St. Ildefonso, it is declared by Spain in 1800, that she retrocedes to France the colony or province of Louisiana, with the same extent that it then had in the hands of Spain, and that it had when France possessed it, and such as it should be after the treaties subsequently entered into between Spain and other States. This latter member of the description has been sufficiently explained by my colleague.[7]

It is said that since France in 1762 ceded to Spain only Louisiana

West of the Mississippi, and the island of New-Orleans, the retrocession comprehended no more—that the retrocession *ex vi termini* was commensurate with and limited by the direct cession from France to Spain. If this were true, then the description, such as Spain held it, that is in 1800, comprising West Florida, and such as France possessed it, that is in 1762, prior to the several cessions, comprising also West Florida, would be totally inoperative. But the definition of the term retrocession, contended for by the other side, is denied. It does not exclude the instrumentality of a third party. It means restoration or reconveyance of the thing originally ceded, and so the gentleman from Delaware acknowledged. I admit that the thing restored must have come to the restoring party from the party to whom it is retroceded; whether directly or indirectly is wholly immaterial. In its passage it may have come through a dozen hands. The retroceding party must claim *under* and in virtue of the right originally possessed by the party to whom the retrocession takes place. Allow me to put a case: You own an estate called Louisiana. You convey one moiety of it to the gentleman from Delaware, and the other to me; he conveys his moiety to me, and I thus become entitled to the whole. By a suitable instrument I reconvey or retrocede the estate called Louisiana to you as I now hold it, and as you held it; what passes to you? The whole estate or my moiety only? Let me indulge another supposition—that the gentleman from Delaware, after he received from you his moiety, had bestowed a new denomination upon it and called it west Florida—would that circumstance vary the operation of my act of retrocession to you? The case supposed is in truth the real one between the United States and Spain. France in 1762 transfers Louisiana west of the Mississippi to Spain, and at the same time conveys the Eastern portion of it, exclusive of New-Orleans, to G. Britain. Twenty-one years after, that is in 1783, Great Britain cedes her part to Spain, who thus becomes possessed of the entire province; one portion by direct cession from France, and the residue by indirect cession. Spain then held the whole of Louisiana *under* France, and in virtue of the title of France. The whole moved or passed from France to her. When therefore, in this state of things, she says, in the treaty of St. Ildefonso, that she retrocedes the province to France, can a doubt exist that she parts with, and gives back to France, the entire colony? To preclude the possibility of such a doubt, she adds, that she restores it, not in a mutilated condition, but in that precise condition in which France had and she herself possessed it.

Having thus shewn, as I conceive, a clear right in the United States to West Florida, I proceed to enquire if the proclamation of the President directing the occupation of property, which is thus fairly acquired by solemn treaty, be an unauthorized measure of war and of legislation, as has been contended.

The act of October, 1803, contains two sections, by one of which the President is authorised to occupy the territories ceded to us by France in the April preceding. The other empowers the President to establish a provisional government there. The first section is unlimited in its duration; the other is restricted to the expiration of the then session of Congress. The act therefore of March, 1804, declaring that the previous act of October should continue in force until the first of October, 1804, is applicable to the second and not the first section, and was intended to continue the provisional government of the President. By the act of the 24th of February, 1804, for laying duties on goods imported into the ceded territories, the President is empowered, *whenever he deems it expedient,* to erect the bay and river Mobile, &c. into a separate district, and to establish therein a port of entry and delivery. By this same act the Orleans territory is laid off, and its boundaries are so defined as to comprehend West Florida. By other acts the President is authorized to remove by force, under certain circumstances, persons settling or taking possession of lands ceded to the United States.

These laws furnish a legislative construction of the treaty, correspondent with that given by the Executive, and they vest in this branch of the government indisputably a power to take possession of the country, whenever it might be proper in his discretion. The President has not therefore violated the constitution and usurped the war making power; but he would have violated that provision which requires him to see that the laws are faithfully executed, if he had longer forborne to act. It is urged that he has assumed powers belonging to Congress in undertaking to annex the portion of West Florida between the Mississippi and the Perdido to the Orleans territory. But Congress, as has been shewn, has already made this annexation, the limits of the Orleans territory, as prescribed by Congress, comprehending the country in question. The President, by his proclamation, has not made law; but has merely declared to the people of West Florida what the law is. This is the office of a proclamation, and it was highly proper that the people of that territory should be thus notified. By the act of occupying the country, the government de facto, whether of Spain, or the revolutionists, ceased to exist; and the laws of the Orleans territory, applicable to the country, by operation and force of law, attached to it. But this was a state of things which the people might not know, and every dictate of justice and humanity required, therefore, should be proclaimed. I consider the bill before us merely in the light of a declaratory law.

Never could a more propitious moment present itself for the exercise of the discretionary power placed in the President, and, had he failed to embrace it, he would have been criminally inattentive to the dearest interests of this country. It cannot be too often repeated, that if Cuba on the one hand, and Florida on the other, are in the possession of a foreign maritime power, the immense country belonging to the United States, watered by streams discharging themselves into the gulph of Mexico—that is one third, nay more than two thirds of the United States, comprehending Louisiana, is placed at the mercy of that power. The possession of Florida is a guarantee absolutely necessary to the enjoyment of the navigation of those streams. The gentleman from Delaware anticipates the most direful consequences from the occupation of the country. He supposes a sally from a Spanish garrison upon the American forces, and asks what is to be done? We attempt a peaceful possession of the country, to which we are fairly entitled. If the wrongful occupants under the authority of Spain assail our troops, I trust they will retrieve the lost honor of the nation in the case of the Chesapeake.[8] Suppose an attack upon any portion of the American army within the acknowledged limits of the United States by a Spanish force? In such event there would exist but a single honorable and manly course. The gentleman conceives it ungenerous that we should at this moment, when Spain is encompassed and pressed on all sides by the immense power of her enemy, occupy West Florida. Shall we sit by passive spectators, and witness the interesting transactions in that country—transactions which tend to jeopardize, in the most imminent degree, our rights, without interference? Are you prepared to see a foreign Power seize what belongs to us? I have heard in the most credible manner that, about the period when the President took his measures in relation to that country, the agents of a foreign power were intriguing with the people there, to induce them to come under his dominion.

Whether this be the fact or not, it cannot be doubted, that if you neglect the present auspicious moment—if you reject the proffered boon, some other nation, profiting by your errors, will seize the occasion to get a fatal footing in your southern frontier. I have no hesitation in saying, that if a parent country will not or cannot maintain its authority in a colony adjacent to us, and there exists in it a state of misrule and disorder, menacing our peace, and if moreover such colony, by passing into the hands of any other power, would become dangerous to the integrity of the Union, and manifestly tend to the subversion of our laws; we have a right, upon eternal principles of self preservation, to lay hold of it. This principle alone, independent of any title, would warrant our occupation of West Florida. But it is not necessary to resort to it, our title being in my judgment incontestibly good. We are told of the vengeance of resuscitated Spain. If Spain, under any modification of her government, chuse to make war upon us, for the act under consideration, the nation, I have no doubt, will be willing to meet the war. But the gentleman reminds us that Great Britain, the ally of Spain, may be obliged by her connexion with Spain to take part with her against us, and to consider this measure of the President as justifying an appeal to arms.

Sir, is the time never to arrive when we may manage our own affairs without the fear of insulting his Britannic majesty? Is the rod of British power to be forever suspended over our heads? Does Congress put on an embargo to shelter our rightful commerce against the piratical depredations committed upon it on the ocean? We are immediately warned of the indignation of offended England. —Is a law of non-intercourse proposed? The whole navy of the haughty mistress of the seas is made to thunder in our ears. Does the President refuse to continue a correspondence with a minister who violates the decorum belonging to his diplomatic character, by giving and deliberately repeating an affront to the whole nation?[9] We are instantly menaced with the chastisement which English pride will not fail to inflict. Whether we assert our rights by sea or attempt their maintenance by land—whithersoever we turn ourselves, this phantom incessantly pursues us. Already has it had too much influence on the councils of the nation. It contributed to the repeal of the embargo—that dishonorable repeal which has so much tarnished the character of our government. Mr. President, I have before said on this floor, and now take occasion again to remark, that I most sincerely desire peace and amity with England; that I even prefer an adjustment of all differences with her before one with any other nation. But if she persist in a denial of justice to us, or if she avails herself of the occupation of West Florida to commence war upon us, I trust and hope that all hearts will unite in a bold and vigorous vindication of our rights. I do not however believe in the prediction that war will be the effect of the measure in question.

It is asked, why, some years ago, when the interruption of the right of depot took place at New-Orleans, the government did not declare war against Spain; and how it has happened that there has been this long acquiescence in the Spanish possession of West Florida? The answer is obvious. It consists in the genius of the nation which is prone to peace; in that desire to arrange, by friendly negociation, our disputes with all nations, which has constantly influenced the present and preceding administrations; and in the jealousy of armies with which we have been inspired by the melancholy experience of free states. But a new state of things has arisen. Negociation has become hopeless. The power with whom it was to be conducted, if not annihilated, is in a situation that precludes it; and the subject matter of it is in danger of being snatched forever from our power. Longer delay would be construed into a dereliction of our right, and would amount to treachery to ourselves: May I ask, in my turn, why certain gentlemen, now so fearful of war, were so urgent for it with Spain when she withheld the right of deposite? and still later, when in 1805 or 6 this very subject of the actual limits of Louisiana was before Congress? I will not say, because I do not know that I am authorized to say, *that the motive is to be found* in the change of relation between Spain and other European powers since those periods.

Does the honorable gentleman from Delaware really believe that he finds in St. Domingo a case parallel with that of West Florida? and that our government, having interdicted an illicit commerce with the former, ought not to have interposed in relation to the latter? It is scarcely necessary to consume your time by remarking that we had no pretensions to that island; that it did not menace our repose, nor did the safety of the United States require that they should occupy it. It became therefore our duty to attend to the just remonstrance of France against American citizens supplying the rebels with the means of resisting her power.

I am not, sir, in favor of cherishing the passion of conquest. But I must be permitted to conclude by declaring my hope to see, ere long, the *new* United States (if you will allow me the expression) embracing not only the old thirteen States, but the entire country East of the Mississippi, including East Florida and some of the territories to the north of us also.

Washington *National Intelligencer,* January 8, 1811. Published also in *Annals of Cong.,* 11 Cong., 3 Sess., XXII, 55-64; Lexington *Kentucky Gazette,* January 22, 1811; Lexington *Reporter,* January 26, 1811; [Swain], *Life and Speeches of Henry Clay,* I, 3-14; Mallory, *Life and Speeches of Henry Clay,* I, [256]-265; Colton, *Life, Correspondence, and Speeches of Henry Clay,* V, 12-21. President Madison in his annual message of December 5, 1810, had referred to his October proclamation under which the United States had occupied West Florida to the Perdido River, and he had expressed confidence that Congress would react promptly with whatever legislation might be necessary. On December 18, a special committee appointed to consider this part of the presidential message had reported a bill extending the Territory of Orleans to the Perdido. On December 28, Senator Outerbridge Horsey, Federalist from Delaware, spoke in opposition to the measure. Clay's speech followed.

1 Stephen R. Bradley.

2 Senator Horsey.

3 Cf. Clay's notes of same date.

4 Here Clay read such parts of the patent as were applicable to the subject.

5 In 1719 a French force had captured Pensacola from the Spaniards, lost it, recaptured it, and then restored it to the original occupants. No treaty of that year has been found.

6 François, Marquis de Barbé-Marbois, French Minister of Finance under Napoleon.

7 Clay's fellow Kentuckian, John Pope, had opened the debate with a speech on December 27.

8 The *Chesapeake-Leopard* affair of 1807.

9 During the period that Francis James Jackson remained in the United States after his recall had been requested, he had engaged in extensive propaganda through the Federalist press, defending his position.

Resolution Censuring Timothy Pickering

[December 31, 1810]

Resolved that the public perusal in the Senate of certain papers with open galleries by the Gentleman from Massachusets [*sic*], Mr. Pickering, in his seat, without a special order of the Senate removing the injunction of secrecy, which papers had been confidentially Communicated to the Senate by the President of the U. States, was a palpable violation of the rules of this body.

AD. DNA, RG46, S11A-B5 (5). Published in Washington *National Intelligencer,* January 1, 1811; *Annals of Cong.,* 11 Cong., 3 Sess., XXII, 66. On December 31 Timothy Pickering, joining the debate on the occupation of West Florida, read a letter written in 1804 by Talleyrand to the American Minister at Paris. Samuel Smith of Maryland, after gaining from Pickering an admission that the letter had been communicated confidentially to the Senate, pointed out that permission of that body was necessary before such a document could be read publicly. The galleries were cleared and the Senate sat behind closed doors for an hour. When the doors were again opened, further consideration of the bill relative to West Florida was postponed, and Clay submitted this resolution. For further action on the measure see below, Amended Resolution, January 2, 1811.

Amended Resolution and Remarks on Censure of Timothy Pickering

[January 2, 1811]

Resolved that Timothy Pickering, a Senator from the State of Massachusets [*sic*], having on this Day whilst the Senate was in session with open doors, read from his place certain documents confidentially communicated by the President of the U. States to the Senate the injunction of secrecy not having been removed has in so doing committed a[1] violation of the rules of this body.

MR. CLAY said he wished that it was consistent with his duty to forbear pressing it; but from the best consideration he could give the subject, he was obliged to ask a decision on it. With respect to the act having been a violation of the rule, there could be but one opinion. The rule seemed to have been made for the precise occasion. If the Senate did not express their disapprobation, it would be inferred from their silence that they had given their approbation of the gentleman's conduct; and any individual would hereafter, if inclined, follow his example without hesitation. Again —if the President could not have some degree of security that the documents confidentially communicated to Congress, and on the preserving which in confidence perhaps the safety of the nation depended, would not be disclosed; must not all reliance on the Senate be lost? These considerations induced him to press a decision.

. . . .

MR. CLAY wished to be allowed to trespass on the attention of the Senate one moment in reply to some remarks not before noticed. If indeed there had been such repeated violations of the rule, and even within one week, that the gentleman was to lose the responsibility of it in consequence of its frequency, it seemed the more necessary to revert to the original rules and give to them the force which they had lost. If any gentleman feels at liberty to disclose at will Executive communications, it is necessary to give some pledge that we will henceforward pay more regard to them. The gentleman from Connecticut,[2] if I mistake not, has told us, sir, that the secrecy imposed by communications in confidence depends on the individual honor of each member—[Mr. Dana said, he had said it depended on the honor of the members as composing this body.] Mr. Clay continued. I did not mean to impute to the gentleman an opinion that each member was at liberty to disclose matters communicated confidentially, but I did understand him that the honor of the individual members was a sufficient pledge that they will not disclose that which is communicated in confidence. It is not simply on that bond, forcible as it ought to be, that the President ought to have entire reliance that his communications will not be divulged; but in my mind on a solemn compact between the President & Senate which ought to be inviolable. The following is the rule in relation to this subject: "All confidential communications made by the President of the U. States to the Senate, shall by the members thereof be kept inviolably secret; and all the treaties which may hereafter be laid before the Senate shall also be kept secret until the Senate shall by their resolution take off the injunction of secrecy." Relying with confidence on the honor of the body and the rule before me which promises secrecy, could the President anticipate the unpleasant event of a disclosure of confidential papers, not only contrary to his wish, but to the will of the Senate, and to our rules? Will the gentleman from Connecticut contend that a casual incidental reference, in the course of a detail of circumstances, to communications of this kind, is to be compared to the deliberate act of taking a file of papers, unfolding them, reading paper after paper, and commenting on its language? Surely there is all possible difference between the character of the two acts. I certainly, sir, do not recollect all the circumstances detailed by the gentleman from Vermont.[3] He went into a particular detail of circumstances attending the acquisition of Louisiana, & possibly, though I do not recollect it, he might have glanced incidentally at these papers. When these communications were made I was not a member, and till the day before yesterday did not know that they were communicated confidentially. Every view requires of us, in justice to the character of the Senate, to afford a pledge that confidential communications hereafter made shall not be indiscreetly disclosed.

[William H. Crawford moved to erase from Clay's resolution the word "palpable." Clay acceded. James Lloyd moved to insert the word "unintentional" before the word "violation."]

MR. CLAY expressed his surprize at this motion. If it was persisted in, he should feel himself bound to move to strike out of the word the syllable *"un."* If he was compelled to vote at all upon the subject, he would say that the gentleman's conduct had been intentional. But when all were willing to soften the censure; when a gentleman on the same side had admitted that the gentleman's conduct was inexcusable, & the gentleman himself did not say that his act was unintentional, would it not be improper in the House to say that it was? If the thing be persisted in, if the gentleman urges us to decide a fact to which I was willing to have given the go-by, I must feel myself bound to pronounce it an intentional violation.

The resolution, AD (DNA, RG46, S11A-B5[6]); the remarks (as well as the resolution) in Washington *National Intelligencer,* January 12, 1811. Published also in *Annals of Cong.,* 11 Cong., 3 Sess., XXII, 73-74, 80. Clay's resolution led to a lively debate in which he participated intermittently as indicated.

1 At this point word "palpable" crossed out.

2 Samuel W. Dana, who had spoken after having made an unsuccessful effort to postpone consideration of Clay's resolution.

3 Stephen R. Bradley.

Motion to Refer President's Message

[January 3, 1811]

Resolved, That the Message from the President of the United States, of this day, which has been just read, be referred to a committee, with leave to report by bill or otherwise.

Annals of Cong., 11 Cong., 3 Sess., XXII, 370. Noted as a memorandum journal entry, not in Clay's hand, DNA, RG46, 11B-B2. The Senate in secret session received from the President a message enclosing several documents relative to the Floridas and recommending "to the consideration of Congress, the seasonableness of a declaration that the United States could not see, without serious inquietude, any part of a neighboring territory, in which they have . . . so deep and so just a concern, pass from the hands of Spain into those of any other foreign Power." Madison also asked for authority to take temporary possession of part of East Florida "in pursuance of arrangements which may be desired by the Spanish authorities." The resolution was adopted and the committee appointed with Clay as chairman. Their report was filed on January 7.

Declaration Concerning East Florida

[January 7, 1811]

The United States of America, in Congress assembled, having had their attention imperiously drawn to the present situation of the territory, adjoining their Southern border, not included in the purchase of Louisiana; & considering the influence which the destiny of that territory may have upon their security, tranquillity and commerce;[1] Declare that they could not see with indifference the said territory pass into the hands of any other foreign power; and that they feel themselves called upon, by the peculiar circumstances of the existing crisis, to provide under certain contingencies for the temporary occupation of the said territory. Whilst they thus yield to what is demanded of them by their own safety, they further declare that the said territory in their hands shall remain, subject to future arrangement[2] between them and Spain.

AD. DNA, RG46, 11B-B2. For the committee appointed January 3, which also included William H. Crawford, Stephen R. Bradley, Samuel Smith, and Joseph Anderson, Clay reported this Declaration and the Bill of same date, which were read and passed to second reading. No further action was taken on the Declaration; a resolution of similar content from the House was amended and adopted. 3 *U. S. Stat.,* 471.

1 The following words deleted: "and moreover the connection it has with negociations with Spain contemplating provision for just claims of indemnity from her to the United States."

2 Deleted at this point: "that may be made of the matter in difference."

Bill Authorizing Occupation of East Florida

[January 7, 1811]

1. Be it enacted by the Senate and House of Representatives of the U. States of America in Congress assembled, That the President of the U. States be and he is hereby authorized to take possession of and occupy all or any part of the Territory lying East of the River Perdido. & South of the State of Georgia and the Mississippi territory or in the event of an attempt to occupy the said territory or any part thereof[1] by any foreign government.[2] And he may, for the purpose of taking possession & occupying the territory aforesaid, and in order to maintain therein the authority of the U. States, employ any part[3] of the army and navy of the United States which he may deem necessary.

3. Be it further enacted that be appropriated[4] for defraying such[5] expences as the President may deem necessary. for obtaining possession as aforesaid &[6] the security of the said territory,[7] to be applied under the direction of the President out of any money in the Treasury not otherwise appropriated.

4.[8] And be it further enacted[9] that in Case possession of the Territory aforesd shall be obtained by the United States as afore-

said that, until other provision be made by Congress, the President be and he is hereby authorized to establish within the territory afd. a temporary government, and the military civil and judicial powers thereof shall be vested in such person and persons, & be exercised in such manner as he may direct, for the protection and maintenance of the inhabitants of the said territory in the full enjoyment of their liberty, property and religion
[Marginal note on first page][10]
In Case an Arrangement has been or shall be made with the Local Authority of the said Territory for delivering up the Possession of the same or any part thereof to the United States.

AD. DNA, RG46, 11B-B2. For other members of the drafting committee, see Declaration, of same date. The bill was read a second time on January 8. On changes noted below, cf. Amendment to Bill, January 9, 1811.

1 The last four words inserted above the line, not in Clay's hand.

2 Deletion at this point: "2. Be it further enacted that the President of the U. States be and he is hereby further authorized, whenever he shall judge it expedient, to require of the Executives of such of the States and territories as from their local situation he shall deem most proper, to take effectual measures to organize arm and equip, according to law, and hold in readiness to march at a moment's warning a detachment of militia not exceeding officers included."

3 Deletion: "of the said detachment and."

4 Deletion: "for paying and subsisting such part of the detachment afd. as may be required for actual service, and."

5 Deletion: "other."

6 The last five words inserted above the line, not in Clay's hand.

7 Deletion: "and the territory of the United States."

8 Deletion: "3."

9 All between the word "enacted" and the second word "that" inserted above the line, not in Clay's hand.

10 Not in Clay's hand; inserted in the first section of the final bill, after the words "Mississippi territory" and before the words "or in the event."

Amendments to Bill on Occupation of East Florida

[January 9, 1811]

On motion, by MR. CLAY, it was agreed to amend the first section of the bill, by inserting the words, "or any part thereof," between the words "same" and "to."[1]

On motion, by MR. CLAY, it was agreed to amend the bill, by striking out all the words, in the second section, preceding the words, "and he may for, &c.;" also, by striking out of the same section the words, "of the said detachment, and."

On motion, by MR. CLAY, it was agreed further to amend the bill, by striking out of the third section the words, "for paying and subsisting such part of the detachment as may be required for actual service, and;" also, the word "other," between the words "such" and "expenses;" also, by inserting after the words "necessary for," the words, "obtaining possession as aforesaid, and;" and, also, by striking out the words, "and the Territories of the United States."

On motion, by MR. CLAY, it was agreed further to amend the bill, by adding to the first section the remainder of the original second section; and by adopting the original third and fourth sections, as the second and third sections of the bill.

Annals of Cong., 11 Cong., 3 Sess., XXII, 373. Cf. above, Bill, January 7, 1811. Clay's action at this time was doubtless occasioned by the opposition to the measure evidenced in several earlier votes. The measure, as amended, was finally enacted January 15. 3 *U. S. Stat.*, 471-72.

Clay also proposed that the following words be inserted after the word "Governor" at the end of the first section: "either in its own name, or under colour of any Spanish power." AD. DNA, RG46, 11B-B2. This motion he subsequently withdrew.

A further Clay motion, offered January 10, supplied the figure $100,000 for expenditure in any action under the legislation. This proposal carried only by the vote of the President of the Senate, George Clinton. *Annals of Cong.*, 11 Cong., 3 Sess., XXII, 374.

1 The reporter must have misunderstood a part of the motion.

To Caesar A. Rodney

My Dear Rodney Senate Chamber 11 Jan. 1810 [*i.e.* 1811]

Before I recd. your favor[1] I had heard of your loss, in which I sincerely sympathize with you.[2] I regret it the more because, as you will not find it practicable to repair it in the course of the Session, I shall not have an opportunity of seeing Mrs. Rodney and at the same time making Mrs. Clay, who is with me, acquainted with her. You see that I am selfish.

We have commenced the political campaign in this body with the Florida bill, in opposition to which Horsey made a sensible speech.[3] The occasion was not propitious to a first display, which on his account personally I am sorry for, tho' as it respects the party with whom he participates it ought to excite with us no dissatisfaction. That subject is merged or rather suspended by one of still more importance which now agitates us in conclave, & with which you are I presume acquainted.[4]

Besides these matters Congress occupies itself with the momentous subject of creating new empires or states (Orleans & the Mississippi Territory for example) in the West, and with the question of renewal of the charter of the National Bank &c &c. Orleans will probably be made a state, possibly the Mississippi T. also, and as to the Charter its friends & its enemies about equally divide the Legislature. Upon the whole the political atmosphere is much more agreeable (the natural one by the bye until yesterday has been more dense heavy & disagreeable than I ever felt it) than it was last year. The President has certainly manifested proper energy in relation to Florida, and if we look abroad we shall find less embarrassment than attended our foreign affairs last winter.

I am anxious to have the pleasure of seeing you; & take it for granted that I shall be shortly indulged in the happiness of saying to you personally how much I am Yr friend H. CLAY

ALS. DLC-Rodney Family Papers (DNA, M212, R22). Directed to Wilmington, Delaware. [1] Not found.

[2] Rodney's household furniture, the greater part of his library, and many important papers had been on board a chartered vessel, bound for Washington, which had been driven ashore and wrecked on November 22. The misfortune had caused Rodney to abandon plans to move his family to Washington at that time. Rodney to Gallatin, December 1, 1810. NHi-Gallatin Papers.

[3] See above, Speech, December 28, 1810, note.

[4] The bill authorizing occupation of East Florida.

Motion to Reconsider Vote on Postponement of Bill

[January 21, 1811]

Clay, as one of the majority, moved to reconsider the vote for postponement of the bill providing for establishment of a Quarter Master Department. Washington *National Intelligencer,* January 24, 1811; cited also in *Annals of Cong.,* 11 Cong., 3 Sess., XXII, 100-101. His motion was defeated.

Presentation of Memorial on Protective Tariff

[January 22, 1811]

Clay presented the memorial of Lewis Sanders and 112 others, mechanics and manufacturers of Lexington, Kentucky, asking encouragement by protective duties and otherwise. Washington *National Intelligencer,* January 24, 1811; cited also in *Annals of Cong.,* 11 Cong., 3 Sess., XXII, 101. See also *Memorial of the Mechanics and Manufacturers of Lexington, Kentucky, to Congress, January 22, 1811. . . .* (Washington City, 1811).

Presentation of Memorial on Rechartering Bank

[January 24, 1811]

Clay presented the memorial "of a great number of citizens of Kentucky, praying a renewal of the charter of the Bank of the United States." Washington *National Intelligencer,* January 26, 1811; cited also in *Annals of Cong.,* 11 Cong., 3 Sess., XXII, 102. For Clay's personal views on the subject see below, Speech, February 15, 1811.

To Adam Beatty

Dr Beatty Senate Chamber 24 Jan 11.

The last mail put into my hands your obliging favor of the 9h. inst.[1] I derive pleasure and information always from your views of our public affairs. In respect to France, her failure to restore the property seized under the Rambouillet decree, but more particularly her new tariff, which amounts to a prohibition of some valuable articles of our produce, creates some embarrassment as to the line of conduct we ought to pursue. Nevertheless, ascribing the latter measure to that municipal power of regulating Commerce which belongs to all nations, and trusting to negociation on the subject of the former, I shall be disposed on our part faithfully to enforce the Non-intercourse agt. G. Britain, unless she repeals her orders in Council, and with them her paper blockade. Whether she will do this or not remains uncertain. My own opinion is that it will not be done during the life of the reigning monarch. As it is announced however that the Prince of Wales has been appointed Regent—an event which will probably be followed by a ministerial change, we ought not to lose all hopes of an abandonment of her iniquitous policy.[2]

The H. of R. this day on a proposition to postpone indefinitely the bill to renew the Charter of the Bank of the U. S. decided agt. the Bank 65 to 64. It is not unlikely that this nice division may occasion the subject to assume some new shape, and that the Corporation may yet accomplish its object.

It is probable that we shall make a State of N. Orleans. As to the Mississippi Territory I think it will hardly be recd. during the present Session.

I had intended to purchase two or three Merinos if I could have gotten them at about $100 or $120 a piece; but I have not been able to ascertain as yet the practicability of procuring them at those prices, and beyond that I will not go.

I will pay for you the subscription as you request for the Intelligencer.[3] Yr. friend H. CLAY

P. S. With regard to Hemp I feel all the solicitude that belongs to this great staple of our Country[4] In the Senate we are precluded constitutionally from introducing a bill which would impose a duty. The other House has had its attention slightly drawn to the subject, and it will be pressed upon them again by our delegation. But such are the jarring interests & views which pervade the National Legislature that I fear nothing effectual will be done.

H C

ALS. NHi. Addressed to Beatty at Washington, Kentucky. [1] Not found.

[2] George III's mental derangement had recurred in October 1810; but the Regency Act was not passed until February 5, 1811, and the Prince Regent, later George IV, then continued his father's ministry until the assassination of the Prime Minister on May 11, 1812. [3] The Washington, D. C., *National Intelligencer*.

[4] Hemp was an important crop in Kentucky, particularly in the Inner Bluegrass area and in Mason County. Clay produced it on his own farm.

To Francis T. Brooke

My Dear Sir Washington 26 Jan. 1811

I recd. your favors[1] inclosing a statement relative to Garlands debt, and bank notes amounting to $35, being three dollars more than was the balance agreeably to the statement. I have since recd. a letter from Mr. Hoomes,[2] in which he acknowledges that I have overpaid the proportion of the purchase of Buzzard coming from me; but as I have the collection in Kentucky of some monies for his father's Estate there will be no difficulty in adjusting the excess. I am much indebted to the kindness of your brother[3] and yourself for your attention to this matter, and I cannot agree that he shall be without compensation for his trouble. I must therefore request that you will pay him $20, for which as well as for the 3 doll. above mentd. you shall be credited in the taxes upon your land.[4] I do not think the present a very favorable period for selling your land, which I have no doubt is gradually rising in value. If you are however desirous to effect a sale your object would probably be facilitated by such a descriptive survey of it as you mention. I can hardly suppose a resurvey necessary to the perpetuation of the boundaries, surveys in that that [*sic*] Country having been generally made in connections in such manner that they tend to prove each other, and the removal of the corners of one would derange the whole block. Instances have indeed occurred there of such fraudulent attempts, but I believe they are rare. Should you desire to possess such an account of the quality of your land as will enable you to satisfy the enquiries of purchasers I need not say that, on this, as well as any other matter interesting to you, I shall take pleasure in promoting your wishes. Yr's truly

HENRY CLAY

ALS. KyU. Addressed to Brooke at Fredericksburg. Published in Colton (ed.), *Private Correspondence of Henry Clay*, 17-18.

1 Not found. The statement probably related to John Garland of Hanover County, Virginia. 2 John, son of Col. John Hoomes. The letter has not been found.
3 John Taliaferro, twin brother of Francis Taliaferro Brooke. 4 In Kentucky.

Receipt from Thomas and Robert Barr

Lexington, Jany 29, 1811.

Rec'd of Mr. John Hart payment in full for a note[1] drawn by Alfred W. Grayson & endorsed by Mr H Clay & E. Noble for Three Hundred & sixteen Dollars. $316 THOS & ROBT BARR

DS, in Hart's hand. Fayette Circuit Court, File 203 (1811).

1 The note, drawn by Grayson on June 12, 1810, payable to Elijah Noble 226 days after date (ADS. Fayette Circuit Court, File 203), and by him transferred to the Barrs, had been protested when presented for payment. Hart was acting as agent for Clay, who served as Grayson's security. Cf. below, Bill of Complaint, March 30, 1811.

To [William W. Worsley]

Senate Chamber, Jan. 30. [1811]

An arrival at New York has put us in possession of information from France as late as the 1st inst. The President's proclamation announcing the revocation of the Berlin and Milan Decrees,[1] had been received, and is said to have diffused great joy throughout the empire. Several American vessels had arrived at Bordeaux with cargoes of cotton and other articles.

The same arrival brings intelligence from England down to the 16th ult.—At that time the king was said to be slowly recovering; but a regency was spoken of, and in the event of its formation, it was asserted, that it would be followed by a total change of ministry. Grenville, Grey, Ponsonby, Holland, &c. &c. it was alledged would supplant the present occupants of power.[2] What to us, however, is much more important—*no disposition was manifested to withdraw the orders in council.*

Extract. Lexington *Reporter,* February 9, 1811. Published also in Lexington *Kentucky Gazette,* February 12, 1811. Identified as from Clay to the *Reporter* editor.

1 The Milan decree, issued by Napoleon on December 17, 1807, had extended the ban upon British goods inaugurated by the Berlin ruling, and had also forbidden neutrals to trade in goods imported from British dominions.

2 See above, Clay to Beatty, January 24, 1811, note.

Tax Bill, 1810

[*ca.* February 1, 1811]

1810 Henry Clay Dr — — — — — — — — — — — —	Cents
To tax on 380 acres 1st. rate Land at 50 Cents pr. hd.	1—90
To do on 4000 acres 2d. rate Do at 37½ cents —— —	15— 00
To Do on 3000 acres 3d. rate Do at 12½ Cents	3 - 75
To Do on 19 Slaves at 12½ Cents each — — —	2 - 37½
To Do on 60 horses at 4 Cents each — — — —	2 - 40
To Do on one 4 wheale Carrage at 24 Cents pr. wheale	1 . 00
To 12 tithes at 50 Cents each —— —— —— —	6 ..00
To £3080 valuation town Lots at 50 Cents pr. £100	15 ..40
[Endorsement][1]	$47 ..82½

Sept 18t 1811 Recd. the above in full

Fee bils [*sic*] ——	$9-.01	
	47..82½	RICHD. SHARPE DS[2]
	56--83½	for W Dudley SFC[3]

D. DLC-TJC (DNA, M212, R15).

1 AES. 2 Early settler in Lexington, subsequently town jailer.

3 William Dudley, Sheriff of Fayette County.

To [Thomas Smith]

WASHINGTON, 1st FEB. [1811]

The enclosed documents[1] were yesterday communicated by the

President to Congress. It is conjectured that the sequestration, under which the vessels therein mentioned, have been placed, results from the French government not having then heard of the President's proclamation.[2] If this supposition should prove incorrect, we shall have another mortifying proof of the total want of good faith on the part of the belligerents.

Extract. Lexington *Kentucky Gazette,* February 12, 1811. Published also in Lexington *Reporter,* February 16, 1811. Identified as to the editor of the *Gazette.*
1 Relating to the seizure of American vessels in French ports during the previous December. 2 Announcing the revocation of the Berlin and Milan decrees.

From Albert Gallatin

Treasury Department February 6th. 1811.

Honorable Mr. Clay in Senate, Sir,

Mr. Gallatin presents his respects to Mr. Clay, whose note[1] he has not answered sooner because it was necessary to examine the correspondence. It is believed that the construction given to the law by Mr Clay is correct, but that it is owing to an accidental omission of the word "agents" in the limitation clause, that they can be considered as yet entitled to pay. That omission was not adverted to by the Treasury, nor it is believed by the Agents. They were considered as no longer in service (at the Treasury) after the expiration of the time limited for the Officers by the Act; and it is presumed that they thought so themselves at the time, for they ceased from that date to draw for their salaries, which they had before done regularly at the end of each quarter. If a claim shall now be set up for compensation, the objection will arise, that, although the agents were not, for the reasons above mentioned, officially informed that they were no longer employed, no instructions or letter of any kind shewing that they were considered as employed, were written to them after that date by the Treasury. But if it shall appear that during any part of that period, services have been actually rendered, the law authorizes and justice requires compensation to be made for the same. [End]

Copy. DNA, RG56, Series E, vol. 5, pp. 319-20. Gallatin was at that time Secretary of the Treasury. 1 Not found.

Speech on Bill to Recharter the Bank of the United States

[February 15, 1811]

Mr. President—When the subject involved in the motion now under consideration was depending before the other branch of the legislature, a disposition to acquiesce in their decision was evinced.[1] For although the committee who reported this bill had been raised many weeks prior to the determination of that House on the proposition to re-charter the bank, except the occasional reference to it of memorials and petitions, we scarcely ever heard of it. The rejection, it is true, of a measure brought before either branch of Congress does not absolutely preclude the other from taking up the same proposition; but the economy of our time, and a just deference for the opinion of others, would seem to recommend a delicate and cautious exercise of this power. As this subject, at the memorable period when the charter was granted, called forth the best talents of the nation—as it has, on various occasions, undergone the most thorough investigation, and as we can hardly expect that it is susceptible of receiving any further elucidation, it was to have been hoped that we should have been spared an useless debate. This was the more desirable because there are, I conceive, much superior claims upon us for every hour of the small portion of the session yet remaining to us. Under the operation of these motives, I had resolved to give a silent vote, until I felt myself bound, by the defying manner of the arguments advanced in support of the renewal, to obey the paramount duties I owe my country and its constitution; to make one effort, however feeble, to avert the passage of what appears to me a most unjustifiable law. After my honorable friend from Virginia (Mr. Giles) had instructed and amused us with the very able and ingenious argument which he delivered on yesterday, I should have still forborne to trespass on the Senate, but for the extraordinary character of his speech. He discussed both sides of the question, with great ability and eloquence, and certainly demonstrated to the satisfaction of all who heard him, both that it was constitutional and unconstitutional, highly proper and improper to prolong the charter of the bank. The honorable gentleman appeared to me in the predicament in which the celebrated orator of Virginia, Patrick Henry, is said to have been once placed. Engaged in a most extensive and lucrative practice of the law, he mistook in one instance the side of the cause on which he was retained, and addressed the court and jury in a very splendid and convincing speech in behalf of his antagonist. His distracted client came up to him whilst he was progressing, and interrupting him, bitterly exclaimed, "you have undone me! You have ruined me!"—"Never mind, give yourself no concern," said the adroit advocate; and turning to the court and jury, continued his argument by observing, "May it please your honors, and you, gentlemen of the jury, I have been stating to you what I presume my adversary may urge on his side. I will now shew you how fallacious his reasoning & groundless his pretensions are." The skilful orator proceeded, satisfactorily refuted every argument he had advanced, and gained his cause! A success with which I trust the exertion of my honorable friend will on this occasion be crowned.

It has been said by the hon. gentleman from Georgia, (Mr. Crawford) that this has been made a party question, although the law incorporating the bank was passed prior to the formation of parties, and when Congress was not biassed by party prejudices. {Mr. Crawford explained. He did not mean that it had been made a party question in the Senate. His allusion was elsewhere.} I do not think it altogether fair to refer to the discussions in the House of Representatives, as gentlemen belonging to that body have no opportunity of defending themselves here. It is true that this law was not the effect, but it is no less true that it was one of the causes of the political divisions in this country. And, if, during the agitation of the present question, the renewal has, on one side, been opposed on party principles, let me ask if, on the other, it has not been advocated on similar principles? Where is the Macedonian phalanx, the opposition in Congress? I believe, sir, I shall not incur the charge of presumptuous prophecy, when I predict that we shall not pick up from its ranks one single straggler! And if, on this occasion, my worthy friend from Georgia has gone over into the camp of the enemy, is it kind in him to look back upon his former friends, and rebuke them for the fidelity with which they adhere to their old principles?

I shall not stop to examine how far a representative is bound by the instructions of his constituents. That is a question between the giver and receiver of the instructions. But I must be permitted to express my surprise at the pointed difference which has been made between the opinions and instructions of state legislatures, and the opinions and details of the deputations with which we have been surrounded from Philadelphia. Whilst the resolutions of those legislatures—known, legitimate, constitutional and deliberative bodies—have been thrown into the back ground, and their interference regarded as officious, these delegations from self-created societies, composed of whom no body knows, have been received by the committee with the utmost complaisance. Their communications have been treasured up with the greatest diligence. Never did the Delphic priests collect with more holy care the frantic expressions of the agitated Pythia, or expound them with more solemnity to the astonished Grecians, than has the Committee gathered the opinions and testimony of these deputies, and, through the gentleman from Massachusetts, pompously detailed them to the Senate![2] Philadelphia has her immediate representatives, capable of expressing her wishes upon the floor of the other House. If it be improper for States to obtrude upon Congress their sentiments, it is much more highly so for the unauthorised deputies of fortuitous congregations.

The first singular feature that attracts attention in this bill is the new and unconstitutional veto which it establishes. The constitution has required only, that after bills have passed the House of Representatives and the Senate, they shall be presented to the President for his approval or rejection, and his determination is to be made known in 10 days. But this bill provides, that when all the constitutional sanctions are obtained, & when according to the usual routine of legislation it ought to be considered as a law, it is to be submitted to a new branch of the legislature, consisting of the President and twenty-four Directors of the Bank of the United States, holding their sessions in Philadelphia, and if they please to approve it, why then it is to become a law! And three months (the term allowed by our law of May last, to one of the great belligerents for revoking his edicts, after the other shall have repealed his) —are granted them to decide whether an act of Congress shall be the law of the land or not![3] An act which is said to be indispensably necessary to our salvation, and without the passage of which universal distress and bankruptcy are to pervade the country. Remember, sir, that the honorable gentleman from Georgia has contended that this charter is no contract. Does it then become the representatives of the nation to leave the nation at the mercy of a corporation? Ought the impending calamities to be left to the hazard of a contingent remedy?

This vagrant power to erect a bank, after having wandered throughout the whole constitution in quest of some congenial spot whereupon to fasten, has been at length located by the gentleman from Georgia on that provision which authorises Congress to lay and collect taxes, &c. In 1791, the power is referred to one part of the instrument; in 1811, to another. Sometimes it is alleged to be deducible from the power to regulate commerce. Hard pressed, here it disappears, and shews itself under the grant to coin money. The sagacious Secretary of the Treasury in 1791[4] pursued the wisest course—he has taken shelter behind general, high sounding, and imposing terms. He has declared, in the preamble to the act establishing the bank, that it will be very *conducive* to the successful *conducting* of the national *finances;* will *tend* to give *facility* to the obtaining of loans, and will be *productive* of considerable advantage to *trade* and *industry* in general. No allusion is made to the collection of taxes. What is the nature of this government?

It is emphatically federal, vested with an aggregate of specified powers for general purposes, conceded by existing sovereignties, who have themselves retained what is not so conceded. It is said that there are cases in which it must act on implied powers. This is not controverted, but the implication must be necessary, and obviously flow from the enumerated power with which it is allied. The power to charter companies is not specified in the grant, and I contend is of a nature not transferable by mere implication. It is one of the most exalted attributes of sovereignty. In the exercise of this gigantic power we have seen an East India company created, which has carried dismay, desolation and death throughout one of the largest portions of the habitable world. A company which is, in itself, a sovereignty—which has subverted empires and set up new dynasties— and has not only made war, but war against its legitimate sovereign!

Under the influence of this power, we have seen arise a South Sea Company and a Mississippi Company, that distracted and convulsed all Europe, and menaced a total overthrow of all credit and confidence, and universal bankruptcy. Is it to be imagined that a power so vast would have been left by the wisdom of the constitution to doubtful inference? It has been alleged that there are many instances, in the constitution, where powers, in their nature incidental, and which would have necessarily vested along with the principal power, are nevertheless expressly enumerated; and the power "to make rules and regulations for the government of the land and naval forces," which it is said is incidental to the power to raise armies and provide a navy, is given as an example. What does this prove? How extremely cautious the convention were to leave as little as possible to implication. In all cases where incidental powers are acted upon, the principal and incidental ought to be congenial with each other, and partake of a common nature. The incidental power ought to be strictly subordinate and limited to the end proposed to be attained by the specified power. In other words, under the name of accomplishing one object which is specified, the power implied ought not to be made to embrace other objects, which are not specified in the constitution. If then you could establish a bank to collect and distribute the revenue, it ought to be expressly restricted to the purpose of such collection and distribution. It is mockery, worse than usurpation, to establish it for a lawful object, and then extend it to other objects which are not lawful. In deducing the power to create corporations, such as I have described it, from the power to collect taxes, the relation and condition of principal and incident are prostrated and destroyed. The accessory is exalted above the principal. As well might it be said that the great luminary of day is an accessory, a satellite to the humblest star that twinkles forth its feeble light in the firmament of heaven!

Suppose the Constitution had been silent as to an individual department of this government, could you under the power to lay and collect taxes establish a judiciary? I presume not; but if you could derive the power by mere implication, could you vest it with any other authority than to enforce the collection of the revenue? A bank is made for the ostensible purpose of aiding in the collection of the revenue, & whilst it is engaged in this, the most inferior and subordinate of all its functions, it is made to diffuse itself throughout society, and to influence all the great operations of credit, circulation and commerce.

Like the Virginia justice, you tell the man, whose turkey had been stolen, that your book of precedents furnishes no form for his case, but then you will grant him a precept to search for a cow, and when looking for that he may possibly find his turkey! You say to this corporation, we cannot authorise you to discount—to emit paper—to regulate commerce, &c. No! Our book has no precedents of that kind. But then we can authorise you to collect the revenue, and, whilst occupied with that, you may do whatever else you please!

What is a corporation such as the bill contemplates? It is a splendid association of favored individuals, taken from the mass of society, and invested with exemptions and surrounded by immunities and privileges. The honorable gentleman from Massachusetts (Mr. Lloyd) has said that the original law, establishing the bank, was justly liable to the objection of vesting in that institution an exclusive privilege, the faith of the government being pledged that no other bank should be authorized during its existence. This objection he supposes is obviated by the bill under consideration; but all corporations enjoy exclusive privileges—that is the corporators have privileges which no others possess; and if you create fifty corporations instead of one, you have only fifty privileged bodies instead of one.

I contend that the states have the exclusive power to regulate contracts, to declare the capacities and incapacities to contract, and to provide as to the extent of responsibility of debtors to their creditors. If Congress have the power to erect an artificial body and say it shall be endowed with the attributes of an individual—if you can bestow on this object of your own creation the ability to contract, may you not, in contravention of state rights, confer upon slaves, infants and femes covert, the ability to contract? And if you have the power to say that an association of individuals shall be responsible for their debts only in a certain limited degree, what is to prevent an extension of a similar exemption to individuals? Where is the limitation upon this power to set up corporations? You establish one, in the heart of a state, the basis of whose capital is money. You may erect others whose capital shall consist of land, slaves and personal estate, and thus the whole property within the jurisdiction of a state might be absorbed by these political bodies. The existing bank contends that it is beyond the power of a state to tax it, and if this pretension be well founded, it is in the power of Congress, by chartering companies, to dry up the whole of the sources of state revenue. Georgia has undertaken, it is true, to levy a tax on the branch within her jurisdiction, but this law, now under a course of litigation, is considered as invalid. The U. States own a great deal of land in the state of Ohio; can this government, for the purpose of creating an ability to purchase it, charter a company? Aliens are forbidden, I believe, in that state, to hold real estate—could you in order to multiply purchasers, confer upon them the capacity to hold land, in derogation of the local law? I imagine this will hardly be insisted upon; and yet there exists a more obvious connexion between the undoubted power, which is possessed by this government, to sell its land, and the means of executing that power, by encreasing the demand in the market, than there is between this bank and the collection of a tax. This government has the power to levy taxes—to raise armies —provide a navy—make war—regulate commerce—coin money, &c. &c. It would not be difficult to shew as intimate a connection between a corporation, established for any purpose whatever, and some one or other of those great powers, as there is between the revenue & the Bank of the U. States.

Let us enquire into the actual participation of this bank in the collection of the revenue. Prior to the passage of the act of 1800, requiring the collectors of those ports of entry, at which the principal bank or any of its offices are situated, to deposite with them the custom house bonds, it had not the smallest agency in the collection of the duties. During almost one moiety of the period to which the existence of this institution was limited, it was noways instrumental in the collection of that revenue, to which it is now become indispensable! The collection, previous to 1800, was made entirely by the collectors; and even at present, where there is one port of entry, at which this bank is employed, there are eight or ten at which the collection is made as it was before 1800. And, sir, what does this bank or its branches when resort is had to it? It does not adjust with the merchant the amount of the duty, nor take his bond; nor, if the bond is not paid, coerce the payment by distress or otherwise. In fact it has no active agency whatever in the collection. Its operation is merely passive; that is, if the obligor, after his bond is placed in the bank, discharges it, all is very well. Such is the mighty aid afforded by this tax-gatherer, without which the government cannot get along! Again, it is not pretended that the very limited assistance which this institution does in truth render, extends to any other than a single species of tax, that is duties. In the collection of the excise, the direct and other internal taxes, no aid was derived from any bank. It is true, in the collection of those taxes, the farmer did not obtain the same indulgence which the merchant receives in paying duties. But what obliges Congress to give credit at all? Could it not demand prompt payment of the duties? And in fact does it not so demand in many instances? Whether credit is given or not, is a matter merely of discretion. If it be a facility to mercantile operations (as I presume it is) it ought to be granted. But I deny the right to ingraft upon it a bank, which you would not otherwise have the power to erect. You cannot *create the necessity* of a bank, and then plead *that necessity* for its establishment. In the administration of the finances, the bank acts simply as a payer and receiver. The Secretary of the Treasury has money in New York and wants it in Charleston; the bank will furnish him with a check, or bill, to make the remittance, which any merchant would do just as well.

I will now proceed to shew by fact, actual experience, not theoretic reasoning, but by the records themselves of the Treasury, that the operations of that department may be as well conducted without as with this bank. The delusion has consisted in the use of certain high sounding phrases, dextrously used on the occasion. "The collection of the revenue"—"The administration of the finance"—"The conducting the fiscal affairs of the government," the usual language of the advocates of the bank, extort express assent, or awe into acquiescence, without enquiry or examination into its necessity. About the commencement of this year there appears, by the report of the Secretary of the Treasury of the 7th of January, to have been a little upwards of two millions and $400,000 in the Treasury of the U. States; and more than one-third of this whole sum was in the vaults of local banks. In several instances, where an opportunity existed of selecting the bank, a preference has been given to the state bank, or at least a portion of the deposites has been made with it. In New York, for example, there was deposited with the Manhattan Bank $188,670, although a branch bank is in that city. In this district, $115,030 were deposited with the Bank of Columbia, although here also is a branch bank, and yet the state banks are utterly unsafe to be trusted! If the money, after the bonds are collected, is thus placed with these banks, I presume there can be no difficulty in placing the bonds themselves there, if they must be deposited with some bank for collection, which I deny.

Again, one of the most important and complicated branches of the Treasury Department is the management of our landed system. The sales have some years amounted to upwards of half a million of dollars, are generally made upon credit, and yet no bank whatever is made use of to facilitate the collection. After it is made, the amount in some instances has been deposited with banks, and according to the Secretary's report which I have before adverted to, the amount so deposited was in January upwards of three hundred thousand dollars, not one cent of which was in the vaults of the Bank of the United States, or in any of its branches, but in the Bank of Pennsylvania, its branch at Pittsburg, the Marietta Bank, and the Kentucky Bank. Upon the point of responsibility, I cannot subscribe to the opinion of the Secretary of the Treasury, if it is meant that the ability to pay the amount of any deposites which the government may make under any exigency, is greater than that of the state banks; that the *accountability* of a ramified institution, whose affairs are managed by a single head, responsible for all its members, is more simple, than that of a number of independent and unconnected establishments, I shall not deny; but, with regard to safety, I am strongly inclined to think it is on the side of the local banks. The corruption or misconduct of the parent, or any of its branches, may bankrupt or destroy the whole system, and the loss of the government in that event will be of the deposites made with each; whereas in the failure of one state bank the loss will be confined to the deposite in the vaults of that bank. It is said to have been a part of Burr's plan to seize on the Branch Bank at New-Orleans. At that period large sums, imported from La Vera Cruz, are alledged to have been deposited with it, and if the traitor had accomplished his design, the Bank of the United States, if not actually bankrupt, might have been constrained to stop payment.

It is urged by the gentleman from Massachusetts (Mr. Lloyd) that as this nation progresses in commerce, wealth, and population, new energies will be unfolded, new wants and exigencies will arise, and hence he infers that powers must be implied from the constitution. But, sir, the question is shall we stretch the instrument to embrace cases not fairly within its scope, or shall we resort to that remedy, by amendment, which the constitution prescribes?

Gentlemen contend that the construction which they give to the constitution has been acquiesced in by all parties and under all administrations; and they rely particularly on an act which passed in 1804 for extending a branch to New Orleans, and another act of 1807 for punishing those who should forge or utter forged paper of the bank. With regard to the first law, passed no doubt upon the recommendation of the Treasury Department, I would remark, that it was the extension of a branch to a territory over which Congress possesses power of legislation almost uncontrolled, and where, without any constitutional impediment, charters of incorporation may be granted. As to the other act it was passed no less for the benefit of the community than the bank—to protect the ignorant and unwary from counterfeit paper, purporting to have been emitted by the bank. When gentlemen are claiming the advantage supposed to be deducible from acquiescence, let me inquire what they would have had those to have done who believed the establishment of the bank an encroachment upon state rights? Were they to have resisted, & how? By force? Upon the change of parties in 1800 it must be well recollected that the greatest calamities were predicted as consequences of that event. Intentions were ascribed to the new occupants of power of violating the public faith, and prostrating national credit. Under such circumstances, that they should act with great circumspection was quite natural. They saw in full operation a bank, chartered by a Congress who had as much right to judge of their constitutional powers as their successors. Had they revoked the law which gave it existence, the institution would, in all probability, have continued to transact business notwithstanding. The judiciary would have been appealed to, and from the known opinions and predilections of the judges then composing it, they would have pronounced the act of incorporation, as in the nature of a contract, beyond the repealing power of any succeeding Legislature. And, sir, what a scene of confusion would such a state of things have presented—an act of Congress, which was law in the statute book, and a nullity on the judicial records! Was it not wisest to wait the natural dissolution of the corporation rather than accelerate that event by a repealing law involving so many delicate considerations?

When gentlemen attempt to carry this measure upon the ground of acquiescence or precedent, do they forget that we are not in Westminster Hall? In courts of justice, the utility of uniformity of decision exacts of the judge a conformity to the adjudication of his predecessor. In the interpretation and administration of the law, this practice is wise and proper; and without it, everything depending upon the caprice of the judge, we should have no security for our dearest rights. It is far otherwise when applied to the source of legislation. Here no rule exists but the constitution, and to legislate upon the ground merely that our predecessors thought themselves authorised, under similar circumstances, to legislate, is to sanctify error and perpetuate usurpation. But if we are to be subjected to the trammels of precedents, I claim, on the other hand, the benefit of the restrictions under which the intelligent judge cautiously receives them. It is an established rule that to give to a previous adjudication any effect, the mind of the judge who pronounced it must have been awakened to the subject, and it must have been a deliberate opinion formed after full argument. In technical language it must not have been sub silentio. Now the acts of 1804 and 1807, relied upon as pledges for the rechartering this company, passed not only without any discussions whatever of the constitutional power of Congress to establish a bank, but I venture to say without a single member having had his attention drawn to this question. I had the honor of a seat in the Senate when the latter law passed, probably voted for it,[5] and I declare with the utmost sincerity that I never once thought of that point, and I appeal confidently to every honorable member who was then present to say if that was not his situation.

This doctrine of precedents, applied to the legislature, appears to me to be fraught with the most mischievous consequences. The great advantage of our system of government over all others, is, that we have a *written* constitution defining its limits, and prescribing its authorities; and that, however, for a time, faction may convulse the nation, and passion and party prejudice sway its functionaries, the season of reflection will recur, when calmly retracing their deeds, all aberrations from fundamental principle will be corrected. But once substitute *practice* for principle—the expositions of the constitution for the text of the constitution, and in vain shall we look for the instrument in the instrument itself! It will be as diffused and intangible as the pretended constitution of England. And it must be sought for in the statute book, in the fugitive journals of Congress, and in reports of the Secretary of the Treasury! What would be our condition if we were to take the interpretations given to that sacred book, which is or ought to be the criterion of our faith, for the book itself? We should find the Holy Bible buried beneath the interpretations, glosses and comments of Councils, Synods, and learned divines, which have produced swarms of intolerant and furious sects, partaking less of the mildness and meekness of their origin than of a vindictive spirit of hostility towards each other! They ought to afford us a solemn warning to make that constitution, which we have sworn to support, our invariable guide.

I conceive then, sir, that we are not empowered by the constitution, nor bound by any practice under it, to renew the charter of this bank, and I might here rest the argument. But as there are strong objections to the renewal upon the score of expediency, and as the distresses which will attend the dissolution of the bank, have been greatly exaggerated, I will ask your indulgence for a few moments longer. That some temporary inconvenience will arise, I shall not deny; but most groundlessly have the recent failures in New-York been attributed to the discontinuance of this bank. As well might you ascribe to that cause the failures of Amsterdam and Hamburg, of London and Liverpool.[6] The embarrassments of commerce—the sequestration in France—the Danish captures—in fine, the belligerent edicts are the obvious sources of these failures. Their immediate cause is the return of bills upon London, drawn upon the faith of unproductive or unprofitable shipments. Yes, sir, the protests of the notaries of London, not those of New-York, have occasioned these bankruptcies.

The power of a nation is said to consist in the sword and the purse. Perhaps at last all power is resolvable into that of the purse, for with it you may command almost everything else. The specie circulation of the United States is estimated by some calculators at ten million of dollars: and if it be no more, one moiety is in the vaults of this bank. May not the time arrive when the concentration of such a vast portion of the circulating medium of the country in the hands of any corporation, will be dangerous to our liberties? By whom is this immense power wielded? By a body, who, in derogation of the great principle of all our institutions, responsibility to the people, is amenable only to a few stockholders, and they chiefly foreigners. Suppose an attempt to subvert this government—would not the traitor first aim by force or corruption to acquire the treasure of this company? Look at it in another aspect. Seven-tenths of its capital are in the hands of foreigners, and these foreigners chiefly English subjects. We are possibly upon the eve of a rupture with that nation. Should such an event occur, do you apprehend that the English premier would experience any difficulty in obtaining the entire control of this institution? Republics, above all other nations, ought most studiously to guard against foreign influence. All history proves that the internal dissentions excited by foreign intrigue have produced the downfall of almost every free government that has hitherto existed; and yet gentlemen contend that we are benefited by the possession of this foreign capital! If we could have its use, without its attending abuse, I should be gratified also. But it is in vain to expect the one without the other. Wealth is power, and, under whatsoever form it exists, its proprietor, whether he lives on this or the other side of the Atlantic, will have a proportionate influence. It is argued, that our possession of this English capital gives us a certain influence over the British government. If this reasoning be sound, we had better revoke the interdiction as to aliens holding land, and invite foreigners to engross the whole property, real and personal, of the country. We had better at once exchange the condition of independent proprietors for that of stewards. We should then be able to govern foreign nations, according to the arguments of gentlemen on the other side. But let us put aside this theory, and appeal to the decisions of experience. Go to the other side of the Atlantic and see what has been atchieved for us there by Englishmen holding 7/10ths of the capital of this bank. Has it released from galling and ignominious bondage one solitary American seaman, bleeding under British oppression? Did it prevent the unmanly attack upon the Chesapeake? Did it arrest the promulgation, or has it abrogated the orders in council—those orders which have given birth to a new æra in commerce? In spite of all its boasted effect, are not the two nations brought to the very brink of war? Are we quite sure, that on this side of the water, it has had no effect favorable to British interests. It has often been stated, and although I do not know that it is susceptible of strict proof, I believe it to be a fact, that this bank exercised its influence in support of Jay's treaty—and may it not have contributed to blunt the public sentiment, or paralyse the efforts of this nation against British aggression?

The Duke of Northumberland is said to be the most considerable stockholder in the Bank of the U. States. A late Lord Chancellor of England, besides other noblemen, was a large stockholder. Suppose the Prince of Essling, the Duke of Cadore & other French dignitaries owned seven-eighths of the capital of this bank, should we witness the same exertions (I allude not to any made in the Senate) to recharter it? So far from it, would not the danger of French influence be resounded throughout the nation?

I shall give my most hearty assent to the motion for striking out the first section of the bill.

Washington *National Intelligencer,* May 25, 1811. Published also in *Annals of Cong.,* 11 Cong., 3 Sess., XXII, 209-19. Lexington *Kentucky Gazette,* June 11, 1811; Lexington *Reporter,* June 18, 1811; Chambers, *Speeches of Henry Clay,* 24-35; Mallory, *Life and Speeches of Henry Clay,* I, [266]-277; and Colton, *Life, Correspondence, and Speeches of Henry Clay,* V, 22-23. A summary, with extended quotation from the speech, reprinted from the Baltimore *Whig,* appeared in the Lexington *Kentucky Gazette,* March 19, 1811. On February 5 Senator William H. Crawford had reported a bill to amend and continue in force the act of 1791 creating the Bank of the United States. Several Senators had already spoken before Clay joined the debate.

1 On January 24 the House of Representatives had voted an indefinite postponement of a bill to extend the charter of the bank.

2 Senator James Lloyd had during the debate referred to testimony given by two

delegations from Philadelphia, one representing the "master manufacturers and mechanics," the other the merchants of that city.

3 Section 13 of Crawford's bill provided that the act was to be void if its terms were not accepted within three months by the Bank itself.

4 Alexander Hamilton.

5 Individual votes on the measure were not recorded.

6 From July, 1810, until 1812 England experienced severe depression, with many bank failures and severe unemployment in manufacturing districts. Willard Long Thorp, *Business Annals* (New York, 1926), 154.

To ——————

Sir Washington 18 Feb. 1811

I recd. your favor of the 14h. instant.[1] I am sorry that I am not able to give you a more satisfactory account of the Judgment agt. Chambers.[2] He is perfectly solvent from what I have understood, but he resides sixty or seventy miles from where I do, and when I first got the Judgment, Mr. Barr,[3] who placed the account in my hands, was to have superintended the collection. The Sheriff committed some blunder, which has been the source of all the delay. Prior to my leaving home, I think the execution was placed in a train for collection, but lest I shd. be mistaken I will immediately write out again, and order it to be issued. The money ought to be made in five or six months.

I wish you would do me the favor to send me by mail my letter,[4] in which the name as you write it of Mr. Grine[5] is mentd. I have no recollection of such a name, and presume you must have mistaken it; nor have I here any memoranda or data to supply my want of recollection. Yrs. H. CLAY

ALS. ViU-Coles Collection.

1 Not found. 2 Probably James Chambers, Maysville, Kentucky, merchant.

3 Possibly Attorney Thomas T. Barr of Lexington. 4 Not found.

5 Not identified.

To William Taylor

Dr Sir S. Chamber 19h. Feb. 1811

I recd. your favor of yesterday.[1] I had before recd. that to which it refers mentioning the arrangement you had made with Kelly,[2] and shall endeavor to do what is necessary on my part to its effectuation.

Montgomery County lies about thirty miles East of Lexington, and comprizes parts of what you will find laid down in your map as Bourbon and Clarke. I had some years ago an intimate knowledge of its inhabitants & still know many of them. I know several of the name of Lane, but am not certain that I am acquainted with the man mentd. by you.[3] I will with pleasure take charge of your papers & do the best I can with them.

Should I pass through Baltimore (wh[ich][4] I have not positively determined on) I wil[l] have the pleasure of seeing you Yrs.
Wm. Taylor Esqe[5] H. CLAY

ALS. DLC-HC (DNA, M212, R1). Endorsed: ". . . Henry Clay—March 21. 1811. June 8. 1812." [1] Not found.
[2] Joseph Kelly. The earlier communication has not been found.
[3] Robert G. Lane. [4] MS. torn. [5] Not in Clay's hand.

From John Swan

Dear Sir Baltimore February 26h 1811

The Session of Congress drawing near to a Close, have thought it well to enquire while you are so near whither I shall have the pleasure of seeing you here before your return Home, & if not to ask when you think I may with any degree of Certainty Calculate on a decision of the long winded Suit at [*sic*] Genl Massey,[1] its most material to me that immediate determination take place a State of Suspence you know of all others is most disagreeable— I have been lately told, Mr Fox[2] who removed my Locations said He was authorized so to do by me inclos'd you have a Copy of his first application to me[3] of a subsequent date as I am informed to the removal of the first interies and if I am now to judge from appearances Calculated to draw some thing from me to justifie the act, as after his specious promises He did nothing in the only transaction He was employed, to execute, I can find no Copy of my answer but you have nothing to apprehend from that, the transaction He was to investigate was a Contract with Paul Froman[4] & Locating 1400 as[5] part of one of Lord Dunmores[6] Warrants for 3000 acres, demand Fox's authority for removing my interies, without shewing that Colo Anderson[7] must be answerable for suffering the removal, the extent of his authority as to my military warrant was to Call at the Office for the Certificates of survey pay the fees &ca & send them to me. I had no doubt they were ready in the Office, my warrant was placed in the late Colo Carringtons[8] Hands of [*sic*] sent it by his Brother or Nephew to Colo Anderson who promised him It should be located & surveyed, He drew on me for $60 how then could I suppose the warrant not located or authorize him to remove the Location—I observed before that I had no Copy of my Letter to Fox, but on examining my Letter Book found one in reply to Mr. John Machir[9] (an extract from which is annexd to the Copy of Mr. Fox's Letter) who had Solicted [*sic*] the transaction of my Affairs in that Country from which you will perceive I considered my Military Warrants as Located & Surveyed, that impression remained unimpared untill the year 1800 when Captn Shepherd[10] who had been examining his Military Lands informed me of the Actual Situation of mine on which I immediately wrote to Mr. Creighton[11] on the Subject with great respect I have the Honor to be Your very Obedt Servt J SWAN

NB is Mr. John Machir yet a resident of Kentuckey if so Can you give me his address J S

ALS. DLC-TJC (DNA, M212, R12). Addressed to Clay at Washington.

1 Nathaniel Massie.

2 Probably Arthur Fox of Mason County, Kentucky, who in 1784 had been sent as a surveyor to explore the Virginia Military Tract north of the Ohio River.

3 Not found.

4 A native of New Jersey who had settled in the Valley of Virginia, then moved to Kentucky, where he had died in 1783.

5 Acres.

6 Royal Governor of Virginia, 1771-1775.

7 Richard C. Anderson.

8 Edward Carrington, Revolutionary officer, brother of Paul Carrington, had died October 28, 1810.

9 Of Mason County, a member of the Kentucky General Assembly, 1792-1800.

10 Abraham Shepherd, a Revolutionary officer of Berkeley County, Virginia, who in 1787 had entered 1000 acres of land in Brown County, Ohio, on a Virginia Military Warrant.

11 William Creighton of Virginia had begun the practice of law in Chillicothe, Ohio, in 1798, and in 1803 had become the first Secretary of State of Ohio. He later served several terms in Congress.

From William Eustis

War Department, Feby. 28th. 1811.

Honble. Henry Clay. (S.U.S.) Sir,

agreably to the Request which you communicated to me in behalf of *Andrew Allison,*[1] who now stands a Pensioner of the United States on the Roll of the No. Carolina Agency, order is taken that his name be transferred to the Kentucky Roll, to be paid his stipend in future at the Seat of Government: but any arrearages of Pension that may be due him up to the 4th. of March next, he must receive from the Agent for the payment of Pensions in No. Carolina.

Examination has been made in the Office of the Accountant of this Department relative to Captain *Leonard Helm;*[2] but no information on the points in question can be found. The Documt: respecting him is enclosed.[3] I am, Sir, &c. &c. &c. W. EUSTIS.

Copy. DNA, RG15, Letter Books: General, vol. 2 (1806-1812), p. 249. Eustis was Secretary of War.

1 No communication found. Allison was a resident of Paris, Kentucky.

2 One of the officers of George Rogers Clark's Northwest Expeditionary Force in 1778.

3 Not found.

Committee Report Relative to the Bank of the United States

[March 2, 1811]

MR. CLAY, *from the committee to whom was referred the me-*

morial of the stockholders of the Bank of the U. States, praying that an act of Congress might be passed, to continue the corporate powers of the Bank, for a further period, to enable it to settle such of its concerns as may be depending on the 3d of March, 1811, respectfully offers, for the consideration of the Senate, the following

REPORT:

"THAT your committee have duly weighed the contents of the memorial, and deliberately attended to such explanations of the views of the memorialists as they have thought proper to present through their agents: That holding the opinion (as a majority of the committee do) that the constitution did not authorise Congress originally to grant the charter, it follows, as a necessary consequence of that opinion, that an extension of it, even under the restrictions contemplated by the stockholders, is equally repugnant to the constitution. But, if it were possible to surmount this fundamental objection, and if that rule which forbids, during the same session of the Senate, the re-agitation of a proposition once decided, were disregarded, your committee would still be at a loss to find any sufficient reasons for prolonging the political existence of the corporation, for the purpose of winding up its affairs. For,

As it respects the body itself, it is believed that the existing laws, through the instrumentality of a trust properly constituted, afford as ample means as a qualified continuance of the charter would, for the liquidation of its accounts, and the collection and final distribution of its funds. But should any inconvenience be experienced on this subject, the committee are persuaded it will be very partial, and such as the state authorities, upon proper application, would not fail to provide a competent remedy for. And

In relation to the community, if the corporation, stripped of its banking powers, were to fulfil bona fide the duty of closing its affairs, your committee cannot see that any material advantage would be derived. Whilst, on the contrary, if it should not so act, but should avail itself of the temporary prolongation, in order to effect a more durable extension of its charter, it might in its operations become a serious scourge.

Your committee are happy to say that they learn, from a satisfactory source, that the apprehensions which were indulged, as to the distress resulting from a non-renewal of the charter, are far from being realised in Philadelphia, to which their information has been confined. It was long since obvious, that the vacuum, in the circulation of the country, which was to be produced by the withdrawal of the paper of the Bank of the U. States, would be filled by paper issuing from other banks. This operation is now actually going on: The paper of the Bank of the U. S. is rapidly returning, and that of other banks is taking its place. The ability to enlarge their accommodations is proportionately enhanced, and when it shall be further increased by a removal into their vaults of those deposits which are in the possession of the Bank of the United States, the injurious effects of a dissolution of the corporation will be found to consist in an accelerated disclosure of the actual condition of those who have been supported by the credit of others, but whose insolvent or tottering situation, known to the bank, has been concealed from the public at large.

Your committee beg leave to present the following resolution:

Resolved, That the prayer of the memorialists ought not to be granted."

Washington *National Intelligencer,* March 5, 1811. Published also in *Annals of Cong.,* 11 Cong., 3 Sess., XXII, 361-62. A memorial had been presented by Senator Michael Leib of Pennsylvania, and referred to a committee composed of Clay, Leib, Jessee Franklin (North Carolina), Joseph Anderson, and James A. Bayard. The report was tabled, without further action.

Resolution to Regulate Publication of Act on Occupation of East Florida

[March 3, 1811]

Resolved by the Senate and H. of Representatives of the U. S. of America in Congress assembled[1] that the act passed during the present Session of Congress entitled "An act to enable the President of the U. States, under certain contingencies, to take possession of the Country lying east of the river Perdido, and South of the State of Georgia, and the Mississippi Territory, &c. for other purposes," and the declaration accompanying the same be not printed or published.,* any law or usage to the contrary notwithstanding.

*unless directed by the P of the US[2]

AD. DNA, RG46, 11B-B2. Published in *Annals of Cong.,* 11 Cong., 3 Sess., XXII, 378. Read three times by unanimous consent, the motion was approved by both Houses of Congress and signed by the President before the end of the day.

1 Last nine words not in Clay's hand.

2 Supplementary note not in Clay's hand.

From John Swan

Dear Sir Balto. March 5h 1811

I have examined my Letter Books from 1786 to 1801 & can find the Copy of no Letter from me to Mr Andw Hynes[1] in that period, at same time its not my intention to disclaim writing him so far from that, it appears by a Letter from Mr Hynes dated March, 1800

I had wrote him a short time prior to that date, my Son & Mr. Ferguson[2] examined my Letters for the same period of time the Letter books were examined by myself two Letters from Him are all that Can be found & I may fairly presume all He ever wrote me You have annexd a Copy of them.[3] It appears by the first I had some suspicion of the injustice done me in the Location of my Military Warrant & by the second that Colo Anderson had endeavoured to wipe off the impression. I am still impress'd with an Opinion that I never Committed myself in authorizing a removal of my first Locations or entiries. I have thought it well to say this much least your time will not permit you to Call a[s] You proposed, with great respect & high esteem I remain Your Obedient Servt

J SWAN

ALS. DLC-TJC (DNA, M212, R12). Cf. above, Swan to Clay, February 26, 1811.

1 One of the trustees appointed in 1780 to lay off the town of Louisville; a founder of Elizabethtown, Kentucky; and a member of the State Senate from Nelson County in 1800.

2 Not identified.

3 DLC-TJC (DNA, M212, R12). Written from "Bairds Town," Kentucky, September 15, 1797, and March 19, 1800.

Receipt from Kennedy and Cox

6h. March 1811

Received of H. Clay Seven hundred and twenty five dollars to be credited to the debt due from William Taylor & Company to Kennedy & Cox. $725 JNO KENNEDY & COX

DS, in Clay's hand. DLC-TJC (DNA, M212, R15). See above, Agreement, May 12, 1809.

Receipt from Cornelius and John Comegys

[March 6, 1811]

Recd Baltimore March 6. 1811 of Henry Clay Esqr. One hundred and two Dollars on amt. of our Claim against William West of— Kentucky—— $102— CORNS. & JNO. COMEGYS

DS. DLC-TJC (DNA, M212, R15).

To Caesar A. Rodney

My Dear Rodney, Frederick Town. 7 Mar. 1811

When I called on saturday last to bid you adieu, and leave with you my good wishes I was unfortunate enough not to find you at home. The City has by this time become free from Congressional bustle and noise, & assumed its wonted tranquillity.[1] And so, Eppes and Randolph accommodated their difference![2] I was glad to hear it, altho' I could not but admire the felicity with which an affair was arranged that I thought admitted of but one mode of adjustment.

We came by the route of Baltimore, and reached here this evening on our way to Pittsburg, where I expect to arrive some 12 or 14 days hence. It has been rumored that, in consequence of the demise of the old King, the Prince of Wales has ascended the throne, and that one of his first acts has been to revoke the orders in Council.[3] If you can find leisure from the cares of State, now devolved wholly upon the Executive, it would give me pleasure to receive at Pittsburg a letter from you on this and any other subject you may think proper to communicate. Suffer me also to enquire if you had any success in relation to the application of my brother.[4] Yr's Sincerely H. CLAY

ALS. DLC-Rodney Family Papers (DNA, M212, R22). Addressed to Rodney at Washington.

1 Congress had adjourned March 3.

2 In the heat of debate in the House of Representatives on the evening of February 27, John Randolph had accused his colleague from Virginia, John W. Eppes, of lying. Eppes had immediately challenged him.

3 George III lived until 1820. The rumors were apparently based upon the passage of the Regency Act.

4 See below, Clay to Rodney, March 9, 1811.

To Caesar A. Rodney

My Dear Rodney Hagers town 9h. Mar. 11.

Since my arrival at this place I recd. the inclosed letter,[1] the object of which you will perceive is to solicit the appointment of Marshall for the Orleans District in favor of my brother. You will give to the application such weight as you may think it deserves. The place would be preferred to the other which he desired.[2] Thruston and Pope[3] are both well acquainted with John Clay.

Yrs truly H. CLAY

ALS. DLC-Rodney Family Papers (DNA, M212, R22).

1 Not found.

2 The appointment desired earlier by John Clay is not known. Later in the year he was recommended for the office of Register in the Orleans Territory.

3 Buckner Thruston and John Pope.

To [Robert Smith]

Sir Hagers town 9h. March. 11.

Since my arrival at this place letters which I have received from New Orleans state that Mr. Robinson,[1] the present Atto. for that District, intends to resign, and recommend as his successor Mr.

Robert Breckenridge.[2] I am acquainted with this gentleman, who is the nephew of the late Atto. Genl. of the U. S., and is a very interesting promising young man, and whom I should be glad to see appointed.

I was prevented, on my departure from the City, from saying to you personally, what I am persuaded you are fully sensible of, how much I feel for your private & public prosperity. Yr. ob. Servt.

HENRY CLAY

ALS. DNA, RG59, R1.
1 Tully Robinson, who was succeeded in office by John R. Grymes.
2 Son of James Breckinridge of Virginia.

Trustees' Bond

[March 9, 1811]

Know all men by these presents that we Henry Clay of Kentucky and Dr. Richard Pindell of Hagers town in Maryland are held and firmly bound unto The State of Maryland in the just and full sum of fifty thousand dollars; to be paid to the said State or its assigns; to which payment well and truly to be made we bind ourselves our heirs executors and administrators jointly & severally firmly by these presents. Sealed with our seals and dated this 9h. day of March 1811

The Condition of the above obligation is such that whereas by an order made by the Chancellor of the State of Maryland on the 27th day of February last in a case between the Creditors of Samuel and Robert Purviance against the Estates of the said Samuel & Robert Purviance, the said H. Clay was appointed a trustee as in and by the said order will more fully and at large appear: Now if the said H. Clay shall duly and faithfully perform the trust reposed in him by the order or decree aforesaid, or that may be reposed in him by any future order or decree made in the premises, & virtue.

Sealed & Delivered
In presence of
WM. O. SPRIGG
THOMAS COMPTON[1]

AD, signatures removed. KyLxT. Endorsed: "Bond approved W. Kilty Chr March 18th 1811." See above, Moale to Clay, October 9, 1810; and below, Draft of Report, July 12, 1813.
1 Witnesses not identified.

To Samuel Hopkins

Dr Sir Hagers town 9 Mar. 11.

I have only time to say that I am thus far on my way home,

and that the Chancellor of Maryland has appointed me a Trustee of the Estates of the Mess. Purviances with full powers &c. &c. If you will meet me at Lexington (the sooner the better) I will endeavor to make with you such arrangement on the subject of the several purchases under Henry Purviance as will be equitable & do justice to all parties concerned. I have no news. Yr. friend

H. CLAY

ALS. Fayette Circuit Court, Hopkins *vs.* Purviance, File 414, Bundle 691. Addressed to Hopkins at Henderson, Kentucky.

To [Benjamin] Howard

Dr. Howard. Bedford[1] 12h. March 11.

Just before I left the City I made a contract with Mr. Richard Parrott of Geo. Town (Rope maker) for the sale to him of Twenty tons of Yarns,[2] upon credit. At the time, I thought him perfectly secure, and such are my present impressions, but since I sat out on my journey I have heard a suggestion to the contrary. Will you do me the favor to make enquiry into his solvency and punctuality, and write me immediately the result? I have supposed you could obtain information entirely to be relied upon through General Mason,[3] and I will only add that I wish the enquiry conducted with the utmost delicacy towards Mr. Parrot [*sic*], of whom I have a very favorable opinion. You will be pleased to address your letter to me at Lexington (K) where it will arrive about the time I shall.

The weather has greatly favored us during this part of our journey, and indeed the roads have been much better than we anticipated. Yr. friend HENRY CLAY

ALS. MiU-C. Recipient identified by Clements Library. Although Howard had resigned his seat in Congress in 1810 and served as Governor of Louisiana Territory thereafter to 1812, he returned to the eastern States for his marriage on February 14, 1811, to Mary Thomson Mason, daughter of Stevens Thomson Mason, deceased, at her family's home in Loudoun County, Virginia.

1 Pennsylvania.

2 Spun from hemp.

3 John Mason, cousin of Stevens Thomson Mason.

From Richard Parrott

Hon Henry Clay GeoTown March 13th 1811

Dear Sir Your esteemed favr. of the 7th[1] I received on Monday and on Yesturday received advice of the whole of the yarns having been shiped. and Messr Howell & Co[2] inform me that at your request they have been well selected by a Judicious hand, for which attention please to accept my thanks. I was yesturday at the Office and find the impression is that we shall have but little to do this Season. but Sir. I will take your crop in yarns at Seventeen Cents per lb. in yarns to run 20 tho I wd much rather have them 22 and I believe the expence to you would be no more payable when you come next to Congress, or at furthest when the next appropration is made for the Navy. I will take every means in my power to get our yarns introdused in the Navy. and I know it is the wish of the Secretary. should there be more business than I expect and I can contract further I will certainly write you and tender you the first offer for yourself or friend. I will upon my return from the Eastern shore of Md (where I am going) advise you of the quality of the yarns as I hope they will be recvd before that time—

Your Obt St RICHD PARROTT.

ALS. DLC-TJC (DNA, M212, R12). Addressed to Clay at Pittsburgh, forwarded to Lexington.

1 Not found.

2 Possibly A. B. Howell and Company of Philadelphia, who were purchasers of Kentucky hemp.

From James C. Williamson

Henry Clay Esqr. New Orleans 21st. march 1811.

Sir

Your Brother[1] has handed to me the enclosed seven notes of hand, drawn by Paul SKidmore[2] of $50 Dollars Each, Viz—

One, dated, New York, 1st. Nov 1803, pble in 21 mo. to J. Foley
One — — " — — — — " — — — — — — — " — — — — — — " — — — 24 — — " — — — — — — "
One — — " — — — — " — — — — — — — " — — — — — — " — — — 27 — — " — — — — — — "
One — — " — — — — " — — — — — — — " — — — — — — " — — — 30 — — " — — — — — — "
One — — " — — — — " — — — — — — — " — — — — — — " — — — 33 — — " — — — — — — "
One — — " — — — — " — — — — — — — " — — — — — — " — — — 36 — — " — — — — — — "
One — — " — — — — " — — — — — — — " — — — — — — " — — — 39 — — " — — — — — — "

making altogether the Sum of $350. which are endorsed, blank by John Foley & I presume ought to bear Interest from the time they are severally due—He informs me that the drawer, is now in Kentucky & in such Circumstances as will enable him, without inconvenience to pay them I will thank you to take such means, as you may think proper to collect the amount—but as we don't know the person, I wish to avoid any expence, which cannot be covered from the receipt of money on the notes.—Three notes of of [*sic*] a Similar Kind & of $50 Each were Some time ago Sent to John Jordan for Collection but he has never accounted for them—Will you have the goodness to make enquiry about them & recover the amount with those enclosed. If you should get this money, please remit it to me in Lexington Bank notes or a bill on this place.—

I will thank you to present my respects to Mrs. Clay—I am Sir
Your Obedt. Servt. JAMES C WILLIAMSON

ALS. DLC-TJC (DNA, M212, R12). Williamson, born in the United States, had settled in New Orleans before 1803.
1 John Clay.
2 Of Louisville.

From William Taylor

Dear Sir, Baltimore March. 21. 1811.

I hope this will find you safe home and that you had as agreeable a Journey as The Season cou'd admit of. I regreted that your stay in Baltimore was so short.

I am advised that The Debt due by Robert G. Lane to Elisha Thatcher & Co. (myself The Company and since its dissolution The property all assigned me) is on Bond dated 1803 for about 4000$ principal—and security to another bond of Robert Walkers[1] for 700$.

Lane made assignments of Debts & accounts—suits were brought, very little has been recovered—something may yet be depending but very Doubtful. He also gave some Deed of Trust on property & assignment on his Interest in his father's estate at The Decease of his mother—this last Interest was in Culpepper County[2] and the Witnesses cou'd never be got into That County to get it recorded —his mother died about Two years ago and he Immediately went There sold his Interest for £100 and got off before my agent heard of it. A Statement of all These things shall be shortly sent you— in The mean time enquire for The man—he may have changed his name or Bought land in some other persons name—Cannot you bring suit, hold him to Bail and get a Commission to take evidence if necessary—Had I better send you The Original Bond.

Inform me of W F Simrall of Louisville—if he does not pay soon I certainly must use coersive measures—allow me to hear from you soon, I am Dear Sir Yr mos obt Svt WM. TAYLOR

ALS. DLC-TJC (DNA, M212, R12). Addressed to Clay at Lexington.
1 Of Mt. Sterling, Montgomery County, Kentucky.
2 Virginia.

Bill of Complaint against Alfred W. Grayson

Fayette Circuit Sct. [March 30, 1811]

H. Clay complains of Alfred W. Grayson in custody &c of a plea of trespass on the case For that whereas on the day of 1811 at the parish of in the County aforesaid the said deft was indebted to the plt in the Sum of $1500[1] for so much money by the said plaintiff before that time had and advanced to and for the use of the said deft at his special instance & request; & being so indebted afterwards to wit on the same day & year afd. at the Circuit afd. the said deft promised to pay to the said plt the said sum of money whenever after he should be thereunto required: Yet the said deft tho' often required fraudulently intending to deceive & defraud the said plt, the said sum of money nor any part thereof to the said plt hath not paid but the same to him to pay hitherto hath refused and still doth refuse to the damage of the plt $ and therefore he brings suit &c

Pledges H. CLAY
J Doe
R. Roe

[Endorsement on verso][2]

One note for	$600.[3]	
Cost of protest	1:66	
	601:66	with interest from the 31 Decr. 1810
One other note for	$316[4]	
Cost of Protest	1:66	
from 29 Jan. 1811	317:66	
	$919:32	with

int thereon from the 15 Jan. 1811 (which is abt. the intermediate time).

ADS. Fayette Circuit Court, File 203 (1811). Filed March 30, 1811.
1 Superimposed on $1000.
2 AE. In addition to the notes here listed, Clay had a claim growing out of a note for $140 which Grayson had given Elijah Noble on July 12, 1810. When the obligation remained unpaid, Charles Carr, to whom it had been assigned, won a judgment against Grayson, which Clay as security for the latter was forced to pay. Fayette Circuit Court, File 203.
3 Above, October 27, 1810.
4 See above, Receipt, January 29, 1811.

Power of Attorney from Joshua Gist

[April 1, 1811]

[Joshua Gist of Frederick County, Maryland, appoints Henry Clay, William Kelly, and Rezin H. Gist[1] (or any two of them) his attorneys, authorizing them to manage his estate in Kentucky, to sell his lands, and to substitute one or more attorneys under them. Acknowledged before two justices of the peace of Frederick County, Maryland, April 1, 1811; recorded by the Clerk of the Kentucky Court of Appeals, June 22, 1811.]

Ky. Court of Appeals, Deed Book O, 61-63.
1 Of Montgomery County, Kentucky.

Power of Attorney from Independent Gist

[April 1, 1811]

[Independent Gist of Frederick County, Maryland, appoints Henry Clay, William Sudduth, and Rezin H. Gist (or any two of them) his attorneys, authorizing them to manage in all respects his estate in Kentucky, to sell his lands, and to substitute one or more attorneys under them. Acknowledged before two justices of the peace of Frederick County, Maryland, April 1, 1811; recorded by the Clerk of the Kentucky Court of Appeals, June 22, 1811.]

Ky. Court of Appeals, Deed Book O, 65-67. Independent Gist was a nephew of Joshua Gist.

Receipt to Charles Humphreys and Thomas Bodley

3 Apl. 1811.

Recd. of C. Humphreys and Thomas Bodley Trustees of James Hughes, on account of Usher's debt, in cash six hundred and sixty six dollars and eighteen Cents; and negociable notes as follows: Two for two hundred and fifty dollars due 1/4h. May; three others for two hundred and eighty eight dollars & 90 Cents due 3/6 April; one for one hundred and forty three dollars and forty two Cents due 5/8 April; and one for four hundred and eight dollars and fifty Cents due 7/10h. May: which said notes if paid are to be credited to the said debt at the times of payment; if not paid may be returned by said Clay if he thinks proper. H. CLAY

ADS. DLC-TJC (DNA, M212, R15). Cf. above, Usher to Clay, May 7, 1809.

Deed of Trust from Micajah Harrison

[April 4, 1811]

[Whereas on January 17, 1807, Micajah Harrison, with Hezekiah Harrison as his security, executed bond to Wilson C. Nicholas for the payment of $1670, besides interest, the consideration of which bond was four slaves, namely, Jube, Nancy, Absalom, and Billy, and the bond being unpaid, now for the purpose of indemnifying the executors of Hezekiah Harrison, who is since deceased, and in consideration of five shillings, paid and acknowledged, Micajah Harrison conveys to Henry Clay the afore-mentioned slaves, in trust that Clay may proceed whenever in his judgment necessary to sell all, or any, of the slaves, for cash or on credit, with or without previous advertisement, to pay the expenses of the aforesaid debt with such interest and costs as may have accrued. Clay agrees to execute his trust faithfully and to pay over to Harrison any residue of proceeds. Signatures of M. Harrison and Clay witnessed by William T. Banton; that of Harrison also acknowledged before Thomas Triplett, Jr., Deputy Clerk of Montgomery County, April 6, 1811.]

Montgomery County Court, Deed Book 5, pp. 284-85.

Rental Agreement with J. L. Downing

[April 5, 1811]

H. Clay has this day rented to J. L. Downing the small house attached to the Establishment of the Kentucky Hotel together with the stables belonging to that establishment for the term of one year to commence on the 13th. instant. The said Clay agrees that the said Downing shall have the use of the pump in the yard of the Hotel, and the liberty of passing from the said small house through the yard to the stables.

In consideration whereof the said Downing covenants & agrees to pay to the said Clay at the end of the year the sum of five hundred and fifty dollars.

The said Downing further covenants that unless he gives the said Clay three months written[1] notice previous to the expiration of the said year, the said Clay shall be at liberty to consider him as tenant for the succeeding year, & so on for successive years.

The said Downing further covenants to surrender the premises in as good order & condition as he receives them, natural decay & inevitable accidents excepted.

It is further understood & agreed by the parties that the said Clay is to be at liberty & he hereby reserves the power of distraining & re entering on the premises if default is made in payment of the rent.

Witness the seals of the parties this 5th. day of April 1811

Sealed & Delivered In presence of H. Clay {L.S.}
(written being first interlined) J. L. Downing {L.S.}
B. Gaines[2]

ADS, signed also by Downing. KyLxT. Downing was probably Josiah L., son of Samuel Downing, Lexington merchant. Josiah L. and his brother, Richard, established for a time a trade in horses with South Carolina.

1 Interlined.

2 Bernard Gaines, a native of Virginia, an early settler and surveyor in Fayette County, Kentucky, and a United States Army officer from 1791 to 1797. He kept a boarding house in Lexington for some years after 1810, but later removed to a farm in Woodford County, where he died in 1839.

Receipt from Tandy and Castleman

6 Apl. 1811.

Recd. of H. Clay Three hundred and twenty one dollars and

sixty two Cents the amt. of a note & Costs of protest given by J. P. Wagnon on the 10h. Septr. last & indorsed by said Clay.[1]

TANDY & CASTLEMAN

DS, in Clay's hand. DLC-TJC (DNA, M212, R15).
[1] Cf. above, Lease, September 1, 1801.

Bill of Sale from George Slaughter, Jr.

[April 6, 1811]

Know all men by these presents that I have this day sold and delivered to Henry Clay a negro slave named Sam thirty one years of age on account of the rent which I owe him for the Hotel; which said slave I warrant and defend agt. all persons whatsoever. Witness my hand & seal this 6h. Apl. 1811. GEO. SLAUGHTER JUR {L.S.}
GEO G ROSS[1]

DS, in Clay's hand. DLC-TJC (DNA, M212, R15).
[1] Who announced the beginning of legal practice in June of this year. He was the husband of Eliza Pindell, Mrs. Clay's niece.

Agreement with George Slaughter, Jr.

[April 6, 1811]

An agreement entered into this 6h. day of April 1811 between H. Clay and Geo. Slaughter.

Whereas the said Clay did on the 14h. day of Nov. 1810 lease to the said Slaughter for the term of one year the establishment of the Kentucky Hotel & premises together with a certain quantity of furniture to be received, and which has been since received from Cuthbert Banks, as in and by the lease will appear: And whereas a conversation has been since had between the said Clay & Slaughter relative to the surrender of the said property, in consequence whereof the said Clay has leased to J L Downing the stables and small dwelling house heretofore attached to the establishment of the Hotel, and also the priviledge of using the pump & yard of the Hotel: Now it is this day further agreed between the parties aforesaid as follows:

The said Clay leases to the said Slaughter for the term of one year to commence on the first day of May next all the residue of the Establishment of the Hotel, with the exception of the lower front room, commonly used as a bar room, which the said Clay hereby reserves to himself.

The said Clay further leases to the said Slaughter the amount of furniture which he the said Slaughter received of Cuthbert Banks under the aforesaid lease of 14h. day of Novr: last; but the said

Clay retains to himself the priviledge of removing whenever he pleases the Chandeliers which he has suspended in the Ball room.

In consideration whereof the said Slaughter covenants & agrees to pay to the said Clay at the rate of five hundred dollars per annum, to be paid quarterly; and to return to the said Clay at valuation the like amount of furniture that he recd. from said C. Banks at the end of the year. And it is further understood and agreed that if the said rent as it becomes due shall not be paid by the said Slaughter the said Clay is to be at liberty to distrain therefor and re-enter on & take possession of the premises.

The said Clay further agrees that the said Slaughter may have a light cheap petition run across the big dining room so as to separate it into two apartments, the expence of which shall be deducted out of the rent, and which petition is to be so run and constructed as to leave the door which opens into the passage in the back room.

And the said Slaughter doth hereby covenant and agree that the said Clay shall have a lien upon all the furniture in the Hotel which belongs to him, or which he recd. from Banks as afd. or which he may place there, & all other property which he may have on the premises for his the said Slaughters compliance with this Contract.

In witness whereof we hereunto set our seals & hands.

Sealed & Delivered H. CLAY {L.S.}
In presence of GEO. SLAUGHTER JUR {L.S.}
JOHN HART.
GEO G ROSS

ADS, signed also by Slaughter. DLC-TJC (DNA, M212, R15).

Deed of Trust from Micajah Harrison

[April 9, 1811]

[Indenture whereby Micajah Harrison, as security for payment of certain specified debts, amounting to a total of approximately $9,000, grants to Henry Clay and Joseph H. Hawkins[1] "the exclusive right title and interest in a new Invented, 'Brick Machine' which the said Harrison purchased of the patentee, Daniel French, resident of the City of New York,[2] by writing bearing date the thirtieth Day of July eighteen hundred and ten granting and assigning to said Harrison his heirs or assigns the exclusive priviledge of using, and transfering the right to others to use in the County of Fayette and State of Kentucky—and the said Harrison for himself his heirs Executors, administrators, warrants the exclusive right and title of said right to use the same in the County aforesaid together with all such of the machinery either in part or in whole that the said Harrison has and may prepare for the working the same and to carry it into full and complete Operation." Harrison also conveys to Clay and Hawkins 7,895 acres of second rate land in Montgomery County and the "ballance or overplus" in certain mortgages he has given to his creditors.[3] Clay and Hawkins are authorized to manage the brick machine according to their best judgment for the discharge of the debts and to hold the land also in trust or to dispose of it as they think best. All "overplus after paying principal Interest and Costs" on the debts is to be returned to Harrison. Clay and Hawkins covenant to execute the trust "faithfully and to the best of their abilities." Signature of Harrison acknowledged before H. Lane, Deputy Clerk of Montgomery County, April 11, 1811.]

Montgomery County Court, Deed Book 5, pp. 285-88.

1 Lexington lawyer, son-in-law of George Nicholas. He was a member of the Kentucky House of Representatives from Fayette County, 1810-1813, and Clay's successor in Congress, 1814-1815. After removing to New Orleans in 1819, he was associated with the Austin venture in Texas until his death four years later.

2 A rival of Robert Fulton in the construction and operation of steamboats.

3 Cf. above, Deed of Trust, April 4, 1811.

Advertisement, by Executors of Thomas Hart, Jr., of Land for Sale

[*ca.* April 20, 1811]

Lexington *Reporter,* April 20, 1811. The tract, lying near Lexington, contained 1,000 acres of first rate land.

Property Deed to William M. Nash

[April 27, 1811]

[Indenture by which Henry and Lucretia Clay for an unstated sum, paid and acknowledged, sell to William M. Nash a tract on the waters of Cane Run, in Fayette County, containing 228 acres and 20 poles, bounded beginning at a stake at Pond Spring, the deeded tract being part of a pre-emption granted to Francis Patterson and by him devised to Arthur and Francis Patterson, who conveyed it to Clay by deed recorded in the Fayette County Clerk's Office.[1] Premises on the property included in the transfer. General warranty of title. Signatures of Henry and Lucretia Clay acknowledged before John D. Young, Clerk of Fayette County, November 2, 1815.]

Fayette County Court, Deed Book N, 57-59. Cf. Agreement, September 3, 1808.

1 See above, Property Deed, November 9, 1807.

Assignment of Bond by Edward West

27 Apl. 1811

For value recd. I assign one other third of the within bond to H. Clay. EDWARD WEST

ES, in Clay's hand. Fayette Circuit Court, File 238 (1812). On the bond, from James Morrison to West, cf. above, Putnam to Clay, August 22, 1804, note. See also above, Assignment of Bond, October 20, 1804.

To Caesar A. Rodney

Lexington 29h. Apl. 1811.

I recd. my dear Rodney, your obliging favor of the 13h. March.[1] I have directed the letters, in recommendation of my brother, suggested by you, to be procured and transmitted to you.[2]

You enquire if I should like an extra session? It would be personally very inconvenient to me, and yet I fear it may become necessary; for I find by information with which the mail was charged this day, that it is still questionable whether the decrees of Berlin & Milan are revoked, and I have always supposed that the call of Congress depended upon their being continued:[3]

The recent change in the Cabinet has excited here much attention and speculation.[4] It is highly approved, the Aurora[5] &c. to the contrary notwithstanding. It would have been gratifying to me (altho' I am aware it is hardly to be expected) that the measure was brought about, without offence to the ex-secretary and his friends. If however they choose to make the event the occasion of hostility to the administration I am persuaded, in this quarter, their efforts will be unavailing.

Rumor ascribes to the President the intention of farther changes, but I have placed no confidence in it.[6]

Our journey out was better than I anticipated. We reached home several weeks ago, and since our return the event which occasioned us so much solicitude, on the way, has occurred & has put me in possession of the stoutest son[7] we ever had, with less inconvenience to Mrs. Clay than she ever before experienced.

I hope you will find leisure to drop me a line occasionally.

Yr friend H. CLAY

ALS. NHi-Gallatin Papers.

1 Not found.

2 See above, Clay to Rodney, March 9, 1811.

3 On July 24 President Madison called for the first session of the Twelfth Congress to begin on November 4, 1811.

4 On April 1 James Monroe became Secretary of State, succeeding Robert Smith, who resigned under pressure from President Madison.

5 Edited by William Duane in Philadelphia.

6 The next change occurred when Rodney, himself, resigned on December 5, 1811.

7 Henry Clay, Jr., born April 10.

Notice of Trustees' Sale

3d. May 1811.

Likely slaves for sale

In virtue of a deed of trust made the first day of September last, by John Wilkinson and Thomas Pickett, which is recorded in the office of the County Court of Clarke, the subscriber, appointed by the said deed Trustee, will proceed, on saturday the sixth day of July next, in the town of Lexington, before the door of the Kentucky Hotel, to sell at public auction, for ready money, upwards of twenty likely slaves, being men women girls and boys, the property of the said Wilkinson and Pickett,[1] to satisfy the two finl [*sic*] instalments of a debt due from the said Wilkinson & Pickett to Abraham [Stout][2] Barton and John Hart surviving partners of Hart Barton and Hart, to secure payment of which debt the said deed of trust was given. HENRY CLAY

Trustee.

ADS. NN. Not found in newspapers; probably printed as a handbill. See Account, *ca.* April 12, 1815.

1 At this point the following words written and then deleted: "or so many of the said slaves as may be necessary."

2 MS. torn.

Property Deed to Henry Watkins

[June 7, 1811]

This Indenture made this 7h. day of June 1811 between Henry Clay of the one part and Henry Watkins of the other part Witnesseth that whereas John Watkins deceased did by his last will and testament bearing date the first day of April 1807 devise to the following effect "my will and desire is that after the decease of my wife the land whereon I now live may be sold to the highest bidder at one or two years Credit as my executors may Judge best and the money arising from such sale be equally divided among my three Children to wit: Samuel Phebe and Patsey with this express condition that Patsey pay out of her part of the said money to my son John and to my daughter Polly twenty five pounds to each of them in cash" and whereas the said Samuel Watkins did by deed bearing date the 11th. day of March 1809 convey to the said Henry Clay all the benefit for him intended whether the same might be received in money or land under the Clause of the will of the said John Watkins herein before recited: now this indenture witnesseth that the said Henry Clay for and in consideration of the sum of twelve hundred dollars to him paid or secured to be paid by the said Henry Watkins hath Granted bargained and sold and by these presents doth grant bargain and sell unto the said Henry Watkins all the interest by him acquired from the said Samuel Watkins under the clause in the will of his father herein before recited whether the same be receivable in the land itself or the proceeds thereof with the appurtinances. To have and to hold the said land or money, as the case may be to the said Henry Watkins his heirs and assigns forever And the said Henry Clay for himself and his heirs doth covenant agree to and with the said Henry Watkins that he will warrant and defend the right and title in the land or money as the case may be hereby intended to be transferred and conveyed against all and every person whatsoever claiming by through or under him the said Henry Clay

In testimony hereof the said Henry Clay hath hereunto set his hand and affixed his seal the day and year first written

HENRY CLAY {SEAL}

Woodford County Court, Deed Book E, 268-69. Recorded June 7, 1811. See above, Assignment, December 5, 1808; Property Deed, March 11, 1809.

To ——————

Dr Sir Ashland 10 June 1811

I have prevailed on Mr. Church[1] to call on you. He is introduced to me in a very particular manner by a friend of mine in New York, and I have had great pleasure in his acquaintance. He has spent about the last 20 years in Europe, altho' a native of America, and now contemplates fixing himself permanently in this Country. Knowing that you will derive much gratification from seeing & becoming acquainted with him, I have indulged the hope that you may be instrumental in detaining him amongst us. Yr's respectfully HENRY CLAY

ALS. Boone Tavern of KyBB.

1 Possibly Edward Church, a native of Massachusetts, who had served with the French army in Spain and, shortly afterward, had been appointed United States Consul at L'Orient, France. Many years later he moved to Lexington, where he died on April 22, 1845. Lexington *Observer and Reporter,* April 30, 1845.

Property Deed from John W. Wooldridge

[June 10, 1811]

[Whereas Edmund Wooldridge, deceased, by will of April 28, 1791, devised to his four sons 4000 acres to be equally divided, and John Wooldridge having for a valuable consideration sold his interest to Henry Clay—now for five shillings, paid and acknowledged, John conveys to Clay all right and title in this legacy; but it is expressly understood and agreed that Clay is to have the thousand acres hereby conveyed laid off out of the lands belonging to the heirs of Edmund Wooldridge south of the Tennessee River and within the State of Kentucky, on which lands the Indian title remains unextinguished. Title warranted only against claimants under John Wooldridge, "it being distinctly understood that if the title of the said Edmund Wooldridges Heirs to the said lands south of Tennessee river should prove bad the said Clay is to have no recourse upon him the said John W. Wooldridge–" Signature of Wooldridge acknowledged before Achilles Sneed, Clerk of the Court of Appeals, June 12, 1811.]

Ky. Court of Appeals, Deed Book O, 83-85.

Check to John Moore

13 June 1811

Pay to John Moore or bearer One hundred dollars. $100
Cashier of the K.I.Co.[1] H. CLAY

ADS. DLC-TJC (DNA, M212, R15). See Receipt, of same date.
[1] Kentucky Insurance Company.

Receipt and Bill of Sale from John Moore

[June 13, 1811]

Received 13 June 1811 of Henry Clay Two hundred and fifty dollars for the negro woman Fanny whom I have sold to said Clay, and the title to whom I do hereby warrant. JOHN × MOORE

Teste
WILL JORDAN

DS, in Clay's hand. DLC-TJC (DNA, M212, R15). Moore probably resided in southern Fayette County.

From Alexander Stephens

June 14th 1811.

I have recd. your letter[1] stating that your hopes of my success against Brenham &c.[2] are much strenghened on exammonation of the subject. I have also recd. a letter from Hardin the Register[3] advising me to a comprimise &c Upon reflection since the receipt of Hardin letter, I have formed the following Opinions 1st. That my property is in the midst of scoundrels, of whom I may expect, forgeries, purjuries, subornations and every other diabolical means to effect their purpose and in this declaration I hope I do not want charity–for what kind of a being must that be who could take property worth $6000 for 716 or in other words take a mans estate from him without the smalest consideration–I therefore am willing to give $750 to those Marauders if they will release me entirely—you will please make the best bargain you can for me,—not exceeding the above sum, Should I suceed finally against this man, perhaps Craig[4] would bring suit against me for damages in consequence of the ejectment, It is left with you however whether the offer of comprimise is to be made at all, If they accept the offer of comprimise they must be paid out of the money which I am to recd from Craig in payment for the land,—

write me when ere you deem it necessary and much Oblige yours Very Sincerly ALEXR. STEPHENS

I red. neither of your letters until a few days ago;

ALS. DLC-TJC (DNA, M212, R12). Stephens was probably the Pennsylvania veteran of the French and Indian and the Revolutionary wars who died a resident of Taliaferro County, Georgia, in 1813. He was the grandfather of Alexander H. Stephens, Vice-President of the Confederacy. [1] Not found.
[2] Not identified. [3] Mark Hardin. [4] Not identified.

Check to ——— Baylor

15 June 1811.

Pay to Mr. Baylor or bearer Twenty seven & a half dollars. $27:50
Cashier of the K.I.Co. H. CLAY

ADS. DLC-TJC (DNA, M212, R15). Probably to John W. Baylor.

To William Lytle

Dr Sir Lex. 22d. June 1811.

I was greatly disappointed in not seeing you when you were over at this place. Having been ready for sometime past to convey you the Falls' estate according to my contract[1] I have been desirous to receive deeds for the Lexington property. This is the more necessary because I have sold the Stable lot,[2] and as the purchase money will shortly become due I fear some difficulty in the payment of it on the score of the title. Are you prepared to make me deeds? And when will it suit your convenience to execute them?

Mr. Parker[3] has communicated his and your wish to purchase a part of the Land, in his neighbourhood belonging to Mr. Hart's estate. I presume we can so divide it as to accommodate him. Our price for the land is fifteen Dollars per acre, one third payable at Christmas & the residue in two years carrying interest from the Sale.

Yrs. H. CLAY

ALS. OCHP-Lytle MSS. [1] Above, Agreement, June 18, 1808.
[2] Clay had sold the stable and lot on the Kentucky Hotel grounds to John P. Wagnon on November 9, 1808. [3] John Parker.

Check to Porter Clay

26 June 1811

Pay to Porter Clay or bearer forty dollars. $40.
Cashier of the K.I.Co. H. CLAY

ADS. DLC-TJC (DNA, M212, R15).

Property Deed to Thomas Helm

[June 28, 1811]

[For $2460, paid and acknowledged, Peyton Short of Lexington and Henry Clay and Robert Alexander, as trustees of Short, convey to Thomas Helm of Woodford County a tract in the district reserved for officers and soldiers of the Virginia Continental line on the Cumberland River, 615 acres adjacent to Leroy Edwards'[1] survey no. 41, together with appurtenances. General warranty of title. Signatures of Short and Clay acknowledged before John D. Young, Clerk of Fayette County, July 3, 1811, and recorded by Achilles Sneed, Clerk of the Court of Appeals, July 11, 1811. Alexander's signature acknowledged before Sneed on July 12, 1811.]

Ky. Court of Appeals, Deed Book O, 71-72. Helm had moved from Frederick County, Virginia, to Woodford County, Kentucky, about 1800.

1 A captain in the Virginia line during the Revolutionary War, he had lived and died (1800) in Northumberland County, Virginia.

From John Graham

Dear Sir Washington 5th July 1811—

I should sooner have had the pleasure to reply to your Letter of the 12th. Ulto.[1] but I could not until yesterday get an answer from Mr King,[2] whether he could or could not, make a Drawing of Mr Millers Machine, from the Papers deposited in the Patent Office—I am sorry to say, he tells me he cannot. I had them sent to his House and he made an effort to do something with them; but he tells me they do not convey to his Mind a distinct idea of the Machine they are intended to describe; and that therefore he should not be able to do justice to Mr Millers Invention—This being the case Mr. M. will do well to get a rough Draft of his Machine made out with such explanations as will make it perfectly intelligible and from that Mr King can make a Drawing to be deposited in the Patent Office.[3]

I have seen Mr Parrot[4] he tells me your yarns were very wet whe[n] they came to him—He has had them warped &c. They are very strong but not such as are used for the Navy—I told him what was the purport of your Letter to me and that I was ready to comply with it.

You will have seen Mr Smith's "address to the People of the U States"[5] It is no doubt intended to produce a great effect; but so far as I can learn it will produce very little which can be gratifying to him It gives a false view of almost every transaction to which it relates, and if I mistake not, will be a cause of deep regret to its author.

The Public are not yet informed as to the Character of the Despatches by the Essex—Private Letters by that vessel say that we must not expect any change of System in either of the Belligerents favorable to neutral [*rights*][6]

With very sincere Regard & Esteem I am Dear Sir Your Most Obt Sevt JOHN GRAHAM

ALS. DLC-TJC (DNA, M212, R12). Addressed to Clay at Lexington. Graham, a native of Virginia, had served in succession as a representative from Mason County in the Kentucky legislature, as a diplomat in Spain, as Secretary of Orleans Territory, and as President Jefferson's agent to inquire into Burr's activities. From 1807 to 1817 he was Chief Clerk in the United States Department of State; he was afterward a member of a special commission to gather information on the rebellious Spanish colonies; and in 1819, for less than a year, he was Minister to Portugal.

1 Not found.

2 Nicholas King, Surveyor of the City of Washington from 1803 to 1812, or Robert King, Jr., who held the same post from 1813 to 1815.

3 On July 13, 1811, a patent was issued to Robert Miller, of Lexington, for a machine for breaking hemp and flax.

4 Richard Parrott.

5 In June, 1811, Robert Smith published a pamphlet, entitled *Address to the People of the United States,* relative to his dismissal from the post of Secretary of State.

6 Word obliterated by seal.

From James Adams, Per James Ekin

Honble Henry Clay Pittsburgh 6 July 1811

Sir I beg leave to inform you that since Writing you I have forwarded agreeable to your instruction Eighteen reels of your yarn to Mr. Richard Parrott Geo Town Carriage at three dollars thirty Seven & One half cent p 100 lbs which is lower than any has been forwarded for a Length of time—there remains now only One reel on hand which Shall be forwarded first opportunity

I remain Sir your Obdt Servt JAMES ADAMS
p JAS. EKIN

ALS, by Ekin. DLC-TJC (DNA, M212, R12). Ekin was presumably an employee of Adams, Pittsburgh shipper.

To [James Ogilvie]

LEXINGTON, July 9, 1811.

DEAR SIR,—In acknowledging the receipt of your favor of the

7th inst., covering $100 for the Lexington Library, I must say you have furnished, what was not wanted, an additional evidence of that devotion to literature, and that disinterested liberality, which you have invariably so eminently displayed. I fear that, in this instance, your munificence has exceeded the bounds of self-justice, by the appropriation of a sum not warranted by the proceeds of the orations, with which you have favored us.[1] Under this impression, I was about to obey my first impulse of soliciting you to permit me to return your benevolent donation. But apprehensive that, in so doing, I might excite some unpleasant sensation, I determined to give it the direction which your goodness has prescribed, and invest it in such of the books contained in your list, as are not already in the Library, which will be not more appreciated for their enlightened contents than by a recollection of the distinguished source whence they have proceeded.

Colton (ed.), *Private Correspondence of Henry Clay,* 18. Ogilvie, born and educated in Scotland, had emigrated to the United States, where for a time he conducted a school in Richmond, Virginia. He then enjoyed a successful career as a public lecturer, particularly in Washington, until his return in 1817 to the British Isles, where he is said to have committed suicide three years later.

1 Earlier in the month Ogilvie had delivered two "of those orations which have procured for him so much celebrity." The third lecture was postponed owing to "the exhaustion occasioned by the extreme heat of the weather." Lexington *Reporter,* July 2, 13, 1811.

To ———

Sir Lex. 9h. July. 1811.

I recd your favor of the 15h Apl.[1] which I delayed answering in the hope that a trial of the cause between Mr. Pringle as trustee of Mr. Russell and the University would have taken place at the term of the Fœd. Court lately closed, and that I should be able to communicate the result.[2] In this however I was disappointed, the cause being again continued. I cannot but believe that it will certainly be tried in the fall. My opinion of the event remains unchanged. Altho' the success of Mr. Pringle is not free from doubt I am persuaded we shall prevail.

When Mr. Johnson[3] placed in my hands the small claim agt Mr. Purviance,[4] to which I presume you allude, he requested me not to bring suit upon it, whilst a prospect existed of obtaining the amt. in any other manner. Payment of it has been repeatedly promised me, but has not yet been made I shall therefore make one further effort, which if not successful, will fully justify the resort to law.

Yrs. H. CLAY

ALS. Dr. Sam Gilmore Collection, Somerset, Kentucky, Board of Education.

1 Not found.

2 See above, Samuel Johnston to Clay, March 26, 1805.

3 Possibly Samuel Johnston, who had died in 1810.

4 Henry Purviance.

To [Directors of the Lexington Library]

Gent 12h. July 1811

Mr. James Ogilbie, on the 7h. inst., inclosed to me $100, the proceeds of two of his orations recently pronounced in Lexington, deducting incidental charges, with a request to apply the same to the use of the Lexington Library. Accompanying his letter was a list of books which he recommended as worthy of a place on your shelves. I have taken measures to procure immediately such of them as you do not already possess, and when received I will have the pleasure of delivering them to the Librarian & submitting a statement of their cost &c. Yr. ob. Servt. H. CLAY

ALS. Owned by Thomas D. Clark, Lexington, Kentucky. Cf. above, Clay to Ogilvie, July 9, 1811.

Bill of Sale from the Executors of Thomas Hart, Jr., to William Short

[July 13, 1811]

Fayette County Court, Deed Book E, 495-96. Transfers ten slaves conveyed to Hart by Peyton Short with the privilege of re-purchase under agreement of October 2, 1809. William Short, American diplomat to France, Holland, and Spain between 1789 and 1795, was an older brother of Peyton, and was himself a heavy investor in Kentucky lands.

From John Graham

Dear Sir Washington 13th July 1811

I had the pleasure yesterday to receive your Letter of the 3d Inst.[1] covering a Post Note for $200 payable in Phia early in Sept—I took it to the Bank in which I keep my accounts and I believe they will pass it to my Credit at once.

Before I got your Letter Mr Parrot[2] had been with me and told me he would pay the waggonage of your yarns—Perhaps he is not aware of what may be the amount and may call on me as your agent to aid him—In that case I shall do so; but until then I understand it to be your wish that I am to say nothing to him about the money you have sent me—

as yet none of the yarns have arrived. when they come he is to send for me to see them weighed and to note the order in which they come—

I am under some apprehension that my last Letter[3] may lead you to suppose that your yarns had arrived in bad order—as Mr Parrot had not received your Letter advising him of the shipment of these yarns he concluded that your Instructions to me had been given in relation to those which he purchased from you last winter belonging to Hart & Bartlet[4]—They were damaged—and as I knew not that you had made more than one contract with him, I naturally fell in to the error which you will find in my Letter.

I hope the difficulty about Mr Millers Patent is now at an end, for the Person who assists Doctor Thornton[5] in his office called on me the other day to inform me that there was a model of Mr Millers Machine in the Patent office which it seems, had been placed there so long ago that it was forgotten.—

Do not be under any apprehension that you impose upon me services that I am not quite willing to render you—I shall always find pleasure in being useful to you.

We have nothing new here as yet the Public are not informed whether "The Essex" or Mr Foster[6] have brought anything pleasant or otherwise. With great Respect & Rega[rd] I am Dear Sir Your Most Obt Sevt JOHN GRAHAM

Henry Clay Esqr
Lexington—

ALS. DLC-TJC (DNA, M212, R12). Addressed to Clay at Lexington.
1 Not found.
2 Richard Parrott.
3 Dated July 5.
4 No record of this transaction has been found.
5 Robert Miller and Dr. William Thornton.
6 Augustus John Foster, newly appointed British minister to the United States.

From Matthew Walton

D Sir, Washington County 15th. July 1811

Shortly after I saw you in Frankfort I made (as I thought) an arrangement to pay you for the land purchased of Purviance[1] & made no doubt but the money was paid you Shortly after, till last mail I understood it was not, & now not having any other opportunity inclose you by post 200 Dollars a Draught on Messrs. Morrison Fisher & Sutton[2] payable at the end of sixty days which I must get you to present for acceptance & by deducting the Interest for the sixty days which I am willing to loose I expect you can get the money, you will oblige me by attending to this Business I want you to Receive this money in part for the debt due for the purchase of the land from Purviance, By the next mail unless a more favourable opportunity offers I Expect I inclose you about 200 Dollars more, or perhaps a Little more & the whole of the first payment in a short time unless I am in lexington in two or three weeks if so I Shall not send only the 200 & odd Dollar by the next mail till I come up I hope Sir you will excuse this Delay in the payment of this money please to let me hear from you on the Rect. of this & let me know the fate of the Bill on Morrison &C— Yours with every sentiment of esteem

MATTHEW WALTON

ALS. DLC-TJC (DNA, M212, R12). Addressed to Clay at Lexington.
1 Henry Purviance.
2 James Morrison, Maddox Fisher, and David Sutton were at this time in partnership as Lexington merchants.

Promissory Note from George Slaughter

[July 15, 1811]

Attached to Agreement, November 14, 1810.

From James Smith, Jr.

Esteemed Friend 19 July 1811—

I have received your favour of 5 Inst[1] with my accot current annexed which accounts for my not hearing from you before, and in some measure, for my kinsman Richard R Smith not having received any answer to his letter[2] written you—I had given this Debt of Millers[3] to him to pay him money advanced for me, he being on my paper—& I expected you would have kept it entirely distinct from my business, having no Idea that my Account would appear as you have made it Miller wrote me 3 March last (,of his own accord) that the Notes were paid that he had assigned you in part—say 2000 Dollars, consequently Richard has been looking ever since to receive this money and altho' 4 months has passed away, it appears the money is not yet received, except 452.70. in November last, of which we had before no account—I have no doubt from Miller's statement that the money was paid & has been waiting for you to send for it all this time—& if you only knew the necessity there is for it I am confident you would have got it long since—I am teazed & worried every day about it, having assured him that it was a Debt perfectly secured (as you had informed me) and would be soon got—This is more than twelve months ago & more than nine months since I begged you to proceed without delay to get it—Miller mentions the sum as 2000 & you say 1700 I hope it will be found to be the former, & which I trust it will be in your power to send to Richd R Smith on receipt hereof that is, all but the 452.70. blended in my account—& which I shall actually have to dispose some Furniture &c. to pay him—having bonafide given him this Debt—Please to correspond with him with respect to the remainder of this Debt & you will oblige both him & me, by being particular & saying for what amount you have taken the Note with a good endorser & what time it will become due, as we may reasonably conclude, it has been some time since its date & as there must be considerable Interest due on the Notes—I hope & expect you have included the same—so that he will eventually receive the amount I mentioned to him that these 2 Notes of Miller's would produce which was 3000 Dollars with 2 years Interest being together 3360 $—You will understand that I have paid him the 452.70. & therefore let me request that you will accot with him for the remainder & not let it interfere with my account—as you must receive enough of Owens[4] to pay this—if not, I pledge my honour you shall be paid if any Ballance should appear—Richard will confidently look for the remainder of this money soon & let me beg it may be sent him if possible & as it may be in his power to negociate the Note you say you have taken for Miller's ballance, please to mention to him the Date of it, the endorser, and the Amount—I must now take the liberty of mentioning some charges in your Acct—which you have overlooked & I feel confident will not charge when I point them out to you—One is the Expences on Wrens[5] debt which you say in your letter of 26 Nov 1809,[6] that he left a Note with you upon a good man for enough to pay all the costs consequently I could not expect to be & ought not to be charged—

You now charge me with – – – – – – – – $48.53
You charge a Commission on money of Barry & Garrets say – 40—

this I feel confident you did not advert to when this charge was made That no suit was commenced—and they merely handed you the post Note as you were going to write me & they paid the premium—This circumstance I before noted to you—With respect to the Land I scarcely know what to say[7]—I had no Idea that so heavy a charge would have been made if nothing was got—I understood that all expences were to be paid—& that if the land was recovered you were to have a handsome compensation—It does not appear that the 100 Dollars you mention in one of your Letters having been offered to Boone[8] was ever paid—and therefore let me ask whether upon consideration of the whole of the circumstances you will not be of opinion that 100 Dollars for what you have done will not be sufficient—You know my situation and will believe that I even would not mention these things were I differently circumstanced—But every thing I have had in expectation seems frittered away, & I am left destitute I have now given up the Land (finding nothing to be got and Charles Copeland Esqr of Richmond is now negociating for me with Norvell to endeavor to get something for it. Therefore please to send me the Deed, if not already sent P first Opportunity—The two first Items, I conceive to be certainly oversights—as you never would with propriety charge a

Commission of 5 P-Cent on 800 Dollars, when no trouble whatever was had but merely enclosing the post Note—I observe a charge of 20 Dollars said to be for fee in a suit commen[ced] against me in Chancery by Owings—I cannot conceive [what] this can mean—Is it not possible for you to make som[e] settlement with the Owings—Will it not be better to endeavour a compromise and allow him for what he claims for damage so as to have the business settled & let me receive the ballance I may perhaps be able to get what is allowed from W. Smith[9] but if I do not it will be best to have the business settled—I want as speedily as possible to have every thing settled that I may get to doing something —& let me beg that you will attend to this & have it settled somehow—I observe it is more than two years since Judgment was obtained—Having written with freedom & with that friendship which I feel for you, Let me hope that you will take into consideration those things I have mentioned—.I make at least 188.53 Cents what I call charged more than I conceive (upon mature consideration you will be satisfied with) —but if you should not be of the same opinion—Let us consent that the present account should be squared, & I will be content—You will consider, that I have never received a shilling of Norvell for principal or Interest of a heavy Debt—I now loose the land & shall get but a small compensation for all my trouble (if any) I wish to look over these things and do what may appear to you to be just & right considering all circumstances— [Continued in margins]

I may note one other circumstance for your consideration, which is that you credit no Interest as being received on Jordan & Seits[10] Debt—there must have been some—Please to write me soon—Get all you possibly can from Owens—and as I have given W. Wren's debt to my Son John[11] for money advanced me & which I have assured him will be good—please to say exactly how it is circumstanced—the amount & if the security is good—I take it for granted that you will at least consent that

that [*sic*] this account you have handed me be now squared, or at least revised—that you will correspond with Rich R Smith with respect to Miller's debt, charging him with the 452.70 paid by me—that you will without delay give him every information with respect to it the amot &c—& the money as soon as possible for reasons before given—That you will settle Owens business for me—&c—& I can truly say I am with respect Yr Friend JAS SMITH JR

please to write me, & to Richd R Smith as soon as leisure will permit

ALS. DLC-TJC (DNA, M212, R12). Addressed to Clay at Lexington.

1 Not found. 2 Not found. 3 Robert Miller.

4 Thomas Deye Owings. 5 Woodson Wren. 6 Not found.

7 See above, Smith to Clay, *ca.* November 2, 1805; December 26, 1810.

[8] Letter not found. Several Boones, including Daniel and Squire (both of whom lost heavily in this connection), had claims to Kentucky lands.
[9] William W. Smith. When James Smith, Jr., had brought suit to collect the Owings note (see above, James Smith, Jr., to Clay, January 6, 1807, note; and Fayette Circuit Court, File 196), Owings had apparently filed a cross action (the latter suit not found). [10] John Jordan, Jr., and John A. Seitz. [11] John J. Smith.

From Ralph Peacock

Dear Sir Philadelphia 23rd July 1811

I have just recd. your favr of the 2nd Inst. to Mr. Wrenshall[1] and observe your proposal with respect to P. W & Cos.[2] demand against Pigman & Crow[3] I shall esteem it a particular favor your recovering my part of that debt on the conditions you propose—I hope in Octr. next you will give me a good Account of the final result of the controvercy with *Morrison*[4] as all the Estate of P W & Co. is transfer'd to me I shall thank you to give me an Acct. of any other claims belonging to them which may be under your Care Judge Allen and other in Paris have not finally settled their Acct.—

I have a demand for About $10,000 against Jno. Duhamel formerly a Doctor but of late a Store Keeper in Beards Town Kentucky his notes became due in 1806 & 7 since which I have not seen him thoh. he was in this City he slipt off to Baltimore where he vested his funds in a new supply for his store instead of paying his notes, since which I am informd he is gone down the river—some say he is in New Orleans[5] if you can secure this debt you shall have One Thousand Dollars of the proceeds waiting the pleasure of hearing fm you soon I am Dr. Sir Yrs most respectfully RALPH PEACOCK

Henry Clay Esqr.

ALS. DLC-TJC (DNA, M212, R12). Addressed to Clay at Lexington.
[1] Not found. [2] Peacock, Wrenshall and Company.
[3] Ignatius Pigman and Joshua Crow, at one time partners in a mercantile firm in Ohio County, Kentucky. Pigman had become a Methodist preacher in 1782 and moved to Kentucky about six years later, settling in that part of Hardin County from which Ohio County was formed. He had engaged heavily in land speculations until his failure in that business, after which he had moved to New Orleans around 1806. Crow remained in western Kentucky. [4] James Morrison.
[5] In 1802 Dr. John Duhamel had been a resident of Mississippi Territory; in 1813 he lived in Louisiana.

From John Graham

Dear Sir Washington 31st July. 1811.

I have had the pleasure to receive your Letters of the 18th and 19th July[1]—The first containing a Post Note of 300 Dol. payable to my order, came to hand last week:—the other, I did not get until yesterday after noon—I regret that I did not get it the day before, as it would have prevented me from doing what I now fear you will think wrong—

On that day I was called on by Mr Parrot[2] to act for you in relation to two waggon loads of your yarns which came on in bad order. The waggoners declared they had done all in their power to preserve them from injury and Mr Parrot told me the waggons and the covers to them were in good order—yet the yarns were wet. the waggoners assigned as the cause the irresistable violence of the "Rain storms" by which they were overtaken.

What to do I knew not. The waggoners appeared in forma pauperis and Mr Parrot seemed to think that in Justice they ought not to be made to pay for the damage done—as he thought, part of it must have been done before the yarns were put in their waggons and that the residue was the necessary and unavoidable consequence of exposure to such Rains as we have had during this month, with such a shelter as could be expected from a waggon—

I requested Mr P— to consult some of the principal Merchants of Geor. Town to know what was the usage there in cases of this kind—and I rode over myself to apply to Mr Ringgold[3] with a like view—He seemed to think the waggoners were bound to pay all damage—but Mr Coxe & Mr Smith[4] to whom Mr Parrot spoke on the subject were of a different opinion and they have both of them much to do with the transportation of goods. My own opinion was, that altho the waggoners were bound in Law there [*sic*] were not in equity and that had you have been here yourself you would have agreed to divide the loss with them. Under these circumstances I told Mr Parrot that he might settle with them upon that principle—and he tells me this morning that he has deducted from each of them 30 Dollars—

I am so much occupied this morning that I haven t time to give you the statement you ask for relative to Mr Ervings accounts[5]—I will therefore refer you to a "review" of Mr Smiths[6] address—which you will doubtless have seen in the National Intelligencer before this reaches you—

When you draw upon me for the Money you have sent me—make your Bill payable here—about the time the Post notes are payable at Phia— very truly Yours JOHN GRAHAM

ALS. DLC-TJC (DNA, M212, R10). Addressed to Clay at Lexington.
1 Not found.
2 Richard Parrott.
3 Tench Ringgold, a large landholder near Hagerstown, Maryland, one of the founders (at Georgetown in 1809) of the Columbian Society for the Promotion of Domestic Economy. Late in 1810 he and Nathaniel K. Heath, under the firm name, Ringgold and Heath, Washington, D. C., began manufacturing rope for the Navy. The partnership was dissolved on December 31, 1812.
4 Apparently Georgetown merchants.
5 George William Erving of Massachusetts, who had been sent abroad to adjust claims for spoliations on American commerce, submitted from Copenhagen on June 23, 1811, a report on his mission.
6 Robert Smith. See above, Graham to Clay, July 5, 1811.

Order from John Marshall

Lexington 5th. August 1811

Sir please to pay Mr. John Ferguson[1] the Amount of Any Sum that may remain In your hands, that I am intitled to, after paying Mr Coyle[2] 15$ . . and oblige yrs. &C JOHN MARSHALL

Mr Henry Clay

[Endorsement on verso][3]

Recd. of H. Clay the sum of seven pounds seven shillings and two pence which I have been credited with as on 20h. Sept. 1810 in a settlemt. with said Clay—30h. Sept. 1813 JOHN FERGUSON

ADS. DLC-TJC (DNA, M212, R15). Marshall was possibly Humphrey Marshall's brother who had moved to the Missouri country several years earlier.

1 Of Fayette County. 2 Probably Cornelius Coyle. 3 ES, in Clay's hand.

From Cornelius and John Comegys

Henry Clay Esqr. Baltimore August 8 1811

Dear Sir;

We have recd your favor of the [. . .] Ulto,[1] since when have recd. this letter from Wm Bradford which is handed to you for perusal[2]—Having fallen into bad hands we must get out of them as well as we can and must request that you will get the debt secured in any manner you may think proper by Land or otherwise and shall be satisfied if you will act for us as you would for yourself was the debt your own—if the Land he offers is unencumbered perhaps it may be worth something at some future day, and as you can judge better than we can at this distance we leave the affair entirely to your own judgment promising to confirm whatever you may do on our behalf—if Land is taken let the Deed be in the name of Cornelius Comegys only, John having no Interest in this debt, unless the Land will sell in this case sell it for whatever it will bring, unless you think it will be worth more by & by—with respect to Mr West[3] let the business rest, our CC. as Executor of B.C[4] will use his endeavor to have it adjusted to the satisfaction of Mr W with as little trouble to him as possible, beleiving [*sic*] from the view he has taken of it that some error has taken place in the Entries made by the late B.C. and we have no wish to prosecute the business to the prejudice of Mr West & only regret that the affair was not investicated before B.C died, persuaded that he intended what was right—yours truly C & J COMEGYS

PS. We hope you will be able to bring on the money from Clark & anderson in November—As soon as We can see the judges of the orphans Court will write Mr West & you

ALS. DLC-TJC (DNA, M212, R12).

[1] Date illegible. The letter has not been found.
[2] Writing from Greenville, Kentucky, July 18, 1811, to inform the Comegyses that he was bankrupt, Bradford offered to give up to $2,000 for his debt and pay the costs of the suit they had brought against him or, as an alternative, to give land as security until he could raise funds to pay his obligation in full. He stated that he had already talked to Clay, their attorney. ALS. DLC-TJC (DNA, M212, R12).
[3] Probably William West. [4] Benjamin Comegys.

Tax Refund

[August 12, 1811]

On the motion of Henry Clay who made it appear to the Court that he had paid five Dollars for the tax on one tract of land in 1809 which he ought not to have paid. It is ordered that he be entitled to a Credit with the Sheriff of this County for that sum to be deducted out of his tax for the present year.

Fayette County Court, Order Book 2, p. 408.

Guardians' Bond

[August 12, 1811]

[Bond for $20,000, signed by Clay, James B. January, and Manzey Q. Ashby, guaranteeing that "the above bound Moanzey Q Ashby his Heirs, Executors and Administrators, shall well and truly pay and deliver to John G. & Anne Ashby Orphans of Nathl. Ashby.—deceased, of whom he is appointed Guardian, all such Estate as now is or shall hereafter appear to be due from him to the said Orphan [*sic*], when he shall attain to lawful age."]

DS. Fayette County Guardians Bonds, 1803-17, p. 159. Nathaniel Ashby, who had died a month or so previously, was a Virginia veteran of the Revolution, an early settler near Lexington on the Woodford road. Dr. Manzey Q. Ashby was his eldest son and James B. January was the husband of Betsy, Nathaniel's eldest daughter.

Receipt from Porter Clay

13 Aug. 1811

Recd. of H. Clay exor of Tho. Hart one hundred and two dollars being compensation for forty five days attending to the Sale of a tract of land in Tennessee for said Hart's estate, and also the expence of advertizing the said land and laying off the same for purchasers. $102. PORTER CLAY

DS, in Clay's hand. DLC-TJC (DNA, M212, R15). Porter Clay for several years acted as agent for his brother in connection with lands belonging to the estate of Col. Thomas Hart.

Agreement with Robert Poage

[August 14, 1811]

An agreement between Robert Poague and H. Clay.

The said Poague hereby covenants & agrees to sell to the said

Clay his farm near Lexington on the waters of Hickman, at present in the possession of Nicholas Izard containing upwards of one hundred acres, for which he agrees to make the said Clay a clear title free from incumbrance with general warranty on demand.[1]

The said Clay agrees to pay the said Poague twenty dollars per acre for the said land, according to an actual survey thereof which is to be made, seven hundred dollars of which the said Clay agrees to pay in hand, and the balance in two years from this date.

The said Poague agrees to deliver possession of the said farm on or before the first day of March next, or sooner if the time of the said Izard shall be out sooner.

Witness our hands & seals this 14 Aug. 11. ROBT POAGE {L.S.}
Teste H. CLAY {L.S.}
THOS. TIBBATTS

ADS, signed also by Poage. DLC-TJC (DNA, M212, R15). Upon coming to Kentucky as a boy in 1775, Poage had settled in Harrodsburg. Later he lived for a time in Fayette County before moving to Mason. He was the commander of Poage's Regiment of Kentucky militia in the War of 1812.

1 Below, September 17, 1811.

To Caesar A. Rodney

My Dear Rodney Lex. 17 Aug 11.

The call of Congress will afford me an opportunity of having the pleasure to see you at a period somewhat earlier than I expected. We contemplate setting out for the City about the middle of October. The state of our foreign affairs has of course occasioned the call; and I presume it has arisen from the intimation of England that a total & absolute revocation of the French decrees will alone satisfy her, and that she will retaliate our non-importation law, if persisted in.[1] The fact of the revocation of those decrees seems now well established as to us. And, as the instructions on which Mr. Foster[2] has been negociating must have been made out when that fact was [certai]nly not known in England but was disbelieved, I can not but suppose now that it is ascertained, a revocation of the orders in Council as to us will follow.[3] I say *as to us,* for England will regulate her measures exactly by those of her adversary. If however she persists in them, and France is honest and sincere in her recent measures, I look upon War with G. Britain inevitable.

The papers have suggested that you are to be translated to the Bench, and Mr. Pinkney to be placed in your situation.[4] I need not say that if you desire a change of office if I can in any way promote your wishes it will give me great satisfaction. I have no doubt that your appointment will give in this quarter the most sincere

& general satisfaction. I transmit you some papers in relation to my brother, of which you may make such use as you think proper. I wish not to be understood as at all urgent or importunate. He writes me that letters of recommendation from Mess. Morgan[5] and Claiborne have been or will be forwarded.[6] He is married to a sister of the present Marshall of the District of Orleans, the daughter of a French gentleman, wealthy and respectable, residing in the Western District of that Territory;[7] and if the office of Register or Receiver of public monies in that quarter could be conferred upon him it would be agreeable. Yr friend H. Clay

ALS. DLC-Rodney Family Papers (DNA, M212, R22).

1 On August 5, 1810, the French foreign minister, the Duc de Cadore, had stated in a letter to the American Minister in Paris that the Berlin and Milan decrees were revoked and would have no effect after November 1, provided that the English should revoke their Orders in Council or that the United States should force England to respect American rights. President Madison had accepted the Cadore letter as evidence of revocation of the decrees and, in accordance with the terms of Macon's Bill No. 2, on November 10, 1810, had proclaimed a restoration of non-intercourse with Great Britain if that country failed to repeal its Orders in Council within three months. The French decrees actually had not been revoked, and England refused to repeal her Orders on the basis of the Cadore note. By an act of Congress, March 2, 1811, non-intercourse had been renewed with Great Britain.

2 Augustus John Foster.

3 The British Orders were revoked, but not until June 23, 1812, five days after the United States had declared war.

4 The death of Justice Samuel Chase, June 19, 1811, had created a vacancy on the Supreme Bench, which President Madison filled in November by the appointment of Gabriel Duval of Maryland, who had been serving as Comptroller of the Treasury. Rodney, angered by the apparent slight, resigned the post of Attorney General on December 5 and was succeeded by William Pinkney.

5 George W. Morgan, Treasurer of the Territory of Orleans.

6 William C. C. Claiborne's letter recommending John Clay for the post of Register in Orleans Territory is found in Rowland (ed.), *Official Letterbooks of W. C. C. Claiborne,* VI, 4.

7 John Clay's wife was Julie, daughter of Martin Duralde of Attakapas, and sister of Martin Duralde, Jr., United States Marshal of Orleans Territory. Another sister was the wife of Governor Claiborne.

From James Smith, Jr.

My Friend Philada 20h Augt 1811—

I shall very much regret that any thing I may have said in my last letter to you[1] should be so construed as a wish on my part to withhold any reasonable compensation for attending to my business —I wrote freely & perhaps more so than I ought, or should have done had my situation been differen[t] I had been been [*sic*] for sometime in daily expectation of receiving money from you supposing that you might have received Owings[2] & instead of which your Accot appeared against me with not only a ballance due you; but upwards of 450 Dollars I had to pay for money received for Miller's[3] Debt which I had assigned to R R Smith—This came heavy, because from the small Debts which I have reserved to pay my borrowed monies I very much fear I shall not be able to collect sufficient for the purpose previous to the time it must be done—for I am sorry to inform you that one Cross Creditor has brought suit against me & Judgment will be obtained the first week in October—consequently in order to put every body on a footing and disappoint him I shall previous to this make an assignment. & therefore all will then be out of my power—I was in hopes. that I should have been able by making comprises [*sic*] & acting in the most honourable manner possible to have satisfied every body considering the nature of my situation—& should have easily accomplished it had it not been for this unfeeling Creditor, who has really less reason to complain than any other having had thousand of pounds Sterling of my mony & has frequently overcharged me very considerably in Goods shipped—however to these things we must submit—I observe in your favour of 3d Inst[4] you say that you do not think it practicable with safety to me to make a compromise with Owings—If it is meant by this, that it will destroy any liens I have on W W Smith,[5] it will amount to nothing as he has again failed & nothing from him is to b expected— he being a man so devoid of principle or common honesty, as to have with held from me the payment of a Note he gave me in settlement when he first failed & gave me Millers & Owens Notes—He drew the Note payable whenever he was able & altho' he has been since many times able I never could find him willing & in hopes that some day I might so find him, no suit was ever brought & so the Debt of 1600 remains—I mention this merely by way of shewing that it is not worth while to protract a settlement with Owings on this Accot.—Perhaps they may be as anxious as we are to make a settlement. by making them an Allowance for the damaged Callicoes—if so—I should like it done in the best manner you possibly can, so that I may receive what may be coming previous to the time above mentioned—as my honour is pledged to return borrowed money which I fear it will not be in my power to do & this will distress more than any other circumstance as this was one of the Debts reserved for this particular purpose—You see my situation & will do what you can for me —If you think it best that this compromise be not attempted will you be kind enough to say in your next what amount you think I may caculate [*sic*] on being recovered—so that if nothing better can be done I may assign it your hands to somebody—but this I shall not do untill I hear from you & therefore if the money can possibly be got you will send it to me—As I before mentioned to you, I beg you will correspond with Richd R Smith with respect to Miller's Debt—I have paid him the sum mentioned in my Accot & charged to me & do hope he will soon receive the remainder from you, as he is at this moment in advance for me—& he desires me to request you will give him a statement of how the Debt stands and has been liquidated & also the amount of the Note you have taken for the ballance & when it will fall due that may [*sic*] calculate upon it

I am very sensible that you must have had trouble with Norvells[6] landed business, but I never knew you had expended monies—I knew you had offered monies to bring people forward—With respect to my looking to Norvell it is all in vain I fear—I must confess that I never had myself more trouble & vexation with any similiar circumstance or Debt. I note what you say with respect to the abatement of Commissn. on Barry & Garretts 800—this I believed to have been an over sight because as near as I can recollect this sum was handed to you by them to send to me without any suit &c—I trust when Owing's money is got, you will look over the Accot again & considering my situation make any further deducttion that may with propriety be made & if none such strikes you I am satisfied—You will gather from what I have said in this lengthy epistle how necessary it is for me to have the money from Owings if it can be got—& if not in time for me to know what amount I may calculate upon I am very respectfully Yr friend

JAS SMITH JR

If you have any Debt under your care to collect for[7] W. W. Smith (which I have reason to believe is the case) or if Mr Price[8] has—I wish you will (in confidence) say so, for I believe, were this the case I might prevail on him to give me an Order as he seems to regret not having paid me the Note mentioned—

ALS. DLC-TJC (DNA, M212, R12). Addressed to Clay at Lexington.
1 Above, July 19, 1811. 2 Thomas Deye Owings. 3 Robert Miller.
4 Not found. 5 William W. Smith. 6 Thomas Norvell.
7 The word "for" written over "from." 8 Andrew F. Price.

Property Deed from Henry Watkins

[September 3, 1811]

[Indenture by which Henry Watkins for five shillings sells to John Watkins and Henry Clay a tract of 1500 acres in Scott County, the property having been patented to Henry Watkins by the Commonwealth of Virginia. Title warranted only against claimants under Henry Watkins. Recorded in the office of the Clerk of the General Court, Frankfort, Kentucky, December 10, 1811.]

Bourbon Circuit Court, File 453. The property in this deed formed the subject of litigation in the suit of the heirs of Alexander McKinney *vs.* Clay and Isham Talbot, begun in Scott Circuit Court in April, 1814, continued through change of venue to the Bourbon Circuit Court in 1818, and finally decided in favor of Clay and Talbot by the

Court of Appeals in April, 1821. 10 Ky. *Reports* (3 A. K. Marshall) 569-70. McKinney (or McKenney), who had been attached to a regiment from Albemarle County, Virginia, during the Revolution, claimed 500 acres on a Treasury Warrant of later entry and survey than the Watkins claim.

To William Lytle

Dr Sir Lex. 10h. Sept. 1811.

Mr. Parker[1] presented us[2] with some bonds executed by you for the 300 Acres of land we were to sell to him. They are not drawn according to the intention of the parties, and I have in consequence drafted one, which will be sent you. We shall give our obligation to Mr. Parker to make him a title when your bond is paid. Acting as executors, we cannot part with the title until the consideration is paid, unless approved personal security residing in this State is given, in which case we shd. not object to making a deed.

I am extremely desirous to receive & give deeds for the property we exchanged.[3] I am now entirely ready to convey the Louisville estate according to contract, and I apprehend that unless I can get titles from you for the Lexington property I shall have some difficulty in receiving the purchase money *for a lot I have sold.* I shall set out about the 12*h. of Oct.* to *Washington.* Yrs.

H. CLAY

ALS. OCHP-Lytle MSS.
[1] John Parker. [2] The executors of Thomas Hart, Jr.
[3] See above, Clay to Lytle, June 22, 1811.

From David Trimble

Henry Clay Mount Sterling Sept 11th 1811—
Sir

I have been reflecting on the Subject of a Sale of the Sandy-Licks &c.[1]

The Sheriff will call a Jury, to find the right of property &c; and if they, should find for the trustees; and a Sale is not forced; the Sheriff will then return, levied on the land &c; and a Jury called &c who found the right of property in the trustees &c, and therefore no Sale—upon which return, you will loose your prior Lien on the Land in case the Graysoms [*sic*] should levy their 7,000 Dollar Executions before you levy again—.[2]

This will certainly be the result in Case my Idea is well founded, that an Execution does not bind the property after the return-day unless a Ven. Ex.[3] can issue thereon—I therefore conclude that you and the other Creditors will resolve to force a Sale at all hazards whether we purchase or not—To effect that purpose, it will be necessary for the Creditors to have security ready to offer to indemnify the Shff, and force a Sale; and to avoid disappointment it would be well to take one or more affidavits to prove that the persons offered as Securities, are fully sufficient and able to pay the Damage &c

If I go up, it will be, necessary for me to be empowered to direct a sale, execute any bond, and do any act which the creditors could do personally &c. Any omission in not being prepared to give security, or want of power to execute bonds will certainly prevent a sale, because, ("inter-nos.") the sheriff will do just as they tell him, unless compelled to do right—I know him well, and have no faith in him—he is under the controle of the Graysons—and besides they could *buy* him up for a trifle—

If we buy, the Licks, it will be necessary to have security ready, to give bond & security for the payment of the money in three months—

I mention these things now, fearing we may forget some of them when I come down—

Capt Geo. Johnston [*sic*] is here, just from Sand[y,][4] he thinks that the Graysons are not ab[le] to give bond and Security to the Amou[nt] of $5,000,—I think it is very probable the Licks will sell very Low— Johnston Says that A W Grayson has sold out none of his part of the Land, and he thinks that Alfreds[5] one fourth is worth double as much—as either of the other three fourths—

Inclosed you will find G. J. calculation &c—

I have examined the Act of assembly you alluded to in our last conversation—you will find it in Little's Edition 1 Vol page 572„ 3-§.13[6] —Let me request you to examine the Second Section of the Statute of frauds & perjuries Same Vol page 371[7]— Yours &c D. Trimble

P.S. I must request you not to omit bestowing some attention on the probability of your loosing your prior lien by not forceing a Sale at this time—

[Enclosure][8]

Capt. Geo. Johnstons Calculation and estimate of the Value of A. W. Graysons part of the Sandy Licks—Viz.

A W Graysons part (say one fourth) of the Land, exclusive of Salt Water, is worth at the least Lowest valuation $12,000—taking the same as he held it, at the date of his Deed to the trustees—

At a fair Sale Alfreds part ought to sell for 10 years purchase— The present rent is at least to be set down at 4,000 bushels—which at fifty cents per-bushel, will be two thousand Dollars—of course, at ten years purchase the property ought to be worth $20,000—If salt is worth one Dollar per-bushel, it will be worth double that sum—And the property ought not to be sold at less than ten years purchase—because that is the Lowest rate at which sales of perishable [*sic*] have been made—.

This calculation is made upon the Licks, as they are now worked by the proprietors—and tenants—

From the best information the Kenhawa works[9] will not (in three years from this time) be able to produce salt at less than $1„50 per bushell—, While at Sandy there is no probable cause operating which will increase in any great degree the expense of making salt, but It may be greatly decreased—in all probability—

I have at Mr Trimbles request dictated the above for him and H. Clay. If I could use my hand to write, I would make one more at length—Sept 11th 1811— GEO: JOHNSON

P.S. I wrote down Geo' Johnstons calculation without telling him how, or at what rate I myself estimated the property—You can Judge how far we agree—&c—&c—

After conversing with him on the subject I have resolved to buy at all events,—I am well satisfyed that I shall never have an equal chance to get property of the same value as Low—If you conclude not to make a purchase with me, I must intreat you to let me know as soon as possible, that I may make some arrangement to effect my object; I will try to buy the whole myself if you do not join me—

If we can force a sale of George's part[10] also—it is probable that he would sell out to us, for 6,000 or 7,000 Dollars—perhaps less— If not he will give us a handsome sum to sell him our title under the purchase— —

ALS. DLC-TJC (DNA, M212, R10). Trimble, a Virginian and a graduate of William and Mary College, practiced law in Mount Sterling, Kentucky. He later served in the War of 1812 and was a member of five successive Congresses, beginning in 1817.

1 See Property Deed, May 11, 1802.

2 Members of the Grayson family of Washington, Mason County, Kentucky, claimed from the time of the earliest surveys a large tract of land in this area.

3 A writ of *Venditioni Exponas,* under which the sheriff is bound to sell property in his hands.

4 MS. torn. 5 Alfred Grayson.

6 "Estates . . . holden or possessed in trust, shall be subject to like debts . . . of the persons, to whose use, . . . they were . . . holden or possessed, as they would have been subject to, if those persons had owned the like interest in the things holden or possessed."

7 Relative to fraudulent conveyances of land and other property.

8 DS, in Trimble's hand.

9 Extensive salt works were in operation along the Kanawha River in western Virginia. Their product actually sold for much less than the figure mentioned here. Maryida W. Mosby, "Salt Industry in the Kanawha Valley," (M. A. thesis, University of Kentucky, 1950), 21-22.

10 Probably George Grayson.

Bill of Sale from Squire M. and Elizabeth Barrett

[September 13, 1811]

Know all men by these presents that we Squire M. Barrett and

Elizabeth his wife administratrix of William Bacon[1] deceased have for value received bargained sold and delivered unto Henry Clay one slave named Maria, a mulatoe girl about ten or eleven years old. Burt [*sic*] we do not warrant the said slave against the claim of Christians heirs who have brought a suit for her amongst other slaves which is now depending in Fayette Circuit Court agt. the said Elizabeth.[2] Witness our seals this 13h. Septr. 1811.

Teste SQUIRE M. BARRETT {L.S.}
JOHN C. BACON[3] ELIZABETH BARRETT {L.S.}

DS, in Clay's hand. DLC-TJC (DNA, M212, R15). Squire M. Barrett and Elizabeth Bacon were married in Fayette County, Kentucky, February 9, 1811. Elizabeth had been the wife of William Bacon and one of the heirs of John Christian.

1 Scott County farmer, probably deceased in the fall of 1808.

2 John Christian's heirs *vs.* Elizabeth Bacon. Fayette Circuit Court, Order Book G, 310; H, 294.

3 Probably the son of William and Elizabeth Bacon.

Promissory Note from Edward Trabue

[September 14, 1811]

On demand I promise to pay to Henry Clay One hundred dollars for value recd. Witness my hand & seal this 14h. Septr. 1811.

EDWARD TRABUE {L.S.}

DS, in Clay's hand. Woodford Circuit Court, File 69. Trabue, an officer in the Revolutionary War, had come to Kentucky from Chesterfield County, Virginia, and settled in Woodford County near Tyrone, on the Kentucky River. In September, 1812, Clay won a judgment in a suit to collect this note.

Property Deed from Robert and Nancy Poage

[September 17, 1811]

[Indenture by which Robert Poage and Nancy, his wife, for the sum of $20 per acre, paid and acknowledged, sell to Clay a tract on the headwaters of Hickman Creek in Fayette County, the former residence of Poage, containing 124 acres by survey of Price Curd, made August 27, 1811, adjacent to properties of John H. Morton, Elijah Poage, and James Morrison. General warranty of title. Signatures of the Poages acknowledged in the Office of the Clerk, Fayette County, September 17, 1811.]

Attached to Tax Bill, *ca.* February 1, 1811.

Receipt from William Dudley

[September 18, 1811]

Attached to Tax Bill, *ca.* February 1, 1811.

Promissory Note to Robert Poage

[September 20, 1811]

Two years after date for Vallue received I promise to pay to Robert Poague [*sic*] Or Order, seventeen hundred And eighty Dollars, Witness my hand and seal this 20th day of September 1811

Teste HENRY CLAY {L.S.}

THOS CRAIG[1]

Fayette County Court, Deed Book F, 46. Signature of Clay acknowledged before the Fayette County Clerk the same date.

1 Probably of Woodford County.

Assignment by Robert H. McNair

30h. Sept. 1811.

For value recd. I do hereby assign to H. Clay two Judgments recovered by me against A. W. Grayson in Fayette Circuit Court, & direct all officers to observe his directions accordingly; but this assignment is without recourse to me or my representatives.

ROBT H MCNAIR

DS, in Clay's hand. DLC-TJC (DNA, M212, R15). McNair was a son of John McNair.

Land Patent

[September 30, 1811]

[Charles Scott, Governor of Kentucky, by virtue of an act for endowment of certain seminaries of learning and for other purposes,[1] grants to Henry Clay, assignee of William Bradford, who was assignee of the Justices of the County Court of Henderson, a tract of land containing 800 acres by survey dated January 27, 1810, in Hopkins County on the waters of Flat Creek, a branch of Pond River, together with appurtenances. Signed by Scott and by J. Bledsoe, Secretary of State.]

Ky. Register of Lands, Old Kentucky Grants, Book 17, pp. 451-52.

1 Enacted in 1798, the measure had appropriated 6000 acres south of the Green River to each of certain academies, the trustees of which were empowered to sell a portion of their respective grants. A supplementary statute on February 11, 1809, had extended the program to Henderson and several other counties, providing that the justices of the county courts should be authorized to procure like grants under similar regulations "for the use of seminaries of learning." Littell (comp.), *Statute Law of Kentucky,* II, 107-109; IV, 66.

Land Patent

[September 30, 1811]

[Charles Scott, Governor of Kentucky, by virtue of an act for endowment of certain seminaries of learning and for other purposes, grants to Henry Clay, assignee of William Bradford, who was assignee of the Justices of the County of Henderson, a tract of 400 acres, surveyed January 25, 1810, in Hopkins County on both sides of a branch of the Crab Orchard fork of Drakes Creek, a branch of Pond River, together with appurtenances. Signed by Scott and by J. Bledsoe, Secretary of State.]

Ky. Register of Lands, Old Kentucky Grants, Book 17, pp. 452-53.

Receipt from Nathaniel S. Porter

[*ca.* October 1, 1811]

Received of H. Clay esq. five Dollars for selling by auction Land belonging to the estate of H. Purviance deceased.
Sept 31st [*sic*] 1811. N S PORTER auctr.

ADS. DLC-TJC (DNA, M212, R15). Several months later Porter was named Captain of the Watch and Tax Collector for the town of Lexington.

Agreement with John Murphy

[October 1, 1811]

An agreement between John Murphy and H. Clay.

The said Murphy agrees to sell to said Clay his farm adjoining the said Clay's on Boone's road, supposed to contain about 25 Acres, with the appurtenances, for which he is to make the said Clay a deed with general warranty;[1] he also agrees to assign to said Clay a lease he procured from Mrs. Russell for the Acre of land on which the Horse mill stands, which Mill he hereby also covenants to sell to said Clay[2]—Of all which property he will deliver possession, with the appurtenances on or before the first day of March next, except the acre & horse mill, of which he will deliver immediate possession.

In consideration whereof the said Clay agrees to sell & convey by deed with general warranty to said Murphy, the farm he bought of Robert Poague [*sic*],[3] containing about 124 Acres, possession whereof he will deliver on or before the first day of March next, and he further agrees to pay said Murphy in merchandize at the difference of Currency & carriage six hundred dollars (including a bale of Cotton) immediately. No waste is to be done or permitted on either farm in the interim.

Witness our seals this first day of Oct. 1811.

JOHN MURPHY {L.S.}
H CLAY {L.S.}

ADS, signed also by Murphy. DLC-TJC (DNA, M212, R15). Murphy, a Methodist lay-leader in Lexington, later moved to Indiana, where he died in 1854.

1 Clay actually received fifteen acres, which became part of his estate, "Ashland." Property Deed, July 2, 1816.

2 On September 22, 1804, Murphy had rented from Mary Owen Russell one acre of land on which Murphy was to construct a mill for grinding grain. The land lay on the Boonesborough Road, opposite Murphy's home.

3 See above, Property Deed, September 17, 1811.

Assignment from John Murphy

1st. Oct. 1811.

I do hereby assign the within to H. Clay JOHN MURPHY

ES, in Clay's hand, KyLxT. Endorsement on verso of the agreement, dated September 22, 1804, between Murphy and Mary Owen Russell.

Bill of Exchange on Samuel Hopkins

Exchange for $4000. Lexington (K). 1st. Octr 1811

One hundred and thirty eight days after date pay to John Hart or order at the Union Bank in Baltimore this my second of exchange (the first of the same tenor and date not being paid) the sum of four thousand dollars, for value received.

Genl. Sam. Hopkins HENRY CLAY

Accepted Octor. 1st. 1811

SAML HOPKINS

[Endorsements on verso][1]

Pay to H. Clay or order value recd. JNO. HART.

10h. Oct. 1811.

Pay to Ralph Higginbothom Cashier of the Union Bank, or order for my use. 3 Feb. 1812. H. CLAY

ADS. Fayette Circuit Court, Hopkins *vs.* Purviance, File 414, Bundle 691.

1 The first, ES, in Clay's hand; the second, ADS. Despite Hopkins' initial acceptance of the bill, it was protested when the Union Bank of Maryland presented it for payment on February 19, 1812.

Bill of Exchange on Samuel Hopkins

Exchange for $9504. Lexington (K) 1st. Octr. 1811.

Two hundred and fifty eight days after date pay to John Hart or order at the Union Bank in Baltimore this my first of exchange (the second of the same tenor and date not being paid) the sum of nine thousand five hundred and four dollars, for value received.

Genl. Sam. Hopkins. HENRY CLAY

[Endorsement][1]

Accepted Octor. 1st. 1811

SAML HOPKINS

18 June 1812. JGN.P.[2] nonPayment–

[Endorsements on verso][3]

Pay to H. Clay or order Value recd. JNO. HART.

Pay to Ralph Higinbotham [*sic*] Esqr. Cashier of the Union Bank or order for my use. 6 June 1812. H. CLAY

ADS. Fayette Circuit Court, Hopkins *vs*. Purviance, File 414, Bundle 691.
1 AES. 2 John Gill, Notary Public of Baltimore.
3 The first, ES in Clay's hand; the second, AES. The bill was protested when the Union Bank of Maryland presented it for payment on June 18, 1812.

Deed of Trust from Samuel Hopkins

[October 1, 1811]

[Whereas Henry Clay has this day drawn on Samuel Hopkins of Henderson County two bills of exchange payable at the Union Bank in Baltimore, one for $4000 payable 138 days after date, and the other for $9504 payable in 258 days, which bills are accepted by Hopkins, now on these premises and for five shillings, paid and acknowledged, Hopkins conveys to Clay 1700 acres in Henderson's grant, being part of lots no. 40 and 41, on which Hopkins now resides, together with appurtenances; also the slaves Lewis, aged about 42, Winney, Ormond, Lydda, Kessey, Crissey, Dick, Linda, John, Rose, Nancy, and Fanny, which ten last named are the children of Lewis and Winney; also George and Linda and their children, Charlotte and her child China, Matty, Letty, Clarissa, Sam, Nicholas, Aaron, and Obay; also James and Clarissa and their children, Fanny, Crilla, Phebe, William, Jim, Dolly, Milly, and Patsey; also Richard and his children, Peter, Richard, Phil, Isaac, and Lucy, with the increase of the females—In trust that if Hopkins fails to pay either or both of the bills of exchange according to tenor, Clay is to sell at public auction the land and the slaves as necessary to pay the bills, rendering any balance to Hopkins. Hopkins agrees to produce the slaves at the place of sale as required, and Clay agrees to execute the trust to the best of his ability. Signatures of the parties witnessed by Robert Crockett[1] and Robert Wickliffe, who acknowledge the act before Achilles Sneed, Clerk of the Court of Appeals, October 7, 1811.]

Ky. Court of Appeals, Deed Book O, 170-71.
1 Of Jessamine County, later captain of a militia company in the War of 1812.

Receipt for Bill of Exchange on Presley Neville

[October 1, 1811]

Recd. a bill of exchange on Col. Neville of Pittsburgh for the within land purchased at the sale of Moale agt Purviance 1st. Octr. 1811—(A quit claim sale) H. CLAY

AES. DLC-TJC (DNA, M212, R15). On verso of a memorandum of a document, dated January 17, 1809, whereby Henry Purviance of Lexington agreed to sell to Robert Pollard of Jefferson County 200 acres of land in that County and, in return, Pollard agreed to pay $600, with interest, to Samuel Moale of Baltimore, who held a mortgage on the land.

Order Drawn by Joseph Beard

Sir/ Octr. 2d. 1811

Please To pay the Bearer Mr. Charles Mc.Gowan one Hundred Dollars & Charge the above To F.. Cosby & you Will oblige your Obt. Huml. Servt. JOSEPH BEARD Ex.

Henry Clay Esqr. for Sarah Beard-dd[1]

$100

DS. DLC-TJC (DNA, M212, R15). See above, Agreement, December 8, 1806.

1 Joseph Beard, executor for Sarah Beard, deceased.

Memorandum from Jesse Bledsoe

Octobr. 4th. 1811

In a negotiable note this day given by myself & H. Clay for $300 to Isaac Shelby. payable at the Lexington Branch Bank in twelve months he is my scecurity [*sic*] J: BLEDSOE

ADS. DLC-TJC (DNA, M212, R15).

Receipt from Hawes Graves by David Todd

Lexington October 4th. 1811.

Received of John Hoomes of Virginia at the Bowling Green by the hands of Henry Clay Esq. forty four dollars eighty cents amount of order and interest drawn by James Shelby[1] on Cuth. Banks and received by said Hoomes herewith enclosed—Which credit I was entitled to on a Judgment by Hoomes against me.[2]

HAWES GRAVES
by his atto. DAVID TODD

ADS. DLC-TJC (DNA, M212, R15). Graves, a resident of the northern district of Fayette County, was a brother of Benjamin, George, and Thomas C. Graves.

1 Eldest child of Governor Isaac Shelby.

2 The following crossed out at this point: "(which is paid up)."

Receipt from Reuben Bailey

5 Oct. 1811.

Recd. of H. Clay Twelve dollars for bringing from Bedford or thereabouts in Pennsylvania four Merinos being the same four which James Adams brought from N. York for said Clay.

REUBEN BAILEY.

DS, in Clay's hand. DLC-TJC (DNA, M212, R15). Bailey was possibly a Kennett, Pennsylvania, farmer, brother of Joshua Bailey, Philadelphia merchant.

From Humphrey Marshall

October 7th 1811.

H. Marshall, has received the note of Mr. Clay,[1] on the subject of Mr. Priestmans business[2]—and is compelled to say (with what reluctance it is needless to express) that he is not Just now ready to settle that business—owing to his being obliged to divert his funds to calls more closely pressed—nor will it be in his power before Mr. Clay leaves the state. Without a positive pledge, he will presume to say the money shall be remitted to Mr. Clay by Christmas next, should this meet the views or answer the purpose of Mr. Clay.

AN. KyLxT. Addressed to Clay at Frankfort.
1 Not found. 2 Possibly involving William Priestman, Philadelphia merchant.

Promissory Note from Alexander Macy and Will Trigg

[October 9, 1811]

Two years after date for value received we promise to pay to H. Clay one thousand dollars with interest from the date; but if punctual payment is made of the principal, the interest is to be remitted.

Witness our hands & seals this 9h. Oct.—1811

his
ALEXR. × MACY {L.S.}
Mark

Teste.
W. P. GREENUP[1]

WILL TRIGG {L.S.}

DS, in Clay's hand. DLC-TJC (DNA, M212, R15). Macy and Trigg were residents of Franklin County. 1 Son of ex-Governor Christopher Greenup.

Order Drawn by John Hart

[October 10, 1811]

Attached to Bill of Exchange for $4000, October 1, 1811.

Receipted Account with Benjamin Stout

Henry Clay Esqr. [October 10, 1811]

1809	To Benjn. Stout	Dr
July 15th	To 1 Carriage whip pr J P Wagnon — —	0.. 6..0
Sepr 5 — —	1 bridle 7/6, 1 halter 6/ — — —	..13..6

Date	Item	Amount	Total
26 --	1 buckskin Saddle with housin and Plated Irons --	12.. 0..0	
" --	1 Plated Sharp bridle -----	2.. 2..0	
Octr 17 --	1 blindbridle 7/6, 2 hame-strings 1/6 ---------	0.. 9..0	
" --	1 backband 9/. 1 Crooper & hipstraps 13/6 -------	1.. 2..6	
			15..13..6
24 --	1 bridle 22/6. girth Hoops 4/6 } pr W T Banton		
"	1 Sirsingle & altering 1 do 8/9 } pr W T Banton	1..15..3	[*sic*]
"	1 girth Strap & Repairs -- 1/6 } pr W T Banton		
27 --	Silk lash to whip --------	.. 1..1	
1810			
Jan 10 --	new pad 12/ lineing pillion 3/	..15..0	
"	Portmanteau girth & Strap --	.. 5..3	
" --	Martingail brestplate & Straps	.. 7..6	
" --	buckle on Sturrup ------	.. 0..9	
" --	2 Crooper @ 3/. 1 bridle 7/6	..13..6	
			3..18..4
16 --	1 pair of portmanteau Straps -	.. 5..3	
" --	1 Sirsingle 9/. 1 do 6/. ----	..15..0	
Feb 3 --	1 Martingail pr T Pindle[1] --	..16..6	
27 --	2 backbands pr yor overseer[2]	.. 7..6	
" --	1 blind bridle 9/. 4 hame-strings 2/ ---------	..11..0	
Mar 31 --	1 blindbridle ---------	..12..0	
Apr 12 --	1 Collar ----------	..15..0	
			4.. 2..3
Octr 2 --	2 Carriage bits ---------	2..10..3	
Nov 14 --	1 Martingail brestplate ----	6 0	
" --	1 pair of Stirrup leathers 4/6 Stufing pad 1/6 ------	.. 6..0	
" --	1 pair of trunk straps 9/ 1 bridle 30/	1..19..0	
" --	1 Martingail & Collar 16/6. 1 bridle 7/6 ---------	1.. 4..0	
" --	1 pair Suspenders 3/. 1 girth 3/ ---------	6 0	
1811 " --	1 Sirsingle 6/. Strap to tar bucket 1/6 ---------	.. 7..6	
			6..18..9

May 6 --	Mending whip ---------	6..9	
July 22 --	1 girth 3/9. Sirsingle 6/. Sturrups 4/6 --------	..14..3	
26 --	1 pair of brich bands ----	2 14 0	
" --	2 blind bridles 21/. 2 belly bans 10/6 ---------	1. 11..6	
" --	6 hamestrings 4/6. 1 whip 7/6	..12..0	
" --	1 pair of Check lines ----	18 0	
" --	1 bridle 12/. 1 halter 6/ ---	..18..0	
" --	1 Collar ----------	..12..9	
			8.. 1..3
Augt 16 --	1 girth 3/9. 1 sirsingle 6/. 1 pair of Sturrups 4/6 ------	..14..3	
Sepr 6 --	1 [. . .][3] ----------	2.. 5..0	
26 --	Peasing Carriage lines ---	7 6	
			3.. 6..9
			£ 43.. 0..4
Octr 9th	1 pair of Sturrup leathers	4 6	
"	Repairs to Saddle & Martingail	.. 2..3	
"	1 portmanteau girth -----	5 3	
	1 sirsingle ---------	6 0	18 0
			£ 43..18..4

[Endorsement on verso][4]
Recd. payment. 10 Oct. 1811 BENJN. STOUT

D. DLC-TJC (DNA, M212, R15).

1 Thomas Hart Pindell, the son of Dr. Richard Pindell and a nephew of Lucretia Clay. The young man had come to Lexington in 1807 and had been graduated from Transylvania University in 1809. He was subsequently active as a merchant, speculator in real estate, manufacturer of hempen products, and banker.

2 James Glenn. 3 Word illegible. 4 ES, in Clay's hand.

Property Deed from William and Elizabeth Lytle

[October 10, 1811]

[Indenture by which William Lytle and Elizabeth, his wife, of Hamilton County, Ohio, for $20,000 current money of Kentucky, paid and acknowledged, convey to Henry Clay a tract in Fayette County on the waters of Elkhorn, in Lexington, bounded as follows: beginning on Short Street at the western corner of James Morrison's brick house, which he now occupies, thence northeast at right angles to Short Street 75 feet, thence at right angles northwest 32 feet 10 inches, thence at right angles northeast 156 feet to First, or Middle, Street, thence with the latter street northwest 59 feet 10 inches to Tibbatts' lot, thence with Tibbatts' line southwest 231 feet to Short Street, thence with Short Street southeast

92 feet 8 inches to the beginning, including the building now known as the Kentucky Hotel, occupied by William Satterwhite, which tract was conveyed to Lytle by four separate deeds, one from William Morton and wife dated January 4, 1797, one from Frederick Ridgely and wife dated March 28, 1799, one from James Morrison and wife dated October 9, 1811, and one from Thomas January and wife dated October 10, 1811. General warranty of title. Signatures of the Lytles acknowledged before J. D. Young, Clerk of Fayette County, October 11, 1811.]

Fayette County Court, Deed Book F, 116-17.

Agreement with William Satterwhite

[October 10, 1811]

An agreement between W. Satterwhite & H. Clay.

The said Clay has heretofore leased to the said Satterwhite a part of the establishment called the Kentucky Hotel,[1] and the said Satterwhite has by the assent of the said Clay taken that part of the said establishment which Jo. Downing rented of the said Clay,[2] so that he has now the entire possession of the whole establishment with the exception only of the office occupied by the said Clay.[3] For the part so leased and possessed by the said Satterwhite he covenants to pay the paid Clay six hundred and ten dollars and thirty three Cents, for the use thereof until the 15h. day of April next, which said sum the said Satterwhite is to pay on the said 15h. day of April next.

And the said Clay covenants and agrees to rent to the said Satterwhite the whole establishment of the Kentucky Hotel (including the afd office) for the term of one year, commencing the 15h. day of April next. For which the said Satterwhite agrees to pay to the said Clay the sum of One thousand dollars in equal quarterly payments.

It is further agreed & understood that the said Clay retains the liberty or right of distraining or re-entering the premises, if non-payment should be made of the rents.

The said Satterwhite also agrees to surrender the premisses on the expiration of the term in as good order as he receives them, natural decay & fire excepted. Witness our seals this 10h. Oct. 1811.

H. CLAY {L.S.}
WM SATTERWHITE {L.S.}

[Endorsements on verso][3]

Upon a settlement this day made of all accounts whatever (except H. Clay's tavern account from the 18h. day of last month) the rent due said Clay on the 15h. day of April last is paid and satisfied, and the rent commencing on that day remains unpaid. 18h. Septr. 1812.

H. CLAY
WM SATTERWHITE

We have this day settled all accounts whatever (except the repairs which the said Satterwhite is to have done upon the Hotel, the manure which he is to have cleared away in front of the stable &c) and he has paid me up in full for the rent. 15h. April 1813.

H. CLAY
WM. SATTERWHITE

ADS, signed also by Satterwhite. Fayette Circuit Court, File 823.

1 The lease, probably drawn early in June, 1811, has not been found. Several years earlier Satterwhite had operated the Eagle Tavern, apparently in the buildings that became successively Travelers' Hall and the Kentucky Hotel.

2 Rental Agreement, April 5, 1811. 3 See above, Agreement, April 6, 1811.

4 Both AES, signed also by Satterwhite.

Assignment from Joseph Pollard, Jr., and William Meriwether

[October 11, 1811]

Pay the within to H. Clay or order 11th Octr 1811

JOSEPH POLLARD JR.
WM. MERIWETHER

True copy. DLC-TJC (DNA, M212, R15). Endorsement on bill of exchange for $696, drawn at Lexington, October 11, 1811, by Benjamin R. Pollard on Presley Neville in favor of Joseph Pollard and William Meriwether.

Property Deed by Executors of Thomas Hart, Jr., to John Parker

[October 11, 1811]

[Hart's executors, including Clay, convey to John Parker for $15 per acre, current money of Kentucky, 300 acres of land on Thomas's Run, a branch of the South Elkhorn.]

Fayette County Court, Deed Book F, 124-25.

Property Deed by Executors of Thomas Hart, Jr., to David Bryant

[October 11, 1811]

[Hart's executors, including Clay, convey to David Bryant of Fayette County for $324 current money of Kentucky, 27 acres of land on South Elkhorn and Thomas's Run.]

Fayette County Court, Deed Book F, 126-27.

Property Deed from Thomas and Catharine Bodley

[October 11, 1811]

This Indenture made this Eleventh day of October in the year of Our Lord, One thousand eight hundred & Eleven Between Thomas Bodley & Catharine his wife of the County of Fayette And Commonwealth of Kentucky, On the One Part, And Henry Clay of the County and Commonwealth aforesaid, of the other Part. Witnesseth: That the Said Thomas Bodley & Catharine his wife for, And in Consideration of the sum of One thousand pounds Current Money of Kentucky, to them in hand Paid the receipt whereof is hereby acknowledged: have granted, bargained & sold And by these Presents do grant, bargain. Sell & Confirm Unto the Said Henry Clay his heirs and assigns all that tract Or Parcel of land Situate & being in the County of Fayette On the waters of Elkhorn & Hickman near Lexington Containing One hundred & twenty three acres be it more or less And bounded as follows Towit: Beginning at a large honey locust On the Side of Boons road. nearly opposite the house formerly Occupied by Thomas Irvin[1] for a Still house, thence south thirty degrees west. Eighty Six Poles to a Stake. On the line of Mansfield Tract & Corner to the land formerly the Property of George Nicholas decd. (now Sd Clays)[2] thence with the line thereof South forty five degrees west. One hundred & ninety two poles to a locust Post, thence North thirty One And A half degrees west Sixty four Poles to a Stake, thence North forty five degrees East. Sixty five Poles to a Stake on Boons road. thence with Said road South forty five degrees East. two hundred & thirty Poles to the Beginning. being the same land Conveyed to Said Bodley by Thomas Hart & wife by deed dated the 2nd day of April 1800. duly recorded in the Clerks Office of Fayette County, & was Sold by Said Bodley to Cuthbert Banks, who transfered it to Said Clay—Together with all and Singular the Premises thereunto belonging Or in any wise appertaining, to have and to hold the land hereby Conveyed with the appurtenances Unto the Said Henry Clay his heirs & assigns forever: &. the Said Thomas Bodley and Catharine his wife for themselves their heirs, Executors, And Administrators the aforesaid tract of land & Premises. Unto the said Henry Clay his heirs Or Assigns. against the Claim Or Claims of all and every Person Or Persons whatsoever do & will forever defend by these Presents. In Witness whereof, the Said Thomas Bodley & Catharine his Wife have hereunto Set their hands & Seals the day & date first above written.

Acknowledged
in Presence of

THOS BODLEY {SEAL}
CATHARINE H BODLEY {SEAL}

Fayette County Court, Deed Book F, 120-21. Recorded October 12, 1811. This was part of the estate, "Ashland." See above, Agreement, September 13, 1804.
1 Irwin. 2 See above, Bill, June 18, 1810.

To Thomas Bodley

[October 12, 1811]

I have sold to Thomas Bodley all my Interest in a Survey of Darby and Marie of 30,000 acres on Johnsons fork of Licking[1] which was allotted to me in a division amongst the Creditors of Robert Morris[2] &c. and I will at any time make said Bodley a Conveyance or relinquishment, without makeing myself liable in any respect whatever.

Witness my hand & Seal this 12th day of October 1811.

Teste. H. Clay {Sealed}

ADS. KyHi.
1 The survey for Daniel Darby and John Marie, both of Philadelphia, had been made March 16, 1784. Johnson's Creek joins the Licking River in Robertson County.
2 The Philadelphia financier, who suffered great losses from land speculations.

From Peyton Short

Dear Sir: [October 21, 1811]

Since putting into your hands my reflections on the subject of the Mobille navigation &c. I have thought that it might be in my power to afford you some information in regard to the country through which that navigation would pass; and with that view have sent you the above extract from my Journal of the tour, which was made in the years 1809 and 1810. Should the remarks, which I have made on that subject afford any additional intelligence beyond which [*sic*] you already possess, I shall be happy in having communicated it to you, if not, I pray you to excuse the trouble, which I shall have given you in the perusal of the foregoing sheets.

In the course of my observations on the resources of that country I forgot to mention two important articles in the commercial world —I mean staves and headings (and many others no doubt have been pretermitted which might have been mentioned) with which that country could supply the world as the white oak of immense bulk forms one of the principal growths on the bottoms of the Tombeckbee and Alabama rivers as well as the low grounds emptying into the river and I might also add of all the most fertile highlands. It will afford me great pleasure to hear from you whenever you can make it convenient to write to me. I probably may descend the Mississippi this winter. If I should Mr. Wilkins[1] will know where to forward any communications with which you may be so good as to favor me. I am dear sir Your friend &c. Peyton Short.

Reuben T. Durrett, [Peyton Short's Journal of a Tour to Mobile, Pensacola, etc., November 12-December 31, 1809], a paper read before The Filson Club, April 4, 1904, pp. 13-15. Published in Ohio Historical and Philosophical Society, *Quarterly Publications,* V (1910), 13-15. The letter addressed to Clay is included at the end of the account.

1 Charles Wilkins.

To James Madison

[*ca.* November, 1811]

H. Clay presents his respects to Mr. Madison, & sends him a bottle of wine made from the grape of the Island of Madeira, which has been cultivated in Kentucky. He regrets that the specimen is not more ample, but it is all that he could have conveniently brought in his carriage.

H. C. had the mortification to have been present some years ago at the exhibition at Mr. Jefferson's table of some Kentucky wine which, having been injured in the process of fermentation, was of a most wretched quality. The sample now sent will he flatters himself restore in some degree the credit of the wine of that State.

Wednesday morning

AN. Owned by Thomas D. Clark, Lexington, Kentucky. Undated, but endorsed, presumably by Madison: "Clay H. 1811."

Speech Accepting Speakership of the United States House of Representatives

GENTLEMEN [November 4, 1811]

In coming to the station which you have done me the honor to assign me—an honor for which you will be pleased to accept my thanks—I obey rather your commands than my own inclination. I am sensible of the imperfections which I bring along with me, and a consciousness of these would deter me from attempting a discharge of the duties of the chair, did I not rely confidently upon your generous support.

Should the rare and delicate occasion present itself when your Speaker should be called upon to check or control the wanderings or intemperance in debate, your justice will, I hope, ascribe to his interposition the motives only of public good and a regard to the dignity of the house. And in all instances, be assured, gentlemen, that I shall, with infinite pleasure, afford every facility in my power to the despatch of public business, in the most agreeable manner.

Washington *National Intelligencer,* November 6, 1811. Published also in *Annals of Cong.,* 12 Cong., 1 Sess., XXIII, 330-31; and *Niles' Weekly Register,* I (November 9, 1811), 153. When the House assembled on November 4, Clay was elected Speaker on the first ballot.

From Bartlet and Cox

Henry Clay Esqr. New Orleans 11 Novr. 1811.
Dear Sir

We received early in Octo: a note on Pigman & Crow for 90. odd £ which was presented for Payment, and the amount acknowledged & of course assumed, conditioned that a payment Pigman beleivd had been made, but if that payment could not be established to our satisfaction, he would pay us the whole amount but subsequently on receipt of an account claiming upwards of £400.,, My. Cy.[1] Pigman appeared astonished at the demand & assures us he is well convinced a large proportion if not the whole debt was arranged many years since with Peacock, Wrenshall & Co. you have annexed a Copy of his reply to a note demanding payment.

a Copy

"Messrs. Bartlet & Cox—New Orleans novr. 7. 1811.—On the Subject of Peacock & Wrenshalls claim—I can only say that a transaction stated to have taken place in the last century and bought [*sic*] forward at the end of the 11: year of the present & my not having heard of such a claim by word or letter I am fully persuaded for the last 12 years, and having no person or papers with me which can throw any light on the subject—I can only add what I said to you in conversation that I have appropriated a claim of about $5000 to pay sundry claims in Philadelphia & Said claim of $5000 not having been returned to me, nor any information given of its failure I considered that claim settled." Your's

(Signed) "Ignatius Pigman"

the above claim was at the request of Pigman & Crow's creditors (as Pigman states) given in trust to & and when he left the state of Maryland he fully believed all the Creditors were satisfactorily paid—He has now wrote to some friend in Philadelphia requesting special information on the subject, on receipt of which further communications will be made to us & of course to you—As we have a good opinion of Pigman's honesty think there will be no difficulty in recovering the claim if not already settled which we almost believe is the case.

General Hopkins advises that on the strength of funds in our hands he has given an acceptance at the Union Bank of Baltimore for $4000. Pble the 15. Feby. next—altho he will not have that sum in our hands we have assured him of a remittance to you for the purpose of taking the same up provided Bills of Exchange can be purchased, which at this time cannot be done on any terms—Such is the state of the commercial world that, not a merchant can be found in New Orleans who will execute an order to be drawn for without a stong [*sic*] guarratee [*sic*]

Our convention met on monday the 4h Novr. Inst:[2] but owing to the Sickness adjourned until the 18h.—One member Bernard Marigny about 24 or 25 years of age & having more understanding than all the other members protested against the adjournment & called a meeting on the 7h. when 17 members met but not forming a Quorum dispersed—& of course nothing is [. . .][3] done in constitution making—When one is fram[ed] it will be no doubt on the Nepolean System & such I hope your Honble body will reject

The occurrances at Washington would be thankfuly received by Dear Sir Your Ob. Sts BARTLET & COX.

ALS. DLC-TJC (DNA, M212, R12). The firm, Bartlet and Cox, had been Hart, Bartlet and Cox.

1 Maryland currency.

2 The Louisiana Constitutional convention met in New Orleans.

3 MS. torn; one or two words missing.

Presentation of Petition for Matthew Lyon

[November 13, 1811]

Washington *National Intelligencer,* November 16, 1811. Clay, as Speaker, communicated numerous petitions to the House of Representatives not noted in these volumes; however, in presenting that of Matthew Lyon, seeking reimbursement of a heavy fine inflicted under the Sedition Act, Clay was representing a Kentuckian. Lyon, an Irish immigrant who had served as an officer in the Revolution, had edited for a brief period an ultra-democratic newspaper, served in the Vermont legislature for some ten years, and entered Congress in 1797 as an anti-Federalist. His opposition to the Adams Administration had brought him conviction for libel, with a fine of $1000 and jail confinement for four months. In 1801 he had moved to Livingston County (now Lyon), Kentucky, where he had founded the town of Eddyville. He had acquired large land and slave holdings, served in the Kentucky legislature, 1802, and returned to Congress, 1803-1811. He petitioned for the refund of his fine immediately after his retirement from Congress, but legislation meeting the request was not enacted until July 4, 1840, many years after his death.

Ruling on House Discussion of a Tax Resolution

[November 15, 1811]

Ruling on a protest against comment in the House of Representatives on a resolution relating to a provision for an additional duty on coarse hemp and flax, Clay, as Speaker, decided that although all tax proposals were required to be discussed in Committee of the Whole, the restriction did not apply in this case, since the resolution was merely an instruction to a committee to inquire into the expediency of laying an additional tax. Washington *National Intelligencer,* November 16, 1811; *Annals of Cong.,* 12 Cong., 1 Sess., XXIII, 351.

Property Deed from Samuel Smith and Wilson Cary Nicholas

[November 16, 1811]

This Indenture made this 16th. day of November, 1811 Between Samuel Smith of Maryland, and Wilson C. Nicholas of Virginia of the one part and Henry Clay of Kentucky of the other part Witnesseth that the said Smith and Nicholas, for and in consideration of the sum of twenty five dollars per acre heretofore agreed to be paid by the said Clay for the land hereafter described, have granted bargained sold & delivered and by these presents do grant bargain sell and deliver unto the said Henry Clay a certain farm and tract of land near the town of Lexington in the State of Kentucky, purchased by George Nicholas deceased of Charles Wilkins, & conveyed by Commissioners to the said Smith and Nicholas, under a decree of the Circuit Court of Fayette[1] in the said State of Kentucky, containing Two hundred and fifty five acres and bounded as follows, to wit, Beginning at a stake hickory and walnut corner to Elisha Winter's land,[2] thence running along James Trotter's line South thirty degrees West 194 perches to a blue ash corner of Trotter's line, thence along Hall's[3] line South 63 degrees East twenty two perches to a blue ash the corner of said Hall's line and on Tate's creek road, thence along said road South 23 degrees East fifteen perches to a post, thence along Poage's[4] line South 60 degrees East 278 perches to two hickories corner to the heirs of John Todd deceased settlement and preemption land, then with the said settlement and preemption North 30 degrees East 85½ poles to a post the corner of Elisha Winter's land thence with said Winter's line North 45 degrees West 195½ poles to a post corner to said Winter's, thence with said Winter's line to the place of beginning North thirty one and a half degrees West one hundred and thirty one poles, with the appurtenances: To have, and to hold, the said tract of land with the appurtenances to the said H. Clay his heirs and assigns forever in fee simple: And the said Smith and Nicholas do covenant and agree to and with the said Clay that they will make to him such further or other conveyance better to secure to him the title hereby conveyed or intended to be conveyed as Counsel may advise. And the said Nicholas doth covenant and agree to and with the said Clay that he will warrant and defend the right and title to the tract of land before described to the said Clay his heirs and assigns against the claim of all and every person whatsoever.

In testimony whereof the said Smith and Nicholas have hereunto set their hands and seals the day and year first mentioned.

Sealed & Delivered S. SMITH {L.S.}
In presence of WILSON C. NICHOLAS {L.S.}
JAMES MORRISON
GEO: M. BIBB.
as to the ackt. of Gen. Smith.

DS, in Clay's hand. DLC-TJC (DNA, M212, R10). Signature of Nicholas acknowledged in the Court of Hustings of Richmond, Virginia, March 19, 1812; signature of Smith identified by the witnesses to the indenture, in Fayette County Court, April 13, 1812. Recorded in Fayette County Court on the latter date. Clay already had possession of this property, part of "Ashland."

1 See above, Bill, June 18, 1810, note.

2 Which Clay now owned, by deed of October 11, 1811.

3 Moses Hall, who had come to Kentucky as a young man around 1780 and invested heavily in land. In addition to his Fayette County holdings, he owned extensive property adjacent to the town of Shelbyville, where he resided after 1792. Hall had sold his land adjoining Clay to John McNair, into whose estate the property had now passed. Clay subsequently by deed of December 7, 1830, purchased part of the tract from George W. Morton, McNair's son-in-law.

4 Robert Poage.

From William Plumer

Dear Sir, Epping[1] November 20, 1811.

Permit me sincerely to congratulate you & the nation upon your elevation to the Speaker's chair. An office you did not want, but an office that wanted you. Every well informed man, conversant with a numerous legislative assembly feels the necessity of having a man of talents, extensive information, & prompt decision to preside over their discussions & proceedings. Without such a presiding officer neither the dignity of the house, can[2] be supported, or the business of the public performed, with propriety & dispatch. From the acquaintance I had with you during the last session I was in the Senate, I feel confident you will reflect back upon the house with usury, the honor they have conferred upon you.

If you should find leisure from your important duties, at this eventful era, to communicate to me any information relative to men or measures, or transmit any public documents, they will be gratefully received, & applied to proper & useful purposes.

I am with much respect & esteem, Dear Sir, your friend & servant.

WILLIAM PLUMER

Hon. Henry Clay, Speaker of the House of Representatives in Congress, Washington.

ALS copy. Plumer Letterbook, 158-59, DLC (DNA, M212, R22).

1 Plumer's home town in New Hampshire.

2 The word "can" superimposed on "nor."

To John Parker

Dr Sir Washington 7h. Decr 1811

I recd. your favor of the 19h. Nov.[1] on the subject of a commission for Robert Todd your nephew.[2] I shall take pleasure in promoting his wishes. In the event of War (of which there is much probability) there will be certainly an augmentation of the Army. Indeed we have now before us propositions for such an increase and if they are carried, Mr. Todd's prospect of success will be very good.

The occurrences on the Wabash have excited much sensation here. Poor Daviess's death I most sincerely regret.[3] I indulge the hope that, as the Indians were repulsed, they will not be disposed to prosecute the War. It will certainly add to our embarrassments if we have to carry on a war with them, as well as their good friends, the English. Yr's Sincerely H. CLAY

ALS. KyHi. Addressed, not in Clay's hand: "John Parker, Esq. Near Lexington, Ky. Via Marietta."

1 Not found. 2 Robert Smith Todd, son of Levi Todd.

3 Joseph Hamilton Daveiss, wounded during the Battle of Tippecanoe, November 7, 1811, died the next day.

From Benjamin Henry Latrobe

The Honble Henry Clay. Washington, Decr. 11h. 1811

Dear Sir,

I herewith send you a hasty translation of the letter of my excellent friend Godefroi.[1] It is not a true image of the original, for it wants its elegance as well as its force, & that marked a deceded [*sic*] character which is stamped upon the style as well as the substance of the writings of genius, which always possess an individuality of which they cannot be deprived, & which of course is lost when they are translated.

I have also ventured to soften the expression of disapprobation which this old Soldier uses when censuring a mistake of the importance of which his experience in the Vendean War[2] has made him a competent judge. Perhaps I ought to have omitted these passages, but the truth of his remarks, as well as my confidence in your care that they shall not injure him, forbad it.—

During the presidency of Mr. Jefferson, & the Secretaryship of Genl Dearborne,[3] I tried to serve this [ex]cellent Officer of whose talents & experience our Country might make such important use. But from the Secretary of War I received a short reply, that *"we cannot & will not employ foreigners,"*[4] & from Mr Jefferson's remark that he heard he was *a good draughtsman,* I [s]aw through the impression which the President had received at one glance,—namely that Godefroi was a a [*sic*] good Engineer *on paper.* In fact, my own importance was, & is, too small to enable me to serve my country by serving Godefroi,—but could I procure for him the good opinion of yourself and & others to whose talents, penetration, & *influence* [i]t is intrusted to decide who shall be the subordinate [a]gents in promoting the public welfare, I should [in]deed deserve public thanks.—

Let me n[o]w intreat you, by your connexions at [Le]xington to endeavor to effect the wishes of my friend [to] procure the portrait of Col. Davies,[5] and at least to se[cu]re his papers from piracy.— Every service rendered him, binds me by a double obligation

Mr Godefroi, will probably spend a few days with me at Christmas when I will have the honor to introduce him to him [*sic*] Yours very respectfully B H LATROBE.

I must beg you to excuse the marks of haste on the note as well as on the translation.

ALS copy. Latrobe Letterbook, 602-604, owned by Mrs. Ferdinand C. Latrobe, Baltimore, Maryland.

1 Not found. Maximilian Godefroy, painter, architect, and military engineer, was at this time a resident of Baltimore.

2 An uprising of French Royalists against the Republic, 1793-1795.

3 Henry Dearborn, Jefferson's Secretary of War.

4 Godefroy was a Frenchman, though born outside France.

5 Possibly Joseph Hamilton Daveiss. No connection between Daveiss and Godefroy has been discovered.

To [James Morrison]

Dr. Major Washington 21st Decr. 1811

Agreeably to the request contained in your favor from Sidling Hill[1] I called on Mr. Gallatin,[2] who never heard any thing whatever on the subject of Ballinger's[3] bond, except what you stated to Mr. Sheldon, the principal Clerk,[4] when you called on the Secretary. Mr. Ballinger, whom I have also seen, declares himself equally ignorant of the source of information on which Mr. Eustis[5] bottomed his inquiries; and he added that the insinuation to your prejudice was as far as his knowledge extends utterly destitute of truth. He professed himself to have a high regard for you. I dined in company with Eustis a few days ago and casually hinted the affair to him. He did not state on what information it was he put the queries to you, but seemed to regret that they had occasioned you any such concern as you have manifested. I think your standing here is so good that it cannot be easily affected. Should I hear any thing further on the subject of the bond it shall be communicated to you. Perhaps the publication of the proceedings of the Court at Frederick may develope the cause of Mr. Eustis's enquiries.

The War preparations are advancing with the support of an immense majority; and I think the spirit you witnessed in their favor when you were here is not at all diminished. Our greatest difficulty will be revenue, and I do not well see how we can dispense with internal taxes. This is the delicate and trying topic, and that I fear on which we shall have the greatest desertion. Rumors are afloat that the orders in Council will be repealed, and they are even traced up to the British Minister or his Secretary, but I do not think they ought to command attention.[6]

I transmitted to John Hart[7] the statement by which we settled our travelling account. I think you will find we committed an error.

Yr friend H. CLAY

P.S. The hint given in your letter relating to myself is recd. in the spirit of amity which dictated it.

ALS. NcD.

1 The letter, not found. Sideling Hill, in Fulton County, Pennsylvania, was a way-station on the Cumberland road.

2 Albert Gallatin.

3 Probably John Ballinger, a member of the Kentucky legislature from Knox County in 1806, subsequently a resident of Cape Girardeau, Louisiana Territory, and still later a leader in the movement to separate West Florida from Spanish rule. He had come to Washington in the fall of 1811 as representative of the supporters of the Feliciana Convention, seeking governmental recognition of their land claims and assumption of their debts, the latter owed primarily to Kentucky and Tennessee backers who had supplied horses, provisions, and military supplies. Isaac Joslin Cox, *The West Florida Controversy, 1798-1813, A Study in American Diplomacy* (Baltimore, 1918), 599-604.

4 Daniel Sheldon, of the Treasury Department.

5 William Eustis, Secretary of War.

6 The Orders in Council were revoked on June 23, 1812.

7 Of Lexington.

To Benjamin R. Pollard, Joseph Pollard, Jr., and William Meriwether

Messrs. Benjamin R. Pollard
Joseph Pollard jr
Wm. Meriwether

Decr. 27th. 1811

Gent. Take notice that the original Bill of Exchange, of which the above is a copy,[1] was on the fourth Instant at Pittsburgh presented to presley neville esqr. by Isaac Craig a notary Public, and duly protested for non acceptance and non payment—The reason assigned by neville for the non-acceptance and non payment, is that the only funds placed in his hands by Benjn. R Pollard was a quantity of Lead, the sales of which amounted only to three hundred and forty-six dollars and eighty seven Cents which sum said neville was ready to pay But could not accept the Bill or thereafter pay it

HENRY CLAY

True copy, by Thomas Joyes, DLC-TJC (DNA, M212, R15). The original was sent by Clay to Worden Pope, clerk of both the county and the circuit courts of Jefferson County, who employed Thomas Joyes (later a State representative from Jefferson County) to serve notices on the addresses. An endorsement by Joyes notes that he left true copies of the document with Benjamin Pollard on December 30, 1811, with Joseph Pollard on December 31st, and with William Meriwether on January 1, 1812.

1 See above, Assignment, October 11, 1811.

To [Henry J. Randall]

Dr Sir: Washington, 11 o'clock, 28 Dec. 11.

We have this moment heard of the melancholy catastrophe which occurred at Richmond, and the whole city participates in the distress which it must have occasioned with you.[1] How many hearts are wrung with distress by the horrible events which are evolved in one short hour! My poor friend Col. Clay, by whose side I write you this letter, is among the number who are penetrated with grief by this sad misfortune. He has just learnt that his unhappy child, the pride of his life, has perished in the flames. The accounts which have as yet reached us, left you when all was consternation, and of course are less satisfactory those [*sic*] could be desired. The object of this letter therefore is to interest you so far as to collect & transmit to me the particulars connected with her destruction. The afflicted bosom sometimes derives partial relief from dwelling on the sorrowful detail of circumstances attending the death of the object whose loss it deplores. Yr friend H. CLAY.

Magazine of American History, XIX (Jan., 1888), 80 (copy of original from the collection of the Hon. T. Romeyn Beek, of Albany, then in the possession of Mrs. Pierre Van Cortlandt). Randall, named as the addressee in this source, has not been identified.

1 On December 26, 1811, a fire destroyed the Richmond Theater. Mary, daughter of Matthew Clay, was one of the victims of the disaster.

Amendment to, and Speech on, the Bill to Raise an Additional Military Force

[December 31, 1811]

"Provided, however, That officers for eight regiments only shall be appointed, until three fourths of the privates of such eight regiments shall be enlisted, when the officers for the remaining five regiments shall also be appointed:"

Mr. *Clay* observed, that a difference of opinion had arisen yesterday, whether the additional military force proposed to be raised ought to be 15,000 or 25,000 men not so much, he believed, from a conviction that 25,000 men would be too many; but from a dislike to the appointment of officers for the whole before they would be wanted, so as to have an army of officers, without the requisite number of men for them to command. This objection would be obviated by the adoption of this amendment, for the officers for eight regiments would not be more than would be required for 15,000 men had the friends of that number carried their point. And, as the whole 25,000 men could not be got at once, the expense of the officers whose appointment was proposed to be deferred, would be saved; and the officers for eight regiments would be fully sufficient for the recruiting service. He hoped, therefore, the amendment would be adopted.[1]

Mr. CLAY (the Speaker) said, that when the subject of this bill was before the House in the abstract form of a resolution, proposed by the Committee of Foreign Relations, it was the pleasure of the House to discuss it whilst he was in the Chair. He did not complain of this course of proceeding; for he did not at any time wish the House, from considerations personal to him, to depart from that mode of transacting the public business which they thought best. He merely adverted to the circumstance, as an apology for the trouble he was about to give the committee. He was at all times disposed to take his share of responsibility, and under this impression he felt that he owed it to his constituents and to himself, before the Committee rose, to submit to their attention a few observations.

He saw, with regret, diversity of opinion amongst those who had the happiness generally to act together, in relation to the quantum of force proposed to be raised. For his part, he thought that it was too great for peace, and he feared too small for war. He had been in favor of the number recommended by the Senate, and he would ask gentlemen, who had preferred 15,000, to take a candid and dispassionate review of the subject. It was admitted, on all hands, that it was a force to be raised for the purposes of war, and to be kept up and used only in the event of war. It was further conceded, that its principal destination would be the provinces of our enemy. By the bill which had been passed, to complete the peace establishment, we had authorized the collection of a force of about 6000 men, exclusive of those now in service, which, with the 25,000 provided for by this bill, will give an aggregate of new troops of 31,000 men. Experience, in military affairs has shewn, that when any given number of men is authorised to be raised, you must, in counting upon the effective men which it will produce, deduct one-fourth or one-third for desertion, sickness, & other incidents to which raw troops are peculiarly exposed. In measures relating to war, it is wisest, if you err at all, to err on the side of the largest force, and you will consequently put down your 31,000 men at not more than an effective force in the field of about 21,000. This, with the 4,000 now in service, will amount to 25,000 effective men. The Secretary of War has stated, in his report, that for the single purpose of manning your forts and garrisons on the seaboard, 12,600 men are necessary. Although the whole of that number will not be taken from the 25,000, a portion of it, probably will be. We are told that in Canada there are between 7 and 8 thousand regular troops. If it is invaded, the whole of that force will be concentrated in Quebec, and will you attempt that almost impregnable fortress with less than double the force of the besieged? Gentlemen who calculate upon volunteers as a substitute for regulars, ought not to deceive themselves. No man appreciated higher than he did the spirit of the country. But, although volunteers were admirably adapted to the first operations of the war, to the making of a first impression, he doubted their fitness for a regular siege, or for the manning and garrisoning of forts. He understood it was a rule, in military affairs, never to leave in the rear a place of any strength undefended. Canada is invaded; the upper part falls, and you proceed to Quebec. It is true there would be no European enemy behind to be apprehended; but the people of the country might rise; and he warned gentlemen who imagined that the affections of the Canadians were with us against trusting too confidently on a calculation, the basis of which was treason. He concluded, therefore, that a portion of the invading army would be distributed in the upper country, after its conquest, amongst the places susceptible of military strength and defence. The army, considerably reduced, sets itself down before Quebec. Suppose it falls. Here again will be requisite a number of men to hold and defend it. And if the war is prosecuted still farther, and the lower country and Halifax are assailed, he conceived it obvious that the whole force of 25,000 men would not be too great.

The difference between those who were for 15,000, and those who were for 25,000 men, appeared to him to resolve itself into the question merely of a short or protracted war—a war of vigor—or a war of languor and imbecility. If a competent force be raised in the first instance, the war on the continent will be speedily terminated. He was aware that it might still rage on the ocean. But where the nation could act with unquestionable success, he was in favor of the display of an energy correspondent to the feelings and spirit of the country. Suppose one-third of the force he had mentioned (25,000 men), could reduce the country, say in three years, and that the whole could accomplish the same object in one year; taking into view the greater hazard of the repulsion and defeat of the small force, and every other consideration, do not wisdom and true economy equally decide in favor of the larger force, and thus prevent failure in consequence of inadequate means? He begged gentlemen to recollect the immense extent of the U. States; our vast maritime frontier, vulnerable in almost all its parts to predatory incursions, and he was persuaded they would see that a regular force of 25,000 men was not much too great, during a period of war, if all design of invading the provinces of the enemy were abandoned.

Mr. C. proceeded next to examine the nature of the force contemplated by the bill. It was a regular army, enlisted for a limited time, raised for the sole purpose of war, and to be disbanded on the return of peace. Against this army all our republican jealousies and apprehensions are attempted to be excited. He was not the advocate of standing armies; but the standing armies which excite most his fears, are those which are kept up in time of peace. He confessed he did not perceive any real source of danger in a military force of 25,000 men in the United States, provided for a state only of war, even supposing it to be corrupted and its arms turned by the ambition of its leaders against the freedom of the country. He saw abundant security against the success of any such treasonable attempt. The diffusion of political information amongst the great body of the people constituted a powerful safeguard. The American character has been much abused by Europeans, whose tourists, whether on horse or foot, in verse and prose, have united in depreciating it. It is true that we do not exhibit as many signal instances of scientific acquirement in this country as are furnished in the old world; but he believed it undeniable that the great mass of the people possessed more intelligence than any other people on the globe. Such a people, consisting of upwards of seven millions, affording a physical power of about a million of men capable of bearing arms, and ardently devoted to liberty, could not be subdued by an army of 25,000 men. The wide extent of country over which we are spread was another security. In other countries, France and England for example, the fall of Paris or London is the fall of the nation. Here are no such dangerous aggregations of people. New York, and Philadelphia, and Boston, and every city on the Atlantic, might be subdued by an usurper, and he would have made but a small advance in the accomplishment of his purpose. He would add a still more improbable supposition, that the whole country east of the Alleghany was to submit to the ambition of some daring chief, and, he insisted, that the liberty of the Union would be still unconquered. It would find successful support from the west. We are not only in the situation just described, but a great portion of the militia—nearly the whole, he understood, of that of Massachusetts—have arms in their hands; and he trusted in God that that great object would be persevered in until every man in the nation could proudly shoulder the musket which was to defend his country and himself. A people having, besides the benefit of one general government, other local governments in full operation, capable of commanding and exerting great portions of the physical power, all of which must be prostrated before our constitution is subverted. Such a people has nothing to fear from a petty, contemptible force of 25,000 regulars.

Mr. C. proceeded more particularly to enquire into the object of the force. That object, he understood, distinctly to be war, and war with Great Britain. It had been supposed by some gentlemen improper to discuss publicly so delicate a question. He did not feel the impropriety. It was a subject in its nature incapable of concealment. Even in countries where the powers of government were conducted by a single ruler, it was almost impossible for that ruler to conceal his intentions when he meditates war. The assembling of armies—the strengthening of posts—all the movements preparatory for war, and which it was impossible to disguise, unfolded the intentions of the sovereign. Does Russia or France intend war, the intention is almost invariably known before the war is commenced. If Congress were to pass a law, with closed doors, for raising an army for the purpose of war, its enlistment and organization, which could not be done in secret, would indicate the use to which it was to be applied; and we cannot suppose England would be so blind as not to see that she was aimed at. Nor could she, did he apprehend, injure us more by thus knowing our purposes than if she were kept in ignorance of them. She may, indeed, anticipate us, and commence the war. But that is what she is in fact doing, and she can add but little to the injury which she is inflicting. If she choose to declare war in form, let her do so, the responsibility will be with her.

What are we to gain by war, has been emphatically asked? In reply, he would ask, what are we not to lose by peace? commerce, character, a nation's best treasure, honor! If pecuniary considerations alone are to govern, there is sufficient motive for the war. Our revenue is reduced by the operation of the belligerent edicts to about six millions of dollars, according to the Secretary of the Treasury's report. The year preceding the embargo it was sixteen. Take away the orders in council, it will again mount up to sixteen millions. By continuing therefore in peace, if the mongrel state in which we are deserve that denomination, we lose annually in revenue only, ten millions of dollars. Gentlemen will say, repeal the law of non-importation. He contended that if the U. States were capable of that perfidy, the revenue would not be restored to its former state, the orders in council continuing, without an export trade, which those orders prevent, inevitable ruin woud ensue, if we imported as freely as we did prior to the embargo. A nation that carries on an import trade without an export trade to support it, must in the end, be as certainly bankrupt, as the individual would be, who incurred an annual expenditure without an income.

He had no disposition to swell, or dwell upon the catalogue of injuries from England. He could not however overlook the impressment of our seamen; an aggression upon which he never reflected without feelings of indignation, which would not allow him appropriate language to describe its enormity. Not content with seizing upon all our property, which falls within her rapacious grasp, the personal rights of our countrymen—rights which forever ought to be sacred, are trampled upon and violated. The orders in council were pretended to have been reluctantly adopted as a measure of retaliation. The French decrees, their alledged basis, are revoked. England resorts to the expedient of denying the fact of the revocation, and Sir William Scott, in the celebrated case of the Fox and others, suspends judgement that proof may be adduced of it.[2] And at the moment when the British Ministry, through that judge, is thus affecting to controvert that fact, and to place the release of our property upon its establishment, instructions are prepared for Mr. Foster[3] to meet at Washington the very revocation which they were contesting. And how does he meet it? By fulfilling the engagement solemnly made to rescind the orders? No, sir, but by demanding that we shall secure the introduction into the continent of British manufactures.

England is said to be fighting for the world, and shall we, it is asked, attempt to weaken her exertions? If indeed the aim of the French Emperor be universal dominion (and he was willing to allow it to the argument,) what a noble cause is presented to British valor. But how is her philanthropic purpose to be atchieved? By scrupulous observance of the rights of others; by respecting that code of public law which she professes to vindicate—and by abstaining from self-aggrandizement. Then would she command the sympathies of the world. What are we required to do by those who would engage our feelings and wishes in her behalf? To bear the actual cuffs of her arrogance, that we may escape a chimerical French subjugation! We are invited—conjured to drink the potion of British poison actually presented to our lips, that we may avoid the imperial dose prepared by perturbed imaginations. We are called upon to submit to debasement, dishonor and disgrace—to bow the neck to royal insolence, as a course of preparation for manly resistance to gallic invasion! What nation, what individual was ever taught, in the schools of ignominious submission, the patriotic lessons of freedom and independence? Let those who contend for this humiliating doctrine, read its refutation in the history of the very man against whose insatiable thirst of dominion we are warned. The experience of desolated Spain, for the last 15 years, is worth volumes. Did she find her repose and safety in subserviency to the will of that man? Had she boldly stood forth and repelled the first attempt to dictate to her councils, her Monarch would not now be a miserable captive at Marseilles. Let us come home to our own history; it was not by submission that our fathers atchieved our independence. The patriotic wisdom that placed you, Mr. Chairman,[4] said Mr. C. under that canopy, penetrated the designs of a corrupt Ministry, and nobly fronted encroachment on its first appearance. It saw, beyond the petty taxes with which it commenced, a long train of oppressive measures terminating in the total annihilation of liberty; and contemptible as they were, did not hesitate to resist them. Take the experience of the last four or five years, and which he was sorry to say exhibited, in appearance at least, a different kind of spirit. He did not wish to view, the past further than to guide us for the future. We were but yesterday contending for the indirect trade—the right to export to Europe the coffee & sugar of the West Indies. To day we are asserting our claim to the direct trade—the right to export our cotton, tobacco and other domestic produce to market. Yield this point, and to-morrow intercourse between New-Orleans and New-York—between the planters on James river and Richmond will be interdicted. For, sir, the career of encroachment is never arrested by submission. It will advance whilst there remains a single privilege on which it can operate. Gentlemen say that this government is unfit for any war, but a war of invasion. What, is it not equivalent to invasion, if the mouths of our harbors and outlets are blocked up, and we are denied egress from our own waters? Or, when the burglar is at our door, shall we bravely sally forth and repel his felonious entrance, or meanly skulk within the cells of the Castle?

He contended that the real cause of British aggression, was not to distress an enemy, but to destroy a rival. A comparative view of our commerce with England and the continent, would satisfy any one of the truth of this remark. Prior to the embargo, the balance of trade between this country and England was between eleven and fifteen millions of dollars in favor of England. Our consumption of her manufactures was annually increasing, & had risen to nearly fifty millions of dollars. We exported to her what she most wanted, provisions and raw materials for her manufactures, and received in return what she was most desirous to sell. Our exports to France, Holland, Spain and Italy, taking an average of the years 1802, 3 and 4, amounted to about $12,000,000 of domestic, and about $18,000,000 of foreign produce. Our imports from the same countries amounted to about $25,000,000. The foreign produce exported consisted chiefly of luxuries from the West Indies.[5] It is apparent that this trade, the balance of which was in favor, not of France, but of the United States, was not of very vital consequence to the enemy of England. Would she, therefore, for the sole purpose of depriving her adversary of this commerce, relinquish her valuable trade with this country, exhibiting the essential balance in her favor—nay more, hazard the peace of the country? No, sir, you must look for an explanation of her conduct in the jealousies of a rival. She sickens at your prosperity, and beholds in your growth—your sails spread on every ocean, and your numerous seamen, the foundations of a power which, at no very distant day, is to make her tremble for naval superiority. He had omitted before to notice the loss of our seamen, if we continued in our present situation. What would become of the 100,000 (for he understood there was about that number) in the American service? Would they not leave us and seek employment abroad, perhaps in the very country that injures us?

It is said, that the effect of the war at home, will be a change of those who administer the government, who will be replaced by others that will make a disgraceful peace.[6] He did not believe it. Not a man in the nation could really doubt the sincerity with which those in power have sought, by all honorable pacific means, to protect the interests of the country. When the people saw exercised towards both belligerents the utmost impartiality; witnessed the same equal terms tendered to both; and beheld the government successively embracing an accommodation with each in exactly the same spirit of amity, he was fully persuaded, now that war was the only alternative left to us by the injustice of one of the powers, that the support and confidence of the people would remain undiminished. He was one, however, who was prepared (and he would not believe that he was more so than every other member of the committee) to march on in the road of his duty, at all hazards. What! shall it be said that our *amor patricæ* is located at these desks—that we pusillanimously cling to our seats here, rather than boldly vindicate the most inestimable rights of the country? Whilst the heroic Daveiss[7] and his gallant associates, exposed to all the perils of treacherous savage warfare, are sacrificing themselves for the good of their country, shall we shrink from our duty?

He concluded, by hoping that his remarks had tended to prove that the quantum of the force was not too great—that in its nature it was free from the objections urged against it, and that the object of its application was one imperiously called for by the crisis.

Washington *National Intelligencer,* January 2, 7, 1812. Published also in *Annals of Cong.,* 12 Cong., 1 Sess., XXIII, 596-602; *Niles' Weekly Register,* I (January 4, 1812), 332-34; Lexington *Kentucky Gazette,* January 14, 1812; Lexington *Reporter,* January 25, 1812; Swain, *Life and Speeches of Henry Clay,* I, [15]-21; Mallory, *Life and Speeches of Henry Clay,* I, [278]-85; Colton, *Life, Correspondence, and Speeches of Henry Clay,* V, 35-41. The House, in Committee of the Whole, was considering a bill from the Senate to raise an additional military force.

1 The amendment was accepted, whereupon the chairman was about to put the question on the return to regular House session when Clay arose to speak.

[2] Scott in June, 1811, had rendered a decision that the French decrees were still in effect and that American vessels seized under provisions of the British Orders in Council were subject to condemnation.
[3] Augustus John Foster.
[4] James Breckinridge, of Virginia, who had served in General Greene's regiment during the Revolution. Though a leader of the Federalist Party, Breckinridge was an associate of Jefferson in the founding of the University of Virginia and a brigadier general in the War of 1812. He was a lawyer and an active proponent for construction of the Chesapeake and Ohio Canal.
[5] Under a favorable decision of a British prize court in the case of the *Polly*, re-exportation of French West Indian goods from the United States had flourished from 1802 until 1805, when in the case of the *Essex* a prize appeal court had ruled that such re-exportation violated the British Rule of 1756 if remission of duties accompanied re-shipment of goods.
[6] The Federalist group led by Josiah Quincy of Massachusetts voted for war measures and welcomed the approaching conflict in the expectation that it would be brief and would bring about the overthrow of the administration. The Federalists then would be able to make peace with Great Britain. In a letter written November 26, 1811, Quincy claimed that "Clay our Speaker told me yesterday with some naiveté, 'the truth is I am in favour of war and so are some others—*but some of us fear that if we get into war you will get our places*.'" Samuel E. Morison, *The Life and Letters of Harrison Gray Otis, Federalist, 1765-1848* (2 vols., Boston and New York, 1913), II, 34.
[7] Joseph Hamilton Daveiss.

From Worden Pope

Dr Sir Louisville Jany. 3rd. 1812

I was out of Town when your letter of the 15th of last month[1] reached this place—On my return I took it out of the post-office, and lost no time in effecting the object of it—I drew a notice (enclosed) [2] and procured a young man of business to serve copies of it on B. R. Pollard Joseph Pollard and Mr. Wm. Meriwether—I also return you the Protest which you forwarded me.[3] The young man Mr. Tho. Joyes of this place states to me that Jo. Pollard, wishes you to receive the sum which Neville is willing to pay, and that he will secure the balance to be paid at Bank in this Country.

I had a personal conversation with Mr. Meriwether, whom I would be glad to serve, and he wishes that you will secure the money in Neville's hands and endeavor to get the residue of the Pollards for whom he is only security B. R. Pollard lives in shelby County near the mouth of Brashear's Creek, Jo Pollard seems to be a transient person and Meriwether lives 8 or 9 miles from Town—It was therefore a very troublesome business to serve notice on those persons: Indeed it was a mere accident to meet with Jo Pollard—and as the weather was extreamly bad I have agreed to pay Mr. Joyes ten dollars for his trouble and expence; and my fee for attending to the business is five dollars—which you will please forward to me. Yr. mo obdt WORDEN POPE

ALS. DLC-TJC (DNA, M212, R12). Addressed to Clay at Washington.
[1] Not found.
[2] Above, December 27, 1811.
[3] Not found.

To [William W. Worsley]

WASHINGTON, Jan 4. [1812]

The bill from the Senate authorising to be raised an additional military force of 25,000 men, has been ordered by the House of Representatives to a third reading by a majority of 90 to 35, and will undoubtedly pass.[1] I consider it as the strongest war measure that could be adopted, short of an actual declaration of war, which I have no doubt will be made before we rise, unless England ceases her aggressions.[2]

Extract. Lexington *Reporter,* January 18, 1812. Identified as from Clay to the editor.

1 On January 3 the bill was read a third time. The debate which followed continued until January 6, when the amended bill was passed by the House. When the Senate refused to accept the amendments, the House withdrew all save one, and on January 10 the Senate receded from its disagreement to that one.

2 The declaration of war came on June 18.

Speech against Resolution to Bar Exception of Certain Claims from the Statute of Limitations

[January 7, 1812]

Mr. *Clay* (the Speaker) hoped the committee would disagree to this resolution. It appears that the officers of the treasury are of opinion that provision may be made for this description of claims without that danger of fraud which might possibly arise from a total repeal of the statute of limitation; that their whole amount does not exceed $300,000, and the probability is, that one-fifth will never be applied for, should they be authorised to be paid. What, said Mr. C. is this statute of limitations, which, whenever mentioned in this House, seems to make every body tremble? It is a general rule prescribed by the government for the direction of its accounting officers in order to exclude unjust claims. What are statutes of limitation as applicable to individual cases? A rule under which individuals claim protection whenever they chuse to do so, and when, from the lapse of time, or loss of evidence, they would be injured, were they not to take this advantage. But in these statutes of limitation, there are always exceptions in favor of cases of disability, infancy, coverture, insanity, absence beyond sea, &c. But what is the course which an individual would take who found himself protected by a statute of limitation? He would examine the justice of the claim brought against him, if the claim were just, if he had been deprived of no evidence by the delay, if as able to pay it as if it had been presented at an earlier day, he will not hesitate to discharge the claim, and scorn to take advantage of the statute. And, said Mr. C. shall the government be less willing to discharge its just debts than an honest individual? Shall we turn a deaf ear to the claims of individuals upon government because of this statute? He trusted not. The committee of claims ought to examine the merit of every claim which comes before it, and if it be just, decide in its favor. But what, said Mr. C. has been the history of claims, for four or five years past? When a solitary claim was presented, the House would say, we cannot legislate upon individual cases. They occupy too much of our time. The claim is put aside. The same individual, some time after, appears in company with others. We then say there are too many of these claims—their amount is too large, and the treasury too poor—that there are a great many other claims equally well founded—that justice cannot be done to them all. Sometimes there is a division between the two Houses.—This House passes a bill in favor of some particular claim—the other tells you, they will not legislate for particular cases; that if they act, they wish to take up the subject generally. Mr. C. said, it was his wish, both in his public and private character, as far as possible, to do justice; he therefore hoped the course proposed by the Chairman of the committee of Claims would be agreed to.

Washington *National Intelligencer,* January 9, 1812. Published also in *Annals of Cong.,* 12 Cong., 1 Sess., XXIII, 696. On December 21, 1811, Thomas Gholson of Virginia, chairman of the Committee of Claims, submitted in accordance with earlier House action a resolution disapproving a proposal to suspend or repeal the acts of limitation in connection with certain claims. When, on January 7, the House took up the report in Committee of the Whole, Gholson expressed opposition to the resolution. Clay's remarks followed. The resolution was then defeated.

From Robert Wickliffe

Dr Clay Lexington Jany 9th 1811 [*i.e.* 1812]

Genl Hopkins[1] told me the other day that he wished to pay (on account Kenedy & Cox) (for Barbour)[2] the amt of Barbours debt upon execution I told him to deposite the money subject to my check in the state Bank. this I did that I might facilitate your wishes upon the subject Will you write me if he should make the deposite How I shall dispose of it—If it will not materially affect the interest of your client I would prefer its remaining in Frankfort untill your return here but if it will I will remit it to them or as you shall direct. Upon the subject of Those suits for money, the collections of which you had undertaken before you declined practice—you once named to me that you would divide the profits with me &c but I hope you will permit to declare to you that I should reproach myself were I to take One Cent for closing them for you—No my dear fellow I wish it were in my power to shew you how much I consider my self your debtor in something else than closing a few plain suits permit me to assure you that you need feel no uneasiness about them I will I trust ultimately close them to your satisfaction & any monies that you may wish remitted shall be done with as little delay as possible—Hart & Watson it is said have settled after a fire & it is reported to the disgrace of Watson but I think it likely the thing is mistated or exaggerarated [*sic*].[3] The parties have not returned The Legislature is in Session & have just broke upon the Congressional Districts.[4] In hast I am dear Sir Your Sv ROBERT WICKLIFFE

Write me if I must prepare for Lee & Breckenridge before you return[5]

ALS. DLC-HC (DNA, M212, R1). Cover endorsed by Clay: "R. Wickliffe 1811 [*sic*]."

1 Samuel Hopkins. 2 Philip Barbour.

3 Clay's brother-in-law, Nathaniel G. S. Hart, and Samuel E. Watson, both of Lexington, fought a duel across the Ohio River from Louisville on January 7. After each had fired one shot without effect, the encounter was ended. Lexington *Reporter,* January 11, 1812.

4 Redistricting had become necessary because of the increase from six to ten in Kentucky's representation in the lower house of Congress.

5 The case of the executors of John Lee against the administrators and heirs of John Breckinridge, relating to payment and transfer of title for a tract of nearly 10,000 acres on Slate Creek, a southern branch of the Licking River, in Kentucky, stemmed from a conditional sale of the property by Lee to Breckinridge and George Nicholas in 1795. The litigation was begun in 1811 and not finally settled until 1867. Clay was at this time involved as the guardian of Breckinridge's heirs. See Fayette Circuit Court, Order Book E, 60.

To ————

[*ca.* January 10, 1812]

The Secretary of the Treasury has given us his budget.[1] It comprizes a number of taxes, and some not of the most agreeable description. But taxes must be laid, and we shall have to make a just selection amongst those suggested.

Dearborn is recommended as a Major General in the supplemental army. I suppose he will be the commander in chief, if appointed. The Senate has not yet decided upon the nomination.[2]

Extract. Lexington *Reporter,* February 4, 1812. Identified as from Clay *"to a gentleman in this place."*

1 Dated January 10, taken up in the House on January 20.

2 Henry Dearborn became the senior major general of the Army on January 27, 1812.

Speech Supporting Bill to Raise Volunteers

[January 11, 1812]

MR. CLAY (the Speaker) observed, that he had stated to the committee of the whole, on a former occasion, that he was in favor of an exertion of the national energies in every form, in prosecution of the war in which we are about to engage. He was consequently in favor of authorising the President to accept of the service of a volunteer corps. The difference of opinion on this subject arises from the structure of this force, or rather as to the manner of commissioning its officers.

Mr. C. acknowledged he had not fully investigated the subject, but his present impressions were, that, in cases of emergency, the nation is at liberty to use the best security of the people, whether in the form of ordinary militia or volunteers, in any manner that may appear best calculated to preserve the public interest. He did not think full justice had been done to the able view taken of this subject by his intelligent friend from South Carolina (Mr. Cheves).[1] The power of declaring war, of making war, would seem to carry with it all the attributes of making war.

The gentleman from Georgia (Mr. Troup)[2] to whom he always listened with pleasure, objected to the power contended for, because it might possibly be abused, by sending the militia to a distant foreign country. What the government had the power to do, and what might be deemed expedient, were very different.

What is the argument? The militia cannot be sent out of the U. States, because there is no power given in the constitution of the general government for this purpose. Will gentlemen give a satisfactory answer to this question? The constitution declares Congress shall have power to raise armies and navies; but there is no power given to the government to send them beyond the jurisdiction of the United States—yet no one will say that it was the intention of the framers of the constitution to restrict the government in the use of the army and navy. Whence, then, is the power derived, but from the general power of making war, and of course effective war? And if the general power of making war gives to government the right of using the army and navy without the limits of the U. States, why may not the same general power give the same authority with respect to the militia? He desired those gentlemen who contend that the militia cannot be sent out of the U. States, to answer this question.

But gentlemen say that the government has not power to send the militia out of the U. States, because the constitution defines the purposes for which alone they shall be used, viz. "to suppress insurrections, execute the laws and repel invasions."

Mr. C. said he would call the attention of the committee to two clauses in the constitution already noticed, but not for the same purpose. Congress is "to provide for organizing, arming and disciplining the militia, and for governing such part of them as may be employed in the service of the U. States." What service? For repelling invasion? Does not "the service of the United States," mean any service to which that particular force is applicable? If not, the language would have been, "as may be employed in executing the laws of the Union, suppressing insurrections and repelling invasions."

Again, the constitution says "The President shall be commander in chief of the army and navy of the United States and of the militia of the several states, when called into the actual service of the United States." What service? The service is spoken of generally, and means, no doubt, any service to which physical force is applicable. If intended only to apply to the three cases above specified, why were they not enumerated, instead of speaking of the service of the United States generally?

In one of the amendments to the constitution, it is declared, "that a well-regulated militia is necessary to the security of a free state." But if you limit the use of the militia to executing the laws, suppressing insurrections and repelling invasions; if you deny the use of the militia to make war, can you say they are "the security of a state"? He thought not.

Gentlemen ask, will you carry the militia out of the U. States, for the purpose of making foreign conquest? That is not the purpose for which this volunteer force is wanted. They are wanted in a war of defence. In making the war effective, conquest may become necessary; but this does not change the character of the war—there may be no other way of operating upon our enemy, but by taking possession of her provinces which adjoin us.

The single difference between the two bills, is who shall have the power of making the officers. The proposition for vesting the power of appointing the officers in the President, considering the volunteers as militia, is unconstitutional, as the power is vested in the several states. But gentlemen say, call the force what you will, call it a militia force, or a regular force; let the officers be appointed by the respective states or the President, it matters but little. No man, Mr. C. said, had a higher opinion of the exalted virtues and eminent patriotism of the President of the United States than he had. But we ought to be cautious in setting precedents; bad precedents are always imposed in good times. Though the power might not be abused at present, it might hereafter be made use of for the worst purposes. He should have no fear from placing 100,000 men under the present Executive of the United States; but, as our constitution declares that "a well-regulated militia is the best security of a free state," he should chuse rather to leave the appointment of the officers of these volunteers in the states respectively.

The difficulty which the gentleman from Vermont[3] had suggested, as to the appointment of officers to fill the places of such as may become vacant, might be provided for, by an amendment.

Washington *National Intelligencer*, January 30, 1812. Published also in *Annals of Cong.*, 12 Cong., 1 Sess., XXIII, 743-45. The bill, brought in by Peter B. Porter of New York on December 26, 1811, authorized the President to accept and organize companies of volunteers not exceeding 50,000 men, with the pay of regular troops, for one year's service. Questioning of the extent of federal authority over the militia in war entered into the extensive debate that followed. The bill became law on February 6, 1812.

1 Langdon Cheves, one of the "Warhawks," chairman of the House Select Committee on Naval Establishment. He succeeded Clay as Speaker of the House during the latter's mission to Ghent and later served as president of the Bank of the United States, 1819-1822, while Clay was counsel for that institution in Kentucky and Ohio.

2 George Michael Troup. 3 James Fisk, a Democrat.

Bill from Thomas Deye Owings

Henry Clay Esqr— Lexington Jany. 15th. 1812

Bot. of Thos D. Owings

1 Sett of Carriage harness
for the leading horses &c &c £ 66.0.0

E E. THOS DEYE OWINGS

ADS. DLC-TJC (DNA, M212, R15).

From Ralph Peacock

Henry Clay Esquire Philadelphia 18th Jany. 1812

Dr. Sir

I recd. your favour a few weeks ago dated at Washington[1] respecting the Claim of P. W. &. Co[2] agt. Pigman & Crow as to the plea put up by Pigman of having appropriated a Claim of $5,000 to satisfy sundries in Phila. and ours amongst the rest is a pretext without foundation; and can be only considered a subterfuge for delay as such you will take steps best calculated to recover the Amount of our demand with as little delay as possible on the terms & conditions proposed, provided you should be successfull I can get you other demands agt. them to a large Amount but not at so great a discount I wish you could find Dr. Jno. Duhamel and I would send his notes for Abt. $10,000. our other affairs in Kentucky I respectfully request you will have the goodness to close on the best terms you can and forward me the proceeds I am Dr. Sir Yrs. truly RALPH PEACOCK

ALS. DLC-HC (DNA, M212, R1).

1 Not found. 2 Peacock, Wrenshall and Company.

Memorandum of Account as Attorney for Kennedy and Cox

[*ca.* January 20, 1812]

Kennedy & Cox vs Philip Barbour &c. $6500 with int from the

25h. day of Decr. 1809. Subject to a credit of $2500 with int. from the same time.

Same vs Same–$400 damages.

Same vs Jonathan Taylor &c. $5000 with int from the 10h. March 1810.–Return $1930„61 made exclusive of Commns on that sum–Exon returnable to Apl 1811

Same vs Same–Return $1500 paid to H. Clay 15 July. 1811

Same vs Same–Debt $1000 with int from the 1st. March 1811 until paid–Return Replevied.

Same vs Same–$1093„25 with int thereon from the 20h. Jany 1812 Return–Satisfied & money paid to H Clay–

Same vs Eastland[1] Return upon Exon on Replevy bond–Recd. $200–bal. stayed by an injon–

Same vs Same–Stayed by injunction–

Same vs William Taylor Francis Taylor[2] &c. Judgt. for $5883„21 with int. from the 10h. March 1810 till paid.

Memo–Indorsed on one exon in Mr. Wickliffe's hand writing –Recd. by R. Wickliffe for H. Clay–

AD. DLC-TJC (DNA, M212, R15).

1 Thomas Eastland. 2 Brother of William Taylor.

From Gideon Granger

SIR, *General Post Office, Jan.* 21*st,* 1812.

I have the honor to observe in reply to the letters of Messrs. — — — — —, addressed to you under date of the 3rd and 5th instant,[1] that with a view more fully to accommodate the merchants and other citizens of Lexington in their southern correspondence, I have this day directed the Post-Master of Lexington to make a contract for transporting the mail between his office and Frankfort via Versailles.–The mail is to leave Lexington immediately after the arrival of the eastern mail on Friday, and return on Saturday morning, with Southern, or New-Orleans mail–this arrangement will justly accommodate the citizens of Versailles as well as Lexington. Mr. ——— observes that the mail goes three times weekly to Pittsburg; it does–and I wish it was consistent with my duty to send it three times to Lexington; but we now send two mails weekly from this city via Marietta, Ohio, to Chillicothe with the southern intelligence, where it meets two other mails with eastern intelligence, and from thence they are immediately forwarded to the seat of government in Kentucky. As soon as the funds of this office will justify me in sending additional mails to and from your state, I shall, with great pleasure, establish them.

I have the honor to be, &c. GID'N. GRANGER.

Hon. H. Clay.

Lexington *Reporter*, February 4, 1812. Granger was Postmaster General under Presidents Jefferson and Madison. [1] Not found.

Speech on Increase in the Naval Establishment

[January 22, 1812]

Mr. CLAY (the Speaker) rose to present his views on the bill before the committee. He said that as he did not precisely agree in opinion with any gentleman who had spoken, he should take the liberty of detaining the committee a few moments, while he offered to their attention some observations. He was highly gratified with the temper and ability with which the discussion had been hitherto conducted. It was honorable to the House, and, he trusted, would continue to be manifested on many future occasions.

On this interesting topic a diversity of opinion has existed almost ever since the adoption of the present government. On the one hand, there appeared to him to have been attempts made to precipitate the nation into all the evils of naval extravagance, which had been productive of so much mischief in other countries; and, on the other, strongly feeling this mischief, there has existed an unreasonable prejudice against providing such a competent naval protection for our commercial and maritime rights as is demanded by their importance, and as the encreased resources of the country amply justify.

The attention of Congress has been invited to this subject by the President in his message delivered at the opening of the session. Indeed, had it been wholly neglected by the chief magistrate, from the critical situation of the country, and the nature of the rights proposed to be vindicated, it must have pressed itself upon our attention. But, said Mr. C. the President in his message observes: "Your attention will, of course, be drawn to such provisions on the subject of our naval force as may be required for the service to which it is best adapted. I submit to Congress the seasonableness also of an authority to augment the stock of such materials as are imperishable in their nature or may not at once be attainable." The President, by this recommendation, clearly intimates an opinion that the naval force of this country is capable of producing some effect; and the propriety of laying up imperishable materials, was no doubt suggested for the purpose of making additions to the navy, as convenience & exigencies might direct.

It appeared to Mr. C. a little extraordinary that so much, as it seemed to him, unreasonable jealousy should exist against the naval establishment. If, said he, we look back to the period of the formation of the Constitution, it will be found that no such jealousy was then excited. In placing the physical force of the nation at the disposal of Congress, the Convention manifested much greater apprehension of abuse in the power given to raise armies, than in that to provide a navy. In reference to the navy, Congress is put under no restrictions; but with respect to the army—that description of force which has been so often employed to subvert the liberties of mankind—they are subjected to limitations, designed to prevent the abuse of this dangerous power. But it was not his intention to detain the committee by a discussion on the comparative utility and safety of these two kinds of force. He would, however, be indulged in saying, that he thought gentlemen had wholly failed in maintaining the position they had assumed, that the fall of maritime powers was attributable to their navies. They have told you, indeed, that Carthage, Genoa, Venice, and other nations had navies, and not withstanding were finally destroyed. But have they shewn, by a train of argument, that their overthrow was, in any degree, ascribable to their maritime greatness? Have they attempted even to shew that there exists in the nature of this power a necessary tendency to destroy the nation using it? Assertion is substituted for argument; inferences not authorised by historical facts are arbitrarily drawn; things wholly unconnected with each other are associated together—a very logical mode of reasoning! In the same way he could demonstrate how idle and absurd our attachments are to freedom itself. He might say, for example, that Greece and Rome had forms of free government, and that they no longer exist; and, deducing their fall from their devotion to liberty, the conclusion, in favor of depotism, would very satisfactorily follow! He demanded what there is in the nature and construction of maritime power to excite the fears that have been indulged? Do gentlemen really apprehend that a body of seamen will abandon their proper element, and, placing themselves under an aspiring chief, will erect a throne to his ambition? Will they deign to listen to the voice of history, and learn how chimerical are their apprehensions?

But the source of alarm is in ourselves. Gentlemen fear that if we provide a marine it will produce collisions with foreign nations —plunge us into war, & ultimately overturn the constitution of the country. Sir, if you wish to avoid foreign collision you had better abandon the ocean—surrender all your commerce; give up all your prosperity. It is the thing protected, not the instrument of protection, that involves you in war. Commerce engenders collision, collision war, and war, the argument supposes, leads to despotism. Would the counsels be deemed wise of that statesman who should recommend that the nation should be unarmed—that the art of war, the martial spirit, and martial exercises, should be prohibited— and that the great body of the people should be taught that national happiness was to be found in perpetual peace alone? No, sir. And yet every argument in favor of a power of protection on land applies, in some degree, to a power of protection on the sea. Undoubtedly a commerce void of naval protection is more exposed to rapacity than a guarded commerce; and if we wish to invite the continuance of the old or enaction of new unjust edicts, let us refrain from all exertion upon that element where they operate and where, in the end, they must be resisted.

For his part, (Mr. C. said) he did not allow himself to be alarmed by those apprehensions of maritime power which appeared to agitate other gentlemen. In the nature of our government he beheld abundant security against abuse. He would be unwilling to tax the land to support the rights of the sea, and was for drawing from the sea itself the resources with which its violated freedom should at all times be vindicated. Whilst this principle is adhered to, there will be no danger of running into the folly and extravagance which so much alarms gentlemen; and whenever it is abandoned—whenever Congress shall lay burthensome taxes to augment the navy beyond what may be authorised by the increased wealth, and demanded by the exigencies of the country, the people will interpose, and removing their unworthy representatives, apply the appropriate corrective. Mr. C. could not then see any just ground of dread in the nature of naval power. It was on the contrary free from the evils attendant upon standing armies. And the genius of our institutions—the great representative principle, in the practical enjoyment of which we are so eminently distinguished—afforded the best guarantee against the ambition and wasteful extravagance of government.

What maritime strength is it expedient to provide for the United States? In considering this subject three different degrees of naval power present themselves. In the first place, such a force as would be capable of contending with that which any other nation is able to bring on the ocean—a force that, boldly scouring every sea, would challenge to combat the fleets of other powers however great. He admitted it was impossible at this time, perhaps it never would be desirable, for this country to establish so extensive a navy. Indeed he should consider it as madness in the extreme in this government to attempt to provide a navy able to cope with the fleets of Great Britain, wherever they might be met.

The next species of naval power to which he would advert is that which, without adventuring into distant seas, and keeping generally in our own harbors and on our coasts, would be competent to beat off any squadron which might be attempted to be permanently stationed in our waters. His friends from S. Carolina

(Messrs. Cheves and Lowndes[1]) had satisfactorily shewn, that to effect this object, a force equivalent only to one third of that which the maintenance of such squadron must require would be sufficient —that if, for example, England should determine to station permanently upon our coast a squadron of 12 ships of the line, it would require for this service 36 ships of the line, one third in port repairing, one third on the passage, and one third on the station. But that is a force which it has been shewn that even England, with her boasted navy, could not spare for the American service, whilst she is engaged in the present contest. Mr. C. said he was desirous of seeing such a force as he had described, that is, about 12 ships of the line and 15 or 20 frigates, provided for the U. States; but he admitted that it was unattainable in the present situation of the finances of the country. He contended, however, that it was such as Congress ought to set about providing, and he hoped in less than ten years to see it actually established. He was far from surveying the vast maritime power of G. Britain with the desponding eye with which other gentlemen beheld it. He could not allow himself to be discouraged at the prospect even of her thousand ships. This country only required resolution and a proper exertion of its immense resources to command respect, and to vindicate every essential right. When we consider our remoteness from Europe, the expense, difficulty and perils to which any squadron would be exposed stationed off our coasts, he entertained no doubt that the force to which he referred would insure the command of our own seas. Such a force would avail itself of our extensive seaboard and numerous harbors, every where affording asylums, to which it could safely retire from a superior fleet, or from which it could issue for the purpose of annoyance. To the opinion of his colleague (Mr. M'Kee,) [2] who appeared to think that it was in vain for us to make any struggle on the ocean; he would oppose the sentiments of his distinguished connexion, the heroic Daveiss, who fell in the battle of Tippacanoe.

{Here Mr. C. read certain parts of a work written by Col. Daveiss[3] in which the author attempts to shew that, as the aggressions upon our commerce were not committed by fleets but by single vessels, they could in the same manner be best retaliated; that a force of about 20 or 30 frigates would be capable of inflicting great injury on English commerce by picking up stragglers, cutting off convoys and seizing upon every moment of supineness, & that such a force, with our seaports and harbors well fortified, and aided by privateers, would be really formidable and would annoy the British navy and commerce, as the French army was assailed in Egypt, the Persian army in Scythia and the Roman army in Parthia.}

The third description of force, worthy of consideration, is that which would be able to prevent any single vessel, of whatever metal, from endangering our whole coasting trade, blocking up our harbors or laying under contribution our cities—a force competent to punish the insolence of the commander of any single ship and to preserve in our own jurisdiction the inviolability of our peace and our laws. A force of this kind is entirely within the compass of our means, at this time. Is there a reflecting man in the nation who would not charge Congress with a culpable neglect of its duty, if, for the want of such a force, a single ship were to bombard one of our cities? Would not every honorable member of this committee inflict on himself the bitterest reproaches, if, by failing to make an inconsiderable addition to our little gallant navy, a single British vessel should place N. York under contribution? Yes, sir, when the city is in flames, its wretched inhabitants begin to repent of their neglect in not providing engines and water buckets. If, said Mr. C. we are not able to meet the wolves of the forest, shall we put up with the barking impudence of every petty fice that trips across our way? Because we cannot guard against every possible danger shall we provide against none? He hoped not. He had hardly expected that the instructing but humiliating lesson was so soon to be forgotten which was taught us in the murder of Pearce[4] —the attack on the Chesapeake;[5] and the insult offered in the very harbor of Charleston which the brave old fellow that commanded the fort in vain endeavored to chastise.[6]

It was a rule with Mr. C. when acting either in a public or private character, to attempt nothing more than what there existed a prospect of accomplishing. He was therefore not in favor of entering into any mad projects on this subject; but for deliberately and resolutely pursuing what he believed to be within the power of government. Gentlemen refer to the period of 1798, and we are reminded of the principles maintained by the opposition at that time. He had no doubt of the correctness of that opposition. The naval schemes of that day were premature, not warranted by the resources of the country, and were contemplated for an unnecessary war into which the nation was about to be plunged.[7] He always admired and approved the zeal and ability with which that opposition was conducted by the distinguished gentleman now at the head of the Treasury.[8] But the state of things is totally altered. What was folly in 1798 may be wisdom now. At that time we had a revenue only of about six millions. Our revenue now, upon a supposition that commerce is restored, is about sixteen millions. The population of the country too is greatly increased, nearly doubled, and the wealth of the nation is perhaps tripled. Whilst our ability to construct a navy is thus enhanced, the necessity for maritime protection is proportionately augmented. Independent of the extension of our commerce, since the year 1798, we have had an addition of more than five hundred miles to our coast, from the bay of Perdido to the mouth of the Sabine—a weak and defenceless accession, requiring, more than any other part of our maritime frontier, the protecting arm of government.

The groundless imputation, that those who were friendly to a navy were espousing a principle inimical to freedom, should not terrify him. He was not ashamed when in such company as the illustrious author of the notes on Virginia,[9] whose opinions on the subject of a navy, contained in that work, contributed to the formation of his own. But the principle of a navy, Mr. C. contended, was no longer open to controversy. It was decided when Mr. Jefferson came into power. With all the prejudices against a navy which are alleged by some to have been then brought into the administration—with many honest prejudices he admitted—the rash attempt was not made to destroy the establishment. It was reduced only to what was supposed to be within the financial capacity of the country. If, ten years ago, when all those prejudices were to be combatted, even in time of peace, it was deemed proper, by the then administration, to retain in service ten frigates, he put it to the candor of gentlemen to say, if now, when we are on the eve of a war, and taking into view the actual growth of the country, and the acquisition of our coast on the Gulph of Mexico, we ought not to add to the establishment?

Mr. C. said he had hitherto alluded more particularly to the exposed situation of certain parts of the Atlantic frontier. Whilst he felt the deepest solicitude for the safety of N. York and other cities on the coast, he would be pardoned by the committee for referring to the interests of that section of the union from which he came. If, said he, there be a point more than any other in the U. States demanding the aid of naval protection, that point is the mouth of the Mississippi. What is the population of the Western country, dependent upon this single outlet for its surplus productions? Kentucky, according to the last enumeration, has 406,511, Tennessee 261,727 and Ohio 230,760. And when the population of the western parts of Virginia and Pennsylvania & the territories which are drained by the Mississippi or its waters, is added, it will form an aggregate equal to about one-fifth of the whole population of the U. States, resting all their commercial hopes upon this solitary vent! The bulky articles of which their surplus productions consist can be transported no other way. They will not bear the expense of a carriage up the Ohio and Tennessee and across the mountains, and the circuitous voyage of the lakes is out of the question. Whilst most other states have the option of numerous outlets, so that if one be closed resort can be had to others, this vast population has no alternative. Close the mouth of the Mississippi and their export trade is annihilated. He called the attention of his western friends, especially his worthy Kentucky friends (from whom he felt himself with regret constrained to differ on this occasion) to the state of the public feeling, in that quarter, whilst the navigation of the Mississippi was withheld by Spain; and to the still more recent period when the right of depot was violated. The whole country was in commotion; and at the nod of government would have fallen on Baton Rouge and New Orleans and punished the treachery of a perfidious government.[10] Abandon all idea of protecting, by maritime force, the mouth of the Mississippi and we shall have the recurrence of many similar scenes. We shall hold the inestimable right of the navigation of that river by the most precarious tenure. The whole commerce of the Mississippi—a commerce that is destined to be the richest that was ever borne by a single stream—is placed at the mercy of a single ship lying off the Balize!

Again. The convulsions of the new world, still more perhaps than those of Europe, challenge our attention. Whether the ancient dynasty of Spain is still to be upheld or subverted, it is extremely uncertain, if the bonds connecting the parent country with her colonies are not forever broken. What is to become of Cuba? Will it assert independence or remain the province of some European power? In either case the whole trade of the the western country, which must pass almost within gun shot of the Moro Castle, is exposed to danger. It was not however of Cuba he was afraid. He wished her independent. But suppose England gets possession of that valuable island. With Cuba on the south and Halifax on the north—and the consequent means of favoring or annoying the commerce of particular sections of the country—he asked if the most sanguine amongst us would not tremble for the integrity of the union? If along with Cuba G. Britain should acquire East Florida, she will have the absolute command of the gulph of Mexico. Can gentlemen, particularly gentlemen from the western country, contemplate such possible, nay probable, events without desiring to see at least the commencement of such a naval establishment as would effectually protect the Mississippi? He intreated them to turn their attention to the defenceless situation of the Orleans Territory, and to the nature of its population. It is known that whilst under the Spanish government they experienced the benefit of naval security. Satisfy them that under the government of the

U. States they will enjoy less protection, and you disclose the most fatal secret.

The general government receives annually for the public lands, about $600,000. One of the sources whence the Western people raise this sum, is the exportation of the surplus productions of that country. Shut up the Mississippi and this source is in a great measure dried up. But suppose this government to look upon the occlusion of the Mississippi without making an effort on that element, where alone it could be made successfully, to remove the blockading force, and at the same time to be vigorously pressing payment for the public lands; he shuddered at the consequences. Deep-rooted as he knew the affections of the Western people to be to the Union, (and he would not admit their patriotism to be surpassed by any other quarter of the country) if such a state of things were to last any considerable time, he should seriously apprehend a withdrawal of their confidence. Nor, sir, could we derive any apology for the failure to afford them protection from the want of the materials for naval architecture. On the contrary, all the articles entering into the construction of a navy; iron, hemp, timber, pitch, abound in the greatest quantities on the waters of the Mississippi. Kentucky alone, he had no doubt, raised hemp enough the last year for the whole consumption of the United States.

If, as he conceived, gentlemen had been unsuccessful in shewing that the downfall of maritime nations was ascribable to their navies, they had been more fortunate in shewing, by the instances to which they had referred, that without a marine no foreign commerce could exist to any extent. It is the appropriate—the natural (if the term be allowable) protection of foreign commerce. The shepherd and his faithful dog are not more necessary to guard the flocks that browse and gambol on the neighboring mountain. He considered the prosperity of foreign commerce indissolubly allied to marine power. Neglect to provide the one and you must abandon the other. Suppose the expected war with England is commenced, you enter and subjugate Canada, and she still refuses to do you justice—what other possible mode will remain to operate on the enemy but upon that element where you can then alone come in contact with him? And if you do not prepare to protect there your own commerce and to assail his, will he not sweep from the ocean every vessel bearing your flag, and destroy even the coasting trade? But from the arguments of gentlemen it would seem to be questioned if foreign commerce is worth the kind of protection insisted upon. What is this foreign commerce that has suddenly become so inconsiderable? It has, with very trifling aid from other sources, defrayed the expences of government ever since the adoption of the present constitution—maintained an expensive and successful war with the Indians—a war with the Barbary powers[11] —a quasi war with France—sustained the charges of suppressing two insurrections,[12] & extinguished upward of forty-six millions of the public debt! In revenue it has, since the year 1789, yielded one hundred & ninety-one millions of dollars. During the first four years after the commencement of the present government the revenue averaged only about two millions annually—during a subsequent period of four years it rose to an average of fifteen millions annually, or became equivalent to a capital of two hundred and fifty millions of dollars, at an interest of six per cent. per annum. And if our commerce is re-established it will, in the course of time, nett a sum for which we are scarcely furnished with figures in arithmetic. Taking the average of the last nine years (comprehending of course the season of the embargo) our exports averaged upwards of thirty-seven millions of dollars, which is equivalent to a capital of upwards of six hundred millions of dollars at six per cent. interest, all of which must be lost in a destruction of foreign commerce. In the abandonment of that commerce is also involved the sacrifice of our brave tars, who have engaged in the pursuit from which they derive subsistence under confidence that the government will afford them that just protection which is due to all. They will be driven into foreign employment, for it is in vain to expect that they will renounce the habits of their life.

The spirit of commercial enterprise so strongly depicted by the gentleman from New-York (Mr. Mitchill),[13] is diffused throughout the country. It is a passion as unconquerable as any with which nature has endowed us. You may attempt to regulate—you cannot destroy it. It exhibits itself as well on the waters of the western country, as on the waters and shores of the Atlantic. Mr. C. had heard of a vessel built at Pittsburgh, having crossed the Atlantic, and entered an European port (he believed that of Leghorn). The master of the vessel laid his papers before the proper custom-officer, which, of course, stated the place of her departure. The officer boldly denied the existence of any such American port as Pittsburgh, and threatened a seizure of the vessel, as being furnished with forged papers. The affrighted master procured a map of the U. States, and, pointing out the gulph of Mexico, took the officer to the mouth of the Mississippi—traced the course of the Mississippi more than a thousand miles to the mouth of the Ohio; and, conducting him still a thousand miles higher, to the junction of the Alleghany and Monongahalia—there, he exclaimed, stands Pittsburgh, the port from which I sailed! The custom-house officer, prior to the production of this evidence, would have as soon believed that the vessel had performed a voyage from the moon.

In delivering the sentiments he had expressed, Mr. C. considered himself as conforming to a sacred constitutional duty. When the power to provide a navy was confided to Congress, it must have been the intention of the convention to submit only to the discretion of that body the period when that power should be exercised. That period had, in his opinion, arrived, at least for making a respectable beginning. And whilst he discharged what he conceived to be his duty, he derived great pleasure from the reflection that he was supporting a measure calculated to impart additional strength to our happy Union. Diversified as are the interests of its various parts, how admirably do they blend together and harmonise! We have only to make a proper use of the bounties spread before us, to render us prosperous and powerful. Such a navy as he had contended for will form a new bond of connexion between the States, concentrating their hopes, their interests, and their affections.

He concluded by enquiring of the chairman of the naval committee, if there were seasoned timber on hand, to enable him to judge whether it was best now to vote for immediately building some additional frigates, or to provide the requisite materials.

Washington *National Intelligencer,* March 19, 1812. Published also in *Annals of Cong.,* 12 Cong., 1 Sess., XXIII, 910-19; Lexington *Reporter,* April 4, 1812; Lexington *Kentucky Gazette,* April 7, 1812; Chambers, *Speeches of Henry Clay,* 35-43; Swain, *Life and Speeches of Henry Clay,* I, [22]-32; Mallory, *Life and Speeches of Henry Clay,* I, [286]-95; Colton, *Life, Correspondence and Speeches of Henry Clay,* V, 43-51. Langdon Cheves on December 17, 1811, had presented a bill concerning the Naval establishment and, later, had offered amendments to specify the number and kinds of vessels to be added. He found himself opposed by members of his own party, including some of the "War Hawks," and on January 27 the House struck out his proposal to build new frigates. Clay's remarks, delivered in Committee of the Whole following proposal to set the number of new frigates at ten, were not successful in carrying support for such construction; but following Senate action to restrict the appropriation for timber purchase to that necessary to rebuild four old frigates, the House agreed to a compromise proposal that this reconstruction should have first claim on the money allotted. 1 William Lowndes. 2 Samuel McKee.

3 Joseph Hamilton Daveiss, *The Sketch of a Bill For an Uniform Militia of the United States, With Reflections on the State of the Nation: Addressed to the Secretary at War* (Frankfort, 1810), 61-63.

4 John Pierce, helmsman of a coasting-sloop, had been killed by a ball from the British warship *Leander* just outside New York harbor on April 25, 1806.

5 By the *Leopard,* June 22, 1807.

6 On April 20, 1807, the British sloop of war *Driver,* a vessel interdicted by Presidential proclamation of May 31, 1805, from entering a port of the United States, had anchored in Charleston harbor. The "venerable" Michael Kalteisin, commandant at Fort Johnson in the harbor, had demanded the departure of the vessel within twenty-four hours. Captain William Love of the *Driver* had replied that he intended to leave within the period, but with an arrogance that was widely publicized.

7 The United States had engaged in naval hostilities with France from 1798 to 1800.

8 Albert Gallatin. 9 Thomas Jefferson.

10 The West had become greatly agitated late in 1802 upon learning that Spain, in violation of the Pinckney Treaty, had suspended the right of deposit at New Orleans.

11 From 1801 to 1805. 12 The Whisky Rebellion and the Burr Conspiracy.

13 Samuel Latham Mitchill.

Ruling on Use of Improper Language in the House

[January 28, 1812]

The *Speaker* declared, that in future, when he discovered that any paper presented to the House was couched in disrespectful and improper language, he should consider it his duty to take the sense of the House on the propriety of suffering the reading to progress.

Washington *National Intelligencer,* January 30, 1812. Published also in *Annals of Cong.,* 12 Cong., 1 Sess., XXIII, 1001. Richard Jackson, Jr., of Rhode Island, had presented a long memorial and remonstrance reflecting upon the measures of the Government. After a part had been read, he withdrew the paper in the face of objections that it was indecorous.

Tax Bill, 1811

[*ca.* February 1, 1812]

1811 Henry Clay Esqr. - - - - - - - - -	Dr -- --
To tax on 380 acres 1st rate Land at 50 Cts	$ 1.90
To 7000 acres 2d. rate Do. at 37½ Cents pr. hd.	26.25
To 3080 £ Town Lots at 5$ pr. thousand Lb.	15.36
To one 4 wheal Carrage at 25 Cts pr. wheal - - - - - - -	1.00
To 11 tithes at 50 Cents each - - - - - - - - -	5.50
To 18 Slaves at 12½ Cents each - - - - - - - -	2 25
To 65 horses at 4 Cents each - - - - - - - - -	2.60
	$54.86

Tax & Levy	$54.86
the half of feebill	20.88
	75.74
Howard Clay & C.[1]	2.21
	$77.95

D. DLC-TJC (DNA, M212, R15).
[1] Probably the directors of the Madison Hemp and Flax Spinning Company.

Receipt from Fortunatus Cosby

[February 1, 1812]

Recd. 1 Feby. 1812 of H. Clay One thousand & Seventy five dollars on a/c. of his purchase of me of an interest in the Falls Estate bought of Sarah Beard by me. FORTS. COSBY

DS, in Clay's hand. DLC-TJC, 2d Series, vol. 13. See above, Agreement, December 8, 1806.

Endorsement on Draft to John Hart

[February 3, 1812]

Attached to Bill of Exchange for $4000, October 1, 1811.

From Thomas Backus

Sir.. Kaskaskia Feby. 4th. 1812

I am told by Govr. Edwards[1] of this Territory that you hold a claim against the estate of Elijah Backus Esquire deceased—The estate is now in a train of settlement, and as it is desirable to have knowledge of the claims against it as soon as possible and as I cannot ascertain from any papers which Mr. Backus has left the amount of the claim which you hold or even to whom it is due, I take the liberty to request of you a specification of it, which I will thank you to direct to me at Franklinton[2] Ohio— I am respectfully Sir Yr hbl Svt THOMAS BACKUS.

The Hone Henry Clay Esqr.

ALS. DLC-TJC (DNA, M212, R12). Addressed to Clay at Washington. Thomas was the son of Elijah Backus, who had published the first newspaper at Marietta, Ohio, and who in 1804 had been appointed receiver of public monies at Kaskaskia, Illinois Territory. 1 Ninian Edwards. 2 Now Columbus.

To [James Morrison]

Dr Major H. of R. 6 Feb. 1812.

I recd. your favor[1] in which you request to know if I ordered the suits recently brought agt. you in Mr. Wests name.[2]

Mr. Hardin and Mr. Wickliffe[3] argued with me the cause in the Ct. of Appeals. As a compensation to them and to myself, Mr. West thought proper to make us three equally interested (to the best of my recollection) in your bonds with himself. After the decision lately pronounced, Mr. Hardin and Mr. Wickliffe or one of them, wrote me requesting to know where the bonds were.[4] In a letter to Mr. W. I pointed out the place where they were in my office. You will see that having no greater interest than the other gentlemen I had no greater Control than they over the bonds or proceedings upon them. Nevertheless I suggested to Mr. W. the propriety of conferring with you on the subject before he took any proceeding. This he wrote me he intended to do, but found you so much out of humor about the decision, that he did not choose to subject himself to be hurt by speaking to you on a topic on which you appeared to feel & display so much Sensibility, & therefore concluded to give the law its course.[5]

Your heart Majr. on cool reflection can give me no just reproaches in this affair. Not an event has occurred in the course of this litigation that I did not distinctly foretell to you. After the determination of that branch of the cause in which I was most particularly concerned I intreated you to accept of the terms of compromise proposed by M. West, and giving up your recourse for the amt. of the sum paid P.W.&Co,[6] take a surrender of your bonds. You rejected them—urged on the controversy, hopeless as it was even if you were successful agt West only, and you have been defeated—I can only repeat that I have nothing to do in the future progress of the business more than any one of the other parties concerned.

We have no news. The appointment of officers in the New Army will pretty generally take place I expect next week—Barry and Worseley are here—The latter goes to Philad. to day. Yrs

H. CLAY

ALS. ViU-Alderman Library. [1] Not found.

[2] Cf. above, Wrenshall to Clay, June 13, 1807, note. One suit (no other located), filed in Fayette Circuit Court on December 28, 1811, was based on the failure of Morrison to pay the bond he had given Edward West, which had been assigned to Clay on October 20, 1804. [3] Martin D. Hardin and Robert Wickliffe.

[4] Letters not found. [5] Letters to and from Wickliffe not found.

[6] Peacock, Wrenshall and Company.

[7] Probably William T. Barry and William W. Worsley of Lexington.

To [William W. Worsley]

Washington City, Feb. 9th, 1812.

The Committee of Foreign relations is understood to have fixed upon the period of the return of the Hornet[1] for recommending their ulterior measures—not because that vessel went out charged with any negociation (which she did not) but because, when she arrives, the Prince Regent, being then untrammelled, we shall know whether he will shun or imitate the errors of his infatuated father.[2] Circumstances may however accelerate a declaration of war.

Taxes are indispensibly necessary in the event of hostilities. The only duty left to the representative, it seems to me, is to select those that are least burthensome to the people. That they will, when such a selection is made, be borne with chearfulness I have no doubt. When the most inestimable interests of the country are at stake, the nation would be unfaithful to itself if it withheld the requisite supplies.—Surely no man will hesitate to contribute his just *part* when *all* is at hazzard.

Extract. Lexington *Reporter,* February 22, 1812. Identified as from Clay to the editor.

[1] An American sloop-of-war, sent abroad with dispatches late in 1811 and detained pending the outcome of unsuccessful negotiations for a commercial treaty with France. It finally returned to the United States in May, 1812.

[2] See above, Clay to Beatty, January 24, 1811, note.

To General John Mason

Dr Sir Washington 10h. Feb. 12.

Will you be pleased to inform me in what manner the bill lodged at your bank mentioned in the inclosed letter,[1] which I recd. last evening, can be paid in Philadelphia? If upon its face it purports to be payable at the Bank of Philadelphia (which I do not recollect) I presume you would of course transmit it there that it may be there discharged. But supposing that not to be the case, would not this letter, which is written by a very respectable house, authorize the transmission of the bill to the B. of P. with or without my guarrantee of its payment? Or if that cannot be done, will not my draft on Mess Scott Trotter & Co. payable at sight be recd. in payment of the bill? The favor of a reply by my servant is requested.[2]

Yrs. H. CLAY

ALS. PPL-R. Addressed: "Genl. John Mason (In his absence) The Cashier of the B. of Columbia Geo. Town." Endorsed: "The Bill mentioned by Mr Clay is at our office for collection & came from the Bank of Penna—my impression is, that. the only way we can accomodate Mr Clay is to take his Bill at Sight on Scott Trotter & Co. for the Sum—by our Books it is due 9/12 & is payable here by Mr Clay—"

1 The letter, from Scott, Trotter and Company, enclosing a bill drawn by John Hart, has not been found.

2 Mason's reply, not found, was written that day or the next.

Remarks on Taxing Marriage Licenses

[February 11, 1812]

Mr. *Clay* (the Speaker) knew not which most to admire, the conduct of the opposer or supporter of this bill. If he understood the gentleman last up, there is at present a law taxing marriages, but no authority to collect the tax, which is the same as if there was no law on the subject. As he thought with the gentleman first up, that marriages ought not to be taxed, but promoted, he should vote with him for striking out the first section of the bill.

Washington *National Intelligencer*, February 13, 1812. Published also in *Annals of Cong.*, 12 Cong., 1 Sess., XXIII, 1041. On December 26, 1811, the Committee for the District of Columbia, to which had been referred two petitions from residents of Washington praying that the Maryland tax on marriage licenses be revived in Washington County to provide financial aid for schools, had presented a bill in line with the wishes of the petitioners. After brief and somewhat jocular debate, the bill was rejected.

To Scott, Trotter and Company

Gent. H. of R. 11 Feb 1812

In reply to your favor of the 6h. inst.[1] I observe that the bill drawn by Mr. Hart[2] on me was transmitted to the B. of Columbia for collection. I have this day paid the bill, to enable me to do which it became necessary for me to draw at sight on you for the amt. placed in your hands by M[r]. Hart to discharge it. I hope my draft will be duly honored. I send you inclosed Mr. Hart's bill.[3] Yrs. H. CLAY

ALS. ViU-Alderman Library. Addressed: "Mess Scott Trotter & Co. Merchants Philadelphia."
[1] Not found. [2] John Hart. [3] Not found.

To Richard Smith

[February 11, 1812]

H. Clay presents his respects to Mr. Smith & incloses him the letter of Gen. Mason[1] accompanied by a set of Exchange on Mess Scott-Trotter & Co. of Philadelphia in paymt. of the bill of Hart, which he will be pleased to send by the servant. Tuesday morning.

AN. PPL-R. Addressed: "Mr. Richd. Smith Agent B[ank]. C[olumbia]. Treasury Office."
[1] Replying to Clay's letter of February 10, 1812. Not found.

From [Albert Gallatin]

Treasury Department, February 18, 1812.

Hon: H. Clay, Speaker of the House of Representatives . . .

Sir, The Treasury has no controul over the prosecutions instituted for presumed infractions of the laws prohibiting the slave trade; nor has even the Secretary of that department the power to remit penalties in cases arising under the said acts. The papers relative to the Apollo are therefore returned.[1] The only mode of obtaining relief (without the interference of Congress) is by application to the President for a pardon or nol. pros. . . . . As orders to that effect are always transmitted by the Secretary of State, the applications for relief are generally made through him. I have, &c. [End]

Copy. DNA, RG56, Series E, vol. 5, p. 386. [1] Not found.

Deed of Trust from John Wilkinson

[February 28, 1812]

[Whereas John Wilkinson with Thomas Pickett by deed of September 1, 1810, conveyed in trust to Henry Clay for settlement of sundry debts due from Wilkinson and Pickett to Abraham S. Barton and John Hart, surviving partners of Hart, Barton & Hart, the following land and negroes: one tract of land in Fayette County on Howard's Creek, amounting to 305 acres; negroes Dick, Joseph, Tom, Whitley, Poll, Old Betty, Young Betty, China, and Patty— And whereas Wilkinson on November 15, 1807, by written agreement promised to pay Thomas Hart, Jr., the sum of $2000, four years after date, with two years' interest thereon, which obligation by various assignments has become the property of William Frye, who has commenced suit for its collection,[1] but has agreed to suspend recovery providing Wilkinson procures the approbation of the executors of Thomas Hart, which consent Wilkinson has obtained upon his agreeing to secure the executors against claim by reason of the assignment upon his bond—and for the purpose of indemnifying the executors, Wilkinson hereby conveys to Clay the further trust and use of the above-described property:

Wilkinson agrees that if the executors of Thomas Hart, Jr., suffer in any manner by reason of the assignment of the agreement with Hart, or by reason of any engagements made by Hart or his representatives with Frye, then Clay shall be at liberty to sell all of Wilkinson's claim to the above-conveyed property for the best price that may be obtained, in such manner and at such times as Clay may deem proper, or so much as will sufficiently indemnify the executors of Thomas Hart, Jr.; and Clay engages to execute the trust in good faith. Signature of Wilkinson acknowledged in Fayette County Clerk's Office, February 29, 1812.]

Fayette County Court, Deed Book F, 358-59. The name is recorded here as Wilkerson.

1 Earlier in February, 1812. Fayette Circuit Court, File 235.

To ———

Washington, Feb. 28, 1812.

On yesterday the House of Representatives, in committee of the whole, concurred with the Committee of Ways and Means in all the taxes recommended by them, without any change whatever.[1] There were large majorities in almost every instance. With respect to the Still tax and the Stamp tax there can be no objection on principle, as they are proposed to be laid. The former is free from the vexatious incidents [*sic*] of an Excise, and the other is confined to bank notes (a very fit subject of taxation) and negotiable paper, leaving the great body of country transactions exempt from its operation. The whole system is to take effect in event only of the war into which we are about to be driven by the aggressions of England, and is limited in its duration to one year after the restoration of peace.

The arrival of the Constitution[2] has placed us in possession of very little information as to our foreign affairs. Those of France wore a favorable aspect, while, on the part of England, no change was indicated when she left those countries.

Extract. Lexington *Reporter,* March 7, 1812. Identified as from Clay; the recipient not named.

1 *Annals of Cong.,* 12 Cong., 1 Sess., XXIII, 1105-12.

2 United States frigate, just returned from Europe.

From David Trimble

H Clay, Mount Sterling March 12th 1812.
Dr Sir

On the fifth of this month, the whole of A. W. Graysons interest in the Sandy-Salt-works and the 70,000 acres of Land, including the same, was sold by the Sheriff, under the Executions &c, &c, and you and myself being the highest bidders, became the purchasers, at the Sum of $4,000—

I sent word to R. H. Grayson[1] that his propositions could not be received, unless he would make the debts sure by giving better security than he proposed; he had previously found that he could not raise the first payment, and had declined all intention of buying; and never made any further communication to me on the subject— He was not at the Licks when the Sale was made—

I wrote to the Trustees that, I would with your concurrance, give them a generous price, for their interest under the Deeds-of-Trust—I think, it is probable that they will make us an offer, to buy or sell—If they do, I should be glad to know your mind on the subject before I give them a reply—Instruct me if you please, what further I shall do, and whether you are willing to buy out the Trustees; and if so, at what price &c &c?—

Have not leasure to write in detail—Shall expect to hear from you soon—With Sentiments of respect I am &c D TRIMBLE.

ALS. DLC-TJC (DNA, M212, R10). Postmarked March 20.
[1] Robert H. Grayson of Greenup County, Kentucky.

Amendment to, and Remarks on, Bill for Admission of Mississippi Territory

[March 12, 1812]

"*Provided,* That nothing herein contained shall be so construed as to prevent that portion of the territory comprehended within the said boundary, formerly composing a part of the country known by the name of West Florida, being subject to future negociation on the part of the United States."

. . . .

Mr. CLAY (Speaker) said that in offering this amendment to the committee, he confessed he was actuated rather by a disposition to accommodate the views of other gentlemen, than from any difficulty which he felt on the subject himself; for, with respect to our title to West Florida, he thought it utterly impossible that any gentleman could examine that question, without suffering other considerations to mingle in the investigation, and not be thoroughly convinced that the title was in the United States; and he confessed, that were he to consult his own views only, he should not hesitate a moment in making an unqualified annexation of that territory to the states to be formed of the Orleans and Mississippi territories. But as some gentlemen, adverting to the President's proclamation for taking possession of that country, had supposed that some difficulty might arise under it from such a procedure, in order to quiet these apprehensions, he had submitted this proviso. The right of the general government to destroy the integrity of a state having been questioned, it would be well to guard against any difficulty on that score by a reservation to the general government of the power to negociate on the subject of this territory. At the same time that he made this proposition, Mr. C. utterly disclaimed the idea that in any possible state of things ought this country to be ceded away. He considered the possession of West-Florida as indispensable to the interests and prosperity of the western states, and so far to the integrity of the Union; and he should as soon see a part of the state which he represents ceded away as this territory. What, he asked, was the extent of the country in question? In breadth about twenty miles; in length about 200, binding to that extent our southern frontier. The danger of having provinces of a foreign power on our frontier is too well disclosed by the late communication of the President (concerning Henry's mission) [1]—a disclosure which must combine, in the execration of the project it developed, every man in the country, and every honest man in every country. Suppose the former dynasty of Spain to be reinstated on the throne, it could not desire, for honest purposes, the possession of West-Florida. In proposing the amendment, Mr. Clay said it was merely his object to make the acts of the Legislative Body tally with the proclamation of the President. If, therefore, contrary to his firm conviction, it should be determined that we have not the title, he had no idea that even in that state of things the territory would be given up, but that an equivalent should be given for it.

Mr. C. said he fully approved the boundary established for the new state of Mississippi by the section just agreed to, so far as it operated on the Florida territory. It gave to the state of Louisiana about three-fourths, perhaps four-fifths, of the *population* of the whole territory—a population homogeneous to the character of the country—American in principle and feeling; and with pleasure he had seen the Convention of the Orleans territory, in requesting this annexation, display a liberality of sentiment in desiring a further American population, which he trusted would be reciprocated by Congress.[2] Although the state of Louisiana could not be gratified by the annexation of the whole territory, their desires would be gratified to a considerable extent by giving them all that portion of it lying west of Pearl river. The acquisition of the valuable settlements on the high lands, and their hardy population, would satisfy all the material wishes of the state. By this addition they would give to the new state of Louisiana the entire control of the Lakes Maurepas and Ponchartrain [*sic*], by which the city of New-Orleans may be most easily approached; you thus enable the state to take all necessary means to repel invasion. You effect another object, said Mr. C. There is not any very great natural connexion between the people immediately on the bay of Mobile and Tombigby river, and those on the Mississippi. If there be any connexion, it is an artificial one, resulting from the preponderancy of capital at New-Orleans, and will be lessened whenever there shall be a commercial capital at Mobile. I am therefore anxious to unite the territory east of Pearl river, including the bay of Mobile, to the Mississippi territory to which it is naturally connected; and, Mr. C. said, he had no hesitation in declaring that either Pearl river or the Pascagoula ought to be the boundary which is to separate the two parts of country respectively to be attached to the states of Louisiana and Mississippi—the Pearl river, upon the whole, would be the best, as dividing the territory in about equal portions. Mr. C. concluded by expressing his satisfaction that this subject had been taken up, and that the amendment proposed by the delegate from Mississippi had obtained, which he hoped would finally pass, &c.

Washington *National Intelligencer,* March 14, 24, 1812. Published also in *Annals of Cong.,* 12 Cong., 1 Sess., XXIV, 1204-1206. Toward the end of the previous year George Poindexter, delegate from the Mississippi Territory, had presented a bill for admission of that Territory as a State. On March 12, 1812, he offered in Committee of the Whole an amendment fixing the boundaries to include that part of West Florida east of the Pearl River. Clay then moved adoption of the amendment here presented, to follow after the boundary proposal. Both amendments were adopted. The bill in this form passed the House, but on April 22 was indefinitely postponed by the Senate. Later in the session the boundaries of the Territory were expanded to the limits set in Poindexter's amendment, but without Clay's proviso.

[1] On March 9, President Madison had presented to Congress documents purchased with secret service funds from John Henry, a spy employed by the Governor-General of Canada to report on disaffection in New England. The documents are published in *Annals of Cong.,* 12 Cong., 1 Sess., XXIV, 1162-81.

[2] See below, Remarks, March 18, 1812.

To ———

City of Washington, March 15, 1811 [*i.e.* 1812].

The WASP has gone to *France.*[1]—There exists however not the slightest intention of delaying our declaration of WAR until her return.

Extract. Lexington *Reporter,* March 24, 1812. Identified as from Clay *"to a gentleman in this place."*
[1] The American sloop-of-war bore instructions to our Minister in France.

To [James Monroe]

Dr Sir Wash. 15h. Mar. 1812.

Since I had the pleasure of conversing with you this morning, I have concluded, in writing, to ask a consideration of the following propositions:

That the President recommend an Embargo to last say 30 days, by a confidential message:[1]

That a termination of the Embargo be followed by War: and,

That he also recommend provision for the acceptance of 10.000 Volunteers for a short period, whose officers are to be commissioned by the president.

The objection to an embargo is, that it will impede sales. The advantages are, that it is a measure of some vigor upon the heels of Henry's[2] disclosure—that it will give tone to public sentiment—operate as a notification, repressing indiscreet speculation and enabling the prudent to look to the probable period of the commencement of hostilities and thus to put under shelter before the storm. It will above all powerfully accelerate preparations for the War.

By the expiration of the Embargo the Hornet will have returned with good or bad news, and of course the question of War may then be fairly decided.

The acceptance of such a Corps of Volunteers as is described will get rid of all constitutional embarrassment, furnish a force in itself highly useful and leave a certain quarter of the Country disposed to fly off without even a pretext for dereliction. Yr friend

H. CLAY

[Endorsement in margin][3]

Altho' the power of declaring War belongs to Congress, I do not see that it less falls within the scope of the President's constitutional duty to recommend such measures as he shall judge necessary and expedient than any other which, being suggested by him, they alone can adopt.

ALS. DLC-James Monroe Papers (DNA, M212, R22).
[1] See below, Speech, April 1, 1812.
[2] John Henry.
[3] AE, by Clay.

To [William Eustis]

Dr Sir Wash. 16 Mar. 1812.

Inclosed is a letter from our mutual friend Majr. Morrison,[1] in which he authorizes me to contract with your department for the purchase of a quantity of Nitre and Lead. Will you be so obliging as to let me know if you are disposed to purchase those articles? in which case I will have the pleasure to call & see you.

I was much gratified at the nomination of Wm. Wilkins,[2] with which the Pennsylvania delegation in the H. was also well pleased. I understand that the nomination is laid over or committed in the Senate at the instance of Mr. L.[3] and that an effort is to be made to prevail on you to withdraw it. Should such an experiment be made I take it for granted that it will be repelled, and that the Executive will not expose itself to the censure of indecision which such conduct would be thought to indicate.

The President has nominated a character for an office whose pretentions every way are entirely unquestionable. It is impossible that calumny itself shall detract from the fairness of his reputation or his capacity for the office. At such a nomination a particular individual may bluster, but the Senate must have too much good sense to reject it. They will not take upon themselves such respon- [. . . .]

AL. DNA, RG107, Letters Received, (6) C-211. Mutilated: a part of the letter, including the signature, is missing.

1 James Morrison's letter, directed to Eustis, may be found in the above source.

2 Of Pittsburgh, younger brother of Charles Wilkins of Lexington. William was later a Federal judge, United States Senator, and Secretary of War in Tyler's Cabinet. The appointment here cited it not known. The name "Wm." is superimposed on "Mr."

3 Probably Senator Michael Leib of Pennsylvania.

To [Paul Hamilton]

Sir Wash. 16h. Mar. 1812.

I take the liberty of recommending Richard Lee Smith, son of the late Govr. of Virginia, who unfortunately perished in the theatre at Richmond, as a Mid shipman in the Navy.[1] He is a young gentleman of about 18 years of age whom I do not personally know, but who is highly spoken of by a friend on whom I can rely.

I will add also the name of Dr. John McCullough as a Surgeon's mate.[2] He resides in the town of Lexington, Kentucky, and is strongly recommended to me. Yrs. H. CLAY

ALS. DNA, RG45, Misc. Letters Received, 1812, vol. 2, p. 86. Endorsed: "Appoint him P. H"; and on verso: ". . . Richd L Smith appd Mids: Dr. J McCullough Surgs. mate The latter seems not to have been apptd." (The last sentence is in the same hand as the first endorsement.) Hamilton, a former Governor of South Carolina, had become Secretary of the Navy in 1809.

1 The victims of the Richmond theater fire of December 26, 1811, had included Governor George Smith.

2 John Lawson McCullough had been graduated from the Transylvania University Medical Department in 1809. He was commissioned regimental surgeon's mate in General William Henry Harrison's army on July 29, 1813.

Remarks on Admission of Louisiana

[March 18, 1812]

Mr. *Clay*, (speaker) could not view the subject in the same light, he said, as the gentleman from Virginia; and although there had been a division of sentiment in the select committee, there certainly were some members of that committee in favor of the motion. But could the gentleman imagine any difficulty growing out of making this section a part of the present bill, which would not equally arise if it were put in a separate bill? There could be no difficulty in either way; and in point of propriety, it appeared to him the course now proposed ought to be pursued. They were about to admit a new state into the Union. Should not the bill, which recognised it, present the whole limits of the state in one view, or would it be better to subject enquirers to the necessity of wading through two or three acts to find out the boundary of a single state? He hoped the motion would prevail.

[The motion was approved, 47 to 25.]

Mr. *Clay* said he observed there had been no ordinance passed by the convention recognising the freedom of navigation of the Mississippi. He had no idea that under any circumstances, the Legislature of the new state would impede the navigation; but the object was one so dear to the people of the western country generally, that he wished to place it beyond the possibility of doubt.

[An amendment to this effect was adopted.]

Mr. *Clay* said he had understood that a memorial was in the city, and would be presented to the House at the first opportunity, from the convention of Orleans, praying the annexation of the territory in question to the new state.[1] When that was before them, the committee would be better able to understand how far they could now proceed in sanctioning the representation of that territory in the Louisiana Legislature. He therefore moved that the committee now rise, report progress, and ask leave to sit again.[2]

Washington *National Intelligencer*, March 19, 1812. Published also in *Annals of Cong.*, 12 Cong., 1 Sess., XXIV, 1217-18. During consideration by the House of a bill for the admission of Louisiana, Poindexter of the Mississippi Territory had offered an amendment outlining the boundaries of the new State in such a manner as to include that portion of West Florida west of the Pearl River. John Dawson of Virginia had observed that the select committee believed that the addition of this territory should be considered apart from the bill accepting Louisiana's constitution.

1 The memorial was presented on the following day.

2 Clay spoke again on the subject on March 19.

Remarks on Amendment to the Louisiana Bill

[March 19, 1812]

Mr. *H. Clay* spoke in favor of the amendment. He could see no real obstacle to its adoption. The Convention of Orleans had framed a constitution for the state in conformity to the law of Congress imposing certain conditions as preliminary. The Convention had annexed to their acceptance of these conditions another proposition viz. that the Florida territory should be incorporated in that state. Can we not, said Mr. C. accept or reject this proposition? If we accept, may we not do it with or without qualification? We agree to give only a certain part instead of the whole of the territory; and it is proposed to do this on certain conditions. In alienating a whole territory, an entire people, an exercise of one of the highest attributes of sovereignty, we are about to take care of their rights, and to secure to them the same political rights, privileges and immunities as are enjoyed by the people of the territory to which it is to be annexed. If the present amendment was adopted, the question how these rights shall be invested, by the Legislature, or by a new convention to be called for the purpose, was very properly left to the decision of those concerned.

Washington *National Intelligencer,* March 21, 1812. Published also in *Annals of Cong.,* 12 Cong., 1 Sess., XXIV, 1225-26. Thomas Gholson of Virginia had proposed an amendment to the bill to admit Louisiana, which would guarantee to the people of that part of West Florida now being incorporated into the State all the rights and privileges of residents in the other portion of the State.

From John McKim, Jr.

Dear Sir Baltimore March 20th. 1812

Your esteemed favour dated the 15th. Inst. came duly to hand.[1] Agreeable to your directions, I now enclose you Thomas Dye Owings note dated the 18th. July 1809 Payable on the 7th. of October following, for Dolls. 14315.95—I have two other notes of Mr. Owings Amtg—to about $1800, but I have laid an Attachment on 95 Hhds of his Tobacco laying here, on this Tobacco there is upwards of $1500 Freight, due, with Storage & other Charges, that I am afraid the Tobacco will never pay the whole, Mr. Owings has limited this Tobacco at $6 pr Hundred, which it will never bring.

I would suggest the propriety of holding the Original note, & forwarding a Copy for fear the Original should be lost, on the way out.

I feel myself under great obligations to you, for undertaking the Collection of this money for me, yourself, & I shall rest satisfyed that you will attend to my Interest. I am Respectfully Your Obt. Sert.

JNO MCKIM JR

ALS. DLC-TJC (DNA, M212, R12). Addressed to Clay at Washington. McKim was a merchant, active in business and civic enterprises in Baltimore, and some years later one of the incorporators of the Baltimore and Ohio Railroad.

1 Not found.

To [Paul Hamilton]

Dr Sir Wash. 27h. Mar. 1812.

I recommend Mr. Richardson Buck[1] for the appointment of a Mid-Shipman. He resides in Kentucky, is of very respectable family and connexions, and is a promising young gentleman. with great respect I am Yr. obt. Servt. H. Clay

ALS. DNA, RG45, Misc. Letters Received, 1812. Endorsed: "To be appd & warrt. to be sent to Mr Clay."

[1] Of Woodford County, Kentucky.

Speech Urging Passage of the Embargo Bill

[April 1, 1812]

Mr. Clay (the speaker) then warmly expressed his satisfaction and full approbation of the message, and the proposition now before the committee. He approved of it, because it is to be viewed as a direct precursor to war. He did not wish upon this occasion to hear of the opinion of Brockholst Livingston[1] or any other man. No gentleman can question the propriety of the proposition. Gentlemen who said so much about the want of preparation are not for war. He considered this as a war measure, and as such he should discuss it.[2] Sir, said Mr. Clay, after the pledges we have made, and the stand we have taken, are we now to cover ourselves with shame and indelible disgrace by retreating from the measures and ground we have taken.—He then stated our measures, our pledges, and the great injuries and abuses we have received. He said, what would disgrace an individual under certain circumstances would disgrace a nation.—And what would you think of one individual who had thus conducted to another, and should then retreat. He did not think we were upon this occasion in the least embarrassed by the conduct of France in burning our vessels—that may be a subject of future consideration.[3]—We have complete evidence as to the enemy whom we have selected: As weak and imbecile as we are, we would combine France if necessary. He said there was no intrinsic difficulty or terror in the war; there was no terror except what arises from the novelty. Where are we to come in contact with our enemy? On our own Continent. If gentlemen please to call these sentiments Quixotic, he would say he pitied them for their sense of honor. We know no pains have been spared to vilify the government. If we now proceed we shall be supported by the people. Many of our people have not believed that war is to take place. They have been wilfully blinded. He was willing to give them further notice. It remains for us to say whether we will shrink or follow up the patriotic conduct of the president. As an

American and a member of this house, he felt a pride that the executive had recommended this measure.

[John Randolph of Virginia here spoke at length, questioning the current need for the proposed action.]

Mr. Clay (the speaker) said the gentleman from Virginia need not have reminded us, in the manner he has, of that Being who watches and surrounds us.[4]

He thought from this sentiment we ought to draw very different conclusions than what the gentleman had.—It ought to influence us to that patriotism, to that spirit and display of those qualifications, which are so honorable to the human character. The gentleman asks, what *new* cause of war? He would ask what old cause of war is avenged? He agreed the affair of the Chesapeake is settled[5] —but why? to paralize the spirit of the country. Has Great Britain abstained from impressing our seamen—from depredating upon our property? He had in his hands a paper giving an account of the capture of the ship Hannibal,[6] worth, with the cargo, three hundred, thousand dollars, a short time since, and near our coast, on a voyage to France. He had no doubt but the late Indian war on the Wabash, was excited by the British—and what is to be thought of the emissary who was sent to one of our principal cities, to excite civil war?[7] Is this not a cause of war? We have complete proof that she will do every thing to destroy us—our resolution and spirit are our only dependence. Although he felt warm, he prided himself upon his feelings, and should despise himself if he was destitute of them. The gentleman says, there is no cause of war—

[Randolph said he had never asserted there was no cause of war, but that there was no new cause of war.]

Mr. Clay said, those who voted for the former embargo, are bound now to vote for war. It ought to have succeeded the termination of that measure, which would have been the true policy. He said he was at issue with the gentleman as to the public sentiment.—That it is with us, is proved by the glowing and patriotic resolutions of fourteen legislatures. He said there was no division in the southern and western states—Federalists and republicans were united for war.

[Debate continued, for and against the proposition of war.]

The speaker (Mr. Clay) called Mr. Randolph to order, for charging the House with spending five months in idle debate.

[The chairman's decision that Randolph's expression was not out of order was, upon appeal, confirmed by a vote of 50 to 49.]

Niles' Weekly Register, II (April 18, 1812), 105-106, reprinted from the Philadelphia *Political and Commercial Register*. Published also in *Annals of Cong.,* 12 Cong., 1 Sess., XXIV, 1588-89, 1591, 1593-94. Upon receipt of a confidential message from the President, recommending passage of an act to impose a sixty-day embargo, the House had gone into secret session. Before the day was over a bill embodying Madison's proposal had been reported, debated, and passed in the House. Two days later that body acceded to Senate amendment fixing the term of the embargo at ninety days, and President Madison signed the measure on April 4. 2 *U. S. Stat.*, 700-701.

1 New York lawyer, associate justice of the United States Supreme Court, 1806-1823. Clay's speech followed a statement by Silas Stow, of New York, who had cited a letter by Livingston in support of a charge that the fortifications in New York were unmanned and unarmed.

2 Felix Grundy had already taken the same position.

3 During the previous month it had become known that French naval vessels carried orders to burn all American ships sailing to or from a British port. Not until 1831 did the United States and France come to an agreement relative to payment for these Napoleonic spoliations on American commerce.

4 Referring to the secrecy of the deliberations, Randolph had said: "We are shut up here from the light of Heaven; but the eyes of God are upon us. He knows the spirit of our minds."

5 During the previous November, Secretary Monroe had accepted a British offer, conveyed by Augustus J. Foster, to restore to the *Chesapeake* the surviving seamen impressed from her and to compensate them and their families.

6 Sailing out of Baltimore, built for Christophe of Haiti, reported to carry 30 guns and sail "remarkably fast." She had fallen to two British frigates after a three-day chase. *Niles' Weekly Register*, II (April 4, 1812), 86.

7 John Henry.

To [William W. Worsley]

City of Washington, April 4, 1812.

I transmit you a copy of an act laying an Embargo for ninety days.[1] This measure is not designed as the substitute of War, but as a component part of that system which government is deliberately forming.[2] Its value consists in the notification it gives to preserve property at home, to bring in as much as is practicable from abroad, and to make preparations for that contest which cannot be much longer deferred. It fixes a period beyond which the present state of things will not continue. An incidental advantage (which however by no means constitutes a leading motive in the adoption of the measure) is that it will deprive Great Britain of those supplies so essential to her continental operations.

Extract. Lexington *Reporter*, April 14, 1812. Identified as from Clay to the editor.

1 The measure had been signed by President Madison on this day.

2 See above, Clay to Monroe, March 15, 1812.

To John Darby

[April 10, 1812]

Dr. F. Ridgley[1] Security of James Hughes
In a/c. with John Darby

To amount of one Judgmt. agt. you in the Fayette Circuit Court, which includes Cost interest and damages	$1259:95.
To interest upon $1000, the principal of the above Judgt., from the 27th Oct. 1809 until the 12 Oct 1811	117:50
	1377„45

By Cash paid H. Clay 12th. Oct 1811	1500:
	: 122:55
To amt. of second Judgt. agt. you in the Fayette Circuit Court, which also includes Cost interest & damages	$2437:28.
To interest upon $2000, the principal thereof from the 27h Oct. 1809 until the 10h. Apl. 1812	294:35
	2731:63
Deduct the above	122:55
	2609: .8
By the bal. in full paid H. Clay. 10h. Apl. 1812	

AD. DLC-TJC (DNA, M212, R15). Endorsed on verso by Clay: "Copies of statements Sent to John Darby." Cf. above, Deed of Trust, November 12, 1810.
[1] Frederick Ridgely.

Bill of Exchange Drawn by John Hart

Exchange for $1.200.98/100. Lexington, April 10, 1812.

At sight of this my first of exchange, (second unpaid) pay Nat. G. S. Hart, or order, one thousand, two hundred dollars, 98/100, value recd., which charge, as advised, to Yr. Mo. Ob.,

Henry Clay, JNO. HART.
Washington City.

[Endorsements on verso][1]

Pay to M. T. Scott Cashier of the Lexington Branch Bank or order.
NAT: G. S HART

Pay to the Cashier of the Bank of Pennsylvania[2] or order.
M. T. SCOTT Cashr.
Lexn Br Bank.

Pay Wm Whann Esqr Cashr[3] or order JONO SMITH Casr

Recd. paymt. from H. Clay 1 May 1812 WILLM. WHANN Casr

ADS. DLC-TJC (DNA, M212, R15).
[1] All AES except the last, ES in Clay's hand.
[2] Jonathan Smith.
[3] William Whann was cashier of the Bank of Columbia, Georgetown, D. C.

To [Thomas Smith]

City of Washington, April 11, 1812.

The rumor as announced in the Intelligencer[1] of this day, that the Hornet has arrived, is not ascertained to be well founded.[2] But the Post Master General has this day received, by a private vessel arrived at Baltimore, after a quick passage, a letter from Mr.

Barlow,[3] under date the 12th Feb. in which that minister writes, among other things, that it is probable he will send out by the Hornet a good commercial treaty. Upon the envelope of this letter, there is, on the 3d March, written a note as follows:—"I detain the Hornet a few days longer to take out the treaty."

A vote took place in the House on yesterday, manifesting a disposition for a short recess. Should it take place, which notwithstanding that vote I think doubtful, it is not contemplated to extend it to above six or seven weeks.[4]

Extract. Lexington *Reporter,* April 25, 1812. A note prefacing the letter says, "We have been politely favored by Mr. Smith with the following letter from the Hon. H. Clay. . . ." Smith was the brother-in-law of William Worsley, editor of the *Reporter.*

1 Washington *National Intelligencer.*
2 The rumor was erroneous.
3 Joel Barlow, American Minister to France.
4 No recess occurred.

Newspaper Editorial

[April 14, 1812]

The public attention has been drawn to the approaching arrival of the Hornet, as the period when the measures of our government would take a decisive character, or rather their final cast. We are among those who have attached to this event a high degree of importance, and have therefore looked to it with the utmost solicitude.

But if the reports which we now hear are true, that with England all hope of honorable accommodation is at an end, and that with France our negotiations are in a forwardness encouraging expectations of a favorable result, where is the motive for longer delay? The final step ought to be taken; and that step is WAR. By what course of measures we have reached the present crisis, is not now a question for freemen and patriots to discuss. It exists; and it is by open and manly war only that we can get through it with honor and advantage to the country. Our wrongs have been great; our cause is just; and if we are decided and firm, success is inevitable.

Let war therefore be forthwith proclaimed against England. With her there can be no motive for delay. Any further discussion, any new attempt at negotiation, would be as fruitless as it would be dishonorable. With France we shall still be at liberty to pursue the course which circumstances may require. The advance she has already made by the repeal of her decrees; the manner of its reception by our government; and the prospect which exists of an amicable accommodation, entitle her to this preference. If she acquits herself to the just claims of the U States, we shall have good cause to applaud our conduct in it, and if she fails we shall always be in time to place her on the ground of her adversary. And on that ground, in that event, it is hoped she will be placed.

But it is said that we are not prepared for war, and ought therefore not to declare it. This is an idle objection, which can have weight with the timid and pusillanimous only. The fact is otherwise. Our preparations are adequate to every essential object. Do we apprehend danger to ourselves? From what quarter will it assail us? From England, and by invasion? The idea is too absurd to merit a moment's consideration. Where are her troops? But lately, she dreaded an invasion of her own dominions, from her powerful and menacing neighbor. That danger, it is true, has diminished, but it has not entirely, and forever, disappeared. A gallant effort, which called forth the whole energies of the nation, has put it at a distance, but still it is one of those sparks which peer above the horizon, & excite alarm even in those least liable to it. The war in the peninsula, which lingers, requires strong armies to support it. She maintains an army in Sicily; another in India; and a strong force in Ireland, and along her own coast and in the West Indies. Can any one believe, that, under such circumstances, the British government could be so infatuated, or rather mad, as to send troops here for the purpose of invasion? The experience and the fortune of our revolution, when we were comparatively in an infant state, have doubtless taught her an useful lesson which cannot have been forgotten. Since that period our population has increased three-fold, whilst her's has remained almost stationary. The condition of the civilized world, too, has changed. Although G. Britain has nothing to fear, as to her independence, and her military operations are extensive and distant, the contest is evidently maintained by her rather for safety than for conquest. Have we cause to dread an attack from her neighboring provinces? That apprehension is still more groundless. Seven or eight millions of people have nothing to dread from 300,000. From the moment that war is declared, the British colonies will be put on the defensive, and soon after we get in motion must sink under the pressure. Little predatory incursions on our frontier will not be encouraged by those who know that we can retort them ten-fold, and pursue and punish the authors, retire where they may, if they remain in this hemisphere. Nor is any serious danger to be apprehended from their savage allies. Our frontiers may be easily protected against them. The colonial governments, aware of our superiority, and of the certainty of their subjugation in case of war, will feel their responsibility for the conduct of the Indian tribes, and keep them in order. But should the war lately terminated be renewed, the struggle will be short. Numberless expeditions from different quarters may be led forth against them. A single campaign would drive these unfortunate people into the most distant and desart wilds.

But our coast and seaport towns are exposed and may be annoyed. Even this danger, which exists in a certain degree, has been much exaggerated. No land force can be brought to bear against them, because G. Britain has none to spare for such a service; and without a land force, no great impression can be made. Ships of war cannot approach near the coast, except at the entrance of our great bays and rivers. They cannot annoy the sea coast generally by their cannon; and if detachments of marines should be sent on shore, they may be repelled by the militia where they land. It is, however, unusual for incursions to be made on land from ships of war by sailors or marines. The law of nations forbids, and humanity revolts, at the idea of mere wanton desolation; and in that light only can such incursions be viewed. In the present war between G. Britain and France, which has been prosecuted with so much violence and animosity, no example of this kind, on either side is recollected. In our revolutionary war, in which the object of G. Britain was conquest, no great injury was sustained in this mode. Some of our towns, it is admitted, may be exposed to danger from ships of war, but with suitable precautions it will soon vanish. No ship of war can stand long before a good battery well manned and well supplied with heavy artillery. An attack by ships of war only, on any of our towns, could have no object but that of distressing the inhabitants; and if those towns are put in such a state of defence, as to enable them to repel the attack, as all of them are, or soon may be, it is not probable that the experiment would be made, or, if once made, that it would be repeated. The importance of the protection of our seaport towns is sensibly felt. It is a subject which claims the particular attention of the government, and that attention has doubtless been already bestowed on it.

The great question on which the United States have to decide, is, whether they will relinquish the ground which they now hold, or maintain it with the firmness and vigor becoming freemen. That the sense of the nation favors the latter course, is proved by a series of important and solemn facts, which speak a language not to be misunderstood. From the first attack by Great Britain on our neutral rights in 1805, to the present day, these facts have been multiplied, yearly, by the acts of Congress, by the proceedings of the state legislatures, and by the voice of the people. Let not the Representatives of the People, therefore, in either branch of the government, disappoint their reasonable wishes and just expectations.

The pretensions of Great Britain, so unjustly set up, and pertinaciously maintained, by her orders in council, not to enumerate other wrongs, particularly the impressment of our seamen, arrogate to her the complete dominion of the sea, and the exclusion of every flag from it, which does not sail under her license, and on the conditions which she imposes. These pretensions involve no local interest, nor are they of a transient nature. In their operation they violate the rights, and wound deeply the best interests, of the whole American people. If we yield to them, at this time, the cause may be considered as abandoned. There will be no rallying point hereafter. Future attempts to retaliate the wrongs of foreign powers & to vindicate our most sacred rights, will be in vain. The subject must be dismissed from the debates of Congress, and from our diplomatic discussions. An allusion to it will excite contempt abroad, and mortification and shame at home. Should any of our vessels be hereafter seized and condemned, however unjustly, and that all will be seized and condemned may be confidently expected, we must be silent, or be heard by foreign powers in the humble language of petition only.

Washington *National Intelligencer,* April 14, 1812. On Clay's authorship see Mayo, *Henry Clay,* 504 and note.

To Paul Hamilton

20 Apl. 1812.

H. Clay presents his compliments to Mr. Hamilton and respectfully solicits his attention, if it has not been already given, to the subject matter of the inclosed letter.[1] Mr. Legrand can comply with any contract into which he may enter, and can give ample security for his fulfilment.

AN. DNA, RG45, Misc. Letters Received, 1812, vol. 3, p. 28.
[1] Not found. Probably from Abner Legrand, Lexington merchant.

To [Harry Innes]

Dr Sir Wash. 21st. Apl. 1812.

I beg you to believe that the delay in answering your favor of the 12t. Feb.[1] has proceeded from no intentional neglect.

I recollect very distinctly that when the trial of your cause took place at Jessamine you left it to your Counsel to exercise their discretion, in releasing the damages, assessed by the Jury against Mr. Street;[2] and, before the motion for a new trial, it was certainly contemplated by you and them to release all the damages, except what would reimburse the Costs you had incurred. But when that motion was made, and attempted to be supported by an affidavit manifesting the most determined and continued hostility towards you—an affidavit perverting and misrepresenting the true state of facts, we advised you to release no part of the damages.

Throughout the whole course of the Cause your sole motive appeared to me to be to vindicate your character; and I am confident, as far as one man can be of the intentions of another, that it never for a moment entered into your views to pocket one Cent of what should be ultimately recovered from the defendant.

The Vice President[3] expired yesterday. The period of our adjournment remains uncertain. The earliest time to which any one looks will not allow me to get home until some time in June. Yr friend H. Clay

ALS. DLC-Harry Innes Papers (DNA, M212, R21).

1 Not found.

2 Following attack by the Frankfort *Western World* in connection with its exposure of the "Spanish Conspiracy," Judge Innes had brought suit in Jessamine Circuit Court in 1806 against Editor Joseph M. Street for libel. Clay and Robert Wickliffe had been employed by Innes as counsel. After long continuance the case had been tried in October, 1810. Unable to pay the damages assessed, Street left the state and settled in Illinois Territory in 1812.

3 George Clinton.

To [Paul Hamilton]

Sir Wash. 22 Apl. 1812.

I recommend Legrand F. Rucker of Kentucky, the son of a respectable revolutionary officer, as a fit young gentleman to be appointed a Mid-Shipman in the Navy.[1] Yr. ob. Servt.

H. Clay

ALS. DNA, RG45, Misc. Letters Received, 1812, vol. 3, p. 45. Endorsed on the same page: "No vacancies at present but &c—P. H."

1 The young man, son of Elliott Rucker of Shelby County, Kentucky, did not receive an appointment.

Receipt from Wilson Allen

[April 22, 1812]

Received 22d. Apl. 1812 of H Clay five hundred dollars collected by him from W. T. Banton for the Estate of John Hoomes late of Caroline—

Recd. at Washington City—Said Estate to be charged with two per Cent premium for difference of exchange between here and Kentucky, where said money was collected. Wilson Allen

DS, in Clay's hand. DLC-TJC (DNA, M212, R15). Allen was Clerk of the General Court, Richmond, Virginia.

From Thomas Deye Owings

Honble. H. Clay Lexington Apl: 24th. 1812—

On yesterday our friend Captn. Hart[1] presented me with a letter[2] from you to his brother John inclosing my note to Mr. Jno. McKim

Jnr with instructions to commence suit unless I give my negotiable note with an indorser payable in Six Months—

The amt. being so great I was not willing to involve a friend by procuring his indorsement for so great an amt. *all* payable at so short a period—But in lieu thereof proposed to the Capt. to give my notes with an indorser payable in six and twelve months—To relieve Capt. Hart from any responsibility, as your instructions appear positive. I have told him that should your client not be satisfied with that arrangement I will confess judgment at our next term *reserving equity*—And there is sufficient time between now and the 2d. Monday in June at which period our next term commences. to have any kind of legal precept you think proper served on your—Obt Servant. THOS DEYE OWINGS.

You know well my harrassed situation and that it has not been from want of exertion on my part that Mr. McKim s Debt. has stood so long—And to coerce the payment in the summary way proposed in your favour can not benefit your client and may tend to the *ruin* of T. D. OWINGS

I know well Mr. McKims Debt ought long since to have been discharged & it being out of my power I authorized my brother in Law Mr Nesbitt to secure Mr. McKim s Debt to his satisfaction which I observe has not been done—I should like to know what has passed between them and what has become of my Tobacco, which I understood Mr. McKim had in possession—pray Sir do make that enquiry of Mr. McKim for me. THOS. D. O—GS

and adwise [*sic*] as early as possible, so that I may be prepared for my fate—

ALS. DLC-TJC (DNA, M212, R10).
1 Nathaniel G. S. Hart.
2 Not found.

Receipt from John Kennedy

[April 25, 1812]

Recd. Washington City 25 Apl. 1812. of H. Clay One thousand and twenty dollars (which includes premium for difference of exchange) on account of debts in his hands for collection in Kentucky for Kennedy & Cox— JNO KENNEDY

DS, in Clay's hand. DLC-TJC, 2d Series, vol. 13.

Assignment from Robert Holmes

[*ca.* April 27, 1812]

pay to Henry Clay ROBERT HOLMES

Copy. Fayette Circuit Court, File 341 (1816). Endorsement on note for $125 from Robert Grinstead, Lexington bricklayer, to Holmes, April 27, 1812, payable 48 months after date. Clay won a suit for collection of this note in 1816. Fayette Circuit Court, File 341.

Receipt from William Whann

[May 1, 1812]

Attached to Bill of Exchange, April 10, 1812.

From Bartlet and Cox

Henry Clay Esqr. New Orleans 4' May 1812

Dear Sir,

Since writing you on the 27 ulto: your favour of the 24 March is at hand.[1] We shall with much pleasure receive and remit you you [*sic*] Jno. Ballenger's balance should he offer paymt. but as his credit does not stand very high with us we have some apprehensions of his proving a delinquent

Messrs. Joseph Gray & Co of Bayou Sarah[2] remitted us a draft a few days since, with [orde]rs when paid to pass the sum of 81 25/100 Dols. recd. of [. . .][3] [to] your credit, which shall be done accordingly & remited with any other monies we may receive on your account, respectfully your Ob. Sts BARTLET & COX.

ALS. DLC-TJC (DNA, M212, R12).

1 Neither letter has been found.

2 Plaquemines Parish, Louisiana.

3 Name illegible.

Property Deed from Executors of Thomas Hart, Jr., to Thomas Tibbatts

[May 4, 1812]

[Under authorization to sell for the benefit of the estate of Thomas Hart, Jr., the lot on which the Old Rope Walk is situated, Clay with the other executors conveys to Thomas Tibbatts a lot at the northeast corner of Market and Third streets in Lexington, for $954.75, payable in three years. Signature of Clay acknowledged on October 4, 1823, those of the other executors, on April 25, 1822; and the deed recorded in the Office of the Fayette County Clerk on March 15, 1832.]

Fayette County Court, Deed Book 8, pp. 30-31. A mortgage deed covering this property was also transacted between these parties on May 4, 1812. Fayette County Court, Deed Book G, 164-66.

From Charles Humphreys

Sir Lexington May 4h 1812

My brother Joshua Humphreys at new Madrid informs me that

they are in great distress there— —The earth quake has ruined many of them[1]—and many more have fled out of the country that in the event of an Indian War they are in danger of all being cut off—. He is the only civil officer who has not fled from the country[2]—previous to the earth quakes the population was 3000—now only about 400 remain and those the most helpless—such as could not get away—He therefore requests that the troops at Massack[3] where there is no settlement to protect, be sent to Madrid—or that some other troops be stationed there until the Indian War be over—respecfully your

CH. HUMPHREYS—

ALS. DNA, RG107, Letters Received, (6) C-303.

1 The first shock of the destructive New Madrid (Louisiana Territory) earthquake had occurred on December 16, 1811; it had been followed by others at irregular intervals. Tremors of lessening intensity were felt for several years afterward.

2 In 1806 he had been appointed Clerk of the Sessions and Prothonotary, as well as Clerk of the Court of Probate, in the District of New Madrid.

3 Fort Massac, on the Ohio River in Illinois Territory.

To [John W. Hunt]

Washington, 9th, May 1812.

Dear Sir:—I recd your favor on the subject of a building for the University.[1] I immediately addressed a note to Mr. Latrobe to engage him to execute his promise.[2] Owing to the extreme illness of his lady, I have not yet been able to have a personal interview with him. Allow me to entreat the Board not to proceed with the building until they have a judicious design prepared by some architect I would defer the erection a year, rather than not be in the possession of such a plan. The miserable building put up for a Court House in Lexington—the disgrace of the town and the derision of everybody—ought to admonish us to proceed with more discretion in our public edifices.[3]

The present is a date of most painful suspense as to public affairs. All our measures have tended to one issue, but uncontrollable causes have delayed the final steps. I am persuaded they will not continue to operate longer than the first of next month. The Hornets[4] not yet arrived is inexplicable.

Lucretia talks of accompanying Dr. Pindall[5] (who is now here) to E,[6] the first of the June [*sic*]. As for myself I do not expect the pleasure of seeing you before July. She joins in respects to Mrs. Hunt. Your,

H. CLAY.

Lexington *Transcript*, November 6 (year missing)—clipping in KyU.

1 Not found. The Board of Trustees of Transylvania University, of which Hunt was a member, was considering the erection, on the University lot below Mechanic Street, of a building to cost from $15,000 to $20,000.

2 To Benjamin H. Latrobe, *ca.* May 1, 1812, not found.

3 Fayette County's third courthouse, a brick structure built by Hallett M. Winslow and Luther Stephens in 1806, was razed in 1883.
4 Charleton Hunt, brother of John W., had been captain of this vessel for several years through 1810.
5 Dr. Richard Pindell.
6 Probably a misprint for "K" or "L".

To Thomas Bodley

D Sir Washington 12h. May 1812

I do not believe that the resolution to which you refer in your favor of the 3d. inst.[1] for satisfying V. M. Land warrants will be adopted & the measure carried into effect, but should it take place, contrary to my expectations, I will notify you.[2] I am glad to learn that the people are satisfied with the course their government is pursuing. That course will I am persuaded eventuate in War in a short time—a war brought upon us by the continued aggressions of a foreign government, and to avoid which every honorable effort has been made on the part of ours. God grant us a happy result to this new & untried experiment to which the only free government upon earth is about to be subjected! That such will be the issue of the contest I entertain no doubt if the people possess the fortitude and firmness which I believe they do.

The proposition of Mr. Pope in the Senate to repeal the non-importation [clause was this day] negatived by 15 to 8.[3] The measure has been strongly reprobated. I hope every facility will be given to the recruiting service, and that your apprehensions on this subject will not be realized. Great use may be made of the Land bounty.[4] It is really an important thing. At the lowest estimate it is worth $320.

I feel every possible disposition to serve Mr. Carneal.[5] But the number of applicants has been great [. . .][6] extremely embarrassing. I submitted his name to the delegation at our meeting when we made out the recommendation for our quota of officers. It was thought that others ought to be proposed. Perhaps it may be yet practicable to promote his wishes & if the occasion arises I shall not fail, he may be assured, to embrace it. Would he accept a Lieutenancy in the Marine Corps? It is not a service that I would advise him to enter into but opportunities of getting into it are more frequent than in the Army.

I do not expect to reach home until some time in July. Yr friend H Clay

ALS. KyHi. Addressed to Bodley at Lexington.
1 Not found.
2 During the previous November, on motion of Samuel McKee of Kentucky, the House Committee on Public Lands had conducted an inquiry respecting the location

of Virginia military land warrants between the Scioto and the Little Miami rivers. A bill embodying the Committee's resolutions had been passed by the House in February, 1812, but it was amended prior to adoption by the Senate on May 21. Several weeks elapsed before the two Houses could adjust their differences. The "Act to ascertain the western boundary of the tract reserved for satisfying the military bounties allowed to the officers and soldiers of the Virginia Line on Continental Establishment" was approved June 26, 1812. 2 *U. S. Stat.*, 764-65.

3 Senator John Pope of Kentucky had introduced his motion on May 8. (Several words in this line defaced by tear in MS.)

4 Both the "Act for completing the existing Military Establishment," approved December 24, 1811, and the "Act to raise an additional Military Force," approved January 11, 1812, provided that each non-commissioned officer and soldier, when honorably discharged from the service, should receive three months' pay and 160 acres of land. 2 *U. S. Stat.*, 669-70, 672.

5 Probably Thomas D. Carneal of Fayette County, son of Thomas Carneal.

6 MS. torn.

From John McKim, Jr.

Dear Sir Baltimore May 13th. 1812

Your favour dated the 9th. Inst. covering a letter from Mr. Owings,[1] came to hand on the 12th. Inst., I am perfectly satisfyed With the arangement you have made, and I hope the Endorser [*sic*] of Mr. Owings Notes are men of undoubted stability.

Mr. Nesbitt, Mr. Owings Brother in law, has Informed him respecting the Tobacco, it remains in the hands of the Owner of the Ship, that brought it from New Orleans, as the Freight Amts. to upwards of $1500—and not Paid,

My Dear Sir, I feel much for the Honor and Interest of the United States, and it Grives me to See so much unsteadyness in the Councils of the Nation. We are an Humbled & degraded Nation and If the Stand that is now Taken is departed from, Without bringing England to Justice, we may as well give up our Republican Government & have a Despot to rule over us, A great Cry is made respecting the large amt. of Property Owned by Americans in England, I deny that the ¼ of What is Stated to be in England is there, and If Speculators have sent money to England calculating on Our Government Submiting, are they to be Indulged at the Expense of every thing Dear to the united States, we Know verry well, that the 19 Parts out of 20 have been sent to England since the Presidents proclimation, and With their Eyes Open, Some say that they shipped Flour, and Other produce to Lisbon, & Cadis, and was obliged to Take Bills on England, I deny that, they could have had Dollars, but to get Dollars they had to give a premium, And they recd. Bills of Exchange at a Discount, calculating & Speculating Either on the Submition of the American Government or that the English Would take off the Orders of Council, And then they would get par for their Bills, but I deny that If the Non Importation Act was repealed, that Bills would bring par, the depresiation of Bank notes in England being 25 pr Ct. the Specie would be sent to England to purchase Goods—

If I might offer, What I think would be both popular, and proper, If the Hornet dos not bring Satisfactory Accounts from France, War Should be Declared—Against both, that would be putting them on a footing, and the non Importation Act Kept on against both— With my best Wishes for Your Health, I am Respectfully Your obt. St. JNO. MCKIM JR.

P. S. When you have time, you Would much oblige me by Droping me a line J McK

I meant to say in my letter, that those that brought Dollars from Lisbon & Cadis saved from 4 to 5 pr Ct. more than by bringing Bills of Exchange

ALS. DLC-HC (DNA, M212, R1). Addressed to Clay at Washington.
[1] Thomas Deye Owings. The letter not found.

From Benjamin H. Latrobe

The honorable Henry Clay Washington May 16h. 1812

Dear Sir,

I received your note with its enclosure[1] on the 1st. of May & immediately called at your lodgings, & also the next day but did not find you at home. You were afterwards sick, so that my third attempt to see you, altho' you were within was not successful. I have since made a copy of the plan of Dickinson Colledge of Carlisle,[2] which I presented to that institution 10 or 12 Years ago and have digested generally my ideas for Lexington, but my duties for the Navy dept. have so entirely occupied me for the last week, that I have not proceeded & have been indeed entirely unable to repeat my call at your lodgings.[3]

I now submit to you a few questions on the subject of the College at Lexington[4] on points which it is important to know, & to which I beg the favor of your answers or remarks, & will endeavor to see you to receive you [*sic*] answer tomorrow. I would call today, but the weather prevents it.—

1. What is the *aspect* of the square intended for the University? Which point of the Compass does the longest side (300. ft) face.—

2.) Is the building proposed to be now built & which is not to cost more than 18,000$ to be calculated to lodge *only 30 or 40 Students,* & yet contain 15 lodging rooms. Because in the first part of the letter it is said that the house should be so constructed as to accomodate 200 Students. 15 lodging rooms are two [*sic*] few for that number, & more than necessary for 40 Students.—

3. Is it intended that the whole plan shall be executed at once, or will it be sufficient to lay down a plan for the whole building calculated for 200 Students, & to contrive it that only a part may be now executed, sufficient for the limited number with which the institution may commence.—This seems to me to be the most rational system on which to proceed, For nothing is so certain as that 18000$ will not cover more than 3,000 to 4000 superficial feet of 3 stories high, if the utmost oeconomy should be used in the construction, making a building of perhaps 80 feet by 40 at most,—into which it will be difficult to get all the rooms required.

4. I ought also to know something of the ideas of lodging the students which the Trustees entertain. In Princeton they lodge three or two in a room of 16 or 12 by about 15 (if I recollect right) the room being divided into 3 or two cells. for study, thus: [. . .][5] If you will have the goodness to give or procure me the necessary information on this head it will facilitate my endeavors to to [*sic*] meet the wishes of the Trustees.—

5 I could also wish to know whether from the character of the streets in the vicinity as well as the aspect, it would be preferable to give to the House its principal front the length way (300 ft.) or the breadth of the square (160).—

It is I think probable that you may have to refer back to the Trustees for some of this information. I wish to request you in this case to press them for as early information as possible.

I will only add, that I shall be exceedingly proud of their acceptance of any design of mine. The renovation of Princeton, the College of Carlisle, the medical schools of Philadelphia, are among the most gratifying exertions of my art which I have ever made; and the power to promote institutions on which so much of human happiness depends, consoles for the many mortifications which are inseparable from the practice of my profession.—I enclose the letter which you sent to me that you may refer to it to understand what I allude to in my enquiries. With the truest respect I am Yrs.

B H LATROBE

ALS copy. Latrobe Letterbook, 379, 383-86, owned by Mrs. Ferdinand C. Latrobe, Baltimore, Maryland.

1 Not found. See above, Clay to Hunt, May 9, 1812. 2 Pennsylvania.

3 Latrobe's employment by the Navy Department, at first in connection with a building program at the Washington Navy Yard, had begun in 1804. Talbot Hamlin, *Benjamin Henry Latrobe* (New York, 1955), 296-300.

4 Transylvania University. 5 Diagram omitted by editors.

To [Robert Alexander]

Dr Sir Wash. 17h. May 1812.

I have been unable to hear of any Astronomical Circle, except one in the possession of Mr. Ellicot,[1] altho' I have extended my enquiries to Philadelphia. Mr. Gallatin[2] has directed to be purchased in England a set of instruments, for taking observations, of the best quality, for public use; but their arrival in this Country will not probably be for some time to come.

The Loan has produced $6.118.900. of which $4.190.000 were subscribed by Banks and $1.928.900 by individuals.[3] It is the most favorable experiment ever made in this Country, notwithstanding the discouragements thrown in the way. It is believed it will be yet filled without difficulty.

Accounts from England as late as the 13h. Apl. represent the most painful apprehensions of scarcity and even famine. They had not then of course heard of our Embargo, which must heighten the distress.

The final measure, to which all our acts have pointed, will probably be decided about the first of next month.

As I hope to see you in July I defer till then saying any thing about the Green river business.[4] Yrs. H. CLAY

ALS. Owned by Dr. A. J. and James H. Alexander, Lexington, Kentucky.

1 Andrew Ellicott, 3rd, eminent scientist, inventor, and engineer. In 1813 he became professor of mathematics at West Point.

2 Albert Gallatin.

3 For a report of the Secretary of the Treasury on this loan, which had been authorized by act of Congress of March 14, 1812, see *Annals of Cong.*, 12 Cong., 1 Sess., XXIV, 1432, 2093-2102.

4 Probably Hopkins *vs.* Purviance. Alexander had been appointed one of the commissioners to sell the lands of Henry Purviance.

To [William W. Worsley]

WASHINGTON CITY, MAY 24, 1812.

The Hornet has at length arrived at New-York, and the dispatches from Mr. Barlow with which she was charged have been received by the president.[1] Contrary to the expectations of that minister, as communicated by the Constitution, she brings no treaty, nor any information authorising the belief that any arrangement whatever will be effected with France.

The government is now in possession of a full view of our foreign relations, and will be able to adopt the measure recommended by its best judgment. That I am still persuaded will be war; whether against one or both the Belligerents, the only point on which I find any diversity of opinion, will be determined in the course of a few days.

Extract. Lexington *Reporter,* June 6, 1812. Recipient identified in Frankfort *Palladium,* June 3, 1812.

1 The vessel reached New York on May 19.

From Benjamin H. Latrobe

The Honorable Henry Clay
Speaker H of Rep. Washington, May 24h. 1812
Dear Sir,

I am mortified & ashamed beyond expression that I did not, agreeably to your invitation dine with you yesterday.—The truth is always the best apology, even where no very good one can be made.

When I called on you in the morning my engagement was perfectly in my recollection. About an hour afterwards however I was apprized of the arrival in the Eastern brank [*sic*] of a Vessel which is to take my steam-engine &c as far as it is finished, to Baltimore for the purpose of being shipped to New Orleans.[1] The urgency of the case and the shortness of the notice, together with the great importance to me that the machine should go out soon, & while the navigation is safe, so occupied my mind & time,—that when I again recollected how I was engaged, the time was passed in which I might have availed myself of your politeness. I hope I shall be forgiven by you, on consideration at least of my frankness. I am very respectly. Yrs B HENRY LATROBE

Turn over

PS. I have recd. from Mr Barlow[2] a duplicate of his letter of the 29h. of Feby. by the Hornet. Mrs. L. has recd a letter from Mrs. Barlow also d. Aprl. 21st. Having promised Mr Cheves[3] a copy of the political passage of the letter, I have sent him the duplicate, & requested him to show it to you—There is a report that I had exhibited this letter to the federalists while I had carefully concealed it from the republi[c]an members.—This is not true. The first person to whom I showed the letter was Mr. Hamilton, Secy. Navy. —I afterwards showed it to Mr. M. Clay, Mr. Macon, Mr. Roan,[4] & I think to yourself: at least I stated to you its contents. A week afterwards Mr. E. B. Caldwell[5] (the first federalist) saw it, on enquiry,—at my house.—From that time, till Mr Pope[6] called on me, I refused to exhibit it, repenting that I had so far violated a private communication, as to give [i]t a publicity which might injure the writer, or at least [s]ubject him to the censure of duplicity. —It is how [*sic*] probably true, that the *federalists only* have talked of its contents, as their view of the subject could be but supported [by] them.—

ALS copy. Latrobe Letterbook, 516-17, owned by Mrs. Ferdinand C. Latrobe, Baltimore, Maryland.

1 Latrobe had obtained a charter authorizing him to construct a water works for the City of New Orleans, and he was now engaged in building a steam engine for the project. Because of the imminence of war his machinery got no farther than Baltimore at that time. Hamlin, *Latrobe*, 354-58.

2 Joel Barlow.

3 Langdon Cheves.
4 Representatives Matthew Clay and John Roane of Virginia and Nathaniel Macon of North Carolina.
5 Elias B. Caldwell, Washington businessman.
6 Senator John Pope of Kentucky.

To [William Eustis]

Sir 25h. May 1812

I transmit you the inclosed letter[1] that you may judge of the propriety of a removal of the troops at Massac to New Madrid, where Mr. Joshua Humphreys referred to in the letter resides.

Yrs. H. CLAY

ALS. DNA, RG107, Letters Received, (6) C-303.
1 From Charles Humphreys, above, May 4, 1812.

Order on William T. Barry

D Sir Washington 26h. May 1812

Be pleased to pay to James B. January Esq. five hundred and thirty dollars and oblige yr's. H. CLAY

W. T. Barry Esqr

ADS. Fayette Circuit Court, File 823. Accepted June 15, 1812, by Barry, who paid $300 immediately. Endorsed (not dated): "Recd in full James B. Januar[y]."

To ———————

WASHINGTON, May 27, 1812.

That we shall have war, I still believe. The dispatches brought by the Hornet were yesterday laid before congress.[1] Although not as favorable as we had a right to expect, or could have wished, they are more so than they had been rumoured to be. They shew the practical observance of the repeal of the Berlin and Milan decrees, as to us. The Rambouillet spoliations, it is true, are not yet indemnified, but they are a subject of discussion and negotiation—and with regard to the recent burnings (which by the bye however execrable, they do not fall within those decrees) Mr. Barlow had presented a strong note, but had received no reply.[2] Throughout the whole of Mr. Barlow's intercourse with that government, they appear to have treated him with prompt attention and good manners at least. In short after the dispatches were read yesterday, there was general disappointment manifested at their being much better than they had been rumoured to be, and the universal sentiment was "we will go on in our intended course as to England, and wait a little longer with France." I think it therefore highly probable that about the time this letter will be with you, War will be declared in due form against England.

Extract. Lexington *Kentucky Gazette,* June 9, 1812. Identified as from Clay "to a gentleman of this place."

1 The documents may be found in *American State Papers, Foreign Relations,* III, 500, 512-21.

2 Early in 1812, French warships, under orders to destroy neutral vessels bound to or from enemy ports, had burned numerous American ships on the high seas.

To John Jordan Crittenden

Dr Sir Wash. 28h. May 1812.

I transmit you Mr. Jordan's letter to me,[1] in relation to the credit claimed by Dr Rumsey.[2]

Despatches are recd. from France and are laid before Congress. Altho they fall short of our just expectations before the Hornet's arrival they are not found to be as bad as they were rumored to be. The Govt. will proceed in its course agt. England, waiting a while longer before it takes any measure of a hostile character agt. France. The question of Peace or War will probably have been decided before you receive this, and the decision will I am persuaded not disappoint the Country. Yrs. H. CLAY

ALS. DLC-Crittenden Papers (DNA, M212, R20). Addressed to Crittenden at "Russellsville Kentucky." Born in Woodford County, Kentucky, and educated at William and Mary College, Crittenden had settled in Logan County, where he had opened a successful law practice and entered politics. His legislative career had begun in 1811, when he was elected to the General Assembly. He was closely associated with Clay for nearly forty years.

1 Not found. Probably written by John Jordan, Jr.

2 Dr. Edward Rumsey.

Verbal Exchange with John Randolph

[May 29, 1812]

The SPEAKER (who had resumed the chair) said, that unquestionably in the opinion of the chair, the proposition might be required to be submitted in writing, because it was made the duty of the chair to require the application of observations made on the floor to the subject debated; and this duty certainly could not be performed unless the chair were apprised of the terms of the proposition.

Mr. CALHOUN. I then call upon the gentleman to submit his proposition.

Mr. RANDOLPH. The gentleman has no right to call upon me; you, Mr. Speaker, unquestionably have. My proposition is one respecting our relations with the two great belligerents, and goes to affect the question of peace or war. Whilst up, sir, permit me to observe, that if I were wide of the mark, I might have been permitted to go on—

The SPEAKER. The gentleman will please to take his seat, the chair having decided that his motion must be submitted before further debate.

Mr. RANDOLPH said he had not understood the Speaker as making any such decision.

The SPEAKER said he certainly had so decided.

Mr. RANDOLPH. My proposition is, that it is not expedient at this time to resort to a war against Great Britain.

The SPEAKER. Is the motion seconded?

Mr. Randolph, or some other gentleman, expressed his surprise that a second in such a case should be required.

The SPEAKER said he conceived that every motion must receive a second before it could be announced from the chair. He also required that the motion be reduced to writing.

Mr. RANDOLPH. I then appeal from that decision.

The SPEAKER stated the grounds of his decision, and read the rules requiring motions when made to be seconded before put to the vote, and when demanded to be reduced to writing.

Mr. RANDOLPH said he would only remark that this right of prefacing a motion by remarks was almost the last vestige of the freedom of debate; if it were destroyed, there would be none left but under the permission of the majority.

[Several other Representatives questioned the Speaker's decision. Wright retorted that Randolph was out of order on grounds both of the parliamentary practice and the content of his remarks.]

The SPEAKER said that the question of order submitted involved a matter of fact, that is, whether the gentleman from Virginia (Mr. R.) did or did not use the words ascribed to him by the gentleman from Maryland (Mr. W.) conveying an imputation of French influence, which (not having been in the chair) he could not decide. He could only say that if the gentleman did use such words they were highly improper; if he did not, the gentleman from Maryland (Mr. W.) was out of order in attributing them to him.

[Wright quoted the offending words, and Randolph replied that his accusers were now out of order in discussing a question ruled out of debate.]

The SPEAKER said he did not perceive the direct application of the gentleman's remarks, but he appeared to be speaking in explanation of the expressions for using which he had before been called to order.

Mr. WRIGHT continued. Sir, said he, I do not admire the doctrine of recrimination, nor will I charge that honorable gentleman with being under British influence; although we see the British licensed spies within this hall to hear this *understood* debate—

Mr. RANDOLPH said the gentleman was again out of order.

The SPEAKER. The gentleman from Maryland will please to take his seat. If the Chair understood him correctly, he is certainly out of order. If he meant to say that there was an understanding between a member of this House and a foreign agent out of it, in relation to proceedings to take place in the House, he was undoubtedly out of order.

[After House vote upheld the Speaker in his ruling that the motion be offered in writing, Randolph said he would comply under compulsion.]

The SPEAKER. There is no compulsion in the case; because the gentleman may or may not offer it, at his option.

[A point of order was now raised on the permission of debate prior to House agreement to consider the motion.]

The SPEAKER said he had not before adverted to the imperative terms of the rule which required a previous question of consideration, and which rule, on further reflection, he was of opinion applied to this case.

[Randolph appealed the decision of the chair and cited his long experience in the House in support of his interpretation of the rules.]

The SPEAKER requested the gentleman to confine his remarks to the question whether or not the decision of the chair was correct. Priority of seat on this floor, said the Speaker, gives to the senior members of the House *no* right to which the junior are not *equally* entitled.

. . . .

The SPEAKER said, that he would take the occasion to remark that, at the commencement of the session, he had doubted the propriety of the rule requiring a previous determination of the House to consider a proposition, before it could be debated and decided. But he was then informed that it had been the practice of the House, & to that usage he had conformed. Whatever doubts he had entertained originally of its utility had been removed by subsequent experience.

In regard to the decision, requiring a second to a motion before it was received, of which there was some complaint, he understood it to be the established practice of the British Parliament. As to the alleged violation of the freedom of debate he remarked, that he should be extremely sorry, if any decision which it became his duty to make should produce unnecessarily its abridgement. He was a great friend to a legitimate and decorous freedom of debate. And whether, by the House, or any determination of his, its liberty had been infringed, in the instance of any member, and particularly in reference to the gentleman from Virginia, the discussions and proceedings of the House during the present session would illustrate & attest.

The right to regulate its own proceedings, he observed was a right inherent in every public deliberative body. It was a right necessarily attaching to every body, composed of human beings, independent of positive prescription. It was a right, without the existence & exercise of which it would be impossible to proceed in business at all, or to arrive at any conclusion. But strong as was the natural basis upon which this right stands, it did not depend upon that alone. The constitution had expressly secured to each branch of the national legislature the power to regulate its own proceedings. Whilst in the place with which he was honored, it was his pleasure no less than his duty to enforce, as far as depended upon him, the rules which the House of Representatives in the exercise of this constitutional power, had thought proper to prescribe. He could have no interest but to perform, with the utmost impartiality, this trust, and in doing it he should always consult every source of information which was accessible to him.

Washington *National Intelligencer*, June 16, 1812. Published also in *Annals of Cong.*, 12 Cong., 1 Sess., XXIV, 1452, 1462-63, 1465-69. See below, Reply, June 17; Randolph's Reply, July 2, 1812. Randolph, speaking of rumors that war was to be declared, had been called to order by Robert Wright of Maryland, who had pointed out that no motion was before the House. Clay had overruled Wright's objection on the ground that Randolph had declared his intention to make a motion and that it was usual to permit prefatory remarks. Clay had then for a time relinquished the Speaker's chair. Meanwhile Randolph had extended his remarks until John C. Calhoun, of South Carolina, finally requested that the motion be submitted in writing.

From [William Eustis]

Honle H Clay — War Department
House of Represent. — May 30th. 1812.

Sir,

I have the honor to acknowledge your Letter of the 25th. Instant, and to inform you that it is not considered expedient at present to remove the small Garrison at fort Massac.—

Copy. DNA, RG107, Military Books, vol. 5, p. 415.

From Robert Wickliffe

Lexington May 31st 1812—

Dear Clay,—the Federal Court have adjourned to the 4th Monday in July & will do business untill the 2nd. Monday in Augt I hope you will be able to be out by that time, it was all I could obtain for you Allen & Talbott[1] seemed I thought indisposed to it. Mr Innis[2] Claims one day to be appropriated to the broaching his Kentucky wine of which I promised to give you information. Volunteer Corpse are going out, daily to the protection of Indianna[3] In fact the State was prepared to take the field, If required, Humphrey Marshall has volunteered his services as a light dragoon in Capt. (Doctor) Marshalls[4] *Troop* *Shelby* is a candidate & will beat Slaughter but cant you help him by making some statement in the Intelligencer[5] which *will be copied here.* In which you may state the military ardour of the state & something handsome of Shelby as a military man & the hopes that America may indulge from Kentucky with such a commander in chief of her militia let the piece appear to be either the act of the editor or some disinterest [*sic*] corrospondent I am confident of Shelbys election but The d.n creature *Slaughter* is so industrious that all Shelbys friends will have to be on the Alert.[6] I have in all remitted you I think 29, 12 $ for Kenedy & Cox Have you received it If so please to acknowledge it in your next A few days past a man of the name of Kelly paid me $600 on acct of some one whose name I forget as I was just leaving Frankfort & failed to take a minute but I will ascertain & hold it subject to your order.[7] I have dissolved the injunctions of Fitzhugh & Rose & McMeeken agst Bolton Jackson[8] But Barbour[9] has continued his agst Kenedy & Cox & I was afraid of the one of Eastland[10] & laid it over untill I could see you I had not forgot Stewarts business[11] as you supposed I have been trying Sneed[12] in vain to reduce his Claim & also to acquire Certain information of the value of the land in which I have also failed, some suppose That it is valuable on account of a lead mine mine [*sic*] but others speak of the prosp[e]ct as chimerical When you come out I think it [p]ossible that we can between us manage Sneed. Craig & Preston is decided favourable[13]

I have dismissed the writ of Error & supersedeas that I wrote you had been sued out for Heydelt agst Hazlehurst[14] but I shall not be able, perhaps, now to effect a sale untill you arrive In great hast I am your very sincere friend &c ROBERT WICKLIFFE

ALS. DLC-HC (DNA, M212, R1).

1 Probably attorneys John Allen and Isham Talbot. 2 Judge Harry Innes.

3 During the month of May, William Henry Harrison, victor in the Battle of Tippecanoe, November 7, 1811, organized a force to put an end to Indian troubles along

the Wabash. A Franklin County unit of about seventy men joined him but were sent home when the War Department refused to authorize the expedition. [Robert B. McAfee], *History of the Late War in the Western Country* (Lexington, 1816), 42.

4 Dr. Louis Marshall.

5 Washington *National Intelligencer*.

6 Isaac Shelby, the first Governor of Kentucky, was elected again to that office in August, 1812, defeating Gabriel Slaughter. If Clay wrote such a statement as Wickliffe requested, it has not been found.

7 The money from Joseph Kelly was probably intended for William Taylor of Baltimore.

8 Cases not found. Fitzhugh and Rose were a Louisville firm.

9 Philip Barbour.

10 See above, Memorandum of Account, *ca.* January 20, 1812.

11 Possibly three suits in chancery brought in the name of John Stewart, a Virginia veteran of the French and Indian War. The litigation, involving a military grant of 2,000 acres on Licking Creek, continued from 1798 until 1817, when the suits were dismissed "for lack of security for costs." Fayette Circuit Court, File 394; *ibid.*, Order Book R, 6.

12 Achilles Sneed.

13 See above, Clay to Breckinridge, December 22, 1804.

14 Isaac Hazlehurst and Company, Philadelphia merchants, in 1804 had won by default a suit against George Heytel, Lexington tanner. To secure payment of his debt, Heytel had executed a mortgage on a tract of land, and in time Hazlehurst had brought suit to foreclose. When Heytel failed to answer the bill, a decree had been pronounced in favor of the plaintiff. The Kentucky Court of Appeals in 1815 refused, however, to sustain the judgment and remanded the case for new proceedings. Fayette Circuit Court, Order Book A (1803-1804), 496; 7 *Ky. Reports* (4 Bibb) 19.

Remarks on Bill Concerning American Seamen

[June 1, 1812]

Mr. *Clay* (*the Speaker*) made a motion for the committee to rise. He objected to some of the provisions of the bill, though he applauded and fully coincided in its object. He submitted to the gentleman from Maryland whether, as it was in contemplation to take a measure still more strong,[1] and which would supersede the necessity of the present, they ought not to suspend the decision of the weaker measure till the other was disposed of. At the same time, he pledged himself, for one, if the stronger measure should fail from any cause, that he would agree in the principle of the bill, and afford any aid of his to make its details as perfect as possible.

Washington *National Intelligencer,* June 2, 1812. Published also in *Annals of Cong.,* 12 Cong., 1 Sess., XXIV, 1481. The House had resolved itself into a Committee of the Whole to consider a bill, introduced on February 19 by Robert Wright of Maryland, "for the recovery, protection, and indemnification of American seamen."

1 That is, a declaration of war on Great Britain, the power against whom American sailors needed protection. On June 30 the House refused further consideration of Wright's bill.

Receipt from John Hoomes

6 June 1812.

Recd. of H. Clay Two hundred dollars, which with five hundred dollars paid by him to Wilson Allen, and two per Ct. premium on the whole for difference of exchange, makes Seven hundred and fourteen dollars on a/c. of money collected by said Clay of W. T Banton for my father's Estate. JOHN HOOMES. Exor. of J Hoomes

DS, in Clay's hand. DLC-TJC (DNA, M212, R15).

Endorsement on Draft from John Hart

[June 6, 1812]

Attached to Bill of Exchange for $9504, October 1, 1811.

Receipt from Baker and French

[June 7, 1812]

Attached to Bill, *ca.* December 13, 1810.

From Will Anderson, Jr.

Honorable Sir 10th. June 1812

On a subject like the present I assure you I would not presume to solicit your favour were I not impelled by the most powerful motives. The question shall I apply to you in the present instance amounts to the same as the one shall I exert myself in a period probably the most critical of my life, or contemptibly without an effort Sink under adversity. When a boy at school I was assiduous and successful in application to my studies. But unfortunately bad health for two or three years past had almost extinguished the flattering hopes I then con- conceived [*sic*]. I feel an energy that cannot in any way exert itself under my present circumstances. I have felt my situation unfortunate in being destitute of influential friends or in not being able to satisfy the claim my feelings persuaded me I possessed to a small appointment in the navy, a situation particularly suited to the nature of my indisposition, that would at once make me master of myself and satiate that restless craving for exertion, which in my present situation, it seems impossible to satisfy. One or two of my classmates Rich. Buck and Will Madison[1] have obtained situations of this kind without any peculiarities in their cases as in mine. You now see how important to me is my request and therefore, whatever may be the result, will pardon me for the trouble I give you. If you favour me I cannot soon forget so great a kindness. Wi[th] the highest respect your Hle. St.

WILL ANDERSON JUN
Jessamine County Ky.

ALS. DNA, RG45, Misc. Letters Received, 1812, vol. 4, pp. 95-96. Addressed to Clay at Washington. Postmarked: "Lexington Kentucky June 11." Endorsed on margin: "Appoint him. P. H[amilton]."

1 William was the second son of George Madison.

From Dr. Frederick Ridgely

June 9th: [*i.e.* 10] 1812

Mr.[1] Anderson who writes above, is the Nephew of Captain William Allin—your neighbour & friend—He has been as I understand, an industrious Student with Mr. Wilson:[2] with whom he obtaind a general Classical Education & a pretty complete course of the sciences —He is quite a youth: about 18 yers old: is strong, vigorous, & sprightly—He is such an one as I would expect to become a bold enterprizing Officer:

His Education better than generally those who devote themselves to the naval service possess—My acquaintance with him has resulted from his calling on me for professional aid—and the intercourse in consequence has impress'd me favorably of the independance & capacity of his mind—His private Character is unexceptionable—Dear Sir Yr: friende &c. FR: RIDGELY

ANS. DNA, RG45, Misc. Letters Received, 1812, vol. 4, pp. 95-96. Dr. Ridgely began his note on the bottom of Anderson's letter, above, and continued it on a second page.

1 The word "Mr." superimposed on "The."

2 Probably Samuel Wilson, who conducted Forest Hill Academy at his home in Jessamine County.

Property Deed from Executors of Thomas Hart, Jr., to Peter Paul, Jr.

[June 11, 1812]

[Indenture by which the executors of Thomas Hart, Jr., sell to Peter Paul, Jr., for the sum of $575, current money of Kentucky, a tract in Lexington, beginning 210½ feet from the corner of Second and Market streets, at the corner of a lot sold by the executors to John Anderson, running thence along Market Street 50 feet to a lot sold by the executors to Robert Grinstead, and extending back 97 feet, to an alley. General warranty of title. Signatures of all the executors, that of Clay acknowledged on September 8, 1812, before John D. Young, Clerk of Fayette County.]

Fayette County Court, Deed Book F, 534-535.

Mortgage Deed from James Coleman to Executors of Thomas Hart, Jr.

[June 11, 1812]

[Indenture by which James Coleman of Fayette County conveys to the executors of Thomas Hart, Jr., for the sum of $575, current money of Kentucky, a tract in Lexington, fronting 32 feet on Upper Street, beginning at the southeastern corner of a lot belonging to, and now occupied by, James Coleman, running with it 104 feet in depth to Major Thomas Bodley's line, thence with the latter 32 feet, thence parallel to the first mentioned line 104 feet to Upper Street, and along the latter to the beginning—being the lot conveyed by Henry and Lucretia Clay to Peter Paul, Jr., on August 22, 1808, and by him to Coleman on June 8, 1812—together with the premises appurtenant. General warranty of title. Whereas James Coleman executed note on February 22, 1812, to the abovementioned executors for $575, payable within three years from the date of the note, if the note is paid when due, this obligation is to be void. Recorded by the Clerk of Fayette County, June 15, 1812.]

Fayette County Court, Deed Book G, 63-65.

Reply to John Randolph's Pamphlet Attack

Washington, 17th June, 1812.

TO THE EDITOR OF THE N. INTELLIGENCER.

Some printed sheets, consisting of an address of the hon. John Randolph of Roanoke, to the freeholders of certain counties in Virginia, and of what purports to be the 'fragment' of a speech of that gentleman delivered in the House of Representatives, have fallen into my hands. The author appears to think that particular decisions of that body, of which he undertakes to present an account, have unwarrantably restricted the freedom of debate. However reluctant I may be to offer myself, in this way, to your notice, when a Member of the House of Representatives lends the high authority of his name to an incorrect statement of a transaction, and which, by the omission of material circumstances, exhibits only a partial view of the case, I think it due to the public, whose judgment and interposition have been invoked, to have the matter set fully and accurately before them. It is my intention to aim at the accomplishment of this object. It is not my purpose to notice particularly the manner or the substance of the residue of those compositions. How far the political speculations and sentiments of the author are just, the world may judge.

In the commencement of the observations of Mr. R. after announcing his purpose to make a motion, it is true that, Mr. Wright having called him to order, because there was no motion before the House, it was stated by me that, as he had signified his intention, it was usual to admit *prefatory* remarks. Mr. R. proceeded, and having gone very much at large into the question of the repeal of the French decrees, the subject of blockades, and other topics, I left the Chair for a few minutes, placing there my friend Mr. Bibb,[1] as my substitute. I will not say what was the case upon which that gentleman, whilst he was so kind as to represent me, was called upon to decide, my attention not having been particularly directed to the point. It is said by the 'fragment,' and I will suppose it to have been, on a call to order by Mr. Calhoun because "the question of war was not before the House." I shortly after resumed the chair, and Mr. Calhoun again called Mr. R. to order and submitted, whether he was not bound to specify his proposition and procure a second before he proceeded further. It was decided that he was bound to state it, that it must be seconded, reduced to writing, according to a particular rule of the House, if required, and announced from the chair. At the time this decision was made Mr. R. had been speaking I think at least one hour. An appeal was taken to the House, who confirmed the decision. He was then requested to reduce his motion to writing, which he did and presented it to the chair, remarking that he did it under the compulsion of the House, to which it was replied that it depended upon his own pleasure to withhold or offer his motion. After it was stated from the chair, Mr. R. was proceeding in his argument, when he was called to order upon the ground that the House must, previous to the discussion, determine whether it would at that time consider the proposition. I observed that that rule did not apply to the case, but immediately correcting this impression, it was declared that the House must come to such a resolution, or he would not be at liberty to proceed. Mr. R. again appealed from the decision, but subsequently withdrew his appeal and thereby manifested his acquiescence in it. The House then refused to consider the motion by Ayes & Noes. Other questions of order, having no material bearing on this subject, were decided.

Such were the circumstances of the case. It results that, between the decisions of Mr. Bibb and mine, certainly between my own, there existed no discrepancy; unless it is to be found in the momentary error, rectified almost as soon as it was committed, relative to the necessity of the House determining to consider the motion. Not between the former, because the points on which we decided were different. Not between the latter, because the first decision, at the instance of Mr. Wright, recognised only the admissibility of prefatory remarks, a quality which those of Mr. R. had, when the last determination took place, long ceased to possess.

Two principles are settled by these decisions; the first is, that the House has a right to know, through its organ, the specific motion which a member intends making, before he undertakes to argue it at large; and in the second place that it reserves to itself the exercise of the power of determining whether it will consider it at the particular time when offered, prior to his thus proceeding to argue it.

It would seem to be altogether reasonable that, when a member intends addressing a copious argument to a public body, for the purpose of enforcing a motion, he should disclose the motion intended to be supported. It is the practice of the British parliament, and of several if not all of the state assemblies, to require not only that this should be done, but that it should be seconded; thus affording a protection against the obtrusion upon the body of the whimsical or eccentric propositions of a disordered or irregular mind, by the coincidence in opinion of at least two individuals. At what particular period the proposition ought to be submitted is perhaps not exactly defined or definable. Certainly in the courtesy of all bodies will be found a sufficient safeguard against the exclusion of matter properly introductive, explanatory, or prefatory to the motion. The line separating matter of this character from arguments in chief is not susceptible of accurate description. It does not however present more practical difficulty than to discriminate between observations which are relevant or otherwise, decorous or reprehensible. When a member rises to make a motion, it is indeed not often that the rule is applied of requiring its specification, because the necessity of such application rarely occurs. But its non-existence is no more to be inferred from its non-application than the non-existence of other rules, the actual enforcement of which does not take place in every special case to which in terms they apply. The best demonstration of the utility of the rule is afforded in the very case complained of. Mr. R. had addressed the House not less than an hour. The general tenor of his arguments would have conducted equally well to almost any other conclusion than that to which he was carried, or at least to several others—to war, for example, or some other measure of a hostile character against France—that the law of non-importation ought to be repealed as to England—or put on against her enemy. Any man who will now read seven-eighths, if not the whole of his speech, keeping out of mind the motion with which it terminated, will, I apprehend, find it extremely difficult to conjecture that *such* was or *what* was to be the concluding motion. Now it is made the duty of the presiding officer (by the usages of all deliberative bodies, and moreover by express rules* of the House of Representatives) to keep the member, addressing the chair, to the point. How, that officer being ignorant of the motion intended to be offered, was that duty to be performed? How was the House itself to apply the arguments? In point of fact, I was entirely uncertain (others have assured me they were) as to what motion would be submitted, and even after it was reduced to writing it was believed not to be the one originally contemplated by the mover. I think then I am justified in saying that there is nothing unreasonable in the requisition, on the part of a body addressed to illustrate, enforce and establish a given proposition, that the mover of it shall specify it, that it shall be seconded, and, to prevent misconception of its precise import, that it shall be reduced to writing & distinctly announced from the chair, before he advances into a boundless field of argument. Indeed I understand from the address, as well as from what transpired on the occasion, that the real source of complaint is not in such a requisition, but that Mr. R. would have been satisfied had he not, after a compliance with it, by a subsequent refusal of the House to consider his motion, been prevented from continuing his argument.

Various are the expedients resorted to by deliberative bodies to conduct the business on which they are called upon to act. Among the instruments provided for regulating the time of transacting it are the motions for the previous question, to postpone—to adjourn—to lie upon the table—to consider. These in some instances are differently used by different bodies. In England a motion to 'proceed to the orders of the day' puts by whatever subject is under consideration, and the rule is not used there to consider. In the House of Representatives we practice the rule to consider and do not the motion to proceed to the orders of the day. The object of all bodies, on this subject, is the same—so to arrange the subjects of deliberation as best to promote the public interest. Their experience will, from time to time, suggest the defects in pre-existing rules and the necessity of adapting new ones to new exigencies as they arise. This rule to consider was a novel one to me when I came into the House of Representatives. I found most of the old members clinging to it with great tenacity, and subsequent observation has satisfied me of its wisdom, and removed whatever doubts I entertained originally of its propriety. *It has been indiscriminately applied by the House to members of all parties.* The right of one or two members to compel a body to consider a proposition which, on account of the time, its manner, or its matter, they do not think proper to deliberate upon, can only be maintained by a reversal of the rule that the plurality of the members is to govern, and would, *as to that particular subject,* make the mover and his second superior to the whole body. It may indeed be alleged that, unless such a privilege be recognised, great abuse may be practised—that the body may refuse to consider the most imperious and momentous subject of national interest. The obvious reply is, that an indulgence of such a privilege exposes the body to great abuse by any member who can obtain a second; and, in the danger of opposite abuses, it is believed there is greater safety or [*sic*][2] the side of greater numbers. The responsibility of a Representative body for what is not done exists no less than for what is done. It is not, therefore, probable that it will refuse to consider, and consequently to adopt, a measure presented for its deliberation under circumstances unexceptionable as to time, form and nature of the proposition. The abuse, however, of a rule, in its practical operation, is best tested by an examination of the cases to which it has been applied. I will content myself with that furnished by Mr. Randolph's own record. An extraordinary session of Congress is convoked: various laws are passed with the avowed purpose of war. During their pendency, both in their incipient and matured forms, the subject is discussed at great length. Every topic calculated to excite the passions, alarm the fears, or enlighten the judgment, is exhausted. More than any other member of the House, (often, I own, with admiration on my own part of his talents, however much I disapproved his sentiments) is Mr. R. patiently and repeatedly heard to develope his views on that solemn question. The period at length arrives when, by every previous indication, a declaration of war would seem to be absolutely inevitable. Of that very committee from which it was expected such a declaration is to emanate, Mr. R. is a member. It is admitted by himself on the 30th May,[3] that on the succeeding Monday it was believed it would be presented to the House. It is admitted by himself that it was intended to be discussed with closed doors. Yet on that day (the 30th of May) what does he attempt? Forestalling the friends of the measure, with open doors, without disclosing his particular motion, he engages in an argument which, after consuming one hour, is now denominated a fragment only; and, when required by the House, reluctantly submits the *negative* proposition that it is not expedient at this time, under existing circumstances, to go to war with Great-Britain! Can I be mistaken in believing that the refusal of the House to consider such a proposition, so brought forward, will be approved by the good sense of an intelligent public? It is said that a precedent for such a motion is to be found in the motion of Mr. Sprigg, made in 1798.[4] That gentleman, when the House was in committee of the whole on the state of the Union, offered three resolutions, of which one was negative, and the other two affirmative. The subject before the committee was the President's message of 19th March, 1798. At that time the practice (now no longer existing) prevailed to discuss such messages in full. That message was a war message. Being under consideration, it was the [*sic*] nature of an affirmative proposition for war, to which Mr. Sprigg's motion, in the nature of an amendment, was the negative. The message was the text, the primary subject; his motion was incidental and ancillary. But Mr. R.'s motion was primitive, and not appurtenant to any pending question. In the instance of Mr. Sprigg no point was made whether the committee would consider the proposition. Perhaps, being a direct response to the message, they were bound to consider it, or not to act upon the message. Out of Mr. R.'s motion, supposing it adopted, no positive act could grow. It would be as if the House should formally adopt an original resolution that they would *not* pass a particular law. The cases of Mr. R. and Mr. S. are not analogous. Supposing, however, that they were, in all their material circumstances, what would be proven? Only that a body, having the power to prescribe the time when it will consider the subjects brought before it, has seen fit at one time (no reason then existing against it) to deliberate upon a question, which at another time (when there are cogent reasons against it) it has not thought proper to consider.

The right of the House of Representatives to regulate its own proceedings is quite manifest, whether we advert to the express provision of the Constitution, or to the nature and properties of a deliberative body. It is undoubtedly responsible for the abuse of that right, no less than it is for the abuse of any other power with which it is invested. Whether, in the instance under consideration, it has so abused its authority as to excite alarm or justify censure, will be justly determined by the candor of the public, to whom alone it is amenable. H. CLAY.

*"When a motion is made and seconded, it shall be stated by the Speaker, or, being in writing, it shall be handed to the chair, and read aloud by the clerk, *before debated*."—"When any member is about to speak in debate, or deliver any matter to the House, he shall rise from his seat, and respectfully address himself to Mr. Speaker; *and shall confine himself to the question under debate,* and avoid personality."—*Rules of the House*. In England, still greater restraints have been imposed. "If any man speak impertinently, or beside the question in hand, it stands with the Orders of the House for the Speaker to interrupt him; and to know the pleasure of the House; whether they will further hear him."—"If any superfluous motion or tedious speech be offered in the House, the party is to be directed and ordered by Mr. Speaker."—*Hatsell's Precedents*.[5]

Washington *National Intelligencer*, June 18, 1812. Published also in *Annals of Cong.*, 12 Cong., 1 Sess., XXIV, 1469-73, note. Following the verbal exchange of May 29, Randolph had addressed a letter to his constituents deploring the proscription of freedom of speech in the House of Representatives, stating the grounds of his opposition to war with Britain, and intimating that those who favored war were subservient to France. Hugh A. Garland, *The Life of John Randolph of Roanoke* (13th ed. New York, 1866), I, 299-303. The pamphlet was dated May 30.

1 Dr. William Wyatt Bibb of Georgia.
2 See below, Clay to Worsley, June 18, 1812.
3 Actually, May 29. *Annals of Cong.*, 12 Cong., 1 Sess., XXIV, 1451.
4 For the resolutions offered by Richard Sprigg Jr., of Maryland, on March 27, 1798, see below, p. 692; *Annals of Cong.*, 5 Cong., 2 Sess., VIII, 1319-20.
5 John Hatsell, *Precedents of Proceedings in the House of Commons with Observations* (4 vols., London, 1781).

To William W. Worsley

D Sir Wash. 18h. June 1812.

Look for important news by the next mail. I send you an Intr. in which you will find an address of mine to the public.[1] Will you have the goodness my friend & ask Mr. Smith[2] also to be particular in having it correct, if you publish it. One hates to be mangled. In two particulars Mr. Gales[3] has committed errors towit 'Or' is used in one place instead of 'On'. and in the fifth line of the last column he has left out between 'was' and 'the' the word 'in.' Yrs.

H. CLAY.

ALS. KyLx. Addressed to Worsley at Lexington.
1 His reply to Randolph, June 17, 1812.
2 Thomas Smith.
3 Joseph Gales, Jr., editor of the Washington *National Intelligencer*.

To ———

[June 18, 1812]

I am not at liberty to disclose the subject of secret deliberation on the part of Congress.[1] You must draw your conclusions from what you see in the prints. Foster[2] has lately poured out a flood of letters upon the Secretary of State. Every step he takes displays more glaringly the ingenuity of British pretensions. The open undisguised ground is at length explicitly assumed that a repeal of the French decrees *as to us,* no matter how authentic the evidence of the fact may be, will not induce England to repeal even *as to us* the British orders. The fact, of which you wanted in Kentucky no evidence, but which here was boldly denied, is fully verified, that the Indians are instigated by the British, as you will see from the accompaniments of a letter of Mr. Monroe.[3]

We shall have war, and war against England alone. As to France, the negociation is not yet absolutely broken off, however hopeless we may be of a favourable result. As to France we have no complaint, on the score of violation of neutral rights, but of the past. Of England we have to complain in all the tenses. The one has in some measure ceased her blows, the other is every where pounding us. The one we can strike, the other we cannot reach. A correct view of this subject is taken in a sensible piece which I read in the Gazette and Reporter, (The VOLUNTEER.)[4]

I think it highly probable we shall adjourn on Saturday week.

Extract. Lexington *Reporter,* June 27, 1812.

1 The declaration of war against England. Madison signed the measure on the day this letter was written.

2 Augustus J. Foster.

3 See Monroe to Foster, June 10, 1812, and accompanying documents, in *Annals of Cong.,* 12 Cong., 1 Sess., XXIV, 1856-62.

4 An argument, signed " A VOLUNTEER," for war with England alone at that time, printed in the Lexington *Kentucky Gazette,* June 2, 1812; Lexington *Reporter,* June 6, 1812.

To Jesse Bledsoe

Wash. 18th June 1812.

I hear, My dear Bledsoe, with great pleasure that your political prospects are flattering.[1] No man has fortune more completely in his grasp than yourself, if you will discretely use the blessings of a kind providence. And why should you not, seeing before you a splendid fame, and the happiness of a beloved wife and children?

I am not at liberty to gratify that laudable curiosity which is excited by the closing of the doors of Congress. By the next mail an account of our doings will be transmitted. *We shall have War, and, as I think it ought to be at present, War with England alone.* France has done us much injury, but she has foreborne, except as to her tariff, which we cannot complain of as an infraction of the public law. The balance with her is struck; tho' not paid. England has a running account with us, which every passing moment swells with the most enormous items. The blows of the one, tho' heavy and severe, are at least intermitted. With regard to the other, behind and before us is exhibited but one boundless prospect of wrong & of insult. Let us give, in return for the insolence of British cannon, the peals of American thunder. Silencing her, we can then speak to the hushed batteries of French aggression.

Yr. friend, H. CLAY.

[Marginal addendum opposite the second paragraph]

You may make any use of this.

Typed copy, from the original owned by the late Charles R. Staples, Lexington, Kentucky. KyU-Samuel M. Wilson Collection. Extract published in Lexington *Reporter,* June 27, 1812. Addressed to Bledsoe at Lexington.

1 In the next year he became United States Senator from Kentucky, succeeding John Pope.

Notice of Protest by John Gill

Baltimore, 18 June 1812

PLEASE to take notice that a Bill of exchange dated Lexington

(K) 1 Oct. 1811 for $9504 payable 258 days after date drawn by Henry Clay on Gen. Sam. Hopkins due and by you indorsed, is delivered to me by the Cashier of the Union Bank of Maryland for Protest; and the same not being paid is Protested, and will be returned to the said Cashier and that you are held responsible for payment. *Your Humble Servant.* JNO. GILL Not. Pub
To H. Clay

DS. DLC-TJC (DNA, M212, R15).

From Benjamin H. Latrobe

The honorable Henry Clay,
Dear Sir Washington June 20h. 1812

As you come every morning to Dr Otts fountain,[1] will you be so good as to breakfast with me tomorrow (Sunday) morning between 7 & 8. I have the plan of the College[2] ready for your inspection & should be sorry to send it off without consulting You. I hope you will find this convenient, as I fear I shall not have time to wait upon you on the hill Yrs. truly B H LATROBE

ALS copy. Latrobe Letterbook, 507, owned by Mrs. Ferdinand C. Latrobe, Baltimore, Maryland.
1 Dr. John Ott, of Georgetown, who sold mineral waters and medicines.
2 Transylvania University.

To [William W. Worsley]

CITY OF WASHINGTON, JUNE 20, 1812.

Owing to the occupation of Congress in confidential deliberations, I had foreborne to communicate with you on political subjects for several mails. I am now at liberty to announce that War is declared against England. On the first inst. the President sent us an able message recommending the measure. On the 4th the House of Representatives passed the bill, by a majority of thirty votes, exclusive of my own, and of others who were absent. On the 17th the bill passed through the Senate, with some unessential amendments. It was reported to the House on the 18th, when an attempt being renewed to defeat the bill, it was repelled, 85 to 44. The House concurred in the Senate's amendments, and on that day the President approved the bill. Every patriot bosom must throb with anxious solicitude for the result. Every patriot arm will assist in making that result conducive to the glory of our beloved country.

Extract. Lexington *Reporter,* July 1, 1812. Identified as from Clay to the editor.

From James H. Lynch

H, Clay *Esqr* Richmd. 20h June 1812

Sir I have this moment yr letter.[1] and must say in reply—I feel myself much pleasd, at its Contents and that I really think yr offer very liberal, therefore Conclude to put and [*sic*] end to it by requesting of you to remit the money to me—the amount of the debt originally $449 with about four & half years interest If I am not Correct you will I have no doubt be so I shall Only Once more say that I have given you much trouble and hope you will satisfy yr. self—If you feel at liberty we would, like to hear something from Congress which could, be believd, I am with much respect yrs JAMES H LYNCH

ALS. DLC-TJC (DNA, M212, R12). Endorsed by Clay: "Lynch—Fowler's debt." James Head Lynch was a resident of Richmond.

1 Not found.

To [Paul Hamilton]

Dr Sir Washn. 20h. June 1812.

You will much oblige me by sending me a Mid-Shipman's warrant for the young gentleman mentioned within, if there be any vacancies. Dr. Ridgley who speaks of him in the manner you will see has my entire confidence. I am much interested for the young man. Respctfy. yrs. H. CLAY

ALS. DNA, RG45, Misc. Letters Received, 1812, vol. 4, p. 96. Two enclosures: Anderson to Clay, and Ridgely to Clay, June 10, 1812.

To Adam Beatty

Dr. Beatty Wash. 21st. June 1812.

War was declared agt. G. Britain on the 18h. inst. by Congress. The measure was adopted in the H. of R. on the 4h. It did not get through the Senate until the 17th.. I think a reconsideration of the opinions contained in your favor of the 7th.[1] will eventuate in a belief that we had better not at this time take an hostile attitude towards France. It is in vain, by such a step, to attempt the conciliation of the Feds. It was in fact proposed to the H. of R. ten only voted for it, and of these there were but two feds.

The British Premier was assassinated on entering the H. of Comm. on the 11h. May, by an individual for a private injury.[2] The mob attempted to rescue the assassin but was quelled. So says a Boston account, which is credited here.

I had not paid for the Register for you. I told Gales to put your subscription in my a/c.[3]

We shall adjourn I think in less than two weeks. Yrs. H. CLAY

ALS. MB. Endorsed: "Answd. 26th. July 1812." The answer has not been found.
1 Not found.
2 Sidney Perceval had been shot by John Bellingham.
3 The Raleigh, North Carolina, *Register* was owned and edited by Joseph Gales, Sr., father of the editor of the Washington *National Intelligencer*.

From Benjamin H. Latrobe

The Honorable Henry Clay
Sp. H. Rep. U States. Washington June 24h. 1812
Dear Sir,

You will herewith receive the plans of the College which I respectfully present to the Trustees of the University of Lexington in Kentucky.[1]—In these plans I have endeavored to accomplish all the objects stated in their letter, which you have transmitted to me.[2]—

As I cannot be present when the propriety of adopting this plan will be discussed, I will endeavor to anticipate and to answer the remarks & objections which are likely to be made to it, & at the same time give such explanations as are necessary to understand the principle & the details of the design.

The system of lodging the Students, and the mode of study and instruction which shall be actually adopted in the College, must more than any other consideration determine the plan of arrangement on which the building is to be constructed.—

In Princeton, Carlisle,[3] & other places of instruction the students are lodged in seperate cells, or closets, in wh[ich] also they study their Lessons & prepare their Exercises preparatory to public recitation.—

In the College at Baltimore,[4] & in all those I believ[e] [w]hich are conceived on the German & French plan, the [stu]dents are divided into bands or Classes, each of which [is] either lodged together in a Dormitory, or they sleep in a [gen]eral dormitory, and they study together in Class rooms [fu]rnished with desks & materials to accomodate them [in] Masses more or less numerous,—under constant inspection by the Master of the Class. Having been myself sent when a boy to be educated in Germany at Colleges [co]nducted on the latter principle, I cannot help, from [ha]bit perhaps, considering it as superior to that of P[r]inceton. The latter method renders it practicable [to] subject the students to constant inspection both at [s]tudy & in the night. In the former this cannot well [be] done, it being impossible to have a tutor to each room. [I] know however by experience that young men, & boys [ca]n evade the vigilance of the best organized system [o]f inspection, if they are so inclined: & that more de[p]ends on the personal character & talents of the prin[ci]pal & subordinate Officers of a College, than on any o[t]her circumstance, or even on the excellence of the [es]tablished system of instruction or discipline.

The College of Lexington, being (as the letter indicates) or[g]anized according to the system of Princeton, I have regulated my design to answer its objects.—

Each student, of which 44 may be lodged, in the College is furnished with a Cell 8 feet by 8, large enough to contain commodiously his bed & desk. Of these Cells there are alternately 3 & two in a room. The space round the fireplace or stove, if stoves are used is 10 feet wide, by 24 or 16, according to the number accomodated in the room.

Besides these lodging rooms there are in each of the two upper stories a recitation room in the Center of the house In the principal story are two Lecture rooms each containing space equal to a circle of 36 feet diameter. They occupy also the lower story, & consist of rising seats, Each room might contain an audience of 200 persons, & more might be crouded into them.—Over these lecture rooms in the upper story are two rooms to accomodat[e] those Societies which have been found in many points so useful at Princeton.—

Dark passages ought never to exist in Colleges, I have therefore in this design, as at Carlisle, placed all the rooms on the South side of the house, & an airy & light passage on the North.—

The Offices of the College I have placed altogether on the ground floor, on whi[ch] I propose that no student shall lodg[e or] have any business whatever excepting at the time of meals. [On] this floor the Steward of the College has his appartments [fr]om whence he can have constant & convenient super[in]tendance over the servants at all times.—

If two recitation rooms are insufficient, the dining [r]oom, the lecture rooms, or the Society's rooms may supply the rest.—

I have not devoted any particular apartment to a [li]brary, or a room to deposit the Philosophical appa[r]atus. One of the public rooms may answer this pur[p]ose, untill it becomes necessary to enlarge the build[in]g or erect further accomodation for the growing [w]ants of the Institution.

Under a small part of the West end of the building it will be necessary to provide Cellars. The space under the N.W. Lecture room may probably be sufficient to hold the provisions requisite for the establishment.—There will be a considerable space for stores under the Upper [s]eats of the lecture rooms. One of the rooms appropriated to the servants of the house may be made a Storeroom

[o]r be occupied by the Steward should his family re[q]uire more than two rooms.—

One of the most essential & natural enquiries on the view of every first design for a public building respects its expense.—

The expense of a building must depend upon its *size* the *nature* of its materials, and the difficulty of its workmanship,—provided no extraordinary expense be occasioned by want of skill or fidelity in those who have to execute the work, or to direct it.—

Of two buildings executed in the same manner that which covers the least ground will cost the least money.—The examination of a proposed plan ought therefore to begin with an enquiry into the space allotted to the purposes which are had in view in its erection.

To this examination, I will endeavor to submit the plan which I now propose to You.

The principal part of the space on the two principal or upper floors is occupied by the rooms of the students—

This number of these rooms is ad[a]pted to lodge 44 students, which is about the extent of accomodation proposed You say in your letter d. May 17h.[5] & the Trustees in theirs of April 15th.—that from 30 to 40 students should be lodged in the house.—& further ("*letter of the Trustees*") that [the]re should be

15 lodging rooms
5 recitation do.
1 Hall for public Exhibition
3 Rooms to accomodate a family
1 dining room for the students.—

Now the rooms provided in my plan are.—

16 lodging rooms.—
5.— { 2 Recitation rooms
2 society's Rooms
1 Lecture room (smaller) on the NW. }
1 Hall for public Exhibitions
3 Rooms for a family
1 Dining room for the Students

[an]d there are besides, the following rooms which [th]ough not mentioned are equally essential, & must [be] provided of course—

1 Kitchen
2 servants room
1 Kitchen pantry (cold meat, Flour &c)
1 Dining room pantry (Bread, plates, T[a]ble linnen & dry stores)

[So] that in fact the requisition of the Trustees is exacty [*sic*] [co]mplied with excepting that there is *one lodging* [ro]om more than they require, making room for 4 [s]tudents more than the extent proposed to their number. This excess it is not easy to correct, because it arises out of the symmetry of the plan, which makes an *even* number of rooms (16) requisite, and in a building of three Stories, one single room is not easily omitted, altho' the whole ground plan may be contracted so as to diminish the size of each apartment.

If then the number of rooms is not too great, it then must be enquired whether each room may not be contracted.—

To do this we must begin by the Cells of the students which are 8 feet square.—In these cells the bed will occupy a space of 5 [f]t. 9 [i]n in length & 3 feet in width. The bed may be perhaps 6 feet long.—At the side of the bed then remains a space of 5 feet, or (deducting the partition) 4 [f]t. 6 in by 8 feet—which is to contain a desk, a chair, a set of drawers an [*sic*] small book case at the least,—according to the liberality of the friends of the Student or his own industry.—I believe this space will not be found more than sufficient for convenience, altho' less might certainly be made to answer the purpose, and probably 8 [f]t. by 7 [f]t. including the partition would do. This contraction would save 10 feet in the length of the house, [an]d 5 feet in its breadth, or rather in the length of its [wi]ngs. It would contract the building 5 feet at each [en]d within the ground of the Institution, the whole of [w]hich it now occupies.—

The next question relates to the two recitation rooms [in] the Center which are 32 feet long by 19 wide.—[It] is not my opinion that these can be well contracted. [Bu]t if the Trustees think otherwise I will observe [tha]t not more than 3 feet out of 32 can be gained [wi]thout very much deranging the design.—

The next question is as to the lecture or Exhibition [ro]oms occupying a space of 36 feet diameter.

These are surely quite small enough; but they [mi]ght be diminished 2 feet each without rendering [th]e staircase & adjoining rooms, —(which this alterati[on] would affect) too narrow.

The general passage or Corridor is 10 feet wide.—[If] it were wider it would not be amiss, when we [co]nsider that 200 boys may require the range of [t]his part of the house.—Here I think nothing can be [p]ared.—

There are 10 feet allowing in the open space of the Stu[d]ents rooms. Into this space the Chimney jaumbs will project 1 [f]t. 2 inches leaving 8 [f]t. 10 in the front. This is I thin[k] not two much: But one foot perhaps could be spared.—

The length of the kitchen & dining room results from tha[t] of the rooms above. If they are contracted the others follo[w] of course. But I cannot think them too long. Nothin[g] is so essential as a roomy Kitchen, especially, as the[re] will be much washing done in the house. The kitch[en] must be vaulted to shut out *steam, smell,* & *fire* & be sunk 3 feet lower than the other floor, so as to be 12 feet high. The expence will be little more than of at[. . .][6] floor.

I have put the kitchen at a distance from the Dini[ng] room; the latter being the resort of Students. The doors leading to the kitchen from the passage may all be locked excepting at dinner time, there being a sep[a]rate communication from thence to the kitchen Yar[d.] If the steward occupies as his parlor the room mar[ked] *House servants or Steward,* it would be best.

But if it is thought best, the three rooms next to the Kitchen may be thrown in to one for a dining room, & the dining room be occupied by the Steward & Servant[s.] But I think the change would be for the worse—From the above remarks it results that the size of the house [m]ay be reduced 12 feet in length, perhaps even 15 feet, [an]d the wings 5 feet. The saving might be 1000 to 1500. [B]ut then, should the Institution flourish, (as it as[s]uredly will in such a growing city as Lexington [y]et in her infancy) it would be always subject of [re]gret that for such a sum so much room in details [h]ad been lost, and the means of admitting more stu[d]ents without encreasing the build [*sic*] thrown away.

For in the students rooms which are 24 feet long, and which accomodate 3 students each, 4 may be put, making their cells only 6 feet by 8 which is the *minimum* of accomodation. This would in 12 rooms of that size admit 12 additional students.

On comparing the plan before me with that of Dickinson College at Carlisle, I cannot help thinking the latter very inferior in accomodation to the former I enclose a sketch of D. College, but I am ignorant of the manner in which it is fitted up & occupied not having seen it since it has been erected.—

The next consideration as to expenses is as to the manne[r] of building and the materials.—

In all public buildings, durability should certainly be the first consideration, after good arrangement

I propose the College to be of plain brick,—the lower story 2½ bricks thick 9 feet high, the two upper ones 2 bricks thick 12 feet high each.

The upper story, if it is thought an object, may be made only 1½ bricks thick, & the highth of each may be diminished.—I leave this to the Trustees but should not advise a less highth than 10 [f]t 6 [i]n at the very least,—for it must be considered, that 3 students or 4, sleep in the rooms.

I propose a stone or Marble fascia of 8 inche[s] at each story, and a Marble water table, Marb[le] window heads, and a Marble blocking in the Center.—As the fascia is on the line of the upper window selles much will be thereby saved.

As to the expense of the whole building, if, as you say, the bricks & all Materials can be found & laid at 7.$—or 7.$50 which here cost 12.$50 Then I think the hous[e] [a]nd grounds, fence Walls, privies, &c cannot possibly [be] built for less than 30.000 dollars, & it ought not [to] cost more than 32.000.—

The idea of the Trustees that 15 or 18000$ will give them [th]e accomodation they want is very unfortunate. [L]et them consider what I have above said attentively: let them not be flattered by Men who desire the Job;—to a belief [t]hat they can do as Trustees, what they never could do as individuals: let any one of them who has [bu]ilt calculate the number of superficial feet [his] house covers, & dividing his whole expense by [tha]t number, find out what each foot has cost, & [he] will discover that it has cost him from 4 to [. . .][7] dollars P foot at least. If then the College covers [as] it does 7.440 feet, it will cost at 4$ P foot 29.$760. [Le]t them then calculate the saving they can make [by] the curtailments which I have suggested, and they [w]ill find them at the utmost to amount to 2 to 3000.

If however you have not the funds, to build the [w]hole house, stop at the Center, or omit the N.E wing. [Th]is may be easily done & 8 to 12000$ be saved or rather postponed: I will willingly show them how it may be done.—

My time is now at an end. I began, intending these remarks merely as the sketch of a letter I intended to write to you, but I must send you them rough as they are.—I have only to request that if my plan is adopted I may be apprised of it as early as possible & that nothing may be done untill they receive a regular working drawing for the ground floor & so on for the rest. If I am obliged to *hire* & pay for assistance to the amount of 40 or 50$ to hasten the drawings I shall let you know. But all that I can do myself and without any expenditure I shall think myself highly honored if the Trust[ees] will accept as a small contribution to an inst[it]ution in the success of which every good ma[n] must feel interested. Perpetua esto. With high respect I am Yours B H LATROBE

ALS copy. Latrobe Letterbook, 526-38, owned by Mrs. Ferdinand C. Latrobe, Baltimore, Maryland. Margins obscured in photostatic reproduction.

1 Transylvania University. 2 Not found.

3 Dickinson College, Carlisle, Pennsylvania. 4 St. Mary's College.

5 Not found. 6 Word illegible. 7 Figure illegible.

To ———————

WASHINGTON, 28th June, 1812.

Commodore Rogers[1] is said to have [had] an action with the British frigate [Bel]videre;[2] but if it did take place, it [is n]ot yet known here. It is certain [that] a heavy cannonade was heard off New-York.

We are now told that the commodore is in pursuit of a large Jamaica fleet of merchantmen, under convoy of a single frigate. God grant that he may come up with them. We look with great anxiety for the arrival of every eastern mail. We hope to close the session by at least to-morrow week.

Extract. Frankfort *Palladium,* July 8, 1812.

1 Commodore John Rodgers was the senior American naval officer in command during the War of 1812. He was outranked only by Commodore Alexander Murray, who was too old for active service at sea. Charles O. Paullin, *Commodore John Rodgers; Captain, Commodore, and Senior Officer of the American Navy, 1773-1838* (Cleveland, 1910), 243-44.

2 Commodore Rodgers' ship, the *President,* and the British frigate *Belvidera* had engaged in a running fight on June 23, beginning early in the morning and lasting until the *Belvidera* escaped from her pursuer before midnight. Casualties on both vessels were light.

From Benjamin H. Latrobe

The honbl Henry Clay
The House of Rep. U. S. Washington June 29h. 1812

Sir,

When the Lamps & other furniture were imported by my agency for the house of Representatives, from England, I wrote to my brother there in London[1] to select for me certain articles for my own use & to superintend the execution of the order.—He did so, but unfortunately my articles were mixed with those of the public tho' marked for me in the invoice. Mr. Pleasants[2] to whom they were consigned drew upon me for the amount, & I have received them all excepting part of my lamp glasses, which still remain among the stores of the house of representatives.—Mr Claxton[3] does not think himself at liberty to deliver to me these Glasses without your order. I therefore enclose the Invoice, for your inspection, which I beg you to return to me, and respectfully request you to give such orders as you may think fit in the case.

My wish is only for the ground glasses;—the plain ones are now [*sic*] difficult to be got, and I have supplied myself. I therefore do not ask for more of these,—but the others are quite useless to the public & fit only for a private family. I am with high respect Yrs.

B HENRY LATROBE.

ALS copy. Latrobe Letterbook, 8, 11, owned by Mrs. Ferdinand C. Latrobe, Baltimore, Maryland. 1 Christian I. Latrobe.

2 Probably of the Baltimore mercantile firm John P. Pleasants & Son.

3 Thomas Claxton, doorkeeper of the United States House of Representatives.

To Edward Tiffin

Sir Wash. 1st. July 1812.

At the commencement of the present Session of Congress I deposited a number of plats & Certificates of survey with the proper officer to obtain patents. Altho. I made repeated applications I was unsuccessful in procuring them. I recollect amongst others some for a Mr. Basey[1] & some for Thomas Carneal's representatives or Mr. Coleman. Will you do me the favor to say if I can procure them before or by tuesday next? Yrs. H. CLAY

ALS. DNA, RG49, Misc. Letters Received, C. Addressed: "Edward Tiffin Esqr. Commr. &c. T. Departmt." Endorsed at bottom of page: "2740 Acres Coleman admr of Carneal 100 Acres Do. John McAdams 2666 2/3." Endorsed on cover: "Genl. Scotts patents to be Trans to G Scott Frankfot." Tiffin, the first governor of Ohio and, later, United States Senator from Ohio, had become the first Commissioner of the General Land Office in 1812. Two years later he became Surveyor General. James Coleman of Lexington had married a daughter of Thomas Carneal. John McAdams was probably of Nelson County, Kentucky; Scott was Governor Charles Scott.

1 Not identified—there were several persons of that surname resident in Kentucky and the newly opened Territories at this time.

To Edward Tiffin

Sir H. of R. 2 July 1812—

I recd. your favor of this morning[1] in reply to mine of yesterday. The other plats and Certificates of survey not noticed in your's which I deposited for patents were a bundle I think of Dr. Basey's, and were left either with Mr. Cutting[2] in the office of War, or in the office of State with Mr. Colvin.[3] Should you not be able to complete the patents prior to my departure you will have the goodness to transmit them to me at Lexington. (K.) Yrs. H. CLAY

ALS. DNA, RG49, Misc. Letters Received, C. Addressed to Tiffin.

1 Not found.

2 Nathaniel Cutting, a clerk in the War Department.

3 John B. Colvin, at this time a State Department clerk, formerly an unsuccessful newspaper publisher, and later a Washington lawyer.

To [William W. Worsley]

WASHINGTON, July 2. [1812]

I understand that an express has this moment arrived to the Secretary of the Navy with the intelligence that Com. Rodgers, in the *President,* has taken the *British frigate Belvidere,* after a most severe action of 2 hours and 40 minutes. The two vessels, which are of equal force, fought alone. The Belvidere had 90 men killed, the President 40. The action was fought off Rhode-Island, and the Belvidere is brought into New-Port. Such is the information, which in the main I have no doubt is correct.[1]

Extract. Lexington *Reporter,* July 11, 1812. Identified as from Clay to the editor.

1 Cf. above, Clay to ———, June 28, 1812.

John Randolph's Reply to Clay's Public Letter

FOR THE NATIONAL INTELLIGENCER. *July* 2, 1812

In the National Intelligencer of the 18th of June there appeared a production signed "H. Clay," which purports to supply "the omission of material circumstances, in relation to a late transaction in the House of Representatives," and to "set fully and accurately" before the *public that matter,* which the writer more than insinuates to have been *partially and incorrectly represented,* in the fragment of a speech dedicated to my constituents. When this publication first appeared, I was content to let it pass without notice. The facts (as I believed) were too notorious to be distorted. The very circumstance that the Speaker of the House of Representatives should feel himself reduced to a defence of his decisions in the public prints seemed to me, *of itself,* enough to satisfy all reflecting men, that there must be something wrong at bottom: and my ambition did not aspire to the honor of a news-paper-contest with any man, however high his dignity in the state. I was therefore content to let the matter rest where it stood. But my friends have urged me not to permit this publication—although it derives its sole claim to consideration from its official character—to pass unnoticed: lest the public mind, so habituated to AUTHORITY, should be misled by it.

In deference to their judgment, I enter on this task, with a reluctance, the evidence of which will be found in the cold and sluggish manner in which it is executed.

Of all men it especially behoves him, who brings a charge against his neighbor, to avoid the error which he reprehends. There is something repugnant to our natural sense of justice to behold any man, however high his station—or great his claims to knowledge—reproving in another that failing, of which he himself, in his own person, affords a striking example. We would not endure even from Solomon himself—a king and the wisest of mankind—a reproof to the meanest of his subjects, because he did not confine himself to a single wife. This repugnance will be heightened when the example is exhibited in the very act of rebuke; and we reach the last stage of disgust, when we discover that the accused is innocent of the charge laid at his door—the accuser alone guilty.

But I will close my "prefatory remarks" and proceed to specify some of the instances of omission of material circumstances, or of unfairness of statement on the part of Mr. Clay.

It was not "in the *commencement* of his observations that Mr. R. was called to order by Mr. Wright." Mr. Randolph had been speaking some time—had read several extracts from the correspondence of our government with its agent at Paris, and had advanced considerably into the case of the New-Orleans Packet,[1] when he was interrupted by Mr. Wright. The Speaker's decision that Mr. R. had a right to proceed, in as much as he had declared his intention to submit a motion—and his permitting that gentleman to proceed, according to his own statement, "for at least one hour," are facts conclusive of the point of order.

It does not become me to question the ignorance, pleaded by the Speaker, of "the case on which his friend Dr. Bibb decided, whilst acting as his substitute in the chair." Although the circumstance is certainly an extraordinary one, I shall not insinuate a doubt that the Speaker was so disengaged, or engaged, whilst out of the chair, that he did not observe an occurrence, which attracted the general attention of the house and of the Spectators. This transaction took place on the 29th of May, Mr. Clay's publication bears date the 17th of June. I cannot sufficiently admire his want of that dangerous quality, *curiosity,* manifested by his refraining for three weeks from making himself acquainted with the decision of Dr. Bibb, who lodges next door to him & under the same roof.

"I will not say what was the case upon which that gentleman" {Dr. Bibb} "whilst he was so kind as to represent me, was called upon to decide"—Mr. Clay's letter, 1st column. Again—"It results that between the decisions of Mr. Bibb and mine, certainly between my own, there existed no discrepancy." What! No *"discrepancy"* proved to exist between an unknown and a known decision? The train of reasoning which leads to *results* like this is a new and invaluable discovery in logic. It far surpasses the old method of reasoning from the known to the unknown, and is even an improvement upon the modern practice of reasoning to things unknown from things *more* unknown: *ignotum per ignotius.*

Mr. Bibb's decision, on the repetition of the call to order by Mr. Calhoun, was substantially the same with that of the Speaker, on the interruption by Mr. Wright. And as Mr. Clay may not have "particularly directed his attention to this point," also—I beg leave to inform him that the *"discrepancy,"* between himself and Dr. Bibb, may be found in the recorded vote of the latter gentleman on the journals of the house, affirming the Speaker to have decided contrary to order. But what reasonable man will, for a moment, attach any blame to the Speaker, for ignorance of the *"discrepancy"* which existed between Dr. Bibb's and his own decision, when he appears unconscious of his "discrepancy" with himself. That he should forget his own repeated decisions, on former occasions, is not so much to be wondered at, as that he should appear insensible to the manifest fact, that twice within the space of an hour he should have reversed his own opinions. Yet such unquestionably was the case.

On the subject of those former decisions I will refer members of the house to the debate in conclave on the embargo bill, when at a very late hour Mr. Stanford and Mr. Randolph were both sustained by the chair in the same right against the impatience of the House;[2] and I would call the general recollection to the case of Mr. Randolph's motion to amend Mr. Macon's[3] proposition to afford relief to the people of Caraccas. In this case, the Speaker himself interrupted Mr. Randolph, but as soon as he understood he was about to make a motion, withdrew his objection—and sustained Mr. Randolph's right to the floor against repeated calls to order from different quarters of the House. After delivering his sentiments on the motion which he contemplated to make, Mr. R concluded by submitting it to the house.

It behoves me to admit that when I presented my motion "under the compulsion of the House"—the Speaker did reply "that it depended upon my own pleasure to withhold, or offer it." which reply is not stated, it seems, in the "fragment," and appears to constitute one of the omissions, on my part, of which Mr. Clay complains. Reader! I was not unconscious of the omission at the time, but I had no disposition to inform the world, that mockery was added to the injustice with which I had been treated; nor can I comprehend the interest which Mr. Clay can feel in making the fact public.

There was no compulsion, mark you!—"It depended entirely upon my own pleasure to offer the motion or to withhold it" & *take my seat in silence*. In like manner, there was no compulsion used upon those unhappy people of old, who obstinately and perversely imagined themselves to be exiled from Rome. They were *only interdicted the use of fire and water so long as they should remain there*. No compulsion, at all, in the case! "It depended entirely upon their own pleasure whether they would *go or stay*"—and yet these wayward objects of the tender regard of the majority for their rights, fancied themselves under compulsion, and vented their party spleen by leaving their homes in disgust.

When the decision was given in favor of Mr. Calhoun's appeal to the chair, and the motion was submitted in writing, Mr. Randolph asked if he was at liberty to proceed? The Speaker decided that he was. Mr. Randolph did accordingly proceed for about a minute, when he was again called to order, and the Speaker, declaring that he had given a hasty opinion, reversed his decision. From this an appeal was taken by Mr. R. but withdrawn out of respect to his friend Mr. Macon—who said, that "he had no doubt the decision to reduce the motion to writing and submit it (against which he had voted) was wrong, but the house having established"— Here Mr. Randolph interrupted him, and said that out of respect to his friend he would withdraw his appeal. This he did under a mistaken idea that Mr. Macon would support by his vote the subsequent decision of the chair. He regretted very much the withdrawal of the appeal, when he afterwards discovered that he had misapprehended the vote, which that gentleman was about to have given.

It will not escape attention, that the facts stated in the "fragment" of Mr. R's. speech are few and scarcely accompanied by comment. Let me recapitulate them:

1. The call to order by Mr. Wright; whereupon the Speaker decided that Mr. R. was at liberty to proceed, and accordingly he did proceed, "at least one hour," by Mr. Clay's own statement.

2. The repetition of the call to order, by Mr. Calhoun, when Mr. R. was again supported in his right to the floor, by Dr. Bibb.

3. Mr. Calhoun's second call to order; "whereupon the Speaker reversed his own and Dr. Bibb's decision."

4. The Speaker's declaration that it was not necessary to take the vote "to consider," and that Mr. R. was at liberty to continue his argument; and his retraction and reversal of that opinion.

Let any man read Mr. Clay's letter to the Editor of the National Intelligencer, and then pronounce how far these facts are denied or disproved? I shall not defend the speech against the charge of irrelevancy of the arguments to the motion, brought against it by Mr. Clay. It shall defend itself. Neither shall I stoop to repel the insinuation conveyed in the following passage of the letter—"even after it {the motion} was reduced to writing, it was believed not to be the one originally contemplated by the mover." Such insinuations it is in the power of any man to make. A witty writer—one of the most shrewd observers upon human life & character has said, that "a certain class of politicians should speak impersonally, to avoid compromitment." Thus, one of this race ought never to say "I hear, or I am told, so and so:" because the question immediately occurs, *who told you?* And he may be called upon for his authority—But put it impersonally, *it is said, it is reported, it is believed,* and he is quite safe from any such disagreeable consequences.

The manner in which Mr. Clay speaks of my being acquainted with the projected measure, inasmuch as I am a member of the committee of Foreign Relations, is calculated to make an impression upon persons unacquainted with the state of affairs at Washington. Most certainly "on the 30th of May *it* was *not* expected," by *me* at least, or any body else with whom I conversed, that any such measure as "a declaration of war" would "emanate from that committee." On the contrary, *"it* was expected" that a confidential message would be received from the President, recommending the measure, and the chief of my information was derived, at second hand, from Mr. Clay himself, who, in one of his morning rides to Geo. Town[4] a day or two before, communicated the intelligence to one of my colleagues, from whom I received it. The authority was good—the thing happened accordingly. The President's message was referred to the committee of Foreign Relations—by them, to a sub-committee of three (of whom I was not one) and all the agency which I had in the transaction (even *subsequently* to the 1st of June) was to help to make up a quorum whilst the manifesto was reading.

It is not possible to make out any other difference between Mr. Sprigg's resolution and mine, except the substitution of *Great Britain* for the words "French Republic." The circumstances too were similar. The minority apprehended war and were anxious to avert it from the country. Would Mr. Clay's decision have been affected, in case I had added two other resolutions; "one to prevent the arming of merchant vessels, and the other to provide for the defence of the coast?"*

But what at last is the TRUE QUESTION in which the public are interested? It is, whether, after having been *quibbled* into a war by distinctions between "conditions *precedent* and conditions *subsequent*;" between "decrees affecting our *neutral* rights and decrees affecting our rights *municipally*;" we shall now, under the mask of *form,* be deprived of the *substance* of freedom of speech in the popular branch of the Legislature; whether we are content to be *cast,* and lose forever this invaluable privilege, for some alleged want of nicety in special pleading?

The right of illustrating and enforcing his motion, violated for the first time in the case of Mr. Randolph, was the last relic of freedom of debate, which new rules and forced constructions had left untouched. The present practice of the House of Representatives is an anomaly in legislative proceedings. It is new in this country, and there is nothing similar to it in England, or in any of our state governments, as far as I am acquainted. The use made of this "*rule* to consider, which we practice in the House of Representatives" {which *rule* does not exist in the *Rules and Orders* of the House} and the abuse of "the † *previous question"* are utterly subversive of the rights of the minority, for the preservation of which rules are chiefly instituted, if we are to credit a high authority {Mr. Onslow;}[5] the majority by their numbers being always able to protect themselves.

By these, a member of the minority may be and is prohibited from making any motion whatsoever—and all discussion precluded at their pleasure, on such measures as the majority choose to bring forward. It is notorious that *the previous question*—instead of being applied to its legitimate objects, that is "when a subject is brought forward of a delicate nature, as to high personages, &c. or the discussion of which may call forth injurious observations" ‡—is brought into play altogether on those great topics which especially demand discussion; and hence the recent change of the rule which requires a majority to demand the "previous question," instead of *"any five members"* as heretofore. Fortunately, the Constitution secures that "the yeas and nays shall be taken at the requisition of one-fifth of the members present;" but even this provision is greatly evaded by secret sessions, which lock the vote and the subject from the public eye.

But the practice of the British Parliament is quoted in justification of the conduct of the House of Representatives. I defy any man to shew an instance in which a member of that Parliament has been subjected to the coercion exercised in the case of Mr. Randolph. "A motion to proceed to the orders of the day puts by whatever subject is under consideration"—because the orders of the day have there, as they have here, a preference over ordinary questions. But there is no mode in that Parliament, analogous to the one lately devised and set up here, of preventing a member from bringing forward a motion on any subject fit for legislative deliberation, and illustrating and enforcing it by every argument in his power. Such tyranny would not be borne. Neither would they endure that a member of the opposition should be repeatedly interrupted upon the same plea of order, and by the same member of the court-party, after repeated decisions of the chair in his favor. The British House of Commons present their Speaker to the crown for its {nominal} approbation, they even ask for the confirmation of their ancient privileges; but under this exterior of humility and deference towards the throne, they have sturdily maintained their rights since the restoration, and in no legislative assembly is the freedom of speech enjoyed in greater latitude, or security. With all their venality and devotion to ministers, the members of that House know full well, that upon the jealous preservation of their privileges depends their weight in the constitution. It remains to be seen whether an American Congress shall be justified by the public sentiment in out-stripping a British House of Commons in ministerial devotion; in prostrating, from motives of caprice, temporary convenience, or party spirit, any one of those great fundamental principles, without a religious observance of which no free government can endure. JOHN RANDOLPH *of Roanoke.*

* *Mr. Sprigg's motion, March* 26 [*sic*], 1798

Resolved, That it is the opinion of this committee that under existing circumstances it is not expedient for the United States to resort to war against the French Republic.

Resolved, That provision ought to be made by law for restricting the arming of merchant vessels except in cases in which the practice was heretofore permitted.

Resolved, That adequate provision be made by law for the protection of our sea coast and the internal defence of the country.

† On the 25th of May, 1604, is the first instance that I have found of putting the previous question. Sir Thomas Littleton was therefore mistaken, when he says, in Grey's Debates,[6] vol. II, page 113, "Sir Henry Vane was the first that ever proposed putting a question whether the question should be now put? and since, it has always been the fore-runner of putting the thing in question quite out." Sir Robert Howard, in the same debate says, "This previous question is like the image of the inventor, a perpetual disturbance." 2 Hatsell, p. 80.

‡ See Jefferson's Manuel[7] under the head "Previous Question."

Washington *National Intelligencer,* July 8, 1812. Published also in *Annals of Cong.,* 12 Cong., 1 Sess., XXIV, 1473-79. Clay's letter was dated June 17.

1 An American merchant vessel seized at Bordeaux late in 1810 after the Berlin and Milan decrees had supposedly been repealed.

2 As reported, the incident had not conformed with Randolph's account. The Chair had ruled against both Randolph and Stanford, and had been sustained by vote of the House. *Annals of Cong.,* 12 Cong., 1 Sess., XXIV, 1613.

3 Nathaniel Macon, of North Carolina, who had recommended that the President be authorized to purchase and export flour for the relief of those suffering from an earthquake in Caracas. The discussion is reported without reference to the Randolph-Clay interchange in *Annals of Cong.,* 12 Cong., 1 Sess., XXIV, 1348.

4 Probably to Ott's Fountain.

5 Arthur Onslow (1691-1768), noted Speaker of the British House of Commons.

6 Anchitell Grey (comp.), *Debates of the House of Commons from 1667 to 1694* (10 vols., London, 1796).

7 Thomas Jefferson, *A Manual of Parliamentary Practice; for the Use of the Senate of the United States* (2d. ed., With the Last Additions of the Author, Washington, 1812). This edition included "Rules and Orders for Conducting Business in the House of Representatives of the United States."

Answer to Boston *Repertory*

[July 2, 1812]

It has been our lot heretofore frequently to witness the wild and extravagant effusions of disappointed & frantic ambition. But we have never yet beheld with more mingled emotions of regret,[1] and detestation, any such evidence of the madness and desperation of an unprincipled incendiary, as that which is presented in the Boston Repertory of the 26 of June. It wants only the overt act to consummate the worst of all crimes; or rather, to speak more correctly, it wants only the formality of an inquest to place the maniac under a regimen & restraint which would restore him to his senses.

Does Dr. Parke allow himself for one moment to believe that he can persuade the patriotic people of Massachusetts to raise the paricidal arm? to imbrue a brother's hand in a brother's blood? to plunge that sword, which should be pointed against the enemies of our Country, into the bosoms of our own people? to divert the combined energies of a free people from a noble and manful vengeance[2] upon a foreign foe, to a rash and diabolical resistance of their own government? Resistance! Resistance for what? The fathers of our Country, with the immortal founder of its liberties at their head, presented us with a free government. The people deliberately accepted it. It is the admiration of the world. Under its mild administration every blessing of which we are susceptible is enjoyed. Property protected—liberty secured—religion tolerated—every art encouraged—every science prospering. A government under the benign influence of which man is unfolding all his noblest qualities. Against the lawful mandates of such a government the people of Massachusetts are summoned to rebel. And for what? The constituted authorities of the Land have proclaimed War against G. Britain. The majority of the people themselves, acting through their representatives,—that majority without recognizing the legitimacy of whose acts, all free rule is at an end—have announced this state of things. And the people are solemnly called upon, in the face of open day, to oppose by force of arms, the decree which the people themselves have thus promulgated! And to what would such fatal opposition lead? The long train of horrors lies before us. We may in imagination contemplate the dreadful picture. It is impossible there should be folly and wickedness enough to bring it into actual existence. Suppose a few ambitious demagogues, lost to their Country's happiness and unmindful of their own safety, should attempt to organize force to oppose that Constitution which they have sworn to support? Can they cherish the false and delusive hope that they would[3] disseminate the contagion through the uncontaminated yeomanry of Massachusetts? No! The virtuous people of that State would deny to their fellow Citizens of the adjacient States, a part cipation in the honor of putting down the Treason. Rising in the majesty of their strength they would expel from their bosom the wretches who, by civil war, would bring down upon their Country the most horrible[4] of all calamities. Let us indulge the further supposition, that these leaders should call to their assistance the myrmidons of a foreign power—that the fleets and armies of that nation against which our undivided energies ought to be exerted, should be introduced into Massachusetts to abet the traitor

& subvert his government. The gallant militia of that State would be still competent to crush the treason and to drive from their hallowed shores the insidious invader. But should the contest prove doubtful; should the men of Massachusetts who are true to themselves and to their country be in danger of being overcome by the united force of traitors and British minions, then should we behold the noble spectacle of myriads of freemen in other States starting up, as it were, with one soul and with one arm, flying to the assistance of the faithful militia of Massachusetts, and overwhelming the domestic traitor and his foreign auxiliary.

We might extend our improbable[5] suppositions still farther. We might suppose that a misguided faction in[6] Massachusetts really desired separation; that in other States in New England similar views were entertained,[7] and that an abruption of that section was actually effected. What then would be the situation of the new government in reference to the political parties which would still continue to exist in its own limits; in reference to the residue of the Union; and in reference to foreign powers. But we will not indulge in a course of reasoning upon premises, the possible existence of which we cannot believe. We have already detained our readers too long with the ravings of this bedlamite. If there be any who can imagine him not bereaved of his intellect, let them read with merited execration the following abominable production:[8]

AD. InU. Published in Washington *National Intelligencer,* July 2, 1812. The editor of the Boston *Repertory & General Advertiser* (until July 7, 1812) was Dr. John Park.

1 The word "contempt" was crossed out after the comma.

2 This word substituted for "opposition."

3 Substituted for "will."

4 Substituted for "dreadful."

5 This word interlined.

6 Last four words interlined.

7 This clause substituted for the following: "that other States in New England entertained the same wish."

8 The article, reprinted in the *National Intelligencer* as the heading to Clay's answer, constituted a vigorous diatribe against the war "to place Bonaparte where he never can be, with his foot upon the necks of all mankind." It pointed to the possibility of "*physical force,*" as a means of opposing the measure. "*Let the people see that though forsaken, or rather cruelly persecuted by our national government, we have a* ROCK OF SALVATION, *under God,* IN THE EXECUTIVE AND LEGISLATURE OF MASSACHUSETTS. If the Senate are abandoned; if they are lost to all feelings of honor, justice and the obligations of self-preservation, *let a direct appeal be made to the people, and a correspondence be established throughout the state,* to ensure concert, firmness and promptitude."

To Noah Webster

Sir Wash. 7h. July 1812.

I recd. your's of the 29h. Ulto.[1] I am altogether at a loss to account for the delinquencies you impute to Mess. Maccoun Tilford & Co.: Their standing was correctly represented by me, and when

I left Kentucky about nine months ago they continued to maintain it. I am yet persuaded that a little stimulus which I will apply when I go out will bring up arrears.

Your note upon Charless[2] I placed in the hands of a respectable Atto. and will probably have the amt. next winter. Yrs.

H. CLAY

ALS. NN-Ford Collection. Addressed: "Noah Webster Junr. New Haven."
1 Not found.
2 Joseph Charless.

Receipt from Ringgold and Heath

8h July 1812.

Recd. of H. Clay Seven hundred dollars to be applied to paymt. of the Waggonage from Pittsburgh of the yarns he has contracted to deliver us; the balance of the Waggonage we will advance out of the price of the yarns RINGGOLD & HEATH

DS, in Clay's hand. DLC-TJC (DNA, M212, R15). Late in 1811 Ringgold and Heath had begun advertising in the Lexington *Reporter* their desire to contract for water-rotted hemp and yarns to be delivered at their rope walk in Washington, D.C., during the next two years.

Mortgage Deed from Thomas H. Pindell to Executors of Thomas Hart, Jr.

[July 10, 1812]

[Whereas Thomas H. Pindell on February 22, 1812 gave the executors of Thomas Hart, Jr., a note for $2001, payable within three years from the date of the note,[1] now by this indenture to secure the above obligation, Thomas Pindell and his wife grant the aforesaid executrix and executors a lot in Lexington bounded beginning at the intersection of Second and Market streets, running with Market Street 168½ feet to the corner of a lot sold by the executors to John Anderson,[2] thence with Anderson's line 97 feet, thence at right angles to his line 168½ feet to Second Street, thence with Second Street to the beginning—provided that if Pindell, his executors, or his administrators pay the above-mentioned note, this document shall be void. Certification of signature acknowledgement before John D. Young, Clerk of Fayette County, October 20, 1812.]

Fayette County Court, Deed Book G, 244. The property deed from Hart's executors to Pindell was dated July 31, 1812.
1 Not found.
2 Deed dated July 31, 1812.

To [William W. Worsley]

CHILLICOTHE, 21st July, 1812.

I transmit you a paper, published at Franklinton, in this state, containing some late information from Detroit.

By an express arrived from Gen. Hull,[1] it is ascertained that he passed the river Detroit into Canada on the 11th and 12th inst. and occupied Sandwich, a small town nearly opposite to Detroit. I have read a proclamation issued by the General to the Canadians, promising to those of them who remain neutral, protection and security, and to those who may be found fighting with the Indians, denouncing a denial of the rights of war. It contains no direct invitation to join his standard, having as he declares a force sufficient for the attainment of his object. I cannot procure a copy of the proclamation, having seen but one here.

Lexington *Reporter,* July 25, 1812. Identified as from Clay to the editor.

1 Governor William Hull, of Michigan Territory, was one of the two brigadier generals appointed for service in the Northwest. The other was James Winchester, of Tennessee.

After Dinner Remarks

[July 27, 1812]

Mr. *Clay* (the *Speaker*) rose, and thanked the company for this expression of confidence in the XIIth Congress. He explained in a concise manner the views of the majority in declaring war, and in adopting other important measures.

[A total of seventeen pre-arranged toasts followed. The first of the "volunteer" toasts was then addressed to Clay.]

HENRY CLAY, our immediate Representative in Congress—The course he has pursued meets the applause of his constituents—We are but the more confirmed that his heart is with his country.

Mr. CLAY said, language was inadequate to express the feelings of his heart. On many previous occasions he had been honoured with the too partial regard of the very respectable portion of his fellow citizens before him, but never was the meed of applause so grateful as at the present. After an absence of many months, employed in acting for them in the national legislature, on affairs of the last importance; he was hailed at his return by their hearty approbation—the approbation of those who from his first outset in life had sweetened its progress by their friendship and confidence.

He said that his conduct during the late session of Congress was the dictates [*sic*] of his own judgment. Our multiplied wrongs—the peaceful farmer bleeding beneath the tomahawk—the mariner no longer finding sanctuary under our national flag—the shackles imposed on our commerce, imperiously called upon him to act—he was convinced of the urgent necessity.

On the assistance of the citizens, said he, government must depend for carrying into execution what they propose; and when the citizen remembered how much he is interested in the success of the government, his aid, he was persuaded, would not be found wanting—the general expression, not only in word but deed, convinced him it would not.

Mr C. concluded by expressing his reliance on our proving victorious in the end—saying that his warmest wishes and humble exertions should in nothing be found wanting.

[Bibb was toasted and made his response in turn. The following toast was then proposed.]

By Mr. Clay—The great cause of our country.

Lexington *Kentucky Gazette,* August 4, 1812. At a dinner given by citizens of Lexington in honor of Clay and Senator George M. Bibb, Clay first rose in response to a toast to the twelfth Congress.

To [James Monroe]

My Dr Sir Lexington 29h. July 1812.

On my return home, where I arrived on friday last,[1] I found the public sentiment in Pennsylvania and Ohio entirely in favor of the War. In Kentucky the measure has been received with an enthusiasm, which has been demonstrated by some of the strongest evidences of public feeling and sensibility. Indeed I have almost been alarmed at the ardor which has been displayed, knowing how prone human nature is to extremes. As one mean of preserving the present tone of public opinion here I am extremely desirous that Govt. should, if they can be possibly applied to any use, employ the volunteers or at least some portion of them. The recruitng service has been conducted with a success which, tho' it has not equalled my wishes, has surpassed my expectations. About 400 have been recruited, and if these could be kept together for a time and some assurance existed that those who enlisted would command them, it would advance much more rapidly. It has been somewhat injured by the volunteering to supply our quota under the 100.000 act.[2] More than the quota was made up by volunteers. There have been I believe no tenders of service under the 50.000 Act,[3] which it seems was not well understood here. Such is the structure of our society however that I doubt whether many can be engaged for a longer term than six months. For that term any force whatever which our population can afford may be obtained. Engaged in agricultural pursuits you are well aware that from about this time (when the crop is either secured in the barn or *laid by* in the field) until the commencement of the Spring there is leisure for every kind of enterprize.

Some of the Companies and Regiments of Volunteers have gone to a very considerable expence in their equipment, & have provided themselves with every thing but Camp equipage. John Allen Esqr. who is at the head of the bar and who stands as high as any man in the U. S. for integrity and devotion to the Cause has raised a rifle regiment, composed of as fine men as ever drew a trigger.[4] I know many of them personally, most all of the officers. They would do credit to any service. Col. Simral[5] of Shelby has also raised several Companies of Cavalry that are spoken of in the highest terms. In Lexington, a brother in law of mine, Capt. Hart[6] has a Company of infantry of 100 who are as fine fellows as ever shouldered a musket. Many of them are young men who have actually abandonned their avocations that they might be prepared to march on that moments warning which they hourly looked and wished for. Now it is understood to be extremely doubtful whether any portion of our quota will be called upon, which is likely to create a degree of disappointment & mortification which it is impossible for me to describe, and I dread will eventuate in an utter disgust for volunteering. Indeed the consequences may be more injurious. If a part only of our quota, say the regiment & Companies I have mentioned could be called into service, these effects would be prevented. They are men who did not step forward for the mere shew of patriotism but for effective service. They are ready to march wherever the Government may order them; and I entreat you my dear Col. to use your best exertions to prevent their disappointment. They never will stop to enquire whether they are on this or the other side of the line. The only enquiry they will make will be "where is the enemy." Some of them holding offices under the State authority it would be inconvenient to take Commissions from the President, as they are incompatible by our Laws. But even if this should be required (which however I hope will not be) the sacrifice would be made. Mr. Allen informs me that he has written to the President. Will you do me the favor to say to Mr. Madison that any communication from that gentleman deserves the most respectful attention & may be implicitly relied upon?

You will allow me again to remind you of Govr. Harrison. He was received in this State just before my arrival with a cordiality and an attention which no public character ever before experienced in this Country. Public dinners in the towns, eschorts [*sic*] of Citizens on his approach to them and various other tokens of regard were given. No military man in the U. States combines more general confidence in the Western Country than he does. Every where I have been asked "how come Harrison overlooked"? I hope the President will find it proper to bestow on him one of the brigadier's appointments lately authorized.[7]

I ought to have written this letter perhaps to Mr. Eustis.[8] I intend him however no disrespect, and you my dear Col will excuse me to him, as also accept an apology for its being in this rough form, having really not time to transcribe it. Yr. friend, H. CLAY

ALS. DLC-James Monroe Papers (DNA, M212, R22).

1 July 24. Congress had adjourned on Monday, July 6.

2 Which authorized the raising of militia, to be apportioned among the States, for six months service.

3 See above, Speech, January 11, 1812, note.

4 Allen, commissioned as Colonel of the First Rifle Regiment, Kentucky Militia, was killed at the River Raisin in January, 1813.

5 James Simrall during the ensuing month completed the organization of the First Regiment, Kentucky Light Dragoons, which joined General Harrison at Fort Wayne in September.

6 Nathaniel G. S. Hart, killed in the Battle of the River Raisin.

7 William Henry Harrison, victor of the Battle of Tippecanoe, was highly popular in Kentucky. For his appointment as a major general of Kentucky militia see below, Clay to Monroe, August 25, 1812.

8 William Eustis.

To Edward Tiffin

Sir Lexington 29h. July 1812.

When Mr. Barry,[1] my predecessor, was in Congress he deposited a plat and Certificate of survey in the proper office to procure a patent, but not having procured it, I endeavored to get it but the survey could not be found. The warrant No. 2655 upon which it was made issued to Wm. Lawson,[2] in which The Survey No. 1260 was made, for 1000 Acres of land, and the entry was made in his name. Robert Lawson bought the land of William, and Byrd Price[3] bought it of Robert. Price, to whom the patent ought to issue, obtained a decree of some Court in Virginia agt. the heirs of Lawson for the title. That decree was sent to Washington. Alexander Dunlap,[4] the father in Law of Mr. Senator Campbell[5] from Ohio, obtained some patents for land the winter before last under circumstances similar to Mr. Prices; and possibly the decree to which I allude, if not found with the papers of Mr. Price, may be found with those of Mr. Dunlap.

The object of this letter is to request the favor of you to have the patent made out & sent to me at this place for Mr. Price, who is my neighbour. Yrs. H. CLAY

ALS. DNA, RG49, Misc. Letters Received, C. Addressed to Tiffin at Washington. Postmarked: "Frankfort K. August 2d." Endorsed on cover: ". . . Recd. 20th: Sept: 1812 Ansd. 24 Do—See letter to him. On the subject of Bird Prices Patent. Issd. 22 Decr. 1812." Answering letter of September 24 not found.

[1] William T. Barry, filling an unexpired term, had served in Congress from August 8, 1810, to March 3, 1811.
[2] A lieutenant in the Continental Line from Halifax County, Virginia, who had later moved to Hancock County, Georgia.
[3] Of Fayette County.
[4] Formerly of the Pisgah area of Woodford County, Kentucky, Dunlap in 1804 had moved to Ohio where he held extensive land claims.
[5] Dr. Alexander Campbell, educated at Pisgah (Woodford County) and in the Transylvania Medical Department, had also moved to Ohio in 1804. He had been elected to the United States Senate to complete the term of Edward Tiffin and served from December 11, 1809, to March 3, 1813.

From Langdon Cheves

Dr Sir, Washington (Davis's Hotel) 30 July 1812

Your's of the 15 July inst: Recd: yesterday,[1] at Philadelphia, at the very moment I was getting into the Stage on my way to Carolina—After meeting my family & finding them well & Comfortably situated, I felt it duty as well to my private Concerns as to my Constituents to visit Carolina as I have now been nearly a year & an half absent—

I could not have expected that the Judge[2] would travel in a Style of less magnifence [*sic*] than you mention—I had Ordered your Carriage a few days before I left Philadelphia,[3] tho' I had rec'd no answer, when I left it, to my letter—The only particular in which I have erred is that of having directed the maker to have it finished by the *10*th of October: But I will endeavour to get him to have it finished by the 1st.—

You ask me "What notice you ought to take of Randolph's reply"[4] —Certainly none—none whatever were you to notice it he would reply again & it would never terminate—*He* spoke with great truth in the begining of the last Session when he said the "Speaker of the Ho of Representatives was the second man in the Nation" & if this be true, as I think it is, it does not become the Speaker to enter into altercations any [*sic*] member of the House or even of the Nation in a public Justification of his conduct, any more than it does the *first* man in the Nation—The President—I therefore thought you Originally Wrong[5]—But if any notice of Mr R's first publication was right, it was taken by you exactly in the manner, temparate & dignified, in which it ought to have been noticed—I think as the Question stands you have entirely the advantage of the *argument* & I think you would egregiously err, as the Speaker of the Ho of Representatives (it would be entirely different were it a question between Mr Clay & Mr R) to put it on any other footing than that of argument—I have not heard one sentence on the Subject of his reply, of any kind, from any person, except one in my own family, wh. resulted from my having recd. a Copy of it, through the post Office, from himself—it was not one to your prejudice—

On this Subject, altho' about the latitude of debate we differ, I am entirely & decidedly of Opinion you are right & *that* I think is enough for You as Speaker—I am sure of this whether you think me right or wrong you will be Certain that I give you Candid advice—

I have not a doubt of your willingness to put the question personally on any footing whatever that might be deemed proper; But any such notice of it on your part would be most *inexcusely* [*sic*] *Wrong*—& is always to be remembered that it is the Speaker &c & Mr R who are engaged & really I should be afraid myself of the Freedom of Speech, if the Chair were supported in that way—No—If you had any feelings leading you that way it would be a sacred public duty to suppress them* Present my most respectful Complts to Mrs. Clay—I have only arrived here 15 minutes & go away on my journey in 15 more—I am therefore in great haste., very sincerely, & Wth great respect & esteem Yr's LANGDON CHEVES

* I ought to have said, besides, that there is not even a plausible reason & occasion for any such notice were you viewed merely as any other individual of the Community.

ALS. DLC-HC (DNA, M212, R1). Addressed to Clay at Lexington. Published in Colton (ed.), *Private Correspondence of Henry Clay*, 18-19.

1 Not found.

2 Probably Senator George M. Bibb, who had resigned as Chief Justice of the Kentucky Court of Appeals in 1810.

3 See below, Receipt, November 28, 1812.

4 Of July 2, 1812.

5 To publish the letter of June 17, 1812.

Property Deed from Executors of Thomas Hart, Jr., to Robert Grinstead

[July 31, 1812]

[Indenture by which the executors of Thomas Hart, Jr., for the sum of $650, paid and acknowledged, convey to Robert Grinstead a lot in Lexington bounded beginning on Market Street at the corner of a lot sold by the said executors to Peter Paul and running thence 50 feet with Market Street to the corner of Mechanic Street, thence with the latter thoroughfare 97 feet, thence at right angles 50 feet to another corner of the lot sold to Paul, thence with Paul's line 97 feet to the beginning, together with the premises appurtenant. General warranty of title. Certification of signature acknowledgment by John Hart on October 22, 1812, and by John W. Hunt, Abraham S. Barton, and Eleanor Hart on December 2, 1812, before John D. Young, Clerk of Fayette County.]

Fayette County Court, Deed Book G, 236-37. A mortgage deed on this property, securing payment of the $650 within three years from February 22, 1812, was also negotiated (recorded December 5, 1812). Fayette County Court, Deed Book G, 242.

Property Deed from Executors of Thomas Hart, Jr., to John Anderson

[July 31, 1812]

[Indenture by which the executors of Thomas Hart, Jr., for the sum of $192.60 current money of Kentucky, paid and acknowledged, convey to John Anderson a lot in Lexington bounded beginning on Market Street at the corner of a lot sold by the excutors to Thomas H. Pindell and running with the street 33 feet to the corner of another lot sold by the executors to Peter Paul, thence with Paul's line at right angles to the street 97 feet, thence at right angles with Paul's line 33 feet to another corner of Pindell's lot, thence with Pindell's line 97 feet to the beginning. General warranty of title. Certification of signature acknowledgement by Clay on September 8, 1812, by Barton, Hunt, and John and Eleanor Hart on December 2, 1812, before John D. Young, Clerk of Fayette County.]

Fayette County Court, Deed Book G, 235-36.

Property Deed from Executors of Thomas Hart, Jr., to Thomas H. Pindell

[July 31, 1812]

Fayette County Court, Deed Book G, 240. For definition of the property, see the correlative Mortgage Deed, July 10, 1812.

To William Eustis

Dr Sir Lexington 31. July 1812.

I have promised Majr. Morrison,[1] our mutual friend, to write to you on the subject of the course of exchange between this Country and the Eastern States. Heretofore bills of exchange upon the Eastward have been generally purchased by the banks, which have remitted them to other banks in the Eastern Cities, and thus created a fund, on the faith of which they draw what are termed post notes, with which the merchants of this Country pay their debts to the Eastern merchants. At present, from various causes, such is the quantity in the market & so little the demand, that the banks have ceased purchasing bills, not being able afterwards to sell the post notes which they would be authorized to draw upon them, and being apprehensive of draining their vaults of specie. The consequence is that Maj. Morrison is unable to sell his bills, and experiences great inconvenience. He wishes therefore that you would procure for him from the Treasury, which has a credit with the

Bank of K., a check upon that institution, or in some other way, to relieve him from his present difficulty.

Can you not my Dr. Sir give employment to some of the Volunteers, who have tendered their services under the 100:000. Act as our quota? Great disgust and mortification will ensue if some portion of them are not some how employed. They have gone to great expense in equipping themselves, and are panting for an opportunity of distinguishing themselves somewhere (and they care not where but would prefer Canada) in the service of our Country. For God's sake give them something to do. Yrs.

H. CLAY

P.S. I inclose a Certificate of the Presidents of the Banks of Lexington and Frankfort testifying the fact relative to the scarcity of specie and their ceasing to buy bills.[2] H. C

ALS. DNA, RG107, Letters Received, (6) C-419. Addressed: "The Honble William Eustis Sec. of War. Washington." Postmarked: "Frankfort K. August 2d." Endorsed: "Recd. August: 11. 1812."

[1] James Morrison was contractor for the Northwestern Army and Quartermaster-General during the War of 1812.

[2] The enclosure, dated July 28, 1812, and signed by Alexander Parker, president of the Kentucky Insurance Company, Charles Wilkins, president of the Lexington Branch Bank, and Robert Alexander, president of the Bank of Kentucky, reads: "We Certify, that from the Scarcity of Specie, and Inconsiderable demand for bills of Exchange, we have ceased purchasing, for some time, having already more light money, & drafts on hand, than we can dispose of—"

Property Deed from Executors of Thomas Hart, Jr., to Mathew Kennedy and James W. Brand

[August 6, 1812]

[Indenture by which the executors of Thomas Hart, Jr., for the sum of $456.25, paid and acknowledged, convey to Mathew Kennedy and James W. Brand a lot in Lexington bounded beginning at the northeastern corner of a lot sold by the aforesaid executors to James Hamilton[1] on Market Street, running thence with the street 50 feet to the corner of the lot sold by the said executors to Alexander Gibney,[2] thence with Gibney's line 97 feet, more or less, to Cherry Alley, thence at right angles 50 feet to the corner of the lot sold by the executors to Hamilton, thence at right angles with Hamilton's line to the beginning, with the premises appurtenant. General warranty of title. Certification of signature acknowledgement by all the executors but Clay on January 8, 1813, before John D. Young, Clerk of Fayette County.]

Fayette County Court, Deed Book G, 281. Kennedy and Brand, partners until the latter's death in 1816, were Lexington house-joiners. A mortgage deed correlative to this transaction was apparently not recorded. On March 6, 1815, the executors in Clay's absence conveyed to Kennedy and Brand a relinquishment of the mortgage. *Ibid.* Deed Book M, 403-404 [413-14].

1 Grammar school teacher, who also taught languages at Transylvania University.
2 Plasterer. The deed dated this same day.

Property Deed from Executors of Thomas Hart, Jr., to Mathew Kennedy

[August 6, 1812]

[Indenture by which the executors of Thomas Hart, Jr., for $462.50 current money of Kentucky, paid and receipt acknowledged, convey to Kennedy a lot in Lexington purchased by James Hamilton and transferred to Kennedy, bounded beginning at the corner of a lot on Market Street sold by the above-mentioned executors to John Springle, thence with the street 50 feet to the corner of another lot sold by the said executors to Kennedy and James Brand, thence at right angles from the street with the line of Kennedy and Brand 97 feet, more or less, to Cherry Alley, thence at right angles from the line of Kennedy and Brand 50 feet to another corner of the lot sold to Springle, thence with Springle's line 97 feet, more or less, to the beginning, with the premises appurtenant. General warranty of title. Certification of signature acknowledgment by all the executors but Clay, January 8, 1813, before John D. Young, Clerk of Fayette County.]

Fayette County Court, Deed Book G, 280. On the same date a mortgage deed from Kennedy to Hart's executors was negotiated, covering this property as security for payment of the above-mentioned sum within three years from February 22, 1812. On March 6, 1815, Hart's executors in Clay's absence conveyed a relinquishment of the mortgage. *Ibid.*, 228-29; M, 404-405 [414-15].

Property Deed from Executors of Thomas Hart, Jr., to Alexander Gibney

[August 6, 1812]

[Indenture by which the executors of Thomas Hart, Jr., for the sum of $406.25, paid and acknowledged, convey to Alexander Gibney a lot in Lexington bounded beginning at the northeastern corner of the lot sold by the above-mentioned executors to Mathew Kennedy and James W. Brand on Market Street, running thence with the street 50 feet to the corner of another lot sold by the executors to Thomas Tibbatts, thence at right angles from the street with Tibbatts' line 97 feet, more or less, to Cherry Alley, thence at right angles 50 feet to another corner of the lot sold to Kennedy and Brand, thence with the line of Kennedy and Brand to the beginning, with the premises appurtenant. General warranty of title. Certification of signature acknowledgment by Abraham Barton on September 3, 1812; by John Hart on September 5; by Clay on September 8; and by John W. Hunt and Eleanor Hart on December 2—all before John D. Young, Clerk of Fayette County.]

Fayette County Court, Deed Book G, 241. On the same date a mortgage deed was negotiated, covering this property as security for payment of the above-mentioned sum within three years after February 22, 1812. On March 12, 1815, in Clay's absence, Hart's executors granted Gibney a relinquishment of mortgage. *Ibid.*, 243; N, 130-32.

From William Coleman to Clay and Robert Wickliffe

Mrss. Clay & Wiakliff [*ca.* August 7, 1812]

Gentlemin I am bound to Starte on Tusday next to Virgina & would be very much oblige to you if you Could Except & pay for me to Mr. Har[twell] Boswill[1] fifty dollars Hundred dollars is my due Mr. Wiaklif has paid me fifty in your Exceptance you will much oblige yours &c WM. COLEMAN

☞ for further information I am authorised to Say Clay & Wiakliff Shall be intitled to the one fourth of Henry Coleman Debt proven under the Commission which is —— — —— — — $30
also Jacob duglas[2] — — — 5
also the two hundred pounds in the name of Johnson & wood[3] which Bonds was assighned to them from me — — $666.66 2/3
„66 [*sic*]
$[701].66

the one fourthe of the $701 & 66 2/3 you bouth are to have of all you Can get from Edward[4] there is plenty of property if you Can brake the deed of gift George Edwards[5] has got his & five hundred & od pound oute there fathers Esstate Soe he is not to have any parte oute of the west property I Sirs yours &c

WM COLEMAN

[Endorsement][6]

Recd of H. Clay this 7 Aug. 1812 for W. Coleman fifty dollars on this letter. H. BOSWELL & CO
7th. August 1812

ALS. DLC-TJC (DNA, M212, R15). Endorsed on verso by Clay: "Letter shewing my interest in the debt of Edwards & other debts."

1 At this time a resident of Cynthiana, Kentucky. He later moved to Arkansas Territory. 2 Not identified. 3 Not identified.

4 Possibly Edward Coleman, William's brother. 5 Of Bourbon County.

6 ES, in Clay's hand, excepting date.

Merchandise Account with John Hart and Company

Dr. Henry Clay M/A To Jno. Hart & Co. [August 7, 1812]

1811

Sep 9. To Mdse paid Eads[1] pr. order — — — — 7.50

		To 10 3/4 lb. verdigrease pr. Grant[2]	24.40
	11.	To Mdse pr Lady — — — —	30.43
		To Do paid Chinn[3] pr order	30.—
	13.	To Do. pr Lady	35.12
	14.	To Do " Miss Hall[4] (pepper cotton & drugs)	" .98
	17.	To Do. paid Mr. Pogue[5] pr order — —	5.—
	25.	To Do pr. Miss Hall	3.39
	27.	To Do " Lady — — — — —	64.49
Oct.	1.	To Do " do.	1.—
	2.	To Do " Miss Hall	5.33
		To Do. dress for race rider — — —	4.76
	3.	To Do " Do	.56
	5.	To Do pr. Lady	6. 8
		To Do. " Miss Hall — — — —	.81
	7.	To Do " George[6] (a hat)	5.—
	9.	To Do " Miss Hall — — — —	4.82
		To Do. " family	1.—
		To Do " Ede (a hat) — —	4.—
	10.	To Do " family — — — —	" .19
	11.	To Do. " Order augers &c.	1.75
			$236.61
1811.			236,61
Oct	12.	To Mdse pr. family . . — —	6.—
		To Do pd Grinstead & Davis[7] pr ord.	88.75
	15.	To Do pr family . .	1.62
		To Do. pd Glen's[8] son pr reqt. a coat	7. 8
		To Do " Jno. Jordan pr ord.	60.—
	16.	To Do pr family — — — — —	5.33
		To Do pd Ben. Stout pr order	18.20
	19.	To Do " negroes pr Glen's order	2.50
	21.	To Do " Ben. Stout pr order	37.—
	30.	To Do pr family	2.30
Nov	7.	To Do " Do	" .87.
	9.	To Do " Do — — — — —	1.—.
	11.	To Do paid Jno. W. Stouts bill filed	28.17
	14.	To Do a hat for Peter[9] — —	1.—
	21.	To Do. pr. Glen 5 pr shoes — —	12:50.
	23.	To Do " family	4.54.
	26.	To Do " Priors boy Isaac[10]	5.37.
Dec	2.	To Do " family — —	3:50
	4.	To Do " Glen nails — — — — — —	.50
	7.	To Do " family — — — — — — — —	2.62
	11.	To Do " Do — — — — — — — — — —	".98
			$ 526.44

1811		526,44
Dec 16.	To Mdse p family	" .25
25.	To Do " Do — — —— ———	2.31
1812		
Jan 11.	To Do " Do. — — — —	" .43
13.	To Do. " Bill[11] (Shoes) — —	2.—
25.	To Do " Major (Do)	2.—
29.	To Do " family —. —. —. —. —	.74
Feb 3.	To Do " Cuthb. Shoes — — —	2.—.
6.	To Do " Peter Do	2.—
7.	To Do " Jonathan & Jim[12] ——————	4.—
26.	To Do " family — — —— —— ——	16.23
		$558.40

Cr.

Mar. 20.	By H. C. cash/acct transfd	558.40[13]

Save Errors, Aug 7, 1812.

JNO. HART & CO.

ADS. DLC-TJC (DNA, M212, R15). There were two successive partnerships under the name "John Hart & Co." Clay was formally identified with the second, organized in 1816. His precise relationship with the first has not been ascertained.

1 Probably John Eads, Lexington blacksmith. 2 Probably Thomas Grant.

3 Probably Richard Chinn, Lexington lawyer, who acted occasionally for Clay in personal suits. He later moved to Louisiana, where he attained prominence in his profession at New Orleans.

4 Sarah Hall. 5 Possibly Robert Poage. 6 One of Clay's slaves.

7 Robert Grinstead and Allen Davis. 8 James Glenn. 9 A slave.

10 See below, Cash Account, August 7, 1812, debit item of November 23, 1811.

11 A slave. 12 Slaves.

13 See Cash Account, August 7, 1812, debit item of March 20.

Cash Account with John Hart and Company

Dr. Henry Clay c/a In a/c with JNO HART & CO. [August 7, 1812]

1811.			
Octo	4.	To Invoice goods paid Jno Murphy . .	540,16
		To McCouns[1] bill cotton " Do	59.84
	9.	To Cash paid for a horse pr T Pindells[2] order	60.—
	11.	To Do pd. Grinsteads order in fav. Mrs. Price[3]	37.45
		To Do pd. your note to Jno W Baylor & interest	75.59
	12.	To Do pd. Mrs. Hart[4] for plank furnished David Megowan out of the hemp vats	26. "
		To Do pd for a hat cover	1.25
		To Do pd Thomas Harts Ex & Co, balance due them for sping yarns	479.68
	14.	To Do pd. for ink powder & pencils for the children	" .50
	16.	To Do pd. Ben. Stout, pr order	18.19

	17 . To	Jno Hart for a box claret, cost 12 freight & Carriage 2	14.—
	18 . To	Cash paid Postlethwaits[5] a/c filed . .	51.34
	24 . To	Do pd. Nat. Harts[6] Do . Do . .	125.30
	25 . To	Do pd. disct. on yr note at I. O.[7] 1500$	16.64
	30 . To	Do. pd. Jonathan pr Glens[8] order .	1.50
Nov	2 . To	Do. pd. Bywaters[9] bill plastering the house occupied by Humphreys[10]	4.—
	8 . To	Do pd. for glass for do	3.14
	9 . To	Do pd. Wallers[11] dft for reduction of yr note at Bk Ky — — .	200. "
	13 . To	Do pd. postage	" .62
		$	1715.22

An Error in this addn. 2 cts. corrected 4 page[12]

1811			1,715.22
Nov.	13 . To	Cash pd. for a blanket for Jonathan	3.—
	14 . To	Do. " " Do " Peter . . .	3.—
	15 . To	Do " Humphreys pr rect for judgmt. Todd [*sic*] v Clay &c.[13]	61.—
	16 . To	Do pd. yr note at the In. Office . .	149.35
	To	Do pd for Grays [*sic*] fables[14] pr Mad. Ment.[15]	.75
	To	Do pd for a blanket for Jim	3.—
	19 . To	D pd for glass for Humphreys' house	.69
	22 . To	Do pd 2 discts on Springles[16] note continued for your benefit	3.20
	23 . To	D paid your stake in the match race with Jno T Hawkins,[17] lost ,	150.—
	To	Do. paid Thornton Pryors do, to secure which you have his bill of Sale for Isaac, to be returned when the money is refunded[18]	300.—
	25 . To	Do paid for a barrel salt	8.50
Dec	2 . To	Do paid disct at B Bank[19]	4.80
	7 . To	Do paid Library[20] Contribution on 1 share	1.—
	14 . To	D pd. disct. at B. Bank	8.53
	17 . To	Do pd. for a yd. white flan. pr Tom[21]	" .75
	19 . To	Do. pd. " flannel	.56
	21 . To	Do. pd " 100 brls corn pr. Glens rect to Allen[22]	100.—
	23 . To	Do " freight 6407 lb yarns up the river pr. Adams's[23] rect to Jones[24] . .	80. 9
			2593.44
1811			2593.44
Dec.	27 . To	Cash pd. disct at In. Office . .	16.64

	30. To Do. pd. yr nego. note to T. January[25] — —		72.—
1812			
Jan.	4. To Do pd for 17 barrels corn pr Glen's rect		17.—
	9. To Do pd for 26 " Do " Do "		26.—
	To Do pd for a blanket for Isaac		2.50
	10 To Do pd for 10 barrels Corn pr Glens rect		10.—
	11 To Do pd Hawkins for ice . . .		10.75
	To Do. for 9 barrels Corn		9.—
	16. To Do for 3 barrels salt		22.50
	17. To Do pd. January's[26] storage a/c . . .		13.54
	20. To Do pd W. Harts[27] Blacksmiths bill pr rect		134. 6
	21. To Do pd. January & Stephens[28] a/c for glass		6.—
	To Do pd Disct		4.80
	25. To Do pd. for linen to make shirts for Isaac & bill — — — —		2.—
	27. To Do. paid Lex. Library pr. Treasrs. rect.		100.—
	29. To Do " for paper & pencils for the boys		.42
	31. To Do " disct. on Springle's note . .		1.60
Feb.	6. To Do " Lewis Sanders's a/c pr rect		10.31.
	14. To Do " disct. at B Bank — — —		8.53
	28. To Do " do " I. Off. . — —		16.64
Mar	2. To Do " Jno. T. Hawkins for you		75.—
		$	3.152.73
1812			3152.73
March	4. To Cash paid Madam Mentelle		5.—
	14. To Do paid Cuthb. for breakg hemp pr ord.[29]		1:37
	20. To Amo. your merchandise account accompanying this		558.40[30]
	" To Jno Hart for 6 Mo Salary pr Agrt.[31]		250.—
	" To Balance in your favor this day as Cash — —		4277.99[32]

On this day an interest account was made on the several accts. of Jno. Hart & H. Clay, which exhibited a balance against the former of 160,66, with which he is charged according to agreement.

$8.245.47[33]

Continued on a second sheet.

1812		Time	Int.	
Mar. 24	To Cash paid for removing yr papers	—	—	" 25
27	To Do paid Cuth. & Jonathan pr Glens order for breaking hemp	—	—	3 75
28	To Cash paid Mr Glen, as requested in yr letter to him[34] . . .	4.10	1. 8	50 —
30	To Do paid disct on Springles note	—	—	1 60

Ap.	4	To Do paid for trimg trees pr Glens ord	—	—	1	50
	16	To Do paid yr note at B. Bank	3.22	14.92	800	–
	17	To Do paid Humphreys balce Costs of Judgmt. Todd &c	—	—	1	25
		To Do paid Cuthbert pr Glens order for breakg hemp	—	—	2	12
	18	To Balance this day in yr. favor			5000	"
					5.860	47
	25	To Sam. Owens for Jockey Suit	—	—	2	25
June	19	To Ro. Bywaters goods paid him last dec. & Jan. — — —	—	—	84	69
		To Cash pd. Major for breakg hemp.	—	—	1	12
July	3	To Do pd. disct. at In. Off	—	—	16	64
	10	To Do pd. for hawling from Limestone[35] .	—	—	2	95
Aug	7	To Balance in your favor this day — —		118.83	5,826	35
				134.83	5,934	"

1811. Contra Cr.

Octo.	7	. By Cash recd for Fowler's[36] check		200.–
	12	. By Do Recd in notes		280.–
	14	. By Do recd. of James Miller[37]		15.–
	15	. By Do " a check . . .		352.60
	24	. By Do " for Tom Craigs note . .		653.87
	"	. By Do " " Jemmy O Payne's[38] Do.		250.–
	28	. By Do " of Leavy[39] on a/c W. T Banton		250.–
Nov.	28	. By Do " of Bodley & Coleman[40] in pt their note, balce renewd 30 days		200.–
Dec.	5	. By Do recd for Hughes's[41] two notes		270.–
	9	. By Do " of H. Watkins[42] . — —		100.–
		By Do. " of Do — — — —		20.–
	26	. By Do " of Wilkins[43] in part Pauls[44] note		180.–
1812				
Jan	8	. By Do. " of Morrison (James) — —		42.–
Feb.	3	. By Do " of Charles Carr . . —		275.–
	6	. By Do " for Bell Lee & Wards[45] note		174.–
	10	. By Do " of H. Watkins . . .		154.70
	25	. By Do " of Do — — — —		3.–
Mar.	18	. By 14 Loads wood	1,25	17.50
	20	. By Amo. yr stock account accompanying this		4.807.80[46]
		Continued on next side.		$ 8,245.47

			Time	Int.	
1812					
Mar.	20	By Balce pr contra, as Cash,	4.18	98.39	4277 99[47]

	25	By Cash Recd. of H. Watkins bal. Stephens's[48] note, put into his hands for collection	4.13	" .37	17 50
Ap.	16	By Cash Recd. of Wickliffe[49]	3.22	4.81	258 50
		By Do. " of Branch Bank the balance due you there	3.22	" .89	48 22
		By Do. Check on In. Co.	3.22	9.32	500 –
	18	By Do Do " Do – –	3.20	13.89	758 26
					5.860 47
	"	By Balance pr Contra			5.000 "
July	10	By Cash recd. bal. Paul's note	" .28	.16	34 –
	"	By Do paid Ringgold & Heath in part the Carriage of our yarns – –	2.–	7. "	700 –
Aug	7	By Cash . . – –	——	——	200 –
				134,83	5,934 "
	"	By Balance pr. Contra – –		118,83	5,826 35

v Save Errors. Aug 7, 1812.

JNO HART & CO.

[Enclosure]

Dr. Henry Clay's Stock a/c. To Jno. Hart & Co.

1812			
March.	20.	To H. C. cash/acct transferd	$ 4807, 80-
		Cr.	
1811			
Nov.	22.	By Cash recd. for 2 post notes of the Bank of Washington of 1000 $ each & 2 pr Ct prem thereon	2040. –
Dec.	2.	By Do. recd. for balance Bodley & Coleman's note (200$ where of was as creditted in yr c/a)[50] . – –	878. 22
1812			
Mar.	18.	By Do. Recd. for Millers[51] note	1889. 58
			$ 4,807: 80

Save Errors, Aug 7, 1812. JNO. HART & CO

ADS. DLC-TJC (DNA, M212, R15). 1 Probably James and David Maccoun.
2 Thomas Hart Pindell. 3 Probably Robert Grinstead, Susannah Price.
4 Probably Eleanor, widow of Thomas Hart, Jr. 5 John Postlethwait.
6 Nathaniel G. S. Hart. 7 Insurance Office (Kentucky Insurance Company).
8 James Glenn. 9 Robert Bywaters. 10 Charles Humphreys.
11 William Smith Waller. 12 See below, this account, note 33.

13 At the September Term of Fayette Circuit Court, 1811, William Tod had won an action for debt against Clay and others, amounting to $300 and one cent damage, the defendants having failed to appear. Fayette Circuit Court, Order Book H, 520.

14 John Gay's *Fables,* first published in London in 1726, appeared in numerous editions. A one-volume edition had been published by Mathew Carey, Philadelphia, in 1808. 15 Madame Mentelle.

16 Probably John Springle. 17 Clay's neighbor on the Mansfield tract.

18 Thornton was the brother of Samuel Pryor, trainer and part owner of the horse, Truxton, which raced under Andrew Jackson's colors. Pryor's pledge of Isaac seems not to have been redeemed. 19 Lexington Branch of the Bank of Kentucky.

20 The Lexington Library. 21 Probably a slave; possibly Clay's son Thomas.

22 Probably William Allen, who lived on the Henry's Mill Road, Fayette County.

23 James Adams. 24 Possibly John Jones. 25 Thomas January.

26 Samuel January, who earlier had lived in Lexington, operated Traveler's Inn, two large warehouses, and a commission business in Maysville, Kentucky.

27 Will Hart.

28 January, Stephens and Company, a Lexington mercantile firm composed of Thomas January, Luther Stephens, and Hallett M. Winslow.

29 The process of separating hemp fiber from the stalk was called "breaking hemp." Under the task system, after a slave had broken out a specified amount of fiber during a day's work, he was paid for any additional output.

30 See above, Merchandise Account, August 7, 1812.

31 No agreement found relating to this firm.

32 See below, credit entry of same date, this account.

33 The figure "7" written over "9." 34 Not found.

35 Goods from the eastern States were transported by water from Pittsburgh to Limestone (Maysville, Kentucky), then by wagon to Lexington.

36 Probably John Fowler. 37 Of Fayette County. 38 James Payne.

39 William Leavy. 40 Possibly Thomas Bodley and James Coleman.

41 Probably James Hughes. 42 Henry Watkins. 43 Charles Wilkins.

44 Peter Paul, either the father or the son.

45 Possibly Montgomery Bell; Lee and Ward not identified.

46 See below, enclosure with this document.

47 See above, debit entry of same date, this account.

48 Possibly Merriman Stephens, of Woodford County. 49 Robert Wickliffe.

50 See above, credit entry of November 28, this account. 51 Robert Miller.

Receipt from John Happy

[August 10, 1812]

Recd. 10 Aug. 1812. of H. Clay thirty five dollars in full, for doing one half of the new fence on Todds road, and for resetting the whole of the old.[1]

JOHN HAPPY

DS, in Clay's hand. DLC-TJC (DNA, M212, R15). Happy was a resident of Lexington.

1 On Clay's "Ashland" estate.

To [James Monroe]

My Dr. Col. Lexington 12h. Aug. 1812

Since I wrote you a few days ago[1] a requisition has been made of a reinforcement for Genl. Hull.[2] A detachment of about 2000, consisting of volunteers under the 100.000 act, being part of our quota, and regulars is in consequence under marching orders, and will rendezvous at New port[3] on the 20h. inst. Altho. I lament the necessity which has obliged Genl. Hull to make this demand, I rejoice at the opportunity of employment to our Volunteers in a way best corresponding with their wishes. We feel at the same time great solicitude for the fate of Genl. Hull's army. His suspension of offensive operations, after his bold and confident entry into Canada, was much to be deprecated.[4] It will I fear present him in the ridiculous attitude of a gasconader, whilst it affords to the enemy the substantial advantage of assembling his before fugitive forces and strengthening himself in Malden.[5] When we add to this the fall of the important post of Michilimackinack, and duly estimate the use which will be made of it in exciting the Indians against us, and drawing them down from the Northern extremity of Lake Michigan and the Westward of Detroit to the relief of Col. St. George[6] and the annoyance of our frontiers, you will I think agree that our apprehensions are not destitute of foundation. The detachments destined for Genl. Hull are far from being free from danger before they can form a junction with him. On the line of their march you will see, from a momentary glance of the map, there are several points at which an enterprizing enemy might issue from Malden and attack them with great advantage. Should Hull's army be cut off the effects on the public mind would be, especially in this quarter, in the highest degree injurious. Why did he proceed with so inconsiderable a force? was the general enquiry made of me. I maintained that it was sufficient. Should he meet with a disaster the predictions of those who pronounced his army incompetent to its object will be fulfilled; and the Sec. of War[7] (in whom already there unfortunately exists[8] no sort of confidence) can not possibly shield Mr. Madison from the odium which will attend such an event.

Within these few days past I have had the pleasure of meeting with Govr. Harrison.[9] The favorable sentiments I before entertained of him, and which I endeavored to communicate to you at Washington, are fully confirmed by the repeated conversations I have had with him. His merit cannot be too highly appreciated. He is full of devotion to the cause in which we are embarked. No other man in the U. States enjoys more highly the confidence of the Western people as a military character. I was the other day a passive spectator of a very large body of Citizens assembled in Lexington to express their opinion on public affairs.[10] A number of resolutions were proposed and carried. One affirmed our ability to bring the Indian war to a speedy conclusion under the guidance of W. H. Harrison. The people were all enthusiasm when his name was pronounced. It was carried by the loudest acclamation. I notice the fact as illustrative of general feeling and sentiment in the Western Country.

Govr. Harrison has addressed a letter to the Sec. of War, in which he describes several plans of expeditions against the hostile indians, and which I wish you could see. That which proposes marching an army to Fort Wayne appears to me, under existing circumstances, to be entitled to the preference. A slight survey of the geography of the Country will at once exhibit the great advantages of that position. The great body, perhaps nine tenths, of the unfriendly indians are between the Wabash and Lake Michigan on the East and the Mississippi on the West. An army at Fort Wayne would afford powerful assistance to Genl Hull, as a covering army, by preventing indian succor, or carrying on offensive operations agt. the hostile tribes to the Westward, and if necessary by actual co-operation under him. It would at the same time be the means of protecting Chicago. An army for this object to be commanded by Harrison might be raised with the greatest promptitude. At Washington you have much fuller, if not better, information than we can be presumed to possess here, where perhaps we may yield too much to our fears and our anxieties. If however I am not greatly deceived this expedition deserves immediate attention. The Indians will amuse us until their Corn being ripe subsistence can be easily procured. They will then fall upon our frontier with all their fury, unless in the mean time there is some vigorous blow aimed at the British and themselves.

The only difficulty that occurs to me in assigning the command to Harrison is that he may be called upon to act out of his Territory. If this can be obviated he would be content to retain his present official station. If it cannot, rather than not engage in active military service he would relinquish it, (if that condition be deemed necessary) & accept a Brigadier's command, which it would be extremely gratifying to the friends of the Administration in this quarter he should receive. If the President thought proper he might I presume be appointed a Majr. Genl. by brevet—a rank which would be highly beneficial if an expedition of any magnitude is authorized, and particularly in the event of our whole quota of the 100.000. militia being called for. Yr. friend.

H. CLAY

13h. Aug.

P. S. A report has just reached us that Hull has taken Malden, which he is said to have done on the first. On the 29h. however the express who was sent on to require a detachment for his relief left the army at Sandwich. I do not think the report probable, altho' it may be true.[11]

H. C.

ALS. DLC-James Monroe Papers (DNA, M212, R22). Endorsed: ". . . Mr Clay answd. 28."

1 On July 29. 2 William Hull. 3 Newport, Kentucky.

4 News of the fall of Michilimackinac, July 17, 1812, had caused Hull to turn back from his invasion of Canada and fortify himself at Detroit.

5 South of Detroit, but on the Canadian side of the river.

6 Lieutenant-Colonel Thomas Bligh St. George had been in command at Malden. Clay had not yet learned that Colonel Henry A. Procter had taken charge of the fort late in July.

7 William Eustis. 8 At this point the word "here" was crossed out.

[9] Who had been in Lexington from August 8 to August 12. Harrison to William Eustis, August 12, 1812, in Logan Esarey (ed.), *Governors' Messages and Letters: Messages and Letters of William Henry Harrison* (2 vols. *Indiana Historical Collections*, VII, IX; Indianapolis, 1922), II, 84-88.

[10] In response to a previous notice a large meeting had convened at the court house in Lexington on county court day, Monday, August 10, 1812. Lexington *Reporter*, August 15, 1812.

[11] The report was erroneous.

Speech to Troops at Lexington

[August 14, 1812]

Not found. Mentioned in Lexington *Kentucky Gazette*, August 18, 1812, as addressed to the Kentucky Volunteers at Lewis Sanders' garden, three miles from Lexington, en route to Georgetown.

From [William Eustis]

Hon: H Clay
Lexington.

War Department
August 14th. 1812.

Sir,

Your Letter of July 31st. has been received.—General Winchester has been directed to accept Volunteers, with the advice of the Governor of Kentucky, as part of the Detachment to reinforce General Hull—Other Volunteers will immediately be required for a Campaign against the Indians.—Money has been placed to the Credit of Mr. Morrison[1] in the Bank of Kentucky.—

Copy. DNA, RG107, Military Books, VI, 80.

[1] James Morrison.

Speech to Troops at Georgetown, Kentucky

[August 16, 1812]

Mr. Clay in his address adverted to the cause of the war—the orders in council and previous aggressions on our commerce—the impressment of our seamen—and the instigation of the savages to hostilities. Mr. Clay then told the soldiers, that much was expected of them from abroad. Kentucky was fam'd for her bravery:—they had the double character of Americans and Kentuckians to support.

The Kentuckians by the very foe they were marching against, said Mr. C. have been reproached as savages—Now, he said, was the opportunity to avenge themselves of the insult, not only by a salutary vengeance, but by shewing their calumniator that they were not only brave, but humane and merciful when circumstances permitted.

Lexington *Kentucky Gazette*, August 18, 1812. Clay spoke to the Kentucky Volunteers at their muster ground at Georgetown, shortly before their departure under General John Payne to join the forces of General Hull. The last clause of the first paragraph served as the order of the day issued by Colonel William Lewis prior to the bloody Battle of River Raisin, January 22, 1813.

Credentials as United States Congressman

[August 17, 1812]

ADS, by Peter B. Atwood, deputy for Will Vawter, Sheriff of Woodford County; signed also by Charles Carr, deputy for William Dudley, Sheriff of Fayette, and John McKinney, deputy for Manoah Singleton, Sheriff of Jessamine County. DNA, RG233, HR13A-J1. Similar to Credentials, above, August 21, 1810.

Lease to Alexander Linn

[August 21, 1812]

An agreement between H. Clay & Alex. Linn.

The said Clay leases to the said Linn for one year commencing on the first day of October next, the Brick house lately occupied by Murphy,[1] the yard, stables and barn (exclusive of the house now occupied by Sally English) [2] and also the pasture lot on Todds road adjoining Trotter and next to town.[3]

In consideration whereof the said Linn covenants and agrees to pay to the said Clay at the end of the year the sum of sixty dollars, for recovery of which he reserves the right of distress.

It is understood that the said Clay does not grant any priviledge to cut wood from any part of his Estate.

The said Clay agrees that the said Linn may have the said house glazed, in which case the said Clay will allow him the price of every pain of glass remaining when he surrenders possession.

Witness our seals this 21st. Aug. 1812. H. CLAY {L.S.}
Teste JAMES GLENN ALEXR. LINN {L.S.}

ADS, also signed by Linn. KyLxT. Heretofore Linn had lived in the northern district of Fayette County.

1 John Murphy.

2 Not otherwise identified. She lived for several years in this house.

3 James Trotter's land lay on the west side of the "Ashland" estate.

Bill of Sale from William M. and Joseph Fauntleroy

[August 21, 1812]

We William M. Fauntleroy and Joseph Fauntleroy have this day bargained & sold unto H. Clay a negro man slave named Isaac,[1] now in the possession of the Mess. Trotters,[2] but which we are to deliver to-day, for and in consideration of the sum of five hundred dollars; and we do hereby warrant that the said slave is sound and healthy and that his age does not exceed twenty five—And we do further warrant and defend the title to the said Clay his heirs and assigns.

Witness our hands & seals this 21st. Aug. 1812.

Teste WM. M. FAUNTLEROY {L.S.}
CYRUS CURTIS[3] J FAUNTLEROY {L.S.}
JIMMY PAYNE

DS, in Clay's hand. DLC-TJC (DNA, M212, R15). The Fauntleroys, of a Virginia family, were then living near Bryan Station, a few miles out of Lexington.

1 Apparently not Thornton Pryor's boy but another slave of that name.

2 Samuel and George Trotter.

3 Of Fayette County.

To William Eustis

Sir Lexington 22 Aug. 1812

I transmitted you by the last mail a hand bill published here containing among other things a letter of Genl. Hulls to Col Wells under date the 11h. inst.[1] It represents the army under his command in a most perilous condition—his communications cut off almost entirely by the enemy—in danger of want of provisions, and instead of carrying on offensive operations reduced to act on the defensive. The detachment destined for his relief from this State will, if not prevented by two or three days of the most rainy unpleasant weather I have experienced at this Season, reach New port tomorrow evening; but the strongest apprehensions are entertained here that it will not arrive in time to succor him. That detachment will consist of between 2000 and 2500 men instead of 1500 as ordered.[2]

The D-Commissary (Mr. Buford)[3] is ordered to procure supplies for three months for 1500 men only, and consequently the detachment will shortly after their junction with Hull (if it ever take place) be constrained to draw upon his exhausted Stock, which I fear cannot be replenished through Lake Erie.[4] I have advised the Commissary to shape his supplies to the increased force of the detachment. He doubts his powers; and I fear will not conform to my advice. Can you not take measures agt. the danger, more perhaps to be dreaded than the enemy himself, of a scarcity. But few of the detachment carried with their [*sic*] winter cloathes. Is it not possible in season to provide them with some covering agt. a Canadian winter?

Mr. Robert McNair of this place informs me that he means to present himself to you to be employed in carrying despatches to Canada. You may place entire confidence in his fidelity activity and enterprize, qualities in which he is excelled by no one.

I heard it said here to day that your letter giving Hull information of the War came to Pittsburgh without any superscription; and that the invelope did not supply the omission. The person to whom it was sent had, it is alledged, to guess at its destination. Yr's respectfly. H. CLAY

P.S. I suggested the impropriety of publishing Hulls's letter to Wells, and the hand bills were suppressed, two or three copies only getting out. H. C.

ALS. DNA, RG107, Letters Received, (6) C-448. Addressed to the Secretary of War, Washington. Postmarked from Lexington, "AU 21 [*sic*]." Endorsed: "Recd. 1 Sept. 1812. . . ."

1 Not found. Colonel Samuel Wells was commander of the Seventeenth Infantry Regiment of the United States Army, composed of "regulars" recruited in Kentucky.

2 Five regiments under the command of Brigadier General John Payne had been ordered to the relief of Hull at Detroit.

3 Thomas Buford of Garrard County.

4 Then under British control.

From George Trotter, Jr.

D Sir, Lexington Aug 25th. 1812.

However you and myself may have differed in opinion on minor political subjects, yet I have ample reason to belive you have on various occasions been friendly to me—I have a strong desire to be in some active situation, on the Epedition [*sic*] under Govr. Harrison, who has honorned [*sic*] me with a situation in his family[1]—but as it may not at all times be an active one, (tho' one of the most desireable & honorable in the army) I should wish to have a command also in the line,—When the Lexington Volunteer Troop was first raising, I was solicited to command it by some of the members—My brothers absence at that time precluded my accepting—Colo. Js. McDowell then whoom there is not a more worthy Officer was chosen—his Troop was the first that was mustered, recd and commissioned[2]—& of course the first for promotion,—It indeed was observed by Colo. Simrill[3] that he would in all probability be promoted—there is 4 Troops in His Volunteer Regmt,—& by a law passed at the last Session of the Legislature, 4 Troops are to compose a Regiment at home, & entitled to a Colo. & 2 Majors—Whether any good reason exists to adopt a different plan in the Volunteer Regmt of Cavalry It is not for me to say,—If practicable & right should wish McDowell promoted & in that case would be a candidate (with the Troop) for the Captaincy[4]—both the Lieutenants wish it,[5]—If you can with propriety, do any thing in the arrangement for the promotion of Capt McDowell, you will confer another obligation on Sir Your Most Obt Servant GEO. TROTTER JR

P.S. This letter is confidential

The Honbl. Henry Clay.

ALS. DLC-HC (RNA, M212, R1). Addressed to Clay at Frankfort.

1 Trotter was aide-de-camp to Harrison.

2 At the approach of the War of 1812 James McDowell, a Virginia veteran of the

Revolutionary War, who had settled in Fayette County in 1783, had organized a company of light horse which had volunteered for service at the first opportunity.

3 James Simrall.

4 Two days later the First Regiment of the Kentucky Light Dragoons was organized with McDowell as Major under Col. Simrall, and Trotter as Captain of the First Company.

5 John M. Fisher and James Gabriel Trotter (son of Colonel James Trotter and brother of Samuel and George, Jr.).

To James Monroe

Dr Sir Frankfort 25 Aug. 1812

We have entertained in this quarter the most alarming apprehensions for the safety of Genl. Hulls army. A letter from himself (of which I transmitted a Copy to the Sec. of War) under date the 11h. inst.[1] represents that almost all the Indians had become hostile; that owing to the tardy operations of the army at Niagara, and the fall of Michilimackinack, the prospects of his army had entirely changed; that his provisions were scarce, and that unless speedily relieved by a respectable reinforcement, he anticipated the most fatal consquences. Still more recent advices exhibit his condition more critical than it is represented even by himself. They shew that he has lost all confidence with his army; that he is cooped up in Detroit surrounded by enemies, who are preparing batteries on the opposite bank of the river to play upon that fortress; and that the discontents prevailing amongst his officers have amounted to almost a total subversion of all subordination. Indeed such appears to be his situation that the arrival of succors [*sic*] in time to relieve him is almost hopeless.

In this posture of affairs Govr. Scott, upon the eve of retiring from office, was called upon to act.[2] Still animated by that patriotism which has never ceased to distinguish his highly useful life, he felt disposed to do whatever was in his power, and in this extremity to take upon himself even the responsibility of exceeding his authority. He chose, however before he adopted any final measure to confer with a number of friends in whose judgments he could repose confidence. Having honored me, by selecting me as one of them, we assembled in this place to day[3] and after weighing and deliberating upon the whole circumstances of the case, gave him the written advice which we signed, and which he will cause to be transmitted to Govr. [*sic*][4] with a transcript of a number of letters which constituted in part the informatoin on which our opinions were formed.

The Govr. will, in consequence, Commission Govr. Harrison a Majr. Genl. by brevet,[5] and authorize the augmentation of the detachment, which this evening will reach N. Port on its march, from about 2000, of which it is now composed, to about 3400.

We were sensible that there existed no orders for this increase of force, and that the extreme necessity of the case must alone justify the measure. If we have mis judged of that necessity our zeal for the service and success of our Country must furnish our apology.

As to the appointment of Govr. Harrison there existed some doubts of the Governor's powers.[6] But when it was seen that throughout all parts of the W. Country there has been the strongest demonstrations of confidence in him given, and when he was called for by the very army itself to be relieved, as their last hope, we could not hesitate, especially when the popular sentiment entirely accorded with our own. If you will carry your recollection back to the age of the Crusades, and of some of the most distinguished leaders of those expeditions, you will have a picture of the enthusiasm existing in this country for the expedition to Canada, and for Harrison as the commander.

The governors arrangements, predicated upon our advice, are altogether provisional, depending upon the President, who will revoke or vary them as he pleases. It was thought that the Governor's Communication would reach Washington in about nine days from this time—that in ten more the Presidents orders might reach Detroit, by about which time the detachment under Govr. Harrison will have arrived, & the orders of the President, whatever they may be, will take their effect.

As to Govr. Harrison himself he is so zealously devoted to the country that he will be perfectly satisfied with whatever post may be assigned him. The Commission granted to him was intended only under any contingency, to ensure respect to his command, until the pleasure of the President is made known.

The orders of Mr Eustis were framed upon a supposition that the detachment to be sent to Hull was to consist of 1500 men only; and the Deputy Commissary was directed to provide them contingently subsistence on their march, and absolutely, a stock of provisions for three months. The detachme[nt] being more than doubled, we have advised the Com[missary] to make a correspondent augmentation of his supplies.

Whatever may be the Presidents decision as to the measures generally taken by Govr. Scott, I hope all expenditures that may grow out of them will be sanctioned and justified.

I write you this letter, instead of sending it to Mr Eustis, to multiply the chances of information reaching you. Be pleased to make my respects acceptable to the President & believe me my dear Col. Yr friend &c H. CLAY

ALS. DLC-James Monroe Papers (DNA, M212, R22). Addressed: "Col James Munroe Sec. of State Washington City." Postmarked August 30.

[1] See above, Clay to Eustis, August 22, 1812.
[2] Charles Scott's term as Governor of Kentucky ended on the day this letter was written.
[3] In addition to Scott and Clay, the group had included William Henry Harrison, Isaac Shelby (Scott's successor as Governor), former Governor Christopher Greenup, Judge Thomas Todd of the Court of Appeals, General Samuel Hopkins, and Congressman Richard M. Johnson. Freeman Cleaves, *Old Tippecanoe: William Henry Harrison and His Time* (New York, 1839), 116. A few days later Johnson, of Scott County (member of the State legislature, 1804-1806, 1819, 1841-1842, of the United States Congress, 1807-1819, 1819-1837, and Vice President of the United States, 1837-1841), organized a troup of mounted volunteers and subsequently held the rank of colonel of Kentucky militia, serving with particular distinction in the Battle of the Thames, October 5, 1813. He was the son of Robert Johnson and the brother of James.
[4] Government. [5] The commission was issued on this same day.
[6] Since Harrison was not a citizen of Kentucky.

To Isaac Shelby

[August 25, 1812]

My Dr Sir Judge Todds Tuesday evening

I disclosed so fully to Mr. Hadin [*sic*],[1] who promised to submit to you, the subject on which I engaged to write you from here that it is scarcely necessary to give you the trouble of this letter.

Col. Simral's[2] regiment of Cavalry consists of 4 or 5 Companies. By the act of the last Session of the K. Legislature, when 4 Companies of Cavalry are formed. The Govr. may proceed to appoint a Col. Commandr & two majors, one to each battalion. There is no major yet appointed to Col. Simrals Regiment. I understand that James McDowell's troop was first tendered & first accepted. That circumstance, exclusive of other considerations, would seem to give him a claim to a majority, if there be one. Should you think the Law will warrant it, and entertain the favorable opinion that I do of Mr. McDowell, I should be glad to see him promoted.

Yr friend H. CLAY

ALS. MH. Addressed: "His Excelly. Isaac Shelby Frankfort."
[1] Martin D. Hardin, who had just been appointed Secretary of State for Kentucky by Governor Shelby.
[2] James Simrall.

To [William Eustis]

Dr Sir Lexington 26 Aug. 1812

Communications from Frankfort of yesterday to different branches of the Executive of the U States will apprize you of the highly critical condition of Genl. Hull on the 12h. inst, and of the measures which the Govr. of this State thought himself justified from the extremity of the case in taking. I refer you to those communications, and hope that the President will see fit to approve substantially what was done, which however with respect to the appointment of Govr. Harrison &c. altogether provisional [*sic*].

It is with regret that I have to add that reports are every where prevalent in this State & Ohio imputing to Genl. Hull more than incapacity. It is alledged, by way of color to the imputation, that his family have in several instances intermarried with the very enemy he is encountering. Confidence in him is utterly and irretrievably gone. I have endeavored at least to prevent the formation of opinions of his alledged treachery until further information is obtained. The most sober and deliberate are doubting his fidelity.

One of the steps taken at Frankfort was to increase the detachment from this State (exclusive of Regulars) to about 3000. Your orords [*sic*] for supply of subsistence to the D. Commissary were on a supposition that the detachment would not exceed 1500. As it is now extended to about 3400 including the Regulars, the Commissary has been advised to make a proportionate augmentation of of [*sic*] his stock of provisions. The communication between the N. Eastern and S. W. extremities of Lake Erie being interrupted by the superior naval force of the enemy, the strongest apprehensions are entertained on the score of subsistence. Yrs. H. CLAY

ALS. DNA, RG107, Letters Received, (6) C-453. Endorsed: ". . . Recd. Sept. 4, 1812."

From James Monroe

My dear Sir Washington Augt 28. 1812

Yours of the 29. ulto. & 12. instant have been receiv'd. The former should have been answered sooner had I not been absent in Virga. where I had gone to take my family for the advantage of our mountain air.

We have just heard with equal astonishment & concern, that Genl Hull, has surrendered by capitulation the army under his command at Detroit, to the British force opposed to him. The circumstances attending this most mortifying & humiliating event are not known, but so far as we are informed on the subject, there appears to be no justification of it. I can not suspect his integrity; I rather suppose that a panick had seized the whole force, & that he & they became victims, of his want of energy, promptitude of decision & those resources, the characteristic of great minds in difficult emergencies. we understand that after passing the river, he sufferd his communication to be cut off with the States of Ohio & Kentucky, and without making any active movment in front to strike terror into the enemy, he remain'd tranquil, thereby evincing a want of confidence in his own means, and giving it time to collect its forces together. no intelligence justifies the belief that he gave battle in a single instance. It appears that he surrenderd on a summons from fort Sandwich on the opposite side of the river, after the firing of some cannon or mortars which did no great mischief.

Before this disastrous event was known, the force, now I presume on its march, was orderd from Kentucky, and the appointment of Brigr. had been conferr'd on Govr. Harrison.[1] Your letters had produc'd all the effect on those subjects, which their solidity justly merited.

I most sincerely wish that the President could dispose of me, at this juncture, in the military line. If circumstances would permit, and it should be thought that I could render any service, I wod. in a very few days, join our forces assembling beyond the Ohio, & indeavor to recover the ground which we have lost. He left this to day for Virga., as did Mr Gallatin for N. York, but expresses being sent for them, they will probably both return to morrow. Your friend JAS MONROE

ALS. DLC-HC (DNA, M212, R1). Published in Colton (ed.), *Private Correspondence of Henry Clay,* 19-20.

1 The commission in the regular Army, signed by President Madison on August 22 and delivered to Harrison as his army marched from Cincinnati toward Fort Wayne, was not accepted immediately. It meant not only a reduction from his militia rank, but also a subordination of the command to General James Winchester.

From William Henry Harrison

Cincinnati Augt. 29th. 1812.

I write to you my dear Sir amidst a thousand interruptions & I do it soly [*sic*] for the purpose of shewing you that you are present to my recollection under circumstances that would almost justify a suspension of every private feeling—The rumoured disasters upon our northwestern frontier are now ascertained to be correct—The important point of Macinac was surrendered without an effort, An Army captured at Detroit after receiving 3 shots from *a distant* battery of the enemy (& from the range of which it was easy to retire) A fort (Chicago) in the midst of hostile tribes of Indians ordered to be evacuated & the garrison Slaughtered. The numerous north western tribes of Indians (with the exception of two feeble ones) in arms against us is the distressing picture which presents itself to view in this part of the country. To remedy all these misfortunes I have an army competent in numbers & in spirit equal to any that greece or Rome have boasted of but destitute of Artillery, of many necessary equipments & absolutely ignorant of every military evolution, nor have I but a Single individual capable of assisting me in training them. But I beg you to believe my dear Sir that this retrospect of my Situation far from producing dispondency produces a contrary effect. And I feel confident of being able to surmount them all—The grounds of this confidence are reliance in my own zeal and perseverance & a perfect conviction that no such *Materials* for forming an invincible army ever existed as the volunteers which have marched from Kenty. on the present occasion

Fort Wayne is in eminent danger—Govr. Meiggs[1] is collecting a body of Mounted Men at Urbanna & I suppose will send them to releive fort Wayne before I can get up with the Infantry. I dispatched Garrards troop[2] this morng. with orders to join any corps (at Piqua) which may be destind for that object—The 3 Regiments of Infantry marched also this morng—I shall follow & overtake them tomorrow. Should the releif of Fort Wayne not have been attempted or the attempt have failed, it will be my first object upon my arrival at Piqua

I have made every arrangement in my power to facilitate the march of the Regiments which are expected from Kentucky after they shall arrive here but I fear that I shall be obliged to advance from Piqua without them—with the assistance of a number of Mounted Men however which Govr. Meiggs can supply I may do pretty well—With troops that are awkward & who of course manoevure slowly—Mounted Men are absolutely indispensible to mask their evolutions—

I am so much interrupted that I can only add that I am yr. friend & Hum Servt WILLM. H HARRISON

Honbl H. Clay

ALS. DLC-HC (DNA, M212, R1). Published in Colton (ed.), *Private Correspondence of Henry Clay,* 20-21. Delivered by "Mr LeGrand" (probably Abner LeGrand).

1 Return Jonathan Meigs, Governor of Ohio from 1810 to 1814.

2 State dragoons, volunteers enlisted for twelve months' service, under the command of Captain William Garrard of Bourbon County, Kentucky.

From William Henry Harrison

My dear Sir— Cincinnati 30th. Augt. 1812

After having been absent from home for so many months you will no doubt think it unreasonable that you should be asked to take a considerable journey & that on an occasion entirely foreign to yr. ordinary public duties—I know you however too well not to believe that sacrifices of private convenience will be always made to render service to yr. country Without further preamble then I inform you that in my opinion yr. presence on the frontier of this State would be productive of great advantages. I can assure you that your advice & assistance in determining the course of operations for the army (to the command of which I have been designated by yr recommendation) will be highly useful—You are not only pledged in some measure for my conduct[1] but for the success of the war—for gods sake then come on to Piqua as quickly as possible—& let us indeavour to throw off from the administration that weight of Reproach which the late disasters will heap upon them. If you come bring on McKee[2] with you whom you will overtake upon the road—an extract from this letter will be authority for the Commanding officer of his regt. to let him come—Yours

Honble. H Clay Esqr. WILLM. H HARRISON

ALS. DLC-HC (DNA, M212, R1). Published in Colton (ed.), *Private Correspondence of Henry Clay*, 22.

[1] See above, Clay to Monroe, August 25, 1812.

[2] Upon the outbreak of war in 1812 Congressman Samuel McKee had volunteered as a private in the Kentucky militia.

To [Paul Hamilton]

Sir Lexington 5 Septr. 1812

Mr. Castleman,[1] the bearer of this letter, contemplates visiting Washington, and in that case may call upon you on business. He is a merchant of the highest respectability, in whom you may place entire confidence. Yrs. H. CLAY

ALS. DNA, RG45, Misc. Letters Received, 1812, vol. 6, p. 91.

[1] David Castleman.

Receipt from John H. Morton

7 Septr. 1812—

Recd. of H. Clay four hundred and fifty dollars the price of negro man Billy or Butler now in said Clay's possession sold by me to him, and which said negro I do hereby warrant & defend to said Clay agt. all persons whatever. JOHN H. MORTON

DS, in Clay's hand. Elsie Jackson Kelly Collection, Henry Clay Memorial Foundation, Lexington, Kentucky.

Property Deed from Thomas and Mary B. January to Clay and John Hart

[September 11, 1812]

[Indenture by which Thomas January and Mary B., his wife, for the sum of $3000, current money of Kentucky, paid and acknowledged, convey to John Hart and Henry Clay a tract in Lexington beginning at the intersection of Main Cross and Second streets and running North 45° East on the former street 197½ feet to a stake corner to Andrew McCalla's lot, thence with his line South 45° East 134 feet to a stake corner to an alley of 10 feet, thence with the alley South 45° West 197½ feet to a stake on Second Street, thence with that thoroughfare North 45° West 134 feet to the beginning, being part of Out-Lot no. 4 in the plan of the town, together with all premises appertaining. General warranty of title. Signatures of the Januarys acknowledged before John D. Young, Clerk of Fayette County, September 21, 1812.]

DS. DLC-TJC (DNA, M212, R15). Endorsed: "Recorded book G page 31 and Examd. Att John D Young clk."

From Woodson Wren

Sir, Attacapas Church Sep. 14. 1812.

I have made sale of two prime negroes to meet the balance of Mr. Smith's[1] demand against Me. The payments for them will be $400. on the 10 Decr. next and $400 in 3 mo. thereafter. As those monies come in they will be paid to Messrs. Bartlett & Cox agreeable to your appointment. This will not come quite as soon as due, but it is the best I could possibly do in a time as hard as the present. The whole amount will be paid in the course of six months, which I hope will answer Mr. Smith's purpose. I think the money is sure.

Please inform Major Uriel Sebree[2] not be uneasy, and for God's sake do not proceed against him—I had rather pay twice the amount, than that my bail should suffer.

Please write me. I am Sir very respectfully your Obt. Servant

WOODSON WREN

N. B. Please inform me of the fate of D. M. Sharpe's[3] debt of $192.

ALS. DLC-TJC (DNA, M212, R12). Addressed to Clay at Lexington. Postmarked: "St Martin's Ville Louisiana State 15th. Sept. 1812."

[1] James Smith, Jr.

[2] Member of the Kentucky legislature from Boone County, 1806-1807, 1813-1817; one of the founders of Covington, Kentucky; later a merchant in Lexington.

[3] David M. Sharp of Fayette County.

From James Monroe

My dear Sir— Washington Spr 17. 1812

I have had the pleasure to receive several letters from you in relation to our affairs to the westward, and I hope that one which I wrote you on the rect[1] of the first two has long since reached its destination.[2] Every effort has been made by the govt. to remedy the shameful and disastrous loss of the army and fort at Detroit, & I hope the best effects will result from them. In aid of the force which has so generously volunteer'd it [*sic*] service from Kentuckey & Ohio, 1500. are order'd from Penna & a like number from Virga. so that I think you will have on the borders of Lake Erie early in the next month, 8 or 10 000 men, well equipped, prepared to march on to recover the ground lost & resume the conquest of upper Canada. I have the utmost confidence in the success of the expedition which is set on foot, because the spirit of the people appears to be roused to that state which is best adapted to manly & heroick achievements. I am willing to trust to their sense of honor & to their patriotism, to efface the stigma which has been fix'd on our national character. I hope they will exhibit a noble contrast to that degenerate spirit, which has of late, & continues to exhibit itself to the Eastward, in the dominant party there. The command of this force is committed to Govr Harrison,[3] who it is believed will justify the favorable expectation entertaind of him, by those who are best acquainted with his merit. You & our other friends in Kentuckey will find that the utmost attention has been paid to your opinions & wishes, on all these subjects.

A large park of heavy artillery is sent on to Pittsburg to be forwarded thence towards Cleveland, for the use of the army, whose duty it will be to retake Detroit & expell the British from Malden & upper Canada. In short every arrang ment is made to give effect to our operations in that quarter, that has appeared to be necessary.

On the intelligence of the surrender of Detroit the President expressd a desire to avail himself of my services in that quarter, & had partly decided so to do. He proposed that I shd. go in the character of a Volunteer with the rank of Major Genl. to take the command of the forces. I expressed my willingness to obey the summons, altho. it was sudden, and unexpected, as indeed the event which suggested the idea was. On mature reflection however he concluded that it would not be proper for me to leave my present station at the present juncture. I had no opinion on the subject but was prepar'd, to act in any situation in which it might be thought I might be most useful.

From the northern army we have nothing which inspires a confident hope, of any brilliant success. The disaffection in that quarter has paralised every effort of the govt., & render'd inoperative every law of Congress; I speak comparatively with what might have been expected.[4] On the public mind however—a salutary effect is produced even there, by the events which have occurr'd. Misfortune & success, have alike diminished the influence of foreign attachments, & party animosities, and contributed to draw the people closer together. The surrender of our army excited a general grief, and the naval victory a general joy.[5] Inveterate torysm itself was compelled in both instances, to disguise its character & hide its feelings, by appearing to simpathise with those of the nation.

If G Britain does not come forward soon and propose honourable conditions, I am convinced that the war will become a national one, & will terminate in the expulsion of her force & power, from the continent.

Should you see my old & venerable friend Genl Scott[6] I beg you to present my best regards to him. I am dear sir sincerely your friend JAS MONROE

ALS. DLC-HC (DNA, M212, R1). Published in Colton (ed.), *Private Correspendence of Henry Clay*, 22-24.

1 MS. torn; this word not clear.

2 Probably referring to his letter of August 28.

3 The War Department order was issued on the day this letter was written.

4 In northern New York and eastward there appeared to be little enthusiasm for military service. Enlistments for the regular army and volunteering under the recent acts of Congress had fallen far below expectations.

5 The battle between the *Constitution* and the *Guerriere* had occurred on August 19.

6 Ex-Governor Charles Scott.

Settlement with William Satterwhite

[September 18, 1812]

Attached to Agreement, October 10, 1811.

To [James Monroe]

Lexington 21st. Septr. 1812.

I recd. My Dr Sir your favor of the 29h. Ulto.[1]

It is impossible to give you an adequate idea of the sensations excited in this Country by the mortifying event at Detroit. Altho' our previous intelligence had in some degree prepared us for unfavorable occurrences, the disaster so far exceeded our worst anticipations, that it was som[e] time after the fact was first announced before it was credited. Of Hull's treachery scarcely a doubt is entertained in this Country. For my own part as it respects the man I do not think it worth investigation whether the act is to be attributed to treachery or cowardice. It was so shameful, so disgraceful a surrender, that whether it proceeded from the one or the other cause he deserves to be shot.

Our letters from Frankfort have informed you of the measures adopted by Genl. Scott to afford relief to Hull.[2] Altho that part of their object has failed, the force sent out under Harrison will produce the most beneficial effects. After the fall of Deitroit [*sic*] the indians, probably aided by the British, penetrated as far into the Country as Fort Wayne, and a most formidable body of them laid siege to that place. The approach of Harrison towards Fort Wayne has relieved it and the indians have disappeared, declining to give him battle. Such is our information. Harrison will push on from Fort Wayne to Detroit and endeavor to regain the ground lost by Hull, or he will shape his course towards Pioria, on the river Illinois, a place of general rendezvous for the N. W. Indians, whence their parties sally out in all directions. But I am inclined to think (and indeed it is rumored) that he will proceed directly to Detroit, notwithstanding his want of artillery. The force he has under his command from this State alone is about 5000, and the total ca[nno]t be less than 8000.

Whilst Harrison is directing his Army towards the N. W. Majr. Genl. Hopkins is moving to Vincents,[3] with a force of upwards of 3000 men from this State, besides the Rangers and the militia of Indiana and Illinois that will co-operate with him. He will I presume proceed up the Wabash or Illinois and destroy the Indian towns. Should Harrison not go to Pioria, Hopkins probably will. And whether they ultimately form a junction, or how far they may assist and co-operate with each other will depend upon circumstances.

The capitulation of Detroit has produced no despair. It has on the contrary awakened new energies and aroused the whole people of this State. Kentucky has at this moment from 8 to 10.000 men in the field. It is not practicable to ascertain the precise number. Except our quota of the 100.000. militia, the residue is chiefly of a miscellaneous character, who have turned out without pay or supplies of any kind, carrying with them their own arms and their own subsistence. Parties are daily passing to the theatre of action. Last night 70 lay on my farm, and they go on from a solitary individual to companies of 10 - 50 - 100 &c. The only fear I have is that the savages will as their custom is elude them, and upon their [r]eturn, fall upon our frontiers. They have alre[ad]y shocked us with some of the most horrid murders. Within 24 miles of Louisville, on the head waters of Silver creek, 22 were massacred a few days ago.

Our policy, my dear Sir, must be changed towards these savages. They have commenced an unprovoked War. They must be made to feel the utmost vigor of Government. The President, I have no doubt, has been deceived as to their dispositions. They are not of the pacific or amicable character which certain Gentlemen would represent them. The fact is our frontiers have enjoyed one of the longest intervals of Indian peace that have occurred since the first settlement of Virginia. The progression of the Whites Westward–the death of the old warriors–the springing up of a new race of young ones–the natural propensity of savage man to War, are sufficient to account for Indian hostilities, without recurring to that most fruitful source of them, British instigation.

I expect to set out by the time this letter will reach you for the City, probably taking Richmond in my way. Yr friend &c

H. CLAY

ALS. DLC-James Monroe Papers (DNA, M212, R22).
1 Monroe's letter was written on August 28.
2 See above, Clay to Monroe, August 25, 1812.
3 In response to a proclamation issued by Governor Shelby about 2,500 thirty-day volunteers had rendezvoused at Louisville on September 18. Under the command of Samuel Hopkins the troops had set out for Vincennes and a campaign against the northwest Indians.

Receipted Account with George Trotter, Sr.

Lexington 25th Septr. 1812

Mr. Henry Clay Bot. of George Trotter Senr.

3½ Yds Blue Cloth	@ 31/6		£ 5..10..3
8½ " Bar Skin	10/6		4.. 9..3
2 doz 4/12 Buttons -----------	2/.. . .		4..8
2 " 4/12 ditto ---------	1/6		3..6
1 " 4/12 ditto ----------	1/.........		1..4
3½ " Bleach Linn .-------	3/. -------		10..6
3½ " Bro. holland . . .	3/ -----		10..6
14 hanks Sewing Silk . .	6d		7 –
6 Sticks twist @ 9d			4..6
Thread ----	2/ ------		2 –
1 Yds pading	7/6 ------		7..6.
			£ 12"11"0

Received payment for G Trotter Senr EDMUND B. PEARSON[1]

ADS. DLC-TJC (DNA, M212, R15).
1 A young clerk, later a proprietor of a mercantile business on Main Street, Lexington.

Fire Insurance Policy

[September 25, 1812]

[Policy on Buildings, No. 16, drawn by Kentucky Mutual Assurance Society, against fire. The insurance amounts to $8000, on brick building and out houses occupied by Henry Clay as a dwelling, valued at $10,000. Premium $1.50 a hundred.]
[Endorsement on verso][1]

J Hart will go to the office and examine what notice, if any, is to be given of my having built a wing or wings to my house since the date of this policy and if any be necessary give it accordingly, and take out a new policy and do all other needful acts.

H. CLAY

DS, by James Morrison. DLC-HC (DNA, M212, R1).
1 AES. Probably written the winter of 1813-1814, before Clay left for Ghent. Cf. below, Agreement, April 28, 1813; Insurance Policy, July 27, 1814.

Agreement with Daniel Bradford

[September 26, 1812]

An agreement made this 26h. day of September 1812
Between Daniel Bradford & H. Clay.

The said Bradford agrees to sell & convey or cause to be conveyed to the said Clay forty three Acres and one quarter of an acre of land, lacking a few poles, according to a survey of Richard Higgins, being that part of the tract of land lying near Lexington on which B. Thruston formerly resided & on which the said Bradford now resides. Possession of which said land the said Bradford covenants to deliver to the said Clay on the 25h. day of Decr. 1813. As the said Bradford holds William Challen[1] bound to him for a title to the said land, and is also bound to make a title to certain property in Lexington to the said Challon [*sic*] he agrees with the said Clay to give him, as a security for the title to the said land, the title to the said Lexington property, to be conveyed to Challon whenever he makes good the title to the said land.

The said Bradford further covenants that during the period which he reserves for the occupancy of the said land no waste of any kind shall be committed thereon, nor any standing timber or wood cut, nor any that is down except for the use of the farm. He also agrees to have the grape vines planted out last Spring cultivated.

In consideration of the said property the said Clay agrees to give the said Bradford three thousand and twenty seven dollars, that is seventy dollars per acre, payable as follows: The following horses at one thousand & twenty seven dollars, to wit: The said Clay's Arabian mare & Colt, Short mare & Colt,[2] a Buzzard Filly; the Hurd mare,[3] a Young horse colt of her's three year old by Buzzard, & a young mare put to Knosley:[4] The further sum of one thousand dollars, for which the said Clay will give his negociable note payable on the 24h. of Octr. next, and one thousand dollars in N. B. Bealls note for eight hundred & odd dollars & some other note making the afd. sum of three thousand & twenty seven dollars.

The conveyance to the above land the said Bradford covenants shall be made with general warranty in March 1814

Witness our Seals this 26 Sept. 1812.

Teste	DAN BRADFORD. {L.S.}
JOHN WINN	H. CLAY {L.S.}

ADS, signed also by Bradford. KyLxT.

1 Lexington chairmaker.

2 Possibly acquired from Peyton Short.

3 Not identified.

4 Knowsley, a stallion imported from England in 1801 by William Lightfoot, of Virginia, which as the property of William Woods, Albemarle County, Virginia, had stood on the farm of Benjamin Graves in the spring of 1812. John T. Hawkins purchased an interest in the horse in the fall of 1812 and offered him at stud in Fayette County again the following spring.

Receipt from John Morton

[September 26, 1812]

Attached to Promissory Note, January 1, 1809.

Agreement by James Hughes

Lexington Septr ye 26th. 1812—

In consequence of Henry Clay Esqr. having undertaken to join as Attorney at law, in the investigation & establishment of Mastersons Survey of 22,277½ Acres[1] on the Waters of Huston, & a claim in the name of Shores[2] depending on it of 16,000 a part of which had been sold by Jno Fowler before I became interested, I do engage to divide with the said Clay, One fourth of the said land which I am entitled to by Agreement, on the same terms I received it—

J. HUGHES {SEAL}

ADS. DLC-TJC (DNA, M212, R15).

1 Entered in 1784 by Richard Masterson, a Virginian who had settled in Gallatin County, Kentucky.

2 Thomas Shores of Chesterfield County, Virginia.

Agreement with David Trimble

[September 27, 1812]

Whereas we H Clay and D Trimble have purchased in partnership the Sandy Licks, late the property of A. W. Grayson, which were sold in virture of sundry executions issuing from Fayette Circuit Court; and the said Clay having an execution in his own name from the same Court agt. the said Grayson for nine hundred & odd dollars, which it was agreed between us should stand upon the same footing of those which issued in behalf of Tandy & Castleman, Mess Barrs[1] & Coyle.[2] It is now therefore covenanted by the said David T[rimble th]at he will pay to the said Clay [. . .] of hi[s] said execution [. . .][3] terms and in the same manner as the said Trimble and Clay have become bound to pay to the said Tandy & Castleman, Barrs and Coyle the amount of their executions.[4]

And as owing to the absence of the said Clay from K. the said Trimble will incur further expense and be at more trouble in attending to the purchase afd. for the joint interest of the parties, the said Clay agrees that he shall be reasonably compensated for his extra expenses and trouble beyond the said Clays. Witness our seals this 27 Sept. 1812.

Teste H. CLAY {L.S.}

DAN. BRADFORD D. TRIMBLE {L.S.}

ADS, signed also by Trimble. DLC-HC (DNA, M212, R1).

[1] Thomas T. and Robert Barr.
[2] Cornelius Coyle.
[3] MS torn.
[4] The contract by Clay and Trimble with Tandy and Castleman, the Barrs, and Coyle has not been found.

Receipt from John Parker

30 Sept. 1812.

Recd. paymt. of the within of H Clay. JNO. PARKER

ES, in Clay's hand. DLC-TJC, 2d Series, vol. 5. On verso of promissory note from John Clay to Parker, dated March 28, 1804, for £50/8/6, payable in five to seven years from January 1, 1804.

From Fortunatus Cosby

Dear Clay Louisville Octr. 1st. 1812

I had intended to set out for Lexington on saturday last, but the unfortunate situation of my family has prevented it—the whole of which have been very sick—My wife and eldest daughter, have been at the point of death—my daughter is recovering, but the recovery of my wife is yet doubtful, Thus situated all hope of seeing you before you take your departure is gone, as Mr Gwathmey[1] informs me you will start on Sunday next—I am exceedingly anxious to see you—I will thank you to inclose to me the amount of payments made by you to Mr Beard[2] with the respective dates of each payment—and write me also as to the matters of my letter to you by Mr Vernon[3]—

—General Lytles[4] disappointment to me, has greatly embarrassed me in my pecuniary matters—I trust it will be convenient for you to pay Mr Beard at least 500$. before you go—the Balance I must endeavor speedily to adjust I do not know that I can ask this as matter of right—but I am persuaded I can venture to do it as matter of favor—As soon as you return from the Federal City I will immediately see you—when I hope to be able to come to a final settlement of all our concerns—Upon inquiry I find that you had neglected to prosecute a writ of error in the Case Myself vs Satterwhite[5] This Circumstance together with your neglect to file the Bill against all the Assignors I fear will lose me that debt—I shall be glad to hear from you whilst in Congress Yr friend FORT. COSBY

ALS. DLC-HC (DNA, M212, R1).
[1] Probably John Gwathmey of Louisville.
[2] Joseph Beard.
[3] Probably William S. Vernon, who had moved from Rhode Island to Louisville in 1807 and shortly became a prominent citizen of the community.
[4] William Lytle.
[5] Cosby had brought suit in Fayette Circuit Court in 1805 against Mann Satterwhite for the collection of certain debts. Fayette Circuit Court, File 83 (1805).

Receipt to David Todd

Lexington Octo 2. 1812

Received of David Todd administrator of the estate of Levi Todd deceased, eighty dollars a fee due to me in a land suit between The Trustees of the Transylvania University against Levi Todd and others, this fee was paid. in 1810 by said D. Todd.

The above received in the hire of a negro. H. CLAY

DS (the last line in Clay's hand). Owned by Henry H. Harned, Frankfort, Kentucky.

From Thomas Hart Benton

Dear Sir, Franklin, Octr. 3d. 1812.

By some mis management of the post masters yours of the 4th ult.[1] did not reach me until the 23d. to this circums tance you will please to ascribe the delay you have met with in receiving this answer.

In the course of the past week I had an opportunity of speaking to Col. Sandford.[2] He informed me that he had just sent on by a neighbor the money he had on hand, and that in the month of Nov. he would be ready to make you a more considerable remittance. I will keep him in mind of this engagement; and facilitate its conveyance to you.

I count upon being in the city of Washington soon after the opening of the session. Possibly additional troops will be raised to serve during the war: I should like extremely to have an appointment among them.

We are waiting here with impatience, but with full confidence, to hear that the Ken. and O. volunteers have effaced the stain of Gen. H.s abandoned conduct. Respectfully, &c.

THOMAS H. BENTON

ALS. DLC-HC (DNA, M212, R1). Addressed to Clay at Lexington.

1 Not found.

2 James T. Sandford, a Virginian who had settled at Columbia, Tennessee, and later (1823-1825) represented that district in Congress, was indebted to the estate of Col. Thomas Hart for land purchases.

Receipted Account with Redd and Womack

Lexington 4th October 1812

Henry Clay Esqr. To Redd & Womack	—	Dr
Amount of repairg Carriage & bill		$220
A new Oyl cloth covr lined with baize —		28 —
a new Double tree & clip — —		1 — 25
2 new Swingletree braces for the Tandum harnis		2 — —

a new Drawn for the boddy ————————————	1 — 2-5
4 new Squabs for the quarters of your carrige —	12= 50
2 mew [*sic*] collars made of the best leather —	6 — 50
Repairing two Setts of harnis complete —	11 — —
Cleaining & oyling boddy Braces check traces Swingle Braces &C. with fish oyl —————	1 — —
Mending a lock chain ———————————	0 — 25
	283 — 75
Cr . By one bay horse — —	— 65 — —
	$ 218 — 75
James Weirs Note[1]	68 " 54
	150 " 21

[Endorsement]
Recd. Payment. 5 Oct — 1812 — REDD & WOMACK

D. DLC-TJC (DNA, M212, R15). Samuel Redd and John Womack were carriage makers in Lexington. [1] This line and the endorsement in Clay's hand.

Promissory Note to John Hart

Lexington, 5 October 1812

56.91 DOLLARS Due 5/8 Apl No. 66

Six Months *after date,* I *promise to pay to* John Hart *or order,* Fifty Six *Dollars,* 91 *Cents, negotiable and payable at the office of the* Lexington Branch Bank, *without defalcation, for value received.*

H. CLAY

[Endorsements on verso][1]
10. Note. $56.91
H. Clay. pd. 8 ap. 1813. JNO. HART
Recd for Lex B. Bank F DEWEES[2]

DS. DLC-TJC (DNA, M212, R15). [1] Both AES.
[2] Farmer Dewees, a young man who later became prominent as a Lexington banker and businessman.

Tax Receipt

Lexington, Octo 8, 1812.

Recd. of Jno Hart & Co eighty five dollars, 20 cts., the amo. of H. Clay's town taxes for the present year. NL. S. PORTER

[1] DS, in Clay's hand. DLC-TJC (DNA, M212, R15).

Account Rendered to John Darby

Dr John Darby in a/c with H. Clay [November 7, 1812]
To amt. of Costs in the original suit agt. James

Hughes and in the Court of Appeals which are included in the Judgt. agt. Ridgley[1] — — — —		$ 15„32.
To do. in the second suit do . do .		15„32.
To my fee in the Ct. of Appeals . — —		20„.
To do. in do. (second suit)		20:.
To Costs in Fayette Circuit Court & Ct. of Appeals in Taliaferro assee. agt. Hughes[2]		15: 32.
To my fee in Court of Appeals in Taliaferro's suit — —		20:.
To my Commission on $4109: 8 collected of Ridgley at five per Cent — . .		205: 45.
To post note drawn by the Bank of Washn remitted to you 14 Novr. 1811 . for —		500:.
To premium for difference of exchange 2½ PCt.		12: 50
To four post notes drawn by the K.I.Co.[3] on the 14h. Decr. 1811 for $200 each .		800:.
To 24 post notes of $100 each drawn by the Lex. Branch Bank on the 10h. Apl. 1812 sent you 2d. May 1812 .		2400. .
		4023: 91
By amt. recd. of Ridgley in a bill & Cash on the 12h. Oct. 1811 . . .	1500.	
By Cash recd. of do. 16 Apl. 1812	2609: 8.	
		4109: 8
To a post note of the Bank of Washn. remitted to you this 7h. Nov. 1812 for — — —		:85: 17

AD. DLC-TJC (DNA, M212, R15).

1 Dr. Frederick Ridgely. Cf. above, Deed of Trust, November 12, 1810.

2 Darby had assigned a note of James Hughes to John Taliaferro, who had brought suit to collect. Fayette Circuit Court, File 159 (1808). Taliaferro, of Fredericksburg, Virginia, served in the United States House of Representatives for nearly twenty years, at various periods between 1801 and 1843.

3 Kentucky Insurance Company.

To General John Mason

13h. Nov. 1812

H. Clay presents his respects to Genl. Mason and begs that he will accept his acknowledgments for his obliging politeness in indorsing his note offered for discount to the Bank of Columbia. H. C. was of course altogether ignorant of the rule adopted by that institution which requires two resident indorses [*sic*].

AN. NRU.

From Robert Breckinridge

Dear Sir Lexington Novr. 15th. 1812

At the time I received your & Mr. Trimbles letter[1] on the subject of entering upon terms for the settlement of your and the demands of some other creditors of A. W. Grayson I had hopes of making a sale to Mr. Ward[2] of so much of the Sandy estate as would enable the Trustees[3] to meet fully the demands of all his creditors, and the principal reason for not answering your & Trimbles letter with the promptitude which the subject seemed to require was in consequence of Mr. Ward & myself not having closed the negotiation and therefore could not give a satisfactory answer.—Shortly after your departure for the city of Washington the contract with Mr. Ward was made by which the trustees are to receive $10,000 on the first day of March next ensuing which they intend to apply in discharge of your demand, & the other Exon[4] Creditors which have been levied upon the Sandy estate. I have been the more induced to enter into this arrangement with Mr. Ward in consequence of the repeated & liberal offers you have from time to time made to receive your own demand and relieve you from your engagements for others—This you may rely upon being done in a satisfactory manner to the creditors. May I therefore beg the favour of an answer to this from you signifying your approbation of the arrangement I am respectfully your Obt. Servt. RO BRECKINRIDGE

ALS. DLC-HC (DNA, M212, R1). Addressed to Clay at Washington.
1 David Trimble. The letter not found.
2 David L. Ward of Louisville.
3 Breckinridge was one of Grayson's trustees.
4 Execution.

To [William Taylor]

Sir Wash. 20h. Nov. 1812.

I recd. your favor of the 18h. inst.[1]

I have to apologize to you for the inattention which has taken place on the subject of the payment made by Mr. Kelly to Mr. Wickliffe[2] referred to in your letter. However unaccountable it may appear the fact is it wholly escaped my recollection during the very short time I was at home. Having my family with me last Session as well as this and being consequently under the necessity of travelling much slower, the truth is I had scarcely time to turn around me when I got home before it became necessary for me to set out again. I have, since the receipt of your letter, written to that gentleman, & hope in a few weeks to give you a more satisfactory account.

I can add nothing to the information heretofore communicated relative to Lane & Simral.[3] Yrs. H. CLAY

ALS. DLC-HC (DNA, M212, R1).
1 Not found. 2 Joseph Kelly; Robert Wickliffe.
3 Robert G. Lane and William F. Simrall.

Power of Attorney to John Hart

[November 25, 1812]

Know all men by these presents that I Henry Clay have made, constituted and appointed, and by these presents do make, constitute and appoint, John Hart my true and lawfull attorney, for me and in my name to set a side and annul a contract entered into by David Trimble and my self of the one part and Messrs. Tandy and Castleman, Thomas & Robert Barrs and Cornelius Coyle of the other part,[1] on such terms and conditions as my said attorney may think proper, and for this purpose I do empower my said attorney to execute in name such instrument or Deed as may be requisite. And I do further authorise and empower my said attorney to relinquish and give up all interest acquired by me in the interest of A. W. Grayson in the Sandy Lick property, under a purchase made by the said Trimble & myself at the Sheriffs sale,[2] upon such Terms as my said attorney may think proper: and for this purpose I do authorise my said attorney to execute such Deed or instrument of writing as may be deemed proper: Hereby ratifying and confirming whatsoever my said attorney shall or cause to be done in the premises. In Testimony whereof I have hereunto set my hand and seal this 25th. day November 1812. H. CLAY {SEAL}

Ky. Court of Appeals, Deed Book P, 550. Recorded by the Clerk of the Court of Appeals, October 24, 1814, upon testimony by James Hughes, Martin D. Hardin, and Isham Talbot identifying Clay's handwriting.

1 Cited above, Agreement, September 27, 1812.

2 See above, Trimble to Clay, March 12, 1812.

Receipt from Robert B. Campfield

[November 28, 1812]

Recd. 28h. Nov. 1812 of H. Clay six hundred and thirty dollars the price of a Carriage made by me for him at New Ark and the price of delivery ROBT. B CAMPFIELD

DS, in Clay's hand. DLC-TJC (DNA, M212, R15).

Speech Opposing Remission of Penalties to Violators of the Non-Importation Act

[December 7, 1812]

Mr. CLAY (Speaker) said, that he had participated with the Committee in the pleasure which they must have derived from the splendid exhibition of eloquence made by the gentleman from South Carolina (Mr. CHEVES.) He wished it had been unmingled with regret. But when he saw the honorable gentleman assailing, with his powerful talents, what he deemed an essential system of policy, he felt constrained, however incompetent to the task, to attempt its vindication. The gentleman appeared, indeed, to arraign the whole of the measures pursued by this Government for several years past, in reference to foreign Powers, though he knew his private sentiments to be in favor of the embargo. {Here Mr. CHEVES stated that, in speaking of the restrictive system, he did not mean to include the embargo, which he always thought a wise measure.} Mr. C. thought a concession in its favor admitted the propriety of the law of non-importation.

What is the principle of these restrictive measures? It is to create such a pressure on the foreign nation as would compel it to revoke its anti-neutral edicts. The embargo aimed to accomplish this purpose, by not only withholding supplies of the first necessity, but, at the same time, shutting up our market against the manufactures of the aggressors. The act of non-importation was, upon certain contingencies, substituted for it, and it left the export trade free, whilst it pressed upon the foreign nation, by an exclusion of her manufactures. In this respect, he thought it a measure fraught with more wisdom than the embargo, which, however, he had no doubt would have produced its effect, if it had been persisted in. Neither was designed to impair commercial enterprise. Far from it. The friends of both contemplated the emancipation of commerce from its unjust shackles. Commerce was suspended for the moment, that it might revive with more freedom and energy. The bow was unstrung, that it might acquire fresh vigor and new elasticity. And he considered that the proudest triumph which the friends of the restrictive system could enjoy, was the recent revocation of the orders in council—a revocation which neither regard for the laws of nations, nor a desire to preserve the peace and harmony of the two countries, could effect, but what that very pressure produced by the law of non-importation had achieved. Yes, the distresses, the cries of the manufacturers—their haggard looks, produced by the operation of that law, had at length ascended to a corrupt ministry, and occasioned a reluctant abandonment of those orders. Every deposition given in the House of Commons, on the late examination before that body, on this subject, was a panegyric on our interdiction of British manufactures. He would trouble the committee with one which he had just laid his hands upon.[1] And yet we are now called upon to abandon this system!—We wanted firmness. We are deficient in the virtues of patience and perseverance. The embargo would have attained its object. It was, in a moment of panic, prematurely abandoned. And now, that the non-importation law has been demonstrated, by unerring experience, as capable of effecting its original design, we are asked to relinquish that also. He feared we should, in the same manner, get tired of the war.—He viewed the restrictive system as a powerful auxiliary of the war. You may be defeated by sea and land. Your northwestern army may be ingloriously surrendered, (it did not become him here to say from what causes.) In another quarter of the union your army, by fraud and chicanery, may be robbed of its recruits. The physical force of the country may be withheld, upon novel and dangerous constructions of the Constitution, menacing the total subversion of government. Opposition, transcending all legitimate bounds, may be carried to the very confines, themselves, of treason. That base, degenerate spirit may exist, which, incapable of patriotic struggles itself, questions and derides the motives of those who nobly step forth in their country's cause—a flagitious spirit, which has been seen to assail the standing of two of his honorable colleagues, because they exhibited the more than Roman example in shouldering their muskets and flying to the protection of the frontiers, against a most savage alliance.[2] But if you cling to the restrictive system, it is incessantly working in your favor.

But his friend from South Carolina had contended that we had thrice this session decided against this system, by refusing to entertain the proposition for an embargo. Mr. C. could not agree with him. He admitted, that a trade, in exportation only, could not subsist without a corresponding import trade, either in specie or commodities. But he denied that it must, necessarily, be in the forbidden fruit; English manufactures. He was free to declare that the exact limit to which he wished to see the export trade carried (until our rights are acknowledged) was the specie and commutables, other than British, into which its proceeds could be converted. What that limit was, congress must determine. It must be left to regulate itself. He was opposed, therefore, to the embargo recently proposed. He was desirous that the merchants, acquiescing in the policy of their government, should not continue heedlessly taking in payment for their cargoes to the peninsula bills on London—thus placing their capital in the power of the enemy. If they persisted in it, he was for their doing it at their peril. Taking nothing but specie or merchandise other than of British production, the restrictive system would distress the enemy, not only by closing an important market for his manufactures, but by exhausting his specie. For whilst he keeps up his large armies upon the continent, subsistence must be obtained for them at any sacrifice, and if bills will not procure it, specie must be employed. A stream of specie, equal to twenty millions of dollars, the estimated amount of our exports to the peninsula, continually flowing from any country would soon exhaust it of the precious metals. Much less than this would endanger the stability of the paper system in Great Britain.

The gentleman from South Carolina says, that the manufacturing class in that country is inconsiderable—that the American consumption is not more than one-sixth of the exports of British manufactures. My friend's error consists in separating that class from, and carrying it against, the whole mass of British population. It is unfair, in estimating its consequence, to look only to the divided effect of which it is capable. It ought to be viewed as a co-operating portion of opposition. In that country there will always exist an opposition. And the question is, what quantum of weight will be thrown by the discontents of the manufacturers, into the scale of that opposition, which is made up of the friends of Irish emancipation—the friends of parliamentary reform—those who are opposed to the Continental war, and that system of corruption and burthen of taxes existing in that country. He believed, if persisted in, the restrictive system, aiding the war, would break down the present ministry, and lead to a consequent honorable peace.

The gentleman deplores the gloom and distress which hover over our cities, and which he attributes to the restrictive system. Indeed had a stranger, unacquainted with their actual condition, heard his lamentations, he would have concluded that the melancholy state of ruin which they present is but little short of that of the famed Balbec and Palmyra. But what is the fact? Their growth and prosperity are without example.[3] Where are to be found your magnificent palaces—your splendid equipages—your sumptuous villas—all the luxury of wealth? In these same pining, desolated cities, and their vicinities. It was however, due to candor to say, that perhaps, next to New Orleans, the city of Charleston (of which his friend was the representative) has suffered more than any other by the shackles upon commerce. But he denied it resulted from the measures of our government. No, the gentleman has mistaken the cause of the disease. It flowed from the anti-neutral edicts. It proceeded from cutting off the market for the staple commodity of South Carolina. If it be true, as he has already admitted it was, that an export trade could not exist without an import trade, the converse of the proposition was no less undeniable. Suppose then the non-importation law not to have existed, how would Charleston or South Carolina have been able to sustain a trade in importation only? Cut off as she has been from a market for her cotton, where would she have found the means to pay for foreign articles? The immutable laws of trade would have created for that state a natural non-importation, if the legislature had not prescribed it.

If it be urged that she has enjoyed, in her rice and indigo, (though the culture of this latter article has almost ceased) some export trade, it is no less true that she has had the benefit of a corresponding, and probably an equivalent trade in importation from other countries than Great Britain.

It was remarkable to observe the inconsistency of the opponents of the restrictive system. Sometimes it was said to operate exclusively on the mercantile class. Then it was the agricultural class that bore its whole burthen. He admitted that if the export trade were limited in the manner he had suggested, this system would ultimately re-act upon agriculture. It was, however, but a temporary sacrifice, which that class was prepared to make for the permanent freedom of trade. We have heard of no complaints,—received no petitions from that quarter. The great agricultural state of Pennsylvania, and other similar sections, were patient and patriotic. The time when it was proposed to relinquish this system, was not less impolitic than the proposition itself. If the benefits expected from it were even doubtful, this certainly was the period best calculated to test its value.—Perhaps, at this moment, the fate of the North of Europe is decided, and the French emperor may be dictating the law from Moscow.[4] The British trade shut out from the Baltic—excluded from the continent of Europe, possibly expelled the Black Sea—perishing in South America—its illicit avenue to the United States through Canada closed; was this the period for throwing open our market, by abandoning our restrictive system?

He would next proceed to examine the claim of the petitioners to relief. And here he felt himself constrained to acknowledge that he had never been more embarrassed in the consideration of any subject whatever. He was impelled, on the one hand, by an almost irresistible disposition to grant the relief asked for; and on the other, he had the strongest conviction of the utility of the restrictive system, and the necessity of clinging to it. The difficulty lay in reconciling an act of liberality to individuals with the public interest. Their case undoubtedly presented powerful pretensions to the generosity of government.—What was it? The repeal of our non-importation law had been made to depend upon the revocation of the orders in council. If they were so revoked or so modified as that they ceased to violate our neutral rights, the president was required to declare the fact, by his proclamation, and then our law ceased. It was immaterial whether Great Britain repealed or modified her orders.[5] It was immaterial what was the manner of repealing or modifying them. All that our law demanded was, whether the one or the other, in whatever form the repeal or modification was ordained, the repealing or modifying instrument should produce a given effect. It was not to be denied that the order of the Prince Regent, of the 23d June last, would have produced this effect. It satisfied our law. It was quite a different question, whether independent of the law, it was such an abandonment of their system as he would require.—He entertained no doubt that it would have been the bounden duty of the chief magistrate, if the two countries had remained at peace, to have issued the proclamation enjoined by our law. He would have had no discretion upon the subject. He had only to look at the operation of the Prince Regent's order, and it was such as our law had required. Mr. C. did not doubt that the British government intended, by the condition with which it was coupled, to urge hereafter our implied consent to those orders in council, whenever it might determine to revive them. But the president could not have been restrained, by any such sinister design, from the performance of a positive duty. In the case of the arrangement, first with Mr. Erskine, and afterwards with the French government, the manner in which the aggressive edicts of the respective countries was discontinued, was far from being unexceptionable.[6] The president, however, looking to the substance of things, issued on both those occasions his proclamation, and he was right in doing so. Whether, therefore, the American merchant or his agent in England, prior to a knowledge there of the declaration of war, adverted to the terms of the law, the practice of our government, on similar occasions, or the correspondence between Mr. Monroe and Mr. Foster,[7] he would have been equally brought to the conclusion that the revocation of the orders in council in England, would have been followed by the repeal here of our non-importation law. Under these circumstances shipments were made. And, what puts the question beyond dispute, is that the president, in the message delivered at the opening of the present session, has said that the order of revocation was susceptible of explanations satisfying this government.

Mr. C. thought that, in all cases where the departure of the vessels from British ports was prior to a knowledge there of the war relief ought to be afforded. Official information of that event, it appears, was received on the 1st[8] of August. The shipments made prior to that time, were made when the repeal of our law might have been fairly anticipated, and under ignorance of its continued existence. A still stronger class of cases is that which consists of purchasers prior to the 2d of February, 1811. They bought when the trade was unrestricted, and of course violated neither the prohibitory provisions of the law, nor the policy of the government. When, by the president's proclamation of the 2d of November, 1810, it became unlawful to introduce their goods subsequent to the 2d of

February, they abstained from their introduction. Whilst they ordered their goods not to be shipped from Great Britain, and thus abided by and conformed to the law, as good citizens, others violated the law and introduced their goods after the 2d of February, 1811. These were relieved from the forfeitures and penalties which they had incurred by the law of the ensuing month, prescribing as the rule the time of departure from the British ports and not the arrival in America of the vessel. Shall we then, thus suffer the violators of the law to escape, and punish its observers?

With regard to all who shipped after the 1st of August, the plea of ignorance of the continuance of the non-importation cannot be urged. They knew they were acting contrary to law. They were fully apprized of the fact too, that this house had refused, before the declaration of war, to suspend the operation of the law. They were probably also informed, that after that event, propositions to repeal and modify it were rejected. The state of war itself rendered the trade unlawful. It was in vain to say they did not intend to violate the law. It was a palpable, wilful, undisguised violation. Remit the forfeitures in their case, and your law is virtually repealed. What is the present course of the trade, said Mr. C., to the Peninsula? It is to place American capital in Great Britain, which is constantly accumulating there. Its return can only be effected in British commodities. Having said to one class of shippers, after the war, that they shall be exonerated, how will you hereafter refuse another when they shall present themselves before you? Precedents are dangerous. The human mind, in a state of difficulty and embarrassment, was prone to take refuge under them.—Remit, in all cases, as had been contended for, and you let in a flood, deluging the empire of the law, against which your utmost wisdom and sagacity will be unable to provide a competent embankment.

As to the terms on which relief was to be afforded or withheld, he was decidedly of opinion that there ought to be no conditions. The law ought to be enforced or not. He thought a compromise in the case dangerous and undignified. Indeed he felt shocked at the idea of an equivalent. Already are our laws too openly violated or fraudulently eluded. Shall we degrade them still farther by carrying them into the market, and fixing a price upon their violation? Extend the principle of an equivalent from cases of prohibition merely to instances of moral turpitude—to fèlony and homicide; and every gentleman will see its enormity. No, sir, let us not pollute our hands with this weregild.

The proposed equivalent contemplates taking from the merchant his extraordinary profit, leaving him the ordinary profit; fixing, therefore, a rule for future violations. Now the ordinary profit is exactly that with which the merchant, in a regular course of trade, will be contented. He will trade with alacrity under the firm of the United States & Co. if you will leave him his customary profits, taking only the excess. But he would ask, if the firm gets into complete operation, what would become of the extra profit? Holding the opinion that he did in favor of the law of non-importation, he felt himself under the necessity of defending it no less against the open assaults of its avowed enemies, than the effects of the principle contended for by its professed friends. He was alone the solitary (he feared feeble) advocate of the law. The consequence of a general remission of the forfeitures was its virtual repeal. The consequence also of the equivalent contended for, by fixing as a standard the extraordinary profit, was its virtual repeal. He was for a remission in the specified cases, where remission appeared to him to be due.—He was for an enforcement of the law in all other cases—He was opposed to the establishment of a principle which if practised upon, and he did not see how it was not to be, if once adopted, under the delusive idea of taking the extraordinary profit, most completely prostrated the law.

But this principle of an equivalent was unjust or impracticable in operation. One merchant has imported a gainful cargo, another a losing one.—The same merchant has imported one parcel of merchandise on which he has made profit, and another on which he has sustained a loss—will you estimate the profit only, or take into view both profit and loss? How can you adapt any general rule to this variety of cases? Again—The extraordinary profits made upon the late importations result from the demand being greater than the supply. They will be divided between the importer, the jobber, and the retailer. Will each be compelled to relinquish his portion? And if not, upon what principle of equality can you take from the one and not the other? If it be urged, that the importers only have violated the law, it must be allowed, that the others are in the condition of accessaries after the fact.

He would touch an incidental question which had been started, and cease with, he feared, his unprofitable discourse. It had been questioned, whether congress had the power to remit the moiety of forfeitures claimed by the officers making the seizure. The law which creates the forfeiture reserves the unqualified power of remitting the whole or any part.—It is true that it has vested that power, for convenience sake, in the secretary of the treasury. Congress may, however, abolish that office entirely, and place all its functions in some new institution, or, without abolishing the office, it may transfer the remitting power, or resume it themselves. In all these instances, it would be a mere change of tribunal. The principles which would guide in a decision of the question of remission, it is to be presumed, would be those of justice, and that is all the parties affected have a right to expect. If there be cases in England, where the Crown is supposed not to be authorized to remit the informer's part of a penalty, he apprehended on investigation—it would be found to proceed from the power of remission not being reserved to the government in the law denouncing the penalty, as it is in our laws.

Mr. C. concluded by submitting the following resolution:

"*Resolved,* That as far as respects the case of citizens of the United States who purchased goods, wares and merchandise, the growth, production or manufacture of Great Britain, prior to the 2d of February, 1811—and of citizens of the United States who shipped similar goods between the 23d day of June, and the first day of August, the petitioners ought to be relieved by a remission of the forfeitures and penalties which they have incurred, upon payment of legal costs; and that on all other cases of the petitioners, a recovery of the forfeitures and penalties incurred ought to be enforced."[9]

Lexington *Kentucky Gazette,* January 12, 1813. Published also in *Annals of Cong.,* 12 Cong., 2 Sess., XXV, 298-304. In his annual message, on November 4, 1812, President Madison had referred to the fact that a large number of American vessels, in England when the Orders in Council were revoked, had loaded with British manufactures, "under an erroneous impression that the non-importation act would immediately cease to operate." Upon their arrival in the United States the cargoes had been seized by customs officials. Madison had commented in presenting the matter, that "it did not appear proper to exercise, on unforeseen cases of such magnitude, the ordinary powers vested in the Treasury Department to mitigate forfeitures, without previously affording to Congress an opportunity of making on the subject such provisions as they may think proper."

In the House of Representatives the Committee on Ways and Means, after considering this portion of the President's message, had offered on November 25 a resolution which would leave the problem and the decisions in the hands of the Secretary of the Treasury. Langdon Cheves, though chairman of the committee, opposed the resolution and in the debate in Committee of the Whole argued that Congress ought to act to remit all penalties to which the vessels were liable. Clay's speech followed.

1 Here Clay read the deposition of one W. Thompson.

2 Richard M. Johnson and Samuel McKee.

3 Last two sentences not given in the *Gazette* version.

4 Napoleon was in fact engaged in the crushing retreat from Moscow.

5 This sentence not given in *Gazette.*

6 Under the terms of an agreement made in April, 1809, by David M. Erskine, British Minister to the United States, the Orders in Council were to have been withdrawn on June 10, 1809. A proclamation fixing that date for the end of non-intercourse with Great Britain had been issued by President Madison; but upon reception of the Erskine agreement in England, it had been repudiated and its author recalled for exceeding his instructions. For the arrangement with the French government see above, Clay to Rodney, August 17, 1811, note.

7 Augustus John Foster.

8 Date given as August 10 in *Annals of Congress.*

9 On December 10 Clay again spoke (his remarks not reported) in opposition to a total remission of the merchants' bonds, but "advocating a partial remission of a certain description of the bonds." He renewed his resolution on December 11 and

December 21. *Annals of Cong.*, 12 Cong., 2 Sess., XXV, 361, 364, 441. On each occasion it was rejected. Finally on December 23 the House by a close vote passed a Senate bill directing remittance of fines and forfeitures on goods shipped from Great Britain between June 23 and September 15, provided that the benefits of the act were not to apply in cases where the purchase of the merchandise was made after war was known to exist between the United States and Great Britain, "at the port or place where such purchase was made."

To Callender Irvine

Sir Washington 19h. Dec. 1812.

I am requested by a Gentleman in Kentucky to ascertain from you if you are disposed to contract in behalf of Government for a quantity of Salt petre deliverable in 1813 & 1814 not exceeding 200.000 lb. Bairdstown in K. or Louisville would be preferred as the place of delivery. But if you wish to make the contract, you can specify the price you will give if delivered at either of those places, or in Philadelphia or Baltimore; the Gentleman wishes also to know whether you would make any and what advances. He can be altogether relied upon for the integrity and punctuality with which he would fulfill any contract he may make. Yrs.

H. CLAY

ALS. InHi-Mitten Collection. Addressed: "Callender Irvine Esq. Commissary Genl. &c. Philadelphia."

To Noah Webster

Sir Washington Decr. 19h. 1812

During my very short stay at home in the vacation of Congress I spoke to Mess McCoun Tilford & Co. & urged them to transmit you the account of the books published under your contract with them, and the arrears due to you. I had supposed this was done, according to their promise, until I recd. your favor of the 10h. Ulto.[1] Upon the receipt of that I wrote to them, pressing them in the most earnest manner to comply with their contract. I presume I shall hear from them in the course of a few weeks and as soon as I do I will again address you.

I received just before I sat out for this place, the letter to which you refer, but had not an opportunity of making the overture to them which it authorized. In my letter from this place I have enquired of them what sum they will be disposed to give in gross for the books they may hereafter publish & thus close the contract.[2]

Yrs. H. CLAY

ALS. NN-Ford Collection. Addressed to Webster at Amherst, Massachusetts.

1 Not found.

2 These letters also not found.

To Edward Tiffin

Sir Wash. 19h. Decr. 1812.

I had occasion during the last Session[1] to trouble you on the subject of the Patent described in the inclosed letter. Will you suffer me again to call your attention to it & to request that as soon as convenient you will furnish me with it.? Yrs. H. CLAY

ALS. DNA, RG49, Misc. Letters Received, C. Addressed to Tiffin at the Treasury Office. Endorsed on cover: ". . . Requesting the issuing & delivery to him of Bird Price's Patent for 1000 acres. Patent issd. 22 Decr. 1812."

[1] By letter of July 29, 1812.

Remarks on, and Amendment of, Navy Bill

[December 21, 1812]

Mr. *H. Clay* explained the reasons why, though decidedly in favor of an increase of the navy, he was opposed to seventy-four gun ships.

[Four other speakers followed Clay. The House then rejected an amendment to the bill which would have eliminated the seventy-fours.]

Mr. H. Clay proposed then to amend the bill by striking out the word "forthwith" and substituting the following clause: "As soon as suitable materials can be provided therefor;" so that, if the materials were on hand, these vessels might be built; and, if not, that the materials should be first procured. This, he said, would remove a great objection in his mind to the bill, arising from the doubt, whether suitable materials were on hand forthwith to build these vessels.[1]

Washington *National Intelligencer,* December 22, 1812. Published also in *Annals of Cong.,* 12 Cong., 2 Sess., XXV, 436-37. During the debate on a bill to increase the Navy, received from the Senate on December 15, the main point at issue was the provision authorizing the construction of four ships of not less than seventy-four guns each.

[1] Clay's amendment was agreed to and became a part of the act approved on January 2, 1813. 2 *U. S. Stat.,* 789.

To James Monroe

Dr Sir Washington 23d. Decr. 1812

Of the Campaign proposed by Mr. Johnson[1] I would say, that, considered in reference to a re-inforcement of Genl. Harrison, upon the experation of the term of service of the forces now under his command, it does appear to me entitled to encouragement. What is the actual state of the Genls. forces? The service of the Kentucky & Ohio detachments terminates in less than sixty days from this time, about the 20h. Feb. That of the Pennsylvania and Virginia detachments about twenty days later, say the 10h. March. What will be his condition when these corps shall have returned? He will have a nominal force of about 600 regulars and 12 months Volunteers, which will be wholly incompetent for any offensive movement, and will be exposed to the most imminent danger both in their front and rear, that is if they remain at the Rapids of The Miami of the Lake. If they shall have advanced to Detroit, they will not be able to maintain themselves there for the want of subsistence, their communication with Ohio and Kentucky being wholly cut off. Unless therefore it is determined immediately to abandon the whole expedition and to order the return of Harrison's whole army provision, without delay, ought to be made for reinforcing it, upon the expiration of the term of service of the militia. However much it is to be regreted that his force has been so cumbersome, and whatever measure may be taken for its reduction, it will not do to abandon the object of the expedition. altogether. His re-enforcement therefore is indispensible. It cannot be with regulars, and no other resource than volunteers or militia presents itself.

I think two mounted regiments not to exceed 1200 men might be raised upon Mr. Johnsons plan. Let them supply themselves with every thing but arms and receive a per diem allowance. Let them rendezvous at Cincinati and report themselves to Harrison. Proceed to Piqua or Fort Wayne and there receive his orders. If they should not be immediately wanted by him they may file off to the left and pass over to Chicago, scour the Country thereabouts, proceed from thence to the St. Joseph's, break up the settlements there, and advance from thence to Detroit or to Harrisons head quarters. I think it very possible that the party might surprize Detroit and take it by a coup de main, from the St. Josephs. Let their junction with Harrison be formed about the time when the service of some of the Militia expires. They could give up their horses to them and take their places..

The single obstacle to the execution of the plan is Subsistence for the horses. I think it possible with what they would carry and what could be taken from the enemy, that they might be subsisted. I suppose that the enterprize from Ft. Wayne round by Chicago, St. Josephs, Detroit, and to the Rapids of the Miami could be accomplished in about 30 days.

I have thrown these ideas together in great haste. Yrs.

H. CLAY

ALS. DNA, RG107, Letters Received, (7) C-41. Addressed to Monroe. Endorsed: ". . . Recd Jany 15. 1813." Upon the resignation of William Eustis on December 3, Monroe, still Secretary of State, became acting Secretary of War.

1 Richard M. Johnson had taken leave from his military duties in time to assume his seat in Congress on November 3. On November 10 he offered in the House a proposal for a campaign of mounted volunteers against the hostile Indians during the winter months. General Harrison, whose opinion was requested by the War Department, opposed anything more than occasional forays against particular villages, and the project was not adopted. *Annals of Cong.*, 12 Cong., 2 Sess., XXV, 146-48; Leland W. Meyer, *The Life and Times of Colonel Richard M. Johnson of Kentucky* (New York, 1932), 98-100.

To Caesar A. Rodney

Wash. 29h. Decr 1812

I have intended, my dear Rodney, twenty times to write you, but really such have been the mortifying incidents of the last Campaign on that theatre where all our strength was supposed to lay, that I have not had the courage to attempt to pourtray my feelings to you. Your agreeable favor of the 27th.[1] imposed on me an imperious duty to overcome this apathy. And however little I shall be able to impart as to the past or future satisfactory to either of us the claims of a friendship which I will never cease to cherish shall not be slighted.

Yes! too many errors have been committed. It was a great one to have neglected the command of the Lakes. To that and to the disgraceful events at Detroit are to be attributed all our subsequent misfortunes. The acquisition of the one or the success of Genl Hull would have preserved us from all our disgrace.

It is in vain to conceal the fact—at least I will not attempt to disguise with you—Mr. Madison is wholly unfit for the storms of War. Nature has cast him in too benevolent a mould. Admirably adapted to the tranquil scenes of peace—blending all the mild & amiable virtues, he is not fit for the rough and rude blasts which the conflicts of Nations generate. Our hopes then for the future conduct of the War must be placed upon the vigor which he may bring into the administration by the organization of his new Cabinet. And here again he is so hesitating, so tardy, so far behind the National sentiment, in his proceedings towards his War Ministers, that he will lose whatever credit he might otherwise acquire by the introduction of suitable characters in their places. One of them, unfit by Nature, has resigned;[2] the other incapable now by habit, is still permited to hold his station to the astonishment of every one. He will probably vacate it, if not by Mr. Ms. resolution perhaps by his own kindness & pity.[3]

On the part of the Legislature never was there a body assembled more disposed to adopt any and every measure calculated to give effect and vigor to the operations of the War than are the Members of the 12th. Congress.

You see & can appreciate the state of my feelings. I do not despair.

The justness of our cause—the adequacy of our means to bring it to a successful issue—the spirit & patriotism of the Country—the Chapter, if you please, of chances {you know Rodney that I have always paid peculiar homage to the fickle goddess} will at last I think bring us honorably out. When I speak of the Country I do not see in the result of the Northern elections any cause to distrust its patriotism. Our Land disaters [*sic*] and the incompetence which we have too unfortunately exhibited are sufficient to account for that result. The ensuing campaign conducted with the energy which it ought to be would bring back the heads, as I believe we now have even in that quarter, the hearts of a great majority of the people. In the South & in the West the Republican cause remains firm and unshaken.

Who will be our Secy. of War is undecided. Many are talked of. Still more hazardous would be any conjecture in relation to the Navy Department, if its present incumbent shall go out, as is believed.[4]

The pay and bounty of the Army will be increased. A new and probably more efficient form will be given to the Volunteer System, giving it the character and vigor of Regulars. In short even the Executive itself feels the necessity of recovering in the ensuing Campaign the honor we have lost in the last. And I hope with the means which will be provided this fond expectation will be realized.

I concur with you as to our Naval atchievements. Brilliant as they are however they do not fill up the void created by our misfortunes on Land. I was in favor of an increase of the Navy. I doubted as to 74s. but was satisfied that they were retained.

Mrs. Clay is with me and reciprocates to you the sentiments you have kindly expressed towards her. I have also with me three of my children. Yr. sincere friend H. CLAY.

ALS. PHi. Addressed to Rodney at Wilmington, Delaware.
1 Not found.
2 William Eustis.
3 Paul Hamilton, Secretary of the Navy, resigned on December 31.
4 See below, Clay to Taylor, April 10, 1813, note; Clay to Jones, July 12, 1813, note.

Motion to Repeal Laws Authorizing Land Bounty to Recruits

[December 29, 1812]

Mr. CLAY (Speaker) congratulated the committee and the nation on the system which had been presented to their consideration, and the prospect of prosecuting the next campaign with a vigor which should insure a successful result. He rose at this time, however, to propose an amendment to the bill, the object of which was to repeal so much of former laws as authorizes a bounty of land to the recruits. He was satisfied that, as respected the nation, this was a waste of its capital without producing a single provident result. As to the recruiting service, he was convinced, from what he had heard, that it added scarcely any inducement to the recruit— that it had not added an hundred men to the army. He confessed he had been much mistaken as to the effect it had been expected to produce, &c. Mr. C. added many remarks going to support his positions, stating, among other things, that the land would in the end get into the hands of speculators, and the individuals for whose benefit it was intended would derive no advantage from it. Now, that it was proposed to increase the bounty in money, he tho't it would be a proper occasion to repeal so much of the existing laws as allowed a bounty in land, on which the recruits set generally as much value as if it were located in the moon. Mr. C. concluded by making a motion to that effect.

Washington *National Intelligencer,* January 4, 1813. Published also in *Annals of Cong.,* 12 Cong., 2 Sess., XXV, 466. Clay's motion, offered in Committee of the Whole during debate on a bill "supplementary to the act for the more perfect organization of the Army," was agreed to by the Committee but rejected by the House the next day.

Bill to William T. Banton

[1812]

1811 Mr. William T. Banton To Henry Clay Esqr. Dr.,

		s d		£ s d
	To 6 Loads Wood	at 10/6	-- --	3„3„0
1812	To 12 Loads Wood	10/6	--	6„6„0
				£ 9„9„0

D. DLC-TJC, 2d Series, vol. 14.

To Richard H. Wilcocks

Richard H Wilcocks Philadelphia

Washington 2nd January 1813.

Sir

I received your favor of the 30th ultimo.[1] Prior to my departure from Kentucky I wrote you in reply to your letters stating the amount of the tax &c due upon your Land and presume my letter must have miscarried.[2] altho' I did not consider myself as your agent for paying taxes annually as they accrue (my agency for you having been limited to a particular object long since accomplished)[3] I certainly would have prevented the sale of your lands had I been present when it was about to take place or apprehended that such an event was to occur. It would not however be convenient for me to undertake such a general agency because independent of other considerations I am generally in this City or on my way here when the Sales of Land for taxes take place in Kentucky. The sale which has taken place of your land is subject to a redemption on your part by paying the amount at any time within two years, with 100 per Cent per annum interest thereon. The tax is 25 Cents per hundred acres (unless the Legislature has recently made an alteration of which I am unaware) so that you can ascertain the amount by the number of acres to which must be added the per centum above-mentioned and some trifling cost of advertizing. If you choose I will write to some friend to have the redemption redemption [*sic*] effected for you. As you will wish to avoid the recurrence of a similar event you had better employ an agent on the Spot, and I would recommend to you Mr. Achilles Sneed of Frankfort, who is in the habit of doing this kind of business and may be relied upon. Indeed Mr. Sneed would negotiate the redemption also. Yrs H CLAY

Copy. NHi.
1 Not found.
2 Not found.
3 Cf. above, Wilcocks to Clay, December 9, 1808. Documents concluding the transaction have not been found.

Rebuke to John Randolph

[January 4, 1813]

Mr. *Speaker* said he did not think the remarks of the gentleman, reflecting upon the House for the mode of transacting business, proper in themselves or relevant to the proposition to postpone the resolution until Wednesday. In point of fact, he would observe that there was no difference in the opportunity enjoyed by gentlemen on all sides of the House, of submitting their motions. If there were not greater extension of the time for receiving motions, it proceeded from the inability to make a House, in consequence of the non-attendance of some members, at the hour to which the House is adjourned.

Washington *National Intelligencer,* January 5, 1813. Published also in *Annals of Cong.,* 12 Cong., 2 Sess., XXV, 511. Immediately after John Randolph had proposed a resolution, John Rhea of Tennessee moved that it be tabled. In the brief debate that followed, Randolph complained of the manner in which the business of the House was conducted, charged that the lips of members not among the House leadership were virtually sealed, and stated that the floor should be open to one side of the House as well as to the other. Clay interrupted him at this point. Shortly afterward the motion for tabling was adopted.

Rebuke to Adam Boyd of New Jersey

[January 5, 1813]

The *Speaker* observed, that it was unpleasant to the chair that the gentleman should indulge in such remarks; he had certainly no wish not to give full latitude to debate.

Washington *National Intelligencer,* January 14, 1813. Published also in *Annals of Cong.,* 12 Cong., 2 Sess., XXV, 534-35. Boyd had begun a speech by asking the indulgence of the House for an old man, unaccustomed to public speaking, without the ability to organize his argument "in so connected a form as a lawyer's special pleadings." After Clay had finished, Boyd "said he stood corrected, and was allowed to proceed."

Comments on Speech by Josiah Quincy

[January 5, 1813]

The *Speaker* said, that the relations of amity certainly did subsist between this country and France, and that he did not conceive the gentleman from Massachusetts to be out of order in his expressions. That it was impossible to prevent gentlemen from expressing themselves so as to convey an *inuendo.*

[Quincy continued speaking until again called to order.]

The Speaker said, that really the gentleman laid his premises so remote from his conclusions, that he could not see how his observations applied to the bill.[1]

Washington *National Intelligencer,* January 22, 23, 1813. Published also in *Annals of Cong.,* 12 Cong., 2 Sess., XXV, 544, 564. During the debate on a bill for raising an additional military force, Josiah Quincy of Massachusetts was called to order by Bolling Hall of Georgia for intimating that the American Cabinet were friends of the French Emperor. Quincy replied that he understood that amicable relations existed between this country and France and that, under the circumstances, he had a right to refer to the Cabinet as friends of France.

1 Retorting, "I maintain that both my premises and conclusions are very proximate to each other, and intimately connected with the bill on the table, and with the welfare of this people," Quincy resumed his speech.

Speech on Bill to Raise an Additional Military Force

[January 8, 9, 1813]

Mr. H. CLAY (Speaker) said he was gratified yesterday by the recommitment of this bill to a committee of the whole House, from two considerations; one, since it afforded to him a slight relaxation from a most fatiguing situation; and the other, because it furnished him with an opportunity of presenting to the committee his sentiments upon the important topics which had been mingled in the debate. He regretted, however, that the necessity under which the chairman had been placed of putting the question,[1] precluded him from an opportunity he had wished to have enjoyed of rendering more acceptable to the committee anything he might have to offer on the interesting points it was his duty to touch. Unprepared, however, as he was to speak on this day, of which he was the more sensible from the ill state of his health, he would solicit the attention of the committee for a few moments.

I was a little astonished, I confess, said Mr. C. when I found this bill permitted to pass silently through the committee of the whole, and that, not until the moment when the question was about to be put for its third reading, was it selected as that subject on which gentlemen in the opposition choose to lay before the House their views of the interesting attitude in which the nation stands. It did appear to me that the loan bill, which will soon come before us, would have afforded a much more proper occasion, it being more essential, as providing the ways and means for the prosecution of the war. But the gentlemen had the right of selection, and having exercised it, no matter how improperly, I am gratified, whatever I may think of the character of some part of the debate, at the latitude in which for once, they have indulged. I claim only, in return, of gentlemen on the other side of the House, and of the committee, a like indulgence in expressing, with the same unrestrained freedom, my sentiments. Perhaps in the course of the remarks which I may feel myself called upon to make, said he, gentlemen may apprehend that they assume too harsh an aspect: I have only now to say that I shall speak of parties, measures, and things, as they strike my moral sense, protesting against the imputation of any intention, on my part, to wound the feelings of any *gentleman.*

Considering the situation in which this country is now placed—in a state of actual war with one of the most powerful nations on the earth—it may not be useless to take a view of the past, of various parties which have at different times appeared in this country, and to attend to the manner by which we have been driven from a peaceful posture. Such an inquiry may assist in guiding us to that result, an honorable peace, which must be the sincere desire of every friend to America. The course of that opposition, by which the administration of the government had been unremittingly impeded for the last twelve years, was singular, and, I believe, unexampled in the history of any country. It has been alike the duty and the interest of the administration to preserve peace. Their duty, because it is necessary to the growth of an infant people, their genius, and their habits. Their interest, because a change of the condition of the nation brings along with it a danger of the loss of the affections of the people. The administration has not been forgetful of these solemn obligations. No art has been left unessayed; no experiment, promising a favorable result, left untried to maintain the peaceful relations of the country. When, some six or seven years ago, the affairs of the nation assumed a threatening aspect, a partial non-importation was adopted. As they grew more alarming, an embargo was imposed. It would have attained its purpose, but it was sacrificed upon the altar of conciliation. Vain and fruitless attempt to propitiate! Then came a law of non-intercourse; and a general non-importation followed in the train. In the meantime, any indications of a return to the public law and the path of justice, on the part of either belligerent, are seized with avidity by administration—the arrangement with Mr. Erskine[2] is concluded. It is first applauded and then censured by the opposition. No matter with what unfeigned sincerity administration cultivates peace, the opposition will insist that it alone is culpable for any breach between the two countries. Because the President thought proper, in accepting the proffered reparation for the attack on a national vessel, to intimate that it would have better comported with the justice of the King (and who does not think so?) to punish the offending officer,[3] the opposition, entering into the royal feelings, sees in that imaginary insult abundant cause for rejecting Mr. Erskine's arrangement. On another occasion, you cannot have forgotten the hypercritical ingenuity which they displayed to divest Mr. Jackson's[4] correspondence of a premeditated insult to this country. If gentlemen would only reserve for their own government half the sensibility wihch is indulged for that of Great Britain, they would find much less to condemn. Restriction after restriction has been tried—negociation has been resorted to, until longer to have negociated would have been disgraceful. Whilst these peaceful experiments are undergoing a trial, what is the conduct of the opposition? They are the champions of war—the proud—the spirited—the sole repository of the nation's honor—the exclusive men of vigor and energy. The administration, on the contrary, is weak, feeble, and pusillanimous—"incapable of being kicked into a war." The maxim, "not a cent for tribute, millions for defence," is loudly proclaimed. Is the administration for negociation? The opposition is tired, sick, disgusted with negociation. They want to draw the sword and avenge the nation's wrongs. When, at length, foreign nations, perhaps, emboldened by the very opposition here made, refused to listen to the amicable appeals made, and repeated and reiterated by administration, to their justice and to their interests—when, in fact, war with one of them became identified with our independence and our sovereignty, and it was no longer possible to abstain from it, behold the opposition becoming the friends of peace and of commerce. They tell you of the calamities of war—its tragical events—the squandering away of your resources—the waste of the public treasure, and the spilling of innocent blood. They tell you that honor is an illusion! Now we see them exhibiting the terrific forms of the roaring king of the forest. Now the meekness and humility of the lamb! They are for war, and no restrictions, when the administration is for peace. They are for peace and restrictions, when the administration is for war. You find them, sir, tacking with every gale, displaying the colors of every party, and of all nations, steady only in one unalterable purpose, to steer, if possible, into the haven of power.

During all this time the parasites of opposition do not fail by cunning sarcasm or sly inuendo to throw out the idea of French influence, which is known to be false, which ought to be met in one manner only, and that is by the lie direct. The administration of this country devoted to foreign influence! The administration of this country subservient to France! Great God! how is it so influenced? By what ligament, on what basis, on what possible foundation does it rest? Is it on similarity of language? No! we speak different tongues, we speak the English language. On the resemblance of our laws? No! the sources of our jurisprudence spring from another and a different country. On commercial intercourse? No! we have comparatively none with France. Is it from the correspondence in the genius of the two governments? No! here alone is the liberty of man secure from the inexorable depotism which everywhere else tramples it under foot. Where then is the ground of such an influence? But, sir, I am insulting you by arguing on such a subject. Yet, preposterous and ridiculous as the insinuation is, it is propagated with so much industry, that there are persons found foolish and credulous enough to believe it. You will, no doubt, think it incredible (but I have nevertheless been told the fact), that an honorable member of this House, now in my eye, recently lost his election by the circulation of a story in his district, that he was the first cousin of the Emperor Napoleon. The proof of the charge was rested on a statement of facts which was undoubtedly true.[5] The gentleman in question, it was alleged, had married a connexion of the lady of the President of the United States, who was the intimate friend of Thomas Jefferson, late President of the United States, who some years ago was in the habit of wearing red French breeches. Now, taking these premises as established, you, Mr. Chairman, are too good a logician not to see that the conclusion necessarily followed!

Throughout the period he had been speaking of, the opposition had been distinguished, amidst all its veerings and changes, by another inflexible feature—the application of every vile epithet which our rich language affords to Bonaparte. He has been compared to every hideous monster, and beast, from that of the revelations to the most insignificant quadruped. He has been called the scourge of mankind, the destroyer of Europe, the great robber, the infidel, and Heaven knows by what other names. Really, gentlemen remind me of an obscure lady in a city not very far off, who also took it into her head, in conversation with an accomplished French gentleman, to talk of the affairs of Europe. She, too, spoke of the destruction of the balance of power, stormed and raged about the insatiable ambition of the Emperor; called him the curse of mankind, the destroyer of Europe. The Frenchman listened to her with perfect patience, and when she had ceased, said to her, with ineffable politeness: Madam, it would give my master, the Emperor, infinite pain, if he knew how hardly you thought of him.

Sir, gentlemen appear to me to forget that they stand on American soil; that they are not in the British House of Commons, but in the chamber of the House of Representatives of the United States; that we have nothing to do with the affairs of Europe, the partition of territory and sovereignty there, except in so far as these things affect the interests of our own country. Gentlemen transform themselves into the Burkes, Chathams and Pitts, of another country, and forgetting from honest zeal the interests of America, engage with European sensibility in the discussion of European interests. If gentlemen ask me if I do not view with regret and horror the concentration of such vast power in the hands of Bonaparte? I reply that I do. I regret to see the Emperor of China holding such immense sway over the fortunes of millions of our species. I regret to see Great Britain possessing so uncontrolled a command over all the waters of our globe. And if I had the ability to distribute among the nations of Europe their several portions of power and of sovereignty, I would say that Holland should be resuscitated and given the weight she enjoyed in the days of her Dewitts.[6] I would confine France within her natural boundaries, the Alps, the Pyrenees, and the Rhine, and make her a secondary naval power only. I would abridge the British maritime power, raise Prussia and Austria to first rate powers, and preserve the integrity of the empire of Russia. But these are speculations. I look at the political transactions of Europe, with the single exception of their possible bearing upon us, as I do the history of other countries or other times. I do not survey them with half the interest that I do the movements in South America. Our political relation is much less important than it is supposed to be. I have no fears of French or English subjugation. If we are united we are too powerful for the mightiest nation in Europe, or all Europe combined. If we are separated and torn asunder we shall become an easy prey to the weakest of them. In the latter dreadful contingency, our country will not be worth preserving.

Next to the notice which the opposition has found itself called upon to bestow upon the French Emperor, a distinguished citizen of Virginia, formerly President of the United States, has never for a moment failed to receive their kindest and most respectful attention. An honorable gentleman from Massachusetts (Mr. Quincy),[7] of whom I am sorry to say it becomes necessary for me, in the course of my remarks, to take some notice, has alluded [to him] in a remarkable manner. Neither his retirement from public office, his eminent services, nor his advanced age, can exempt this patriot from the coarse assaults of party malevolence. No, sir, in 1801, he snatched from the rude hands of usurpation the violated constitution of his country, and *that* is his crime. He preserved that instrument in form, and substance, and spirit, a precious inheritance, for generations to come, and for *this* he can never be forgiven. How impotent is party rage directed against him! He is not more elevated by his lofty residence, upon the summit of his own favorite mountain, than he is lifted, by the serenity of his mind, and the consciousness of a well spent life, above the malignant passions and the turmoils of the day. No! his own beloved Monticello is not less moved by the storms that beat against its sides than he hears with composure, if he hears at all, the howlings of the whole British pack set loose from the Essex kennel![8] When the gentleman to whom I have been compelled to allude shall have mingled his dust with that of his abused ancestors, when he shall be consigned to oblivion, or if he lives at all, shall live only in the treasonable annals of a certain junto, the name of Jefferson will be hailed as the second founder of the liberties of this people, and the period of his administration will be looked back to as one of the happiest and brightest epochs in American history. I beg the gentleman's pardon; he has secured to himself a more imperishable fame. I think it was about this time four years ago that the gentleman submitted to the House of Representatives an initiative proposition for an impeachment of Mr. Jefferson. The House condescended to consider it. The gentleman debated it with his usual *temper, moderation and urbanity*. The House decided it in the most solemn manner, and although the gentleman had some how obtained a second, the final vote stood, one for the proposition, 117 against it! The same historic page that transmitted to posterity the virtues and the glory of Henry the Great of France, for their admiration and example, has preserved the infamous name of the fanatic assassin of that excellent monarch. The same sacred pen that pourtrayed the sufferings and crucifixion of the Saviour of mankind has recorded, for universal execration, the name of him who was guilty, not by betraying his country, but (a kindred crime) of betraying his God.

In one respect there is a remarkable difference between administration and the opposition—it is in a sacred regard for personal liberty. When out of power my political friends condemned the surrender of Jonathan Robbins;[9] they opposed the violation of the freedom of the press, in the sedition law! they opposed the more insidious attack upon the freedom of the person under the imposing garb of an alien law. The party now in opposition, then in power, advocated the sacrifice of the unhappy Robbins, and passed those two laws. True to our principles, we are now struggling for the liberty of our seamen against foreign oppression. True to theirs, they oppose the war for this object. They have indeed lately affected a tender solicitude for the liberties of the people, and talk of the danger of standing armies, and the burden of taxes. But it is evident to you, Mr. Chairman, that they speak in a foreign idiom. Their brogue betrays that it is not their vernacular tongue. What, the opposition, who in 1798 and 1799, could raise an useless army to fight an enemy 3000 miles distant from us, alarmed at the existence of one raised for a known specified object—the attack of the adjoining provinces of the enemy. The gentleman from Massachusetts, who assisted by his vote to raise the army of 25,000, alarmed at the danger of our liberties from this very army!

I mean to speak of another subject, which I never think of but with the most awful considerations. The gentleman from Massachusetts, in imitation of some of his predecessors of 1799, has entertained us with cabinet plots, presidential plots, which are conjured up in the gentleman's own perturbed imagination. I wish, sir, that another plot of a much more serious kind—a plot that aims at the dismemberment of our union, had only the same imaginary existence. But no man, who had paid any attention to the tone of certain prints, and to transactions in a particular quarter of the union for several years past, can doubt the existence of such a plot. It was far, very far from my intention to charge the opposition with such a design. No, he believed them generally incapable of it. He could not say as much for some who were unworthily associated with them in the quarter of the union to which he referred. The gentleman cannot have forgotten his own sentiment, uttered even on the floor of this House, 'peaceably if we can, FORCIBLY if we must;' in and about the same time Henry's[10] mission to Boston was undertaken. The flagitiousness of that embassy had been attempted to be concealed by directing the public attention to the price which the gentleman says was given for the disclosure. As if any price could change the atrociousness of the attempt on the part of G. Britain, or could extenuate in the slightest degree the offence of those citizens, who entertained and deliberated upon the infamous proposition! There was a most remarkable coincidence between some of the things which that man states, and certain events in the quarter alluded to. In the contingency of war with G. Britain, it will be recollected that the neutrality and eventual separation of that section of the union was to be bro't about. How, sir, has it happened, since the declaration of war, that British officers in Canada have asserted to American officers that this very neutrality would take place? That they have so asserted can be established beyond controversy. The project is not brought forward openly, with a direct avowal of the intention. No, the stock of good sense and patriotism in that portion of the country is too great to be undisguisedly encountered. It is assailed from the masked batteries of friendship to peace and commerce on the one side, and by the groundless imputation of opposite propensities on the other. The affections of the people there are to be gradually undermined. The project is suggested or withdrawn; the diabolical parties, in this criminal tragedy, make their appearance or exit, as the audience to whom they address themselves are silent, applaud, or hiss. I was astonished, sir, to have lately read a letter, or pretended letter, published in a prominent print in that quarter, written not in the fervor of party zeal, but cooly and deliberately, in which the writer affects to reason about a separation, and attempts to demonstrate its advantages to different sections of the Union, deploring the existence now of what he terms prejudices against it, but hoping for the arrival of the period when they shall be eradicated. But, sir, I will quit this unpleasant subject; I will turn from one, whom no sense of decency or propriety could restrain from soiling the carpet on which he treads,*[11] to gentlemen who have not forgotten what is due to themselves, the place in which we are assembled, nor to those by whom they are opposed. The gentleman from North Carolina, (Mr. Pearson), from Connecticut, (Mr. Pitkin), and from New-York, (Mr. Bleecker),[12] have, with their usual decorum, contended that the war would not have been declared, but for the duplicity of France, in withholding an authentic instrument of repeal of the decrees of Berlin and Milan; that upon the exhibition of such an instrument the revocation of the orders in council took place; that this main cause of the war, but for which it would not have been declared, being removed, the administration ought to seek for the restoration of peace; and that upon its sincerely doing so, terms compatible with the honor and interest of this country may be obtained. It is my purpose, said Mr. C. to examine, first, into the circumstances under which the war was declared; secondly, into the causes for continuing it; and lastly, into the means which have been taken or ought to be taken to procure peace. But, sir, I really am so exhausted that little as I am in the habit of asking of the House an indulgence of this kind, I feel that I must trespass on their goodness.

[Clay at this point sat down. The Committee reported progress, and was granted leave to meet again. On the following day, Clay continued his remarks.]

I am sensible, Mr. Chairman, that some part of the debate to which this bill has given rise, has been attended by circumstances much to be regretted, not usual in this House, and of which it is to be hoped there will be no repetition. The gentleman from Boston had so absolved himself from every rule of decorum and propriety, had so outraged all decency, that I have found it impossible to suppress the feelings excited on the occasion. His colleague, whom I had the honor to follow (Mr. Wheaton),[13] whatever else he might not have proven, in his very learned, ingenious, and original exposition of the powers of this government—an exposition in which he has sought, where nobody before him has looked, and nobody after him will examine, for a grant of our powers, the preamble to the constitution—has clearly shewn, to the satisfaction of all who *heard* him, that the power is conferred of defensive war. I claim the benefit of a similar principle, in behalf of my political friends, against the gentleman from Boston. I demand only the exercise of the right of repulsion. No one is more anxious than I am to preserve the dignity and the liberality of debate—no member more responsible for its abuse. And if, on this occasion, its just limits have been violated, let him, who has been the unprovoked cause, appropriate to himself exclusively the consequences.

I omitted yesterday, sir, when speaking of a very delicate and painful subject, to notice a powerful engine which the conspirators against the integrity of the Union employ to effect their nefarious purpose—I mean Southern influence. The true friend to his country, knowing that our constitution was the work of compromise, in which interests apparently conflicting were attempted to be reconciled, aims to extinguish or allay prejudices. But this patriotic exertion does not suit the views of those who are urged on by diabolical ambition. They find it convenient to imagine the existence of certain improper influences, and to propagate with their utmost industry a belief of them. Hence the idea of Southern preponderance—Virginia influence—the yoking of the respectable yeomanry of the north, with the negro slaves, to the car of southern nabobs. If Virginia really cherished a reprehensible ambition, and aimed to monopolize the chief magistracy of the country, how was such a purpose to be accomplished? Virginia, alone, cannot elect a President, whose elevation depends upon a plurality of electoral votes and a consequent concurrence of many states. Would Vermont, disinterested Pennsylvania, the Carolinas, independent Georgia, Kentucky, Tennessee, Ohio, Louisiana, all consent to become the tools of an inordinate ambition? But the present incumbent was designated to the office before his predecessor had retired. How? By public sentiment—public sentiment which grew out of his known virtues, his illustrious services, and his distinguished abilities. Would the gentleman crush this public sentiment—is he prepared to admit that he would arrest the progress of opinion?

The war was declared because Great Britain arrogated to herself the pretension of regulating our foreign trade under the delusive name of retaliatory orders in council—a pretension by which she undertook to proclaim to American enterprize—"Thus far shalt thou go, and no farther"—Orders which she refused to revoke after the alledged cause of their enactment had ceased; because she persisted in the practice of impressing American seamen; because she had instigated the Indians to commit hostilities against us; and because she refused indemnity for her past injuries upon our commerce. I throw out of the question other wrongs. The war in fact was announced, on our part, to meet the war which she was waging on her part. So undeniable were the causes of the war—so powerfully did they address themselves to the feelings of the whole American people, that when the bill was pending before this House, gentlemen in the opposition—although provoked to debate, would not, or could not, utter one syllable against it. It is true they wrapped themselves up in sullen silence, pretending that they did not choose to debate such a question in secret session. Whilst speaking of the proceedings on that occasion, I beg to be permitted to advert to another fact that transpired, an important fact, material for the nation to know, and which I have often regretted had not been spread upon our journals. My honorable colleague (Mr. M'Kee)[14] moved, in committee of the whole, to comprehend France in the war; and when the question was taken upon the proposition, there appeared but ten votes in support of it, of whom seven belonged to this side of the House, and three only to the other!

It is said that we were inveigled into the war by the perfidy of France; and that had she furnished the document in time, which was first published in England, in May last,[15] it would have been prevented. I will concede to gentlemen every thing they ask about the injustice of France towards this country. I wish to God that our ability was equal to our disposition to make her feel the sense we entertain of that injustice. The manner of the publication of the paper in question, was undoubtedly extremely exceptionable. But I maintain that, had it made its appearance earlier, it would not have had the effect supposed; and the proof lies in the unequivocal declarations of the British government. I will trouble you, sir, with going no further back than to the letters of the British minister,[16] addressed to the Secretary of State, just before the expiration of his diplomatic functions. It will be recollected by the committee that he exhibited to this government a despatch from Lord Castlereagh,[17] in which the principle was distinctly avowed, that to produce the effect of the repeal of the orders in council, the French decrees must be absolutely and entirely revoked as to all the world, and not as to America alone. A copy of that despatch was demanded of him, and he very awkwardly evaded it. But on the 10th of June, after the bill declaring war had actually passed this House, and was pending before the Senate (and which, I have no doubt, was known to him), in a letter to Mr. Monroe, he says: "I have no hesitation, sir, in saying that Great-Britain, as the case has hitherto stood, never did, nor ever *could* engage, without the greatest injustice to herself and her allies, as well as to other neutral nations, to repeal her orders as affecting America alone, leaving them in force against other states, upon condition that France would except singly and especially America from the operation of her decrees." On the 14th of the same month, the bill still pending before the Senate, he repeats: "I will now say, that I feel entirely authorised to assure you, that if you can at any time produce a *full and unconditional* repeal of the French decrees, as you have a right to demand it in your character of a neutral nation, and that it be disengaged from any question concerning our maritime rights, we shall be ready to meet you with a revocation of the orders in council. Previously to your producing *such* an instrument, which I am sorry to see you regard as unnecessary, you cannot expect of us to give up our orders in council." Thus, sir, you see that the British government would not be content with a repeal of the French decrees as to us only. But the French paper in question was such a repeal. It could not, therefore, satisfy the British government. It could not, therefore, have induced that government, had it been earlier promulgated, to repeal the orders in council. It could not, therefore, have averted the war. The withholding of it did not occasion the war, and the promulgation of it would not have prevented the war. But gentlemen have contended that, in point of fact, it did produce a repeal of the orders in council. This I deny. After it made its appearance in England, it was declared by one of the British ministry, in Parliament, not to be satisfactory. And all the world knows, that the repeal of the orders in council resulted from the inquiry, reluctantly acceded to by the ministry, into the effect upon their manufacturing establishments, of our non-importation law, or to the warlike attitude assumed by this government, or to both. But it is said, that the orders in council are done away, no matter from what cause; and that having been the sole motive for declaring the war, the relations of peace ought to be restored. This brings me into an examination of the grounds for continuing the war.

I am far from acknowledging that, had the orders in council been repealed, as they have been, before the war was declared, the declaration would have been prevented. In a body so numerous as this is, from which the declaration emanated, it is impossible to say with any degree of certainty what would have been the effect of such a repeal. Each member must answer for himself. I have no hesitation, then in saying, that I have always considered the impressment of American seamen as much the most serious aggression. But, sir, how have those orders at last been repealed? Great-Britain, it is true, has intimated a willingness to suspend their practical operation, but she still arrogates to herself the right to revive them upon certain contingencies, of which she constitutes herself the sole judge. She waives the temporary use of the rod, but she suspends it in terrorem over our heads. Supposing it was conceded to gentlemen that such a repeal of the orders in council, as took place on the 23d of June last, exceptionable as it is, being known before the war, would have prevented the war, does it follow that it ought to induce us to lay down our arms, without the redress of any other injury? Does it follow, in all cases, that that which would have prevented the war in the first instance, should terminate the war? By no means. It requires a great struggle for a nation, prone to peace as this is, to burst through its habits and encounter the difficulties of war. Such a nation ought but seldom to go to war. When it does, it should be for clear and essential rights alone, and it should firmly resolve to extort, at all hazards, their recognition. The war of the revolution is an example of a war began for one object and prosecuted for another. It was waged, in its commencement, against the right asserted by the parent country to tax the colonies. Then no one thought of absolute independence. The idea of independence was repelled. But the British government would have relinquished the principle of taxation. The founders of our liberties saw, however, that there was no security short of independence, and they achieved our independence. When nations are engaged in war, those rights in controversy, which are not acknowledged by the Treaty of Peace, are abandoned. And who is prepared to say that American seamen shall be surrendered, the victims to the British principle of impressment? And, sir, what is this principle? She contends that she has a right to the services of her own subjects; that, in the exercise of this right, she may lawfully impress them, even altho' she finds them in our vessels, upon the high seas, without her jurisdiction. Now, I deny that she has any right, without her jurisdiction, to come on board our vessels upon the high seas, for any other purpose but in pursuit of enemies, or their goods, or goods contraband of war. But she further contends, that her subjects cannot renounce their allegiance to her and contract a new obligation to other sovereigns. I do not mean to go into the general question of the right [of] expatriation. If, as is contended, all nations deny it, all nations at the same time admit and practise the right of naturalization. G. Britain herself does. Great-Britain, in the very case of foreign seamen, imposes, perhaps, fewer restraints upon naturalization than any other nation. Then, if subjects cannot break their original allegiance, they may, according to universal usage, contract a new allegiance. What is the effect of this double obligation? Undoubtedly, that the sovereign having the possession of the subject would have the right to the services of the subject. If he return within the jurisdiction of his primitive sovereign, he may resume his right to his services, of which the subject by his own act, could not divest himself. But his primitive sovereign can have no right to go in quest of him, out of his own jurisdiction, into the jurisdiction of another sovereign, or upon the high seas, where there exists either no jurisdiction, or it belongs to the nation owning the ship navigating them. But, sir, this discussion is altogether useless. It is not to the British principle, objectionable as it is, that we are alone to look;—it is to her practice—no matter what guise she puts on. It is in vain to assert the inviolability of the obligation of allegiance. It is in vain to set up the plea of necessity, and to allege that she cannot exist without the impressment of HER seamen. The naked truth is, she comes, by her press-gangs, on board of our vessels, seizes OUR native seamen, as well as naturalized, and drags them into her service. It is the case, then, of the assertion of an erroneous principle, and a practice not conformable to the principle—a principle which, if it were theoretically right, must be for ever practically wrong. We are told by gentlemen in the opposition, that government has not done all that was incumbent on it to do to avoid just cause of complaint on the part of Great-Britain—that, in particular, the certificates of protection, authorized by the act of 1796,[18] are fraudulently used. Sir, government has done too much in granting those paper protections. I can never think of them without being shocked. They resemble the passes which the master grants to his negro slave, "Let the bearer, Mungo, pass and re-pass without molestation." What do they imply? That Great-Britain has a right to take all who are not provided with them. From their very nature they must be liable to abuse on both sides. If G. B. desires a mark by which she can know her own subjects, let her give them an ear mark. The colors that float from the mast head should be the credentials of our seamen. There is no safety to us, & the gentlemen have shewn it, but in the rule that all who sail under the flag (not being enemies) are protected by the flag. It is impossible that this country should ever abandon the gallant tars, who have won for us such splendid trophies. Let me suppose that the Genius of Columbia should visit one of them in his oppressor's prison and attempt to reconcile him to his wretched condition. She would say to him, in the language of gentlemen on the other side, 'Great Britain intends you no harm; she did not mean to impress you, but one of her own subjects; having taken you by mistake, I will remonstrate, and try to prevail upon her, by peaceable means, to release you, but I cannot, my son, fight for you.' If he did not consider this mockery, he would address her judgment and say, 'You owe me, my country, protection; I owe you, in return, obedience. I am no British subject, I am a native of old Massachusetts, where live my aged father, my wife, my children. I have faithfully discharged my duty. Will you refuse to do yours?' Appealing to her passions, he would continue, 'I lost this eye in fighting under Truxtun, with the Insurgente;[19] I got this scar before Tripoli; I broke this leg on board the Constitution, when the Guerriere struck." If she remained still unmoved, he would break out, in the accents of mingled distress and despair.

Hard, hard, is my fate! once I freedom enjoyed,
Was as happy as happy could be!
Oh! how hard is my fate, how galling these chains![20]

I will not imagine the dreadful catastrophe to which he would be driven by an abandonment of him to his oppressor. It will not be, it cannot be, that his country will refuse him protection!

It is said, that Great Britain has been always willing to make a satisfactory arrangement of the subject of impressment; and that Mr. King[21] had nearly concluded one prior to his departure from that country. Let us hear what that minister says upon his return to America. In his letter dated at New York in July, 1803, after giving an account of his attempt to form an arrangement for the protection of our seamen, and his interviews to this end with Lords Hawkesbury and St. Vincent;[22] and stating that, when he had supposed the terms of a convention were agreed upon, a new pretension was set up (the *mare clausum*), he concludes: 'I regret not to have been able to put this business on a satisfactory footing, knowing as I do its very great importance to both parties; but I flatter myself that I have not misjudged the interests of our own country, in refusing to sanction a principle that might be productive of more extensive evils than those it was our aim to prevent.' The sequel of his negociation, on this affair, is more fully given in the recent conversation between Mr. Russell[23] and Lord Castlereagh, communicated to Congress during its present session. Lord Castlereagh says to Mr. Russell:— —

'Indeed there has evidently been much misapprehension on this subject, and an erroneous belief entertained that an arrangement, in regard to it, has been nearer an accomplishment than the facts will warrant. Even our friends in Congress, I mean those who were opposed to going to war with us, have been so confident in this mistake, that they have ascribed the failure of such an arrangement solely to the misconduct of the American government. This error probably originated with Mr. King, for being much esteemed here, and always well received by the persons in power, he seems to have misconstrued their readiness to listen to his representations, and their warm professions of a disposition to remove the complaints of America, in relation to impressment, into a supposed conviction on their part of the propriety of adopting the plan which he had proposed. But Lord St. Vincent, whom he might have thought he had brought over to his opinions, appears never for a moment to have ceased to regard all arrangement on the subject to be attended with formidable, if not insurmountable obstacles. This is obvious from a letter which his Lordship addressed to Sir William Scott at the time.' Here Lord Castlereagh read a letter, contained in the records before him, in which Lord St. Vincent states to Sir William Scott the zeal with which Mr. King had assailed him on the subject of impressment, confesses his own perplexity and total incompetency to discover any practical project for the safe discontinuance of that practice, and asks for counsel and advice. 'Thus you see,' proceeded Lord Castlereagh, 'that the confidence of Mr King on this subject was entirely unfounded.'

Thus it is apparent, that, at no time, has the enemy been willing to place this subject on a satisfactory footing: I will speak hereafter of the overtures made by administration since the war.

The honorable gentleman from New York (Mr. Bleecker), in the very sensible speech with which he favored the committee, made one observation that did not comport with his usual liberal and enlarged views. It was that those who are most interested against the practice of impressment did not desire a continuance of the war on account of it, whilst those (the southern and western members) who had no interest in it, were the zealous advocates of the American seaman. It was a provincial sentiment unworthy of that gentleman. It was one which, in a change of condition, he would not express, because I know he could not feel it. Does not that gentleman feel for the unhappy victims of the tomahawk in the Western country, although his quarter of the union may be exempted from similar barbarities? I am sure he does. If there be a description of rights which, more than any other, should unite all parties in all quarters of the Union, it is unquestionably the rights of the person. No matter what his vocation; whether he seeks subsistence amidst the dangers of the deep, or draws it from the bowels of the earth, or from the humblest occupations of mechanic life: whenever the sacred rights of an American freeman are assailed, all hearts ought to unite and every arm should be braced to vindicate his cause.

The gentleman from Delaware[24] sees in Canada no object worthy of conquest. According to him, it is a cold, sterile, and inhospitable region. And yet, such are the allurements which it offers, that the same gentleman apprehends that, if it be annexed to the United States, already too much weakened by an extension of territory, the people of New England will rush over the line and depopulate that section of the Union! That gentleman considers it honest to hold Canada as a kind of hostage, to regard it as a sort of bond, for the good behaviour of the enemy. But he will not enforce the bond. The actual conquest of that country would, according to him, make no impression upon the enemy, and yet the very apprehension only of such a conquest would at all times have a powerful operation upon him! Other gentlemen consider the invasion of that country as wicked and unjustifiable. Its inhabitants are represented as unoffending, connected with those of the bordering states by a thousand tender ties, interchanging acts of kindness, and all the offices of good neighborhood; Canada, said Mr. C. innocent! Canada unoffending! Is it not in Canada that the tomahawk of the savage has been moulded into its death-like form? From Canadian magazines, Malden and others, that those supplies have been issued which nourish and sustain the Indian hostilities? Supplies which have enabled the savage hordes to butcher the garrison of Chicago, and to commit other horrible murders? Was it not by the joint cooperation of Canadians and Indians that a remote American fort, Michilimackinac, was fallen upon and reduced, [while the garrison was] in ignorance of a state of war? But, sir, how soon have the opposition changed. When administration was striving, by the operation of peaceful measures, to bring Great Britain back to a sense of justice, they were for old-fashioned war. And now that they have got old fashioned war, their sensibilities are cruelly shocked, and all their sympathies are lavished upon the harmless inhabitants of the adjoining provinces. What does a state of war present? The united energies of one people arrayed against the combined energies of another—a conflict in which each party aims to inflict all the injury it can, by sea and land, upon the territories, property and citizens of the other, subject only to the rules of mitigated war practised by civilized nations. The gentlemen would not touch the continental provinces of the enemy, nor, I presume, for the same reason, her possessions in the W. Indies. The same humane spirit would spare the seamen and soldiers of the enemy. The sacred person of his majesty must not be attacked, for the learned gentlemen, on the other side, are quite familiar with the maxim, that the king can do no wrong. Indeed, sir, I know of no person on whom we may make war, upon the principles of the honorable gentlemen, but Mr. Stephen,[25] the celebrated author of the orders in council, or the board of admiralty, who authorise and regulate the practice of impressment!

The disasters of the war admonish us, we are told, of the necessity of terminating the contest. If our achievements upon the land have been less splendid than those of our intrepid seamen, it is not because the American soldier is less brave. On the one element organization, discipline, and a thorough knowledge of their duties exist, on the part of the officers and their men. On the other, almost every thing is yet to be acquired. We have however the consolation that our country abounds with the richest materials, and that in no instance when engaged in an action have our arms been tarnished. At Brownstown and at Queenstown the valor of veterans was displayed, and acts of the noblest heroism were performed.[26] It is true, that the disgrace of Detroit remains to be wiped off. That is a subject on which I cannot trust my feelings, it is not fitting I should speak. But this much I will say, it was an event which no human foresight could have anticipated, and for which administration cannot be justly censured. It was the parent of all the misfortunes we have experienced on land. But for it the Indian war would have been in a great measure prevented or terminated; the ascendency on lake Erie acquired, and the war pushed perhaps to Montreal. With the exception of that event, the war, even upon the land, has been attended by a series of the most brilliant exploits, which, whatever interest they may inspire on this side of the mountains, have given the greatest pleasure on the other. The expedition under the command of Gov. Edwards and

Colonel Russell, to lake Pioria, on the Illinois, was completely successful.[27] So was that of Captain Craig, who it is said ascended that river still higher.[28] General Hopkins destroyed the Prophet's town.[29] We have just received intelligence of the gallant enterprise of Colonel Campbell.[30] In short, sir, the Indian towns have been swept from the mouth to source of the Wabash, and a hostile country has been penetrated far beyond the most daring incursions of any campaign during the former Indian war. Never was more cool deliberate bravery displayed than that by Newnan's party from Georgia.[31] And the capture of the Detroit, and the destruction of the Caledonia, (whether placed to our maritime or land account) for judgment, skill, and courage on the part of Lieutenant Elliott,[32] has never been surpassed.

It is alleged that the elections in England are in favor of the ministry, and that those in this country are against the war. If in such a cause (saying nothing of the impurity of their elections) the people of that country have rallied around their government, it affords a salutary lesson to the people here, who at all hazards ought to support theirs, struggling as it is to maintain our just rights. But the people here have not been false to themselves; a great majority approve the war, as is evinced by the recent reelection of the chief magistrate. Suppose it were even true, that an entire section of the Union were opposed to the war, that section being a minority, is the will of the majority to be relinquished? In that section the real strength of the opposition had been greatly exaggerated. Vermont has, by two successive expressions of her opinion, approved the declaration of war. In New-Hampshire, parties are so nearly equipoised that out of 30 or 35 thousand votes, those who approved, and are for supporting it, lost the election by only 1,000 or 1,500 votes. In Massachusetts alone have they obtained any considerable accession. If we come to New-York, we shall find that other and local causes have influenced her elections.

What cause, Mr. Chairman, which existed for declaring the war has been removed? We sought indemnity for the past and security for the future. The orders in council are suspended, not revoked; no compensation for spoliations, Indian hostilities, which were before secretly instigated, now openly encouraged; and the practice of impressment unremittingly persevered in and insisted upon. Yet administration has given the strongest demonstrations of its love of peace. On the 29th June, less than ten days after the declaration of war, the Secretary of State writes to Mr. Russell, authorising him to agree to an armistice, upon two conditions only, and what are they? That the orders in council should be repealed, and the practice of impressing American seamen cease, those already impressed being released. The proposition was for nothing more than a *real* truce; that the war should in fact cease on *both* sides. Again on the 27th July, one month later, anticipating a possible objection to these terms, reasonable as they are, Mr. Monroe empowers Mr. Russell to stipulate in general terms for an armistice, having only an informal understanding on these points. In return, the enemy is offered a prohibition of the employment of his seamen in our service, thus removing entirely all pretext for the practice of impressment. The very proposition which the gentleman from Connecticut (Mr. Pitkin) contends ought to be made has been made. How are these pacific advances met by the other party? Rejected as absolutely inadmissible, cavils are indulged about the inadequacy of Mr. Russell's powers, and the want of an act of Congress is intimated. And yet the constant usage of nations I believe is, where the legislation of one party is necessary to carry into effect a given stipulation, to leave it to the contracting party to provide the requisite laws. If he failed to do so, it is a breach of good faith, and a subject of subsequent remonstrance by the injured party. When Mr. Russell renews the overture, in what was intended as a more agreeable form to the British government, Lord Castlereagh is not content with a simple rejection, but clothes it in the langauge of insult. Afterwards, in conversation with Mr. Russell, the moderation of our government is misinterpreted and made the occasion of a sneer, that we are tired of the war. The proposition of Admiral Warren is submitted in a spirit not more pacific.[33] He is instructed, he tells us, to propose that the government of the United States shall instantly recall their letters of marque and reprisal against British ships, together with all orders and instructions for any acts of hostility whatever against the territories of his Majesty or the persons or property of his subjects. That small affair being settled, he is further authorised to arrange as to the revocation of the laws which interdict the commerce and ships of war of his Majesty from the harbors and waters of the United States. This messenger of peace comes with one qualified concession in his pocket, not made to the justice of our demands, and is fully empowered to receive our homage, the contrite retraction of all our measures adopted against his master! And in default, he does not fail to assure us, the orders in council are to be forthwith revived. Administration, still anxious to terminate the war, suppresses the indignation which such a proposal ought to have created, and in its answer concludes by informing Admiral Warren, "that if there be no objection to an accommodation of the difference relating to impressment, in the mode proposed, other than the suspension of the British claim to impressment during the armistice, there can be none to proceeding, *without the armistice*, to an immediate discussion and arrangement of an article on that subject." Thus it has left the door of negotiation unclosed, and it remains to be seen if the enemy will accept the invitation tendered to him. The honorable gentleman from North Carolina (Mr. Pearson) supposes, that if Congress would pass a law, prohibiting the employment of British seamen in our service, upon condition of a like prohibition on their part, and repeal the act of non-importation, peace would immediately follow. Sir, I have no doubt if such a law were passed, with all the requisite solemnities, and the repeal to take place, Lord Castlereagh would laugh at our simplicity. No, sir, administration has erred in the steps which it has taken to restore peace, but its error has been not in doing too little but in betraying too great a solicitude for that event. An honorable peace is attainable only by an efficient war. My plan would be to call out the ample resources of the country, give them a judicious direction, prosecute the war with the utmost vigor, strike wherever we can reach the enemy, at sea or on land, and negotiate the terms of a peace at Quebec or Halifax. We are told that England is a proud and lofty nation that disdaining to wait for danger, meets it half way. Haughty as she is, we once triumphed over her, and if we do not listen to the councils of timidity and despair we shall again prevail. In such a cause, with the aid of Providence, we must come out crowned with success; but if we fail, let us fail like men, lash ourselves to our gallant tars, and expire together in one common struggle, fighting for "*seamen's rights and free trade*."

Washington *National Intelligencer,* February 5, 6, 1813. Published also in *Annals of Cong.,* 12 Cong., 2 Sess., XXV, 659-76; Lexington *Kentucky Gazette,* March 2, 1813; Lexington *Reporter,* February 27, March 6, 1813; Chambers, *Speeches of Henry Clay,* 44-61; Colton, *Life, Correspondence, and Speeches of Henry Clay,* V, 52-70; [Swain], *Life and Speeches of Henry Clay,* I, 33-54; Mallory, *Life and Speeches of Henry Clay,* I, 240-58. On December 24, 1812, David R. Williams of South Carolina had presented a bill to enlist for one year an additional twenty regiments of infantry. After having been considered in Committee of the Whole, reported, and debated for several days, the measure had been recommitted on January 7. It finally passed the House on January 14, the Senate on January 25, and was signed by the President on January 29.

1 The Chairman had arisen to put the question, which action would have returned the bill to the House, thus preventing Clay, the Speaker, from discussing the measure.

2 David M. Erskine.

3 The American note which accepted the tardy British offer of reparation for the attack upon the *Chesapeake* in June, 1807, at the same time had expressed dissatisfaction that Admiral Berkeley, the officer responsible, had merely been transferred to another command.

4 Francis James Jackson.

5 Richard Cutts, a Democrat of Massachusetts and the husband of Anna Payne, sister of Dolly Payne Madison, had served in the House from 1801 to 1813. Defeated in the election of 1812, he was appointed superintendent general of military supplies, 1813-1817, and the second comptroller of the United States Treasury, 1817-1829.

6 Jan and Cornelius De Witt, Dutch statesmen of the seventeenth century, opponents of William II, Prince of Orange.

7 Josiah Quincy.

8 The "Essex Junto," arch-Federalists in New England, bitterly opposed the Administration and the war.

9 Alias of an Irish seaman, Thomas Nash, who in 1799 had been surrendered to the British, tried for murder, and hanged. The prisoner's claim to American citizenship had formed the basis for sharp Jeffersonian attacks upon the Adams Administration's recognition of the British extradition request.

10 John Henry.

11 Editorial comment by the journalist at this point: "It is due to Mr. C. to observe, that one of the most offensive expressions used by Mr. Q., an expression which produced disgust on all sides of the House, has been omitted in that gentleman's reported speech, which in other respects has been much softened."

12 Joseph Pearson, Timothy Pitkin, Harmanus Bleecker.

13 Laban Wheaton.

14 Samuel McKee.

15 A note from Napoleon's Foreign Minister to the American Chargé in London in May, 1812, had enclosed a decree, dated April 28, 1811, exempting American commerce from application of the Berlin and Milan decrees after November 1, 1810.

16 Augustus J. Foster.

17 Robert Stewart, second Marquis of Londonderry, known as Viscount Castlereagh, was British Foreign Secretary from 1812 to 1822.

18 By which qualified seamen might obtain from collectors of the various districts certificates of citizenship. 1 *U. S. Stat.*, 477.

19 During the undeclared war with France, 1798-1800, the American frigate *Constellation,* under Commodore Thomas Truxton, had overcome *L'Insurgente,* the fastest ship in the French navy, in an engagement off St. Kitts in the West Indies.

20 Editorial comment on the emotional effect of the speech here deleted.

21 Rufus King, a member of the Constitutional Convention from Massachusetts, United States Senator from New York (1789-1796, 1813-1825), and Minister to Great Britain (1796-1803, 1825-1826).

22 Charles Jenkinson, first Earl of Liverpool and first Baron Hawkesbury, long influential in English politics, and John Jervis, Earl of St. Vincent, first lord of the admiralty, 1801-1804.

23 Jonathan Russell, a native of Rhode Island, had been appointed to the diplomatic service in 1811 and was Chargé d'Affaires in England when the war began. On January 18, 1814, he was appointed Minister to Sweden and one of the Commissioners to negotiate peace with Great Britain. Upon his return to the United States in 1818 he settled in Massachusetts and later represented that State in Congress, 1821-1823.

24 Henry M. Ridgely, who had spoken on January 4.

25 A pamphlet, *War in Disguise,* published in 1805 by James Stephen, a British lawyer, supposedly had suggested the orders in council.

26 On August 5, 1812, a detachment of 200 men, sent by General William Hull to afford protection for supplies intended for his army, had been ambushed and thrown back by Indians at Brownstown, some 25 miles below Detroit at the mouth of the Huron River.

At Queenston, Ontario, on October 13, 1812, an American detachment had been defeated and captured when the New York militia refused to cross the Niagara River to reinforce their countrymen.

27 Governor Ninian Edwards of the Illinois Territory and Colonel William Russell of the Seventh United States Infantry Regiment had led a small body of United States Rangers and mounted militia in a foray into the Indian country in October, 1812.

28 Captain Thomas E. Craig, of Shawneetown, Illinois Territory, had led a force of 80 men up the Illinois River with the intent of joining Colonel Russell. Failing to find him, Craig had proceeded to the old Peoria town, which he destroyed.

29 After an abortive effort in October, General Samuel Hopkins had led another, more successful expedition against the Indians on the upper Wabash in November, 1812.

30 A force commanded by Lieutenant Colonel John B. Campbell of the 19th United States Regiment had proceeded to Greenville and on into the Indian country in December, 1812.

31 In the fall of 1812 an expedition under Colonel Daniel Newnan had invaded East Florida and fought several engagements with the Seminoles.

32 In a daring venture in the fall of 1812 Lieutenant Jesse Duncan Elliott, a native of Maryland, had endeavored to recapture the American ship *Adams* (renamed as the *Detroit* by the British following her surrender after Hull's defeat), and also to take a smaller brig, the *Caledonia,* as they lay off Fort Erie, Canada. When, because of light winds and heavy current, boarding parties could not sail the vessels, they had cut the cables and set them adrift. The *Detroit* had been destroyed under the British batteries and the *Caledonia* had run aground on the American shore at Black Rock.

33 Admiral Sir John Borlase Warren, commander of the British fleet operations along the American coast until the summer of 1814.

To Noah Webster

Sir Washington 16h. Jan. 13.

I transmit you a post note for $300 drawn by the Bank of K. payable at the Bank of Pennsya. It was forwarded to me by J. & D. Maccoun. The letter enclosing it contains the following paragraph: "I regret that from the business we have had to attend to we have not yet found time to make out the a/c of Mr. W. This may apologize to you but I fear will not be recd. as such by him. We shall therefore as soon as practicable send the statemt.. This remittance will certainly over pay him considerably." The letter is signed by James Maccoun. Yrs. H. CLAY

ALS. NN-Ford Collection. Addressed to Webster at Amherst, Massachusetts.

Speech Opposing Bill on Compensation for Captures at Sea

[January 18, 1813]

Mr. H. Clay (*Speaker*) spoke in opposition both to the principles and details of the bill. He was disposed to believe the principle unprecedented in any other country; but even if it were not, he thought it ought not to exist in this country. It would have the effect to make it the interest of the captor, unless the vessel should be immediately on the coast, or in the very mouth of our rivers, to destroy the captured vessel. On consulting the underwriters, gentlemen would find the premium required on bringing in a vessel of any description from any considerable distance, would be equal to one half her value; and as proof of it, Mr. Clay instanced the high insurance even from Charleston and New Orleans, along our own coast, to a northern port. The strongest possible temptation would therefore be offered by giving half the value of the destroyed vessel to the captors in case of her destruction. Mr. Clay moved to strike out the first section of the bill.

Washington *National Intelligencer,* January 19, 1813. Published also in *Annals of Cong.,* 12 Cong., 2 Sess., XXV, 850-51. Introduced on December 21, 1812, and committed to Committee of the Whole, the bill provided compensation for officers and crews of United States vessels which, after having captured enemy vessels, should find it necessary to destroy the prizes instead of bringing them to port. After the brief debate in which Clay participated, the bill was recommitted and dropped.

Opposition to Report on Captured Property

[January 21, 1813]

Mr. Clay (*Speaker*) thought with Mr. Bibb that the right had vested in the captors; but it appeared that the Sec'y of the Treasury for the government had interposed a claim to it. Mr. C. then said he was opposed to the report of the Committee of Ways and Means, because he was willing to place the question out of doubt as to the property, to which the captors had in his view a just title.[1]

Washington *National Intelligencer,* January 22, 1813. Published also in *Annals of Cong.,* 12 Cong., 2 Sess., XXV, 862. After considering a petition "praying that certain property on board American ships bound here from England, sent in by privateers, shall be delivered to the captors for their benefit," the Committee on Ways and Means had reported a resolution that no action be taken. Representative William Wyatt Bibb of Georgia favored the report because he believed the courts would decide in favor of the petitioners and therefore no legislation was needed.

1 On the following day the resolution was rejected in favor of a substitute which specified that any claim of the United States to the property in question should "be relinquished for the benefit of the captors." A bill to that effect was presented on February 6 and was passed by the House twelve days before the session ended.

Promissory Note from William Shepard

[January 23, 1813]

On demand I promise to pay to H. Clay or order Two hundred dollars. Witness my hand & seal this 23d. Jan. 1813.

Teste WILLIAM SHEPARD {L.S.}

GEO: M, BIBB

DS, in Clay's hand. Woodford Circuit Court, File 62. Shepard was a resident of Woodford County. In December, 1813, Clay by his attorney, Porter Clay, brought suit to collect on this note. The outcome of the case has not been found.

To John Hart

Dr. John Wash. 24 Jan. 13.

I have recd. your favors of the 10h. & 13th. inst.[1] & thank you for your kind attention to my interests.

Anxious to bring Graysons business to a close, I will accede to the terms proposed, that is will relinquish any interest I may have acquired in the Licks upon the payment or securing to be paid in some short time the several debts due to me and for which I am bound, and you may assure Genl. Breckenridge that such shall be the basis of a Compromise to be completed by you or when I come out.[2] In the mean time it is desirable to receive as much as you can on my account from him which I pray you to do.

Mr. Adams[3] has been slow in sending forward the Yarns, only about 12 thousand weight having been delivered to R. & H.[4] since my arrival, no part to Parrot,[5] and about 10 or 12 thousand weight yet wanting to complete R. & Hs. quantity. I have not yet recd. one cent from them, tho' I still hope to close our business with them before the end of the Session. Our general affairs can be arranged when I go out. Yarns are still looking up.

I look daily for Mr. & Mrs. Brown.[6] Yrs. H. CLAY

ALS. DLC-TJC (DNA, M212, R10). Addressed to Hart at Lexington.
1 Not found. 2 See above, Breckinridge to Clay, November 15, 1812.
3 James Adams. 4 Ringgold and Heath. 5 Richard Parrott.
6 James Brown, appointed a Senator from Louisiana to replace John N. Destréhan (who had resigned), took his seat on February 5.

From Solomon P. Sharp

Dear Sir Bowling green January 27th 1813

according to your request I have obtained from the clerk a statement of the case you wished and here enclose it;[1] The credits show what has been paid; $360. I received and paid over to your Brother P. Clay or your order; part of the balence received by the sheriff he informed me he paid to your brother also, about the same time; how much I do not know.. when I see him I will be able to assertain. The sheriff has indulged the Deft., by the order or direction of your Brother, as he stated, or the money might have been had long since. on the receipt of your letter I have directed the balence to be collected, and expect to have it all settled shortly. We have no Inteligence of any importance more than you see in our prints. Conciderable intrust is excited here on the appointment of the new members of the Cabinet. We have received no certain information who they are yet.

Great hopes are entertained that the increas of our gallent Navy, and the liberal encouragement of the recruiting Servise by inreas [*sic*] of Wages and bounty; will give an aspect to our military affairs; next season much more congenial to the feelings of every true american than they have heretofore worn

To hear from you will ever be pleasing to your friend &c.

SOLOMON P. SHARP

ALS. DLC-TJC (DNA, M212, R12). Addressed to Clay at Washington; postmarked at Bowling Green, Kentucky. Sharp, a native of Virginia, had begun the practice of law in Russellville, Kentucky, in 1809, served several terms in the State legislature, was a member of Congress from March 4, 1813, to March 3, 1817, and filled the post of Attorney General of Kentucky from 1820 to 1824. On November 7, 1825, he was assassinated at his home in Frankfort by Jereboam O. Beauchamp, a young lawyer of Simpson County, Kentucky, whose action purportedly in defense of his wife's honor, a *cause celebre* of Kentucky history, carried political overtones because of Sharp's identification with the New Court Party in that time of heated political controversy.
1 Not found.

To Edward Tiffin

Dr Sir Wash. 6 Feb. 13.

Will you do me the favor as early as convenient to make out and send me the Patents upon the inclosed?[1] Yrs. H. CLAY

ALS. DNA, RG49, Misc. Letters Received, C. Addressed: "Edward Tiffin Esqr. Commr. &c." Endorsed on cover: "Patent issd, Same Day."
1 Enclosure not found.

Motion to Postpone Action on Yazoo Land Claims

[February 15, 1813]

Mr. *Clay* moved that the committee rise and report progress, with a view to lay the subject over for the session, which he supported on the ground that there was not time to discuss the subject fully during the present limited session, without neglecting business of immediate and pressing importance.

Washington *National Intelligencer,* February 16, 1813. Published also in *Annals of Cong.,* 12 Cong., 2 Sess., XXV, 1073; *Niles' Weekly Register,* III (February 20, 1813), 394. A Senate bill to carry into effect a report made to Congress in 1803 relative to the Yazoo land claims had been read and committed on January 20, reported on February 1, and brought up for consideration in Committee of the Whole two weeks later. Clay's motion was approved; and, after the Committee rose, the bill was tabled.

Speech on a Bill to Prohibit Exportation of Certain Articles in Foreign Vessels

[March 2, 1813]

Mr. *Clay* spoke at considerable length in favor of this bill, as forming a complete system, connected with one which passed the house the other day, prohibiting the use of foreign licences on board vessels of the United States—suited to the present relations of the U. States, and to the proper action on the enemy.

Washington *National Intelligencer,* March 3, 1813. Published also in *Annals of Cong.,* 12 Cong., 2 Sess., XXV, 1153. Representative John C. Calhoun from the Committee on Foreign Relations had reported the bill on February 26. After Clay's speech, delivered in Committee of the Whole, the bill passed the House; but in the Senate it was indefinitely postponed.

Resolution of Thanks from the House of Representatives

[March 3, 1813]

Resolved, unanimously, That the thanks of this House be presented to Henry Clay, in testimony of their approbation of his conduct in the discharge of the arduous and important duties assigned him whilst in the Chair.

U. S. H. of Reps., *Journal,* 12 Cong., 2 Sess., VIII, 733. Published also in Washington *National Intelligencer,* March 4, 1813; *Annals of Cong.,* 12 Cong., 2 Sess., XXV, 1167-68. Introduced by Representative Lemuel Sawyer of North Carolina at the close of the session.

Response to Resolution of Thanks

[March 3, 1813]

I thank you, gentlemen, for the testimony you have just so

kindly delivered in approbation of my conduct in the chair. Amidst the momentous subjects of deliberation which undoubtedly distinguished the 12th Congress as the most memorable in the annals of America, it has been a source of animating consolation to me, that I have never failed to experience the liberal support of gentlemen in all quarters of the House. If in the moment of ardent debate, when all have been struggling to maintain the best interests of our beloved country as they have appeared to us respectively, causes of irritation have occurred, let us consign them to oblivion, and let us in the painful seperation which is about to ensue, perhaps for ever, cherish and cultivate a recollection only of the many agreeable hours we have spent together. Allow me, gentlemen, to express the fervent wish that one and all of you may enjoy all possible individual happiness, and that in the return to your several homes you may have pleasant journies.

Washington *National Intelligencer,* March 4, 1813. Published also in *Annals of Cong.,* 12 Cong., 2 Sess., XXV, 1167-68.

From J[ames] G[allatin]

Treasury Department, General Land Office, 6th. March, 1813.

Sir,

By desire of John Graham, Esqr. (department of state) I send herewith a certified copy of a patent, issued 6th. May, 1805, in favor of George Rice,[1] for 300 acres of land, in the United States' military tract, and have the honor to be, &ca. J. G. clerk.

Hon. H. Clay, Lexington, Kentucky.

ALI copy. DNA, RG49, Misc. Letters Sent, vol. 5 (1812-1814), p. 129. Probably from James Gallatin, then a boy of sixteen who had recently left Mt. Airy College to join his father, the Secretary of the Treasury, in Washington. The boy accompanied Albert Gallatin as a private secretary to Russia in May, 1813, and later to Ghent.

1 Probably of Frederick County, Virginia.

To [William Taylor]

Dr Sir Wash. 8h. March 1813.

William Taylor Jr. of Philadelphia[1] having, after compelling me to resort to certain menaces of exposure of his conduct, paid me the $450. intended for you, and which came into his hands through the mistake already noticed to you, I now have the pleasure to remit you an order of the B. of Washington on the Commercial & Farmers' Bank for that sum.

If you will have the goodness to transmit me to Lexington (K) a statement of this business of Kelly's[2] exhibiting the balance to which you are entitled, I will on my return in May have this matter closed, if practicable. Yrs. H. CLAY

ALS. NcD.

1 Possibly the son or grandson of William Taylor, a Philadelphia shipwright about the middle of the eighteenth century.

2 Joseph Kelly.

Receipt from Cornelius and John Comegys

[March 11, 1813]

Recd. 11h. March 1813 of H. Clay One hundred & twenty eight dollars and 15 Cents being the bal. of a debt of Cornelius & John Comegys upon Clarke & Anderson &c. collected by said Clay, deducting costs commissions &c. CORNS & J COMEGYS

DS, in Clay's hand. DLC-TJC, 2d Series, vol. 14.

Account with James Adams

H Clay Esq	Bot. of James Adams	Pittsburg 24th March 1813
1 Boat 51 feet @ 1.75c . .		$ 89.25
Carpenter's Bill for Repairs on do		12 13
		$101.38
Cable — — — — — — — — — — — — —		2 21
		$103-59

[Endorsement][1] Recd. paymt. JAMES ADAMS

D. DLC-TJC (DNA, M212, R15).

1 ES, in Clay's hand.

To Adam Beatty

LIMESTONE, March 31, 1813.

Henry Clay presents his respectful compliments to Mr. Beatty. His solicitude to reach home prevents him from having the pleasure to see Mr. Beatty, whose favors he ought to have acknowledged at the city. With every disposition to serve Colonel C. B.,[1] he regrets his inability to have done so. Under the regular establishment of the military there were no vacancies worthy his notice. Under the act for raising twenty thousand infantry for the term of one year, when Henry Clay left Washington it was understood that but one regiment would be allotted to K., and the field officers of that regiment were determined upon prior to Mr. B.'s application, although not announced. Henry Clay could not interfere with the contemplated arrangement.

Henry Clay paid Mr. Beatty's last year's subscription to the "Intelligencer," and was reimbursed before he left K. What is due he forgot to pay, but will discharge on his return to the city. He can add no news to the public prints.

Colton (ed.), *Private Correspondence of Henry Clay*, 48.
1 Probably Adam Beatty's brother, Cornelius.
2 Washington *National Intelligencer*.

Advertisement of Property for Sale

April, 1813.

THE Subscriber would sell the House and Lot now occupied by W. W. Worsley, Esq. in Lexington;[1] the houses and lots on the same street, occupied by Mr. Owings and Mr. Lowes;[2] and forty odd acres of land near Lexington, late the property of Buckner Thruston, Mann Satterwhite, and Daniel Bradford, Esquires, successively, and now in the possession of the latter.[3] The terms of sale would be easy and accommodating to the purchasers. H. CLAY.

Lexington *Reporter*, April 13, 1813.
1 On Upper Street, purchased by Clay from Benjamin Davis under Deed, below, April 14, 1813.
2 Thomas Deye Owings and Thomas Lowes. This property had been purchased from William M. Nash by Agreement and Deed, above, September 3, 1808.
3 See above, Agreement with Bradford, September 26, 1812.

To Felix Grundy

Dear Sir, Lexington, 7th April, 1813.

I congratulate you upon your safe arrival at home,[1] and hope you found your family well, and your political prospects bright.

Messrs Stanford and Turner[2] are owing me between four and five thousand dollars, which I am very desirous to receive and which the estate of Col. Hart stands in need of. May I ask the favor of you to apply or to cause application to be made to them in my behalf as surviving executor of Col Hart for the debt? I hold their notes (James T. Stanford and A. J. Turner) which I would send enclosed but for the hazard of the mail. Any payment made to you may be considered fully authorized by this letter. Should you receive the debt or any part of it in time for it to be transmitted to me by the first of May (when I purpose setting out for Washington) I will thank you to remit it to me in a post note upon some Eastern or Kentucky Bank; if not you will be pleased to carry it with you to the city. Yours truly, H. CLAY.

P. S. Will you favor me with a letter whatever success may attend the application?

The Hon. Felix Grundy, Nashville Tenn.

American Historical Magazine, V (April, 1900), 132.
1 From Congress.
2 James T. Sandford and Anthony J. Turner, the latter a major of Tennessee militia in the Creek War later that year.

Receipt from John Hart

[April 8, 1813]

Attached to Note, October 5, 1812.

Advertisement of Resort for Sale or Lease

April 9, 1813.

THE OLYMPIAN SPRINGS,[1]

ARE offered for Sale, or to be leased for one or more Years. Immediate possession may be obtained of the property. H. CLAY,
Surviving Executor of Thos. Hart, Senr. deceased.

Lexington *Reporter,* April 10, 1813.
1 Under order by the Fayette Circuit Court in chancery action to discharge the mortgage held by the estate of Colonel Thomas Hart against Cuthbert Banks, the Olympian Springs had been sold at commissioners' auction in September, 1812, and apparently bought in by Clay as executor. Thomas Deye Owings acquired the resort at the close of the War of 1812 and operated it for the next fifteen years.

To [James Taylor]

Ashland 10h Apl. 1813.

I am greatly indebted, my dear Sir, by your obliging favor of the 26h. Ulto.[1] Profiting as you always do by the opportunities which your intercourse with the President & Secretaries affords, its contents were particularly gratifying

Our detachment of 1500 men marched from Lexington &c. on the 31st. March, and is hastening on to the relief of Harrison. Rumors afloat here represent him as besieged, and his situation highly perilous, but I do not think they are in a shape entitling them to credit. Genl. Green Clay commands the detachment, consisting of two regiments commanded by Dudley & Boswell.[2]

There is I find on coming home unfortunately a state of the public mind to be much regretted. There seems to be general dissatisfaction with the conduct of the War, without an accusation agt. any one in particular. These discontents will I fear, unless removed, ultimately concentrate & fall somewhere with a dreadful concussion. I do what I can to allay public feeling, and not being able to defend our Washington friends as fully as I could wish in the past, I point to the future and endeavor to place the hopes and attention of the public there. I pray you, whatever influence you may have, to exert it in realizing these favorable predictions. Of the importance of the command of the Lakes. they were sufficiently aware, but I apprehend there may have been some omissions as to that great point. At Pittsburg I saw a number of artisans who I was told had been there weeks waiting for tools from Philadelphia, or Washington, which could have been as well if not better and cheaper supplied in the borough. The recruiting officers tell me that never until a few days ago did they receive instructions to use the additional bounty. Do suggest these things to the Secretaries of the War & Navy Departments and to them only.

I shall be glad to hear frequently from you. Yr friend

H. Clay

P. S. You may add to Genl. Armstrong[3] that it has been asserted that the moving of our detachment was not warranted by him.

H. C.

ALS. NcU-Southern Historical Collection. Taylor, Quartermaster-General and Paymaster-General attached to General Hull's army, had been captured at Detroit and paroled. He appears to have been in Washington for several months in 1813.

1 Not found.

2 Early in 1813 General Harrison had built Fort Meigs, below the rapids of the Maumee River in Ohio, where he endeavored to form an army. Faced with great difficulties, including expiration of terms of enlistment of his forces, he had appealed to Kentucky for aid. The Kentucky legislature had responded by calling into service 3,000 militia under the command of General Green Clay. The regiments of Colonels William Dudley and William E. Boswell had been ordered to march to Fort Meigs, which was besieged by forces under Tecumseh and General Henry Proctor on April 28. The Kentucky troops reached their objective on May 5, when Dudley and many of his men were killed.

3 John Armstrong had become Secretary of War in January, 1813.

Property Deed from John Hart

[April 13, 1813]

[Indenture by which John Hart for the sum of five shillings, paid and acknowledged, conveys to Clay all interest in a tract in Lexington at the intersection of Main Cross and Second streets, on the southeast side of Main Cross and running with it North 45° East 197½ feet to a stake at the corner of Andrew McCalla's lot, thence with his line South 45° East 134 feet to a stake at the corner of an alley of ten feet, thence with the line of the alley South 45° West 197½ feet to a stake on Second Street, thence with that street North 45° West 134 feet to the beginning—being part of Out Lot no. 4 in the plan of Lexington, which parcel was conveyed to Hart and Clay by deed of September 11, 1812, from Thomas January and wife. Certification of signature acknowledgement before John D. Young, Clerk of Fayette County, April 13, 1813.]

DS, in Clay's hand. DLC-TJC (DNA, M212, R15).

To [John Armstrong]

Dr Sir Lex. (K) 13h. April 1813

In consequence of what passed in your Departmt. with me, Dr. Ridgley,[1] the Contractor for supplying the troops of the U. S. tates [*sic*] the ensuing year, in K., is about to draw for $8000. in advance, to enable him to make those preparations requisite to ensure the certainty of the Supply. Independent of what was stated to me at your office as to the practice of making advances, and as to what would be done, in this particular case, the necessity of public assistance in these large contracts is quite obvious; and I hope therefore he will meet with no disappointment in the payment of his drafts. My sole motive for giving you the trouble of perusing this letter is, that the Dr. is my neighbour & particular friend, and one in whose integrity I have the most unbounded confidence. Yr's H. CLAY

ALS. DNA, RG107, Letters Received, vol. 7, C-99. Endorsed: ". . . Recd.. April 23rd.. 1813."

1 Dr. Frederick Ridgely of Lexington.

From John Evans

Henry Clay Esq Philada. April 13h. 1813

The peculiarly unpleasant & exercising circumstances attending my business with Craig in the Estate at Frankfort[1] will I hope excuse my application to thee as my Attorney at Law on the occasion & that my application may induce thy kind attention thereto. I am lately informed by one of my Attornies Thomas T Barr of date the 21t of March last, just received, of the necessity of an application to Fields in order to have a power of Attorney from them to recover the money or property adjudged in Craigs Estate my name not appearing in the suit against him. He also requests my sending out my Deed for the property, which has already been sent out & recorded and is I suppose in his Fathers or some of the Counsels' hands

Annexed I hand Copies of several letters—first a Letter from John Field to me dated 5 mo (May) 1. 1802—My letter to Thomas Todd Esq, August 12. 1802 & his answer thereto of Novemb. 11. 1802, which give a full statement of facts as relates to this business & by the dates thou may observe it has lain now about Eleven years & of course the length of time creates difficulty—but as it is my property & by Deed acknowledged and Recorded & also publickly known that the Suit is carried on at my expense, I hope there will be sufficient testimony by the Deed & circumstances attending to recover the same and as Judge Todd is acquainted with the circumstances if necessary to apply I expected [*sic*] it can be effected—I am doubtful if I was to apply to John Field, I could not get a power of Attorney & the application to him might affect my title—

There is also another circumstance—since they conveyed the property they have taken the benefit of the Bankrupt Law & though there were assignees appointed, they have never qualified nor acted in the business, and though Strange as it may appear John Field has advertized his agency, under those assignees, & acted in the receipt of money, but never Accounted for one farthing, by a dividend to his Creditors

This Estate being sold previous to their taking the benefit of the Bankrupt L[aw] it could not be returned in the Schedule of their property—this being the state of the business, & the most extraordinary character of Field the Elder I hope my Attorney at Law will endeavour, if possible to have the business so placed as it may be had without applying to Field, as I much doubt if I could get a power of Atty from him, and his Son John is a mere nullity in the business—It may be necessary to inform that the property was Struck off at Auction, to my Attornies for my Account, & I never knew 'till within these few days that there was any difficulty in the Settlement of it—And as thou was so oblidging as to write me a long time ago that it only wanted the Executive part to recover it—the legal part being settled in my favour—[2]

Please to inform me on the occasion, and any attention I shall hold myself bound to satisfy— Am respectfully JOHN EVANS

P. S. I have wrote my Attornies Robert Barr & Thomas Barr a few lines by this conveyance & informed them of my writing thee with copies of them [*sic*] letters which please to hand them for their information. J. EVANS

LS. DLC-TJC (DNA, M212, R12).
[1] In 1794 Joseph Craig, of Frankfort (brother of John, Lewis, and Elijah, and father of Thomas), had conveyed to John Field and Son, of Philadelphia, certain Frankfort property which, in 1802, had been transferred to Evans by the Fields.
[2] Letter not found.

Property Deed from Benjamin Davis

[April 14, 1813]

[Indenture by which Benjamin Davis for the sum of $1000, paid and acknowledged, sells to Henry Clay a lot in Lexington fronting on Upper Street 66 feet, thence at right angles southeast between the lots of Simon Hickey and James Brown ten poles to the lot lately occupied by (name missing) and James Wilson's lot, the property here conveyed having been transferred to Moses Bledsoe[1] by the heirs of Hugh McDermid, together with a small farm house built by George N. Camper,[2] and from Bledsoe and his wife to Ann Barker[3] by deed of October 10, 1804, recorded in Fayette County, and from Mrs. Barker to Davis by two deeds, dated October 25, 1804, and May 29, 1807, also recorded in Fayette County[4] —together with all appurtenances. General warranty of title. Davis' signature acknowledged before John D. Young, Clerk, April 30, 1813.]

Fayette County Court, Deed Book G, 407-408. Davis, a carpenter and a veteran of the Lexington Light Infantry campaigns of the preceding winter, kept tavern for a year or two in Butler County, Kentucky, following the war, then returned to Lexington as a retailer of liquors.

1 Pioneer Baptist minister who had settled in Montgomery County, possibly the uncle of Jesse Bledsoe.

2 Not identified.

3 A widow who, with her small family, lived in Lexington.

4 Fayette Circuit Court, Deed Book B, 33-34, 59-60; C, 278-79.

Bill of Sale for Slave, from William Satterwhite

[April 15, 1813]

I have this 15h. day of April 1813 bargained Sold and delivered unto Henry Clay one negro slave named George,[1] whom I do hereby warrant to be sound and free from disease, and the title to whom I do hereby warrant & defend to the said Clay his heirs and assigns forever. Witness my Seal the day and year first mentd.

Teste WM SATTERWHITE {L.S.}

HUGH CARLAN[2]

DS, in Clay's hand. DLC-TJC (DNA, M212, R15).

1 The slave was apparently already in Clay's possession. See above, p. 706.

2 Of Lexington.

Settlement with William Satterwhite

[April 15, 1813]

Attached to Agreement, October 10, 1811.

Rental Agreement with William Satterwhite

[April 15, 1813]

H Clay and William Satterwhite agree as follows:

The said Clay agrees to rent the said Satterwhite for the term of one year commencing this day the small house now occupied by his family, being part and parcel of the Establishment called the Kentucky Hotel in Lexington, and including the Kitchen immediately back and adjoining the said small house and the smoak house, and exclusive of all other parts of the said establishment.

For the above property the said Satterwhite covenants & agrees to pay the said Clay three hundred dollars payable quarter yearly.

The said Satterwhite further covenants so to use the said property as not to interfere with the residue of the said Establishment of the K. Hotel, and at the end of the term to surrender the demised premises in good tenantable order, natural decay & unavoidable accidents excepted.

It is agreed that the said Clay reserves the right of distress and of re entry &c.

Witness our hands & seals this 15h. April 1813

Teste H. Clay {L.S.}

C" Coyle[1] Wm. Satterwhite {L.S.}

[Endorsements][2]

Recd. of Mr. John Crittendon seventy five Dollars the 2d. quarters rent above for the year 1813.[3] 1st. Janry 1814

For H. Clay. John Watkins

[Verso]

Recd. Forty three Dollars thirty seven and one half Cents in part of the third quarter Recd.

Recd. sixty four Dollars seventy five Cents in part of the 4th. quarters rent. For H. Clay John Watkins

ADS, signed also by Satterwhite. Fayette Circuit Court, File 823. At this point the property which Satterwhite had operated as a single establishment under the Agreement of October 10, 1811, was subdivided, Satterwhite briefly retaining the westernmost unit. The remainder was rented to Garrett, Payne and Underwood (by lease of same date) and to McCullough and Foster (April 24, 1813).

1 Cornelius Coyle.

2 AES by John Watkins.

3 John Crittenden (not John J. Crittenden's father, who had died in 1806) for a time offered for sale in this house an assortment of general merchandise.

Rental Agreement with Thomas J. Garrett, Jimmy Payne, and Richard Underwood

[April 15, 1813]

An agreement Between Henry Clay and Thomas J. Garrett Jimmy Payne and Richard Underwood.

The said Clay agrees to rent to the said Garrett, Payne and Underwood the Stables attached to the establishment called the Kentucky Hotel in Lexington and also the small house called the Billiard house,[1] for the term of four years commencing this day.

The said Clay further agrees that they shall have the use of the pump for the Stables, in common with other tenants of the said property called the Kentucky Hotel.

In consideration of the above demised premises the said Garrett, Payne and Underwood agree to pay the said Clay five hundred dollars per annum for the use of the premises, payable quarter yearly, in part pay of which the said Clay agrees to receive the grey horse of the said Payne now at Ba[n]ton's[2] at two hundred [. . . .][3] seals this 15h. day of Ap[ril 1813.]

H. CLAY {L.S.}
Teste THOS. J. GARRETT {L.S.}
THA [. . .] [JI]MMY PAYNE {L.S.}
[. . .] UNDERWOOD {L.S.}

[Endorsements][4]
Recd. of [. . . do]llars the amount in full [. . .] Novr. 30th. 1813
For H. Clay JOHN WATKINS
[. . .] rent. For H. Clay JOHN WATKINS
[Verso]
Recd. Fifty Dollars in part of the 4th. quarters rent.
For H. Clay JOHN WATKINS
Recd. the ballance in full of the 4th. quarter
Recd. the 1st. quarter of the second year.
Recd. the 2d. quarter of the 2d. year
Recd. the 3d. quarters Rent of the 2d. yr.

ADS, signed also by Garrett, Payne, and Underwood. KyLxT.
1 This was the central section of the establishment as it had been operated by William Satterwhite.
2 William T. Banton.
3 MS. incomplete; one sixth of page missing.
4 The first three, AES; the remainder, AE, by John Watkins.

Receipt from Thomas Todd

21 April. 1813.

Recd. of H. Clay Thirty dollars recd. by him from Government for John Brown,[1] a Pensioner of the U. States. THOMAS TODD.

DS, in Clay's hand. DLC-TJC, 2d Series, vol. 14.
1 A resident of Kentucky who had held the rank of sergeant in the Revolutionary forces; not the former Kentucky Senator.

Rental Agreement with Lawson McCullough and Hugh Foster

[April 24, 1813]

An agreement between Lawson McCullough and Hugh Foster under the firm of McCullough and Foster of the one part and H Clay of the other

The said Clay doth hereby agree to rent to the said McCullough and Foster that portion of the establishment called the Kentucky Hotel in the town of Lexington which Consists of what was lately used as a dining room and the rooms above, being the house adjoining Majr. Morrison, and which was built by Robert Bradley,[1] for and during the term of four years, the term to commence as soon as certain repairs which McGowan and Bull[2] are now making are so completed that the said McCullough & Foster can occupy the same, and of which the said Megowan and Bull will notify them.

In consideration whereof the said McCullough & Foster agree to pay the said Clay five hundred dollars per annum, for and during every year of the term aforesaid, to be paid quarter yearly.

And the said McCullough and Foster agree to surrender the premises at the end of the term in as good order as they receive them natural decay, and inevitable accidents excepted.

It is understood and agreed that the said Clay reserves the right of distress.

Witness our seals this 24h. April 1813.

L MCCULLOUGH {L.S.}
HUGH FOSTER {L.S.}
H. CLAY {L.S.}

Teste
JOB MESSICK[3]

[Endorsements on verso][4]

It is agreed that the period when the term within mentioned commenced was the 7h. June 1813. Witness our seals this 17h Sept. 1813.

MCCULLOUGH & FOSTER {L.S.}
H. CLAY {L.S.}

Teste DAVID MEGOWAN

Recd. the first quarter's rent of the first year. H CLAY

Recd. the Second quarters rent of the 1st. year. For H. Clay.
Dr. 7th. 1813 JOHN WATKINS

Recd. the third quarters rent of the 1st. y[ear.] JOHN WATKINS
For H. Clay

Recd. the last quarter of the 1st. year–June 7th. 1814.

Red. the 1st. quarters Rent of the 2d year. For H. Clay
JOHN WATKI[NS]

Recd. the 2d. quarter's Rent

ADS, signed also by McCullough and Foster, Lexington tailors. DLC-TJC (DNA, M212, R15).

1 This was the easternmost section of the hotel as it had been operated by William Satterwhite.

2 David Megowan and John P. Bull, Lexington carpenters.

3 A young resident of Lexington.

4 All AES (the first signed also by McCullough and Foster), except the last, AE, by Watkins.

From Nathaniel Hart

Dear Sir Spring Hill April 25th 1813

In the course of the fall of last year Albert Gallatin Esq Secry of the Treasury of the United States made proposals to the President and Directors of the Bank of Ky to pay over to them (or such agent as they should appoint,) $200,000 in Specie either in the City of Baltimore or Philadelphia, for which he would allow the company expences of transportation, or 2 Pr. Ct. on the amount, which was intended to cover all expences and the risque, The Board of Directors concluded to take it upon the latter proposals, and immediately employed me to go in and take charge of it. I arrived at the City of Washington on the 29th October, and was informed by Mr. Gallatin that in consequence of the urgent necessities of the Government, he had paid the money over to the Secry at War, who had taken steps to forward it on, and that it had left Philad, on the 23d, October.

Mr. Gallatin informed me that the Bank of Kentucky should be indemnifyed for their expences and trouble in sending in, and proposed to me to delay 8 or 10 days and then proceed on to Philad, & take charge of $300,000 in Treasury Notes which he proposed sending out to the State of Ohio & Kentucky, and that the Government would compensate me for my expenses and trouble.

I complyed with his request, went on to Philad, took charge of the Notes and delivered them to the Cashiers of the Bank at Chilacotha and Frankfort as directed, and forwarded duplicate rects to Mr. Gallatin. The Bank of Kentucky was to give me $500 for the trip and pay my expences, which amounted to $150, I have felt unwilling to receive any compensation from the Bank of Kentucky, as they were not chargable with the disappointment.

Will You be pleased to lay this claim before the Secry of the Treasury of the U, States with a request that he will make me such compensation for my expences and trouble as shall appear reasonable,

And in so doing You will oblige Your Humble Servant

The Honbl Henry Clay Esq. NATHL. HART

ALS. KyBgW-Kentucky Library. Hart, owner of the estate called "Spring Hill," near Versailles, Kentucky, was the eldest son of Captain Nathaniel Hart of the Transylvania Company and a cousin of Mrs. Henry Clay.

Order on Thomas Bodley

To Majr. Tho. Bodley— 26 April 1813

Ten days after sight be pleased to pay James Fisher[1] or order in horses One hundred dollars on account of your note to me for horses. for value received & oblige Yrs. H. CLAY

ADS. KyLoF. Endorsed on verso: ". . . Paid Majr Fisher by W. Banton 100$ on this Ord T Bodley."

1 A veteran of the Revolution and a pioneer settler in Kentucky, Fisher lived in the northern part of Fayette County.

From Abraham Buford

Sir April 26h 1813

Having understood that you have some money for me If so please to pay Mr John Jouit[1] three hundred dollars for which he Mr Jouit will be accountable to me A. BUFORD

[Endorsement][2]

Recd. payment. 27 April 1813. JOHN JOUITT

ALS. KyLxT. Addressed to Clay at Washington.

1 Revolutionary War veteran from Virginia, member of the Kentucky legislature from Mercer County in 1792, from Woodford County, 1795-1797; afterward a resident of Bath County. Matthew Jouett, the artist, was his son.

2 ES, in Clay's hand.

Agreement with John Fisher

[April 28, 1813]

An agreement between John Fisher and H. Clay.

The said Fisher agrees to build for the said Clay at Ashland the brick part of a wing to his dwelling house, according to a plan of Mr. Latrobe which has been shewn to him.[1] For the brick and laying of them when counted in the house (openings excluded) the said Clay is to pay the said Fisher at the rate of eight dollars and a quarter per thousand for the brick actually laid; but the said Clay is at liberty to haul or procure to be hauled any portion of the brick from the Yard of the said Fisher, and for all such is to be allowed Seventy five Cents per thousand. All the exterior of the building is to be finished with Sand brick, and the said Clay is to pay two dollars extra[2] per thousand for all the Sand brick, except those used on the front next to Boone's road. The said Fisher is to be allowed one dollar for all double and ½ dollar for all single arches over the windows &c. The said Fisher is to procure the Stone and have the foundation of the building laid at two dollars per perch estimated in the building.[3] The said Fisher covenants that the whole work shall be done in a workmanlike manner, and that he will pay as agreed damages one hundred and fifty dollars for every fire place that may smoak. The said Fisher covenants that the above work shall be executed in all the month of June next.

The said Clay has paid the said Fisher three hundred and forty five dollars and eighty nine Cents on account of the above: He is further to pay two hundred dollars in horses next fall, and the residue in money, one hundred and fifty dollars when the foundation is completed, and the balance upon the finishing of the work.

The said Clay agrees to board the hands of the Fisher [*sic*] that is to give them two meals a day, without lodging, of plain substantial dieting, whilst they are at work at Seven shillings and six pence per hand, the amt. to be deducted from the two hundred dollars above-mentioned which the said Clay is to pay in horses

Witness our hands & Seals this 28th. April 1813.

Teste (being interlined in two places) H. CLAY {L.S.}
JOHN P BULL JOHN FISHER {L.S.}

ADS, signed also by Fisher. DLC-TJC (DNA, M212, R15). See above, Contract with Fisher, January 22, 1805.

1 Cf. below, Latrobe to Clay, August 15, September 5, 1813. For plan, see Hamlin, *Latrobe*, 382.

2 This word interlined.

3 Last nine words interlined.

Property Deed to Robert Holmes

[April 30, 1813]

[Indenture by which Henry Clay as executor of Thomas Hart, deceased, for the sum of $1000, current money of Kentucky, paid and acknowledged, sells Robert Holmes a tract in Lexington, two and a half acres, more or less, bounded beginning at the corner of Main Cross and Third streets, running with the former North 45° East 22½ poles to Robert Grinstead's lot this day conveyed by Clay, thence with Grinstead's line North 45° West 17½ poles, more or less, to Out Lot no. 37, thence with the latter South 45° West 22½ poles, more or less, to Third Street, thence with that street to the beginning, being one half of Out Lot no. 36, together with appurtenances. General warranty of title. Clay's signature acknowledged before John D. Young, Clerk, April 30, 1813.]

Fayette County Court, Deed Book G, 411.

Property Deed to Robert Grinstead

[April 30, 1813]

[Indenture by which Henry Clay as executor of Thomas Hart, deceased, for the sum of $1000, current money of Kentucky, paid and acknowledged, conveys to Robert Grinstead a tract in Lexington, two and a half acres, more or less, bounded beginning on Main Cross Street at the corner of a lot this day conveyed by Clay to Robert Holmes, thence with the street North 45° East 22½ poles, more or less, to Fourth Street, along the latter North 45° West 17½ poles, more or less, to Out Lot no. 37, thence South 45° West 22½ poles, more or less, to the corner of Holmes' lot, and along Holmes' line to the beginning, being one half of Out Lot no. 36, together with all appurtenances. General warranty of title. Clay's signature acknowledged before John D. Young, Clerk, April 30, 1813.]

Fayette County Court, Deed Book G, 412.

Property Deed from Adam and Martha Rankin

[April 30, 1813]

[Indenture by which Adam Rankin and Martha, his wife, of Fayette County for one dollar current money of Kentucky, paid and acknowledged, convey to Clay a tract on Mulberry, or Limestone, Street, part of Out Lot no. 32, granted to Rankin by the Trustees of Lexington, beginning at the upper corner of a lot sold to Linden Comstock[1] by Rankin under deed of September 14, 1808, thence running with Limestone Street 86½ feet, more or less, to an alley or street intended to be laid off in the center of the Out Lot 20 feet in width and at right angles to the aforementioned street, thence with the alley North 45° West 144 feet, more or less, to an alley in the middle of the Out Lot and parallel with Limestone, thence with the latter alley 86½ feet, more or less, to the corner of the Comstock lot, along this line South 45° East to the beginning—together with premises appurtenant. Title warranted only against claimants through Rankin. Adam Rankin's signature certified on April 30, 1813, his wife's, on September 3, 1813, before John D. Young, Clerk of Fayette County.]

Fayette County Court, Deed Book G, 593-94. Rankin had come to Lexington in 1784 as pastor of the community's first church, organized by the Presbyterians earlier in that year.

1 A manufacturer and, during the winter of 1812-1813, a lieutenant in the Lexington Light Infantry.

Receipted Account, as Executor of Thomas Hart, Sr.

[*ca.* May, 1813]

H. Clay, Ex'r. of Thomas Hart dec. To W. W. Worsley — Dr.

1812.		
Septr.	To advertising Olympian Springs in the Reporter[1] 3 times 2 squares	$ 2.00
Decr.	To publishing in the Reporter, an order of Fayette Circuit Court, "Exr. of Thos. Hart dec. *vs.* John Hart's heirs & als"[2]	2.50
1813.		
May.	To advertising Olympian Springs 8 times	2.25.
		$ 6.75

(Duplicate)

Recd. payment of H. Clay

THO. SMITH
(last charge not paid) For W. W. Worsley

ADS. DLC-TJC (DNA, M212, R15).
[1] In connection with the commissioners' sale, cited above, Advertisement, April 9, 1813, note.
[2] As Hart's executor, Clay had brought the suit at the September Term, 1812. Court order had then required the appearance of the out-of-state defendants the following January. Fayette Circuit Court, Order Book K, 274, 278; Lexington *Reporter,* October 10, 1812.

Account with William T. Banton

[May 4, 1813]

1812	Mr Henry Clay To Wm. T Banton Dr	
August 13	To 43 nights Stabling at 25 Cts P night	$ 10..75
Sept 1	To 20 nights Stabling @ 25 Cts P night	5..00
	To 4 Dollars for backing of too colts & driving a brown horse to carrage	4..00
	To keeping a gray horse one night that Willis Bush[1] rode from Frankford	37½
1813		$ 20 .12½
May 4	To Season of five mares to North Starr[2] at 12 P mare — — — — —	60
		$ 80 .12½

D. DLC-TJC (DNA, M212, R15). [1] Not identified.
[2] North Star, an imported stallion, stood at Banton's stables in the spring of 1813.

Agreement with Robert Grinstead and Allen Davis

[May 4, 1813]

An agreement between Robert Grinstead & Allen Davis of the one part & H. Clay of the other.

The said Grinstead and Davis covenant with the said Clay to do brick work for him in a house or houses which he intends building in Lexington to the amount of eight hundred dollars, at the customary prices; to cause to be done for him Carpenters work to the amount of twelve hundred dollars; to furnish for such house or houses Scantling and plank to the amount of four hundred dollars; nails locks hinges and other English materials to the amount of two hundred dollars; & in plaistering three hundred dollars, all the above articles & work of a good quality and in a workmanlike manner: And the aforesaid work of every kind to be done & the articles to be furnished by September 1814. They also covenant to furnish Stone and do paving therewith to the amount of one hundred dollars, in the course of the present summer.

The said Clay covenants to pay the said Grinstead & Davis the aforesaid Several sums amounting together to three thousand dollars in the following manner: Six hundred dollars in the said Grinstead & Davis' bond,[1] which he has this day given up to them: Five hundred dollars in John Dillon's[2] note which he has this day assigned to them; five hundred and Twenty dollars in the following horses, the Lucretia[3] mare and Colt, a grey horse, and a Mendoza[4] filly, which the said Clay has this day delivered to them, but which he permits to remain on his farm at their risk for three or four weeks; in Bail rope at five Cents P lb. to the amt. of three hundred and eighty dollars; in geldings at valuation next fall to the amount of five hundred dollars; and the balance of five hundred dollars upon the completion of the work aforesaid.

Witness our Seals this 4h. May 1813.

ROBERT GRINSTEAD {L.S.}
Teste ALLEN DAVIS {L.S.}
JAMES GENN [*sic*][5] H. CLAY {L.S.}

ADS, by Clay, signed also by Grinstead and Davis. Fayette Circuit Court, File 412 (1818). Endorsed on verso by Clay: "Delivered 11 Oct. 1813 by valuation of W. R. Morton and Majr. Quarles $755 on a/c of the within." The reference is probably to Roger Quarles. In 1818 Clay brought two suits for covenant broken relating to this agreement and another, below, September 17, 1813. On the first contract Clay was awarded $1600 and on the second, $1500. *Ibid.*

1 Not found. 2 Lexington shoemaker. The note has not been found.
3 Not identified. 4 An imported English stallion, foaled in 1778.
5 James Glenn.

Agreement with John Keiser

[May 4, 1813]

An agreement entered into this 4h. day of May 1813. Between John Keizer and Henry Clay.

The said Keizer covenants and agrees to sell the lot which he at present occupies in the town of Lexington, including the Brick house adjoining William Ross, the corner house used as a tavern, the new house which the said Keizer is building and all other houses and appurtenances on the said lot which fronts Short street about sixty-six feet and two thirds and adjoins the lot of the said Ross back to a street or Ally and including the Stable of the said Keizer thence along the said Street or Ally to Market street and with the same to Short street.[1]

The said Keizer covenants to make the said Clay a deed for the above property, free from incumbrance, with general warranty on demand.

The said Keizer further covenants to have completely finished plaistered and glaized the new house he is now building as soon as may be, of which the said Clay is to have possession as soon as finished.

The said Keizer covenants to deliver possession of all the above described property on or before the first day of October next.

In consideration whereof the said Clay sells & agrees to convey by deed free from incumbrance the two houses he purchased of Nash occupied at present by Owings and Lowes.[2]

He also agrees to convey to the said Keizer the lot he purchased of Ben. Davis adjoining the aforesaid houses purchased of Nash, which the said Keizer takes subject to an incumbrance of Mrs. Barker.

He also further agrees to convey the forty three acres or thereabouts of land purchased by him of Daniel Bradford, on which Buckner Thruston formerly resided.

He further agrees to convey to the said Keizer all that part of a lot lying on Main Cross Street purchased by said Clay and John Hart of Thomas January which was not sold to John D. Dillon.[3]

The said Clay is to make to the said Keizer deeds with general warranty for the aforesaid property on demand, except the land purchased of Bradford, for which he will make a similar deed as soon as he procures the title.

He is to deliver possession to the said Keizer of all the aforesaid property on or before the first day of October next, except the land, of which he is to deliver the possession on Christmas next.

He is finally to pay to the said Keizer on demand three thousand dollars.

Witness our Seals this 4h. May 1813.

Sealed & Delivered — JOHN KEISER {L.S.}
In presence of — H CLAY {L.S.}
ALLEN DAVIS
ROBERT BYWATERS

[Endorsement on verso][4]

Recd. 4h. May 1813 the three thousand dollars within mentd. in two Checks on the Branch Bank and Insurance Company.

JOHN KEISER

ADS, signed also by Keiser. DLC-TJC (DNA, M212, R15). Keiser's copy of the document (KyLxT) was assigned, August 10, 1815, by Keiser to Benjamin Stout and on July 5, 1820, by Stout to Dr. Frederick Ridgely.

1 This property was located on the northwest corner of Short and Market Streets.

2 This and the two following properties had been advertised for sale by Clay, above, p. 781.

3 See above, deeds from the Januarys to Hart and Clay, September 11, 1812, and from Hart to Clay, April 13, 1813. No deed to Dillon recorded.

4 ES, in Clay's hand.

Agreement with John Keiser

Memo. [May 5, 1813]

H. Clay has become my Security in five Notes for five hundred dollars each to John D. Young. They are given for a lot in Lexington the title to which is to pass through said Clay on payment of what is due to them.[1] I agree that the said Clay shall hold the title and also the title upon 43 Acres of land he has sold me near Lexington purchased of Daniel Bradford as an indemnity for his suretyship Witness my seal this 5 May 1813. JOHN KEISER

Teste (interlined)
FRS. MCCONNELL[2]

DS, in Clay's hand. KyLxT. Cf. above, Agreement with Keiser, May 4, 1813.
1 Last eight words interlined.
2 Francis McConnell of Fayette County, son of Kentucky pioneer James McConnell.

Power of Attorney to John Hart

[May 5, 1813]

Whereas I did in conjunction with David Trimble purchase all the interest of A. W. Grayson in the Sandy Salt Works and Land & appurtenances, at a Sheriffs Sale,[1] made in virtue of sundry executions which issued from Fayette; which I have agreed to relinquish to the Trustees of the said Grayson upon certain terms and conditions, among which was the payment on the part of said Trustees of a debt due from the said Grayson to Smith & Vonphul,[2] and which was assigned to Geo. Caldwell:[3] Now upon payment being made by them of [*sic*] or security given to the satisfaction of the representatives of the said Caldwell for the said debt, I do hereby authorize and empower John Hart as my attorney to convey to the Trustees of the said A. W. Grayson or to any person they may direct all interest acquired by me in the property afd. under the said Sheriffs Sale; or, if the Sheriff has not yet conveyed to the said Trimble & myself I empower my attorney to give directions to him to whom to convey, agreeably to the request of the said Trustees.

In testimony whereof I do herewith set my hand & seal this 5h. day of May 1813 H. CLAY {L.S.}

ADS. Fayette Circuit Court, File 488 (1820).
1 See above, Trimble to Clay, March 12, 1812.
2 William Smith, Lexington hatter, and Henry Von Phul, a Philadelphian who around 1801 had come to Lexington and found employment as clerk for John Jordan, Jr., and, later, for Thomas Hart, Jr. In 1810 or 1811 Smith and Von Phul had become partners in a mercantile business which they shortly afterward had moved to St. Louis.
3 Resident of the southern district of Fayette County.

Property Deed to Trustees of Alfred W. Grayson

[May 7, 1813]

[Whereas Alfred W. Grayson having been indebted to Clay for

about $1600, and Clay having been answerable to several persons for large sums due them by Grayson, and whereas on judgments obtained for these debts *Fiere Facias* were levied on Grayson's interest in the salt works on Sandy River, which were sold by authority thereof and purchased partly for Clay's benefit for the purpose of satisfying the debt due him and of protecting him against loss as Grayson's security—now in consideration that Robert Breckinridge, Frederick W. S. Grayson,[1] and Joseph Cabell Breckinridge,[2] trustees of Alfred W. Grayson, have paid or secured to be paid to Clay the debt due him, with all costs, and to others all sums due by Grayson for which Clay was responsible, Clay relinquishes to Grayson's trustees all right to the Sandy Salt Works. Title is warranted against claims through Clay, but against no others—"nor is the Said Henry Clay to be answerable for any Consequences Except as to those claiming under him." Signed by John Hart, attorney in fact for Clay. Recorded in the office of the Fayette County Clerk, May 31, 1813.]

Fayette County Court, Deed Book G, 468. Erroneously dated in court record as "March." Cf. above, Power of Attorney, May 5, 1813.

1 Of Bullitt County, later a resident of Louisville.

2 Son of John Breckinridge. After a promising career as a lawyer and politician, he died in 1823 at the age of thirty-five.

Receipt from William C. Dunn

18h. May 1813.

Recd. of H. Clay one hundred and thirty six shillings and six pence for two hundred and seventy three pannels of fence repaired by me between H. Clay and Mr. Erwin;[1] and also fifty six shillings for one hundred and twelve pannels of fence repaired by me between Mrs. Morrison and said Clay,[2] being the bal. in full of all accounts.

W C DUNN

DS, in Clay's hand. DLC-TJC (DNA, M212, R15). Dunn lived in the southern district of Fayette County.

1 After his marriage to Jane Todd, Thomas Irwin lived at "Mansfield," her daughter's estate adjoining "Ashland" on the east.

2 James Morrison owned 250 acres adjoining "Ashland" on the southeast.

Acceptance of Speakership of House of Representatives

[May 24, 1813]

GENTLEMEN: In returning to the station in which I am replaced by a continuance of your favor, whilst I am sensible of the honor which I have received, I am sensible also of my inability to fulfil the expectations justly raised by so elevated a distinction; but, gentlemen, the experience I have had, limited as it is, has satisfied me that, in the maintenance of the order of the House, less depends upon the presiding officer than upon the sense of the necessity of decorum being generally diffused throughout the body. Then only will a deliberative assembly be well governed, and its business agreeably transacted, when each member, identifying the reputation of the body to which he belongs in his own, shall make the preservation of its order an affair of personal and individual concern, and shall render to the Chair a candid, liberal, and unbiassed support. Under the hope and persuasion that you participate with me in these sentiments, I shall proceed to administer the duties you have been pleased to assign me.

Annals of Cong., 13 Cong., 1 Sess., XXVI, 106-107.

To Martin D. Hardin

Dr Sir Wash. 26h. May 1813.

Mr. Grundy[1] paid me $110 which you were good enough to forward by him on a/c. of Pollard's draft.[2] The balance, together with the amount of Hanna's[3] note, which I will thank you to get discounted, you will deposit, after deducting your Commission, in the Bank and send me on a certificate of its being there deposited to my credit.

It appears that we have been destined to experience another severe loss in Genl. Clay's detachment.[4] I am not in possession of facts to determine to whom the misfortune is attributable. My present impressions are unfavorable to Harrison.[5] But justice requires that we shd. not hastily decide.

The president's message is a plain temperate and sensible paper.[6] It does not add however to the stock of information previously possessed by the public except in one particular, and that is, our commissioners are sent to Russia upon the presumption only that the enemy will accede to the mediation.[7] Yrs. H. CLAY

ALS. ICHi. Addressed to Hardin at Frankfort.

1 Felix Grundy.

2 Joseph Pollard, Jr.

3 Probably John H. Hanna.

4 See above, Clay to Taylor, April 10, 1813, note.

5 General William Henry Harrison.

6 Delivered May 25, 1813.

7 The Russian Minister in Washington had communicated to President Madison on March 8, 1813, an offer of the Czar to mediate for peace between the United States and Great Britain. Without waiting to learn of the British response, Madison had accepted and sent Secretary of the Treasury Albert Gallatin and Senator James A. Bayard of Delaware to join John Quincy Adams, American Minister to Russia, in negotiations for peace.

Remarks and Resolution Relating to Presidential Message on Atrocities

[May 26, 1813]

Mr. Clay (Speaker) rose and adverted to that part of the message which alludes to the inhumanity of the enemy, expressed his abhorrence of the enormities committed by them, as well in the massacre of our citizens on the Western frontier, as the conflagration of our little towns on the maritime border. The latter outrage had not been pretended to be denied, but had been *apologised for* (by whom he did not say) on the pretence that our people had first fired on one of their flags.[1] Although he believed the allegation false, he was glad that it was thought necessary to make *any* apology for it. The facts, however, in both cases ought to be enquired into and distinctly ascertained. If found to be as public report had stated them, they called for the indignation of all Christendom, and they ought to be embodied in an authentic document which might perpetuate them on the page of history. These were substantially the remarks, as written from memory with which Mr. Clay prefaced the following resolution:

"*Resolved,* That so much of the Message of the President of the U. States as relates to the spirit and manner in which the war has been waged by the enemy, be referred to a Select Committee."

Washington *National Intelligencer,* May 27, 1813. Published also in *Annals of Cong.,* 13 Cong., 1 Sess., XXVI, 109; *Niles' Weekly Register,* IV (May 29, 1813), p. 214; Lexington *Reporter,* June 12, 1813. In his message to Congress on the previous day President Madison had accused the enemy of adding to the "savage fury" of war on one frontier "a system of plunder and conflagration on the other." Clay's resolution was adopted without opposition.

1 British raiding parties had burned and sacked Havre de Grace, Maryland, on May 3, Fredericktown and Georgetown on Sassafras River on May 5.

To Martin D. Hardin

Dr Sir Washington 28h. May 1813

The Mail brought me to day your favor of the 19h. inst.[1] with William Taylor's[2] draft for $300. on a/c. of the protested bill of Pollard.[3] Yr. friend H. CLAY

ALS. ICHi. Addressed to Hardin at Frankfort.

1 Not found. 2 Of Kentucky. 3 Joseph Pollard, Jr.

Remarks on Seating of Federalist Newspaper Reporter

[May 31, 1813]

Mr. *Clay* (Speaker) after observing that, in his opinion, an importance had been given to this petition which did not well comport with the dignity of the House, stated the ground on which the decision had been made by him of which the petitioner complained; which was simply this: that in consequence of the recent alterations in the House seats had been arranged for but four stenographers—and to those places he had assigned the applicants according to seniority; all of whom having been of longer standing than Mr. R. he had by this arrangement been excluded. If the House should deem it proper to admit others than those now on the floor, he hoped they would designate the stations they should occupy, &c.

Washington *National Intelligencer,* June 1, 1813. Published also in *Annals of Cong.,* 13 Cong., 1 Sess., XXVI, 119. Representative Thomas Peabody Grosvenor of New York had presented a petition for George Richards, a reporter of House proceedings during the previous session for a Federalist journal, who had been denied access to the floor of the House during the current session and who now prayed "to be admitted as heretofore for the purpose of reporting debates." The petition brought on a debate which ended on June 3 with a decision to refer the matter to a special committee authorized to recommend changes in House rules concerning stenographers.

From [John Armstrong]

Hon H: Clay. Sir, War Department, June 9th. 1813.

Your Letter of May 25th. has been received.[1] The vast issues of Arms which have been made to the Volunteers & militia of the Western Country since the declaration of War, render it impracticable to furnish the Company of Cap: McCulla.[2] Whenever Arms are furnished to the militia in future, it must be under the provisions of the Act for arming the whole body of the militia of the United States. In that act no provision is made for supplying ordnance.—

Transfers of Officers from one Corps to another in the service of the United States, cannot be made in ordinary cases without the consent of the parties, and when the transfer would not prejudice the rights of other Officers.—I suggested that an exchange of Service might be made between Hopkins & Cummings,[3] if agreeable to the latter—the transfer to be temporary.—

Copy. DNA, RG107, Military Books, vol. 6, pp. 451-52. [1] Not found.

[2] A volunteer artillery company organized by Captain (later, General) John M. McCalla of Lexington, who had served as sergeant-major in Captain Nathaniel G. S. Hart's company earlier in the war. Afterwards, McCalla practiced law in Lexington, Kentucky, and Washington, D. C.

[3] Captain Samuel Goode Hopkins, of the United States Light Dragoons, and Captain Alexander Cummings, of the Pennsylvania Light Dragoons.

To Martin D. Hardin

Dr Sir Wash. 10h. June 1813.

The bills which you did me the favor to inclose in your letter of the 26h. Ulto.[1] for the balance of what you collected from Merewether[2] arrived in safety.

The British posts from Fort George to Fort Erie inclusive are in our possession.[3] But we have a mortifying offset in the Capture of the Chesapeake by the British frigate Shannon off Boston—an event about which, altho' there is not complete information, I entertain no doubt.[4] Yrs. H. CLAY

ALS. ICHi. Addressed to Hardin at Frankfort.

1 Not found. 2 William Meriwether.

3 These posts, located between lakes Erie and Ontario, had been taken on May 27 and 28. They were abandoned in the face of an approaching British army in December.

4 The fate of the *Chesapeake,* captured on June 1, was not known with certainty in the United States until more than two weeks after the event.

Promissory Note to John Hart

$450. Lexington, June 10, 1813.

Sixty days after date, for value received, I promise to pay Jno. Hart, or order, four hundred and fifty dollars, without defalcation; negotiable and payable at the Lexington Branch Bank.

H. Clay, by

No 1267 due 12 Augt JNO. HART.

ADS, by Hart. DLC-TJC, 2d Series, vol. 14. Endorsed on verso: ". . .H. Clay's note Pd. & chd. 12 aug 1813." Probably to John Hart, Sr.

To Edward Tiffin

Dr Sir Wash. 16h. June. 13.

Six patents have been issued by the U. S. Government to John Joseph and Richd. Campbell as devisees of Richd. Campbell deced,[1] for 1000 Acres each., A party interested in the enquiry has desired me to ascertain on what authority the patents were issued to those persons? Was there a transcript of the will filed? I will thank you to enable me to comply with his request, and furnish me with a Copy of the instrument on which the office proceeded. Yr's respectfy. H. CLAY

ALS. DNA, RG49, Misc. Letters Received, C. Addressed to Edward Tiffin, "Present." Endorsed: ". . . recd June 16th. 1813 . . . requesting copies of papers in Virga military district—answered June 18th, 1813." Answer not found.

1 A lieutenant colonel of the Virginia Continental line, killed at the Battle of Eutaw Springs, September 8, 1781.

To [William W. Worsley]

Washington City, June 17, 1813.

The Committee of Ways and Means has presented a system of

taxation contemplating the provision of a nett additional revenue of $5,600,000. It does not essentially vary from that which was before the House of Representatives during the session before the last. Of this sum, three millions of dollars are proposed to be raised by a direct tax, of which the quota assigned to Kentucky, according to the principles of the constitution, is $168,928 76. The committee has apportioned each state's quota among the several counties of which it is composed. In Kentucky, the basis of the apportionment has been the state tax paid in each county. The proportion allotted, upon this principle, to the district to which I belong is $22,598 55, of which Fayette is to pay $14,585 28, Jessamine $3,305 97, and Woodford $4,707 30.—The subject is not yet acted upon in the House, but will be in a day or two.[1]

Extract. Lexington *Reporter,* June 26, 1813. Identified as from Clay to the editor.
[1] The figures given here were incorporated in the act, approved August 2, 1813.

Property Deed, Clay and Others to John L. May and Polly Epes

[June 18, 1813]

[Whereas Benjamin Netherland on July 24, 1784, entered into an agreement with John May, deceased, and Joseph Jones,[1] whereby they became entitled to one fourth of all Netherland's right, title, and interest in several tracts of land, land warrants, and locations therein described, among which were several claims mentioned below, and on the same day Netherland assigned his interest in the aforesaid property in accordance with the terms of the agreement; and thereafter on November 9, 1787, Netherland conveyed to May and Jones his right, title, and interest to the whole of the aforesaid lands in trust as stated in the conveyance, empowering them in the first place to reserve for their own benefit one fourth of the several lands and claims, then to sell the residue for payment of Netherland's debts—and in the latter action first to sell so much of the lands as would reimburse a large sum of money paid for Netherland by May, and second, to sell so much as would reimburse May and Jones for their advance to Netherland;

And whereas Netherland subsequently transferred to George Walker and Henry Clay his whole interest in the aforesaid land and claims,[2] but by decree of the United States Circuit Court for the District of Kentucky at the May Term, 1812, in a suit brought by Jones and by John L. May and Polly Epes, the legal representatives of John May, against Netherland, Walker, and Clay[3] the plaintiffs were awarded one fourth part of all right, title, and interest which Netherland had on November 9, 1787, or at the time of the issuance of the decree and also all interest which Walker and Clay had in the aforesaid claims, the conveyances to be made by August 1, 1812—And the decree further requiring execution of all the aforesaid trusts and for that purpose a public sale of three undivided fourth parts of all interest to which Netherland was entitled by law or equity on November 9, 1787, or at the time of issuance of the said decree, which sale was held under commissioners appointed by the court, and John L. May and Polly Epes became the purchasers of three fourths part of the several tracts and claims below described;

And the report of the said commissioners having been confirmed by the court at the November Term, 1812, and it further appearing that Netherland, Clay, and Walker had failed to convey their respective interests in the lands as required, the court proceeded to a final decree and appointed Christopher Greenup, William Trigg, Willis A. Lee,[4] and Jephthah Dudley,[5] commissioners to convey to the above purchasers by deed with special warranty against Netherland and those claiming under him the whole of the lands and claims sold as aforesaid—also to convey to Jones and the devisees of John May by deed with like warranty the one undivided fourth part of all tracts patented in Netherland's name or jointly to him and others, as well as one fourth part of all his right, title, and claim in lands entered or patented in the name or names of others as hereafter described—and also to convey with special warranty against Netherland, Clay, and Walker, and all under them, such lands patented to them as are included in the commissioners' report, with one fourth undivided part to be conveyed to the complainants, Jones and the devisees of John May, and three fourths undivided part to the respective purchasers under the reported commissioners' sale:

Now by this indenture of June 8, 1813, between Netherland, Clay, Walker, and Jones by Greenup and Trigg, two of the commissioners, of the first part—and John L. May and Polly Epes of the second part—and Netherland, Clay, Walker, and the commissioners of the third part, and under the premises aforementioned, Netherland, Clay, Walker, and Jones convey to John L. May and Polly Epes all interest in the three fourths undivided part of the several tracts described, which were devised to the grantors by Netherland:[6]

Netherland, Clay, and Walker also grant to Jones and the devisees of May all interest in the remaining undivided one fourth part of the several tracts above described as well as their one fourth interest in 960 acres patented to Jones and John May by assignees of Netherland on December 2, 1785; one fourth of one half of two tracts of 500 acres each in the name of John Hawkins, one on Treasury Warrant no. 6499 and the other on Treasury Warrant no. 6498; one fourth of 1800 acres an unsurveyed part of an entry of 2400¼ acres in Netherland's name on the Kentucky River opposite Cedar Run; and one fourth of an undivided one half of William Bradshaw's entry for 1668 acres on Treasury Warrant no. 14154,[7] joining John Curd's 5000 acres on the waters of Hickman's Creek.[8]

Special warranty of title. Signatures of Netherland, Walker, Clay, Jones, Trigg, and Greenup witnessed by John Rennick and Giles M. Samuel.[9] Trigg's signature acknowledged before J. McKinley and Benjamin Logan,[10] June 12, 1813; Trigg's and Greenup's, before Achilles Sneed, March 29, 1814.]

Kentucky Court of Appeals, Deed Book P, 367-79.

1 Probably of Shelby County, Kentucky. 2 Not found.

3 Suit not found. John May was the father of John L. May and Polly Epes.

4 At various times clerk of Franklin County and Circuit courts and of the State Senate.

5 Brother of William Dudley. In May, 1813, Jephthah resigned as magistrate of Franklin County, Kentucky, to accept a commission in the 28th Regiment, United States Infantry. He later became a member of the State Senate, 1824-1828, and in 1853, ten years before his death, was the principal property-owner in the city of Frankfort.

6 Eighty-seven tracts, amounting to approximately 50,000 acres, are here delineated.

7 Entered in 1783. Bradshaw also owned land in Clark County.

8 Also entered in 1783. Curd, of Mercer County, owned land near the confluence of the Dix and Kentucky rivers and operated a ferry on the latter stream.

9 Both of Frankfort.

10 Probably John McKinley of Frankfort and Dr. Benjamin Logan (son of General Benjamin Logan) of Shelby County.

From Thomas Hart Benton

My dear Sir, Crawfords. Geo. Town. June 22d. 1813.

I should have call'd to have said farewel to you, but did not know precisely the state of your family.

I am now a soldier for the war, and have an unbounded desire to make some figure in it.[1] My younger brothers[2] have also entered: they will do something, or they will perish.

I am apprehensive this conflict will last several years. The enemy will keep it alive to make it an instrument of dividing the Union, and of pulling down those who are now in power; and the heads of the opposition will secretly encourage its continuance with the last of those same veiws. Shall I give you my opinion? Then press on vigorously. Spare neither men nor money: make the war successful and glorious, and the people will bear with pride the burthens it imposes.

There are many honest Federalists in our state. They will be filled with horror when I tell them what I have seen here; for they have no idea of treason and of civil war. And my testimony will go far, because I have been of that soil, but not of the New England school.

With the sincerest wishes for your welfare.

Hon. H. Clay. THOMAS H. BENTON.

ALS. DLC-HC (DNA, M212, R1). Benton, aide-de-camp to General Andrew Jackson and a colonel of Tennessee volunteers, had been in Washington on official business. While there he obtained a commission as lieutenant colonel of the 39th United States Infantry Regiment, to be recruited in Tennessee.

1 Benton's hope for military glory was not realized. His regiment, not ready for action until 1814, saw limited service.

2 Jesse, Nathaniel, and Samuel Benton.

To [John Armstrong]

Sir Wash. 24h. June 1813.

At the request of Tho. Bodley Esqr., Quarter Master General of the K. Militia, I will thank you to inform me if you recd. his letter of the 20h. of April last, upon the subject of his pay and the liquidation of his accounts. He is very desirous to know how his accounts are to be settled, and if you will favor me with the requisite information it shall be communicated to him. Yrs.

H. CLAY

ALS. DNA, RG107, Letters Received, vol. 7, C-155.

To John Armstrong

Sir Washington 25h. June 1813.

Mr. A. Logan, a respectable Citizen of Kentucky,[1] who will present you this letter, is brought to this place at great personal inconvenience to himself, to ascertain the causes of protest of certain bills of Exchange drawn upon your Department by Mr. Shaumberg,[2] a government agent at N. Orleans, and which were taken by Mr. Logan in a regular course of trade. The unexpected dishonor of these bills has subjected him to great embarrassment, and I have advised him to lay his case at once before you, under a full persuasion that the injustice which he feels to have been done him will be corrected.

You will excuse me for submitting to your consideration a few observations growing out of this case. The supply of money in the Western Country, comprehending N. Orleans, for the public service has been heretofore principally and is now altogether through the medium of bills of exchange. Such have been the effects of the War, and the military operations in that quarter, that altho' good bills prior to its commencement, drawn upon the Eastward, commanded a premium, they are now frequently sold at a discount, and the competition is no longer between the buyers but between the sellers. In other words the demand by the Western Country upon the Atlantic for money is much greater than the demand of the Atlantic upon the Western Country. The course of Exchange is altogether changed and is in favor of the Westward. The consequence has been already stated, bills sell at a discount, and even then the purchasers have great scope of selection. To maintain therefore an equal competition on the part of the Government with individuals their bills must be duly honored. But the traders in this article are not in the habit (indeed they have not the means) of discriminating between the bills drawn by one Quarter Master General or another or by different Government agents. The protest of the bills therefore of one of them brings all into discredit. And I am informed, by a president of one of the Banks in Kentucky, that at this period, & owing to the above cause, whilst the bills of individuals, drawn at 60 days sight, readily command in Lexington cash at a discount of one per cent, Government bills, drawn at five or ten days sight, are with difficulty negociated at two per Cent discount. It is altogether unnecessary with you to dilate upon the injuries to which the public service may be exposed by bringing their bills into disrepute. An enterprize of the first consequence may be defeated, an army starved, or a whole Campaign lost.[3]

The injustice done to the holder of the protested bill deserves also serious consideration. If the agent improperly draws, displace him at once; deprive him of the power in future of injuring individuals. But it is altogether intolerable that they are to suffer, because an accredited agent of the government draws upon an improper fund, or violates a secret instruction, locked up from the eyes of all, except it be him who gives and him whom [*sic*] receives it.

Yr. ob. Servt. H. CLAY

ALS. DNA, RG107, Letters Received, vol. 7, C-182. Addressed to Armstrong.
1 Probably Archibald Logan, Lexington tanner and currier.
2 Colonel Bartholomew Shaumburgh, Deputy Quartermaster General.
3 A similar warning was expressed by Governor Claiborne of Louisiana to President Madison, July 9, 1813. Rowland (ed.), *Letter Books of W. C. C. Claiborne,* VI, 238.

From Martin D. Hardin

The Honble Henry Clay Secys Office—July 6th 1813
Dr Sir,

During the spring of the last year the Indians Commenced Stealing horses on the South Western border of this State and gave such indications of Hostillities that the settlements South of the Cumberland river near its mouth were about breaking up—To afford protection to the inhabitants thus exposed small Guards were Ordered out from the militia of this State by Governor Scott to range out side of the settlement in order to repel any substantial Act of hostillity or to give notice to the settlers if they were likely to be overpowered;—That this measure was then proper can admit of but little doubt, and that it was highly beneficial in giving repose to the Settlers is evident. It had also the effect of keeping off those Straggling Indians who were disposed to involve their Tribes in War with us—The Legislature of this State Sensible of this and finding no provisions made by Congress on the Subject passed a Law at their last Session, making compensation to those who were out at the rate of $8. per month for pay & $5. pr. mo. for rations, they having furnished themselves.[1] A Copy of this law I have the honor of enclosing to you. Under it there has been paid from the Treasury of this State $5047.22 as will appear by the Statement of the Auditor of Public Accounts inclosed.

It must be acknowledged that this sum is larger than it was expected to have been, when the law was passed, it was owing to the guards having been kept out by the Commandants of Regiments longer than was expected, and perhaps in some few instances longer than was necessary.

During the last spring the neighbourhood in those quarters became again alarmed and very generally petitioned for relief and so apprehensive were those a small distance inside of the frontiers that the Outer settlements would break up and leave *them* exposed that they in several instances formed voluntary associations to go out on duty before the measures taken by the Governor[2] for their relief were carried into effect.—He had upon receiving these petitions directed the General and Field Officers in that quarter to convene and after collecting what information could be obtained to order out for thirty days a guard Consisting of not more than two Subalterns and forty privates if they found it necessary—This was accordingly done,—and on the like representations a similar guard was ordered out for thirty days longer, after the expiration of the services of the first—Of these steps the Secretary of War was duly notified.—The term of Service of those last Ordered out has expired and we have reason to believe that there will not be occasion for any others.

I have been instructed by the Governor (who is now absent)[3] to make this Communication to you, and to desire you to bring the subject before Congress,[4]—For it is presumed no doubt can be entertained but that expences of this kind should be paid by the General Government and not by the States.

I beg leave to refer you to my predecessor in Office, Mr. Bledsoe[5] now in the Senate of Congress, for more particular information should it be required as to the measures taken by Governor Scott on this subject.——

The Documents are on the files of this office upon which Governor Scott and Governor Shelby have made their orders—They are voluminous, but if required I will have them copied and forwarded to you. I have the honor &c. M D HARDIN

Copy. KyHi-Isaac Shelby, Letter Book A, 114-17.
1 The act, concerning the militia of Caldwell, Livingston, and Christian counties, had been approved January 4, 1813. 2 Isaac Shelby. 3 On military service.
4 The matter was brought to the attention of the House of Representatives on July 23, 1813, by Samuel McKee, who introduced a resolution instructing the Committee on Military Affairs to inquire into the expediency of refunding to Kentucky the money expended. The resolution, in amended form, was adopted; but the subject was tabled after committee report authorized payment only in cases where militia calls were sanctioned by the President. *Annals of Cong.*, 13 Cong., 2 Sess., XXVI, 797, 816, 980, 1432. 5 Jesse Bledsoe, Secretary of State under Governor Scott.

From Martin D. Hardin

Frankfort Kentucky.
Dr Sir. Secretarys Office July 7th 1813.

I am instructed by the Governor to Communicate to you; and through you to the representatives from this State in Congress, that the militia who served in the north western Army during the last fall and winter, have not yet been paid for the retained Componant Parts of Rations. I need not repeat to you what those men suffered by Privations, The World knows it; They were assured by their General that they should be Speedily Paid.—

An Order was issued by Genl Harrison in February last, directing the mode of liquidating those Accounts, and Authorising the Field Commissary General to make the Payments.—Upon application to him, he says he has not been furnised [*sic*] with the funds by the Secretary at War.—The Governor Cannot Conceive why any difficulty is thrown in the way of Closing this subject and requests your Particular Attention and good Offices in relation to it.

I have the honour to be very respectfully Sir Your mo. Obt.
The Honble Henry Clay M. D. HARDIN
Congress

ALS. DLC-William Henry Harrison Papers (DNA, M212, R21).

From Hugh and William Young

Henry Clay Esqr Baltimore 9 July 1813
Sir

We were last evening favor'd with Yours of 7 Currt[1] covering a Bank Post Note for Seven Hundred Dollars which We have placed to the Credit of Our claim against Messrs. Clark & Anderson

On 14 July 1808 You advised having settled Our claim against Clark & Anderson with Interest to 10 June following & payable on that day by their Note indorsed by Geo Greer for $706 50/100[2] The Bond You afterwads [*sic*] took in exchange payable 1 Octr. 1809 was, We suppose, for about $719 56/100

In Our two last letters to You[3] We mentiond a small balance due Us on the money You collected from Aiken & Eastland We now annex You a Copy of the Accots. You furnishd Us under date of 8 Decr. 1807 & request Your attention to the same. With respect We are Sir Your Obt Sts HU & WM. YOUNG

(Copies)

Dr. Eastland & Aikin in a/c with Hugh & Wm Young

1806		
Augt. 11	To Balance due on Your Notes this day	$706 .44
	To Interest thereon to 11 Novr 1806	10„59
		717„03
	By Cash paid H. Clay as per his receipt	240„
		477„03
	To Interest thereon to 26 Decr 1807	32„19
		$509„22

Dr H. Clay in A/c with Hugh & Wm. Young

To Cash Recd. of Messrs. Eastland & Aikin ------	$749„22	
By Commission at 5 per Ct ------	37„48	
	711„74	
By Cash which it is supposed Mr Kennedy[4] will pay on application ----	250	$461„74

[Endorsed in margin above: "Turn Over."]

of the Balance of $461 74/100 as stated on the other side We recd 11 Octr 1808 from Messrs. Luke Tiernan & Co $394 which with 1½ pr Ct paid by You for Bill is equal to $400. The Money You paid Mr. Kennedy by mistake we did not receive from him untill March 1809

ALS. DLC-TJC (DNA, M212, R12).
1 Not found. 2 Letter not found.
3 Not found. 4 Probably John Kennedy of Kennedy and Cox.

To [John Cleves Short]

Dr Sir Wash. 11h. July 1813.

I have recommended you to both the President and Mr. Monroe for the office of U. S. Atto. in the In. Territory. There has been as yet no decision as to the person who will be appointed. The practice is to file the applications, and when the subject is acted upon to take them into consideration. It will be very gratifying to me if I can be instrumental in promoting your wishes. I apprehend the chief obstacle will be your not residing in the Territory.

Will you excuse me for saying that I think you act unwisely in not settling in K.? I would go at once to Lexington or Frankfort & instead of being dismayed by the competition to be met with there, I would derive from that circumstance fresh motives for exertion. In truth, however, there was never a more fortunate moment, owing to the death and discontinuance in the practice, of many gentlemen of the Bar. You will find in Ohio & Indiana so little incentive, that you will become disgusted with a profession yielding neither honor nor profit.[1] Yrs. H. CLAY.

ALS. DLC-Short Family Papers (DNA, M212, R22). John Cleves, son of Peyton Short, had attended Transylvania University and studied law; in 1814 he married a daughter of General William Henry Harrison.

[1] Failing to obtain the appointment he sought, Short began the practice of law in Cincinnati.

To William Jones

Dr Sir Wash. 12h. July 1813

Mr. McNair[1] of Lexington (K.) who will present you this letter, and to whom I beg leave to introduce you, informs me that he has a quantity of Kentucky yarns lying at Philadelphia of an excellent quality and adapted to the use of the Navy. I have said to him that I was well assured you felt every disposition to give encouragement to the production of native hemp, and that if you wanted yarns of the description of his, you would purchase them. I added that it was probable they might be wanted at Philadelphia or to the North of it for the public service.

Mr. McNair is a neighbour of mine, and one on whose veracity and probity you may safely rely. Yr. ob. Servt. H. CLAY

ALS. DNA, RG45, Misc. Letters Received, 1813, vol. 4, p. 156. Addressed to Jones. Endorsed on cover: ". . . State the substance of this lette[r] to Mr Harrison N A & direct him to have the yarns caref[ully] examined by a competent jud[ge] and inform me of the quality and lowest value—

"They will not answer for th[e] Navy unless they are of the b[est] topt hemp of which qual[ity] he says about 2/3 of his parce[l] consists—"

Jones, a Philadelphia merchant and former Congressman, had succeeded Paul Hamilton as Secretary of the Navy on January 12, 1813, and served until December 2, 1814. He was later (1816-1819) the first president of the second Bank of the United States. George Harrison was Navy Agent at Philadelphia.

[1] Probably Robert H. McNair.

Report to Chancellor of Maryland

Washington City 12 July 1813

To the Honble the Chancellor of Maryland.

The Report of Henry Clay of Kentucky, trustee appointed by

your honor in behalf of the Creditors of Samuel and Robert Purviance, concerning the sale of the lands belonging to the said Purviance's Estate lying in the said State of Kentucky.

That in September 1811 certain Commissioners appointed by the Circuit Court of the U. States for the K. District, attended by your trustee and acting by his advice and directions, proceeded to sell certain parts of the lands conveyed to Samuel Moale by the late Henry Purviance, in mortgage:[1] That on this occasion the said Commissioners made sales to the amount of twenty thousand seven hundred and eighty seven dollars (as by a Certified Copy of their report hereto annexed) from which sum however is to be deducted two thousand three hundred, being the amount of the purchase of two tracts of land stricken off to your trustee for the benefit of the trust, and which he was induced to buy because he believed them to be about to be most unreasonably sacraficed: That making that deduction there will remain eighteen thousand four hundred and eighty seven dollars as the nett amount of the sales, of which sum he has now in money five thousand dollars ready to be applied as your honor may direct: That what remains due of the amt. of said sales is well secured by note, deed of trust &c. and is in a progress of collection: That your trustee intends causing a sale to be made the ensuing fall of the residue of the lands in Kentucky.[2]

Your trustee prays your Honor to direct to whom he shall pay over the said sum of five thousand dollars &c. H: CLAY

ADS draft. DLC-TJC (DNA, M212, R15). Endorsed by Clay on verso: "Rough sketch of Report to Chancellor of Md." See above, Moale to Clay, October 9, 1810; Trustees' Bond, March 9, 1811.

1 Crossed out at this point: "to secure payment of the purchase money which he had agreed to pay for the lands bought by him."

2 See below, Hopkins to Clay, September 25, 1813.

Amendment to Bill on Stamp Tax

[July 14, 1813]

Mr. (Speaker) *Clay* then moved so to amend the bill as to confine the tax on notes, &c. to those negociated at Banks, with a view to except from stamp duties the ordinary country transactions by notes, &c.; which motion Mr. C. supported by a luminous and comprehensive view of the expediency and policy of the course he proposed.

Washington *National Intelligencer,* July 15, 1813. Published also in *Annals of Cong.,* 13 Cong., 1 Sess., XXVI, 441-42. The House, in Committee of the Whole, was engaged in consideration of a "bill laying a duty on bank notes, notes of hand, and foreign bills of exchange of certain descriptions." Clay's motion was approved without a division.

To [William Jones]

Sir Washington 17th. Juy 1813

We beg leave to recommend John Tompkins of Kentucky as a Mid-shipman in the navy of the U. States.[1] Yrs. H. CLAY

J. BLEDSOE

ALS, signed also by Bledsoe. ICHi.

[1] John, son of Gwyn R. Tompkins, died in the naval service.

To John Armstrong

To the Honble Secy. of War. [*ca.* July 20, 1813]

Col. William Lewis of Kentucky is now a prisoner in the hands of the enemy in Canada, having been taken at Winchesters defeat on the 22d. January last. He commanded the 5th. Regiment. He was in the actions both of the 18th. and 22d. January, and to his good conduct chiefly our success on the former of those days was attributable.[1] No man who was out in that unfortunate detachment acquired more reputation than Col. Lewis. And in no commander of a Regiment would the people of Kentucky (and we believe we may add many of those of Ohio) have more confidence. We understand that to the command of one of the two Regiments assigned to Ohio, under the act authorizing 20 additional regiments, no officer has been yet appointed, and that the Regiment is far from being filled. We beg leave respectfully to suggest the expediency of the Exchange of Col. Lewis and his being appointed to the command of that Regiment. We are fully persuaded that the confidence inspired by his name would ensure an immediate completion of the Regiment. Whilst referring to the subject of the unfortunate action of the 22d. Jan., we beg leave to add, that it is extremely desirable that an exchange of the Americans, surrendered on that occasion, should be effected as early as it can possibly be done consistent with the public interest. And we cannot forbear saying that Majr. Madison's[2] distinguished merits and peculiar *situation entitle him to an early notice. Capt. John Hamilton[3] has been recommended also to us as an officer of merit, who ought to be early exchanged.

H. CLAY THOMAS MONTGOMERY
SOLOMON P. SHARP. STEPN. ORMSBY
SAML. HOPKINS. WM. P. DUVAL
SAML, MCKEE J. BLEDSOE
JAMES CLARK GEO: M BIBB[4]

* He is the Auditor of public accounts of Kentucky—a highly important and respectable post, to the duties of which he is obliged to attend by deputy.

ALS, signed also by nine other members of the Kentucky delegation to the Thirteenth Congress. DNA, RG107, Letters Received, vol. 7, C-181. Endorsed: ". . . What of this letter relates to exchanges of prisoners is referred to Gen. Mason for his information & decision. J. Armstrong. This letter to be returned." General John Mason was serving as Commissary General of Prisoners.

1 The Americans had won the first battle at Frenchtown, on the River Raisin, on January 18, but had been soundly defeated four days later. General Winchester also had been among those captured by the British.

2 George Madison.

3 Hamilton had commanded the Sixth Company in Lewis' Regiment.

4 Bledsoe and Bibb were Senators; the others were members of the House of Representatives.

From [John Armstrong]

Hon: Mr. Clay Speaker. War Department
Sir, July 21st. 1813.

I had the honor of receiving the Letter addressed to me by the Senators & Representatives from the State of Kentucky.[1] What of that letter relates to the Exchange of Major Madison & others has been referred to the commissary General of Prisoners, to whom that business has been specially assigned by the President.—

Copy. DNA, RG107, Military Books, vol. 7, p. 17.

1 See above, *ca.* July 20, 1813.

Speech Favoring an Embargo on Exports

[July 21, 1813]

Cited in *Annals of Cong.*, 13 Cong., 1 Sess., XXVI, 500. The speeches of Clay and other participants in the debate were not reported. On the previous day President Madison had recommended to Congress an "effectual prohibition of exports, . . . removable . . . in the event of a cessation of the blockade of our ports." Clay's speech supported a proposal that the House consider the measures suggested by the President. A bill laying an embargo was passed by the House on July 22 but rejected by the Senate.

Deed of Trust from William Shellars and Wife

[July 21, 1813]

[Indenture by which for $1200, paid and acknowledged, William Shellars and Mary, his wife, convey to Clay a lot in Lexington, part of In Lot no. 35, beginning at the corner of Main and Spring streets, running with Main Street South 45° East 40 feet to a lot deeded by Shellars to Lewis Pigg,[1] thence at right angles with Pigg's line South 45° West 133 feet, more or less, to Englehard Yeiser's[2] lot, purchased from Shellars, thence at right angles along Yeiser's line 40 feet to Spring Street, thence with the latter street to the beginning, together with the premises appurtenant—In trust that whereas Daniel Bradford has sold and is bound to convey to Clay 43¼ acres of land, lacking a few poles, according to a survey of Richard Higgins, being that part of a tract of land lying near Lexington on which Buckner Thruston formerly and Bradford lately resided, for a conveyance of which free from incumbrance and with general warranty William Challen stands bound to Bradford, now further to secure to Clay the title for the aforesaid tract, this deed is executed; and when Clay receives his title in accordance with a contract between Challen and Bradford, then Clay is to convey the above-mentioned lot to Challen. Shellars and his wife pledge general warranty of title. Certification of signature acknowledgement before John D. Young, Clerk of Fayette County, July 21, 1813.]

Fayette County Court, Deed Book G, 483. Shellars (or Shellers) formerly a shoemaker on Main Street, Lexington, was now a resident of Georgetown, Kentucky.
1 House joiner on Main Cross Street.
2 Tanner and currier at the corner of Main and Main Cross streets.

To [William Jones]

Dr Sir Wash. 22 July 13

Inclosed is Morrisons bill about which I spoke to you last evening. If convenient, I would be glad that you could send me a check for the amt. in favor of the Mess Gratz's[1] on some Bank in Philadelphia. Yrs. respectfly H. CLAY.

P. S. The bill was sent to the Bank of Columbia solely for collection.

ALS. DNA, RG45, Misc. Letters Received, 1813, vol. 5, p. 26.
1 In 1798 Michael Gratz, prominent Philadelphia merchant, had turned his business over to two of his sons, Simon and Hyman. After expiration of the co-partnership in 1806, the firm had been known as Simon Gratz and Company until 1813, when it became Simon Gratz and Brother (s). Simon and Hyman Gratz had three brothers, Joseph, Jacob, and Benjamin, of whom the last named settled in Lexington, Kentucky, in 1819, where he became prominent in the business and cultural life of the community. His daughter, Anna, became the wife of Thomas Hart Clay, grandson of Henry Clay.

To [John Armstrong]

Sir Wash. 23d. July 1813

Will you do me the favor to inform me if the Non payment for the retained component parts of rations, as mentioned in the inclosed letter,[1] proceeds from any defect in the Law, or in the administration of the Law? If the former, Congress being now in session, a remedy may be applied; if the latter I am sure your sense of the services and sufferings of the Corps in question will not allow you to hesitate for a moment in ordering the proper corrective. Yrs. H. CLAY

ALS. DLC-William Henry Harrison Papers (DNA, M212, R21).
1 See above, Hardin to Clay, July 7, 1813.

To Simon Gratz and Brothers

Gent. H. of R. 24h. July 1813

I recd. two or three days ago your letter[1] covering the protested bill drawn by Majr. Morrison[2] on the Navy Department, and shortly after called upon the Secy. on the subject of it.[3] He stated to me that the reason of the protest was the failure of Majr. M. to exhibit his accounts shewing the necessity of the application of the money to the public service, and for some other reasons not necessary to be detailed. Upon a strong representation which I made to him as to the prejudice likely to be done to the credit of Government bills by its return, and my assurance of the solidity of the drawer, he consented to pay the bill. As it was not endorsed to me but to Mr. Whann,[4] you will perceive from the inclosed letter that the Secy. deems it the proper course to make the payment to him, which I presume will be entirely satisfactory, and which indeed I prefered. The warrant will be handed over to Mr. Whann today.

Yrs. H. CLAY

ALS. PHi. Addressed to Simon Gratz & Brothers.
1 Not found. 2 James Morrison.
3 See above, Clay to Jones, July 22, 1813. 4 William Whann.

From [John Armstrong]

Honle. H: Clay. H of Reps. War Department
Sir, July 29th. 1813.—

I have had the honor to receive your note inclosing a communication from the Governor of Kentucky,[1] relative to retained rations & parts of rations, stated to be due to the militia who served with the North Western Army during the last fall & winter.—

It appears that the subject was referred to the Commanding General by the Executive of Kentucky—& your Communication to this Department shall be transmitted to him with instructions to have these demands adjusted & paid.—

Copy. DNA, RG107, Military Books, vol. 7, p. 25.
1 See above, Hardin to Clay, July 7, 1813; Clay to Armstrong, July 23, 1813.

To [Martin D. Hardin]

Dr Sir Wash. 1 Aug. 1813

I transmit you the inclosed letter from the War Department.[1]

As I apprehended, your communication as to the reimbursement expected by Kentucky of advances made to repel the incursions of the Savages on our S. W. frontier arrived too late to be acted on this Session.[2]

I have not yet obtained the desired information relative to the rifles.

A law has passed entitling the families of our friends Allen, Hickman &c. to pensions.[3] Measures ought to be taken to get them allowed at the next Session. Yrs. H. CLAY

ALS. NcD.
[1] See above, Armstrong to Clay, July 29, 1813.
[2] See above, Hardin to Clay, July 6, 1813.
[3] "An Act to provide for the widows and orphans of militia slain, and for militia disabled in the service of the United States" was approved on August 2. 3 *U.S. Stat.*, 73-74. Colonel John Allen and Captain Paschal Hickman of Franklin County had been among those killed at the River Raisin in January, 1813.

To [William Jones]

Dr Sir 2 Aug. 1813.

Mr. Parrott[1] has furnished me with the inclosed Certificate as to the quality &c. of the yarns about which I spoke to you yesterday. I found that I had a surplus of but nine thousand weight instead of ten thousand as I had supposed

If you choose to purchase them (by which I shall be much obliged) they can be continued in Mr. P.s. possession, or removed elsewhere, at your pleasure.

I have indorsed an order upon the back of the Certificate for the delivery of them to your order. Yr's respectfy H. CLAY

ALS. DNA, RG45, Misc. Letters Received, 1813, vol. 5, p. 62.
[1] Richard Parrott.

Statement of William West's Account

[*ca.* August 3, 1811]

Amt. of William West's Note Principal & Int. due 15h. Decr. 1811 —		$542„33.
Int thereon say to 15 Apl 1813.		43„36:
		585„69
By Com. at five per Cent	$29„25	
By remittance 5h. June	450„	
„ 2 Pr. Cent premium for diffce. of Exchange	9„	488„25
		97„44
By post note sent 3 Aug. 1813.	$96	
2 PCent premium for diffence [*sic*] of Exchange (say)	1„44	97„44

AD, by Clay. DLC-TJC (DNA, M212, R15).

From Benjamin H. Latrobe

The Honorable Henry Clay
Lexington Kentucky Washington Augt. 15h. 1813
Dear Sir,

I returned hither only on the 12th. having been detained at New York & also at Philadelphia and Baltimore, by a violent Diarrhoea, which lengthened my absence near a fortnight beyond my intentions. —I have on my return received your very polite letter of the 4h. of Augt, with its enclosures;[1] and shall immediately attend to the business they explain.—As to your *house*,[2] I think you said that you had reversed the use of the wings, putting the kitchen on the stair case side of the house, & the nursery on that of the parlor. I also understood you to say, that you are at present engaged in building the Wing containing the Chambers & Nursery; & that you are not at a Loss at present how to communicate them with the parlor, by removing the door nearer to the Wall. The opposite side then only requires to be so arranged, as that, when you proceed with it, n[o] alteration of the Staircase shall be necessary:—and that you mean to postpone the building of this wing till spring. I shall however lose no time in attending to this part of the plan, after having devised a design for the range of buildings in Lexington of which you have now sent me the exact dimensions as far as regards the ground plan.[3] The information however which was most essential to the design of the external front is still wanting, namely the highths of the stories, the place of the fascia if any,—in fact a compleat *elevation* of the buildings now on the ground. Nothing is mentioned but the size of the Windows as far as it can be found from that of the glass.—I beg you therefore to be so good as to procure me [t]hese dimensions & to direct them to me at Pittsburg, where I intend to be, the middle of September [a]t latest.[4] In the mean time I shall make my design without regard to the corner houses, guessing [a]s well as I can from the ground plan, as to their external appearance, & shall send you the drawing from hence, before I go.—

Mrs. Latrobe joins me in expressing our sense of your politeness,—or rather kindness, in inviting us to visit you at Lexington. If I succeed in finishing my first steam boat in spring, I will come down with it to the falls, & then we will certainly avail ourselves of the pleasure you offer us. I hope to be very busy, & also a little useful as a citizen of the *Transalpine* part of the Union,—and on your influence & support in any project which shall unite public with individual advantage I know I may safely count.—

My good old father in law, Mr. Hazlehurst begs me to remind you of his concerns.[5] I had stated to him that you would perhaps remit to him part of the amount recovered before the close of the Session, [as] you desired.—He requests his best respects to you & hopes in your more important public concerns you will find leisure for his affairs.

Mrs L joins in sincere respects to Mrs. Clay with Your obt. hble Servt. B. H LATROBE

ALS copy. Latrobe Letterbook, 588-90, owned by Mrs. Ferdinand C. Latrobe, Baltimore, Maryland.

1 Not found.

2 See above, Agreement, April 28, 1813.

3 For the site of the proposed buildings see above, Agreement with Keiser, May 4, 1813.

4 For nearly two years Latrobe lived in Pittsburgh; then, financially ruined, he returned to Washington.

5 Latrobe's second wife was Mary Elizabeth, daughter of Isaac Hazlehurst.

To Isaac Shelby

Lexington, 22d August, 1813.

MY DEAR SIR,—I have seen by the public prints that you intend leading a detachment from this state.[1] As you will want a sword, I have the pleasure to inform you that I am charged by Governor Turner and Mr. Macon[2] with delivering to you that which the State of North Carolina voted you in testimony of the sense it entertained of your conduct at King's Mountain.[3] I would take it with me to Frankfort, in order that I might personally execute the commission and at the same time have the gratification of seeing you, if I were not excessively oppressed with fatigue. I shall not fail, however, to avail myself of the first safe conveyance, and if any should offer to you, I will thank you to inform me.[4] May it acquire additional lustre in the patriotic and hazardous enterprise in which you are embarking! Your friend, H. CLAY.

Archibald Henderson, "Isaac Shelby, Revolutionary Patriot and Border Hero," *The North Carolina Booklet,* XVIII (July, 1918), 33.

1 Governor Shelby was acting under authorization of a resolution passed by the Kentucky legislature.

2 Senator James Turner and Representative Nathaniel Macon were members of the North Carolina delegation to the Thirteenth Congress. Turner had been Governor of his State from 1802 to 1805.

3 In 1781 the North Carolina legislature had voted its thanks to Shelby and other officers, and directed that a sword be presented to each, for their heroism at the Battle of Kings Mountain in the previous year. Shelby's sword had not been delivered.

4 Both the sword and this letter were conveyed to the Governor by William T. Barry, one of Shelby's aides in the forthcoming military campaign.

From Thomas Hart Benton

My dear Sir, Franklin [Tennessee], Aug. 23d. 1813.

I have seen Mr. Turner and Mr. Sandford.[1] They promise $1500.

in the month of September; and would, on any day, deliver several negroes at valuation, if you would receive them. I have undertaken to make known to you this last proposition, and to let them know your determination upon it. I have also spoken to them about the taxes: Mr. Sandford thought that you should pay them: Mr. Turner thought it had been otherwise agreed between themselves and your agent, Mr. Porter Clay. Finally it was understood between us that they were to pay the taxes. If a bill on the Pay master General at Washington, ten days sight, would answer your purpose, I could easily purchase it, and remit you in that way whatever may be received from these gentlemen.

Mr. Jesse Benton has recovered of his wound.[2] My best wishes attend you. THOMAS HART BENTON

ALS. DLC-HC (DNA, M212, R1). Addressed to Clay at Lexington.

1 Anthony J. Turner and James T. Sandford.

2 On June 14, 1813, while Thomas Hart Benton was in Washington, his brother, Jesse, had been shot in the buttocks in a duel with Major William Carroll of Tennessee. As a result of the ill-feeling engendered by this affray, on September 4 in Nashville a wild and somewhat ludicrous encounter occurred between the Benton brothers on one side and Andrew Jackson, who had served as Carroll's second, and Colonel John Coffee on the other. The fight, in which Jackson was seriously wounded, terminated when Thomas Hart Benton accidentally tumbled down a flight of stairs. William Nisbet Chambers, *Old Bullion Benton, Senator from the New West: Thomas Hart Benton, 1782-1858* (Boston, [1956]), 50-51.

From Benjamin H. Latrobe

Henry Clay Lexington K. Washington Augt. 24h. 1813

Dear Sir,

I herewith send you the drawing[1] for the ground in Lexington, which I hope will arrive in time & meet your ideas. It has taken me some time to satisfy my own wishes, & a few days delay have resulted from my unwillingness to send you a project with which I was myself displeased. I believe I have now made the most of the space.

I have no copy of the drawing, & should be glad, if you proceed to have this or a copy returned that I may make the working drawings Yours in haste B H LATROBE

ALS copy. Latrobe Letterbook, [612], owned by Mrs. Ferdinand C. Latrobe, Baltimore, Maryland.

1 Not found, but see above, Latrobe to Clay, August 15, 1813.

Property Deed to James B. January

[August 26, 1813]

This Indenture Made this 26th day of August in the year of our Lord, one thousand eight hundred and 1813 between Henry Clay and Lucretia his Wife of the County of Fayette and Commonwealth of Kentucky, on the one part, and James B. January of the County aforesaid and Commonwealth aforesaid, of the other part, Witnesseth: That the said Henry Clay & Lucretia his Wife for, and in consideration of the sum of Five Thousand Dollars Current money of Kentucky, to them in hand paid, the receipt whereof is hereby acknowledged; have granted, bargained and sold, and by these presents do grant, bargain, sell and confirm, unto the said James B. January & his Heirs and Assigns, all that tract or parcel of Land, situate and being in the county of Fayette on the waters of the Town Fork of Elkhorn Beginning on the North West side of Mill Street in the Town of Lexington Two Hundred feet South West from the Corner of John Bradfords House Erected by the late Coll Thomas Hart Thence North West with Asa Blanchards line Eighty two feet Thence South west with Asa Blanchard's back line Forty three feet nine inches to Asa Blanchards line Thence North West with said Blanchards line to a Ten foot Aley Thence North East with said Alley One Hundred & Forty three feet nine inches to said John Bradford's line Thence with said John Bradfords line to Mill Street Thence down Mill Street South West One Hundred feet to the beginning.

Together with all and singular, the premises thereunto belonging, or in any wise appertaining: to have and to hold the Land hereby conveyed, with the appurtenances, unto the said James B. January & his Heirs and Assigns forever: And the said Henry Clay & Lucretia his Wife for themselves their Heirs, Executors, and Administrators, the aforesaid tract of Land and Premises, unto the said James B. January & his Heirs or Assigns, against the claim or claims of all and every person, or persons whatsoever do and will forever defend, by these presents. *In Witness* whereof, the said Henry Clay & Lucretia his Wife have hereunto set their Hands and Seals the day and date first above written.

ACKNOWLEDGED IN PRESENCE OF

H. CLAY
LUCRETIA CLAY

Teste
LEVI L. TODD[1]
WILL S. DALLAM
DAVID R STOUT[2]

DS. Owned by Henry H. Harned, Frankfort, Kentucky. Endorsement on verso notes recording of deed in Fayette County Clerk's office, Book H, p. 62, September 6, 1813, with relinquishment of Mrs. Clay's dower rights on November 2, 1815. Cf. above, Property Deed, February 10, 1802.

1 Young Lexington lawyer, who had served with the Lexington Light Infantry at the River Raisin. He was the son of General Robert Todd.

2 A young man of Fayette County.

To Richard Parrott and Company

Gent. Lex. 2d. Septr. 1813.

I wrote you a few days ago stating my purchase for you of a quantity of sugar, agreeably to the request contained in your letter.[1] On the 30h. Ulto. I drew upon you for $4000, at ninety days sight, in favor of Mr. John Hart, who had made the purchase for me. That sum was drawn for to cover the amt. of the price of the article, to wit $3.661:54, including barrels, and the probable expence of transportation to Pittsburg, the precise account of which will hereafter be rendered. The sugar has been sent on from here to Limestone to the care of Mr. Sam. January, by whom it will be forwarded to Mr. James Adams of Pittsburg. From the diligence of those gentlemen, I have every reason to believe it will not be permitted to be delayed in their hands in its passage to you. Yrs.

H. CLAY

ALS. ViU. Addressed: "Mess Richard Parrott & Co, George town, Distt. of Columbia."
1 These letters not found.

Rental Agreement with John Keiser

[September 3, 1813]

An agreement entered into this 3d. day of September 1813 Between H. Clay and John Keizer.

The said Clay hereby rents to the said Keizer the brick house which the said Keizer at present occupies on the lot which he sold to said Clay in Lexington in May last,[1] of which lot the said Clay has the entire possession on the first day of October next; and the said Clay also rents to the said Keizer the new brick house, which he is building on the said lot and which he is bound to finish by the said first day of October next. The said Clay rents to the said Keizer the above mentioned two houses for the term of one year, commencing on the said first day of October next.

In consideration whereof the said John Keizer hereby covenants to pay to the said Clay the sum of seven hundred dollars payable in equal quarterly payments, beginning on the said first day of October next.

The said Keizer further covenants to surrender the demised premises on the first day of October 1814, in as good order and condition as they are or ought to be on the first day of October next, natural decay only excepted.

The said Clay further agrees that the family of the said Keizer may continue to occupy the small house which they are at present in, on Market Street,[2] free from rent.

The said Clay reserves the right to destrain for arrears of rent, and of re-entry on the premises.

Witness our seals. H. CLAY {L.S.}

Sealed & Delivered In presence of JOHN KEISER {L.S.}

BENJN. DAVIS

ADS. signed also by Keiser. Fayette Circuit Court, File 823. Endorsements by John Watkins indicate that Keiser paid the first three quarters' rent in full and $120 on the fourth.

1 See above, Agreement, May 4, 1813.

2 Cf. below, Rental Agreement, September 22, 1813.

Receipt from Abraham Buford

[September 3, 1813]

Recd. 3 Septr. 1813 of H. Clay Two Hundred and seventy one dollars paid by him to John Jouitt for me amounts to $571„92/100 recd. by him from Government for A. BUFORD

DS, in Clay's hand. DLC-TJC, 2d Series, vol. 13.

From Benjamin H. Latrobe

The Honorable Henry Clay
Lexington Kentucky Washington Septr. 5 1813

Dear Sir

The last post brought me yours of the 20h. of Augt.[1] to which my letters of the 15h. & 24h. of August will impart the answers. The latter enclosed the design for your houses in Lexington which I hope will give you satisfaction. If not, any alteration you may desire will most cheerfully be made.—

I confess myself a little at a loss on the subject of the wing of your house. I have an impression on my mind that the Kitchen wing has been placed by you on the Stairca[se] side of the house, & that that is the wing you have carried up. If so, the Parlor which i[s] between the Kitchen & the body of the house will be affected in shape by the position of the door from the stairs. The corners may be take[n] off either square or diagon[al]ly, giving a useful Closet o[n] one side, & room for the doo[r] from the Stairs on the other [. . .][2]

I had an idea that the wo[rk]ing plans of both wings w[ere] in [y]our possession. If not you shall have them immediately after my arrival in Pittsburg. I am with true respect Yours

B H. LATROBE

ALS copy. Latrobe Letterbook, 634-35, owned by Mrs. Ferdinand C. Latrobe, Baltimore, Maryland.

1 Not found. 2 Diagram omitted by editors.

Account with John Fisher

Mr H Clay Dr To John Fisher [September 10,] 1813

Sept 10	To furnishing and Laying 24 purch Stone at your farm in foundation of wing at at [*sic*] $2 pr purch (See bills)	$ 48 -00
	To furnishing and Laying 70-500 Bricks in wing at $8-25 cents pr thous — —	586 -62 [*sic*]
	To 8000 Sand Bricks $2 . . . — — —	16„ —
	To 11 — Doubel arches at — 6/each — —	11„ — [*sic*]
	To 10 — — single do at — — —	5„ —
		$ 666„62

[Endorsements][1]

To credit claimed by Beauchamp[2] upon his note assigned to me — — — — — — — . 15„

681„62

By notes &c assigned as per my receipt of 10 April 1813[3]	$345„89.	
By Cash paid me by John Hart . . .	150„	
By boarding of hands say 24 Weeks @ 7/6	30„	
By 1100 Shingles	3„	528„89
		$152„73

Recd. H. Clay's note for the above bal. in full of all accounts. 10h. Septr. 1813. JOHN FISHER

D. DLC-TJC (DNA, M212, R15). See above, Agreement, April 28, 1813.
1 The first, AE, by Clay; the second, ES, in Clay's hand.
2 Not identified. 3 Not found.

Memorandum to Agreement with Humphrey Marshall

[September 10, 1813]

Attached to Bond, July 18, 1805.

Bill of Sale for Slave, from William Heron

[September 13, 1811]

Know all men by these presents that I William Heron of Culpepper County in Virginia in consideration of five hundred dollars to me in hand paid[1] have bargained sold and delivered and do bargain sell & deliver hereby one negro man slave named Joe, twenty four or five years of age; which said slave I do hereby war-

rant and defend to be free from all incumbrance or claim of any other person whatsoever. In testimony whereof I do hereunto set my hand & Seal this 13h. Septr. 1813. WILLIAM HERON {L.S.}
Sealed & Delivered In presence of
(Consideration first interlined.)
D WATTS[2]

DS, in Clay's hand. DLC-TJC (DNA, M212, R15).
[1] Last eleven words interlined. [2] David Watts.

Agreement with Grinstead and Davis

[September 17, 1813]

An agreement between Grinstead and Davis & H. Clay

The said Clay has sold & delivered to the said Grinstead & Davis a negro man named Joe at six hundred dollars. He covenants to assign to them John Dillon's note payable next fall for five hundred dollars; and also to deliver to them horses this fall not exceeding eight years old to the amt. of five hundred dollars, making sixteen hundred dollars in the whole—In consideration whereof the said Grinstead & Davis agree to do brick work, furnishing all the materials &c. for the said Clay upon the lot he purchased of John Keizer[1] to the amt. of the said sum of sixteen hundred dollars; at eight dollars the thousand; the brick counted in the houses exclusive of openings.

It is understood that the said Grinstead & Davis are also to do the requisite Stone work on account of the said sixteen hundred dollars, for which they are to be allowed the customary prices.

Witness our Seals this 17h. Sept. 1813.

Teste ROBERT GRINSTEAD {L.S.}
ROBERT CLARK[2] H. CLAY {L.S.}
ALLEN DAVIS {L.S.}

[Endorsement on verso][3]
Recd. 11 Oct. 1813 Dillon's note within mentioned.
GRINSTEAD AND DAVIS

ADS, signed also by Grinstead and Davis. Fayette Circuit Court, File 412 (1818). Cf. above, Agreement with Grinstead and Davis, May 4, 1813.
[1] See above, Agreement with Keiser, May 4, 1813.
[2] Of Clark County, Kentucky; nephew of Judge James Clark.
[3] ES, in Clay's hand.

Agreement with Lawson McCullough and Hugh Foster

[September 17, 1813]

Attached to Rental Agreement, April 24, 1813.

Order on Thomas Bodley

Tho. Bodley Esq. 17h. Septr. 1813

Be pleased to deliver to Mess. Grinstead & Davis,[1] ten days after sight, a horse of sixty seventy or eighty dollars value, on account of your bond to me for horses. Yrs. H. CLAY.

ADS. KyHi. An endorsement by Davis assigned "Eighty of the within" to William T. Banton, and Bodley noted this payment.

1 Robert Grinstead and Allen Davis.

Rental Agreement with Elizabeth Keiser

[September 22, 1813]

An Agreement entered into this 22d day of Septr. 1813 between H. Clay and Elizabeth Keiser.

The sd. Clay hereby rents to the sd.—Keiser the new Brick house and small weather-boarded house[1] she now occupies in Lexington on Markett street of which the sd. Clay has the entire possession the 1st day of Octr. next for the term of one year commencing on the sd. first day of Octr. next.

In consideration whereof the sd. Elizabeth Keiser hereby Covenants to pay to the sd. Clay the sum of two hundred & fifty Dollars payable in equal quarterly payments, beginning on the sd. first day of October next.

The sd. Elizabeth Keiser further Covenants to surrender the demised premises on the first day of October 1815, in as good order and condition as they are or ought to be on the first day of October next, natural decay and inevitable accidents excepted—

It is understood between the parties that the little weather boarded house is to be given up at any time the sd. Clay may want it, but it's not to deminish the Rent afd—

The said Clay further Covenants to have the lower rooms and passage of the sd. Brick house painted and latches or other fastening fixed to the doors and two locks put on the Closets in the lower Rooms—

He further agrees to have the garrett laid with loose plank on such portion as will answer for a lumber Room—

The said Clay reserves the right to distrain for arrears of Rent, and of re-entry on the premises.

Witness our seals

Sealed & Deld. in presence of JAMES DOUGHERTY[2]

For H. CLAY {L.S.}
JOHN WATKINS
For E. KIESER
BENJ. KIESER [*sic*] {L.S.}

ADS by John Watkins, signed also by Benjamin Keiser. Fayette Circuit Court, File 823. Endorsements (undated) by Watkins show that three quarters' rent and $30 on the fourth quarter were paid. Elizabeth Keiser, sister of John, operated a boarding house; Benjamin, nephew of Elizabeth, once a clerk for John Jordan, Jr., was a bookbinder "at the sign of the Ledger" on Main Street.

1 Behind the tavern house on the corner of Short and Market sold by John Keiser to Clay by Agreement, May 4, 1813.

2 Of Fayette County.

From Samuel Hopkins

My dear sir.— Henderson 25th. Sept. 1813.

I got home 31st. ulto. after a dusty dry journey,[1] & a Little rested Went down to Andrew McFaddins & deliver'd your letter myself, as I would leave the old Man without Excuse in not answering it. Yesterday he was to have attended at my House, with satisfactory Documents, but has not Come, this delay'd thus long my writing to you. I think it probable the old Man is sick, he lives on the bank of Ohio 25 Miles below me, & the people are Sickly in the Neighbourhood he lives in; I will again endeavor to obtain from him an answer to your letter.

In the Sales of Purviance Land soon to take place, I beg you to Notice in Lott No. 6, the sales made to Jaril Willingham, Thomas Willingham, & Martin Friely,[2] Vizt.

Jaril Willingham — — — — — — — — — — — — — — —	acres	579.
Thos. Willingham — — — — — — — — — — — — — —		239.
Martin Friely — — — — — — — — — — — — — — — —		250 —
		1068
Leaving a Ballance from 1875 of — — — — — —		807. for sale

also in Lott No. 24 . to Felty Hay 100 acres.
in Lott No. 23 to David Stevens 100 acres. to be deducted

All which Lands were sold & Contracted for previous to the Sale made to H. P.[3] by his Family—the three first Tracts H. P. made Deeds to, in his own Name, but after the Discovery of of [*sic*] the Mortgage, the purchasers, would only rely upon Titles made by him as atto. & agent, agreably to the Contract. the two last Tracts were Contracted for in the same Manner, but no Deeds were Made for all These lands, H. Purviance receiv'd every Cent of the Paymts. & the People Expect Titles made by the Heirs of Saml. & Robt. Purviance. in Lott No. 1 North of Green River, H. P. sold to Wm. James 100 acres fifteen years ago, & receiv'd Payment as agent & atto. for the Heirs of S. & R. Purviance &c. this Tract has been by James's Heirs sold to Eneas McCalister, They say no Deed has been Made,—as this was a Contract of H. P. himself I never had any agency in it, I was with Mr. P. when He Survey'd the land to James, & Know he receiv'd the Money. I thought it best to apprise you of it.—

Mr. Callands 1500 acres is Deeded & paid for long ago, as Mr. P. inform'd me & as the recorded Deed in my possession declares. this land lies in Lott No 46.—

I am Hard at Work preparing Shipments to Orleans, in Six weeks I expect to set out, Tobo.[4] & other Articles to the amount, of $8000, reconing [*sic*] upon the prices now Current, & which will Hold untill the Spring Shipments.—my Son-in-law Mr. Towles[5] goes With my property, & without some Unforeseen disaster I hope to be able to Extinguish the Claims against me in the Months of January & Feby..—I think it will be 15th. Novr. before I can set out for Washington, & 10th. Decemr before I reach it. Accept the sincere affection Of Your Friend SAM. HOPKINS

Mr. Clay.

ALS. DLC-TJC (DNA, M212, R10). Addressed to Clay at Lexington.

1 From Washington, where he had served in the first session of the Thirteenth Congress, which adjourned on August 2.

2 Jarrell Willingham, Martin Friley—all of Henderson County. On the land sales see above, Report, July 12, 1813.

3 Henry Purviance.

4 Tobacco.

5 Thomas Towles, a young lawyer who had emigrated to Henderson County from Virginia. For a short time (1815-1818) he was a judge of Illinois Territory, after which he resided in Henderson for the remainder of his life.

Bond from Thomas Hamilton and Sureties

[September 29, 1813]

Know all men by this presents that We Thomas Hamilton William Martin & John Harris of Floyd County are held and firmly bound unto Henry Clay in the sum of fourteen hundred Dollars to be paid to the said Clay his heirs or assigns to which payment well & Freely to be made we bind ourselves our heirs Executors & Administrators firmly by these presents sealed with our seals and dated the 29th day of September 1813

The Condition of the above obligation is such that if the said Hamilton shall pay to the said Clay on or before the 16th day of September next One hundred Dollars and on or before the 16th day of each September for six succeeding years thereafter shall pay to the said Clay annually the further sum of One hundred Dollars making in the whole Seven hundred Dollars then this Obligation to be void otherwise to remain in full force

Signed sealed & Delivered in Presence of
WM. J. MAYO[1]
JOHN FRANKLIN[2]

THOMAS HAMILTON {SEAL}
WILLIAM MARTIN {SEAL}
JOHN HARRIS {SEAL}

[Endorsement][3]

Recd. of Mr. Thomas Hamilton one hundred Dollars the 1st payment mentd above. Septr. 14th. 1814. For H. Clay
JOHN WATKINS

DS. DLC-TJC (DNA, M212, R15). Cf. below, Rental Agreement, October 7, 1813.
1 County Clerk of Floyd County.
2 Formerly of Madison County, probably at this time of Floyd.
3 AES.

Receipt from John Ferguson

[September 30, 1813]

Attached to Order, August 5, 1811.

Property Deed to William Lytle

[October, 1813]

[Indenture under which in exchange for title to certain houses and lots in Lexington, which Lytle has conveyed to Clay by deed with general warranty duly recorded,[1] and for the further consideration of one dollar current money of Kentucky, Clay and his wife convey to Lytle all those several parcels of land lying in Jefferson County, Kentucky, adjoining the town of Louisville, which were conveyed to Clay by deed of October 29, 1807, from Fortunatus Cosby, to whom the property was granted by Sarah Beard under deed of July 7, 1806, both of which deeds are recorded in Jefferson County Court, "it being Clearly agreed and understood that the said Clay And Wife Convey All their Intrest in Said Lands being One third Part of the said Lands as Expressed in the Deed from the said Cosby to the said Clay Subject to the Exception therein Specifyed to said William Lytle And it being also Clearly agreed And understood that the said Clay And Wife Convey only *their right And title such as it is* derived from said Cosby And Beard to the said Clays intrest in what is generally termed the Lower thousand Acre tract or survey pattented in the name of John Conally And Charles Wonsdorf[2] upon which there is supposed to be incumberances And that the said Clays intrest in said One thousand Acres aforesaid be Lost the said Clay And his Heirs are in no event to be liable therefor or responsible in Any manner to the said Lytle for such Loss"—with the appurtenances. The Clays warrant title against claimants through them. Signatures of Henry and Lucretia Clay, with note as follows: "Memo. Mrs. Clay is to relinquish her dower as soon as Mrs. Lytle relinquishes her dower in the Lexington property H Clay." Certification of signature acknowledgement by Henry Clay before John D. Young, Clerk of Fayette County, October 12, 1813.]

Fayette County Court, Deed Book H, 47-48.
1 See above, October 10, 1811.
2 John Connolly and Charles de Warnsdorff.

Bill from Gerard and Berry

Hon. H. Clay [*ca.* October 1, 1813]

To Gerard & Berry Dr.

1812.	To advertising by your direction Purviances[1] Lands for sale, 2 squares ½ sqr. 6 weeks	$5.00
1813	To Do. do— 8 weeks—	5.00
		$10.00

Sir,

Pay the amo't. of the above account to Mr. G. Lewis,[2] and this shall be your receipt. Mr. Clay directed the above advertisements to be made and directed them to be charged to him.

Mr. Clay or his agent GERARD & BERRY
Lexington

ADS. DLC-TJC, 2d Series, vol. 14. William Gerard, founder of the Frankfort *Argus of Western America,* had Elijah C. Berry as his partner for about four years, until late 1816. Brigham, *History and Bibliography of American Newspapers, 1690-1820,* I, 151.

1 Henry Purviance.

2 Gabriel Lewis.

From Joseph Kelly

D Sir Christian County 1st. Octr. 1813

Some few days pas'd I recievd a note from Mr. Thruston (Deputy Marshall) stating that he had an Execution in his hands agst. me at the suit of Wm Taylor of Baltimore to the amount of about $400—but agreable to my statement (here annexd) if correct there is a balance due me of *$18..29* if you will Examine the Record on which the Judgment agst. me was founded you will find a credit for $252.40, which sum with the Intt. would amount to about the Balance of the Execution.

Feby. 9th. 1810 Replevin Bond		$1599..40[1]
Deduct from Bond a credit	$252.40	
deduct Intt. on do. 3 ys. 7. M. 13. Days .	54„75.	
deduct Marshall's Commision $307.15 @ 2½ PCt. is	7„71	314„86
What the Amount of the Bon [*sic*] augt. to be		$1284.54
Intt. on $1284.54 from the 9th. Feby. 1810 untill 29th. Jany. 1813 is 2 Years 11 2/3 Month		229. 7
1810		$1513:61
Octr. 26th. By Wm Taylors Recpt for	$740	
Intt. untill 29th. Jany. 1813. 2 Years 3 Monts [*sic*]	99..90	

1812		
April 28 By Robt. Wickliffs Recpt.	$600.–	
Intt. untill 29th. Jany. 1813. 9 Months ..	27	
1813		
Jany. 29th. By R. Wickliffs Recpt.	65	$1531.90
Bal. due	[J.] Kelly	$18.29

I wish the affair dismis'd therefore you will be so good as to examin the record make a Statement (if mine shold not be correct) and forward it to me as quick as you can make it convenient—I expect to be in Lexington some time the last of this Month if you should be from home you will have the business so stated that I can settle with Mr. Wickliff I am with Esteem Yours &C &C

Joseph Kelly

PS. You will be so good as to favour me with a Reply to this as soon as you can[2] Your Obt. St. J. Kelly

ALS. DLC-TJC (DNA, M212, R15). Addressed to Clay at Lexington. Postmarked: "Hopkinsville, Oct 9th."

[1] See above, Clay to Taylor, May 28, 1810. [2] No reply found.

Receipt from Richard Downton

[October 2, 1813]

Recd. of H. Clay four dollars for crying the Lands of Purviance[1] at public sale this 2d. October 1813 Richd Downton

DS, in Clay's hand. DLC-TJC, 2d Series, vol. 14.

[1] Henry Purviance.

Receipt from John Hart

Octr. 3. [1813]

Recd. 2d. Oct. of H. Clay N. B Beall's bond for eighteen hundred dollars worth of Land for which I am to deliver him of the best quality of Seine twine three thousand pounds properly put up in bundles for transportation. Jno. Hart.

DS, in Clay's hand. DLC-TJC (DNA, M212, R15).

Rental Agreement with Thomas Hamilton

[October 7, 1813]

An agreement entered into this 7h. day of October 1813 between H. Clay in behalf of himself and the others who are interested with him in the Salt works on Middle creek, a branch of Big Sandy, of the one part, and Thomas Hamilton of the other.

The said Clay doth hereby lease to the said Hamilton the said Salt works for the term of seven years, which said term is to be considered as commencing on the 10h. day of November next.

In consideration where of the said Hamilton covenants to pay to the said Clay the sum of one hundred dollars per annum, on the 16h. day of September next, and on the 16h. day of each succeeding September during the afd. term, for which he the said Hamilton with William Martin and John Harris his sureties have executed their bond to the said Clay.[1]

The said Clay reserves also the right of distress and the right of re-entry, upon default in the payment of the said yearly rent as it accrues.

It is agreed that the said Clay is not to be accountable for any repairs or improvements which the said Hamilton may make.

The said Hamilton covenants to surrender the premises at the end of the term to the said Clay. Witness our Seals.

Sealed & Delivered H. CLAY {L.S.}
In presence of THOS. HAMILTON {L.S.}
ROBERT CLARK

ADS, signed also by Hamilton. DLC-TJC (DNA, M212, R15).
1 See above, September 29, 1813.

Receipt from Grinstead and Davis

[October 11, 1813]

Rec'd 11 Oct. 1813 of H. Clay One Sorrel mare at One hundred and twenty five dollars on a/c of his contracts with us.

Test GRINSTEAD & DAVIS
ROBERT BYWATERS

DS, in Clay's hand. Fayette Circuit Court, File 442 (1818). See also receipt of this date attached to Agreement, September 17, 1813.

Receipted Bill from Asa Payne

October 11th 1813—

Henry Clay & John Watkins Dr
To D Surveyor of Scott County

To runing 2916 poles @ 3 poles 1 cent	$9.72
To 3 platts & notes of Refferance — — — — — — —	1.50
	$11.22

$11.22 Received the above accunt in full of Henry Clay.
ASA PAYNE DSSC

ADS. DLC-TJC (DNA, M212, R15). Asa was the son of John Payne.

Bond from Nathaniel S. Porter and Samuel Long

[October 11, 1813]

Know all men by these presents that we Nathl. S. Porter and Samuel Long are held and firmly bound to H. Clay in the just and full sum of eighteen hundred dollars; to be paid to the said Clay his heirs executors administrators and assigns; to which payment well and truly to be made we bind ourselves our heirs executors & admors. jointly and severally firmly by these presents Sealed with our seals and dated this 11h. October 1813.

The Condition of this obligation is such that whereas the said Clay hath this day rented to the said Porter for the term of three years commencing on the 15h. day of April next the small house adjoining the Kentucky Hotel at present occupied by John Crittenden,[1] for which the said Porter hath agreed to pay three hundred dollars per annum payable in equal quarterly payments: Now if the said Porter shall pay the said rent as it accrues this bond is to be void otherwise to remain in full force and virtue.

Sealed & Delivered N. S. PORTER {L.S.}
In presence of SAML LONG {L.S.}
Teste—
ROBERT CLARK

DS, in Clay's hand (except for names other than Clay's in body of document). DLC-TJC (DNA, M212, R15). Samuel Long was a Lexington house-joiner.

1 That is, the section of the establishment leased to William Satterwhite, April 15, 1813.

Power of Attorney to John Watkins

[October 12, 1813]

I do hereby constitute John Watkins my attorney for me and in my name to demand and receive any money now due or which may become due to me; and for this purpose to do all lawful and necessary acts; to sell my negro man George, & to sell any stock on my farm or other produce thereof; and in general to superintend manage and control my farm—

Witness my hand & Seal this 12h. Oct. 1813. H. CLAY {L.S.}

ADS. DLC-TJC (DNA, M212, R15). Notarial certification on verso by John D. Young, dated December 24, 1814, on the testimony of James E. Davis, Sheriff of Fayette County, and Hubbard B. Smith and John M. Smith, Lexington grocers and flour merchants (Hubbard also being Town and County Clerk), as witnesses to Clay's handwriting.

Settlement with James Dunn

[October 13, 1813]

We have this day settled all accounts whatever; whereupon the subscriber H. Clay gives up the Judgt. he has recovered agt James Dunn in Fayette Circuit Court; and the said Dunn admits the balance to be due from him according to the decree of the Court in the suit in Chy Clay agt. Dunn in Fayette Circuit Court.[1]

Witness our hands & seals this 13h. Oct. 1813.

Teste H. CLAY {L.S.}
D. WATTS J. DUNN. {L.S.}

ADS, signed also by Dunn. KyLxT.
[1] The court on September 25, 1813, had ordered that Dunn pay the sum of $1750, with interest, and that the lots involved (see above, Promissory Note, June 17, 1805) be sold at auction to satisfy the debt. Dunn was to receive credit for $286, paid in 1810, and $124.74, for work done at the Kentucky Hotel in 1811. Fayette Circuit Court, Order Book L, 197-98.

Conditional Promise to Give Property Deed

13h Oct. 1813.

Upon payment to me of the balance due me according to the decree of Fayette Circuit Court in my suit agt James Dunn & the costs of suit; and the production of my bond or contract[1] for the title to the lots decreed by said Court to be sold, I will make the title to the said lots. H. CLAY

ADS. Fayette Circuit Court, File 266 (1813).
[1] Not found.

Receipt from John Barker

[November 1, 1813]

Recd. of H. Clay, Nov 1, 1813, seventeen bales of seine twine as below,[1] which I promise to deliver to Sam January, Limestone, in good order, and without delay, sd. Clay paying 50 cts pr. 100wt. carriage JOHN BARKER

DS, in Clay's hand. DLC-TJC (DNA, M212, R15). Barker not identified, apparently a wagoner.
[1] The list, here omitted, included 13 bales of 9-thread twine and 4 bales of 12-thread, weighing a total of 1802 pounds.

From Benjamin H. Latrobe

The Honble Henry Clay
Washington Pittsburg, Novr. 2d 1813
Dear Sir,

I recd. Your favor d. Washington Pensa. Octr. 22d.[1] today by a Gentleman who informed me that you were at Bedford last Tuesday week,[2] the very day on which I was also there. It is vexatious that I had not then the pleasure to see You.—I am now fully at Your service here, & shall be very happy in any way to be serviceable to Your objects. When I have been so, & not before, I shall think of that compensation which you request me now to name. In the mean time, I shall have great pleasure in performing any task You assign me.

Permit me now candidly to explain to you a subject of some delicacy.

I have understood from Mr Hazlehurst my father in law,[3] that Mr. James Eakin called upon You to stop the payment of any monies recovered by You on behalf of the house of Isaac Hazlehurst & Co., producing an assignment to himself Mr. Eakin is a cousin of my wifes, being the son of the younger sister of her Mother. He is a proof that the human character may be, & generally is, a compound of good & evil. His near relationship to us, and his solid worth, has attached us to him, and a plate at our table has always been set for him on Sunday. In the confidence of family intercourse, it was mentioned to him that you were likely to recover some money for our unfortunate parent. He expressed great pleasure to hear it, but made no other remark. The next day he called upon You with his assignment, & not being satisfied with Your answer to him, he wrot[e] Mr. Hazlehurst a very acrimonious letter on the subject.

Now we are all very anxious that you should not suppos[e] that our virtuous & respectable father is capable of the injustice of defrauding his nephew, by concealment of his effects, a charge implied by Mr Eakin's conduct, & I therefore beg your attention to what I shall now say.

Mr. Eakin's father was a prebyterian [*sic*] Clergyman from the state of Delaware. His Mother was the daug[hter] of old Saml. Purviance, & once the first beauty in Philadelphia. During the Synods of the Presbyterian Church, Mr Purviance always invited to his house some of the Clergy, & among the rest the Revd Mr. Eakin. In return [. . .][4] invited to his house, his daughter, who, without her [p]arents leave went with Mr Eakin to Delaware as his wife. This offence was never forgiven by Mr Purviance, [w]ho therefore struck her out of his will, & left her to [s]truggle with poverty & sickness, & to nurse a consumptive & peevish husband as long as he lived.—Mr. Hazlehurst however did not desert his wife's sister & her family. He fitted out one of her Sons for France [a]s a merchant, & opening his house to *James* he promoted his interests till he at last procured him a situation in the public Offices which he now holds. Mrs. Eakin married a second time more imprudently than the first,—& became the wife of a Young man, Dr. Greenman.[5] He also died, & she was reduced to the utmost distress. Mr. Hazlehurst however did not let her want, but assisted her in all her embarrassments.—In the mean time James Eakin grew up, & no Son ever acted more dutifully to his mother. Living parsimoniously himself, he not only supported his mother & Sisters as soon as his Salary permitted but accumulated for their use the sum of I believe 8,000 dollars which he placed in the hands of Mr. Hazlehurst, the interest of Jersey (7 Cent) being pd. into the hands of his mother. When the house of Isaac Hazlehurst & Sons failed, Mr. Hazlehurst Assigned of the debts due to Isaac Hazlehurst & Robert Morris double the amount of the sum due to James Eakin Mr. Saml. Riddle[6] was attorney to recover the principal part of these debts, & the debts *specially* assigned were those to be recovered by him, *at his own risk*, Mr. Hazlehurst, to secure the recovery or payment by Mr Riddle if not recovered, having made an arrangement with him, in the nature of an assurance for a limited sum. When Mr. Eakin called on You there was due to him only 1.500$ of the original sum. His mother had notwithstanding the failure of the house, regularly received the interest from Mr Saml. Hazlehurst,[7]—altho' Mr. H. held & holds a bond of Mrs. Greenman, Eakin's mother of 1000$ & upwards for money advanced for the outfit & support of his [*sic*] Children twenty years ago which he has forborne to demand, & still forbear[s] to set off against the balance due to her Son. [An]d further,—Mr. Riddle has now in his hands [go]od securities for Mr. Eakin's use to the amount [o]f treble the balance due Mr Eakin,—which securities were mentioned to us as good by Mr Eakin on the [ve]ry day on which we stated your success in recovering other debts for our good father.

I make no apology for this long detail, for it is addressed to a Man highly sensible of the delicacy due to the character & feelings of such a Man as Isaac Hazlehurst. Very respectfully Yrs

B H LATROBE—

ALS copy. Latrobe Letterbook, 675-79, owned by Mrs. Ferdinand C. Latrobe, Baltimore, Maryland. Margins partially hidden on photostatic transcript.

1 Not found.

2 En route to Washington to attend the second session of the Thirteenth Congress.

3 Isaac Hazlehurst.

4 One or two words obscured.

5 Not identified.

6 Of Bedford, Pennsylvania.

7 Son of Isaac Hazlehurst.

From William Jones

Sir Navy Department Novr. 4, 1813.

Our verbal agreement this day is understood to have been as follows Viz. That you as Agent for the Rope manufacturing concern

of Messrs. Hart & Co of Kentucky engage to deliver at Philadelphia for the use of the Navy of the United States on or before the 20th Feby next One hundred and fifty tons of yarns made of the best top't & rooted Kentucky Hemp the yarns to be of fineness and quality equal to any that the same concern has hitherto delivered in this district for the use of the Navy of the U States and that this Department engages to pay for the same at the rate of thirteen Cents per pound on delivery: In order to render the contract obligatory you will please sign your agreement to the counterpart of this letter—I am respectfully Your Obd Servt W JONES
The Hon Jos. [*sic*] Clay.

ALS. DNA, RG45, Naval Records Collection. Misc. Letters Received [*sic*], 1813, vol. 7, p. 23. Addressed: "Honble Henry Clay Washington City." An accompanying document in Clay's hand (*ibid.*, p. 24), from [Jones] to the [Navy Agent at Philadelphia], [November, 1813], indicates that the contract for 150 tons of yarns was to be filled by "Mrs. [*sic*] Hart and some other manufacturers of hemp in K."

Receipted Account with John H. Barney

Honbl. H. Clay — Balto. 30th Novbr. 1813
To John H. Barney

29th.	Barber 12½ Cash 2.62½ ———————	2„75
"	Segars 37½— Mada.[1] 3.75 Porter 37½—	4„50
"	fire & Candles 2.00.., Swt Gin 12½	2 12½
30.	Segars 12½. Sirt's[2] bitters 12½ — — — — .	„25
"	1 Day's Board 5.00	5 —
"	Dinner's 2.00 . — — — — — — .	2 —
"	3 Sirt's. Board 112½ Each ———————	3„37½
"	Mada. 1.25 — — — — ———————	1„25
"	5 Horses Hay & Oats. ———————	5 —
"	11 Go. (Extra) Oats . . . — —	1„37½
		$ 27„62½
"	Mr. M. Jinkin's[3] Bill ———	$254„50
		$282„12½

[Endorsement][4]
Recd payment, for J H Barney JAMES THOMPSON

D. DLC-TJC (DNA, M212, R15). Barney, brother of Commodore Joshua Barney, also of Baltimore, operated the Fountain Inn.
1 Madeira. 2 Servant's.
3 Michael Jenkins, Baltimore cabinet maker.
4 ES. Thompson not identified.

Receipt to Garrett, Payne, and Underwood

[November 30, 1813]

Attached to Rental Agreement, April 15, 1813.

Receipt to Lawson McCullough and Hugh Foster

[December 7, 1813]

Attached to Rental Agreement, April 24, 1813.

Resolution Relating to Reference of President's Message

Wednesday, December 8. [1813]

Mr. *Clay, of Kentucky* (Speaker) remarked that the resolutions adopted appeared to embrace all the principal topics adverted to in the message, with the exception of one which had no doubt escaped the gentleman's observation. The subject to which he referred was embraced in the following resolution, which Mr. Clay offered for consideration:

6.[1] *Resolved,* That so much of the Message of the President as relates to the expediency of such legal provisions as may supply the defects, or remove the doubts of the Executive authority to allow to the cruizers of other powers, at war with the enemies of the United States, such use of the American ports and markets as may correspond with the privileges allowed by such powers to American citizens, be referred to a select committee.

[Taylor stated "that he had not overlooked this important recommendation, but had supposed it would fall within the province of the committee on naval affairs; inasmuch as its declared object was 'to give to our vessels of war, public and private, the requisite advantage in their cruizes.'"]

Mr. *Clay* observed, in reply, that, if it belonged to any of the committees proposed in the resolutions just agreed to, it appeared to him to belong to the committee of Foreign Relations, the object being a reciprocation to a foreign power of certain privileges in our ports which it granted to us on its part. It was at least doubtful to which committee it properly belonged, and it would therefore be better to refer it to a special committee.

[Taylor withdrew his opposition to Clay's resolution, which was then adopted.]

Washington *National Intelligencer,* December 9, 1813. Published also in *Annals of Cong.,* 13 Cong., 2 Sess., XXVI, 785. Representative John W. Taylor of New York had previously submitted six resolutions, referring to various committees certain parts of President Madison's message of the previous day.

[1] Should be "7."

To [James Madison]

Sir Washington 11h. Decr. 1813.

I should not venture to take the liberty of addressing this letter to you, if you had not have done me the honor of mentioning the subject of the appointment of a P. Master in Lexington, nor if I were quite sure that you would yourself exercise the right of selecting, from among the applicants, the individual to be appointed. But as I have perceived in the P. Office Department a most unaccountable reluctance to appoint the person who I think is entitled to the office, and as at all events a delay has arisen injurious to the public, you will I am persuaded excuse the trouble the perusal of this letter may give you.[1] John Fowler appears to me to have claims to the office, in his early migration to Kentucky, in his integrity, in his capacity, and in his invariable adherence to republican principles, which I had supposed would have been at once recognized by Mr. Granger.[2] The truth is I cannot help suspecting a bias towards another gentleman, Mr. Pope,[3] to whom I have no personal objection, but whose appointment, under existing circumstances, would give I am persu[ad]ed much and just umbrage. It would indeed imply th[at] the forfeiture of the confidence of the people was [. . .][4] passport to Executive favor; and that the preserva[tion of] that confidence was an insuperable obstacle to th[e receipt] of an Executive appointment. Nor Sir would you escape the obloquy of such a proceeding, altho' you had not, as I am sure you wd. not have, any participation in it.

I do not believe that Mr. Fowler ever before asked or received any mark of the confidence of the General Govt. In such estimate were his pretensions held in Lexington that I know that gentlemen, well qualified for the office, were prevented from applying for it, because they believed he ought to obtain it. Yr. ob. Servt. H. CLAY

ALS. ViU-McGregor Library.

1 John Jordan, Jr., Lexington postmaster since 1802, had died September 9, 1813. Clay's nominee, John Fowler, received the appointment early in the next year.

2 Gideon Granger. 3 John Pope.

4 MS. torn; one or two words missing.

To Caesar A. Rodney

My Dear Rodney. Wash. 11h. Decr. 1813.

Your favor of the 27h. Ulto.[1] not reaching Philadelphia, until my departure thence, found me here.[2]

The great fall of rain which took place the day before we sat out from that City, and the reputed badness of the roads by Wilmington, constrained us, with great reluctance, to deny ourselves the pleasure of seeing you on our return. I wish indeed that we could have been able to realize your conjecture that we were waiting to bear you the tidings of the reduction of Montreal. That event was wanted to enable the President to give to his message a finishing stroke, & why it was not permitted to him to announce it I confess has not been satisfactorily explained.[3]

We have been engaged several days on [confidential] subjects [which I] am not at [liberty] to disclose.[4] I have nothing [further] to offer you. Sincerely Yrs H. CLAY.

ALS. DLC-Rodney Family Papers (DNA, M212, R22).
[1] Not found.
[2] Clay had visited Philadelphia for two weeks, possibly in relation to the receipt of a shipment of navy yarns on the account of Hart and Company.
[3] An incursion down the St. Lawrence for the purpose of capturing Montreal had ended with the defeat of American forces under General James Wilkinson on November 11, 1813.
[4] On December 9 Congress had received from the President a confidential message requesting an embargo on exports. After considering the matter behind closed doors, Congress responded with an embargo act, which was approved on December 17. The injunction of secrecy was removed three days later.

To ———

Dr Sir H of R. 11h. Decr. 1813.

Inclosed is a letter of the Honble Mr. Duval[1] recommending a substitute for Mr. Strother.[2] Coming from the District for which Mr. S. was appointed, and being much better acquainted there than I am, Mr. Duval's recommendation is entitled to the highest consideration.

Mr. Clarke[3] is expected this or tomorrow evening, and I still wish that he may be consulted. Indeed there would be hazard that any person I might name, wd. not be disposed to accept; whereas Mr. Clarke is no doubt acquainted with the fact of Mr. Hanigan's[4] declining to accept, and is prepared to name a suitable successor who will.

If however you cannot wait, I would propose Mr. Hubbard Taylor, Winchester (K.) whose qualifications, in every respect, will ensure a faithful discharge of his duty, if he will accept. Yrs. H. CLAY

ALS. Lincoln Memorial University, Harrogate, Tennessee.
[1] William Pope Duval, a Bardstown lawyer, represented his district in the Thirteenth Congress (1813-1815). After serving briefly as United States Judge in East Florida, he became Governor of the Territory of Florida, a position which he filled from 1822 to 1834.
[2] Not identified.
[3] James Clark.
[4] Possibly Edward B. Hannegan of Lexington, who for many years operated a successful "English School and Academy" and subsequently for a brief period engaged in the grocery business.

To James Trotter

Dr Sir Wash. 12h. Decr. 1813.

Inclosed is the letter of Mr. Nott, in which I am sorry to find he declines accepting the proposal of the Trustees.[2] You will be pleased to lay it before the Board, together with a Copy of our letter to him in the hands of Mr- Young.[3] Yrs. H CLAY

ALS. PPPrHi. Addressed to Trotter, long a member of the board of trustees of Transylvania University. The letters mentioned in this document have not been found.

1 Clay was a member of a committee appointed some three months earlier by the Transylvania board of trustees to employ as president of the University the Reverend Eliphalet Nott, president of Union College, Schenectady, New York.

2 John D. Young, another member of the board of trustees.

To Martin D. Hardin

My Dr Sir Wash. 14h. Decr. 1813.

The papers relative to Mrs. Allen's pension[1] are now under examination, and appear to me to be sufficient.

There is a vacant Brigadier Generals Commn. and will probably be another. I think we may get Genl. Adair appd.[2] A strong letter from the Governor will aid us much. Harrison[3] is now here, speaks hily of Adair, and will support it. Whatever I can do shall be done with great pleasure—In haste Yr friend H. CLAY

ALS. ICHi. Addressed to Hardin at Frankfort.

1 Mrs. John Allen.

2 John Adair, in spite of the strong recommendations in his favor, failed to obtain the commission.

3 General William Henry Harrison.

To Thomas Bodley

Dr. Bodley Wash. 18h. Decr. 1813

When your favor[1] giving me an account of the glorious result of the Campaign in the N.W.[2] reached me, I was in Philada. where we spent very agreeably two weeks. I had heard of your success on my way to this place from K. and heard of it with emotions of pleasure which it is impossible for me to describe. In another quarter our success has not been equal to our expectations,[3] but we must have patience, and all will turn out well.

You describe that portion of the Country which Kentucky has conquered as extremely fine, and say that a very unpopular opinion has been attributed to me that it ought to be given up, as the price of peace. During the last summer when, so far from having reduced any portion of the Territories of the enemy, the enemy had possession of the Michigan Territory, I did say that if we could make a peace securing to us all the points in controversy, I should for one be willing not to give up Canada (for we had it not to give up) but to forego for the present its conquest. I was totally unapprized of the views of Administration on this subject, and expressed the sentiment in casual conversation. When the War was commenced Canada was not the end but the means; the object of the War being the redress of injuries, and Canada being the instrument by which that redress was to be obtained. But it has ever been my opinion that if Canada is conquered it ought never to be surrendered if it can possibly be retained. Relations and connexions will take place which ought not to be broken, in the event of its conquest. You know however that I do not belong to that branch of the Government with which the power of making peace is lodged; and perhaps after all it is premature to say any thing at present about the terms of a peace, which may not be made for years to come. The *state* of things is undergoing continual changes, and we must judge of the conditions of peace, when peace comes, not by the present state, but by that state of things which shall exist when it is negociated. That government is sensible of the advantages which will accrue from the possession of Canada, you may be well assured; and that it will get all it can in making a peace its desire of fame, to say nothing of its love of country, affords a sufficient guarrantee.

Congress has been chiefly engaged in confidential business, since it met. I am not yet at liberty to say what it is, but it will be disclosed in a day or two.[4]

Judge Todd[5] is here. He and Genl. Harrison dine with me to day.

We shall have to pay $2.000 as Jordan's sureties. That is the penalty of our bond. When Granger arrives (for he has been detained on the road to this place by illness) I shall get him to direct the Atto. of the U.S. to investigate Jordan's circumstances. I hope our friend Fowler has by this time got the appointment of P. Master.[6]

I have recommended Davis and Young for subaltern commissions in the army.[7]

There is a rumor that one of our frigates has arrived to the Eastward. Genl. Floyd[8] and the Georgia Militia have defeated a party of the creeks killing 200 of them, besides the wounded, and losing only 11 killed and 54 wounded Yr frie[nd][9] H [CLAY]

ALS. KyHi. Addressed: "Majr. Tho. Bodley Lexington (K)."

1 Not found.

2 William Henry Harrison's army had invaded Canada after Commodore Oliver H. Perry's victory on Lake Erie in September and, at the Battle of the Thames, October 7, 1813, had destroyed the British forces under Colonel Henry Procter and Tecumseh.

3 The expedition under General James Wilkinson against Montreal.

4 The embargo act, approved December 17.

5 Thomas Todd.

6 See above, Clay to Madison, December 11, 1813, note.

7 Benjamin Davis and Thomas B. Young were appointed ensigns in the 17th Regiment of Infantry (Kentucky), May 14, 1814, then transferred to the 24th Regiment (Tennessee) as third lieutenants.

8 John Floyd, in command of the First Brigade, Georgia Militia, in the campaign against the Indians, later a member of the Georgia legislature and, for one term (1827-1829), of the United States House of Representatives.

9 MS. defaced.

Receipt from James Adams

Pittsburgh 21 Decr 1813

Recd from Benjamin Cole[1] in good order Seventeen Bales Twine the property of the Honl H. Clay Weighing Eighteen Hundred and nine pounds. Freight at one Dollar fifty cents p 100 payable by sd. Clay in Lexington Kenty

For James Adams

17 Bales 1809— M. ALLEN[2]

DS. DLC-TJC (DNA, M212, R15).
1 Of Mason County, Kentucky.
2 Possibly a member, subsequently, of the Pittsburgh firm of Allen and Grant, commission merchants and forwarders.

To Martin D. Hardin

My Dear Sir Wash. 22d. Decr. 1813.

The rate of pension which has been fixed at the Accountant's office of the War Dept. for Mrs. Allen[1] is thirty dollars per month, or $360 per annum, being one half the monthly pay to which, according to their construction of the law Col Allen was entitled at his death. This pension commences on the 22d. Jan. last and will be payable half yearly, during the continuance of the five years, that is to say on the 22d. July and 22d. Jan. Proof must be exhibited and accompany the power of Atto. on each application at the Accountant's office that Mrs. Allen remains a widow; for if she marries the pension for the residue of the term goes to her children.

According to this construction of the law the Accountt has been governed by the pay of a Lieut. Col. in the army of the U. States, and not that of a Col. I have contended with him (and the point is not finally decided) that substance and not names ought to guide, and consequently Col Allen being the actual commander of a regiment, his pay ought to have been the same as that of a Col. in the regular service, notwithstanding in the K. organization of the Militia he is called Lieut. Col. Commandant. The Accountt. seemed to think that the pay and Muster rolls of the Regimt. would throw some light on the subject I do not think it of much consequence because the question is not what did he receive, but what was he entitled to receive? However I have promised to endeavor to procure them from Mr. Dudley,[2] and you must enable me to comply with it, for it seems that Mr. Dudley has not settled his accounts, and has not returned a single pay roll.

I have recd. $180 the first six months' pension, ending on the 22d. July last, but without prejudice to Mrs Allen's claim to a higher rate of pension. For that sum she will be pleased to draw on me at sight. She will also forward me proof that on the 22 Jan. next she remains a widow, and I will obtain the accruing half year's pension. The pay rolls you will attend to.

We have laid an embargo for one year, and made the measure as strong as we could.[3] Not one syllable has been recd. from our Commissioners in Russia.[4] It is supposed their letters have been intercepted. I think we ought to square ourselves for a protracted War.

Yrs. H. CLAY

ALS. ICHi. Addressed to Hardin at Frankfort.

1 Mrs. John Allen.

2 Peter Dudley, brother of William and Jephthah, and paymaster of the First Rifle Regiment, Kentucky Militia, organized under Colonel John Allen (Frankfort) and Majors Martin D. Hardin and George Madison, August 15, 1812.

3 See above, Clay to Rodney, December 11, 1813, note.

4 See above, Clay to Hardin, May 26, 1813, note.

To Dr. William Thornton

Sir 24h. Decr. 1813.

I recd. your favor of to day with its inclosures.[1] I have examined the Copies from the originals in Majr. Graves's[2] hand writing and find them correctly made. I do not know who are the personal representatives of the Majr. but if you choose I will transmit your letter to a friend who will present it to them, whoever they may be.

As to the duel, I have heard, with infinite regret, the rumor that such a thing is contemplated.[3] The House of R. cannot I fear make any interference to prevent it. What prospective regulation on such subjects might be adopted is another question; but I fear, in spite of all the efforts of Legislation, we shall go on to fight, in single combat, and go on to condemn the practice. The remedy lies deeper than in legislative acts—public opinion must be corrected. Yrs.

H. CLAY

ALS. NBuHi. Addressed to Thornton, for local delivery.

1 Not found.

2 Benjamin Graves, killed at the River Raisin.

3 A possible encounter between Representatives Thomas P. Grosvenor of New York and John C. Calhoun, following a dispute in the House, was forestalled by the intervention of their friends, including Clay. The press was thereupon authorized "to announce that the affair has been arranged in a manner entirely honorable to both parties." Washington *National Intelligencer*, December 28, 1813.

To William Jones

Sir Washington City 28h. Decr. 1813

Inclosed is a letter of Mr. Hunt,[1] a manufacturer of Hemp in K., directing his correspondents in Philadelphia to deliver to the Navy Agent there between 20 and 40 tons of yarns, in consequence of what has passed between us. You will observe that some of them are of a finer quality (to wit No. 26) than was contemplated. I have added a postscript to the letter stating that Mr. Hunt will be satisfied with payment when an appropriation is made. You will be good enough to have the letter forwarded to Mr. Harrison[2] with directions to receive the yarns, if upon inspection they are found to be of the quality described.

I am requested by Capt. Hunt,[3] formerly the Commander of the Hornet, to offer for sale to you an excellent Chronometer, well calculated for one of our Ships of War. He is willing to take for it what it cost him six hundred dollars. It is in New York. Do you want such an instrument? Yrs H. CLAY

ALS. DNA, RG45, Misc. Letters Received, 1813, vol. 7, p. 136. Addressed to Jones. Endorsed on cover: "Forward the enclosed letter to the Navy agent Philad. & direc[t] him to cause the yarns to be carefully inspected and if fou[nd] to accord with the description [of] the letter to receive this quantity as part of the parcel to be deliv[ered] agreeably to my letter of (see my last letter to him)." See above, Jones to Clay, November 4, 1813.

1 John W. Hunt. 2 George Harrison. 3 Charleton Hunt.

Opposition to Motion Granting Federal Aid to the Delaware-Raritan Canal

[December 29, 1813]

Cited in Washington *National Intelligencer,* December 30, 1813; *Annals of Cong.,* 13 Cong., 2 Sess., XXVI, 815. During consideration of a bill authorizing the Secretary of the Treasury to purchase shares in the stock of the Chesapeake and Delaware Canal Company, an amendment had been offered to grant similar aid to a canal between the Delaware and Raritan rivers in New Jersey. Clay, with Charles Jared Ingersoll of Pennsylvania and Robert Wright of Maryland, opposed the proposal (speeches not reported) on the ground that it would tend to defeat the basic bill. In April, 1814, the Committee of the Whole was discharged from further consideration of the entire project.

Receipt to John Crittenden

[January 1, 1814]

Attached to Rental Agreement, April 15, 1813.

Speech on Resolutions Commending American Naval Heroes

[January 4, 1814]

Mr. *Clay, of Ky.* (Speaker) said, that before the question was put, the Chairman must allow him an opportunity of expressing the high satisfaction he felt at the very handsome and eloquent manner in which the gentleman from S. Carolina had acquitted himself in the observations he had just made. It would indeed have ill become the

Representatives of the People, when every city on the continent had almost literally blazed with joy on the occasion of these victories, to have remained silent on this subject. Our ships on the ocean, commanded by the most gallant officers in the world, had already shewn what American tars could do, ship to ship. It remained for the Hero of Erie[1] to exhibit to them an awful lesson of our capacity to fight in squadron, against not only an equal but superior force. If he were to relate the circumstance which in his opinion most distinguished the hero of that battle, Mr. Clay said, he should certainly refer to that mentioned by the gentleman from South Carolina. Imagine to yourself (said he) this valuable officer in the hour of peril, his vessel a wreck, her deck strewed with the mangled bodies of his dead and dying comrades—and admire, with me, the cool intrepidity and consummate skill with which he seized the propitious moment, changed his station, and, aided by his gallant second in command,[2] and only second in merit, pressed forward to fame and victory. Such an action, it has been well said, has scarcely its parallel in history. The importance of victory can be more readily realized, when we look at its consequences. It led to the victory on land, by which a territory was delivered, and a province conquered. No longer is the patriotic soldier, whose safety ought to be guarded by all the principles of honor and of modern warfare, to be delivered over in cold blood to the merciless tomahawk. No longer the mother wakes to the agonizing spectacle of her child torn from her breast, and immolated to savage brutality. Here, sir, said he, the consequences of that victory are most conspicuous; and, coming from a country in the vicinity of the scene of action, and so sensibly alive to its consequences, I could not forbear expressing my high satisfaction at giving my vote in favor of these propositions. Mr. C. could not sit down, he said, without expressing his pleasure at finding that the name of Elliott was coupled with that of Perry. Lt. Elliott had given, in the capture of the British brig Detroit, last winter,[3] a promise of future greatness in the line of his profession. The admirable manner in which he had in the battle of Erie seconded his brave commander, attested the propriety of connecting his name in their resolve with that of the Hero of the Lake.

Washington *National Intelligencer*, January 5, 1814. Published also in *Annals of Cong.*, 13 Cong., 2 Sess., XXVI, 847-48. On January 4 the House resolved itself into a Committee of the Whole to consider resolutions on the conduct of officers and seamen who had distinguished themselves in recent naval actions. Clay's remarks followed a speech by William Lowndes, of South Carolina, chairman of the House Committee on Naval Affairs.

1 Commodore Oliver Hazard Perry.

2 Jesse Duncan Elliott, whose conduct at the Battle of Lake Erie, September 10, 1813, at which time he was the ranking officer under Perry, had become the subject of prolonged controversy.

3 See above, Speech, January 8, 9, 1813, note.

To Gales and Seaton

Mess. Gales and Seaton. 4 Jan. 1814

I send you substantially a sketch of what I said to day in relation to Perry's victory, which if you mean to publish any thing that I did say, you may put in your paper—I do not wish however that it should appear, if it appear at all, before the much more interesting remarks of Mr. Lowndes. Yrs. H. CLAY

[Enclosure][1]

Mr. Clay (the Speaker) said, he rose to express his satisfaction with the resolutions under consideration, and his thanks to the honble Chairman of the Committee on Naval affairs (Mr. Lowndes) for the very handsome and eloquent manner in which he had just performed the duties of his station. It was impossible for the representatives of the people, when our Cities from one end of the Union to the other had blazed with the most spendid [*sic*] illuminations, when the whole Country had been filled with transports of joy, to remain silent, without manifesting their[2] participation in the universal gladness. The gallant commanders of our ships had taught the proud mistress of the Seas what American tars are[3] capable of effecting in single and equal combat. It was reserved for Captain Perry to give the more impressive lesson of what they are able to atchieve[4] in conflicts between Squadron and Squadron. This he has nobly done in the action of the 10th. of September, in which there was not an equality of force between the respective squadrons, but a decided superiority on the part of the enemy. If, said Mr. C. he were to point to one circumstance which more than any other distinguished, on that memorable day, the Hero of Lake Erie, it was undoubtedly that to which his honorable friend had adverted—the cool and collected intrepidity which enabled him, amidst the heat of the action, his vessel completely riddled, her deck strewed with the mangled bodies[5] of the dead and the[6] dying, to quit the unmanageable hulk and assume the command of the Niagara. Rushing again with this ship into the midst of the enemies[7] fleet, and being admirably seconded by the gallant officer next in command, the contest was at once brought to the most glorious termination.

But the victory, great as it was, when viewed by itself, challenges also our admiration and gratitude in the important consequences by which it was followed. Paving the way to the total defeat of the British and their allies which soon after occurred on the Thames, it brought the whole of the N. Western tribes of savages to our feet, suing for that peace which they so illy deserve. No longer is the brave and patriotic soldier who, by the fortunes of War, has been[8] surrendered up to British faith and whose safety ought to have had all the guarranties of modern civilized warfare,[9] delivered over or wantonly seized a victim to the merciless tomahawk. No longer is the fond mother waked from her dreadful midnight dreams to behold the agonizing spectacle of her bleeding infant, torn from her breast, dashed, by the ferocious savage, in pieces before her eyes. A territory delivered; a province conquered—Such are, or might have been, some of the fruits of the gallant conduct of which the house is called upon to express its sense.

He was particularly pleased at the name of Capt. Elliott being coupled, in the resolutions, with that of Capt. Perry. That valuable officer had, in the capture of the Brig Detroit, on the same theatre, given a previous pledge of what on greater occasions his Country might expect of him. He has nobly redeemed the pledge, and shewn that second in command he was only second in the glory with which the officers and men have covered themselves.

Coming from that quarter of the Country which had been so signally benefited by the victory of the 10h. of September, he (Mr. C. said) took the greatest delight in endeavoring to give utterance to his feelings. He should have lamented the more his total inadequacy to do them or the subject justice but for the masterly manner in which it had been treated by his honorable friend from South Carolina.

ALS. NN-Ford Collection. Joseph Gales, Jr., editor of the Washington *National Intelligencer*, announced on October 31, 1812, that he had taken into partnership William W. Seaton, formerly associated with Joseph Gales, Sr., of the Raleigh, North Carolina, *Register*.

1 AD by Clay, including word substitutions.
2 This word substituted for "any."
3 The word substituted for "were."
4 The phrase substituted for "capable of atchieving."
5 The word substituted for "limbs."
6 Word inserted.
7 Word inserted, as spelled.
8 Word inserted.
9 Last fourteen words interlined.

From Benjamin H. Latrobe

The Honorable Henry Clay
Washington- Pittsbs. Pa. Jany. 4h. 1814
Dear Sir

By the papers I observe that the State house of your State at Frankfort is burnt down.[1] I am so ambitious as to wish to design a new one for the State & as I shall go down the Ohio in May in my steam boat to Louisville, & probably ride over to Lexington and Frankfort, I might perhaps find thro' your means, the gratification of my ambition. I propose making an application to the Kentucky legislature for a Charter for a Steam boat Company on the Cumberland,[2] & I confess that I should look to the success of my present idea, for the means of a better acquaintance with the leading Men of Your State, & of course for a better prospect of success in my application. —I mention these things to you as a friend.—

On your own affairs your silence is easily accounted for from the pressure of your public business; for you have always considered the public, as your paramount interest. And yet a few lines of *decision* on what I am to do for you, would be very acceptable Yours truly

B. H Latrobe

ALS copy. Latrobe Letterbook, 15, owned by Mrs. Ferdinand C. Latrobe, Baltimore, Maryland.

1 Constructed in 1793-1794, the building had been destroyed by fire on November 25, 1813.

2 Latrobe's plans were upset by the failure, later in the year, of his boat building venture in Pittsburgh.

To [Francis T. Brooke]

My Dr Sir Wash. 8h. Jan. 14.

It will be satisfactory to you to know that before I left K. I paid the taxes on your land.

Some years ago you were good enough to place (I think I so understood you) a small claim of mine on the Estate of Warner Lewis of Gloster in the hands of a Mr. Sanders of Williamsburg.[1] I have never known its fate. Last Session I addressed a letter[2] to Mr. Sanders but had not the good fortune to obtain any reply. Will you allow me to trouble you with ascertaining the present condition of that demand? Yr's truly H. Clay

ALS. NcD. A draft copy is found in DLC-TJC (DNA, M212, R10).

1 Robert Saunders.

2 Not found.

Account with John Hart

Dr. Henry Clay In a/c with Jno. Hart. [*ca.* January 10, 1814]

1813			
Decr.	23.	To Cash paid John Fink & Co[1] freight 2 reels yarns (J Ht Co)[2]	$ 25.65
	29.	To Do. Paid Ridgely's a/c agt. Do.[3]	13.—
	30.	To Do. " disct at BB[4]	4.80
1814			
Jan.	4.	To Do. " McCullough & Pointz[5] tare of 12 ct. ea on the 40 reels ship'd by them the nett freight of which only I charged in my last a/c[6] @ 1$	4.80
	6.	To Do. paid Jno. Hart & Co's order on J. Pitt's[7] to M B & Sutton[8] he being insolvent — —	58.40

10.	To Cash pd. stamp tax on my dft of today — —		" .75
"	To [. . .][9] J. H. & Co note to Th. Hart's Ex[. . .] 1 Jan. for sping[10] tow		864.67
"	To Balance due you —		239.20
			$1211.27

1813		Cr.	
Decr.	18.	By Balce due you pr. a/c forwarded	$11.27
1814			
Jan.	10.	By My dft favor R Megowan & Co[11] 60 ds	1200.—
			$1211.27
	"	Due you this day $239.20	

AD, by Hart. DLC-TJC (DNA, M212, R15).

1 Not identified.

2 John Hart and Company.

3 Dr. Frederick Ridgely.

4 Lexington branch of the Bank of Kentucky.

5 Operators of a line of boats on the Ohio River, with offices at both Maysville (Kentucky) and Pittsburgh.

6 Not found.

7 Josiah Pitts, a Virginian who had settled in Georgetown, Kentucky, about 1806 and carried on an extensive shipping trade in Kentucky produce until his failure after the outbreak of the War of 1812. He was a son-in-law of Elijah Craig.

8 Morrison, Boswell, and Sutton, successors in 1812 to Morrison, Fisher, and Sutton. The firm now included James Morrison, Dr. Joseph Boswell, Bushrod Boswell, and David Sutton. Dr. Boswell had come to Lexington from Virginia in 1786 and served as an army surgeon, 1799-1800. Thereafter, except for a brief residence in Paris, Kentucky, beginning in 1805, he practiced his profession in Lexington until his death in the cholera epidemic of 1833. Among his various business enterprises was another mercantile firm, Joseph and George Boswell, in which he and a nephew were partners. Bushrod, brother of Joseph, was a Lexington merchant, at first with his brother and later as a partner in the firm, Thomas E. Boswell and Company.

9 MS. defaced; one or two words missing at each of the indicated points in this line.

10 Spinning.

11 Robert Megowan, Lexington merchant, son of Robert Megowan the tavern keeper of an earlier day.

Guardians' Bond

[January 10, 1814]

KNOW all men by these presents, that we Henry Clay & John Hart are held firmly bound unto the Commonwealth of Kentucky in the just and full sum of three thousand dollars current money; to the payment of which well and truly to be made to the said Commonwealth, we and each of us bind ourselves and every of our Heirs, Executors and Administrators, jointly and severally, firmly by these presents, sealed and dated this 10th day of January 1814

THE CONDITION of this Obligation is such, that if the above bound Henry Clay his Heirs, Executors and Administrators, shall well and truly pay and deliver Eliza & Nannette Price Orphans of Saml. Price deceased, of whom he is appointed Guardian,[1] all such Estate as now is or shall hereafter appear to be due from him to the said Orphan [*sic*], when he [*sic*] shall attain to lawful age, to demand the same, or when thereunto required by the Justices of the said county for the time being; and also faithfully execute his office herein in such a manner as to save harmless and indemnify the first above-mentioned Justices, their Heirs, Executors and Administrators, from all trouble or damage that may arise about the said Estate—then this Obligation to be void, else to remain in full force.

JNO. HART, Atto in {L.S.}
fact for H. Clay.
JNO. HART. {L.S.}

Fayette County, Guardians Bonds, 1803-1817, p. 195.
1 At the session of Fayette County Court of this date the Misses Price chose Clay, their uncle, as their guardian.

From Benjamin H. Latrobe

The Honble H. Clay
Speaker of the house of Rep. Pittsburg Jany. 16h. 1814
Dear Sir

Your favor of the 11h I received two days ago,[1] returning me at the same time my project for your Lexington buildings.[2] On your own house you say nothing.—I take it for granted therefore that all is right, & that what I said in former letters[3] has been found sufficient. But if you are seriously about building the bed chamber wing, I much wish to give you the drawings in detail.—To return now to Lexington:—

1. There will be no difficulty I think is [*sic*] taking a passage of 3 feet wide off of the large house in Short street, by making the passage instead of 10 feet only 6.6, with a six inch brick *nogged* pan partition without touching the Wall of the house excepting perhaps to open a door thro' it. How this will affect the Staircase I cannot tell, but as the new buildings will have their ground floors within 6 inches level with the streets, the narrow new passage will probably be so much lowered as that the stairs may remain, & the passage pass under the landing; unless they commence rising on the right hand,—in which case they must be shifted to the left. The front door will require also to be new modelled something in the manner drawn here.—[. . .][4] The only difficulty will arise from the staircase, & of that I can form no judgement unless I knew the manner of its construction.

2. You say, (with the air of an objection), that I have given to the houses on Market street all the conveniencies of a family.—It is true, I have done so, because I found that the space admitted it, —that is I have given them separate privies and Yards.—By putting privies into a block,—for 4 houses, immediately behind the bac[k] buildings of the large house on Short street, for the use of the small

tenements, you appear not to have contemplated that this house shall have any Yard at all, because if it has, this block of privies must be in it, & of cou[rse] it must be passed thro' by the neighbors; or a separa[te] passage must be contrived to reach them; while the[y] might in fact with more oeconomy of space be placed in the separate Yards of the tenements. If this block however is intended for the use of the tenements in the angle on Short street the Yard for the great house is inevitably, & I think *unnecessarily* lost, while the small tenements will each have a Yard,—because nothing else can be made of the space behind them There will be no difficulty in making two tenements of 16 feet about in the clear, besides the great house on Short street, having one good room & a staircase on the floor: & the Alley taken thro' the great house will serve to go to all the Yards. The first tenement on Market street will then be curtailed to one room & a staircase. If there are to be three tenements at the corner of Short street, on Short street they can only be 10ft. wide each in the Clear for the whole space is only 32[f]t. 6in.—

To the rest of the plan you make no objection, & therefore, not seeing how I can improve it, I shall adhere to it, giving it the passage thro.' a central alley, which you suggest, and which will be a great improvement.

The front you like least is the Collonade. Your fears lest there should be a want of light, are not, I believe well founded, & if they were, it would be a recommendation to Shop Keepers, who prefer a very moderate light as more favorable to the appearance of their goods.

But before the Colonade can be executed, please to inform me whether your municipal regulations permit it to be placed on the pavement, & how far out. In Philadelphia 4 ft. 6 is the utmost.—

As soon as I have your answer to these points, I will immediately transmit to you a fair drawing. I am very respectfully Yrs

B H LATROBE

ALS copy. Latrobe Letterbook, 31-33, owned by Mrs. Ferdinand C. Latrobe, Baltimore, Maryland.

1 Not found.

2 See above, Latrobe to Clay, August 15, 24, 1813.

3 Dated August 15, September 5, 1813.

4 Diagram omitted by editors.

Full Powers to Commissioners to Negotiate a Treaty of Peace

[January 18, 1814]

James Madison, President of the United States of America,
To all to whom these presents shall come, Greeting.

Reposing especial Trust and Confidence in the Integrity, Prudence and Ability of John Quincy Adams, at present the Minister Plenipotentiary of the United States at the Court of his Imperial Majesty, the Emperor of all the Russias, James A. Bayard, late a Senator of the United States, Henry Clay, Speaker of House of Representatives of the United States, and Jonathan Russell, one of their distinguished Citizens, I have nominated, and by and with the advice and consent of the Senate appointed them jointly and severally Ministers Plenipotentiary and Extraordinary of the United States, with authority to meet, a Minister, or Ministers, having like authority from the Government of Great Britain, and with him or them to negotiate and conclude a settlement of the subsisting differences, and a lasting peace and friendship between the United States and that power; transmitting the Treaty or Convention so to be concluded, for the ratification of the President of the United States, by and with the advice and consent of the Senate of the United States.

In Testimony whereof, I have caused the Seal of the United States to be hereunto affixed.

Given under my hand at the City of Washington, the Eighteenth day of January Anno Domini 1814: and of the Independence of the United States, The Thirty Eighth. JAMES MADISON

By the President JAMES MUNROE [*sic*], Secretary of State.

Copy. DNA, M36, R2. Having rejected the Russian offer of mediation (above, Clay to Hardin, May 26, 1813, note), the British in November, 1813, had proposed direct negotiations with the United States. President Madison had accepted the offer and on January 14 had nominated Clay and Jonathan Russell to serve with Adams and Bayard on the peace commission. The appointments had been promptly confirmed.

Full Powers to Commissioners to Negotiate a Treaty of Commerce

[January 18, 1814]

James Madison President of the United States of America.

To all whom these Presents shall concern—Greeting.

Know Ye, that for the purpose of confirming between the United States and His Britannic Majesty perfect harmony and a good correspondence, and of removing all grounds of dissatisfaction, and reposing special trust and confidence in the Integrity, prudence and abilities of John Quincy Adams, Minister Plenipotentiary of the United States at the Court of his Majesty the Emperor of all the Russias, James A. Bayard, late a Senator of the United States, Henry Clay, Speaker of the House of Representatives of the United States, and Jonathan Russell, one of their distinguished Citizens, I have nominated, and by and with the advice and consent of the Senate appointed them jointly & severally, Ministers Plenipotentiary and Extraordinary of the United States, with full and all manner of power and authority for and in the name of the United States to meet and confer with a Minister or Ministers of his said Britannic Majesty, being furnished with the like power and authority, and with Him or them, to agree, treat, consult and negotiate of and concerning the general commerce between the United States and Great Britain and its dominions or dependencies, and of all matters and subjects connected therewith, which may be interesting to the two nations, and to conclude and sign a Treaty or Treaties, Convention or Conventions touching the premises; transmitting the same to the President of the United States for his final ratification, by and with the advice and consent of the Senate of the United States.

In Testimony whereof, I have caused the seal of the United States to be hereunto affixed: Given under my hand at the City of Washington the Eighteenth day of January A.D 1814, and of the Independence of the United States of America, the Thirty Eighth

JAMES MADISON

By the President JAMES MUNROE [*sic*] Secretary of State.

Copy. DNA, M36, R2.

Resignation as Speaker of the United States House of Representatives

Gentlemen, [January 19, 1814]

I have attended you to-day to announce my resignation of the distinguished station in this House, with which I have been honored by your kindness. In taking leave of you, gentlemen, I shall be excused for embracing this last occasion to express to you personally my thanks for the frank and liberal support the Chair has experienced at your hands. Wherever I may go, in whatever situation I may be placed, I can never cease to cherish, with the fondest remembrance, the sentiments of esteem and respect with which you have inspired me.

[Representative John Findlay of Pennsylvania then moved adoption of the following resolution, which was approved by vote of 149 to 9.]

Resolved, That the thanks of this House be presented to Henry Clay, in testimony of their approbation of his conduct in the arduous and important duties assigned to him as Speaker of this House.

Washington *National Intelligencer,* January 20, 1814. Published also in *Annals of Cong.,* 13 Cong., 1 Sess., XXVI, 1057; *Niles' Weekly Register,* III (January 22, 1814), 350.

From Cornelius Comegys and Peter Hoffman and Son

H Clay Esquire Baltimore 19th Jany 1814

Sir.

We were on yesterday honoured with your letter of the 17th inst,[1] instructing us to value on you for $3144 on the Acct of both our claims vs Doct. E Rumsey of Christian Co Kentucky. We have accordingly, this day, drawn on you for the said amount, in the favour of James Sterett Cashr.[2] which please pass to our debit in said Acct.

It was foreign from our intention, as seems to have been infered by you, to comprise any offensive ambiguity in our joint letter to you of the 15th. inst.[3]—Our design was simply to convey our solicitude for a closure, at length, of our unmeasureably protracted demands vs Rumsey, and our determination, if by any means practicable, to coerce payment from the debtor, who at no period for ten years past, was entitled to any indulgence from our abused confidence

We are Sir most respectfully Your very Ot H Sts.

CORNS. COMEGYS actg Executor
Estate of B Comegys
PETER HOFFMAN & SON

LS. DLC-TJC (DNA, M212, R12).

1 Not found.

2 Cashier of the City Bank of Baltimore.

3 Not found.

Receipt from Peter T. January

Jan. 24, 1814.

Recd. the amo. of the within freight viz twenty seven dollars 13 Cents of John Hart. PETER T JANUARY

DS, in Hart's hand. DLC-TJC (DNA, M212, R15). Endorsed: "Pay to Peter T. January or Order John Fink & Co." January, a resident of Maysville, had served in the Thames campaign of the War of 1812 the preceding autumn. He may now have become partner with Samuel January in the firm January, Winans, and January.

Toast at Dinner Honoring Commodore Oliver H. Perry

[January 25, 1814]

The policy which looks to peace as the end of war—and to the war as the means of peace.

Niles' Weekly Register, V (February 5, 1814), 381. The celebration was held at Washington, D.C.

To Andrew Allison

Sir Wash. 27h. Jan. 1814

I drew for you the sum of eighteen dollars (18$) which was all that was coming to you for your pension. Being among the transferred pensioners from No. Carolina, you were charged with whatever you recd. there. It is probable that there will be shortly due to you something more. If you will call on John Hart at Lexington and shew him this letter he will pay you for me the above sum of eighteen dollars. Yrs. H. CLAY

ALS. DLC-TJC (DNA, M212, R12). Addressed to Allison at Paris, Kentucky. Endorsement acknowledges receipt of the sum from John Hart, March 7, 1814.

To ———

CITY OF WASHINGTON, Jan. 27. [1814]

You will have seen that I am going to Europe. Having a decided preference for a seat in the House of Representatives over any other station under the government I vacated it with great reluctance. But I did not feel myself at liberty to decline a service, however delicate and responsible, which the President, without solicitation on my part, has been pleased to assign me. I shall leave this city in two or three days, and in about a fortnight shall embark at New-York.

Extract. Lexington *Reporter,* February 5, 1814. Identified as from Clay to a friend in Lexington.

From David Parish

Dear Sir New York the 28 Jany 1814.

I wrote you a few hurried Lines by yesterday's mail[1] & now beg leave to enclose the promised Letters for Europe: With regard to pecuniary arrangements you will observe that I have opened you credits with my friends in Amsterdam Hamburg & London which will enable you to chuse the place thro' which the negociation of bills may prove most advantageous to your interest—If you could take a Sum in Portugeese or English Gold Coins out with you to which there can be no possible objection in your Case, the Embargo Law to the Contrary notwithstanding the profit would be considerable, Say from 30 to 40 pct—Spanish Dolls. will answer better yet.

As I think it probable that you will spend some days in this City, I have annexed introductory Letters to Mr Gracie[2] & Mr. Astor[3] two very particular friends of mine & merchants of great intelligence & respectability—I am very desirous that you should make their Acquaintance, as I think you will be gratified in conversing with them on Some commercial Subjects about which you may wish to obtain information, previous to your departure.

Wishing you a pleasant passage & full Success in the important Mission confered to you, I am dear sir with Sentiments of great Regard Your very hble. & obedt Servt. David Parish

The Hone. H. Clay Esqre.

ALS. DLC-TJC (DNA, M212, R12). Addressed on verso: "The Honourable Henry Clay Esqre. expected at New York." Parish, member of a family of Hamburg financiers, had come to the United States in 1805 and established his home in Philadelphia.

1 Not found.

2 Probably Archibald Gracie, one of New York's most prominent merchants, or his son, William.

3 The merchant, financier, and fur trader, John Jacob Astor.

James Monroe to the American Commissioners

Gentlemen Dept. of State. 28th. Jany. 1814.

The British Government having declined the Russian mediation and proposed to treat directly with the United States, the President has, on due consideration, thought proper to accept the overture. To give effect to this arrangement, it was necessary that a new Commission should be formed, and for that purpose, that a new nomination should be made to the Senate, by whose advice and consent, this important trust is committed to you.

You will consider the instructions given to the Commission to treat under the mediation of Russia,[1] as applicable to the negotiation with which you are now charged, except as they may be modified by this Letter. The objects are the same, and the reasons for maintaining them, have gained great additional weight, by the vast amount of blood and treasure, which have been expended in their support.

I shall call your attention to the most important grounds of the controversy with Great Britain, only, and make such remarks on each, & on the whole subject, as have occurred since the date of the former instructions, and are deemed applicable to the present juncture, taking into view the negotiation in which you are about to engage.

On impressment, as to the right of the United States to be exempted from it, I have nothing new to add. The sentiments of the President have undergone no change on that important subject. This degrading practice must cease; our flag must protect the crew; or the United States, cannot consider themselves an independent Nation. To settle this difference amicably, the President is willing, as you are already informed by the former instructions, to remove all pretext for it, to the British Government, by excluding, all British Seamen from our Vessels, and even to extend the exclusion to all British Subjects, if necessary, excepting only the few already naturalised, and to stipulate likewise the surrender of all British Seamen, deserting in our ports, in future, from British Vessels public or private. It was presumed by all dispassionate persons, that the late law of Congress, relative to Seamen would effectually accomplish the object.[2] But the President is willing, as you find, to prevent a possibility of failure, to go further.

Should a Treaty be made, it is proper, and would have a conciliatory effect, that all our impressed Seamen, who may be discharged under it, should be paid for their services by the British Government, for the time of their detention, the wages which they might have obtained in the merchant service of their own Country.

Blockade is the subject, next in point of importance, which you will have to arrange. In the instructions bearing date on the 15th. of April 1813, it was remarked, that, as the British Government had revoked its Orders in Council, and agreed that no blockade could be legal, which was not supported by an adequate force, and that such adequate force should be applied to any blockade which it might thereafter institute, this cause of controversy seemed to be removed. Further reflection, however, has added great force to the expediency and importance of a precise definition of the public law on this subject. There is much cause to presume, that if the repeal of the Orders in Council had taken place in time to have been known here, before the declaration of war, and had had the effect of preventing the declaration, not only that no provision would have been obtained against impressment, but that under the name of blockade the same extent of coast would have been covered by proclamation, as had been covered by the Orders in Council. The war, which these abuses, and impressment, contributed, so much, to produce, might possibly prevent that consequence. But it would be more satisfactory, if not more safe, to guard against it by a formal definition in the Treaty. It is true should the British Government, violate again the legitimate principles of blockade, in whatever terms, or under whatever pretext it might be done, the United States would have in their hands, a correspondent resort; but a principal object in making peace, is to prevent, by the justice and reciprocity of the conditions, a recurrence again to war, for the same cause. If the British Government sincerely wishes to make a durable peace with the United States, it can have no reasonable objection to a just definition of blockade, especially as the two Governments have agreed in correspondence in all its essential features. The instructions of the 15th. of April 1813, have stated in what manner the President is willing to arrange this difference.

On the other neutral rights enumerated in the former instructions,

I shall remark only, that the catalogue is limited, in a manner to evince a spirit of accomodation; that the arrangement proposed in each instance is just in itself; that it corresponds with the general spirit of Treaties, between commercial powers, and that Great Britain has sanctioned it, in many treaties, and gone beyond it in some. The reasons given in my Letter of the 23rd. of June, and of the first of this month in favor of a cession of the Canadas to the United States have also gained much additional force from further reflection.[3] Experience has shewn that Great Britain cannot participate in the dominion and Navigation of the Lakes, without incurring the danger of an early renewal of the War. It was by means of the Lakes that the British Government interfered with, and gained an ascendency over the Indians, even within our own limits. The effect produced by the Massacre of our Citizens, after they were made prisoners, and of defenceless women and children along our frontiers, need not be described. It will perhaps never be removed while Great Britain retains in her hands the government of those provinces. This alone will prove a fruitful source of controversy; but there are others. Our settlements had reached before the War, from our northern boundary, with lower Canada, along the St. Lawrence, to the South-western extremity of Lake Erie, and after peace it cannot be doubted that they will soon extend by a continued population to Detroit, where there is now a strong establishment & to the banks of the Michigan, and even of the other Lakes, spreading rapidly over all our vacant territory. With the disposition already existing, collisions, may be daily expected between the Inhabitants on each side, which it may not be in the power of either Government to prevent. The cupidity of the British Traders, will admit of no controul. The inevitable consequence of another war, and even of the present, if persevered in by the British Government, must be to sever those provinces by force from Great Britain. Their inhabitants themselves, will soon feel their strength, and assert their independence. All these evils had therefore better be anticipated and provided for, by a timely arrangement between the two Governments in the mode proposed.

Should the British Government decline a cession of territory to an extent to remedy the evils complained of, you will not fail to attend to the injunctions, contained in my Letter of the 15th. of April last, as the means of mitigating them, so far as we may be able.

On the claim to indemnity for spoliations, I have only to refer you to what was said in the former instructions. I have to add, that should a Treaty be formed, it is just in itself, and would have a happy effect on the future relations of the two Countries, if indemnity should be stipulated, on each side, for the destruction of all unfortified Towns, and other private property, contrary to the Laws and usages of war. It is equally proper that the Negroes taken from the Southern States, should be returned to their owners, or paid for, at their full value. It is known that a shameful trafic [*sic*], has been carried on in the West Indies, by the sale of these persons there, by those who professed to be their deliverers. Of this fact, the proof which has reached this Department, shall be furnished you. If these Slaves are considered as non-combatants they ought to be restored, if as property they ought to be paid for. The Treaty of peace[4] contains an article which recognises this principle.

In the view which I have taken of the conditions on which you are to insist, in the proposed negotiation, you will find on a comparison of them, with those stated in the former instructions, that there is no material difference, between them, the two last mentioned claims, to indemnity, excepted, which have originated since the date of those instructions. The principal object of this review has been, to shew that the sentiments of the President are the same in every instance, and that the reasons for maintaining them, have become more evident and strong since the date of those instructions.

I shall proceed to notice the conduct of the British Government in declining the Russian Mediation, and proposing to treat directly with the United States. It's policy in so doing cannot be mistaken. Indeed the British Minister explains it himself, in stating that his object was to keep the business, unmixed, with the affairs of the Continent. Whence this desire, supposing it to be the real & only object, unless it be founded, in an opinion that in the most important questions, on which we have to treat with the British Government, Russia, and all the other powers of the Continent, have a common interest with the United States against Great Britain, and a dread thence arising, if a negotiation should be carried on under the auspices of the Emperor of Russia, that it might produce a concert, between parties having a common interest? To this cause, alone, as is presumed, is the conduct of the British Government to be imputed. It is therefore the interest of the United States to avoid becoming its victims, & to improve the occurrence, to their advantage, so far as it may be practicable.

It is believed that there is not a power in Europe that would give the slightest countenance to the British practice of impressment. Had that practice been brought into discussion under the auspices of Russia it may reasonably be presumed that it would have been treated by the Emperor, so far as he might have expressed an opinion on it, as novel, absurd, and inadmissible in regard to other Nations, and that the British Ministers, would have been forced to support it against the United States by arguments drawn from their former connection with, and dependence on Great Britain. Had the British Government supported the practice on the ground of a maritime right applicable to all Nations, it would have offended and might have excited all, against Great Britain. Had it supported it as a right applicable to the United States only, thereby degrading them below the condition of other Nations, it was easy to anticipate the effect here.

The objection of the British Government to a negotiation which formed an appeal, on any question of neutral right, to the impartial judgement of Russia, or of any other power, tho' not as an umpire, would be still stronger, for all Europe has long known, & suffered, under British violations of neutral rights. It must have been on this view of the subject that the British Government declined a negotiation, which could not fail to shew, in their naked deformity, the injustice of the British claims, & usurpations.

In accepting the overture of the British Government to treat independently of the Russian Mediation the United States, have acted on principles, which have governed them, in every transaction, relating to peace, since the war. Had the British Government accepted the Russian Mediation, the United States would have treated for themselves, independently of any other power, and had Great Britain met them on just conditions, peace would have been the immediate result. Had she refused to accede to such conditions, & attempted to dictate others, a knowledge of the views of other powers, on those points might have been useful to the United States. In agreeing to treat directly with Great Britain, not only, is, no concession contemplated, on any point in controversy, but the same desire is cherished to preserve a good understanding with Russia and the other Baltic Powers, as if the negotiation had taken place under the mediation of Russia. By meeting this overture in the manner it has been done, those powers will see, the manifestation of a desire, to keep open the door of communication with them; and to this communication great facility will be afforded by Mr. Adams and Mr. Russell, who while joined in the commission to treat with England, may preserve a direct correspondence with the Governments to which they are respectively appointed.[5]

It is probable that the British Government may have declined the Russian Mediation, from the apprehension of an understanding between the United States & Russia, for very different purposes, from those which have been contemplated, in the hope that a much better Treaty might be obtained of the United States, in a direct negotiation, than could be obtained, of them, under the Russian mediation, and with a view to profit of the concessions which might thus be made by the United States, in future negotiations with the

Baltic powers. If this was the object of the British Government & it is not easy to conceive any other, it clearly proves the advantage to be derived, in the proposed negotiation, from the aid of those powers, in securing from the British Government, such conditions as would be satisfactory to all parties. It would be highly honorable as well as advantageous to the United States, if the negotiation with which you are charged, should terminate in such a Treaty.

In availing yourselves of the good Offices of Russia & Sweden, so far as it may be practicable, on any of the points in question, in the proposed negotiation, you will always recollect that the object is to secure to the United States by means thereof, a safe and honorable peace, and not to combine with any power, in any object of ambition, or in claiming other conditions more favorable than those proposed, which may tend to prolong the war.

I have the honor to be, with high consideration, Gentlemen, Your most obedient humble servant. JAS. MONROE

John Quincy Adams Esqe.
Jas. A Bayard Esqe.
Henry Clay Esqe.
Jonathan Russell Esqe.
Albert Gallatin Esqe.[6]
&c. &c. &c.

ALS, "Duplicate." NHi-Gallatin Papers (MR8). Published in part (confidential paragraphs omitted) in *American State Papers, Foreign Relations,* III, 701-702.

1 The instructions, dated April 15, 1813, may be found in *American State Papers, Foreign Relations,* III, 695-700.

2 The act, approved March 3, 1813, had provided that after the end of the war no American vessel, public or private, might employ as seamen persons not citizens of the United States (or in the case of Negroes, natives of the United States). Naturalized citizens were to be required to produce certified copies of the records as proof of their citizenship.

3 Monroe to Gallatin and Bayard, June 23, 1813, in Elizabeth Donnan (ed.), *Papers of James A. Bayard 1796-1815* (American Historical Association, *Annual Report . . . 1913,* II), 228; January 1, 1814, in *American State Papers, Foreign Relations,* III, 701.

4 Treaty of Paris, 1783. Slaves had been seized in a series of naval raids along the Southern coast.

5 That is, Russia and Sweden.

6 Gallatin was not a member of the commission until February 9. See below, Clay to Monroe, February 13, 1814, note.

James Monroe to the American Commissioners

[January 30, 1814]

[Calling attention to the seizure of American vessels in British ports when war was daclared and referring to the act of Congress that allowed British subjects six months after the beginning of the conflict to remove their property from the United States, Monroe suggested the possibility of "A general reciprocal provision" in this connection.]

LS, "Duplicate." NHi-Gallatin Papers (MR8). Published in *American State Papers, Foreign Relations,* III, 702-703.

To Martin D. Hardin

Dr Sir Wash. 1 Feb. 1814

Inclosed is a post note drawn by the B. of Washington for $180, being the amt recd. by me for Mrs Allen.[1] Her half year's pension due 23 Ulto. is not drawn. You will transmit a Certificate or affidavit of her widowhood on that day to some person here, who will draw it.

I regret that I am unable, on a/c. of my departure from this place, to attend to having what I conceive her proper rate of pension fixed. I am thoroughly convinced that injustice has been done her, and I am persuaded that it will be corrected by a proper representation.

I leave here to day for N. York, whence I embark for Europe.

Yr's sincerely H. CLAY

ALS. ICHi. Addressed to Hardin at Frankfort.

[1] Mrs. John Allen.

Passport for Clay and Party to Gottenburg

To all who shall see these Presents, Greeting: [February 4, 1814]

The President of the United States of America having appointed the Honorable Henry Clay, late Speaker of the House of Representatives, a Minister Plenipotentiary and Extraordinary, in conjunction with John Quincy Adams, James A. Bayard, and Jonathan Russell, Esquires, to negociate and sign a treaty of Peace with Great Britain; and the said Henry Clay, who is the Bearer hereof, being now on his way to Gottenburg, in the Kingdom of Sweden, for the purpose of fulfilling the objects of his mission; These are to request all officers of the United States aforesaid, civil and military, the officers and subjects of powers in amity with the said United States, and all others whom it may concern, not to offer to the said Henry Clay any hindrance or molestation whatsoever; but, on the contrary, to afford to him and to his Secretaries and attendants, with their baggage, all necessary aid, comfort and protection.

In faith whereof, I, James Monroe, Secretary of State for the United States of America, have hereunto subscribed my name and affixed the seal of my office.

given at Washington City, this 4th day of February, A.D. 1814; and in the thirty-eighth year of American Independence.

JAS. MONROE

DS. DLC-HC (DNA, M212, R1). Published in Colton (ed.), *Private Correspondence of Henry Clay,* 24.

Russian Passport, drawn by André de Daschkoff

[February 4, 1814]

Par Ordre de Sa Majésté Impériale,
Alexandre Premier,
Empereur et Autocrateur de toutes les Russies,
&c. &c. &c.

NOUS ANDRÉ DE DASCHKOFF, Conseiller de Cour, Envoyé Extraordinaire et Ministre Plénipotentiaire près les Etats Unis d'Amérique

Savoir faisons à qui il appartiendra que le Sieur Henry Clay, Envoyé Extraordinaire et Ministre Plénipotentiaire des Etats-Unis d'Amérique, se rend à Gottenbourg en Suède, ou en Russie, accompagné de ses Sécrétaires et de sa suite.

En consequence nous prions tous ceux qui sont à prier et qui les presentes verront de laisser passer librement le dit Sr. H: Clay et sa suite et de lui prêter aide et assistance au besoin, à l'effet de quoi, nous lui avons délivré le present Passe-port, muni de notre signature et du sceau de nos armes.

Fait à Washington, ce 4. de février 1814.

GRATIS. {SEAL} ANDRÉ DE DASCHKOFF

DS. DLC-HC (DNA, M212, R1). Accompanying document:

By order of His Imperial Majesty Alexander the First, *Emperor and Autocrator of all the Russias, &c, &c, &c.*

BE it known by these presents to all whom it may concern, that the bearer of this, Henry Clay Esqr. Minister Plenipotentiary & Extraordinary from the United States, is proceeding with his Secretaries & Attendants to Gottenburgh or to Russia

All persons to whom this may be presented are therefore requested to permit the said H. Clay & his Attendants freely to pass to Said places and to aid and assist.

In faith of which have I delivered to him this passport under my signature and my seal. Washington the *4th* of february 1814. HIS IMPERIAL MAJESTY'S my MOST GRACIOUS SOVEREIGN'S Envoy Extraordinary and Minister Plenipotentiary to THE UNITED STATES OF AMERICA.

{L.S.} A. DASCHKOFF

By the Minister. The Secretary of Legation GEORGE ELLISEN.

Swedish Passport, drawn by John Albert de Kantzou

No. 2. [February 5, 1814]

We John Albert de Kantzou:

His Swedish Majesty's, Minister Resident, near the United States of America, Councellor of His Majesty's Röyal Chancery
&te &t &te.

Do hereby request, in the Name of His Majesty, all Admirals, Generals, Governors, Commanders, Magistrates, and other Officers, both Civil and Military, whoever they may be, belonging to Princes and States in friendship and Alliance with His Majesty, not only to lett [*sic*] pass:

The Honble. Mr. Henry Clay, appointed Commissioner by the President of the United States of America, to treat for Peace with great Brittain [*sic*]; His Secretaries, Attendants and baggage, going from the Port of New York to Gottenburg, in the American Corvette of War, John Adams:

without hindrance or molestation whatsoever, but to render Him, the said Honble. Mr. Henry Clay, all the aid and assistance He may require.—

Given in Philadelphia this 5th. Day of February 1814, and sealed with the Seal of our Arms

Gratis DE KANTZOU

DS. DLC-HC (DNA, M212, R1). Endorsed: "reprist; Kongl. Guarantains Commissionen; Gotheborg den 13, April 1814. Vestor Ex officio Adolph Helberg."

Decretal Order to Convey Property

[February 8, 1814]

It is now decreed and ordered that the proceedings and report of the commissioners herein returned an [*sic*] affirmed—That the Complainant Clay Convey on request to Lewis Sanders and Robert Bywaters; that part of the Lott, Sold them, agreeably to the report,[1] and that he Convey to the Defendant Dunn, the residue thereof by Deed in fee Simple, with Covenant of General Warranty,[2] and that the Defendant have leave to Withdraw the note filed for $481 12/100 and that the Defendant Pay to the Complainant his Costs &C.

D. Fayette Circuit Court, Order Book L, 362-63. On November 3, 1813, commissioners appointed to sell the property involved in the chancery suit Henry Clay against James Dunn had reported sale of one lot, to Lewis Sanders and Robert Bywaters, for $1718.88, "the am't of H. Clay's claim, with interest, but no costs of suit included." *Ibid.*, File 266 (1813).

1 Deed (below) dated November 1, 1815. 2 Not found.

James Monroe to the American Commissioners

[February 10, 1814]

[Should the commissioners conclude a treaty without a satisfactory provision for neutral rights, they are instructed "to provide that the United States shall have advantage of any stipulations more favorable to neutral nations, that may be established between Great Britain and other Powers."]

LS, "Duplicate." NHi-Gallatin Papers (MR8). Published in *American State Papers, Foreign Relations*, III, 703.

James Monroe to the American Commissioners

Gentlemen, Department of State February 10—1814.

Mr. William Shaler[1] it is believed possesses qualities which may be very useful in the course of the negotiation with Great Britain, as the bearer of written and verbal communications to our Ministers at the different courts in Europe, which circumstances may render necessary; and with this view he is attached to the Mission. He is to be allowed a compensation at the rate of 2000 dollars a year, from the time of his leaving the United States, and you will accordingly, on your arrival at Gottenburg, draw on the Bankers at Amsterdam, at this rate, from time to time as it may be due him, *as a contingency of the Mission.* I have the honor to be with great respect, Gentln your ob Set.

To the Gentlemen composing the joint Mission JAS. MONROE

LS. NHi-Gallatin Papers (MR8). Published in Donnan (ed.), *Papers of James A. Bayard,* 256. Addressed: "Henry Clay & Jonathan Russell Esqrs."

[1] Born in Connecticut, Shaler had already traveled to Europe and the Far East as a sea captain. In 1810 he had become United States consul at Havana, a post to which he returned in 1828 after having served for more than a decade as consul to Algiers. Under his assignment to the Peace Mission he carried instructions from Monroe directing him to act as confidential agent reporting to the American Commissioners and Government on any Congress which might be held for the effectuation of a general European peace. Adams, *Memoirs,* III, 53.

To [James Monroe]

Dr Sir (Private.) N. York. 13h. Feb. 1814.

I perceive that great changes have taken place in the structure of the Cabinet since I parted with you.[1] I derive much satisfaction from that by which our mission has acquired the benefit of Mr. Gallatin's services,[2] tho'. I confess I am sometimes afraid that we shall find neither him nor Mr. Bayard at Gottenburgh.[3]

Wonderful events in Europe are almost daily announced. A continental peace to the exclusion of G. Britain.—A general peace comprehending her—the revival of all the powers of Europe, as they existed prior to the French revolution, with some slight territorial modification—A congress for a general peace, which will break up without arranging it—The defeat of Lord Wellington[4]—and the defeat of the French force by which he is opposed, are among the occurrences which are asserted in the public prints. The *facts* are too confused, contradictory, and uncertain to authorize any speculations as yet on the subject of their effect on our own affairs.

Mr. Hughes[5] and Mr. Shaler have joined me. We wait only the arrival of Mr. Russell and your orders to take our departure. I understand that a Mr. Weir[6] is to go out with us, as consul at Riga. Are you quite sure that you have not been imposed upon in the appointment of this gentleman? Yr's sincerely H. CLAY

ALS. DLC-James Monroe Papers (DNA, M212, R22).

[1] See below, Clay to Crawford, April 14, 1813.

[2] After Gallatin had sailed for Europe as a member of the peace commission in 1813,

the Senate had refused to confirm his nomination because he continued as Secretary of the Treasury. He had remained abroad, however; and when his cabinet post had been declared vacant, February 9, 1814, he had been added to the newly constituted commission to negotiate directly with Great Britain.

3 Bayard and Gallatin had in fact begun on January 25 the long journey from Russia to London, where they arrived in early April.

4 Arthur Wellesley, Viscount (later Duke of) Wellington, having virtually cleared Spain of French troops during the previous year, early in 1814 resumed his victorious march into France. Meanwhile, following the Battle of Leipzig in October, 1813, the Napoleonic Empire disintegrated and the Allies occupied Paris on March 31, 1814. The Congress of Vienna assembled in the following September.

5 Christopher Hughes, Jr., of Baltimore, secretary to the mission. Afterward he was with American diplomatic posts in London, Stockholm, and the Netherlands.

6 Edward Wyer of Massachusetts, friend of John Quincy Adams and a minor diplomatic functionary.

James Monroe to the American Commissioners

[February 14, 1814]

[Should the war end in Europe, eliminating the need for impressment, the British would presumably "have less objection to a stipulation to forbear that practice for a specified term." It is important to the United States that such a stipulation be included in a peace with Great Britain.]

LS, "Duplicate." NHi-Gallatin Papers (MR8). Published in *American State Papers, Foreign Relations,* III, 703.

To [James Monroe]

Dr Sir N. York 14 Feb. 1814

The Commissions for Mr. Gallatin, your instruction of the 30h. Ulto. and sundry other papers and packets for the mission, for Mr. Crawford,[1] and for other agents abroad have been duly recd. By your letter of the 11h. inst.[2] I understand that, without waiting for other communications or orders from the Department, it is desired that we should take our departure with the utmost promptitude. Yet I doubt whether we shall get off before sunday next, the 20h. instant. Mr. Russell has not arrived, nor do I expect him before wednesday or thursday next, and I presume after he joins me he will require one or two days for preparation. So that I think that sunday may be considered as the day of our departure. Yr's truly

H. CLAY

ALS. DLC-James Monroe Papers (DNA, M212, R22).

1 William H. Crawford of Georgia, United States Senator from 1807 to 1813; Minister to France from 1813 to 1815; Secretary of War, 1815-1816; Secretary of the Treasury, 1816-1825; and candidate for the Presidency of the United States, 1824.

2 Not found.

From John Mason

Washington Feby 15. 1814

Sir Office of Commissary-Genl of Prisoners

I take the liberty of transmitting herewith, three unsealed Packets for Reuben G Beasley Esqr, the United States Agent for Prisoners, in London, which I have thought proper to submit to your inspection, in order to possess you of the most prominent points, at this moment, at issue between the two Governments of the United States and Great Britain, as relate to the Prisoner-Intercourse, namely, the system of Retaliation, and the unusual restrictions which have been imposed, by the Officers of that Government, on the Agents of ours, at Halifax, and in Canada.

I have to request, that, after perusal, you will be pleased to forward them, sealed, to their destination, together with the two other Packets now also enclosed for Mr. Beasley.

I pray you to receive, Sir, my best wishes for a pleasant passage on the Sea, and for a happy result of the important mission, in which you are engaged. I have the honor to be With very great respect Sir, Your most Obnt. Servt. J MASON

The Honble. Henry Clay. &c. &c. &c.

ALS. DLC-HC (DNA, M212, R1).

From Samuel Moale

Henry Clay Esqr

Dr Sir, Balto Feby 18h. 1814.

Your Letter of the 12th. Feby Instant[1] enclosing a Check drawn by W. Fish Cashier of the Mechanics Bank in the City of New York dated the Twefth [*sic*] day of February Eighteen hundred and fourteen drawn to your Order for five thousand Dollars and indorsed by you to Mr John Purviance[2] and myself for the purpose of lodging the same in the Chancery Court of Maryland to the Credit of your Trusteeship of Messrs Purviances Estate,[3] reached us and we will lodge the said Sum of Money in the Chancery Court accordingly— We hope you will instruct your agent to pay any other Sums of Money on this Trust during your absence from America—

I wrote to you on the 16h. Instant[4] and I assure you with great reluctance because I conceived you had been so often troubled on this subject but I am sure you will excuse me for reasons assigned in my two last Letters to you—respectfully S MOALE

ALS. DLC-TJC (DNA, M212, R12). 1 Not found.
2 Baltimore attorney, later a judge of the Baltimore County Court.
3 See above, Report, July 12, 1813. 4 Letter not found.

From James Monroe

Sir Dept. of State Feby 18th. 1814.

Should Mr Russell, in consequence of the attention due to his

and should not be an uncertainty as
private affairs, not have returned to New York, at the time you receive
to the time of his ar[rival, or a certainty that he will not arrive in
this letter, the President thinks it best that you will immediately sail
a day or two][1]
for Gottenburg, in execution of the trust committed to you. It is con-
will be provided as soon as possible to
templated to provide another vessel, to take duplicates of your instruc-
in which Mr Russell may sail with the chance of arriving as soon
tions, which it is presumed will be ready for sea, by the time Mr.
as yourself.
Russell is prepard [*sic*] to sail. There is danger, by the delay of
particularly of the former
losing the services of Mr Gallatin and Mr Bayard, in the proposed
not to lose sight of the very great importance of not
negotiation, which would be cause of serious regret. By the arrange-
being ready in time to meet the Comrs. of the other party to
ment proposed, it is hoped, that the public will be availed, of the services, of all the gentlemen who are included in the joint mission.

I have the honor to be with great respect your very obt servant

JAS MONROE

In case you sail without Mr Russell send to him a copy of this letter.
by any unnecessary delay
of not being instrumental to the commencment [sic] *of negotiations for peace.*

ALS draft. DLC-James Monroe Papers (DNA, M212, R22). Interlineations italicized by editors. Endorsed on verso: "Mr Clay 1814."

1 Bracketed words written in margin as a continuation of the interlinear text.

To [James Monroe]

My Dr Sir (Private) N. York 23 Feb. 1814

Your surprize will not be greater than my mortification at the delay which has arisen in our departure. It terminates however to day, and I derive some consolation from the assurance I have recd. here, on all hands, that owing to the state of the wind and weather we have not really lost any time.

I fear I may have occasioned unintentionally a slight misconception of each other's views between you and Mr. Russell. Speaking on the subject of pecuniary arrangement at Philada. I observed to him that a part of an outfit had been allowed to Mr Adams, in consequence of his association in the mission at St. Petersburg, with the approbation I believed of Congress; and that if any thing were allowed him for repairing to Gottenburg I was persuaded he (Mr.

R.) wd. be placed on a footing of equality. At all events I Advised him, from your known character, to write you with the utmost freedom and frankness. I am sure that Mr. Russell was altogether uninfluenced by avaricious motives, and that he had no other feeling than such as would arise from the supposition that an equality of compensation ought to follow an equality of service and responsibility. However he perfectly acquiesces in the views of the President, and I now write on this subject (confidentially) merely to maintain between you the best understanding

It seems that Capt. Angus[1] having no instruction from the Navy Dept. declines admitting Mr. Wyer[2] on board the ship, and he of course does not go out. He appears to regret it very much. I confess freely that I am not myself sorry that we have not the honor of his Company. The public interest I am persuaded will not suffer by *his* absence from Riga; and if one half of what I have heard from a respectable source is true his Commission ought to be instantly revoked.

In taking leave of you allow me to present you my thanks for the repeated instances of your kindness and friendship which I have experienced; and to express my wishes for your private & public prosperity. Yr friend H. CLAY

By the desire of Mr. Dashkoff I return through you a passport which being unnecessary, he wished to recall under cover to you.[3]

H. C.

ALS. DLC-James Monroe Papers (DNA, M212, R22).
1 Samuel Angus, Captain of the United States corvette, *John Adams*.
2 Edward Wyer. 3 Above, February 4, 1814.

From Lucretia Clay

WASHINGTON, MARCH 10. [1814]

MY DEAR HUSBAND,—Mr. Barker[1] called to-day to let me know that he has an opportunity of sending letters to Gottenburg, and offered to take charge of one for you. I heard the other day from Lexington that it is more sickly than it ever has been. Nelly Hart[2] had twelve negroes sick; Theodore[3] wrote me that all our family were well. The children that I have with me are all well,[4] and Henry is always talking of you, he comes up and kisses me for his papa. I long very much to be at home with my family, for I am very dreary here as I do not pay visits; indeed I found I could not go out without you in the evening, but I do all in my power to keep me from being melancholy. Our suit in this court was tried the other day; I have not heard that it is decided.[5] Mr. Wickliff[6] started on Sunday last for Kentucky. Mrs. Brown[7] has at last made up her mind to go home with me and spend the summer. Judge Todd and his lady[8] have been very polite to me since you left this; the Judge called the other day to examine the light wagon we were to have got from Mr. L.[9] but he found it so completely worn out that I determined not to take it; we shall I hope get on without it. Mr. Bibb[10] paid me the $500 as soon as he got here. You need not make yourself the least uneasy on our account, for I believe we shall do very well. Mr. Granger[11] has been turned out of office. A great many blame Mr. Madison. Susan and Ann send their love to you. May God spare you to us. Do take care of yourself for our sakes.

Colton (ed.), *Private Correspondence of Henry Clay,* 24-25.

1 Jacob Barker, a native of Maine, who as a young man had joined his brother Abraham in New York. Both attained wealth as merchants and helped finance the War of 1812. Jacob, who suffered heavy reverses during the war, made and lost several fortunes. In 1834 he moved to New Orleans, where he began to practice law.

2 Widow of Thomas Hart, Jr.

3 Theodore Wythe Clay, eldest son of Henry and Lucretia Clay, born in 1802; at this time a student at Transylvania University.

4 Thomas Hart (born 1803), Susan Hart (born 1805), Ann Brown (born 1807), Lucretia Hart (born 1809), and the baby, Henry Clay, Jr. (born 1811).

5 Suit not found. 6 Robert Wickliffe.

7 Mrs. Clay's sister, Mrs. James Brown.

8 Judge Thomas Todd was married to Lucy Payne, sister of Dolly Madison.

9 Not identified. 10 George M. Bibb. 11 Gideon Granger.

James Monroe to the American Commissioners

[March 21, 1814]

[The loan bill has passed both houses of Congress, and acts for augmenting the military forces have been adopted. There is, however, a sincere desire for peace on just and honorable terms. The success of the Baltic powers in the war will free them "to look to the great object of the maritime rights, for which we contend." In view of the common interest of these powers with the United States in this connection "their friendly interposition has been invited, & a fair opportunity offered to secure to it the best effect. It is hoped that this opportunity will be improved."

If peace can be made, the sooner the better. "If such an arrangement cannot be obtained, it is important to the United States to be acquainted with it without delay."]

Copy (Extract). NHi-Gallatin Letterbook, II, 242-43 (MR19). Published in *American State Papers, Foreign Relations,* III, 703, with confidential paragraph (summarized in the first above) omitted.

James Monroe to the American Commissioners

[March 22, 1814]

[The commissioners, in case "a reciprocal restitution of territory be agreed on," are to remember that the United States had before the war a post at the mouth of the Columbia River. "On no pretext can the British Government set up a claim to territory south of the northern boundary of the United States." Should an attempt be made to define a boundary, no British pretension to territory south of that line should be countenanced.]

Copy. NHi-Gallatin Letterbook, II, 243-44 (MR19). Published in *American State Papers, Foreign Relations,* III, 731.

William H. Crawford to the American Commissioners

Gentlemen. Paris 8th. April 1814.

The events which have within a few days passed in this city, and in its neighborhood, have changed every thing in France, but the character of the Parisians, and perhaps of French-men in general.

On the 30th ult a battle was fought in the vicinity of Paris by the French troops under the Duke of Ragusa,[1] amounting to between fifteen & twenty thousand men, and the grand allied army. The loss was considerable on both sides, but that of the Allies was more than double—It is estimated from eight to ten thousand men. The disparity in the loss, was the result of the strong positions of the French troops, and the desire of the Allies to get possession of the Capital before the arrival of the Emperor Napoleone, who was advancing by rapid marches upon their rear. This desire was so predominant that they made no attempt to turn these positions, but marched directly up to the intrenchments, where they were repulsed four or five times. The battle commenced about 4 o clock A M, & finished about the same time, in the evening. The Duke of Ragusa entered into a convention by which he agreed to evacuate the city, taking with him all his baggage, ammunition & artillery.

The next day The Emperor of Russia & King of Prussia, entered Paris at the head of about 50,000 of the finest troops in the world. The remainder of their immense army either defiled on the north or south side of the city, or remained in their positions on the East, which was the field of battle. The Emperor of Russia with his minister of Foreign Relations went directly to the house of the Prince of Benevento,[2] who convened the Senate the same evening, & had himself & three of his friends, with one devoted Bourbonite named to the provisional government. The Senate have deposed Napoleone Buonaparte, and directed the provisional government to form A constitution, which has been accomplished and accepted by the Senate & the small portion of the Legislative corps who are now in Paris. The monitor[3] of this day contains this constitution which you will probably see before you receive this letter. The monarchy is declared to be Hereditary in the House of Bourbon in the male line. The present Senators remain Senators of the Realm by the same tenure. The Senate to consist of 150, at least, & not more than 200. The ancient & new nobility to remain. All French men to be capable of filling all the offices of the government. The members of the legislative corps to hold their offices for five years, and to be elected directly by the people.

The proceedings of the Senate and of the provisional government, has overturned the authority of the Emperor with his army, and especially with his ablest generals. He seems to have sunk without an effort, at least without an effort corresponding in any degree with his former fame. Such at least is the conclusion which I draw from the facts which are communicated to the public. It is possible that these facts may be misrepresented. I believe however that it is certain, that he has agreed to retire with his family to the Isle of Elba, upon a pension of six millions of Livres. From the moment that he saw it was impossible for him to reign, he ought to have died. The manner was in his election. A strange infatuation seems to have influenced his conduct during the last six months. Still relying upon his talents and his power, he refused at Prague to secure at least the neutrality of Austria, by giving her every thing she required. After having retreated across the Rhine, he reluctantly accepted the bases which the Allies proposed, and which there is some reason to believe they were sincerely disposed to adopt. Lord Castlereagh's mission however, according to the best view of the subject which I have been able to take, was intended solely to prevent this accommodation.[4] Time will prove the accuracy or inaccuracy of this opinion. There must have been great addressed [*sic*] employed in managing the Emperor of Austria,[5] who had rejected all idea of overthrowing the reigning dinasty. The infatuation of the Emperor and his arrogance to his father in Law, (if we are to credit reports apparently well founded) greatly contributed to the success of the arts employed by the British Secretary. That the Emperor of Austria has been duped, is clearly established, by the declaration of the Allies after the breaking up of the Congress at Chatillon and by the conduct of Lord Wellington. This declaration states that up to the 15th of March they were ready to make peace with the Emperor Napoleone,[6] whereas the address of Lord Wellington on the 2d of February declares Louis the 18th. and raises the Bourbon standard. The introduction of the ancient dinasty is not acceptable to the great body of the people of Paris. Even now after the Senate & provisional government have declared for that dinasty there is not one man in an hundred who puts on the white cockade. On the day of the entry of the Allied Sovereigns, all the persons devoted to their ancient

Kings endeavored to make themselves as conspicuous as possible, and to conceal the smallness of their numbers by continual change of place. Exertions were made to excite popular feeling and popular tumult but without effect. But for the national guard popular tumult would have been excited perhaps, but not in favor of the Bourbons. If the mob of Paris had been put in motion, it would have been in favor of a free government.

The men now in power would, as far as I have been able to judge, have preferred the succession of the King of Rome,[7] with a regency presided by the Empress; but the Emperor Alexander[8] who under the modest exterior of submitting every thing to the will of the French people dictates to the Senate & provisional government at least this article of their constitution.
1385.103.1576.1385.21.1576.68.1517◊.1592.1385.530.1361.1242.1576. November. 222.801.1501.118.1503.818.871.1426.1385.44. Every declaration made 792.1385.981.639.21.668.792.184.385.1022.908.500. 1003.1061.1458.801.569.1426.1279.68.569.1310.880.282.1384. reparation 1179.1310.488.880.1310.718.216◊. 1264.1385.21.1505.1501.1116. 1318.169.1087.938.981.1385.171.704◊ 1576.1385. 1538◊. 692.395.520. 628.1384.169.1244.605.1501.747.569.1385.16.1176. contained every 1149.1426.121.1486.463.399.1331.1385.775.1229.637◊. 1401.1259.235. learned that it recommended 1426.821.449.981.1044.821.411◊.480. 1385.1325.886.668.647.1549.809.1054◊—1318. their operation was known to the 49.—981.1535. confiscations, by 1054◊—668.981.1535 1002.1075.1067.1576.785.446.699.1076×.[9] These conditions were short of what we had a right to claim, but they were such as to require much consideration, before they ought to be rejected. The new state of things will probably change the ground on which the demand will be contested. In the mean time, I shall have an opportunity of hearing from the government before I am compelled to proceed in the discussion. I am fearful that 664.1426.24.1433◊. 684. 360. calculated 981 1385.289.1436.564.1201.264.1576.1395◊. However, I presume that a peace in Europe must have been anticipated 792.1385.78.1318.664.826.490.301. I endeavored to convince 1385. 1229.637.1384.1501.287.1549.1118. would certainly take place, early in the campaign, and that it would be unfavorable to France. 1416. 167.879◊.1259.360.1317.310.594.1431.1385.1249◊.1576.1385.550. 1385.78.1436 1426. possession of 167.74.1429.668.906◊.488.1399.384. 1411. It is however true that I did not anticipate precisely the manner in which this European peace was to be consummated. I most sincerely wish you complete success in your negociations, altho I apprehend that great difficulties will be presented.

Under existing circumstances if peace is made, I presume that the treaty will very [*sic*] short, concluding nothing but peace, and the restoration of what territory that may be in the hands of either party by conquest, if there is any such. I am Gentlemen most sincerely your most obt. & very humble servt

Wm. H. Crawford.

P.S. I send this by the Secty of the Danish legation who sets out immediately for Copenhagen, which gives me no opportunity for reflection or revision of this hasty scrawl, as I have just been informed of the fact of his setting out. W H C

ALS. DLC-HC (DNA, M212, R1).

1 Auguste Frederic Louis Viesse de Marmont, Marshal of France, Duke of Ragusa, had been associated with Napoleon since Toulon.

2 Napoleon had conferred the title, Prince of Benevento, on Talleyrand in 1806.

3 *Le Moniteur Universelle,* French journal, official organ of the Government.

4 For several months Castlereagh had been on the Continent urging the Allies to a determined effort to overthrow Napoleon.

5 Emperor Francis I of Austria, the father of Marie Louise, Napoleon's second wife.

6 The Châtillon Conference, February 4 to March 19, 1814, had been an effort to bring an end to the war by means of a negotiated peace. Neither side, however, had been willing to compromise. The declaration to which Crawford refers had been intended to place on Napoleon the responsibility for continuing the war.

7 Napoleon's son. 8 Of Russia.

9 Cipher, not found, same as that used below, Crawford to the American Commissioners, October 14, 1814. Clay was not able to read the coded portion of this letter until Russell deciphered it for him. See below, Clay to Russell, May 9, Russell to Clay, May 16, 1814.

Clay and Jonathan Russell to James A. Bayard and Albert Gallatin

Gentlemen Gottenburg 14 April 1814

The President of the United States with the approbation of the Senate, having appointed Mr. Adams, you and us, jointly & severally to treat at this place with a minister or ministers appointed by Great Britain, of the differences subsisting between the two countries, we sailed from New York on the 25h February last, in the United States Corvette John Adams, and reached here last night to proceed to the execution of the trust confided to us. No British Commissioners have arrived nor do we know of the appointment of any. We have communicated to Mr. Adams, who is also absent, information of our arrival. It will give us much pleasure to be joined by you as early as your convenience may admit. We do not send by the bearer, Mr. Shaler,[1] any packets or letters with which we are charged for you, lest he might be prevented from delivering them, by your having left Amsterdam, before he reaches it. We have the satisfaction however, to inform you of the health of your respective ladies and families when we sailed, shortly before which they were seen by one or both of us.

You will find by a copy of the enclosed note from the Secretary of State that Mr. Shaler is attached to the mission.[2] We have sent by him dispatches from the government for Mr. Crawford,[3] and, subject to your approbation we have assigned to him the execution of a confidential service which he will explain to you. Under the same restriction we have drawn on Mess Willinks & Van Staphorst[4] at Amsterdam for one years compensation in his behalf. If you approve of it you will subjoin your signatures to the draft.

Your Obedient Servants H. CLAY
JONA RUSSELL

ALS copy by Russell. RPB-Russell Letterbook, 174-75. Published in Donnan (ed.), *Papers of James A. Bayard,* 283-84.
1 William Shaler.
2 See above, Monroe to American Commissioners, February 10, 1814 (2).
3 William H. Crawford.
4 Wilhem Van Willink and N. and Joseph van Staphorst, Amsterdam bankers.

Clay and Russell to John Quincy Adams

Sir Gottenburg 14 Apl. 1814.

You will have learnt through Mr. Strong[1] of the accession by the President of the U. States to a British overture to treat of peace between the two countries at this place; and of your appointment with Mr. Bayard and us to represent our government. Subsequent to the departure of Mr. Strong from America Mr. Gallatin was associated in the commission. We sailed from N. York on the 25th. Feb. last in the U. States Corvette John Adams and reached here yesterday to be in readiness to proceed to the execution of our duty. We have communicated to Mess. Bayard and Gallatin supposed to be at Amsterdam, information of our arrival; and it will give us much pleasure to be joined by them and yourself as soon as your convenience may admit. We know nothing of the measures which the British Government may have adopted to give effect to the negotiation.

We are charged with sundry packets and letters for you which we shall retain until you join us, or direct what disposition we shall make of them. This letter is committed to the Mail. We are Sir with much consideration Yr. ob. Servts. H. CLAY
John Q. Adams Esqr. JONA RUSSELL

LS, the concluding paragraph in Clay's hand. MHi-Adams Family Papers. Published in Donnan (ed.), *Papers of James A. Bayard,* 284.
1 Nathaniel H. Strong, recently appointed United States Consul at Gottenburg, had carried dispatches from America to St. Petersburg.

To [William H. Crawford]

My Dr Sir Gottenburg 14h. Apl. 1814.

Mr Shaler is charged with the delivery to you of sundry packets and letters, public and private, which with the oral communications you will receive from him will put you in complete possession of American affairs up to the period of our departure from N. York. Among the letters you will find several from our friends at Mrs. Dowson's mess No. 2, all of whom I am happy to inform you were well.

The success with which our operations on the Lakes, in the N.W. and in the South had been attended gave to the administration a strength, of which they were not deprived, altho' it was somewhat diminished, by the failure of Genl. Wilkinson's enterprize agt. Montreal.[1] The causes of that failure you will be able to collect from a document, called for by Congress, and with which Mr. Shaler will supply you. Laws had been passed offering increased incentives to the recruiting service, which was going on with much spirit; so that sanguine hopes were entertained of our ability to enter the field, on the opening of the campaign, with an imposing force. The Embargo law was enforced, without any of those violations which characterized the execution of the former one. The effect of this measure most regretted, as it respects its operation upon ourselves, was the probable diminution of the revenue. On the other hand, it was believed that the product of the Internal taxes had been placed at much too low an estimate.

You will have heard of the acceptance, by the President of the British overture to treat of peace at this place. The unexpected continuance of Mr. Gallatin in Europe rendered it necessary to supply his place at the head of the Treasury, and G. W. Campbell[2] was appointed to that station, and Mr Gallatin associated in this mission, after I left Washington: The Cabinet experienced a further change in the resignation of Mr. Pinkney,[3] and the appointment of Mr. Rush[4] to the office of Atto. General. His place as Comptroller was filled with E. Bacon, formerly of the House of Representatives.[5]

Upon leaving America it was my wish to have visited France, and altho' it is somewhat weakened by the late visit which Paris has received; or rather is said to have recd. (for the fact is not yet confirmed)[6] I have not entirely abandoned the intention. Will you do me the favor to inform me if there be any difficulty in my executing this purpose; and if I shall not trespass too much upon your goodness, may I further ask that you would obtain for me any facilities that may be necessary to my *safety* in travelling? The *time* is of course altogether uncertain, depending upon the termination of my public duties here; but I should hope it would not be longer than July or August.

If Paris has been really occupied by the allies, I presume your public character has protected you from any inconvenience. As to your success in the object of your mission[7] I apprehend that is not to be counted upon. With sincere wishes for your prosperity I remain very truly Yrs. H. CLAY

ALS. DLC-William H. Crawford Papers (DNA, M212, R20).

1 See above, Clay to Rodney, December 11, 1813, note.

2 George Washington Campbell, a Scotch immigrant, who resigned as United States Senator from Tennessee to become Secretary of the Treasury. Eight months later he left the Cabinet because of ill health and in 1815 returned to the Senate. He was subsequently, 1818-1821, United States Minister to Russia.

3 William Pinkney.

4 Richard Rush, former Attorney-General of Pennsylvania, who had served as Comptroller of the United States Treasury since 1811. He became the United States Minister to Great Britain in 1817, was Secretary of the Treasury, 1825-1828, and Minister to France, 1847-1849.

5 Ezekiel Bacon, Massachusetts Congressman from 1807 to 1813, who served slightly more than a year as Comptroller.

6 Clay had not yet seen the letter written on April 8 by Crawford to the American Commission, summarizing recent events in France.

7 Crawford had been sent to France in the summer of 1813 to demand repeal of the Berlin and Milan decrees, to seek redress for violation of American shipping interests, and, if possible, to negotiate a treaty of commerce.

Rental Agreement with Asa Wilgus and William Clarke

[April 15, 1814]

An agreement entered into this 15th. day of Apl. 1814 Between H. Clay, Asa Wilgus and Wm. Clarke.

The said Clay hereby rents to the said Clarke and Wilgus the ballance of the Hotel including the lower room and the rooms above that part of the Hotel between the tenements of McCullough & Foster and Porter[1] including all the rooms except that heretofore rented, which is now in the occupancy of said Clarke and which was leased to J. O. Payne[2] for the term of three years commencing on this day.

The said Clay also leases to the said Clarke and Wilgus at the end of three months from this date the kitchen and smoke house attached to the said establishment and now in the occupancy of Porter. The possession of which Can't be obtained until the expiration of three months according to the lease given to said Porter.

In consideration whereof the the [*sic*] said Wilgus and Clarke hereby Covenants to pay to the said Clay the sum of two hundred and fifty Dollars for the first year, four hundred Dollars for the second and four hundred Dollars for the third payable in equal quarterly payments. And the said Wilgus and Clarke agree to surrender the premises at the end of the term in as good order as they recieve them, natural decay and inevitable accidents excepted.

The said Clay further agrees to have each and all the rooms hereby leased white washed, and new glass put into the windows that wants it—

The said Clay reserves the right to distrain for arrears of rent and of reentry on the premises.

Witness our hands and seals the day and Date afd.

Sealed and Delivered	For H. Clay
in the presence of	JOHN WATKINS {L.S.}
JAMES G. TROTTER	ASA WILLGUS [*sic*] {L.S.}
JAMES MCCONNELL[3]	WM CLARKE {L.S.}

[Endorsement on sheet attached to first page][4]

Bradford substituted for these tenants by agreemt. with J. Watkins—[5]

DS. KyLxT. Clarke was probably the son of William Clarke, Lexington hatter who had died in 1808. Shortly after this agreement was drawn, Wilgus opened the "Columbian Inn," in the building rented from Clay. Unsigned endorsements by Watkins indicate payment of the rent through three quarters of the first year.

1 Nathaniel S. Porter.

2 See above, Rental Agreement, April 15, 1813. Clarke apparently occupied the premises under an agreement with Payne.

3 Fayette County farmer, brother of Francis.

4 ES, in Clay's hand.

5 Daniel Bradford used the building for a time as an auction house.

Clay and Russell to Crawford

Sir Gottenburg 16th. April 1814

Having been appointed by the President of the U. States, with Messrs Gallatin, Adams & Bayard, to negociate at this place, treaties of peace & commerce with Great Britain, we beg leave to announce to you our arrival in this Country & our expectation of being at an early day joined by our Colleagues.

As it may be in your power to communicate to us important information, useful to us in the execution of our trusts, we beg leave to call your attention to this object & to assure you of the great respect & high consideration with which we are Sir Yr. faithful & obedient Servants

The honble. William Crawford &c. &c. &

Paris.

L, in hand of an amanuensis, signatures removed. DLC-William H. Crawford Papers (DNA, M212, R20).

Clay and Russell to Willink and Van Staphorst

Gentlemen Gottenburg 16h April 1814

According to the power vested in us by the President of the United States we have this day drawn on you, at sight, in favor of William Shaler Esqr for two thousand dollars which we desire you to pay and charge to the account of the United States as a contingent expense of this mission for one years salary of the said Shaler. Very Respectfully Your Obedt Servt H. CLAY

JONA RUSSELL

ALS copy by Russell. RPB-Russell Letterbook, 178. Published in Donnan (ed.), *Papers of James A. Bayard,* 285.

Clay and Russell to Adams

Sir, Gottenburg 16th. April 1814—

To multiply the chances of your obtaining information of our arrival, and to ensure a safe delivery of sundry despatches for the American Consul at St. Petersburg[1] and for the Russian government, we have engaged the bearer hereof Mr. Lewis[2] to proceed to St. Petersburg somewhat earlier and with more expedition than he would otherwise have done. We enclose herein a copy of a letter which we forwarded to you by mail.[3] We still retain your letters &c because of the probability of your having left Russia before Mr. Lewis's arrival, and the uncertainty of his meeting with you.[4] We take great pleasure in recommending this young countryman of ours to your notice. He accompanied us on the voyage, and interested us extremely by his amiable and obliging disposition. Yr. obt. Servts.

H. CLAY

Honbl. Mr. Adams JONA RUSSELL

ALS by Russell, signed also by Clay. MHi-Adams Family Papers. Published in Donnan (ed.), *Papers of James A. Bayard,* 284-85.

1 Levett Harris, United States Consul at the Russian capital, had been appointed secretary to the earlier peace mission, in 1813.

2 William Davis Lewis of Philadelphia, who, through Clay, had obtained an appointment as one of the secretaries of the peace commission to enable him to join his brother, a commission merchant in Russia. After reaching Gottenburg on the *John Adams,* Lewis continued to St. Petersburg. His friendship with Clay continued; in 1850 Clay was instrumental in securing Senate confirmation of his nomination as Collector of the Port of Philadelphia.

3 Their letter of April 14.

4 Adams remained in St. Petersburg until April 28.

Clay and Russell to Bayard and Gallatin

Gentlemen Gottenburg 20th. April 1814

We despatched a Messenger to Amsterdam, by the way of Copenhagen, on the 17th. Inst. to inform you of the appointment of each of you, with Mr. Adams and us to conduct, on the part of America, the proposed negotiations at this place with Great Britain; and of our arrival here, in the Corvette John Adams, on the 14th. Inst. We did not send the Letters &c. which we brought for you, and do not now, because we thought the most certain, if not the most speedy, delivery of them; would be ensured by their remaining here.

We have the pleasure of informing you of the health of your families, when we left America, your ladies having been seen by one, or both of us, just before we sail'd.

We are unadvised as to the movements of Mr. Adams.

We are, with high consideration Yr. obedt. Sevts.

to H. Clay
J. A. Bayard Jona Russell
A. Gallatin Esqrs. &c. &c. &c.

ALS by Russell, signed also by Clay. NHi-Gallatin Papers (MR8). Published in Donnan (ed.), *Papers of James A. Bayard,* 287.

Clay and Russell to Monroe

Sir Gottenburg 20th April 1814.

We reached this place on the 14th. inst. The ice not admitting of the John Adams coming up the river, she came to anchor in a harbour near its mouth, about 12 miles from Gottenburg, where we were landed.

We understand that our Colleagues Mess. Bayard and Gallatin are in England. Of Mr. Adams' movements we are unadvised. We have conveyed them intelligence of their appointments.

We commit this despatch to the chances of finding a conveyance to America through England without knowing the direction it may take.

With high consideration we are Sir Yr. obt. Servts. H. C.
J. R.

ALI copy by Clay. NHi-Gallatin Papers (MR8). Published in Donnan (ed.), *Papers of James A. Bayard,* 285.

Bayard to Clay and Russell

Gentlemen— London 20 [*i.e.* 22] April 1814.

The mail of last evening brought the intelligence of your arrival at Gottenburgh[1]

I present you my congratulations upon your safe passage across the Atlantic.

Mr. Gallatin & myself left St. Petersberg on the 25th. of January and arrived at Amsterdam on the 4th. of March

In that city we received the first advice of the direct negociation proposed to be held between the U States & Great Britain at Gottenburgh and of the intention of our Government to send additional Commissioners from America. Knowing that some time would elapse before your arrival in Europe and also before the appointment of Commissioners on the part of this Government, we thought it likely that more good might result from spending the interval in this Country rather than in Holland

We came over on the 9th inst. at a moment not very propitious for the objects we had in view. The Allies had taken possession of Paris, and the next day brought the news of Bonaparte's formal abdication of the thrones of France & Italy. The intelligence completely turned the heads of all ranks who seem to have thought of nothing since but the means of manifesting their joy on the occasion.

It is much to be apprehended that this great & unexpected event will have an unfavorable influence upon the state of affairs between the U States & G. Britain

There is reason to think that it has materially changed the views of the British ministry. In fact the sudden reduction of their naval & military establishments would create much embarrassment and the American war furnishes too good a pretense to avoid it. and the great augmentation of their disposeable force presents an additional temptation to prosecute the war. You must also know that the temper of the Country is highly excited against us & decidedly expressed in favor of the continuance of hostilities.

I do not pretend however to speak at present with any certainty of the intentions of the government, for we have had no communication with any member of it

I think they have avoided any intercourse with us, but this may be attributed to the absence of Lord Castlereagh[2] and the indisposition of the other ministers to interfere with the affairs of his Department

We cannot learn that any step has yet been taken towards the selection of characters to be charged with the negociation on the part of this Government. It is stated and upon such authority as to deserve credit that no appointment will be made till the government is officially notified of the appointment of the American Commissioners & of their arrival at the place of rendezvous. Mr. G. & myself have thought it therefore of sufficient importance to dispatch a special messenger to apprize you of the fact & to enable you by his return without loss of time to make the official communication.

If there be a discretion on the subject we would though recommend that some Town in Holland should be substituted in lieu of Gottenburgh as the seat of the negociation. There can be no doubt that the change would facilitate and accelerate the result. You may rely upon the friendly dispositions of the Prince of Orange,[3] of which we had distinguished proofs during a short residence at Amsterdam.

One of the first acts of the Government of the Prince was to nominate a minister to the United States.

I shall remain in London, till I have the pleasure of hearing from you, unless (which is not to be expected) in the meantime Commissioners should be appointed on the part of this Government

This letter will be delivered to you by Colonel Milligan[4] who accompanied me as private secretary to St Petersberg. He is deserving of your confidence and I beg leave to recommend him to your attentions. I have the honor to be with the highest respect Gentlemen Your very obt. Sert. J. A. Bayard

The Honorable Henry Clay & Jonn. Russell &c &c

ALS. DLC-HC (DNA, M212, R1). Published in Colton (ed.), *Private Correspondence of Henry Clay*, 28-29; Donnan (ed.), *Papers of James A. Bayard*, 285-87. On the dating of this letter, cf. Bayard, "European Diary," in Donnan (ed.), *op. cit.*, 507; Gallatin to Clay, same date.

1 Not by the letter, Clay and Russell to Bayard and Gallatin, April 14, 1814, which was delivered by Shaler.

2 From April 10 to May 30 Castlereagh was in Paris.

3 William, son of William V of Orange, had arrived in Holland from England on November 30, 1813. In March, 1815, he was crowned as King William I of the Netherlands.

4 George B. Milligan, Bayard's private secretary. The young men who accompanied the peace mission to St. Petersburg in 1813 had received commissions in the United States Army.

From Albert Gallatin

Dear Sir London 22d. April 1814

We have just heard of your arrival, but have received no letters, and I am yet ignorant whether I am one of the new commission to treat of peace. My arrangements must depend on that circumstance & I wait with impatience for the official account which you must have brought. For that reason Mr Bayard addresses you & Mr Russel in his own name;[1] but I coincide fully with him in the opinion that the negotiations should by all means be opened here or at least in Holland, if this is not rendered impracticable from the nature of the commission. If this has unfortunately been limited to treating of peace at Gottenburg, which seems highly improbable, there is no remedy. But if the commission admits of a change of place, I would feel no hesitation in removing thence at least to any other neutral place, whatever may be the language of the instructions. For their spirit would be fully answered by treating in any other friendly country as well as if at Gottenburg. On that point I feel great anxiety, because on account of the late great changes in Europe & of the encreased difficulties thence arising in making any treaty, I do believe that it would be utterly impossible to succeed in that corner, removed from every friendly interference in our favour on the part of the European powers, and compelled to act with men clothed with limited authorities & who might at all times plead a want of instructions.

You are sufficiently aware of the total change in our affairs produced by the late revolution & by the restoration of universal peace in the European world, from which we are alone excluded. A well organised & large army is at once liberated from any European employment, and ready, together with a super abundant naval force, to act immediately against us. How ill prepared we are to meet it in a proper manner no one knows better than yourself, but above all our own divisions and the hostile attitude of the Eastern States give room to apprehend that a continuance of the war might prove vitally fatal to the United States.

I understand that the Ministers, with whom we have not had any direct intercourse, still profess to be disposed to make an equitable peace. But the hope not of ultimate conquest but of a dissolution of the Union, the convenient pretence which the American war will afford to preserve large military establishments, and above all the force of popular feeling may all unite in inducing the Cabinet in throwing impediments in the way of peace. They will not certainly be disposed to make concessions, nor probably[2] displeased at a failure of negociations. That the war is popular, and that national pride inflated by the last unexpected success cannot be satisfied without what they call the chastisement of America, cannot be doubted. The mass of the people here know nothing of American politics but through the medium of federal speeches & news papers faithfully transcribed in their own journals. They do not even suspect that we have any just cause of complaint, & consider us altogether as the aggressors & as allies of Bonaparte. In those opinions it is understood that the Ministers do not participate: but it will really require an effort on their part to act contrary to public opinion; and they must, even if perfectly sincere, use great caution & run some risk of popularity. A direct or at least a very near intercourse with them is therefore highly important as I have no doubt that they would go farther themselves than they would be willing to entrust any other person. To this must be added that Lord Castlereagh is, according to the best information I have been able to collect, the best disposed man in the cabinet & that coming from France & having had intercourse with the Emperor Alexander, it is not improbable that those dispositions may have been encreased by the personal expression of the Emperor's wishes in favor of peace with America. Whatever advantage may be derived from that circumstance & from the Emperor's arrival here would be altogether lost at Gottenburg.

I have confined my letter to this single point, and hoping soon to hear from you & from Mr Russel to whom you will present my best compliments, I remain, Dear Sir, respectfully & affectionately

Your friend & Servt. ALBERT GALLATIN

H. E. Henry Clay of the U. States Gottenburg.

ALS. DLC-HC (DNA, M212, R1). Delivered by George B. Milligan. Published in Colton (ed.), *Private Correspondence of Henry Clay,* 30-31; Henry Adams (ed.), *The Writings of Albert Gallatin* (3 vols; Philadelphia, 1879), I, 606-608.
[1] Letter dated April 20. [2] This word a marginal addendum by Gallatin.

To James Monroe

Sir Gottenburg 23d. Apl. 1814.

I avail myself of the opportunity afforded by a Swedish vessel[1] bound to Boston to transmit to you the inclosed copy of a dispatch from Mr. Russell & myself.[2] Since its date that gentleman has proceeded to Stockholm,[3] where he will remain until he is notified of the necessity of his attendance here. A letter from Mr. Gallatin to Capt. Jones of the Neptune,[4] which wintered here, directs that vessel to proceed to Harwich in England, where he and Mr. Bayard had arrived on the 8th. inst. I presume that there, or at London, Mr. Gallatin heard of his appointment, and that in a few days I shall have the satisfaction of being joined by him and Mr. Bayard.

Of the wonderful events which have occurred in France you will have been informed through a channel less circuitous than this. The capture of Paris by the Allies on the 31st. of March appears to have been followed by a declaration, on the part of the Senate, headed by Talleyrand, that Buonaparte had forfeited the throne, and no doubt exists of the acquiescence of France in this declaration. His power may be therefore considered as at an end, & Louis the 18th. is I presume at this moment quietly seated on the throne. Indeed it is *rumoured* here that Buonaparte has acceded to a proposition of the allies to retire to the Island of Elbe, upon an establishment suited to his fallen condition. A new epoch has thus arisen, the first effect of which will be an European peace. It will doubtless lead to totally new relations political as well as commercial. It remains for us to see if Great Britain will insist upon retaining or surrender her conquests, and admit other nations to a fair participation in the general commerce of the world. Whilst the sole principle that actuated the allies was the reduction of French power, there appears to have been a hearty concurrence between them. We shall see if sentiments of harmony and moderation will continue to guide their councils, when delicate and difficult arrangements are to be made among themselves.

It will cost Sweden some trouble to possess herself of her new acquisition.[5] The people of Norway are said to be extremely averse to the annexation, and countenanced, as Sweden suspects, by Denmark, are preparing to resist it. From the scanty resources of Norway I should suppose however that the resistance must be entirely ineffectual, unless the aid now covertly given by Denmark, if given at all, should lead to a war between the two Countries, and unless also Great Britain, in the new circumstances in which she may find herself, sees it her interest to support the Norwegians.

I rely upon your goodness for excusing the liberty I take in inclosing these letters to my family to your care, that they may be put into the Post-office at Washington.

With due consideration I am Sir Yr. Obd Servt. H. CLAY

James Monroe Esqr. &c &c &c.

LS. DLC-James Monroe Papers (DNA, M212, R22). Published in Donnan (ed), *Papers of James A. Bayard*, 287-88.

1 The *Fortuna*. 2 Dated April 20. 3 To his ministerial post.

4 Lloyd Jones, brother of the Secretary of the Navy. His vessel had transported the earlier peace commission to Europe in 1813.

5 In the Treaty of Kiel, January, 1814, following the collapse of Napoleon's power outside France, Denmark had ceded Norway to Sweden.

Order Drawn by Porter Clay

Henry Clay Esquire April 25h. 1814

Sir

Please to pay John McKinney junr. or order Five hundred dollars on or before the 1st. day of February next and charge the same to the account of yrs. PORTER CLAY

[Endorsements][1]

Accepted Apl. 30th. 1814. For H. Clay JOHN WATKINS

Recd. bal. in full 2 Nov 1815. JNO. MCKINNEY JUNR.

ADS. DLC-TJC (DNA, M212, R15). Endorsed by Clay: "On a/c. of the legacy given to Sophia Clay by Tho. Hart in Col. Harts Estate. H. C."

1 The first, AES by Watkins; the second, ES, in Clay's hand.

From Jonathan Russell

Dear Sir, Stockholm 26th April 1814

I did not reach this place until yesterday a little before noon—The roads were very fine but the weather, after the first day, exercrable [*sic*] I have announced my arrival to the Minister & he has assigned one OClock tomorrow for our first interview when I shall probably learn when I may expect to be presented to the King—

This place, as far as I have yet seen it, promises to be agreeable—

Mr Speyer[1] received this morning a letter from Mr. Adams, dated the 11h of this month, in which he says he proposes to leave St Petersburg about the 20h of this month & hopes to arrive *somewhere* in Sweden by the first of May—probably at Stockholm—His *route,* he he [*sic*] says, will depend on the thermometer of the next ten days—

I shall endeavour to complete my preparatory errand here, in season, to join Mr Adams in his progress towards Gottenburg, should he come this way—

If you hear any thing of our wandering colleagues please communicate it to me as well as every thing else of an interesting nature at your residence—

Please say to our worthy secretary[2] & to Capt Angus[3] that I think Stockholm will fully indemnify them for the fatigue & expense of a visit—

I shall occasionally report progress & give you a sketch of the times here—Make my compliments to Mr Carroll[4]——Yours respectfully & cordially JONA RUSSELL

His Excellency Henry Clay &c &c &c

ALS. DLC-HC (DNA, M212, R1). Published in Colton (ed.), *Private Correspondence of Henry Clay*, 31-32.

1 John Speyer, American Consul at Stockholm. 2 Christopher Hughes, Jr.
3 Samuel Angus. 4 Henry Carroll, Clay's private secretary.

Statement of John Watkins' Account

[*ca.* April 30, 1814]

D. DLC-TJC (DNA, M212, R15). The account notes debits against Watkins for cash received of Lotty (Charlotte Dupuy) for butter, amounting to $95.50 in small payments every few days from October 13, 1813, through April 27, 1814; and a credit for the full amount in cash paid Mrs. Clay on April 30, 1814.

To Jonathan Russell

My Dr. Sir Gottenburg 1st. May 1814

Mr. Milligan, private secretary of Mr. Bayard, arrived here last evening from London, in the packet, charged with a dispatch from him to us, and with a private letter from Mr. Gallatin to me,[1] of each of which I have the pleasure to inclose you a copy herein. You will perceive from the perusal of them, that they have for their object mainly a change in the theatre of the proposed negotiation with Great Britain. On this delicate question I have regretted extremely that I could not have the benefit of your and Mr. Adams' opinion and advice.

The first enquiry is as to our power to take the step, and the nature of our instructions.[2] Our commissions oppose no obstacle to it, not being at all limited as to place. I recollect, before the Commissions were made out, asking the President if they would restrict us to this place and his observing that they had been presented to him for his signature, so prepared, but he had ordered them to be changed, which was accordingly done to their present unrestricted form. Neither are we limited by the instructions to Gottenburg; but they certainly contemplate Sweden as the scene of the negotiation. The motives which led to this selection undoubtedly were the neutrality of the territory, the friendly dispositions of the Crown Prince towards us, and the facility of keeping up a correspondence, which might be deemed expedient, through yourself and Mr. Adams with the Courts of Stockholm and St. Petersburg—All these reasons would equally apply to Holland, unless the removal of the place of negotiation would create coolness on the part of the Swedish Government. There are additional reasons, indeed, to recommend Holland. It would be a compliment to the new Government,[3] manifesting our confidence in its friendship, and merited by the step which it hastened to take, immediately after its establishment, of sending a Minister to America. It would afford us more frequent opportunities, direct and indirect, of communicating with our Government; and giving also much greater facility to the communications between the British Ministers and theirs, would thereby accelerate the termination of the Mission. Still, if the substitution of Holland cannot be made without dissatisfaction to the Swedish Government, I think we ought not to take the step. Of this you are the best judge. I can hardly however suppose it possible that this effect would be produced, if it were understood that the change was at the instance of England. I shall therefore say to Mess. G. and Bayard, by Mr. Milligan, who returns on tuesday in the packet, that they have my consent to go to Holland, if the arrangement can be so made that the responsibility of desiring it, whatever it may be, shall be assumed by the British Ministry.[4] Of course I shall not, because I cannot, commit either yourself or Mr. Adams on the occasion. I shall not consent to go to London.

American papers have been recd. in England, Mr. Milligan informs me, down to the 12th. of March, from Boston and N. York. He says that he understood from them that a flag was to sail on the 15th. of Apl. with dispatches for us—that Granger[5] was removed from the office of P. Master General and Govr. Meigs of Ohio appointed[6]—& that it was rumoured that Wilkinson was arrested—[7]

We took on Monday last a trip to Trolhatta,[8] and although [the w]eather was bad felt ourselves abundantly compensated for the jaunt in a view of the canal.[9] I got into my rooms last evening.

Mr. Hughes will proceed to London with Mr. Milligan. I fear my detention here will be much longer than I expected.

Do me the favor to present my respects to Mr. Lawrence[10] and to Master George—[11] Yr's sincerely H. CLAY

LS. RPB-Russell Papers. Addressed to Russell at Stockholm. Endorsed: "... recd 6h May." Published in Donnan (ed.), *Papers of James A. Bayard*, 288-90.

1 Both, above, April 20, 1814.

2 See above, the instructions, Monroe to the American Commissioners, January 28; the commission, Full Powers, January 18, 1814.

[3] See above, Bayard to Clay and Russell, April 22, 1814, note.
[4] See below, Clay to Bayard and Gallatin, May 2, 1814.
[5] Gideon Granger.
[6] The appointment of Return Jonathan Meigs had been confirmed March 17.
[7] Following the failure of the expedition against Montreal, Wilkinson, at his own request, had been summoned to a court of inquiry.
[8] Trollhättan, on the Göta River about 45 miles north of Gottenburg.
[9] The Göta Canal.
[10] John L. Lawrence, of New York, Russell's Secretary of Legation.
[11] Russell's son, then about twelve years old.

To James A. Bayard and Albert Gallatin

Gentlemen Gottenburgh 2d. May 1814.

Col. Milligan arriving here the evening before last delivered to me Mr. Bayard's letter of the 20th. Ulto. to Mr. Russell and myself, and that of Mr. Gallatin of the 22d. to me alone. I was much gratified in being relieved by them from the uncertainty in which I was placed as to your movements and prospects. On your part you will have been extricated, prior to the receipt of this letter, from a more perplexing embarrassment (particularly in respect of Mr. Gallatin as to the new commission, by the dispatch forwarded by Capt. Jones in the Neptune.[1]

It would have been highly satisfactory to me to have been assisted by our Colleagues Mess. Adams Russell [*sic*], in deliberating upon the contents of your letters. But the latter gentleman left this place on the 21st. of April for Stockholm, where I am informed by a letter this moment received from him he arrived on the 25th. The object of his visit was to present his credentials, and to establish those relations with the Swedish Government which may be deemed expedient, intending to return to this place the moment he should learn by your arrival that his presence was necessary. Of Mr. Adams I have no information except what is contained in the following paragraph of Mr. Russell's letter:[2] Mr. Speyer[3] received this morning (26th. Apl.) a letter from Mr. Adams, dated the 11th. of this month, in which he says he proposes to leave St. Petersburg about the 20th. of this month and hopes to arrive somewhere in Sweden by the first of May, probably at Stockholm. His route, he says, will depend on the thermometer of the next[4] ten days." Mr. Russell adds that he shall endeavor to be ready to accompany Mr. Adams, should he pass by Stockholm to Gottenburg.

Being thus without the benefit of consulting with either Mr. Adams or Mr. Russell I have given to the subject of your letters the best consideration in my power. With regard to chaning [*sic*] the place of negotiation it appears to me to be a measure attended with some difficulty and requiring on our part great delicacy. Before Mr. Russell left this place we learnt that the British Chargé d'Affaires at Stockholm had presented on the 9th. April a note to the Swedish Government, informing it of the contemplated negotiation here, and asking its sanction to the measure. It was an obvious duty, on the part of the Representative of our Government to solicit also from Sweden the hospitalities requisite to our condition here; and altho' Mr. Russell had no particular instruction to that effect, he intended with my advice to present a note on the occasion the moment he was accredited. This I have no doubt he has done. The Swedish Government thus officially informed by both parties of the intended negotiation here, must see with surprize, if with no other emotion, another place so quickly substituted for Gottenburgh. I need not inform you that our Government counts much upon the friendship of the Northern powers particularly Russia and Sweden. And altho' I have no doubt that the Crown Prince[5] has lost, in the scale of European affairs, much of his weight by the events which he has himself contributed to produce, we ought not lightly to jeopardize his friendship. But it is highly probable that the President, had he foreseen what has occurred since the date of our instructions, would have deemed Holland equally eligible with this place, if not more so. And I am prepared in this instance and in all others to give to our instructions a liberal interpretation, with a view to the wonderful revolutions which have recently occurred. If therefore any place in Holland can be substituted for Gottenburg in such manner as that the change shall be understood to be at the instance of Great Britain, you have my consent to make it. Being thus brought about such explanations may be made to Sweden as will not only retain us her friendship, but cast upon the other party all the unfriendly consequences, should there be any, growing out of the measure. I enclose herein an extract from a letter I forwarded this morning to Mr. Russell to put him in possession of the proposed change, and my views of it.[6]

With regard to going London [*sic*], with great deference for the opinion of Mr. Gallatin, I really cannot concur in that measure. If there be a doubt as to what our Government has done to restore peace, it cannot be on the side of its having done too little. A power of less pretensions than the U. States might, with great propriety, after the rejection of the Russian mediation, have demanded that its own seat of Government should be the theatre for discussing propositions for peace. Having waived this, and acceded to one of the alternatives offered by the other party, I do not think that we ought to submit to further condescension, especially when we have yet to see the example in British history of that haughty people having been conciliated by the condescension of their enemy. I am deeply sensible of the magnitude of the present crisis which I have endeavoured to view in all its immediate and remote consequences. And the result of my reflections is, that we shall best promote the objects of our Mission, and acquit ourselves of our duty, by presenting a firm and undismayed countenance. We have the chances in our favor of the continental negotiations, which are now, or will be shortly going on. It is impossible that Europe, liberated as it is from the despotism of Buonaparte, should be indifferent to the enormous power and the enormous pretensions of G. Britain on the ocean. It will assuredly, I presume, impose some limits on her. If she is wise she will readily acquiesce in them—The sympathy which she derived from the world generally, under the supposition that she was contending for her existence, and struggling for their liberties, has ceased. If, intoxicated by her present prosperity, she reject the councils of moderation and prudence, that which Bonaparte attempted by compulsion will be accomplished by the voluntary consent of Europe—But I forbear—Indeed I ought to apologize for touching at all upon a subject on which you are so much more competent to judge.

From the letter of Mr. Bayard I remark that it is thought by you proper that we should make some official communication to the British Government of our arrival here. The embarrassment, which even if Mr. Russell had been here a minority of the commission must have felt on this subject is greatly increased by my standing alone. It seems to me in the first place, that having been invited here by the British Govt., that Government ought by the promptitude of its own measures to have rendered unnecessary such a notification on our part. Waiving however this point of etiquette (and I certainly am not going during this negotiation to give consequence to any affair of mere etiquette) what could I alone, one of five who compose the Commission, say to accelerate the movements of the other party? It has therefore appeared to me most advisable to transmit to you, which I now do, copies of the new Commissions, and of the new Instructions which our Government has issued,[7] and to submit to you the making of such communication as may be adapted to the occasion and I authorize, if you deem it at all necessary, any use whatever of my name in relation to it.

The packages and letters which we brought for you from America are sent by Col. Milligan and Mr. Hughes, the Secretary of the Mission who accompanies him. I regret now very much that they were not sent by Capt. Jones, but they were kept for reasons contained in the letter which he bore for you. The fine qualities of Mr. Hughes cannot fail to interest you, as they have me, very highly

I have the honor to be, Gentlemen, With great respect, Your obedient Servant H.C.

LI copy. RPB-Russell Papers. Published in Adams (ed.), *Writings of Albert Gallatin*, I, 608-11; Donnan (ed.), *Papers of James A. Bayard*, 290-93.

1 See above, Clay and Russell to Bayard and Gallatin, April 20; Clay to Monroe, April 23, 1814.

2 Of April 26. 3 John Speyer. 4 Word substituted for "last" in MS.

5 Since Charles XIII of Sweden was childless, Jean Bernadotte, one of Napoleon's marshals, had been chosen Crown Prince in 1810. Founder of the present dynasty, he had begun at once to exert a strong influence in the affairs of his adopted country. Clay referred to Sweden's need for Allied support to maintain her claim to Norway.

6 Clay to Russell, May 1.

7 See above, Full Powers, January 18; Monroe to the American Commissioners, January 28, 1814.

To Albert Gallatin

Dr Sir Gottenburg 2d. May 1814.

I am rejoiced at finding you in Europe. We had great fears that you would have left it before our arrival and proceeded to America. Your rejection last summer in the Senate[1] was very generally condemned by the people, and produced a reaction highly favorable to you. The total uncertainty in which the Government was left as to your movements (for on the first of Feb. when I left Washington not one syllable had been received from either yourself or Mr Bayard) And the increased and complicated concerns of the Treasury produced a state of things highly embarrassing to the President, so much so that he could no longer resist the pressure to fill the Treasury. After this measure was determined on it became more than ever desirable that the public should have the benefit of your services here. Had it not been confidently believed when the new commission was formed that you were on your way to America, and would be there shortly, you would have been originally comprehended in it.

I have not time to say what I wish to communicate on American affairs. Peace, necessary to our Country before the astonishing events which have recently occurred on this side of the Atlantic,—events with which the imagination can scarcely keep pace—will doubtless be now more than ever demanded. I think however you attach more consequence than belongs to the indications in the Eastern States. I have no doubt that a game of swaggering and gasconade has been played off there, without any serious intention to push matters to extremity. After a great deal of blustering about raising 20 000 men, and declaring the freedom of the port of Boston, a meeting of the malcontents there determined it inexpedient to take any such measure during the last Session of the Legislature. The truth is they want men—they want money—the principal actors want courage. Yet I would not despise these appearances. If the British Government should determine to land a considerable force in the Eastern States, avowing friendship to them, and an intention only to war with the Southern States, or with the Administration, certainly very serious consequences might ensue, though I believe they would fall far short of conquest or dissolution.

I have brought with me some gold for my expences.[2] Will you do me the favor to inform yourself of the most advantageous use I can make of it in exchange. Yr. friend &c. H. CLAY

P.S. Your nomination in the Senate was approved by all but two or three.

ALS. NHi-Gallatin Papers (MR8). Addressed to Gallatin at London in response to the latter's letter of April 22.

1 See above, Clay to Monroe, February 13, 1814, note.

2 Cf. above, Parish to Clay, January 28, 1814.

To [Jonathan Russell]

Dr Sir Gottenburg 4h. May 1814.

I have been favored with your letter of the 26h. Ulto. You have no doubt before this passed through the ceremonial of presentation to the King, and become quietly located in your quarters. Yesterday Mr. Milligan and Mr. Hughes, *whose health I feared would be impaired* by any further opposition to his visit to London, sailed in the packet and the wind this morning promises them a speedy passage. To enable you to understand exactly the result of my deliberation upon the contents of Mess. Gallatin and Bayards letter's[1] brought by Mr. Milligan (copies of which I transmitted to you in a letter[2] by the Portug ese [*sic*] Consul who left here the day before yesterday) I inclose you a transcript of my communication to them.[3] What course they will take, on receiving it, as to changing the place of negotiation, I cannot pretend to say; but I apprehend their chief difficulty will be in not knowing your and Mr. Adams's opinion. Mr. Gallatin appears to have the subject so much at heart that I think it highly probable that your consent will be *presumed*. Undoubtedly public considerations concurring in the measure, we have every motive belonging to personal accommodation and comfort for desiring the change; for I suppose there can be no comparison between this place and Amsterdam, or the Hague.

Would it not be advisable to improve the opportunity which your presence at Stockholm affords by a frank communication with the Swedish Government on the nature of the principal ground of dispute between G. Britain and America? If the amicable interposition of other powers is to be obtained in our favor it can only be expected after a clear understanding of the nature of the controversy. With that, it is not to be doubted, that Sweden is already somewhat acquainted, but it can hardly understand much of the nature and provisions of the Act passed by Congress.

The good people of Gottenburg are becoming more civil to us than they were when you were here. I have dined at Count Rosen's,[4] and we have been invited to dine at several other houses. We find ourselves too much more agreeably situated in the rooms I have taken than we were at the inn.

Mr. Beasely[5] sent us by Mr. Milligan a pretty extensive file of the Morning Chronicle and the Courier,[6] which I should have forwarded by the Portugese Consul if I had not feared it would have trespassed too much upon his politeness. English papers have been recd. here as late as the 26h. Ulto. They contain nothing of importance but the account of a battle between Soult and Wellington before Toulouse[7] and of a sortie made by the garrison of Bayonne.[8] In the former the English claim the victory, but admit great loss. In the latter they were surprized, much cut to pieces and their Commander in chief Hope[9] taken prisoner.

My respects to Mr. Lawrence and Master George[10]—Yr's truly

H. CLAY

ALS. RPB-Russell Papers.
1 Bayard to Clay and Russell, April 20; Gallatin to Clay, April 22, 1814.
2 Dated May 1.
3 Dated May 2.
4 Governor of the administrative district composed solely of the city of Stockholm.
5 Reuben G. Beasley.
6 London newspapers.
7 April 10, 1814.
8 April 14, 1814.
9 Sir John Hope, considered by Wellington his ablest general.
10 John L. Lawrence and George Russell.

From Jonathan Russell

My Dear Sir, Stockholm 8h May 1814

I received, day before yesterday, your communication,[1] by the Consul General of Portugal, but not in season to return an answer by the mail of that day—

With regard to our power to enter into the negociation elsewhere than at Gottenburg, I think the view which you have taken is quite satisfactory—A restriction of this power having been omitted in the commission, by the express direction of the President, appears to explain sufficiently his intentions and to leave us at liberty, notwithstanding the incidental insertion of "Gottenburg" in the instructions,[2] to treat wherever we may have the most promising prospect of success—

The only point therefore which remains for consideration is that of expediency & the reasons urged by Mr Gallatin Mr Bayard and yourself have great weight—

The apprehension of any *serious* evil from this quarter, occasioned by our change of position, is I trust without foundation—I regret however that I had not known the opinions of Mess Gallatin & Bayard in season to have shaped my communications here accordingly—Something like a retrograde movement will now be necessary and it may require some address to reconcile this Government to the new arrangement—I hope it may be in our power to throw the responsibility on the British Government—but am somewhat afraid the original proposition will appear to have come from our Colleagues—

My personal convenience & inclination are, indeed, opposed to the change but considerations of this kind must yield to those of public utility—

I am placed rather in an awkward predicament, by your communication, as the uncertainty, in which it leaves our ultimate location, disqualifies me from adapting my movements here, with sufficient precision, to either alternative—This is a situation truly diplomatic but I pray you to relieve me from its embarrassments the first moment it is in your power to do so—

I had on the 29h ulto my presentations, successively, to the King[3] —the Queen—the Duke of Sudermania and the Princess Sophia—The early day assigned for this ceremony may be considered as some proof of a friendly disposition towards us—

The Crown Prince[4] was to leave Paris on the 23rd ulto and will probably be here by the 20h of this month. I hope therefore to have an opportunity of seeing him before my departure from Stockholm

I wrote you soon after my arrival here but my letter[5] does not appear to have been received at the date of yours—I hear nothing more of Mr. Adams but as the navigation is now open from Abo he will probably soon be in Sweden—

Granger,[6] it seems, is at last removed—It is well His successor I presume is a good man & true—

I am glad that Mr. Hughes has, at length, attained his *summum bonum*

It is impossible to obtain here a piece of plate such as we want without waiting to have it made for which there is not time—

Please remember me kindly to Mr Carrol & Capt Angus & his officers and believe me truly Yrs JONA RUSSELL

His Excellency Henry Clay &c &c &c

ALS. DLC-HC (DNA, M212, R1). Published, in part, in Colton (ed.), *Private Correspondence of Henry Clay*, 32-33.

1 Of May 1.

2 In his instructions of February 14, Monroe had referred to acceptance of "the British overture to treat at Gottenburg and not at London."

3 Charles XIII.

4 Bernadotte.

5 Dated April 26.

6 Gideon Granger.

To Jonathan Russell

My Dr Sir Gottenburg 9h. May 1814.

I transmit you the inclosed copy of a letter addressed to the joint mission by Mr. Crawford,[1] and received yesterday through Mr. Forbes,[2] supposing you might take an interest in the perusal of it. The parts in cypher I have not been able to interpret, the key with which I have been furnished not being adapted to them—a misfortune which I hope will be remedied by that in your possession, or by one with which our other colleagues have been provided.

From a private letter which I have recd. from Mr. Crawford[3] it appears not to be very certain that the French King will ratify the Constitution, especially that part of it in which the Senate has taken care of itself, with so much disinterestedness.[4] He says that those few Parisians who allow themselves to speak at all of the recent events declare that they knew long ago that Bonaparte possessed neither genius talents or courage!

Nothing material has occurred here since my last. No packet has arrived from England since that which brought over Mr. Milligan; of course I am still in the most painful uncertainty as to the duration of my probation. Yr's Sincerely H. CLAY

H. E. J. Russell &c. &c. &c.

ALS. RPB-Russell Papers.
1 Dated April 8.
2 John M. Forbes, United States Consul at Copenhagen.
3 Not found.
4 See above, Crawford to American Commissioners, April 8, 1814.

To William H. Crawford

Gottenburg 10h. May 1814

I was rejoiced, my dear Sir, to find by your favor of the 8h. Ulto. recd. through Mr. Forbes, that you were in Paris and well. I knew that your public character ought to have protected you, but I feared, amidst the confusion inseparable from a vast military force, that you might have experienced some indignity or inconvenience. When I left America a general peace in Europe was anticipated, but no human sagacity could then have foreseen the astonishing events which have since occurred in France—events which have put the mind more in that state of amazement which attends a deep dramatic performance, or an agitating dream, than belongs to the sober condition of real transactions. Our expectation was that the allies, having reached the Rhine, would tender to Bonaparte such terms of peace as he would find it his interest to accept, or if some of them were disposed to press too severely upon him, that Austria would secede from the coalition and leave him a more equal contest. That she has been led on, step by step, to concur in measures from which she would have recoiled in the first instance, I do not entertain a doubt. The arts of some of the allies and the infatuated obstinacy of the ex-Emperor alike tended to produce that effect. I concur with you in the hope that France and her new monarch will acquiesce in the constitution which the Senate has adopted. Her condition, after all the vicissitudes which she has experienced, will be greatly improved by it; and perhaps it secures to the people as much liberty as they are capable of enjoying. But Charles the second when he got firmly seated on the throne (and still more his successor) forgot the moderation professed at Breda.[1] And when Louis comes to be surrounded by the exiled nobility, stript of their estates, and restored only to empty honors, it will be wonderful if Talleyrand and his friends are not made to feel the insecurity of mere paper guards.

You will have been relieved I trust long! ere this from the unpleasant state of uncertainty in which you have remained as to your family and American affairs, by the arrival of Mr. Shaler at Paris. He left here on the 18th. Ulto. to proceed to that City, by the way of Copenhagen, charged with sundry dispatches, public and private, for you. No law had passed authorizing the appointment of a Lieut. General nor when I left Washington was there a disposition to urge the adoption of that measure. It is possible however it may be revived if (as I see suggested in the prints) Wilkinson[2] be arrested. That I think is highly probable; for the failure of the expedition agt. Montreal—an expedition which he dissuaded, prefering an attack upon Kingston, and which Armstrong[3] advised—had produced a state of things between the Commander in Chief and the Secretary at War which it was believed must eventuate in the dismission of one of them. You will have learnt, from the papers delivered to you by Mr. Shaler, that all the operations of the last campaign were attended with much success, except that directed agt. Montreal. The concentration of our forces at the North end of Ontario, in prosecution of that object, leaving the Niagara frontier unprotected, it was exposed to the incursions of the enemy and the Western part of N. York had to feel some of the enormities which were practised on the little villages of the Chesapeak [*sic*].[4]

Since my arrival here I see that Granger's removal is announced in the papers. I think it highly probable, in consequence of his appointing Leib to the post office of Philadelphia, become vacant by the death of the former incumbent. The appointment of Dr Leib was opposed by the whole Pennsylvania delegation; notwithstanding which it was made, contrary too to the wishes of the Administration.[5]

I have examined the list of lands belonging to the Estate of Mr. Vail[6] inclosed in your letter. I have no particular information of the title or value of any of the tracts contained in the list, and any remarks I make must be understood, with this qualification, and as having a general reference to the subject. 1st. As to the title. It is impossible to form any opinion as to its validity without I had a view of the title papers and knew whether there were any interferences of other claims, and had a view also of the papers appurtaining to them. You have no doubt heard that our lands in Kentucky are frequently covered by two or three or more original patents granted by the State. When that is the case (and it is almost always so in the quarter of the Country in which these lands are situated) one can only form a satisfactory judgment after a view of all the papers, and obtaining much local knowledge of facts connected with them. In the case of these lands the patents I observe are late, which is unfavorable. I do not much like the character of the persons through whose hands the titles have passed; most of them being Land Speculators. Besides the inherent difficulties attending original titles, many embarrassments have grown out of sales made for taxes. If these lands were entered for taxes (as they ought to have been) it is more than probable that the taxes have not been regularly paid, and in that case they have been sold, and very probably twice sold, once for the State, and once for the direct tax formerly imposed by the General Government.[7]

By a law of Kentucky, where lands in possession of one man are claimed by a person out of possession, this latter claimant is required to bring his Suit for the recovery of them within seven years from the date of the law, or he is barred.[8] I think there are only about two years remaining of this period of limitation. The temper of the State being much in favor of the possessor I do not think there is a liberal provision, if there be any (of which I am not certain) for the usual disabilities. If therefore the lands of Mr. Vail's family are occupied by others, and there are ten chances to one that they are, you will see that they are in much danger from this law.

2d. As to the quality, all I can observe is that in the quarter where these lands are, mountainous and broken land prevails, though intermixed with much good land. It is not however like the region of Country about Lexington which is in an immense plain, where you may find perhaps 100.000 Acres of land in a body, of which one acre will be as good as any other. Where Mr. Vails lye, lands vary from 1 Cent to $10 per acre in value.

My advice then to the family would decidedly be to take the 150 thousand francs which you say they have been offered, especially if they can make the sale without responsibility if the lands are not got;

a condition so advisable that they had better reduce the price very much if they cannot otherwise secure it. Interested extremely by the flattering account you have given of the family I have regretted very much that I could not give a more encouraging answer to your enquiries. You will see however that I have to indulge mostly in conjecture. My greatest fear is that the title will be found insecure.

I am here entirely alone keeping the ground until my scattered colleagues are assembled. Two of them you know are in England, Mr. Russell is at Stockholm, and Mr. Adams is somewhere between here and St. Petersburg. It is however probable that we shall be collected together early enough for the British Government, which has not, as far as I have yet learnt, taken any step towards opening the negotiation. As to its probable issue, when opened, you are more competent than I am to determine. The general peace will doubtless have much influence upon it. I cannot but hope that the Continent will provide, in the general peace, some limits to the enormous maritime power and pretensions of G. Britain. Indeed it appears to me that the allies have matters amongst themselves to arrange not less difficult than the overthrow of Bonaparte, and I confess I shall not be surprized to find soon some who are now very good friends very inveterate foes. Let what will happen, we must not despair of the Republic. If G. Britain rejecting the counsels of moderation, determine to persevere in the War, and to chastise America, as is impudently proclaimed by some of her prints to be her purpose or her policy, I cannot but cherish the belief that she will find the energies of a free people equal to the crisis. I sincerely hope that she may not be thus unwise, and that our mission may terminate in the extension to America of that peace in which all Europe, it would at this moment seem, are about to participate.

I adhere to my intention of paying you my respects at Paris as communicated by Mr. Shaler, as soon as I shall be released from my public duties.

I shall forward this letter to Mr. Beasley at London, from whence I presume it will find without difficulty a conveyance to you. Through that or some other eligible channel I hope to have the pleasure of hearing frequently from you.

very sincerely Yr friend &c H. CLAY

H. E. Wm. H. Crawford Minister &c &c. &c.

ALS. MeHi.

1 In 1660 Charles II had issued from Breda, in the Netherlands, a declaration designed to make the Restoration more palatable to the people of England.

2 James Wilkinson.

3 John Armstrong.

4 In December, 1813, the British had captured Fort Niagara, then burned Black Rock and Buffalo and plundered the countryside. Cf. above, Resolution, May 26, 1813.

5 Michael Leib, a surgeon during the Revolutionary War, Congressman (1799-1806) and United States Senator (1808-1814) from Pennsylvania, had resigned from the

Senate to accept the Philadelphia appointment. Although a strong Jeffersonian, he had turned against the Madison administration.

[6] Aaron Vail, New York merchant, American commercial agent at L'Orient, France.

[7] "Direct" taxes levied by the Federal government under State apportionment had been enacted on July 14, 1798, and again in the summer of 1813. The tax under the latter measure was doubled the following year.

[8] Littell (comp.), *Statute Law of Kentucky,* IV, 55-57 (February 9, 1809).

Man Coursin to Clay and Bayard

The Honble Mess. Clay & Bayard. Dronthiem[1] May 10. 1814
Gent.

Hearing of your arrival at Gottenburg I hasten to lay my case before you, in hopes that you will be enabled to extricate me from the difficulties I labour under.

The American private armed Brig Rattlesnake commanded by David Maffitt and owned by Andrew Cowsric of Philada.[2] captured and sent to this port nineteen British prizes in August last, and likewise captured a valuable Brig loaded with Dry goods which vessel arrived here the 1st. of Jan. 1814.

Great exertions have been made to get this property condemned in this Country both by our merchants here, and by Mr. Forbes Consul at Copenhagen, but without effect.

The Government of Norway will not allow these prizes to be condemned here. nor allow us to dispose of the property. The difficulties of procuring condemnation from America you no doubt are well aware of. I request you gentlemen will please take my case into consideration and if possible condemn these prizes or allow the American Consul to do the same.

My only object in making this request is that the property may be distributed to those who by the right of conquest it belongs to.

With the highest consideration & respect I am Gentlemen Yr. obt. Servt.

MAN COURSIN
Agent for the Brig Rattlesnake.
The address of Messrs Hans Knudtzon & Co.
Drontheim

Copy, in Clay's hand. RPB-Russell Papers. Name of writer uncertain, not clearly legible.

[1] Trondheim, in Norway.

[2] The *Rattlesnake,* a 16-gun brig, the second privateering vessel commanded by Maffitt, preyed with notable success on British commerce in European waters until captured on June 3, 1814. Maffitt in 1819 was made master warden of the port of Philadelphia. Cowsric (or Coursin—not clearly legible) has not been identified.

Promissory Note from Oliver Hart

\$500. No. 658—due 9/12 July Lexington 10 May 1814

Sixty days after date I promise to pay to James Morrison, Henry

Clay, Thomas Tibbatts & Andw McCalla[1] without defalcation, Five hundred dollars—negotiable and payable at the office of the Kentucky Insurance Compy value received. OLIVER HART

DS. DLC-TJC (DNA, M212, R15). Endorsed on verso: "James Morrison Henry Clay by Jno. Hart. Thos. Tibbatts John M. McCalla for Andrew McCalla." Oliver Hart, not a member of the family that included Mrs. Clay, had lived for a time in Lexington, where he had been married in 1812. At the time of his death, 1836, he was a resident of Nashville, Tennessee.

When payment was not made at the appointed time, the note was protested. (DS by John D. Young. *Ibid.*)

1 Morrison, Clay, Tibbatts, and McCalla were all property owners on the north side of Short Street between Market and Upper.

From Jonathan Russell

My dear Sir Stockholm 12h May 1814

Immediately after closing my answer[1] to your favor of the 1rd I received that of the 4h inst—

If Mess Gallatin & Bayard consider the condition on which you have consented to remove to Holland, viz—that the change shall be understood to be at the instance of Great Britain, to be a sine qua non we shall undoubtedly be fixed at Gottenburg, for on reading again the copies of their letters to you[2] no doubt remains in my mind at whose instance the change will take place—As my consent to the new arrangement will, however, as you say, probably be presumed, I suspect that your condition will not stand very immoveably in the way of their zeal—I do not indeed think this condition to be of so much importance as you appear to consider it; altho what I have done since my arrival here is of a nature rather to increase than to diminish that importance On the 30h. ulto the day after my presentation to the King I addressed a note to the minister announcing the contemplated negociation at Gottenburg & asking the necessary permission & customary immunities—A copy of his answer of the 6h. instant I enclose to you[3]—Not wishing in my note formally to state what my government hoped & expected from the good offices of Sweden I obtained an interview with the minister on the 3rd instant for this purpose. I explained the nature & objects of our controversy with England & our sincere desire, with the aid of Sweden to bring this controversy to a satisfactory termination

In the absence of the Crown Prince[4] I could not expect to receive any very precise assurances on the subject I was not therefore disappointed that none were given, but I must confess that a comparative view, in which the minister thought proper to indulge himself on this occasion, between the period of Mr. Jay's negociation & the present times, highly in favor of the former with relation to neutral pretensions, had rather an inauspicious aspect—[5]

If we remain at Gottenburg or repair to Holland I begin to believe we shall be equally sure of the good wishes of this government, but at neither, can we, I fear, calculate on very positive advantages from the weight or direct exertion of its influence—America is of less importance to Sweden & Sweden to Europe than twelve months ago—

It is not prudent to commit to the post all which may be said on this point—

In the absence of the Crown Prince, nothing can be done with effect here & I am sorry to learn by the last courrier that he has deferred his departure from Paris until the 10h or 15h of this month—I am very desirous to see him before I leave Stockholm, as being from the great theatre of the pacification of Europe he will know & probably not be averse to saying how far the rights of maritime states have been discussed & secured—Should he not return hither before I am summoned hence I will leave the act of Congress[6] with the minister here accompanied by an explanatory act of my own—

I am glad to learn that Gottenburg begins to brighten & that more comfort at home & hospitality abroad enable you to pass your time agreably—

I begin to believe that Mr Adams has left Stockholm out of his route to Gottenburg—I learn nothing further of his movements—Our worthy young friend Lewis,[7] after much fatigue & beating Robert C. Porter[8] all hallow in hair breadth 'scapes, reached Abo safe & soun[d] on the 28h. ulto—

Mr Lawrence & George wish me to present their respects to you & join me in best wishes to Capt Angus & Mr Carrol—

faithfully yours JONA RUSSELL

His Excellency Henry Clay &c &c &c

ALS. DLC-HC (DNA, M212, R1).

1 Dated May 8. 2 Dated April 20 and 22.

3 Not found. 4 Bernadotte.

5 John Jay, in his treaty with England in 1794, had won no concessions regarding neutral rights.

6 Probably the act regulating seamen on American vessels. See above, Monroe to American Commissioners, January 28, 1814.

7 William Davis Lewis.

8 Sir Robert Ker Porter, British painter and traveler, had published in 1809 his two-volume work, *Travelling Sketches in Russia and Sweden During the Years 1805-1808.*

To Jonathan Russell

My Dr Sir Gottenburg 13h. May 1814

The Cartel Chauncey[1] arrived here yesterday from N. York, from which place she sailed on the 10h. Ulto., bringing Mr. Weyer[2] with dispatches from Government for the joint mission and for our other foreign ministers. Mr. Lang, the Russian Consul, sending an express to Stockholm, I avail myself of his politeness in tendering the facility it affords, to send to you your separate dispatch from the Government. The objects in sending out this vessel appear to have been mainly to guard agt. any accident which might have befallen the John Adams, and to put the American Commissioners in possession of the state of things as existing at her departure. We are made acquainted, by the Secty. of State, with the important facts that the President had on the 31st. of March recommended to Congress a repeal of the Embargo, and of the Non-importation system; that a report favoring the repeal had been made by the Committee of Foreign relations to the House of Representatives; and that the repeal would in all probability take place.[3] I transmit you some of the latest prints which have been recd. in which you will find the President's message and the report of the Committee. Our instructions do not vary essentially the ground before taken in the negotiation contemplated here. They display much solicitude that its result, whatever it may be, should be accelerated as much as possible and communicated to the President.[4]

One of the principal considerations which induced a recommendation of the repeal of the above measures appears to have been the liberation of the commerce of so many friendly powers from the shackles under which it had been placed by French regulations, and the consequent desire of our Government to place the commerce between America and those powers on the most liberal footing.

It appears that they had recd in America intelligence of the progress the allies were making in France, and of their approach towards its Capital within sixty miles.

An act had passed both houses of Congress to quiet the Yazoo claims, which adopts as its basis the compromise formerly recommended.[5] A proposition to establish a National bank was pending before Congress and had acquired much additional strength.[6] It does not appear that Wilkinson[7] has been arrested.

A *private* letter recd. from N. York[8] states that Sir George Prevost[9] had proposed an armistice; that listening to his proposition the Government had sought an explanation as to the extent of his powers, that is whether they extended to maritime operations as well as those on Land; and the writer adds his belief, if they are thus extensive, that it will be acceded to. No countenance is given to this letter by any of the public dispatches. It however bears a much later date than any of them.

I have recd. a regular file of the Intellr[10] from the period of or rather before our sailing down to the 5h. Apl. but as I know not at what moment some of our Colleagues may arrive I have thought it best to retain it here—From those in England[11] I have heard nothing since my last. It is said however that a packet is in sight which may have something for me. Mr. Adams was to leave St. Petersburg about the 28h. Apl. for this place—and expected, as he wrote Mr. Hall,[12] to reach it about the 10h. instant; so that I am in hourly expectation of the pleasure of being joined by him.

Yr's Sincerely H. CLAY

H.E. J. Russell Minister &c &c

P.S. Since writing the above I have recd. from the Cartel a file of the Intellr. intended for my individual use, which I have the pleasure to forward to you, as also sundry letters brought by her for you. H.C.

ALS. RPB-Russell Papers.
1 An American schooner, sailing under a flag of truce.
2 Edward Wyer.
3 The repealing act had been signed on April 14.
4 See above, Monroe to American Commissioners, March 21, 1814.
5 The act had been approved March 31, 1814. Cf. above, Motion, February 15, 1813.
6 On April 15, the House bill to establish a National Bank had been postponed indefinitely.
7 James Wilkinson.
8 Not found, but see below, Clay to Crawford, May 14; Clay to Bayard and Gallatin, May 16, 1814.
9 Governor-General of Canada.
10 Washington *National Intelligencer*.
11 Bayard and Gallatin.
12 Joseph Hall, Jr., American Vice Consul at Gottenburg.

William H. Crawford to the American Commissioners

The Ministers of the United States at Gothenbourg — Paris 13th. May 1814.

Gentlemen.

The Dispatches from the Government & the letters of Messrs. Clay and Russell[1] have been delivered to me by Mr Shaler.

I shall endeavour from time to time to inform you of every thing which passes here, which can have any influence on your deliberations.=I presume however that my communications will be of no real utility to you. Expectations have been entertained by the Government, and you no doubt have participated in them, that the Emperor Alexander would interest himself in the negociation between us and our enemy. This expectation I am convinced will be wholly disappointed. Shortly after the arrival of the allies in Paris I called upon Count Nesselrode[2] but but [*sic*] was informed that he was attending the Emperor in council. I left my card; and proceeded to the hotel of the King of Prussia and carded the person whose duty it was to present persons of distinctions [*sic*] to the King. Sometime after I called on Count Nes lerode [*sic*] again, who sent me word by my valet, that he was engaged at the Council table and was quite in despair at not being able to see me. Pursuant to the advice and opinion of the Danish Minister, I addressed a Note to the Count, requesting an interview and foreseeing that his *engagements might prevent his compliance with this request,* I desired him to communicate to the Emperor, my wish to be presented to a Monarch who had given such strong proofs of friendship to the United States. To this note I have received no answer. In my Interviews with the Count la Forest,[3] I thought I discovered the most friendly disposition towards the United States. I asked him whether I should have to wait for new letters of credence, before I could engage seriously in the discussion of our claim to indemnity,[4] with the new Government. He thought there would be no necessity for this delay; but said the question would be settled immediately after the King[5] arrived. This day week the Monitor announced that, on the next day, the King would receive, in the hall of his throne, the Ambassadors near his Majesty. I had an interview with la Forest in the course of the day, who thought I ought to attend, I told him that he was the proper person to decide that question, and that I could not go without an express invitation from him. He insisted that the Grand Master of Ceremonies was the proper person to whom I ought to address myself.

He desired me to send him a note simply by way of informing him of my name and station, and that I would be presented of course. I refused to go to the Palace unless I was assured in writing that I should be presented. I finally agreed to write a note to the G.. M.. of Ceremonies, and request an answer. This was done and no answer was received. I mention these circumstances to shew that the King and his Minister do not feel the same friendly disposition to the U.S.—Some time since the Minister told me that Lord Castlereagh had submitted to him observations upon the difference of treatment between American and British vessels in the ports of France. He afterwards read to me a report which he intended to submit to the King, proposing that the prizes of both Belligerents might be condemned and sold in the ports of France. He said he was afraid this proposition would not be acceptable to the English Minister. If the proposition should be rejected, he would propose that the prizes of both Belligerents should be brought in and remain without adjudication until peace. I saw him two days ago, when he informed me that every interview between him and the British Minister, afforded new proofs of the most extreme hostility, on the part of the Minister to the United States. In the course of the conversation, I mentioned as wholly unworthy of credit the reports circulated in Paris; of engagements on the part of the King, to aid

England in the prosecution of the war against the United States. He said that in an interview with the King, he undertook to amplify the bad effects resulting from the fabrication of false reports, by refering to the paragraph in the news papers stating that the allied powers had by a secret convention engaged not to interfere in the affairs of the United States,, and that the King of France was to make the same engagement. The King promptly replied that he came to the throne as free from all conditions from foreign powers, as was the crown which he wore. The Count said that he did not care what effect these reports might have upon the minds of the few Americans in the trading cities of France, but he should deeply regret that they should reach the United States and have a tendency to depress the public mind. He is extremely anxious that the negociation should open immediately and progress rapidly. He believes the duration of the European peace depends substantially upon the adjustment of our difference with England. After I had failed in obtaining access to the Emperor of Russia and to his Minister, I requested Genal. La Fayette[6] to endeavour thro' Colo La Harpe[7] to have the proper representations made to Neslerode, or to the Emperor. Every effort to effect this object, has been abortive. It seems as if there had been a settled determination to prevent the approach of every person who is suspected of an attachment to the U..S.. The General has however, come in contact several times with Baron Humbolt[8] the Prussian Minister who has imbibed already the British misrepresentations.

The General asked him, if his particular friend should have a quarrel with a man who was known to be engaged in a contest which indirectly affected his interests, and, notwithstanding this circumstance, this person should propose to make him the umpire in the case, and his friend should refuse this proposition, whether he should not without further enquiry or knowledge of the circumstances suspect that his friend was wrong. He replied certainly he should. The General then said that such was the case with the United States and England. England had refused the mediation of Russia at the moment he was receiving her money. After the publication of the paragraph before alluded to, the Baron told the General that the paragraph was untrue, but admitted that they could not get England to treat, until they agreed that the question of maritime rights should not be brought into discussion of the General Peace. He insisted however that nothing had been settled in relation to the United States, and that, that question was entirely open. Mr Poletica[9] called on me yesterday evidently for the purpose of contradicting the same statement, but he spoke of it as though we had conversed upon the subject before. I had not seen him since saturday and the paragraph did not appear until sunday. I took no notice of this mistake; admitted that it might be incorrect, but stated what I believed to be the fact, which he seemed disposed to admit. I stated to Count la Forest in my last interview with him, my conviction that this statement was not without foundation, and that its publication in the Monitor was something like an official declaration of the policy which the French Government intended to pursue. He said by way of repelling this Idea, that the Monitor consisted of three parts—That under the Interior head, it was official; but under the Foreign and Litterary heads, the Editor acted on his own responsibility. I have discovered no change in the character of the Monitor, except that it now eulogises Louis the 18th. instead of the Emperor Napoleon; and every body knows that nothing ever appeared under the foreign head without authority.= These details I think will convince you that there is no reason to expect any interference on the part of the Emperor of Russia. I observe in the French papers the appointment of Lord Gambier and Mr Hamilton to treat with you.[10] It is stated that their Instructions relative to the boundaries of Canada will make it necessary to wait new Instructions from the United States. I beleive this to be impossible. If any material change of this line to the disadvantage of the U.. S.. is proposed, there is no serious intention of making a peace, which the Government can accept. If the alteration is immaterial, or advantageous, and the other conditions of the treaty shall be acceptable, you ought not to jeopardize the negociation by waiting new instructions. There are occasions when a public officer should not hesitate to jeopardize his own reputation rather than the national Interest.—This I think, would be one of them. I beleive however, there will be no necessity of this kind.—I understand the instructions under which you are to act are substantially those which were given under the Russian Mediation.[11] These Instructions according to my interpretation of them requires [*sic*] the relinquishment of the principle of impressment on board American vessels at sea. The British Ministry under circumstances much more unfavourable than those which now exist, refused to suspend the practise of impressment during the armistice which it had proposed. There can therefore be no reasonable ground to expect that they will now by treaty relinquish the principle. I think that there will be no disposition on their part to accept, as a substitute for this principle, any security which we can offer for the exclusion of their seamen from our employment. If my construction of your powers and my opinions of the sentiments by which the British Ministry are actuated, should prove to be correct, there is no possibility of making peace at the present moment.

If your Instructions will permit you to make peace by excluding the question of impressment altogether, or by pos po ning it for future discussion, I should still hope for peace. In the two propositions for an armistice, which have been made, the American Government said "suspend the practice of impressment, during the armistice, and we accept the proposition." This was refused. At the present moment the practice of impressment is suspended. The British Government instead of impressing has now to discharge a great number of her seamen.—The state of things required by the American Government, as preliminary to an armistice; now exists. —We can therefore consistantly with the whole of our conduct, consent to an armistice.—We can make peace provided the British Minister [*sic*] do not insist upon admitting by treaty their right of impressment.—In that event the war must be prosecuted until the right of the strongest, or mutual fatigue and exhaustion shall effect a change of opinions in one or both parties.. I can not beleive that any Administration will feel itself at liberty, to admit the legality of the enemy's claim to impress on board an American vessel at sea. I cannot beleive that peace upon this condition will be acceptable to the nation. In a contest prosecuted for the attainment of this great principle, I shall support the Government without regard to the political character of the men who administer it.—I trust that the situation in which the nation is placed, will awaken every honest man to a sense of his duty, and of his interests. If this takes place we cannot fail of success.—I do not expect to force our enemy to relinquish the principle by treaty, but I am confident we shall be able to make peace, without admitting the legality of their claim.—This is all we can expect in the present state of the world. —This will leave us at liberty to apply the proper remedy when the evil shall be felt.—I have two days ago written to the Secretary of State with a view to induce the administration to authorize you to negociate on this principle.—The opportunity is a safe one but the distance is so great and the time necessary for the transmission of new Instructions so long; that I expect the negociation will be concluded before they will arrive, if they should be given. If any thing should transpire in the capital which can be of service to you, or even amuse you, it will afford me much pleasure to communicate it.

May Heaven prosper your efforts in the work of peace I am gentlemen with sentiments of respect. Your Obedient and very humble Servant. WM.: H: CRAWFORD

Their Excellencies the Ministers.
of the United States at Gothenburg.

ALS. NHi-Gallatin Papers (MR8). Published in part in Adams (ed.), *Writings of Albert Gallatin,* I, 614-17.

1 Dated April 14, 16, 1814.

[2] Count Karl Robert Nesselrode, Russian Minister of Foreign Affairs.
[3] Count René de la Forest, French Minister of Foreign Affairs in the provisional government established in April, 1814.
[4] See above, Clay to Crawford, April 14, 1814, note.
[5] Louis XVIII.
[6] After having lived for some years in retirement, LaFayette had returned to public life with the overthrow of Napoleon.
[7] Frederic César La Harpe, Swiss politician, former tutor of Czar Alexander I.
[8] Baron Karl Wilhelm von Humboldt, Prussian author and diplomat.
[9] Pierre de Polética, who in 1812 had returned to Europe from the United States, where he had been Secretary of the Russian Legation. Later, from 1819 to 1823, he was Russian Minister to the United States.
[10] Admiral James Gambier, first Baron Gambier, was one of the commissioners appointed by the British to negotiate with the Americans; William R. Hamilton, British Under-Secretary of State for Foreign Affairs, was not.
[11] See above, Monroe to American Commissioners, January 28, 1814.

To William H. Crawford

My D Sir Gottenburg 14h. May 1814.

On the 12h. inst. the Cartel Chauncey arrived at this place from N. York, whence she sailed on the 10h. Ulto. charged with dispatches for the joint mission here, and for you. The mode of transmitting those intended for you was not indicated by the Governmt. but presuming, from the importance of the present crisis, that it must be essential that you should receive them as early as possible, and a vessel being about to sail from this port for Amsterdam, I have determined to despatch Mr. Carrol with them. I imagine that the relations between Holland and France will be found by him to be such as to offer no impediment to his reaching Paris.

This arrival brings information from Washington down to the 7th. and from N. York to the 9h. of April. It appears that the President on the 31st. of March had recommended a repeal of the Embargo and Non-importation system—that the Committee of foreign relations had shortly after reported a bill to the H. of R. in pursuance of the recommendation—and a private letter I have recd. from N. York adds that the bill passed the House 115 to 37. The motives which led to this measure you will be able to collect from the President's message, the report of the Committee and a speech of Mr. Calhoun.[1] I confess I fear that England, in her present intoxication, will not see the repeal in the light in which it ought to be viewed.

An act to quiet the Yazoo claims had passed Congress upon the basis of the Compromise formerly recommended. It does not appear to be true that Wilkinson has been arrested. The elections in N. England, altho favorable in their event to the Fœderalists, shew that this party has lost some ground there.

A private letter which I have recd. from N. York states that a proposition has been made by Sir George Prevost for an armistice—

that the Government, listening to the proposition, had sought from him an explanation of the extent of his powers, that is whether they embraced a cessation of hostilities upon both elements—and if they be thus comprehensive it adds the belief of the writer that an armistice will take place. Nothing of this sort is hinted at in any of the dispatches I have recd., but their dates is [*sic*] not so late, as the letter from Washington, on the foundation of which my N. York correspondent writes me. Abraham Barker writes the letter, on the authority of information recd. from his brother Jacob at Washington. I am inclined to credit it.

I refer you to the papers, and to Mr. Carrol for further details. I have engaged with him that the public shall defray the expences of his journey to Paris and back again to this place, via London, if he can take that route. But there being no provision made (at least none with which I am acquainted) by Govt. for this expenditure, I shall have to advance it out of my private resources, unless you have public funds at your disposal for such an object. If you have I must request you to perform my engagement with Mr. Carrol. I beg leave to present him to you as a very amiable and respectable young gentleman, who has attended me as my private secretary and who has my most unqualified confidence. He is the son of my particular friend Charles Carrol Esq. at whose house, if I mistake not, I once had the pleasure of dining with you.[2]

With much consideration I am your's &c—

His Excelly. Wm. H. Crawford. Minister &c &c.

AL (signature removed). DLC-William H. Crawford Papers (DNA, M212, R20). Cf. above, Clay to Russell, May 13, 1814.

1 John C. Calhoun of South Carolina, chairman of the House Committee on Foreign Relations, on April 4 had reported a bill to repeal the embargo and non-importation acts and two days later had spoken in support of the proposed measure.

2 Charles Carroll "of Bellevue," a resident of western New York, had formerly lived near Hagerstown, Maryland.

From William H. Crawford

Dear Sir Paris 15th May 1814

Your favor of the ult[1] was handed me by Mr. Shaler, together with the dispatches of which he was the bearer. I had previously learned the general history of the last campaign, and was prepared to believe that the eclat of the events upon the upper lakes would be overlooked in the disgraces of Northern army at the close of the campaign. The events which have occurred in this quarter have had the effect of placing all the continental powers under the direct influence of our enemy. How long it will continue, and to what extent it will be carried, cannot be more than a subject of conjecture at present. The appointment of Lord Wellington as ambassador at this court furnishes the strongest evidence of the importance the ministry attach to the influence which it now possesses, and of their desire to extend its duration as much as possible. A rupture, or an expected rupture between Ferdinand the 7th and the Cortes has caused this nobleman[2] to set out suddenly for Madrid. The particulars of what has taken place have not yet transpired. The detailers of news in this capital have circulated as authentic, the speech of the President of the Cortes to the King upon his induction to the regal chair, in which the feelings of the King are not consulted. The speech is the strongest evidence of the want of respect for the King, and of the confidence of the Cortes, that the King was entirely at their mercy, that they could possibly give. It tells him that owing to the mis rule, and pusillanimity of his father, and to his premature desire to reign, the Crown had fallen from their heads. That the nation had roused, and kept itself erect. That it was it [*sic*] liberty to have conferred this Crown on some one of its warriors, or civil rulers who had most distinguished themselves. That its duty and its interest pointed out this course; but that the oaths they had taken to him had replaced the crown on his head. That his whole life and that of his posterity would be too short to discharge the debt of gratitude which he owed that nation. Reign, says the President, according to the Constitution & laws, & remember, that on the day you violate them, you become the subject of the law.

The English newspapers hold out threats that Spain will attempt to resume her right to Louisiana. There can be no doubt, but the Counsels of England will be to resume it; but I presume Spain will have more to do than she will be able to accomplish in her colonies for some years to come, even if she escapes a civil war at home. This I hope she will avert by the energy of the Cortes. I feel some interest in the success of the experiment which the Cortes is making. Their Constitution is the first in Europe; if they have intelligence and virtue to support it, I shall look forward to more friendly and intimate connexions between them, & the United States, than with any other European nation.

France is now a political volcano, ready to explode whenever the match shall be applied. It is said, that the march of the Foreign troops has been Countermanded. The King seems to be in a dilemma. He fears to trust his own troops; and to retain foreign troops, unless in sufficient numbers to look down opposition, will be the most certain means of producing the explosion. It seems to me to be impossible for him to retain a sufficient number for this purpose, if the allied sovereigns were disposed to oblige him. The most deadly animosity exists between the French troops and those of the Allies. The exertions of the Superior officers on both sides, are insufficient to prevent the most sanguinary combats. Duels between the officers produce a daily mortality principally on the side of the Allies. These duels are decided with the sword, at which the French officers greatly excel.

I refer you to my letter in Cypher to the embassy for confidential information.[3]

From what I have understood, I expect the scene of your negociations will be transferred to the Hague. If so I think it probable that I shall pay you a visit. The Prince of Benevent [*sic*],[4] is announced by yesterday's monitor minister of foreign Affairs. From what has taken place, I presume I shall not be able to broach our claim for indemnity with new government, until I receive new letters of credence.

I will obtain, and send you a pass port to come to Paris, as soon as the place of negociation shall be known to me. When you arrive in Paris enquire for No. 56. Rue St Lazare. I can furnish you with Apartments in my hotel during your stay in Paris. Owing to an immense concourse of English I am told it is almost impossible to obtain furnished apartments at any price

I am dear sir with sentiments of esteem Your friend &C.

His Excellency Henry Clay WM. H. CRAWFORD.

ALS. DLC-HC (DNA, M212, R1).
1 April 14, 1814. 2 Wellington. 3 Dated April 8, 1814.
4 Talleyrand.

From William Shaler

Sir, Paris. 15 May 1814

As it seems to me certain that you will visit this capital before your return home, when you will as certainly want a carriage I have thought that it would be advantageous & agreable to you that I should purchase one for you here and bring it on. The great affluence of travellers from all parts in this city offers a better opportunity of procuring a good one on moderate terms than allmost anywhere else. I think such a one as would suit you could be had for from 200 to 300 dollers & that might be resold again for nearly the Same amount. I write this proposal however in the expectation of the place of negotiation being changed to the Hague which I have been led to believe probable. in the contrary wise I must indeavor to to [*sic*] find out some more oeconimical way of returning to Gothenburg than the way I came, thro' England for instance. I wish you would do me the favor to write me, for really I do not know what to do with myself; my stay here seems to me superfluous, as I cannot flatter myself with being able to add any thing to the information you will constantly receive from Mr Crawford. and at the same time it seems to me improper that I should return without your approbation. If you cover a letter by Mail to Nathl. G. Ingraham Jr.[1] at the New England coffee House London, it will come safe, as he is a young man in whom I can confide. In case of not hearing from you I shall act as I am advised by Mr Crawford.

Tho' I presume you are well informed of what is passing by Mr Crawford. I shall continue to communicate Such events as appear interesting. Please to remember me to Mr Russel and the other gentlemen of the Mission & I have the honor to be with great respect and consideration Sir your most humble Servant WM. SHALER
His Excelleny [*sic*] Henry Clay. Minister of the U.S. &c &c &c.

ALS. DLC-HC (DNA, M212, R1).
1 An American courier attached to the embassy at London.

From Christopher Hughes, Jr.

London Sunday Evening 16th. [*i.e.* 15th] May 1814

I arrived at Harwich, my dear Sir, on Tuesday morning the 9th. [*sic*] and proceeded to London immediately, getting here at 7 OClock that Evening. Mr. Milligan was detained three days until a passport could be sent him from France: this was occasioned by my name being inserted as Bearer of dispatches & not his.

I was charmed with the country, from Harwich here: the cultivation is beautiful, beyond any description I can command: indeed, I beleive no one could conceive of its perfection, who did not see it: it is a range of beautiful gardens & lawns attached to neat, & in many instances, magnificent dwellings: to call them *farms,* with *our* view of *what are farms,* would be not giving a correct idea of the country.

The size of this place, astonished me: the interest excited by it was not comparable to that which the view of the country inspired: my intimacy with Philadel. & New York was a key to comprehend an immense mass of houses, but my mind was not prepared for the perfect state of cultivation & ostensible comfort over so large a tract of country.

Of course I can say nothing interesting to you, concerning missionary affairs: I know nothing: and I am not directed to write: I am lodging in the House in which Mr. Bayard has Rooms & I Breakfast with Him: I have seen Mr. Gallatin twice since I have been here. They appear to have many engagements of which I know nothing: as to leaving this place, when I came it was talked of; but not since.

Mr Harris,[1] a very neat little man, who was formerly Secretary to the mission, & pending it, is to be Chargé des affaires at St. Petersburg, informed Mr. Bayard, that Admiral Gambier had told him, that a Mr. Golsby (or Goldburn)[2] & Mr. Adams,[3] were appointed with himself to meet the American Commissioners: since, I have heard nothing of it, until to day, when I have heard it, as said, from high authority denied.

I have an infinitude of little things to talk to you about, and long, my dear sir, to see you. I have felt more *from home*, since I have lost your society, than I have felt, during my absence from America. I say this because I feel it.

I am to go a few miles in the country to morrow, to see two Cousins, young Virginians, who are educating here: I will not close this until I return: I am sitting up on sunday night to write to you: It gives me pleasure to do any thing, in which you are connected: but do not be surprised, if I ask your leave to return to America very soon.

My Dr. Sir. noon. Tuesday morning 17th.

I will add a line, or two; I am in Bed, and have been quite ill: I have had a billious attack, but having gone through a surgeon's depletion, & taken some medicine, hope to be well in a day or two; yesterday I was very, very ill.

On my arrival, the arrival of the Jno. Adams &c. &c. was officially communicated by Messrs. B. & G. to the Foreign office here: to day, they received an answer, Mr. B. tells me, saying that commrs would be appointed by this Government "& suggesting" Ghent as the seat of negotiation.

The paper announces the appointment of the Gentlemen mentioned on the other page as the Commissioners. I suppose it is so. I am informed that Ghent is a most delightful place, in every respect.

I beg to be most particularly remembered to Mr. Carroll. I hope you have missed me, from the establishment. I say so, because I have myself so much missed the solace of our domestic society at such times of the day, when ones own family is the most agreable company one can enjoy! & you know, my dear Sir, it would be mortifying to be alone in this feeling.

I hope John[4] has behaved so as to deserve Mr. Carrolls approbation—Believe me, my dear Sir, very truly your friend

C. HUGHES JR.

P.S. Mr. Milligan left his best respects to you.

I am just told by Mr. B. that Ghent is aggreed to: the nature of this change has taken the course anticipated by you as the only admissible one in which a change could be acceded to: your opinion and intentions were very decidedly given in your letter brought by me. I shall not, I think, return from hence to Gottenburg. The rout would be very circuitous. May I ask of your goodness to instruct Frederick[5] to put up the things I left in my trunk, of which he has the key, and to take them & John under his special care, during the transit from Gothenb. to Ghent. You will believe, I am afraid, that we all mean to impose our troubles on you, this being the second instance of the kind. I must beg you to find an excuse for me in my [. . .][6] disposition to be useful to you. I remain &c. C. H. JR.

I have written a letter to Mr. Hall,[7] giving him some directions, or rather making some requests of him, about one or two little things I wish arranged. As you may not wish the change of place to be known so immediately, I take the liberty of enclosing it to you; his receiving it, you will please to regulate.

ALS. DLC-HC (DNA, M212, R1).

1 Levett Harris, who had reached England from St. Petersburg late in March.

2 Henry Goulburn, British Under-Secretary for War and the Colonies. He later became a member of the Privy Council and, in 1828, Chancellor of the Exchequer.

3 William Adams, British expert on maritime law.

4 Probably a servant.

5 Clay's servant, Frederick Cana, who had previously operated a grocery in Washington.

6 MS. illegible; one word omitted.

7 Joseph Hall, Jr.

To James A. Bayard and Albert Gallatin

Gent. Gottenburg 16h. May 1814

On the 12h. inst. the Cartel Chauncey arrived here from N. York, whence she sailed on the 10h. Ulto. charged with dispatches for the joint mission and for our foreign ministers. She was originally engaged by Government to guard against any casualty which might have attended the John Adams, but before her departure a messenger arriving with dispatches from Mr. Crawford she was detained to afford an opportunity of transmitting an answer to them, and any comments, which they might authorize, to us. She brings Washington dates to the 7th, N. York to the 9th. Ulto. The date of the last dispatch to us is the 4h. of April. I should transmit you Copies of the dispatches which she has brought, if it were not for the uncertainty of this letter finding you in England. But they are not very material, making no essential change in our former instructions.

The intelligence which she brings is however highly important. It appears that the President had on the 31st. March recommended to Congress a repeal of the Embargo and Non-importation system—that very shortly after the Committee of foreign affairs made a report to the H. of Representatives in favor of it, and Mr. Monroe says it is highly probable that it will pass. A private letter addressed to me states its actual passage through that house by 115 to 37. I transmit to you a copy of the President's message, and news papers containing the report of the Committee, and the speech of their Chairman, from which you will be able to collect the motives which dictated this interesting measure. I would have forwarded to you a complete file of the N. Intellr from about the period of the sailing of the John Adams to the 5h. of April, with which I have been furnished, but for the reason assigned in relation to the dispatches, and that I hourly expect Mr. Adams, who counted upon reaching this place on the 10h. instant.

A bill has passed Congress to quiet the Yazoo claims upon the basis of the compromise formerly recommended. A proposition to establish a National bank was pending before Congress and appeared to have gathered much strength. The elections in Massachusetts and N. Hampshire, though they eventuated in favor of the Fœderalists, demonstrate that that party has lost ground in N. England.

The engagement of the Government with the owner of the Chauncey terminates here, unless we choose to take her again, which of course I shall not do. A vessel being ready to sail for Amsterdam the moment the wind will admit of her getting out I shall send Mr. Carroll to Paris with the dispatches for Mr. Crawford. On this, as on other occasions, I should have been highly gratified to have had it in my power to confer with some of my colleagues. Denied that advantage, it appeared to me eligible to send a special messenger with these dispatches.

When the Chauncey sailed from America information had been recd. there of the advance of the allies within 60 miles of Paris. Opposite views, the result probably of opposite wishes, appeared to be taken of their further progress. The expectation however seemed general of a general peace by the fall or by the consent of Bonaparte.

Having been without any packet from Harwich for more than a fortnight, one arrived yesterday, which I hoped would bring something to throw a little chearful light around me. I was disappointed in not receiving a line from any body on any subject. A vague report, traceable to no authentic source, circulates that Admiral Gambier and some body else are appointed to treat with us.

Mr. Russell, in a letter from Stockholm dated the 8h. inst. expresses his concurrence in the proposed change of the place of negotiation, and writes: "The apprehension of any serious evil from this quarter occasioned by our change of position, is I trust without foundation. I regret however that I had not known the opinions of Mess. Gallatin and Bayard in season to have shaped my communications here accordingly. Something like a retrograde movement will now be necessary, and it may require some address to reconcile this Government to the new arrangement. I hope it may be in our power to throw the responsibility on the British Government" &c "I am placed rather in an awkward predicament by your communication as the uncertainty in which it leaves our ultimate location disqualifies me from adapting my movements here to either alternative."

The last like the former instructions display great solicitude on the part of the President to hasten the result of our mission, be it what it may.

I am gentlemen with great consideration Your's H. CLAY

Their Ex. Mess Bayard & Gallatin.

[Enclosure][1]

In a letter, dated at N. York 9h. Apl. addressed to Mess. Gallatin and Clay by Abraham Barker & Co. they say: "Jacob Barker (who was at Washington City) requests us to say Government have recd. a letter from Sir George Prevost on 5h. inst. dated in Canada March 22d. proposing an Armistice and offering to appoint a Commissioner to meet one they may appoint to negotiate the terms. The Governmt. believing from the tenor of the letter that the proposition was made with an honest desire to effect the object proposed with a view to peace, determined yesterday 6h. inst. in a Cabinet Council to open a negotiation with Sir George provided he was authorized to conclude an armistice *by sea* as well as by land. They wrote on the 7h. inst. enquiring on that point, and as Sir George proposed it without saying a word about sea or land it is to be presumed that he has full authority, in which case we shall have an armistice in a very short time."[2]

ALS. NHi-Gallatin Papers (MR9). Published in Donnan (ed.), *Papers of James A. Bayard,* 295-97. Cf. above, Clay to Russell, May 13; Clay to Crawford, May 14, 1814.

1 AD by Clay.

2 These preliminary exchanges had led to a fruitless conference between an American and a British representative at Champlain on May 1. Donnan (ed.), *Papers of James A. Bayard,* 297 note.

From Jonathan Russell

My dear Sir Stockholm 16h May 1814

I announced to you on friday[1] the arrival of Mr Strong[2] from St Petersburg—since when I have received a letter from our friend Lewis[3] dated at that place on the 5 instant stating that he reached it on the 2nd & found that Mr Adams had taken his departure four days before for Revel[4] & Gottenburg. I think therefore he must be already with you, in which case please present him with my best respects—

I have deciphered the figures of Mr Crawford & herein send you the English of them & if you will insert between the crotchets () the word in the original you will have his whole meaning—[5]

His concluding sentence might as well have been a cipher for whatever the ultimate necessity may be perhaps it might be proper to make our first stand on higher ground—

It is now *twenty* days since the date of the last London accounts received here & I am very impatient to learn the course which our Colleagues, there, have decided finally to pursue—

Pray do you hear any thing of our melancholy friend the Owhyen Ambassador?[6] There is certainly now much field for his diplomatic labors at Paris & I hope he may find a zealous fellow laborer in Mr Crawford—The knight of the woeful countenance will hardly be able to hold plough & drive alone—The ground is too difficult—It is apparently of much importance to us to know if our affairs have been at all considered in the general arrangements—whether any stipulation has been insisted on in favor of maritime rights or their protection be abandoned to us—

The arrival of the crown Prince is still uncertain—Count D'Engestrom[7] informed me last evening that two or three days would probably settle that point

With compliments to Capt Angus & Mr Carrol I remain faithfully Yours

J R

If you have a spare copy of Hay's Pamphlet on impressment[8] I should like to obtain for [*sic*] the minister *here*

ALI draft. RPB-Russell Papers.

1 No communication of that date found. 2 Nathaniel H. Strong.

3 William D. Lewis. 4 Now Tallinn, Russian port.

5 Russell's transcription of the coded portion of Crawford's letter (to the American Commissioner, April 8) has not been found.

6 William Shaler, who had visited the Hawaiian Islands in 1804.

7 Swedish Minister of Foreign Affairs.

8 George Hay, lawyer, who as United States Attorney for the District of Virginia had prosecuted Aaron Burr for treason, had published earlier in 1814 *A Treatise on Expatriation.*

To Jonathan Russell

Gottenburg 16h. May 1814

I recd. my dear Sir your's of the 8h. inst. I regret that it is not in my power yet to relieve you from the embarrassment under which you have been placed about the removal of the seat of negotiation. There has been but one packet since that which brought over Mr. Milligan, which arrived yesterday but did not bring me one line from our London colleagues. It brought no news except a vague rumor, which I have not been able to trace to any authentic source, that Admiral Gambier & some other persons were appointed to treat with us. The latest London print I have seen is the 6h. I am glad to hear of your flattering reception. Can you not obtain at Stockholm information of the truth of the article which you have no doubt seen, stating that the Allies on the 1st. of March, besides the public treaties, entered into a secret stipulation with G. Britain that they wd. not interfere in the American controversy?[1] I cannot credit it. Such a stipulation wd. have been dishonorable on the part of any of them, disgraceful to the Emperor Alexander–

A vessel being about to sail to Amsterdam the moment the wind will let her get out I have determined to send Mr. Carroll in her with Mr. Crawford's dispatches.

You will have recd. I trust before this reaches there important communications brought by the Cartel Chauncey from N. York–

My respects to Mr. L. & master Geo. Yr's truly
H.E. J. Russell. H. CLAY

ALS. RPB-Russell Papers.
1 Cf. above, Crawford to American Commissioners, May 13, 1814.

Bayard and Gallatin to Adams, Clay, and Russell

London 17th May 1814

We have the honor to acknowledge the receipt of Messrs. Clay & Russel's joint letter of 26th April,[1] and of Mr Clay's of the 2d of May written in answer to that of Mr Bayard of the 20th April. In conformity with the view of the subject, taken by Mr Clay, we simply communicated to this Governmt. our joint appointment & your arrival at Gottenburgh, leaving to them to make any proposal they might think proper for a change in the place of negotiation. Copies of our note, of Lord Bathurst's[2] answer, and of our reply are inclosed.[3] You will perceive that, thinking Ghent free from objection, and not less convenient than a place in Holland, we have acceded to Lord Bathurst [*sic*] proposal. Some advantage may be derived from having evinced a conciliatory disposition on that subject; and we felt no hesitation in preferring any place in the Netherlands to Gottenburg. A prompt communication, between the British Commissioners and their Government, may have the effect to facilitate & shorten the negotiations.

In regard to Sweden we beg leave to observe that, however favorable her general disposition may be, she cannot at this moment interpose any good offices on our behalf, being no longer wanted by the allies, whilst she needs the active assistance of this country, in order to obtain the possession of Norway. We will thank you to favor us with an early answer directed under cover of Mr Beasley, and to inform us of the time at which you expect to reach Ghent; which may probably enable us to hasten the departure of the British Commissrs., and prevent any delay in the opening of the negotiations. In case we should have left London before the arrival of your letter, Mr Beasley will transmit it to us on the Continent.

Copy. NHi-Gallatin Letterbook, 17-18 (MR19). Published in Adams (ed.), *Writings of Albert Gallatin,* I, 617-18. 1 Copyist's error. This letter is dated April 20.

2 Henry, third Earl Bathurst, Secretary for War and the Colonies.
3 These documents published in Donnan (ed.), *Papers of James A. Bayard,* 306-308.

From Jonathan Russell

Dear Sir Stockholm 17 May 1814

After closing my letter of yesterday, which I send herewith by Mr Strong I received your letter of the 9h by the Russian courier. I thank you sincerely for the newspapers—There are so many views in which the repeal of the embargo may be considered that I will not pretend to decide, at once, on its expediency—I can but regret however that it seems to furnish new proof of want of perseverance & systym—As it regards our negociation, it has perhaps a conciliatory character towards neutral powers & may persuade Russia & Sweden to interpose their good offices in our favor, but it affords some temptation also to these powers, by the interest it gives them in the carrying trade, to wish for a continuance of the war—It so happens too that the repeal of the embargo is most opportune for feeding the force which the enemy has in our neighbourhood & comes exactly in season to encourage him to increase that force for the ensuing campaign—An embargo is indeed rather inefficient which commences with the ice & is raised the first great thaw.

If an armistice has been proposed by Sir George Provost,[1] & your letter makes it highly probable, I should be inclined, from the circumstances of the moment at which it was made, to infer good—At any rate as a measure of relaxation it corresponds with the repeal of the embargo & I hope they may together lead to the restoration of peace—

You have, undoubtedly, seen S. Dexter's address to the people of Massachusetts[2]—He is sufficiently explicit against commercial restrictions—If his opinions have had no influence in terminating the last embargo yet that event renders them completely triumphant—He appears well to understand the proper time when to attack & when to retire—& while he heroically drags at his horse's tail expiring embargo & non-importation acts & orders in council, long since dead, he prudently avoids all encounter with a stout & living adversary & shuns the question of impressment, the great surving [*sic*] cause of the war, with most admirable dexterity*—Discretion may indeed be the better part of valor but had Mr Dexter been a true knight he would, when he affected to take the lists against all comers, have broken a lance, either in our favor or against us with this redoubtable giant—

As I said yesterday, I wish much before I leave Stockholm to see the Prince, but I shall promptly obey your summons when I shall have received it—Cordially & faithfully yours JONA RUSSELL

* I had written *modesty* first, but thinking of our friend Hughes I could not resist a pun & so interlined *dexterity*

ALS draft. RPB-Russell Papers.

1 Prevost.

2 Samuel Dexter, Secretary of War and Secretary of the Treasury under John Adams, unsuccessful candidate for Governor of Massachusetts in 1814 and, again, in 1815. Though he approved of the war, he had opposed the embargo and non-intercourse acts.

From Jonathan Russell

My dear Sir Stockholm 22 May 1814

I have now to thank you for your letter of the 16th inst—I received, by the same mail which brought it, letters from England & they are of a most melancholy complexion in relation to our affairs Mr. Beasley sent me a copy of a letter of the 20th ulto which he had just received from Mr Crawford. As I find Mr C accords with me concerning the naturalisation of pedlars & petty-chapman [*sic*]. I transmit to you the copy of his letter[1]—it is interesting also in other respects—

With regard to the engagement of the Allies on the 1st march not to interfere in the American controversy I am rather inclined to believe it to be true[2]—The circumstances of the moment at which this engagement is said to have taken place must have facilated [*sic*] very much a a [*sic*] desertion of us by the allies & rendered even their own maritime[3] rights comparatively unimportant—Indeed Austria & Prussia could not be expected at any time to feel a very lively interest in our concerns or the cause in which we are engaged—But Russia is indeed without apology—It is certain that the article in question appeared in a newspaper printed at Vienna & the Austrian chargé d'affaires confessed to me last evening, that altho the publication was not to be considered strictly official, yet it could not well have been made without the countenance of the local authorities & was therefore probably true—Well—notwithstanding all these discouraging events it is best to give the heart free motion—If we cannot make an honorable peace I trust at least we shall be able to put the enemy so completely in the wrong that we shall unite every honest American in the vigourous prosecution of the war—

It appears you are left quite alone by the departure of Mr Carrol —Perhaps never was a joint mission so disjointed & scattered—

The enclosed letter for Leiutt. Thomas W. [. . .][4] came to me yesterday under cover from his father with a request that it might be *safely* delivered—Will you have the goodness to cause this to be done—faithfully yours

AL draft. RPB-Russell Papers. Endorsed by Russell: "Henry Clay 22nd May 1814."

1 Not found.

[2] See above, Crawford to American Commissioners, May 13, 1814.
[3] This passage originally written: "The circumstances of the moment at which this engagement is said to have been made must have induced the allies to have consented to allow a desertion of us by the allies & considered even their own commercial & maritime. . . ."
[4] Name illegible.

From William Shaler

Sir, Paris 23 May 1814.

Since I had the honor to address you on on [*sic*] the 15 instant there has been no remarkable occurrence here within the sphere of my observation.

The general treaty of peace has been much expected lately, but it seems certain that its conditions are not yet agreed on. It is now said and I suppose is certain that the allied sovereigns are preparing to depart for England,[1] where I presume the influence that enshrouds their councils here will rather increase than diminish. It is also reported that the allied troops will evacuate france immediately, and leave them to the free discussion of a constitution: at present every thing seems profoundly quiet, and it is certain that the King has greatly recommended himself to the public by the firmness he is believed to have shewn in the discussions for peace, but from the heterogeneous character of the persons and parties who will assemble on the first of June to deliberate on a new constitution for france there appears to me much apprehension that Paris may again become the theatre of political discord. In Spain the attempt to obtain a constitution has entirely failed for the present but on this subject you must be better informed from London than I can be here.

for my own part I am anxious to hear where you are to negotiate, and to know your wishes as to myself. I also take the liberty of asking at what time you think of dispatching one of the vessels at your disposal for the U. S. Please to remember me to Mr. Russell, and all my late fellow passengers, and believe me to be with high consideration and respect Sir Your most faithfull humble servant

To His Excelency Henry Clay &c &c. &c. WM. SHALER

ALS. DLC-HC (DNA, M212, R1).
[1] The London Conference, meeting at the invitation of the Prince Regent of Britain, was attended by the Czar of Russia, the King of Prussia, and Metternich, representing the Emperor of Austria.

Crawford to the American Commissioners

Paris 24th. May 1814.

Their Excellencies the Ministers of the United States
Gentlemen

The return of Mr. Poletica to London offers a safe conveyance for this communication.—I have but little to add to my letter of the 13th Instant. A few days past, I was informed by a friend, that, if I would draw up a short statement of the reciprocal causes of complaint, between the United States and England, that he would cause it to be laid before the Emperor of Russia.—This statement would not be communicated to the Count Neslerode [*sic*], or to any of the Emperors officers as they are beleived to be in the interests of England—In consequence of this intimation I drew up a statement, a copy of which is enclosed[1]—It was to have been presented to the Emperor yesterday.—I do not expect any beneficial result from it—The in injunction [*sic*] of brevity, which was thought to be indispensible to secure its perusal, and a sense of national dignity prevented the introduction of observations tending to repel the charge of subserviency to the views of the Emperor Napoleon. I understand that the ministers of the three allied powers have affected to consider the war between America and England as the result of this subserviency.—I will not intrude upon your time, by enquiring whether this oppinion is real, or only affected to cover the apathy which is affected by them for the event of the contest for maritime rights, in which we are engaged.—Perhaps I should not have excluded this topic, if I had anticipated any beneficial result from the measure.—It seems to be generally understood that the conditions granted to France by the allies, have been settled definitely but what the conditions, are has not yet transpired.—The Paris journals are labouring to console the nation for "the Sacrifices" which the peace imposes upon it, by ridiculing the Idea of national boundaries—The nation, however derives but little consolation from these attempts. It is impossible to ascertain with correctness the true state of public Feeling in France; at least whilst the presence of foreign troops continues to insult and mortify the national pride.—From the addresses which are deposited at the foot of the throne, no conclusion can be safely drawn—The same fulsome adulation; and in many instances signed by the same individuals, were deposited at the foot of the throne during the months of January, Febuary [*sic*], & March last. —As little dependance can be placed on the effusions and enthusiasm which the papers of the capital state to burst forth from the people on the appearance of the King, or of Royal Family. The same demonstrations attended the appearance of the members of the late Imperial family up to the 28th March. It is true that the journals declare the demonstrations of joy, *now*, to be the spontaneous emotions of hearts overflowing with love and joy, whilst those which were manifested for Bonaparte were only from the lips. This is nothing but the assertion of hireling editors, who, before and since the 30th of March, prostituted the presses under their direction to the vilest purposes.—

The only changes which these presses have undergone is that they have changed the object of their Idolatry. The Idolatrous worship is as notorious and unprin- principled [*sic*] at this day, as it was on the 29th. of March. No dependance can therefore be placed on facts resting alone unpon [*sic*] their declarations. It is generally admitted that a state of general discontent exists throughout the military establishment. The young and enterprising officers of the army are most conspicious [*sic*] for their disatisfaction [*sic*]. The commission taken from the body of the Senate and Corps Legislatif are at work upon the constitution. The events which are said to have taken place in Spain give much uneasiness to the true friends of civil liberty in this country. They apprehend that they may have an unfortunate influence upon the constitution which they have now under consideration. They [*sic*] fall of the patriotic Spaniards must excite the sympathy of every feeling and philanthropic mind. After emerging from a foreign invasion, attended by the horrors of a civil war, brought upon them by the imbecility of their own Monarch, and the wickedness of a foreign enemy, to see themselves driven into another civil war by the same imbecile Ruler, in order to preserve their rights and secure their liberties, is a fate which is cruel, in the extreme.

The news from the United States which is contained in the late English newspapers is unintellegible to me.—The new state of things which has arisen in Europe ought to produce a change in the Embargo law. But I can not conceive the reason of any considerable change in the non importation act. So far as these events can have an influence upon this measure it seems to me to strengthen it.—Perhaps the act, which we were informed had passed into a law, prohibiting the importation of cotton and woolen goods generally, has embraced other articles and has rendered the original non Importation act unnecessary.—

I beg you Individually to accept my best wishes for your heath [*sic*] and happiness and my most devout prayers for the success of your labors in the work of peace.

Their Excies. The Ministers of the U.S. WM: H: CRAWFORD

ALS. NHi-Gallatin Papers (MR9). Published in part in Adams (ed.), *Writings of Albert Gallatin,* I, 619.

1 A 16½-page memorandum entitled "Reflections upon the War between the United States & England. . . ." D. NHi-Gallatin Papers (MR9).

From Jonathan Russell

My dear Sir Stockholm 25th May 1814

I have not had the pleasure to hear from you since my last.[1] I am at length able to announce to you the arrival of Mr Adams at this place, he reached here yesterday evening—

I have laid before him the actual circumstances of the mission & we both expect with much solicitude to learn from our Colleagues in England the result of their preliminary arrangements & the appointment of the British negociators—On the receipt of this information we shall be prepared to act accordingly—very truly yours

His Excellency Henry Clay &c &c J RUSSELL

ALS draft. RPB-Russell Papers.

1 Dated May 22, 1814.

To Jonathan Russell

My Dr Sir Gottenburg 27h. May 1814.

I have deferred acknowledging the receipt of your two favors by Mr. Strong,[1] in the hope that I could, at the same time, communicate something to you of an interesting nature, about the prospects of the joint mission; but this I am not yet permitted to do. It is now nearly two weeks since a packet has arrived from England, and although the wind is fair I have looked in vain for one for the last four or five days. The demand for packets created by the renewal of intercourse between England and Holland and France is such that I am told we are to expect them here much less frequent [*sic*] than before that event. I am equally without information as to the movements of Mr. Adams, whose arrival here has been expected, on his own information, since the 10h. inst. In this state of painful ignorance and solicitude I have to put into requisition every resource to bear me up against ennui. Indeed the delay in opening the negotiation, whose result, be it what it may, is so anxiously looked for at home, is inexpressibly distressing.

I thank you for the interpretation, with which you have favored me of the part of Mr. Crawford's letter in cypher—He will be fortunate to obtain from the new government the terms of adjustment which he counted upon from the old. I observe that the provisional governt. has promulgated a new tariff which is highly favorable to the article of Cotton.

I have heard nothing from Shaler. He will come upon us like a ghost at some unexpected moment. Through him or Mr. Carroll, if our Colleagues have not already obtained the information, we shall probably learn the dispositions of the Allies as to Neutral rights and the American War. From the conversation which you had with the Swedish minister of foreign affairs it does not seem likely that this government will interest itself much in the question. The Blockade of Norway, unsustained as it must be by any adequate force, does not proclaim the purpose of adherence or return to the old principles.

I send you the Copy of a letter[2] addressed to Mr. Bayard and myself from the agent of the owner of the Rattlesnake, whose case seems rather to fall within your jurisdiction. I wish to God we could, as he requests, condemn the 20 prizes which he has taken. If Norway is now to be considered as belonging to Sweden, the affair of course claims your interposition. I fear however, I confess, that the relations between England and Sweden are such, particularly in regard to Norway, that you will not be able to do any thing. At all events it may perhaps afford you the occasion of touching on the subject of the reception & hospitality which this Governmt. may feel willing to extend to our Cruizers and their prizes.

I will send you by the first opportunity one of Hay's pamphlets. My respects to Mr Lawrence. Yr's truly H. CLAY

P.S. Capt. Angus has been extremely ill, having violent fever with mental derangement. But he is getting better.

ALS. RPB-Russell Papers.
[1] Nathaniel H. Strong. The letters are dated May 16 and 17.
[2] Dated May 10.

Crawford to the American Commissioners

Gentlemen Paris 28th May 1814.

Since my letter of the 24th Instant I have received the enclosed letter from General la Fayette.[1] 634. 211. 1313. 453. 1556. which may be of some use to you.—He feels very confident that the exertion will be made.—I presume there is no rational ground to doubt it.

I think the strongest argument he could urge, would be the certainty of enlisting all the maritime states against England, in a very short time, if this war continues—So far as the Interest of English commerce is likely to be directly involved in the question, I imagine it has been well understood and has been maturely considered.

The French Government has revoked the decision of the late Emperor, permitting American armaments in the ports of France. The general complexion of the of this [*sic*] official note communicating this change of measures is friendly, and I am still in hopes that if the war continues, the condemnation and sale of prizes will be permitted in the ports of France to both belligerents. Mr. Poletica who will hand you this, will possibly be able to inform you something of the nature of the treaty, which has been, or will be signed before the departure of the allied Sovereigns. Its contents have not transpired—The French nation will be probably dissatisfied with it, even if it is reasonable and just.—The attempt in the French journals of Paris, to reconcile them to it, has a tendency to irritate the national feelings, not simply against the treaty but against the King. The object of the journals is to give the King the whole credit of the peace, by representing the nation as being conquered and imploring the mercy of the allied Sovereigns.

This is wholly indigestible to French Stomacks. You can not make a frenchman beleive that he is conquered as long as he can walk.—Europe seems to be engaged in making and breaking constitutions.—England and Russia are perhaps the only nations who are not engaged in forming or overturning constitutions.—Certainly great changes of opinion have taken place upon this subject within the last twenty years.—The news from Spain is of a distressing nature.—Perhaps it is not very truly represented, as it is at least probable that there is something like concert between the Sovereigns of this and that country.—I am Gentlemen your most Obedt and very humble St. WM: H: CRAWFORD.

Their Excellencies the Ambassadors of the United States at Gothenbourg.

ALS. NHi-Gallatin Papers (MR9). Published in Adams (ed.), *Writings of Albert Gallatin*, I, 622-23.

1 My Dear Sir. May 26. 1814

I past the last evening in company with the Emperor Alexander who, however prepossessed in his favour, has surpassed my expectations. He really is a great, good, sensible, noble minded man and a sincere friend to the cause of liberty.—We have long conversed upon American affairs.—It began with his telling me, that he had read with much pleasure and interest, what I had sent him.—I found Ideas had been suggested, that had excited a fear that the people of the United States had not properly improved their internal situation.—My answer was an observation upon the necessity of parties in a Common wealth, and the assertion that they were the happiest and free est people upon earth.—The transactions with France and England were explained in the way that altho' the U.S. had to complain of both, the British outrages came nearer home particularly in the affair of Impressments—He spoke of the actual preparation and the hostile dispositions of England.—I of course insisted on the rejection of his mediation, the confidence reposed in him by the United States, who hastened to send Commissioners, chosen from both parties, which he very kindly acknowledged.—He said he had twice attempted to bring on a peace.—"Do Sir said I "make a third attempt—it must succeed—ne vous arretez pas en si beau chemin." all the objects of a war at an end. the reestablishment of their old limits can the less be opposed, as the Americans have gained more than they have lost.—A protraction of the war would betray intentions quite perverse & hostile to the cause of humanity.—Your personal influence must carry the point—I am sure your Majesty will exert it. "Well" says he I promise you I will my journey to London affords opportunities and I will do the best I can."—I told him I had received a letter from Mr. Gallatin now in London—and we spoke of him, Mr. Adams, Mr. Bayard, and the two new Commisioners. I had also other occasions to speak of America.—one afforded me by the Sweedish Marshall Stadinck, who mentioned my first going over to that country.—another by a well intentioned observation of Madme de Stael that she had received a letter from my friend Mr. Jefferson of whom he [*sic*] spoke with great regard. This led to observations relative to the U.S. and the spirit of monopoly in England, extending even to liberty itself. The Emperor said they had been more liberal in Sicily than I supposed them —I did not deny it but expressed my fears of their protecting Ferdinand against the Cortes.—His sentiments on the Spanish affairs were noble and patriotic. The slave trade became a topic upon which he spoke with philanthropic warmth—Its abolition will be an article in the general peace.

You see my dear Sir, I had fully the opportunity we were wishing for.—If it has not been well improved, the fault is mine—but I think some good has been done—and upon the promise of a man so candid and generous, I have full dependance. If you think proper to communicate these details to Mr Gallatin, be pleased to have them copied—He spoke very well of him, and seemed satisfied with the confidence of the U.S. and the choice of their Representations to him—By his last accounts Mr Adams was at St Petersburg.—The particulars of this conversation ought not of course to be published—but you will probably think it useful to communicate to the Commissioners—Most truly and respectfully Yrs L F

To Russell and Adams

Gentlemen Gottenburg 31st May 1814

I had the satisfaction to learn from Mr Russell's letter of the 25h inst. received this morning that Mr. Adams reached Stockholm on the 24h.

A packet arriving this morning from England, I have also had the pleasure to receive dispatches from our Colleagues there,[1] which I have deemed of a nature sufficiently important to justify sending Mr. Connell[2] as a special messenger with them to you. Besides the casualties incidental to a conveyance by the mail he will anticipate its arrival in Stockholm two or three days—

You will see from these dispatches the negotiation is transferred to Ghent. I have ordered Capt Angus to be in readiness with the John Adams to transport you to such port as you may think proper to direct, the moment you may arrive here. The officers inform me that she could sail this evening, if it were necessary, so that if you choose to go in her, you will probably be subjected to no detention here. I shall myself proceed by land—will set out tomorrow and expect to get to Ghent before you.

If you do not choose to employ on this service the Corvette, you will have the goodness to inform Capt. Angus accordingly, and direct him to proceed to the port the most convenient to Ghent which I presume will be Antwerp or Ostend—He may in that case require some documentary protection.

Such packages and letters (and there are a number) brought from America for Mr. Adams, as Mr. Connell could not conveniently take charge of I shall place with some of Mr. Russell's goods & chattels under the care of our excellent acquaintance Mr Hall,[3] to whom if you do not come here you will give the needful directions. Most of my baggage I shall put on board the John Adams.☞

I have engaged with Mr Connell that his expenses to Stockholm and back again shall be borne by the government. As they cannot now be ascertained, if you will advance him the amount it will be reimbursed on our meeting at Ghent. We may expect from America at this place other dispatches. A flag was, it is alleged, to sail in twenty days after the Chauncey. I have directed the consul here in the event of one arriving to detain it until you get here. It will

I presume be necessary for you to leave some general order with him for the future I am Gentn Your Ob Servt H. CLAY

☞ I send you a second set of commissions for the joint mission to guard against any accident which may attend me, which were brought by the Chauncey.

Admiral Gambier, Mr Golsby[4] and Mr Adam [*sic*] are the British Comm appointed to treat with us. Mr Bayard left London on the 23d May for Ghent via Paris. Mr. Gallatin remained there on the 24.

Copy. RPB-Russell Letterbook, 221-24. Published in Donnan (ed.), *Papers of James A. Bayard*, 298-99.
[1] Dated May 17.
[2] John Connell, an American who had been residing in Copenhagen. At Gran on June 3 he met John Q. Adams, who had set out from Stockholm on the previous day for Gottenburg. Delivering the letters and dispatches addressed to the latter, Connell then continued to Stockholm. [3] Joseph Hall, Jr. [4] Goulburn.

To Jonathan Russell

My Dr Sir Gottenburg 31st. May 1814.

I congratulate you most heartily upon the prospect of once more seeing Land. Indeed the passage through the North sea was not more insupportable than my imprisonment here—My letter to yourself and Mr. Adams[1] explains all—

I owe you ten thousand obligations for your kind and frequent letters during my residence here. They have served to sustain my spirits.

We thought that poor Hughes would have died if we had kept him from London. It has been otherwise with him—he has been confined eight days there by severe fever. He was however getting better—

I send you the pamphlet you desired.[2]

I shall go by the way of Copenhagen, and thence by Hamburgh and the most direct route to Ghent, where I hope soon to meet you.

Give my respects to Mr. Lawrence and Master George. Yr's Sincerely H. CLAY

Will you do me the favor to deliver the inclosed and apologize for its detention which has proceeded from mistake?

ALS. RPB-Russell Papers. Addressed to Russell, in care of Connell.
[1] Also dated May 31. [2] George Hay's *Treatise on Expatriation*.

To Bayard and Gallatin

GOTTENBURG, *1 June 1814*.

GENTLEMEN: I had the satisfaction yesterday to receive your letter of the 17 ult. addressed to Mr. Adams, Mr. Russell and myself. These Gentlemen being in Stockholm which place Mr. Adams reached on the 24 ult. I sent off last evening a special messenger with your communication to them who will anticipate the arrival of the mail at Stockholm several days. I have directed the Corvette *John Adams* to be in readiness (and she will be so accordingly) to take them to Antwerp or any other port convenient to Ghent, the moment they arrive here, if they choose to go by sea. I shall proceed tomorrow by the way of Copenhagen and Bremen to Ghent and I hope to get there in three weeks at farthest. I should imagine by the solicitude manifested by Mr. Russell to open the negociation with which the Joint Mission is charged he will lose no time in hastening to Ghent in company I presume with Mr. Adams.

Other Commissions having been sent out for the Mission by the *Chauncey* to guard against the loss of the *John Adams* I have placed them at the disposal of Mr. Adams and Mr. Russell to provide for any contingency happening to me.

The passport with which the *Chauncey* was furnished by the British Admiral off the American coast is limited in its terms to the outward voyage. It was an unintentional omission to which our attention is called by Mr. Monroe who requests us to obtain from the British Commissioners presumed to be here the requisite protection for her return. Not being able to make application to them and there being no commander off this station within my knowle[d]ge who would be likely to grant the proper document you will see the propriety of procuring it at London. Some of the Passengers in that vessel have endeavoured to make the impression here that she violated her flag during the voyage. And as it is more than probable that the imputation may reach the British Government, the agent of the owner has put into my hands to refute it the enclosed extract from the log book which discloses the whole transaction in which the violation is alleged to have occurred.[1]

Donnan (ed.), *Papers of James A. Bayard,* 300-301.
[1] Not found.

Account with Joseph and Olof Hall

Gothenburg 2d. June 1814.

His Excellency Henry Clay

dr.	in account Current with Jos & Olof Hall			Cr
1814			1814	
April 18.	To Cash paid You . .	800.—.	April 21.	By 100.
" 25.	—. Paid Washer-womans acct.	7.27.—.		Guineas c 16 R Ks 20 . . 1641.32

"	.— —.	do. for Sugar & Tea as pr. do.	51.12.—.	May	2.	—. Cash recd. from Segerlinds by error in his Bill..	25. —.
May	2. —	do. Stolpes account	144.36.—.				
"	" —	do. L. Segerlinds dito	270.38.—.	June	2.	—.Balance in our favour ..	62. —.
"	" —	do. for 10. lb Coffee ....40....	8.16.—.				
"	16. —.	Cash paid You..	300. —.—.				
"	17. —.	do.A.W. Bissmaik for 5¼ Ells blue Cloath, 1¼ Ells Casimir, 2¼ dozens Buttons as pr. account	116.24.—.				
"	21. —.	Paid to the Amaranthe	24. —.—.				
"	31. —.	Governor's Passport	1.24.—.				
"	" —.	Postage	3.47.—.				
		Rl K	1728.32.—.[sic]			Rl Ks	1728.32.—
		E. & O.E.				JOSEPH & OLOF HALL.	

DS. DLC-TJC (DNA, M212, R15). Endorsed: "Left in my hands by His Exclly H. Clay—653⅔ Guineas Joseph Hall Jr—"

Commission to Clay and Russell for Examination of Witnesses

[June 4, 1814]

Fourth Circuit, District of Delaware, ss. The President of the United States,

To Jonathan Russell and Henry Clay in Europe Esquires *Greeting*:

Know Ye, That in confidence of your prudence and fidelity you are appointed, and by these presents is given unto you and each of you full power and authority diligently to examine all witnesses whatsoever upon certain interrogatories to be exhibited to you and each of you on the part of Alexander Murray Esqr. plaintiff and Allen McLane Esqr. defendant[1] AND THEREFORE it is commanded you and each of you That at certain days and places to be appointed by you for that purpose you do cause the said witnesses to come before you, and then and there examine each of them apart upon the said interrogatories on their respective corporal oaths or affirmations first taken before you or one of you AND that you do take such their examinations and reduce them into writing, and when you shall have so taken them you are to send the same to the Justices of the Circuit Court of the United States for the Fourth Circuit and District of Delaware, to be holden at Dover in the said District, on the twenty seventh day of October next, Closed up under your and each of your seals, distinctly and plainly set together with the said interrogatories, and this writ. *And it is further commanded* you and each of you that before you act in, or be present at the swearing or examining any witness or witnesses you do severally take the oath first specified in the Schedule hereunto annexed,[2] and full power and authority is hereby given to you severally to administer such oath to each other respectively. *And it is further commanded* that all and every the clerk and clerks employed in taking, writing, transcribing, or engrossing the deposition or depositions of witnesses to be examined by virtue of these presents shall before he or they be permitted to act as clerk, or clerks aforesaid, or be present at such examination, severally take the oath specified in the said Schedule annexed, and full power and authority is hereby given to you and each of you to administer such oath to such clerk, or clerks. WITNESS the Honourable Gabriel Duvall Esquire, at New Castle the fourth day of June in the year of our Lord one thousand eight hundred and fourteen. A JOHNS—Clk. Cir. Ct. D. D.

DS. DLC-HC (DNA, M212, R1).

1 Murray, a naval officer, was in command of the Philadelphia navy yard; McLane was Collector of the Port of Wilmington. Both had engaged in mercantile business.

2 Accompanying schedule of prescribed oaths omitted by editors.

Receipt to Lawson McCullough and Hugh Foster

[June 7, 1814]

Attached to Rental Agreement, April 24, 1813.

From William H. Crawford

My dear Sir Paris 10th. June 1814.

Mr. Carroll arrived a few days ago and brought me your letters of the 10th & 14 ult. The change in the place of the negociation for peace will enable me to write to you frequently, and will afford me the pleasure of receiving from you the most interesting details upon the advances which you shall make from day to day in the work of peace. My expectations of a happy result are not strong. The arrogance of the enemy was never greater than at the present moment. The infatuation of that nation excludes almost the possibility of peace. The ministry are represented as being very temperate and moderate. In my former communications I have stated the reasons which I have for doubting the sincerity of their professions of moderation. I may have been wrong in my inferences. I wish that the result may convict me of this error. Admitting the possibility that the British ministers will consent to make peace, without deciding any thing upon the question of impressment, will your instructions justify you in accepting it. So far as I am acquainted with the nature of those instructions, their letter will not. But these instructions were given at a time when the great changes which have intervened in Europe, were not only unknown, but wholly unexpected. What will be the effect which these changes will produce, upon the determinations of the government? Will the government, after they are informed of these changes, give directions to conclude peace, leaving the question of impressment open to further negociation? Will it consent to a peace which shall make no mention of this question? I presume it will. If the negociators shall be of this opinion, ought they to hesitate, to accept in the most prompt manner, of a peace, which they are convinced the government will instruct them to make, as soon as it is informed of the actual state of things? I should answer promptly no. A peace which omits the question of impressment entirely, will leave the American government at perfect liberty, to Apply the proper remedy, whenever the evil shall be felt. I do not believe that you will be placed in a situation to determine this question. I believe they will insist upon the unqualified admission of their right to impress on board American vessels at sea. This I trust will never be conceded. It would be better to return to our colonial relations with *our mother country*, than submit to this condition. If it must be conceded, a federal President must make the concession. As there is but a faint glimmering of hope, that the negociation will terminate in peace, the next important point to be obtained, is that it shall break off upon principles which will convince the American people, of all parties, that peace can be obtained only by the most vigorous prosecution of the war. I have the most unlimited confidence in the skill and address of our negociators. I am perfectly satisfied that the negociation will be conducted with a view to affect this important point. I have seen and conversed with several Englishmen in Paris, upon the question of impressment, & find the most of them, very ignorant, and arrogant. Sir Thomas Baring[1] is an exception to this remark. But his mode, of adjusting this question, is wholly inadmissible. He proposes that no impressment shall be made in vessels engaged in the coasting trade—that no impressment shall take place in Vessels engaged in the Foreign trade, in sight of the American coast. He thinks the ministry will hardly go so far. A merchant of the name of Wilson[2] says that an arrangement of a different nature would be satisfactory to the nation. It is that, that [*sic*] when a British officer should visit an American vessel, and designate any one of the crew as a British subject, & he should admit the fact, that the master or Capt. of the American vessel should deliver him up. If the man should deny that he is an Englishman, & the captain should refuse to deliver him that the visiting officer should endorse the ships papers with the name of the sailor and with his allegation The question of nationality shall be inquired into, at the first port, at which, the vessel shall touch, where there is a British Consul—if found against the sailor, the Capt. shall pay a fine, or the expences of the investigation, and the sailor shall be delivered up. If for him, the British Consul, or if in England the British government, should be subject to the same payment. He says, that in the case of an admitted British subject, if the American Captain shoul[d] declare that the loss of the man would endanger the Vessel, that he should be kept on board; until the vessel entered the port of destination, when the Capt shoul[d] be bound to deliver him over to the British Consul, or officer authorized to receive him. I see no objection to this plan, except that the Captain should not be permitted to deliver any man, who denies the charge, until it is established against him. This arrangement will give the enemy the absolute control over their own se[a]men, as fast as the fact of nationality can be established. It at the same time secures American sailors from arbitrary impressment. If the vessel should be bou[nd] to the ports of a nation at war with Englan[d] it might be made the duty of the American consul at such port, to ship him on board of an American vessel bound to England, to the United States, or to a neutral port, where the fact should be promptly settled. I do not believe that this arrangement will be acceptable to the government of England; because I do not believe, they will be satisfied with any arrangement, which will prevent their seizing upon the sailors of other nations. If I am correct in my conjecture, the proposition will embarrass them, and the rejection will prove to the most prejudiced mind, that they are determin'd to make the American Sailors fight the battles which are to rivet the chains of slavery which they have been forging for all maritime states, and especially for the seafaring men of those states, for a Century past. I have thought that this arrangement ought to be suggested to you, because it may not have occurred to any one of our ministers. I think it highly improbable that the English negociators will make any proposition of this nature. If their pretensions shall be so moderate as to afford rational ground for discussion, this arrangement may be proposed with advantages—If their views are so unreasonable as to exclude discussion, that of itself will have the happy effect of convincing all parties, that the peace must be obtained by the sword alone. But even in this case, when the rejection of the arrangement will be certain, I am inclined to believe, that the proposition Coming from the American ministers, will have a tendency to elucidate the extent of the concessions, which they demand upon this point, more satisfactorily than any other mode which has been presented to my mind. Mr Wilson is a true John Bull, but I believe a very honest man, and I am sure, sincerely desirous of peace. The rejection of the arrangement will probably have some effect upon the English nation itself. If this principle will be satisfactory to Mr Wilson, it is probable, that it will be acceptable to many others—in fact to all reasonable men—to all men who have not formed the foolish, & extravagant idea of recolonizing the U S.

I have felt that it was my duty to present this subject to you, in its fullest extent. I have verbally communicated it to Mr Bayard. It is possible that Mr Wilson may have communicated this idea to Mr Gallatin, as he made his acquaintance, and that of Mr Bayard's also in London. He had not suggested it to the latter.

I will obtain the necessary passports for you, and send them on to Ghent, as the monitor of yesterday has notified that it is necessary to have them to leave the Kingdom. I suppose it is equally necessary to enter it. From the letters which I have written to you, you will perceive that some of my inferences have been proved by subsequent events to be incorrect. I reasoned from the facts as they were presented to my mind, & I feel no mortification at the result. If it was my duty to communicate every thing to you, which I knew, or believed, at the moment of writing, I do not feel any mortificatio[n] that Some of my conjectures, some of my inferences have proved to be incorrect.

I have authority to draw on the bankers of the the [*sic*] U.S. for diplomatic intercourse, and for disbursements for distressed seamen. Under the first head I can satisfy Mr Carroll's expences and shall do it with great pleasure on his own account, as well as upon your request. I am well acquainted with his father and entertain the highest esteem for him.

This letter will be delivered to you by Mr Bayard, who I am happy to inform you, coincides with me in every question relative to the peace. He believes with me that if the nation can be united in the prosecution of the war, that the interest of the United States will be promoted. by the failure of the negociation. He will heartily unite with you in bringing the discussions to a close that will secure this great object. I think from the English papers that no Armistice has been agreed upon. I rejoice that it has failed. It might have done us much injury, but could not possibly do us any good. God bless you my dear Sir & bless your labors, & make them useful to your Country—mine I believe are like water spilled on the ground that can never be gathered. Adieu

His Exccey. H Clay. WM H CRAWFORD

ALS. DLC-HC (DNA, M212, R1). Published in Colton (ed.), *Private Correspondence of Henry Clay*, 33-37; John E. D. Shipp, *Giant Days or the Life and Times of William H. Crawford* (Americus, Ga., 1909), 120-22.

1 Eldest son of the founder of the financial house, Baring Brothers and Company.

2 Probably Thomas Wilson of London.

James Monroe to the American Commissioners

[June 25, 1814]

[The letter encloses the *projet* of an article (to be proposed in case the British should refuse a stipulation to give up impressment) providing for a future meeting of commissioners from the two powers to negotiate with regard to commerce and impressment.]

Copy. NHi-Gallatin Papers (MR9); RPB-Russell Papers. Published in *American State Papers, Foreign Relations*, III, 703-704.

James Monroe to the American Commissioners

[June 27, 1814]

[The Secretary authorizes the omission of "any stipulation on the subject of impressment, if found indispensably necessary to terminate" the war, and the transfer of negotiations from Gottenburg to any more desirable place.]

Copy. NHi-Gallatin Papers (MR9). Published in part in *American State Papers, Foreign Relations*, III, 704-705.

Rental Agreement with Elijah Noble

[June 29, 1814]

An Agreement entered into this 29th. day of June 1814 Between H. Clay and Elijah Noble.

The said Clay hereby rents to the sd. Noble, the brick house, Kitchen and Cellars now in the occupency of John Keiser for and dureing the term of five years, subject to the Condition herein after named.

If at any time within the 1st and second years of the said lease the sd. Clay should sell the afd. property, the s[d]. Noble hereby Covenants to deliver peacible possession of the sd. premises; upon the sd. Clay giving said Noble thirty Days notice of his intention to sell.

The sd. Clay Covenants (if such sale should take place within the time above mentd.) that he is to defray one half of the expence of the following additions and repairs towit Repairs of Cellar's, Cutting a Door, shelving, the raising of the Kitchen and a porch extending from the house to the Kitchen, but after the lapse of the two years afd. the said Clay may sell upon giving notice as afd. without paying one half the expence as afd.—In the repairs specified to be made the sd. Noble Covenants that no injury shall be done to the house——

It is understood, that the time when this lease is to commence is on the 1st. day of Octr. next, at which time the lease with Keiser expires

In consideration whereof the sd. Noble agrees to pay the sd. Clay his heirs &c. for the 1st. year five hundred Dollars, the second year five hundred and twenty five Dollars, the third, fourth and fifth years six hundred Dollars each to be paid quater [*sic*] yearly.

The said Noble agrees to surrender the premises at the end of the term, and at the time sd. Clay sells (should he do so) in as good order as he receives it, natural decay and inevitable accidents excepted.

The sd. Clay reserves the right to destrain for arrears of rent, and of re entering on the premises.

Witness our hands and seals the date afd.

Sealed and Deld. in the presence of — For H. Clay
TEREN[CE] COONEY[1] — JOHN WATKINS {L.S.}
WM. TAYLOR[2] — ELIJAH NOBLE {L.S.}

ADS by John Watkins, signed also by Noble. Fayette Circuit Court, File 823. Endorsed by Watkins: "Recd. 1st. & 2d. quarters Rent 1st. year."

1 Of Fayette County, for a time partner in the mercantile firm of Castleman and Cooney.

2 Of the northern district of Fayette County.

To [William H. Crawford]

My Dr Sir — Ghent 2d. July 1814

I reached this place on tuesday last after a journey for the most part excessively unpleasant, and found here three of my colleagues,[1] from one of whom I had the pleasure to receive your agreeable favor of the 10h Ulto.. I also had for the first time an opportunity of reading your interesting communications to the joint mission,[2] and I beg you to accept my individual thanks, as you deserve those of Country, for the exertions you have made in promoting the [*success*][3] of our labours. On the subject of our instructions, in relation to the great question on which the War has turned my opinion is, that they do not leave us at liberty to conclude a treaty without a relinquishment on the part of the enemy of the pretension complained of. Still I do not believe, in the actual condition of things, that if the continuance of the War depended on that single point, the American Government would persist in their demand of the abandonment of what is now a mere theoretic pretension, the practical evil having for the present ceased; and if I were persuaded that the interests of our Country demanded of me the personal risk of a violation of instructions I should not hesitate to incur it. But the determination of this question depends on the enquiry whether *now* or a few months hence, when we could certainly hear from home is the most favorable time for us to negotiate. A more unfavorable moment than the present certainly never could occur, and in this statement you appear to concur, as every other person must. Will our condition be worse a few months hence? On the other side of the Atlantic every thing we hear is cheering—the Creek war terminated[4]—10 millions of the loan filled on terms highly encouraging[5]—rapid progress made on Ontario in the construction of vessels which will give us the ascendancy there;[6] and every reasonable prospect, from these and other circumstances which I will not trouble you with enumerating, of a successful issue to the Campaign. I do not believe, whatever efforts the British Government may make, that they can throw any considerable force into America so as to affect materially the present Campaign. No treaty that we can now conclude can arrest the progress of this campaign.

On this side of the Atlantic is the aspect of affairs likely, by the delay I have supposed, to become worse for us? I think, my dear Sir, affairs here are far from being settled. This Country (I mean the Low Countries) appears to be about to be occupied by the British. For what? It will at least as to us have the effect of giving occupation to a portion of that force which might be sent agt. us. We know that all the great interests of Germany are unsettled. Altho' peace has been made, all the difficult points seem to have been put over to the Congress at Vienna? [*sic*] Is even France, conquered France, satisfied? When she has heaved from her bosom the immense foreign armies that now weigh her down, and her own shall have taken their place, will she not seek to efface the disgrace which her Arms have incurred?

If the negotiation is brought to the single issue, all other question [*sic*] being disposed of, that we must now, without waiting to hear from America, sign a treaty, waiving the relinquishment of the pretension of impressment, I confess I should pause before I consented to a total rupture of the negotiation. But my friend it appears to me, holding the opinion that I do, on the subject of a short delay, that it will be our interest so to manage the negotiation as to take advantage in the turn of events here or at home—I should like to have your views on this matter, which it is not necessary to add, would have great influence with me—I confess I am inclined to think that the British Governmt. will have no difficulty in making a peace leaving Impresst untouched. They will doubtless set up many claims—they will lay their d[. . .]pict,[7] but rely upon it ultimately (and that even without any change here or in America) they will be content to cast us and make us go hence &c. Why shd. they not? Undoubtedly, if we say nothing about impressment, they triumph in the contest.

As to acknowledging their right, our governmt. would neither permit us to sign, nor would I ever sign, a treaty embracing such a stipulation.

Mr Wilson's project is very much that which Mr. Jeffrey, Editor of the E. Review, when in America,[8] suggested. Altho' it would probably be better for the victims of this tyranny than the existing practice, my opinion is that as it respects the nation, it is not a subject of compromise—there is no midway point on which honor can rest between abandonment of the practice, and total silence in relation to it.

I agree heartily with you that if we can make no peace it is a solemn duty enjoined by our situations so to conduct the negociation as to satisfy the nation that a vigorous and united exertion alone will procure it—

I thank you for your attention to my request relative to my purposed visit to Paris, and to my friend Mr. Carrol. I long much to see you, but I cannot yet say when I shall have that gratification—

This place is quite comfortable, infinitely more so than Gottenburg. But what think you of our being surrounded by a British garrison?

I confide this letter, which I wd. not trust to the mail, to Mr. Connell,[9] whom I have found a genuine, intelligent & confidential American. Yr friend H. CLAY

ALS. DLC-William H. Crawford Papers (DNA, M212, R20).
1 Adams, Bayard, and Gallatin.
2 Dated May 13, 24, 28, 1814.
3 MS. torn.
4 Following General Andrew Jackson's victory over the Indians at Horseshoe Bend, March 29, 1814.
5 Actually, less than half of the loan of $25,000,000 authorized in March, 1814, was raised, and that under terms disadvantageous to the government.
6 The Americans were successful in increasing the size of their fleet on the lake, as evidenced in action the following month.
7 MS. torn—two or three words missing.

[8] During the winter of 1813-1814 Francis Jeffrey, editor of the *Edinburgh Review,* had visited the United States, where he had married an American girl.
[9] John Connell.

From Jonathan Russell

My dear Sir Stockholm 2nd July 1814

I have had the pleasure to receive your letter of the 27h ulto—

My distress at the delay which our joint errand has encountered had almost become intolerable & the kind of comfort I have received from Mr. Adams has afforded very little relief. His apprehensions are rather of a gloomy cast with regard to the result of our labours, in which I hope however he will be disappointed:—He will show you a letter to Lord Castlereagh which I have signed—I have done this in the expectation that the letter will not be delivered without the signatures of the other gentlemen composing the mission & solely in the case that the conferences be not transferred to Holland on the terms which you proposed—that is—if Mess Gallatin & Bayard, not being able to obtain your condition & declining a removal without it, should again recur to you at Gottenburg with new propositions—I think indeed that the condition itself was not of importance altho you had certainly reason to beleive it to be so—Things have however come to my knowledge since my arrival here which have entirely altered my view of the disposition & policy of this cabinet—Altho the condition be not important yet I find Mr Adams, who also believes it not to be important, has definitively made up his mind not to remove without it & it was uncertain if he will go with it. His reasons are that our present instructions will not admit of a negociation on the basis which will be proposed by the adverse party & therefore the sooner we meet the sooner shall we know the result & be able to act accordingly. He is decided therefore that Gottenburg is to be preferred unless Holland should already be agreed on—I have signed the above note to prevent the delay of applying to me or the necessity of acting without me should the circumstances occur in which it can be properly used—

I sincerely wish with you that the twenty prizes of the Rattlesnake in Norway could be condemned[1] but to this procedure there are insuperable difficulties—I do not recollect a single instance of a sovereign having freely consented to the institution of a foreign court of admiralty within his dominions & the peculiar situation of Norway at this moment presents additional difficulties—Both the contending parties must consider the freindship of England to be indispensable to their success & so far from consenting to an extraordinary measure for the condemnation of the property in question I am not without alarm that either of them would be willing to conciliate that friendship by a violation of the rights of the captor—

The prince will be here tomorrow & I shall follow Mr. Adams, who will hand you this letter, as soon as I learn the definitive location of the mission—I regret very much to learn the serious indisposition of Capt Angus please present my respects to him & assure him of my best wishes for a speedy & perfect recovery.

very truly yours JONA RUSSELL

It seems that a mail from England has at length arrived at Gottenburg but I have not yet learnt if it brought you any thing of a decisive character—a letter from Mr. Beasley of the 13 May informs me that Admiral lord Gambier, Mr Adam [*sic*] & Mr Gouldsbourn [*sic*] are the persons who are to meet us & that the place of the conference would be ascertained the next day—

ALS. DLC-HC (DNA, M212, R1). Published in Colton (ed.), *Private Correspondence of Henry Clay*, 37-39.
[1] See above, Clay to Russell, May 27, 1814.

From William H. Crawford

My dear Sir. Paris 4th July 1814

I have but little to add to the contents of my preceding letters. Mr Gallatin & the gentlemen who accompany, or follow immediately after him, will give you the ephemeral news of this Capital. There is but little doing here which can interest an American Citizen.

I am not sanguine in my expectations of peace. If the failure of your exertions to put an end to the war shall succeed in producing unanimity at home we shall have no cause to lament that failure. I am thoroughly Convinced, that the U S. can never be called upon treat [*sic*], under circumstances less auspicious than those which exist at the present moment, unless our internal bickerings shall continue to weaken the efforts of the government. I sincerely trust that this will not be the case. In your letter to Messrs. Gallatin & Bayard[1] you state that the elections in the East had terminated against the government, but by smaller majorities than on the preceding elections. I have not yet recd. any other information upon this subject than what is contained in that letter. There is a chasm in my news-papers delivered by Mr Carroll[2] from the 19th. of March to the 5th of April. If you can supply this chasm you will greatly oblige me.

From what I have lately discovered of the Councils of this nation, and of the temper of the principal maritime states, of Europe, I am inclined to believe that the time at which they may be disposed to oppose the maritime usurpations of our enemy will be more distant than I had previously imagined. At all events, I am fearful, that it will be more distant than we shall be disposed to prosecute the war, to avoid concessions which they will feel as severely as we shall.

In the prosecution of the war, the great difficulty we shall have to encounter, will be the raising of money. The war will give us soldiers, & point out the officers qualified to Command, but it will neither Coin money, or increase our Credit. If we can get thro this campaign without any signal defeat, and without the loss of any of our principal Commercial cities, and can raise for the ensuing year, the sums necessary for the prosecution of the war, we shall find ourselves in much more eligible circumstances at the Close of the next campaign than we are at present.

I do not look forward with dismay; I believe we shall rise superior to all the difficulties with which we are surrounded. I trust we shall live to enjoy many happy celebrations of this anniversary of our national existence.

Give my best respects to your Colleagues and accept for yourself the assurances of my warmest friend ship.

His Excellency H. Clay. WM: H: CRAWFORD

P.S. I will send by Mr Todd[3] the pass port necessary to enable you to Come to Paris, after you Close your diplomatic function. I repeat my request that you will make my house your home during your residence here.

If you wish to take a disciple of Pestalozzi[4] with you to the U S, one can be obtained. Upon him you can impose the condition of teaching the Greek and Latin—You will have however to maintain him until he learns English enough to teach—The economy of Switzerland makes this expense very inconsiderable. I have learned with great pleasure from the enemy's of the system that it has overcome the prejudices even of the priest hood. W H C

ALS. DLC-HC (DNA, M212, R1). Published in Colton (ed.), *Private Correspondence of Henry Clay*, 39-40.

1 Dated May 16.

2 Henry Carroll.

3 John Payne Todd, son of Mrs. James Madison by her first husband, had accompanied Bayard and Gallatin to Europe in 1813 as a private secretary.

4 Johann Heinrich Pestalozzi, Swiss educational reformer.

From William H. Crawford

My Dr. Sir Paris. 9th. July 1814

I acknowledge with much pleasure your very interesting letter of the 2d. inst by the hands of Mr Connell.

It appears that we differ in opinion upon two points. You believe that the British government will not hesitate to make peace, leaving the question of impressment wholly out of view. You appear also to believe, that, the events of the present campaign will have a favorable effect upon your negociation. I sincerely wish you may be right, but I am strongly inclined to believe, that the result will prove your opinions to be incorrect.

When I foresaw that peace would probably take place in Europe, in the early part of the Year, I did not expect that the manner in which the war has terminated would so inflate the arrogance of the enemy, as it manifestly has done. I thought as you now think, that England would not hesitate to make peace by waving [*sic*] the question of impressment. I am even now convinced, that her interest requires that this course should be adopted. There are however occasions in which nations, like individuals, blinded by some momentary, but predominant passion turn a deaf ear to the view of interest. This I presume to be the case with our enemy at the present moment.

Various facts which have come to my knowledge have led me to believe, that she will now decidedly any [*sic*] proposition, which you can make, which does not admit the legality of her practice of impressment, on board American vessels at sea.

At the moment however when I presented to the joint Embassy,[1] the idea of making peace, by omitting this question, even, if your instructions did not literally warrant it, I still believed that England would consent to this course. At that time I expected the negociation to open at Gottenburg about the 1st of May. I did not expect that instructions could be received from the government, founded on the recent changes in Europe, before the month of August. At the date of my letter to you of the 10th ult. my opinion of the views of the British government had in some degree changed, but even then, I expected the negociation to open a month sooner, than it probably will. I also expected that the change of the seat of negociations would probably postpone the receipt of the instructions expected from the United States. These reasons, together with those which arise from the expectation of a different result from our military operations, from that which you entertain, aided by the express wish of Mr Bayard, that I should present the question anew to you individually, must plead my apology for its intrusion upon your attention.

If there was any rational ground to expect, that by a longer prosecution of the war, we should ultimately succeed in compelling the enemy to relinquish by treaty, the practice of impressment, I would not hesitate to continue the war. I believe there is no such reasonable ground of expectation, unless we are disposed to bequeath this war as a legacy to our sons.

In that event, I believe that ultimate success would attend their exertions, if they were made with zeal, and union. Even in this case, I presume, that they would be in a better situation to command this result, by the enjoyment of peace three fourths of the intervening years. I am fearful that if peace can be obtained by omitting the question of impressment, and should be declined by the government, that the nation will decide differently. I am not alarmed at the idea of the downfal of the majority. It is an evil of minor importance, compared with the rights and honor of the nation. But I am unwilling that the administration should determine to continue the war, upon a point in which it will not be supported by the nation, which will place the federal party in a situation to make the peace which ought to have been made by the majority. My impression is decidedly, that this dilemma will not be presented to you, because I am confident, that the enemy so far from conceding, will insist upon concession from you.

It cannot be denied that the conclusion of peace, without settling the question of impressment in our favor, will be likely to place us in worse ground than we were before. If the question is not mentioned in the written discussions we shall certainly stand upon worse ground, than we occupied before the war. If it should be introduced by us, our situation will not be improved. If on the contrary the British ministers should in writing formally demand the recognition of their right to impress, as I presume they will, and should afterward conclude the treaty omitting the question entirely, we shall stand upon the same ground which we occupied antecedent to the war. If peace is made, I trust that the written discussions will be conducted with a view to this point. The arrogance of the enemy, the idea of superiority—the impression that we are panic struck, & that the Eastern people are ripe for a dissolution of the union, will certainly lead them to demand a full and explicit recognition of their right to impress on board our ships at sea.

You have no doubt heard the number of troops sent by England to America very differently estimated. I have endeavored to ascertain the number, but have not succeeded. This has arisen from some of the troops being sent to England & more to Ireland. I believe however that I shall not be far from the truth when I state them at twenty thousand. This force aided by the complete command of the water will be able to do immense mischief upon any point where it shall present itself. The facility of withdrawing this force when a superior force shall present itself on our side, and of debarking at some point less prepared for defence gives it an efficiency which it would be difficult for us to restrain, even if our troops were disciplined and our officers possessed the military skill which many active campaigns have given to the enemy. From this view of the subject I am fearful that your expectations will not be realized. I am fearful that the events of the Campaign will diminish, rather than increase, the force of your diplomatic efforts.

If the battle on lake Ontario shall prove to be as decisive in our favor, as was that upon Lake Erie last year, and a vigorous effort is immediately made by land, so as drive [*sic*] the enemy below Montreal before the arrival of the reinforcements from Europe, there will then be reasonable ground to hope, that the general result of the Campaign will aid you in your negociations. We have done so little on land, when we ought to have done so much, & our officers have shewn themselves so deficient in military skill, to say nothing worse, that I am afraid your expectations are too sanguine. The contest on lake Champlain ought to be closed also before the arrival of the troops from Europe upon our Coast.[2] Our inactivity in the winter seems to have lost us more, than we gained in the summer and Autumn.

The cold of winter does not prevent the British commanders from active operations whilst it appears to throw ours into a state of torper which renders them incapable of self defense.

I agree with you, that Europe generally, was never more unsettled than at the present moment. England and Russia are perhaps the only countries which do not contain within their bosoms the Seeds of discontent, and perhaps of revolution. The probable result of the Congress at Vienna will be general discontent. Will this discontent—will the war, or wars which may possibly proceed from this state of discontent operate in our favor?

I am afraid not. Here the government is so feeble; the temper of the military so bad; & the disposition of the Court so pacific, that nothing but positive constraint, can force into [*sic*] hostilities with any power, and more especially with England. The army it is true will seek to involve the nation in war; but its opportunities will be few and feeble, unless indeed it should be a civil war. Even this will be difficult, as the troops are cantonned thro' the whole Kingdom in small bodies, and are commanded by officers in whom the greatest confidence is reposed. Spain will engage in the war against us if she engages in the war at all. My impression is, that a state of peace in Europe, for two or three years, will be more favorable to our cause, if peace is not made, than a premature war which may, & probable [*sic*] will arise from the general discontent growing out of the division of the spoil wrested from France. Such a war can have no connexion with our contest with England, & can only postpone the moment when the maritime states of Europe will have leisure to attend to their marine, and feel the practical effect of British usurpation on the Ocean. I shall therefore regret rather than rejoice at the breaking out of a war among the continental powers in Europe. Such an event will tend to the advantage rather than disadvantage of England. In a state of peace her trade will be more limited than in a state of war. I am confidently of opinion that her revenue derived from her customs will be less during the year after the signing of the peace, than it was the preceding year. If the maritime states of Europe remain at peace, they will be successful competitors with her in every branch of commerce.

They will not be compelled by pecuniary embarrassments to sacrifice their own manufactures to the wants of their treasury. During the Continental system these manufactures have acquired a degree of perfection and stability that renders British connection of but little value, except for colonial productions. These productions can now be obtained from other hands upon as good terms as from the British capitalists, and in twelve months upon much better. We always over rate what we are deprived of—this is the true cause of the discontent which existed on the continent during the Continental system. Instead of sighing for British manufactures, you will see every nation in Europe, Spain & Portugal, perhaps excepted, prohibiting directly, or by high duties, indirectly, all these manufactures. I therefore sincerely hope that the discontents which will probably grow out of the arrangements made at Vienna may not break out in war. One or two years of peace will lead the maritime states to breathe from the exertions which they have just made. It will give them time to feel the practical effect of the "Maritime rights of the Britannic Empire. It will also give them time to recruit their navy. I rejoice that the Dutch marriage has failed.[3] I hope Holland will recieve all that part of Belgium which wishes to be united to her. Any further accession will weaken, rather than strengthen her. The Russian officers now in Paris who have been in England are highly disgusted with that nation. They speak of a war with Austria as certain. In this I think they are mistaken. If war breaks out on the Continent, I presume England in her present temper must have a finger in it. In this question however as she has no resentments to gratify she will be governed by her interest. She will therefore be against that power who is most commercial, and the destruction of whose commerce will tend most directly to her interest

I must really apologize to you for the length of this letter.

Present me most respectfully to your Colleagu[es] and accept yourself the assurance of my most sincere friend ship

WM: H: CRAWFORD.

PS. Mr Carroll leaves Paris sooner than I expected I will send your passport by Mr. Todd. W.H.C.

remember me to the young gentlemen of the mission

ALS. DLC-HC (DNA, M212, R1). Published in part in Colton (ed.), *Private Correspondence of Henry Clay,* 40-42.

1 In his letters of April 8 and May 13.

2 Only on Lake Champlain, where Lt. Thomas Macdonough won a remarkable naval victory on September 11, 1814, were Crawford's hopes realized.

3 The British Government in 1813 had undertaken to arrange a marriage between Princess Charlotte of Wales and the Prince of Orange. Castlereagh had obtained the assent of the latter, but the Princess had rejected the proposal.

American Commissioners to Monroe

[July 11, 1814]

[The dispatch reports activities of the commissioners, the removal of the seat of negotiations, arrival of the commissioners at Ghent, and their wait for arrival of the British negotiators.]

DS. DNA, M36, R1. Published in Donnan (ed.), *Papers of James A. Bayard,* 305-306.

From Baring Brothers and Company

The Honble. H. Clay London—12 July 1814
Commissioner from the United States &c &c &c at Ghent
Sir

We had the honor of addressing you on the 1st. Instant, in reply to your Letter of the 24th. June from Amsterdam, with a remittance inclosed for £500—on S. Williams, the acceptance of which we advised you.[1] The expected remittance from Mr Hall at Gottenburg[2] is not yet received: But we are in possession of your esteemed favor of the 5th. Instant,[3] with an inclosure from our mutual friend David Parish Esqr, which, was any inducement wanting would have great weight with us in claiming for you our best services. Begging that you will freely command us on all occasions we remain very respectfully Sir Your most obedient Servants

BARING BROTHERS &C

LS. DLC-TJC (DNA, M212, R12). Addressed to Clay, "Care of Mess De Meulemeester & Co Ghent." Baring Brothers and Company, a London banking house founded by Francis Baring, was after 1810 under the control of Alexander Baring (later known as Lord Ashburton), nephew of the founder. Jean de Meulemeester van Aken was a banker in Ghent.

1 None of these letters has been found. Samuel Williams was a London merchant who handled many American accounts.

2 Joseph Hall, Jr.

3 Not found.

From William H. Crawford

My dear Sir, Paris. 19th. July 1814

The departure of Messrs. Blanchard & Elliot[1] for Ghent enables me to send you the pass port which I have obtained for you. They will be able to give you the ephemeral news of this capital.

I see, with regret, that Mr. Adam[2] argued a cause before the house of Lords on the 13th.. This systematic delay is ominous of the result of your labors. This however is not the cause of my regret. I have never entertained much hopes of peace from this attempt to bring it about. It is the insult which is practised by this delay that gives me pain. The appointment of Mr. Baker, is of the same character.[3] The appointment could have been made with no other design than that of injuring the feelings of the American ministers.

I dined a few days ago in Company with the Marquis of Buckinghamshire.[4] We Conversed long and freely upon the subject of the approaching negociation. The result of our conversation was that there can be no peace. He insists absolutely that the question of impressment shall be settled in this treaty, and of course that it shall be settled entirely in their favor. He attempted to derive their right to take (for he insisted upon dropping the word *impressment*, to which I assented) their seamen from our vessels, from the law of nations. To this I replied that if any writer of celebrity had ventured an assertion of this kind, I would admit the legitimacy of his derivation, but that this was too important a principle to rest upon implication. If no writer of reputation had expressly treated of this question the inference was irresistible that it formed no part of this Code. He admitted that he did not recollect any express recognition of this principle. Mr. Bayard mentioned to me a conversation which he had had with Lord Holland[5] who endeavored to distinguish the right of impressment from the right of searching or seizing property. If he succeeds in establishing this distinction he cannot by it support the legitimacy of impressment on board foreign vessels at sea. To put him on the strongest possible ground, we will admit the men impressed are deserters. A belligerent cannot arrest deserters within a neutral territory: Merchant vessels at Sea, are the territory of the nation to which they belong, and this territory will be violated by the seizure of any person on board having the character of deserters. This conclusion is sound even admitting the right to arrest deserters should be derived from the law of nations. The right to impress sea-faring men merely as such, is founded merely on the municipal laws of England & cannot be derived from the law of nations. The practice of impressment on board foreign vessels at sea, is an extension of the jurisdiction of the municipal laws of England throughout every sea at the expense of every other maritime power. At the present moment, I believe the maritime states of Europe will Submit to this abridgement of their rights, or to any other which the enemy Shall find it useful to practice against them.

The French papers have not announced the arrival of the Wasp in the port of L'Orient, altho' they have published the British account of the capture of the Rein-deer.[6] I mentioned the capture of the vessel, and the arrival of the Wasp to the Marquis of B. who replied, that she would not be permitted to remain in port. I told him that I could not suppose that the French government would act so individious [*sic*] a part. That the laws of neutrality did not require it, and that the expulsion of the vessel from the port, would under existing circumstances, be an act of hostility against the United States. The British account of the Capture states that the Wasp had probably gone into the ports of Norway. This they have published, without stating the truth of the case,–

The motive of this silence, no doubt, is, the hope tha[t] the Wasp may leave port before the British minister shall know it, & pester Mr T[7] with his importunities. I believe the treaty does not stipulate the time within which the French Colonies shall be given up. From the exertions which have been made by the Parliament in relation to the slave trade, it is probable that these Colonies will under various pretexts, be retained, until after the Congress at Vienna, which it seems now settled, will not b[e] opened before the 1st. Oct. Until these colonies a[re] in the hands of the French, they will be extreme[ly] cautious of giving offense to England. But the general state of discontent in the army, will of itself, be sufficient, to render this government extremely supp[le] to its neighbors. This dis content is increasing every day, and rapidly extending itself among all ranks and classes of men, and even of *Women,* who almost universally hated Napoleone. The attempt to restore the fripperies of the Roman Catholic religion have disgusted every class of the Parisians

Present me respectfully to your Colleagues and accept my best wishes for your health & happiness

His Exclcy. H Clay. WM: H: CRAWFORD

ALS. DLC-HC (DNA, M212, R1). Brief extract published in Colton (ed.), *Private Correspondence of Henry Clay,* 42.

1 Neither has been identified. 2 William Adams.

3 Anthony St. John Baker, secretary to the British peace commission, formerly secretary to Augustus J. Foster.

4 Robert Hobart, fourth Earl of Buckinghamshire.

5 Henry Richard Vassal Fox, third Baron Holland.

6 The earlier *Wasp* had been captured by the enemy in October, 1812. A second vessel bearing this name, a 22-gun sloop of war completed in 1814, had sailed into the English Channel and on June 28, 1814, defeated the British sloop, *Reindeer.* The *Wasp* had then put into L'Orient for repairs.

7 Talleyrand.

Deed of Trust from Samuel B. Smith

[July 20, 1814]

I Saml. B. Smith of Lexington Kentucky hath for the Consideration of four hundred & five dollars to me paid by H. Clay of the same place. have sold to him his heirs &C. One negro boy named George thirteen or fourteen Yrs. old. Which I warrant and defend against the Claim or Claims of all persons whatsoever It is understood by the parties that if the said Smith pays to the said Clay the above mentioned sum. within ninety days from the date herof [*sic*] a negotiable note for which I have this day given the Said negro is to be returned to the said Smith Witness my hand &C. this 20. day of July 1814.

Att SAML. B. SMITH {SEAL}

ROBT. T. CAMPBELL.[1]
JOHN WATKINS

Fayette County Court, Deed Book M, 146. Recorded March 4, 1815.
1 Of Lexington.

To William H. Crawford

My D Sir Ghent 25h. July 1814.

I take great pleasure in introducing to your acquaintance Mr. Benson,[1] who will deliver you this letter. I am sure you will derive as I have much satisfaction from it. He is very well informed, and particularly on the concerns of Europe. Married to a daughter of Mr. Astor of N. York and having resided in America a long time we have some claims to consider him a Countryman I will only add that he loves our friends the British quite as well as you and I do.[2]

Yr's truly

AL, signature removed. DLC-William H. Crawford Papers (DNA, M212, R20).
1 Adrian Benjamin Bentzon, a Dane, husband of John Jacob Astor's eldest daughter.
2 Bentzon had been Governor of the Island of Santa Cruz until the British had seized the Danish West Indies in 1807.

Fire Insurance Policy on Wing to "Ashland"

KENTUCKY MUTUAL ASSURANCE SOCIETY, [July 27, 1814]
AGAINST FIRE.
POLICY ON BUILDINGS. *No.* 38

This Policy of Assurance witnesseth, That Henry Clay Esqr. residing near Lexington ha[s] entered for assurance, against loss or damage by fire, in the KENTUCKY MUTUAL ASSURANCE SOCIETY against Fire on Buildings and other Property, contained therein, as per Declaration *No.* 38—filed and recorded in the Society's Office, the following Building situated near the Boonborough [*sic*] Road near Lexington—Wing to his Brick House Containing Three Rooms & a Bath & passage valued at $2500 of which 2000 Dollars is hereby Insured @ 2 P Cent

Which sum of Two Thousand dollars, the real sum insured, and on which the said H Clay Esqr has this day paid Forty dollars — cents Premium, and the said assured having by his above mentioned Declaration agreed for himself and his heirs, executors, administrators and assigns, to abide by, observe and adhere to the Constitution, Rules and Regulations of this Society which are already, or may hereafter be established for the said Assurance Society.[1]

DS. DLC-TJC (DNA, M212, R10). Cf. above, Fire Insurance Policy, September 25, 1812.

[1] The remainder of the document, here omitted, is a formal statement of the company's liability, signed by Richard Higgins, director, in the absence of James Morrison, president, and by W. Macbean, clerk.

Receipt from Richard Higgins for Insurance Premium

[July 27, 1814]

[Receipt to Clay for $10, part of premium of $40 on Kentucky Mutual Assurance Society Policy for $2,000.]

DS. DLC-TJC (DNA, M212, R10).

Receipted Bill from F. G. Dutalis

[July 31, 1814]

Doit Mr H: Clay à Dutalis Fabricant Orfevre Jouaillier & Bijoutier.[1]
rue de la Madeleine No. 398.
— — — à Bruxelles.— — —

1814		
31 Juillet	1 Boulloire d'argent,[2] prix convenu	
	a 33 napoleons	660= 00
	pour l'Emballage	5= 00
	Total francs—	665= 00

Pour aquit [*sic*]
F. G. DUTALIS

ADS (printed script billhead). RPB.

[1] Manufacturer of, and dealer in, gold and silver jewelry and diamonds.

[2] Silver coffeepot.

Receipt from John Hoomes

Lexington Augt. 5th. 1814.

Received of Mr. Watkins Agent for Henry Clay Esq. Seventy five Dollars which I promise to refund with Interest provided such ballance should not appear due J. Hoomes: on settlement

JOHN HOOMES:

ADS. DLC-TJC (DNA, M212, R15). See above, Clay to Brooke, January 26, 1811.

Journal of Ghent Negotiations

[August 7-10, 1814]

Ghent 7th. August 1814.

Thinking it possible that I may take hereafter some interest in reviewing the transactions of the Mission with which I am connected, I have determined to commit to writing a brief account of the conferences, whether between ouselves [*sic*], or with the British Commissioners, and other occurrences, from time to time as they shall take place.

On this day, after all of us had been here a month, and some of us longer, Mr. Bayard was called upon by the Secretary of the British Commissioners, Mr. Baker, and informed that they had arrived last evening, and would be glad to see us, and exchange copies of our powers, at their lodgings on tomorrow at 1 o'clock. He was informed by that gentleman that his message should be communicated to the rest of us, and an answer sent in the course of the evening.

Upon considering this message, we sent Secretary Mr. Hughes to Mr. Baker to communicate to the British Commissioners that we should be very happy to meet and confer with them, and to exchange our full powers, at any time that would suit their convenience, and at any place that should be mutually agreed upon; but that it would be more agreeable to us to us [*sic*] to meet them at some place other than their lodgings. If any difficulty should be suggested in relation to a suitable place, Mr. Hughes was instructed to suggest a Hotel, at which neither party lodged. Mr. Hughes delivered the message accordingly, and was promised a reply before one o'clock tomorrow. Mr. Baker called in the evening and informed us that the Hotel des Pays-Bas, the inn suggested by Mr. Hughes was assented to as the place of meeting by the British Commissioners, and that they would meet us there tomorrow at one o'clock.

August 8th. We attended accordingly at the hour appointed at the Pays-Bas, and found the British Commissioners already assembled. After the ceremony of introduction was over, we seated ourselves at a table, and Lord Gambier, the first named British Commissioner, proceeded to state the regret which the British Nation felt at the existence of the war between the two countries, and the sincere desire which the Prince Regent had for its termination; that he felt himself, as did his Colleagues, no less anxious for this disirable object; and that he hoped we should be able to put an end to a state of things so contrary to the interests of the two Nations, and restore again those amicable relations, which he hoped under the blessing of divine Providence might advance the happiness of both nations. The other British Comms stated that Lord Gambier had expressed their sentiments, and all the gentlemen accompanied these professions with a great deal of civility. Mr. Adams, in our names, declared that we felt, as did the American Government and people, the most sincere desire to put an end to a war, so contrary to the interests of both nations and reciprocated the sentiments so cordially expressed by Lord Gambier. We then proceeded to exchange copies of our full powers, which each party thought satisfactory.

Mr. Goulburn then stated that his colleagues had devolved upon him the task of opening on their part the conference. That, in execution of this duty, it appeared to him proper that those points should be mentioned which are likely to be brought into discussion, during the negotiation, and that he would proceed, on their part, to mention such as they supposed would arise in the negotiation; adding that, if any which they should enumerate should be deemed by us unnecessary to be discussed, we would say so, or that if they should omit any, which we thought ought to be discussed, we could supply the omission.

The 1st. point, he continued, which they supposed would arise respected "the forcible seizure of mariners, and the claim incident to it of the King of Great Britain to the allegiance of all his native born subjects.

2dly. Great Britain was disirous that the peace to be made should embrace their Indian allies and that, in order that the peace with them should be equally permanent as the peace with her, there should be fixed a boundary for the Indians, which should not be liable to be encroached upon; and this, they were instructed to say, was a sine qua non to the conclusion of any treaty of amity and peace.

3dly. That a partial revision of the boundary between the Provinces of Great Britain and the U. States should take place, with a view to such modifications & alterations as would be mutually accommodating.

4. He observed that it was necessary in candor to add, that the privilege which had been accorded to the U. States, by the treaty of peace,[1] so far as it depended upon treaty, relative to the fisheries, would not be continued to the U. States, without an equivalent.

After having closed this enumeration of points for the discussion, Mr. Goulburn stated that he would be glad to know from the American Commissioners if they were enabled by their instructions to entertain a discussion of them; disclaiming any intention of enquiring into the nature of those instructions.

Mr. Adams proceeded to repeat the points suggested by the other party, with a view to ascertain if he correctly understood them. He observed, "if I understand you, Gentemen [*sic*], G. Britain thinks the impressment of Seamen and the incidental claim of allegiance which she asserts a point proper for discussion." No, said the gentlemen, G. Britain does not think it a point necessary to be discussed; but it was impossible not to advert to that subject in stating the subjects of discussion which we supposed were likely to come up in this negotiation.

Mr. Adams having gone through the several points, observed that it would be individually & personally agreable to him to have some time to confer with his colleagues, before an answer was given to the enquiry as to our instructions, and before the other points were furnished which we might think proper to be brought forward, which was promptly assented to by the British Commissioners, and tomorrow morning at 11 O'clock was fixed on for this purpose.

In the course of this conference the B. Commrs. stated that the British Government was disposed to make a peace, having a view to the state of things existing at the time Lord Castlereagh made the proposition for a direct negotiation[2] and without regard to subsequent events. That they did not desire an augmentation of territory for themselves or the Indians. And that they did not mean any change in the Country to be reserved for the Indians, any change in the nature of the sovereignty of those Savages over the Country set apart for them.

It was agreed that our interviews should be had alternately at each others lodgings, and that the B. Commrs should call on us at our's tomorrow morning at 11 o'clock.

Upon deliberating between ourselves, on the preceeding conference, we determined to say to the British Commrs as to the points suggested by them,

1st. That we were instructed as to the first point to discuss the subject.

2. That we had no instructions on this point; but that we had reason to believe our Government had taken measures and actually appointed Commissioners to treat of Peace with the Indians; but that at all events the War with them would fall with the war with Great Britain.

3. That we were instructed on this point.

4. That we had no instructions whatever on this point.

We also determined to state to the British Commissioners that we suggested, as subjects proper to be brought into the discussion 1st. A definition of Blockade and as far as can be agreed upon other neutral and belligerent rights. and 2dly. Certain claims to indemnity arising from captures both before and since the war. That we should further state to them, that we were desirous of abridging as much as possible the points in this preliminary notice, with a view only to present those we deemed essential, and to the end of making peace if possible; but that we were instructed upon several other minor points, which might be afterwards suggested, or if more convenient reserved for the treaty of Commerce which we were instructed to negotiate, if their Government was disposed to enter upon that subject.

Most opportunely for us on this evening we recieved our instructions of the 25th. and 27th. June last, given by our Government, after a knowledge of the recent changes in Europe, and containing an enlargement of our powers. Still they were silent on the two points before mentioned, and did not render any change necessary in the communication which as above we had agreed to make to the British Commrs.

9th. Aug: On this day, according to appointment, we met the British Commissioners at our lodgings, and Mr. Adams made to them the communication as we had agreed upon. They were at the same time informed that we presumed it would excite no surprize with them, at finding us uninstructed upon two points, which had never heretofore formed any subject of controversy between the two Countries, which were not at all grounds of the war, and which therefore could not have been anticipated by our Government. That, altho' our instructions were thus silent on those topics, we had no objection to hear what they had to say upon them, and we could afterwards determine whether they came at all, under any possible modification which they could be made to assume, within the scope of our discretionary power. We thought it proper, at the same time, in candor, to tell them that we did not think it likely that any provisional form whatever which they could receive would obtain for them our assent. This we stated in answer to an inquiry of theirs if we could not under our general power agree upon a provisional arrangement, subject to the future decision of our Government.

In this conference they were reminded that, not only for the reasons before assigned, but that from the tenor of Lord Castlereagh's proposition of this negotiation, it was not to be expected that these topics would arise; and that in point of fact so late as the 27th. of June (down to which time we had received despatches from our Government) they had not the remotest expectations of any such points. The B. Commrs confessed that they did not feel any surprize at our not being instructed on those matters; that however Lord Castlereagh's despatch was not a place for an intimation of them, as that could not have contemplated ulterior events, and that it could not be expected that Great Britain should make peace without including her allies.

As to a peace with them we observed that we wanted nothing from them; that a peace between them and America would follow inevitably, if it did not precede, a peace with G. Britain; that there had always existed a boundary line between them and the U. States; that there would be one of course at the conclusion of peace with them; and that we could not understand the difference between a line agreed upon by themselves, and one by G. Britain and America for them.

The British Commissioners were again asked if they meant an acquisition of territory for the Indians, or any change in the attributes of that Sovereignty which Indians had heretofore exercised; and, in answer to an enquiry if any restriction were intended as to our purchasing their lands, replied that they did not. Subsequently however they said that they wanted the Country which was to be set apart, by this boundary for the Indians, to be a barrier between the provinces of G. Britain and the U. States and both parties restrained from purchasing from the Indians, who might however sell to others.

The British Commrs observed that as our instructions did not authorize us to discuss the points mentioned, particularly that which they had already informed us was a sine qua non, and as we did not think it likely even that we could on that subject agree to any provisional article, it was useless to entertain the discussion at all, and that they saw no course left to them but to report to their Government and await their orders. We expressed the sincere regret we felt at the danger of the negotiation breaking off thus at the threshold, and although we could not press any discussion on the point of greatest difficulty, we felt strongly persuaded that a disclosure of their views on that subject, with a communication to them of our's, would lead to a satisfactory understanding. We could not however object to the reference which they proposed to make to their Government, but hoped that as little time would be lost as possible.

To prevent misconception of the points which had been suggested by the parties respectively as those which were likely to be brought into the discussion it was agreed that a protocol should be made of them, and that for this purpose each party should prepare a written statement, according to their impressions of what had passed, and that we should again meet tomorrow morning at 12 o'clock at our lodgings, and compare them.

10th. Aug. We again met this morning at our lodgings, and each party produced a sketch of the proposed protocol. Our's was much fuller than their's, and a good deal of conversation arose on the contents. The British Commrs conceived it ought to be limited to a simple statement of the points proposed by either side as subjects of discussion in the negotiation, and of facts, without containing argumentative matter offered by either side. They objected therefore to any assignment by us, in the instrument, of the reasons why we were not instructed on the two points relative to the Indian boundary and the fisheries. We admitted that it ought not to contain reasons at large which might be urged during the conference, but that important facts ought to enter into it, and that if these facts imported reasoning, that was no objection to their insertion.

It was agreed that the statement of each party as made by himself, of the points which he supposed would arise in the negotiation, should be taken for the protocol; and hence that we should receive the British Commissioners' statement of the points suggested by themselves, in the first day's conference, in their own language; and that, on the other hand, our statement, in answer to their enquiry relative to our instructions, and of the two additional points which appeared to us as proper for discussion should be taken as we had made it in the sketch prepared by us.

Our sketch stated that the B. Commrs, in explanation of their second point, had said, that the boundary which they proposed to run for the Indians, was to mark off a district of country which was to form a barrier between the U. S. and the Provinces of Great Britain; that the Indians were not to be permitted to Sell to either party within that district, tho' they might Sell to others; and that the U. S. was not to be permitted, as heretofore, to purchase of the Indians within that district. The British commissioners without at all objecting to the truth of this Statement, objected to its insertion in the protocol, on the ground that it was not matter for such an instrument, and that it was a gratuitous discloSure [*sic*] of their views made in a spirit of frankness on their part. We endeavored to retain this Statement in the instrument but finally consented to Strike it out upon their agreeing to modify their Statement of the Second point in the manner in which it now Stands in the Protocol. Our Sketch also Stated that we offered to discuss all the points Suggested by the British commissioners, in order that on their two, as to which we had no instructions, we might See if it were possible that they could be made to assume any form admissible within the Scope of our general discretionary powers; and that if they could not, we might know and put our government in possession of the precise views and intention of the British government; and that we might on the other hand possess them of our objections to those points. Our Sketch continued that the British commissioners declined to enter upon the discussion, and Said they must refer the matter to their government, and await their orders.[3]

The British commissioners objected with much earnestness to the Protocols Stating that they declined to enter upon the discussion, and the reference to their government, they conceived it ought not to be inserted at all in that instrument; that they were under no necessity to have announced to us their intended reference to their Government, which which [*sic*] they had merely communicated to us in conse-[*sic*] of that spirit of candor and mutual confidence, which, on their part, they desired should guide the negotiation; and that if we pressed them in this way, it would certainly make them more reserved in future. When the last sentiment was thrown out, we instantly agreed to strike out the objectionable matter. This we had the less hesitation to do, because it was clearly and distinctly understood that, the protocol notwithstanding, we were both at liberty to communicate in the fullest manner to our respective governments, what should occur from time to time at the conferences. The matter for the protocol being finally arranged, our Secretaries were directed to prepare it from the two sketches, which they accordingly did in the following form;

"Protocol of conference.

8th. August. The British and American Commissioners having met, their full powers were respectively produced, which were found satisfactory, and copies thereof were exchanged.

The B. Commrs stated the following subjects as those upon which it appeared to them that the discussions between themselves and the American Commrs would be likely to turn:

1st. The forcible seizure of mariners from on board merchant ships on the high seas, and in connection with it the right of the King of Great Britain to the allegiance of all his native subjects.

2dly. That the peace be extended to the Indian allies of Great Britain and that the boundary of their territory be definitively marked out as a permanent barrier between the dominions of Great Britain and the U. States. An arrangement on this subject to be a sine qua non of a treaty of peace.

3dly. A rivision of the boundary line between the British and American Territories, with the view to prevent future uncertainty and dispute.

The British Commrs requested information whether the American Commrs were instructed to enter into negotiation on the above points; but before they desired any answer they felt it right to communicate the intentions of their Government as to the North American fisheries, viz. that the British Government did not intend to grant to the U. States gratuitously the privileges formerly granted by treaty to them, of fishing within the limits of the British sovereignty, and of using the shores of the British Territories for purposes connected with the fisheri[es.]

The meeting being adjourned to the 9th. of August the Commrs met again on that day.

The American Commrs at this meeting stated, that upon the first and third points proposed by the British Comm[rs] they were provided with instructions from their Government and on the second and fourth of those points they were not provided for in their instructions. That in relation to an Indian pacification they knew that the Government of the U. States had appointed Commrs to treat of peace with the Indians, and that it was not improbable peace had been made with them.

The American Commrs presented, as further subjects considered by the Government of the U. States as suitable for discussion,

1st. A definition of blockade, and as far as may be agreed, of other neutral and belligerent rights.

2dly. Certain claims of indemnity to individuals for captures and seizures preceeding and subsequent to the war.

3dly. They further stated that there were various other points to which their instructions extended, which might with propriety be objects of discussion either in the negotiation of peace, or in that of a treaty of commerce, which in the event of a propitio[us] termination of the present conferences they were likewise authorized to conclude. That for the purpose of facilitating the first and most essential object, of peace, they had discarded every subject which was not considered as peculiarly connected with that, and presented only those points which appeared to be immediately relevant to this negotiation.

The A. Commissioners expressed their wish to receive from the B. Commrs a statement of the views and objects of Great Britain upon all the points, and their willingness to discuss them all.

They (the A. C.) were asked whether, if those of G. Britain should enter further upon this discussion, particularly respecting the Indian boundary, the A. C. could expect that it would terminate by some provisional arrangement which they could conclude subject to the ratification of their government?

They answered that, as any arrangement to which they could agree upon the subject, must be without specific authority from their Government, it was not possible for them, previous to discussion, to decide whether an article on the subject could be formed which would be mutually satisfactory, and to which they should think themselves, under their discretionary powers authorized in acceding.

The meeting was adjourned."

D, in hand of Christopher Hughes Jr. (except one page, probably by William Shaler), amended by Clay. DLC-William H. Crawford Papers (DNA, M212, R20). Enclosed in Clay to Crawford, August 22, 1814. Another copy, substantially the same as this, was enclosed with the letter of August 18 to James Monroe. A continuation of the journal appears below, August 19.

1 At the end of the American Revolution.

2 November 4, 1813.

[3] Most of this paragraph and the beginning of the next probably in hand of William Shaler.

To William H. Crawford

My Dear Crawford Ghent 11th. Aug. 1814.

The deep interest you have taken, and I have no doubt continue to feel, in the result of our negotiation induces me to communicate to you the present state of it, as briefly as possible, reserving for a future occasion more ample details.

British C instructed in sist si
The 666. 1132. are 1348. 73. 113 [*sic*] to 1348. 296. upon as a 1547.
ne qua non to the con clus ion of any
1166. 232. 105. 1554. 1355. 1209. 1132. 366. 652. 1397. 1472.
treaty of peace that the pa cification
884. 1275. 1397. 882. 284. 1355. 1190. 1470. 75 shall include the
In di an allies G B In di
1348 161. 1516. 1115. 249 of 1107. 1450.; and that an 1348. 161.
an bound ary fixed treaty
1516. 419. 410. 1376. 390 shall be 1452. 1133 by the 884. 1275.,
setting country for them to create a per ma
562. 1111. 1107. apart a 971. 1390. 456., 1554. 214. 1215. 1314. 413.
ne nt bar ri er between British provin ces U S
1166. 1399. 138. 463. 133. 737. the 666. 409. 1102. 439. and the 98.
with In which neither U S. nor GB at liberty
240. 324. 803 the 98. 1444. 3. are to be 1413. 249. 218. 1095. to
purchase Indians.
1493. 1425. 557. 404. from the 1348. 161.◊1516.

rights fishing
They have further informed us that the 780. of 1276. 317 &c.
jur is di c tion G B
within the 591. 588. 161. 1132. 601. of 3., which were granted to
America Treaty peace not contin u ed
14 by the 884. 1275 of 882. will 1412 be 532. 1348. 509. 1133.
an equivalent
without 1516. 153. 708. 1329. 174.

They have asked if we are in structed
1121. 713. 1101. 1133. 1483. 1207. 770. 1348. 73. 1133. on those
two we
1087. points, to which 1207. answered in the negative. Nevertheless
we
1207 expressed a willingness to take up those subjects, with the other matters of negotiation, and receive the 666. views upon them,
our own return they
and to communicate 1512. 190. in 1379. 200. 410. This 1121 declined

we *we* *would not give*
doing, without 1207. would give, what 1207. 687. 1412. 1241. an
discussion *pro vis*
assurance that a 318. 1225. 1027. 652. might lead to some 409. 573.
ion al *article* *subject*
708. 531. 1115. 1418. 101. 448. which we would agree upon, 939. 314
fu ture de ci sion our government
to the 1201. 777. 1556. 1548. 1470. 652. of 1512. 916. 1441. In this
they re fer red sub ject their gov
state of things, 1121 have 1228. 604. 542. the 939. 314 to 800. 916.
ernment further orders our conferences
1441. for its. 173. 175. 852, and in the mean time 1512. 155. 642 are
suspended
699. 469. 380.

From the expressions and manner of the B. C. I inferred a
pass over silence
willingness on their part to 1357. 1027. 993. in 1547. 943. if we
the sub ject of im press ment
were willing to do so, 1355. 939. 314. 1397. 149. 1581. 1441. This
now even tually
we are 260 authorized 227. 1329. 400. to do by our late instructions.

ins tructed
I think it probable that the B. C. will be 1348. 73. 1133.
per sist sine qua non
to 1314. 296. in their 279. 1556. 232. 105 with the view of getting
our government
us to 1228. 604. the subject to 1512. 916. 1441. On such a state of things an important question will arise, upon which I should like
break off the negociation
to have your opinion, Shall we 459. 1377. 1397. 1355. 93.?

I recd. your kind letter by Mr. Myers.[1] I shall never cease to retain the most lively sense of your very friendly offer in relation to myself. Upon that and other subjects I will hereafter communicate with you.

The John Adams will sail in the course of ten or twelve days, if we receive her passport, now daily expected from London. You will do well to prepare the dispatches which I presume you intend to expedite by her

The B. C. have taken a house in town Yr friend. H Clay

P.S. The cypher used is that of which Mr. S.[2] informs me he lately furnished you a Copy.

ALS. DLC-William H. Crawford Papers (DNA, M212, R20). Interlineations in unknown hand; italics by editors. Cf. Clay's Journal, above, August 7-10.

1 Probably Christopher Meyer, United States Consul at Bordeaux.

2 William Shaler.

Monroe to the American Commissioners

[August 11, 1814]

[The President approves the transfer of negotiations from Gottenburg to Ghent. The question of impressment may be disposed of either in the manner suggested in the instructions of June 25, which is to be preferred, or by omitting it from the treaty as authorized by the instructions of June 27. If Great Britain does not end the war on the terms Americans are authorized to offer, "she has other objects in it than those for which she has hitherto professed to contend." Such objects will be resisted by the United States, and the resulting severe conflict "will be borne with firmness."]

Extract. *American State Papers, Foreign Relations,* III, 705.

The American Commissioners to James Monroe

[August 12, 1814]

LS (signed by all but Gallatin). DNA, M36, R1. Published in *American State Papers, Foreign Relations,* III, 705-708. Summarizes discussions reported above, Clay's Journal, August 7-10.

From Joseph Hall, Jr.

Gothenburg 17th August 1814.

His Excellency Henry Clay &c &c &c
Ghent.
Sir,

My last respects were of the 27th ulto.[1] informing you of your Guineas remaining unsold.—Inclosed Letters have since come to hand—those for Mr. Hughes & Capt Angus you'll have the goodness to deliver to them.—

The Consulate is again left with me—Mr. Strong[2] has taken Passage for Amelia Island[3] and it is very doubtful if he intends to return here.—At your convenience may I request you to have the goodness to recommend to the Hon the Secretary of State, in case Mr. Strong resign his Commission.——[*sic*]

The Swedes are not advancing in Norway as fast as was expected.

Respectfully I remain Sir Your Mo Obet. Servt.

JOSEPH HALL J—

ALS. DLC-HC (DNA, M212, R1).
1 Not found. 2 Nathaniel H. Strong. 3 Off the northeast coast of Florida.

To James Monroe

My Dr Sir (Private) Ghent 18th. Aug. 1814.

The great solicitude which you no doubt feel as to the result of our mission, and my wish to contribute any thing in my power towards the means of your forming on that subject a correct opinion, have determined me, though it is perhaps somewhat irregular, to address to you this separate letter. I have felt less repugnance at doing this, because communications (not it is true very essential, but still possessing a certain degree of interest) may properly enough enter into a private confidential letter which could not find a place in a joint despatch.

We were prepared, by the events which have occurred in Europe, by the temper manifested in English pamphlets and prints, and by the well known arrogance of the British character, for the most extravagant pretensions to be brought forward in our negotiation. Unhappily we have not been disappointed in this expectation, as you will see from our despatch.[1] In such a state of mind, we have been all strongly impressed that, next to our first and greatest duty of making an honorable peace, if practicable, was that of so conducting ourselves, and the negotiation, as to demonstrate that, if the War were to be continued, this calamity was ascribable to the enemy.

After all had been here a month and some of us longer, waiting for the B. Commissioners to enter upon a negotiation invited by their own government, at a place of its own choice, they at length presented themselves upon the ground on the 6th. inst. Their Secretary Mr. Baker (formerly secretary to Mr. Foster)[2] called on Mr. Bayard next morning to notify us of their arrival, and to say that they would be glad to see us at their lodgings on the next day at one oClock, when they would exchange their full powers with us. It appeared to us that, according to established usage, we were entitled to the first visit; and that there was, both in the place fixed on and in the precision of the time designated, the evidence of an assumption of superiority on their part, which we could not admit. At the same time we felt how painful it would be, in an affair of mere ceremonial, that any serious difficulty should arise in the very threshold of the negotiation. Waiving therefore our own right, and putting aside altogether matters of etiquette, we sent Mr. Hughes to communicate to the British Commissioners that we should be happy to meet them at any time that would suit their convenience, and at a place mutually agreed upon, to confer with them and to exchange our full powers. This proposal obtained their assent, and a Hotel at which neither party resided was assigned as the place of our interview.

We accordingly met them on the next day (the 8th) and on the two following days. The meeting on the third day was only for the purpose of arranging the contents of a protocol of our two first days conferences. Having for my private use committed to writing the substance of these conferences, immediately after they took place, I transmit to you a copy of it.[3]

Their proposition that the pacification should embrace their Indian allies, and that a definite boundary, separating their possessions from our territories, should be fixed in the treaty, was brought out in a manner that betrayed much ignorance of the political nature of that relation which has subsisted between the Indians and the U. States, or more probably it was intentionally announced in obscure and ambiguous terms. It was not until after we had put many questions to them, on both of the two first days of conference, that we acquired a distinct knowledge of their meaning. It at first appeared that their design was simply not to abandon their allies, but to provide for their peace in the same instrument which secured their own; and in order to ensure its permanency to have ascertained for them a certain boundary. Thus, in answer to a question which I put on the first day, it was expressly stated by them that they meant neither accession of territory to the Indians, nor change in the attributes of Indian sovereignty. It was not until the second day's conference that the intention of a barrier was unequivocally avowed, and that, in answer to a question put by Mr. Bayard as to the operation of the contemplated boundary, it was admitted to be their design that neither the U. States, nor G. Britain were to be at liberty to purchase lands from the Indians, who were at the same time to be left free to sell them to any third party.

This ignorance or affectation on their part was my sole motive for the willingness which we expressed to receive a communication of their views, and to discuss all the topics suggested by them as likely to come up in the negotiation. If it were the first, I hoped that we should be able, in the progress of the negotiation, to satisfy them and their government through them, that there was no such necessity for British interference between the Indians and us as, on that account, to continue the War; that the branch would fall with the trunk; and that, as a matter of course some suitable line would be established between the Indians and the U. States. If it were the last, I thought we could lose nothing by knowing precisely their whole design. We saw the proposition, as soon as we clearly understood it, in all its enormity—a proposition to sever our Country—made under the guise of a generous and disinterested attention to the welfare of their allies,—but urged in fact for the purpose of security to the British provinces—and amounting in effect to a cession of territory by the U. States to G. Britain. On such a proposition it is quite unnecessary to add that not one of us, for a single moment, harboured the idea that it was possible for us to come to any agreement. Nor will I dwell upon the absurdity, to say the least of it, of G. Britain attempting, without powers, to treat for savage tribes, scattered over our acknowleged [*sic*] territory, the very names of which she probably does not know.

We could have as little difficulty as to the surrender of any of our rights connected with the Fisheries. From the manner in which they adverted to this subject, it would seem to be the British doctrine, that certain privileges enjoyed by us, under the treaty of peace, in their waters and on their shores, ceased with the declaration of War, and are revivable only by convention. Whether, on the contrary, our rights in this respect do not stand on the same firm basis as that on which our Independence rests, will demand our serious examination, if we proceed in the negotiation.

Much anxiety was shewn by the B. Commissioners at our first interview to ascertain if our instructions extended to all the points brought forward by them; and at the second when they were informed that we were not instructed to treat on two of them, but were nevertheless willing to hear what they had to say on those subjects, they appeared I thought extremely desirous to obtain from us an admission, that the discussion might lead to the formation of a provisional article which we would agree upon, in relation to the Indian boundary, subject to the ratification of our Government. Without any intimation whatever of a wish for it on our part, they proposed a temporary adjournment for an hour, that we might consult among ourselves and see if we could not admit the practicability of such a result. This we promptly declined as being altogether unnecessary.

When, on the second day's meeting, we were informed by the B. Commissioners that our conferences must be suspended, until they obtained the orders of their Government as to the course which it became them to pursue, in the state in which they found our instructions, we were assured that a Courier should be that evening sent off, and that his return might be expected in four or five days. Nine days have however already elapsed without any intimation being given to us of the receipt of those orders.

What will be their purport when they do arrive can only be matter of conjecture. I am inclined to think that the Ministry has been attempting an experiment upon us, under the supposition that a panic has seized us, and that their policy is to consume as much time as possible before the termination of the negotiation, under the hope that they will strike some signal blow, during the present campaign. If this opinion be correct the B. Commissioners will probably be instructed to insist on their sine qua non, in expectation that we will refer the subject to our Government. In that case should we determine not to make such reference, as being wholly useless, and should they not in the mean time hear of some decisive advantage gained over us, I think the Ministry will pause before they break off the negotiation on the points in question. Such a rupture, it is evident, would entirely change the whole character of the War, would unite all parties at home, and would organize a powerful opposition in Great Britain. It is difficult to believe that they should not have foreseen such a state of our instructions as we have communicated to them, and therefore if they intended a rupture on those points, I presume their Commrs would have needed no fresh instructions. It would at the same time seem somewhat improbable that they should suddenly abandon ground which, in such an early stage of the negotiation, they so earnestly occupied. This they can only avoid by prevailing on us to refer the subject to our Government.

We took care, during our second day's conference, to throw out incidentally, that we had received despatches from Washington as late as the 27th. of June, and that up to that period the President had not the slightest anticipation that any such subjects as those in question would be brought into our conferences.

I have great satisfaction in informing you that the most entire harmony prevails between my colleagues on the subjects of our mission. No former diversity of opinion here shews itself in the smallest degree. All are deeply sensible of the solemn nature of our duty. All are animated solely by the desire of advancing the interests of our common Country. All are equally tenacious of its rights and its honor. No one, in our most free and confidential consultations among ourselves, has ventured to suggest, even as matter of consideration, the expediency of subscribing to the demands of the other party in any possible shape which could be given to them.

Our residence is in a Hotel which we have taken for the occasion. The B. Commissioners have also established themselves in a Hotel in the City. They have dined with us.

Many Englishmen and other foreigners of distinction pass through this City to different parts of the Continent. Mr. Whitebread[4] is now in town. He said to our Banker[5] yesterday that it was well for us that we had gained an advantage lately on the Niagara frontier.

The opposition in England has been extremely reserved on our subject. Towards the close of the Session of Parliament Mr. Whitebread indeed did reproach the Ministry for the delay in meeting the American Commissioners; and some of the Gazettes have rather leant towards us. But they have not committed themselves, and I think it very probable that the Ministry feels extremely embarrassed by knowing that whether peace is made or the War is continued they are equally exposed to attack at home.

If the War is to be continued, we must rely for its prosecution exclusively upon our own resources. Continental Europe is too much exhausted, and has yet too much to do to arrange its own complicated affairs to authorize the expectation of any immediate succor from this quarter. Besides, much misconception has prevailed on the Continent, particularly in Germany, of the views of our Government in declaring War. This has been owing to the activity of the British influence & the state of the press. The British side of the question has alone reached the public. We have nevertheless many friends, and our cause is daily acquiring more. Still we cannot at present calculate upon any thing but good wishes. France is occupied in consolodating her new government. She would be very unwilling to renew the War with G. Britain until she gets back her Colonies. In that Country the materials sufficiently abound for internal explosion, which will only be prevented by the difficulty of their combination. Every body is dissatisfied, but every body is wearied, and this perhaps is the best guarrantee for the continuance of the present order of things. The Military is the most discontented class, and they are represented to be anxious for War. Austria is however the power upon which they wish to fall; and it is not unlikely that Louis the 18th. will find, in the indulgence of this passion, the means of preserving domestic tranquility and strengthening his throne.

The prospect of renewed War is the greatest in the North; Poland the bone of contention, and Russia and Austria the great parties. The arrangement of the concerns of Germany, and the future condition in particular of Saxony, will afford serious occupation to the Congress at Vienna, and will very likely result in War. Such is the martial character, stamped upon Europe by the last twenty years, that it will be wonderful if the habits and the pursuits of peace are resumed without further struggle.

The final disposition of this Country (the Netherlands) is said to depend upon the deliberations of Vienna. In the mean time it is occupied nominally by the Prince Sovereign of the U. Netherlands & in fact by British and Hanoverian troops. The people are extremely averse from a Dutch connexion, and would greatly prefer one with France or Austria. I am My Dr Sir very sincerely Yrs.

H. Clay

19h. August

P.S. After finishing my letter, but before I had sealed it, we received this morning an invitation from the B. Commissioners to a conference with them at 3 OClock. We accordingly attended and I transmit you a copy of the journal I have kept of the substance of what occured on that occasion.[6] From our despatch & the paper sent us by the British Commissioners, you will see that there is no room for comment. The prospect of peace has vanished. In the state in which their claims now appear, I should consider that it would be offering an unpardonable insult to our Government to ask of them any instructions. The pretensions of G. Britain do not admit of deliberation.[7] I ought perhaps, after what has transpired, to suppress altogether this letter, but as with my erroneous speculations relative to the course which I supposed would be taken by the B. Commrs there may be mixed some matter not absolutely useless I give it to you for what it is worth. It is indeed not impossible that our decision to make no reference for instructions to our Government of the inadmissible claims which they have brought forward, and as far as depends upon us to finally terminate the negotiation, may yet occasion a pause. But the hope of their retracting their demands is to remote to warrant the smallest calculation upon it. The reliance will be much better on the firmness and energy of the American people, to conquer again their Independence. H. C.

The Honble James Monroe.

ALS. DLC-James Monroe Papers (DNA, M212, R22). [1] Dated August 12.
[2] Augustus John Foster. [3] See Clay's Journal, August 7-10.
[4] Samuel Whitbread, member of Parliament from Bedford, long an advocate of peace. [5] Jean de Meulemeester. [6] See Clay's Journal, August 19.
[7] An additional clause here crossed out as follows: "and I could not consent to be the degraded medium of a proposition involving the disgrace of my Country."

Journal of the Negotiations (Continued)

19th. Aug. [1814]

Mr. Baker called on us this morning and stated that the B. Commrs requested an interview to day at three o'clock at their Hotel. We accordingly waited upon them, and Mr. Goulburn on their part opened the conference by stating that they had received that morning the orders of their Government, and desiring to avoid the loss of any time had requested this interview. They were instructed to say, that their Government was surprized that we should be unprovided with instructions from our's in relation to the Indian pacification and boundary, as it must have been foreseen, that they could not consent to terminate the war leaving their weaker allies engaged in the contest. That in this state of things the least they could require was that we should, on that subject, agree to a provisional article, to be subject to the future decision of our Government. If rejected by it the whole treaty to fall. That as we had, in our former conferences, complained of their want of explicitness, they were instructed to afford us a full explanation of their views. That these were, as before intimated, to make the peace with the Indians durable, and to this end to fix a permanent boundary for them, which should form a neutral barrier between the provinces of G. Britain and the U. States, and prevent them from being conterminous. That both parties were to be restricted from purchasing lands from the Indians. That they were willing to take as the basis of this boundary, the line established by the treaty of Greenville between the Indians and the U. States,[1] subject to such modifications as might be agreed upon during the negotiation. That upon our refusal or consent to such an article depended the continuance or suspension of the negotiation. That to enable us to decide this point, they would explain more at large their views and intentions in relation to the revision of the boundary line between the U. S. and the British provinces. That considering on the N. American Continent that G. Britain was the weaker power; that she had no desire or motive whatever for conquest or aggrandizement there; and that different views had been represented to be entertained by the American Government, they might have required the exclusive possession of the Lakes, and for their security the cession of a certain extent of territory along their southern shores. That they were however disposed to be more moderate. That as an equal right to the occupation of the Lakes would lead to a contest for the ascendancy[2] in peace as well as war, and would occasion a great expense, which neither party might be disposed to incur, G. Britain would require that the U. S. should build or retain no vessels of war on the lakes, that is from Ontario to Superior inclusive; and that they should erect or maintain no fort or military post on the shores of the Lakes; but that the military occupation thereof should be exclusively with G. Britain, who was to be under no restriction. That the commercial navigation of the Lakes was to remain as heretofore.

G. Britain would further require the line between the two Countries to be revised from Superior to the Mississippi, and that the treaty right of G. Britain to the navigation of that river should be continued to her.[3] That G. Britain would also require, that as the communication between Halifax and Quebec was interrupted by the intervention of a part of the province of Maine, there should be a cession of so much thereof as would secure a facile intercourse between those places.

They were asked that as beyond the line which they proposed as a basis, many of the Citizens of the United States had migrated and settled in the state of Ohio, and in the Territories of Indiana Illinois and Michigan what was to be their condition? They replied that might be a subject of con- consideration [*sic*] for the U. States, and might induce us to propose modifications; but that the people not provided for must shift for themselves.

They were asked what was understood by the British Government as to Moose island and the other islands in Passamaquoddy Bay, the military occupation of which by the arms of Great Britain we had recently heard of. To which they answered that as to them she had always considered them as her's, that her intention was to keep them; that they were considered as much a part of her Territory as Northamptonshire; and that they could not be a subject of discussion.

In reply to a question whether the character of a sine qua non was to be considered as attached to their demand relative to the Lakes, they replied pettishly, that they had given us one sine qua non, and when we had disposed of that it would be time enough to talk about another.

They informed us that if the negotiation were now suspended, and we referred to our Government for further instructions, they were required to notify us, that they would not consider themselves bound to make peace upon the terms now offered; but would, upon the renewal of the negotiation, hold themselves at liberty to regulate their conduct by the then state of events.

They were asked when they spoke of the line from Superior to the Mississippi, if they did not mean the Lake of the Woods instead of Superior?[4] They said No. We requested from the importance of their communication, and that we might be exposed to no misconception of their views, that they would reduce its substance to writing, which they promised to do. They accordingly sent the following paper:[5]

Note. The paper being now in use, I regret that I cannot send a Copy of it. If it varies from the conference, it is in being stronger. Thus, we are required by it to have no armed vessels on waters emptying into the Lakes.

D, in Christopher Hughes' hand, amended by Clay. DLC-William H. Crawford Papers (DNA, M212, R20). Cf. above, Journal, August 7-10.

1 Signed August 3, 1795, after General Anthony Wayne's successful campaign against the Indians in the Northwest, the treaty had provided for the cession to the United States of Indian lands east and south of a line along the watershed dividing the flow of streams into Lake Erie from the tributaries of the Ohio River, that is, all but the northwestern quarter of the State of Ohio.

2 Last three words inserted by Clay.

3 The right had been guaranteed by the Treaty of Paris, 1783.

4 The Treaty of 1783, reflecting ignorance of the geography of the area, had provided that the boundary should run westward from the most northwestern point of the Lake of the Woods to the Mississippi River.

5 This line and the following "Note" are in Clay's hand. The paper to which Clay refers is the note, of this date, from the British to the American Commissioners.

The British to the American Commissioners

[August 19, 1814]

True copy, by Christopher Hughes, Jr. DNA, M36, R1. Published in *American State Papers, Foreign Relations,* III, 710. Summarized in Clay's Journal, same date.

The American Commissioners to James Monroe

[August 19, 1814]

[The *John Adams* has been detained in Europe owing to the necessity of obtaining from the British a second passport, the first having excluded passengers from the vessel "without an exception even for a bearer of dispatches." The new passport has been received, and the Commissioners have requested Captain Angus to be ready to sail on August 25.

Enclosed is a copy of an order recently received by Mr. Beasley.[1]]

DS. DNA, M36, R1.

1 From the British Transport Office to Reuben G. Beasley, August 6, 1814. Since the British agent for prisoners in the United States has been ordered to reside in Bladensburg (Maryland) and to come to Washington only with special permission, Beasley must immediately take up residence in Brentford (Middlesex County, England) and must apply for passports to return to London.

The American Commissioners to James Monroe

[August 19, 1814]

[The letter reports the conference of this date with the British Commissioners and encloses the note of same date from the British to the American Commissioners.]

LS. DNA, M36, R1. Published in *American State Papers, Foreign Relations,* III, 708-709. Cf. Clay's Journal, same date.

To William H. Crawford

My Dear Sir: GHENT, 22d August, 1814.

Your letter[1] by Mr. Todd apprising [*sic*] me of what I had before only feared, that my letters to you transmitted by the mail, have been intercepted. I had written you two, but the latter and the more important one was altogether in cipher,[2] so that the robbers will make but little of their booty. I regret the larceny, however, on your account and my own. In [*sic*] yours because you have been so long kept out of information, which you have been, no doubt, exceedingly anxious to possess; and on mine because I had asked what I should liked [*sic*] much to have received, and what would be now too late for any practical effect—your opinion upon some important topics. I should not have ventured to commit my letters to so treacherous a medium, but that no other conveyance offered or as far as I knew was likely to offer.

To repair as much as possible the loss, I now have the pleasure of enclosing to you a copy of a private journal I have kept at our conferences with the British commissioners.[3] From its perusal you will see that the prospect of peace has disappeared, and that nothing remains for us but to formally close the abortive negotiations. The regret you will feel for the continuance of the war will be mitigated, however, by the evidence you will have, that this unhappy issue is attributable solely to the extravagant demands of the enemy; and by the consoling reflection that these demands, affecting as they do every section and every interest in the Union, must arouse, if anything can arouse, all parties into a vigorous resistance.

My journal is so full that I will not accompany it now with any illustrative details. These I will supply when I have the pleasure to see you at Paris. I will, however, add, that we are preparing, and will probably deliver tomorrow, our answer to their paper,[4] and if anything turns up before I seal this letter (which I do not expect to send until tomorrow or next day) worthy of your knowledge it shall be communicated.

You will also derive much satisfaction from seeing that as the enemy will not make peace, all the old grounds of difference and impressment of course among them, are put altogether in the background. Our late instructions[5] authorized us to pass this subject over in silence.

I ought, perhaps, to mention to you that throughout the whole of the negotiations I have been inclined to think that the other party has been practicing upon our supposed fears, and that he would ultimately abandon his pretensions. In this impression (I will not call it opinion) what [*sic*] I do not yet absolutely abandon, I stand alone. If it be well founded when our paper is received and it is known that we will not refer to our government for further instructions, he may possibly yet pause.

We have sent off Mr. Dallas[6] with the dispatches for our Government, which include the note of the British commissioners.[7] The John Adams will sail the 25th inst., and I hope will reach America in time for the President to lay the subject, or such part of it as he may think proper, before Congress.[8]

We propose to sail for Cherbourg, Brest or L'Orient, and ordering the Neptune to one of those ports, and the period we have talked of is first of October.

Whatever of the intervening period of time I can command after the cessation of our labors here I shall spend with you in Paris.

Your kind offer to recommend me to the Government for the place which you now fill will be forever remembered by me with the sincerest gratitude. As I hope soon to see you, I will then inform you of my views on that subject, and will at the same time arrange the affair of Mr. Carroll's expenses.[9] Your friend, etc.,

Wm. H. Crawford, Esq. H. CLAY.

Shipp, *Giant Days, or the Life and Times of William H. Crawford,* 123-24.

1 Not found. 2 Dated August 11. The earlier letter has not been found.

3 Dated August 7-10, 19, 1814.
4 The American answer is dated August 24.
5 From Monroe, June 25, 27, 1814.
6 George M. Dallas, son of Secretary of the Treasury Alexander J. Dallas, had gone to Europe in 1813 as secretary to Gallatin. He was later United States Senator from Pennsylvania, Minister to Russia, Vice-President of the United States, and Minister to Great Britain. 7 Dated August 19.
8 Dallas reached New York early in October, and on October 10 copies of the dispatches were laid before Congress.
9 See above, Clay to Crawford, May 14, 1814.

The American to the British Commissioners

[August 24, 1814]

[Reply to the British note of August 19. The American negotiators reject the proposals for the creation of an Indian barrier state above the Ohio River and for the cession of the military sovereignty of the Great Lakes to Great Britain. They have been instructed to agree to the termination of the war, "both parties restoring whatever territory they may have taken, and both parties reserving all their rights, in relation to their respective seamen."]

DS. MiU-C. Published in *American State Papers, Foreign Relations,* III, 711-13.

The British to the American Commissioners

[September 4, 1814]

[Reply to the American note of August 24. The British accuse the United States of a policy of territorial aggrandizement. They insist on the need for American disarmament on the shores of the Great Lakes and for an Indian boundary to be fixed by further negotiation. They announce that the American Commissioners must now decide whether to continue the negotiations, refer to their government for further instructions, or "take upon themselves the responsibility of breaking off the negotiation altogether."]

True copy, by C. Hughes, Jr. DNA, M36, R1. Published in *American State Papers, Foreign Relations,* III, 713-15.

To Henry Goulburn

Ghent 5h. Sept. 1814.

Mr. Clay presents his Compliments to Mr. Goulburn and takes the liberty of reminding him of the promise which he was polite enough to make on saturday relative to the passport for himself and Henry Carroll his private Secretary.

Mr. Clay intends returning to America in the U. States Ship Neptune and wishes, after the termination of his public duty here, to avoid any delay in taking his departure.

He has been requested at the same time to apply for passports for

Christopher Hughes, Secretary to the mission, and for William Shaler who is attached to it.

Mr. Clay requests Mr. Goulburn to accept the assurance of his high respect.

AN. MiU-C. Upon the receipt of the British note of September 4, Clay favored breaking off negotiations and returning home.

The American to the British Commissioners

[September 9, 1814]

[Reply to the British note of September 4. The Americans deny charges of territorial aggrandizement, assert that the United States from the beginning of hostilities has been willing to make peace on the basis of a satisfactory arrangement of maritime questions, and firmly repeat that the two propositions regarding an Indian boundary and exclusive British military possession of the Great Lakes are inadmissible.]

DS. MiU-C. Published in *American State Papers, Foreign Relations,* III, 715-17.

From William H. Crawford

My dear Sir; Paris. 10th. Sept. 1814

Mr Adams's letter of the 29th. ult with a post cript [*sic*] of the 31st. is the latest information that I have recd. from Ghent. I have been for several days expecting to see you at my hotel, but the note which Mr Connell[1] shewed me this morning has induced me to suppose that it may yet be some time before I have that pleasure. I cannot believe that the Sine qua non has been withdrawn, and I do not see how your abode at Ghent, can be rendered necessary, if that is not done. Genl La Fayette came to Paris to day with an expectation of seeing you all in this city on your way to the port of embarkation. He will remain during the next week with his friends in the hope of seeing you and your Colleagues.

The Wasp sailed the 27th ult with a fair wind—no sail in sight. On the 29th in the latitude in which she probably then found herself the master of a French vessel saw an action, between two vessels, one under American, the other under British Colors, which terminated in the sinking of the latter. The action is believed to have been between the Wasp & the Andromeda of 24. 42-pounders which was known to have been cruising in that latitude for the Wasp with orders to bring her into port.[2] After the action, the American vessel stood in for the French Coast. Previous to the action, she was seen to capture two letters of marque. I have not yet heard of her arrival in a French port.

On the 8th inst I answered Mr Adams' letter of the 29th ult which I hope has come to hand. I would have sent a duplicate of it, but for the short notice which I have had of Mr Connell's departure for Ghent. Your letter of the 22d. ult is the last I have recd, from you. I recd. letters from Mr Bayard & Mr Russel of the same date. They have all been answered, and I presume the answers have been regularly rend.[3]

Present my respects to your Colleagues and accept the assurance of my warmest friendship. WM H CRAWFORD

P.S. I have understood that Mr. Todd[4] did not embark in the John Adams—I hope my dispatches have not remained with him.

W H C

ALS. DLC-HC (DNA, M212, R1). 1 John Connell.

2 No engagement with the *Andromeda* had occurred. After leaving L'Orient, the *Wasp* had destroyed three enemy vessels before engaging in a victorious battle with the British brig, *Avon*, on September 1.

3 Crawford's answer to Clay's letter has not been found. For his answer to Bayard see Donnan (ed.), *Papers of James A. Bayard*, 325-26.

4 John Payne Todd.

Crawford to the American Commissioners

Paris 13h Sept. 1814

Their Excellencies The Envoys of the United States at Ghent—

Gentlemen

The English newspapers continue to speculate on the probable result of the negotiation. They assert that you have submitted a counterproject and have demanded an armistice by sea and land until it shall have been definitively accepted or rejected. I can hardly believe that the negotiation has taken this direction. I cannot conceive how with a sine qua non, which closed the door of discussion at the very threshold of the negotiation, you can have had the address to present to the consideration of the British Envoys, questions which they had determined not to discuss. If this is the case the views of the British Ministry must materially have changed since the commencement of the negotiation. Perhaps I can give a clue to the labyrinth in which you may be involved. Erick Bolman[1] is now at Paris. He came direct from England with a letter from Arbuthnot,[2] a subordinate member of the British ministry, to Lord Castlereagh. He follows him to Vienna. This philosophic & science-loving man, it seems, has undertaken a voyage from the United States to impart to the chymists and mecanicians of Europe his discoveries in rendering zinc maleable, and is going to Austria, which he has been forbidden to enter, and where patents have never been granted to establish steam-boats on the Danube—This man asserts that he had an interview, the first of this month, with A— at which Vansitart[3] was to have been present, but was prevented by business. He says that he insisted upon the necessity of making peace with the United States, upon liberal terms, and that if the war was continued on account of the extravagant demands of England that all parties will be united, and the expectations of the ministry completely disappointed. That this course will effectually put down the federal party and exalt the present administration. That the latter has always contended that the British nation was jealous of the prosperity of the United States, and sought every occasion to destroy it, while the other party had a more favourable opinion of her amity; That the further prosecution of the war will verefy all the assertions of the former and disappoint all the expectations of the latter. He represented himself as the enemy of the administration and desirous of removing them from power. Being a Hanoverian by birth, and inimical to the republican party, he conceives gave his representations more weight than those which the ministry are in the habit of receiving. He contrived that this interview should be sought by the ministry. Mr. A— appeared to be convinced by his statements and reasoning, and expressed a strong desire that he would see lord C—[4] and make the same communcation [*sic*] to him. For this purpose the letter, previously mentioned, was written. This is the history which he has given under circumstances which induce me to believe that he intended it should reach me. In stating to a friend of his in this city that the further prosecution of the war would unite all parties and call into activity all the activity [*sic*] all the talents of the country he suggested the probability of Colo. Burr's employment in a military capacity. This suggestion naturally presents to the mind the probability that he may yet be the infatuated tool of that restless and unprincipled man. That he has had an interview with Mr R. [*sic*] A. I readily believe, that if the nature of the demands which have been made in the negotiation were disclosed to him he remonstrated against them and endeavoured to convince the ministry that they were defeating their own views, may reasonably be admitted; but it is highly improbable that he made any exertions to promote the interests of the United States. This I can hardly believe. He expressed a hope that he had done something for America and says that the Neptune has not been ordered to Brest as was intended. This he attributes to a change of views in the British Cabinet effected by his representations. Haec credeat Judaes appella sed non ego. I cannot give credit to this zinc & steam boat story. I cannot believe that this is the reason that induces him to expose his person to the danger which he would incur by venturing to Vienna, unprotected by the British ministry. No—the thing is impossible. He is the minister of mischief to the United States. If my conjectures are correct you will be kept in a state of suspence or will be amused with various projects and devices until the propositions with which he is charged shall have been decided. Believing as I do that your exertions cannot be successful and that the negotiation cannot be broken off upon propositions more favourable to the interest of our country than upon their sine qua non I shall rejoice to hear of your leaving Ghent—

With my best wishes for the success of your efforts accept those for your individual happiness— WM. H. CRAWFORD—

Copy. RPB-Russell Letterbook, 428-32.
1 Bollman. 2 Charles Arbuthnot, an official in the Treasury.
3 Nicholas Vansittart, first Baron Bexley, was Chancellor of the Exchequer.
4 Castlereagh.

The American Commissioners to Baring Brothers and Company

[September 13, 1814]

[Alexander Glennie, Son and Company, navy agents of the United States in London have informed Albert Gallatin that they have protested bills for £1900 drawn by Captain Angus of the *John Adams* and that, with proper authority, Baring Brothers would be willing to advance funds for the bills.

The Commissioners therefore request that Baring Brothers take up the bills and charge the amount to the United States.]

Copy. DNA, M36, R1.

The American Commissioners to James Monroe

Ghent, 13th. Septr. 1814

[The note covers copies of letters from Alexander Glennie, Son and Company and from the American Commissioners to Baring Brothers and Company.[1] The commissioners have caused Captain Angus' bills to be honored but do not consider themselves authorized to give directions regarding funds needed for the support of American seamen imprisoned in England.]

LS. DNA, M36, R1. 1 Above, same date.

Jean-Guillaume Hyde de Neuville to the American Commissioners

[September 13, 1814]

[The letter covers a packet containing letters and other documents, the most important of which is permission for a cartel to return refugees from the United States to France.]

ALS. NHi-Gallatin Papers (MR9). De Neuville, French politician and adherent of the Bourbons, was Minister to the United States from 1816 to 1821.

Receipt to Thomas Hamilton

[September 14, 1814]

Attached to Bond, September 29, 1813.

The British to the American Commissioners

[September 19, 1814]

[Reply to the American note of September 9. Proclamations of Generals William Hull and Alexander Smyth are cited as evidence of the American desire to conquer and annex Canada. The British plenipotentiaries have been instructed not to sign a treaty "unless the Indian nations are included in it, and restored to all the rights, privileges, and territories which they enjoyed in the year 1811." Indian boundary is offered as a subject for discussion, but neither that question nor the exclusive military control of the lakes is included in the *sine qua non.*]

Copy, partly by Hughes, completed by Clay. DNA, M36, R1. Published in *American State Papers, Foreign Relations,* III, 717-18.

To William H. Crawford

My Dr Sir Ghent 20h. Septr. 1814

I have just heard of, what I have long wished, an opportunity of writing to you, by some American Gentlemen, Mess. Lewis and Geron,[1] who propose leaving here tomorrow morning for Paris.

I have recd. your favors' both of the 28h. Aug. and 13th. inst.[2] In relation to Mr. Vanderlyn[3] it would give us much pleasure to provide for his conveyance to America in the Neptune, but really so many are to go in that vessel that I regret to say he cannot be accommodated in her. Mr. Smith and his family from St. Petersburg[4] now here are to take a passage in her, and with those who were previously to go in her constitute so great a number that Capt. Jones has been already obliged to make considerable sacrifices in the œconomy of his Ship to provide for us all. An application has been made by us for a Cartel from Amsterdam in which he might probably be provided for. But as, if it should be granted, she is a private vessel, he would have to make his arrangements with her commander. The Chauncey is also in possession of a passport, but this vessel is entirely without our control, and the man who has the direction of her[5] has acted in so strange a manner that I am utterly ignorant even of the fact whether she will return at all as a flag of truce.

I have been greatly shocked at the infamous calumny of which Bollman has allowed himself to be the medium implicating us in certain speculations founded on the state of our negotiation here. You will of course expect from me no denial on that subject. What unfortunately tended perhaps to give some colour to the falsehood was Mr. Milligan[6] (who is I believe wholly blameless) having travelled from this place to England in company with a person, who it is alleged did engage in some speculations.

There is a long story about our negotiations which I have not now time to tell. We have received three papers from the B. P.[7] The first I noticed in my last letter.[8] Our ansr. to that containes [*sic*] a rejection of their demands and a refusal to refer them to our Govt. In their second, they somewhat varied the state of the case, but still in effect adhered to their former pretensions. We still rejected and refused to refer. Their third and last note has just been received this day. According to this their sine qua non has dwindled down to a demand that the Indians shall be included in the peace and put in the condition they stood in prior to the battle of Tippacanoe. But, coupled with this subject, they are instructed to propose for *discussion* an article providing that within a certain described boundary within the Indian territory neither party shall purchase lands from the Indians.

They now say that as to the military possession of the Lakes they never meant that as a sine qua non, and in substance wave the demand. Still they declare that as soon as we admit the principle of Indian pacification, they are instructed to propose to us in relation to Canadian boundary an article, so moderate and reasonable, that they think we cannot reject it. What it is we are left to conjecture.

We are now deliberating on the contents of this last note. I am (and I believe all my colleagues will be) agt. the principle of British interference with our Indian affairs. Should we reject that principle, you may expect us in Paris in the course of the next week, if any reliance is to be placed on the principles of British diplomatists.

I regret that I have time only to send you this hasty sketch. When I have the pleasure to see you I will fill up the lines with all details. 'Till then Yr Sincere friend

AL, signature removed. DLC-William H. Crawford Papers (DNA, M212, R20).

1 Not identified.

2 Letter of August 28, not found. Crawford addressed that of September 13 to the Commissioners; he wrote to Clay on September 10.

[3] John Vanderlyn, the American artist, who, after twelve years in Europe, returned to the United States in 1815.
[4] William Steuben Smith, nephew and private secretary of John Quincy Adams. He was also a brother-in-law of William Shaler.
[5] Elias M. Stilwell, agent for the owner. See below, American Commissioners to Monroe, October 26, 1814.
[6] George B. Milligan.
[7] The British Plenipotentiaries.
[8] Dated August 22.

The American to the British Commissioners

[September 26, 1814]

[Reply to the British note of September 19. The Americans suggest that commissioners be appointed by the two governments to extend the Maine boundary line in conformity with the Treaty of Paris of 1783. The proclamations of American generals, to which the British have alluded, were no more the acts of their government than were the proclamations of Admiral Cochrane (enclosed with this note) the acts of the British government. Peace with the Indians, and their reinstatement in the situation that existed before the war, would follow peace with Great Britain, but the United States cannot consent to any inclusion of the Indians in the treaty in a manner that would recognize them as independent nations. The Americans are willing to discuss any proposals, based on "moderation and justice," that may be offered by the British.]

LS. MiU-C. Published in *American State Papers, Foreign Relations,* III, 719-21.

From William H. Crawford

Dear Sir, Paris 26th. Sept. 1814

Your letter of the 20th & Mr Russel's of the 21st. have been recd. The conclusion which I have drawn from the facts which have been disclosed me connected with this negociation, is that you will remain at Ghent until Lord Castlereagh discovers the probable result of the negociation at Vienna. I Regret that the negociation was not broken off after the first interchange of official notes. This however I presume was impossible. From the news papers which I have recd. it appears that the Savage Allies of the Prince Regent had by treaty of the 16th of July become our Allies and had engaged to raise the war hatchet against their former insidious friends.[1] The great difficulty is then removed. It is true the information is not official. Perhaps you may have official information of the fact.

The reasons which induced me to request that the appointment of Mr Erving may not be made public, are [t]hat upon examining the dispatches which accompany his appointment we discover that our [g]overnment has no information of the disposition of Spain to receive a minister.[2] Private advices from that country induce a belief, that no minister will be received. In this state of things I think the government alone ought to give publicity to this appointment.

You have no doubt recd. the English account of the battle of Bridgewater.[3] It is not worse than might have been expected. Their subsequent details prove its falsehood. They assert that they had only 2800 men in the action, & that their loss exceeded 800 men. Yet within three days after they state their force at 4000 men. In the mean time they assert that the sedentary militia had been discharged. It appears that their news is a few days later than ours, & that they have made an attack à la Congreve[4] upon Stonnington in which they have failed.[5] This attack however they say was only a feint to cover a more serious one upon New London. I believ[e] the spirit of the nation will rise in proportion to the emergency, & that the hostile views of the enemy will be entirely, & ultimately defeated.

Present my respects to Messrs. Bayard and Russell & accept for your self the assurance of my highest regard.

His Excellency H. Clay. WM H CRAWFORD.

P.S. You will discover that Wilkinson[6] is at Washington scribbling in the news-papers & discussing the orders & views of the war department. The mode of dismission recommended by Genl. Brown in the case of [. . .][7] ought to be applied to this man. If this mode is not resorted to, the officers will be employed half the year in trying culprits. W.H.C.

ALS. DLC-HC (DNA, M212, R1).

1 On July 22 a large number of northwestern Indians, in council at Greenville, Michigan Territory, had signed a treaty binding themselves to aid the United States in the war against the British and those Indians who remained hostile.

2 George W. Erving had been named United States Minister to Madrid.

3 On July 25, 1814, usually referred to as the Battle of Lundy's Lane or of Niagara Falls.

4 Sir William Congreve, developer of the Congreve rockets used by the British in both land and naval warfare.

5 A British naval squadron had shelled the village of Stonington, Connecticut, for three days (from August 9 to 12) before withdrawing.

6 James Wilkinson.

7 Initial illegible. General Jacob J. Brown was commander of American forces in western New York.

The American to the British Commissioners

[September 30, 1814]

[The note requests a passport for the return of the *Transit,* with a bearer of dispatches, to the United States.]

LS. MiU-C. The *Transit,* a fast-sailing Baltimore schooner, had just arrived from the United States, bringing George Boyd, brother-in-law of John Quincy Adams, with dispatches for the mission.

From Henry Goulburn

Private [*ca.* October 3, 1814]
Dear Sir, Sunday morng.

If you find Brussells as little interesting as I have done you will not be sorry to have the occupation of reading the latest Newspapers which I have received I therefore inclose them to you & should be glad to have them back by to morrow evening.[1] I take this opportunity of mentioning that I do not propose leaving this late [*sic*] Tuesday morning in case you should be desirous of extending your excursion Believe me Dear Sir Yours ever most faithfully

HENRY GOULBURN

ALS. DLC-HC (DNA, M212, R1).

[1] On September 30 Clay, Russell, and Hughes had left Ghent for a visit of several days at Brussels. The newspapers so thoughtfully provided by Goulburn brought to the Americans the unwelcome news of the sacking of Washington on August 24.

The British to the American Commissioners

[October 8, 1814]

[Reply to the American note of September 26. The British present as an ultimatum an article by which the United States would bind itself, upon ratification of a treaty of peace, to put an end to the war with the Indians and to restore them to "all the possessions, rights, and privileges, which they may have enjoyed, or been entitled to, in 1811," provided the Indians desist from hostilities with the United States. The same provision would apply to Great Britain with regard to the Indians at war with her.]

True copy, by C. Hughes, Jr. DNA, M36, R1. Published in *American State Papers, Foreign Relations,* III, 721-23.

The American to the British Commissioners

Ghent October 13th. 1814.

The Undersigned have the honour to acknowledge the receipt of the Note of the Plenipotentiaries of His Britannic Majesty, dated on the 8th. Instant.

Satisfied of the impossibility of persuading the world that the Government of the United States was liable to any well grounded imputation of a spirit of conquest, or of injustice towards other nations, The Undersigned, in affording explanations on several of the topics adverted to by the British Plenipotentiaries, during this negotiation, were actuated by the sole motive of removing erroneous impressions. Still influenced by the same motive, they will now add, that, at the time when the Spanish Minister was remonstrating at Washington against the transfer of Louisiana, orders were given by His Government for its delivery to France; that it was in fact delivered a short time after that remonstrance; and that, if the Treaty, by which the United States acquired it, had not been ratified, it would have become, of course, a French Colony. The Undersigned believe that the evidence of the assent of Spain to that transfer, has been promulgated. They neither admit the alleged disability of the Spanish Monarch, nor the inference which the British Plenipotentiaries would seem to deduce from it; on the contrary, the assent was voluntarily given in the year 1804, by the same King, who, about the same time, ceded Trinidad to Great Britain, and prior to the time, when he was again engaged in War with Her. The Cession by France was immediately communicated to Great Britain, no circumstance affecting it, and then within the knowledge of the United States, being intentionally concealed from Her. She expressed Her satisfaction with it, and, if in any possible state of the case, She would have had a right to question the transaction, it does not appear to the Undersigned, that She is now authorized so to do.

After having generally stated that the Proclamations of Generals Hull and Smythe [*sic*] were neither authorized nor approved by their Government, the Undersigned could not have expected, that the British Plenipotentiaries would suppose, that their Statement did not embrace the only part of the Proclamations, which was a subject of consideration.

The Undersigned had indeed hoped that, by stating in their Note of the 9th. Ulto., that the Government of the United States, from the commencement of the war, had been disposed to make peace, without obtaining any cession of territory, and by referring to their knowledge of that disposition and to Instructions accordingly given from July 1812 to January 1814, They would effectually remove the impression that the annexation of Canada to the United States, was the declared object of their Government. Not only have the Undersigned been disappointed in this expectation, but the only inference which the British Plenipotentiaries have thought proper to draw from this explicit Statement has been that, either the American Government, by not giving instructions subsequent to the pacification of Europe, or the Undersigned, by not acting under such instructions, gave no proof of a sincere desire to bring the present negotiation to a favourable conclusion. The Undersigned did not allude, in reference to the alleged intention to annex Canada to the United States, to any instructions given by their Government subsequent to January last, because asking at this time for no accession of territory, it was only of its previous disposition that it appeared necessary to adduce any proof. So erroneous was the inference drawn by the British Plenipotentiaries, in both respects, that it was in virtue of the instructions of June last, that the Undersigned were enabled, in their Note of the 24th. of August, to state, that, the causes of the War between the United States and Great Britain, having disappeared by the maritime pacification of Europe, they had been authorized to agree to its termination upon a mutual restoration of territory, and without making the conclusion of the peace to depend on a successful arrangement of those points on which differences had existed.

Considering the present state of the negotiation, the Undersigned will abstain, at this time, from adducing any evidence, or remarks, upon the influence which has been exerted over the Indian Tribes, inhabiting the Territories of the United States, and the nature of those incitements which have been employed by British Traders and Agents.

The arguments and facts already brought forward by the Undersigned, respecting the political condition of those Tribes, render it unnecessary for them to make many observations on those of the British Plenipotentiaries on that subject.

The Treaties of 1763 and of 1783, were those principally alluded to by the Undersigned to illustrate the practice of Great Britain. She did not admit in the first, nor require in the last, any stipulations respecting the Indians who, in one case, had been her enemies, and, in the other, her Allies, and who, in both instances, fell, by the peace, within the dominions of that power, against whom they had been engaged in the preceding War.

The negotiation of 1761 was quoted for the purpose of proving what appears to be fully established by the answer of England to the Ultimatum of France, delivered on the first of September of that year, that His Britannic Majesty would not renounce his right of protection over the Indian Nations and Countries reputed to be within his dominions, that is to say, between the British Settlements and the Mississippi. Mr. Pitts letter, cited by the British Plenipotentiaries far from contradicting that position, goes still farther. It states that "the fixation of new limits to Canada, as proposed by France, is intended to shorten the extent of Canada (which was to be ceded to England:) and to lengthen the boundaries of Louisiana (which France was to keep:) and in the view to establish what must be not admitted, namely, that all which is not Canada is Louisiana, whereby all the intermediate nations and countries, the true barrier to each province, would be given up to France." This is precisely the principle uniformly supported by the Undersigned, to wit, that the recognition of a boundary gives up to the Nation, in whose behalf it is made, all the Indian Tribes and Countries within that boundary. It was on this principle that the Undersigned have confidently relied on the Treaty of 1783, which fixes and recognizes the boundary of the United States, without making any reservation respecting Indian Tribes.

But the British Plenipotentiaries utterly unable to produce a solitary precedent of one European power treating for the Savages inhabiting within the dominions of another, have been compelled, in support of their principles, to refer to the Germanic Empire, a Body, consisting of several independent States, recognized as such by the whole world, and separately maintaining, with foreign powers, the relations belonging to such a condition. Can it be necessary to prove, that there is no sort of analogy between the political situation of these civilized communities, and that of the wandering tribes of North American Savages?

In referring to what the British Plenipotentiaries represent as alarming and novel pretensions, which Great Britain can never recognize, the Undersigned might complain that those alleged pretensions have not been stated either in terms, or in substance as expressed by themselves. This, however, is the less material, as any further recognition of them by Great Britain is not necessary nor required. On the other hand, they can never admit nor recognise the principles or pretensions asserted, in the course of this correspondence by the British Plenipotentiaries, and which to them appear novel and alarming.

The Article proposed by the British Plenipotentiaries, in their last Note, not including the Indian Tribes, as parties, in the Peace, and leaving the United States free to effect its object, in the mode consonant with the relations which they have constantly maintained with those Tribes, partaking also of the nature of an amnesty, and being, at the same time, reciprocal, is not liable to that objection, and accords with the views uniformly professed by the Undersigned, of placing those Tribes precisely and in every respect, in the same situation, as that, in which they stood, before the commencement of hostilities. This Article thus proposing only what the Undersigned have so often assured the British Plenipotentiaries would necessarily follow, if indeed it has not already, as is highly probable, preceded, a peace between Great Britain and the United States, the Undersigned agree to admit it in substance as a provisional article, subject in the manner originally proposed by the British Government, to the approbation or rejection of the Government of the United States, which, having given no instructions to the Undersigned, on this point, cannot be bound by any article they may admit on the subject.

It will of course be understood that, if unhappily peace should not be the result of the present negotiation, the Article thus conditionally agreed to shall be of no effect, and shall not, in any future negotiation, be brought forward, by either party, by way of argument or precedent.

This Article having been presented as an indispensable preliminary, and being now accepted, The Undersigned request the British Plenipotentiaries to communicate to them a projet of a Treaty, embracing all the points deemed material by Great Britain, the Undersigned engaging, on their part, to deliver, immediately after, a Counter projet, with respect to all the articles to which they may not agree, and on the subjects, deemed material by the United States, and which may be omitted in the British projet.

The Undersigned renew to the British Plenipotentiaries the assurance of their high consideration.

To the Plenipotentiaries of His Britannic Majesty—&c. &c. &c.

JOHN QUINCY ADAMS.
J. A. BAYARD
H. CLAY
JONA RUSSELL
ALBERT GALLATIN

LS. MiU-C. Published in *American State Papers, Foreign Relations,* III, 723-24. This note, in specific answer to the British papers of September 19 and October 8, was drafted by Clay. Although Adams disliked it, he was able to make only minor changes in the original draft. Adams, *Memoirs,* III, 52.

Crawford to the American Commissioners

Gentlemen Paris 14th Oct: 1814

As it is wholly uncertain when I shall have the pleasure of seeing either of you or indeed whether I shall have the pleasure of seeing you at all in Europe, I think it my duty to communicate to you certain propositions which have been made and which it is believed *has* [*sic*] been made with a sincere desire to fulfil them. It is also believed that engagements of the same kind may be offered to a considerable extent and that the demand for advances may be greatly diminished relinqued [*sic*].[1] In the latter event I cannot see any objection which can be offered to *it* on our part. The difficulty of executing these engagements excludes the idea that they can be very extensive but the advantages which they offer even upon a contracted scale ought not to be overlooked. The proposition is that
go dan first aid to mar ec hal other of
1225. 806 345 . 1528 . 569 . 617 . 516 . 1246 Augerau[2] and 925 . 1576
fi cers of dist. in ct ion with mi cha long Captain
330.1021◊.1576.851.1426.1060.1433.1190.643.1024.888.1011.
letter mark propose to se lect a copy ps [sic][3]
of a 879 of 620 . 227 . 569 . 1075 . 590 . 1501 . 1045 . 1101 . 1067 .

of two hundred vet er an so l di ers
1576 . 775 . 43 . 465 . 1300 . 1549 . 249 . 1452 . 833 . 1300◇.
to serve in the U. S M has contrary[4] *three ves. sels*
569 . 1086 . 1426 . 1385 . 49 . 601—125 . 555 . 465 . 1080◇.
now ready of them a fast sa il
366 . 733 . He will employ one 1576 . 1387 . 1501 . 315 . 1068 . 1421
or to trans: port them to the U S. 4 00 franks
908 . 569 . 752 . 1153 . 1387 . 569 . 1385 . 49 . He demands 987 . 43 993◇.
for each pas sa ge an half at the em. bar cation
981 . 503 . 1112 . 1068 . 1205 . 1549 . 1247 . 699 . 1385 . 539 . 1307 1014 .
and the other upon lan din g proposes to adv
668 . 1385 . 925 . 488 . 1454 . 843 . 1201 . G—227◇ . 569 1515 .
ance one 00 franks to the men to them
1550 . 1594 . 43 . 993◇ . 569 . 1385 . 636 . 569 clothe 1387 An indemnity will
adv. ance and for the pas. sa ge in the
be found for this 1515.1550.668.981 1385.1112.1068.1205.1426.1385.
bou. nty of a hundred and 20 four dollars and the
1350 . 370 . 1576 . 1501 . 43 668 . 773 . 987 . 794◇ . 668 . 1385
the adv. ance two 00 frank for each man in france
land. 1385 . 1515 . 1550 of 775 43 . 993 . 981 503 . 129 . 1426 . 992 is the
on the part of the U S.
only risk to be run 1592 1385 1110 1576 1385 . 49 . I have already stated that this will probably be much diminished, if not entirely
to these propos it ions I have re plied
abandoned 569 . 1392 . 227 . 1440 . 1433◇. 1401 . 1259 731 1145
the[sic] until the negocn. at gh ent is ter min ated
1385 483 1385 44 699 . 1215 . 1293 1436 . 1379 . 649 . 863
that it would be extremely imprudent to engage in an enterprise
the res ult of that negocn. should ren
of this nature. That when 1385 . 748 477 1576 1384 44 90 744.
der the of the war cer tain
828 *1325* [*sic*] indefinite continuance 1576 1385 498 1021 1364 it
and to
would become my duty to examine into the proposition 668 . 568 .
give it a final an sw er as I have no
1219 1440 1501 342 1549 398 1300 . 692 1401 1259 352 authority
in this case I to consul t you upon it they can
1246 1399 1015 1401 569 120 1361 . 663 488 1440 If 1393 1006
be trans ported safe ly to the U S they will be
1310 752 1153 1069 897 569 1385 49 . 1393 1186 1310 extremely
use a few foreign of fi
492 . 87 This will be a means of introducing 1501 329 68 1576 330
cers into our ser ice[sic] without giv ing cause of dis cont
1021◇ 1431 934 1086 1405 1192 1219 1429 1015 1576 845 121

ent to our own foreign tr
1293 569 934 943 It is certainly our interest to employ 68 754 .
oops to as great an ext ent as they can be had at
903 569 692 1233 1549 298 1293 692 1393 1006 1310 1244 699
this time
1399 563 I wish you would deliberate upon it and give me your
upon the propos it ion which has been made
opinion 488 1385 227 1440 1433 1176 1254 1317 605 I learned
with regret from Mr Boyd[5] that the prejudice against the employ-
foreign of fi cers had not dim in ished in
ment of 68 1576 330 1021◊ 1244 360 842 1426 1438 1426
the U S. en light en ed nation acts upon differ ent
1385 49 Every 545 881 545 520 411 1510◊ 488 837 1293
principals Lord Well ing ton cap ture of
216 890 1167 1429 571 says that the 1009 768 e [*sic*] 1576
Washington will not noth ing but the
32 1186 360 increase their demands 361 1429 790 1385
Indi an bou nd ary at the
restoration of the 1428 1549 1350 416 691 as it existed 699 1385
peace of G[6] from whom this in form
1118 1576 1783 I told Mr 1201 —st 999 1181 I recd 1399 1426 983
ation that unless it did change them there could be no peace
864 1384 482 1440 834 103 1387 1391 1047 1310 352 1118—

I am Gentlemen with sentiments of respect your Most obt. & very humble Servt. WM. H CRAWFORD

P S. My last letter from Ghent was from Mr. Russel under date of the 21st Ulto: W H. C.

ALS. DNA, M36, R1. Interlineations in unknown hand; italics by editors.

1 A true copy of this letter, by Christopher Hughes, Jr. (*ibid.*), inserts the phrase, "if not entirely," before the word he copies as "relinquished."

2 Pierre François Charles Augereau, Duke of Castiglione, Marshal of France under Napoleon.

3 Hughes' copy transliterates this as "corps."

4 This word, omitted in Hughes' copy, is interlinear under "has."

5 George Boyd.

6 Not identified.

To William H. Crawford

Ghent 17h. Octr. 1814

I wish, my dear Crawford, it were possible to pass over in silence, & bury in oblivion, the distressing events which have occurred at home. But it would be in vain to attempt to conceal that they have given me the deepest affliction. The enemy, it is true, has lost much in character, at least in the estimation of the impartial world. And the loss of public property gives me comparatively no pain. What does wound me to the very soul is, that a set of pirates and incendiaries should have been permitted to pollute our soil, conflagrate our Capital, and return unpunished to their ships![1] No consolation is afforded us by the late intelligence from America. It appears that by the unfortunate failure of Chauncey to co-operate with Brown the campaign is lost; and we are compelled every where to act upon the defensive. Drummond, who I thought was caught, will escape, if he does not take Gains, and consequently Chauncey's whole flotilla is seriously menaced.[2] I tremble indeed whenever I take up a late News paper. Hope alone sustains me.

My last letter[3] apprized you that we had rejected the proposition, made a sinaqua [*sic*] non, to include the Indians in the peace, as the allies of G. Britain; and expressed the expectation that a rupture of the negotiation, or an abandonment of the principle by the other party must probably ensue. Neither alternative has occurred. Still coming down, they have changed again their ground, and sent in an article of which the inclosed is a Copy,[4] which they declared to be their ultimatum, and that upon our acceptance of it depended their remaining in Ghent. As this article strips their principle of some of its most exceptionable features, and as we did not like a rupture upon such ground, especially as it was highly probable that the article itself would be inoperative, by a previous pacification with the Indians, we concluded to accept it, with the full knowledge by the other party that our Government, having given no instructions on the subject, was free to adopt or reject it. We invited at the same time the presentation to us of a projet of a treaty, offering immediately after to furnish a counter-projet. Our answer to this effect[5] was delivered on friday last, and we have since been informally told that it has been sent to London; and that no reply will be given until the return of the messenger, which will be about the first of next week.

There is much reason to believe that the other party has aimed to protract the negotiation here so as to make it subservient to his views at Vienna. Under this persuasion I urged the propriety of placing the true state and prospects of the whole business in possession of the French and Russian Governments; and had actually prepared a letter which was agreed to be sent to you from the mission. But the complexion of the last note seems to render this course somewhat questionable, especially at this late period, and when there is so little reason to hope for co-operation from any part of Europe.

We have however deemed it eligible, in consonance with views entertained by the Govt. when I left America, in relation to a Congress which it was supposed would be held upon the Rhine, to send Mr. Shaler to Vienna to collect what information he can. He will go in no official known character, and will observe all practicable secrecy. If you can furnish him any letters calculated to promote the object of his mission or can facilitate, after arriving at Vienna, his correspondence with us, you will oblige us. Perhaps this latter aid may be obtained through the French Couriers.

You have been apprized of the 25h. inst being fixed for the sailing of the Chauncey. I think it probable that it may be a day or two later.

I hope my omitting to communicate heretofore to you my decision as to the mission which you fill[6] has subjected you to no inconvenience; indeed I cannot suppose that any such effect could happen. When you first mentioned your kind offer to me I expected very soon to be with you in Paris, and hence delayed making it. I find, by a letter which Mr. Boyd brought me,[7] that the District I formerly represented in Congress has again returned me. I cannot therefore accept of any situation which would disable me from fulfilling the expectations of those who have so honorably noticed me. Had not that event occurred Europe has no attractions for me sufficient to detain me here beyond the termination of my present duties or to bring me back again, when I shall be so happy as once more to see our native land.

P.S. Since writing the preceding, we have abandoned the intention of sending Mr. Shaler. H C.

ALI, signature removed. DLC-William H. Crawford Papers (DNA, M212, R20). Christopher Hughes, Jr., added a brief personal postscript.

1 Six days after burning the public buildings in Washington, the British had reembarked on their transports.

2 Commodore Isaac Chauncey, in command of American naval forces on Lakes Erie and Ontario, did not consider support of the land forces to be a part of his mission and had refused the pleas of General Jacob J. Brown for help. Meanwhile, after the Battle of Lundy's Lane, in which Generals Brown and Winfield Scott had been wounded, General Edmund Pendleton Gaines had taken command until August 29, when he had become a casualty and Brown had returned to his post. The campaign ended with Sir Gordon Drummond, civil and military Governor of Upper Canada, strongly established on a line anchored at Fort Niagara. In early November the Americans, now under General George Izard, blew up Fort Erie and abandoned Canada.

3 Dated September 20.

4 Enclosure, a copy of the British note of October 8, not found.

5 Dated October 13.

6 See above, Clay to Crawford, August 22, 1814.

7 The letter, from Mrs. Clay (Adams, *Memoirs,* III, 43), has not been found.

The American Commissioners to Crawford

His Excellency W. H. Crawford. Ghent 19. October 1814.

Sir

We have received your favour of the 14th. instant, and are of opinion that if an immediate decision upon the propositions referred to in it should be necessary, they ought to be accepted; especially if the advances suggested as being required should be relinquished. The objection to these advances is twofold—first, that there might be some difficulty in providing for them; and secondly, that in case of failure in the transportation of the men, they would not be covered by law. But if you can conveniently postpone for ten days or a fortnight the final determination on the subject, we may within that time have it in our power to give you a more positive opinion with regard to the prospect of the continuance or termination of the War.

We are very respectfully, your very humble and obedt. Servts

AL by Adams, signatures removed. DLC-William H. Crawford Papers (DNA, M212, R20).

James Monroe to the American Commissioners

[October 19, 1814]

[The Secretary acknowledges receipt of dispatches by the *John Adams,* expresses approval of the rejection of the terms proposed by the British, encloses copies as printed for distribution at home and in Europe of part of the instructions to the American Commissioners and the documents received from them, and grants authority to agree to the *status quo ante bellum* as the basis of a treaty.]

Copy. NHi-Gallatin Letterbook, II, 247-48 (MR19). Published in *American State Papers, Foreign Relations,* III, 732.

The British to the American Commissioners

[October 21, 1814]

[Reply to the American note of October 13. The British refer to the first conference between the negotiators for a statement of matters yet to be settled in a treaty. They argue that European peace renders any reference to maritime rights and impressment unnecessary. Their views in regard to the fisheries remain unchanged. On the question of boundaries they suggest in the northwest the line from the Lake of the Woods to the Mississippi and, elsewhere, that the doctrine of *uti possidetis* apply.]

True copy, by C. Hughes, Jr. DNA, M36, R1. Published in *American State Papers, Foreign Relations,* III, 724-25.

From Wilhem Van Willink and N. and Joseph van Staphorst

Sir Amsterdam 21. October 1814.

We have the honor to acknowledge receipt of your esteemed favor

19: inst:[1] advising your drafts for f10625. of de Meulemeester & Co. which will be duly honored to the debit of the United States.

We have the honor to be with respect Sir Yr mo Obedt hble Serts

WILHEM VAN WILLINK

N. & JOSEF VAN STAPHORST.

The Honorable H. Clay Esqr.
Minister Extraordinary of the U.S. Ghent.

LS. DLC-TJC (DNA, M212, R12).

1 Not found.

The American to the British Commissioners

My dear Sir. Paris. 24th Oct: 1814

[Acknowledging receipt of the British note of October 21, the Americans refuse to negotiate on the basis of *uti possidetis.* The British are requested to communicate a *projet* of all other proposals they intend to offer.]

LS. MiU-C. Published in *American State Papers, Foreign Relations,* III, 725.

From William H. Crawford

My dear Sir. Paris. 24th Oct: 1814

I congratulate you most sincerely upon the favorable issue of the late military and naval operations in the U.S. Some thing of this nature must have been more necessary to you than to me. My mind has been made up all the year for an uninterrupted series of defeats and repulses. The information we had received anterior this pleasing intelligence was better than I had anticipated. Your expectations were more sanguine, & I am happy to see them gratified in so high a degree. I am now of opinion that the enemy upon the Niagara will not escape. Izzard's[1] movement must have that object in view. 4000 militia are ordered by the governor of N. York to march upon the same point. The Capture of this force is so important, that the safety even of Sackets harbour ought to yield to it. The naval victory on Champlain[2] must have been as splendid and decisive in its consequences as that of the last year upon lake Erie. The enemy sought the battle, he must therefore have felt himself superior to our naval hero. The defeat of Genl Prevot [*sic*] seems not to be well explained. It is incredible that a militia force should have defeated 10 or 12000 regular troops. McCombs says that he had but 1500 regulars, & from the representation of the affair they fought in the works only, whereas the enemy appears to have pushed a body of our militia two miles in the rear of the fort, where being joined by the Greene Mountain boys they turned like the hunted lion upon their pursuers, and drove them back with immense slaughter.[3] If the Veterans who *conquered* France, have in the United States suffered themselves to be defeated by Militia, the prosecution of the war with a view to conquest, must be hopeless indeed.

These Veterans were commanded by generals formed under the *first Captain of this,* or *any other age,*[4] whilst our republican Militia were commanded by men who in most cases never saw an action. I am afraid the result of the battle on land, has been a little exagerated [*sic*]. The official report will elucidate all the doubts which at present hang over & obscure the subject. The English news papers say the Fingal[5] has brought you dispatches, if this is true I suppose I shall recieve some likewise. They also state that the Fingal brings the Presidents message.

I do not like the manner in which Genl. Armstrong has been removed, admitting his statement to be correct.[6] From every thing I have been able to learn, I am inclined to believe that it had become necessary. Upon this point you are no doubt a better judge than I can possibly be. The Spirit manifested in New York is worthy of a free government. It appears to equal the best period of the American revolution. If this resolution could be completely infused into the Bostonians the further prosecution of the war would be of the greatest importance to the nation. However after Drummond[7] is captured, I shall be content to have peace. That event will place the reputation of our army upon the same high ground upon which our navy has stood, from the first naval Combat. The British papers however assert that the Army in fort Erie will certainly be captured. Ten days ago they asserted, that they had a decided Superiority upon lake Champlain, but after the destruction of their naval force, they have discovered that our fleet was very superior to theirs. I hope they will discover a real superiority upon the Niagara. The fate of that part of the campaign has been definitely settled some time ago. I am glad that Brown has resumed the command aga[in.] I regret that he, by implication, censured the conduct of Ripley,[8] & still more that he and Chauncey[9] are openly bickering about their mis understandings, & mis conceptions

I think it will be found that Ripley acted judiciously in not seeking an action the next morning. The disorganization which the loss of officers in the preceding battle must have occasioned, especially in Scott's briga[de] was of itself a sufficient reason for his conduct. This might not have occurred to Genl Brown when he gave the advice, but it ought to have occurred to him before he made his official report. He ought to have had magnanimity enough to have suppressed that part of his report, or to have acknowledg[ed] that the advice was in itself improper.

I am sorry you decline remaining in Europe, tho I know your services will be very important at home.[10] If you had been disposed to remain here, it would ha[ve] been important for me to have known it before the sailing of the John Adams. As it is, it is of no kind of importa[nce] and produces no inconvenience. Mr Monroe in his last dispat[ch]es has withdrawn the consent which had been previousl[y] given.[11] I am dear Sir with Sentiments of esteem & friendship yours WM H CRAWFORD

His Excellency H. Clay

ALS. DLC-HC (DNA, M212, R1).

1 General George Izard.

2 September 11, 1814.

3 A formidable army of veterans of the European war, commanded by Sir George Prevost, had reached Plattsburg, on Lake Champlain, September 6, 1814. Finding General Alexander Macomb's small American force well fortified and Macdonough's vessels at anchor in the bay, Prevost had delayed action until the arrival of the British fleet on the Lake. Even then he had failed to launch an assault; and, on September 12, the day after the American naval victory, the British Army had retreated toward Canada. For his conduct in this campaign Prevost was ordered home to a court martial but died before the trial could be held.

4 The Duke of Wellington.

5 The *Fingal* did not leave New York until October 23. Bayard to Harris, December 6, 1814, in Donnan (ed.), *Papers of James A. Bayard,* 357.

6 After the burning of Washington, President Madison had forced the resignation on September 3, 1814, of John Armstrong as Secretary of War.

7 Sir Gordon Drummond.

8 General Eleazer Wheelock Ripley, commander of the Second Brigade on the Niagara frontier, had been briefly the ranking American officer on the field after Generals Jacob J. Brown and Winfield Scott had been wounded at the Battle of Lundy's Lane. When Ripley had failed to carry out orders to regroup his men and resume action the next morning, Brown had summoned General Gaines to come from Sackett's Harbor and take command. Brown was subsequently highly critical of Ripley, and the bitterness between the two continued after the war. Ripley was later (1835-1839) a member of Congress from Louisiana.

9 Commodore Isaac Chauncey.

10 See above, Clay to Crawford, October 17, 1814.

11 For Crawford's return to America.

Promissory Note from Charles R. Thompson and Benjamin Eliott

[October 24, 1814]

Eighteen months after date we or either of us promise bind and oblige ourselves our heirs &c. to pay Henry Clay or order Seventy one Dollars value Recd. Witness our hands and Seals this 24th. day of Oct: 1814. CHAS. R THOMPSON {L.S.}

Att: BEN ELIOTT {L.S.}

ADS, by Thompson. Woodford Circuit Court, File 103. Clay, by his attorney, Porter Clay, brought suit on this note in 1816. At the March Term, 1817, Woodford Circuit Court, the jury found against Thompson, a resident of Lexington. Benjamin Elliott [*sic*] had paid taxes in Bourbon, Nelson, and Scott counties of Kentucky at the turn of the century, but he could not be located by court officers at the time of Clay's suit.

The American Commissioners to James Monroe

[October 25, 1814]

[Transmitting copies of correspondence with the British plenipotentiaries to that date, the Americans see no hope for a successful termination of the negotiations. "The British plenipotentiaries have invariably referred to their Government every note received from us, and waited the return of their messenger before they have transmitted to us their answer, and the whole tenor of the correspondence, as well as the manner in which it has been conducted on the part of the British Government, have concurred to convince us that their object has been delay" pending the settlement of European affairs at the Congress of Vienna and the anticipated success of British arms in America.]

LS, "Duplicate." DNA, M36, R1. Published in *American State Papers, Foreign Relations,* III, 710-11.

The American Commisioners to James Monroe

[October 26, 1814]

[Although having received a passport to carry dispatches, the *Chauncey* has been detained for several weeks by the owner's agent. The agent has now been asked to return the passport or dispatch the vessel. Copies of the correspondence with him are enclosed.[1]

Mr. Connell,[2] bearer of the present dispatches, will take them to the seat of government, where his expenses are to be paid.]

DS, "Triplicate." DNA, M36, R1.

1 Christopher Hughes, Jr., Secretary of Legation, to Elias M. Stilwell, October 16, 1814; Stilwell to Hughes, October 18, 1814. In his reply Stilwell states that the *Chauncey* is now at the disposition of the Ministers.

2 John Connell.

To [James Monroe]

My Dr Sir (Private) Ghent 26th. Oct. 1814.

We have had no conference with the British Commissioners since the departure of the John Adams; and as every thing that has passed between us is on paper, and will be delivered to you by Mr. Connell, I have but little to add.

Our last note was presented on the 24h. inst., and, as has been invariably the case with all preceding ones, will be sent to England for the answer, which we may receive next monday or tuesday. I am inclined to think they will abandon the uti possidetis, and stick on the islands of Passamaquody, and perhaps the way to Halifax from Quebec. This may depend on intervening events. If they shall have obtained any success on the Mobile or at New Orleans we shall have more difficulty in driving them from their ground. Even if they abandon it, they will probably do it slowly and by piece meal, as in the case of Indian pacification. The attitude which France is said to be taking at Vienna will undoubtedly help us, but not so much as the events at Baltimore and on Champlain: for in our own Country, my dear Sir, at last must we conquer the peace.

The pending obstacle removed, others still remain of a serious and difficult character. So that the safest opinion to adopt is that contained in our despatch, that our Mission will terminate unsuccessfully.

You will observe that the English papers which we send you are marked by increased acrimony against us. The ridiculous idea of recolonization is more than hinted at in the Times. Still it is remarkable that the Courier, said to be the most ministerial print, has constantly and with apparent anxiety maintained, in opposition to the Morning Chronicle, that the negotiation here was not broken off.

The British Government continues to pour [. . .][1] troops into this Country. And it has been humorously, and with some appearance of truth, asserted that Lord Wellington has his head quarters in Paris and his army in Flanders.

Nothwithstanding [*sic*] the memoir of Mr. Talleyrand presented at Vienna,[2] and the desire which France feels to efface her recent disgrace, I think the best calculation will be upon a continuance of the European peace. A warlike chief no longer guides the power of France, and Louis dreads, justly if the military favor the ex-Emperor as much as they are alleged to do, the condition of war still more than that of peace, exposed as even the latter is to the danger of commotions.

On the other hand I do not think Spain is in a situation to give us any trouble, whatever may be her disposition. She has her hands full with her own internal distractions. Several of her provinces are alleged to be in actual revolt, and every where the spirit of discontent reigns.

The same harmony that I had the satisfaction of communication to you in my former letter continues to prevail amongst us.

I am requested by Mr. Bayard to say to you that a reputed extract of a letter from him, published in some of the American papers, in which he is made to say that the conduct of our rulers has drawn down upon us the vengeance of the sovereigns of Europe, is totally false, he never having written any such letter.[3] I have not the least doubt but that it is a forgery, from the uniform tenor of this gentleman's conduct since I have had the pleasure of being associated with him. There is not a more genuine American in the mission. There is not one who would go farther in maintaining the honor of the Country. And I know, from the honorable structure of his mind, that if he could not praise he would not censure, in the slighest [*sic*] degree, the administration, whilst he is in its service.

On the painful subject of Washington I will make no comments. I was glad to see the President's proclamation, which puts it on the same ground that it had been placed on in Europe.[4] Every where, as far as my information extends, the destruction of the public buildings, has excited the most pointed reprobation. This sentiment has been strongly expressed in Paris, in several of the public journals.

The great effort of the enemy this winter will most probably be directed towards the Southern parts of the U. States, and particularly New Orleans. If we could hear shortly of their being beaten in that quarter, and no new disaster occurs in the North, I think we should make peace. I am My Dr Sir Yr. friend &c. H. CLAY

ALS. DLC-James Monroe Papers (DNA, M212, R22).

1 Word illegible.

2 Arriving at Vienna late in September, Talleyrand had refused to accept the arrangements decided on by the Allies for the Congress. In an informal conference on October 5 he had submitted a proposal regarding eligibility for membership in the Congress, which had been rejected. Subsequently, however, he was able to turn dissensions among the Allies to the advantage of France.

3 The New York *Commercial Advertiser* of August 29, 1814, had carried a letter from a correspondent who claimed to have seen extracts from Bayard letters. After prodding by Bayard's cousin, the editor later stated that the "correspondent" had been one "A. Stevenson," whom he was unable to locate. Donnan (ed.), *Papers of James A. Bayard,* 328, 330-32.

4 Madison on September 1, 1814, had enjoined Americans to chastise and expel the invader whose recent activities had exhibited "a deliberate disregard of the principles of humanity and the rules of civilized warfare."

Lease to Phillip Dunn

[October 26, 1814]

Henry Clay hereby leases to Philip Dunn the Brick house yard and garden late in the occupancy of Thomas Church[1] on the Boonsborough Road for one year commencing on the 27th. of the present month (Octr)[2]

In consideration whereof the Sd. Dunn hereby Covenants to pay to Sd. Clay his heirs &c. one hundred and twenty Dollars—

It is understood between the parties that Miss English[3] is to enjoy the use of the yard and well in common with Said Dunn —— Said Dunn further Covenants to Surrender the premises in as good order as recd. natural decay &c. excepted.

The Sd. Clay reserves the right to distrain for arrears of rent and of re-entry on the premises. Witness our Seals &c this Twenty Sixth day of Octr. 1814. For H. Clay {L.S.}

Teste JOHN WATKINS.

[Endorsement on verso][4]

Upon a settlement of all accounts whatever with H. Clay this 23d. Oct. 1815 there remains due to the said Clay fourteen dollars.

Teste PHILLIP DUNN

JOHN WATKINS

ADS, by Watkins. DLC-TJC (DNA, M212, R15). Dunn, a private in the Lexington Light Infantry Company early in the War of 1812, was a Fayette County farmer.

[1] Long a resident of Fayette County.
[2] Earlier this property had been leased to Alexander Linn.
[3] Sally English. [4] ES, in Clay's hand.

The American Commissioners to James Monroe

[October 27, 1814]

DS, "Duplicate" and "Triplicate." DNA, M36, R1. A letter of transmittal covering letters from Crawford to the American Commissioners, October 14; the Commissioners to Crawford, October 19, 1814. An added note, dated December 25, covers transmittal of the letter from the Commissioners to Crawford, December 2, 1814.

The American Commissioners to Crawford

Wm. H. Crawford Esqr. Ghent 28th octr. 1814
Minister Plenipotentiary
U. States at Paris—
Dr. Sir
We enclose herewith copies of the Notes which have passed between the British Plenipotentiaries and us, since we had the honour of writing to you by Mr. Boyd.[1] The tenour of the last communication received from them, confirms us in the opinion which we then gave you, with regard to the proposal on which you had consulted us.
We are &c. &. JOHN QUINCY ADAMS
J. A. BAYARD
HY. CLAY
JONA. RUSSELL
A. GALLATIN

True copy, by Christopher Hughes, Jr., M36, R1. [1] George Boyd.

The British to the American Commissioners

[October 31, 1814]

[Reply to the note of October 24, in which the Americans had objected to *uti possidetis*. The British state that their note of October 21 included "all the points upon which they were instructed to insist" and request that the Americans deliver a *contre-projet* before discussion of the objection to *uti possidetis* shall begin.]

True copy, by C. Hughes, Jr. DNA, M36, R1. Published in *American State Papers, Foreign Relations*, III, 726.

The American Commissioners to James Monroe

[October 31, 1814]

[The negotiators enclose the note of same date, just received from the British Commissioners.]

LS. DNA, M36, R1. Published in *American State Papers, Foreign Relations,* III, 726.

To [Sylvanus Bourne]

Sir Ghent 2d. Nov. 1814

I recd. your favor of the 27th. Ulto.[1] Mr. Harris's[2] despatches are too late for the Chauncey, which has probably sailed this day, if not yesterday. The Transit, for which a passport is obtained, will sail in 5 or 6 weeks, and if you will send them to this place, without expence to this mission, they will be forwarded from here with our despatches. We have heard nothing about the Herald.[3]

Our late intelligence from America presents a more flattering prospect of things. I am still however extremely anxious to hear from there on three subjects, Drummonds Army, Chauncey & Sacketts harbour, and New Orleans. If the first is taken, and the two last are safe, the Campaign will terminate upon the whole quite brilliantly.

Altho the French article to which you refer may be liable to some of your objections, the general complexion of the late French prints has been as favorable for us as could be expected. Yrs. H. CLAY

P.S. If a good private opportunity offers you will oblige me by sending me 200 or 300 of the best Spanish Segars in Amsterdam. H.C

ALS. DLC-HC (DNA, M212, R1). Probably to Bourne, United States Consul General at Amsterdam.

1 Not found. 2 Levett Harris.

3 United States vessel, which later carried one of the copies of the treaty to America.

The American to the British Commissioners

[November 10, 1814]

[Surprised to learn from the note of October 31 that the British consider their note of October 21 "as containing the *projet* of a treaty," the Americans enclose their own *projet,* accompanied by comments on certain of the articles included.]

In answer to the declaration made by the British Plenipotentiaries respecting the Fisheries, The Undersigned, referring to what passed in the conference of the 9th. Augt. can only state, that they are not authorized to bring into discussion any of the rights or liberties which the United States have heretofore enjoyed in relation thereto. From their nature, and from the peculiar character of the Treaty of 1783, by which they were recognized no further stipulation has been deemed necessary by the Government of the United States, to entitle them to the full enjoyment of all of them.

[The Americans repeat their refusal to treat on the basis of *uti possidetis.* They agree to discuss a boundary running from the Lake of the Woods to the Mississippi, provided a boundary for Louisiana can also be arranged; and they propose that the whole subject of other boundary revisions be referred to commissioners.

On the subject of impressment they suggest a temporary agreement.]

LS. MiU-C. Published in *American State Papers, Foreign Relations,* III, 733-34. For Clay's authorship of the paragraph relating to the fisheries, see Adams, *Memoirs,* III, 64-65.

Article 11 of American *Projet*

[November 10, 1814]

Each party shall effectually exclude from its Naval and commercial service, all Seamen, Sea-faring, or other persons, subjects or citizens of the other party, not naturalized by the respective Governments of the two parties before the day of .

Seamen or other persons, subjects of either party, who shall desert from public or private Ships or Vessels, shall, when found within the jurisdiction of the other party, be surrendered, provided they be demanded within from the time of their desertion.

No person whatever shall, upon the High Seas, and without the jurisdiction of either party be demanded or taken out of any Ship or Vessel belonging to subjects or Citizens of any [*sic*] of the parties, by the public or private armed Ships or Vessels belonging to, or in the service of the other, unless such person be, at the time, in the actual employment of an enemy of such other party.

This Article shall continue in force for the term of years. Nothing in this Article contained, shall be construed thereafter to affect or impair the rights of either party.

True copy, by C. Hughes, Jr. DNA, M36, R1. Published in *American State Papers, Foreign Relations,* III, 735-40. The *projet* accompanied the note of same date. For Clay's authorship of this article, see Adams, *Memoirs,* III, 64.

Crawford to the American Commissioners

Gentlemen. Paris 22d. Nover. 1814

Mr. Shaler will deliver you the dispatches which Mr. P.[1] has been charged to deliver. The govt. has not even sent me a file of the newspapers of Washington Mr. Perviance [*sic*] thinks that my dispatches and private letters are under cover to you, as it was intended that the Fingal[2] should have sailed for Ostend or some other port in the neighborhood of Ghent. This determination was changed after the arrival of the J. Adams. If any private letters should be found under your cover, directed to me, I will thank you to transmit them by the mail.

Upon the return of Mr. S., it may be proper to transmit the stock which Mr. Boyd delivered to you,[3] unless I should previously state it to be unnecessary. I expect in a few days to have an interview with La Fitte & Co.[4] upon this subject. This interview has been requested by them, & may terminate in something. I have had application for above $80,000 by two individuals wholly unconnected with any banker.

I enclose a copy of a letter from Mr. Dallas to Messrs Gallatin, Adams & myself.[5] This letter was a cyph[er.] I have sent you a decyphered copy as I supposed you would derive no pleasure from the act of decyphering it. W. H. CRAWFORD

P. S. Mr. Adams letter of the 19th. inst. has been recd.

Copy. NHi-Gallatin Papers (MR9).

1 John Henry Purviance, a courier for the United States Government.

2 Which had sailed for the United States August 28.

3 George Boyd had brought from the United States a message empowering Gallatin to negotiate a loan of $6,000,000.

4 Perregaux, Laffitte et Cie, French bankers.

5 From Alexander J. Dallas, dated October 19, 1814. Copy. NHi-Gallatin Papers (MR9).

The British to the American Commissioners

[November 26, 1814]

[Returning the American *projet* of November 10 (to which they wish to confine further discussion), the British make marginal alterations in the various articles. Abandoning *uti possidetis,* they accept the proposal for restoration of the *status quo ante bellum* with the exception of certain islands claimed by both in the Bay of Fundy. They reject articles pertaining to the use of Indians in any future war between the two countries, to impressment, to blockade, and to indemnity for British spoliations on American commerce during the war between Great Britain and France. Changes are suggested in articles relating to the notification of cessation of hostilities, boundaries, and prisoners of war. A provision is added guaranteeing to the British access to, and free navigation of, the Mississippi River. The Indians are restored to the rights they had enjoyed before the war.[1]]

True copy (letter and projet), by C. Hughes, Jr. DNA, M36, R1. Published in *American State Papers, Foreign Relations,* III, 735-41.

1 Already approved (above, note of October 13). The issues of an Indian boundary and exclusive military control of the Great Lakes are not mentioned.

The American to the British Commissioners

[November 30, 1814]

[Consenting to some of the alterations suggested by the British communication of November 26, relative to the *projet* of a treaty, the Americans state opposition to others, including the article on the Mississippi River. They request a conference to discuss the differing views.]

LS. MiU-C. Published in *American State Papers, Foreign Relations,* III, 741.

The British to the American Commissioners

[November 30, 1814]

[The British acknowledge receipt of the note of this date and invite the Americans to the Chartreux[1] on the next day for the requested conference.]

True copy, by C. Hughes, Jr. DNA, M36, R1. Published in *American State Papers, Foreign Relations,* III, 742. The protocol of the conference held on December 1 may be found *ibid.,* 742.

1 Where the British plenipotentiaries were lodged.

The American Commissioners to Crawford

D. Sir. Ghent 2 December 1814

We duly received your favor of the 22d. ulto by Mr. Shaler who now returns to Paris with dispatches from the Dept. of State for you which have been received by us. Most of them were brought by the Ajax, which arrived on the 21st. ulto. at the Texel[1] from Boston. Under the present circumstances of the negotiation at this place, we think it expedient to revoke the opinion which we had given you in our former letters[2] by Mr. Boyd & Shaler, on the subject concerning which you had consulted us. It may be advisable to suspend for the present all further proceedings of the kind which we had recommended.

Copy. NHi-Gallatin Letterbook, II, 253 (MR19).

1 Dutch island in the North Sea.

2 Dated October 14, 19, 28, 1814.

The British to the American Commissioners

[December 7, 1814]

[The note requests proofs of the claim, as asserted by the American Secretary of State in a letter lately made public, that British subjects had engaged in traffic in slaves, by the sale of Negroes taken from the Southern States, and assures the American Plenipotentiaries that upon receipt of such proof, the British Government will attempt to bring the British subjects to justice.]

Copy. NHi-Gallatin Letterbook, II, 229 (MR19).

Proposed Note to the British Commissioners

[December 13, 1814]

The Undersigned, Ministers &c, have the honor of recalling to the attention of his B. M. P. the note of the undersigned of the 30th. Ulto. and to so much of what has passed in the subsequent conferences as is deemed material to the present communication.

In that note they stated, that they objected to one of the alterations proposed by the B. P. in the first article,[1] and to the modification which they also proposed of the eighth article,[2] of the projet which the undersigned had submitted for consideration.

By the first article of their projet, the undersigned had proposed that there should be a mutual restitution of all territories, places and possessions, taken by either party during the War, without exception. The alteration in question, proposed by the B. P., contemplates a restitution of what belongs to either party. The alteration would be free from objection, if there were no places in the occupation of either party, which are claimed by the other. In that case the execution of the treaty would depend upon the single fact of who was the possessor at the moment when war was declared. But there are certain islands in the bay of Fundy, the title to which is claimed by both parties, and other portions of territory from that bay to the Lake of the Woods, the whole line between which is more or less liable to dispute, may by each party be supposed to belong to him. For the settlement of the respective pretensions of the two parties to those islands and for other purposes, a mode of decision, suggested by G. Britain, has been assen[ted] to by the undersigned.

They cannot consent to the proposed alteration first, beca[use] by constituting each party the sole judge of what belongs to him, it makes the restitution to depend upon his uncertain exercise of judgment, and not on the precise principle of status before the War, on which alone in this respect they have repeatedly stated they can treat, and which has been agreed to by G. Britain; and secondly because it is repugnant to the principle on which it has been agreed to waive at this time the determination of the claims of the parties to the disputed islands, and to submit it to an impartial tribunal erected for the purpose. These objections apply equally to [t]he alteration as proposed in general terms, and to the qualification by which it would be limited in its operation to the territories in dispute, or to the islands in Passamaquoddy bay. It may be added, that it is further objectionable as sowing, in the very instrument of pacification, the seeds of an immediate misunderstanding, the moment it is carried into practical execution.

On the other remaining subject of difference the undersigned must observe, that the demand of G. Britain of the navigation of the Mississippi, brought forward in the form of a modification of the eighth article of the projet of the undersigned, was wholly unexpected by them, after the explicit declaration made by the B. P. that their government had no demands to make other than what were contained in their notes of the &c.[3] of which this was not [o]ne. As to that modification the undersigned have offered three alternatives, first to strike out the article altogether, or to strike out the clause which grants the navigation of the Mississippi, or lastly, retaining that clause, to place the exercise of the right under restrictions to prevent its abuse or perversion, in consideration of the recognition by G. B. of that liberty in the fisheries [w]hich she considers abrogated by the War. To either of these [a]lternatives the undersigned are yet willing to assent. And it [is] with some surprize that they have been acquainted in conference [with] B. P. that their Govt. declines to accept either of them, [an]d offers as a substitute for the second a claus[e] refering to a future negotiation the adjustment of the proper equivalent to be given by the U. States for the enjoyment of the liberty in the Fisheries refered to; and of the proper equivalent to be given by G. B. for the navigation of the Mississippi.

The undersigned cannot consent to this substitute because it is either useless in itself, in providing for a future negotiation which the two governments, without any such provision, will at all times, if it be necessary, have it in their power to take up, or because it supposes, what the undersigned have declared their Govt. does not admit, that the liberty in the fisheries alluded to has been lost by the War.

To a general stipulation similar to the article of the treaty of 1794[4] the undersigned will not object—

All other points having been substantially arranged either by the correspondence or in the conferences between the P. of the two Countries, it remains only to dispose of the two existing topics of difference to conclude, so far as depends on the undersigned, a treaty of peace. For this happy result it is quite unnecessary to dwell on the testimony wh[ich, at] every stage of the ne[go]tiati[on], th[ey] have constant[ly given of the]ir anxious desire.

[Endorsement on verso][5]

Proposed by me in lieu of the note which we sent on the 14h. day of Decr. 1814. H.C.

AD. DLC-HC (DNA, M212, R1). Published in Colton (ed.), *Private Correspondence of Henry Clay*, 42-44. Clay's draft and one prepared by Adams were discussed by the American Commissioners on December 13. Later in the day Gallatin offered a substitute which, after some changes, was presented to the British on December 14.

1 Relative to the restoration of territory and property.

2 The addition of the provision regarding access to and navigation of the Mississippi

River. Throughout the negotiations Clay had vigorously opposed any concession on this point.
[3] October 21.
[4] Probably Article 4 in which the United States and Great Britain agreed to a joint survey in connection with the disputed boundary from the Lake of the Woods, following which "the two parties will . . . proceed, by amicable negotiations, to regulate the boundary line in that quarter, as well as all other points to be adjusted between the said parties, according to justice and mutual convenience, and in conformity to the intent of the said treaty [of 1783]." Cf. Adams, *Memoirs*, III, 109.
[5] AEI.

The Baron de Brockhausen to the American Commissioners

[December 13, 1814]

[The Prussian Minister to the Netherlands requests the aid of the Commissioners in recovering a statue of the late Queen of Prussia, which was on board an English vessel captured by an American privateer.]

ALS. DNA, M36, R1. After the capture, the privateer attempted to send his prize to the United States; but before reaching its destination it was retaken by a British vessel. The statue eventually was delivered to Prussia unharmed.

The American to the British Commissioners

[December 14, 1814]

[Replying to proposals offered by the British in a conference on December 10, the Americans agree to allow the British to retain possession of islands in Passamaquoddy Bay pending a decision as to ownership, and to accept an article recognizing both the British right to navigation of the Mississippi and American rights in the fisheries. They also accede to a proposal to promote abolition of the slave trade but reject as unnecessary an article declaring that the courts of each country shall be open to the citizens or subjects of the other.]

LS. MiU-C. Published in *American State Papers, Foreign Relations,* III, 743-44.

The British to the American Commissioners

[December 22, 1814]

[Accepting with slight modification the American proposal of December 14 regarding the islands in Passamaquoddy Bay, but objecting to the American request for a fixed time of settlement, the British also agree to adopt a suggestion, offered by the Americans in the conference of December 1, to omit the articles relating to the boundary west of the Lake of the Woods and navigation of the Mississippi River and to the fisheries.]

True copy, by C. Hughes, Jr. DNA, M36, R1. Published in *American State Papers, Foreign Relations,* III, 744-45.

The Treaty of Ghent

[December 24, 1814]

[Hostilities shall cease upon ratification of this treaty by both parties, and all "territory, places, and possessions" taken by either party from the other during the war, with the exception of certain islands in Passamaquoddy Bay, claimed by both, shall be restored immediately. Prisoners of war shall be restored as soon as possible.

Commissions are to be established to settle the question of disputed claims to islands in Passamaquoddy Bay, the northeast boundary, and the river and lakes boundary from the Iroquois River to the most northwestern point of the Lake of the Woods.

Each party is to end hostilities with the Indians with whom it may be at war at the time of ratification of this treaty, and to restore to the tribes "the possessions, rights, and privileges which they may have enjoyed, or been entitled to," in 1811. "Both the contracting parties shall use their best endeavors" to abolish the traffic in slaves. Ratifications are to be exchanged in Washington within four months.]

ADS by Clay, signed also by the other American and British Commissioners. MiU-C. Published in *American State Papers, Foreign Relations,* III, 745-48. At a conference of the British and American Commissioners on December 23 final agreement on terms was reached, and each group of negotiators undertook to prepare three copies of the treaty for signature the following day. Clay made one of the American copies, which after the ceremony of signing were exchanged for the documents prepared by the British. Adams, *Memoirs,* III, 122-26.

Power of Attorney to John Pollard

[December 24, 1814]

Know all men by these presents that I John Watkins of the County of Fayette and State of Kentucky as attorney in fact for Henry Clay of the same County and State have constituted and appointed and do hereby nominate constitute and appoint John Pollard of the City of Philadelphia the true and lawful Attorney of the said Henry Clay to demand, reclaim and retake a negroe boy George, a Slave, aged about twenty five years old, the property of the said Henry Clay, now in the State of Pennsylvania as is supposed, and in the name of the said Henry Clay to issue or cause to be issued any legal process, or prosecute any suit or suits at law which may be deemed necessary to that end, and the said slave [*sic*] to sue for and in the name of the said Clay to such [*sic*] person and at such price as he may deem expedient and such bill of Sale as may be required for that purpose to execute to the purchasor, or to bring back the said Clay slave to this Comwealth provided he shall not be able to dispose of him by sale—Hereby ratifying and confirming every thing which the said

Attorney shall do or cause to be done touching the Premises afsd. In Testimony where of I have hereto set my hand and affixed my seal this twenty fourth day of December one thousand eight hundred & fourteen— JOHN WATKINS {SEAL}

DS. DLC-TJC (DNA, M212, R10). Endorsement presents notarial certification of Watkins' action as attorney in fact for Henry Clay, December 24, 1814.

The American Commissioners to James Monroe

[December 25, 1814]

Attached to letter from the Commissioners to Monroe, October 27, 1814.

The American Commissioners to James Monroe

[December 25, 1814]

DS. DNA, M36, R1. Published in *American State Papers, Foreign Relations,* III, 732-33. In a long letter the Commissioners transmit the Treaty of Peace, "signed last evening," and explain certain details of the negotiations.

The American Commissioners to James Monroe

[December 25, 1814]

DS. DNA, M36, R1. A letter of transmittal covering the letter from Baron Brockhausen, above, December 13.

To [James Monroe]

My Dr Sir (Private) Ghent 25h. Decr. 1814

According to opinions which I have before communicated to you, our negotiation has terminated in a Treaty of peace, which was signed yesterday.

The terms of this instrument are undoubtedly not such as our Country expected at the commencement of the War. Judged of however by the actual condition of things, so far as it is known to us, they cannot be pronounced very unfavorable. We lose no territory, I think no honor. If we lose a particular liberty in the Fisheries, on the one hand, (which may be doubted) we gain, on the other, the exemption of the Navigation of the Mississippi from British claims. We gain also the right of exemption from the British practice of trading with the Indians.

Judged of by another standard, the pretensions of the enemy at the opening of the negotiation, the conditions of the peace certainly reflect no dishonor on us.

We propose sailing in the Neptune for America on the first of

April. I observe that I am again returned to Congress, and as I presume it will become necessary to have an Extra Session in the Spring to make the arrangements belonging to a state of peace, I am anxious to reach home, to be at my post. Still it does not seem convenient to take our departure from Europe before the time I have mentioned. That will enable me I suppose to get to Washington before the 20h. of May, about which time I conjecture the Extra Session will be convened.[1]

I intend to employ the three months before me at Paris and in England to see whatever is curious or instructive—I am Dr Sir Yr's Sincerely H. CLAY

ALS. DLC-James Monroe Papers (DNA, M212, R22).

[1] Proceeding to England to serve with Gallatin and Adams as negotiator for a treaty of commerce, Clay did not return to the United States until early September, 1815.

The American Commissioners to Crawford

Sir Ghent 25h December 1814

We have the honour to inform you that we yesterday signed a treaty of peace with the British Ministers. Mr. Hughes will communicate it to you—

We have &c

JOHN QUINCY ADAMS
J. A BAYARD
H. CLAY
JONA RUSSELL
ALBERT GALLATIN

To William H. Crawford
Minister of the United States at Paris

Copy. RPB-Russell Letterbook, 556.

The American Commissioners to Henry Carroll

Ghent 26th Dec. 1814

[Instructions relative to his bearing a copy of the treaty to America.]

Copy. NHi-Gallatin Papers (MR9).

The American Commissioners to Baring Brothers

Gent. Ghent 26 Dec 1814

We request you to advance to Henry Carroll Esqre. the bearer of a copy of the Treaty of peace between G. B & the U. S. of America, one hundred & fifty pounds sterling, for which he will be accountable to the Treasury of the said States, & to charge the same to the U S. on account of the contingent expences of this Mission.

Messrs. Baring brothers & Co.
London

Copy. NHi-Gallatin Papers (MR9).

To [James Monroe]

My Dr Sir Ghent 26th. Decr. 1814

Mr. Carroll carries a Copy of the Treaty of Peace which was signed on the 24th. inst., of which Mr. Hughes has also taken out another Copy.

This opportunity allows me to say how much I have been gratified by my relation with Mr. Carrol [*sic*]. Throughout the Negotiation he has enjoyed my entire confidence, and has invariably shewn himself worthy of it. The opinion which my intimate acquaintance with him has enabled me to form justifies me in saying that if a Secretary should be appointed to the English or French Legation, Mr. Carroll's qualifications render him a person whom the Government may employ with great advantage to its interests. Should he desire either of those places you will place me under great obligations if you will zealously employ your good offices in his behalf.

Yr's Sincerely H. CLAY

ALS. DNA, RG59, Applications and Recommendations (State Department).

To James Monroe

My Dr Sir Ghent 26h. Decr. 1814

I cannot permit Mr. Hughes, the Secy. of our legation, to return to America, without testifying my sense of his merits. With all the qualifications requisite for the place, the duties of which he has performed with unremitting care and prompitude [*sic*], and fidelity, he combines the accomplishments of a polished gentleman. In his society, during a long and fatiguing voyage, at Gottenburg, and here pending an arduous negotiation, I have found consoling resources which have made on my heart the most permanent impression. Although I shall always regard him in the attitude of a friend, still I can judge I think of his merits without prejudice, and the estimate I have formed of these induces me earnestly to recommend him to your notice as a person who may be engaged in the service of the Government, in some honorable and respectable situation, highly advantageous to its interests. Yr. friend & Servt.

The Honble James Monroe. H. CLAY

ALS. PHi-Dreer Collection. See Hughes to Clay, November 27, 1844, for a description of the parting scene between the two friends at Ghent.

The American to the British Commissioners

Ghent 28. December 1814.

The Undersigned have the honor to inform the Plenipotentiaries of His Britannic Majesty that, for the purpose of confirming between the United States and His Majesty perfect harmony and a good correspondence, and of removing all grounds of dissatisfaction, the Undersigned have been vested with full powers to treat and negotiate for and in the name of the United States, with a Minister or Ministers of His Britannic Majesty, furnished with the like power, concerning the general commerce between the United States and Great Britain and its dominions or dependencies, and concerning all matters and subjects connected therewith which may be interesting to the two Nations; and to conclude and sign a treaty or Convention touching the same.[1]

The Undersigned had the honor to give an intimation to that effect in the conference held on the 9th. of August with the Plenipotentiaries of His Britannic Majesty.[2] The Negotiations for the restoration of peace between the two Countries having now been brought to a happy conclusion, they renew the Communication, and avail themselves of this opportunity to reiterate to the British Plenipotentiaries the assurance of their high consideration.

JOHN QUINCY ADAMS.
J. A. BAYARD
H. CLAY
JONA RUSSELL,
ALBERT GALLATIN

ALS by Adams, signed also by the other Commissioners. MiU-C.
1 See above, Full Powers, January 18, 1814.
2 See Clay's journal of August 8 and 9.

From ——— de Rauville

Monsieur Paris, le 28 Décembre 1814.

Un jeune homme auquel je m'interesse beaucoup ce qui est le fils d'une la plus respectable famille de la Lorraine voudrait passer aux Etats unies; mais comme ses parens [*sic*] ont été totalement ruinés par suite des derniere événement [*sic*] de la guerre, il desireroit qu'une personne de distinction voulut bien l'acheter pour servir en quelque qualité que ce soit, le prix de son achat serait employé à soulager ses infortunés parens; enfin il veut se sacrifier pour eux. Ce jeune homme a 22 ans, il est auteur de plusieurs pièces de Théatre qui ont eu beaucoup de succès et qui ont fait concevoir de lui les plus belles esperances il vieut de terminer une Comédie en 3 actes et en vers qu'il m'a lu ces jours derniers et qui est pleine de chaleur. Mais tout cela ne peut l'écarter de son plan. J'aurais facilement trouvé en france l'occasion de remplir l'objet de sa demande, mais il veut passer en Amérique. Daignez, Monsieur, je vous prie, prêter une oreille favorable à la demande de ce jeune infortuné qui sacrifierait sa vie pour adoucir la position déplorable de sa famille. il suffira, sans doute, Monsieur, de vous apprendre Monsieur, qu'il s'agit de rendre une famille entiere au bonheur, pour être certain du succès de ma demarche auprès de votre Excellence: je la supplie de vouloir bien m'honorer de deux mots de réponse pour me faire connoitre ses intentions à cet égard. Si votre Excellence daigne acheter ce jeune homme, il la servira en quelque qualité que ce soit.

J'ai l'honneur d'être, Monsieur, de votre Excellence, Le très humble et obeissant Serviteur DE RAUVILLE

Rue Meslée[1] No. 52 à Paris.

Si votre Excellence ne pouvait pas accéder à la demande de mon jeune ami, je la supplie de s'interesser en sa faveur pour le même moi, près de leurs Excellences, Messieurs Adams, Gallatin, Bayard et Russel.

ALS. DLC-HC (DNA, M212, R1). Addressed to Clay at Ghent. Writer not identified.
1 Possibly a variant spelling of Meslay; not clearly legible.

The American to the British Commissioners

Ghent 29h Decr 1814.

The undersigned, ministers plenipotentiary, and extraordinary from the United States of America, have had the honor of receiving the Note of his Britannic Majesty's Plenipotentiaries of the seventh instant, requesting a communication of the proofs that a shameful traffick in slaves has been carried on by British subjects in the West Indies, by the sale of negroes taken from the Southern States of North America, by those who professed to be their deliverers; and containing an assurance that, upon receiving the proofs in question, the British Government will adopt every means in its power of bringing to justice any British subjects, who may be found chargeable with such offence.

This proof was furnished to the undersigned, by their Government, to enable them to demand compensation to the injured American [Citiz]ens for their loss of property. Having failed in [gain]ing that object, and not being instructed to communicate it to the British Government for the purpose which it appears to have in contemplation, the undersigned will transmit the note of the Plenipotentiaries of his Britannic Majesty to the American Government, which is alone competent to decide upon the propriety of its co-operation in the object which the British Government now has in view.

The Undersigned renew to His Britannic Majesty's Plenipotentiaries assurances of their high consideration.

JOHN QUINCY ADAMS.
J. A. BAYARD
H. CLAY.
JONA. RUSSELL
ALBERT GALLATIN

ANS by Clay, signed also by the other Commissioners. MiU-C. Drafted by Clay (Adams, *Memoirs,* III, 132).

Clay, Bayard, and Russell to Adams

Sir Ghent 30h. Decr. 1814.

According to the resolution which was adopted, by a majority of the Board of American Commissioners, this day assembled at their Hotel, we request you to have packed up all books, maps, and other articles which have been purchased, at the public expence, for the use of the mission; as also all the original notes, papers, and communications which have been received by the American Commissioners from the British Government, from the British Plenipotentiaries, and from other persons; and cause the said books, maps, and other articles, and notes papers and communications to be transmitted to the Neptune, at the public expence, to be carried to America and deposited with the Department of State.

We are, with much consideration, Yr's
His Excelly. John Quincy Adams.

J. A. BAYARD
H. CLAY.
JONA. RUSSELL

ALS by Clay, signed also by Bayard and Russell. MHi-Adams Papers. Delivered by Clay on December 31. A controversy over disposition of the papers of the Ghent mission had arisen on December 28 when Clay wished them sent to the United States by the *Neptune* (on which he expected to travel) and deposited in the Department of State. Adams thereupon had stated his own determination to take charge of them, basing his contention on precedent and the fact that he was the "first named in the mission." On December 30 Adams agreed to give them up "to any person named to me in writing by a majority of the mission and authorized to give me a receipt for them; the papers which I should deliver being also specified." Clay declared that he would draw up a document such as Adams required, and the present letter, to which Gallatin expressed opposition, resulted. Adams, *Memoirs,* III, 129-34.

The British to the American Commissioners

[December 30, 1814]

[Acknowledging receipt of the American notes of December 28 and 29, the British Plenipotentiaries state that, in consequence of the expiration of their powers, they are unable to return any answer but that they will transmit the communications to His Majesty's Government at the earliest opportunity.

They give assurance that their government "will endeavour to facilitate the transmission of intelligence to the Government of the United States of the signing of the treaty of peace," and that Mr. Carroll will be allowed to travel on the ship which will carry Mr. Baker,[1] bearer of a copy of the treaty ratified by the Prince Regent. A duplicate act of ratification will also be sent to the United States "without loss of time."]

Copy. NHi-Gallatin Letterbook, II, 231-32 (MR19).

1 Anthony St. John Baker. At a conference on December 23, Clay had asked that this permission be granted. Adams, *Memoirs,* III, 125.

The American Commissioners to James Monroe

[December 30, 1814]

ADS by Adams, signed also by the other Commissioners. DNA, M36, R1. A letter of transmittal for copies of the notes of December 28, 29, from the American to the British Plenipotentiaries. A postscript added January 6, 1815, states that the British reply of December 30 to these two communications is also included.

INDEX

ABOUT THE PAPERS OF HENRY CLAY

THE EDITORS: James F. Hopkins is professor of history in the University of Kentucky, where he received the M.A. degree in 1938. He received the B.A. degree from the University of Mississippi in 1929 and the Ph.D. degree from Duke University in 1949. He is the author of A HISTORY OF THE HEMP INDUSTRY IN KENTUCKY and THE UNIVERSITY OF KENTUCKY—ORIGINS AND EARLY YEARS.

Mary W. M. Hargreaves received the A.B. degree from Bucknell University (1935), the M.A. degree from Harvard University and Radcliffe College (1936) and the Ph.D. degree from Harvard University and Radcliffe College in 1951. Mrs. Hargreaves is the author of DRY FARMING IN THE NORTHERN GREAT PLAINS.

FORMAT: The text is set in Linotype Baskerville, a revival of the classic typeface cut about 1760 by John Baskerville of England, the greatest printer and typefounder of his time. The pattern for the cutting by the Mergenthaler Linotype Company is a complete font cast from Baskerville's own matrices and exhumed at Paris, France in 1929. The paper is "1854," a text stock made to order for these volumes by the S. D. Warren Company, founded in 1854 at Boston, Massachusetts. The binding fabric is Bradford Buckram, manufactured in a gray-blue color designed for this set by the Columbia Mills of Syracuse, New York.

The book was composed and printed in the University of Kentucky printing plant. It was bound by the C. J. Krehbiel Company, Cincinnati, Ohio.

www.ingramcontent.com/pod-product-compliance
Lightning Source LLC
LaVergne TN
LVHW010347080826
844660LV00003B/209

* 9 7 8 0 8 1 3 1 0 0 5 1 7 *